The Relative Importance of the National Debt

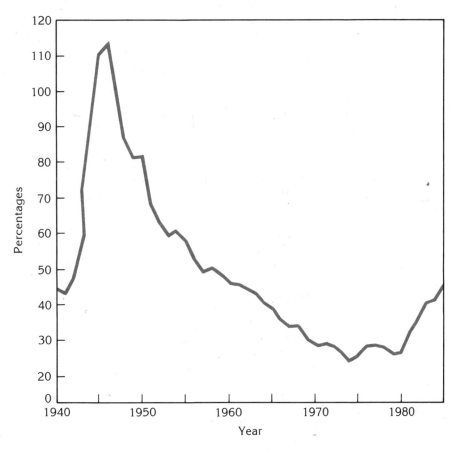

(i) National debt as proportion of GNP

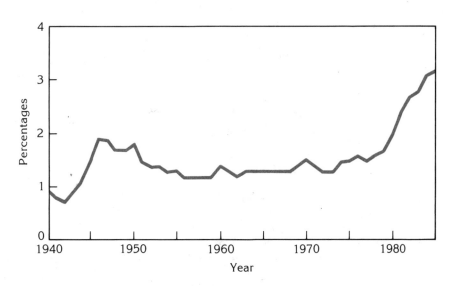

(ii) Net interest paid on national debt as proportion of GNP

ECONOMICS

Eighth Edition

ECONOMICS

Richard G. Lipsey
Queen's University

Peter O. Steiner
The University of Michigan

Douglas D. Purvis
Queen's University

1817

HARPER & ROW, PUBLISHERS, New York
Cambridge, Philadelphia, San Francisco, Washington,
London, Mexico City, São Paulo, Singapore, Sydney

Sponsoring Editor: John Greenman
Development Editor: Mary Lou Mosher
Project Editor: Lenore Bonnie Biller
Cover Design and Illustration: Tomoko Miho
Text Design: Leon Bolognese
Text Art: Vantage Art, Inc.
Production Manager: Jeanie Berke
Production Assistant: Paula Roppolo
Compositor: Ruttle, Shaw & Wetherill, Inc.
Printer and Binder: Arcata Graphics/Kingsport Press

Economics, Eighth Edition

Library of Congress Cataloging-in-Publication Data

Lipsey, Richard G., 1928–
  Economics.

  Includes index.
  1. Economics.   I. Steiner, Peter Otto, 1922–
II. Purvis, Douglas D.   III. Title.
HB171.5.L733   1987   330   86-29422
ISBN 0-06-043917-3
Harper International Edition
ISBN 0-06-350427-8

87 88 89 90 9 8 7 6 5 4 3 2 1

Brief Contents

v

Detailed Contents

vii

487

Preface

Economics is a living discipline. Through eight editions of *Economics,* our basic motivation has been to provide a text that reflects the tremendous changes in that discipline over the decades.

The first major theme of this book is to reflect the gradual movement of economics today toward becoming a science, exhibiting the key characteristic that marks any science: the systematic confrontation of theory with observation. Today most economists agree that their subject is more than a stage for parading pet theories. Nor is economics just a container for collecting masses of unrelated institutional and statistical material. Economists are expanding the frontiers of knowledge about the economic environment and learning to understand and often to control it. But new problems and new events are always challenging existing knowledge. Economists are therefore continually concerned with how theory, institutions, and facts relate to each other. Every theory is subject to empirical challenge.

A second major theme of this book concerns the relations between economic theory and economic policy. Decades of systematic observations have provided an ever-growing understanding of how things relate to one another quantitatively. This knowledge has increased economists' ability to make sensible and relevant statements about public policy. True, there remain many areas where economists' knowledge is painfully sparse, as current debates about supply-side economics and the nature of an appropriate monetary policy remind us.

The third major feature of the book has to do with the way we view students. We have tried to be as honest with them as possible within the limits of an introductory textbook. No subject worth studying is always easy, and we do not approve of slipping particularly hard bits of analysis past students without letting them see what is happening and what has been assumed, nor do we approve of teaching them things they will have to unlearn if they go on in economics (a practice sometimes justified on the grounds that it is important to get to the big issues quickly). In short, we have tried to follow Albert Einstein's advice: make things as simple as possible, but not simpler.

Effective criticism of existing ideas is the springboard to progress in science. We believe that introductory economics should introduce students to methods for testing, criticizing, and evaluating the present state of the subject. We do not believe that it is wrong to suggest to students the possibility of criticizing current economic theory. Students will always criticize and evaluate their course content, and their criticisms are more likely to be informed and relevant if they are given practice and instruction in how to challenge what they have been taught in an effective, constructive manner.

Major Revisions in This Edition

Our main theme in this revision has been teachability. Every sentence, the structure of every argument, and every figure has been reviewed. Minor inconsistencies, and passages that our own and other teachers' experiences have told us are unnecessarily difficult, qualifications that belong only in more advanced treatments, unnecessary variations in the labelling of graphs, and a host of other smaller but significant problems have all received our attention. We hope that the result is a smoother and more teachable treatment throughout.

Some dramatic content changes have been made. The most important are listed below.

Changes in Microeconomics

1. We have shortened substantially the micro half of the book by reducing the number of examples, second-order qualifications, and other "fringe mate-

rial." We believe that the new treatment has tightened the presentation while omitting nothing essential.

2. We have introduced Chapter 15 on oligopoly with an illustrative discussion of the rise and fall of OPEC. The rest of the chapter has been reworked to reflect many of the changes in economists' views about oligopoly that are being developed in the literature on the "new industrial organization theory."

3. Our surveys show that many instructors, hard pressed for time, omit the entire distribution section. We feel that this is a shame, since some of the ideas found in this section, such as the distinction between economic rents and transfer earnings, are fundamental to all of economics. To remedy this situation, we have written a wholly new introductory chapter to Part Five that contains the minimum that we think every student should know. We believe all students should read Chapter 18, even if they skip the more detailed material that follows.

4. Major microeconomic policy changes of three additional years of the Reagan administration are given extended treatment. These include a continuing trend to deregulation, a major retreat from antitrust enforcement, modifications in poverty and social service programs, and a thorough and sweeping reform of the tax structure that may well be the most important long-run achievement of the Reagan years.

Changes in Macroeconomics

1. The detailed treatment of index numbers has been combined with national income accounting into Chapter 25, "Measuring Macroeconomic Variables," to present these topics more simply and more comprehensively than in previous editions.

The second half of Chapter 25, which deals with the meaning of the basic income concepts as defined by national income accountants, has been thoroughly reworked so as to reduce the discussion to its important and easily understood essentials.

2. Chapter 28 on aggregate supply has been thoroughly revised and, where possible, simplified. The chapter treats in detail the factors influencing the slope of the $SRAS$ curve and the forces that cause the $SRAS$ curve to shift. The distinction, important for most of the remaining chapters, between the

short-run aggregate supply curves ($SRAS$) and the long-run aggregate supply curves ($LRAS$) is met and carefully explained.

We feel that it is worth making the effort required to establish this distinction because, as economists, we are concerned about the many textbooks that carry out the bulk of their analysis with a single, stable AS curve. This simplifies teaching, but it risks serious confusion. The alert student, faced with a fixed AS curve and an AD curve that can be shifted by policy, will wonder why anyone would hesitate to pay the price of a once-and-for-all increase in the price level in order to obtain a permanent increase in output and employment. And who would hesitate, faced with such a trade-off?! To avoid such serious confusions, we introduce the shifting, short-run AS curve and the vertical, long-run AS curve at the outset.

3. The structure of Chapter 30, "Fiscal Policy," is mostly unchanged from the seventh edition but the material has been extensively rewritten to increase its relevance and its teachability. The AD and AS apparatus are now fully integrated into the chapter. The historical discussion of fiscal policy in action has been considerably shortened in order to make room for an extended discussion of the implications of persistent government budget deficits.

4. The chapter on inflation has been reworked and greatly simplified. The emphasis is now more on long-term inflation control and less on the issue—important at the time of writing the previous edition—of how to break an entrenched inflation.

5. The international section has been revised and expanded to reflect the growing importance of international economic issues in American policy formation. The treatments of dynamic comparative advantage, nontariff barriers to trade, particularly voluntary export restrictions, and the longer-term consequences of the overvaluation of the American dollar—which is only being rectified at the time of writing—are all new or greatly expanded.

Teaching Aids

Tag lines and captions for figures and tables. The boldface tag line below or next to a figure or table states briefly the central conclusion to be drawn from the illustration; the lightface caption gives information needed to reach that conclusion. Each title, tag line, and caption, along with the figure or table, forms a self-contained unit, useful for reviewing.

Boxes. The "boxes" contain examples or materials that are relevant extensions of the main text but need not be read as part of the text sequence. They are all optional. Some have further theoretical material. Others contain expansions and applications of points already covered in the text. The boxes give flexibility in expanding or contracting the coverage of specific chapters.

End-of-chapter material. Each chapter has a Summary, a list of Topics for Review, and Discussion Questions. The questions are designed for class discussion or for "quiz sections." Answers appear in the Instructor's Manual.

Appendixes. For several editions, the appendixes that give more detailed discussion of certain economics topics have been gathered in a separate section at the back of the text. In this present edition, for ease of use, we have placed the appendixes directly following the chapters to which they are related.

Mathematical notes. Mathematical notes are collected in a separate section at the end of the book. Since mathematical notation and derivation is not necessary to understand the principles of economics, but is helpful in more advanced work, this segregation seems to be a sensible arrangement. Mathematical notes provide clues to the uses of mathematics for the increasing number of students who have some background in math, without loading the text with notes that are useless and offputting to other readers. Students with a mathematical background have often told us they find the notes helpful.

Glossary. The glossary covers widely used definitions of economic terms. Because some users treat micro- and macroeconomics in that order, and others in the reverse order, words in the glossary are printed in boldface type when they are first mentioned in *either half* of the text.

Endpapers. Inside the front cover on the left is a list of the most commonly used abbreviations in the text; on the right appears a figure representing the relative importance of the national debt. Inside the back cover on the left is an illustration representing the major forms of federal expenditure. At the right is a table of selected time series, useful data on the United States economy since 1929.

Supplements

Our book is accompanied by a workbook, *Study Guide and Problems,* by Professors Dascomb R. Forbush and Fredric C. Menz. The workbook can be used either in the classroom or by the students on their own.

An *Instructor's Manual,* prepared by us, and a *Test Bank* of 2,400 multiple-choice questions prepared under our supervision, are available to instructors adopting the book. The Test Bank is also available in a microcomputerized version called Harper Test, developed for Harper & Row by Economic Research, Inc.

New to this edition are fifty key theory diagrams reproduced from the text in the form of 2-color acetate transparencies; free to adopters. There are also over 100 transparency masters of important text figures available for classroom use.

Also new is the Lipsey Disk: Key Concepts for Review. This computerized student review tool asks fifteen crucial multiple-choice questions for each chapter. If an incorrect answer is given, the student is referred to specific text pages for further study; free to adopters. Available for an IBM PC.

Using the Book

Needs of students differ: some want material that goes beyond the average class level, but others have gaps in their backgrounds. To accommodate the former, we have included more material than we would assign to every student. Also, because there are many different kinds of first-year economics courses in colleges and universities, we have included more material than normally would be included in any single course.

Although teachers can best design their own courses, it may help if we indicate certain views of our own as to how this book *might* be adapted to difference courses.

Sequence

The choice of macro first or micro first is partly a personal one that cannot be decided solely by objective criteria. We believe that in the 1980s there are good reasons for preferring the micro-macro order. The thrust over the last 20 years has been to examine the micro underpinnings of macro functions and to erect macroeconomics on a firmer base of micro behavioral relations. Virtually every current macro controversy turns on some micro underpinning. For "micro-firsters" this poses no problem. For "macro-firsters" it is often hard to explain what is at issue.

Changes occur not only in economic theory but in the problems that excite students. Many of today's problems that students find most challenging—the plight of the cities, poverty, pollution—are micro-economic in character. The micro-macro order, moreover, reflects the historical evolution of the subject. A century of classical and neoclassical development of microeconomics preceded the Keynesian development of macroeconomics.

For those who prefer the macro-micro order, we have attempted to make reversibility easy. The overview chapter that ends Part One provides a base on which to build either the microeconomics of Part Two or the macroeconomics of Part Seven. Chapter 4 should be assigned after Chapter 3, even in macro-first courses. Where further microeconomic concepts are required—as in the macro investment chapter—we have added brief sections to make the treatment self-contained, while providing review material for those who have covered the microeconomic section.

One-Semester Courses

Many first courses in economics are only one semester (or equivalent) in length. Our book can be easily adapted to such courses. Suggestions for using this book in such courses are given on page xxv.

Those Who Helped with This Edition

We are grateful to Robert Dernberger, Richard Porter, and Murray Smith for their detailed reviews of the chapters on China, development, and commercial policy, respectively.

A few individuals provided reviews of the seventh-edition micro chapters: Trudy Cameron, University of California, Los Angeles; Jerry Evensky, Syracuse University; Richard Anderson, Texas A & M University; Gerald M. Miller, Miami University (Ohio); Mark W. Plant, University of California, Los Angeles; and Frank A. Scott, Jr., University of Kentucky. When revising the macro portion of the text, we benefitted greatly from critical readings of draft material by Charles Chittle, Bowling Green State University; Michael Kupilik, University of Montana; W. D. Morgan, University of California, Santa Barbara; Kent Olsen, Oklahoma State University; Laura Tyson, University of California, Berkeley; Pamela Weidler, Iowa State University; William C. Wood, University of Virginia. The final draft of the key macro chapters was read by Phillip Allman, University of the Pacific; Charles Britton, University of Arkansas; Kathleen Carroll, University of Maryland, Baltimore Campus; Richard J. Cebula, Emory University; Patricia Euzent, University of Central Florida; and Scott D. Hakala, University of Minnesota.

The new edition has benefited greatly from the research assistance of Mary Lovely and Patricia O. Steiner. Linda Blakely, Evelyn Chipps, Loretta Forsythe, Ellen McKay, and Danna Miltchen handled with skill and patience our mountains of manuscript and innumerable revisions. Weidenfeld and Nicholson generously gave permission to use material first prepared for the sixth and seventh editions of *An Introduction to Positive Economics* by R. G. Lipsey.

Richard G. Lipsey
Peter O. Steiner
Douglas D. Purvis

Acknowledgments

So many teachers, colleagues, students, and friends contributed to the original book and to its continuing revision that it is impossible for us to acknowledge our debt to all of them individually. Hundreds of users, both teachers and students, have written us with specific suggested improvements, and much of the credit for the fact that the book has become more teachable belongs to them. Those who reviewed the first through the fourth editions were listed in the fourth edition. But to convey a sense of the many more who have helped, we are listing here the names of all those who reviewed the fourth through the seventh editions:

Robert M. Aduddell
Wells Allred
Christine Augustyniak
Douglas A. L. Auld
Bixio Barenco
Peter S. Barth
Maurice C. Benewitz
Robert M. Bernado
Jeff Blais
Tom Bonsor
Charles Brown
Owen M. Broyles
James T. Campen
Ira C. Castles
Robert J. Cheney
Wallace Cohen
John R. Coleman
Cynthia Cross
Robert Crouch
Charles Donahue, Jr.
Kenneth G. Elzinga
Frances Esposito
Francis Flanagan
Dascomb R. Forbush
Dorothy F. Forbush
Virginia L. Galbraith
Louis C. Gasper
J. Fred Giertz
E. Kenneth Grant
Eric Gustafson
Malcom D. Gutter
Hiroaki Hayakawa

Stephen A. Hoenack
Emily Hoffman
Taka Ito
Janice Jacobson
William R. Johnson
Edward J. Kane
Allen C. Kelley
Kenneth J. Kopecky
Arthur Kruger
Rodney H. Mabry
A. McKee
John Madden
James R. Marsden
Gerald M. Miller
Felipe Montt
Theodore J. Morgan
Edward J. Mulholland
Edwin Nadel
Stephen Nord
Gerald T. O'Boyle
Kenji Okuda
Michael Perelman
Charlotte Phelps
George B. Pidot
Joseph E. Pluta
Richard C. Porter
James Price
Joe Rabianski
Maury Rabinowitz
Stephen E. Reynolds
Randolph Rice
Richard Rosenberg

Louis Rossiter
Bernard Saffran
B. Sahni
Arnold W. Sametz
Terrance Sandalow
Joseph L. Sax
W. M. Scammell
Elliot Schlar
Harvey Schwartz
Nancy Schwartz
Stuart O. Schweitzer
Joseph J. Seneca
Donald Shoup
A. P. Simson
Gordon R. Sparks
Dennis Starleaf
M. Stelcner
Courtenay Stone
Kenneth Strand
William J. Swift
Josephine K. Tan
David Terkla
Captain John Throckmorton
John M. Trapani, III
W. R. Trenton
Charles Vars
Gerald Visgilio
Robert F. Wallace
Stanislaw Wasowski
C. R. Winegarden
Jeffrey Wolcowitz
William C. Wood

Suggested Outlines for a One-Semester Course

Core chapters in bold **gold** numerals

Chapters in bold black numerals for courses with micro emphasis

Chapters in light **gold** numerals for courses with macro emphasis

Chapters not given special emphasis by color or boldface numerals seem to us to be of lower priority in a one-semester course.

Note: A full semester course can cover not more than 25 full chapters. The core consists of about 13 chapters. Selections from other chapters, as listed below or according to the instructor's own preferences, can produce courses with various emphases.

* Chapters shown with an * are particularly appropriate for courses with a heavy policy orientation.

To the Student

A good course in economics will give you insight into how an economy functions and into some currently debated policy issues. Like all rewarding subjects, economics will not be mastered without effort. A book on economics must be worked at. It cannot be read like a novel.

Each of you must develop an individual technique for studying, but the following suggestions may prove helpful. It is usually a good idea to read a chapter quickly in order to get the general run of the argument. At this first reading you may want to skip the "boxes" of text material and any footnotes. Then, after reading the Topics for Review and the Discussion Questions, reread the chapter more slowly, making sure that you understand each step of the argument. With respect to the figures and tables, be sure you understand how the conclusions stated in the brief tag lines with each table or figure have been reached. You should be prepared to spend time on difficult sections; occasionally, you may spend an hour on only a few pages. Paper and a pencil are indispensable equipment in your reading. It is best to follow a difficult argument by building your own diagram while the argument unfolds rather than by relying on the finished diagram as it appears in the book. It is often helpful to invent numerical examples to illustrate general propositions. The end-of-chapter questions require you to apply what you have studied. We advise you to outline answers to some of the questions. In short, you should seek to understand economics, not to memorize it.

After you have read each part in detail, reread it quickly from beginning to end. It is often difficult to understand why certain things are done when they are viewed as isolated points, but when you reread a whole part, much that did not seem relevant or entirely comprehensible will fall into place in the analysis.

We call your attention to the glossary at the end of the book. Any time you run into a concept that seems vaguely familiar but is not clear to you, check the glossary. The chances are that it will be there, and its definition will remind you of what you once understood. If you are still in doubt, check the index entry to find where the concept is discussed more fully. Incidentally, the glossary, along with the captions that accompany figures and tables and the end-of-chapter summaries, may prove very helpful when reviewing for examinations.

The bracketed colored numbers in the text itself refer to a series of 51 mathematical notes that are found starting on page 892. For those of you who like mathematics or prefer mathematical argument to verbal or geometric exposition, these may prove useful. Others may ignore them.

We hope that you will find the book rewarding and stimulating. Students who used earlier editions made some of the most helpful suggestions for revision, and we hope you will carry on the tradition. If you are moved to write to us, please do.

PART ONE

The Nature of Economics

1

The Economic Problem

Many of the world's most pressing problems are economic. The dominant problem of the 1930s was the massive unemployment of workers and resources known as the Great Depression. The wartime economy of the 1940s solved that problem but created new ones, especially how to reallocate scarce resources quickly between military and civilian needs. By the late 1950s inflation was becoming a major problem in many countries. A slowdown in economic growth was the focus of much attention in the latter half of the 1960s. The central problems of the 1970s were the rising cost of energy—oil prices increased tenfold over the decade—and the disturbing combination of rising unemployment and rising inflation, called *stagflation*. High unemployment was a major problem of the early 1980s, and remains a problem among workers in the traditional "smokestack industries." Record balance of trade deficits led to a growing concern throughout the first half of the 1980s about the threat to American jobs from foreign competition. Massive government deficits and the growth of the public debt cast a shadow over prospects for the rest of the century. Problems change over the decades, yet there are always problems.

Of course, not all the world's problems are primarily economic. Political, biological, social, cultural, and philosophical issues often predominate. But no matter how "noneconomic" a particular problem may seem, it will almost always have a significant economic dimension.

The crises that lead to wars often have economic roots. Nations fight for oil and rice and land to live on, although the rhetoric of their leaders evokes God, Glory, and the Fatherland. The current rate of world population growth is 2.2 persons a second, or about 70 million a year; the economic consequences are steady pressures on the available natural resources, especially arable land. Unless the human race can find ways to increase its food supply as fast as its numbers, increasing millions face starvation.

Current Economic Problems

Unemployment and Inflation

In 1978 Congress enacted the Humphrey-Hawkins Full Employment and Balanced Growth Act, which officially established full employment and stable prices as twin goals of economic policy. Reasonable as that may sound, the fact is that we have seldom had both full employment and stable prices at the same time, and often during the last decade we have had neither. At the start of 1986 unemployment stood at about 7 percent of the labor force and prices were rising at an annual rate of just over 4 percent.

Are zero unemployment and zero inflation reasonable long-run goals? What is an "acceptable" level of unemployment? Can we be sure that we will never again experience the trauma of the 1930s, when up to a quarter of all those who sought work were unable to find it? What is an "acceptable" amount of inflation? Why do prices in some countries rise 30 percent or 40 percent a year, while in others they rise at a rate of 3 percent or 4 percent? Why did inflation accelerate dramatically over most of the world in the early 1970s? Can a country control unemployment and inflation?

International Trade and Protection

The issue of free trade versus protectionism has been central to international policy discussions throughout this century. In the late 1930s, following the Great Depression, country after country imposed tariffs and other restrictions on imports. Did these measures create jobs, as many politicians claimed? Or did they prolong the worldwide stagnation, as most economists believe? The next 40 years witnessed increased trade liberalization *and* unprecedented economic growth. During the serious worldwide recession in the early 1980s and in the ensuing years, pressures again mounted in the United States and elsewhere to restrict imports in order to save jobs. If acted upon, will these forces lead to a decline in world living standards?

Government and the Individual

Poverty is a dominant problem in the world. It is still a major problem in the United States even though the average American continues to be one of the richest individuals in the world. How can poverty survive in the midst of relative plenty? Who are the poor, and what makes them so? Can poverty ever be eliminated in the United States? Is a more equal distribution of income a desirable or attainable national goal? Do government policies improve or impair the lot of those who are poor?

Do we, as John Kenneth Galbraith once argued, allocate too little to government expenditure for such valuable things as health and education while growing sated on frivolous, privately produced goods such as electric can openers? Or, as charged by Milton Friedman, do we instead invite the government to do badly many things that private groups could do well? Do we, as some "supply-side" economists charge, create *dis*incentives to productive labor by imposing high tax rates in order to pay for all those governmental expenditures while providing a "welfare net" that saps people's initiative even as it protects them from economic hardship?

Government Deficits and the National Debt

Almost everyone running for public office these days calls for a major reduction in government deficits, but large deficits persist and, as a result, the national debt continues to grow. In 1985 the federal government had the biggest deficit in history. Will these deficits cause inflation? Did these deficits contribute to the sustained recovery from the 1982 recession, or did they merely lead to a more rapid increase in the national debt? The national debt in 1986 was over $2 trillion. Does such a number threaten national bankruptcy, or is it within reasonable bounds? Since politicians apparently cannot balance the federal budget on their own, should we compel them to do so by law?

What Is Economics?

The discussion so far has presented only a handful of the important current issues on which economic analysis is designed to shed light. One way to define the scope of economics is to say that it is the social science that deals with such problems. Another, perhaps better known, is Alfred Marshall's: "Economics is a study of mankind in the ordinary business of life." A more penetrating definition might be the following:

Economics is the study of the use of scarce resources to satisfy unlimited human wants.

Scarcity is inevitable and is central to economic problems. What are society's resources? Why is scarcity inevitable? What are the consequences of scarcity?

Resources and Commodities

A society's resources consist of natural gifts such as land, forests, and minerals; human resources, both mental and physical; and manufactured aids to production such as tools, machinery, and buildings. Economists call such resources **factors of production**[1] because they are used to produce those things that people desire. The things produced are called **commodities.** Commodities may be divided into goods and services. **Goods** are tangible (e.g., cars or shoes), and **services** are intangible (e.g., haircuts or education). Notice the implication of positive value contained in the terms *goods* and *services*. (Compare the terms *bads* and *disservices*.)

People use goods and services to satisfy many of their wants. The act of making goods and services is called **production**, and the act of using them to satisfy wants is called **consumption**. Goods are valued for the services they provide. An automobile, for example, helps to satisfy its owner's desires for transportation, mobility, and possibly status.

Scarcity

For most of the world's 4 billion human beings, scarcity is real and ever present. In relation to desires (for more and better food, clothing, housing, schooling, entertainment, and so forth), existing resources are woefully inadequate; there are enough to produce only a small fraction of the goods and services that are wanted.

Is not the United States rich enough that scarcity is nearly banished? After all, we have been characterized as the affluent society. Whatever affluence may mean, it does not mean the end of the problem of scarcity. Most households that earn $50,000 a year (a princely amount by worldwide standards) have no trouble spending it on things that seem useful to them. Yet it would take more than twice the present

[1] The definitions of the terms in boldface type are gathered together in the glossary at the end of the book.

output of the American economy to produce enough to allow all American households to consume that amount.

Choice

Because resources are scarce, all societies face the problem of deciding what to produce and how to divide the products among their members. Societies differ in who makes the choices and how they are made, but the need to choose is common to all. Just as scarcity implies the need for choice, so choice implies the existence of cost.

Opportunity Cost

A decision to have more of one thing requires a decision to have less of something else. It is this fact that makes the first decision costly. We look first at a trivial example and then at one that vitally affects all of us; both examples involve precisely the same fundamental principles.

Consider the choice that must be made by a small boy who has 10 cents to spend and who is determined to spend it all on candy. For him there are only two kinds of candy in the world: gumdrops, which sell for 1 cent each, and chocolates, which sell for 2 cents. The boy would like to buy 10 gumdrops and 10 chocolates, but he knows (or will soon discover) that this is not possible. (In technical language it is not an *attainable combination* given his scarce resources.) There are, however, several attainable combinations that he might buy: 8 gumdrops and 1 chocolate, 4 gumdrops and 3 chocolates, 2 gumdrops and 1 chocolate, and so on. Some of these combinations leave him with money unspent, and he is not interested in them. Only six combinations (as shown in Figure 1-1) are both attainable and use all his money.

After careful thought, the boy has almost decided to buy 6 gumdrops and 2 chocolates, but at the last moment he decides that he simply must have 3 chocolates. What will it cost him to get this extra chocolate? One answer is 2 gumdrops. As seen in the figure, this is the number of gumdrops he must give up to get the extra chocolate. Economists would describe the 2 gumdrops as the *opportunity cost* of the third chocolate.

FIGURE 1-1   **A Choice Between Gumdrops and Chocolates**

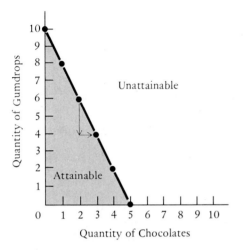

A limited amount of money forces a choice among alternatives. Six combinations of gumdrops and chocolates are attainable and use all of the boy's money. The downward-sloping line provides a boundary between attainable and unattainable combinations. The arrows show that the opportunity cost of 1 more chocolate is 2 gumdrops. In this example the opportunity cost is constant and therefore the boundary is a straight line.

Another answer is that the cost of the third chocolate is 2 cents. But given the boy's budget and his intentions, this answer is less revealing than the first one. Where the real choice is between more of this and more of that, the cost of "this" is fruitfully looked at as what you cannot have of "that." The idea of opportunity cost is one of the central insights of economics.

The **opportunity cost** is the cost of using resources for a certain purpose, measured in terms of the benefit given up by not using them in an alternative way; that is, measured in terms of other commodities that could have been obtained instead.

Every time scarcity forces one to make a choice, one is incurring opportunity costs. These costs are measured in terms of forgone alternatives.

Production Possibilities

Although the choice between gumdrops and chocolates is a minor consumption decision, the essential nature of the decision is the same whatever the choice being made. Consider, for example, the important social choice between military and civilian goods. Such a choice is similar in form to the one facing the boy deciding what candies to buy with his dime. It is not possible to produce an unlimited quantity of both military and civilian goods. If resources are fully employed and the government wishes to produce more arms, then less civilian goods must be produced. The opportunity cost of increased arms production is forgone production of civilian goods.

The choice is illustrated in Figure 1-2. Because resources are limited, some combinations—those that would require more than the total available supply of resources for their production—cannot be attained. The downward-sloping curve on the graph divides the combinations that can be attained from those that cannot. Points above and to the right of this curve cannot be attained because there are not enough resources; points below and to the left of the curve can be attained without using all of the available resources; and points on the curve can just be attained if all the available resources are used. The curve is called the **production possibility boundary.** It slopes downward because, when all resources are being used, having more of one kind of goods requires having less of the other kind.

A production possibility boundary illustrates three concepts: scarcity, choice, and opportunity cost. Scarcity is indicated by the unattainable combinations above the boundary, choice by the need to choose among the alternative attainable points along the boundary, and opportunity cost by the downward slope of the boundary.

The shape of the production possibility boundary in Figure 1–2 implies that more and more civilian goods must be given up to achieve equal successive increases in military goods. This shape, referred to as *concave* to the origin, indicates that the opportunity cost of either good grows larger and larger as we increase the amount produced of the other. A slope that forms a straight line, as in Figure 1-1, indicates that the opportunity cost of one good in terms of the other stays constant, no matter how much of it is produced. As we shall see, there are reasons to believe that the case of rising opportunity cost applies to many important choices.[2]

Four Key Economic Problems

While modern economies are complex, many basic decisions that must be made by consumers and producers are not very different from those made in a primitive economy in which people work with few tools and barter with their neighbors. Nor do capitalist, socialist, and communist economies differ in their need to solve the same basic problems, although they do differ, of course, in how they solve them. Most problems studied by economists can be grouped under four main headings.

1. What Is Produced and How?

The allocation of scarce resources among alternative uses, called **resource allocation**, determines the quantities of various goods that are produced. Choosing to produce a particular combination of goods means choosing a particular allocation of resources among the industries or regions producing the goods because, for example, producing a lot of one good requires that a lot of resources be allocated to its production.

Further, because resources are scarce, it is desirable that they be used efficiently. Hence it matters which of the available methods of production is used to produce each of the goods that is to be produced.

---

[2] The importance of scarcity, choice, and opportunity cost has led some people to define economics as the problem of allocating scarce resources among alternative and competing ends. The issues emphasized by this definition are important, but, as will be seen in the next section, there are also other important issues.

FIGURE 1-2   A Production Possibility Boundary

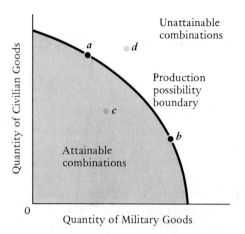

Quantity of Civilian Goods (vertical axis)

Unattainable combinations

Production possibility boundary

Attainable combinations

0

Quantity of Military Goods (horizontal axis)

The downward-sloping boundary shows the combinations that are just attainable when all of the society's resources are efficiently employed. The quantity of military goods produced is measured along the horizontal axis, the quantity of civilian goods along the vertical axis. Thus any point on the diagram indicates some amount of each kind of good produced. The production possibility boundary separates the attainable combinations of goods such as *a, b,* and *c* from unattainable combinations such as *d.* It slopes downward because resources are scarce: More of one good can be produced only if resources are freed by producing less of the other goods. Points *a* and *b* represent efficient use of society's resources. Point *c* represents either inefficient use of resources or failure to use all the available resources.

---

2. What Is Consumed and by Whom?

What is the relation between the economy's production of commodities and the consumption enjoyed by its citizens? Economists want to understand what determines the distribution of a nation's total output among its population. Who gets a lot, who gets a little, and why? What role does international trade play in this?

Questions 1 and 2 fall within **microeconomics,** the study of the allocation of resources and the distribution of income as they are affected by the

workings of the price system and government policies.

3. How Much Unemployment and Inflation Exist?

When an economy is in a recession, unemployed
workers would like to have jobs, the factories in
which they could work are available, the managers
and owners would like to be able to operate their
factories, raw materials are available in abundance,
and the goods that could be produced by these resources are needed by individuals in the community.
But for some reason resources remain unemployed.
This forces the economy within its production possibility boundary, at a point such as *c* in Figure 1-2.

The world's economies have often experienced
bouts of prolonged and substantial changes in price
levels. In recent decades the course of prices has
almost always been upward. The 1970s was a period
of accelerating inflation not only in the United States,
but in most of the world. Inflation slowed in the
early 1980s while unemployment soared. Were these
two events related?

Why do governments worry that short-run reductions in either unemployment or inflation will be
at the cost of increasing the other?

4. Is Productive Capacity Growing?

The capacity to produce commodities to satisfy human wants grows rapidly in some countries, slowly
in others, and actually declines in still others. Growth
in productive capacity can be represented by a pushing outward of the production possibility boundary,
as shown in Figure 1-3. If an economy's capacity to
produce goods and services is growing, combinations that are unattainable today will become attainable tomorrow. Growth makes it possible to have
more of all goods.

Questions 3 and 4 fall within **macroeconomics,**
the study of the determination of economic aggregates such as total output, total employment, the
price level, and the rate of economic growth.

**FIGURE 1-3   The Effect of Economic Growth on
the Production Possibility Boundary**

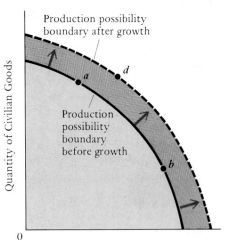

**Economic growth shifts the boundary outward and
makes it possible to produce more of all commodities.** Before growth in productive capacity, points *a* and
b were on the production possibility boundary and point
d was an unattainable combination. After growth, as
shown by the dark shaded band, point *d* and many other
previously unattainable combinations are attainable.

Alternative Economic Systems

This book examines the four basic questions just
outlined in the context of a market economy in
which private firms and households interact in markets with some assistance (and interference) from the
government. We study the market economy for several reasons. First, this is the kind of economy *we*
live in. Second, it is the economic environment in
which the serious study of economics was born and
has grown.

Today, however, a third of the world's population live in the Soviet Union and China, countries
that reject important elements of our kind of economic system. They rely heavily on centrally planned

actions to deal with the four basic questions. At least another third of the world's population live in countries whose economies have not yet developed to the point where they could accurately be described as either *market* or *planned* economies.

To the extent that economics deals with the ways in which people respond to incentives and mobilize scarce means to given ends, the same economic principles are applicable under a variety of different institutional, political, and social arrangements.

All economies face scarcity, and all must decide how to allocate scarce resources and distribute goods and services; all may face problems of inflation, unemployment, and unsatisfactory rates of growth.

Because all economies face many common problems, economic analysis can contribute valuable insights even where familiar institutions are modified or absent.

Differences Among Economies

It is common to speak of only two economic systems, capitalism (or, a market oriented system) and socialism (or, a centrally planned system). But this is at best a simplification and at worst a confusion.

There are dozens of economic systems in existence today, not just two. Just as there are many differences among the United States, Canada, the United Kingdom, Germany, Sweden, Japan, and Brazil, so are there differences among the Soviet Union, China, Poland, Cuba, Czechoslovakia, and Yugoslavia. Countries are dissimilar in many respects, including who owns resources, who makes decisions, and the nature of the incentives offered to people. These three aspects are discussed in the next three sections.

Ownership of Resources

Who owns a nation's farms and factories, its coal mines and forests? Who owns its railways, its streams and golf courses? Who owns its houses and hotels?

One characteristic of capitalism is that the basic raw materials, the productive assets of the society, and the goods produced in the economy are predominantly privately owned. By this standard the United States is predominantly a capitalist economy. However, even in the United States public ownership extends beyond the usual basic services such as schools and local transport systems to include other activities such as electric power utilities and housing projects.

In contrast, in a socialist society the productive assets are predominantly publicly owned. Although the Soviets officially designate their economy as socialist, there are three sectors—agriculture, retail trade, and housing—in which some private ownership exists. However, even though the USSR is not a pure socialist economy, public ownership is sufficiently widespread to place the USSR at one end of a spectrum with predominate public ownership, and the United States at the other end.

Other countries fall between them on the spectrum. Great Britain has six times in this century elected Labor governments that have been officially committed to socialism to the point of nationalizing key industries, including railroads, steel, coal, electricity, postal services, and telephones. However, the bulk of industries that produce goods and services for household consumption and machinery and equipment for firms remains privately owned. Furthermore, a major thrust for privatization, or the return of publicly owned firms to private ownership, has been underway since 1980.

Ownership patterns are generally mixed and variable rather than exclusive and unchanging. Figure 1-4 shows the division of investment between public and private sectors in 11 countries.

The Decision Process (Coordinating Principles)

A distinction is sometimes made between two kinds of systems: a *market system*, in which decisions are made impersonally and in a decentralized way by the interaction of individuals in markets, and a *command system*, in which centralized decision makers decide what is to be done and issue appropriate commands to achieve the desired results.

FIGURE 1-4   An Indicator of Differences in Ownership Patterns for Selected Countries

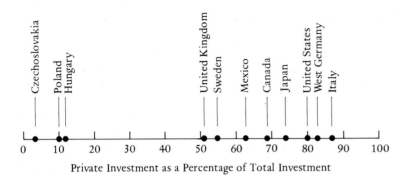

Private Investment as a Percentage of Total Investment

Actual economies never rely solely on private or solely on public investment. These estimates are based on the percentage of gross fixed investment accounted for by the private sector. Such investment provides additions to the stock of productive capital. Private capital investment plays a role even in communist countries; public capital is a significant part of investment in all countries. (*Source*: World Book, *World Tables*.)

Again, no country offers an example of either system working alone. But it is true that some economies, such as those of the United States, Canada, France, and Yugoslavia, rely much more heavily on market decisions than do others, such as the economies of East Germany, the Soviet Union, and Cuba. Yet even in the United States the command principle has some sway. Minimum wages, quotas on some agricultural outputs, and quotas on clothing imports are obvious examples. More subtle examples are public expenditures and taxes that in effect transfer command of some resources from private individuals to public officials.

In the planned economies of the Soviet bloc, where targets, quotas, and directives are important aspects of the decision-making system, the command principle dominates. But the market principle also operates. For example, at the retail level people have considerable discretion in how they spend their income on a wide variety of goods.

Much economic behavior depends more on the decision pattern than on the ownership pattern. Thus in the United Kingdom, while many key industries are publicly owned, their control is vested in semi-autonomous boards over which Parliament exerts little control. By and large, the boards try to make their enterprises profitable, and to the extent that they succeed, their behavior will be similar to that of profit-seeking, privately owned firms. In contrast,

firms in Hitler's Germany were under a high degree of state control, even though they were privately owned. The behavior of these firms was no doubt very different from that of privately owned firms that are managed in order to earn profits for their owners.

Table 1-1, though it makes no subtle distinctions, gives one simple classification of some twentieth century economies according to ownership and decision patterns. Such a classification suggests how communist countries such as the USSR and Yugoslavia differ significantly from one another as well as from the United States.

Incentive Systems

Psychologists know that people (and most other living creatures) respond to incentives. Incentives may be positive or negative—the carrot or the stick—and of almost infinite variety. Among positive incentives, direct monetary rewards, in the form of wages or profits or bribes, are well understood. Indirect monetary rewards, such as special housing, vacations, or subsidized education, are not always as readily identified, but they can be effective. Nonmonetary "carrots" include praise, medals, certificates, and applause. All societies use negative incentives—prison terms, public ridicule, and other penalties—to discourage aberrant behavior; in some societies indirect

---

TABLE 1-1   Comparative Economic Systems: Ownership and Decision Patterns

	Ownership pattern	
Decision pattern	Predominantly private	Predominantly public
Predominantly decentralized with use of market principle	United States	Yugoslavia
Predominantly centralized with use of command principle	Nazi Germany	USSR

Each of these combinations of private and public ownership and centralized and decentralized control has occurred in practice. This table is a simplification that highlights differences among economic systems. It would be an interesting exercise to use a grid that gives several, rather than just two, gradations for each variable and then attempt to place current and past economies in the appropriate cells.

---

negative incentives, such as coercion, fear, and threat of punishment, provide as strong motivation as direct incentives.

Capitalist economies tend to rely heavily on direct monetary rewards. Socialist economies rely more heavily on indirect rewards. Both use negative incentives, but because the command system is relied on in socialist economies, negative nonmonetary incentives are prevalent. In capitalist economies, a major negative monetary incentive that is used is taxation.

Alternative Systems: A Final Word

Perhaps the most important empirical observation about different economies is that a wide variety of economic systems seem able to coexist and to be successful. Three basic points are worth remembering:

1. **All countries have "mixed" economies.**
2. **Among countries the mixture differs in ways that are appreciable and significant.**
3. **Over time, the mixture changes.**

No economic system seems to do everything better than any major competing system; indeed, each has its strengths and weaknesses. To talk of "better" and "worse" in this context may itself be misleading.

Differences of opinion about the answer to the question of which system is best may simply reflect differences in emphasis on particular outcomes. Americans may view their economy as being the reason for their high standard of living and see in their well-stocked stores proof of the superiority of free-enterprise capitalism. Soviet citizens may look at their economy and see the absence of urban unemployment and the availability of comprehensive welfare services as proof of its superiority to the American economy. Sweden's slum-free public housing, nationalized medicine, and high productivity in private industry lead many Swedes to regard their "mixed" economy as more desirable than others.

Ends and means.   In many less-developed countries, ordinary people often put more importance on the ends—higher living standards—than on the means of achieving them. They may regard a change of means as unimportant. The choice between a market and a planned economy may seem to be simply a choice of which group will exploit them—government officials or powerful monopoly interests. If a highly planned, socialist economy offers them a good chance of a 4 percent growth rate, while a market-oriented, democratic society offers 2 percent, they may well choose the planned society. To warn them that in so choosing they may throw away their freedom is likely to evoke the reply: What has freedom meant to us in the past but the freedom to be hungry and exploited?

But many people in Western industrialized societies value the means of the free market and democratic processes even more highly than they value the ends of high and rising living standards. Most Americans distrust the agglomeration of central power and the loss of democratic institutions that accompany a high degree of socialism. It is clear that markets are less personal than bureaucrats, and this makes them more acceptable to many people because they are less arbitrary and less subject to autocratic abuse.

How many Americans would decide to go over to Russian-style socialism, even if there were *proof* that it would produce higher material living standards than the free-market system? In the 1930s some believed that Fascist dictatorships were more efficient than democracies. Mussolini, it was said, "made the Italian trains run on time." It is debatable that the belief was correct, but many people accepted it. Yet few Americans advocated that the United States become a Fascist dictatorship.

Of course, many Americans and citizens of other Western societies believe there is no need to choose. They feel that free markets and democracy produce better results than do alternative systems in terms of both means and ends.

Summary

1. Every generation faces important economic problems. A common feature of such problems is that they concern the use of limited resources to satisfy virtually unlimited human wants.

2. Scarcity is a fundamental problem faced by all economies. Not enough resources are available to produce all the goods and services that people would like to consume. Scarcity makes it necessary to choose. All societies must have a mechanism for choosing what commodities will be produced and in what quantities.

3. The concept of opportunity cost emphasizes the problem of scarcity and choice by measuring the cost of obtaining a unit of one commodity in terms of the number of units of other commodities that could have been obtained instead.

4. Four basic questions that must be answered in all economies are: What commodities are being produced and how? What commodities are being consumed and by whom? What are the unemployment and inflation rates, and are they related? Is productive capacity changing?

5. Not all economies resolve these questions in the same ways or equally satisfactorily. Economists study how these problems are addressed in various societies and the consequences of using one method rather than another to provide solutions.

6. Economies can differ from one another in many ways, and such capsule classifications as "capitalism" and "socialism" represent simplifications of complex matters.

7. Among the important dimensions in which economies can differ from one another are (a) the pattern of ownership of goods and resources, (b) the decision process used, with a particularly important distinction between command and market coordinating principles, and (c) the incentive systems used.

8. All countries have mixed economies in that they exhibit a mixture of public and private ownership, of market and command decision-making systems, and of incentive mechanisms used. The mixtures differ among countries and change over time.

Topics for Review

Scarcity and the need for choice
Choice and opportunity cost
Production possibility boundary
Resource allocation
Unemployed resources
Growth in productive capacity
Alternative economic systems
Public versus private ownership
Market versus command systems

Discussion Questions

1. What does each of the following quotations tell you about the policy conflicts perceived by the person making the statement and about how he or she has resolved them?

   a. Russell Baker, commenting on the decision of Nantucket Island residents to approve a Holiday Inn to cater to oil drillers: "Economics compels us all to turn things into slums. Although it will be too bad, it will be absolutely justifiable. An economic necessity. Another step down the ladder to paradise."

   b. "Considering our limited energy resources and the growing demand for electricity, the United States really has no choice but to use all of its possible domestic energy sources, including nuclear energy. Despite possible environmental and safety hazards, nuclear power is a necessity."

   c. "As growth picks up, beware inflation picking up too. Politicians should resist the temptation to seek faster real growth by inflating nominal demand."

2. What is the difference between scarcity and poverty? If everyone in the world had enough to eat, could we say that food was no longer scarce?

3. Consider the right to free speech in political campaigns. Suppose that the Flat Earth Society, the Communist party, the Republican party, and the Democratic party all demand equal time on network television in a presidential election. What economic questions are involved? Can there be freedom of speech without free access to the scarce resources needed to make one's speech heard?

4. Evidence accumulates that the use of chemical fertilizers, which increases agricultural production greatly, causes damage to water quality. Show the choice involved between more food and cleaner water in using such fertilizers. Use a production possibility curve with agricultural output on the vertical axis and water quality on the horizontal axis. In what ways does this production possibility curve

reflect scarcity, choice, and opportunity cost? How would an improved fertilizer that increased agricultural output without further worsening water quality affect the curve? Suppose a pollution-free fertilizer were developed; would this mean there would no longer be any opportunity cost in using it?

5. "What the world of economics needs is an end to ideology and *isms*. If there is a best system of economic organization, it will prove its superiority in its superior ability to solve economic problems." Do you agree with this statement? Would you expect that if the world survives for another hundred years, a single form of economic system would be found superior to all others? Why or why not?

6. Identify the coordinating principle and the incentive system suggested by each of the following:
   a. Taxes on tobacco and alcohol
   b. Production targets assigned to a Russian factory manager by the state planning agency
   c. Legislation establishing minimum wages to be paid
   d. State government directing its agencies to use local suppliers of goods and services
   e. Legislation prohibiting the sale and use of cocaine

2

Economics As a Social Science

Economics is generally regarded as a social science. What exactly does it mean to be scientific? Can economics ever hope to be "scientific" in its study of those aspects of human behavior with which it is concerned?

The Distinction Between Positive and Normative

The success of modern science rests partly on the ability of scientists to separate their views on *what does happen* from their views on *what they would like to happen*. For example, until the nineteenth century most people in the Western world believed that the earth was only a few thousand years old. About 200 years ago evidence that some existing rocks were millions or even billions of years old began to accumulate. Most people found this hard to accept: it forced them to rethink their religious beliefs. Many wanted the evidence to be wrong; they wanted rocks to be only a few thousand years old. Nevertheless, the evidence accumulated until today most people accept that the earth is neither thousands, nor millions, but 4 or 5 billion years old.

This advance in our knowledge came because the question "How old are observable rocks?" could be separated from the feelings of scientists (many of them devoutly religious) about the age they would have liked the rocks to be. Distinguishing what *is* true from what we would *like* to be true depends on recognizing the difference between positive and normative statements.

Positive statements concern what is, was, or will be. **Normative statements** concern what one believes ought to be. Positive statements, assertions, or theories may be simple or complex, but they are basically about matters of fact.

Disagreements over positive statements are appropriately handled by an appeal to the facts.

Normative statements, because they concern what ought to be, are inextricably bound up with philosophical, cultural, and religious systems. A normative statement is one that makes, or is based on, a *value judgment*—a judgment about what is good and what is bad.

Disagreements over normative statements cannot be handled merely by an appeal to facts.

Some related issues about disagreements among economists are taken up in Box 2-1 on page 16.

The Distinction Illustrated

The statement "It is impossible to break up atoms" is a positive statement that can quite definitely be (and of course has been) refuted by empirical observations, while the statement "Scientists ought not to break up atoms" is a normative statement that involves ethical judgments. The questions "What government policies will reduce unemployment?" and "What policies will prevent inflation?" are positive ones, while the question "Ought we to be more concerned about unemployment than about inflation?" is normative.

The Importance of the Distinction

If we think something ought to be done, we can deduce other things that, if we wish to be consistent, ought to be done, but we can deduce nothing about what is done (i.e., is true). Similarly, if we know that two things are true, we can deduce other things that must be true, but we can deduce nothing about what is desirable (i.e., *ought* to be).

It is logically impossible to deduce normative statements from only positive statements or positive statements from only normative ones.

As an example of the importance of this distinction in the social sciences, consider the question "Has the payment of generous unemployment benefits increased the amount of unemployment?" This positive question can be turned into a testable hypothesis such as "The higher the benefits paid to the unemployed, the higher will be the total amount of unemployment." If we are not careful, however, our attitudes and value judgments may get in the way of our study of this hypothesis. Some people are opposed to the welfare state and believe in an individualist, self-help ethic. They may hope that the hypothesis will be found correct because its truth could then be used as an argument against welfare measures in general. Others feel that the welfare state is a good thing, reducing misery and contributing to human dignity. They may hope that the hypothesis is wrong because they do not want any welfare measures to come under attack. In spite of different value judgments and social attitudes, however, evidence is accumulating on this particular hypothesis. As a result, we have much more knowledge than we had ten years ago of why, where, and by how much unemployment benefits increase unemployment. This evidence could never have been accumulated or accepted if investigators had not been able to distinguish their feelings on how they wanted the answer to turn out from their assessment of evidence on how people actually behaved.

Positive statements assert things about the world. If it is possible for a statement to be proved wrong by empirical evidence, we call it a *testable statement*. Many positive statements are testable, and disagreements over them are appropriately handled by an appeal to the facts.

In contrast to positive statements, which are often testable, normative statements are never testable. Disagreements over such normative statements as "It is wrong to steal" or "It is immoral to have sexual relations out of wedlock," cannot be settled by an appeal to empirical observations. Thus, for a rational consideration of normative questions, different techniques are needed from those used for a rational consideration of positive questions. Because of this, it is convenient to separate normative and positive inquiries. We do this not because we think the former are less important than the latter, but merely because they must be handled in different ways.

The distinction between positive and normative allows us to keep our views on how we would like the world to work separate from our views on how the world actually does work. We may be interested in both. It can only obscure the truth, however, if we let our views on what we would like to be bias our investigations of what actually is. It is for this reason that the separation of the positive from the normative is one of the foundation stones of science and that scientific inquiry, as it is normally understood, is usually confined to positive questions. Some important limitations on the distinction between positive and normative are discussed in Box 2-2 on page 18.

BOX 2-1

Why Economists Disagree

If you listen to a discussion among economists on "Meet the Press" or "The McNeil/Lehrer Report" or if you read about their debates in the daily press or weekly magazines, you will find economists constantly disagreeing among themselves. Indeed, one widespread reason for rejecting economists' advice is that they seldom completely agree on any issue. Why do economists disagree, and what should we make of this fact?

In a recent column in *Newsweek,* Charles Wolf, Jr., suggests four reasons for the disagreement among economists: (1) Different economists use different benchmarks: Inflation is *down* compared with last year, but *up* compared with the 1950s. (2) Economists fail to make it clear to their listeners whether they are talking about short-term or long-term consequences: Tax cuts will stimulate consumption in the short run and investment in the long run. (3) Economists often fail to acknowledge the full extent of their ignorance. (4) Different economists have different values, and these normative views play a large part in their public discussions.

There is surely some truth in each of these assessments. But there is also a fifth reason: the public's *demand for disagreement.* For example, suppose that all economists were in fact agreed on the proposition that unions are not a major cause of inflation. This view would be unpalatable to some individuals. Those who are hostile to unions, for instance, would like to blame inflation on them and would be looking for an intellectual champion. Fame and fortune would await the economist who espoused their cause, and a champion would soon be found.

This fact assures that there will not be unanimity among economists on any issue over which the public or policy makers are split. This forces anyone wanting to know the profession's opinion on a given issue to form a judgment by first assessing what proportion of the profession supports the opinion and how much weight to give to a particular individual's view.

Disagreement does exist, but it can also be exaggerated. Media coverage is a major source of exaggeration. When the media cover an issue, they naturally wish to give both sides of it. Normally, the public will hear one or two economists for each side of a debate, regardless of whether the profession is divided right down the middle or is nearly unanimous in its support of one side. Thus the public will not know that in one case a reporter could have chosen from dozens of economists to present each side, while in a second case the reporter had to spend three days trying to locate someone willing to take a particular side because nearly all economists contacted thought it was wrong. On many issues, the profession overwhelmingly supports one side. In their desire to show both sides of the case, however, the media present the public with the appearance of a profession equally split over all matters.

Thus, anyone seeking to discredit the economists' advice by showing that they disagree will have no trouble finding evidence to support his or her case. But those who wish to know if there is a majority view or even a strong consensus will find one on a surprisingly large number of issues, such as the housing shortages caused by rent control laws and the unemployment caused by minimum wage laws. Of course, there are also genuine disagreements among economists on many issues, especially those that involve recent and incompletely understood events, and there will always be controversies at the frontiers of current research. But there is no evidence to suggest that disagreements among economists are more common now than they have been in the past.

Positive and Normative Statements in Economics

Economics, like other sciences, is concerned with questions, statements, and hypotheses that could conceivably be shown to be false by actual observations of the world. It is not necessary to show them to be either consistent or inconsistent with the facts tomorrow or the next day; it is only necessary to be able to imagine evidence that could show them to be false. Normative questions cannot be settled by a mere appeal to facts. Of course, this does not mean that they are unimportant. Such questions as "Should we subsidize higher education?" and "Should we send food to Afghanistan?" must still be decided somehow. In democracies, such questions are often settled by voting.

Economists need not confine their discussions to positive, testable statements. Economists can usefully hold and discuss value judgments as long as they do not confuse such judgments with evaluations of testable statements.

Indeed, the pursuit of what appears to be a normative statement will often turn up positive hypotheses on which the *ought* conclusion depends. For example, there are probably relatively few people who believe that government control of industry is in itself good or bad. Their advocacy or opposition will be based on beliefs that can be stated as positive rather than normative hypotheses. For example: "Government control reduces efficiency, changes the distribution of income, and leads to an increase of state control in other spheres." A careful study of this subject would reveal enough positive economic questions to keep a research team of economists occupied for many years.

The Scientific Approach

Very roughly, the scientific approach, or the scientific method as it is sometimes called, consists of relating questions to evidence. When presented with a controversial issue, scientists will look for all relevant evidence. If they find that the issue is framed in terms that make it impossible to gather evidence for or against it, they will then usually try to recast the question so that it can be answered by an appeal to evidence.

In some fields scientists are able to generate observations that will provide evidence against which to test their hypotheses. Experimental sciences such as chemistry and some branches of psychology have an advantage because it is possible for them to produce relevant evidence through controlled laboratory experiments.

Other sciences such as astronomy and economics cannot do this. They must wait for natural events to produce observations that can be used as evidence in testing their theories. The evidence that then arises does not come from laboratory conditions where everything is held constant except the forces being studied. Instead, it arises from situations where many things are changing at the same time and great care is therefore needed in drawing conclusions from what is observed.

The ease or difficulty with which one can collect evidence does not determine whether a subject is scientific or nonscientific.

Later in this chapter, we shall consider some of the problems that arise when analyzing evidence that is not generated under controlled laboratory conditions. For the moment, however, we shall consider some general problems that are more or less common to all sciences, and are particularly important in the social sciences.

Is Human Behavior Predictable?

Social scientists seek to understand and to predict human behavior. A scientific prediction is based on discovering stable response patterns. But are such patterns possible with anything so complex as human beings? Sometimes this question is answered "no" on the basis of the following argument. While the natural sciences deal with inanimate matter that is subject to natural laws, the social sciences deal with human beings who have free will and cannot therefore be subject to such laws.

This view implies that inanimate matter will show stable response patterns, but human beings will

BOX 2-2

Limits on the Positive-Normative Distinction

While the distinction between positive and normative is useful, it is not the be-all and end-all of scientific analysis for several reasons.

The classification is not exhaustive.   The classifications *positive* and *normative* do not cover all statements that can be made. For example, there is an important class, called *analytic statements,* whose validity depends only on the rules of logic. Thus the sentence "If all humans are immortal and if you are a human, then you are immortal" is a valid analytic statement. It tells us that *if* two things are true, *then* a third thing must be true. The validity of this statement is not dependent on whether or not its individual parts are in fact true. Indeed the sentence "All humans are immortal" is a positive statement which has been decisively refuted. Yet no amount of empirical evidence on the mortality of humans can upset the truth of the "if-then" sentence quoted above. Analytic statements—which proceed by logical analysis—play an important role in scientific work and form the basis for much of our ability to theorize.

Not all positive statements are testable.   A positive statement asserts something about the universe. It may be empirically true or false in the sense that what it asserts may or may not be true of the universe. If it is true, it adds to our knowledge of what can and cannot happen. Many positive statements are refutable: if they are wrong this can be ascertained (within a margin for error of observation) by checking them against data. For example, the positive statement that

the earth is less than 5,000 years old was tested and refuted by a mass of evidence accumulated in the nineteenth century.

The statement "Extraterrestrials exist and frequently visit the earth in visible form" is also a positive statement. It asserts something about the universe. But we could never refute this statement with evidence because, no matter how hard we searched, believers could argue that we did not look in the right places or in the right way, or that E.T.s do not reveal themselves to nonbelievers, or any one of a host of other alibis. Thus some positive statements are irrefutable.

The distinction is not unerringly applied.   Because the positive-normative distinction helps the advancement of knowledge, it does not follow that all scientists automatically and unerringly apply it. Scientists are human beings. Many have strongly held values, and they may let their value judgments get in the way of their assessment of evidence. For example, many scientists are not prepared to consider evidence that there may be differences in intelligence among races because as good liberals they feel that all races ought to be equal. Nonetheless, the desire to separate what is from what we would like to be is a guiding light, an ideal, of science. The ability to do so, albeit imperfectly, is attested to by the acceptance, first by scientists and then by the general public, of many ideas that were initially extremely unpalatable—ideas such as the extreme age of the earth and the theory of evolution.

not. For example, so goes this argument, if you put a match to a piece of dry paper, the paper will burn, whereas if you subject human beings to torture, some will break down and do what you want them to do and others will not. Even more confusing, the same individual may react differently to torture at different times.

Does human behavior show sufficiently stable

responses to factors influencing it to be predictable within an acceptable margin of error? This is a positive question that can be settled only by an appeal to evidence and not by a priori speculation. (**A priori** may be defined as the use of knowledge that is prior to actual experience.) The question itself might concern either the behavior of groups or that of isolated individuals.

Group Behavior Versus Individual Behavior

There are many situations in which group behavior can be predicted accurately without certain knowledge of individual behavior. The warmer the weather, for example, the more people visit the beach and the higher the sales of ice cream. It may be hard to say if or when one individual will buy an ice cream cone, but a stable response pattern from a large group of individuals can be seen. Although social scientists cannot predict what particular individuals will be killed in auto accidents in the next holiday weekend, they can come very close to knowing the total number who will die. The more objectively measurable data they have (for example, the state of the weather on the days in question and the trend in gasoline prices), the more closely they will be able to predict total deaths.

The well-known fact that pollsters usually do a good job of predicting elections on the basis of surveys provides evidence that human attitudes do not change capriciously. If group behavior were truly capricious, there would be no point in trying to predict anything on the basis of such surveys. The fact that 80 percent of the voters who were surveyed said they intended to vote for a certain candidate would give no information about the probable outcome of the election. Today's information would commonly be reversed tomorrow.

The difference between predicting individual and group behavior is illustrated by the fact that economists can predict with fair accuracy what households as a group will do when their take-home pay is increased. Some individuals may do surprising and unpredictable things, but the total response of all households to a permanent change in tax rates that leaves more money in their hands is predictable within quite a narrow margin of error. This stability in the response of households' spending to a change in their available income is the basis of economists' ability to predict successfully the outcome of major revisions in the tax laws.

This does not mean that people never change their minds or that future events can be foretold by a casual study of the past. The stability discussed here is a stable response to causal factors (e.g., next time it gets warm, ice cream sales will rise) and not merely inertia (e.g., ice cream sales will go on rising in the future because they have risen in the past).

The "Law" of Large Numbers

Successfully predicting the behavior of large groups is made possible by the statistical "law" of large numbers. Broadly speaking, this law asserts that random movements of many individual items tend to offset one another. The law is based on one of the most beautiful constants of behavior in the whole of science, natural and social, and yet it can be derived from the fact that human beings make errors! The law is based on the statistical relation called the *normal curve of error*.

What is implied by this law? Ask any one person to measure the length of a room and it will be almost impossible to predict in advance what sort of error of measurement will be made. Dozens of things will affect the accuracy of the measurement and, furthermore, the person may make one error today and quite a different one tomorrow. But ask a thousand people to measure the length of the same room, and we can predict within a small margin just how this *group* will make its errors. We can assert with confidence that more people will make small errors than will make large errors, that the larger the error the fewer will be the number making it, that roughly the same number of people will overstate as will understate the distance, and that the average error of all individuals will be close to zero.

If a common cause should act on each member of the group, the average behavior of the group can be predicted even though any one member may act in a surprising fashion. If, for example, each of the thousand individuals is given a tape measure that understates "actual" distances, it can be predicted that, on the average, the group will understate the length of the room. It is, of course, quite possible that one member who had in the past been consistently undermeasuring distance because of psychological depression will now overmeasure the distance because the state of his health has changed. But some other event may happen to another individual that will turn her from an overmeasurer into an undermeasurer. Individuals may act strangely for inexplicable reasons. But the group's behavior, when the inaccurate tape is substituted for the accurate one, will be predictable precisely because the odd things that one individual does will tend to cancel out the odd things some other individual does.

Irregularities in individual behavior tend to cancel one another out, and the regularities tend to show up in repeated observations.

The Nature of Scientific Theories

When some regularity between two or more things is observed, we may ask why this should be so. A *theory* is an attempt to answer this question, and by providing an explanation for the regularity, it enables us to predict as yet unobserved events. For example, national income theory predicts that a reduction in tax rates will reduce the unemployment rate. The simple theory of market behavior predicts that, under specified conditions, a partial failure of the potato crop, will cause an increase in the incomes of potato farmers.

Theories are used in explaining observed phenomena. A successful theory enables us to predict behavior.

Any explanation whatsoever of how given observations are linked together is a theoretical construction. Theories are used to impose order on our observations, to explain how what we see is linked together. Without theories there would be only a shapeless mass of meaningless observations.

The choice is not between theory and observation but between better or worse theories to explain observations.

Misunderstanding about the place of theories in scientific explanation gives rise to many misconceptions. One of these is illustrated by the phrase "True in theory, but not in practice." The next time you hear someone say this (or, indeed, the next time you say it yourself) you should immediately reply, "All right then, tell me what does happen in practice." Usually you will not be told mere facts, but you will

be given an alternative theory—a different explanation of the facts. The speaker should have said, "The theory in question provides a poor explanation of the facts (that is, it is contradicted by some factual observations). I have a different theory that does a much better job."

A theory consists of (1) a set of definitions that clearly define the *variables* to be used, (2) a set of *assumptions* that outline the conditions under which the theory is to apply, (3) one or more *hypotheses* about the relationships among the variables, and (4) *predictions* that are deduced from the assumptions of the theory and can be tested against actual empirical observations. We consider these four elements in the following four sections.

Variables

A **variable** is a magnitude that can take on different possible values. Variables are the basic elements of theories, and each one needs to be carefully defined.

Price is an example of an important economic variable. The price of a commodity is the amount of money that must be given up to purchase one unit of that commodity. To define a price we must first define the commodity to which it attaches. Such a commodity might be one dozen grade A large eggs. The price of such eggs sold in, say, supermarkets in Fargo, North Dakota, defines a variable. The particular values taken on by that variable might be $.98 on July 1, 1987, $1.02 on July 8, 1988, and $.99 on July 15, 1989.

There are many distinctions between kinds of variables; two of the most important are discussed below.

Endogenous and exogenous variables. An **endogenous variable** is a variable that is explained within a theory. An **exogenous variable** influences endogenous variables but is itself determined by factors outside the theory.

For example, consider the theory that the price of apples in Seattle, Washington, on a particular day is a function of several things, one of which is the weather in the Yakima Valley during the previous apple-growing season. We can safely assume that the state of the weather is not determined by economic conditions. The price of apples in this case is an endogenous variable—something determined within the framework of the theory. The state of the weather in the Yakima Valley is an exogenous variable; changes in it influence prices because the changes affect the output of apples, but the state of the weather is not influenced by the prices.

Other words are sometimes used for the same distinction. One frequently used pair is *induced* for endogenous and *autonomous* for exogenous.

Stock and flow variables.   A flow variable has a time dimension; it is so much per unit of time. The quantity of grade A large eggs purchased in Fargo is a flow variable. No useful information is conveyed if we are told that the number purchased was 2,000 dozen eggs unless we are also told the period of time over which these purchases occurred. Two thousand dozen per hour would indicate an active market in eggs, while 2,000 dozen per month would indicate a sluggish market.

A stock variable has no time dimension; it is just so much. Thus, the number of eggs in the egg producer's co-op warehouse—for example, 20,000 dozen eggs—is a stock variable. All those eggs are there at one time, and they remain there until something happens to change the stock held by the co-op. The stock variable is just a number, not a rate of flow of so much per day or per month.

Economic theories use both flow variables and stock variables, and it takes a little practice to keep them straight. The amount of income earned is a flow; there is so much per year or per month or per hour. The amount of a household's expenditure is also a flow—so much spent per week or per month. The amount of money in a bank account or a miser's hoard (earned, perhaps, in the past, but unspent) is a stock—just so many thousands of dollars. The key test is always whether a time dimension is required to give the variable meaning.

Assumptions

Assumptions are essential to theorizing. Students are often greatly concerned about the justification of assumptions, particularly if they seem unrealistic.

An example will illustrate some of the issues involved in this question of realism. Much of the theory that we are going to study in this book uses the assumption that the sole motive of all those who run firms is to make as much money as they possibly can, or, as economists put it, firms are assumed to be run so as to *maximize their profits.* The assumption of profit maximization allows economists to make predictions about the behavior of firms. They study the effects that alternatives open to firms would have on profits, and then predict that the alternative selected will be the one that produces the most profits.

But profit maximization may seem like a rather crude assumption. Surely the managers of firms sometimes have philanthropic or political motives. Does this not discredit the assumption of profit maximization by showing it to be unrealistic?

To make successful predictions, however, the theory does not require that managers are solely and always motivated by the desire to maximize profits. All that is required is that profits are a sufficiently important consideration that a theory based on the assumption of profit maximization will produce predictions that are substantially correct.

This illustration shows that it is not always appropriate to criticize a theory because its assumptions seem unrealistic. All theory is an abstraction from reality. If it were not, it would merely duplicate the world and would add nothing to our understanding of it. A good theory abstracts in a useful way; a poor theory does not. If a theory has ignored some really important factors, then its predictions will be contradicted by the evidence—at least where the factor ignored exerts an important influence on the outcome.

Another, sometimes confusing, use of assumptions is to state the conditions that are important to a particular theory. Suppose, for example, that an economic theory starts out: "Assume that there is no government." Surely, says the reader, this assumption is totally unrealistic, and I cannot therefore take seriously anything that comes out of the theory. But this assumption may merely be the economist's way of saying that, whatever the government does, even whether it exists, *is irrelevant for the purposes of this particular theory.*

Now, put this way, the statement becomes an empirical assertion. The only way to test it is to see if the predictions that follow from the theory do or do not fit the facts that the theory is trying to explain. If they do, then the theorist was correct in the assumption that the government could be ignored for the particular purposes at hand. In this case the criticism that the theory is unrealistic because there really is a government is completely beside the point.

Hypotheses

Relations among variables.   The critical step in theorizing is formulating hypotheses. A hypothesis is a statement about how two or more variables are related to each other. For example, it is a basic hypothesis of economics that the quantity produced of any commodity depends upon its own price in such a way that the higher the price the larger the quantity produced. To illustrate, the higher the price of eggs the larger the quantity of eggs that the farmers will produce. Stated in more formal terms, the hypothesis is that the two variables, price of eggs and quantity of eggs, are positively related to each other.[1]

Functional relations.   A **function,** or a functional relation, is a formal expression of a relation among variables.[2]

The particular hypothesis that the quantity of eggs produced is related to the price of eggs is an example of a functional relation in economics. In its most general form, it merely says that quantity produced is related to price. The more specific hypothesis is that as the price of eggs rises, the quantity produced also rises.

In the case of many hypotheses of this kind, economists can be even more specific about the nature of the functional relation. On the basis of detailed factual studies, economists often have a pretty good idea of by how much quantity produced will change as a result of specified changes in price, that is, they can predict magnitude as well as direction.

[1] When two variables are related in such a way that an increase in one is associated with an increase in the other, they are said to be *positively related*. When two variables are related in such a way that an increase in one is associated with a decrease in the other, they are said to be *negatively related*.

[2] The appendix to this chapter gives a more detailed discussion of functional relations and the use of graphs in economics.

Predictions

A theory's predictions are the propositions that can be deduced from that theory. An example of a prediction would be a deduction that *if* firms maximize their profits, and *if* certain other assumptions and hypotheses of the theory hold true, *then* a rise in the rate of corporate tax will cause a reduction in the amount of investment that firms make in new plant and equipment. The prediction is that the rise in the tax rate will be accompanied by a fall in investment. The reasons that lie behind the prediction are contained in the assumptions and hypotheses that constitute the theory in question.

It should be apparent from this discussion that a scientific prediction is not the same thing as a prophecy.

A scientific prediction is a conditional statement that takes the form: *If* **you do this,** *then* **such and such will follow.**

If hydrogen and oxygen are combined under specified conditions, *then* water will be the result. *If* the government cuts taxes, *then* the rate of unemployment will decrease. It is important to realize that this prediction is very different from the statement: "I prophesy that in two years' time there will be a large reduction in unemployment because I believe the government will decide to cut tax rates." The government's decision to cut tax rates in two years' time will be the outcome of many influences, both economic and political. If the economist's prophecy about unemployment turns out to be wrong because in two years' time the government does not cut tax rates, then all that has been learned is that the economist is not a good guesser about the behavior of the government. However, *if* the government does cut tax rates (in two years' time or at any other time) and *then* the rate of unemployment does not decrease, a conditional scientific prediction in economic theory has been contradicted.

Tests

A theory is tested by confronting its predictions with evidence. It is necessary to discover if certain events

BOX 2-3

Can Hypotheses Be Proved or Refuted?

Most hypotheses in economics are universal. They say that whenever certain specified conditions are fulfilled, cause X will always produce effect Y. Such universal hypotheses cannot be proved correct with certainty. No matter how many observations are collected that agree with the hypothesis, there is always some chance that a long series of untypical observations has been made or that there have been systematic errors of observation. After all, the mass of well-documented evidence accumulated several centuries ago on the existence of the power of witches is no longer accepted, even though it fully satisfied most contemporary observers. The existence of observational errors, even on a vast scale, has been shown to be possible, although (one fervently hopes) it is not very frequent. Observations that disagree with the theory may begin to accumulate, and after some time a theory that looked nearly certain may begin to look rather shaky.

By the same token a universal hypothesis can never be proved false with certainty. Even when current observations consistently conflict with the theory, it is still possible that a large number of untypical cases has been selected or systematic errors of observation have been made. For instance, evidence was once gathered "disproving" the theory that high income taxes tend to discourage work. More recent research suggests that economists may have been wrong to reject this theory. As a result of measurement errors and bad experimental design, the conflicting evidence may not have been as decisive as was once thought.

There is no absolute certainty in any knowledge. No doubt some of the things we now think true will eventually turn out to be false, and some of the things we currently think false will eventually turn out to be true. Yet while we can never be certain, we can assess the balance of evidence. Some hypotheses are so unlikely to be true, given current evidence, that for all practical purposes we may regard them as false. Other hypotheses are so unlikely to be false, given current evidence, that for all practical purposes we may regard them as true. This kind of practical decision must always be regarded as tentative. Every once in a while we will find that we have to change our mind: Something that looked right will begin to look doubtful, or something that looked wrong will begin to look possible.

---

are followed by the consequences predicted by the theory. For example, is an increase in the corporate tax rate followed by a decline in business investment? (Box 2-3 gives further discussion of what can be learned from testing theories.)

Generally, theories tend to be abandoned when they are no longer useful. And theories cease to be useful when they cannot predict the consequences of actions in which one is interested better than the next best alternative. When a theory consistently fails to predict better than the available alternatives, it is either modified or replaced. Figure 2-1 summarizes the discussion of theories and their testing.

Refutation or confirmation. The scientific approach to any issue consists in setting up a theory that will explain it and then seeing if that theory can be refuted by evidence.

The alternative to this approach is to set up a theory and then look for confirming evidence. Such an approach is hazardous because the world is sufficiently complex that *some* confirming evidence can be found for any theory, no matter how unlikely the theory may be. For example, the advocates of conspiracy theories, such as the theory that President Kennedy's assassination was a plot involving many persons and at least two gunmen, can always find some confirming evidence. The scientific way to deal with such questions is to set up the simplest theory—in this case that the president was assassinated by Lee Harvey Oswald acting alone—and then see if the evidence can refute it.

FIGURE 2-1   The Interaction of Deduction and Measurement in Theorizing

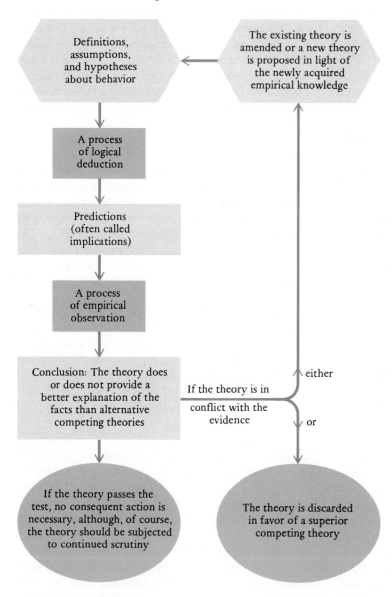

Theory and observation are in continuous interaction. Starting (at the top left) with the assumptions of a theory and the definitions of relevant terms, the theorist deduces by logical analysis everything that is implied by the assumptions. These implications are the predictions of the theory. The theory is then tested by confronting its predictions with evidence. If the theory is in conflict with facts, it will usually be amended to make it consistent with those facts (thereby making it a better theory); in extreme cases it will be discarded, to be replaced by a superior alternative. The process then begins again: The new or amended theory is subjected first to logical analysis and then to empirical testing.

An example of the unfruitful approach of seeking confirmation is frequently seen when a leader—be he an American president or a foreign dictator—surrounds himself with yes-men who feed him only evidence that confirms his existing views. This approach is usually a road to disaster because the leader's decisions become more and more out of touch with reality.

A wise leader adopts a scientific approach instinctively; he constantly checks the realism of his views by encouraging subordinates to criticize them. This tests how far the leader's existing views correspond to all available evidence and encourages amendment in the light of evidence that conflicts with the current views.

Measurement and Testing of Economic Relations

So far we have given an outline of the main elements of theories. Because measurement and testing are so important in evaluating theories, we present below a more detailed discussion of these topics in relation to economic principles.

It is one thing for economists to theorize that two or more variables are related to each other; it is quite another for them to be able to say how these variables are related. Economists might generalize on the basis of a casual observation that when households receive more income, they are likely to buy more of most commodities. But precisely how much will the consumption of a particular commodity rise as household incomes rise? Are there exceptions to the rule that the purchase of a commodity rises as income rises? For estimating precise magnitudes and for testing general rules or hypotheses, common sense, intuition, and casual observation do not take us very far. More systematic statistical analysis is required.

Statistical analysis is used to test the hypothesis that two things are related and to estimate the numerical values of the function that describes the relation.

In practice, the same data can be used simultaneously to test whether a relationship exists and, when it does exist, to provide a measure of it.

We have seen that economics is a nonlaboratory science. It is rarely possible to conduct controlled experiments with the economy. However, millions of uncontrolled experiments are going on every day. Households are deciding what to purchase given changing prices and incomes; firms are deciding what to produce and how to produce it; and the government is involved in the economy by its various taxes, subsidies, and controls. Because all these activities can be observed and recorded, a mass of data is continually produced by the economy.

The variables that interest economists, such as the volume of unemployment, the price of wheat, and the share of income going to wage earners, are generally influenced by many factors, all of which vary simultaneously. If economists are to test their theories about relations among variables in the economy, they must use statistical techniques designed for situations in which other things cannot be held constant.

An Example of Statistical Testing

To illustrate how data may be used to test theories even while other things are not held constant, we take the very simple and intuitively plausible hypothesis that the federal income taxes paid by American families increase as their incomes increase.

A Sample

To begin with, observations must be made of family income and tax payments. It is not practical to do so for all American families, so a small number (called a *sample*) is studied on the assumption that these households are typical of the entire group.

It is important that the sample be what is called a random sample. A **random sample** is chosen according to a rigidly defined set of conditions guaranteeing, among other things, that every member of the group from which we are selecting the sample has an equal chance of being selected. Choosing the sample in a random fashion has two important consequences.

First, it reduces the chance that the sample will be unrepresentative of the population from which it is selected. Second, and more important, it allows us to calculate just how likely it is that the sample will be unrepresentative by any specified amount. For example, if the average amount of income tax paid by the households in our sample is $2,000, then it is most likely that the average tax paid by all American households is in the vicinity of $2,000. But that is not necessarily so. The sample might be so unrepresentative that the actual figure for average tax paid by all American households is only $1,500, or it might be $2,750. If the sample is random, we are able to calculate the probability that the actual data for the whole population differs from the data in our sample by any stated amount.

The reason for the predictability of random samples is that such samples are chosen by chance, and chance events are predictable.

That chance events are predictable may sound surprising, but consider these questions. If you pick a card from a deck of ordinary playing cards, how likely is it that you will pick a heart? An ace? An ace of hearts? You play a game in which you pick a card and win if it is a heart and lose if it is anything else; a friend offers you $5 if you win against $1 if you lose. Who will make money if the game is played a large number of times? The same game is played again, but now you get $3 if you win and pay $1 if you lose. Who will make money over a large number of draws? If you can answer these questions (we will bet that most of you can), you must believe that chance events are in some sense predictable.

To test the hypothesis about taxes, we have chosen a random sample of 212 families from data collected by the Survey Research Center of the University of Michigan. For each family we record its income and the federal income tax it pays.

Graphical and Tabular Analysis

There are several ways in which the data may be used to evaluate the hypothesis.

Scatter diagram.   One is the **scatter diagram.**[3] Figure 2-2 is a scatter diagram that relates family income to federal income tax payments. The pattern of the dots suggests that there is a stong tendency for tax payments to be higher when family income is higher. It thus supports the hypothesis.

There is some scattering of the dots because the relationship is not "perfect"; in other words, there is some variation in tax payments that cannot be associated with variations in family income. These vari-

---

[3] The second half of the appendix to this chapter outlines the elements of graphs and the graphical analysis of economic data. If you find graphical analysis baffling, you might read this appendix now.

FIGURE 2-2   A Scatter Diagram Relating Taxes Paid to Family Income

The scatter pattern shows a clear tendency for taxes paid to rise with family income. Family income is measured along the horizontal axis, and federal income taxes paid are measured along the vertical axis. Each dot represents a single family in the sample and is located on the graph according to the family's income and taxes paid. The dots fall mainly within a narrow, rising band, suggesting the existence of a systematic relationship between income and taxes paid. But they do not fall along a single line, which suggests that things other than family income affect taxes paid. The data are for 1979. (Negative amounts of tax liability arise because of such things as capital losses that may be carried forward.)

---

ations in tax payments occur mainly for two reasons. First, factors other than income influence tax payments, and some of these other factors will undoubtedly have varied among the families in the sample. Second, there will inevitably be some errors in measurement. For example, a family might have incorrectly reported its tax payments to the person who collected our data.

Cross-classification table.   A cross-classification table provides another way to examine the hypothesis that tax payments vary directly with income. Table 2-1 cross-classifies families by their income and their

TABLE 2-1   Federal Tax Payments Cross-Classified by Family Income

Annual family income	Average income tax payment	Number of families
Less than $10,000	$ 70	38
$ 10,000–19,999	893	76
20,000–29,999	2,470	42
30,000–39,999	4,205	28
40,000–99,999	7,755	28
100,000 or more	—	None

Tax payments tend to increase as family income increases. The data on 212 families are grouped into the income classes shown in the first column. The average tax payment for families in each income group is calculated and listed in the second column. When we read down this second column, we find an unbroken rise in tax payments. This cross-classification reduces 212 individual observations to a mere 5. More (or less) detail could have been preserved by varying the size of the income classes used in the first column.

average tax payments. At the loss of considerable detail, the table makes clear the general tendency for tax payments to rise as income rises.

Regression Analysis

While both the scatter diagram and the cross-classification table reflect the general relationship between federal income tax payments and family income, neither characterizes what the precise relationship is. **Regression analysis,** a widely used technique, provides quantitative measures of what the relationship between two variables is and how closely it holds.[4] It employs a **regression equation** that represents the best estimate of the *average* relationship between the variables being tested. The equation can be used in this case to describe the tendency for higher family income to be associated with higher tax payments.[5]

[4] The detailed discussion of techniques and conditions that must hold for the technique to be valid is left to courses in statistics and econometrics.

[5] The equation of a straight line fitted to the data shown in Figure 2-2 is $T = -1,924 + 0.19Y$, where T is taxes paid and Y is income in thousands of dollars per year. The equation shows that for every increase of $1,000 in family income, taxes paid tend to increase by $190.

A measure of how closely the relationship holds can be obtained by calculating the percentage of the variance in federal tax payments that can be accounted for by variations in household income.[6] This measure is called the **coefficient of determination** (r^2). For our sample $r^2 = 0.734$. This number tells us that in this case 73.4 percent of the variance in tax payments can be "explained" by associating it with variations in family incomes.

A *significance test* can be applied to determine the odds that the relation discovered in the sample does not exist for the whole population but has arisen by chance because the families selected happen not to be representative of the entire set of American families. It turns out that in this example there is less than one chance in a million that the rising pattern of dots shown in Figure 2-2 would have been observed if there were no positive association between income and tax payments for U.S. families. We conclude with less than one chance in a million of being wrong that the hypothesis that tax payments and family income are positively related is correct. Statistically the relationship is said to be *significant*.

Extending the Analysis to Three Variables

The scatter diagram and the regression equation show that *all* the variation in income tax payments cannot be accounted for by observed variations in family income. If it could, all the dots would lie on a line, and r^2 would equal 1.0. Since they do not, some other factors must influence tax payments. Why might one family with an income of $12,000 pay 20 percent more in income taxes than another family with the same income?

One reason is difference in family size, for American tax laws provide exemptions based on the number of family members. (There will be other reasons, too, such as differences in itemized deductions for medical expenses or charitable donations.) We anticipate that family size will be an important second reason. The survey also collected data on family size, which we now use.

There are now *three* observations for each of the

[6] *Variance* is a precise statistical measure of the amount of variability (dispersion) in a set of data.

TABLE 2-2   Federal Tax Payments Cross-Classified by Family Income and Family Size

Annual family income	Number of family members		
	3 or less	4 or 5	6 or more
$ 0–9,999	$ 175	$ 142	$ 26
10,000–19,999	1,028	995	507
20,000–29,999	2,950	2,491	935
30,000–39,999	5,349	3,802	2,372
40,000–99,999	9,459	8,624	4,193
100,000 or more	None in the sample		

Tax payments tend to vary positively with family income and negatively with family size.   Each row in the table shows the effect of family size on tax payments for a given level of income. For example, reading across the second row shows that families with incomes between $10,000 and $20,000 paid an average of $1,028 if the family had less than 4 members, $995 if the family had 4 or 5 members, and $507 if the family had 6 or more members. The declining numbers across each row show that for each income group tax payments tend to decline as family size increases. Each column on the table shows the effect of income on tax payments for a given family size. The increase in taxes paid as we move down each column shows that tax payments increase with family income.

---

212 families: annual income, federal income tax payments, and family size. How should these data be handled? The scatter diagram technique is not available because the relation among three sets of data cannot conveniently be shown on a two-dimensional graph.

The data may, however, be classified into groups once again. This time we are testing two variables that are thought to influence tax payments, and the data have to be cross-classified in a more complicated manner, as shown in Table 2-2.

The table can be used to hold one variable roughly constant while allowing another to vary. Reading across each row, we see that income is held constant within a specified range and family size is varied; reading down each column, we see that size of family is held constant within a specified range and income is varied.

To estimate a numerical relation among family income, family size, and tax payments, **multiple**

regression analysis is used.[7] This type of analysis allows estimation of both the separate and joint effects on tax payments of variations in family size and variations in income by fitting to the data an equation that "best" describes them. It also permits the measurement of the proportion of the total variation in tax payments that can be explained by associating it with variations both in income and family size. Finally, it permits the use of significance tests to determine how likely it is that the relations found in the sample are the result of chance and thus do not reflect a similar relationship for all U.S. families. Chance plays a role because by bad luck an unrepresentative sample of families might have been chosen.

The Decision to Reject or Accept

In general, a hypothesis can never be proven or refuted with absolute certainty, no matter how many observations are made. Those who are interested in pursuing this matter will find further discussion in Box 2-3.

Although we can never be certain, we do have to make decisions. To do so it is necessary to accept some hypotheses (to act as if they were proven) and reject some hypotheses (to act as if they were refuted). Just as a jury can make two kinds of errors (finding an innocent person guilty or letting a guilty person go free) so can statistical decision makers make two kinds of errors. They can reject hypotheses that are true, and they can accept hypotheses that are false. Luckily, like a jury, they can also make correct decisions—and indeed they expect to do so most of the time.

Although the possibility of error cannot be eliminated in statistics, it can be controlled.

The method of control is to decide in advance how large a risk to take of accepting a hypothesis

---

[7] Details must be left to a course in statistics. The regression equation for our example is $T = -733 + .197Y - 344F$, where F is the number of family members. On average, an additional family member decreases taxes paid by $344. R^2, the coefficient of determination in multiple regression analysis, is .774. Comparison with the previous $r^2 = .734$ shows that adding family size to the analysis increased the percentage of variance explained from 73.4 percent to 77.4 percent.

that is in fact false.[8] Conventionally in statistics this risk is often set at 5 percent or 1 percent. When the 5 percent cutoff point is used, we will accept the hypothesis if the results that appear to establish it could have happened by chance no more than 1 time in 20. Using the 1 percent decision rule gives the hypothesis a sterner test. A hypothesis is accepted only if the results that appear to establish it could have happened by chance no more than 1 time in 100.

Consider the hypothesis that a certain coin is "loaded," favoring heads over tails. The coin is flipped 100 times and comes up heads 53 times. While this result is not inconsistent with the hypothesis, such an unbalanced result could happen by chance more than 22 percent of the time. Thus the hypothesis of a head-biased coin would not be accepted using either a 1 percent or a 5 percent cutoff. Had the experiment produced 65 heads and 35 tails, a result that would occur by chance less than 1 percent of the time, we would (given a 1 percent or a 5 percent cutoff) accept the hypothesis of a loaded coin.[9]

When action must be taken, some rule of thumb is necessary. But it is important to understand, first, that no one can ever be certain about being right in rejecting any hypothesis and, second, that there is nothing magical about arbitrary cutoff points. Some cutoff point must be used whenever decisions have to be made.

Finally, recall that the rejection of a hypothesis is seldom the end of inquiry. Decisions can be reversed should new evidence come to light. Often the result of a statistical test of a theory is to suggest a new hypothesis that "fits the facts" better than the old one. Indeed, in some cases just looking at a scatter diagram or making a regression analysis uncovers apparent relations that no one anticipated and leads economists to formulate a new hypothesis.

Economics As a Developing Science

Economics is like other sciences in at least two respects. First, there are many observations of the world for which there are, at the moment, no fully satisfactory theoretical explanations. Second, there are many predictions that no one has yet satisfactorily tested. Serious students of economics must not expect to find a set of answers to all their questions as they progress in their study. Often they must expect to encounter nothing more than a set of problems that provides an agenda for further research. Even when they do find answers to problems, they should accept these answers as tentative and ask even of the most time-honored theory, "What observations would be in conflict with this theory?"

Economics is still a young science. On the one hand, economists know a good deal about the behavior of the economy. On the other hand, many problems are almost untouched. Students who decide to specialize in economics may find themselves, only a few years from now, publishing a theory to account for some of the problems mentioned in this book; or they may end up making a set of observations that will upset some venerable theory described in these pages.

A final word of warning: Having counseled a constructive disrespect for the authority of accepted theory, it is necessary to warn against adopting an approach that is too cavalier. No respect attaches to the person who says, "This theory is for the birds; it is *obviously* wrong." This is too cheap. To criticize a theory effectively on empirical grounds, one must demonstrate, by a careful set of observations, that some aspect of the theory is contradicted by the facts. This is a task worth attempting, but it is seldom easily accomplished.

---

[8] Return to the jury analogy: Our notion of a person's being innocent unless the jury is persuaded of guilt "beyond a reasonable doubt" rests on our wishing to take only a small risk of accepting the hypothesis of guilt if the person being tried is in fact innocent.

[9] The actual statistical testing process is more complex than this example suggests but must be left to a course in statistics.

Summary

1. It is possible, and fruitful, to distinguish between positive and normative statements. Positive statements concern what is, was, or will be, while normative statements concern what ought to be. Disagreements over positive, testable statements are appropriately settled by an appeal to the facts. Disagreements over normative statements can never be settled in this way.

2. The success of scientific inquiry depends on separating positive questions about the way the world works from normative questions about how one would like the world to work, formulating positive questions precisely enough so that they can be settled by an appeal to evidence, and then finding means of gathering the necessary evidence.

3. Some people feel that although natural phenomena can be subject to scientific inquiry and "laws" of behavior, human phenomena cannot. The evidence, however, is otherwise. Social scientists have observed many stable human behavior patterns. These form the basis for successful predictions of how people will behave under certain conditions.

4. The fact that people sometimes act strangely, even capriciously, does not destroy the possibility of scientific study of group behavior. The odd and inexplicable things that one person does will tend to cancel out the odd and inexplicable things that another person does.

5. Theories are designed to give meaning and coherence to observed sequences of events. A theory consists of a set of definitions of the variables to be employed, a set of assumptions under which the theory is meant to apply, and a set of hypotheses about how things behave. Any theory has certain logical implications that must be true if the theory is true. These are the theory's predictions.

6. A theory provides predictions of the type "*if* one event occurs, *then* another event will also occur." An important method of testing theories is to confront their predictions with evidence. The progress of any science lies in finding better explanations of events than are now available. Thus, in any developing science, one must expect to discard present theories and replace them with demonstrably superior alternatives.

7. Theories are tested by checking their predictions against evidence. In some sciences these tests can be conducted under laboratory conditions where only one thing changes at a time. In other sciences testing must be done using the data produced by the world of ordinary events. Modern statistical analysis is designed to test hypotheses when many variables are changing at once.

8. Sample data are often used in testing economic theories. If the sample is random, the probability that the measured characteristics of the sample will be misleading (because of the unlucky choice of a nonrepresentative sample) can be calculated.

9. Scatter diagrams or simple cross-classification tables are devices for discovering systematic relationships between two variables. Regres-

sion analysis permits more specific measurement of the relationship: what it is, how closely it holds, and whether or not it is "significant."

10. Hypotheses involving several variables require more sophisticated statistical techniques such as the use of complex cross-classification tables and multiple regression analysis. These techniques attempt to identify the separate and joint effects of several variables on one another.

11. Methods of graphing economic observations and the use of functional relations are discussed in more detail in the appendix to this chapter.

Topics for Review

Positive and normative statements
Testable statements
The law of large numbers and the predictability of human behavior
Variables, assumptions, and predictions in theorizing
Endogenous and exogenous variables
Stock and flow variables
Functional relations
Prediction versus prophecy
The scientific approach
Role of statistical analysis: measurement and testing
Scatter diagrams
Cross-classification tables
Rejection and acceptance of hypotheses

Discussion Questions

1. A baby doesn't "know" of the theory of gravity, yet in walking and eating the child soon learns to use its principles. Distinguish between behavior and the explanation of behavior. Does a business executive or a farmer have to understand economic theory to behave in a pattern consistent with economic theory?

2. "If human behavior were completely capricious and unpredictable, life insurance could not be a profitable business." Explain. Can you think of any businesses that do *not* depend on predictable human behavior?

3. Write five statements about inflation. (It does not matter whether the statements are correct, but you should confine yourself to those you think might be correct.) Classify each statement as positive or normative. If your list contains only one type of statement, try to add a sixth statement of the other type.

4. Each of the following unrealistic assumptions is sometimes made. See if you can visualize situations in which each of them might be useful.
   a. The earth is a plane.
   b. There are no differences between men and women.
   c. There is no tomorrow.
   d. People are wholly selfish.

5. "The following theory of wage determination proceeds on the assumption that labor unions do not exist." Of what use can such a theory be in the United States today?

6. What may first appear to be untestable statements can often be reworded so that they can be tested by an appeal to evidence. How might you do that with respect to each of the following assertions?
   a. The American economic system is the best in the world.
   b. The provision of free medical care for more and more people will inevitably end in socialized medicine for all, and socialized medicine will destroy our standards of medical practice by destroying the doctor's incentive to do his or her job well.
   c. Robotics ought to be outlawed, because it will destroy the future of the working classes.
   d. Inflation is eroding the standard of living of the American worker and undermining the integrity of the family.

7. "The simplest way to see that capital punishment is a strong deterrent to murder is to ask yourself whether you might be more inclined to commit murder if you knew in advance that you ran no risk of ending in the electric chair, the gas chamber, or on the gallows." Comment on the methodology of social investigation implied by this statement. What alternative approach would you suggest?

8. Since 1979, when the data used in Figure 2-2 were collected, federal tax laws have changed, lowering the tax rates that apply to higher incomes. How would you expect this development to change a scatter diagram of income and tax payments? Would you expect it to change the regression results? Do these changes lead you to reject the conclusions of the analysis of the 1979 data?

9. There are hundreds of eyewitnesses to the existence of flying saucers and other UFOs. There are films and eyewitness accounts of Nessie, the Loch Ness monster. Are you persuaded of their existence? If not, what would it take to persuade you? If so, what would it take to make you change your mind?

10. Relate the role of the law of large numbers to the statistical idea that one can test hypotheses by using average relationships based on random samples.

Expressing and Graphing Relations Among Variables

The idea of relationships among variables is one of the basic notions behind all science. Many such relations are found in economics.

Expressing Relations: Correspondences and Functions

When mathematicians want to say that there is a relation between two variables, let us call them X and Y, they say that there is a correspondence between them. When the relation is such that for every value of X there is one and only one value of Y, mathematicians say that Y is a function of X. In what follows we confine ourselves to the subclass of correspondences that are functions.

Consider two examples, one from a natural science and one from economics. The gravitational attraction of two bodies depends on their mass and on the distance separating them, attraction increasing with size and diminishing with distance; the amount of a commodity that people would like to buy depends on (among other things) the price of the commodity, purchases increasing as price falls. Thus gravitational attraction is a function of the mass of the two bodies concerned and the distance between them, and the quantity of a product demanded is a function of the price of the product.

One of the virtues of mathematics is that it permits the concise expression of ideas that would otherwise require long, drawn-out verbal statements. There are two steps in giving compact symbolic expression to functional relations. First, each variable is given a symbol. Second, a symbol is designated to express the idea of one variable's dependence on another. Thus, if G equals gravitational attraction, M equals the mass of two bodies, and d equals distance between the two bodies, we may write

$$G = f(M, d)$$

where f is read "is a function of" and means "is uniquely related to." The whole equation states a hypothesis and is read "gravitational attraction is a function of the mass of the two bodies concerned and the distance between them." The same hypothesis can be written as

$$G = G(M, d)$$

This is read in exactly the same way and means the same thing as the previous expression. Instead of using f to represent "a function of," the left-hand symbol, G, is repeated.[1]

The hypothesis about desired purchases and price can be written

$$q = f(p)$$

or

$$q = q(p)$$

where q stands for the quantity people wish to purchase of some commodity and p is the price of the commodity. The expression says that the quantity of some commodity that people desire to purchase is a function of its price. The alternative way of writing this merely uses a different letter to stand for the same functional relation between p and q.

Functional Forms: Precise Relations Among Variables

The expression $Y = Y(X)$ merely states that the variables Y and X are related; it says nothing about the form that this relation takes. Usually the hypothesis to be expressed says more than that. Does

---

[1] Any convenient symbol may be used on the right-hand side before the parenthesis to mean "a function of." The repetition of the left-hand symbol may be convenient in reminding us of what is a function of what.

Y increase as X increases? Does Y decrease as X increases? Or is the relation more complicated? Take a very simple example, where Y is the length of a board in feet, and X is the length of the same board in yards. Quite clearly, $Y = Y(X)$. Further, in this case the exact form of the function is known, for length in feet (Y) is exactly three times the length in yards (X), so we may write $Y = 3X$.

This relation is a definitional one, for the length of something measured in feet is defined to be three times its length measured in yards. It is nonetheless useful to have a way of writing relationships that are definitionally true. The expression $Y = 3X$ specifies the exact form of the relation between Y and X and provides a rule whereby, if we have the value of one, we can calculate the value of the other.

Now consider a second example. Let C stand for consumption expenditure, the total amount spent on purchasing goods and services by all American households during a year. Let Y_d stand for the total amount of income that these households had available to spend during the year. We might state the hypothesis that

$C = f(Y_d)$

and, even more specifically,

$C = 0.8Y_d$

The first expression gives the hypothesis that the total consumption expenditure of households depends on their income. The second expression says, more specifically, that total consumption expenditure is 80 percent of the total available for spending. The second equation expresses a specific hypothesis about the relation between two observable magnitudes. There is no reason why it *must* be true; it may be consistent or inconsistent with the facts. This is a matter for testing. However, the equation is a concise statement of a particular hypothesis.

Thus the general view that there is a functional relation between Y and X is denoted by $Y = f(X)$, whereas any precise relation is expressed by a particular equation such as $Y = 2X$, $Y = 4X^2$, or $Y = X + 2.0X^2 + 0.5X^3$.

If Y increases as X increases (e.g., $Y = 10 + 2X$), we say that Y is an *increasing function* of X, or that Y and X *vary positively* with each other. If Y decreases as X increases (e.g., $Y = 10 - 2X$), we

say that Y is a *decreasing function* of X or that Y and X *vary negatively* with each other. Y varying negatively with X merely means that Y changes in the opposite direction from X.

Error Terms in Economic Hypotheses

Expressing hypotheses in the form of functions is misleading in one respect. When we say that the world behaves so that $Y = f(X)$, we do not expect that knowing X will tell us *exactly* what Y will be, but only that it will tell us what Y will be *within some margin of error*.

This error in predicting Y from a knowledge of X arises for two distinct reasons. First, there may be other variables that also affect Y. When, for example, we say that the quantity of butter people wish to purchase is a function of the price of butter, $q_b = f(p_b)$, we know that other factors will also influence this demand. A change in the price of margarine will certainly affect the demand for butter, even though the price of butter does not change. Thus, we do not expect to find a perfect relation between q_b and p_b that will allow us to predict q_b exactly from a knowledge of p_b.

Second, variables can never be measured exactly. Even if X is the only cause of Y, measurements will give various Ys corresponding to the same X. In the case of the demand for butter, errors of measurement might not be large. In other cases, errors can be substantial—as, for example, in the case of a relation between the total consumption expenditure of all American households and their total income. The measurements of consumption and income may be subject to quite wide margins of error, and various values of consumption associated with the same measured value of income may be observed, not because consumption is varying independently of income, but because the error of measurement is varying from period to period.

When we say Y is a function of X, we appear to say Y is completely determined by X. Instead of the deterministic formulation

$Y = f(X)$

it would be more accurate to write

$Y = f(X, \epsilon)$

FIGURE 2A-1   A Coordinate Graph

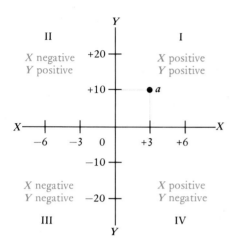

The axes divide the total space into four quadrants according to the signs of the variables. In the upper right-hand quadrant, both X and Y are greater than zero; this is usually called the *positive quadrant*. Point a has *coordinates* $Y = 10$ and $X = 3$ in the coordinate graph. These coordinates *define* point a.

where ϵ, the Greek letter epsilon, represents an **error term**.[2] Such a term indicates that the observed value of Y will differ from the value predicted by the functional relation between Y and X. Divergences will occur both because of observational errors and because of neglected variables. While economists always mean this, they usually do not say so.

The deterministic formulation is a simplification; an error term is really present in all assumed and observed functional relations in economics.

Graphing Relations Among Variables

The popular saying "The facts speak for themselves" is almost always wrong when there are many facts. Theories are needed to explain how facts are linked together, and summary measures are needed to assist

[2] The relationship with the error term in it is frequently written $Y = f(X) + \epsilon$.

in sorting out what it is that facts show in relation to theories. The simplest means of providing compact summaries of a large number of observations is the use of tables and graphs. Graphs play important roles in economics by representing geometrically both observed data and the correspondence among variables that are the subject of economic theory.

Because the surface of a piece of paper is two-dimensional, a graph may readily be used to represent pictorially any correspondence between two variables. Flip through this book and you will see dozens of examples. Figure 2A-1 shows generally how a coordinate grid can permit the representation of any two measurable variables.[3]

Representing Theories on Graphs

Figure 2A-2 shows a simple two-variable graph, which will be analyzed in detail in Chapter 4. For now it is sufficient to notice that the graph permits us to show the relationship between two variables, the *price* of carrots on the vertical axis and the *quantity* of carrots per month on the horizontal axis.[4] The downward-sloping curve, labeled D for a *demand curve,* shows the relationship between the price of carrots and the quantity of carrots buyers wish to purchase.

Figure 2A-3 is very much like Figure 2A-2 but with one difference. It generalizes from the specific example of carrots to an unspecified commodity and focuses on the slope of the demand curve rather than on specific numerical values. Note that the quantity labeled q_0 is associated with the price p_0 while the quantity q_1 is associated with the price p_1.

Straight Lines and Their Slopes

Figure 2A-4 illustrates a variety of straight lines. They differ according to their slopes. **Slope** is defined as the ratio of the vertical change to the corresponding horizontal change as one moves along a curve.

[3] Economics is often concerned only with the positive values of variables, and the graph is confined to the upper right-hand (or "positive") quadrant. Whenever a variable has a negative value, one or more of the other quadrants must be included.

[4] The choice of which variable to put on which axis is discussed in footnote 2 on page 88 and in math note [8] on page 893.

FIGURE 2A-2   The Relationship Between the Price of Carrots and the Quantity of Carrots That Purchasers Wish to Buy: A Numerical Illustration

Quantity of Carrots
(Thousands of Tons Per Month)

A two-dimensional graph can show how two variables are related. The two variables, the price of carrots and the quantity people wish to purchase, are shown by the downward sloping curve labeled D. Particular points on the curve are labeled U through Z. For example, Z shows that at a price of \$120, the demand to purchase carrots is 60,000 tons per month.

FIGURE 2A-3   The Relationship Between the Price of a Commodity and the Quantity of the Commodity That Purchasers Wish to Buy

Quantity

Graphs can illustrate general relationships between variables as well as between specific quantities. Here, in contrast to Figure 2A-2, price and quantity are shown as general variables. The demand curve illustrates a quantitatively unspecified *negative* relationship between price and quantity. For example, at the price p_0 the quantity that purchasers demand is q_0, while at the higher price of p_1 purchasers demand the lower quantity of q_0.

FIGURE 2A-4   Four Straight Lines with Different Slopes

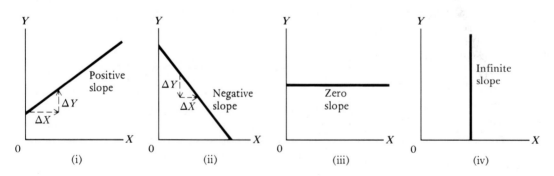

The slope of a straight line is constant, but can vary from one line to another. The direction of slope of a straight line is characterized by the signs of the ratio $\Delta Y/\Delta X$. In (i) that ratio is positive because X and Y vary in the same direction; in (ii) the ratio is negative because X and Y vary in opposite directions; in (iii) it is zero because Y does not change as X increases; in (iv) it is infinite.

FIGURE 2A-5   **Two Straight Lines with Different Slopes**

FIGURE 2A-5   Two Straight Lines with Different Slopes

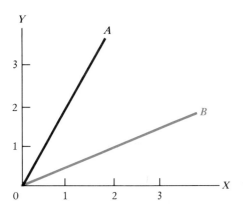

Slope is a quantitative measure. Both lines have positive slopes and thus are similar to Figure 2A-4 (i). But curve *A* is steeper (i.e., has a greater slope) than curve *B*. For each 1-unit increase in *X*, the value of *Y* increases by 2 units along curve *A*, but by only 1/2 unit along curve *B*. The ratio $\Delta Y/\Delta X$ is 2 for curve *A* and 1/2 for curve *B*.

The symbol Δ is used to indicate a change in any variable. Thus ΔX means the change in *X*, and ΔY means the change in *Y*. The ratio $\Delta Y/\Delta X$ is the slope of a straight line. Where both increase or decrease together, the ratio is positive and the line slopes upward to the right, as in (i). Where ΔY and ΔX have the opposite sign, that is, one increases while the other decreases, the ratio is negative and the line slopes downward to the right, as in (ii). Where ΔY does not change, the line is horizontal, as in (iii), and the slope is zero. Where ΔX is zero, the line is vertical, as in (iv), and the slope is often said to be infinite, although the ratio $\Delta Y/X$ is indeterminate. **[1]**[5]

Slope is a quantitative measure, not merely a qualitative one. For example, in Figure 2A-5 two upward-sloping straight lines have different slopes. Line *A* has a slope of 2 ($\Delta Y/\Delta X$ = 2.0); line *B* has a slope of 1/2 ($\Delta Y/\Delta X$ = 0.5).

Curved Lines and Their Slopes

Figure 2A-6 shows four curved lines. The line in (i) is plainly upward sloping and in (ii) downward sloping. The other two change from one to the other, as

[5] Notes giving mathematical demonstrations of the concepts presented in the text are designated by colored reference numbers. These notes can be found beginning on page 892.

FIGURE 2A-6   Four Curved Lines

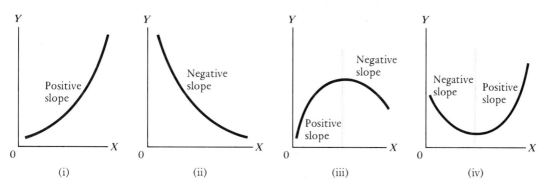

(i)   (ii)   (iii)   (iv)

The slope of a curved line is not constant and may change direction. The slopes of the curves in (i) and (ii) change in size but not direction, whereas those in (iii) and (iv) change in both size and direction. Unlike that of a straight line, the slope of a curved line cannot be defined by a single number because it changes as the value of *X* changes.

FIGURE 2A-7   Defining the Slope of a Curve

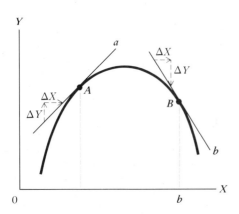

The slope of a curve at any point on the curve is defined by the slope of the straight line that is tangent to the curve at that point. The slope of the curve at point *A* is defined by the slope of the line *a*, which is tangent to the curve at point *A*. The slope of the curve at point *B* is defined by the slope of the tangent line *b*.

the labels indicate. Unlike straight lines, whose slope is the same at every point on the line, the slope of a curve changes. The slope of a curve must be measured at a particular point and is defined as the slope of a straight line that just touches (is tangent to) the straight line at that point. This is illustrated in Figure 2A-7. The slope at point *A* is measured by the slope of the tangent line *a*. The slope at point *B* is measured by the slope of the tangent line *b*.

Graphing Observations

A coordinate space such as shown in Figure 2A-1 can be used to graph the observed values of two variables as well as the theoretical relationships between them. For example, curve *D* in Figure 2A-2 might have arisen as a free-hand line drawn to generalize actual observations of the points labeled *U, V, W, X, Y, Z*. While that graph was not constructed from actual observations, many graphs are. Two of the most important kinds are called *scatter diagrams* and *time series graphs*.

Scatter Diagrams

Scatter diagrams provide a method of graphing any number of *paired* observations made on two variables. In Chapter 2 data for family income and taxes paid for a sample of 212 American families were studied. Figure 2-2 on page 26 shows these data on a scatter diagram. Income is measured on the horizontal axis and taxes paid on the vertical axis. Any point in the diagram represents a particular family's income combined with the tax payment of that family. Thus each family for which there are observations can be represented on the diagram by a dot, the labels indicate.

TABLE 2A-1   Income and Consumption, 1955–1982
(1982 dollars)

Year	Disposable personal income per capita	Personal consumption expenditures per capita
1955	$ 5,714	$5,287
1956	5,881	5,349
1957	5,909	5,370
1958	5,908	5,357
1959	6,027	5,531
1960	6,036	5,561
1961	6,113	5,579
1962	6,271	5,729
1963	6,378	5,855
1964	6,727	6,099
1965	7,027	6,362
1966	7,280	6,607
1967	7,513	6,730
1968	7,728	7,003
1969	7,891	7,185
1970	8,134	7,275
1971	8,322	7,409
1972	8,562	7,726
1973	9,042	7,972
1974	8,867	7,826
1975	8,944	7,926
1976	9,175	8,272
1977	9,381	8,551
1978	9,735	8,808
1979	9,829	8,904
1980	9,723	8,784
1981	9,773	8,798
1982	9,732	8,825
1983	9,952	9,148
1984	10,427	9,462
1985	10,504	9,682

Source: Economic Report of the President, 1986.

FIGURE 2A-8   A Scatter Diagram Relating Consumption and Disposable Income

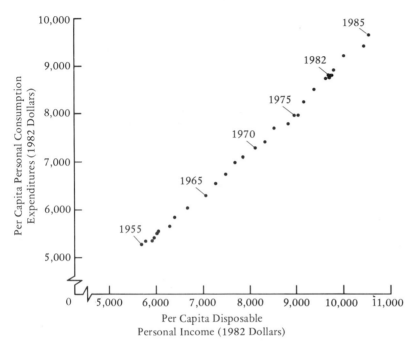

This scatter diagram shows paired values of two variables. The data of Table 2A-1 are plotted here. Each dot shows the values of per capita personal consumption expenditures and per capita disposable personal income for a given year. A close, positive, linear relationship between the two variables is established. Note that in this diagram the axes are shown with a break in them to indicate that not all the values of the variables between $4,000 and zero are given. Since no *observations* occurred in those ranges, it was unnecessary to provide space for them.

the coordinates of which indicate the family's income and the amount of taxes it paid in 1979.

The scatter diagram is useful because if there is a simple relation between the two variables, it will be apparent to the eye once the data are plotted. Figure 2-2, for example, makes it apparent that more taxes tend to be paid as income rises. It also made it apparent that the relation between taxes and income is approximately linear. A rising straight line fits the data reasonably well between about $10,000 and $40,000 of income. Above $40,000 and below $10,000 the line does not fit the data as well, but since more than two-thirds of the families sampled had incomes in the $10,000 to $40,000 range, the straight line provides a fairly good description of the basic relationship for middle income families.

The diagram also gives some idea of the strength of the relation. If income were the only determinant of taxes paid, all of the dots would cluster closely around a line or a smooth curve; as it is, the points are somewhat scattered and particular incomes are

often represented by several households, each with different amounts of taxes paid.

Time-Series Data

The data used in the example of Figure 2-2 are **cross-sectional data.** The incomes and taxes paid of different households are compared over a single period of time—the year 1979. Scatter diagrams may also be drawn for a number of observations taken on two variables at successive periods of time.

For example, if one wanted to know whether there was any simple relation between personal income and personal consumption in the United States between 1950 and 1985, data would be collected for the levels of personal income and expenditure per capita in each year from 1950 to 1985, as is done in Table 2A-1. This information could be plotted on a scatter diagram, with income on the *X* axis and consumption on the *Y* axis. The data are plotted in Figure 2A-8, and they do indeed suggest a systematic linear relation.

FIGURE 2A-9   A Time Series of Consumption Expenditures, 1950–1985

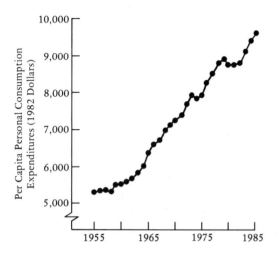

A time series plots values of a single variable in chronological order. The graph shows that, with only minor interruptions, consumption measured in 1982 dollars rose from 1950 to 1985. The data are given in the last column of Table 2A-1.

FIGURE 2A-10   The Difference Between Natural and Ratio Scales

(i) A natural scale

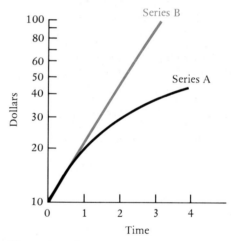

(ii) A ratio scale

On a natural scale equal distances represent equal amounts; on a ratio scale equal distances represent equal percentage changes. The two series in Table 2A-2 are plotted in each chart. Series A, which grows at a constant absolute amount, is shown by a straight line on a natural scale, but by a curve of diminishing slope on a ratio scale because the same absolute growth represents a decreasing percentage growth. Series B, which grows at a rising absolute rate but a constant percentage rate, is shown by a curve of increasing slope on a natural scale, but by a straight line on a ratio scale.

Figure 2A-8 is a scatter diagram of observations taken over successive periods of time. Such data are called **time-series data,** and plotting them on a scatter diagram involves no new technique. When cross-sectional data are plotted, each point gives the values of two variables for a particular unit (say, a family); when time-series data are plotted, each point tells the values of two variables for a particular year.

Instead of studying the relation between income and consumption suggested in the previous paragraph, a study of the pattern of the changes in either one of these variables over time could be made. Figure 2A-9 shows this information for consumption.

FIGURE 2A-11   A Contour Map of a Small Mountain

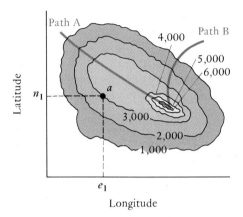

A contour map shows three variables in two-dimensional space. This familiar kind of three-variable graph shows latitude and longitude on the axes and altitude on the contour lines. The contour line labeled 1,000 connects all locations with an altitude of 1,000 feet, that labeled 2,000 connects those with an altitude of 2,000 feet, and so forth. Point *a*, for example, has a latitude n_1, a longitude e_1, and an altitude of 3,000 feet. Where the lines are closely bunched, they represent a steep ascent; where they are far apart, a gradual one. Clearly, path A is a gentler climb from 3,000 to 4,000 feet on this mountain than path B.

FIGURE 2A-12   Three Variables Shown in Two Dimensions

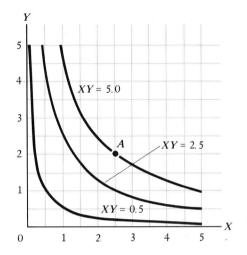

This chart illustrates examples of the three-variable function $XY = a$. The function $XY = a$ is called a *rectangular hyperbola*. The figure shows three members of the family. For example, point *A* represents $Y = 2.0$, $X = 2.5$, and $a = 5.0$

TABLE 2A-2   Two Series

Time period	Series A	Series B
0	$10	$ 10
1	18	20
2	26	40
3	34	80
4	42	160

Series A shows constant absolute growth ($8 per period), but declining percentage growth. Series B shows constant percentage growth (100 percent per period), but rising absolute growth.

Time is one variable, consumption expenditure the other. But time is a special variable; the order in which successive events happen is important. The year 1985 followed 1984; they were not two independent and unrelated years. In contrast, two randomly selected households are independent and unrelated. For this reason it is customary to draw in the line segments connecting the successive points, as has been done in Figure 2A-9.

Such a figure is called a *time-series graph* or a *time series*. This kind of graph makes it easy to see if the variable being considered has varied in a systematic way over the years or if its behavior has been more or less erratic.

Ratio (Logarithmic) Scales

All of the above graphs use axes that plot numbers on a natural arithmetic scale, with distances between two values shown by the size of the numerical difference. If *proportionate* rather than *absolute* changes in variables are important, it is more revealing to use a ratio scale rather than a natural scale. On a **natural scale** the distance between numbers is proportionate to the absolute difference between those numbers. Thus 200 is placed halfway between 100 and 300. On a **ratio scale** the distance between numbers is proportionate to the percentage difference between the two numbers (which can also be measured as the absolute difference between their logarithms). Equal distances anywhere on a ratio scale represent equal percentage changes rather than equal absolute changes. On a ratio scale the distance between 100 and 200 is the same as the distance between 200 and 400, between 1,000 and 2,000, and between any two numbers that stand in the ratio 1:2 to each other. For obvious reasons a ratio scale is also called a **logarithmic scale.**

Table 2A-2 shows two series, one growing at a constant absolute amount of 8 units per period and the other growing at a constant rate of 100 percent per period. In Figure 2A-10 the series are plotted first on a natural scale, then on a ratio scale. The natural scale makes it easy for the eye to judge absolute variations, and the logarithmic scale makes it easy for the eye to judge proportionate variations.[6]

Graphing Three Variables in Two Dimensions

Often we want to show graphically more than two dimensions. For example, a topographic map seeks to show latitude, longitude, and altitude on a two-dimensional page. This is done by using contour lines, as in Figure 2A-11. Now consider the function $XY = a$, where X, Y, and a are variables. Figure 2A-12 plots this function for three different values of a. The variables X and Y are represented on the two axes. The variable a is represented by the labels on the curves. Several examples of this procedure occur throughout the book (see, for example, the discussion of indifference curves in Chapter 8 and isoquants in the appendix to Chapter 11.

---

[6] Graphs with a ratio scale on one axis and a natural scale on the other are frequently encountered in economics. In the cases just illustrated there is a ratio scale on the vertical axis and a natural scale on the horizontal (or time) axis. Such graphs are often called *semi-log* graphs. In scientific work graphs with ratio scales on both axes are frequently encountered. Such graphs are often referred to as *double-log* graphs.

3

An Overview of the Economy

The Evolution of Market Economies

The central economic problem of our times—choice under conditions of scarcity—has been with us about 10,000 years. It began with the original agricultural revolution, when human beings first found it possible to stay in one place and survive. Gradually abandoning their nomadic life of hunting and food gathering, people settled down to tend crops that they had learned to plant and animals that they had learned to domesticate. Since that time all societies have faced the problem of choice under conditions of scarcity.

Surplus, Specialization, and Trade

Along with permanent settlement, the agricultural revolution brought surplus production. Farmers could produce substantially more than they needed for survival. The agricultural surplus allowed the creation of new occupations and thus new economic and social classes such as artisans, soldiers, priests, and government officials. Freed from having to grow their own food, these new classes turned their talents to performing specialized services and producing goods other than food. They also produced more than they themselves needed, so they traded the excess to obtain whatever other goods they required.

The allocation of different jobs to different people is called **specialization of labor.** Specialization has proven extraordinarily efficient compared with self-sufficiency for at least two reasons. First, individual talents and abilities differ, and specialization allows each person to do the job he or she can do relatively best, while leaving everything else to be done by others. Second, a person who concentrates on one activity becomes better at it than could a jack-of-all-trades.

The exchange of goods and services in early societies commonly took place by simple mutual agreement among neighbors. In the course of time, however, trading became centered in particular gathering places called markets. Today we use the term **market economy** to refer to a society in which people specialize in productive activities and meet most of their material wants through exchanges voluntarily agreed upon by the contracting parties.

43

Specialization must be accompanied by trade. People who produce only one thing must trade most of it to obtain all the other things they require.

The earliest market economies depended on **barter,** the trading of goods directly for other goods. But barter can be a costly process in terms of time spent searching out satisfactory exchanges. The evolution of money made trade easier. Money eliminates the inconvenience of barter by allowing the two sides of the barter transaction to be separated. If a farmer has wheat and wants a hammer, he does not have to search for an individual who has a hammer and wants wheat. He merely has to find someone who wants wheat. The farmer takes money in exchange, then finds another person who wishes to trade a hammer and swaps the money for the hammer.

By eliminating the need for barter, money greatly facilitates trade and specialization.

The Division of Labor

Market transactions in early economies mainly involved consumption goods. Producers specialized in making a commodity and then traded it for the other products they needed. The labor services required to make the product would usually be provided by the makers themselves, by apprentices learning to be craftsmen, or by slaves. Over the past several hundred years, many technical advances in methods of production have made it efficient to organize agriculture and industry on a large scale. These technical developments have made use of what is called the **division of labor,** which is a further step in the specialization of labor. This term refers to specialization within the production process of a particular commodity. The labor involved is divided into a series of repetitive tasks, and each individual does a single task that may be just one of hundreds of tasks necessary to produce the commodity. Today it is possible for an individual to work on a production line without knowing what commodity emerges at the end of that line!

To gain the advantages of the division of labor, it became necessary to organize production in large factories. With this development urban workers lost their status as craftsmen and became members of the working class, wholly dependent on their ability to sell their labor to factory owners, and lacking a plot of land to fall back on for subsistence in times of need. The day of small craftsmen who made and sold their own goods was over. Today's typical workers do not earn their incomes by selling commodities they personally have produced; rather, they sell their labor services to firms and receive money wages in return. They have increasingly become cogs in a machine they do not fully understand or control. Adam Smith, the eighteenth century Scottish political economist, was the first to develop the idea of the division of labor, as discussed in Box 3-1.

Markets and Resource Allocation

The term **resource allocation** refers to the distribution of the available factors of production among the various uses to which they might be put. There are not enough resources to produce all the goods and services that could be consumed. It is therefore necessary to allocate the available resources among their various possible uses and in so doing to choose what to produce and what not to produce. In a market economy millions of consumers decide what commodities to buy and in what quantities; a vast number of firms produce these commodities and buy the factor services that are needed to make them; and millions of factor owners decide to whom they will sell these services. These individual decisions collectively determine the economy's allocation of resources.

In a market economy the allocation of resources is the outcome of countless independent decisions made by consumers and producers, all acting through the medium of markets.

Our main objective in this chapter is to provide an overview of this market mechanism.

The Decision Makers

Economics is about the behavior of people. Much that we observe in the world and that economists assume in their theories can be traced back to deci-

BOX 3-1

The Division of Labor

Adam Smith begins *The Wealth of Nations* (1776) with a long study of the division of labor.

The greatest improvements in the productive powers of labour . . . have been the effects of the division of labour.

To take an example . . . the trade of the pinmaker; a workman not educated to this business (which the division of labour has rendered a distinct trade), nor acquainted with the use of the machinery employed in it could scarce, perhaps, with his utmost industry, make one pin in a day, and certainly could not make twenty. But in the way in which this business is now carried on . . . it is divided into a number of branches. . . . One man draws out the wire, another straightens it, a third cuts it, a fourth points it, a fifth grinds it at the top for receiving the head; to make the head requires two or three distinct operations; to put it on, is a peculiar business, to whiten the pins is another; it is even a trade by itself to put them into the paper; and the important business of making a pin is, in this manner, divided into about eighteen distinct operations, which, in some manufactories, are all performed by distinct hands, though in others the same man will sometimes perform two or three of them.

Smith observes that even in smallish factories, where the division of labor is exploited only in part, output is as high as 4,800 pins per person per day!

Later Smith discusses the general importance of the division of labor and the forces that limit its application.

Each animal is still obliged to support and defend itself, separately and independently, and derives no sort of advantage from that variety of talents with which nature has distinguished its fellows. Among men, on the contrary, the most dissimilar geniuses are of use to one another; the different produces of their respective talents, by the general disposition to truck, barter, and exchange, being brought, as it were, into a common stock, where every man may purchase whatever part of the produce of other men's talents he has occasion for.

As it is the power of exchanging that gives occasion to the division of labour, so the extent of this division must always be limited by the extent of that power, or, in other words, by the extent of the market. When the market is very small, no person can have any encouragement to dedicate himself entirely to one employment for want [i.e., lack] of the power to exchange all that surplus part of the produce of his own labour, which is over and above his own consumption, for such parts of the produce of other men's labour as he has occasion for.

Smith notes that there is no point in specializing to produce a large quantity of pins, or anything else, unless there are enough persons making other commodities to provide a market for all the pins that are produced. Thus, the larger the market, the greater the scope for the division of labor and the higher the resulting opportunities for efficient production.

---

sions made by individuals. There are millions of individuals in most economies. To make a systematic study of their behavior more manageable, we categorize them into three important groups: households, firms, and the government.[1] These groups are economic theory's cast of characters, and the market is the stage on which their play is enacted.

[1] Although in basic economic theory we can get away with three sets of decision makers, it is worth noting that there are others. Probably the most important are such nonprofit organizations as private universities and hospitals, charities such as the American Cancer Society, and funding organizations such as the Ford Foundation. These bodies are responsible for allocating some of the economy's resources.

Households

A **household** is defined as all the people who live under one roof and who make, or are subject to others making for them, joint financial decisions. The members of households are often referred to as consumers. Economic theory gives households a number of attributes.

First, economists assume that each household makes consistent decisions, as though it were composed of a single individual. Thus economists ignore many interesting problems of how the household reaches its decisions. Family conflicts and the moral and legal problems concerning parental control over minors are dealt with by other social sciences.[2] These problems are avoided in economics by the assumption that the household is the basic decision-making atom of consumption behavior.

Second, economists assume that each household is consistently attempting to achieve *maximum satisfaction* or *well-being* or *utility,* as the concept is variously called. The household tries to do this within the limitations of its available resources.

Third, economists assume that households are the principal owners of factors of production. They sell the services of these factors to firms and receive their incomes in return. It is assumed that in making these decisions on how much to sell and to whom to sell it, each household seeks to maximize its utility.

Firms

A **firm** is defined as the unit that employs factors of production to produce commodities that it sells to other firms, to households, or to government. For obvious reasons a firm is often called a *producer.* Economic theory gives firms several attributes.

First, economists assume that each firm makes consistent decisions, as though it were composed of a single individual. Thus economics ignores the internal problems of how particular decisions are reached. In doing this, economists assume that the firm's internal organization is irrelevant to its decisions. This allows them to treat the firm as the atom of behavior on the production or supply side of commodity markets, just as the household is treated as the atom of behavior on the consumption or demand side.

Second, economists assume that most firms make their decisions with a single goal in mind: to make as much profit as possible. This goal of *profit maximization* is analogous to the household's goal of utility maximization.

Third, economists assume that in their role as producers, firms are the principal users of the services of factors of production. In markets where factor services are bought and sold, the roles of firms and households are thus reversed from what they are in commodity markets: In factor markets firms do the buying and households do the selling.

Government

The term **government** is used in economics in a broad sense to include all public officials, agencies, government bodies, and other organizations belonging to or under the direct control of federal, state, and local governments. For example, in the United States, the term *government* includes, among others, the president, the Federal Reserve System, city councils, commissions and regulatory bodies, legislative bodies, and police forces. It is not important to draw up a comprehensive list, but one should have in mind a general idea of the organizations that have legal and political power to exert control over individual decision makers and over markets.

It is *not* a basic assumption of economics that the government always acts in a consistent fashion. Three important reasons for this may be mentioned here. First, the mayor of Los Angeles, a Utah state legislator, and a United States senator from Maine represent different constituencies, and therefore they may express different and conflicting views and objectives.

Second, individual public servants, whether elected or appointed, have personal objectives (such as staying in office, achieving higher office, power, prestige, and personal aggrandizement) as well as public service objectives. Although the balance of importance given to the two types of objectives will vary among persons and among types of office, both will almost always have some importance. It would be a rare senator, for example, who would vote against a measure that slightly reduced the "public good" if this vote almost guaranteed his defeat at the next election. ("After all," he could reason, "if I am defeated, I won't be around to vote against *really* bad measures.")

Third, the system of checks and balances is designed to set one part of the government against another, thereby producing the characteristic American division of authority and responsibility among branches of government. (Here American practice differs sharply from that of most of the rest of the

---

[2] In academic work, as elsewhere, a division of labor is useful. However, it is important to remember that when economists speak of *the* consumer or *the* individual, they are in fact referring to the group of individuals composing the household. Thus, for example, the commonly heard phrase *consumer sovereignty* really means *household sovereignty.*

English-speaking world, whose governments are based on the British parliamentary system that was not designed to produce pluralism.)

Decisions on interrelated issues of policy are made by many different bodies. Federal and state legislatures pass laws, the courts interpret laws, the governments decide which laws to enforce with vigor and which not to enforce, the Treasury and the Federal Reserve Board influence monetary conditions, and a host of other agencies and semiautonomous bodies determine actions in respect to different aspects of policy goals. Because of the multiplicity of decision makers, it would be truly amazing if fully consistent behavior resulted. Most Americans believe that there are advantages to this separation of responsibilities, but one of its consequences is that inconsistent decisions will be made.

Another problem arises from the fact that in a democracy legislators and political officials have as important goals their own and their leader's re-election. This means, for example, that any measure that imposes large costs and few benefits obvious to the electorate over the short run is unlikely to find favor, no matter how large the long-term benefits are. There is a strong bias toward shortsightedness in an elective system. Although much of this bias stems from an inability to grasp long-run consequences or a selfish unwillingness to look beyond the present, some of it reflects genuine uncertainty about the future. The further into the future that the economist calculates, the wider the margin of possible error. It is not surprising that politicians, who must worry about the next election, often tend to worry less about the long-term effect of their actions. "After all," they may argue, "who can tell what will happen 20 years hence?"

Markets and Economies

We have seen that households, firms, and the government are the main actors in the economic drama. Their action takes place in individual markets.

Markets

The word *market* originally designated a place where goods were traded. The Fulton fish market in New York is a modern example of markets in the everyday sense, and most cities have fruit and vegetable markets. Much early economic theory attempted to explain price behavior in just such markets. Why, for example, can you sometimes obtain great bargains at the end of the day and at other times get what you want only at prices that appear exorbitant in relation to prices quoted only a few hours before?

As theories of market behavior were developed, they were extended to cover commodities such as wheat. Wheat produced anywhere in the world can be purchased almost anywhere else in the world, and the price of a given grade of wheat tends to be nearly uniform the world over. When we talk about the wheat market, the concept of a market has been extended well beyond the idea of a single place to which the producer, the storekeeper, and the homemaker go to sell and buy.

Economists distinguish two broad types of markets: **product markets,** in which outputs of goods and services are sold, and **factor markets,** in which services of factors of production are sold.

Economies

An **economy** is rather loosely defined as a set of interrelated production and consumption activities. It may refer to this activity in a region of one country (for example, the economy of New England), in a country (the American economy), or in a group of countries (the economy of Western Europe). In any economy the allocation of resources is determined by the production, sales, and purchase decisions made by firms, households, and government.

A **free-market economy** is an economy in which the decisions of individual households and firms (as distinct from the government) exert the major influence over the allocation of resources.

The opposite of a free-market economy is a **command economy,** in which the major decisions about the allocation of resources are made by the government and in which firms and households produce and consume only as they are ordered.

As we saw in Chapter 1, the terms *free-market* and *command economy* are often used to describe economies. No real economies rely solely on either free markets or commands. In practice all economies are **mixed economies** in the sense that some decisions are made by firms, households, and the government acting through markets and some are made by the government using the command principle.

Sectors of an Economy

Parts of an economy are usually referred to as **sectors** of that economy. For example, the agricultural sector is the part of the economy that produces agricultural commodities.

Market and Nonmarket Sectors

Producers make commodities. Consumers use them. Commodities may pass from one group to the other in two ways: They may be sold by producers and bought by consumers through markets, or they may be given away.

When commodities are bought and sold, producers expect to cover their costs with the revenue they obtain from selling the product. We call this type of production *marketed production,* and we refer to this part of the economy's activity as belonging to the **market sector.**

When the product is given away, the costs of production must be covered from some source other than sales revenue. We call this *nonmarketed production,* and we refer to this part of the economy's activity as belonging to the **nonmarket sector.** In the case of private charities the money required to pay for factor services may be raised from the public by voluntary contributions. In the case of production by the government—which accounts for the bulk of nonmarketed production—the money is provided from government revenue, which in turn comes mainly from taxes.

Whenever a government enterprise *sells* its output, its production is in the market sector. But much state output is in the nonmarket sector by the very nature of the product provided. For example, one could hardly expect the criminal to pay the judge for providing the service of criminal justice. Other products are in the nonmarket sector because governments have decided that there are advantages to removing them from the market sector. This is the case, for example, with much of American education. Public policy places it in the nonmarket sector

even though much of it could be provided by the market sector.

Private and Public Sectors

An alternative division of an economy's productive activity is between private and public sectors. The **private sector** refers to all production that is in private hands and the **public sector** refers to all production that is in public hands. The distinction between the two sectors depends on the legal distinction of ownership. In the private sector the organization that does the producing is owned by households or other firms; in the public sector it is owned by the state. The public sector includes all production of goods and services by the government plus all production by government-operated industries that is sold to consumers through ordinary markets.

The distinction between market and nonmarket sectors is economic; it depends on whether or not the producer earns revenue by selling output to users. The distinction between the private and the public sectors is legal; it depends on whether the producing organizations are privately or publicly owned.

Microeconomics and Macroeconomics

As we saw in Chapter 1, there are two different but complementary ways of viewing the economy. The first, *microeconomics,* studies the detailed workings of individual markets and interrelations between markets. The second, *macroeconomics,* suppresses much of the detail and concentrates on the behavior of broad aggregates.[3]

An Overview of Microeconomics

Early economists observed the market economy with wonder. They saw that most commodities were

---

[3] The prefixes *micro* and *macro* derive from the Greek words *mikros,* for small, and *makros,* for large.

made by a large number of independent producers and yet in approximately the quantities that people wanted to purchase them. Natural disasters aside, there were neither vast surpluses nor severe shortages of products. They also saw that in spite of the ever-changing geographical, industrial, and occupational patterns of demand for labor services, most laborers were able to sell their services to employers most of the time.

How does the market produce this order in the absence of conscious coordination? It is one thing to have the same good produced year in and year out when people's wants and incomes do not change; it is quite another thing to have production adjusting continually to changing wants, incomes, and techniques of production. Yet this adjustment is accomplished relatively smoothly by the market—albeit with occasional, and sometimes serious, interruptions.

A major discovery of eighteenth century economists was that the price system is a social control mechanism.

Adam Smith, in his classic *The Wealth of Nations,* published in 1776, spoke of the price system as "the invisible hand." It allows decision making to be decentralized under the control of millions of individual producers and consumers but nonetheless to be coordinated. Two examples may help to illustrate how this coordination occurs.

A Change in Demand

For the first example, assume that households wish to purchase more of some commodity than previously. To see the market's reaction to such a change, imagine a situation in which farmers find it equally profitable to produce either of two crops, carrots or brussels sprouts, and so are willing to produce some of both commodities, thereby satisfying the demands of households who wish to consume both. Now imagine that consumers develop a greatly increased desire for brussels sprouts and a diminished desire for carrots. This change might have occurred because of the discovery of hitherto unsuspected nutritive or curative powers of brussels sprouts.

When consumers buy more brussels sprouts and fewer carrots, a shortage of brussels sprouts and a glut of carrots develop. To unload their surplus stocks of carrots, merchants reduce the price of carrots—in the belief that it is better to sell them at a reduced price than not to sell them at all. Sellers of brussels sprouts, however, find that they are unable to satisfy all their customers' demands for that product. Sprouts have become scarce, so merchants charge more for them. As the price rises, fewer people are willing and able to purchase sprouts. Thus making them more expensive limits the quantity demanded to the available supply.

Farmers see a rise in the price of brussels sprouts and a fall in the price of carrots. Brussels sprout production has become more profitable than in the past; the costs of producing sprouts remain unchanged while their market price has risen. Similarly, carrot production is less profitable than in the past because costs are unchanged while the price has fallen. Attracted by high profits in brussels sprouts and deterred by low profits or potential losses in carrots, farmers expand the production of sprouts and curtail carrot production. Thus the change in consumers' tastes, working through the price system, causes a reallocation of resources—land and labor—out of carrot production and into brussels sprout production.

As the production of carrots declines, the glut of carrots on the market diminishes and their price begins to rise. On the other hand, the expansion in brussels sprout production reduces the shortage and the price begins to fall. These price movements will continue until it no longer pays farmers to contract carrot production and to expand brussels sprout production. When all of the adjustments have occurred, the price of sprouts is higher than it was originally, but lower than it was when the shortage sent the price soaring before output could be adjusted; and the price of carrots is lower than it was originally, but higher than when the initial glut sent the price tumbling before output could be adjusted.

The reaction of the market to a change in demand leads to a transfer of resources. Carrot producers reduce their production; they will therefore be laying off workers and generally demanding fewer factors of production. Brussels sprout producers expand production; they will therefore be hiring workers and generally increasing their demand for factors of production.

Labor can probably switch from carrot to sprout production without much difficulty. Certain types of land, however, may be better suited for growing one crop than the other. When farmers increase their sprout production, their demands for those factors especially suited to sprout growing also increase—and this creates a shortage of these resources and a consequent rise in their prices. Meanwhile, with carrot production falling, the demand for land and other factors of production especially suited to carrot growing is reduced. A surplus results, and the prices of these factors are forced down.

Thus factors particularly suited to sprout production will earn more and will obtain a higher share of total national income than before. Factors particularly suited to carrot production, however, will earn less and will obtain a smaller share of the total national income than before.

Changes of this kind will be studied more fully later; the important thing to notice now is how a change in demand causes a reallocation of resources in the direction required to cater to the new, higher level of demand.

A Change in Supply

For a second example, consider a change originating with producers. Begin as before with a situation in which farmers find it equally profitable to produce either sprouts or carrots and in which consumers are willing to buy, at prevailing prices, the quantities of these two commodities that are being produced. Now imagine that, at existing prices, farmers become more willing to produce sprouts than in the past and less willing to produce carrots. This shift might be caused, for example, by a change in the costs of producing the two goods—a rise in carrot costs and a fall in sprout costs that would raise the profitability of sprout production and lower that of carrot production.

What will happen now? For a short time, nothing at all; the existing supply of sprouts and carrots on the market is the result of decisions made by farmers at some time in the past. But farmers now begin to

plant fewer carrots and more sprouts, and soon the quantities on the market begin to change. The quantity of sprouts available for sale rises, and the quantity of carrots falls. A shortage of carrots and a glut of sprouts results. The price of carrots consequently rises, and the price of sprouts falls. This provides the incentive for two types of adjustments. First, households will buy fewer carrots and more sprouts. Second, farmers will move back into carrot production and out of sprouts.

This example began with a situation in which a shortage of carrots caused the price of carrots to rise. The rise in the price of carrots removed the shortage in two ways: It reduced the quantity of carrots demanded and it increased the quantity offered for sale (in response to the rise in the profitability of carrot production). Remember that there was also a surplus of brussels sprouts that caused the price to fall. The fall in price removed the surplus in two ways: It encouraged consumers to buy more of this commodity and it reduced the quantity of sprouts produced and offered for sale (in response to a fall in the profitability of sprout production).

These examples illustrate a general point:

The price system is a mechanism that coordinates individual, decentralized decisions.

The existence of such a control mechanism is beyond dispute. How well it works in comparison with alternative coordinating systems has been in serious dispute for over a hundred years. It remains today a major unsettled social question.

Microeconomics and Macroeconomics Compared

Microeconomics and macroeconomics differ in the questions each asks and in the level of aggregation each uses. Microeconomics deals with the determination of prices and quantities in individual markets and with the relations among these markets. Thus it looks at the details of the market economy. It asks, for example, how much labor is employed in the fast food industry and why is the amount increasing. It asks about the determinants of the output of brussels sprouts, pocket calculators, automobiles, and Domino's pizzas. It asks, too, about the prices of these things—why some prices go up and others down. Economists interested in microeconomics analyze how prices and outputs respond to exogenous shocks caused by events in other markets or by government policy. They ask, for example, how a technical innovation, a government subsidy, or a drought will affect the price and output of beet sugar and the employment of farm workers.

In contrast, macroeconomics focuses on much broader aggregates. It looks at such things as the total number of people employed and unemployed, the average level of prices and how it changes over time, national output, and aggregate consumption. Macroeconomics asks what determines these aggregates and how they respond to changing conditions. Whereas microeconomics looks at demand and supply with regard to particular commodities, macroeconomics looks at aggregate demand and aggregate supply.

An Overview of Macroeconomics

We can group together all the buyers of the nation's output and call their total desired purchases **aggregate demand.** We can also group together all the producers of the nation's output and call their total desired sales **aggregate supply.** Determining the magnitude of these and explaining why they change are among the major problems of macroeconomics.

Major changes in aggregate demand are called *demand shocks,* and major changes in aggregate supply are called *supply shocks.* Such shocks will cause important changes in the broad averages and aggregates that are the concern of macroeconomics, including total output, total employment, and average levels of prices and wages. Government actions sometimes are the cause of demand or supply shocks, while at other times they are reactions to such shocks and are used in an attempt to cushion or change the effects of such shocks.

The Circular Flow of Income

One way to gain insight into aggregate demand and aggregate supply is to view the economy as a giant set of flows. A major part of aggregate demand arises from the purchases of consumption commodities by the nation's households. These purchases generate income for the firms that produce and sell commodities for consumption. A major part of aggregate supply arises from the production and sale of consumption goods by the nation's firms. This production generates income for all the factors that are employed in making these goods.

The black arrows on Figure 3-1 show the interaction between firms and households in two sets of markets—factor markets and product markets—through which their decisions are coordinated. Consider households first. The members of households want commodities to keep themselves fed, clothed, housed, entertained, healthy, and secure. They also want commodities to educate, edify, beautify, stupefy, and otherwise amuse themselves. Households have resources with which to attempt to satisfy these wants. But not all their wants can be satisfied with the resources available. Households are forced, therefore, to make choices as to which goods and services to buy in product markets that offer them myriad ways to spend their incomes.

Now consider firms. They must choose among the products they might produce and sell, among the ways of producing them, and among the various quantities (and qualities) they can supply. Firms must also buy factors of production. Payments by firms to factor owners provide the factor owners with incomes. The recipients of these incomes are households whose members want commodities to keep themselves fed, clothed, housed, and entertained.

We have now come full circle! The action of this drama involves firms and households interacting with one another.

Payments flow from households to firms through product markets and back to households again through factor markets.

If the economy consisted only of households and firms, if households spent all the income they received on buying goods and services produced by firms, and if firms distributed all their receipts to households either by purchasing factor services or by distributing profits to owners, then the circular flow would be simple indeed. Everything received by

FIGURE 3-1   The Circular Flow of Expenditures and Income

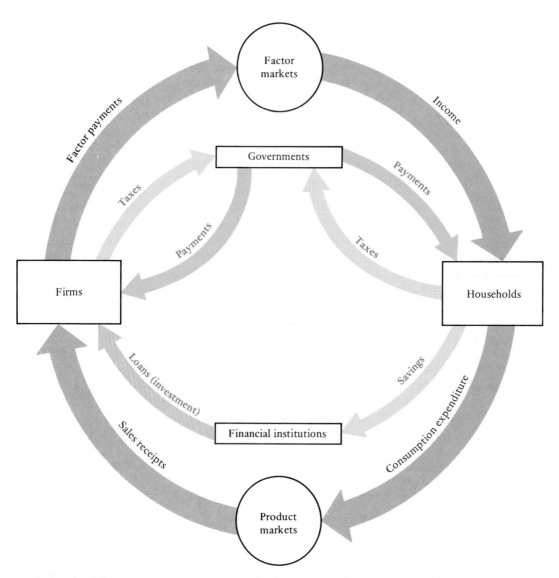

The interaction of firms and households in product and factor markets generates a flow of expenditure and income. These flows are also influenced by other institutions such as governments and the financial system. Factor services are sold by households through factor markets, which leads to a flow of income from firms to household. Commodities are sold by firms through product markets, which leads to a flow of receipts from households to firms. If these primary flows, shown by the black arrows, were the only flows, the circular flow would be a closed system. But other institutions, such as governments and financial institutions, play roles. For example, governments may inject funds in the form of government payments to households and firms, and banks may inject funds in the form of loans to firms for investment expenditures. Such additions or injections are illustrated by the dark color arrows. Similarly, governments may withdraw funds in the form of taxes, and financial institutions may do so by accepting funds that households wish to save. Such leakages or withdrawals are illustrated by the light color arrows.

households would be passed on to firms, and every-thing received by firms would be passed back to households. The circular flow would be a completely closed system; aggregate demand and aggregate sup-ply would consist only of consumption goods; and macroeconomics would involve little more than measuring the flows of production of and expendi-ture on consumption goods.

The circular flow is not, however, a completely closed system. First, households do not spend all their income. Some of their income is saved, and some goes to governments as taxes. As a result, total household demand for consumption goods and ser-vices falls short of total household income. These two *leakages* from the circular flow are shown by the light-colored arrows flowing out of the households in Figure 3-1. As shown in the figure, a third leakage occurs because firms also pay taxes. (Of course, firms may also save, but this leakage is omitted from the figure for simplicity.[4])

A second reason why the circular flow is not a closed system is that there are elements of aggregate demand that do not arise from household spending. The two main additional elements are investment and government expenditure. A major component of aggregate demand stems from firms that borrow in order to purchase such investment goods as plant and equipment. A further major component of ag-gregate demand comes from governments—federal,

[4] Additional elements related to international trade are discussed later in the book.

state, and local. They add to total expenditure on the nation's output by spending on a whole range of goods and services from national defense through the provision of justice to the building of roads and schools. These two major additions to the circular flow of income are shown by the dark-colored ar-rows flowing into the firms in Figure 3-1. As shown in the figure, a third addition arises because house-holds also receive payments from government. (Of course, households may also borrow from financial institutions to finance current consumption expen-diture, but for simplicity this fourth addition is omit-ted from the figure.)

When any of these elements of aggregate demand changes, aggregate output and total income earned by households are likely to change as a result. Thus, studying the determinants of total consumption, in-vestment, and government spending is crucial to un-derstanding the causes of changes both in the nation's total output and in the employment generated by the production of that output.

The Next Step

Soon you will be going on to study micro- or mac-roeconomics. Whichever branch of the subject you study first, it is important to remember that micro-economics and macroeconomics are complementary, not competing, views of the economy. Both are needed for a full understanding of the functioning of a modern economy.

Summary

1. This chapter provides an overview of the workings of the market economy. Modern economies are based on the specialization and division of labor, which necessitate the exchange of goods and ser-vices. Exchange takes place in markets and is facilitated by the use of money. Much of economics is devoted to a study of how markets work to coordinate millions of individual, decentralized decisions.

2. In economic theory three kinds of decision makers—households, firms, and government—interact in markets. Households are as-sumed to maximize their satisfaction and firms to maximize their profits. Government may have multiple objectives.

3. A free-market economy is one in which the allocation of resources is determined by the production, sales, and purchase decisions made

by firms and households acting in response to such market signals as prices and profits.

4. Subdivisions of an economy are called sectors. Economies are commonly divided into market and nonmarket sectors and into public and private sectors. These divisions cut across each other; the first is based on the economic distinction of how costs are covered, and the second is based on a legal distinction of ownership.

5. A key difference between micro- and macroeconomics is in the level of aggregation to which attention is directed. Microeconomics looks at prices and quantities in individual markets and how they respond to various shocks that impinge on those markets. Macroeconomics looks at broader aggregates such as aggregate consumption, employment and unemployment, and rate of change of the price level.

6. The questions asked in micro- and macroeconomics differ, but they are complementary parts of economic theory. They study different aspects of a single economic system, and both are needed for an understanding of the whole.

7. Microeconomics deals with the determination of prices and quantities in individual markets and the relations among those markets. It shows how the price system provides signals that reflect changes in demand and supply and to which producers and consumers react in an individual but nonetheless coordinated manner.

8. The microeconomic interactions between households and firms through markets may be illustrated in a circular flow diagram that traces money flows between households and firms. These flows are the starting point for studying the circular flows of aggregate income that are key elements of macroeconomics.

9. Household purchases of consumption goods generate income for firms whose payments to factors then flow back to the households as income. This circular flow is not a simple closed system because not all income received by households is spent for the output of firms and some receipts of firms are not paid out to households. Also, some payments to firms do not result from the spending of households and some payments to households do not result from the spending of firms. The flows of expenditure in the economy determine total output, total income, and total employment.

Topics for Review

Specialization and division of labor
Economic decision makers
Markets and market economies
Market and nonmarket sectors
Private and public sectors
The price system as a social control mechanism
Relation between microeconomics and macroeconomics

1. Suggest some examples of specialization and division of labor among people you know.
2. There is a greater variety of specialists and specialty stores in large cities than in small towns having populations with the same average income. Explain this in economic terms.
3. Define the household of which you are a member. Consider your household's income last year. What proportion of it came from the sale of factor services? Identify other sources of income. Approximately what proportion of the expenditures by your household became income for firms?
4. "It is not from the benevolence of the butcher, the brewer, or the baker that we expect our dinner, but from their regard to their self-interest. We address ourselves, not to their humanity, but to their self-love, and never talk to them of our necessities, but of their advantages, not to their humanity, but to their self-love, and never talk to them out of our necessities, but of their advantages." Do you agree with this quotation from *The Wealth of Nations?* How are "their self-love" and "our dinner" related to the price system? What are assumed to be the motives of firms and of households?
5. Trace the effect of a sharp change in consumer demand away from cigarettes and toward chewing gum as a result of continuing reports linking smoking with lung cancer and heart disease.
6. Make a list of other decision makers in the economy today that do not fit into the categories of firm, household, and government. Are you sure that the concept of a firm will not stretch sufficiently to cover some of the items on your list?
7. Trace out some significant microeconomic and macroeconomic effects of a baby boom such as occurred following World War II.
8. Which, if any, of the arrows in Figure 3-1 do each of the following affect in the first instance?
   a. Households increase their consumption expenditures by reducing saving.
   b. The government lowers income tax rates.
   c. In view of a recession, firms decide to postpone production of some new products.
   d. Consumers like the new model American cars and borrow money from the banking system to buy them in record numbers.
   e. The Swatch fad dies out as consumers shift their expenditures to other items.

A General View of the Price System

4

Demand, Supply, and Price

Some people believe that economics begins and ends with the "law" of supply and demand. It is, of course, too much to hope for "economics in one lesson." (An unkind critic of a book with that title remarked that the author needed a second lesson.) Still, the so-called laws of supply and demand are an important part of our understanding of the market system.

First we need to understand what determines the demands for commodities and the supplies of them. Then we can see how demand and supply together determine price and how the price system as a whole allows the economy to respond to changes in demand and in supply. Demand and supply help us in understanding the price system's successes and its failures, as well as the consequences of such government interventions as price controls, minimum-wage laws, and sales taxes.

Demand

The American consumer spent about $2,600 billion on goods and services in 1985. Table 4-1 shows the composition of this expenditure and how it has changed over 30 years. Economists ask many questions about the pattern of consumer expenditure: Why is it what it is at any moment of time? Why does it change in the way it does? Why did the fraction of total consumer expenditure for food decline from more than one-third in 1910 to less than one-fifth by 1985? Why did U.S. consumers allocate a negligible percentage of their total expenditure to automobiles in 1920, 4 percent in 1929, only 2 percent in 1932, and 7 percent in both 1972 and 1985? How have Americans reacted to the large changes in fuel prices that occurred in the late 1970s and early 1980s? Why do people who build houses in Norway and the American West rarely use brick, while it is commonly used in England and the eastern United States? Why have the maid and the washerwoman been replaced by the vacuum cleaner and the washing machine?

Quantity Demanded

The total amount of a commodity that all households wish to purchase is called the **quantity demanded** of that commodity.[1] It is important

---

[1] In this chapter we concentrate on the demand of *all* households for commodities. Of course, what all households do is only the sum of what each individual household does, and in Chapters 7 and 8 we shall study the behavior of individual households in greater detail.

TABLE 4-1	Composition of Personal Consumption Expenditures, 1955 and 1985 *(percentages)*	

	1955	1985
Motor vehicles and parts	7.0	6.5
Furniture and household equipment	6.4	4.9
Other	1.8	2.5
Total durable goods	15.2	13.9
Food	26.5	18.4
Clothing and shoes	9.1	6.0
Gasoline and oil	3.4	3.5
Other	9.5	7.4
Total nondurable goods	48.5	35.3
Housing and household operation	19.0	22.4
Other	17.3	28.4
Total services	36.3	50.8
Total all goods and services	100.0	100.0

Source: Economic Report of the President, 1986.

The declining relative importance of food, clothing, and durables and the rising importance of gasoline and oil and services of all kinds stand out.

to notice three things about this concept. First, quantity demanded is a *desired* quantity. It is how much households wish to purchase, given the price of the commodity, other prices, their incomes, tastes, and so on. This may be different from the amount that households actually succeed in purchasing. If sufficient quantities are not available, the amount households wish to purchase may exceed the amount they actually do purchase. To distinguish these two concepts, the term *quantity demanded* is used to refer to desired purchases, and a phrase such as **quantity actually bought** used to refer to actual purchases.

Second, *desired* does not refer to idle dreams but to effective demands, that is, to the amounts people are willing to buy given the price they must pay for the commodity.

Third, quantity demanded refers to a continuous *flow* of purchases. It must therefore be expressed as so much per period of time: 1 million oranges per day, 7 million per week, or 365 million per year. For

example, being told that the quantity of new television sets demanded (at current prices) in the United States is 500,000 means nothing unless you are also told the period of time involved. Five hundred thousand television sets demanded per day would be an enormous rate of demand; 500,000 per year would be a very small rate. (The important distinction between stocks and flows was discussed on page 21.)

What Determines Quantity Demanded?

The amount of some commodity that all households are willing to buy in a given time period is influenced by the following important variables. [2][2]

Commodity's own price
Average household income
Prices of related commodities
Tastes
Distribution of income among households
Size of the population

We cannot understand the separate influence of each of the above variables if we try to consider what happens when everything changes at once. Instead, we consider the influence of the variables one at a time. To do this, we hold all but one of them constant. Then we let that one selected variable vary and study how it affects quantity demanded. We can do the same for each of the other variables in turn, and in this way we can come to understand the importance of each.[3] Once this is done, we can aggregate the separate influences of the variables to discover what would happen if several things changed at the same time—as they often do in practice.

Holding all other influencing variables constant is often described by the words "other things being

[2] Notes giving mathematical demonstrations of the concepts presented in the text are designated by colored reference numbers. These notes can be found beginning on page 892.

[3] A relation in which many variables—in this case average income, population, tastes, and many prices—influence a single variable—in this case quantity demanded—is called a *multivariate* relation. The technique of studying the effect of each of the influencing variables one at a time, while holding the others constant, is common in mathematics and there is a specific concept, the *partial derivative,* designed to do so.

equal" or by the equivalent Latin phrase, ***ceteris paribus.*** When economists speak of the influence of the price of wheat on the quantity of wheat demanded *ceteris paribus,* they refer to what a change in the price of wheat would do to the quantity demanded if all other factors that influence the demand for wheat did not change.

Demand and Price

We are interested in developing a theory of how commodities get priced. To do this we need to study the relation between the quantity demanded of each commodity and that commodity's own price. This requires that we hold all other influences constant and ask: How will the quantity of a commodity demanded vary as its own price varies?

A basic economic hypothesis is that the lower the price of a commodity, the larger the quantity that will be demanded, other things being equal.

Why might this be so? Commodities are used to satisfy desires and needs, and there is almost always more than one commodity that will satisfy any given desire or need. Such commodities compete with one another for the purchasers' attention. Hunger may be satisfied by meat or vegetables, a desire for green vegetables by broccoli or spinach. The need to keep warm at night may be satisfied by several woolen blankets or one electric blanket or a sheet and a lot of oil burned in the furnace. The desire for a vacation may be satisfied by a trip to the seashore or to the mountains, the need to get there by different airlines, a bus, a car, a train. And so it goes. Name any general desire or need, and there will be at least two and often dozens of different commodities that will satisfy it.

Now consider what happens if we hold income, tastes, population, and the prices of all other commodities constant and vary only the price of one commodity. As that price goes up, the commodity becomes an increasingly expensive way to satisfy a want. Some households will stop buying it altogether; others will buy smaller amounts; still others may continue to buy the same quantity. Because many households will switch wholly or partially to other commodities to satisfy the same want, less will be bought of the commodity whose price has risen. As meat becomes more expensive, for example, households may switch to some extent to meat substitutes; they may also forego meat at some meals and eat less meat at others.

Alternatively, a fall in a commodity's price makes it a cheaper method of satisfying a want. Households will buy more of it. Consequently, they will buy less of similar commodities whose prices have not fallen and which as a result have become expensive *relative to* the commodity in question. When a bumper tomato harvest drives prices down, shoppers switch to tomatoes and cut their purchases of many other vegetables that now look relatively more expensive.

The Demand Schedule and the Demand Curve

A **demand schedule** is one way of showing the relationship between quantity demanded and price. It is a numerical tabulation showing the quantity that is demanded at selected prices.

Table 4-2 is a hypothetical demand schedule for carrots. It lists the quantity of carrots that would be demanded at various prices on the assumption that all other influences on quantity demanded are held constant. We note in particular that average household income is fixed at $20,000 because later we will wish to see what happens when income changes. The table gives the quantities demanded for six selected prices, but actually a separate quantity would be demanded at each possible price from one cent to several hundreds of dollars.

A second method of showing the relation between quantity demanded and price is to draw a graph. The six price-quantity combinations shown in Table 4-2 are plotted on the graph shown in Figure 4-1. Price is plotted on the vertical axis and quantity on the horizontal axis. The smooth curve drawn through these points is called a **demand curve.** It shows the quantity that purchasers would like to buy at each price. The slope of the curve, downward to the right, indicates that the quantity demanded increases as the price falls.

TABLE 4-2   A Demand Schedule for Carrots

	Price per ton	Quantity demanded when income is $20,000 per year (thousands of tons per months)
U	$ 20	110.0
V	40	90.0
W	60	77.5
X	80	67.5
Y	100	62.5
Z	120	60.0

The table shows the quantity of carrots that would be demanded at various prices, *ceteris paribus.* For example, row *W*, indicates that if the price of carrots were $60 per ton, consumers would desire to purchase 77,500 tons of carrots per month, given the values of the other variables that affect quantity demanded, including average household income.

FIGURE 4-1   A Demand Curve for Carrots

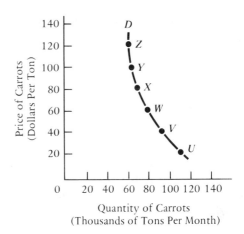

This demand curve relates quantity of carrots demanded to the price of carrots; its downward slope indicates that quantity demanded increases as price falls. The six points correspond to the price-quantity combinations shown in Table 4-2. Each row in the table defines a point on the demand curve. The smooth curve drawn through all of the points and labeled *D* is the demand curve.

Each point on the demand curve indicates a single price-quantity combination. The demand curve as a whole shows more.

The demand curve represents the relation between quantity demanded and price, other things being equal.

When economists speak of the conditions of demand in a particular market as being given or known, they are referring not just to the particular quantity being demanded at the moment (i.e., not just to one point on the demand curve). Instead, they are referring to the entire demand curve—to the relation between desired purchases and all the possible alternative prices of the commodity.

Thus the term **demand** refers to the entire relation between price and quantity (as shown, for example, by the schedule in Table 4-2 or the curve in Figure 4-1). In contrast, a single point on a demand schedule or curve is the *quantity demanded* at that point (for example, at point *W* in Figure 4-1, 77,500 tons of carrots a month are demanded at a price of $60 a ton).

Shifts in the Demand Curve

The demand schedule is constructed and the demand curve plotted on the assumption of *ceteris paribus.* But

what if other things change, as surely they must? What if, for example, households find themselves with more income? If they spend their extra income, they will buy additional quantities of many commodities *even though their prices are unchanged.*

But if households increase their purchases of any one commodity whose price has not changed, the purchases cannot be represented on the original demand curve. They must be represented on a new demand curve, which is to the right of the old curve. Thus the rise in household income shifts the demand curve to the right as shown in Figure 4-2. This illustrates the operation of an important general rule.

A demand curve is drawn on the assumption that everything except the commodity's own price is held constant. A change in any of the variables previously held constant will shift the demand curve to a new position.

FIGURE 4-2   Two Demand Curves for Carrots

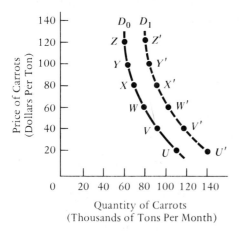

Quantity of Carrots
(Thousands of Tons Per Month)

The rightward shift in the demand curve from D_0 to D_1 indicates an increase in the quantity demanded at each price. The lettered points correspond to those in Table 4-3. A rightward shift in the demand curve indicates an increase in demand in the sense that more is demanded at each price and that a higher price would be paid for each quantity.

TABLE 4-3   Two Alternative Demand Schedules for Carrots

Price per ton p	Quantity demanded when average household income is $20,000 per year (thousands of tons per month) D_0		Quantity demanded when average income is $24,000 per year (thousands of tons per months) D_1	
$ 20	110.0	U	140.0	U'
40	90.0	V	116.0	V'
60	77.5	W	100.8	W'
80	67.5	X	87.5	X'
100	62.5	Y	81.3	Y'
120	60.0	Z	78.0	Z'

An increase in average household income increases the quantity demanded at each price. When average income rises from $20,000 to $24,000 per year, quantity demanded at a price of $60 per ton rises from 77,500 tons per month to 100,800 tons per month. A similar rise occurs at every other price. Thus the demand schedule relating columns p and D_0 is replaced by one relating columns p and D_1. The graphical representations of these two functions are labeled D_0 and D_1 in Figure 4-2.

A demand curve can shift in many ways; two of them are particularly important. In the first case more is bought at *each* price, and the demand curve shifts right so that each price corresponds to a higher quantity than it did before. In the second case less is bought at *each* price, and the demand curve shifts left so that each price corresponds to a lower quantity than it did before.

The influence of changes in variables other than price may be studied by determining how changes in each variable shift the demand curve. Any change will shift the demand curve to the right if it increases the amount people wish to buy, other things remaining equal, and to the left if it decreases the amount households wish to buy, other things remaining equal.

Average household income. If households receive more income on average, they can be expected to purchase more of most commodities even though

commodity prices remain the same.[4] Considering all households, we expect that no matter what price we pick, more of any commodity will be demanded than was previously demanded at the same price. This shift is illustrated in Table 4-3 and Figure 4-2.

A rise in average household income shifts the demand curve for most commodities to the right. This indicates that more will be demanded at each possible price.

Other prices.   We saw that the downward slope of a commodity's demand curve occurs because the lower its price, the cheaper the commodity is relative to other commodities that can satisfy the same needs or desires. Those other commodities are called **substitutes.** Another way for the same change to come about is for the price of the substitute commodity to

[4] Such commodities are called *normal goods*. Commodities for which the amount purchased falls as income rises are called *inferior goods*. These concepts are defined and discussed in Chapter 5.

rise. For example, carrots can become cheap relative to cabbage either because the price of carrots falls or because the price of cabbage rises. Either change will increase the amount of carrots households are prepared to buy.

A rise in the price of a substitute for a commodity shifts the demand curve for the commodity to the right. More will be purchased at each price.

For example, a rise in the price of cabbage could shift the demand curve for carrots to the right in Figure 4-2.

Complements are commodities that tend to be used jointly with each other. Cars and gasoline are complements; so are golf clubs and golf balls, electric stoves and electricity, an airplane trip to Vail and lift tickets on the mountain. Since complements tend to be consumed together, a fall in the price of either will increase the demand for both.

A fall in the price of a complementary commodity will shift a commodity's demand curve to the right. More will be purchased at each price.

For example, a fall in the price of airplane trips to Vail will lead to a rise in the demand for lift tickets at Vail even though their price is unchanged.

Tastes.   Tastes have a large effect on people's desired purchases. A change in tastes may be long lasting, such as the shift from fountain pens to ball-point pens or from slide rules to pocket calculators. Or it may be a short-lived fad such as hula hoops or Billy Beer. In either case a change in tastes in favor of a commodity shifts the demand curve to the right. More will be bought at each price.

Distribution of income.   If a constant total of income is redistributed among the population, demands may change. If, for example, the government increases the deductions that may be taken for children on income tax returns and compensates by raising basic tax rates, income will be transferred from childless

persons to households with large families. Demands for commodities more heavily bought by the childless will decline, while demands for commodities more heavily bought by those with large families will increase.

A change in the distribution of income will shift to the right the demand curves for commodities bought most by those gaining income, and it will shift to the left the demand curves for commodities bought most by people losing income.

Population.   Population growth does not by itself create new demand. The additional people must have purchasing power before demand is changed. Extra people of working age who are employed, however, will earn new income. When this happens, the demands for all the commodities purchased by the new income earners will rise. Thus it is usually true that:

A rise in population will shift the demand curves for commodities to the right, indicating that more will be bought at each price.

The reasons that demand curves shift are summarized in Figure 4-3.

Movements Along the Demand Curve Versus Shifts of the Whole Curve

Suppose you read in today's newspaper that a soaring price of carrots has been caused by a greatly increased demand for that commodity. Then tomorrow you read that the rising price of carrots is greatly reducing the typical household's purchases of carrots as shoppers switch to potatoes, yams, and peas. The two statements appear to contradict each other. The first associates a rising price with a rising demand; the second associates a rising price with a declining demand. Can both statements be true? The answer is that they can be because they refer to different things. The first describes a shift in the demand curve; the second describes a movement along a demand curve in response to a change in price.

Consider first the statement that the increase in the price of carrots has been caused by an increased

FIGURE 4-3   **Shifts in the Demand Curve**

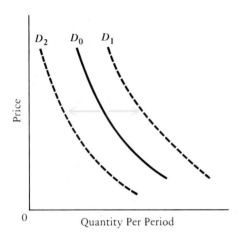

A shift in the demand curve from D_0 to D_1 indicates an increase in demand; a shift from D_0 to D_2 indicates a decrease in demand. An increase in demand means that more is demanded at each price. Such a rightward shift can be caused by a rise in income, a rise in the price of a substitute, a fall in the price of a complement, a change in tastes that favors the commodity, an increase in population, or a redistribution of income toward groups who favor the commodity.

A decrease in demand means that less is demanded at each price. Such a leftward shift can be caused by a fall in income, a fall in the price of a substitute, a rise in the price of a complement, a change in tastes that disfavors the commodity, a decrease in population, or a redistribution of income away from groups who favor the commodity.

demand for carrots. This statement refers to a shift in the demand curve for carrots. In this case the demand curve must have shifted to the right, indicating more carrots demanded *at each price*. This shift will, as we shall see later in this chapter, increase the price of carrots.

Now consider the statement that fewer carrots are being bought because carrots have become more expensive. This refers to a movement along a given demand curve and reflects a change between two specific quantities being bought, one before the price rose and one afterward.

So what lay behind the two stories might have been something like the following.

1. A rise in the population is shifting the demand curve for carrots to the right as more and more are demanded at each price. This in turn is raising the price of carrots (for reasons we will soon study in detail). This was the first newspaper story.
2. The rising price of carrots is causing each individual household to cut back on its purchase of carrots. This causes a movement upward to the left along any particular demand curve for carrots. This was the second newspaper story.

To prevent the type of confusion caused by our two newspaper stories, economists have developed a specialized vocabulary to distinguish shifts of curves from movements along curves.

We have seen that *demand* refers to the *whole* demand curve. Economists reserve the term **change in demand** to describe a shift in the whole curve, that is, a change in the amount that will be bought at *every* price.

shift : ∆ in Demand

An increase in demand means that the whole demand curve has shifted to the right; a decrease in demand means that the whole demand curve has shifted to the left.

Any one point on a demand curve represents a specific amount being bought at a specified price. It represents, therefore, a particular quantity demanded. A movement along a demand curve is referred to as a **change in the quantity demanded.** [3]

movement: ∆ in Q demanded

A movement down a demand curve is called an increase (or a rise) in the quantity demanded; a movement up the demand curve is called a decrease (or a fall) in the quantity demanded.

To illustrate this terminology, look again at Table 4-3. When average income is $20,000, an increase in price from $60 to $80 decreases the *quantity demanded* from 77.5 to 67.5 thousand tons a month. An increase in average income from \$20,000 to \$24,000 increases *demand* from D_0 to D_1.

Figure 4-4 shows the combined effect of a rise in demand, shown by a rightward shift in the whole demand curve, and a fall in the quantity demanded, shown by a movement upward to the left along a given demand curve in response to a change in price.

FIGURE 4-4   Shifts of and Movements Along the Demand Curve

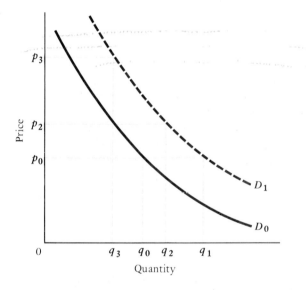

A rise in demand means that more will be bought at each price, but it does not mean that more will be bought under all circumstances. The demand curve is originally D_0 and price is p_0 at which q_0 is bought. Demand then increases to D_1 which implies that at the old price of p_0, there is a larger quantity demanded, q_1. Now assume the price rises above p_0. This causes quantity demanded to fall below q_1. *The shift in the demand curve means that more is bought at each price. A movement upward along the demand curve causes less to be bought in response to a rise in price.* The net effect of these two shifts can be either an increase or a decrease in the quantity demanded. In the figure a rise in price to p_2 leaves the quantity demanded of q_2 still in excess of the original quantity q_0, while a rise in price to p_3 leaves the final quantity of q_3 below the original quantity of q_0.

Supply

America's private sector produced goods and services worth about \$3.5 trillion in 1985. A broad classification of what was produced is given in Table 4-4. The percentages shown in Table 4-4 reflect some of the changes that have taken place over 30 years. Even more dramatic changes can be seen in more detailed data.

Economists have as many questions to ask about production and its changing composition as they do about consumption. For example, why have the country's manufacturing industries declined in relative importance? What is the significance of the rising importance of service industries?

At the more detailed level, economists want to know such things as why the aluminum industry grew faster than the steel industry; why the increase in output of the chemical industries was about 60 times that of the primary metals industries, over 3 times that of the apparel industry, and twice that of the motor vehicle industry in the 30 years since 1955. Why and how do firms and industries come into being, grow, and decline?

All these questions and many others are aspects of a single question: *What determines the quantities of commodities that will be produced and offered for sale?*

Full discussion of these questions of supply will come later (in Part Four). For now it is enough to develop the basic relation between the price of a commodity and the quantity that will be produced and offered for sale by firms, and to understand what forces lead to shifts in this relationship.

Quantity Supplied

The amount of a commodity that firms wish to sell is called the **quantity supplied** of that commodity. Note that this is the amount that firms are willing to offer for sale; it is not necessarily the amount they succeed in selling. The term **quantity actually sold** indicates what they succeed in selling. Quantity supplied is a flow; it is so much per unit of time.

Although households may desire to purchase an amount that differs from what sellers desire to sell, they cannot succeed in buying what someone else

TABLE 4-4   **Composition of National Product by Industry of Origin, 1955 and 1984** *(percentages)*

Industry group[a]	1955	1984
Manufacturing	29.8	20.6
Mining and construction	7.7	7.6
Agriculture, forestry, and fisheries	4.9	2.5
Transport and public utilities	9.0	9.1
Wholesale and retail trade	16.5	16.4
Finance, insurance, and real estate	12.4	15.3
Other services	8.6	15.2
Government and government enterprises	9.6	11.7
Other	1.5	1.6
	100.0	100.0

Source: Economic Report of the President, 1986.

[a] Excluding government and government enterprises.

Over a generation manufacturing, agriculture, forestry, and fisheries have all declined in relative importance, while services have become more important.

does not sell. A purchase and a sale are merely two sides of the same transaction. Looked at from the buyer's side, there is a purchase; looked at from the seller's side, there is a sale.

Since desired purchases do not have to equal desired sales, quantity demanded does not have to equal quantity supplied. But because no one can buy what someone does not sell the quantity actually purchased must equal the quantity actually sold.

What Determines Quantity Supplied?

The amount of a commodity that firms will be willing to produce and offer for sale is influenced by the following important variables. [4]

Commodity's own price
Prices of inputs
Goals of firms
State of technology

The situation is the same here as it is on the demand side. The list of influencing variables is long, and we will not get far if we try to discover what happens when they all change at the same time. So

again we use the convenient *ceteris paribus* technique to study the influence of the variables one at a time.

Supply and Price

Since we want to develop a theory of how commodities get priced, we study the relation between the quantity supplied of each commodity and that commodity's own price. We start by holding all other influences constant and asking: How do we expect the quantity of a commodity supplied to vary with its own price?

A basic economic hypothesis is that, for many commodities, the higher the price of the commodity, the larger the quantity that will be supplied, other things being equal.

Why might this be so? It is because the profits that can be earned from producing a commodity are almost certain to increase if the price of that commodity rises while the costs of inputs used to produce it remain unchanged. This will make firms, which are in business to earn profits, wish to produce more of the commodity whose price has risen and less of other commodities.[5]

The Supply Schedule and the Supply Curve

The general relationship just discussed can be illustrated by a **supply schedule** which shows the quantities that producers would wish to sell at alternative prices of the commodity. A supply schedule is analogous to a demand schedule; the former shows what producers would be willing to sell, while the latter shows what households would be willing to buy at alternative prices of the commodity. Table 4-5 presents a hypothetical supply schedule for carrots.

A **supply curve,** the graphical representation of the supply schedule, is illustrated in Figure 4-5.

---

[5] Notice, however, the qualifying word *many* in the hypothesis stated above. It is used because, as we shall see in Part Four, there are exceptions to this rule. Although the rule states the usual case, a rise in price *(ceteris paribus)* is not always necessary to call forth an increase in quantity in the case of all commodities.

TABLE 4-5   A Supply Schedule for Carrots

	Price per ton	Quantity supplied (thousands of tons per month)
u	$ 20	5.0
v	40	46.0
w	60	77.5
x	80	100.0
y	100	115.0
z	120	122.5

The table shows the quantities that producers wish to sell at various prices, *ceteris paribus*. For example, row *y* indicates that if the price were $100 per ton, producers would wish to sell 115,000 tons of carrots per month.

While each point on the supply curve represents a specific price-quantity combination, the whole curve shows more.

FIGURE 4-5   A Supply Curve for Carrots

Quantity of Carrots
(Thousands of Tons Per Month)

This supply curve relates quantity of carrots supplied to the price of carrots; its upward slope indicates that quantity supplied increases as price increases. The six points correspond to the price-quantity combinations shown in Table 4-5. Each row in the table defines a point on the supply curve. The smooth curve drawn through all of the points and labeled *S* is the supply curve.

The supply curve represents the relation between quantity supplied and price, other things being equal.

When economists speak of the conditions of supply as being given or known, they refer not just to the particular quantity being supplied at the moment, that is, not to just one point on the supply curve. Instead, they are referring to the entire supply curve, to the complete relation between desired sales and all possible alternative prices of the commodity.

Supply refers to the entire relation between supply and price. A single point on the supply curve refers to the *quantity supplied* at that price.

Shifts in the Supply Curve

A shift in the supply curve means that at each price a different quantity will be supplied than previously. An increase in the quantity supplied at each price is shown in Table 4-6 and graphed in Figure 4-6. This change appears as a rightward shift in the supply curve. In contrast, a decrease in the quantity supplied at each price would appear as a leftward shift. A shift in the supply curve must be the result of a change in one of the factors that influence the quantity supplied other than the commodity's own price. The major

TABLE 4-6   Two Alternative Supply Schedules for Carrots

Price per ton p	Quantity supplied before cost-saving innovation (thousands of tons per month) S_0		Quantity supplied after innovation (thousands of tons per month) S_1	
$ 20	5.0	*u*	28.0	*u'*
40	46.0	*v*	76.0	*v'*
60	77.5	*w*	102.0	*w'*
80	100.0	*x*	120.0	*x'*
100	115.0	*y*	132.0	*y'*
120	122.5	*z*	140.0	*z'*

A cost-saving innovation increases the quantity supplied at each price. As a result of a cost-saving innovation, the quantity that is supplied at $100 per ton rises from 115,000 to 132,000 tons per month. A similar rise occurs at every price. Thus, the supply schedule relating p and S_0 is replaced by one relating p and S_1.

FIGURE 4-6   Two Supply Curves for Carrots

The rightward shift in the supply curve from S_0 to S_1 indicates an increase in the quantity supplied at each price. The lettered points correspond to those in Table 4-6. A rightward shift in the supply curve indicates an increase in supply in the sense that more carrots are supplied at each price.

FIGURE 4-7   Shifts in the Supply Curve

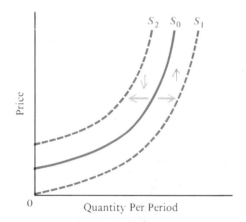

A shift in the supply curve from S_0 to S_1 indicates an increase in supply; a shift from S_0 to S_2 indicates a decrease in supply. An increase in supply means that more is supplied at each price. Such a rightward shift can be caused by certain changes in producers' goals, improvements in technology, or decreases in the costs of inputs that are important in producing the commodity.

A decrease in supply means that less is supplied at each price. Such a leftward shift can be caused by certain changes in producers' goals or increases in the costs of inputs that are important in producing the commodity.

possible causes of such shifts are summarized in the caption of Figure 4-7 and are considered briefly below.

For supply, as for demand, there is an important general rule.

A change in any of the variables (other than the commodity's own price) that affect the amount of a commodity that firms are willing to produce and sell will shift the whole supply curve for that commodity.

Prices of inputs. All things that a firm uses to produce its outputs—such as materials, labor, and machines—are called the firm's inputs. Other things being equal, the higher the price of any input used to make a commodity, the less will be the profit from making that commodity. We expect, therefore, that the higher the price of any input used by a firm, the lower will be the amount that the firm will produce and offer for sale at any given price of the commodity.

A rise in the price of inputs shifts the supply curve to the left indicating that less will be supplied at any given price; a fall in the price of inputs shifts the supply curve to the right.

Goals of the firm. In elementary economic theory, the firm is assumed to have the single goal of profit maximization. Firms might, however, have other goals either in addition to or as substitutes for profit maximization. If the firm worries about risk, it will pursue safer lines of activity even though they promise lower probable profits. If the firm values size, it may produce and sell more than the profit-maximizing quantities. If it worries about its image in society, it may forsake highly profitable activities (such as the production of dioxin) when there is major public disapproval. However, as long as the firm prefers more profits to less, it will respond to changes in the profitabilities of alternative lines of action, and supply curves will slope upward.

A change in the importance that firms give to other goals will shift the supply curve one way or the other, indicating a changed willingness to supply the quantity at any given price and hence a changed level of profitability.

Technology.   At any time what is produced and how it is produced depends on what is known. Over time knowledge changes; so do the quantities of individual commodities supplied. The enormous increase in production per worker that has been going on in industrial societies for about 200 years is largely due to improved methods of production. Yet the Industrial Revolution is more than a historical event; it is a present reality. Discoveries in chemistry have led to lower costs of production of well-established products, such as paints, and to a large variety of new products made of plastics and synthetic fibers. The invention of transistors and silicon chips has radically changed products such as computers, audiovisual equipment, and guidance-control systems, and the consequent development of compact computers is revolutionizing the production of countless other nonelectronic products.

Any technological change that decreases production costs will increase the profits that can be earned at any given price of the commodity. Since increased profitability leads to increased production, this change shifts the supply curve to the right, indicating an increased willingness to produce the commodity and offer it for sale at each possible price.

Movements Along the Supply Curve Versus Shifts of the Whole Curve

As with demand, it is important to distinguish movements along supply curves from shifts of the whole curve. The term **change in supply** is reserved for a shift of the whole supply curve. This means a change in the quantity supplied at each price of the commodity. A movement along the supply curve indicates a *change in the quantity supplied* in response to a change in the price of the commodity. Thus an increase in supply means that the whole supply curve has shifted to the right; an increase in the quantity supplied means a movement upward to the right along a given supply curve.

Determination of Price by Demand and Supply

So far demand and supply have been considered separately. The next question is this: How do the two forces interact to determine price in a competitive market? Table 4-7 brings together the demand and supply schedules from Tables 4-2 and 4-5. The quantities of carrots demanded and supplied at each price may now be compared.

There is only one price, $60 a ton, at which the quantity of carrots demanded equals the quantity supplied. At prices of less than $60 a ton there is a shortage of carrots because the quantity demanded exceeds the quantity supplied. This is often called a situation of **excess demand.** At prices greater than $60 a ton there is a surplus of carrots because the quantity supplied exceeds the quantity demanded. This is called a situation of **excess supply.**

To discuss the determination of market price, suppose first that the price is $100 a ton. At this price 115,000 tons would be offered for sale, but only 62,500 tons would be demanded. There would be an excess supply of 52,500 tons a month. We assume that sellers will then cut their prices to get rid of this surplus and that purchasers, observing the stock of unsold carrots, will offer less for what they are prepared to buy.

Excess supply causes a downward pressure on price.

Next consider the price of $20 a ton. At this price there is excess demand. The 5,000 tons produced each month are snapped up quickly, and 105,000 tons of desired purchases cannot be made. Rivalry between would-be purchasers may lead to their offering more than the prevailing price to outbid other purchasers. Also, perceiving that they could have sold their available supplies many times over, sellers may begin to ask a higher price for the quantities that they do have to sell.

TABLE 4-7   Demand and Supply Schedules for Carrots and Equilibrium Price

(1) Price per ton *p*	(2) Quantity demanded (thousands of tons per month) *D*	(3) Quantity supplied (thousands of tons per month) *S*	(4) Excess demand (+) or excess supply (−) (thousands of tons per month) *D − S*
$ 20	110.0	5.0	+105.0
40	90.0	46.0	+ 44.0
60	77.5	77.5	0.0
80	67.5	100.0	− 32.5
100	62.5	115.0	− 52.5
120	60.0	122.5	− 62.5

Equilibrium occurs where quantity demanded equals quantity supplied—where there is nei-ther excess demand nor excess supply. These schedules are those of Tables 4-2 and 4-5. The equilibrium price is $60. For lower prices there is excess demand; for higher prices there is excess supply.

SHORTAGE

Excess demand causes an upward pressure on price.

Finally, consider a price of $60. At this price producers wish to sell 77,500 tons a month and purchasers wish to buy that quantity. There is neither a shortage nor a surplus of carrots. There are no unsatisfied buyers to bid the price up, nor are there unsatisfied sellers to force the price down. Once the price of $60 has been reached, therefore, there will be no tendency for it to change.

An equilibrium implies a state of rest, or balance, between opposing forces. The **equilibrium price** is the one toward which the actual market price will tend. It will persist once established, unless it is disturbed by some change in market conditions.

The price at which the quantity demanded equals the quantity supplied is called the equilibrium price.

Any other price is called a **disequilibrium price:** the price at which quantity demanded does not equal quantity supplied, and price will be changing. A market that exhibits either excess demand or excess supply is said to be in a state of **disequilibrium.**

Anything that must be true if equilibrium is to

FIGURE 4-8   Determination of the Equilibrium Price of Carrots

The equilibrium price corresponds to the intersection of the demand and supply curves. Equilibrium is indicated by *E*, which is point *W* on the demand curve and point *w* on the supply curve. At a price of $60 quantity demanded equals quantity supplied. At prices above equilibrium there is excess supply and downward pressure on price. At prices below equilibrium there is excess demand and upward pressure on price The pressures on price are represented by the vertical arrows.

BOX 4-1

Laws, Predictions, Hypotheses

In what sense can the four propositions developed for supply and demand be called "laws"? They are not like acts passed by Congress, interpreted by courts, and enforced by the police; they cannot be repealed if people do not like their effects. Nor are they like the laws of Moses, revealed to man by the voice of God. Are they natural laws similar to Newton's law of gravity? In labeling them *laws*, classical economists clearly had in mind Newton's laws as analogies.

The term *law* is used in science to describe a theory that has stood up to substantial testing. A law of this kind is not something that has been proven to be true for all times and all circumstances, nor is it regarded as immutable. As observations accumulate, laws may often be modified or the range of phenomena to which they apply may be restricted or redefined. Einstein's theory of relativity, for one example, forced such amendments and restrictions on Newton's laws.

The laws of supply and demand have stood up well to many empirical tests, but no one believes that they explain all market behavior. Indeed, the range of markets over which they seem to meet the test of

providing accurate predictions is now much smaller than it was 80 years ago. It is possible—though most economists would think it unlikely—that at some future time they would no longer apply to any real markets. They are thus laws in the sense that they predict certain kinds of behavior in certain situations and the predicted behavior occurs sufficiently often to lead people to continue to have confidence in the predictions of the theory. They are not laws—any more than are the laws of natural science—that are beyond being challenged by present or future observations that may cast their predictions in doubt. Nor is it a heresy to question their applicability to any particular situation.

Laws, then, are hypotheses that have led to predictions that account for observed behavior. They are theories that, in some circumstances at least, have survived attempts to refute them and have proven useful. It is possible, in economics as in the natural sciences, to be impressed both with the "laws" we do have and with their limitations: to be impressed, that is, both with the power of what we know and with the magnitude of what we have yet to understand.

---

be obtained is called an **equilibrium condition.** In the competitive market, the equality of quantity demanded and quantity supplied is an equilibrium condition. [5]

This same story is told in graphical terms in Figure 4-8. The quantities demanded and supplied at any price can be read off the two curves; the magnitude of the shortage or surplus is shown by the horizontal distance between the curves at each price. The figure makes it clear that the equilibrium price occurs where the demand and supply curves intersect. Below that price there will be a shortage and hence an upward pressure on the existing price. Above it there will be a surplus and hence a downward pressure on price. These pressures are represented by the vertical arrows in the figure.

The Laws of Demand and Supply

Changes in any of the variables other than price that influence quantity demanded or supplied will cause a shift in the supply curve or the demand curve or both. There are four possible shifts: (1) a rise in demand (a rightward shift in the demand curve), (2) a fall in demand (a leftward shift in the demand curve), (3) a rise in supply (a rightward shift in the supply curve), and (4) a fall in supply (a leftward shift in the supply curve).

Each of these shifts causes changes that are described by one of the four "laws" of demand and supply. Each of the laws summarizes what happens when an initial position of equilibrium is upset by some shift in either the demand or the supply curve

FIGURE 4-9   The "Laws" of Demand and Supply

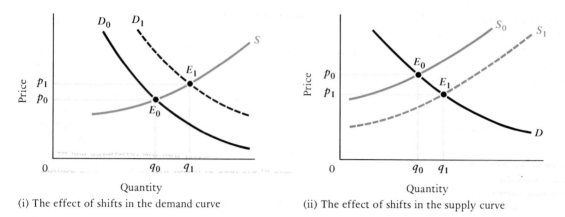

(i) The effect of shifts in the demand curve   (ii) The effect of shifts in the supply curve

The effects on equilibrium price and quantity of shifts in either demand or supply are called the laws of demand and supply.

A rise in demand. In (i) assume that the original demand and supply curves are D_0 and S, which intersect to produce equilibrium at E_0, with a price of p_0 and a quantity of q_0. An increase in demand shifts the demand curve to D_1, taking the new equilibrium to E_1. Price rises to p_1 and quantity rises to q_1.

A fall in demand. In (i) assume that the original demand and supply curves are D_1 and S, which intersect to produce equilibrium at E_1, with a price of p_1 and a quantity of q_1. A decrease in demand shifts the demand curve to D_0, taking the new equilibrium to E_0. Price falls to p_0 and quantity falls to q_0.

A rise in supply. In (ii) assume that the original demand and supply curves are D and S_0, which intersect to produce an equilibrium at E_0, with a price of p_0 and a quantity of q_0. An increase in supply shifts the supply curve to S_1, taking the new equilibrium to E_1. Price falls to p_1 and quantity rises to q_1.

A fall in supply. In (ii) assume that the original demand and supply curves are D and S_1, which intersect to produce an equilibrium at E_1, with a price of p_1 and a quantity of q_1. A decrease in supply shifts the supply curve to S_0, taking the new equilibrium to E_0. Price rises to p_0, and quantity falls to q_0.

and a new equilibrium position is then established. The sense in which it is correct to call these propositions "laws" is discussed in Box 4-1 on page 71.

To discover the effects of each of the curve shifts that we wish to study, we use the method known as **comparative statics.**[6] We start from a position of equilibrium and then introduce the change to be studied. The new equilibrium position is determined

---

[6] The term *statics* is used because we are not concerned about the actual path by which the market goes from the first equilibrium position to the second. Analysis of that path would be described as dynamic analysis.

and compared with the original one. The differences between the two positions of equilibrium must result from changes in the data that were introduced, for everything else has been held constant.

The four laws of demand and supply are derived in Figure 4-9 which generalizes our specific discussion about carrots. Previously, we had given the axes specific labels, but from here on we will simplify. Because it is intended to apply to any commodity, the horizontal axis is simply labeled *Quantity*. This should be understood to mean quantity per period in whatever units output is measured. *Price*, the ver-

B O X   4 - 2

Demand and Supply: What Really Happens

"The theory of supply and demand is neat enough," said the skeptic, "but tell me what really happens."

"What really happens," said the economist, "is that first, demand curves slope downward; second, supply curves slope upward; third, prices rise in response to excess demand; and fourth, prices fall in response to excess supply."

"But that's theory," insisted the skeptic. "What about reality?"

"That is reality as well," said the economist.

"Show me," said the skeptic.

The economist produced the following passages from articles in the *New York Times*.

Increased demand for macadamia nuts causes price to rise above competing nuts. Major producer now plans to double the size of its orchards during the next five years.

*   *   *

OPEC countries once again fail to agree on output quotas. Output soars and prices plummet.

*   *   *

Last summer, Rhode Island officials reopened the northern third of Narragansett Bay, a 9,500-acre fishing ground that had been closed since 1978 because of pollution. Suddenly clam prices dropped, thanks to an underwater population explosion that had transformed the Narragansett area into a clam harvester's dream.

*   *   *

Increasing third world agricultural production threatens the stability of American agriculture. In the 1970s American farm prosperity was built on rising demand due to world prosperity and on falling output in Eastern Europe. Farm experts now worry that the prosperity will prove fragile in the face of major increases in world output.

*   *   *

The effects of [the first year of] deregulation of the nation's airlines were spectacular: cuts in air fares of up to 70 percent in some cases, record passenger jam-ups at the airports, and a spectacular increase in the average load factor [the proportion of occupied seats on the average commercial flight].

The skeptic's response is not recorded, but you will have no trouble telling which clippings illustrate which of the economist's four statements about "what really happens."

---

tical axis, should be understood to mean the price measured as dollars per unit of quantity for the same commodity. The laws of supply and demand are:

1. **A rise in demand causes an increase in both the equilibrium price and the equilibrium quantity exchanged.**
2. **A fall in demand causes a decrease in both the equilibrium price and the equilibrium quantity exchanged.**
3. **A rise in supply causes a decrease in the equilibrium price and an increase in the equilibrium quantity exchanged.**
4. **A fall in supply causes an increase in the equilibrium price and a decrease in the equilibrium quantity exchanged.**

In this chapter we have studied many forces that can cause demand or supply curves to shift. These were summarized in Figures 4-3 and 4-7. By combining this analysis with the four laws, we can link many real-world events that cause demand or supply curves to shift with changes in market prices and quantities.

The theory of the determination of price by demand and supply is beautiful in its simplicity. Yet, as we shall see, it is powerful in its wide range of applications.[7] The usefulness of this theory in interpreting what we see in the world around us is further discussed in Box 4-2.

Prices in Inflation

Up to now we have developed the theory of the prices of individual commodities under the assump-

[7] The laws of demand and supply apply in competitive markets where a supply curve exists and slopes upward. As we shall see later, not all markets satisfy these conditions.

tion that all other prices remained constant. Does this mean that the theory is inapplicable to an inflationary world when almost all prices are rising? Fortunately the answer is no.

The key lies in what are called relative prices. We have mentioned several times that what matters for demand and supply is the price of the commodity in question relative to the prices of other commodities. This is called a **relative price.**

In an inflationary world we are often interested in the price of a given commodity as it relates to the average price of all other commodities. If, during a period when the general price level rose by 40 percent, the price of oranges rose by 60 percent, then the price of oranges rose relative to the price level as a whole. Oranges became *relatively* expensive. However, if oranges had risen in price by only 30 percent when the general price level rose by 40 percent, then the relative price of oranges would have fallen. Although the money price of oranges rose substantially, oranges became *relatively* cheap.

In Lewis Carroll's famous story *Through the Looking Glass,* Alice finds a country where you have to run in order to stay still. So it is with inflation. A commodity's price must rise as fast as the general level of prices just to keep its relative price constant.

It has been convenient in this chapter to analyze a change in a particular price in the context of a constant price level. The analysis is easily extended to an inflationary period by remembering that any force that raises the price of one commodity when other prices remain constant will, given general inflation, raise the price of that commodity faster than the price level is rising. For example, a change in tastes in favor of carrots that would raise their price by 20 percent when other prices were constant, would raise their price by 32 percent if at the same time the general price level goes up by 10 percent.[8] In each case the price of carrots rises 20 percent *relative to the average of all prices.*

In price theory whenever we talk of a change in the price of one commodity, we mean a change relative to other prices.

If the price level is constant, this change requires only that the money price of the commodity in question should rise. If the price level is itself rising, this change requires that the money price of the commodity in question should rise faster than the price level.

---

[8] Let the price level be 100 in the first case and 110 in the second. Let the price of carrots be 120 in the first case and x in the second. To preserve the same relative price we need x such that $120/100 = x/110$, which makes $x = 132$.

Summary

1. The amount of a commodity that households wish to purchase is called the *quantity demanded.* It is a flow expressed as so much per period of time. It is determined by the commodity's own price, average household income, the prices of related commodities, tastes, the distribution of income among households, and the size of the population.

2. Quantity demanded is assumed to increase as the price of the commodity falls, *ceteris paribus.* The relationship between quantity demanded and price is represented graphically by a demand curve that shows how much will be demanded at each market price. A movement along a demand curve indicates a change in the quantity demanded in response to a change in the price of the commodity.

3. A shift in a demand curve represents a change in the quantity demanded at each price and is referred to as a *change in demand.* The demand curve shifts to the right (an increase in demand) if average income rises, if the price of a substitute rises, if the price of a complement falls, if population rises, or if there is a change in tastes

in favor of the product. The opposite changes shift the demand curve to the left (a decrease in demand).

4. The amount of a commodity that firms wish to sell is called the *quantity supplied*. It is a flow expressed as so much per period of time. It depends on the commodity's own price, the costs of inputs, the goals of the firm, and the state of technology.

5. Quantity supplied is assumed to increase as the price of the commodity increases, *ceteris paribus*. The relationship between quantity supplied and price is represented graphically by a supply curve that shows how much will be supplied at each market price. A movement along a supply curve indicates a change in the quantity supplied in response to a change in price.

6. A shift in the supply curve indicates a change in the quantity supplied at each price and is referred to as a *change in supply*. The supply curve shifts to the right (an increase in supply) if the costs of producing the commodity fall, or if, for any reason, producers become more willing to produce the commodity. The opposite changes shift the supply curve to the left (a decrease in supply).

7. The *equilibrium price* is the one at which the quantity demanded equals the quantity supplied. At any price below equilibrium there will be excess demand; at any price above equilibrium there will be excess supply. Graphically, equilibrium occurs where demand and supply curves intersect.

8. Price is assumed to rise when there is a shortage and to fall when there is a surplus. Thus the actual market price will be pushed toward the equilibrium price, and when it is reached, there will be neither shortage nor surplus and price will not change until either the supply curve or the demand curve shifts.

9. Using the method of comparative statics, the effects of a shift in either demand or supply can be determined. A rise in demand raises both equilibrium price and quantity; a fall in demand lowers both. A rise in supply raises equilibrium quantity but lowers equilibrium price; a fall in supply lowers equilibrium quantity but raises equilibrium price. These are the so-called laws of supply and demand.

10. Price theory is most simply developed in the context of a constant price level. Price changes discussed in the theory are changes relative to the average level of all prices. In an inflationary period a rise in the *relative price* of one commodity means that its price rises by more than the price level; a fall in its relative price means that its price rises by less than the price level.

Topics for Review

Quantity demanded and quantity exchanged
Demand schedule and demand curve
Quantity supplied and quantity exchanged
Supply schedule and supply curve
Movement along a curve and shift of a whole curve

Change in quantity demanded and change in demand
Change in quantity supplied and change in supply
Equilibrium, equilibrium price, and disequilibrium
Comparative statics
Laws of supply and demand
Relative price

Discussion Questions

1. What shifts in demand or supply curves would produce the following results? (Assume that only one of the two curves has shifted.)
   a. The price of pocket calculators has fallen over the last few years and the quantity exchanged has risen greatly.
   b. As the American standard of living rose over the past three decades, both the prices and the consumption of prime cuts of beef rose steadily.
   c. Summer sublets in Ann Arbor, Michigan, are at rents of 50 percent or less of the regular rental.
   d. Style changes cause the sale of jeans to decline.
   e. Potato blight causes spud prices to soar.
   f. "Gourmet food market grows as affluent shoppers indulge."
   g. Oil prices tumble as OPEC countries violate production quotas.
2. Recently the Department of Agriculture predicted that this spring's excellent weather would result in larger crops of corn and wheat than farmers had expected. But its chief economist warned consumers not to expect prices to decrease since the costs of production were rising and foreign demand for American crops was increasing. "The classic pattern of supply and demand won't work this time," the economist said. Discuss his observation.
3. Explain each of the following in terms of changes in supply and demand.
   a. Du Pont increased the price of synthetic fibers, although it acknowledged demand was weak.
   b. The Edsel was a lemon when produced in 1958–1960 but is now a best-seller among cars of its vintage.
   c. The decision not to deploy the MX missile in western Utah signaled the collapse in land prices in that area.
   d. Some of the first $10 coins minted in Canada to commemorate the Olympics were imperfectly stamped. These flawed pieces are currently worth as much as $1,000.
4. Suppose that video recorder producers find that they are selling more video recorders at the same price than they did two years ago. Is this a shift of the demand curve or a movement along the curve? Suggest at least four reasons why this rise in sales at an unchanged price might occur.
5. What would be the effect on the equilibrium price and quantity of marijuana if its sale were legalized?
6. The relative price of personal computers has dropped drastically over time. Would you explain this falling price in terms of demand or supply changes? What factors are likely to have caused the demand or supply shifts that did occur?

7. Classify the effect of each of the following as (i) a decrease in the demand for fish, (ii) a decrease in the quantity of fish demanded, or (iii) other. Illustrate each diagrammatically.
   a. The government of Iceland bars fishermen of other nations from its waters.
   b. People buy less fish because of a rise in fish prices.
   c. The Roman Catholic Church relaxes its ban on eating meat on Fridays.
   d. The price of beef falls and as a result households buy more beef and less fish.
   e. In the interests of training marine personnel for national defense, the U.S. government decides to subsidize the American fishing industry.
   f. It is discovered that eating fish is better for one's health than eating meat.
8. Predict the effect on the price of at least one commodity of each of the following:
   a. Winter snowfall is at record high in Colorado, but drought continues in New England ski areas.
   b. A recession decreases employment in Detroit automobile factories.
   c. The French grape harvest is the smallest in 20 years.
   d. The state of New York cancels permission for citizens to cut firewood in state parks.
9. Are the following two observations inconsistent? (a) Rising demand for housing causes prices of new homes to soar; (b) families reduce purchases of housing as prices become prohibitive.

5

Elasticity of Demand
and Supply

Quantitative (#'s)

The laws of demand and supply predict the direction of changes in price and quantity in response to various shifts in demand and supply. But often it is not enough to know merely whether quantity rises or falls in response to a change in price; it is also important to know by how much.

When flood damage led to major destruction of the onion crop, onion prices rose generally. In Hartford, Connecticut, they rose 42 percent in one week. Not surprisingly, overall consumption fell. The press reported that many consumers stopped using onions altogether and substituted onion salt, sauerkraut, cabbage, and other products. Other consumers still bought onions, but in reduced quantities. Were aggregate dollar sales of onions (price times quantity) higher or lower? The data above do not tell, but this is the sort of information that may matter a good deal. A government concerned with the effect of a bad crop on farm income will not be satisfied with being told that food prices will rise and quantities consumed will fall; it will need to know by approximately how much they will change if it is to assess the effects on farmers.

In 1982 the New York City Opera, faced with a growing deficit, cut its ticket prices by 20 percent, hoping to attract more customers. At the same time the New York Transit Authority raised subway fares to reduce its growing deficit. Was one of these two opposite approaches to reducing a deficit necessarily wrong? The answer, as we shall see, is not necessarily.

Measuring and describing the extent of the responsiveness of quantities to changes in prices and other variables is often essential if we are to understand the significance of these changes. This is what the concept of elasticity does.

Price Elasticity of Demand

Suppose there is an increase in a farm crop, that is, a rightward shift in the supply curve. The two parts of Figure 5-1 show the same rightward shift. Because the demand curves are different, the magnitude of the effects on equilibrium price and quantity are different.

A shift in supply will have different quantitative effects depending on the shape of the demand curve.

FIGURE 5-1 - The Effect of the Shape of the Demand Curve

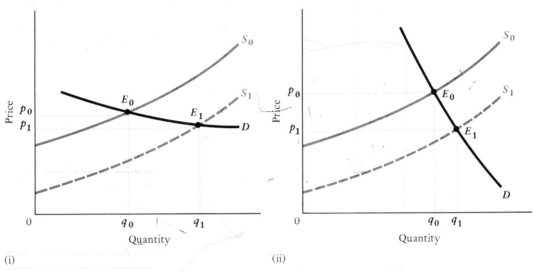

(i)   (ii)

The flatter the demand curve, the less the change in price and the greater the change in quantity. Both parts of the figure show the same shift in the supply curve. In each part initial equilibrium is at price p_0 and output q_0 and the new equilibrium is at p_1 and q_1. In (i) the effect of the shift in supply from S_0 to S_1 is a slight fall in the price and a large increase in quantity. In (ii) the effect of the identical shift in the supply curve from S_0 to S_1 is a large fall in the price and a relatively small increase in quantity.

The difference may have great policy significance. Consider what would happen if the rightward shift of the supply curve shown in Figure 5-1 occurs because the government has persuaded farmers to produce more of a certain crop. (It might, for example, have paid a subsidy to farmers for producing this crop.)

Figure 5-1(i) illustrates a case in which the quantity that consumers demand is very sensitive to price changes. The extra production brings down price, but because the quantity demanded is quite responsive, only a small change in price is necessary to restore equilibrium. The effect of the government's policy, therefore, is to achieve a large increase in the production and sales of this commodity and only a small decrease in price.

Figure 5-1(ii) shows a case in which the quantity demanded is quite unresponsive to price changes. As before, the increase in supply at the original price

causes a surplus that brings the price down. But this time the quantity demanded by consumers does not increase much in response to the fall in price. Thus the price continues to drop until, discouraged by lower and lower prices, farmers reduce the quantity supplied nearly to the level attained before they received the increased incentive to produce. The effect of the government's policy is to bring about a large fall in the price and only a small increase in the quantity produced and sold.

In both of the cases shown in Figure 5-1, it can be seen that the government's policy has exactly the same effectiveness as far as farmers' willingness to supply the commodity is concerned (the supply curve shifts are identical). But the effects on the equilibrium price and quantity are very different because of the different degrees to which the quantity demanded by consumers responds to price changes. If the purpose of the policy is to increase the quantity of this commodity produced and consumed, the policy will be a great success when the demand curve is similar to the one shown in Figure 5-1(i), but it will be a failure when the demand curve is similar to the one shown in Figure 5-1(ii). If, however, the main purpose of the policy is to achieve a large reduction in the price of the commodity, the policy will be a failure when demand is as shown in (i), but it will be a great success when demand is as shown in (ii).

The Measurement of Price Elasticity

In Figure 5-1 a measure of demand responsiveness to a change in price could be obtained by comparing the geometrical steepness of the two demand curves because they were both drawn on the same scale. Thus, for any given price change, the quantity changes more on the flatter curve than it does on the steeper one. However, it can be <u>misleading</u> to inspect a *single* curve and to conclude from its general appearance something about the degree of responsiveness of quantity demanded to price changes. You can make a curve appear as steep or as flat as you like by changing the scales. For example, a curve that looks steep when the horizontal scale is 1 inch = 100 units will look much flatter when the horizontal scale is 1 inch = 1 unit as long as the same vertical scale is used in each case.

[margin note: Prob's when using slope as a measure for demand curve]

Instead of gaining a vague general impression from the shape of demand curves, one could note the actual change in quantity demanded in response to a certain price change. But it would still be impossible to compare degrees of responsiveness for different commodities.

Assume that we have the information shown in Table 5-1. Should we conclude that the demand for

radios is not as responsive to price changes as the demand for beef? After all, price cuts of $.20 cause quite a large increase in the quantity of beef demanded but only a small increase in radios.

There are two problems here. First, a reduction of price of $.20 will be a large price cut for a low-priced commodity and an insignificant price cut for a high-priced commodity. The price reductions listed in Table 5-1 represent different fractions of the total prices. It is usually more revealing to know the percentage change in the prices of the various commodities. Second, by an analogous argument, knowing the quantity by which demand changes is not very revealing unless the level of demand is also known. An increase of 7,500 pounds is quite a significant reaction of demand if the quantity formerly bought was 15,000 pounds, but it is only a drop in the bucket if the quantity formerly demanded was 10 million pounds.

Table 5-2 shows the original and new levels of price and quantity. Changes in price and quantity expressed as percentages of the average prices and quantities are shown in the first two columns of Table 5-3.[1] **Elasticity of demand,** the measure of responsiveness of quantity demanded to price changes, is symbolized by the Greek letter eta, **η**. It is defined as: **[6]**

$$\eta = \frac{\text{percentage change in quantity demanded}}{\text{percentage change in price}}$$

This measure is frequently called *demand elasticity*. When it is necessary to distinguish it from other related concepts, it may, however, be called **price elasticity of demand,** since the variable causing the change in quantity demanded is the commodity's own price.

TABLE 5-1 Price Reductions and Corresponding Increases in Quantity Demanded

Commodity	Reduction in price	Increase in quantity demanded
Beef	$.20 per pound	7,500 pounds
Men's shirts	.20 per shirt	5,000 shirts
Radios	.20 per radio	100 radios

---

[1] The use of averages is designed to avoid the ambiguity caused by the fact that, for example, the $.20 change in the price of beef is a different percentage of the original price, $1.70, than it is of the new price, $1.50 (11.8 percent versus 13.3 percent). We want the elasticity of demand between any two points (*A* and *B*) to be independent of whether we move from *A* to *B* or from *B* to *A;* as a result, using either original prices and quantities or new prices and quantities would be less satisfactory than using averages. In this illustration $.20 is unambiguously 12.5 percent of $1.60 and applies to a price increase from $1.50 to $1.70, as well as to a decrease discussed in the text. Further discussion is found in the appendix to this chapter.

TABLE 5-2   Price and Quantity Information Underlying Data of Table 5-1

Commodity	Unit	Original price	New price	Average price	Original quantity	New quantity	Average quantity
Beef	per pound	$ 1.70	$ 1.50	$ 1.60	116,250	123,750	120,000
Men's shirts	per shirt	8.10	7.90	8.00	197,500	202,500	200,000
Radios	per radio	40.10	39.90	40.00	9,950	10,050	10,000

These data provide the appropriate context of the data given in Table 5-1. The table relates the $.20 per unit price reduction of each commodity to the actual prices and quantities demanded.

Interpreting Numerical Elasticities

Because demand curves slope downward, an *increase* in price is associated with a *decrease* in quantity demanded and vice versa. Since the percentage changes in price and quantity have opposite signs, demand elasticity is a negative number. (We shall follow the usual practice of ignoring the negative sign and speak of the measure as a positive number, as we have done in the illustrative calculations in Table 5-3.) Thus, the more responsive the quantity demanded, for example, radios relative to beef, the greater the elasticity of demand and the higher the measure: 2.0 compared to 0.5.

The numerical value of elasticity can vary from zero to infinity. Elasticity is zero when quantity demanded does not respond at all to a price change. As long as the percentage change in quantity is less than the percentage change in price, the elasticity of demand has a value of less than unity (i.e., less than

one). When the two percentage changes are equal to each other, elasticity is equal to unity. When the percentage change in quantity exceeds the percentage change in price, the value for the elasticity of demand is greater than unity.

When the percentage change in quantity is less than the percentage change in price (elasticity less than one), the demand is said to be **inelastic.** When the percentage change in quantity is greater than the percentage change in price (elasticity greater than one), the demand is said to be **elastic.** This terminology is important, and you should become familiar with it. It is summarized in the first half of Box 5-1.

A demand curve need not, and usually does not, have the same elasticity over every part of the curve. Figure 5-2 on page 83 shows that a downward-sloping, straight-line demand curve does not have a constant elasticity. A straight line has constant elasticity only when it is vertical or when it is horizontal. Figure 5-3 on page 83 illustrates three special cases of demand curves with constant elasticities.

Price Elasticity and Changes in Total Expenditure

The total amount spent by purchasers is also the total revenue received by the sellers. How does this revenue react when the price of a product is changed? The simplest example will show that it may rise or fall in response to a decrease in price. Suppose 100 units of a commodity are being sold at a unit price of $1. The price is then cut to $.90. If the quantity sold rises to 110, the total revenue of the sellers falls from $100 to $99; but if quantity sold rises to 120, total revenue rises from $100 to $108.

What happens to total revenue depends on the

TABLE 5-3   Calculation of Demand Elasticities

Commodity	(1) Percentage decrease in price	(2) Percentage increase in quantity	(3) Elasticity of demand (2) ÷ (1)
Beef	12.5	6.25	0.5
Men's shirts	2.5	2.5	1.0
Radios	0.5	1.0	2.0

Elasticity of demand is the percentage change in quantity divided by the percentage change in price. The percentage changes are based on average prices and quantities shown in Table 5-2. For example, the $.20 per pound decrease in the price of beef is 12.5 percent of $1.60. A $.20 change in the price of radios is only 0.5 percent of the average price per radio of $40.

BOX 5-1

Terminology of Elasticity

Term	Symbol	Numerical measure of elasticity	Verbal description
A. Price elasticity of demand (supply)	$\eta(\eta_S)$		
Perfectly or completely inelastic		Zero	Quantity demanded [supplied] does not change as price changes.
Inelastic		Greater than zero, less than one	Quantity demanded [supplied] changes by a smaller percentage than does price.
Unit elasticity		One	Quantity demanded [supplied] changes by exactly the same percentage as does price.
Elastic		Greater than one, less than infinity	Quantity demanded [supplied] changes by a larger percentage than does price.
Perfectly, completely, or infinitely elastic		Infinity	Purchasers [sellers] are prepared to buy [sell] all they can at some price and none at all at an even slightly higher [lower] price.
B. Income elasticity of demand	η_Y		
Inferior good		Negative	Quantity demanded decreases as income increases.
Normal good		Positive	Quantity demanded increases as income increases:
Income-inelastic		Greater than zero, less than one	less than in proportion to income increase
Income-elastic		Greater than one	more than in proportion to income increase
C. Cross elasticity of demand	η_{xy}		
Substitute		Positive	Price increase of a substitute leads to an increase in quantity demanded of this good (and less of the substitute).
Complement		Negative	Price increase of a complement leads to a decrease in quantity demanded of this good (as well as less of the complement).

UNITY = ONE

FIGURE 5-2   Elasticity Along a Straight-Line Demand Curve

Moving down a straight-line demand curve, elasticity falls continuously. On this straight line a reduction in price of $.10 always leads to the same increase (1,000 units) in quantity. Near the upper end of the curve, however, where price is $2 and quantity is 1,000 units, a reduction in price of $.10 (from $2.05 to $1.95) is only a 5 percent price reduction, but the 1,000-unit increase in quantity is a 100 percent quantity increase. Here, elasticity (η) is 20. At the price of $.50 and quantity of 16,000 units, a price reduction of $.10 (from $.55 to $.45) leads to the same 1,000-unit increase in demand. The 20 percent price decrease combines with the 6.25 percent quantity increase to give an elasticity of 0.31.

price elasticity of demand. If elasticity is less than unity, the percentage change in price exceeds the percentage change in quantity. The price change will then dominate so that total revenue will change in the same direction as the price changes. If, however, elasticity exceeds unity, the percentage change in quantity exceeds the percentage change in price. The quantity change will then dominate so that total revenue will change in the same direction as quantity changes (that is, in the opposite direction to the change in price).

Notice what happened to total revenue when the prices of radios, shirts, and beef fell in our example. (The calculations are shown in Table 5-4.) In the case of beef the demand is inelastic and a cut in price lowers the sellers' revenue; in the case of radios the demand is elastic and a cut in price raises revenue. The borderline case is men's shirts; here the elasticity is unity and the cut in price leaves revenue unchanged.

The general relations between elasticity and change in price can be summarized as follows:

1. If demand is elastic, a fall in price increases total revenue and a rise in price reduces it.
2. If demand is inelastic, a fall in price reduces total revenue and a rise in price increases it.
3. If elasticity of demand is unity, a rise or a fall in price leaves total revenue unaffected. [7]

Consider two real examples. When a bumper potato crop in the United States sent prices down 50 percent, quantity sold increased only 15 percent and potato farmers found their revenues falling sharply.

FIGURE 5-3   Three Demand Curves

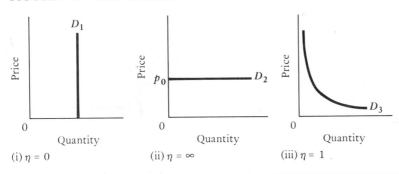

(i) $\eta = 0$ (ii) $\eta = \infty$ (iii) $\eta = 1$

Each of these demand curves has constant elasticity. D_1 has *zero elasticity:* The quantity demanded does not change at all when price changes. D_2 has *infinite elasticity* at the price p_0: A small price increase from p_0 decreases quantity demanded from an indefinitely large amount to zero. D_3 has *unit elasticity:* A given percentage increase in price brings an equal percentage decrease in quantity demanded at all points on the curve.

TABLE 5-4   Changes in Total Revenue (Total Expenditure) for the Example of Table 5-2

Commodity	Price × quantity (original prices and quantities)	Price × quantity (new prices and quantities)	Change in revenue (expenditure)	Elasticity of demand from Table 5-3
Beef	$ 197,625	$ 185,625	− $12,000	0.5
Men's shirts	1,599,750	1,599,750	0	1.0
Radios	398,995	400,995	+ 2,000	2.0

Whether revenue increases or decreases in response to a price cut depends on whether demand is elastic or inelastic.   The $197,625 figure is the product of the original price of beef ($1.70) and the original quantity (116,250 pounds); $185,625 is the product of the new price ($1.50) and quantity (123,750), and so on.

Demand was clearly inelastic. When, some years ago, Salt Lake City's transit authority cut its bus fares by 40 percent for the average journey, the volume of passenger traffic increased from 4.4 million to 14 million journeys within two years and revenues rose sharply. Demand was clearly elastic.

What Determines Elasticity of Demand?

Table 5-5 shows some measured elasticities of demand. Evidently, they can vary considerably. The main determinant of elasticity is the availability of substitutes. Some commodities, such as margarine, cabbage, lamb, and Fords, have quite close substitutes—butter, other green vegetables, beef, and similar makes of cars. A change in the price of these commodities, *the prices of the substitutes remaining constant,* can be expected to cause much substitution. A fall in price leads consumers to buy more of the commodity and less of the substitutes, and a rise in price leads consumers to buy less of the commodity and more of the substitutes. More broadly defined commodities, such as all foods, all clothing, cigarettes, and gasoline, have few if any satisfactory substitutes. A rise in their price can be expected to cause a smaller fall in quantity demanded than would be the case if close substitutes were available.

A commodity with close substitutes tends to have an elastic demand, one with no close substitutes an inelastic demand.

Closeness of substitutes—and thus measured elasticity—depends both on how the commodity is de-

fined and on the time period. This is explored in the following sections.

Definition of the Commodity

Food is a necessity of life. Thus, for food taken as a whole, demand is inelastic over a large price range. It does not follow, however, that any one food, such as white bread or beef, is a necessity in the same sense. Individual foods can have quite elastic demands, and they frequently do.

Durable goods provide a similar example. Durables as a whole are less elastic than individual kinds of durable goods. For example, when the price of television sets rises, many households may replace their lawnmower or their vacuum cleaner instead of buying that extra television set. Thus, while their purchases of television sets fall, their total purchases of durables do not.

Because most specific manufactured goods have close substitutes, studies show they tend to have price-elastic demand. Millinery, for example, has been estimated to have an elasticity of 3.0. In contrast, clothing in general tends to be inelastic.

Any one of a group of related products will tend to have an elastic demand, even though the demand for the group as a whole may be inelastic.

Long-Run and Short-Run Elasticity of Demand

Because it takes time to develop satisfactory substitutes, a demand that is inelastic in the short run may

TABLE 5-5 Estimated Price Elasticities of Demand in the United States[a] *(selected commodities)*

Demand significantly inelastic (less than 0.9)	
Potatoes	0.3
Sugar	0.3
Public transportation	0.4
All foods	0.4
Cigarettes	0.5
Gasoline	0.6
All clothing	0.6
Consumer durables	0.8
Demand of close to unit elasticity (between 0.9 and 1.1.)	
Beef	
Beer	
Marijuana	
Demand significantly elastic (more than 1.1)	
Furniture	1.2
Electricity	1.3
Lamb and mutton (U.K.)	1.5
Automobiles	2.1
Millinery	3.0

[a] For the United States except where noted.

The wide range of price elasticities is illustrated by these selected measures. These elasticities, from various studies, are representative of literally hundreds of existing estimates. Explanations of some of the differences are discussed in the text.

prove elastic when enough time has passed. For example, when the Tennessee Valley Authority (TVA) brought cheap electric power to the rural South in the 1930s, few households were wired for electricity. The initial measurements showed demand for electricity to be very inelastic. Some commentators even argued that it was foolish to invest so much money in bringing cheap electricity to the South because people did not buy it even at low prices. But gradually households became electrified and purchased appliances, and new industries moved into the area to take advantage of TVA's cheap electric power. As this occurred, measured elasticity steadily increased.

Petroleum provides a more recent example. When the first OPEC oil price shock occurred in the mid 1970s, the short-run demand for oil proved highly inelastic. Large price increases were met in the short run by very small reductions in quantity

demanded. In this case the short run lasted for several years. Gradually, however, the high price of petroleum products led to such adjustments as the development of smaller, more fuel-efficient cars, economizing on heating oil by installing more efficient insulation, and replacement of fuel oil in many industrial processes by such other power sources as coal and hydroelectricity. The long-run elasticity of demand, relating the change in price to the change in quantity demanded after all adjustments were made, turned out to be well in excess of one, although the long-run adjustments took as much as a decade to work out.

The degree of response to a price change, and thus the measured price elasticity of demand, will tend to be greater the longer the time span considered.

Because the elasticity of demand for a commodity changes over time as consumers adjust their habits and substitutes are developed, the demand curve also changes; hence a distinction can be made between short-run and long-run demand curves. Every demand curve shows the response of consumer demand to a change in price. For such commodities as cornflakes and pillowcases, the full response occurs quickly and there is little reason to worry about longer term effects. But other commodities are typically used in connection with highly durable appliances or machines. A change in price of, say, electricity and gasoline may not have its major effect until the stock of appliances and machines using these commodities has been adjusted. This adjustment may take a long time to occur.

For commodities whose substitutes are developed over a period of time, it is helpful to identify two kinds of demand curve. A *short-run demand curve* shows the response of quantity demanded to a change in price for a given structure of the durable goods that use the commodity and for the existing sets of substitute commodities. A different short-run demand curve will exist for each such structure.

The *long-run demand curve* shows the response of quantity demanded to a change in price after enough time has passed to assure that all adjustments to the changed price have occurred. The relation between long-run and short-run demand curves is shown in

Figure 5-4. The principal conclusion, already suggested in the above discussion, is:

> The long-run demand curve for a commodity will tend to be substantially more elastic than any of the short-run demand curves.

The importance of this distinction will be evident in the chapters that follow.

Other Demand Elasticities

Income Elasticity of Demand

One of the most important determinants of demand is the income of the potential customers. When the Food and Agricultural Organization (FAO) of the United Nations wants to estimate the future demand for some crop, it needs to know by how much world income will grow and how much of that additional income will be spent on the particular foodstuff. For example, as a nation gets richer, its consumption patterns change, with relatively more being spent on meat and relatively less on staples such as rice and potatoes.

The responsiveness of demand to changes in income is termed **income elasticity of demand** and may be symbolized η_y.

$$\eta_y = \frac{\text{percentage change in quantity demanded}}{\text{percentage change in income}}$$

For most goods increases in income lead to increases in demand and income elasticity will be positive. These are called **normal goods**. Goods for which consumption decreases in response to a rise in income have negative income elasticities and are called **inferior goods**.

The income elasticity of normal goods may be greater than unity (elastic) or less than unity (inelastic), depending on whether the percentage change in the quantity demanded is greater or less than the percentage change in income that brought it about. It is also common to use the terms *income-elastic* and *income-inelastic* to refer to income elasticities of greater or less than unity. See Box 5-1 on page 82 for further discussion of elasticity terminology.

FIGURE 5-4   Short-Run and Long-Run Demand Curves

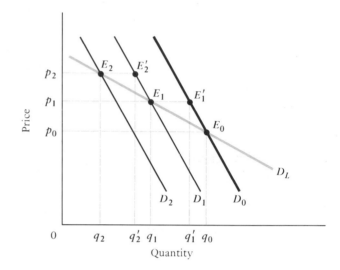

The long-run demand curve is more elastic than the short-run curves. D_L is a long-run demand curve. Suppose consumers are fully adjusted to price p_0. Equilibrium is then at E_0, with quantity demanded q_0. Now suppose price rises to p_1. In the short run consumers will react along the short-run demand curve D_0 and reduce consumption to q_1'. Once time has permitted the full range of adjustments to price p_1, however, a new equilibrium at E_1 will be reached with quantity q_1, leading to a new short-run demand curve D_1. A further rise in price to p_2 would lead first to a short-run equilibrium at E_2', but eventually to a new long-run equilibrium at E_2. The screened long-run demand curve is more elastic than the short-run curves.

The reaction of demand to changes in income is extremely important. We know that in most Western countries economic growth has caused the level of income to double every 20 to 30 years over a sustained period of at least a century. This rise in income is shared to some extent by most citizens. As they find their incomes increasing, they increase their demands for most commodities. But the demands for some commodities such as food and basic clothing, will not increase much, while the demands for other commodities increase rapidly. In developing countries, such as Ireland and Mexico, the demand for durable goods is increasing most rapidly as household incomes rise, while in the United States it is the demand for services that is rising most rapidly. The uneven impact of the growth of income on the demands for different commodities has important effects on the economy and groups in it, and these will be studied at several different points in this book, beginning with the discussion of agriculture in Chapter 6.

What Determines Income Elasticity?

The variations in income elasticities shown in Table 5-6 suggest that the more basic or staple a commodity, the lower is its income elasticity. Food as a whole has an income elasticity of 0.2, consumer durables of 1.8. In the United States pork and such starchy roots as potatoes are inferior goods; their quantity consumed falls as income rises.

Does the distinction between luxuries and necessities explain differences in income elasticities? The table suggests that it does. The case of meals eaten away from home is one example. Such meals are almost always more expensive, calorie for calorie, than meals prepared at home. It would thus be expected that at lower ranges of income restaurant meals would be regarded as an expensive luxury, but the demand for them would expand substantially as households became richer. This is in fact what happens.

Does this mean that the market demand for the foodstuffs that appear on restaurant menus will also have high income elasticities? Generally the answer is no. When a household eats out rather than preparing meals at home, the main change is not in what is eaten but in who prepares it. The additional expenditure on "food" goes mainly to pay cooks and waiters and to yield a return on the restaurateur's capital. Thus, when a household expands its expenditure on restaurant food by 2.4 percent in response to a 1 percent rise in its income, most of the extra expenditure on "food" goes to workers in service industries; little, if any, finds its way into the pockets of farmers. Here is a striking example of the general tendency for households to spend a rising proportion

TABLE 5-6   Estimated Income Elasticities of Demand[a] *(selected commodities)*

Inferior goods (negative income elasticities)	
Whole milk	−0.5
Pig products	−0.2
Starchy roots	−0.2
Inelastic normal goods (0.0 to 1.0)	
Coffee	0.0
Wine (France)	0.1
All food	0.2
Poultry	0.3
Cheese	0.4
Beef	0.5
Housing	0.6
Cigarettes	0.8
Elastic normal goods (greater than 1.0)	
Gasoline	1.1
Wine	1.4
Cream (U.K.)	1.7
Wine (Canada)	1.8
Consumer durables	1.8
Poultry (Sri Lanka)	2.0
Restaurant meals (U.K.)	2.4

[a] For the United States except where noted.

Income elasticities vary widely across commodities and sometimes across countries. The basic source of food estimates by country is the FAO, but many individual studies have been made. Explanations of some of the differences are discussed in the text.

of their incomes on services as their incomes rise and a lower proportion on foodstuffs.

The more basic an item in the consumption pattern of households, the lower its income elasticity.

So far we have focused on differences in income elasticities among commodities. However, income elasticities for any one commodity also vary with the level of a household's income. When incomes are low, households may eat almost no meat and consume lots of starchy foods such as bread and potatoes; at higher income levels they may eat the cheaper cuts of meat and more green vegetables along with their bread and potatoes; at yet higher levels they are likely to eat more (and more expensive) meat, to substitute frozen for canned vegetables, and to eat a greater variety of foods.

What is true of individual households is also true of countries. Empirical studies show that for different countries at comparable stages of economic development, income elasticities are similiar. But the countries of the world are at various stages of economic development and so have widely different income elasticities for the same products. Notice in Table 5-6 the different income elasticity of poultry in the United States, where it is a standard item of consumption, and in Sri Lanka, where it is a luxury.

Graphical Representation

Increases in income shift the demand curve for a normal good to the right and for an inferior good to the left. Figure 5-5 shows a different kind of graph, an **income-consumption curve.** The curve resembles an ordinary demand curve in one respect: It shows the relation of quantity demanded to one variable, *ceteris paribus*. The variable, however, is not price but household income. (An increase in the price of the commodity, incomes remaining constant, would shift the curves shown in Figure 5-5 downward.)

The figure shows three different patterns of income elasticity. Goods that consumers regard as necessities will have high income elasticities at low levels of income, but show low income elasticities beyond some level. The obvious reason is that as incomes rise, it becomes possible for households to devote a smaller proportion of their income to meeting basic needs and a larger proportion to buying things they have always wanted but could not afford. Some of these necessities may even become inferior goods. So-called luxury goods will not tend to be purchased at low levels of income but will have high income elasticities once incomes rise enough to permit households to sample the better things of life available to them.[2]

[2] In Figure 5-5, in contrast to the ordinary demand curve, quantity demanded is on the vertical axis. This follows the usual practice of putting the to-be-explained variable (called the *dependent variable*) on the vertical axis and the explanatory variable (called the *independent variable*) on the horizontal axis. It is the ordinary demand curve that has the axes "backward." This practice dates to Alfred Marshall's *Principles of Economics* (1890), the classic that is one of the foundation stones of modern price theory. [8] For better or worse, Marshall's scheme is now used by everybody, although mathematicians never fail to wonder at this further example of the odd ways of economists.

Cross Elasticity of Demand

The responsiveness of demand to changes in the prices of other commodities is called **cross elasticity of demand**. It is often denoted η_{xy} and defined as

$$\eta_{xy} = \frac{\text{percentage change in quantity demanded of one good } (X)}{\text{percentage change in price of another good } (Y)}$$

Cross elasticity can vary from minus infinity to plus infinity. Complementary commodities such as cars and gasoline, have negative cross elasticities. A large rise in the price of gasoline will lead (as it did in the United States) to a decline in the demand for cars as some people decided to do without a car and others decided not to buy a second (or third) car. Substitute commodities, such as cars and public transport, have positive cross elasticities. A large rise in the price of cars (relative to public transport) would lead to a rise in the demand for public transport as some people shifted from cars to public transport.

Measures of cross elasticity sometimes prove helpful in defining whether producers of similar products are in competition with each other. For example, glass bottles and tin cans have a high cross elasticity of demand. The producer of bottles is thus in competition with the producer of cans. If the bottle company raises its price, it will lose substantial sales to the can producer. Men's shoes and women's shoes have a low cross elasticity. A producer of men's shoes is not in close competition with a producer of women's shoes. If the former raises its price, it will not lose many sales to the latter. This kind of knowledge has been extremely important in antitrust cases where the issue was whether a firm in one industry was or was not in active competition with firms in another industry. Indeed, many of the most interesting studies of cross elasticity have been made during antitrust inquiries to determine whether specific products are substitutes (see Chapter 16.) Whether celophane and Saran Wrap or aluminum cable and copper cable are or are not substitutes may determine questions of monopoly under the law. The positive or negative sign and the size of cross elasticities tell us whether or not goods are substitutes.

FIGURE 5-5   Income-Consumption Curves of Different Commodities

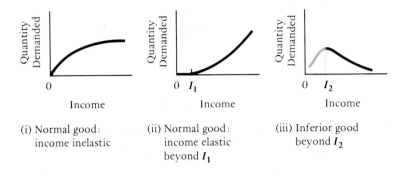

(i) Normal good:
    income inelastic

(ii) Normal good:
    income elastic
    beyond I_1

(iii) Inferior good
    beyond I_2

Different shapes of the curve relating quantity demanded to income correspond to different ranges of income elasticity. Normal goods have rising curves; inferior goods, falling curves. Many different patterns of income elasticity have been observed. The good in (i) is a typical normal good that is a necessity. It is purchased at all levels of income; even at high levels some fraction of extra income is spent on it, although this fraction steadily decreases. The good in (ii) is a luxury good that is income elastic beyond income I_1. The good in (iii) is a necessity at low incomes that becomes an inferior good for incomes beyond I_2.

Elasticity of Supply

The concept of elasticity can be applied to supply as well as to demand. Just as elasticity of demand measures the response of quantity demanded to changes in any of the forces that influence it, so elasticity of supply measures the response of quantity supplied to changes in any of the forces that influence it. We will focus on the commodity's own price as a factor influencing supply.

Elasticity of supply measures the responsiveness of the quantity supplied to a change in the commodity's own price. It is denoted η_S and defined as

$$\eta_S = \frac{\text{percentage change in quantity supplied}}{\text{percentage change in price}}$$

The supply curves considered in this chapter all have positive slopes: An increase in price causes an increase in quantity sold. Such supply curves all have positive elasticities.

There are important special cases. If the supply curve is vertical—the quantity supplied does not change as price changes—elasticity of supply is zero. This would be the case, for example, if suppliers produced a given quantity and dumped it on the market for whatever it would bring. A horizontal supply curve has an infinitely high elasticity of supply: A small drop in price would reduce the quantity

producers are willing to supply from an indefinitely large amount to zero. Between these two extremes elasticity of supply will vary with the shape of the supply curve.[3]

What Determines Elasticity of Supply?

Supply elasticities are important for many problems in economics. We shall discuss them only briefly here for two reasons. First, much of the treatment of demand elasticity carries over to supply elasticity and does not need repeating. For example, the ease of substitution can vary in production as well as in consumption. If the price of a commodity rises, how much more can be produced profitably? This depends in part on whether it is easy to shift from the production of other commodities to the one whose price has risen. If agricultural land and labor can be readily shifted from one crop to another, the supply of any one crop will be more elastic than if they cannot. Here also, as with demand, length of time for response is critical. It may be difficult to change quantities supplied in response to a price increase in

[3] Steepness, which is related to absolute rather than percentage changes, is *not* always a reliable guide. As is shown in the appendix to this chapter, any upward-sloping straight line passing through the origin has an elasticity of +1.0 over its entire range.

a matter of weeks or months, but easy to do so over a period of years. An obvious example concerns the planting cycle of crops. Also, new oil fields can be discovered, wells drilled, and pipelines built over a period of years, but not in a few months. Thus elasticity of oil supply is much greater over five years than over one year.

The second reason for brevity of treatment is that supply elasticity depends to a great extent on how costs behave as output is varied, an issue that will be treated at length in Part Three. If costs of production rise rapidly as output rises, then the stimulus to expand production in response to a price rise will quickly be choked off by increases in costs. In this case supply will tend to be rather inelastic. If, however, costs rise only slowly as production increases, a rise in price that raises profits will elicit a large increase in quantity supplied before the rise in costs puts a halt to the expansion in output. In this case supply will tend to be rather elastic.

Summary

1. *Elasticity of demand* (also called *price elasticity of demand*) is a measure of the extent to which the quantity demanded of a commodity responds to a change in its price. It is defined as the percentage change in quantity divided by the percentage change in price that brought it about. Elasticity is defined to be a positive number and it can vary from zero to infinity.

2. When the numerical measure of elasticity is less than unity, demand is *inelastic*. This means that the percentage change in quantity is less than the percentage change in price that brought it about. When the numerical measure exceeds unity, demand is *elastic*. This means that the percentage change in quantity is greater than the percentage change in price that brought it about.

3. Elasticity and total revenue of sellers are related in the following way: If elasticity is less than unity, a fall in price lowers total revenue; if elasticity is greater than unity, a fall in price raises total revenue; and if elasticity is unity, total revenue does not change as price changes.

4. The main determinant of the price elasticity of demand is the availability of substitutes for the commodity. Any one of a group of close substitutes will tend to have an elastic demand even though the group as a whole may have a highly inelastic demand.

5. Elasticity of demand tends to be greater the longer the time over which adjustment occurs. Items that have few substitutes in the short run may develop ample substitutes when consumers and producers have time to adapt.

6. *Income elasticity* is the percentage change in quantity demanded divided by the percentage change in income that brought it about. Luxuries tend to have higher income elasticities than necessities. The income elasticity of demand for a commodity will usually change as income varies. For example, a commodity that has a high income elasticity at a low income (because increases in income bring it within reach of the typical household) may have a low or negative income elasticity at higher incomes (because with further rises in incomes it can be replaced by a superior substitute).

7. *Cross elasticity* is the percentage change in quantity demanded divided by the percentage change in the price of some other commodity that brought it about. It is used to define commodities that are substitutes for one another (positive cross elasticity) and commodities that complement one another (negative cross elasticity).

8. *Elasticity of supply* is an important concept in economics. It measures the ratio of the percentage change in the quantity supplied of a commodity to the percentage change in its price. It is the analogue on the supply side to the elasticity of demand.

9. An appendix to this chapter, for students with some mathematics training, extends the analysis.

Topics for Review

Elasticity of demand
Significance of elastic and inelastic demands
Difference between inelastic and perfectly inelastic and elastic and infinitely elastic
Relation between demand elasticity and total expenditure
Income elasticity of demand
Short-run and long-run demand curves
Income-elastic and income-inelastic demands
Normal goods and inferior goods
Cross elasticity of demand
Substitutes and complements
Elasticity of supply

Discussion Questions

1. From the following quotations what (if anything) can you conclude about elasticity of demand?
   a. "Good weather resulted in record corn harvests and sent corn prices tumbling. For many corn farmers the result has been calamitous."
   b. "Ridership always went up when bus fares came down, but the increased patronage never was enough to prevent a decrease in overall revenue."
   c. "The 30 percent increase in postal rates has led us [The Narragansett Electric Co.] to have 60 percent of our bills hand delivered instead of mailed."
   d. "Coffee to me is an essential—you've gotta have it no matter what the price."
2. What would you predict about the relative price elasticity of demand of (a) food, (b) meat, (c) beef, (d) chuck roast, (e) chuck roast sold at Safeway? What would you predict about their relative income elasticities?
3. "Avocados have a limited market, not greatly affected by price until the price falls to less than $.25 a pound. Then they are much demanded by manufacturers of dog food." Interpret this statement in terms of price elasticity.

4. "Home computers were a leader in sales appeal through much of the 1980s. But per capita sales are much lower in Puerto Rico than the United States, lower in Mississippi and Arkansas than in Illinois and Texas. Manufacturers are puzzled by the big differences." Can you offer an explanation in terms of elasticity?

5. What elasticity measure or measures would be useful in answering the following questions?
   a. Will cheaper transport into the central city help keep downtown shopping centers profitable?
   b. Will raising the bulk-rate postage rate increase or decrease the postal deficit?
   c. Are producers of toothpaste and mouthwash in competition with each other?
   d. What effect will falling gasoline prices have on the sale of cars that use diesel fuel?

6. Interpret the following statements in terms of the relevant elasticity concept:
   a. "As fuel for tractors has gotten more expensive, many farmers have shifted from plowing their fields to no-till farming. No-till acreage increased from 30 million acres in 1972 to 95 million acres in 1982."
   b. "Fertilizer makers brace for dismal year as fertilizer prices soar."
   c. "When farmers are hurting, small towns feel the pain."

7. It has been observed recently that obesity is a more frequent medical problem for the relatively poor than for the middle-income classes. Can you use the theory of demand to shed light on this observation?

8. Suggest commodities that you think might have the following patterns of elasticity of demand.
   a. High income elasticity, high price elasticity
   b. High income elasticity, low price elasticity
   c. Low income elasticity, low price elasticity
   d. Low income elasticity, high price elasticity

9. Look at Table 5-5. Can you suggest why cigarettes and gasoline are inelastic but electricity is elastic? Why is furniture more elastic than all consumer durables taken together?

10. Look at Table 5-6. Can you suggest why gasoline is more income elastic than cigarettes or housing? Or why coffee is more income elastic than beef?

11. In 1983 the new United States Football League was playing to half empty stadiums. The Michigan Panthers averaged 22,250 people at its regular season games. When the team made the playoffs, its owner Alfred Taubman *lowered* ticket prices about 30 percent and drew a crowd of over 60,000 to the Silverdome, near Detroit. "This crowd gave us a hint," said the Panthers' general manager. "We will sit down and take that turnout into consideration. I think tickets for Panther games will be cheaper next season."

   What does this tell us about price elasticity of demand? Does the fact that Detroit was suffering from 25 percent unemployment at the time have any relevance in evaluating the experience?

Elasticity: A Formal Analysis

The verbal definition of elasticity used in the text may be written symbolically in the following form:

$$\eta = \frac{\Delta q}{\Delta q} \times \frac{\text{average } p}{\text{average } q}$$

used in lecture (also text) *not* $\frac{}{\Delta p}$

where the averages are over the arc of the demand curve being considered. This is called **arc elasticity,** and it measures the average responsiveness of quantity to price over an interval of the demand curve.

Most theoretical treatments use a different but related concept called **point elasticity.** This is the responsiveness of quantity to price at a particular point on the demand curve. The precise definition of point elasticity uses the concept of a derivative, which is drawn from differential calculus.

In this appendix we first study arc elasticity, which may be regarded as an approximation to point elasticity. Then we study point elasticity.

Before proceeding, we should notice one further change. In the chapter text we multiplied all our calculations of demand elasticities by -1, thereby defining elasticity of demand as a positive number. In theoretical work it is more convenient to retain the concept's natural sign. Thus normal demand curves will have negative signs, and statements about "more" or "less" elastic must be understood to refer to the absolute, not the algebraic value of demand elasticity.

The following symbols will be used throughout.

$\eta \equiv$ elasticity of demand
$\eta_s \equiv$ elasticity of supply
$q \equiv$ the original quantity
$\Delta q \equiv$ the change in quantity
$p \equiv$ the original price
$\Delta p \equiv$ the change in price

Arc Elasticity As an Approximation to Point Elasticity

Point elasticity measures elasticity at some point (p,q). In the approximate definition, however, the responsiveness is measured over a small range starting from that point. For example, in Figure 5A-1 the elasticity at point 1 can be measured by the responsiveness of quantity demanded to a change in price that takes price and quantity from point 1 to point 2. The algebraic formula for this elasticity concept is

$$\eta = \frac{\Delta q}{\Delta p} \times \frac{p}{q} \qquad [1]$$

This is similar to the definition of arc elasticity used in the text except that since elasticity is being measured at a point, the p and q corresponding to that point are used (rather than the average p and q over an arc of the curve).

Equation 1 splits elasticity into two parts: $\Delta q/\Delta p$, the ratio of the change in quantity to the change in price, which is related to the *slope* of the demand curve, and p/q, which is related to the *point* on the curve at which the measurement is made.

Figure 5A-1 shows a straight-line demand curve. To measure the elasticity at point 1, take p and q at that point and then consider a price change, say, to

FIGURE 5A-1   A Straight-Line Demand Curve

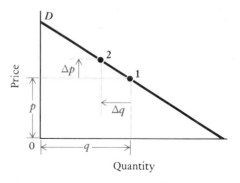

Because p/q varies with $\Delta q/\Delta p$ constant, the elasticity varies along this demand curve, being high at the left and low at the right.

point 2, and measure Δp and Δq as indicated. The slope of the straight line joining points 1 and 2 is $\Delta p/\Delta q$. The term in Equation 1 is $\Delta q/\Delta p$, which is the reciprocal of $\Delta p/\Delta q$. Therefore the first term in the elasticity formula is the reciprocal of the slope of the straight line joining the two price-quantity positions under consideration.

Although point elasticity of demand refers to a point (p,q) on the demand curve, the first term in Equation 1 still refers to changes over an arc of the curve. This is the part of the formula that involves approximation and, as we shall see, it has some unsatisfactory results. Nonetheless some interesting theorems can be derived using this formula as long as we confine ourselves to straight-line demand and supply curves.

1. *The elasticity of a downward-sloping straight-line demand curve varies from zero at the quantity axis to infinity* (∞) *at the price axis.* First notice that a straight line has a constant slope, so the ratio $\Delta p/\Delta q$ is the same everywhere on the line. Therefore its reciprocal, $\Delta q/\Delta p$, must also be constant. The changes in η can now be inferred by inspecting the ratio p/q. Where the line cuts the quantity axis, price is zero, so the ratio p/q is zero; thus $\eta = 0$. Moving up the line, p rises and q falls, so the ratio p/q rises; thus elasticity rises. Approaching the top of the line, q approaches zero, so the ratio becomes very large. Thus elasticity increases without limit as the price axis is approached.

2. *Where there are two straight-line demand curves of the same slope, the one farther from the origin is less elastic at each price than the one closer to the origin.* Figure 5A-2 shows two parallel straight-line demand curves. Compare the elasticities of the two curves at any price, say, p_0. Since the curves are parallel, the ratio $\Delta q/\Delta p$ is the same on both curves. Since elasticities at the same price are being compared on both curves, p is the same, and the only factor left to vary is q. On the curve farther from the origin, quantity is larger (i.e., $q_1 > q_0$) and hence p_0/q_1 is smaller than p_0/q_0; thus η is smaller.

It follows from theorem 2 that parallel shifts of a straight-line demand curve lower elasticity (at each price) when the line shifts outward and raise elasticity when the line shifts inward.

3. *The elasticities of two intersecting straight-line de-*

FIGURE 5A-2   Two Parallel Straight-Line Demand Curves

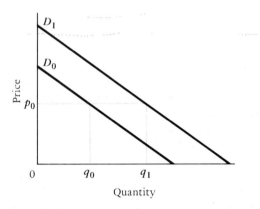

For any given price the quantities are different on these two parallel curves; thus the elasticities are different, being higher on D_0 than on D_1.

mand curves can be compared at the point of intersection merely by comparing slopes, the steeper curve being the less elastic. In Figure 5A-3 there are two intersecting curves. At any point of intersection, p and q are

FIGURE 5A-3   Two Intersecting Straight-Line Demand Curves

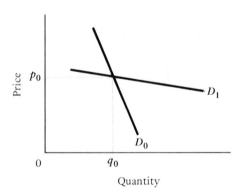

Elasticities are different at the point of intersection of these demand curves because the slopes are different, being higher on D_0 than on D_1. D_1 is more elastic at p_0.

common to both curves and hence the ratio p/q is the same. Therefore η varies only with $\Delta p/\Delta q$. On the steeper curve, $\Delta q/\Delta p$ is smaller than on the flatter curve, so elasticity is lower.

4. If the slope of a straight-line demand curve changes while the price intercept remains constant, elasticity at any given price is unchanged. This is an interesting case for at least two reasons. First, when more customers having similar tastes to those already in the market enter the market, the demand curve pivots outward in this way. Second, when more firms enter a market that is shared proportionally among all firms, each firm's demand curve shifts inward in this way.

Consider, in Figure 5A-4, the elasticities at point b on demand curve D_0 and at point c on demand curve D_1. We shall focus on the two triangles abp_0 on D_0 and acp_0 on D_1, formed by the two straight-line demand curves emanating from point a and by the price p_0.

FIGURE 5A-4 Two Straight-Line Demand Curves from the Same Price Intercept

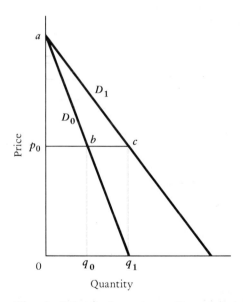

The elasticity is the same on D_0 and D_1 at any price p_0. This situation occurs because the steeper slope of D_0 is exactly offset by the smaller quantity demanded at any price.

The price p_0 is the line segment $0p_0$. The quantities q_0 and q_1 are the line segments p_0b and p_0c, respectively. The slope of D_0 is $\Delta p/\Delta q = ap_0/p_0b$ and the slope of D_1 is $\Delta p/\Delta q = ap_0/p_0c$

From Equation 1 we can represent the elasticities of D_0 and D_1 at the points b and c respectively as

$$\eta \text{ at point } b = \frac{p_0b}{ap_0} \times \frac{0p_0}{p_0b} = \frac{0p_0}{ap_0}$$

$$\eta \text{ at point } c = \frac{p_0c}{ap_0} \times \frac{0p_0}{p_0c} = \frac{0p_0}{ap_0}$$

The two are the same. The reason is that the distance corresponding to the quantity demanded at p_0 appears in both the numerator and denominator and thus cancels out.

Put differently, if the straight-line demand curve D_0 is twice as steep as D_1, it has half the quantity demanded at p_0. Therefore in the expression

$$\eta = \frac{\Delta q}{q} \times \frac{p}{\Delta p}$$

the steeper slope (a smaller Δq for the same Δp) is exactly offset by the smaller quantity demanded (a smaller q for the same p).

5. Any straight-line supply curve through the origin has an elasticity of one. Such a supply curve is shown in Figure 5A-5. Consider the two triangles with the sides p, q, and S curve, and the Δp, Δq, and the S

FIGURE 5A-5 A Straight-Line Supply Curve Through the Origin

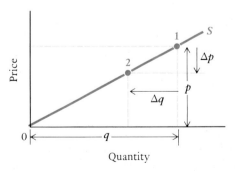

At every point on the curve, p/q equals $\Delta p/\Delta q$; thus elasticity equals unity at every point.

FIGURE 5A-6   Point Elasticity of Demand Measured by the Approximate Formula

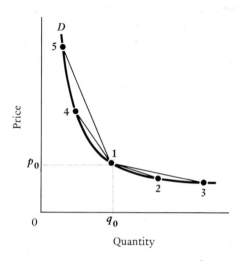

When the approximation of $\eta = \dfrac{\Delta q}{\Delta p} \times \dfrac{p}{q}$ is used, many elasticities are measured from point 1 because the slope of the chord between 1 and every other point on the curve varies.

curve. Clearly, these are similar triangles. Therefore, the ratios of their sides are equal, that is,

$$\frac{p}{q} = \frac{\Delta p}{\Delta q} \qquad [2]$$

Elasticity of supply is defined as

$$\eta_s = \frac{\Delta q}{\Delta p} \times \frac{p}{q}$$

which, by substitution from Equation 2, gives

$$\eta_s = \frac{q}{p} \times \frac{p}{q} \equiv 1$$

6. *The elasticity measured from any point p, q, according to Equation 1 above, is dependent on the direction and magnitude of the change in price and quantity.* Except for a straight line (for which the slope does not change), the ratio $\Delta q/\Delta p$ will not be the same at different points on a curve. Figure 5A-6 shows a demand

curve that is not a straight line. To measure the elasticity from point 1, the ratio $\Delta q/\Delta p$—and thus η—will vary according to the size and the direction of the price change.

Theorem 6 yields a result that is very inconvenient and is avoided by use of a different definition of point elasticity.

Point Elasticity According to the Precise Definition

To measure the elasticity at a point exactly, it is necessary to know the reaction of quantity to a change in price *at that point,* not over a range of the curve.

The reaction of quantity to price change at a point is called *dq/dp,* and this is defined to be the reciprocal of the slope of the straight line tangent to the demand curve at the point in question. In Figure 5A-7 the elasticity of demand at point 1 is the ratio *p/q* (as it has been in all previous measures), now multiplied

FIGURE 5A-7   Point Elasticity of Demand Measured by the Exact Formula

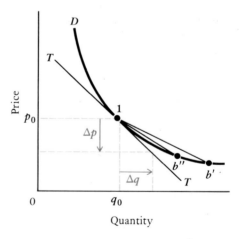

When the exact definition $\eta = \dfrac{dq}{dp} \times \dfrac{p}{q}$ is used, only one elasticity is measured from point 1 because there is only one tangent to the demand curve at that point.

by the ratio of $\Delta q/\Delta p$ measured along the straight line T, tangent to the curve at 1, that is, by dq/dp.

Thus the exact definition of point elasticity is

$$\eta = \frac{dq}{dp} \times \frac{p}{q} \qquad [3]$$

The ratio dq/dp, as defined, is in fact the differential calculus concept of the *derivative* of quantity with respect to price.

This definition of point elasticity is the one normally used in economic theory. Equation 1 is mathematically only an approximation to this expression.

It is obvious from Figure 5A-7 that arc elasticity will come closer to point elasticity the smaller the price change used to calculate the arc elasticity. The $\Delta q/\Delta p$ in Equation 1 is the reciprocal of the slope of the chord connecting the two points being compared. As the chord becomes shorter, its slope gets closer to that of the tangent T. (Compare the chords connecting point 1 to b' and b'' in Figure 5A-7.) Thus the error in using Equation 1 as an approximation to Equation 3 tends to diminish as the size of Δp diminishes.

6

Supply and Demand in Action: Price Controls and Agriculture

Supply and demand have application to many real-world problems. In this chapter we illustrate these applications by studying government policies that involve intervention into competitive markets. In the first half of the chapter we study the general problems involved in the setting of both minimum and maximum prices and then go on to a case study of rent controls. In the second half we study the problems of government intervention in the markets for agricultural commodities.

We use the method of comparative statics, first encountered on page 72. The method, you will recall, is to start from a position of equilibrium in the market and then introduce the change to be studied. The new equilibrium position is then determined and compared with the original one. The difference between the two positions of equilibrium can be attributed to the change introduced, for that is the only change that has occurred.

Controlled Prices

Equilibrium in a free market occurs when the quantity demanded equals the quantity supplied. Government **price control policies** are designed to hold the actual price at some disequilibrium value that could not be maintained in the absence of the government's intervention. Some price control policies hold the market price below equilibrium. In so doing they cause quantity demanded to exceed quantity supplied at the controlled price, creating shortages. Other price control policies are designed to hold prices above equilibrium. In so doing they cause quantity supplied to exceed quantity demanded at the controlled price, creating surpluses.

Disequilibrium Prices

In competitive markets price tends to change whenever quantity supplied does not equal quantity demanded. Thus price will move toward its equilibrium value, at which there are neither unsatisfied suppliers nor unsatisfied demanders.

When price controls hold price at some disequilibrium value, what determines the quantity actually traded on the market? The key to the answer to this question is the simple fact that any voluntary market transaction requires both a willing buyer and a willing seller. This means that if quantity demanded is less than quantity supplied, demand will determine the amount actually exchanged, while the rest of the quantity supplied will remain in the hands of the unsuccessful sellers. On the other hand, if quantity demanded exceeds quantity supplied, supply will determine the amount actually exchanged, while the rest of the quantity demanded will represent desired purchases of unsuccessful buyers. This argument is spelled out in more detail in Figure 6-1, which establishes the general conclusion that:

At any disequilibrium price, quantity exchanged is determined by the *lesser* of quantity demanded or quantity supplied.

FIGURE 6-1 The Determination of Quantity Exchanged in Disequilibrium

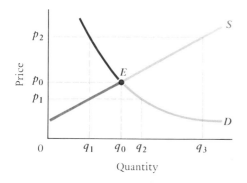

In disequilibrium, quantity exchanged is determined by the *lesser* of quantity demanded or quantity supplied. At p_0 the market is in equilibrium, with quantity demanded equal to quantity supplied at q_0. For prices below p_0, such as p_1, the quantity exchanged will be determined by the supply curve. For example, the quantity q_1 will be exchanged at the disequilibrium price p_1 in spite of the excess demand of $q_1 q_2$. For prices above p_0, such as p_2, the quantity exchanged will be determined by the demand curve. For example, the quantity q_1 will be exchanged at the disequilibrium price p_2 in spite of the excess supply of $q_1 q_3$. Thus the darker portions of the S and D curves show the actual quantities exchanged at different prices.

Price Floors

The government sometimes establishes a minimum price, or **price floor,** for a good or service. Minimum wages for labor and guaranteed prices for some agricultural commodities are well-known examples.

A price floor that is set at or below the equilibrium price has no effect, because equilibrium remains attainable and will not be inconsistent with the legal price floor. If, however, the price floor is set above the equilibrium price, it is said to be *binding* or *effective*.

Price floors may be established by rules that make it illegal to sell the commodity below the prescribed price, as in the case of the minimum wage (examined in Chapter 20). Or, the government may establish a floor by announcing that it will guarantee a certain price by buying any excess supply of the product that emerges at that price. Such guarantees are a feature of much of agricultural policy (examined later in this chapter).

The key result of price floors is illustrated in Figure 6-2.

Effective price floors lead to excess supply. Either an unsold surplus will exist or someone must step in and buy the excess production.

The consequences of excess supply will, of course, differ from commodity to commodity. If the commodity is labor, subject to a minimum wage, excess supply translates into people without jobs. If the commodity is wheat, and more is produced than can be sold, the surplus wheat must accumulate in grain elevators or government warehouses. These consequences may or may not be "worth it" in terms of the other goals achieved. But the consequences are inevitable whenever the price floor is set above the market-clearing, equilibrium price, and nothing further is done.

Why might the government wish to incur these consequences? One reason is that those who actually succeed in selling their commodities at the price floor are better off than if they had to accept the lower equilibrium price. Workers and farmers are among those who have persuaded the government to establish floor prices and so help them raise the prices of what they sell.

FIGURE 6-2   A Price Floor

If a price floor is above the equilibrium price, quantity supplied will exceed quantity demanded. The free-market equilibrium is at E, with price p_0 and quantity q_0. If the government makes it illegal for the price to fall below p_1, it has established an effective price floor. Quantity supplied will exceed quantity demanded by q_1q_2. If the government does nothing, this excess supply will be in private hands and will either go to waste or accumulate in inventories. If the government buys the excess supply, sellers will get rid of the full quantity they wish to produce, q_2, but the government will have the quantity q_1q_2 to store or dispose of.

Price Ceilings

It is common in wartime, and not unknown in peacetime, for the government to fix the *maximum prices* at which certain goods and services may be sold. Price controls on oil, natural gas, and rental housing have been features of the American scene at various times since World War II.

Although frequently referred to as *fixed* or *frozen prices,* most price controls actually specify the highest permissible price that producers may legally charge. This maximum is often called a **price ceiling.** If the ceiling is set above the equilibrium price, it has no effect, since the equilibrium remains attainable. If, however, the ceiling is set below the equilibrium price, the ceiling is binding or effective. The key result for price ceilings is established in Figure 6-3.

Effective price ceilings lead to excess demand, and the quantity exchanged falls below its equilibrium amount.

Allocating a Commodity in Short Supply

The free market eliminates excess demand by allowing prices to rise, thereby allocating the available supply among would-be purchasers. Since this does not happen under price ceilings, some other method of allocation must be adopted. Experience shows that certain alternatives are likely.

If stores sell their available supplies on a first-come, first-served basis, people will rush to those stores that are said to have stocks of any commodity in short supply. In many Eastern European and Af-

FIGURE 6-3   A Price Ceiling and Black Market Pricing

A price ceiling set below the equilibrium price causes excess demand and invites a black market. Equilibrium price is at p_0. If a price ceiling is set at p_1, the quantity demanded will rise to q_1 and the quantity supplied will fall to q_2. Quantity actually exchanged will be q_2. Although excess demand is q_2q_1, price may not rise legally to restore equilibrium. If all the available supply of q_2 were sold on a black market, price to consumers would rise to p_2, with black marketeers earning receipts shown by the shaded areas. The dark shaded area shows the profit of those who buy at the price ceiling and sell at the black market price.

rican countries where prices of "essentials" are subject to effective price ceilings, even the rumor that a shop is selling supplies of a scarce commodity can cause a local stampede. Buyers may wait hours to get into the shop, only to find that supplies are exhausted before they can be served. This is why standing in lines is often a way of life in command economies.

Instead of first-come, first-served, storekeepers may use a different system of allocation of a scarce commodity. They may decide to keep goods "under the counter" and sell only to customers of their own choosing. For example, in the United States in 1978 during a gasoline shortage, some gas station operators sold only to regular customers. When sellers decide to whom they will (and will not) sell scarce supplies, allocation is by **sellers' preferences.**

If the government dislikes the distribution that results from sellers' preferences, it can do at least two things. First, it can pass laws requiring suppliers to sell on a first-come, first-served basis. To the extent that this legislation is effective, it leads to allocation according to willingness to stand in line.

Second and more drastic, the government can ration the commodity. To do so, it prints only enough ration coupons to match the available supply and then distributes the coupons to purchasers, who need both money and coupons to buy the commodity. The coupons may be distributed equally among the population or on the basis of some criterion such as age, family status, or occupation.

Rationing substitutes the government's preferences for the sellers' preferences in allocating a commodity that is in excess demand because of an effective price ceiling.

Black Markets

Price ceilings, with or without rationing, usually give rise to black markets. A **black market** is any market in which goods are sold illegally at prices above a legal price ceiling.

Many manufactured products are produced by only a few firms, but sold by many retailers. Thus, although it may be easy to police the few producers, it is often impossible to enforce the price at which the many retailers sell to the general public. If the government can control the price received by producers but not retailers, production remains at a level consistent with the price ceiling because the producers receive the controlled price for their product. At the retail level, however, the opportunity for a black market arises because purchasers are willing to pay more than the price ceiling for the limited amounts of the commodity that are available.

Effective price ceilings always create the potential for a black market, because a profit can be made by buying at the controlled price and sellng at the black market price.

Figure 6-3 illustrates the extreme case in which all the available supply is sold on a black market.[1]

Does the existence of a black market mean that the goals sought by imposing price ceilings have been thwarted? The answer depends upon what the goals are. A government might be interested mainly in (1) restricting production (perhaps to release resources for war production), (2) keeping prices down, or (3) satisfying notions of equity in the consumption of a commodity that is temporarily in short supply. When price ceilings are accompanied by a black market, only the first objective is achieved. When goods find their way onto the black market, the second objective is frustrated. Effective price ceilings on manufacturers plus an extensive black market at the retail level may produce the opposite of the third goal. There will be less to go around than if there were no controls, and the available quantities will tend to go to those with the most money or the least social conscience.

Rent Controls: A Case Study of Price Ceilings

A widespread use of price ceilings in North America today relates to the rental of houses and apartments

---

[1] This case is extreme because there are honest people in every society and because governments ordinarily have considerable power to enforce their price ceilings. Although *some* of a commodity subject to an effective price ceiling will be sold on the black market, it is very unlikely that *all* of that commodity will be so sold.

for private occupancy. Rent controls have been used the world over, with similar consequences: severe housing shortages, private allocation systems, and black markets.

Controls have existed in New York City, London, Paris, and many other large cities at least since World War II. In Sweden and Britain, where rent controls on unfurnished apartments have existed for decades, housing shortages are chronic. When British controls were extended to furnished apartments in 1973, the supply of such accommodations dried up, at least until loopholes were found in the law. When rent controls were initiated in Rome in 1978, a housing shortage developed virtually overnight. This kind of induced shortage led University of Chicago professors George Stigler and Milton Friedman to point to the conflict between "ceilings" and "roofs."

Rent controls instituted by many cities in the 1970s and early 1980s are still in force today. Economic theory is useful in understanding the current experience with rent controls and in predicting the consequences. Rent controls are just a special case of price ceilings, and Figure 6-3 can be applied to them. It allows us to derive the following predictions, which are straightforward applications to housing of results that apply to any commodity subject to binding price ceilings.

1. There will be a housing shortage in the sense that quantity demanded will exceed quantity supplied.
2. The actual quantity of rental housing will be less than if free-market rents had been charged.
3. The shortage will lead to alternative allocation schemes. Landlords may allocate by sellers' preferences, or the government may intervene. (In the housing market government intervention usually takes the form of security-of-tenure laws, which protect the tenant from eviction and thus give existing tenants priority over potential new tenants.)
4. Black markets will appear. For example, landlords may require large "entrance fees" from new tenants. In general, the greater the housing shortage, the larger the amount the landlord can obtain. In the absence of security-of-tenure laws, landlords may force tenants out when their leases expire, and they may even try to evict them to extract a large entrance fee from new tenants.

Special Features of the Housing Market

Housing has unusual features that make the analysis of rent controls somewhat special. The most important is the nature of the commodity itself. Housing is an example of a **durable good,** a good that yields its services gradually over an extended period of time. Once built, an apartment can be used for decades or even centuries.

The supply of rental accommodation depends on the *stock* of rental housing available, which in any year is composed mainly of buildings built in the past. The stock is augmented by conversions of housing from other uses and construction of new buildings, and it is diminished by conversions to other uses and demolition or abandonment of existing buildings whose economic life is over. The stock usually changes slowly from year to year.

These considerations mean we can draw more than one supply curve for rental accommodation, depending on how much time is allowed for reactions to occur to any given level of rents. We shall distinguish just two such curves. The *long-run supply curve* relates rents to the quantity of rental accommodation that will be supplied after sufficient time has passed for all adjustments to be made. The *short-run supply curve* relates rents to quantity supplied when only a short time—say, a few months—is allowed for adjustments to be made in response to a change in rents.

The Long-Run Supply Curve of Rental Accommodation

If the expected return from investing in new apartments rises significantly above the return on comparable other investments, there will be a flow of investment funds into the building of new apartments. However, if the return from apartments falls significantly below that obtainable on comparable investments, funds will go elsewhere. The construction of new apartments will fall off and possibly stop altogether. Old apartments will not be replaced as they wear out, so the quantity available will fall drastically.

The long-run supply curve of apartments tends to be much more elastic than the short run curve.

The Short-Run Supply Curve of Rental Accommodation

Now consider the supply response over a few months. What if rents rise? Even though investing in new apartments immediately becomes profitable, years may pass before land is obtained, plans drawn up, and construction completed. Of course, some existing housing can be more quickly converted to rental uses, but in many cases even this will take more than a few months. Thus a long time may pass between the decision to create more apartments and the occupancy by tenants of those apartments.

What if rents fall? New construction will fall off, which will surely decrease the supply at some time in the future. It will, however, pay the owners of existing apartments with no attractive alternative use of their rental units to rent them for whatever they will earn, providing that the rentals at least cover current out-of-pocket costs such as taxes and heating. Some rental housing can be converted to other uses, but, again, this will not usually happen very quickly. Thus,

The short-run supply curve tends to be inelastic at the level of the quantity currently supplied.

The longer the time allowed for adjustment, the less inelastic the supply curve will be. For the very short run, however, it is likely to be almost completely inelastic.

Supply Response to Changes in Rents

If rents rise due to a housing shortage, the quantity will initially remain more or less the same because the short-run supply curve is inelastic. For a while existing landlords will make **windfall profits,** profits that bear no relation to current or historical costs. These profits, however, serve as a spur to the long-run allocation of resources. New construction and conversions will begin, and after a year or two new rental units will begin to come onto the market. The

quantity will continue to expand until a new point on the long-run supply curve has been attained and all windfall profits have been eliminated.

If rents decrease, the quantity supplied will also remain more or less unchanged because of the inelastic short-run supply curve. Landlords who were breaking even will now make *windfall losses*. As the profitability of rental accommodations falls, new construction will be curtailed. But it will take time before the stock of rental housing shrinks to its new point on the long-run supply curve. Only then will it again pay to maintain the remaining stock of rental housing.

Short-run windfall profits or losses provide the signals that bring about long-run supply adjustments in a free market.

Because houses are durable, they do not disappear quickly. But owners of rental properties can speed the shrinkage in various ways. Some apartments can be converted into cooperatives or condominiums. Some apartment buildings occupy land with valuable alternative uses. If rents fall far enough, owners may find it profitable to demolish those apartments and use the land for something else.

Many existing apartment buildings have no real alternative uses and stand on land that is worth less than the cost of demolishing the building. These will continue to provide rental accommodation until they are abandoned as useless. The less spent on maintenance and repairs, the shorter the structure's effective life. The lower the rents, the less it will pay landlords to spend on upkeep and thus the faster the apartment will "wear out."

If rental revenues fall below the minimum costs of operation (which include such things as taxes and heating), the owner may simply abandon the apartment. Although this may sound extreme, it has happened repeatedly. When it happens, a stock of housing that might have lasted decades or even centuries is dissipated within a few years.

Having seen how supply responds to price changes we can analyze the supply-side effects of rent control. An effective ceiling on rents drives them below their free-market equilibrium value. As shown in Figure 6-4, the controls lead to a growing housing shortage.

FIGURE 6-4   Effects of Rent Control in the Short and Long Run

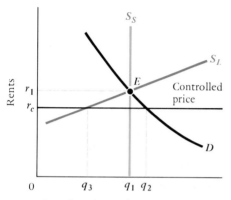

Quantity of Rental Accommodation

Rent control causes housing shortages that worsen as time passes. The controlled rent of r_c forces rents below their free-market equilibrium value of r_1. The short-run supply of housing is shown by the inelastic curve S_S. Thus quantity supplied remains at q_1 in the short run, and the housing shortage is q_1q_2. Over time, the quantity supplied shrinks, as shown by the long-run supply curve S_L. In long-run equilibrium there are only q_3 units of rental accommodation, far fewer than when controls were instituted. Since the long-run supply is quite elastic, the housing shortage of q_3q_2, that occurs after supply has fully adjusted, ends up being much larger than the initial shortage of q_1q_2.

Rent controls that remain in force for a sustained period inevitably lead to a large reduction in the quantity of rental housing available.

Demand Response to Changes in Rents

There are many reasons to expect the demand for apartments and other forms of rental housing to be quite elastic. As the relative price of rental accommodation in an area rises, the following occur.

1. Some people stop renting and buy instead.
2. Some move to where rental housing is cheaper.
3. Some economize on the amount of housing they consume by renting smaller, cheaper accommo-

dations or renting out to others a room or two in their present accommodations.
4. Some double up and others do not "undouble" (for example, young adults do not move out of parental homes as quickly as they might otherwise do).

Such occurrences contribute to an elastic demand for rental housing: Increases in rents will sharply decrease the quantity demanded.

Rent controls prevent such increases in rents from occurring. Thus, even while the supply of rental housing is shrinking for the reasons discussed above, the signal to economize on rental accommodation is *not* given through rising rentals. The housing shortage grows as the stock of rental accommodation shrinks, while nothing decreases the quantity demanded.

When Rent Controls May Work: Short-Term Shortages

Pressure for rent controls seems to arise in response to rapidly rising rents for housing. The case for controlling rising rentals is strongest when the shortages causing the increasing rents are temporary.

Sometimes there is a temporary influx of population into an area. Possibly an army camp is established in wartime, or a pipeline or a power complex is being built, and many workers are required for the time being even though few will remain behind. When the temporary population floods in, market rents will rise. New construction of apartments will not occur, however, because investors recognize the rise in demand and the rise in rentals as temporary. In such a situation rent controls may stop existing owners from gaining windfall profits with few harmful supply effects since a long-run supply response is not expected in any case. After the boom is over, demand will fall and free-market rents will return to the controlled level (their original level). Controls may then be removed with little further effect.

Even when rent controls have no long-run adverse effect, there will be some disadvantages. At controlled rents there will be a severe housing shortage but no incentive for existing tenants to economize on housing and no incentive for potential suppliers to find ways to provide extra short-run accommodation. If rents rise on the free market, existing tenants will economize and some tenants and owners will find it profitable to rent out rooms. Even though the supply of permanent apartments does not change, the supply of casual temporary accommodation (mobile homes, for example) will increase. Such reactions are induced by the signal of rising rents, but inhibited by controls.

Temporary controls are also disadvantageous because political pressures to make them permanent may prove irresistible. During World War II many American cities imposed rent controls because of temporary shortages. Most cities removed controls after the war to allow the housing supply to expand when factors of production were again available for construction. Some cities, among them New York, kept the controls, thus inhibiting the adjustments in supply that were needed to eliminate the shortages. This is illustrated in Figure 6-5.

When Rent Controls Fail: Long-Term Shortages

Long-Run Increases in Demand

Consider a long-term increase in the demand for rental accommodation. An example is provided by areas such as the Sunbelt states, where rapidly increasing population is creating severe local housing shortages and forcing up rents. Such increases in rents give the signal that apartments are highly profitable investments. A consequent building boom will lead to increases in the quantity supplied, and it will continue as long as windfall profits can be enjoyed.

If rent controls are imposed in the face of such long-term increases in demand, they will prevent short-run windfalls, but they will also prevent the needed long-run construction boom from occurring. Thus controls will convert a temporary shortage into a permanent shortage. This is also illustrated in Figure 6-5.

Inflation in Housing Costs

Rent controls also fail when they are introduced to protect tenants from rent increases in an inflationary world. Inflation raises both the costs of construction of new housing and the costs of operating and main-

FIGURE 6-5   Rent Controls in Response to Increasing Demand

Rent controls prevent a temporary skyrocketing of rents when demand rises but also prevent the long-term supply adjustment to demand increases.

Temporary demand fluctuations. The short-run supply curve S_S applies. In the free market a temporary rise in demand from D_0 to D_1 and then back to D_0 will change rents from r_0 to r_1 and then back to r_0. Rent control would hold rents at r_0 throughout; there would be a housing shortage of $q_0 q_1$ due to excess demand as long as demand was D_1, but rent control would not affect the quantity of housing available.

Permanent changes in demand. The long-run supply curve S_L applies. A permanent rise in demand from D_0 to D_1 will cause free-market rents to rise temporarily from r_0 to r_1 and then to fall to r_2 as the quantity of accommodation supplied grows from q_0 to q_2. Controlling the rent at r_0 to prevent windfall profits produces a permanent housing shortage of $q_0 q_1$.

taining existing housing. As we saw in Chapter 4, a rise in costs shifts the supply curve upward and to the left. Rent ceilings in an economy that is experiencing a steady inflation will produce a housing shortage that grows over time. If inflation is combined with growth in demand, the growth in the housing shortage becomes large, as shown in Figure 6-6.

Of course, the housing shortage need not grow if the controlled rent is allowed to rise as fast as the equilibrium rent. But since the usual purpose of controls is to hold rents down in the face of rapid increases in costs and demand, controlled rents have usually been allowed to rise more slowly than market

FIGURE 6-6   An Ever-growing Housing Shortage

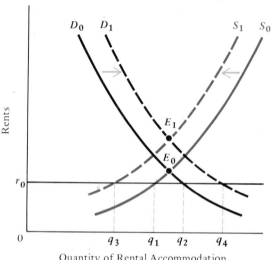

In a growing, inflation-prone economy, rent control will cause the housing shortage to worsen year by year. In a growing economy the demand curve is continually shifting rightward as more people with higher real incomes demand more housing. In an inflationary economy the supply curve is continually shifting leftward because construction, maintenance, and operating costs are rising. Such shifts, when combined with rent control, cause the housing shortage to grow over time. For example, when the curves are D_0 and S_0, rent control at r_0 is accompanied by a housing shortage of q_1q_2. When the curves have shifted to D_1 and S_1, however, the same controlled rent causes an overall housing shortage of q_3q_4.

determined rents. Thus housing shortages grow over the years, although not as fast as they would if controlled rents were *never* changed.

Box 6-1 takes up the interesting question of why, if the consequences are so bad, rent controls are so often resorted to in today's world.

Alternative Responses to the Rising Cost of Housing

Most rent controls today are meant to protect lower-income tenants not only against profiteering by landlords in the face of severe local shortages, but also against the steadily rising cost of housing.

The free market solution is to let rents rise sufficiently to cover the rising costs. If ordinary people (and others) really decide they cannot afford the market price of apartments and will not rent them, then construction will cease. Given what we know about past consumer behavior, however, it is more likely that agonizing choices will be made to economize on housing or to spend a higher proportion of total income on it.

If the government does not wish to accept this free market solution, what alternatives are open to it?

One alternative is to control rents below the cost of new building, with the inevitable consequence of a housing shortage that grows as the stock of rental accommodation wears out and is not replaced.

A second alternative is for government to fill the gap between total demand and private supply with subsidized public housing, financed at the taxpayers' expense (since the high costs of housing must be paid by someone).

A third alternative is to subsidize the housing of the less well-off citizens by providing them with housing vouchers good for paying so much rent and redeemable by landlords in cash paid by the government.

Note that if the housing is built, its resource cost must be met by someone. Either the tenant pays in higher rents, or the taxpayer pays in subsidies to government housing that is rented at less than cost or to finance a scheme of housing vouchers. The only way the cost can be avoided is when, under effective rent control, the housing that costs more than is yielded by the controlled rents is not built at all (which is why a housing shortage develops under this arrangement).

The costs of providing additional housing cannot be voted out of existence; they can only be transferred from one set of persons to another.

Rent Controls: The Future Outlook

Several European countries have been through the whole process of imposing rent controls to protect tenants and ending up with excess demand and an increasingly expensive program of subsidized public

BOX 6-1

The Clamor for Rent Control

In the face of the predicted and observed consequences, why do rent controls persist and even grow? The answer is largely that the primary victims of rent control do not identify themselves as such, while the primary beneficiaries do.

Renting families include a disproportionate fraction of the aged, the unemployed, welfare recipients, and members of minority groups. They also include many students. A high percentage of these groups are paying at least half their money incomes to a landlord (who seems never to be in view except to collect the rent), and these groups are being squeezed by the rising costs of everything. (Of course, not all existing renters are poor, nor landlords rich.) Whatever the long-term consequences of rent control, tenants know that the immediate effect is to hold down the cost of existing housing. Thus tenants constitute an important and sympathetic political constituency for rent controls.

If the beneficiaries of rent control are existing tenants, who are the victims? The housing shortage hurts those who will want rental housing that will not be there in the future. The elderly couples who fight to keep rent control on the apartments they occupy are behaving in their own best interest. But if they succeed they are making life more difficult for the next generation of aged couples, many of whom will not find housing of the same quality if rent controls are kept. The welfare family protected today will have a hard time finding housing if it moves when the opportunity for a job arises or when its present apartment house is abandoned. Minority groups will find that their members are hurt in the long run by the steadily shrinking quantity and quality of available rental housing.

Why do so many people favor rent controls when control-induced shortages will make it more difficult for them to find a suitable apartment? The answer, when it is not an ideological dislike of landlords, seems to be that they do not recognize the link between the lower rents they will pay—if they are lucky enough to find a rent controlled apartment where they want it—and the decreased chance of finding such an apartment. If they knew that rent control was the reason they had to wait so long and search so hard to find accommodation, they might prefer to pay the free-market rent. But they do not know this—and once "in," they will be protected by rent controls.

Thus the call for rent control comes both from existing tenants, who gain at the expense of those who do not have secured leases in rental housing, and from potential tenants, who underestimate the adverse effects control-induced housing shortages may have on them. In contrast, the articulate opposition is the much smaller (and less sympathetic) group of landlords. The silent victims, who are the future unsuccessful searchers for rental units, may never realize the causal link between rent controls and the housing shortage from which they suffer.

That many individuals are either selfish or myopic in calling for rent control is understandable. That their leaders and public representatives do not appreciate and weigh the long-term consequences is less comprehensible except in political terms. Perhaps the politicians are selfish and myopic, too, judging next year's election (and today's constituency) to be more important than adverse, long-run effects.

housing. In the face of other public needs, they are now trying to give more scope to private markets for housing, but policies of rent controls are always politically popular. Only time will tell how far the United States is to travel the same path. Economics cannot tell society which hard choice to make, but it can show what the choices are. The greatest danger is that the long-run costs will be neglected in making the choice.

Agriculture and the Farm Problem

For nearly 80 years the "farm problem" has challenged and troubled U.S. policymakers. It is really two quite different problems of the price system. First, prices fluctuate widely from year to year, causing much uncertainty about farm income. Second, there is a long-run tendency for farm incomes to be depressed below urban incomes in spite of both the extremely rapid rise in agricultural productivity and the long-term shift of labor from the farms.

Today fewer than 6 million people—less than 3 percent of the American population—live on farms, and even for that group less than 40 percent of their income comes from farm sources. Why then has farming and the farm problem loomed so large in American politics and economic policy?

The answer is partly historical. Farmers have not always been so few in number. Farmers in 1910 were 35 percent of the American population and as recently as 1969 were over 5 percent. More importantly, the declining proportion of farmers has not been matched by a comparable decline in their political influence. Family farmers—and those who make their living supplying farmers—constitute the dominant political force in 16 or 17 states. They elect one-third of the 100 U.S. senators. The farm bloc remains a potent political influence in Congress.

American farm problems are important not only because of the importance of farmers in American life, but also because American agriculture is critical to the world's food supply. Although traditionally regarded as a manufacturing nation, the United States now provides two-thirds of all grain and soybeans exported in world trade. American agriculture is the regular supplier to hundreds of millions of people outside the United States and the buffer against crop failure for more than 3 billion others.

To deal with the farm problem, governments have tried a variety of techniques including price supports, crop insurance, transportation and storage subsidies, and payments not to produce. But each of these "solutions" seems to bring problems of its own, often as serious as the original problem they were meant to solve.

Long-Term Trends

In 1935 disposable income of American families who lived on farms was less than one-third that of urban families. By 1950 the ratio had risen to one-half and the gap continued to narrow until it was briefly eliminated in the 1970s. During the 1980s, however, the gap opened again, until farmers' disposable income

in 1985 was only about two-thirds that of urban families. Even allowing for differences in cost of living, there is little doubt that over a lifetime the average farm family achieves a significantly lower level of material prosperity than does the average urban family.

Surprisingly, the gap in farm incomes is not a result of low productivity or poor and depleted soils, but of the reverse. American agriculture is, and has long been, one of the most rapidly innovative industries in the entire world. New seeds and crops, new propagation methods, new mechanical cultivating methods, and computerization have led to rising production per worker and per acre. Since 1900 the output per worker in agriculture has increased tenfold, roughly twice as fast as manufacturing productivity.

Rising productivity in agriculture allows more people to be fed by the same number of workers. The results have been spectacular. Rough estimates of the number of people who can be fed per worker employed on the land are 60 in the United States, 20 in Western Europe, 10 in the Soviet Union, and less than 5 in the underdeveloped countries of the world. Rapid productivity growth has meant that American agricultural output has grown faster than that of any other large producing nation. Therein lies the hope, and the problem, for American agriculture: the rise in productive capacity has been vastly greater than the increase in demand for American farm output.

The historical problem for American agriculture is that its productive capacity has increased faster than its markets.

Lagging Domestic Demand

For most of the last century the average American family has steadily earned more income and enjoyed an increasing standard of living. How do households wish to consume their extra income? The relevant measure, we have seen, is income elasticity of demand. At the levels of income existing in the United States and other advanced industrial nations, most foodstuffs have low income elasticities because most people are already well fed. When these people get extra income, they tend to spend much of it on consumers' durables, entertainment, and travel. Thus, as incomes grow, the demand for agricultural goods tends to increase relatively slowly.

Even if productivity in agriculture had increased at the same rate as that in the rest of the economy, there would have been a tendency for excess supply to develop, owing to lagging demand. Because productivity was increasing much more rapidly than in the rest of the economy, the problem was potentially severe. In economic terms productivity increases were shifting the supply curve of agricultural products to the right, while demand was not increasing nearly as fast. In a sector with increasing supply unmatched by increasing demand, excess supplies will tend to depress prices, profits, and wages and signal the need for resources to move into other industries.

The Required Supply Response

The magnitude of the supply response required if domestic demand is to absorb production is easily shown. In 1929 there were 12.8 million people employed on farms. The output they produced in 1929 could be produced today by 1.5 million people! If resources had not been reallocated out of farming, there would have been enormous increases in output which could hardly have been sold within the United States or exported at any price. Fortunately, resources did move: actual employment on farms was under 3.5 million in 1985.

The movement out of farming has not, however, been as fast as required. Adjusting for both productivity increases and population increases, the number of people working on farms was at least 20 percent higher than was needed to meet domestic needs at prices that were constant in real terms. Either foreign demand had to be counted on to absorb the excess production, or farmers faced chronic oversupply.

Reallocations of resources in a free-market economy take place under the incentives of low prices, low wages, and depressed incomes in sectors where there is excess supply and high prices, high wages, and elevated incomes in expanding sectors. But incentives of this kind prove painful—indeed pain is the spur—to those who live and work on farms,

especially when resources move slowly in response to depressed incomes. It is one thing for the farmer's son or daughter to move to the city; it may be quite another for the farmer and the farmer's parents to be displaced. Because farmers are people—and voters—governments tend to respond to their cries for help in overcoming the depressed conditions in agriculture that free markets often produce.

Notice that the same problem exists for any industry where growth in demand is low while productivity growth is high. Similar problems are beginning to affect such other American industries as automobiles and steel.

The Problem of Long-Term Oversupply

Causes of the rise in productivity.   The continuing growth of agricultural productivity reflects the application of factors other than land and simple labor to farms. Farming is increasingly a vast, capital-intensive, corporate activity. Mechanization, large-scale production, and computerized analysis of day-to-day decisions are common. Many a modern American farmer has a college degree, even a postgraduate degree in business administration, and may spend more time in the office analyzing computer printouts than in the fields. In some ways large-scale modern farming resembles an automobile assembly line more than it does the traditional small and often poor family farm. By 1990 more than half of farm output will be produced on giant farms.

The continuing pace of these changes is reflected in the following average annual growth rates achieved over the last decade. American farm production increased by nearly 3 percent; farm labor input *decreased* by 3.2 percent; machinery use increased 2.5 percent; while use of chemicals increased 4.3 percent.

It is perhaps ironic that the innovations in agriculture that make possible the increase in output with the use of less labor have been encouraged by a long American tradition of government-financed research, agricultural assistance services in every state, and government programs designed to keep farm prices and incomes high even when production is increasing faster than demand.

Of course, increases in productivity, which permit more output to be produced by fewer scarce resources, are desirable. But the displaced resources must find alternative uses before the benefits of the productivity increases can be achieved.

Export demand.   Until the 1970s foreign demand was not very important to American farmers. American exports were heavily industrial and other nations served as breadbaskets for the world. In the 1960s only about 14 percent of the agricultural output of the United States was sold abroad. By 1980 the figure was 30 percent.

While dramatic events, such as the massive sales of wheat to the Soviet Union in 1972 and the normalization of trade relations with China, with its 1 billion population, have underlined America's expanding role as a food exporter, this expansion has come about gradually and is not guaranteed to be permanent. Its underlying causes have been the enormous growth in the world's population and rising incomes in many underdeveloped countries. These countries are at a stage of development where income elasticities of demand for wheat, dairy products, and meat are relatively high; thus, they are prepared to spend a large fraction of their increased income on them. But the United States is but one among many actual or potential sources of supply.

Agricultural exports increased by an average of 20 percent *per year* during the 1970s, and in 1981 they stood at over $43 billion. Over the 1970s when American manufactures seemed expensive in world markets, American farm products became relatively cheap. Drought and hunger in many countries of Asia and Africa led these countries to increase food imports, providing relief from excess supplies of many American farm products.

Much of this growth in foreign demand did not just happen. It was carefully cultivated by such government agencies as the Foreign Agricultural Service, which sought new markets and provided technical and financial assistance to other countries that were taught how to buy and process American agricultural output. Much of the growth, too, has been financed by economic aid to less-developed countries. But the increase in export demand is quite fragile. Between 1980 and 1984 the rising price of American exports (caused by the rising value of the dollar in world markets) led to a sharp downturn in the quantity of farm exports. For corn, it was nearly 20 percent; overall, it exceeded 10 percent.

Government intervention to eliminate excess supply. Through a variety of programs dating from 1929 to the present, the government has bought surplus farm products from farmers at a guaranteed price above the free-market level. Such programs solve the surplus problem for the individual farmer, but they do not do so for the nation, as surplus commodities accumulate in government warehouses.

Eventually, if agricultural surpluses persist, the stored crops have to be destroyed, dumped on the market for what they will bring, or otherwise disposed of at a fraction of their cost. If the crops are thrown on the market and allowed to depress the price, then the original purpose in purchasing them—to stabilize prices and raise farm incomes—is defeated. If the crops are destroyed or allowed to rot, the efforts of a large quantity of the country's scarce factors of production (the land, labor, and capital that went into producing the stored goods) will have been completely wasted.

Destroying crops is a vexing moral problem when millions are starving, but if the stored crops are not to depress the price, they must be kept off the market. Giving crops away to those who would not otherwise buy them is sometimes attempted. See Box 6-2 for one example.

When support schemes begin to produce ever-larger surpluses, often the next step is to try to limit each farmer's production. Quotas may be assigned to individual farmers and penalties imposed for exceeding the quotas. Or bonuses may be paid for leaving the land idle and for plowing crops under. Such measures waste resources because the desired output could be produced with fewer resources and the remaining resources used to produce other goods. All they dispense with is the visible symbol of trouble, the accumulating surpluses.

Indeed, schemes that try to solve the long-run supply problem without creating new markets or inducing resources to shift to other, more productive uses may be self-defeating. The artificially profitable and stable market conditions provide additional stim-

BOX 6-2

Let Them Eat Cheese

Surplus commodities have been accumulating in government warehouses for decades, but every once in a while some aspect of the program catches the public imagination. In December 1981, President Reagan announced a distribution of some surplus cheese to the needy. The commentators had a field day, as the following excerpts suggest.

I was surprised to hear that the Reagan Administration was giving free cheese to the poor. The credo of the Reagan people, if I've heard them right, is "There is no free lunch." I always assumed this included the cheese course.

What bothers me is their giving it away to the poor. This is against everything President Reagan stands for. How are you going to put any backbone into the poor so they'll get out and take care of themselves if you give them free cheese? (Russell Baker, *New York Times*)

Free the cheese! Consumer groups have been beaming that message at the White House in petitions and telegrams for a month, and last week Ronald Reagan agreed to do just that. In an Oval Office ceremony, during which he signed an $11 billion farm price-support bill, the President announced that the Government will give away 30 million lbs. of surplus cheese to states for distribution to the needy. Explained Reagan: "At a time when American families are under increasing financial pressure, their Government cannot sit by and watch millions of pounds of food turn to waste."

As Reagan noted in signing the farm bill last week, "surpluses will continue to pile up" because the Government must keep on buying dairy products at prices that are currently higher than commercial buyers will pay.

Other suggestions for disposing of the surplus range from dumping the cheese in the sea to staging bring-your-own-wine-and-crackers parties at warehouses. Reagan hinted last week that some of the cheese might be sold abroad, at a loss to the Government. The all-too-obvious solution, of course, would be to lower price-support levels until dairy farmers are no longer tempted to produce more cheese than they can sell commercially. But that would be a lot to ask of politicians. Meanwhile, the Government is left with a stockpile that is a mess . . . oh, all right, no matter how you slice it. (*Time* Magazine)

The scene conjured up images of the Great Depression. Thousands of poor people, including pensioners and young mothers with infants swaddled in blankets against the biting chill, stood in line for hours outside Washington's First Rising Mount Zion Baptist Church recently to receive their share of the 30 million pounds of surplus government-owned cheese that President Reagan has agreed to give away to America's poor. . . . But that still represents only a fraction of the 637 million pounds of cheese currently in storage—a glut caused in part by a 33-year-old Federal farm-price-support policy that critics say actually encourages farmers to produce more than the market can bear.

Farmers . . . defend price supports as a necessary cushion against the fluctuations of the market. "Price-support legislation, assures farmers a fair return on basic crops." Critics say that subsidies do more than that: "The support system in this country, . . . allows farmers to produce a product knowing they can sell it even though there isn't a market demand for it." (*Newsweek*)

---

ulus for research and development that further increases productivity in the farm sector. These increases shift the supply curve yet further to the right, increasing the excess of quantity supplied over quantity demanded at given prices.

Short-Term Fluctuations

Why is short-term price volatility typical of many agricultural markets? Farm crops are subject to variations in output because of many factors completely

beyond farmers' control. For example, pests, floods, and lack of rain can drastically reduce farm output, and exceptionally favorable conditions can cause production greatly to exceed expectations. By now you should not be surprised to hear that such unplanned fluctuations in output cause fluctuations in farm prices. There are other less obvious consequences that shed light on farmers' problems.

Consider two examples. In a recent year good weather generated bumper fruit crops in California, where more than half of America's fruit—and almost the entire crop for canning—is grown. At prevailing prices the state director of food and agriculture predicted 100,000 tons of unsold peaches, 50,000 tons of unsold pears, and large surpluses of apricots, cherries, and nectarines. California's canneries would take the surplus, but only at sharply reduced prices, prices that meant lower incomes for fruit growers. While growers cursed a bountiful nature, consumers stood to benefit.

When bad weather destroyed 80 percent of the U.S. soybean crop in a year when most other grains were also in short supply, a series of indirect but predictable results occurred. Soybeans are a primary ingredient of chicken feed for the mass-production broiler chicken industry. The decrease in supply of soybeans (a leftward shift of the supply curve) caused the price of soybeans to triple in two months. Chicken farmers found the cost of soybeans rising so fast that it did not pay to continue feeding baby chicks. Millions were simply killed, and many more millions were not allowed to hatch. This led to a decrease in the supply of chickens (a leftward shift in the supply curve of chickens) and a rise in the price of chickens to households.

Fluctuating Supply with Inelastic Demand

The basic behavior is illustrated in Figure 6-7. Variations in farm output placed on the market cause price fluctuations in the opposite direction to crop sizes. A bumper crop sends prices down, a small crop sends them up. The price change will be larger, the less elastic the demand curve.

Because farm products typically have inelastic demands, price fluctuations tend to be large in response to unplanned changes in production.

What are the effects on the receipts of farmers? If the commodity in question has an elastic demand, increases in the quantity supplied will raise farmers' receipts. If the demand is inelastic, increases in quantity supplied will reduce farmers' receipts.

Wherever demands are inelastic, good harvests will bring reductions in total farm receipts and bad harvests will bring increases.

Most farm products do have inelastic demands. When nature is bountiful and produces a bumper

---

FIGURE 6-7   The Effect on Price of Unplanned Variations in Output Depends on Elasticity of Demand

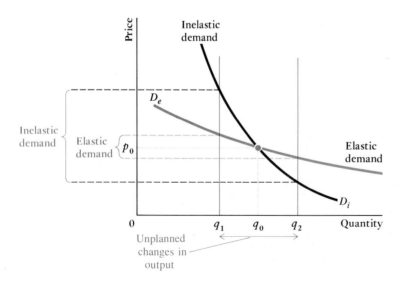

An unplanned fluctuation in output of a given size leads to a much sharper fluctuation in price if the demand curve is inelastic than if it is elastic. Suppose that the expected price is p_0 and the planned output is q_0. The two curves D_i and D_e are *alternative* demand curves. If actual production always equaled planned production, the equilibrium price and quantity would be p_0 and q_0 with either demand curve. Unplanned variations in output, however, cause quantity to fluctuate year by year between q_1 (a bad harvest) and q_2 (a good harvest). When demand is inelastic (shown by the black curve), prices will show large fluctuations. When demand is elastic (shown by the gray curve), price fluctuations will be much smaller.

crop, farmers' receipts dwindle; when nature is moderately unkind and output falls unexpectedly, their receipts rise. The interests of the farmer and the consumer are exactly opposed in such cases. This conflict is dramatically illustrated every time a partial crop failure sends food prices soaring but raises farm incomes, and whenever a bumper crop that brings relief to consumers evokes a cry for help from the farm belt, where incomes are shrinking.

Fluctuating Demand with Inelastic Supply

As the tide of business activity flows and ebbs, demand curves for all commodities rise and fall. The effects on prices and outputs depend on the elasticity of *supply*. Industrial products typically have rather elastic supply curves, so shifts in demand cause fairly large changes in outputs, but only small changes in prices. Agricultural commodities typically have rather inelastic supply curves because land, labor, and machinery devoted to agricultural uses is not quickly transferred to non-agricultural uses when demand falls nor quickly returned to agriculture when demand rises.

Given an inelastic supply curve for agricultural products as a whole, farm prices, farm receipts, and farm income will be sensitive to demand shifts, as Figure 6-8(i) illustrates. A sharp drop in demand (a leftward shift of the demand curve) will cause hardship among those whose income depends on farm crops.

To the public (and to many in Congress) the economic plight of farmers during the Great Depression seemed to be caused by the great fall in prices, which was caused by the fall in demand for commodities with an inelastic supply curve. The notion

FIGURE 6-8   The Effect on Receipts of a Decrease in Demand

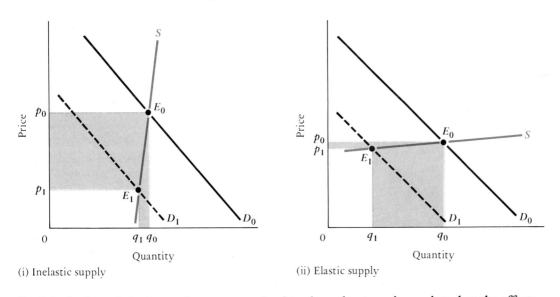

(i) Inelastic supply   (ii) Elastic supply

Both inelastic and elastic supply curves can lead to sharp decreases in receipts, but the effects on prices are very different in the two cases. In each part of the figure, when demand decreases from D_0 to D_1, price and quantity decrease to p_1 and q_1 and total receipts decline by the shaded area. In (i) the symptom is mainly the sharp decrease in price. Output and employment remain high, but the drastic fall in price will reduce or eliminate profits and put downward pressure on wages. In (ii) the symptom is primarily the sharp decrease in quantity. Employment and total profits earned fall drastically, though wage rates and profit margins on what is produced may remain close to their former level.

of **price parity**, the ratio of the prices farmers receive for things they sell to the prices they pay for things they buy, was invoked to measure their hardship. As a result, programs were proposed to restore price parity to farmers.

But this appealing diagnosis is incomplete. It is income earned and wages received, not prices, that determine how much people have to spend. As Figure 6-8(ii) shows, when demand falls a very elastic supply curve can be as much a curse as a very inelastic one. The loss in receipts in this case is due primarily to a decline in *quantity* sold rather than to a decline in *price,* but that does not make it less painful, as the experience in the United States during the Great Depression shows.

Agriculture and industry both suffered in the Great Depression but with different symptoms: farmers via low prices, as in Figure 6-8(i), and industry via low production and high unemployment of workers and resources, as in Figure 6-8(ii).

From 1929 to 1932 agricultural output fell 1 percent while prices fell 56 percent, leaving revenues at about 44 percent of their 1929 levels. Over the same period, manufacturing prices fell only 30 percent but output fell 47 percent, leaving revenues at only 37 percent of their 1929 levels.[2] While farmers clamored for the government to do something about prices, industry and industrial workers clamored for the government to act to overcome unemployment of people and underemployment of factories.

Agricultural Stabilization in Theory

Governments throughout the world intervene in agricultural markets in attempts to stabilize agricultural prices and incomes in the face of short-term and uncontrollable fluctuations in supply and cyclical fluctuations in demand. How may they do so? We shall consider several types of schemes.

To start, assume the supply curve in each case refers to planned (or average) production per year, but actual production fluctuates around that level. In a free market, as we have seen, this causes both prices and farmers' receipts to fluctuate widely from year to year.

The Ever-Normal Granary

One method of preventing fluctuations in prices and gross receipts is for the government to permit individual farmers to form a producers' association that tries to stabilize—to keep "ever normal"—the supply *actually coming onto the market* in spite of variations in production.[3] The association does this by storing a crop, say, grain, in years of above average production and selling out of its storage elevators in years of below average production.

Since one farmer's production is an insignificant part of total production, there is no point in an individual farmer's holding some production off the market in an effort to prevent a fall in price in a year of bumper crops. But if all farmers get together and agree to vary the supply coming onto the market, then, collectively, they can have a major effect on price. The appropriate policy is shown in Figure 6-9.

Since revenues accrue to the producers when the goods are actually sold on the market, total revenues can be stabilized by keeping sales constant at the equilibrium output even though production varies. This can be accomplished by adding to or subtracting from inventories the excesses or shortages of production.

The fully successful ever-normal granary stabilizes both prices and revenues of producers.

The costs of this plan are those of providing storage and organizing and administering the program. A potential danger is that in order to get higher prices the producers' association will sell on average less than is produced and will find itself with ever-increasing stockpiles of the crop.

Government Price Supports at the Equilibrium Price

Because there are many difficulties in organizing and administering private stabilization programs such as

---

[2] Farm income is not simply farm profits, for the wages paid to farm labor are also incomes attributable to farming. Similarly, the incomes earned in industry include the wages and salaries of workers as well as the profits of business people. When output drops greatly, as in Figure 6-8(ii), businesses will lay off workers, and so on. This reduces incomes earned from industrial production.

[3] Government permission is required because of antitrust laws, which are discussed in Chapter 16.

FIGURE 6-9   The Ever-Normal Granary

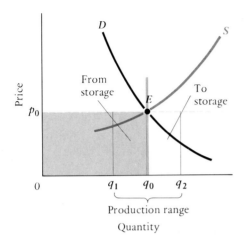

The ever-normal granary scheme stabilizes the
quantity sold by farmers even though actual production varies. The planned supply curve is S; p_0 and
q_0 are the equilibrium price and quantity, respectively.
Actual production varies between q_1 and q_2. When production is q_2, the producers' association sells q_0 and stores
$q_0 q_2$. When production is q_1 it still sells q_0, supplementing
the current production by selling $q_1 q_0$ from its stored
crops. Producers' revenue is stabilized at $p_0 \times q_0$ (the
shaded area) every year.

the ever-normal granary, can government do the
same thing and do it more efficiently? The answer
(perhaps surprisingly) is no.

Suppose the government, instead of the producers' association, enters the market, buying and thereby adding to its own stocks when there is a surplus
and selling and thereby reducing its stocks when
there is a shortage. If it had enough grain elevators
and warehouses, and if its support price were set at
a realistic level, the government could stabilize *prices*
indefinitely. But, as Figure 6-10 illustrates, it would
not succeed in stabilizing farmers' revenues, which
would be high with bumper crops and low with poor
crops.

**Government price supports at the equilibrium
price would not stabilize revenues. They would,
however, reverse the pattern of revenue fluctuation.**

In effect, the government policy imposes a demand
curve that is perfectly elastic at the support price.
This stabilizes price, but it does not stabilize receipts
to producers.

Revenue Stabilization by Government Purchases and Sales

Obviously, there must be a government buying and
selling policy that will stabilize farmers' receipts.
What are its characteristics? As has been seen, too
much price stability causes receipts to vary directly
with production, and too little price stability causes
receipts to vary inversely with production. It appears
that the government should aim at some intermediate
degree of price stability. If the government allows

FIGURE 6-10   Government Price Supports at the Equilibrium Price

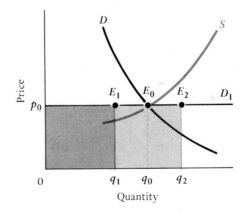

**Government price supports at the equilibrium price
stabilize prices (not quantities sold by farmers) and
do not accumulate surpluses but cause revenues to
vary directly with production.** Actual production
varies around the equilibrium level of q_0. When production is q_2, the government buys $q_0 q_2$ and stores it. When
production is q_1, the government sells $q_1 q_0$ from storage.
The quantity sold to the public is always q_0, and this
stabilizes price at p_0. The government policy converts the
demand curve facing farmers to D_1. If q_0 is average production, there is no trend toward the accumulation of
storage crops.

Farmers' revenue varies from $p_0 q_1$ (the darker shaded
area) when production is q_1 to $p_0 q_2$ (the entire shaded
area) when production is q_2.

prices to vary in inverse proportion to variations in production, then receipts will be stabilized. A 10 percent rise in production should be met by a 10 percent fall in price, and a 10 percent fall in production by a 10 percent rise in price.

To stabilize farmers' receipts, the government must make the demand curve facing the farmers one of unit elasticity. It must buy in periods of high output and sell in periods of low output, but only enough to let prices change in inverse proportion to farmers' output.

Government Price Supports Above the Free-Market Equilibrium Level

In practice stabilization plans involving price supports usually set prices *above* the average free-market equilibrium level. This is due to the fact that stabilization is not the only goal; there is also a desire to assure farmers a standard of living comparable with that of city dwellers. This involves attempting to *raise* farm incomes in addition to stabilizing them.

Here, too, the government buys in periods of high output and sells in periods of low output, but on average it buys much more than it sells, with the result that unsold surpluses accumulate (see Figure 6-2, on page 100). Taxpayers generally will be paying farmers for producing goods that no one is willing to purchase at prices that come near to covering costs.

Fifty-Five Years of American Farm Policy

The American experience in trying to help the large, often poor, and always politically influential farm population illustrates the theory just developed. In particular, it shows the twin difficulties of surplus production and slow resource reallocation out of agricultural production. There is no doubt that a free-market policy would have avoided surplus production, but the human cost would have been immense. The challenge has been to respond to the real hardships of the farm population without intensifying the problems. As of now, American farm policy has not succeeded in doing so. The economic analysis of the previous sections helps us understand why.

Before 1950

The first serious government intervention in agricultural markets was in 1929, when the Federal Farm Board was set up to buy and sell farm produce to promote "orderly agricultural marketing." It specified "support prices" at which it would buy any farm products that could not be sold on the free market. (A brief glossary of terms used in American farm policy is given in Box 6-3.) The board's operations failed when its support prices, set well above the free-market price levels, led to the accumulation of large stocks and a rapid exhaustion of available funds.

The Roosevelt administration (1933–1945) could not, it felt, politically or morally abandon the farmers, who were among the earliest victims of the Great Depression. Thus it did not abandon support prices. Indeed, it established support prices at a level designed to restore "parity" between agricultural crops and manufactured goods in the period before World War I, 25 years earlier. Since farm prices had fallen relative to the prices of manufactured goods, this meant that they were to be supported by the government at levels well above their free-market equilibrium levels.

The government realized that unless output could be restricted, holding prices above the free-market level would require unending injections of federal money to buy crops that could never be sold. In order to prevent the buildup of surplus output, programs were introduced to pay farmers *not to produce* as well as imposing acreage restrictions and marketing quotas on individual farmers.

But supported prices and guaranteed sales, government-financed research, as well as government loans for farm improvements were an enormous incentive to productivity, and output per acre and output per worker soared. Thus total output was not held down in spite of acreage limitations, and the federal costs for buying and storing the resulting surplus crops remained at a high level.

From 1950 to 1970

After 1950 farm policy was modified but not basically changed. In the 1950s the notion of parity with pre-World War I relative prices was finally dropped, and the base for parity was made the average of prices ruling during the previous 10 years. Moreover, actual

BOX 6-3

The Vocabulary of American Farm Policy

Here is a lexicon of some of the basic terms used in discussions of farm policy.

Basic commodities The six crops—corn, cotton, peanuts, rice, tobacco, and wheat—for which government price supports are legally mandated.

Support price The price at which the government will buy farmers' output to assure farmers the income level they would get if market prices were at support price levels.

Parity price The price for a bushel today that would be necessary to buy the same quantity of goods that a bushel bought in the 1910–1914 base period. At one time used as level of support price.

Target price A fictional price set by the government as a benchmark for subsidizing farmers' income. Sometimes used as a basis for setting support prices (e.g., support price at 80 percent of target prices).

Loan rate The price at which the government will provide loans to farmers to enable them to store their crops for later sale. If market price falls below the loan rate, the farmer keeps the loan and forfeits his grain, effectively selling his grain to the government and receiving what amounts to a government-guaranteed minimum price.

Deficiency payment A direct income subsidy paid to the farmer equal to the difference between the target price and the higher of the market price or the loan rate, if the market price falls below the target price.

Acreage reduction program A program under which farmers agree to cut their planted acreage to gain entry into other farm programs.

Soil bank A form of acreage reduction program under which land is left fallow for a specified number of years to restore its quality.

Paid diversion A program under which farmers agree to cut their planted acreage in exchange for cash from the government.

Payments-in-kind (PIK) A payment to farmers of a specified quantity of a commodity in return for their agreement to cut their planted acreage of that commodity.

Guaranteed farm loans Loans that are made by farm banks to eligible farmers and that are guaranteed by the government.

Farm bank A bank with one-fourth or more of its loans for agricultural purposes.

---

prices were allowed to fall to a specified fraction of parity prices before the full price support was given. This modification allowed a slow decline in relative prices over time. The influence on reallocation of even these small price changes was weakened by additional measures that reduced the incentive to shift resources out of farming and encouraged further research and development.

Meanwhile, the "soil bank" and other programs paid farmers not to produce commodities that consumers would not buy at the prevailing prices and to take acreage out of production. Superficially, the policies seemed to be working: The number of farms decreased by over 3 percent per year, and in 1969 there were only 2.7 million farms, half of the 1950 total. But the average size of farms increased from 216 to 389 acres, and thus the acreage under cultivation in 1970 was only about 9 percent less than

two decades earlier. Because of productivity increases, output was actually 30 percent *higher* in 1970 than in 1950, and the problem of excess supply was just as acute as it had been over the preceding decades.

The 1970s

Quite unexpectedly, dramatic shifts in demand changed the entire farm outlook during the first half of the 1970s. Rising world population, growing world income, and some massive crop failures around the world created a worldwide food shortage. Decreases in the value of the dollar relative to many other currencies, along with American productivity gains, made U.S. farm products cheaper abroad. Almost overnight, increased American exports eliminated the historical surpluses. The increasing demand for wheat, cotton, soybeans, and livestock depleted stored reserves and in some cases even led to shortages.

Rising demand and good harvests led to sharp rises in farm incomes. Farmers borrowed heavily to buy newer and bigger farm equipment to take advantage of the boom conditions. Acreage yields rose, and, at the same time, total acreage planted increased by 30 percent over the decade. Needless to say, this rising prosperity slowed the outflow of resources from farming. The number of farms decreased by only 1 percent per year, but farms continued to grow in size and sophistication as their owners substituted machinery for labor.

By 1974 many government officials and some economists were speaking of having solved the farm problem. Direct price supports were replaced by loans to farmers when prices fell below "target prices." These target prices were designed to cover most but not all farm costs, and the loans were secured by the crop which the farmer stored and could sell whenever the market price rose above the target price. The government took over the stored crops only if the farmer defaulted on the interest payments on the loans. Because of the anticipated continuation of high export demand, default did not seem an imminent danger.

Although it did not seem important at the time, the debt burden of farmers was rising steadily to finance massive equipment purchases. But high prices and unlimited demand seemingly justified these expenditures. Such was farm prosperity that for a brief time average farm income rose above non-farm income.

By mid decade, however, the "farm problem" reappeared. In 1974 the world entered the most serious economic recession since the 1930s. Hard times hit every sector of the economy. Buoyant international demand and declining export surpluses elsewhere in the world, however, shielded U.S. agriculture from a repetition of the 1930s. But for farmers who had incurred a heavy debt to expand and mechanize rapidly during the early 1970s, even a mild decline threatened disaster. Between 1974 and 1978, prices *paid* by farmers rose by 31 percent, but prices *received* by them rose only 9 percent. When the market ceased to expand as fast as expected,

farmers faced rising costs and many of them borrowed more in order to keep up the payments on their loans. They marched on Washington for higher support prices to protect their investments. A general economic recovery of 1978 helped, but only temporarily.

From 1980 to 1985

The worldwide recession that began in 1980 revived farmers' demands for protection from the age-old fluctuations in their income. Although the Reagan administration had come to office committed to letting the market, not the federal government, regulate agriculture, political realities dictated otherwise.

1981 to 1984.   Nineteen eighty-one was a bad year for American farming. The 1981 harvest was so large that most farm prices fell far short of predicted levels. Prices for farm commodities rose less rapidly than the prices farmers paid for fertilizer, credit, machinery, and other items. Already in debt, they borrowed more, even while interest rates reached record highs, up to 20 percent in some regions.

The 1981 farm bill was a throwback to pre-1970 policies, increasing major crop price supports and raising target prices. The provisions of the bill were justified as a temporary response to the worldwide recession and the "farm emergency" of 1981.

Many of the expectations and projections underlying the 1981 act proved to be wrong. Export demand did not recover, owing to rising production in other countries and to the rising value of the dollar, which had the effect of making American exports ever more expensive. Farm prices remained depressed. For one example, the market price of a bushel of wheat in 1984 fell to $3.40, over $1.00 below the target price of $4.45 and below the level of $3.65, at which the farmer could borrow from the government with the crop as collateral. Many borrowed and subsequently defaulted on the loans.

Despite new acreage restriction programs the United States ended the year 1982 with surpluses unequaled in magnitude for 20 years. Basic commodities for which there was no commercial demand were estimated at about 150 million metric tons, an amount nearly large enough to meet the nation's domestic needs for a full year. With prices and export volumes down, the number of farm loan delinquencies and bankruptcies rose. Private banks estimated that as many as one-fourth of their farm customers would fail to qualify for financing for the coming year and thus would have to default on their loans.

In 1983 the administration began a new production control program called the Payments-in-Kind (PIK) program. It offered to give farm crops (that had been forfeited to the government as loan repayment) to farmers who removed part of their land from production in accordance with program guidelines.

Under the program an individual farmer could take an entire farm out of production. The Department of Agriculture announced that farmers had signed agreements to idle almost a third of the nation's 231 million acres usually planted in basic commodities. This program solved the government's surplus problem—it depleted its stockpiles of grain. Indeed, the government found that it did not have sufficient stockpiles to meet its PIK commitments at harvest time in 1983!

A combination of acreage reduction under PIK and poorer weather led to price increases through mid 1984. However, as soon as the 1984 crop production returned to pre-PIK levels, prices fell sharply again.

1985.   Early in 1985 stories of the desperate financial conditions of American farms began appearing in the press. Many farmers were unable to obtain the credit needed to pay their bills and to do spring planting; as a result many were going bankrupt.

The source of distress on many farms was the unusually high level of debt as a proportion of farm assets. In the 1970s, as we have seen, agricultural projections had led farmers to expand operations, to mechanize, and to bring more land into production. In so doing they borrowed heavily, using their land as collateral. But, as agricultural prices and incomes fell in the early 1980s, many farmers were unable to renew the loans they had taken out five or six years earlier, when the optimistic farm outlook led them to invest in newer and bigger machinery.

The crisis of 1985 was different from the historical farm problem. It was not a matter of inelastic demands, low income elasticities, and rising productivity. Farmers were suffering from a different problem: overinvestment in new technologies during boom times. Throughout history, new products and new techniques have led to investment. Investment booms often go too far as investors rush to get rich quick. Some investments prove unprofitable, and many investors lose their money, but after a period of "shakeout" the remaining investment is then normally profitable.

But farmers had become used to having the government bail them out and were unprepared for such a shakeout. After a series of marches, protests, and a major lobbying effort, the government once again did so. Both the Reagan administration and Congress responded with new federal loan funds to guarantee commercial farm loans in danger of default and with funds to subsidize new loans to farmers who needed them. As 1985 ended, a new farm bill passed Congress and was signed into law. It provides for $52 billion in aid over three years. Its basic elements—target prices, deficiency payments, acreage limitations, loan guarantees, loan rate subsidies—differ in many details, but are not fundamentally different than the devices of the last 50 years.

Evaluating Farm Policy

American farm policy reflects the central dilemma of government intervention in competitive markets to protect a portion of the population from economic hardship. By doing so it impedes the reallocation of resources that are required in a changing economy.

Box 6-4 discusses some general lessons about resource allocation that apply to farm policy as well as elsewhere. Most economists and many politicians believe that our historical farm policies have proven expensive and wasteful and that they have impeded the long-run adjustments required by changing tastes and technology. Yet the historical policies continue, even under administration that promised to reverse them. The reason is that a generation of farmers would be treated extremely harshly by the free market, and farmers are still considered too politically influential to be left exposed. Few people quarrel with the objectives of protecting farmers from a long period of severe hardship, but many hope for less

BOX 6-4

Four General Lessons About Resource Allocation

We have examined examples of government intervention in markets that might have been left unregulated. Our discussion suggests four widely applicable lessons.

1. Costs May Be Shifted, But They Cannot Be Avoided

Production, whether in response to free-market signals or to government controls, uses resources; thus it involves costs to members of society. If it takes 5 percent of the nation's resources to provide housing at some stated average standard, those resources will not be available to produce other commodities. If resources are used to produce unwanted soybeans, those resources will not be available to produce other commodities. For society there is no such thing as free housing or free soybeans.

The average standard of living depends on the amounts of resources available to the economy and the efficiency with which these resources are used. It follows that *costs are real* and are incurred no matter who provides the goods. Rent controls or subsidies to agriculture can change the share of the costs paid by particular individuals or groups, lowering the share for some and raising the share for others, but they cannot make the costs go away.

Different ways of *allocating* the costs may also affect the total amount of resources used and thus the amount of costs incurred. For one example, controls that keep prices and profits of some commodity below free-market levels will lead to increased quantities demanded and decreased quantities supplied. Unless government steps in to provide additional supplies, fewer resources will be allocated to producing the commodity. If government chooses to supply all the demand at the controlled prices, more resources will be allocated to it, which means fewer resources will be devoted to other kinds of goods and services.

2. Free-Market Prices and Profits Encourage Economical Use of Resources

Prices and profits in a market economy provide signals to both demanders and suppliers. Prices that are high and rising (relative to other prices) provide an incentive to purchasers to economize on the commodity. They may choose to satisfy the want in question with substitutes whose prices have not risen so much (because they are less costly to provide) or to satisfy less of that want by shifting expenditure to the satisfaction of other wants.

On the supply side, rising prices tend to produce rising profits. High profits attract further resources into production. Short-term windfall profits that bear no relation to current costs repeatedly occur in market economies. They cause resources to move into those industries with profits until profits fall to levels that can be earned elsewhere in the economy.

Falling prices and falling profits provide the opposite motivations. Purchasers are inclined to buy more; sellers are inclined to produce less and to move

expensive and less wasteful *means* than those relied upon for half a century. Let us review how these means have been wasteful.

Price parity.   Price parity in effect freezes relative prices. To freeze relative prices at levels existing at any one time prevents the price system from allocating resources in response to changes in tastes and

incomes on the demand side and to costs and availabilities on the supply side. Society progresses by substituting newer, cheaper products for more expensive ones, not by keeping relative prices the same forever.

Support prices above market levels.   Such prices create surpluses that must be stored, given away, or resources out of the industry and into more profitable undertakings.

The price system responds to need for change in the allocation of resources, say, in response to an external event such as the loss of a source of a raw material or the outbreak of a war. Changing relative prices and profits signal the need for change to which consumers and producers respond.

3. Government Intervention Affects Resource Allocation

Governments intervene in the price system sometimes to satisfy generally agreed social goals and sometimes to help politically influential interest groups. Government intervention changes the allocation of resources that the price system would achieve.

Interventions have allocative consequences because they inhibit the free-market allocative mechanism. Some controls, such as rent controls, prevent prices from rising (in response, say, to an increase in demand with no change in supply). If the price is held down, the signal is not given to consumers to economize on a commodity that is in short supply. On the supply side, when prices and profits are prevented from rising, the profit signals that would attract new resources into the industry are never given. The shortage continues, and the movements of demand and supply that would resolve it are not set in motion.

Other controls, such as agricultural price supports, prevent prices from falling (in response, say, to an increase in supply with no increase in demand). This leads to excess supply, and the signal is not given to producers to produce less or to buyers to increase their purchases. Surpluses continue, and the movements of demand and supply that would eliminate them are not set in motion.

4. Intervention Requires Alternative Allocative Mechanisms

Intervention typically requires alternative allocative mechanisms. During times of shortages allocation will be by sellers' preferences, by first-come, first-served, or by some system of government rationing. During periods of surplus there will be unsold supplies unless the government buys and stores the surpluses. Since long-run changes in demand and costs do not induce resource reallocations through private decisions, the government will have to step in. It will have to force resources out of industries where prices are held too high, as it has tried to do in agriculture, and into industries where prices are held too low, as it can do, for example, by providing public housing.

Intervention almost always has both benefits and costs. Economics cannot answer the questions of whether a particular intervention with free markets is desirable, but it can clarify the issues by identifying benefits and costs and who will enjoy or bear them. In doing so it can identify the competing values involved. This will be discussed in detail in Chapter 22.

---

destroyed. They also encourage more production than would otherwise occur.

Loan guarantees to avoid bankruptcy. If people know the government will bail them out if they overinvest in some industry, they will tend to do so. If demand turns out to be unexpectedly strong, they will earn the profits; if it turns out to be unexpectedly weak, the government will pay the bill. While those investing cannot lose, society is sure to lose when overinvestment wastes scarce capital.

Guaranteeing relative incomes by direct payments to farmers. Changes in relative incomes signal the need for resources to move from one occupation to another. By freezing relative incomes, the government not only eliminates the incentive to use resources efficiently, but also reduces incentives for owners or workers to move resources to more productive uses.

The Future

Is there a better way to make farming an occupation in which people can invest and work without being disadvantaged relative to other citizens? Most econ-omists believe it would be more efficient to subsidize farm workers to change occupations and farm producers to change products than to subsidize them to stay where they are not needed and to produce products that are not profitably marketed. Such subsidies would require significant one-time outlays—as do the present schemes—but would eventually allow the market to do the further job of allocating resources to agriculture.

Summary

1. The elementary theory of supply, demand, and price provides powerful tools for analyzing and understanding some real-world problems and policies. The chapter illustrates a few of them.
2. Effective price floors lead to excess supply. Either the potential seller is left with quantities that cannot be sold, or the government must step in and buy the surplus. Effective price ceilings lead to excess demand and provide a strong incentive for black marketeers to buy at the controlled price and sell at the higher free-market price.
3. Rent controls are a persistent and spreading form of price ceiling. The major consequence of effective rent control is a shortage of rental accommodation that gets worse due to a slow but inexorable decline in the quantity of rental housing.
4. Rent controls can be an effective response to temporary situations in which there is a ban on building or a transitory increase in demand. They will almost surely fail when they are introduced as a response to a long-run increase in demand or to inflation in the costs of providing rental housing.
5. Average farm incomes in the United States have lagged behind urban incomes despite the fact that farm products are vital to our economy. The long-term problems of agriculture arise from a high rate of productivity growth on the supply side and a low income elasticity on the demand side. This means that, unless many resources are being transferred out of agriculture, quantity supplied increases faster than quantity demanded year after year.
6. Although the number of farmers has decreased, it has not done so nearly fast enough to keep domestic demand and supply in balance without incurring sharply falling prices. During the 1970s a sharp rise in demand for American farm products by foreign nations temporarily relieved the long-standing supply surplus and led to a burst of prosperity that showed signs of eliminating the income gap of farmers relative to the rest of the population.
7. Agricultural prices and incomes are depressed by chronic surpluses in agricultural markets. Government policies to protect farm incomes have included buying farmers' output at above free-market

prices, limiting production and acreage by quotas, and paying farmers to leave crops unproduced. Such policies tend to inhibit the reallocation mechanism and thus to increase farm surpluses above what they would otherwise be and to lead to accumulating stocks.

8. Agricultural commodities are subject to wide fluctuations in market prices, which cause fluctuations in producers' incomes. This is because of year-to-year unplanned fluctuations in supplies combined with inelastic demand and because of cyclical fluctuations in demand combined with inelastic supplies. Where demand is inelastic, large crops tend to be associated with low total receipts and small crops with high total receipts.

9. Fluctuations in farm income can be reduced by producers' associations that store unsold crops when output is high and sell from inventories when output is low or by appropriate government purchases and sales in the open market.

10. The history of American farm policy illustrates dramatically these theoretical predictions as well as the more general lessons that government intervention to prevent the working of the market mechanisms affects resource allocation and requires alternative allocative mechanisms. While farm policy has protected farmers from certain hardships, it has slowed the required outflow of resources that alone would solve the problem of chronic excess supply.

Topics for Review

Price floor and price ceiling
Allocation by sellers' preferences, rationing, and black market
Windfall profits and their allocative function
Short-run and long-run supply curves
Effects of high productivity growth and low income elasticity
Importance of export demand
Price supports at and above the level of free-market equilibrium
Price stabilization versus income stabilization

Discussion Questions

1. "When a controlled item is vital to everyone, it is easier to start controlling the price than to stop controlling it. Such controls are popular with consumers, regardless of their harmful consequences." Explain why it may be inefficient to have such controls, why they may be popular, and why, if they are popular, the government might nevertheless choose to decontrol these prices.

2. If there is an opportunity for a black market with price ceilings, is there a similar opportunity with price floors?

3. When in the mid 1970s there was a shortage of natural gas, the columnist William Safire called it "the unnatural shortage of natural gas." He wrote: "Be angry at the real villains: the Washington-knows-best Congressmen, the self-anointed consumer 'protectors' and the regulatory bureaucracy. They thought they could protect

the consumer by breaking the laws of supply and demand, and as a result have made a classic case against government intervention." From these remarks what do you judge the policy to have been? Could producers have created the shortage of natural gas? If so, how? How would you define a "shortage"? Is there a useful distinction between a "natural shortage" and an "unnatural shortage"?

4. Medical and hospital care in Britain is provided free to individuals by the National Health Service, with the costs paid by taxation. Some British doctors complain that patients want "too much" medical care; patients complain that they have to wait "too long" in doctors' offices for the care they get, and months or years for needed operations. Use the theory of supply and demand to discuss these complaints. Would you expect a private (pay) medical market to grow up alongside the National Health Service? Can you reconcile your analysis with the fact that polls always show the National Health Service to be very popular in the population at large?

5. The Yarvard Law School, in Princetown, has 1,000 qualified applicants for 200 places in the first-year class. It is debating a number of alternative admission criteria: (a) a lottery, (b) LSAT score, (c) recommendations from alumni, (d) place of residence of applicant. An economist on the faculty determined that if the tuition level is doubled, the excess demand will disappear. Argue for (or against) using the tuition rate to replace each of the other suggested criteria.

6. It is sometimes asserted that the rising costs of construction are putting housing out of the reach of ordinary citizens. Who bears the heaviest cost when rentals are kept down by (a) rent controls, (b) a subsidy to tenants equal to some fraction of their rent payments, and (c) low-cost public housing.

7. "This year the weather smiled on us, God smiled on us and we made a crop," says Don Marble, a grain and cotton farmer in South Plains, Texas. "But just as we made a crop, the economic situation changed." This quotation brings to mind the old saying "If you are a farmer, the weather is always bad." Discuss the sense in which this saying might be true.

8. "This ought to be a time of rejoicing in the vineyards of California. The crop of wine grapes has rarely been richer, the harvest is nearly complete, and Americans are drinking more California wine than ever before." Why then were there falling profits and a record number of bankruptcies in the industry?

9. The Kenya Meat Commission (KMC) decided it was undemocratic to allow meat prices to be out of the reach of the ordinary citizen. It decided to freeze meat prices. Six months later, in a press interview, the managing commissioner of the KMC made the following statements. Do the facts alleged make sense given KMC's policy?
   a. "The price of almost everything in Kenya has gone up, but we have not increased the price of meat. The price of meat in this country is still the lowest in the world."
   b. "Cattle are scarce in the country, but I do not know why."
   c. "People are eating too much beef, and unless they diversify their eating habits and eat other foodstuffs, the shortage of beef will continue."

10. Three million acres of American farmland are being converted each year to other uses (out of about 525 million acres available). The American Farmland Trust calls this "one of the most critical problems facing our country and the world today." It has appealed to the public for contributions on the ground that "steps need to be taken immediately to preserve the prime agricultural land on which the food you eat is now grown." Discuss whether this is a critical problem, and if it is, whether the free market can be expected to solve it.

11. Discuss the following recent headlines in terms of the analysis of this chapter.
    a. "Agriculture's long-run outlook is bleak."
    b. "Boom goes bust: Soviet feast on U.S. grain in 70s leads to disaster on the farm in the 80s."
    c. "Farm children plan for careers off their family land."
    d. "Surging value of the dollar means chaos in Iowa."

12. Compare the following two headlines that appeared within days of each other. Do American consumers benefit or lose when bumper crops occur?
    a. "Bumper potato crop dashes farmers hopes."
    b. "Record high corn crop leaves farmers smiling."
    Hint: Corn is a "basic commodity"; potatoes are not.

13. What do the following quotes tell you about the politics of farm policy?
    a. Farmer Peter de Gravelles, Jr., of Franklin, Louisiana, an ardent supporter of President Reagan's free enterprise philosophy: "I am not asking the government to guarantee me a profit for my sugar cane. I just wanted a safety net so that I would not go bankrupt in bad years like this one."
    b. "The whole Agriculture Committee is biased toward agricultural interests," said Representative George E. Brown, Jr., of California, a senior Democrat on the panel. "We're not evil or anything, just a little one-sided."

PART THREE

Consumption, Production, and Cost

7

Household Consumption Behavior: The Marginal Utility Approach

In Part Two we saw that demand is an important part of the explanation of market prices and that the shape of demand curves has a great influence on the way in which markets behave. But why do market demand curves have the shape they do? To deal with this question, we need to study the individual household behavior on which market demand curves depend.

Market demand curves tell how much is demanded by all purchasers. For example, in Figure 4–1 (page 61) the market demand for carrots is 90,000 tons when the price is $40 per ton. This 90,000 tons is the sum of the quantities demanded by millions of different households. It may be made up of 4 pounds for the McDaniels, 7 pounds for the Gonzaleses, 1.5 pounds for the Wilsons, and so on. The demand curve for carrots also tells us that when the price rises to $60, aggregate quantity demanded falls to 77,500 tons per month. This quantity too can be traced back to individual households. The McDaniels might buy only 3 pounds, the Gonzaleses 6.5 pounds, and the Wilsons none at all. Notice that we have now described two points not only on the market demand curve, but on the demand curves of each of these households.

Aggregate behavior is merely the sum of the behavior of individual households. The market demand curve is the horizontal sum of the demand curves of the individual households.

It is the *horizontal* sum because we wish to add quantities demanded at a given price, and quantities are measured in the horizontal direction on a conventional demand curve graph. This process is illustrated in Figure 7-1.

The question "Why do market demand curves have the shape they do?" becomes "Why do individual demand curves have the shape they do?" Economists have long sought to understand individual household behavior. In this chapter and the next we explore two approaches. Both arrive at the same basic answers, but each offers somewhat different insights.

FIGURE 7-1   The Relation Between Household and Market Demand Curves

(i) Household *A*   (ii) Household *B*   (iii) Households *A* and *B*

An aggregate demand curve is the horizontal sum of the individual demand curves of all households in the market. The figure illustrates aggregation over only two households. At a price of $3, household *A* purchases 2 units and household *B* purchases 4 units; thus together they purchase 6 units. No matter how many households are involved the process is the same.

Marginal Utility Theory

Early economists, struggling with the problem of what determines the relative prices of commodities, encountered what they came to call the *paradox of value:* Necessary commodities, such as water, have prices that are low compared with prices of luxury commodities, such as diamonds. Water is necessary to our existence, while diamonds used as ornaments are frivolous and could disappear from the face of the earth tomorrow without causing any great loss. Does it not seem odd then, these economists argued, that water is so cheap and diamonds are so expensive? It took a long time to resolve this apparent paradox, so it is not surprising that even today the confusion persists and in different forms clouds many current policy discussions. The key to resolving the apparent paradox lies in the important distinction between marginal and total utility.

Marginal and Total Utility

The satisfaction someone receives from consuming commodities is called **utility. Total utility** refers to the total satisfaction from consuming some commodity. **Marginal utility** refers to the change in satisfaction resulting from consuming a little more or a little less of the commodity. For example, the total utility of consuming 10 units of any commodity is the total satisfaction those 10 units provide. The marginal utility of the tenth unit consumed is the additional satisfaction provided by the consumption of that unit, or, in other words, the difference in total utility gained by consuming 9 units and by consuming 10 units.[1]

The significance of this distinction can be seen by considering two questions: (1) If you had to give up consuming one of the following commodities completely, which would you choose: water or the movies? (2) If you had to pick one of the following, which would you choose: increasing your water consumption by 35 gallons a month (the amount required for

---

[1] Here and elsewhere in elementary economics it is common to use interchangeably two concepts that mathematicians distinguish. Technically, *incremental* utility is measured over a discrete interval, such as from 9 to 10, while *marginal* utility is a rate of change measured over an infinitesimal interval. But common usage applies the word *marginal* when the last unit is involved, even if a one-unit change is not infinitesimal. [9]

an average bath) or attending one more movie a month?

In (1) you are comparing the value you place on your total consumption of water with the value you place on all your attendance at the movies. You are comparing the *total utility* of your water consumption with the *total utility* of your movie attendance. There is little doubt that everyone would answer (1) in the same way, revealing that the total utility derived from consuming water exceeds the total utility derived from attending the movies.

In (2) you are comparing the value you place on a small addition to your water consumption with the value you place on a small addition to your movie attendances. You are comparing your *marginal utility* of water with your *marginal utility* of movies. In responding to (2), some might select the extra movie; others might select the extra water. Furthermore, their choice would depend on whether it was made at a time when water was plentiful so that they placed a low value on obtaining a little additional water (*low* marginal utility of water), or when water was scarce, so that they might put quite a high value on obtaining a little more water (*high* marginal utility of water).

Choices of type (1) are encountered much less commonly than are choices of type (2). If our income rises a little, we have to decide to have some more of one thing or another. If we find that we are overspending or if our income falls, we have to decide what to cut down on. Do we have a little less of this or a little less of that?

Real choices are rarely conditioned by total utilities; it is marginal utilities that are relevant to choices concerning a little more or a little less.

The Hypothesis of Diminishing Marginal Utility

The basic hypothesis of utility theory, sometimes called the *law of diminishing marginal utility,* is:

The utility any household derives from successive units of a particular commodity diminishes as total consumption of the commodity in- creases while the consumption of all other commodities remains constant.

Consider water once again. Some minimum quantity is essential to sustain life, and a person would, if necessary, give up all his or her income to obtain that quantity of water. Thus, the marginal utility of that much water is extremely high. More than this bare minimum will be drunk, but the marginal utility of successive glasses of water drunk over a period will decline steadily.

Evidence for this hypothesis will be considered later, but you can convince yourself that it is at least reasonable by asking a few questions. How much money would induce you to cut your consumption of water by one glass per week? The answer is very little. How much would induce you to cut it by a second glass? By a third glass? To only one glass consumed per week? The answer to the last question is quite a bit. The fewer glasses you are consuming already, the higher the marginal utility of one more or one less glass of water.

But water has many uses other than for drinking. A fairly high marginal utility will be attached to some minimum quantity for bathing, but much more than this minimum will be used only for more frequent baths or for having a water level in the tub higher than is absolutely necessary. The last weekly gallon used for bathing is likely to have a low marginal utility. Again, some small quantity of water is necessary for tooth brushing, but many people leave the water running while they brush. The water going down the drain between wetting and rinsing the brush surely has a low utility. When all the extravagant uses of water by the modern consumer are considered, it is certain that the marginal utility of the last, say, 30 percent of all units consumed is very low, even though the total utility of *all* the units consumed is extremely high.

Utility Schedules and Graphs

The schedule in Table 7-1 is hypothetical. It is constructed to illustrate the assumptions that have been made about utility, using our example of movie attendance. The table shows that total utility rises as the number of movies attended each month rises.

TABLE 7-1   Total and Marginal Utility Schedules

Number of movies attended per month	Total utility	Marginal utility
0	0	
1	30	30
2	50	20
3	65	15
4	75	10
5	83	8
6	89	6
7	93	4
8	96	3
9	98	2
10	99	1

Total utility rises, but marginal utility declines as this household's consumption increases. The marginal utility of 20, shown as the second entry in the last column, arises because total utility increases from 30 to 50—a difference of 20—with attendance at the second movie. To indicate that the marginal utility is associated with the change from one rate of movie attendances to another, the figures in the third column are recorded between the rows of the figures in the second column. When plotting marginal utility on a graph, it is plotted at the midpoint of the interval over which it is computed.

Everything else being equal, the more movies the household attends each month, the more satisfaction it gets—at least over the range shown in the table. But the marginal utility of each additional movie per month is less than that of the previous one even though each movie adds something to the household's satisfaction. The schedule shows that marginal utility declines as quantity consumed rises. [10] The same data are shown graphically in the two parts of Figure 7-2.

Maximizing Utility

A basic assumption of the economic theory of household behavior is that households try to make themselves as well off as they possibly can in the circumstances in which they find themselves. In other words, the members of a household seek to maximize their total utility. This assumption of utility

FIGURE 7-2   Total and Marginal Utility Curves

(i)

(ii)

The total utility curve rises, but the marginal utility curve falls as the quantity consumed rises. The dots correspond to the points listed in Table 7-1; smooth curves have been drawn through them.

maximization is sometimes criticized as being obviously unrealistic. Such criticisms are discussed and assessed in Box 7-1.

The Equilibrium of a Household

How can a household adjust its expenditure so as to maximize the total utility of its members? Should it

BOX 7-1

Does Demand Theory Require Households to Maximize Utility Unerringly?

It is tempting to dismiss utility maximization theory with the objection that it is unrealistic. After all, most of us know people who occasionally buy strawberries in spite of, or even because of, a rise in their price, or who spend a week's pay on a binge or a frivolous purchase that they afterward regret.

To judge such an observation, it is helpful to distinguish three possible uses of demand theory. The first is to study the aggregate behavior of all households—as illustrated, for example, by the market demand curve for a product. The second use is to make statements about an individual household's probable actions. The third is to make statements about what each household will certainly do.

The criticism cited in the opening paragraph of this box applies only to the third use of demand theory. Observations of exceptional behavior refute only the prediction that *all* households *always* behave as assumed by the theory. To predict the existence of a relatively stable downward-sloping market demand curve (the first use) or to predict what an individual household will probably do (the second use), we do *not* require that *all* households behave as is assumed by the theory all of the time. Consider two illustrations.

First, some households may always behave in a manner not assumed by the theory. Households whose members are mental defectives or have serious emotional disturbances are obvious possibilities. The inconsistent or erratic behavior of such households will not cause market demand curves to depart from their downward slope, provided these households account for a minority of total purchasers of any product. Their erratic behavior will be swamped by the normal behavior of the majority of households.

Second, an occasional irrationality on the part of every household will not upset the downward slope of the market demand curve so long as these isolated inconsistencies do not occur at the same time in all households. As long as such inconsistencies are unrelated across households, occurring now in one and now in another, their effect will be offset by the normal behavior of the majority of households.

The downward slope of the demand curve requires only that at any moment of time most households are behaving as assumed by the theory. This is compatible with inconsistent behavior on the part of some households all of the time and on the part of all households some of the time.

---

go to the point at which the marginal utility of each commodity is the same, that is, the point at which it would value equally the last unit of each commodity consumed? This would make sense only if each commodity had the same price per unit. But if a household must spend $3 to buy an additional unit of one commodity and only $1 for a unit of another, the first commodity would represent a poor use of its money if the marginal utility of each were equal. The household would be spending $3 to get satisfaction it could have acquired for only $1.

The household maximizing its utility will allocate its expenditure among commodities so that the utility of the last dollar spent on each is equal.

Imagine that the household is in a position in which the utility of the last dollar spent on carrots yields three times the utility of the last dollar spent on brussels sprouts. In this case, total utility can be increased by switching a dollar of expenditure from sprouts to carrots and gaining the difference between the utilities of a dollar spent on each.

The utility-maximizing household will continue to switch its expenditure from sprouts to carrots as long as a dollar spent on carrots yields more utility than a dollar spent on sprouts. But this switching reduces the quantity of sprouts consumed and, given the law of diminishing marginal utility, raises the marginal utility of sprouts; at the same time the switching increases the quantity of carrots consumed and thereby lowers the marginal utility of carrots.

Eventually, the marginal utilities will have changed enough so that the utility of a dollar spent on carrots is just equal to the utility of a dollar spent on sprouts. At this point there is nothing to be gained by a further switch of expenditure from sprouts to carrots. If the household persists in reallocating its expenditure, it will further reduce the marginal utility of carrots (by consuming more of them) and raise the marginal utility of sprouts (by consuming less of them). Total utility will no longer be at its maximum because the utility of a dollar spent on sprouts will exceed the utility of a dollar spent on carrots.

Let us now consider the conditions for maximizing utility in a more general way. Denote the marginal utility of the last unit of commodity X by MU_x and its price by p_x. Let MU_y and p_y refer to the marginal utility of a second commodity Y and its price. The marginal utility per dollar of X will be MU_x/p_x. For example, if the last unit adds 30 units to utility and costs \$2, then its marginal utility per dollar is $30/2 = 15$.

The condition required for a household to maximize its utility is, for any pair of commodities,

$$\frac{MU_x}{p_x} = \frac{MU_y}{p_y} \qquad [1]$$

This says that the household will allocate its expenditure so that the utility gained from the last dollar spent on each commodity is equal.

This is the fundamental equation of the utility theory of demand. Each household demands each good (for example, movie attendance) up to the point at which the marginal utility per dollar spent on it is the same as the marginal utility of a dollar spent on another good (for example, water). When this condition is met, the household cannot shift a dollar of expenditure from one commodity to another and increase its utility.

An Alternative Interpretation of Household Equilibrium

If we rearrange the terms in Equation 1, we can gain additional insight into household behavior.

$$\frac{MU_x}{MU_y} = \frac{p_x}{p_y} \qquad [2]$$

The right side of this equation states the *relative* price of the two goods. It is determined by the market and is outside the control of individual household; the household reacts to these market prices, but is powerless to change them. The left side states the relative ability of the goods to add to the household's satisfaction and is within the control of the household. In determining the quantities of different goods it buys, the household determines also their marginal utilities. (If you have difficulty seeing why, look again at Figure 7-2(ii).)

If the two sides of Equation 2 are not equal, the household can increase its total satisfaction by rearranging its purchases. Assume, for example, that the price of a unit of X is twice the price of a unit of Y ($p_x/p_y = 2$), while the marginal utility of a unit of X is three times that of a unit of Y ($MU_x/MU_y = 3$). Under these conditions it pays the household to buy more X and less Y. For example, reducing its purchases of Y by two units frees enough purchasing power to buy a unit of X. Since one extra unit of X bought yields 1.5 times the satisfaction of two units of Y forgone, the switch is worth making. What about a further switch of X for Y? As the household buys more X and less Y, the marginal utility of X falls and the marginal utility of Y rises. The household will go on rearranging its purchases—reducing Y consumption and increasing X consumption—until, in this example, the marginal utility of X is only twice that of Y. At this point total satisfaction cannot be further increased by rearranging purchases between the two commodities.

Now consider what the household is doing. It is faced with a set of prices that it cannot change. The household responds to these prices and maximizes its satisfaction by adjusting the things it can change—the quantities of the various goods it purchases—until Equation 2 is satisfied for all pairs of commodities.

This sort of equation—one side representing the choices the outside world gives decision makers and the other side representing the effect of those choices on their welfare—recurs in economics. It reflects the equilibrium position reached when decision makers have made the best adjustment they can to the external forces that limit their choices.

When it enters the market, every household faces the same set of market prices. When all households are fully adjusted to these prices, each will have identical ratios of its marginal utilities for each pair of goods. Of course, a rich household may consume more of each commodity than a poor household. However, the rich and the poor households (and every other household) will adjust their *relative* purchases of each commodity so that the relative marginal utilities are the same for all. Thus, if the price of X is twice the price of Y, each household will purchase X and Y to the point at which the household's marginal utility of X is twice its marginal utility of Y.

Derivation of the Household's Demand Curve

To derive the household's demand curve for a commodity, it is only necessary to ask what happens when there is a change in the price of that commodity. To do this for candy, take Equation 2 and let X stand for candy and Y for all other commodities. What will happen if, with all other prices constant, the price of candy rises? The household that started from a position of equilibrium will now find itself in a position in which[2]

$$\frac{MU \text{ of candy}}{MU \text{ of } Y} < \frac{\text{price of candy}}{\text{price of } Y} \qquad [3]$$

To restore equilibrium, it must buy less candy, thereby raising its marginal utility until once again Equation 2 (where X is candy) is satisfied.[3] The common sense of this is that the marginal utility of candy *per dollar* falls when its price rises. The household began with the utility of the last dollar spent on candy equal to the utility of the last dollar spent on all other goods, but the rise in candy prices changes

---

[2] The inequality sign (<) points to the smaller of two magnitudes. When the price of candy rises, the right side of Equation 2 increases. Until the household adjusts its consumption patterns, the left side will stay the same. Thus Equation 2 is replaced by Inequality 3.

[3] For most consumers candy absorbs only a small proportion of total expenditure. If, in response to a change in its price, expenditure on candy changes by $5 per month, this represents a large change in candy consumption, but only a negligible change in the consumption of other commodities. Hence, in the text we proceed by assuming that the marginal utilities of other commodities do not change when the price and consumption of candy change.

this. The household buys less candy (and more of other goods) until the marginal utility of candy rises enough to make the utility of a dollar spent on candy the same as it was originally.

This analysis leads to the basic prediction of demand theory.

A rise in the price of a commodity (with income and the prices of all other commodities held constant) will lead to a decrease in the quantity of the commodity demanded by each household.

If this is what each household does, it is also what all households taken together do. Thus the theory predicts a downward-sloping market demand curve.

Using Marginal Utility Theory

Consumers' Surplus

Assume that you would be willing to pay as much as $100 a month for the amount of a commodity you consume rather than do without it. Further assume that you actually buy the commodity for $60 instead of $100. What a bargain! You have paid $40 less than the top figure you were willing to pay. Yet this sort of bargain is not rare; it occurs every day in any economy where prices do the rationing. Indeed, it is so common that the $40 "saved" in this example has been given a name: *consumers' surplus*. We will define the term later; now let us look at how this surplus arises.

Consumers' surplus is a direct consequence of diminishing marginal utility. To illustrate the connection, suppose we have collected the information in Table 7-2 on the basis of an interview with Mrs. Schwartz. Our first question is: If you were getting no milk at all, how much would you be willing to pay for one glass per week? With no hesitation she replies $3.00. We then ask: If you had already consumed that one glass, how much would you pay for a second glass per week? After a bit of thought she answers $1.50. Adding one glass per week with each

TABLE 7-2   Consumers' Surplus on Milk Consumption by One Consumer

(1) Glasses of milk consumed per week	(2) Amount the consumer would pay to get this glass	(3) Consumers' surplus on each glass if milk costs $.30 per glass
First	$3.00	$2.70
Second	1.50	1.20
Third	1.00	0.70
Fourth	0.80	0.50
Fifth	0.60	0.30
Sixth	0.50	0.20
Seventh	0.40	0.10
Eighth	0.30	0.00
Ninth	0.25	—
Tenth	0.20	—

Consumers' surplus on each unit consumed is the difference between the market price and the maximum price the consumer would pay to obtain that unit. The table shows the value that one consumer, Mrs. Schwartz, puts on successive glasses of milk consumed each week. Because marginal utility declines, she would pay progressively smaller amounts for each additional unit consumed. As long as she would be willing to pay more than the market price for any unit, she obtains a consumers' surplus on it when she buys it. The marginal unit is the one valued just at the market price and on which no consumers' surplus is earned.

question, we discover that she would be willing to pay $1.00 to get a third glass per week and $.80, $.60, $.50, $.40, $.30, $.25, and $.20 for successive glasses from the fourth to the tenth glasses per week. The progressively lower valuation on each additional glass of milk illustrates the general concept of diminishing marginal utility.

But Mrs. Schwartz does not have to pay a different price for each glass of milk she consumes each week; she can buy all the milk she wants at the prevailing market price. Suppose the price is $.30. She will buy eight glasses per week (one each weekday and two on Sunday) because she values the eighth glass just at the market price, while valuing all earlier glasses at higher amounts. Because she values the first glass at $3.00 but gets it for $.30, she makes a "profit" of $2.70 on that glass. Between her $1.50 valuation of the second glass and what she has

to pay for it she clears a "profit" of $1.20. She clears $.70 on the third glass, and so on. These "profit" amounts are called her consumers' surpluses on each glass. They are shown in column 3 of the table; the total surplus is $5.70 per week.

While other consumers would put different numerical values into Table 7-2, diminishing marginal utility implies that the figures in column 2 would be declining for each consumer. Since a consumer will go on buying further units until the value he or she places on the last unit equals the market price, it follows that there will be a consumers' surplus on every unit consumed except the last one.

In general, **consumers' surplus** is the difference between the total value consumers place on all the units consumed of some commodity and the payment they must make to purchase that amount of the commodity. The total value placed by each consumer on the total consumption of some commodity can be estimated in at least two ways. The valuation that the consumer places on each successive unit may be summed, or the consumer may be asked how much he or she would pay to consume the amount in question if the alternative were to have none of the commodity.[4]

The data in columns 1 and 2 of Table 7-2 give Mrs. Schwartz's demand curve for milk. It is her demand curve because she will go on buying glasses of milk as long as she values each glass at least as much as the market price she must pay for it. When the market price is $3.00 per glass, she will buy only one glass; when it is $1.50, she will buy two glasses, and so on. The total valuation is the area below her demand curve, and consumers' surplus is that part of the area that lies above the price line. This is shown in Figure 7-3. Figure 7-4 shows that the same relation holds for the smooth market demand curve that indicates the total amount all consumers would buy at each price.

---

[4]This is only an approximation, but it is good enough for our purposes. More advanced theory shows that the calculations presented here ignore an "income effect." As a result, they slightly overestimate consumers' surplus. Although it is sometimes necessary to correct for this bias, no amount of refinement upsets the general result that we establish here: When consumers can buy all units they require at a single market price, they pay much less for the quantity consumed than they would be willing to pay if faced with the choice between that amount and nothing.

FIGURE 7-3 Consumers' Surplus for an Individual

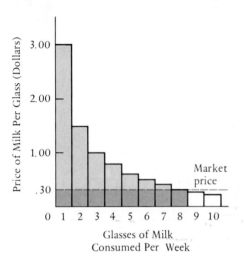

Consumers' surplus is the sum of the extra valuations placed on each unit above the market price paid for each. This figure is based on the data in Table 7-2. Mrs. Schwartz will pay the dark shaded area for the eight glasses of milk she will consume per week when the market price is $.30 a glass. The total value she places on these eight glasses is the entire shaded area. Hence her consumers' surplus is the light shaded area.

FIGURE 7-4 Consumers' Surplus for the Market

Quantity Consumed Per Period

Total consumers' surplus is the area under the demand curve and above the price line. The demand curve shows the amount consumers would pay for each unit of the commodity if they had to buy their units one at a time. The area under the demand curve shows the total valuation consumers place on all units consumed. For example, the total value that consumers place on q_0 units is the entire shaded area under the demand curve up to q_0. At a market price of p_0 the amount paid for q_0 units is the dark shaded area. Hence consumers' surplus is the light shaded area.

The Paradox of Value Revisited

We saw at the beginning of this chapter that early economists found it paradoxical that the market often valued necessary commodities such as water much lower than it valued luxuries, such as diamonds. They distinguished a commodity's *value in use* (its total utility) and its *value in exchange* (its total market value, that is, price × quantity).[5] It seemed reasonable to them that commodities with high use values should have high market values. A precise statement

of what they expected is this: For any two commodities, the ratio of their values in exchange should conform to the ratio of their values in use. In the case of water and diamonds, this led to the *incorrect* prediction that

$$\frac{p \times q \text{ of diamonds}}{p \times q \text{ of water}} = \frac{\text{total utility of diamonds}}{\text{total utility of water}} \quad [4]$$

The paradox of value was resolved when later economists showed that Equation 4 is inconsistent with the assumption that households maximize utility. The reason is that utility-maximizing behavior relates marginal utilities to prices (as shown in Equation 2), not total utilities to total values purchased (as hypothesized in Equation 4).

Thus, for example, the fact that air is free means that people will use it until its marginal utility is zero. However, its zero value in exchange does not preclude its having a high value in use (total utility). To understand the case of water and diamonds, re-

[5] The total utilities of two commodities cannot be simply related to their relative market *prices,* since the prices can be made anything we want by choosing appropriate units. For example, one barrel of diamonds is expensive relative to one barrel of water, but a one-carat diamond is cheap relative to one reservoir full of water.

member that water is cheap because there is enough of it that people consume it to the point at which its *marginal* utility is low; they are not prepared to pay a high price to obtain a little more of it. Diamonds are expensive because they are scarce (the owners of diamond mines keep diamonds scarce by limiting output), and those who buy them have to stop at a point where marginal utility is still high; they are prepared to pay a high price for an additional diamond.

Elasticity of Demand: Necessities and Luxuries

It is common to distinguish necessities and luxuries on the basis of total utilities. *Luxuries* have low total utilities, that is, they can be dispensed with altogether if circumstances require, while *necessities* have high total utilities, that is, certain minimum quantities of them are essential to life.

A frequent error arises when people try to use these commonsense notions of luxuries and necessities to predict demand elasticities. They argue that since luxuries can be given up, they have highly elastic demands; when their prices rise, households can stop purchasing them. On the other hand, necessities have almost completely inelastic demands because when prices rise, households have no choice but to continue to buy them. But elasticity of demand depends on marginal utilities, not total utilities.

Demand theory leads to the prediction that when the price of a commodity, say, eggs, rises, the household will reduce its purchase of eggs enough to increase its marginal utility to the point where the marginal utility per dollar spent on eggs is the same as for other commodities whose prices did not rise. But will the reduction in quantity required to raise the marginal utility be a little or a lot? This depends on the shape of the marginal utility curve in the range that is relevant. If the marginal utility curve is flat, a large change in quantity is required and demand will be elastic. If the curve is steep, a small change will suffice and demand will be inelastic. Figure 7-5 presents two possible responses to a doubling in price. It leads to this important conclusion:

FIGURE 7-5   The Relation of Elasticity of Demand to Utility

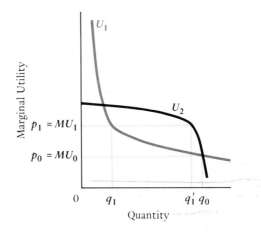

Elasticity of demand is determined by marginal utilities in the relevant range, not total utilities. Consider two different marginal utility curves for a commodity, U_1 and U_2. Suppose price is p_0. Given either utility curve the household consumes the quantity q_0, where the last unit consumed has a marginal utility of MU_0. When the price doubles to p_1, the household must cut its consumption. The marginal utility required to achieve a new equilibrium doubles to MU_1. If the black line U_2 is the household's marginal utility curve, consumption only falls to q_1' and the household will have a very inelastic demand curve for the product. If, however, the colored line U_1 is the household's marginal utility curve, consumption falls to q_1 and the household will have a very elastic demand curve. Although the shape of the marginal utility curve in the relevant range is thus important, its shape outside of this range is irrelevant. But total utility depends upon the whole area under the curve. Depending on what happens between 0 and q_1, the colored curve can show more or less total utility. Thus total utility has no influence on the household's behavior when it seeks to raise marginal utility from MU_0 to MU_1.

The size of the response of quantity demanded to a change in price (i.e., elasticity of demand) depends on the marginal utility of the commodity over the relevant range and has no necessary relation to the total utility of the good.

Free Goods, Scarce Goods, and Freely Provided Goods

A **free good** is one for which the quantity supplied exceeds the quantity demanded at a price of zero. Such goods will therefore not command positive prices in a free-market system. Since a household's total utility can always be increased by its consuming more of any good having positive marginal utility, it follows that free goods will be consumed up to the point at which their marginal utilities are zero. At some times in some places, air, water, salt, sand, and wild fruit have been free goods. Note that a good may be free at one time or place but not at another.

A **scarce good** is one for which the quantity demanded exceeds the quantity supplied at a price of zero. Such goods will therefore command positive prices in a free-market system. Most goods are scarce goods. If all such goods had zero prices, the total amount that people would want to consume would greatly exceed the amount that could be produced by all the economy's resources.

Sometimes a scarce good is *freely provided* to consumers by the government. Whatever the merits of a particular free distribution, the economic consequences are clear. Households will treat it as free to them and consume to the point of zero marginal utility. This point is illustrated in Figure 7-6. Since every unit consumed requires resources to produce, the government in this situation is using scarce resources to produce a good that has a low marginal utility. If some resources were withdrawn from the production of this commodity, total utility would fall very little. Those resources could then be used for producing other goods with a higher marginal utility, thus raising total utility.

People often have strong views about the prices charged for certain commodities. The views are often an emotional reaction to total utilities of goods rather than to their marginal utilities. We often hear an argument such as this: Water is a necessity of life to rich and poor; it is wrong to make people pay for so necessary a commodity. The government, so goes the argument, should freely provide such goods.

The relevant question when deciding between a zero price and a modest price for water is not "Is water so necessary that we do not want to deprive

FIGURE 7-6   Hypothetical Marginal Utility Curve for Water

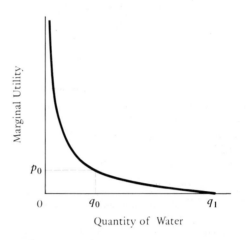

Quantity of Water

The imposition of a modest price may greatly reduce the quantity of water consumed without causing a large total sacrifice in the utility derived from water consumption. Suppose water is a scarce good, not a free good. If water is priced at p_0, consumers will consume q_0 units per month. Lowering the price to zero would increase the consumption to q_1. Much of the water that a household would consume at a zero price has a low marginal utility.

anyone of *all* of it?" but rather "Are the marginal uses of water so important that we are willing to use scarce resources to provide the necessary quantities?" Clearly, the two questions can be given different answers.

Evidence about the consumption of water at various prices suggests that the marginal utility curve for water is shaped like the curve in Figure 7-6. The difference between providing water free and charging a modest price for it may mean a great deal in the quantity of water consumed. The additional water is costly to provide, and its provision requires scarce resources that could have been used to produce other things. If the utility of the commodities forgone is higher than the utility of the extra water consumed, then people are worse off as a result of receiving water free. A charge for water would release resources from water production to produce goods that yield a higher utility. Of course, some

BOX 7-2

What Do Attitude Surveys Measure?

Consider a type of survey that is popular both in the daily newspapers and in sociology and political science. These surveys take the form of asking such questions as:

Do you like the Republicans more than the Democrats?

In deciding to live in area A rather than area B, what factors influenced your choice? List the following in order of importance: neighbors, schools, closeness to swimming area, price and quality of housing available, play areas for children, general amenities.

In choosing a university, what factors were important to you? List in order of importance: environment, academic excellence, residential facilities, parents' opinion, school opinion, athletic facilities, tuition.

You should be able to add other examples to this list. All of the above survey questions, and most of those you might add, *attempt to measure total rather than marginal utilities.* The total value being asked about includes the consumers' surplus. There is, of course, nothing illegal or immoral about this. People are free to measure anything that interests them, and in some cases knowledge of total utilities may be useful. But in many cases actual behavior is determined by marginal utilities, and anyone who attempts to predict such behavior from a knowledge of total utilities, even a correct knowledge, will be hopelessly in error.

Where the behavior being predicted involves an either-or decision, such as a vote for the Democratic or the Republican candidate, total utility attached to each choice will indeed be what matters because the voters are choosing one or the other. But where the decision is marginal, between a little more and a little less, total utility is not what will determine behavior.

A recent newspaper poll in a large midwestern city showed that two-thirds of the city's voters rated its excellent school system as one of its important assets. Yet in a subsequent election the voters turned down a school bond issue. Is this irrational behavior, as the newspaper editorials charged? Does it show a biased sample in the poll? It demonstrates neither. The poll measured the people's assessment of the total utility derived from the school system (high), while the bond issue vote depended on the people's assessment of the marginal utility of a little more money spent on the school system (low). There is nothing contradictory in anyone's feeling that the total utility of the city's fine school system is high, but that the city (or the taxpayer) has other needs that have a higher marginal utility than further money spent on school construction.

A recent survey showed—paradoxically, it claimed—that many Americans are getting more pleasure from their families just at the time that they are electing to have smaller families. There is nothing paradoxical about a shift in tastes that increases the marginal utility of the first one or two children and reduces the marginal utility of each further child. Nor is there any paradox in a parent's getting a high total utility from the total time spent with the children, but assigning a low marginal utility to the prospect of spending additional time with them each evening.

---

minimum quantity of water could be provided free to every household, but the effects of this would be quite different from the effects of making all water free.

Similar considerations apply to food, medical services, and a host of other commodities that are necessities of life, but also have numerous low utility uses which will be encouraged if the commodity is scarce but is provided very cheap or free.

Box 7-2 provides a different example of the distinction between marginal and total utility.

Used Car Prices: The Problem of "Lemons"

It is common for people to regard the huge loss of value of a new car in the first year of its life as a sign that consumers are overly style conscious and will always pay a big premium for the latest in anything. Professor George Akerlof of the University of California suggests a different explanation based upon the proposition that the utility expected from a one-year-old car purchased on the used car market will be lower than the utility of the average one-year-old car. Consider his theory.

Any particular model year of automobiles will include a certain proportion of "lemons"—cars that have one or more serious defects. Purchasers of new cars of a certain year and model take a chance on their car's turning out to be a lemon. Those who are unlucky and get a lemon are more likely to resell their car then those who are lucky and get a quality car. Hence in the used car market there will be a disproportionately large number of lemons for sale. Similarly, not all cars are driven in the same manner. Those that are driven long distances or under bad conditions are much more likely to be traded in or sold used than those that are driven on good roads and in moderate amounts.

Thus buyers of used cars are right to be on the lookout for low quality, while salespeople are quick to invent reasons for high quality ("It was owned by a little old lady who drove it only on Sundays"). Because it is difficult to identify a lemon or a badly used car before buying it, the purchaser is prepared to buy a used car only at a price low enough to offset the increased probability that it is of poor quality.

This is a rational consumer response to uncertainty and may explain why one-year-old cars typically sell for a discount much larger than can be explained by the physical depreciation that occurs in one year in the average car of that model. The large discount reflects the lower utility the purchaser can expect from a used car because of the higher probability that it will be a lemon.

Summary

1. Market demand curves reflect the aggregate of the consumption behavior of the millions of households in the economy.
2. Marginal utility theory distinguishes between the total utility gained from the consumption of all units of some commodity and the marginal utility resulting from the consumption of one more unit of the commodity.
3. The basic assumption made in utility theory is that the utility the household derives from the consumption of successive units of a commodity per period of time diminishes as the consumption of that commodity increases.
4. Households are assumed to maximize utility and thus reach equilibrium when the utility derived from the last dollar spent on each commodity is equal. Another way of putting this is that the marginal utilities derived from the last unit of each commodity consumed will be proportional to their prices.
5. Consumers' surplus arises because a household can purchase every unit of a commodity at a price equal to the value it places on the last unit purchased. Diminishing marginal utility implies that the household places a higher value on all other units purchased and hence that all but the last unit purchased yield a consumers' surplus.
6. It is vital to distinguish between total and marginal utilities because choices concerning a bit more and a bit less cannot be predicted from a knowledge of total utilities. The paradox of value involves a confusion between total and marginal utilities.

Topics for Review

Discussion Questions

1. Why is market demand the horizontal sum of individual demand curves? Is the vertical sum different? What would a vertical sum of individual demand curves show? Can you imagine any use of vertical summation of demand curves?

2. Which of the choices implied below involve a consideration of marginal utilities and which total utilities?

    a. The State Legislature debates whether 17-year-olds should be given the vote.

    b. A diet calls for precisely 1,200 calories per day.

    c. My doctor says I must give up smoking and drinking or else accept an increased chance of heart attack.

    d. When Armand Hammer decided to buy the Rembrandt painting *Juno* for a record $3.25 million, he called it the "crown jewel of my collection."

    e. I enjoyed my golf game today, but I was so tired that I decided to stop at the seventeenth hole.

3. Explain the transactions described in the following quotations in terms of the utility of the commodity. Interpret "worthless" and "priceless" as used here.

    a. "Bob Koppang has made a business of selling jars of shredded U.S. currency. The money is worthless, and yet he's sold 53,000 jars already and has orders for 40,000 more—at $5 a jar. Each jar contains about $10,000 in shredded bills."

    b. "Leonardo da Vinci's priceless painting *Genevra de' Benci* was sold to the National Gallery of Art for $5 million."

4. The *New York Times* called it the great liver crisis. Chopped liver is a delicacy on the table, particularly the kosher table, but not long ago it was a glut on the market. Prices had sunk to a 20-year low as supplies had risen to an all-time high due to a high cattle slaughter. What do the following quotations from the *Times* tell you about the marginal and total utility of liver?

    a. "Grade A-1 liver is being used for cats and dogs instead of people. It's unheard of, it's a waste," says the manager of Kosher King Meat Products. "Even Israel is drowning in chopped liver."

    b. "They're falling all over their feet to sell to me," said the president of Mrs. Weinberg's Kosher Chopped Liver Co., which uses 3,500 pounds of liver daily. "I've been offered prices so low I can't believe them."

c. "The nature of people being what they are, even though they like a good bargain, they're not going to eat something that doesn't agree with their taste."

5. "A survey shows that most people prefer butter to margarine." What exactly might this mean? Supposing it to be true, can you acccount for the facts that many people buy some of both butter and margarine each month and that in total more pounds of margarine are sold than pounds of butter?

6. Discuss the following situation in terms of marginal and total utilities. John was trying to decide between training to be a carpenter or an electrician. When the union rate for carpenters went up slightly while that for electricians stayed the same, he made up his mind in favor of carpentry.

7. Mary is willing to pay $10 for the first widget she purchases each year, $9 for the second, $8 for the third, and so on down to $1 for the tenth and nothing for the eleventh. How many widgets will she buy and what will be her consumer's surplus if widgets cost $3 each? What will happen if the price of widgets rises to $5. Can you state a generalization about the relation between consumer's surplus obtained and price of a commodity?

Household Consumption Behavior: The Indifference Curve Approach

The marginal utility approach to household behavior discussed in Chapter 7 was developed before the indifference curve approach discussed in this chapter. The concept of marginal utility is still valued because of the insights it provides. With the publication in 1939 of Sir John R. Hicks' classic *Value and Capital,* an alternative approach, often called indifference curve analysis, became popular in English-language economics.[1] This is not a competing theory, but a slightly different way of looking at choices by households. Its major innovation was to dispense with the notion of a *measurable* concept of utility that is required by marginal utility theory.

The Budget Line

Consider a household faced with the choice between only two goods, food and clothing. (Simplifying reality by considering a choice between only two goods reveals all the essential points we are interested in.) Suppose that the household has a money income of $120 a week and that the prices for food and clothing are fixed at the outset at $4 a unit for food and $2 a unit for clothing. For the purpose of our example, further suppose that the household does not save; its only choice is in deciding how much of its $120 to spend on food and how much to spend on clothing. We denote food by *F* and clothing by *C* to refer to so many units of each; for example, 20 units as 20*F* or 20*C*.

The household's possible alternatives are shown by the line *ab* in Figure 8-1, which shows the combinations of food and clothing that it can buy. It could spend all its income on clothing and obtain 60*C* and no *F* per week. It could also go to the other extreme and purchase only food, buying 30*F* and no *C*. Or it could go to an intermediate position and consume some of both goods; for example, it could spend $40 to buy 10*F* and $80 to buy 40*C*.

---

[1] Hicks was the first British recipient of the Nobel prize in economics. He received the prize for the contributions to economics that he made in *Value and Capital* and elsewhere. He did not invent indifference curve analysis; he took over, popularized, and extended the use of a concept developed by the great Italian economist Vilfredo Pareto in the first decade of this century. As is so often true in science, it is not the discoverer or the inventor, but the one who makes the timely and insightful application who has the major impact. Thus it was Hicks, not Pareto, who led to the almost universal use of indifference analysis by economists in the 1940s and 1950s.

The line *ab* is called the household's **budget line.** It indicates all the combinations of commodities available to the household if it spends a fixed amount of money, in this case all its income, at fixed prices of the commodities. (It is also sometimes called an **isocost** line since all points on it represent bundles of goods with the same total cost of purchase.)

The budget line has several important properties. (Check enough examples on Figure 8-1 to satisfy yourself that the following statements are true.)

1. Points on the budget line represent bundles of commodities that exactly use up the household's income. (Try the point 20*C* and 20*F.*)
2. Points between the budget line and the origin represent bundles of commodities that use up less than the household's income. (Try the point 20*C* and 10*F.*)
3. Points above the budget line represent combinations of commodities costing more to purchase than the household's present income. (Try the point 30*C* and 40*F.*)

The budget line shows all combinations of commodities that are available to the household given its money income and the prices of the goods that it purchases, if it spends all its income on them.

Shifts in the Budget Line

Change in Money Income

What happens to the budget line when money income changes? If the household's money income is halved from $120 to $60 per week, prices being unchanged, then the amount of goods it can buy will also be halved. If it spends all its income on clothing, it will now get 30*C* and no *F* (point *c* in Figure 8-1; if it spends all its income on food, it will get 15*F* and no *C* (point *d*). All possible combinations now open to the household appear on budget line *cd,* which is closer to the origin than the original budget line.

If the household's income rises to $180, it will be able to buy more of both commodities than it could previously. The budget line shifts outward. If the household buys only clothing, it can have 90*C*; if it

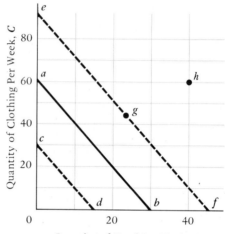

FIGURE 8-1   Budget Lines

Quantity of Food Per Week, *F*

The budget line shows the quantities of goods available to a household given its money income and the prices of the goods it buys. Any point indicates a combination (or *bundle*) of so much food and so much clothing. Point *h*, for example, indicates 60 units of clothing and 40 units of food per week. With an income of $120 a week and prices of $4 per unit for food and $2 per unit for clothing, the household's budget line is *ab.* This line shows all the combinations of *F* and *C* available to a household spending that income at those prices. Neither combination *g* nor *h* is attainable.

An increase in money income from $120 to $180, with money prices of *F* and *C* constant, shifts the budget line outward to the parallel line *ef.* At this level of income, combination *g* is attainable. A decrease in money income to $60 shifts the budget line to *cd.*

buys only food, it can have 45*F*; if it divides its income equally between the two goods, it can have 45*C* and 22.5*F.*

Variations in the household's money income, with prices constant, shift the budget line parallel to itself.

Proportional Change in All Prices

Changing both prices in the same proportion shifts the budget line parallel to itself in the same way that a money income change shifts it. Doubling both prices with money income constant halves the amount of goods that can be purchased. It thus has exactly the same effect on the household's budget line as halving money income with money prices constant. In both cases the household's original budget line is shifted inward. Similarly, a proportional reduction of both prices causes the budget line to shift outward in exactly the same manner that an increase in money income does.

Proportional changes in the prices of all goods, with money income constant, shift the budget line parallel to itself.

It is now apparent that it is possible to have exactly offsetting changes in prices and money incomes. Such a situation leaves the real choices available to the household unchanged.

A change in money income and a *proportional* change of the same amount in all money prices leaves the position of the budget line unchanged.

Changes in Relative Prices

The price of a commodity usually refers to the amount of money that must be spent to acquire one unit of the commodity. This is called the **absolute price** or *money price*. A *relative price* is the ratio of two absolute prices. The statement "the price of F is $4" refers to an absolute price; the statement "the price of F is twice the price of C" refers to a relative price.

A change in a relative price can be accomplished by changing both of the absolute prices in different proportions or by holding one price constant and changing the other. It is useful for our purposes to do the latter. The effects of such a change are shown in Figure 8-2. The basic conclusion that emerges is:

A change in relative prices alters the slope of the budget line.

The economic significance of the slope of the budget line for food and clothing (which we have

FIGURE 8-2   The Effect on the Budget Line of Changes in the Price of Food

A change in the price of one commodity changes relative prices and thus changes the slope of the budget line. The original budget line *ab* arose from a money income of $120, with C priced at $2 per unit and F at $4 per unit. A fall in the price of F to $2 per unit doubles the quantity of F obtainable for any given quantity of C purchased and pivots the budget line outward to *aj*. A rise in the price of F to $8 per unit reduces the quantity of F obtainable and pivots the budget line inward to *ak*.

just seen to be related to the relative prices of the two commodities) is that it reflects the opportunity cost of food in terms of clothing. To increase food consumption with expenditure constant, one must move along the budget line, consuming less clothing. Suppose the price of food (p_F) is $4 and the price of clothing (p_C) is $2. With income fixed, it is necessary to forgo the purchase of two units of clothing to acquire one unit extra of food. The opportunity cost of food in terms of clothing is thus two units of clothing. But it can also be stated as p_F/p_C, which is the relative price.

Notice that the relative price (in our example, $p_F = 2p_C$) is consistent with an infinite number of absolute prices. If $p_F = \$40$ and $p_C = \$20$, it still takes the sacrifice of two units of clothing to acquire one unit of food. This shows that it is relative, not absolute, prices that determine opportunity cost. The general conclusion is that the opportunity cost of F in terms of C is measured by the slope of the budget line or (the equivalent) by the relative price ratio. [11]

Real and Money Income

A household's **money income** is its income measured in money units, so many dollars and cents per week or per year. A household's **real income** is the purchasing power of its money income, that is, the quantity of goods and services that can be purchased with its money income.

If money prices remain constant, any change in money income will cause a corresponding change in real income. If the household's money income rises by 10 percent (say, from $10,000 to $11,000), the household is able to buy 10 percent more of all commodities—its real income has also risen by 10 percent.

If prices change, however, real and money incomes will not change in the same proportion—indeed, they can easily change in opposite directions. Consider a situation in which all money prices rise by 10 percent. If money income rises by any amount less than 10 percent, real income falls. If money income also rises by 10 percent, real income will be unchanged. Only if money income rises by more than 10 percent will real income also rise.

Changes in real income are shown graphically by shifts in the budget line. When the budget line in Figure 8-1 shifts away from the origin, real income rises. When the line shifts toward the origin, real income falls. The household's ability to purchase goods and services is measured by real income, not by money income.

Indifference Curve Analysis

What the household does is determined by both what it can do and what it wants to do. What it *can do* is determined by its budget line; what it *wants to do* is determined by its tastes, which as we shall see can be expressed by its indifference curves.

An Indifference Curve

We start by taking an imaginary household and giving it a bundle of goods, say 18 units of clothing and 10 units of food. Now offer the household an alternative bundle, say, 13 units of clothing and 15 units of food. This alternative combination of goods has 5 fewer units of clothing and 5 more units of food than the first one. Whether the household prefers this bundle depends on the relative valuation that it places on 5 more units of food and 5 fewer units of clothing. If it values the extra food more than the forgone clothing, it will prefer the new bundle to the original one. If it values the food less than the clothing, it will prefer the original bundle. If the household values the extra food the same as it values the forgone clothing, it is said to be *indifferent between* the two bundles.

Assume that after much trial and error we have identified several bundles among which the household is indifferent. In other words, each bundle gives the household equal satisfaction. They are shown in Table 8-1.

There will, of course, be combinations of the two commodities other than those enumerated in the table that will give the same level of satisfaction to the household. All these combinations are shown in Figure 8-3 by the smooth curve that passes through the points plotted from the table. This curve is an indifference curve. In general, an **indifference curve** shows all combinations of goods that yield the same

TABLE 8-1   Alternative Bundles Giving a Household Equal Satisfaction

Bundle	Clothing	Food
a	30	5
b	18	10
c	13	15
d	10	20
e	8	25
f	7	30

These bundles all lie on a single indifference curve. Since all of these bundles of food and clothing give equal satisfaction, the household is "indifferent" among them.

FIGURE 8-3   An Indifference Curve

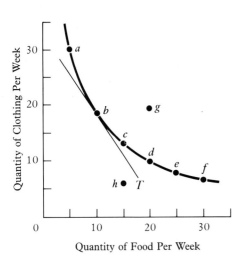

This indifference curve shows combinations of food and clothing that yield equal satisfaction and among which the household is indifferent. Points *a* to *f* are plotted from Table 8-1. The smooth curve through them is an indifference curve; each combination on it gives equal satisfaction to the household. Point *g* above the line is a preferred combination to any point on the line; point *h* below the line is an inferior combination to any point on the line. The slope of the line *T* gives the marginal rate of substitution at point *b*. Moving down the curve from *b* to *f*, the slope flattens, showing that the more food and the less clothing the household has, the less willing it will be to sacrifice further clothing to get more food.

satisfaction to the household. A household is indifferent between the combinations indicated by any two points on one indifference curve.

Any points above the curve show combinations of food and clothing that the household would prefer to combinations indicated by points on the curve. Consider, for example, the combination of 20 food and 18 clothing, represented by point *g* in the figure. Although it may not be obvious that this bundle must be preferred to bundle *a* (which has more clothing but less food), it is obvious that it will be preferred to bundle *c* because there is both less clothing and less food represented at *c* than at *g*. Inspection of

the graph shows that *any* point above the curve will be obviously superior to *some* points on the curve in the sense that it will contain both more food and more clothing than those points on the curve. But since all points on the curve are equal in the household's eyes, the point above the curve must be superior to *all* points on the curve. By a similar argument, points below and to the left of the curve represent bundles that are inferior to bundles represented by points on the curve.

The Hypothesis of Diminishing Marginal Rate of Substitution

How much clothing would the household be prepared to give up to get one more unit of food? The answer to this question measures what is called the marginal rate of substitution of clothing for food. The **marginal rate of substitution (MRS)** is the amount of one commodity a consumer would be prepared to give up to get one more unit of another commodity.

The first basic assumption of indifference theory is that the algebraic value of the *MRS* is always negative.

This means that to gain a positive change in its consumption of one commodity, the household is prepared to incur a negative change in its consumption of a second. The negative marginal rate of substitution is indicated in graphical representations by the downward slope of all indifference curves. (See, for example, the curve in Figure 8-3.)

The second basic assumption of indifference theory is that the marginal rate of substitution between any two commodities depends on the amounts of the commodities currently being consumed by the household.

Consider a case in which the household has a lot of clothing and only a little food. Common sense suggests that the household might be willing to give up quite a bit of its plentiful clothing to get one unit more of scarce food. It suggests, as well, that the household with a little clothing and a lot of food would be willing to give up only a little of its scarce clothing to get one more unit of already plentiful food.

This example illustrates the hypothesis of diminishing marginal rate of substitution. The less of one commodity, *A*, and the more of a second commodity, *B*, the household has already, the smaller will be the amount of *A* it will be willing to give up to get one further unit of *B*. The hypothesis says that the marginal rate of substitution changes systematically as the amounts of two commodities presently consumed vary. The graphical expression of this is that the slope of any indifference curve becomes flatter as the household moves downward to the right along the curve. In Figure 8-3 a movement downward to the right means that less clothing and more food is being consumed. The decreasing steepness of the curve means that less and less clothing need be sacrificed to get one further unit of food. **[12]**

The hypothesis is illustrated in Table 8-2, which is based on the example of food and clothing in Table 8-1. The last column of the table shows the rate at which the household is prepared to sacrifice units of clothing per unit of food obtained. At first the house-

hold will sacrifice 2.4 units of clothing to get 1 unit more of food, but as its consumption of clothing diminishes and that of food increases, the household becomes less and less willing to sacrifice further clothing for more food.[2]

The Indifference Map

So far we have constructed only a single indifference curve. However, starting at any other point in Figure 8-3, such as *g,* there will be other combinations that will yield equal satisfaction to the household. If the points indicating all of these combinations are connected, they will form another indifference curve. This exercise can be repeated as many times as we wish, and as many indifference curves as we wish can be generated. The farther any indifference curve is from the origin, the higher will be the level of satisfaction given by any of the combinations of goods indicated by points on the curve.

A set of indifference curves is called an **indifference map,** an example of which is shown in Figure 8-4. It specifies the household's tastes by showing its rate of substitution between the two commodities for every level of current consumption of these commodities. When economists say that a household's tastes are *given,* they do not mean that the household's current consumption pattern is given; rather, they mean that the household's entire indifference map is given.

The Equilibrium of the Household

Indifference maps describe the preferences of households. Budget lines describe the possibilities open to the household. To predict what households will actually do, both sets of information must be put together. This is done in Figure 8-5. The household's

---

TABLE 8-2   The Marginal Rate of Substitution Between Clothing and Food

Movement	(1) Change in clothing	(2) Change in food	(3) Marginal rate of substitution (1) ÷ (2)
From *a* to *b*	−12	5	−2.4
From *b* to *c*	− 5	5	−1.0
From *c* to *d*	− 3	5	−0.6
From *d* to *e*	− 2	5	−0.4
From *e* to *f*	− 1	5	−0.2

The marginal rate of substitution of clothing for food declines as the quantity of food increases. This table is based on Table 8-1. When the household moves from *a* to *b,* it gives up 12 units of clothing and gains 5 units of food; it remains at the same level of overall satisfaction. The household at point *a* was prepared to sacrifice 12 clothing for 5 food (i.e., 12/5 = 2.4 units of clothing per unit of food obtained). When the household moves from *b* to *c,* it sacrifices 5 clothing units for 5 food units (a rate of substitution of 1 unit of clothing for each unit of food).

---

[2] Movements between widely separated points on the indifference curve have been examined. In terms of a small movement from any of the points on the curve, the rate at which the household will give up clothing to get food is shown by the slope of the tangent to the curve at that point. The slope of the line *T,* which is a tangent to the curve at point *b* in Figure 8-3, may thus be thought of as the slope of the curve at that precise point. It tells us the rate at which the household will sacrifice clothing per unit of food obtained when it is currently consuming 18 clothing and 10 food (the coordinates of point *b*).

FIGURE 8-4   An Indifference Map

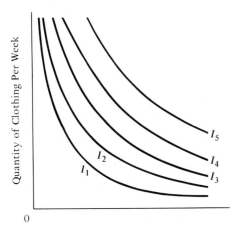

Quantity of Food Per Week

An indifference map consists of a set of indifference curves. All points on a particular curve indicate alternative combinations of food and clothing that give the household equal satisfaction. The further the curve from the origin, the higher the level of satisfaction it represents. For example, I_5 is a higher indifference curve than I_4, which means that all the points on I_5 yield a higher level of satisfaction than do the points on I_4.

FIGURE 8-5   The Equilibrium of a Household

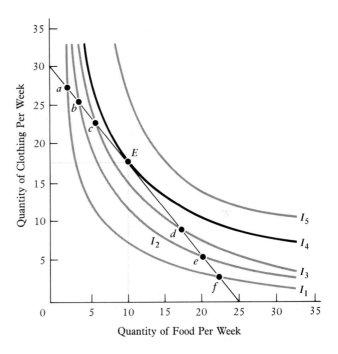

Quantity of Food Per Week

Equilibrium occurs at E, where an indifference curve is tangent to the budget line. The household has an income of $750 a week and faces prices of $25 a unit for clothing and $30 a unit for food. A combination of units of clothing and food indicated by point a is attainable, but by moving along the budget line, higher indifference curves can be reached. The same is true at b and c. At E, however, where an indifference curve is tangent to the budget line, it is impossible to reach a higher curve by moving along the budget line. If the household did alter its consumption bundle by moving from E to d, for example, it would move to the lower indifference curve I_3 and thus to a lower level of satisfaction.

budget line is shown by the straight line in the figure, and the curves from the indifference map are also shown. Any point on the budget line is attainable. But which point will actually be chosen by the household?

Since the household wishes to maximize its satisfactions, it wishes to reach its highest attainable indifference curve. Inspection of the figure shows that if the household purchases any bundle on its budget line at a point cut by an indifference curve, a higher indifference curve can be reached. Only when the bundle purchased is such that the indifference curve is tangent to the budget line is it impossible for the household to alter its purchases and reach a higher curve.

The household's satisfaction is maximized at the point where an indifference curve is tangent to the budget line.

At such a tangency position the slope of the indifference curve (the household's marginal rate of substitution of the goods) is the same as the slope of the budget line (the relative prices of the goods in the market).

The common sense of this result is that if the household values goods differently than the market does, there is room for profitable exchange. The household can give up some of the good it values relatively less than the market and take in return some of the good it values relatively higher than the market does. When the household is prepared to swap goods at the same rate as they can be traded on the market, there is no further opportunity for it to raise its satisfaction by substituting one commodity for the other.

The household is presented with market prices that it cannot change. It adjusts to these prices by choosing a bundle of goods such that, at the margin, its own subjective evaluation of the goods conforms with the valuations given by market prices.

The Household's Reaction to a Change in Income

We have seen that a change in income leads to parallel shifts of the budget line—toward the origin when income falls and away from the origin when income rises. For each level of income there will be an equilibrium position at which an indifference curve is tangent to the relevant budget line. Each such equilibrium position means that the household is doing as well as it possibly can for that level of income. If

---

FIGURE 8-6   The Income-Consumption Line

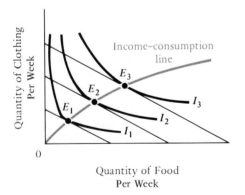

The income-consumption line shows how the household's purchases react to a change in income with relative prices held constant. Increases in income shift the budget line out parallel to itself, moving the equilibrium from E_1 to E_2 to E_3. By joining up all the points of equilibrium, an income-consumption line is traced out.

---

we move the budget line through all possible levels of income, and if we join up all the points of equilibrium, we will trace out what is called an **income-consumption line,** an example of which is shown in Figure 8-6. This line shows how consumption bundles change as income changes, with relative prices held constant.

The Household's Reaction to a Change in Price

We already know that a change in the relative price of the two goods changes the slope of the budget line. Given a price of clothing, for each possible price of food there is an equilibrium consumption position for the household. Connecting these positions traces out a **price-consumption line,** as is shown in Figure 8-7. Notice that as the relative price of food and clothing changes, the relative quantities of food and clothing purchased also change. In particular, as the price of food falls, the household buys more food.[3]

Derivation of the Demand Curve

If food and clothing were the only two commodities purchased by households, we could derive a demand curve for food from the price-consumption line of Figure 8-7. On an indifference map, that line represents how the quantity of food demanded varies as the price of food changes, with the price of clothing unchanged. To use indifference theory to derive the kind of demand curve introduced in Chapter 4, however, it is necessary to depart from the world of two commodities that we have used so far in this chapter.

What happens to the household's demand for some commodity, say, carrots, as the price of that commodity changes, *all other prices being held constant?* In Figure 8-8 a new type of indifference map is plotted in which the quantity of carrots is represented on the horizontal axis and the value of all other goods consumed is represented on the vertical axis. We have in effect used "everything but carrots" as the second commodity. The indifference curves give the rate at

---

[3] There is a rarely encountered, but theoretically possible exception to this rule, a Giffen good, which is described in the last part of this chapter.

FIGURE 8-7   The Price-Consumption Line

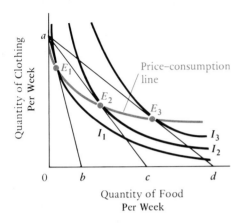

The price-consumption line shows how the household's purchases react to a change in one price, with money income and other prices held constant. Decreases in the price of food (with money income and the price of clothing constant) pivot the budget line from ab to ac to ad. The equilibrium position moves from E_1 to E_2 to E_3. By joining up all the points of equilibrium, a price-consumption line is traced out.

FIGURE 8-8   Derivation of a Demand Curve

Every point on the price-consumption line corresponds to both a price of the commodity and a quantity of the commodity demanded; this is the information required for a demand curve. The household has $\$a$ of income; if it buys no carrots, it can consume $\$a$ worth of all other goods. For each price of carrots there is a single budget line. As the price of carrots falls, the budget line pivots from ab to ac to ad, and the quantity of carrots demanded rises from q_0 to q_1 to q_2. This leads to a downward-sloping demand curve for carrots.

which the household is prepared to swap carrots for money (which allows it to buy all other goods) at each level of consumption of carrots and of other goods.

Given the money price of carrots and the household's income, a budget line can be obtained showing all those combinations of carrots and other goods that the household can consume for its given level of money income and the given price of carrots. Now assume a change in the money price of carrots. By joining the points of equilibrium, we can trace a price-consumption line between carrots and all other commodities in the same way that such a line was traced for food and clothing in Figure 8-7.

Figure 8-8 is similar to Figure 8-7, but notice two differences. First, the axes are labeled differently. Second, the price-consumption line in Figure 8-8 is crowded into the upper part of the diagram, indicating that whatever the price of carrots, the household does not spend a large part of its income on them. Every point on the price-consumption line corre-

sponds to one price and one quantity of carrots demanded. In the figure the quantity of carrots consumed increases as their price falls. These pairs of price-quantity values can be transferred to a new figure, whose axes represent price of carrots and quantity of carrots, and used to plot a downward-sloping demand curve.

The Slope of the Demand Curve[4]

The price-consumption line in Figure 8-8 indicates that as price decreases, quantity of carrots demanded increases. But, as a little experimentation will show you, one can draw indifference curves in such a way

[4] The remainder of this chapter may be omitted without loss of continuity.

that in response to a decrease in price, the quantity demanded remains unchanged, that is, the demand is perfectly inelastic. It is even possible that in response to a decrease in price, less is consumed rather than more. This possibility, which means that a commodity might have an upward-sloping demand curve, has been discussed at length in demand theory. A good with such a demand curve is called a **Giffen good,** after the Victorian economist who is thought to have observed such a case. The conditions that would bring this situation about are not often found in the real world, but we can deepen our understanding of the economic theory of demand by seeing what they are.

Income and Substitution Effects

A fall in the price of a commodity can lead a household to increase purchases of it for two reasons. First, because the commodity's relative price has fallen, people will tend to substitute it for other, more expensive goods, even if the household's total purchasing power remains unchanged. This is called the **substitution effect.** Second, a fall in the price of one commodity with all other prices constant has the effect of a rise in income by making it possible for the household to have more of all goods. This second incentive to increase quantity consumed is called the **income effect** of a price change.

We illustrate these two effects graphically in Figure 8-9, which shows in greater detail part of the price-consumption line shown in Figure 8-8. Points E_0 and E_2 are on the price-consumption line for carrots. The increase in quantity of carrots demanded is the result of both a substitution and an income effect. Figure 8-9 separates the two effects. We can think of this separation as occurring in the following way. The substitution effect is defined by sliding the budget line around a fixed indifference curve until it is tangent at the slope that represents the lower price. This leads to a move from point E_0 to an imaginary equilibrium point such as E_1. The income effect is then defined by a parallel shift of the budget line that is required to move from E_1 to the actual new equilibrium point, E_2. The move from E_1 to E_2 is as if the household's income is increased with no change in price from an initial position of E_1.

In Figure 8-9 income and substitution effects are in the same direction, both tending to increase quantity demanded when price falls. Is this necessarily the case? The answer is no. While it follows from the convex shape of indifference curves that the substitution effect is always in the same direction, income effects can be in either direction. The direction depends on the distinction we drew earlier between normal and inferior goods.

Demand Curves for Inferior Goods

For a normal good an increase in real income due to a decrease in the price of the commodity leads to its increased consumption, reinforcing the substitution effect. Because quantity demanded increases, the demand curve slopes downward.

Figure 8-10, page 154, shows indifference curves for two inferior goods. The income effect is negative in both parts of the diagram. This follows from the nature of an inferior good: as income rises, less of the good is consumed. In both cases the substitution effect serves to increase the quantity demanded as price decreases and is offset to some degree by the negative income effect. The final result depends upon the relative strengths of the two effects. In 8-10(i) the negative income effect only partially offsets the substitution effect and thus quantity demanded increases as a result of the price decrease, though not as much as for a normal good. This is the typical pattern for inferior goods, and it, too, leads to downward-sloping demand curves, often relatively inelastic ones.

In 8-10(ii) the negative income effect actually outweighs the substitution effect and thus leads to an upward-sloping demand curve. This is the Giffen case. For this to happen the good must be inferior, but that is not enough; the change in price must have a negative income effect *strong enough* to offset the substitution effect. A combination of circumstances that makes this possible is not often expected, and therefore an upward-sloping market demand curve is at most an infrequent exception to the rule that demand curves slope downward.

The Shape of Market Demand Curves

The **law of demand** asserts that the price of a product and the quantity demanded in the market vary inversely with each other. Criticisms of the law have

FIGURE 8-9   The Income Effect and the Substitution Effect in Indifference Theory

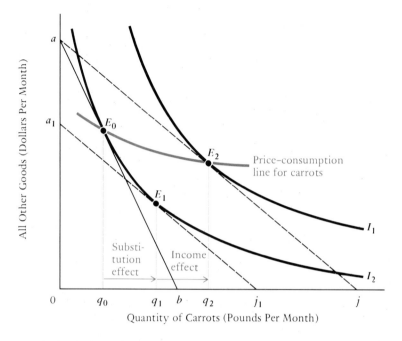

The substitution effect is defined by sliding the budget line around a fixed indifference curve; the income effect is defined by a parallel shift of the budget line. The original budget lines is at ab and a fall in the price of carrots takes it to aj. The original equilibrium is at E_0 with q_0 of carrots consumed, and the final equilibrium is at E_2 with q_2 of carrots consumed. To remove the income effect, imagine reducing the household's income until it is just able to attain its original indifference curve. We do this by shifting the line aj to a parallel line nearer the origin until it just touches the indifference curve that passes through E_0. The intermediate point E_1 divides the quantity change into a substitution effect q_0q_1 and an income effect q_1q_2. It can also be obtained by sliding the original budget line ab around the indifference curve until its slope reflects the new relative prices.

taken various forms, focusing on the Giffen good, the conspicuous consumption good, and the good whose demand is perfectly inelastic. Let us consider each of these in turn.

Giffen Goods

Great interest was attached to Giffen's apparent refutation of the law of demand. He is supposed to have observed that during the nineteenth century a rise in

the price of imported wheat led to an increase in the price of bread, but the consumption of bread by the British working class increased.

While there is some doubt that what Giffen asserted really occurred, Figure 8-10 shows that such an observation would be consistent with our theory. Suppose that bread is the diet staple of a great many people and that its price rises sharply. This may be expected to compel larger expenditures on bread, further impoverishing many households to the point

FIGURE 8-10   Income and Substitution Effects for Inferior Goods

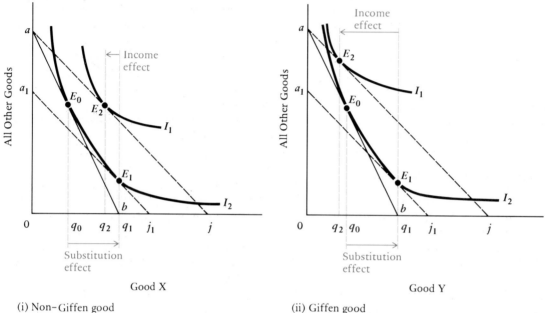

(i) Non–Giffen good   (ii) Giffen good

Inferior goods have negative income effects. A large enough negative income effect can out-weigh the substitution effect and lead to a decrease in consumption in response to a fall in price. In each part of the diagram the household is in equilibrium at E_0, consuming a quantity q_0 of the good in question. The price then decreases and the budget line shifts to aj, with a new equilibrium at E_2 and quantity consumed q_2. In each case the substitution effect is to increase consumption from q_0 to q_1. In (i) there is a negative income effect of q_1q_2. Because this is less than the substitution effect, the latter dominates so that good X has a normal, downward-sloping demand curve. In (ii) the negative income effect q_1q_2 is larger than the substitution effect, and quantity consumed actually decreases. Good Y is thus a Giffen good.

where they are forced to substitute bread (even though it is more expensive than it had been) for more luxurious forms of nourishment. While possible, the fact is that such cases are all but unknown in the real world.

Conspicuous Consumption Goods

Thorstein Veblen in *The Theory of the Leisure Class* (1899) noted that some commodities were consumed not for their intrinsic qualities but because they carried a snob appeal. He suggested that the more ex-

pensive such a commodity became, the *greater* might be its ability to confer status on its purchaser.

Consumers might buy diamonds, for example, not because they particularly like diamonds per se but because they wish to show off their wealth in an ostentatious but socially acceptable way. They are assumed to value diamonds precisely because they are expensive; thus a fall in price might lead them to stop buying diamonds and to switch to a more satisfactory object of conspicuous consumption. They may behave in the same way with respect to luxury cars: they may buy them *because* they are expensive.

People of this sort will have upward-sloping *individual* demand curves for diamonds and cars. However, no one has ever observed an upward-sloping *market* demand curve for such commodities. The reason for this is easy to discover. Consideration of the countless lower-income consumers who would be glad to buy diamonds or Cadillacs if only they were sufficiently inexpensive suggests that upward-sloping demand curves for a few individual wealthy households are much more likely than is an upward-sloping market demand curve for the same commodity.

Perfectly Inelastic Demand Curves

Even if demand curves do not slope upward to the right as the previous cases have suggested, the substantial insight provided by the law of demand would be diminished if there were many important commodities for which changes in price had virtually no effect on quantity demanded.

It is surprising how often the assumption of a vertical demand curve is implicit. A common response of urban bus or subway systems to financial difficulties is to propose a percentage fare increase equal to the percentage their deficit is of their revenues. Even professors are not immune. At a meeting of the American Association of University Professors, a motion was introduced "to raise annual dues by 20 percent, in order to raise revenues by 20 percent"—in spite of the empirical evidence that a previous increase in dues had led (as the theory would predict) to a significant drop in membership.

It was once widely argued that the demand for gasoline was virtually perfectly inelastic on the ground that people who had paid thousands of dollars for cars would never balk at a few pennies extra for gas. The events of recent years have proven how wrong that argument was: Higher gas prices in the 1970s led to smaller cars, to more car pools, to more economical driving speeds, and to less pleasure driving. Falling gas prices in the mid-1980s led to a reversal of these trends.

As we have seen, a mass of accumulated evidence suggests that most demand curves do in fact slope downward to an appreciable degree.

For practical purposes, the hypothesis of the downward-sloping demand curve can be regarded as being supported by the evidence.

Summary

1. The basic constructs of indifference curve analysis are the budget line and the indifference map.
2. The budget line shows all combinations of commodities that are available to the household given its money income and the prices of the goods it purchases.
3. Variations in the household's money income shift the budget line parallel to itself. Changes in relative prices change the slope of the budget line.
4. While the budget line describes what the household *can* purchase, indifference curves describe the household's tastes and, therefore, refer to what it *would like* to purchase. A single indifference curve joins combinations of commodities that give the household equal satisfaction and among which it is therefore indifferent. An indifference map is a set of indifference curves.
5. The basic hypothesis about tastes is that of a diminishing marginal rate of substitution. This hypothesis states that the less of one good and the more of another the household has, the less willing it will be to give up some of the first good to get a further unit of the

second. This means indifference curves are downward-sloping and convex to the origin.

6. The household achieves an equilibrium that maximizes its satisfactions given its budget line at the point at which an indifference curve is tangent to its budget line.

7. The income-consumption line shows how quantity consumed changes as income changes with relative prices constant.

8. The price-consumption line shows how quantity consumed changes as relative prices change. When prices change, the household will consume more of the commodity whose relative price falls. The price-consumption line relating the purchases of one particular commodity and all other commodities contains the same information as an ordinary demand curve. The horizontal axis measures quantity, and the slope of budget line measures price. Transferring this price-quantity information to a diagram whose axes represent price and quantity leads to a conventional demand curve.

9. The effect of a change in price of one commodity, all other prices and money income constant, changes not only relative prices, but also real incomes. A price decrease can affect consumption both through the substitution effect and the income effect.

10. Demand curves for normal goods slope downward because both income and substitution effects work in the same direction, a decrease in price leading to increased consumption.

11. For an inferior good a decrease in price leads to more consumption via the substitution effect and less consumption via the income effect. In the extreme case of a Giffen good the negative income effect more than offsets the substitution effect, and the consumption of the commodity decreases as a result of a price decrease. This is a theoretical possibility that has seldom if ever been observed in fact.

12. The so-called law of demand leads to the prediction that the market demand curve for a commodity will slope downward and to the right except in very special circumstances. A great deal of empirical evidence supports the law of demand.

Topics for Review

Budget line
Real income and money income
Indifference curve and indifference map
Marginal rate of substitution
Tangency of the budget line and an indifference curve
Price-consumption line and income-consumption line
Income effect and substitution effect
Inferior good and Giffen good
The law of demand

Discussion Questions

1. Is a household relatively better off if its money income is decreased by 10 percent or if the prices of all the goods it buys are increased by 10 percent? Does it matter in answering this question whether the household spends all its income?

2. Some people do not care about the difference between two similar products. To see what effect this would have on their behavior, draw a typical indifference curve of a man who values white and whole wheat bread identically. Show his consumption equilibrium position when the price of white bread is held constant at $1.00 a loaf, while that of whole wheat changes from $.80 to $1.00 to $1.20. How does this behavior differ from that of a household that likes both kinds of bread, but has a diminishing marginal rate of substitution between white and whole wheat bread?

3. Between 1980 and 1985 the after-tax money incomes of American households rose by about 45 percent, while the average level of all prices rose by about 30 percent. What happened to real incomes?

4. When no-frills houses came on the market, they were regarded as a response to high prices. But they have captured more of the market than expected. Some builders estimate they may ultimately constitute 80 percent of all houses sold. Suggest alternative explanations of this unexpected success. A leading builder says, "It's just like people driving smaller cars and drinking beer instead of Scotch."

5. A reliable newspaper reports that synthetic motor oil is gaining in sales despite its high price relative to natural oil. What can account for a synthetic oil's selling at $4.95 a quart when the best conventional oils are readily available at about $1.50?

6. Answer question 5 on page 142 (in Chapter 7), using indifference curve analysis.

7. "Indifference curves can never intersect." Can you show that this is so by drawing two intersecting indifference curves and seeing that they would require that the household's tastes be self-contradictory?

9

The Role of the Firm

Ask almost anyone you know to name 10 American business firms. The odds are overwhelming that the list will include some of these firms: General Motors, U.S. Steel, General Electric, American Telephone & Telegraph, Standard Oil, Bank of America, United Airlines, Prudential Insurance, and the National Broadcasting Company. Drive around Ypsilanti, Michigan, and note at random 10 firms that come into view. They will likely include an A & P supermarket, Richardson's Pharmacy, a Shell service station, Schaeffer's Hardware Store, Haabs, and the First National Bank of Ypsilanti. Drive through Iowa or Nebraska and look around you: Every farm is a business firm as well as a home.

Firms develop and survive because they are efficient institutions for organizing resources to produce goods and services and for organizing their sale and distribution. It is not hard to count ways in which General Motors, Haabs, and the Iowa farm are different. But insight can be gained in treating them all under a single heading; that is, seeing what they have in common. This is what economic theory does. Economists usually assume that the firm's behavior can be understood in terms of a common motivation. Whether the firm is Ma and Pa's Bar and Grill or the Ford Motor Company and whether a particular decision is made by the board of directors, the third vice-president in charge of advertising, or the owner-manager is regarded as irrelevant to predicting what decisions are made. Criticisms that economic theory neglects differences among firms will be considered in Chapter 17.

Before studying how the firm is treated in economic theory, we shall examine more closely the firm in America today.

The Organization of Production

Forms of Business Organization

There are three major forms of business organization: the single proprietorship, the partnership, and the corporation. In the **single proprietorship,** a single owner makes all decisions and is personally responsible for everything done by the business. In the **partnership,** there are two or more joint owners. Either may make binding decisions, and each partner is personally responsible for everything done by the business. In the **corporation,** the firm has a legal entity of its own. The owners (the stockholders) are not each personally responsible for everything that is done by the business. Owners elect a board of directors who hire managers to run the firm under the board's supervision.

In the United States today there are about 7 million single proprietorships (not counting farms), 1 million partnerships, and nearly 2 million corporations.

Corporations account for more than two-thirds of the nation's privately produced income.

In manufacturing, transportation, public utilities, and finance, corporations do almost all of the nation's business. In trade and construction they do about half the total business. Only in agriculture and in services (such as hair styling, medicine, and accounting) is the corporation relatively unimportant, yet even here its share of the business is steadily rising.

The Proprietorship and the Partnership

The major advantage of the single proprietorship is that the owner can maintain full control over the firm. The owner is the Boss. The disadvantages are, first, that the size of the firm is limited by the capital the owner can personally raise and, second, that the owner is personally responsible in law for all debts of the firm.

The ordinary (or general) partnership overcomes to some extent the first disadvantage of the proprietorship but not the second. Ten partners may be able to finance a much bigger enterprise than could one owner, but they are still subject to unlimited liability. Each partner is fully liable for all the debts of the firm.

Because of this unlimited liability, people with substantial personal assets will be unwilling to enter a partnership unless they have complete trust in the other partners and a full knowledge of all the obligations of the firm. Also, it is difficult to raise money from persons who wish to invest, but not be active in the business. Investors may be willing to put up $1,000, but unwilling to jeopardize their entire fortune; if, however, they join a partnership in order to do the former, they may also do the latter.

The **limited partnership** is designed to avoid some of these difficulties. General partners in a firm continue to have unlimited liability, but there are also limited partners. The limited partner's liability is restricted to the amount he or she has invested in the firm. Such partners do not participate in the man-agement of the firm or engage in agreements on behalf of the partnership. In effect, the limited partnership permits some division of the functions of decision making, provision of capital, and risk taking.

In most respects this division of responsibility is more effectively achieved through the corporation. But there are certain professions in which general partnership is traditional. These include law, medicine, and (until recently) brokerage. Partnerships survive in these fields partly because they all depend heavily on a relationship of trust with their clients, and the partners' unlimited liability for one another's actions is thought to enhance public confidence in the firm.

The Corporation

The corporation is regarded in law as an entity separate from the individuals who own it. It can enter into contracts, it can sue and be sued, it can own property, it can contract debts, and it can generally incur obligations that are the legal obligations of the corporation, *but not of its owners.* The right of the corporation to be sued may not seem to be an advantage, but it is, because it makes it possible for others to enter into enforceable contracts with the corporation.

Although some corporations are owned by just a few stockholders who also manage the business, the most important type of corporation is one that sells shares to the general public. The company raises the funds it needs for the business by the sale of stock, and the stockholders become the company's owners. They are entitled to share in corporate profits. When paid out, profits are called **dividends. Undistributed profits** also belong to the owners, but they are usually reinvested in the firm's operations. If the corporation is liquidated, stockholders share any assets that remain after all debts are paid.

Diffuse ownership of corporate shares means that the owners cannot all be managers. Stockholders, who are entitled to one vote for each share they own, elect a board of directors. The board defines general policy and hires senior managers who are supposed to translate this general policy into detailed decisions.

Should the company go bankrupt, the personal liability of any one shareholder is limited to whatever money that shareholder has actually invested in the firm. This is called **limited liability.**

From a shareholder's viewpoint, the most important aspect of the corporation is limited liability.

The corporation's advantage is that it can raise capital from a large number of individuals. Each investor shares in the firm's profits, but has no liability for corporate action beyond risking the loss of the amount invested. Thus, investors know their exact maximum risk and may simply collect dividends without needing to know anything about the policy or operation of the firm they own collectively. Because shares are easily transferred from one person to another, a corporation has a continuity of life unaffected by frequent changes in owners.

From the individual owner's point of view, there are disadvantages in investing in a corporation. First, the owner may have little to say about the management of the firm. For example, if those who hold a majority of the shares decide that the corporation should not pay dividends, an individual investor cannot compel the payment of his or her share of the earnings. Second, the income of the corporation is taxed twice. In 1986 the rate at which corporate income, before dividends are paid, was taxed was reduced from 47 percent to 34 percent. Dividends are paid out of the after-tax income. Then individual stockholders are also taxed on any dividends paid to them. This "double taxation" of corporate income is viewed by some as unfair and discriminatory; others see it as the price to be paid for the advantage of incorporation. Judging from the continuing importance of the corporation in the United States, despite a corporate tax rate that has long been around 50 percent, the price has not been prohibitive.

The Rise of the Modern Corporation

The corporate form of organization is employed today wherever large enterprises are found. The principal reason is that it has decisive advantages over any other form in raising the vast sums of capital required for major enterprises. Historically, wherever and whenever large accumulations of capital in a single firm were required, the limited liability company developed. The corporate form has spread even to the service industries and agriculture, as firms in these industries grew in size.

The direct predecessor of the modern corporation was the English chartered company of the sixteenth century. The Muscovy Company, granted a charter in 1555, the East India Company, first chartered in 1600, and the Hudson's Bay Company, chartered in 1609 and still going strong in Canada 375 years later, are famous examples of early joint-stock ventures with limited liability. Their special needs for many investors to finance a ship that would not return with its cargo for years—if it returned at all—made this exceptional form of organization seem desirable.

In the next three centuries the trading company's needs (large capital requirements, the need to diversify risk, the need for long-term investment) were seen to exist in other fields, and charters were granted in the fields of insurance, turnpikes and canals, and banking, as well as foreign trade. The new techniques introduced during the Industrial Revolution made the large firm efficient and so extended the needs for large amounts of capital committed over long periods of time to many more fields. During the nineteenth century the demand for a basis for incorporation other than special privilege became strong. General laws permitting incorporation with limited liability *as a matter of right rather than special grant of privilege* became common in England and the United States during the late nineteenth century.

Today incorporation is relatively routine, although it is subject to a variety of state laws. Moderate fees are charged for the privilege of incorporation, and competition among the states for the incorporation fees has served to liberalize the conditions for incorporation throughout the country. Delaware is an example of a small state that at one time had a highly disproportionate share of incorporations because of its permissive laws. In insurance, Connecticut took the lead; most insurance companies founded before 1930 have Connecticut charters.

Financing of Firms

The money a firm raises for carrying on its business is sometimes called its **money capital** as distinct from its **real capital** (or *physical capital*), the physical assets that constitute plant, equipment, and inventories. Money capital may be broken down into **equity capital,** provided by the owners, and **debt,** which consists of the funds borrowed from persons and institutions who are not owners of the firm.

The use of the term *capital* to refer to both an amount of money and a quantity of goods can be confusing, but it is usually clear from the context which is being referred to. The two uses are not independent, for much of the money capital raised by a firm will be used to purchase the capital goods the firm requires for production.

There are two basic methods by which a firm raises capital: equity financing and debt financing.

Equity Financing

The owners of the firm are its **stockholders,** those who have put up money to purchase shares in the firm. They make their money available to the firm and risk losing it in return for a share of any profits the firm makes.

Stockholders usually have voting rights and have only a residual claim on profits. After all other claims have been met, the remaining profits, if any, belong to the stockholders. There is no legal limit to the profits that may be earned by the company and therefore no limit to potential dividends that may be paid out to common stockholders. Firms are not obliged by law to pay out any fixed portion of profits as dividends, and in fact practices among corporations vary enormously. Firms sometimes pay out a large fraction and hold back only enough to meet contingencies; at other times they pay small or no dividends in order to reinvest retained funds in the enterprise.

As this suggests, there are two ways for the firm to raise equity. One is to issue and sell new shares. Another is to reinvest, or plow back, some or all of its own profits, thus increasing the stake that existing shareholders have in the firm.

Reinvestment has become an extremely important source of funds in modern times. Over $35 billion per year is obtained for investment in this fashion. The shareholder who does not wish his or her profits to be reinvested can do little about it except to sell the stock and invest in a company with a policy of paying out a larger fraction of its earnings as dividends.

Debt Financing

Firms can also raise money by issuing debt, either by selling bonds or by borrowing from banks and other financial institutions. Debtholders are creditors, not owners, of the firm. They have loaned money to the firm in return for a promise to pay interest on the loan and, of course, a promise to repay the principal. Bank loans are often short-term in nature; sometimes the firm even commits to repay the principal *on demand.* A **bond,** on the other hand, is a promise to pay interest each year and to repay the principal at a stated time in the future (say, 20 years hence). In either case the promise to pay is a legal obligation on the firm's part whether or not profits have been made. If these payments cannot be met, the debtholders can force the firm into bankruptcy. Should this happen, the debtholders have a prior claim on the firm's assets. Only when the debtholders and all other creditors have been repaid in full can the stockholders attempt to recover anything for themselves.

Much of the firm's short-term and some of its long-term monetary needs are met through bank loans. This is often true of giant corporations and is particularly the case for small businesses. Banks, however, limit the amounts they are willing to lend companies, typically to specified fractions of the companies' total financial needs.

A major disadvantage to the corporation of raising capital through issuing debt is that interest payments must be met whether or not there are profits. Many a firm that would have survived a temporary crisis had all its capital been equity financed has been forced into bankruptcy because it could not meet its contractual obligations to pay interest to its debtholders.

The Firm in Economic Theory

IBM and the Main Street Deli certainly make decisions in different ways. Indeed, within a single large corporation not all decisions are made by the same people or in the same way. To take an example, someone at IBM decided to introduce a small computer in 1981. Someone else decided to call it the IBM personal computer and market it for home use. Someone else decided how and where to produce it.

BOX 9-1

Different Kinds of Firms

In economic theory the firm is defined as the unit that makes decisions with respect to the production and sale of commodities. This single definition covers a variety of business organizations from the single proprietorship to the corporation, and a variety of business sizes from the inventor operating in his garage and financed by whatever he can extract from a reluctant bank manager to vast undertakings with tens of thousands of shareholders and creditors. We know that in large firms decisions are actually made by many different individuals. We can nonetheless regard the firm as a single consistent decision-making unit because of the assumption that all decisions are made to achieve the common goal of maximizing the firm's profits.

Whether a decision is made by a small independent proprietor, a plant manager, or a board of directors, that person or group is the firm for the purpose of that decision. This is a truly heroic assumption; it amounts to saying that for purposes of predicting those aspects of their behavior that interest us, we can treat a farm, a corner grocery, a department store,

a small law partnership, General Motors, and a giant multinational corporation, all under the umbrella of a single theory of the behavior of the firm. If this turns out to be even partially correct, it will prove enormously valuable in revealing some unity of behavior where to the casual observer there is only bewildering diversity.

You should not be surprised, therefore, if at first encounter the theory appears rather abstract and out of touch with reality. To generalize over such a wide variety of behavior, the theory must ignore many features with which we are most familiar and which distinguish the farmer from the grocer and each of them from the Exxon Corporation. Any theory that generalizes over a wide variety of apparently diverse behavior necessarily has this characteristic because it ignores those factors that are most obvious to us and that create the appearance of diversity. If it were not possible to do this, it would be necessary to have dozens of different theories, one for each type of firm. The task of learning economics would then be much more complex than it now is!

Someone else decided its price. Someone else decided how best to promote its sales. The common aspect of these decisions is that all were in pursuit of the same goal—the manufacture and sale of products to earn profits for IBM.

Economic theory assumes that the same principles underlie each decision made within a firm and that the decision is uninfluenced by who makes it. The assumption that all firms are the same is further discussed in Box 9-1.

Motivation: Profit Maximization

It is assumed that the firm makes decisions in such a way that its profits will be as large as possible. In other words, the firm is assumed to *maximize its profits*. The concept of profits requires careful definition, which will be given later in this chapter. For now we may treat it in the everyday sense of the

difference between the value of the firm's sales and the costs to the firm of producing what is sold.

The assumption of profit maximization provides a principle by which a firm's decisions can be predicted.

Economists predict the firm's behavior by studying the effect that making each choice would have on the firm's profits. They then predict that from these alternatives the firm will select the one that produces the largest profits.

At this point you may well ask if it is sensible to build a theory on such a simple assumption about the motives of business people. Of course, some business people are inspired by motives other than a desire to make as much money as possible. Cases in which they use their positions to seek political influence or pursue charitable objectives are not difficult to document.

This theory does not say, however, that profit is the *only* factor that influences business people. It says only that profits are so important that a theory that assumes profit maximization to be the firm's sole motive will produce predictions that are substantially correct.

Why is this assumption made? First, it is necessary to make *some* assumption about what motivates decision makers if the theory is to predict how they will act. Second, a great many of the predictions of theories based on this assumption have been confirmed by observation. Third, no alternative assumption has yet been shown to yield more accurate predictions. However, the assumption has been criticized, and alternatives have been suggested (see Chapter 17).

Factors of Production

Firms seek profits by producing and selling commodities. Production may be compared to a sausage machine. Certain elements, such as raw materials and the services of capital and labor, are fed in at one end, and a product emerges at the other. The materials and factor services used in the production process are called **inputs,** and the products that emerge are called **outputs.** One way of looking at the process is to regard the inputs as being combined to produce the output. Another equally useful way is to regard the inputs as being used up, or sacrificed, to gain the output.

Hundreds of inputs enter into the output of a specific good. Among the inputs entering into automobile production are, to name only a few, sheet steel, rubber, spark plugs, electricity, machinists, cost accountants, forklift operators, managers, and painters. These inputs can be grouped into four broad classes: (1) those that are inputs to the automobile manufacturer, but outputs to some other manufacturer, such as spark plugs, electricity, and sheet steel; (2) those that are provided directly by nature, such as land; (3) those that are provided directly by households, such as the services of workers; and (4) those that are provided by the machines used for manufacturing automobiles.

The first class of inputs is made up of goods produced by other firms. These products, which may be called *intermediate products*, appear as inputs

only because the stages of production are divided among different firms so that, at any one stage, a firm is using as inputs goods produced by other firms. If these products are traced back to their sources, all production can be accounted for by the services of only three kinds of inputs, which are called *factors of production*. Economists call all gifts of nature, such as land and raw materials, **land.** All physical and mental efforts provided by people are called **labor** services. All machines and other production equipment are grouped in a category called **capital,** defined as manufactured aids to further production.

Extensive use of capital—the services of machines and other capital goods—is one distinguishing feature of modern as opposed to primitive production. Instead of making consumer goods directly with only the aid of simple natural tools, productive effort goes into the manufacture of tools, machines, and other goods that are desired not in themselves, but as aids to making further goods. The use of capital goods renders the production processes *roundabout*. Instead of making what is wanted directly, productive effort first goes to making tools that will subsequently be used to make what is finally wanted.

Economic Efficiency

There is usually more than one way to produce a given product. For example, it is possible to produce agricultural commodities by farming a small quantity of land, combining a great deal of labor and capital with each acre of land, as is done in Belgium. It is also possible to produce the same commodities by farming a great deal of land, using only a small amount of labor and capital per acre of land, as is done in Australia.

Faced with alternative production processes, how does the firm decide which process is best? The firm could choose the process that uses the fewest inputs for producing a given output, that is, the one that is technically most efficient. Alternatively, the firm might choose the process that costs the least for producing a given output, that is, the one that is economically most efficient. **Technological efficiency** (or, *technical efficiency*) measures use of inputs in physical terms; **economic efficiency** measures use in

BOX 9-2

Technological Versus Economic Efficiency: An Example

Suppose, given the state of technology, there are only four known ways to produce 100 widgets per month.

	Quantity of inputs received	
	Capital	**Labor**
Method A	6	200
Method B	10	250
Method C	10	150
Method D	40	50

Method B is technologically inefficient because it uses more of both inputs than does method A. Among the other three methods, method A uses the least capital, but uses the most labor.* Method D conserves labor, but uses much more capital. Method C is intermediate between them. (If you consider method D technologically most efficient because it uses only 90 units of all resources, think again.)

---

*There is yet a third concept of efficiency, "engineering efficiency," which involves the least use of a particular factor. When engineers speak of the efficiency of an engine, they may mean how much of the fuel it turns into power.

Methods A, C, and D are all technologically efficient because no one of them uses more of both resources than either of the others.

Which one is the least costly, that is, is economically efficient? We cannot tell without knowing the costs of capital and of labor. Economic efficiency depends on factor prices. Consider the three cases shown in the table below. As we move from case I to II to III, a unit of labor becomes increasingly expensive *relative to* a unit of capital.

Method A is economically efficient when labor is cheap relative to capital. Method C becomes efficient when labor gets somewhat more expensive relative to capital. Finally, when labor gets very expensive relative to capital, method D, which uses least labor per unit of capital, becomes economically efficient.

To test your understanding, answer these questions:

1. Can a technologically inefficient method ever be economically efficient?
2. Is there a set of factor prices for which both method C and method D will be economically efficient?

	Factor prices per unit			Total cost of factors		
	Capital	**Labor**		**Method A**	**Method C**	**Method D**
Case I	$50	$3		$ 900	$950	$2,150
Case II	20	5		1,120	950	1,050
Case III	15	5		1,090	900	850

---

terms of costs.[1] An example distinguishing the concepts is given in Box 9-2.

The economically most efficient method of producing a given output is the one that minimizes costs. Economic efficiency depends on factor prices and on technological efficiency.

---

[1] Efficiency plays an important role in economic discussions. We shall discuss it at greater length in Chapter 12.

Cost and Profit to the Firm

The Meaning of Cost

Economic efficiency is defined in terms of cost. But what is cost? **Cost,** to the producing firm, is the value of inputs used in producing its output.

Notice the use of the word *value* in the definition. A given output produced by a given technique, say,

6,000 cars produced each week by American Motors with its present production methods, has a given set of inputs associated with it—so many working hours of various types of laborers, supervisors, managers, and technicians, so many tons of steel, glass, and aluminum, so many kilowatt hours of electricity, and so many hours of the time of various machines. The cost of each can be calculated, and the sum of these separate costs is the total cost to American Motors of producing 6,000 cars per week.

Purpose in Assigning Costs

Costs are an important element in business decisions because profit from production is the difference between revenue from the sale of outputs and the cost of inputs. To understand the behavior of profit-maximizing firms, we need to understand how costs change as the firm's production changes.

There are several reasons why an economist may be interested in the behavior of firms: (1) to *describe* actual behavior of firms, (2) to *predict* how the firm's behavior will respond to specified changes in the conditions they face, (3) to *help* firms make the best decisions they can in achieving their goals, and (4) to *evaluate* how well firms use scarce resources.

The same measure of cost need not be correct for all of these purposes. For example, a firm behaves according to the information it has, but that information may be wrong or incomplete. In describing or predicting that firm's behavior, economists should use the information the firm actually uses, even if they know it is incorrect. But in helping the firm to achieve its goals, economists should substitute the correct information.

Economists use a well-established definition of costs in solving problems that involve helping and evaluating firms. If business people use the same definition and have the same information, the economists' definition will be appropriate for problems of description and prediction as well. This will be assumed for the moment.

Opportunity Cost

Although the details of economic costing vary, they are governed by a common principle that is some-

times called *user cost* but is more commonly called *opportunity cost*. We met this concept first in Chapter 1.

> **The cost of using something in a particular venture is the benefit foregone (or opportunity lost) by not using it in its best alternative use.**

An old Chinese merchant's proverb says: "Where there is no gain, the loss is obvious." The sense of this proverb is that the merchant who shows no gain has wasted time, time that could have been used in some other venture. The merchant has neglected the opportunity cost of his time. Box 9-3 considers opportunity cost more generally.

The Measurement of Opportunity Cost by the Firm

To measure opportunity cost, the firm must assign to each input that it has used a monetary value equal to what it has sacrificed to use the input. Applying this principle to specific cases, however, reveals some tough problems.

Purchased and Hired Factors

Assigning costs is a straightforward process when inputs purchased in one period are used up in the same period and when the price the firm pays is determined by forces outside the firm. Many raw material and intermediate product purchases fall into this category. If the firm pays $110 per ton for coal delivered to its factory, it has sacrificed its claims to whatever else $110 can buy, and thus the purchase price is a reasonable measure of the opportunity cost to it of using one ton of coal.

For hired factors of production, where the rental price is the full price, the situation is identical. Borrowed money is paid for by **interest.** An **interest rate** is the money price paid to use $1 for one year. Interest payments measure the opportunity cost of borrowed funds. Most labor services are hired and the cost includes the wages paid and any related expenses such as contributions to social security, pension funds, unemployment and disability insurance, and other fringe benefits.

BOX 9-3

Opportunity Cost More Generally

Opportunity cost plays a vital role in economic analysis, but it is also a fundamental principle that applies to a wide range of situations. It is one of the great insights of economics. Consider some examples:

- George Bernard Shaw, on reaching his ninetieth birthday, was asked how he liked being 90. He is reputed to have said, "It's fine, when you consider the alternative."
- Llewelyn Formed likes to hear both Dan Rather and John Chancellor. If he finally settles on Chancellor, what is the opportunity cost of this decision?
- Link Heartthrob, a 31-year-old bachelor, is thinking about marrying. But, although he thinks Miss Piggy is a lovely girl, he figures that if he marries her, he will give up the chance of wedded bliss with another girl he may meet next year. So he decides to wait a while. What

other information do you need to determine the opportunity cost of the decision?
- Serge Ginn, M.D., complains that now that he is earning large fees he can no longer afford to take the time for a vacation trip to Europe. In what way does it make sense to say that the opportunity cost of his vacation depends upon his fees?
- Retired General William Russ, who is married to a wealthy woman, has decided to contribute $5,000 to a political candidate. His lawyer points out to him that since he is in the 50 percent tax bracket, and since political contributions are not deductible from income, the real cost of his contribution is the same as giving an extra $10,000 to his favorite charity, the Gen. Russ Foundation. Is the opportunity cost of the political contribution $5,000 or $10,000?

Imputed Costs

Cost must also be assessed for inputs that the firm uses but neither purchases nor hires for current use. Since no payment is made to anyone outside the firm, these costs are not so obvious. They are called **imputed costs.** To discover the most profitable lines of production, the opportunity cost of these factors should be assessed as the value the firm might earn from the factors if it shifted them to their next best use. The following examples all involve imputed costs.

Using the firm's own money.   Consider a firm that uses $100,000 of its own money that it could instead have loaned out at 10 percent per year.

Thus, $10,000 (at least) should be deducted from the firm's revenue as the cost of funds used in production. If, to continue the example, the firm makes only $6,000 over all other costs, then one should say not that the firm made a profit of $6,000 by producing, but that it lost $4,000. For if it had closed down completely and merely loaned out its money to someone else, it could have earned $10,000.

Costs of durable assets.   The costs of using assets owned by the firm, such as buildings, equipment,

and machinery, consist of the cost of the money tied up in them and a charge, called **depreciation,** for the loss in value of the asset because of its use in production. Depreciation includes the loss in value due to physical wear and tear and to obsolescence. The economic cost of owning an asset for a year is the loss in value of the asset during the year.

Accountants use several conventional methods of depreciation based on the price originally paid for the asset. One of the most common is *straight-line depreciation,* in which the same amount of historical cost is deducted in every year of useful life of the asset. While historical costs are often useful approximations, they may in some cases differ seriously from the depreciation required by the opportunity cost principle. Consider two examples of the possible error involved.

Assets that may be resold. A woman buys a new automobile for $10,000. She intends to use it for five years and then sell it for $2,500. She may think that, using straight-line depreciation, this will cost her $1,500 per year. But if after one year the value of her car on the used car market is $7,500, it has cost her $2,500 to use the car during the first year. Why should she charge herself $2,500 depreciation during the first year? After all, *she* does not intend to sell the car for five years. The answer is that one of the purchaser's alternatives is to buy a one-year-old car and operate it for four years. Indeed, that is the position she is in after the first year. Whether she likes it or not, she has paid $2,500 for the use of the car during the first year of its life. If the market had valued her car at $9,000 after one year (instead of $7,500), the depreciation would have been only $1,000.

Sunk costs. In the previous example, an active used-asset market was considered. At the other extreme, consider an asset that has no alternative use. This is sometimes called a *sunk cost.* Assume that a firm has a set of machines it purchased some time ago for $100,000. These machines should last 10 years and the firm's accountant calculates the depreciation costs of these machines by the straight-line method at $10,000 per year. Assume also that the machines can be used to make one product and nothing else. Suppose, too, that they are installed in the firm's plant, they cannot be leased to any other firm, and their scrap value is negligible. In other words, the machines have no value except to this firm in its current operation. Assume that if the machines are used to produce the one product, the cost of all other factors utilized will amount to $25,000, while the goods produced can be sold for $29,000.

Now, if the accountant's depreciation "costs" of running the machines are added in, the total cost of operation comes to $35,000; with revenues at $29,000, this yields an annual loss of $6,000 per year. It appears that the goods should not be made!

The fallacy in this argument lies in adding in a charge based on the sunk cost of the machines as one of the costs of current operation. The machines have no alternative uses whatsoever. Clearly, their *opportunity cost* is *zero.* The total costs of producing this line of goods is thus only $25,000 per year (assuming all other costs have been correctly assessed), and the line of production shows an annual profit of $4,000, not a loss of $6,000.

To see why the second calculation leads to the correct decision, notice that if the firm abandons this line of production as unprofitable, it will have no money to pay out and no revenue received on this account. If the firm takes the economist's advice and pursues the line of production, it will pay out $25,000

and receive $29,000, thus making it $4,000 per year richer than if it had not done so. Clearly, production is worth undertaking. The amount the firm happened to have paid out for the machines in the past has no bearing whatever on deciding the correct use of the machines once they are installed on the premises.

Because they involve neither current nor future costs, sunk costs should have no influence on deciding what is currently the most profitable thing to do.

The "bygones are bygones" principle extends well beyond economics and is often ignored in poker, in war, and perhaps in love. Because you have invested heavily in a poker hand, a battle, or a courtship does not mean you should stick with it if the prospects of winning become very small. At every moment of decision, you should be concerned with how benefits from this time forward compare with current and future costs.

Risk taking.   One difficulty in imputing costs is the evaluation of the service of risk taking. Business enterprise is often a risky affair. The risk is borne by the owners of the firm who, if the enterprise fails, may lose the money they have invested in the firm.

Risk taking is a service that must be provided if the firm is to carry on production, and it must be paid for by the firm. If a firm does not yield a return sufficient to compensate for the risks involved, the firm will not be able to persuade people to contribute money to it in return for a part ownership in the firm. The owners will not take this risk unless they receive compensation. They expect a return that exceeds what they could have obtained by investing their money in a virtually riskless manner, say, by buying a government bond.

Suppose, in investing $100,000 in a class of risky ventures, a businesswoman expects that most of the ventures will be successful but some will fail. In fact, she expects about $10,000 worth to be a total loss. (She does not know which specific projects will be the losers, of course.) Suppose further that she requires a 20 percent return on her total investment. To earn a $20,000 profit and recover the $10,000 expected loss, she needs to earn a $30,000 profit on the $90,000 of successful investment. This is a rate of return of 33⅓ percent. She charges 20 percent for the use of the capital plus 13⅓ percent for the risk she takes.

Patents, trademarks, and other special advantages.

Suppose a firm owns a valuable patent or a highly desirable location or produces a popular brand-name product such as Coca-Cola, Chevrolet, or Marlboro. Each of these involves an opportunity cost to the firm in production (even if it was acquired free) because if the firm does not choose to use the special advantage itself, it could sell or lease it to others. Typically, the value of these advantages will differ from their historical cost. Indeed, typically several alternative uses will be open to the owner. The opportunity cost in any one is the value forgone in the *best* alternative use.

The Meaning and Significance of Profits

Economic profits on goods sold are the difference between the revenues received from the sale and the opportunity cost of the resources used to make them. If costs are greater than revenues, such "negative profits" are called *losses*. This definition includes in costs (and thus excludes from profits) the imputed returns to capital and to risk taking.

This definition of the words *profits* and *losses* gives specialized meaning to words that are in everyday use. It is, therefore, a potential source of confusion to the student who has used the words in a more general sense before. Table 9-1 may help clarify terms used in connection with this specific definition.

Some economists, while following substantially the same definitions, label as **normal profits** the imputed returns to capital and risk taking just necessary to prevent the owners from withdrawing from the industry. These normal profits are, of course, what has been defined as the opportunity costs of risk taking and capital. Whatever they are called, they are costs that have to be covered if the firm is to stay in operation in the long run.

TABLE 9-1   The Calculation of Economic Profits: An Example

Gross revenue from sales	$1,000
Less: direct cost of goods sold (materials, labor, electricity, etc.)	650
"Gross profits" (or "contributions to overhead")	350
Less: indirect costs (depreciation, overhead, management salaries, interest on debt, etc.)	140
Normal profits before income taxes	210
Less: imputed charges for own capital used and for risk taking	100
Economic profits before income taxes	110
Less: income taxes payable	100
Economic profits after income taxes	$ 10

Economic profits are less than normal profits. The main difference between economic profits and normal profits, that is, between profits as defined in economics and profits as defined in ordinary speech, is the subtraction of imputed charges for use of capital owned by the firm and for risk taking. Income tax is levied on whatever definition of profits the taxing authorities choose, usually closely related to normal profits.

Other Definitions of Profits

Business firms define profits as the excess of revenues over the costs with which accountants provide them. We explore in the appendix to this chapter some of the differences between accountants' and economists' views of business transactions. Some of these differences affect the meaning of profits. Accountants do not include as costs charges for risk taking and use of owners' own capital, and thus these items are recorded by businesses as part of their profits. When a business says it *needs* profits of such and such an amount to stay in business, it is making sense within its definition, for its "profits" must be large enough to pay for those factors of production that it uses but that the accounting profession does not include as costs.

Economists would express the same notion by saying that the business needs to cover *all* its costs, including those not employed in accounting conventions. If the firm is covering all its opportunity costs, then it could not do better by using its resources in any other line of activity than the one currently being followed.

A situation in which revenues equal costs (economic profits of zero) is a satisfactory one—because all factors, hidden as well as visible, are being rewarded at least as well as in their *best* alternative uses.

With zero economic profits, then, you can do no better, although you might do worse. To reverse the Chinese proverb cited earlier, "Where there is no loss compared to the best alternative use of every input, the gain is obvious."

The income tax authorities have yet another definition of profits, which is implicit in the thousands of rules as to what may and may not be included as a deduction from revenue in arriving at taxable income. In some cases the taxing authorities allow more for cost than accountants recommend; in other cases they allow less.

It is important to be clear about different meanings of the term *profits* not only to avoid fruitless semantic arguments, but because a theory that predicts that certain behavior is a function of profits defined in one way will not necessarily predict behavior accurately given some other definition. For example, if economists predict that new firms will seek to enter an industry whenever profits are earned, this prediction will frequently be wrong if the accountants' definition is used to determine profits. The definition of profits as an excess over all opportunity costs is for many purposes the most useful, but in order to apply it to business behavior or to tax policy, appropriate adjustments must be made. And to apply accounting or tax data to particular theories, the data must be rectified. Henceforth, when we use the word *profits*, unless otherwise noted, we mean *economic* profits.

Profits and Resource Allocation

When resources are valued by the opportunity cost principle, their costs show how much these resources would earn if used in their best alternative uses. If there is an industry in which all firms' revenues exceed opportunity costs, all the firms in the industry will be earning profits. Thus, the owners of factors of production will want to move resources into this industry because the earnings potentially available to them are greater there than in alternative uses of the resources. If in some other industry firms are incurring losses, some or all of this industry's resources are more highly valued in other uses, and owners of the resources will want to move them to those other uses.

Profits and losses play a crucial signaling role in the workings of a free-market system.

Profits in an industry are the signal that resources can profitably be moved into the industry. Losses are the signal that the resources can profitably be moved elsewhere. Only if there are zero economic profits is there no incentive for resources to move into or out of an industry.

Summary

1. The firm is the economic unit that produces and sells commodities. The economist's definition of the firm abstracts from real-life differences in size and form of organization of firms.
2. The single proprietorship, the partnership, and the corporation are the major forms of business organization in the United States today. The corporation is by far the most common wherever large-scale production is required. The corporation is recognized as a legal entity; its owners, or shareholders, have a liability that is limited to the amount of money they have actually invested in the organization.

Corporate ownership is readily transferred by sale of shares of the company's stock in securities markets.

3. Firms can raise money through equity financing or debt financing. The firm's owners provide equity capital either by purchasing newly issued shares or when the firm reinvests its profits. The firm obtains debt financing from creditors either by borrowing from financial institutions or by selling bonds.

4. Economic theory assumes that the same principles underlie each decision made within the firm and that the actual decision is uninfluenced by who makes it. The key behavioral assumption is that the firm seeks to maximize its profit.

5. Production consists of transforming inputs (or factors of production) into outputs (or goods and services). It is often convenient to divide factors of production into categories. One common classification is land, labor, and capital. Land includes all primary products (land and natural resources), labor means all human services, and capital denotes all manufactured aids to further production. An outstanding feature of modern production is the use of capital goods and roundabout methods of production.

6. Because there is more than one way to produce a commodity, the firm must decide *how* to produce. Efficiency measures are based on the relative amounts of inputs necessary to produce a given output. Technological efficiency evaluates units of input in physical terms. Economic efficiency evaluates them in terms of costs.

7. The opportunity cost of using a resource is the value of that resource in its best alternative use. If the opportunity cost of using a resource in one way is less than or equal to the gain from using the resource in this way, there is no superior way of using it.

8. Measuring opportunity cost to the firm requires some difficult imputations in cases involving resources not purchased or hired for current use. Among these imputed costs are those for use of owners' money, depreciation, risk taking, and any special advantages that the firm may possess.

9. A firm maximizing profits, defined as the difference between revenue and opportunity cost, is making the best allocation of the resources under its control, according to the firm's evaluation of its alternatives.

10. Economic profits and losses provide important signals concerning the reallocation of resources. Profits earned in an industry provide a signal that more resources can profitably move into the industry. Losses show that some resources have more profitable uses elsewhere and serve as a signal for them to move out of that industry.

11. The appendix to this chapter introduces balance sheets and profit and loss statements and uses them to discuss some of the differences between the concept of profits used by accountants and that used by economists.

Role of profit maximization
Single proprietorship, partnership, and corporation
Advantages of the corporation
Debt and equity financing
Inputs and factors of production
Economic efficiency
Opportunity costs
Economic profits and normal profits
Profits and resource allocation

Topics for Review

---

1. Can the economic theory of the firm be of any help in analyzing the productive decisions of such nonprofit organizations as governments, churches, and colleges? What, if any, role does the notion of opportunity cost play for them?
2. In *The Engineers and the Price System,* Thorstein Veblen argued that businessmen who made decisions about financing, pricing, and the like were largely superfluous to the operation of a business. In his view, knowledge of the technology would be sufficient to ensure efficient operation of firms. Discuss Veblen's contention.
3. "There is no such thing as a free lunch." Can anything be costless? Gas stations have traditionally provided free services, including windshield cleaning, air pumps for tire inflation, and road maps. Now, many sell road maps and have discontinued free services. Indeed, self-service stations are becoming increasingly popular with motorists who like the lower gas prices of those stations. Under what conditions will profit-maximizing behavior lead to the coexistence of full-service and self-service gas stations? What would determine the proportions in which each occurred?
4. What is the opportunity cost of the following?
   a. Fining a politician $10,000 and sending him to prison for one year
   b. Lending $500 to a friend
   c. Not permitting a $116-million electric power dam to be built because it would destroy the snail darter, a rare 3-inch-long fish found only in that particular river
   d. Towing icebergs to Saudi Arabia to provide drinking water at the cost of $.50 per cubic meter
5. Is straight-line depreciation an appropriate method of assessing the annual cost to the typical American household of using a passenger automobile? Some firms that use trucks allocate the cost on a per-mile basis. Why might this method be more appropriate for trucks than for automobiles owned by households?
6. Having bought a used car from Smiling Sam for $900, you drive it two days and it stops. You now find that it requires an extra $500 before it will run. Assuming that the car is not worth $1,400 fixed, should you make the repairs?
7. "To meet the legislated standard of 3.4 grams of carbon monoxide per mile driven, General Motors has calculated that it will cost $100

Discussion Questions

million and prolong 200 lives by one year each, thus costing $500,000 per year of extra life. Human lives are precious, which is why it is so sad to note another use of that money. It has been estimated that the installation of special cardiac-care units in ambulances could prevent premature deaths each year at an average cost of only $200 for each year of extra life."

Assume the facts in this quotation are correct. If the money spent on carbon monoxide control would have been spent on cardiac-care units instead, what is the opportunity cost of the carbon monoxide requirement? If the money would not have been so spent but simply reduced automobile companies' costs, what is the opportunity cost? In either case, do the facts tell us whether the regulation of carbon monoxide to the 3.4 gram level is desirable or undesirable?

8. Which concept of profits is implied in the following quotations?
   a. "Profits are necessary if firms are to stay in business."
   b. "Profits are signals for firms to expand production and investment."
   c. "Increased depreciation lowers profits and thus benefits the company's owners."

Balance Sheets, Income Statements, and Costs of Production: Two Views

Accounting is a major branch of study in and of itself. Many students of economics will want to study accounting at some stage in their careers. It is not our intention to give a short course in accounting in this appendix, but rather to acquaint you with the kinds of summary statements that are used by both economists and accountants. **Balance sheets** report the status of a firm at a particular time. They balance in the sense that they show the assets (or valuable things) owned by the firm on one side and the claims against those assets on the other side. **Income statements** summarize the flows of resources through the firm in the course of its operations over a specified period of time (for example, a year). Balance sheets thus measure a stock; income statements measure a flow.

To illustrate what balance sheets and income statements are, the same example will be treated from two points of view: that of the accountant and that of the economist.

An Example

Late in 1986, James Maykby, the second vice-president of Acme Artificial Flower Corporation (at a salary of $50,000 per year), decided he would go into business for himself. He quit his job and organized the Maykby Leaf Company. He purchased suitable plant and equipment for $160,000 and acquired some raw materials and supplies. By December 31, 1986, he was in a position to start manufacturing. The funds for his enterprise were $80,000 raised as a bank loan on the factory (on which he is obligated to pay interest of $10,000 per year) and $110,000 of his own funds, which had previously been invested in common stocks. He also owed $10,000 to certain firms that had provided him with supplies.

Maykby, who is a trained accountant, drew up a statement of his company's position as of December 31, 1986 (see Table 9A-1).

Maykby showed this balance sheet to his brother-in-law, an economist, and was pleased and surprised[1] to find that he agreed that this was a fair and accurate statement of the position of the company as it prepared to start operation.

During 1987, the company had a busy year hiring factors, producing and selling goods, and so on. The following points summarize these activities of the 12-month period.

1. The firm hired labor and purchased additional raw materials in the amount of $115,000, of which it still owed $20,000 at the end of the year.[2]
2. The firm manufactured artificial leaves and flow-

---

[1] He usually finds that he and his brother-in-law disagree about everything.

[2] In this example all purchased and hired factors are treated in a single category.

TABLE 9A-1 Maykby Leaf Company, Balance Sheet, December 31, 1986

Assets		Liabilities and equity	
Cash in bank	$ 10,000	Owed to suppliers of factors	$ 10,000
Plant and equipment	160,000	Bank loan	80,000
Raw materials and supplies	30,000	Equity	110,000
Total assets	$200,000	Total liabilities and equity	$200,000

TABLE 9A-2   Maykby Leaf Company, Accountant's Balance Sheet, December 31, 1987

Assets		Liabilities and equity	
Cash in bank	$ 65,000	Owed to suppliers of factors	$ 20,000
(See Exhibit 1)		(See Exhibit 4)	
Plant and equipment	146,000	Bank loan	80,000
(See Exhibit 2)		Equity	141,000
Raw materials and supplies	30,000	(See Exhibit 5)	
(See Exhibit 3)			
Total assets	$241,000	Total liabilities and equity	$241,000

TABLE 9A-3   Maykby Leaf Company, Exhibits to Balance Sheet of December 31, 1987

Exhibit 1. Cash

Balance, January 1, 1987	$ 10,000	
+ Deposits		
Proceeds of sales of goods	200,000	$210,000
− Payments		
Payments to suppliers (1987 bills)	10,000	
Payments for labor and additional raw materials	95,000	
Salary of Mr. Maykby	20,000	
Purchase of new machine	10,000	
Interest payment to bank	10,000	− 145,000
Balance, December 31, 1987		65,000

Exhibit 2. Plant and Equipment

Balance, January 1, 1987	$160,000	
+ New machine purchased	10,000	170,000
− Depreciation charged		− 24,000
Balance, December 31, 1987		146,000

Exhibit 3. Raw Materials and Supplies

On hand January 1, 1987	$ 30,000	
Purchases in 1987	115,000	145,000
Used for production during 1987		− 115,000
On hand December 31, 1987		30,000

Exhibit 4. Owed to Suppliers

Balance, January 1, 1987	$ 10,000	
New purchases, 1987	115,000	125,000
Paid on old accounts	10,000	
Paid on new accounts	95,000	− 105,000
Balance, December 31, 1987		$ 20,000

Exhibit 5. Equity

Original investment	$110,000
+ Income earned during year	31,000
(See income statement)	
Balance, December 31, 1987	$141,000

ers whose sale value was $200,000. At year's end it had sold all of these and still had on hand $30,000 worth of raw materials.
3. The firm paid off the $10,000 owed to suppliers at the beginning of the year.
4. At the very end of 1987, the company purchased a new machine for $10,000 and paid cash for it.
5. The company paid the bank $10,000 interest on the loan.
6. Maykby paid himself $20,000 "instead of salary."

An Accountant's Balance Sheet and Income Statement

Taking account of all these things and also recognizing that he had depreciation on his plant and equipment,[3] Maykby spent New Year's Day 1988 preparing three financial reports (see Tables 9A-2, 9A-3, and 9A-4).

These reports reflect the operations of the firm as described above. The bookkeeping procedure by which these various activities are made to yield both the year-end balance sheet and the income statement need not concern you at this time, but you should notice several things.

1. Some transactions affect the balance sheet, but do not enter into the current income statement. Examples of these are the purchase of a machine, which is an exchange of assets—cash for plant and equipment—and which will be entered as a cost in the income statements of some future periods as depreciation is charged; and the payment of past debts, which entered the income statements in the period in which the things purchased were used in production.[4]
2. The net profit from operations increased the owner's equity, since it was not "paid out" to him. A loss would have decreased his equity.
3. The income statement, covering a year's operation, provides a link between the opening balance

sheet (the assets and the claims against assets at the beginning of the year) and the closing balance sheet.
4. Every change in a balance sheet between two dates can be accounted for by events that occurred during the year. (See the exhibits to the balance sheet, Table 9A-3.)

After studying these records, Maykby felt that it had been a good year. The company had money in the bank, it had shown a profit, and it was able to sell the goods it produced. He was bothered, however, by the fact that he and his wife felt poorer than in the past years. Probably the cost of living had gone up!

An Economist's Balance Sheet and Income Statement

When Maykby's brother-in-law reviewed the December 31, 1987 balance sheet and the 1987 income statement, he criticized them in three respects.

1. Maykby should have charged the company $50,000 for his services, since that is what he could have earned outside.
2. Maykby should have charged the company for the use of the $110,000 of his funds. He computes that had Maykby left these funds in the stock market, he would have earned $11,000 in dividends and capital gains.
3. Maykby's depreciation figure is arbitrary. The

---

[3] The tax people told him he could charge 15 percent of the cost of his equipment as depreciation during 1987, and he decided to use this amount in his own books as well. No depreciation was charged on the new machine.

[4] Beginning students often have difficulty with the distinction between *cash* flows and *income* flows. If you do, analyze item by item the entries in Exhibit 1 in Table 9A-3 and in Table 9A-4, the income statement.

TABLE 9A-4   Maykby Leaf Company, Accountant's Income Statement for the Year 1987

Sales		$200,000
Costs of operation		
Hired services and raw materials	$115,000	
Depreciation	24,000	
Mr. Maykby	20,000	
Interest to bank	10,000	− 169,000
Profit		$ 31,000

TABLE 9A-5   Maykby Leaf Company, Economist's Income Statement for the Year 1987

Sales		$200,000
Cost of operations		
Hired services and raw materials	$115,000	
Depreciation[a]	36,000	
Interest to bank[b]	10,000	
Imputed cost of capital	11,000	
Services of Maykby	50,000	− 222,000
Loss		$(22,000)

[a] Market value on January 1 less market value on December 31.
[b] Because the bank loan is secured by the factory, its opportunity cost seems to the economist as properly measured by the interest payment.

TABLE 9A-6   Maykby Leaf Company Economist's Balance Sheet, December 31, 1987

Assets		Liabilities and equity	
Cash	$ 65,000	Owed to suppliers of factors	$ 20,000
Plant and equipment	134,000	Bank loan	80,000
Raw materials and supplies	30,000	Equity (see Exhibit)	129,000
	$229,000		$229,000

TABLE 9A-7   Exhibit to Balance Sheet, December 21, 1987: Equity to Mr. Maykby

Original investment		$110,000
New investment by Mr. Maykby		
Salary not collected	$30,000	
Return on capital not collected	11,000	41,000
		151,000
Less loss from operations		22,000
Equity		$129,000

TABLE 9A-8   Maykby's Situation Before and After

	(1) As second vice-president of Acme Flower Company	(2) As owner-manager of Maykby Leaf Company	(3) Difference (2) − (1)
Salary paid	$ 50,000	$ 20,000	−$30,000
Earnings on capital, invested in stocks	11,000	0	− 11,000
Assets owned	110,000 (stocks)	129,000 (equity in Maykby Leaf Co.)	+ 19,000
Net change			−$22,000

plant and equipment purchased for $160,000 a year ago now has a *market value* of only $124,000. (Assume he is correct about this fact.)

The brother-in-law prepared three revised statements (See Table 9A-5 on page 175, Table 9A-6, and the exhibit, Table 9A-7.)

It was not hard for Maykby to understand the difference between the accounting profit of $31,000 and the reported economist's loss of $22,000. The difference of $53,000 is made up as follows:

Extra salary	$30,000
Imputed cost of capital	11,000
Extra depreciation	12,000
	$53,000

What Maykby did *not* understand was in what sense he *lost* $22,000 during the year. To explain this, his brother-in-law prepared the report shown in Table 9A-8.

Although Maykby spent the afternoon muttering to himself and telling his wife that his brother-in-law was not only totally lacking in any business sense, but unpleasant as well, he was observed that evening at the public library asking the librarian whether there was a good "teach-yourself economics" book. (We do not know her answer.)

The next day Maykby suggested to the economist that they work out together the expected economic profits for next year. "After all," he said, "dwelling on what might have been doesn't really help decide whether I should continue the Maykby Leaf Company next year." The economist agreed. Because of expected sales increases, they concluded, the prospects were good enough to continue for at least another year. They dipped deep in the bowl of New Year's cheer to toast those stalwart pillars of society, the independent business person and the economist.

10

Production and Cost in the Short Run

Of the four domestic automobile manufacturers, General Motors is year-in and year-out more profitable than Ford, and Ford more profitable than Chrysler and American Motors. The prices charged for comparable models are approximately the same, but the profits *per automobile* are different. A good part of the reason lies in different levels of output. General Motors has about a 55 percent share of the four companies' aggregate sales, Ford 30 percent, Chrysler 12 percent, and American Motors Corporation only about 3 percent. American Motors with dollar sales of nearly $4.1 billion may not sound like a small company, but for the automobile industry it is uneconomically small because the costs of making and selling cars decline sharply with increases in volume of cars sold. Thus the smaller companies are at a big disadvantage relative to GM even if they are as imaginative in design, management, and salesmanship. Over the past 40 years several once-profitable smaller producers, among them Packard, Crosley, Studebaker, and Kaiser-Frazer, were unable to increase their volume and found that costs had become greater than revenues. They left the industry after suffering heavy losses. This experience illustrates one important aspect of the theory of cost of production: Cost of production per unit may differ significantly for different levels of output.

Another aspect of the theory of costs relates to factor prices. For example, when rising feed prices reached the point at which the cost of feeding chickens as they grew exceeded the price of fully grown chickens, farmers killed off their stocks and chicken production fell drastically. Similarly, during a period when price controls were in effect, meat packers were squeezed between the legal maximum price at which they could sell and the rising cost of the livestock they bought. Some of them suspended production.

In the previous chapter we defined costs of production. In this chapter we see how and why costs vary with the level of production and with changes in factor prices.

Choices Open to the Firm

Consider a firm producing a single product in a number of different plants. If its rate of sales has fallen off, should production be reduced correspondingly? Or, should production be held at the old rate and the unsold amounts stored up against an anticipated future rise in sales? If production is to be reduced, should a single plant be closed or should some plants be put on short time? Such decisions concern how best to use *existing* plant and equipment. They involve time periods too short to build new plants or to install more equipment.

Rather different decisions must be made when managers do long-range planning. Should the firm adopt a highly automated process that will greatly reduce its wage bill, even though it must borrow large sums of money to buy the equipment? Or, should it continue to build new plants that use the same techniques it is now using? Should it build new plants in an area where labor is plentiful, but that is distant from its sources of raw materials? These matters concern what a firm should do when it is changing or replacing its plant and equipment. Such decisions may take a long time to put into effect.

In the above examples, managers make decisions from known possibilities. Large firms also have research and development (R&D) staffs whose job is to discover new methods of production. But the firm must decide how much money to devote to R&D and in what areas the payoff for new development will be largest. If, for example, a shortage of a particular labor skill or raw material is anticipated, the research staff can be told to try to find ways to economize on that input or even eliminate it from the production process.

Time Horizons for Decision Making

Economists organize the decisions firms are constantly making into three theoretical groups: (1) how best to employ existing plant and equipment—the *short run*; (2) what new plant and equipment and production processes to select, given the framework of known technical possibilities—the *long run*; (3) how to encourage or adapt to the invention of new techniques—the *very long run*.

The Short Run

The **short run** is a time period in which the quantity of some inputs cannot be varied. A **fixed factor** is

one that cannot be increased in the short run.[1] The firm cannot get more of the fixed factors than it has on hand, and it is committed to make any money payments that are associated with these fixed factors. A fixed factor is usually an element of capital (such as plant and equipment), but it might be land, the services of management, or even the supply of skilled labor. Inputs that can be varied in the short run are called **variable factors**.

The short run does not correspond to a specific number of months or years. In some industries it may extend over many years; in others it may be only a matter of months or even weeks. Furthermore, it may last a different period of time when an industry is expanding than when it is contracting.

In the electric power industry, for example, it takes three or more years to acquire and install a steam-turbine generator. An unforeseen increase in demand will involve a long period during which the extra demand must be met as best it can with the existing capital equipment. In contrast, a machine shop can acquire new equipment or sell existing equipment in a few weeks. An increase in demand will have to be met with the existing stock of capital for only a brief time, after which it will be possible to adjust the stock of equipment to the level made desirable by the higher demand.

The Long Run

The **long run** is a time period in which all inputs may be varied, but the basic technology of production cannot be changed. Again, the long run does not correspond to a specific length of time.

The special importance of the long run in production theory is that it corresponds to the situation facing the firm when it is planning to go into business, to expand the scale of its operations, to branch

---

[1] Sometimes it is physically impossible to increase the quantity of a fixed factor in a short time. For instance, there is no way to build a hydroelectric dam or a nuclear power plant in a few months. Other times it might be physically possible, but prohibitively expensive, to increase the quantity. For example, a suit-manufacturing firm could conceivably rent a building, buy and install new sewing machines, and hire a trained labor force in a few days if money were no consideration. Economists regard prohibitive cost along with physical impossibility as a source of fixed factors.

out into new products or new areas, or to modernize, replace, or reorganize its method of production.

The firm's *planning decisions* characteristically are made with fixed technological possibilities, but with freedom to choose from a variety of production processes that will use factor inputs in different proportions.

The Very Long Run

Unlike the short and long run, the **very long run** is a time period in which the technological possibilities available to a firm may change. A central characteristic of modern industrial society has been the continuously changing technology that leads to new and improved products and production methods.

Some of these technological advances arise from within the firm as part of its own research and development efforts. For example, much of the innovation in cameras and films has been due to the efforts of the Kodak and Polaroid companies. Other firms adopt technological changes developed elsewhere. For example, the transistor and the electronic chip have revolutionized dozens of industries that had nothing to do with developing them. The firm must regularly decide how much to spend in its efforts to change its technology either by developing new techniques or adapting techniques developed by others.

Connecting the Runs: The Production Function

The various "runs" are simply different aspects of the same basic problem: getting output from inputs efficiently. They differ in terms of what the firm is able to change.

The relation between inputs into the production process and the quantity of output obtained is called the **production function.** A simplified production function in which there are only two factors of production, labor and capital, will be considered here, but the conclusions apply equally when there are many factors. The variation of output and cost under the assumption that one of the two factors is fixed is

TABLE 10-1 Variation of Output with Capital Fixed and Labor Variable

(1) Quantity of labor (L)	(2) Total product (TP)	(3) Average product (AP)	(4) Marginal product (MP)
0	0	—	
			15
1	15	15.0	
			19
2	34	17.0	
			14
3	48	16.0	
			12
4	60	15.0	
			2
5	62	12.4	

The relation of output to changes in the quantity of labor can be looked at in three different ways. Capital is assumed to be fixed at four units. As the quantity of labor increases, the rate of output (the total product) increases. Average product increases at first and then declines. The same is true of marginal product.

Marginal product is shown between the lines because it refers to the *change* in output from one level of labor input to another. When graphing the schedule, *MP*s of this kind should be plotted at the midpoint of the interval. Thus, graphically, the marginal product of 12 would be plotted to correspond to quantity of labor of 3.5.

examined. (Capital is taken to be the fixed factor and labor the variable one.) The long-run situation in which both factors can be varied is covered in the next chapter.

Short-Run Choices

Total, Average, and Marginal Products

Assume that a firm starts with a fixed amount of capital (say, 4 units) and contemplates applying various amounts of labor to it. Table 10-1 shows three different ways of looking at how output varies with the quantity of the variable factor. As a first step, some terms need to be defined.

Total product (*TP*) means the total amount produced during a given period of time. If the inputs of all but one factor are held constant, total product will change as more or less of the variable factor is used. This variation is shown in columns 1 and 2 of

FIGURE 10-1 Total Product, Average Product, and Marginal Product Curves

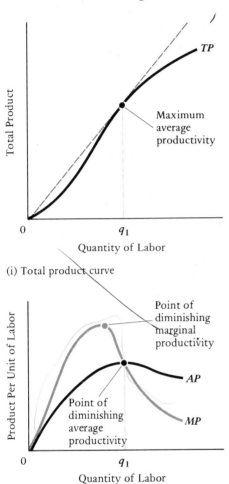

(i) Total product curve

(ii) Average and marginal product curves

Total product (*TP*), average product (*AP*), and marginal product (*MP*) curves often have the shapes shown here. (i) The total product curve shows the total product steadily rising, first at an increasing rate, then at a decreasing rate. This causes both the average and the marginal product curves in (ii) to rise at first and then decline. The point of maximum average productivity (also called the point of diminishing average productivity) is q_1. At this point $MP = AP$.

Table 10-1, which gives a total product schedule. Figure 10-1(i) shows such a schedule graphically. (The shape of the curve will be discussed shortly.)

Average product (*AP*) is the total product per unit of the variable factor, labor. The number of units of labor is denoted by *L*.

$$AP = \frac{TP}{L}$$

Notice in column 3 of Table 10-1 that as more of the variable factor is used, average product first rises and then falls. The level of output where average product reaches a maximum (34 units in the example) is called the **point of diminishing average productivity.**

Marginal product (*MP*), sometimes called **incremental product,** or **marginal physical product (*MPP*),** is the change in total product resulting from the use of one unit more of the variable factor. [13]

$$MP = \frac{\Delta TP}{\Delta L}$$

Computed values of marginal product are shown in column 4 of Table 10-1.[2] The figures in this column are placed between the other lines of the table to stress that the concept refers to the *change* in output caused by the *change* in quantity of the variable factor. For example, the increase in labor from 3 to 4 units ($\Delta L = 1$) raises output by 12 from 48 to 60 ($\Delta TP = 12$). Thus the *MP* equals 12, and it is recorded between 3 and 4 units of labor. Note that the *MP* in the example rises and then falls. The level of output at which marginal product reaches a maximum is called the **point of diminishing marginal productivity.**

Figure 10-1(ii) plots average product and marginal product curves. Although three different schedules are shown in Table 10-1 and three different curves are shown in Figure 10-1, they are all aspects of the same single relationship that is described by the production function. As we vary the quantity of labor, with capital fixed, output changes. Sometimes it is interesting to look at total output, sometimes at

---

[2] Δ is read "change in." For example ΔL is read "change in quantity of labor."

the average output, and sometimes at the marginal change in output.

Finally, bear in mind that the schedules of Table 10-1 and the curves of Figure 10-1 all assume a specified quantity of the fixed factor. If the quantity of capital had been, say, 6 or 10 instead of the 4 units that were assumed, there would be a different set of total product, average product, and marginal product curves. The reason for this is that if any specified amount of labor has more capital to work with, it can produce more output, that is, its total product will be greater.

The Shape of Marginal Product and Average Product Curves

The Hypothesis of Diminishing Returns

The variations in output that result from applying more or less of a variable factor to a given quantity of a fixed factor are the subject of a famous economic hypothesis. Usually it is called the **hypothesis of diminishing returns** (it is sometimes also called the *law of diminishing returns* or the *law of variable proportions*).

The hypothesis of diminishing returns states that if increasing amounts of a variable factor are applied to a given amount of a fixed factor, eventually a situation will be reached in which each additional unit of the variable factor adds less to total product than did the previous unit.

The common sense of diminishing marginal product is that the fixed factor limits the amount of additional output that can be realized by adding more of the variable factor. The hypothesis of diminishing returns predicts only that sooner or later the marginal product will decline. It is conceivable that marginal product might diminish from the outset, so that the first unit of labor contributes most to total production and each successive unit contributes less than the previous unit. (This is the case in what is known as the Cobb-Douglas production function.)

It is also possible for the marginal product to rise

at first and decline later. Thus, what is called the law of diminishing marginal returns might more accurately be described as the law of *eventually* diminishing marginal returns. The reason for such a rise and decline is clear when seen in the context of the organization of production.

Consider the use of a variable number of workers in a manufacturing operation. If there is only one worker, that worker must do all the tasks, shifting from one to another and becoming competent in each. As a second, third, and subsequent workers are added, it is often possible to break the tasks into a large number of separate jobs, with each laborer specializing in one job and becoming expert at it. This process, as we noted in Chapter 1, is called the *division of labor*. If additional workers permit more and more efficient divisions of labor, marginal product will rise. But (according to the hypothesis of diminishing returns) the scope for such economies must eventually disappear and sooner or later the marginal products of additional workers must decline. When this happens, each additional worker will increase total output by less than the previous worker increased it. This sort of case, where marginal product rises at first and then declines, is illustrated in Figure 10-1.

Eventually, marginal product may reach zero and become negative. It is not hard to see why, when you consider the extreme case where there are so many workers in a limited space that additional workers simply get in the way.

The hypothesis is usually described in terms of diminishing marginal returns, but it can equally well be stated in terms of diminishing average returns. The law of diminishing *average* returns states that if increasing quantities of a variable factor are applied to a given quantity of fixed factors, the average product of the variable factor will eventually decrease. [14]

The Significance of the Hypothesis of Diminishing Returns

Empirical confirmation of both diminishing marginal and diminishing average returns occurs frequently. Some examples are illustrated in Box 10-1.

BOX 10-1

Diminishing Returns

The law of diminishing returns applies in a wide range of circumstances. Here are three examples.

When Southern California Edison was required to modify its Mojave power plant to reduce the amount of fly ash emitted into the atmosphere, it discovered that a series of filters applied to the smokestacks could do the job. A single filter eliminated half the discharge. Five filters in series reduced the fly ash discharge to the 3 percent allowed by law. When a state senator proposed a new standard that would permit no more than 1 percent fly ash emission, the company brought in experts who testified that such a requirement would require at least 15 filters per stack and would triple the cost.

Idaho's Salmon River, a noted sport fishing river, has become the center of a thriving, well-promoted tourist trade. As the fishing pressure in the Salmon River has increased, the total number of fish caught has steadily increased, but the number of fish per person fishing has decreased and the average hours fished for each fish caught has increased.

Gallup, Roper, and all other pollsters, as well as all students of statistics, know that you can use a sample to estimate characteristics of a very large population. Even a relatively small sample can provide a useful estimate—at a tiny fraction of the cost of a complete enumeration of the population. However, sample estimates are subject to sampling error. If, for example, 38 percent of a sample approves of a certain policy, the percentage of the population that approves of it is likely to be close to 38 percent, but it might well be anywhere from 36 to 40 percent. The theory of statistics shows that the size of the expected sampling error can always be reduced by increasing the sample size. The 4 percent interval (in the example above) could be cut in half—to 2 percent—by *quadrupling* the sample size. That is, if the original sample had been 400, a new sample of 1,600 would halve the expected error. To reduce the interval to 1 percent, the new sample would have to be quadrupled again—to 6,400. In other words, increasing the sample size yields diminishing marginal returns in terms of accuracy.

One might wish that it were not so. There would then be no reason to fear that the world population explosion will bring with it a food crisis. If the marginal product of additional workers applied to a fixed quantity of land were constant, world food production could be expanded in proportion to the population merely by keeping a constant fraction of the population on farms. But with fixed techniques, diminishing returns dictate an inexorable decline in the marginal product of each additional laborer because an expanding population has a fixed world supply of agricultural land.

Thus, unless there is a continual improvement in the techniques of production, continuous population growth will bring with it, according to the hypothesis of diminishing returns, declining average living standards and eventually widespread famine. This gloomy prediction of the nineteenth century English economist Thomas Malthus is discussed further in Box 11-1 on page 199.

The Relation Between Marginal and Average Curves

Notice that in Figure 10-1(ii) the *MP* curve cuts the *AP* curve at the *AP*'s maximum point. Although the relation between marginal and average curves is a mathematical one and not a matter of economics, it is important to understand how these curves are related. [15]

The average product curve slopes upward as long as the marginal product curve is above it; it makes no difference whether the marginal product curve is itself sloping upward or downward. The common sense of this relation is that if an additional worker is to raise the average product of all workers, his or her output must be greater than the average output of all other workers. It is immaterial whether the new worker's contribution to output is greater or less than the contribution of the worker hired immediately before; all that matters is that his or her

BOX 10-2

Pete Rose's Batting Statistics

The relationship between the concepts of marginal and average measures is very general. An illuminating example comes from the *Baseball Encyclopedia*. The table below gives the average batting percentage, that is, number of hits (output) divided by official times at bat (input), of Pete Rose over his illustrious career in the National League, during which he has set all kinds of batting records. For each year column 1 gives his lifetime batting percentage as of opening day of that season. Column 2 gives his batting percentage during the year. Column 3 gives his lifetime batting percentage at the end of the season; this of course, is also the entry in column 1 for the next year.

The columns of the table provide an interesting example of the general relationship between average and marginal values: *whenever his performance dur-*

ing a season is better than his lifetime average at the start of the season, his lifetime average rises. For example, in the years 1975, 1976, and 1977, Rose raised his lifetime batting average because each was an above-average year. *Whenever his performance during a season is worse than his lifetime average at the start of the season, his lifetime average falls.* For example, during the 1971, 1974, and 1980 seasons his performance was below his lifetime average going into those seasons, and hence in each case his lifetime average fell.

If the average is to rise, all that matters is that the marginal is above the average; if the average is to fall, all that matters is that the marginal is below the average.

Pete Rose's Batting Record*

Year	(Old average) Lifetime batting percentage at start of season	(Marginal) Batting percentage during season	(New average) Lifetime batting percentage at end of season
1963	0.0000	0.2729	0.2729
1964	0.2729	0.2694	0.2713
1965	0.2713	0.3119	0.2863
1966	0.2863	0.3135	0.2935
1967	0.2935	0.3009	0.2949
1968	0.2949	0.3355	0.3019
1969	0.3019	0.3477	0.3085
1970	0.3085	0.3159	0.3095
1971	0.3095	0.3038	0.3088
1972	0.3088	0.3070	0.3087
1973	0.3087	0.3382	0.3116
1974	0.3116	0.2837	0.3092
1975	0.3092	0.3172	0.3098
1976	0.3098	0.3233	0.3108
1977	0.3108	0.3115	0.3109
1978	0.3109	0.3023	0.3103
1979	0.3103	0.3312	0.3115
1980	0.3115	0.2824	0.3099
1981	0.3099	0.3248	0.3104
1982	0.3104	0.2713	0.3084
1983	0.3084	0.2454	0.3061
1984	0.3061	0.2830	0.3054
1985	0.3054	0.2642	0.3042

* Baseball fans will note that in order to allow changes in lifetime percentages to show up in all cases, the figures are reported to four decimal places, rather than the customary three.

contribution to output exceeds the average output of *all* workers hired previously. (The relation between marginal and average measures is further illustrated in Box 10-2.)

Short-Run Variations in Cost

We now shift our attention from the firm's production function to its costs. We consider firms that are not in a position to influence the prices of the inputs they employ. These firms must pay the going market price for all inputs.[3] Given these prices and the physical returns summarized by the product curves, the costs of different levels of output can be calculated.

Cost Concepts Defined

The following brief definitions of several cost concepts are closely related to the product concepts just introduced.

[3] The important problems that arise when the firm is in a position to influence the prices it pays for its factors of production are considered in Chapter 20.

Total cost (*TC*) is the total cost of producing any given level of output. Total cost is divided into two parts, **total fixed costs (*TFC*)** and **total variable costs (*TVC*)**. A **fixed cost** is one that does not vary with output; it will be the same if output is 1 unit or 1 million units. Such a cost is also referred to as an *overhead cost* or *unavoidable cost*. A cost that varies directly with output, rising as more is produced and falling as less is produced, is called a **variable cost** (also a *direct* or *avoidable cost*). In the example of Table 10-1, since labor was the variable factor of production, the wage bill is a variable cost.

Average total cost (*ATC*), also called **average cost (*AC*),** is the total cost of producing any given output divided by that output. Average total cost may be divided into **average fixed costs (*AFC*)** and **average variable costs (*AVC*)** in the same way that total costs were.

Although average *variable* costs may rise or fall as production is increased (depending on whether output rises more rapidly or more slowly than total variable costs), it is clear that average *fixed* costs decline continuously as output increases. A doubling of output always leads to a halving of fixed costs per

TABLE 10-2   Variation of Costs with Capital Fixed and Labor Variable

(1) Labor (L)	(2) Output (q)	Total cost ($)			Marginal cost ($ per unit) (6) (MC)	Average cost ($ per unit)		
		(3) Fixed (TFC)	(4) Variable (TVC)	(5) Total (TC)		(7) Fixed (AFC)	(8) Variable (AVC)	(9) Total (ATC)
0	0	100	0	100		—	—	—
					0.67			
1	15	100	10	110		6.67	0.67	7.33
					0.53			
2	34	100	20	120		2.94	0.59	3.53
					0.71			
3	48	100	30	130		2.08	0.62	2.71
					0.83			
4	60	100	40	140		1.67	0.67	2.33
					5.00			
5	62	100	50	150		1.61	0.81	2.42

The relation of cost to level of output can be looked at in several different ways. These cost schedules are computed from the product curves of Table 10-1, given the price of capital of $25 per unit and the price of labor of $10 per unit. Marginal cost (in column 6) is shown between the lines of total cost because it refers to the *change* in cost divided by the *change* in output that brought it about. For example, the *MC* of $.71 is the $10 increase in total cost (from $120 to $130) divided by the 14-unit increase in output (from 34 to 48). In constructing a graph, marginal costs should be plotted midway in the interval over which they are computed. The *MC* of $.71 would be plotted at output 41.

unit of output. This is a process popularly known as *spreading one's overhead.*

Marginal cost (MC), sometimes called **incremental cost,** is the increase in total cost resulting from raising the rate of production by one unit. Because fixed costs do not vary with output, marginal fixed costs are always zero. Therefore marginal costs are necessarily marginal variable costs, and a change in fixed costs will leave marginal costs unaffected. For example, the marginal cost of producing a few more potatoes by farming a given amount of land more intensively is the same, whatever the rent paid for the land. **[16]**

Short-Run Cost Curves

Take the production relationships in Table 10-1. Assume that the price of labor is $10 per unit and the price of capital is $25 per unit. The cost schedules for these values are shown in Table 10-2 on page 185.[4]

Figure 10-2 plots cost curves that are similar in shape to those arising from the data in Table 10-2. Notice that the marginal cost curve cuts the average total cost curve and the average variable cost curve at their lowest points. This is another example of the relation (discussed above) between a marginal and an average curve. The *ATC* curve, for example, slopes downward as long as the *MC* curve is below it; it makes no difference whether the *MC* curve is itself sloping upward or downward.

Short-run average variable cost. In Figure 10-2 the average variable cost curve reaches a minimum and then rises. With fixed factor prices, when average product per worker is a maximum, average variable cost is a minimum. **[17]** The common sense of this proposition is that each additional worker adds the same amount to cost but a different amount to output, and when output per worker is rising, the cost per unit of output must be falling and vice versa.

The hypothesis of eventually diminishing average productivity implies eventually increasing average variable costs.

[4] If you do not see where any of the numbers come from, review Table 10-1 and the definitions of cost just given.

FIGURE 10-2   Total Cost, Average Cost, and Marginal Cost Curves

(i) Total cost curves

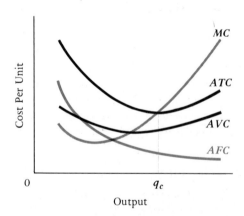

(ii) Marginal and average cost curves

Total cost (TC), average cost (AC), and marginal cost (MC) curves often have the shapes shown here. (i) Total fixed cost does not vary with output. Total variable cost and the total of all costs ($TC = TVC + TFC$) rise with output, first at a decreasing rate, then at an increasing rate. The total cost curves in (i) give rise to the average and marginal curves in (ii). Average fixed cost (*AFC*) declines as output increases. Average variable cost (*AVC*) and average total cost (*ATC*) fall and then rise as output increases. Marginal cost (*MC*) does the same, intersecting *ATC* and *AVC* at their minimum points. Capacity output is q_c, the minimum point on the *ATC* curve.

Short-run average total cost curve.   Short-run ATC curves are often U-shaped. This reflects the assumptions that (1) average productivity is increasing when output is low, but (2) at some level of output average productivity begins to fall fast enough to cause average variable costs to increase faster than average fixed costs fall. When this happens, ATC increases.

Marginal cost curves.   In Figure 10-2(ii) the marginal cost curve is shown as a declining curve that reaches a minimum and then rises. This is the reverse of the usual shape of the marginal product curve as seen in Figure 10-1(ii). The reason for the reversal is as follows. With a fixed price per unit of the variable factor, if extra units of the variable factor produce increasing quantities of output (marginal *product* rising), the cost per unit of extra output must be falling (marginal *cost* falling). If marginal product is falling, marginal cost will be rising. Thus, the hypothesis of eventually diminishing marginal product implies eventually increasing marginal cost. [18]

Total variable cost.   In Figure 10-2(i) total variable cost is shown as a positively sloped curve, indicating that total variable cost rises with the level of output. This is true as long as marginal cost is positive, since the total variable cost of producing any given level of output is just the area under the marginal cost curve up to that level of output. [19]

Definition of Capacity

The output that corresponds to the minimum short-run average total cost is often called by economists and business people the **capacity** of the firm. Capacity in this sense is not an upper limit on what can be produced. Instead, it is the largest output that can be produced without encountering rising average costs per unit. In Figure 10-2(ii) capacity output is q_c units, but higher outputs can be achieved, provided the firm is willing to accept the higher per unit costs that accompany output "above capacity." A firm producing with **excess capacity** is producing at an output smaller than the point of minimum average total cost.

The technical definition gives the word *capacity* a meaning different from that in everyday speech; it is a useful concept that is widely used in economic and business discussions.

A Family of Short-Run Cost Curves

A short-run cost curve shows how costs vary with output for a given quantity of the fixed factor, say, a given size of plant.

There is a different short-run cost curve for each given quantity of the fixed factor.

A small plant for manufacturing nuts and bolts will have its own short-run cost curve. A medium-size plant and a large plant will each have its own short-run cost curve. If a firm expands and replaces its small plant with a medium-size plant, it will move from one short-run cost curve to another. This change from one plant size to another is a long-run change. How short-run cost curves of plants of different size are related to each other is studied in the next chapter.

---

1. The firm's production decisions can be classified into three groups: (a) how best to employ existing plant and equipment—the short run, (b) what new plant and equipment and production processes to select, given the framework of known technical possibilities—the long run, and (c) how to encourage or adapt to technological changes—the very long run.
2. The short run involves decisions in which one or more factors of production are fixed. The long run involves decisions in which all factors are variable but in which technology is given. The very long run involves decisions in which technology can change.

Summary

3. The production function describes the ways in which different inputs may be combined to produce different quantities of output. Short-run and long-run situations can be interpreted as implying different kinds of constraints on the production function. In the short run the firm is constrained to use no more than a given quantity of some fixed factor; in the long run it is constrained only by the available techniques of production.

4. The theory of short-run behavior depends on the productivity of variable factors when combined with fixed factors. The concepts of total, average, and marginal product represent alternative ways of looking at the relation between output and the quantity of the variable factor of production.

5. The hypothesis of diminishing returns asserts that if increasing quantities of a variable factor are combined with a given quantity of fixed factors, the marginal and the average products of the variable factor will eventually decrease. This hypothesis leads directly to implications of eventually rising marginal and average costs.

6. Given physical productivity schedules and the costs per unit of factors, it is a matter of simple arithmetic to develop the whole family of short-run cost curves, one for each quantity of the fixed factor.

7. Short-run average total cost curves are drawn as U-shaped to reflect the expectation that average productivity increases for small outputs but eventually declines sufficiently rapidly to offset advantages of spreading overheads. The output corresponding to the minimum point of a short-run average total cost curve is called the plant's capacity.

Topics for Review

Short run, long run, and very long run
Total product, average product, and marginal product
The hypothesis of diminishing returns
Marginal product curves and average product curves
Relation between productivity and cost
Total cost, marginal cost, and average cost
Short-run cost curves
Capacity and excess capacity

Discussion Questions

1. Is the short run the same number of months for increasing output as for decreasing it? Must the short run in an industry be the same length for all firms in the industry? Under what circumstances might the short run actually involve a longer time span than even the very long run?

2. Use the distinction between long and short run to discuss each of the following.
   a. A guaranteed annual employment contract of at least forty–eight 40-hour weeks of work for all employees
   b. A major economic depression during which there is substantial unemployment of labor and in which equipment is being used at well below capacity levels of production
   c. A speeding up of delivery dates for new easy-to-install equipment
3. Experimenters with chemical fertilizers at the Rothampsted Experimental Station, an agricultural research institute in Hertfordshire, England, in 1921 applied different amounts of a particular fertilizer to 10 apparently identical quarter-acre plots of land. The results for one test, using identical seed grain, are listed in the table. Compute the average and marginal product of fertilizer and identify the (approximate) points of diminishing average and marginal productivity.

Plot	Fertilizer dose	Yield index*
1	15	104.2
2	30	110.4
3	45	118.0
4	60	125.3
5	75	130.2
6	90	132.4
7	105	131.9
8	120	132.3
9	135	132.5
10	150	132.8

*Yield without fertilizer = 100

4. Indicate whether each of the following conforms to the hypothesis of diminishing returns and, if so, whether it refers to marginal or average returns or both.
   a. "The bigger they are, the harder they fall."
   b. As more and more of the population receive smallpox vaccinations, the reduction in the smallpox disease rate for each additional 100,000 vaccinations becomes smaller.
   c. Five workers produce twice as much today as 10 workers did 40 years ago.
5. Consider the education of a human being as a process of production. Regard years of schooling as one variable factor of production. What are the other factors? What factors are fixed? At what point would you expect diminishing returns to set in? For an Einstein, would it set in during his lifetime?
6. Suppose that each of the following news items is correct. Discuss each in terms of its effects on cost. (You will have to decide which concept of cost is most likely to be affected.)

a. The U.S. Office of Education reports that the increasing level of education of our youth has led both to higher productivity and to increases in the general level of wages.

b. During the winter of 1977 many factories were forced by fuel shortages to reduce production and to operate at levels of production far below capacity.

c. NASA reports that the space program has led to development of electronic devices that have brought innovations to many industries.

7. "Because overhead costs are fixed, increasing production lowers costs. Thus small business is sure to be inefficient. This is a dilemma of modern society, which values both smallness *and* efficiency." Discuss.

11

Production and Cost in the Long and Very Long Run

Analyzing the short-run behavior of the firm helps us understand how markets work to allocate resources, but it cannot show us why standards of living have risen over the decades throughout much of the world. Only an analysis of much longer run phenomena can do this. In this chapter we first look at the firm's *long-run* behavior, when it is free to vary all factors of production. Should the firm use a great deal of capital and only a small amount of labor? Should it use less capital and more labor? What do these decisions mean in terms of the firm's costs?

In the second part of the chapter we examine what we have called the *very long run*. Improvements in technology and productivity have dramatically increased output and incomes in the United States during the past 100 years, but recently the rate of increase seems to have slowed. The causes of this rapid growth and the present slowdown are subject to debate. What do we know about them?

The Long Run: No Fixed Factors

In the short run, in which only one factor varies, the only way to produce a given output is to adjust the input of the variable factor until the desired level of output is achieved. Thus, in the short run the firm must make a decision about its desired output, but once it has decided on a rate of output, there is only one technically possible way of achieving it. In the long run, all factors may be varied and so there are multiple technically possible ways to produce output. Thus the firm must decide on a level of output and also on which method to employ. More specifically this means that firms in the long run must choose the nature and amount of plant and equipment.

Long-run planning decisions are important. Today's variable factors are tomorrow's fixed factors. A firm deciding on a new steel mill and the machinery to go into it will choose among many alternatives. But once installed, that equipment is fixed for a long time. If the firm makes a wrong choice now, its survival may be threatened; if it estimates shrewdly, it may reward both owners and farsighted managers with large profits and bonuses.

Long-run decisions are difficult because the firm must anticipate what methods of production will be efficient not only today but in the years ahead, when costs of labor and raw materials may have changed. The decisions are difficult, too, because the firm must estimate how much output it will want to produce. Is the industry of which it is a part growing or declining? Will new products emerge to render its buggy whips less useful than an extrapolation of past sales suggests?

Profit Maximization and Cost Minimization

Any firm that is trying to maximize its profits should in the long run select the method that produces its output at the lowest possible cost. This implication of the hypothesis of profit maximization is called **cost minimization.** From the alternatives open to it, the firm chooses the least costly ways of achieving any specific output.

What can a firm do in the long run to make its costs as low as possible? The firm does not have the least costly method of production if it is possible to substitute one factor for another so as to keep its output constant while reducing its total cost.

Choice of factor mix.   The firm should substitute one factor (for example, capital) for another factor (for example, labor) as long as the marginal product of the one factor *per dollar expended on it* is greater than the marginal product of the other factor *per dollar expended on it*. The firm cannot have minimized its costs as long as these two magnitudes are unequal. Using K to represent capital, L labor, and p the price of a unit of the factor, the necessary condition of cost minimization may be stated:

$$\frac{MP_K}{p_K} = \frac{MP_L}{p_L} \qquad [1]$$

Equation 1 is analogous to the condition for the utility-maximizing household, given on page 133, in which the household equated the marginal utility per dollar of two goods.

Whenever the two sides of Equation 1 are not equal, there are possibilities for factor substitutions that will reduce costs.

To see why this equation needs to be satisfied if costs of production are to be minimized, suppose that the left side of Equation 1 is equal to 10, showing that the last dollar spent on capital added 10 units to output, while the right side is equal to 4, showing that the last dollar spent on labor added only 4 units to output. In such a case the firm, by using $2.50 less of labor, would reduce output by 10 units. But it could regain that lost output by spending $1.00 more on capital.[1] Making such a substitution of capital for labor would leave output unchanged and reduce cost by $1.50. Thus the original position was not the cost-minimizing one.

By rearranging terms in Equation 1 we can look at the cost-minimizing condition a bit differently.

$$\frac{MP_K}{MP_L} = \frac{p_K}{p_L} \qquad [2]$$

The ratio of the marginal products on the left side compares the contribution to output of the last unit of capital and the last unit of labor. If the ratio is 4, this means one unit more of capital will add 4 times as much to output as one unit more of labor. The right side of the equation shows how the cost of one unit more of capital compares to the cost of one unit more of labor. If it is also 4, it does not pay the firm to substitute capital for labor or vice versa. But suppose the right side is 2. Capital, although twice as expensive, is four times as productive. It will pay the firm to switch to a method of production that uses more capital and less labor. If, however, the right side is 6 (or *any* number more than 4), it will pay to substitute labor for capital.

How much should inputs be changed?   We have seen that when the ratio MP_K/MP_L is 4, while the ratio P_K/P_L prices is 2, the firm will substitute capital for labor. But how far does the firm go in making this substitution? There is a limit because as the firm uses more capital, its marginal product falls, while as it uses less labor, the marginal product of labor rises. Thus the ratio MP_K/MP_L falls. When it reaches

[1] The argument in the previous two sentences assumes that the marginal products do not change when expenditure is changed by a few dollars.

2, the firm need substitute no further. The ratio of the marginal products is equal to the ratio of the prices.[2]

This formulation shows how the firm can adjust the elements over which it has control (the quantities of factors used, and thus the marginal products of the factors) to the prices or opportunity costs of the factors given by the market. A precisely analogous adjustment process is involved when households adjust their consumption of goods to the market prices of those goods (see page 133).

Long-run equilibrium of the firm.   The firm will have achieved long-run equilibrium factor proportions when there is no opportunity for cost-reducing substitutions. This occurs when the marginal product per dollar spent on each factor is the same (Equation 1); or, equivalently, when the ratio of the marginal products of factors is equal to the ratio of their prices (Equation 2).

The Principle of Substitution

Suppose that a firm is producing by a method that meets the cost-minimizing conditions shown in Equations 1 and 2, but that the cost of labor increases while the cost of capital remains unchanged. The least-cost method of producing any output will now use less labor and more capital than was required to produce the same output before the factor prices changed.

Methods of production will change if the relative prices of factors change. Relatively more of the cheaper factor and relatively less of the more expensive one will be used.

This prediction called the **principle of substitution** follows from the assumption that firms minimize their costs.

The principle of substitution plays a central role in resource allocation in a market economy since it

relates to the way the individual firm will respond to changes in relative factor prices that are caused by the changing relative scarcity of factors to the economy as a whole. The individual firm is thus motivated to use less of factors that have become scarcer to the economy.

For example, as construction workers' wages have risen sharply relative to the wages of factory labor and the cost of machinery, many home builders have shifted from on-site construction to panelization. Panelization is a method of building standardized modules with wiring, plumbing, insulation, and painting done at the factory. The bulk of the work is performed by machinery and by assembly line workers, whose wages are only half those of on-site construction workers.

Consider another example. One country has a great deal of land and a small population. The price of land will be low, and, because labor is in short supply, the wage rate will be high. Producers of agricultural goods will tend to make lavish use of the cheap land while economizing on expensive labor; thus a production process will be adopted that utilizes a low ratio of labor to land. Suppose a second country is small in area and has a large population. Here the demand for land will be high relative to its supply, and land will be relatively expensive while labor will be relatively cheap. Firms producing agricultural goods will tend to economize on land by using a great deal of labor per unit of land; thus, a productive process will be adopted that uses a high ratio of labor to land.

Once again we see the price system functioning as an automatic control system. No single firm needs to be aware of national factor surpluses and scarcities. These are, however, reflected by market prices, so individual firms that never look beyond their own private profit are led to economize on factors that are scarce to the nation as a whole.

This discussion suggests why methods of producing the same commodity differ among countries. In the United States, where labor is highly skilled and expensive, a large-scale farmer may use elaborate machinery to economize on labor. In China, where labor is abundant and capital scarce, a much less mechanized method of production is appropriate.

[2] The appendix to this chapter provides a graphic analysis of this condition, which is similar to the analysis of household behavior in Chapter 8.

The Western engineer who believes that the Chinese lag behind Westerners because they are using methods long dismissed in the West as inefficient may be missing the truth about economic efficiency in the use of resources. The notion that to aid underdeveloped countries we have only to export Western "know-how" is misleading.

Cost Curves in the Long Run

There is a best (least-cost) method of producing each level of output when all factors are free to be varied. In general, this method will not be the same for different levels of output. If factor prices are given, a minimum achievable cost can be found for each possible level of output; if this cost is expressed as an amount per unit of output, we can obtain the long-run average cost of producing each level of output. When this information is plotted on a graph, the result is called a **long-run average cost (LRAC) curve.** Figure 11-1 shows such a curve.

This cost curve is determined by the technology of the industry (which is assumed to be fixed) and by the prices of the factors of production. It is a "boundary" in the sense that points below the curve are unattainable, points on or above the curve are attainable if sufficient time elapses for all inputs to be adjusted.

The *LRAC* curve divides the cost levels that are attainable with known technology and given factor prices from those that are unattainable.

The Shape of the Long-Run Average Cost Curve

The long-run average cost curve shown in Figure 11-1 first falls and then rises. This curve is often described as U-shaped, although "saucer-shaped" might be more accurate.

Decreasing costs. Over the range of output from zero to q_m the firm has falling long-run average costs. An expansion of output permits a reduction of costs per unit of output. These are referred to as **economies of scale.** (Of course, such economies will be

realized only after enough time has elapsed to allow changes in the methods of production.) Since the prices of factors are assumed to be constant, the reason for the decline in long-run average cost must be that output increases faster than inputs as the scale of the firm's production expands. Over this range of output the firm is often said to enjoy long-run **increasing returns.**[3]

Increasing returns may arise as a result of increased opportunities for specialization of tasks made possible by the division of labor. Adam Smith's classic discussion of this important point is given in Box 3-1 on page 41. Even the most casual observation of the differences in production technique used in large-size and small-size plants shows the greater specialization that larger plants utilize.

These differences arise because large, specialized equipment is useful only when the volume of output that the firm can sell justifies its employment. For example, assembly line techniques, body-stamping machinery, and multiple-boring engine-block machines in automobile production are economically efficient only when individual operations are repeated thousands of times. Using elaborate harvesting equipment (which combines many individual tasks that would otherwise be done by hand and by tractor) provides the least-cost method of production on a big farm but not on a few acres.

Increasing returns may also arise because of substitution of one input for another. Typically, as the level of planned output increases, capital is substituted for labor and complex machines for simpler machines. Robotics is a contemporary example. Electronic devices can handle huge numbers of operations quickly, but unless the level of production requires such a large volume of operations, it does not make sense to use robotics or other forms of automation.

Increasing costs. Over the range of outputs greater than q_m the firm encounters rising costs. An expansion in production, even after sufficient time has elapsed for all adjustments to be made, will be ac-

---

[3] Economists shift back and forth between speaking in physical terms (i.e., *increasing returns* to production) and cost terms (i.e., *decreasing costs* of production).

FIGURE 11-1   A Long-Run Average Cost Curve

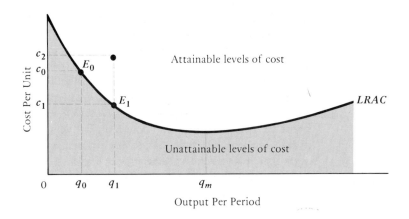

The long-run average cost ($LRAC$) curve provides a boundary between attainable and unattainable levels of cost. If the firm wishes to produce output q_0, the lowest attainable cost level is c_0 per unit. Thus point E_0 is on the $LRAC$ curve. E_1 represents the least-cost method of producing q_1. Suppose a firm is producing at E_0 and desires to increase output to q_1. In the short run it will not be able to vary all factors, and thus costs above c_1, say, c_2, must be accepted. In the long run a plant optimal for output q_1 can be built and cost of c_1 can be attained. At output q_m the firm attains its lowest possible per unit cost of production for the given technology and factor prices.

companied by a rise in average costs per unit of output. If costs per unit of input are constant, this rise in costs must be the result of an expansion in output less than in proportion to the expansion in inputs. Such a firm is said to suffer long-run **decreasing returns.**[4] Decreasing returns imply that the firm suffers some diseconomy of scale. As its scale of operations increases, diseconomies, say, of management, are encountered that increase its per unit costs of production.

Constant returns. In Figure 11-1 the firm's long-run average costs fall to output q_m and rise thereafter. Another possibility should be noted. The firm's $LRAC$ curve might have a flat portion over a range of output around q_m. With such a flat portion, the firm would be encountering constant costs over the relevant range of output. This would mean that the firm's long-run average costs per unit of output do not change as its output changes. Since factor

prices are assumed to be fixed, this must mean that the firm's output is increasing exactly as fast as its inputs are increasing. Such a firm is said to be encountering **constant returns.**

Relation Between Long-Run and Short-Run Costs

The various short-run cost curves mentioned at the conclusion of Chapter 10 and the long-run curve studied in this chapter are all derived from the same production function. Each assumes given prices for all factor inputs. In the long run all factors can be varied; in the short run some must remain fixed. The long-run average cost ($LRAC$) curve shows the lowest cost of producing any output when all factors are variable. The short-run average cost ($SRAC$) curve shows the lowest cost of producing any output when one or more factors are not free to vary.

The short-run cost curve cannot fall below the long-run curve because the $LRAC$ curve represent the *lowest* attainable costs for every output. It might be the same curve if precisely the same size plant was the best for any level of output, but that is not likely. The usual situation is that as the level of output is changed, a different size plant is required to achieve the lowest attainable costs. This is shown in Figure

[4] Long-run decreasing returns differ from the short-run diminishing returns. In the short run, at least one factor is fixed, and the law of diminishing returns ensures that returns to the variable factor will eventually diminish. In the long run all factors are variable, and it is possible that physically diminishing returns would never be encountered—at least as long as it was genuinely possible to increase inputs of all factors.

FIGURE 11-2   Long-Run Average Cost and Short-Run Average Cost Curves

The short-run average cost (*SRAC*) curve is tangent to the long-run average cost (*LRAC*) curve at the output for which the quantity of the fixed factors is optimal. If output is varied around q_0 units with plant and equipment fixed at the optimal level for producing q_0, costs will follow the short-run cost curve. Whereas *SRAC* and *LRAC* are at the same level for output q_0 where the fixed plant is optimal for that level, for all other outputs there is too little or too much plant and equipment and *SRAC* lies above *LRAC*. If some output other than q_0 is to be sustained, costs can be reduced to the level of the long-run curve when sufficient time has elapsed to adjust the plant and equipment.

11-2, where the *SRAC* curve lies above the *LRAC* curve at all outputs except q_0.

We saw in Chapter 10 that an *SRAC* curve such as that in Figure 11-2 is one of many such curves. Each curve shows how costs vary as output is varied from a base output, holding some factors fixed at the quantities most appropriate to the base output. Figure 11-3 shows a family of short-run average cost curves, along with a single long-run average cost curve. The long-run curve is sometimes called an **envelope curve** because it encloses the whole family of short-run curves. Each short-run cost curve is tangent to (touches) the long-run curve at the level of output for which the quantity of the fixed factor is optimal and lies above it for all other levels of output.

Shifts in Cost Curves

The cost curves derived so far show how cost varies with output, given constant factor prices and fixed

technology. Changes in either technological knowledge or factor prices will cause the entire family of short-run and long-run cost curves to shift. Loss of existing technological knowledge is rare, so technological change normally works in only one direction, to shift cost curves downward. Improved ways of making existing commodities will mean that lower-cost methods of production become available. (Technological change is discussed in more detail in the next section of this chapter.)

Factor price changes can exert an influence in either direction. If a firm has to pay more for any factor that it uses, the cost of producing each level of output will rise; if the firm has to pay less, costs will fall.

A rise in factor prices shifts the family of short-run and long-run cost curves upward. A fall in factor prices or a technological advance shifts the entire family of cost curves downward.

Although factor prices usually change gradually, they sometimes change suddenly and drastically. For example, in the mid 1980s oil prices fell dramatically; the effect was to shift downward the cost curves of all users of oil and oil related products.

The Very Long Run

In the long run the nation's producers are assumed to do the best they can to produce known products with the techniques and the resources currently available. The best they can do is to be on, rather than above, their long-run cost curves. *In the very long run the techniques and resources that are available change.* Such changes cause shifts in long-run cost curves. These, along with the development of new products, are major sources of economic growth, the long-run rise in output that accounts for rising living standards.

The decrease in cost levels that can be achieved by choosing wisely among available factors of production, known techniques, and alternative levels of output is necessarily limited, since a firm can never do better in the long run than select the best available technique. But improvements by invention and innovation are potentially limitless. For this reason,

FIGURE 11-3   The Envelope Relation Between the Long-Run Average Cost Curve and All the Short-Run Average Cost Curves

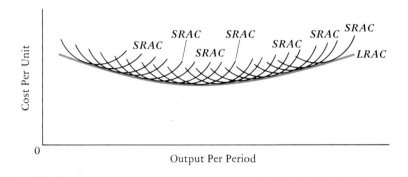

To every point on the long-run average cost (*LRAC*) curve there is an associated short-run average cost (*SRAC*) curve tangent at that point. Each short-run curve shows how costs vary if output varies, with the fixed factor held constant at the level that is optimal for the output at the point of tangency.

---

the long-term struggle to get ever more from the world's limited resources is critically linked to technological change.

Kinds of Technological Change

Three kinds of change tend to dominate production and cost in the very long run. All are related to technology, broadly defined.

New techniques.   Over an average lifetime in the twentieth century, changes in the techniques available for producing existing products have been dramatic. About the same amount of coal is produced today as 50 years ago, but the number of coal miners is less than one-tenth of what it was then. Seventy years ago roads and railways were built by gangs of workers using buckets, spades, and draft horses. Today bulldozers, steam shovels, giant trucks, and other specialized equipment have completely banished the workhorse from construction sites and to a great extent have displaced the pick-and-shovel worker. Generally, capital has been substituted for labor.

New products.   Changes in available goods and services are constantly occurring. Television, polio vaccine, nylon, and many current consumer products did not exist two generations ago. Other products are so changed that the only connection they have with the "same" commodity produced in the past is

the name. A 1986 Ford automobile is very different from a 1936 Ford. It is even different from a 1976 Ford in size, safety, and gasoline consumption. Modern jets are revolutionary compared with the DC-3, which itself barely resembled Lindbergh's *Spirit of St. Louis.*

Improved inputs.   Improvements in such intangibles as health and education raise the quality of labor services. Today's workers and managers are healthier and better educated than their grandparents. Even unskilled workers today tend to be literate and competent in arithmetic, and their managers are apt to be trained in modern scientific methods of business control and computer science.

Similarly, improvements in raw materials occur. For example, the type and quality of metals has changed. Steel replaces iron, and aluminum substitutes for steel in a process of change that makes a statistical category such as "primary metals" seem unsatisfactory and obsolete. Even for a given category, say, steel, today's product is lighter, stronger, and more flexible than the product manufactured only 15 years ago.

Sources of Technological Change

To measure the extent of technological change, economists utilize the notion of **productivity,** defined as a measure of output per unit of resource input. One widely used measure of productivity is output *per hour of labor*.[5] The rate of increase in productivity provides a measure of the progress caused by technical change. The concept of productivity highlights society's ability to get more and better output from the basic resources of the economy. The significance of such changes is further explored in Box 11-1.

Productivity is increased by anything that increases output while maintaining the number of hours worked or that decreases the hours required to attain the same output. Here are some of the major historical sources of productivity increase.

Substitution of Capital for Labor

In manufacturing, transportation, communications, mining, and agriculture, capital has been substituted for labor to a major extent. This substitution can be measured by the **capital-labor ratio,** which determines changes in the amount of capital per worker. The capital-labor ratio increased steadily over the 100 years from 1870 to 1970.

Three reasons for this substitution can be identified. First, the price of labor rose relative to capital goods. As predicted by the principle of substitution, this led to the use of more capital and less labor. Second, more productive machines were developed to replace older ones. Third, the opportunity provided by both population growth and growth in demand enabled businesses to produce larger outputs by using more capital, thereby taking advantage of economies of scale.

Energy Substitution

Related to the substitution of capital for labor has been the increasing reliance on inanimate energy for production. Energy to plow fields, to turn machines, to move goods, to provide heat, and to transform natural resources is a major determinant of the productive power of an economy. In 1900 more than half of all energy requirements in the United States was supplied by human beings, horses, mules, and

oxen. By 1985 human and animal power provided less than 10 percent of all energy; they have been replaced by coal, oil, gas, nuclear, and water power.

Invention and Innovation

Invention is the discovery of something new, such as a production technique or a product. **Innovation** is the introduction of an invention into use. Invention is thus a necessary precondition to innovation.

Invention is cumulative in effect. A useful invention is adopted, a useless one discarded. The cumulative impact of many small, useful devices and techniques may be fully as great or greater than the impact of the occasional dramatic mechanism such as the steam engine, the cotton gin, or the sewing machine. Indeed, none of these famous inventions represented a single act of creative inspiration. Each depended on the contributions of prior inventors. The backlog of past inventions constitutes society's technical knowledge and in turn that backlog feeds innovation.

Innovation depends upon a steady supply of new inventions. However, new methods, machines, materials, and products do not come into use simply "because they are there." They are introduced if and when it appears *profitable* to do so.

The Endogenous Nature of Technical Change

Technical change was once thought to be mainly a random process, brought about by inventions made by crackpots and mad scientists working in garages or basements. We now know better.

Changes in technology are to a major degree *endogenous* responses to changing economic signals, that is, they are responses to the same things that induce the substitution of one factor for another with a given technology. In our discussion of long-run demand curves in Chapter 5, we looked at just such technological changes in response to rising relative prices when we spoke of the development of smaller, more fuel-efficient cars in the wake of rising gasoline prices. Similarly, much of the move to substitute capital for labor in American industry in response to rising wage rates has taken the form of developing labor-saving methods of production.

---

[5] This is the measure we shall use. Other possible measures include output *per worker*, output *per person*, and output *per unit of inputs*, measured by an index number.

BOX 11-1

The Significance of Productivity Growth

Economics used to be known as the dismal science because some of its predictions were dismal. Malthus and other classical economists predicted that the pressure of more and more people on the world's limited resources would cause a decline in output per person. Human history would see more and more people living less and less well, with the surplus population that could not be supported dying off from hunger and disease.

This prediction has proven wrong for the industrial countries for two main reasons. First, the population has not expanded as rapidly as forseen by early economists writing before birth control techniques were widely used. Second, pure knowledge and its applied techniques have expanded so rapidly during the last 150 years that our ability to squeeze more out of limited resources has expanded faster than the population, that is, we have experienced growth in productivity.

Growth in productivity permits increases in output per person and thus contributes to rising standards of living.

Productivity increases are a powerful force for increasing living standards. Our great-grandparents would have regarded today's standard of living in most industrialized countries as unattainable. An apparently modest rate of increase in productivity of 2.5 percent per year leads to a doubling of output per hour of labor every 28 years. Productivity in the United States increased at at least such a rate from 1900 to 1965.

In other countries growth rates have been even higher. Since World War II productivity in Germany has increased at 5 percent per year, doubling output every 14 years. In Japan it has increased at more than 9 percent per year, a rate that doubles output per hour of labor approximately every 8 years! In many countries, including the United States, productivity growth at a stable rate came to be taken for granted as an automatic source of ever-increasing living standards.

Then, after 1965, productivity increases dropped sharply below their historical trends. This slowdown happened worldwide to some degree, but was particularly acute in the United States and Canada. Indeed, from 1977 to 1982 American non-agricultural productivity did not increase at all. Since 1982 productivity growth has resumed at about 2 percent per year. It remains to be seen whether the 1965 to 1982 slowdown was a one-time occurrence or whether the accustomed doubling every generation is a thing of the past.

It matters a great deal. A permanent slowdown in productivity growth would have severe consequences. Lower productivity growth combined with a stable level of employment leads to a lower rate of increase of real output. Combined with declining employment, it may actually contribute to declining output per person. Declining productivity growth surely means that living standards rise more slowly or actually decline.

Decreases in rates of productivity growth also contribute to inflation. For example, if productivity increases at 3 percent per year, all factor prices, and profits, too, can increase 3 percent per year on average without leading to product price increases. But factor price increases in excess of productivity growth become inflationary. Thus lower rates of productivity growth make a given rate of factor price increases more inflationary.

Even invention can frequently be produced on demand. The development of the atomic bomb in the 1940s is a very dramatic example of this fact. Money can buy invention. Major changes in the store of technical knowledge are often the result of expenditures on research and development (R&D). In the United States in 1986 about $100 billion was devoted to such expenditures, of which roughly 40 percent was expended by the federal government, 40 percent by private firms, and the rest by universities and other research institutions.

Current evidence indicates that productivity

growth is to a significant degree a response to investment in research. Those countries, particularly Germany and Japan, that have stepped up R&D expenditures have experienced much higher levels of productivity growth than those countries (the United States, Canada, and the United Kingdom) that have let such expenditures lag. Similarly, industries that are major research and development spenders (chemicals, electrical equipment, air transport) have maintained productivity growth at a much higher level than industries that do little research (steel and construction). Some sectors that do little research, such as coal mining and farming, may buy their equipment, fertilizer, and seed from industries that do a great deal and thus achieve gains in productivity. These sectors buy invention and innovation through the price they pay for inputs.

Innovation has an unmistakably endogenous component, rising as profit incentives increase, declining as they fall. Profit incentives in turn are affected by many aspects of the economic climate, among them the rate of growth of the economy, the level of capacity utilization, the cost and availability of money for investment, and all sorts of government policies from taxes to regulations.

Lessons from the Decline in Productivity Growth

Productivity growth slackened sharply between 1965 and 1980, as Table 11-1 shows. Not surprisingly, this episode raised the specter of a permanent or at least long-lasting condition. Such a gloomy conclusion is not warranted, as the partial recovery since 1980 shows, but important lessons have been learned from the intensive study of the causes of the slowdown.[6] Here are the principal ones.

[6] There is a parallel here to the impact of the Great Depression on the analysis of the causes of persistent unemployment. The nightmare of permanent depression and unemployment was the stimulus to Keynes' *General Theory* and thus to what we now call macroeconomics. The nightmare of an economy without growth has stimulated renewed attention to the causes and stimuli to greater growth.

TABLE 11-1 Productivity Increases in the United States, 1950-1984 *(annual percentage rate of change of output per hour)*

	Farm productivity	Non-farm productivity	Total business sector productivity
1950–1955	6.47	2.20	2.96
1955–1960	7.31	1.69	2.26
1960–1965	7.04	3.34	3.73
1950–1965	6.94	2.41	2.98
1965–1970	4.88	1.52	1.94
1970–1975	6.16	1.78	1.88
1975–1980	4.70	0.73	0.87
1980–1984	3.80	1.95	2.01
1965–1984	4.94	1.47	1.66
1950–1984	5.82	1.88	2.24

Source: Economic Report of The President, Handbook of Labor Statistics.

The historical rate of growth of productivity of about 3 percent per year has declined sharply since 1965. Growth in output per hour declined from about 3 percent per year from 1950 to 1965 to only about 1.7 percent per year over the next 19 years. The late 1970s showed the sharpest decline. Farm productivity has been increasing much more rapidly than non-farm, a fact whose consequences were discussed in Chapter 6.

Exhaustion of growth opportunities. It is easier to grow from a low base than from a high one. When a country starts to industrialize, labor is generally employed in labor-intensive, low-productivity industries. This starting point gives great scope for developing capital-intensive industries and shifting labor into them. As the shift happens, productivity rises. But as a country becomes industrialized, there is less scope for further gains since much less labor is left working with little capital. Thus the opportunities for labor-saving technological changes diminish.

Similarly, the opportunities for improving labor skills may diminish. Over the last 100 years the level of "human capital" investment in the health, training, and education of the population and, consequently, in the work force has steadily increased, contributing to increases in the productivity of labor.

Are these human investment opportunities being exhausted? It is true that most of the population of the United States is now literate and many debilitating diseases have been brought under control. But the opportunities for further education and training, in computer use, for example, still seem large.

Abundance of energy. Cheap energy fueled American productivity growth for a century. As we shall see in Chapter 15, OPEC changed that situation abruptly in the early 1970s. Energy, instead of being plentiful and cheap, became scarce and expensive. Just as falling energy costs meant rising productivity, rising energy costs slowed productivity increases. Now that energy costs are again falling, productivity is rising. Rapid growth depends upon maintaining, finding, or developing cheap fuels.

Demographic changes. Growth is easier with a moderately growing population than with a static or declining one. The end of the postwar baby boom is one of a number of forces currently adversely affecting growth in output. When relatively few industries and firms are expanding, less investment will take place and firms will tend to stick with the plant and equipment in place. A growing industry often has profitable opportunities for investment in additional machines as well as machines geared to a larger scale of output. Every time a firm seeks new invest-

ment, it is likely to look at the latest, most modern technology available. The introduction of that new technology leads to productivity increases.

Similarly, an economy that has stopped growing cannot adapt easily to the changing skill requirements of its labor force. It is much harder to retrain existing workers than to educate and train new entrants into the labor force with the new skills they will need. Moreover, the lack of new occupations and the promotion opportunities that growth generates may discourage young people from acquiring the fresh skills needed for productivity growth.

Changes in the composition of the labor force also affect growth. One of the dramatic demographic and sociological shifts of the last two decades has been the remarkable change in the size and composition of the labor force. Not only has the baby boom generation come of age, with a consequent growth in the labor force from 70 million in 1960 to 114 million in 1984, but women have entered the labor force in ever-increasing numbers. Between 1960 and 1984 the percentage of the labor force consisting of females 20 years old or older increased from 30 percent to 40 percent. The growth in the labor force has lowered the capital-labor ratio and thus tended to decrease productivity.

Shifts in the composition of output. Industries and sectors of the economy differ greatly from one another in what is called their *technological base*, that is, in the opportunities they provide for high and growing productivity. Shifts in the composition of output can decrease productivity in two distinct ways: first, by shifting labor from high productivity to low productivity uses and, second, by shifting output from industries where productivity is increasing rapidly to ones where it is growing only slowly. Both kinds of shift have occurred in recent decades in the United States.

There has been a major shift from manufacturing (high productivity) to services (lower productivity). Many of the commodities we consume in increasing amounts have a low technological base and low productivity. These include items such as fast-food hamburgers and services designed to provide such amenities as garbage collection, clean air, police protection, and libraries. In the same way demands for safety and for medical and hospital care have increased relative to demands for copper, manufactured goods, and transportation. The resulting shifts of labor from sectors with relatively high levels of productivity (largely due to lots of capital per worker) to those with much lower levels has automatically decreased average productivity. This has nothing to do with the skill or dedication of the librarian compared with the factory worker: it is related to the nature of their tasks and the tools at their disposal. In the librarian's production of services, there is no counterpart to the highly automated assembly line where automobiles are produced.

Moreover, many of the sectors to which output is being shifted, especially services, have lower productivity and lower growth potential than sectors such as agriculture or industries such as airlines, where employment is decreasing. Here, too, it is not a matter of effort or energy. It is much harder for social workers to increase their output (cases handled per year) than it is for airline pilots to increase their output (passenger miles flown per year). All the pilots need are bigger, faster airplanes.

Of course, some of the shifts in output have been to high-productivity, high-growth sectors such as electronics. Indeed, such shifts fueled the recovery of productivity growth in the United States in the mid 1980s.

Institutional climate.   The profits from innovation depend, among other things, on tax laws and regulatory requirements. If innovators are allowed to reap large gains from successful innovations, they will be more likely to take the risks of innovating. Innovation can be encouraged by investment tax credits, strong patent laws, low tax rates, government subsidies, and government-assisted research and development. It can be discouraged by regulatory burdens such as environmental impact statements, safety regulation, and the hassles and delays involved in meeting government requirements.

Many believe that the institutional climate in the United States became increasingly hostile to private innovation in the 1960s and 1970s and that high taxes, government regulation, and economic protec-

tion all added to the forces inhibiting innovation and growth. These factors may partly explain a 20 percent decline in R&D expenditures as a percent of national income between 1965 and 1985.

How Much Productivity Growth Do We Want?

There remains an important question about social values. Progress, as measured by productivity growth, is no longer an unquestioned overriding goal of society. Progress has come to mean growth, and growth has meant industrialization. Applied to the economy as a whole, industrialization and its accompanying changes in productivity have vastly increased our material well-being and permitted ever more people to escape the ravages of hunger and poverty. Clearly, we do not wish to remain permanently an economy whose productivity growth is absent or very low. But not all the slowdown in productivity growth is unwanted. The shift to the provision of services with high income elasticities but low productivity levels is the most obvious example. The population evidently does not want more manufactured goods if it means less police protection, or more food at the cost of less recreation, even though such shifts would increase productivity growth.

Moreover, growth in productivity has often been accompanied by increased pollution and more industrial accidents. Nothing is without its cost. In the case of growth this fact is increasingly being recognized. The gasoline engine, the steel mill, the jet airplane, DDT, plastics, and the skyscraper with its hundreds of thousands of electric lights are the artifacts of our progress over the last century. Many believe that they have lowered the quality of life even while raising the standard of living.

Just as members of a society can benefit (at some stage in economic development) from more luxuries and fewer basic necessities, so, too, may they benefit from more amenities and lower productivity growth. To the extent that they can, a slower rate of productivity growth may reflect a better life, not a worse one.

1. There are no fixed factors in the long run. The profit-maximizing firm chooses, from the alternatives open to it, the least costly way of achieving any specific output. A long-run cost curve represents the boundary between attainable and unattainable levels of cost for the given technology.

2. The principle of substitution says that efficient production will substitute cheaper factors for more expensive ones. If the relative prices of factors change, relatively more of cheaper factors and relatively less of more expensive ones will be used.

3. The shape of the long-run cost curve depends on the relationship of inputs to outputs as the whole scale of a firm's operations changes. Increasing, constant, and decreasing returns lead to decreasing, constant, and increasing long-run average costs.

4. The long-run and short-run cost curves are related. Every long-run cost corresponds to *some* quantity of each factor and is thus on some short-run cost curve. The short-run cost curve shows how costs vary when that particular quantity of a fixed factor is used to produce outputs greater than or less than that for which it is optimal.

5. Cost curves shift upward or downward in response to changes in the prices of factors or the introduction of changed technology. Increases in factor prices shift the cost curves upward. Decreases in factor prices or technological advances that make it possible to produce the same amount of output with lower quantities of all inputs shift cost curves downward.

6. Over extended periods, the most important influence on costs of production and the standard of living has been the increases in output made possible by new technology, which has led to new techniques, new products, and improved inputs. These considerations involve the so-called very long run.

7. Major sources of productivity growth in industrializing countries include the substitution of capital for labor (an increasing capital-labor ratio), increased energy use, and invention and innovation.

8. Innovation in one form or another is the key to productivity growth. It requires invention, but also profitable opportunities for the introduction of available knowledge. Thus innovation and the changes in technology it brings are to a major degree endogenous. The economic climate (its growth and level of capacity utilization), institutional climate, and differences in technological possibilities in sectors where demand is growing and declining all affect the opportunities for innovation.

9. The slowdown in productivity growth in the United States from 1965 to 1982, with its consequent reduction in the average growth rate of living standards, was due to a combination of circumstances including sharply rising energy costs, shifts in the size and composition of the labor force, growth in aggregate output, shifts in

Summary

demand from higher productivity to lower productivity activities, and a less encouraging institutional climate.

10. Not all of the slowdown in measured productivity growth represents a worsening of the quality of life. Material progress leads both to more goods and services per person and to opportunities for better living. Yet progress of this kind is not an unmixed blessing; pollution of the environment accompanies growth, and an increased number of injuries and accidents occur. Expenditures to control pollution and increase safety are examples of things that decrease measured productivity, but improve the quality of life.

Topics for Review

Implication of cost minimization
Interpretation of $MP_K/MP_L = p_K/p_L$ and $MP_K/p_K = MP_L/p_L$
The principle of substitution
Increasing, decreasing, and constant returns
Economies of scale
Envelope curve
Distinction between production and productivity
Level of productivity and rate of growth of productivity
Sources of increasing productivity
Invention and innovation
Determinants of innovation
Causes of the slowdown in growth of productivity

Discussion Questions

1. Why does the profit-maximizing firm choose the least costly way of producing any given output? Might a nonprofit-maximizing organization such as a university, church, or government intentionally choose a method of production other than the least costly one?

2. In Dacca, Bangladesh, where gasoline costs $3.00 a gallon and labor is typically paid less than $.20 an hour, Abdul Khan pedals a bicycle-ricksha (pedicab) for his living. It's exhausting work that is coming under increasing attack by those who feel it is an inhumane practice. "We really want to get rid of them and move to motorized taxis, but I'm afraid it will take a long, long time," says the Bangladesh information officer. Ricksha drivers earn $2.00 a day, which is more than a skilled worker gets in Dacca. Explain the use of pedicabs in Dacca, but not in New York or Tokyo. Comment on the information officer's statement.

3. Use the principle of substitution to predict the effect of each of the following:
   a. During the 1960s salaries of professors rose much more rapidly than those of teaching assistants. During the 1970s salaries of teaching assistants rose more than those of professors.
   b. The cost of land in big cities increases more than the cost of high-rise construction.
   c. Gold leaf is produced by pounding gold with a hammer. The

thinner it is, the more valuable. The price of gold is set on a world market, but the price of labor varies among countries.

d. Wages of textile workers and shoe machinery operators rise more in New England than in South Carolina.

4. The long-run average cost curve can be thought of as consisting of points from each of a number of short-run average cost curves. Explain in what sense any point on the long-run curve is also on some short-run curve. What is the meaning of a move from one point on a long-run cost curve to another point on the same curve? Contrast this with a movement along a short-run curve.

5. During the "energy crisis" of the 1970s, the director of federal energy programs urged the American people to make necessary "long-run adjustments to the energy shortage by reducing energy input per unit of output." How exactly might this be done? Is this use of *long-run* the economists' use of that concept?

6. Israel, a small country, imports the "insides" of its automobiles, but manufactures the bodies. If this makes economic sense, what does it tell us about cost conditions of automobile manufacture?

7. Name five important modern products that were not available when you were in grade school. Make a list of major products that you think have increased their sales at least tenfold in the last 30 years. Check your judgment by consulting the *Statistical Abstract of the United States, Business Statistics* (biennial of the U.S. Department of Commerce) or similar sources. Consider to what extent the growth in each series may reflect product or process innovation.

8. Each of the following is a means of increasing productivity. Discuss which groups within the society might oppose each one.

    a. A labor-saving invention that permits all goods to be manufactured with less labor than before

    b. Rapidly increasing growth of population in the economy

    c. Removal of all government production safety rules

    d. Reduction in corporate income taxes

    e. Reduction in production of services and increase in agricultural production

9. Mobil Oil chairman Rawleigh Warner, Jr., has said, "Our government has adopted a gratuitously hostile attitude. Industry has been compelled to spend more and more of its research dollars to comply with environmental, health and safety regulations—and to move away from longer-term efforts aimed at major scientific advance." Suppose this is true. Is it necessarily a sign that government policies are misguided?

Appendix to Chapter 11

Isoquants: An Alternative Analysis of the Firm's Input Decisions

The production function gives the relation between the factor inputs that the firm uses and the output that it obtains. In the long run the firm can choose among many different combinations of inputs that will yield the same output. The production function and the choices open to the firm can be represented graphically using the concept of an isoquant.

A Single Isoquant

Table 11A-1 illustrates a hypothetical example in which different combinations of two inputs (labor and capital) produce a given quantity of output. The data from Table 11A-1 are plotted in Figure 11A-1. A smooth curve is drawn through the points to indicate that there are additional ways, not listed in the table, of producing six units.

This curve is called an **isoquant.** It shows the whole set of technologically efficient possibilities for producing a given level of output—6 units in this case. This is an example of graphing a three-variable function in two dimensions. It is analogous to the contour line on a map that shows all points of equal altitude and to an indifference curve that shows all combinations of commodities that yield an equal utility.

As we move from one point on an isoquant to another, we are *substituting one factor for another* while holding output constant. If we move from point b to point c, we are substituting 1 unit of labor for 3 units of capital. The marginal rate of substitution measures the rate at which one factor is substituted for another with output held constant. Graphically, the marginal rate of substitution is measured by the slope of the isoquant at a particular point. Table 11A-1 shows the calculation of some rates of substitution between various points of the isoquant. [20]

The marginal rate of substitution is related to the marginal products of the factors of production. To see how, consider an example. Assume that at the present level of inputs of labor and capital the marginal product of 1 unit of labor is 2 units of output, while the marginal product of capital is 1 unit of output. If the firm reduces its use of capital and increases its use of labor to keep output constant, it needs to add only ½ unit of labor for 1 unit of capital given up. If, at another point on the isoquant with more labor and less capital, the marginal products are 2 for capital and 1 for labor, then the firm will have to add 2 units of labor for every unit of capital it gives up. The general proposition is

TABLE 11A-1   Alternative Methods of Producing 6 Units of Output: Points on an Isoquant

Method	K	L	ΔK	ΔL	Rate of substitution $\Delta K/\Delta L$
a	18	2			
b	12	3	−6	1	−6.0
c	9	4	−3	1	−3.0
d	6	6	−3	2	−1.5
e	4	9	−2	3	−0.67
f	3	12	−1	3	−0.33
g	2	18	−1	6	−0.17

An isoquant describes the firm's alternative methods for producing a given output. The table lists some of the methods indicated by a production function as being available to produce 6 units of output. The first combination uses a great deal of capital (K) and very little labor (L). As we move down the table, labor is substituted for capital in such a way as to keep output constant. Finally, at the bottom, most of the capital has been replaced by labor. The rate of substitution between the two factors is calculated in the last three columns of the table. Note that as we move down the table, the absolute value of the rate of substitution declines.

FIGURE 11A-1   **An Isoquant for Output of 6 Units**

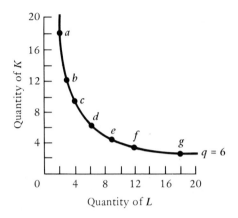

Isoquants are downward-sloping and convex. The downward slope reflects the requirement of technological efficiency. A method that uses more of one factor must use less of the other factor if it is to be technologically efficient. The convex shape of the isoquant reflects a diminishing marginal rate of substitution. The lettered points on the graph are plotted from the data in Table 11A-1. Starting from point *a*, which uses relatively little labor and much capital, and moving to point *b*, 1 additional unit of labor can substitute for 6 units of capital (while holding production constant). But from *b* to *c*, 1 unit of labor substitutes for only 3 units of capital. This diminishing rate is expressed geometrically by the flattening of the slope of the isoquant.

The marginal rate of substitution between two factors of production is equal to the ratio of their marginal products.

Isoquants satisfy two important conditions: They are downward-sloping, and they are convex viewed from the origin. What is the economic meaning of these conditions?

The downward slope indicates that each factor input has a positive marginal product. If the input of one factor is reduced and that of the other is held constant, output will be reduced. Thus, if one input is decreased, production can be held constant only if the other factor input is increased. The marginal rate of substitution has a negative value. Decreases in one

factor must be balanced by increases in the other factor if output is to be held constant.

To understand convexity, consider what happens as the firm moves along the isoquant of Figure 11A-1 downward and to the right. Labor is being added and capital reduced to keep output constant. If labor is added in increments of exactly 1 unit, how much capital may be dispensed with each time? The key to the answer is that both factors are assumed to be subject to the law of diminishing returns. Thus the gain in output associated with each additional unit of labor added is *diminishing* while the loss of output associated with each additional unit of capital forgone is *increasing*. It therefore takes ever-smaller reductions in capital to compensate for equal increases in labor. This implies that the isoquant is convex viewed from the origin.

An Isoquant Map

The isoquant of Figure 11A-1 referred to 6 units of output. There is another isoquant for 7 units, another for 7,000 units, and a different one for every rate of output. Each isoquant refers to a specific output and connects combinations of factors that are technologically efficient methods of achieving that output. If we plot a representative set of these isoquants on a single graph, we get an **isoquant map** like that in Figure 11A-2. The higher the level of output along a particular isoquant, the farther the isoquant is from the origin.

Conditions for Cost Minimization

Finding the efficient way of producing any output requires finding the least-cost factor combination. To find this combination when both factors are variable, factor prices need to be known. Suppose, to continue the example, that capital is priced at $4 per unit and labor at $1. In Chapter 8 a budget line was used to show the alternative combinations of goods a household could buy; here an *isocost line* is used to show alternative combinations of factors a firm can buy for a given outlay. Four different isocost lines appear in Figure 11A-3. The slope of each reflects *relative* factor prices, just as the slope of the budget line in Chapter 8 represented relative product prices. For

FIGURE 11A-2   An Isoquant Map

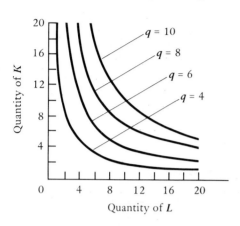

An isoquant map shows a set of isoquants, one for each level of output. The figure shows four isoquants drawn from the production function and corresponding to 4, 6, 8, and 10 units of production.

FIGURE 11A-3   Isocost Lines

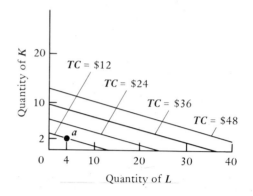

Each isocost line shows alternative factor combinations that can be purchased for a given outlay. The graph shows the four isocost lines that result when labor costs $1 a unit and capital $4 a unit and expenditure is held constant at $12, $24, $36, and $48, respectively. The line labeled $TC = \$12$ represents all combinations of the two factors that the firm could buy for $12. Point a represents 2 units of K and 4 units of L.

FIGURE 11A-4   The Determination of the Least-Cost Method of Output

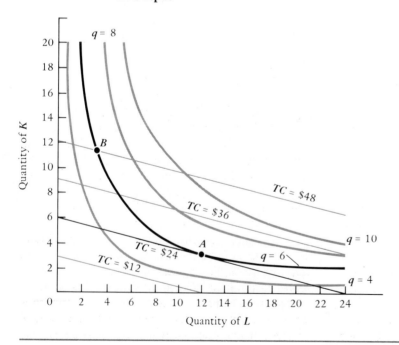

Least-cost methods are represented by points of tangency between isoquant and isocost lines. The isoquant map of Figure 11A-2 and the isocost lines of Figure 11A-3 are brought together. Consider point A. It is on the 6-unit isoquant and the $24 isocost line. Thus it is possible to achieve the output $q = 6$ for a total cost of $24. There are other ways to achieve this output, for example, at point B, where $TC = \$48$. Moving along the isoquant from point A in either direction increases cost. Similarly, moving along the isocost line from point A in either direction lowers output. Thus either move would raise cost per unit.

FIGURE 11A-5   The Effects of a Change in Factor Prices on Costs and Factor Proportions

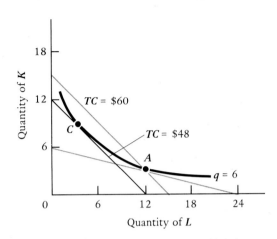

(i) The effect on the isocost line of an increase in the price of labor

(ii) Substitution of capital for labor resulting from an increase in the price of labor

An increase in the price of labor pivots the isocost line inward and thus increases the cost of producing any output. It also changes the slope of the isocost line and thus changes the least-cost method of producing. (i) The rise in price of L from \$1 to \$4 a unit (with price of K constant at \$4) pivots the \$24 isocost line inward to the dashed line. Any output previously produced for \$24 will cost more at the new prices if it uses any amount of labor. The new cost of producing at A rises from \$24 to \$60. (ii) The steeper isocost line is tangent to the isoquant at C, not A. Costs at C are \$48, higher than they were before the price increase, but not as high as they would be if the factor substitution had not occurred.

given factor prices a series of parallel isocost lines will reflect the alternative levels of expenditure on factor purchases that are open to the firm. The higher the level of expenditure, the farther the isocost line is from the origin.

In Figure 11A-4 the isoquant and isocost maps are brought together. The economically most efficient method of production must be a point on an isoquant that just touches (i.e., is tangent to) an isocost line. If the isoquant cuts the isocost line, it is possible to move along the isoquant and reach a lower level of cost. Only at a point of tangency is a movement in either direction along the isoquant a movement to a higher cost level. The lowest attainable cost of producing 6 units is \$24. This cost level can be achieved only by operating at A, the point where the \$24 isocost line is tangent to the 6-unit isoquant. The lowest average cost of producing 6 units is thus \$24/6 = \$4 per unit of output.

The least-cost position is given graphically by the tangency point between the isoquant and the isocost lines.

Notice that point A in Figure 11A-4 indicates not only the lowest level of cost for 6 units of output, but also the highest level of output for \$24 of cost. Thus, we find the same solution if we set out *either* to minimize the cost of producing 6 units of output *or* to maximize the output that can be obtained for \$24. One problem is said to be the "dual" of the other.

The slope of the isocost line is given by the ratio of the prices of the two factors of production. The slope of the isoquant is given by the ratio of their marginal products. When the firm reaches its least-cost position, it has equated the price ratio (which is given to it by the market prices) with the ratio of the marginal products (which it can adjust by varying the proportions in which it hires the factors). In symbols,

$$\frac{MP_K}{MP_L} = \frac{p_K}{p_L}$$

This is equivalent to Equation 2 on page 192. We have now derived this result by use of the isoquant analysis of the firm's decisions. [21]

The Principle of Substitution

Suppose that with technology unchanged, that is, with the isoquant map fixed, the price of one factor changes. Suppose that with the price of capital unchanged at $4 per unit, the price of labor rises from $1 to $4 per unit. Originally, the efficient factor combination for producing 6 units was 12 units of labor and 3 units of capital. It cost $24. To produce that same output in the same way would now cost $60 at the new factor prices. Figure 11A-5, page 209, shows why that is not efficient. The slope of the isocost line has changed, which makes it efficient to substitute the now relatively cheaper capital for the relatively more expensive labor.

This illustrates the principle of substitution.

Changes in relative factor prices will cause a partial replacement of factors that have become relatively more expensive by factors that have become relatively cheaper.

Of course, substitution of capital for labor cannot fully offset the effects of a rise in cost of labor, as Figure 11A-5(i) shows. Consider the output attainable for $24. In the figure there are two isocost lines representing $24 of outlay—at the old and new price of labor. The new isocost line for $24 lies inside the old one (except where no labor is used). The isocost line must therefore be tangent to a lower isoquant. This means that if production is to be held constant, higher costs must be accepted. However, because of substitution, it is not necessary to accept costs as high as would accompany an unchanged factor proportion. In the example 6 units can be produced for $48 rather than the $60 that would be required if no change in factor proportions were made.

This leads to the predictions that

A rise in the price of one factor with all other factor prices constant will (1) shift upward the cost curves of commodities that use that factor and (2) lead to a substitution of factors that are now relatively cheaper for the factor whose price has risen.

Both these predictions were stated in Chapter 11; now they have been derived formally using the isoquant technique.

Markets and Pricing

12

Pricing in Competitive Markets

Market Structure and Firm Behavior

Does Goodyear compete with Goodrich? Does Macy's compete with Bloomingdale's? Does a wheat farmer from Wheatland, Iowa, compete with a wheat farmer from North Platte, Nebraska? In the ordinary meaning of the word *compete,* the answers to the first two questions are plainly yes, and the answer to the third question is probably no.

Goodyear and Goodrich both advertise extensively to persuade tire buyers to buy *their* product. Goodrich once tried to confuse the issue by asking, "See the blimp up there? It's theirs, not ours. If you want Goodrich tires, you'll just have to remember Goodrich." Everyone knows that Macy's and Bloomingdale's watch each other closely and that swarms of comparison shoppers check the other firm's prices and product qualities every day. But nothing the Iowa farmer can do will affect either the sales or the profits of the Nebraska farmer.

Competitive Behavior and Competitive Market Structure

To sort out the questions of who is competing with whom and in what sense, it is useful to distinguish between the *behavior* of individual firms and the *type of market* in which the firms operate. In everyday use the word *competition* usually refers only to competitive behavior; economists, however, are interested both in the competitive behavior of individual firms and in a quite distinct concept, competitive market structure.

The term *market structure* refers to all aspects of a market, such as the number of firms and the type of product sold, that may affect the behavior and performance of the firms in that market.

Competitive market structure. The competitiveness of the market refers to the extent to which individual firms have power over that market—power to influence the price or other terms on which their product is sold. The less power an individual firm has to influence the market in which it sells its product, the more competitive is that market. The extreme of competitiveness occurs when each firm has zero power. In such a case there are so many firms that each must accept the price set by the forces of market demand and supply. This extreme is called the *perfectly competitive market structure.* In it there is no need for individual firms to compete actively with one another since none has any power over the market. One firm's ability to sell its product does not depend on the behavior of any other firm.

For example, the Iowa and Nebraska wheat farmers do not engage in active *competitive behavior* with each other. They are firms operating in a perfectly competitive market over which they have no power. Neither has significant power to change the market price for its wheat by altering its own behavior.

Competitive behavior. In everyday language the term *competitive behavior* refers to the degree to which individual firms actively compete with one another. For example, Goodrich and Goodyear certainly engage in competitive behavior.

It is also true, however, that Goodrich and Goodyear have some power over the tire market. Either firm could raise its prices and still continue to sell tires. Each has the power to decide, within limits set by buyers' tastes and the prices of competing tires, what price consumers will pay for its own product. Thus, although they compete actively with each other, they do not do so within the confines of a perfectly competitive market structure.

Behavior versus structure. The distinction made above explains why it is that firms in perfectly competitive markets (e.g., the Iowa and Nebraska wheat farmers) do not actively compete with each other, while firms that do compete actively with each other (e.g., Goodrich and Goodyear) do not operate in perfectly competitive markets.

The Significance of Market Structure

Before we proceed further, we need to define two important concepts: the market and the industry.

From the point of view of a buyer, the **market** consists of those firms from which a well-defined product can be purchased; from the point of view of a firm, the market consists of those buyers to whom a well-defined product can be sold. A group of firms that sells a well-defined product or closely related set of products is said to constitute an **industry**. The market demand curve is the demand curve for an industry's product.[1]

Consider a firm that produces a specific product for sale in a particular market and competes for cus-

tomers with other firms in the same industry. If the firm knows the demand curve it faces, it knows the price it could charge for each rate of sales and thus knows its potential revenues. If it also knows its costs, the firm can calculate the profits that would be associated with each rate of output and can choose the rate that maximizes its profits.

But what if the firm knows only its costs and the *market* demand curve for its industry's product? Because it does not know its *own* demand curve, it does not know what its own sales would be at any price that it might charge. To know how its own demand would change as its own price changes, the firm needs to know how other firms will respond to its change in price. If it reduces its price by 10 percent, will other sellers leave their prices unchanged, or will they also reduce them? If so, by how much? Obviously, these responses will have an effect on the firm's sales and thus on its revenues and profits.

We have seen that economists define market structure to mean those characteristics that affect the behavior and performance of firms that sell in that market. These characteristics are many of the ones that determine the relation between the market demand curve for the industry's product and the firm's own demand curve.

The number of sellers and the nature of the product are highly significant dimensions of market structure. There are others as well, such as the ease of entering the industry, the nature and number of the purchasers of the firm's products, and the firm's ability to influence demand by advertising. To reduce these aspects to manageable proportions, economists have focused on a few theoretical market structures that they believe represent a high proportion of the cases actually encountered in market economies. In this and the following chapters, we shall look at four market structures: perfect competition, monopoly, monopolistic competition, and oligopoly.

Before considering any of these, it is useful to deal with the rules of behavior common to all firms that seek to maximize profits.

Profit-Maximizing Behavior

Marginal revenue. A firm interested in maximizing its profits must pay attention to both its costs and its revenues. In Chapter 10 we defined *marginal cost* as

---

[1] An industry typically sells many different products and sells them in many different markets. For our elementary treatment, we shall focus attention on the single-product industry and the market (or markets) in which that product is sold.

the addition to the firm's total cost caused by increasing its rate of production by one unit. It is now helpful to define a parallel revenue concept. **Marginal revenue *(MR)*** is the change in the firm's total revenue caused by a change in its sales by one unit. At any level of sales, marginal revenue shows what the firm would gain on the revenue side by selling a bit more, and what revenue it would lose by selling a bit less.

Should the firm produce at all?   The firm always has the option of producing nothing. If it exercises that option, it will have an operating loss equal to its fixed costs. If it decides to produce, it will add the variable cost of production to its costs, and the receipts from the sale of its product to its revenue. Therefore, if there is some level of output for which revenue exceeds variable cost, it will pay the firm to produce; if, however, revenue is less than variable cost at every level of output, the firm will actually lose more by producing than by not producing.[2]

Rule 1: **A firm should not produce at all if the total revenue from selling its product does not equal or exceed the total variable cost of producing it. [22]**

How much should the firm produce?   If a firm decides that, according to Rule 1, production is worth undertaking, it must decide how much to produce. Common sense dictates that on a unit-by-unit basis, if any unit of production adds more to revenue than it does to cost, that unit will increase profits; if it adds more to cost than to revenue, it will decrease profits. If a further unit of production will increase the firm's profits, the firm should expand output. However, if the last unit produced will reduce profits, the firm should contract output. From this it follows that the only time the firm should leave its output unaltered is when the last unit produced adds the same amount to costs as it does to revenue.

Rule 2: **Assuming that it pays the firm to produce at all, the firm should produce where marginal revenue equals marginal cost. [23]**

[2] Formal proofs of the propositions discussed in the text are given in the Mathematical Notes.

These rules refer to each firm's own costs and revenues and they apply to all profit-maximizing firms, whatever the market structure in which they operate.[3] Before we can apply the rules, however, we need to consider particular market structures in order to relate the demand curve for an industry's product to the demand curves facing individual firms.

The Elements of the Theory of Perfect Competition

The theory of the perfectly competitive market structure applies directly to a number of real-world markets. It also provides a benchmark for comparison with other market structures.

The Assumptions of Perfect Competition

The theory of **perfect competition** is built on two critical assumptions, one about the behavior of the individual firm and one about the nature of the industry in which it operates.

The *firm* is assumed to be a **price taker;** that is, the firm is assumed to be able to alter its rate of production and sales within any feasible range without such action having a significant effect on the price of the product it sells. Thus, as stated earlier, a firm operating in a perfectly competitive market has no power to influence that market through its own individual actions. It must passively accept whatever price happens to be ruling.

The *industry* is assumed to be characterized by **freedom of entry and exit;** that is, any new firm is free to set up production if it so wishes, and any existing firm is free to cease production and leave the industry. Existing firms cannot bar the entry of new firms, and there are no legal prohibitions on entry or exit.

[3] There is also a third rule that is needed to distinguish between profit-*maximizing* and profit-*minimizing* positions: The marginal cost curve must cut the marginal revenue curve from below. [24] This rule is not, however, needed in what follows so we say nothing further about it.

The ultimate test of the theory based on these assumptions will be the usefulness of its predictions, but because students are often bothered by the first assumption, it is worth examining whether it is in any way reasonable. To do this, we contrast the demands for the products of an automobile manufacturer and a wheat farmer.

An automobile manufacturer. General Motors is aware that it has market power. If it increases its prices substantially, sales will fall off; if it lowers prices substantially, it will sell more of its products. If GM decides on a large increase in production that is not a response to a known or anticipated rise in demand, it will have to reduce prices in order to sell the extra output. General Motors is *not* a price taker. The quantity that it is able to sell will depend on the price it charges, but it does not have to accept passively whatever price is set by the market. In other words, an auto manufacturing firm such as GM is faced with a downward-sloping demand curve for its product. It may select any price-quantity combination consistent with that demand curve.

A wheat farmer. In contrast, an individual firm producing wheat is just one of a very large number of firms all growing the same product; one firm's contribution to the total production of wheat will be a tiny drop in an extremely large bucket. Ordinarily, the firm will assume that it has no effect on price and will think of its own demand curve as being horizontal. Of course, the firm can have *some* effect on price, but a straightforward calculation will show that the effect is small enough that the firm can justifiably neglect it.

The market elasticity of demand for wheat is approximately 0.25. This means that if the quantity of wheat supplied in the world increased by 1 percent, the price would have to fall by 4 percent to induce the world's wheat buyers to purchase the whole crop. Even huge farms produce a small fraction of the total crop. In a recent year an extremely large Canadian wheat farm produced about 50,000 tons, only about 1/4,000 of total world production of 200 million tons. Suppose a large wheat farm increased its production by 20,000 tons, say from 40,000 to 60,000 tons. This would be a big percent-age increase in its own production, but an increase of only 1/100 of 1 percent in world production. Table 12-1 shows that this increase would lead to a decrease in the world price of 4/100 of 1 percent (4¢ in $100) and give the firm an elasticity of demand of 1,000! This is a very high elasticity of demand; the farm would have to increase its output 1,000 percent to bring about a 1 percent decrease in the price of wheat. Because the firm's output cannot be varied this much, it is not surprising that the firm regards the price of wheat as unaffected by any change in output that it could conceivably make. In other words, the firm is faced with a perfectly elastic demand curve for its product—it is a price taker.

The difference between General Motors and the wheat farmer is one of degree of market power. The firm producing wheat, as an insignificant part of the whole market, has no power to influence the world price of wheat. The automobile firm does have power to influence the price of automobiles because its own production represents a significant part of the total supply of automobiles.

Demand and Revenue for the Perfectly Competitive Firm

The demand curve facing a single firm in perfect competition is horizontal because variations in its production over the range that we need to consider for all practical purposes will have a negligible effect on price. Of course, if the single firm increased its production by a vast amount, a thousandfold say, this might well cause a significant increase in supply and the firm would be unable to sell all it produced at the going price. The horizontal (perfectly elastic) demand curve does not mean that the firm could actually sell an infinite amount at the going price; rather, the variations in production *that it will normally be practicable for the firm to make* will leave price virtually unaffected. Figure 12-1 contrasts the demand curve for a competitive industry and for a single firm in that industry.

Total, average, and marginal revenue. The notions of total, average, and marginal revenue are the demand counterparts of the notions of total, average, and marginal cost that we considered in Chapter 10.

TABLE 12-1 The Calculation of a Firm's Elasticity of Demand (η_F) from Market Elasticity of Demand (η_M)

Given

$\eta_M = 0.25$

World output $= 200$ million tons

Firm's output increases from 40,000 to 60,000 tons, a 40% increase over the average quantity of 50,000 tons

Step 1. Find the percentage change in world price.

$$\eta_M = -\frac{\text{percentage change in world output}}{\text{percentage change in world price}}$$

$$\text{Percentage change in world price} = -\frac{\text{percentage change in world output}}{\eta_M}$$

$$= -\frac{\frac{1}{100} \text{ of } 1\%}{0.25}$$

$$= -\frac{4}{100} \text{ of } 1\%$$

Step 2. Compute the firm's elasticity of demand.

$$\eta_F = -\frac{\text{percentage change in firm's output}}{\text{percentage change in world price}}$$

$$= -\frac{+40\%}{-\frac{4}{100} \text{ of } 1\%} = +1,000$$

Because even a large change in output to the firm is a minute change in world wheat production, the effect on world price is small. Thus the firm's elasticity of demand is high. This table relies on the concept of elasticity of demand developed in Chapter 5. Step 1 shows that a 40 percent increase in the firm's output leads to only a tiny decrease in the world's price. Thus, as step 2 shows, the firm's elasticity of demand is very high: 1,000.

The arithmetic is not important, but understanding why the wheat farm will be a price taker in these circumstances is vital.

FIGURE 12-1 The Demand Curve for a Competitive Industry and for One Firm in the Industry

Quantity (Millions of Tons)

(i) Competitive industry's demand curve

Quantity (Thousands of Tons)

(ii) Competitive firm's demand curve

The industry's demand curve is downward-sloping; the firm's demand curve is virtually horizontal. Notice the difference in the quantities shown on the horizontal scale in each part of the figure. The competitive industry has a price of $3 and an output of 200 million tons. The individual firm takes that market price as given to it and considers producing up to 60 thousand tons. The firm's demand curve in (ii) appears horizontal because of the change in the quantity scale compared to the industry's demand curve in (i). The firm's output variation has only a tiny percentage effect on industry output. If one plotted the industry demand curve from 199,970 thousand tons to 200,030 thousand tons on the scale used in (ii), the D curve would appear virtually horizontal.

TABLE 12-2   Revenue Concepts for a Price-Taking Firm

Price p	Quantity q	$TR = p \cdot q$	$AR = TR/q$	$MR = \Delta TR/\Delta q$
$3.00	10	$30.00	$3.00	
3.00	11	33.00	3.00	$3.00
3.00	12	36.00	3.00	3.00
3.00	13	39.00	3.00	3.00

When price is fixed, $AR = MR = p$. Marginal revenue is shown between the lines because it represents the change in total revenue (e.g., from $33 to $36) in response to a change in quantity (from 11 to 12 units): $MR = (36-33)/(12-11) = \$3$ per unit.

We focus now on the receipts to a seller from the sale of a product.

Total revenue (TR) is the total amount received by the seller. If q units are sold at p dollars each, $TR = p \cdot q$.[4]

Average revenue (AR) is the amount of revenue *per unit* sold. This is the price of the product.

Marginal revenue (MR), sometimes called incremental revenue, has already been defined. It is the change in total revenue resulting from a change in the firm's rate of sales by one unit. [25]

Calculations of these revenue concepts for a price-taking firm are illustrated in Table 12-2. The table shows that as long as the firm's output does not affect the price of the product it sells, both average and marginal revenue will be equal to price at all levels of output. Thus, graphically (as is shown in Figure 12-2(i)), average revenue and marginal revenue are both horizontal lines at the level of market price. Since the firm can sell any quantity it wishes at this price, the same horizontal line is also the *firm's* demand curve.

If the market price is unaffected by variations in the firm's output, then the firm's demand curve, the average revenue curve, and the marginal revenue curve coincide in the same horizontal line. Thus, for a firm in perfect competition, price equals marginal revenue.

---

4 Three common ways of indicating that two variables, p and q in this case, are to be multiplied together are: $p \cdot q$, $p \times q$ and pq.

FIGURE 12-2   Revenue Curves for a Price-Taking Firm

(i) Average and marginal revenue

(ii) Total revenue

This is a graphic representation of the revenue concepts of Table 12-2. Because price does not change, neither marginal nor average revenue varies with output. When price is constant, total revenue is an upward-sloping straight line from the origin.

Total revenue, of course, does vary with output; since price is constant, it follows that total revenue rises in direct proportion to output as shown in Figure 12-2 (ii).

Short-Run Equilibrium

The Firm's Equilibrium Output

In perfect competition the firm is a price taker and can adjust to varying market conditions only by changing the quantity it produces. In the short run it has one or more fixed factors, and the only way to vary its output is by using more or less of those factors that it can vary. Thus, the firm's short-run cost curves are relevant to its output decision.

We saw earlier that *any* profit-maximizing firm will seek to produce at the level of output at which marginal cost equals marginal revenue. In the immediately preceding section we saw that a perfectly competitive firm's demand and marginal revenue curves coincide in the same horizontal line whose height represents the price of the product. It follows that a firm operating in a perfectly competitive market will equate its marginal cost of production to the market price of its product (as long as price exceeds average variable cost).

The market determines the price at which the firm sells its product. The firm picks the quantity of output that maximizes its profits. This is the output for which $p = MC$. When the firm is maximizing profits, it has no incentive to change its output. Therefore, unless prices or costs change, the firm will continue producing this output because it is doing as well as it can do, given the situation. The firm is said to be in **short-run equilibrium,** which is illustrated in Figure 12-3.

In a perfectly competitive market, each firm is a mere quantity adjuster. It pursues its goal of profit maximization by increasing or decreasing quantity until it equates its short-run marginal cost with the prevailing price of its product—a price that is given to it by the market.

In a perfectly competitive market the firm responds to a price that is set by the forces of demand and supply. By adjusting the quantity it produces in response to the current market price, the firm helps to determine market supply. The link between the behavior of the firm and the behavior of the competitive market is provided by the market supply curve.

Short-Run Supply Curves

The supply curve for one firm. Figure 12-4(i) shows a firm's marginal cost curve and four alternative prices. The horizontal line at each price is the firm's demand curve when the market price is at that level. The firm's marginal cost curve gives the marginal cost corresponding to each level of output. We re-

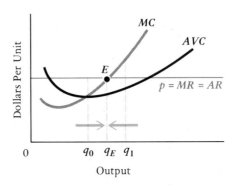

FIGURE 12-3   The Short-Run Equilibrium of a Competitive Firm

The firm chooses the output for which $p = MC$ above the level of AVC. When $p = MC$ as at q_E, the firm would decrease its profits if it either increased or decreased its output. At any point to the left of q_E, say, q_0, price is greater than the marginal cost, and it pays to increase output (as indicated by the arrow on the left). At any point to the right of q_E, say, q_1, price is less than the marginal cost, and it pays to reduce output (as indicated by the arrow on the right). The short-run equilibrium output for the firm is q_E.

quire a supply curve that shows the quantity the firm will supply at every price. For prices below average variable cost, the firm will supply zero units (rule 1). For prices above AVC, the firm will equate price and marginal cost (rule 2 modified by the proposition that $MR = p$ in perfect competition). From this it follows that

In perfect competition the firm's supply curve has the identical shape as the firm's marginal cost curve above average variable cost.

The supply curve of an industry. Figure 12-5 illustrates the derivation of an industry supply curve for an example of only two firms. The general result is that

In perfect competition the industry supply curve is the horizontal sum of the marginal cost curves (above the level of average variable cost) of all firms in the industry.

The reason for this is that each firm's marginal cost curve tells us how much that firm will supply at each

FIGURE 12-4   Derivation of the Supply Curve for a Price-Taking Firm

(i) Marginal cost and average variable cost curves

(ii) Supply curve

For a price-taking firm, the supply curve (ii) has the same shape as its *MC* curve above the level of *AVC* (i). As prices rise from $2 to $3 to $4 to $5, the firm wishes to increase its production from q_0 to q_1 to q_2 to q_3. For prices below $2, output would be zero because there is no positive output at which *AVC* can be covered. The point E_0, where price equals *AVC*, is the shutdown point. If price were $3, the firm would produce output q_1 rather than zero because that output would be making a contribution to fixed costs, as shown by the shaded rectangle.

FIGURE 12-5   Derivation of the Supply Curve for an Industry

(i) Firm A

(ii) Firm B

(iii) Firms A and B

The industry supply curve is the horizontal sum of the supply curves of each of the firms in the industry. At a price of $3, firm A would supply 4 units and firm B would supply 3 units. Together, as shown in (iii), they would supply 7 units. If there are hundreds of firms, the process is the same. Each firm's supply curve (derived in the manner shown in Figure 12-4) shows what the firm will produce at any given price p. The industry supply curve relates the price to the sum of the quantities produced by each firm. In this example, because firm B does not enter the market at prices below $2, the supply curve $S_{A + B}$ is identical to S_A up to price $2 and is the sum of $S_A + S_B$ above $2.

given market price, and the industry supply curve is the sum of what each firm will supply. This supply curve, based on the short-run marginal cost curves of the firms in the industry, is the industry's supply curve of the kind introduced in Chapter 4 and used as an important part of our analysis. It is sometimes called a **short-run supply curve** to distinguish it from a long-run supply curve that is used in more advanced analysis that concerns the relation of long-run equilibrium price and quantities supplied.

Short-Run Equilibrium Price

The market price of a product sold in a perfectly competitive market is determined by the interaction of the industry's short-run supply curve and the market demand curve. Although no one firm can influence market price significantly, the collective actions of all firms in the industry (as shown by the industry supply curve) and the collective actions of households (as shown by the market demand curve) together determine the equilibrium price at the point where the demand and supply curves intersect.

At the equilibrium price each firm is producing and selling a quantity for which its marginal cost equals price. No firm is motivated to change its output in the short run. Since total quantity demanded equals total quantity supplied, there is no reason for market price to change in the short run; the market and all the firms in the industry are in short-run equilibrium.

Short-Run Profitability of the Firm

Although we know that when the industry is in short-run equilibrium the competitive firm is maxi-

FIGURE 12-6   Alternative Short-Run Equilibrium Positions of a Competitive Firm

(i)   (ii)   (iii)

When it is in short-run equilibrium, a competitive firm may be suffering losses, breaking even, or making profits. The diagrams show a firm with given costs faced with three alternative prices p_1, p_2, and p_3. In each part of the diagram equilibrium occurs at the point at which $MC = MR$ = price. Since in all three cases price exceeds AVC, the firm is in short-run equilibrium at E_1, E_2, and E_3, respectively, in (i), (ii), and (iii).

In (i) price is p_1 and the firm is suffering losses, shown by the color shaded area, because price is below average total cost. Since price exceeds average variable cost, it pays the firm to keep producing, but it does *not* pay it to replace its capital equipment as the capital wears out.

In (ii) price is p_2 and the firm is just covering its total costs. It pays the firm to replace its capital as it wears out since it is covering the full opportunity cost of its capital.

In (iii) price is p_3 and the firm is earning profits, shown by the gray shaded area, in excess of all its costs.

mizing its profits, we do not know *how large* these profits are. It is one thing to know that a firm is doing as well as it can in particular circumstances; it is another to know how well it is doing.

Figure 12-6 shows three possible positions for a firm in short-run equilibrium. In all cases the firm is maximizing its profits by producing where $p = MC$, but in (i) the firm is making losses, in (ii) it is just covering all costs, and in (iii) it is making profits in excess of all costs. In (i) it might be better to say that the firm is minimizing its losses rather than maximizing its profits, but both statements mean the same thing. The firm is doing as well as it can, given its costs and prices.

Long-Run Equilibrium

While Figure 12-6 shows three possible short-run equilibrium positions for the profit-maximizing firm in perfect competition, not all of them are possible equilibrium positions in the long run.

The Effect of Entry and Exit

The key to long-run equilibrium under perfect competition is entry and exit. We have seen that when firms are in *short-run* equilibrium, they may be making profits or losses or just breaking even. Since costs include the opportunity cost of capital, firms that are just breaking even are doing as well as they could do by investing their capital elsewhere. Thus there will be no incentive for existing firms to leave the industry; neither will there be an incentive for new firms to enter the industry, for capital can earn the same return elsewhere in the economy. If, however, existing firms are earning profits over all costs, including the opportunity cost of capital, new capital will enter the industry to share in these profits. If existing firms are making losses, capital will leave the industry because a better return can be obtained elsewhere in the economy. Let us consider the process in a little more detail.

If all firms in the competitive industry are in the position of the firm in Figure 12-6(iii), new firms will enter the industry, attracted by the profitability of existing firms. Suppose that in response to high profits for 100 existing firms, 20 new firms enter.

The market supply curve that formerly added up the outputs of 100 firms now must add up the outputs of 120 firms. At any price more will be supplied because there are more producers.

This shift in the short-run supply curve, with an unchanged market demand curve, means that the previous equilibrium price will no longer prevail. The shift in supply will lower the equilibrium price, and both new and old firms will have to adjust their output to this new price. This is illustrated in Figure 12-7. New firms will continue to enter and equilibrium price will continue to fall until all firms in the industry are just covering their total costs. Firms will then be in the position of the firm in Figure 12-6(ii), which is called a *zero-profit equilibrium*.

Profits in a competitive industry are a signal for the entry of new capital; the industry will expand, forcing price down until the profits fall to zero.

If the firms in the industry are in the position of the firm in Figure 12-6(i), they are suffering losses.

FIGURE 12-7   The Effect of New Entrants on the Supply Curve

New entrants shift the supply curve to the right and lower the equilibrium price. Initial equilibrium is at E_0. If the supply curve shifts to S_1 by virtue of entry, the equilibrium price must fall to p_1 while output rises to q_1. At this price before entry only q_0 would have been produced. The extra output is supplied by the new productive capacity.

They are covering their variable costs, but the return on their capital is less than the opportunity cost of this capital; the firms are not covering their total costs. This is a signal for the exit of firms. As plant and equipment are discarded, they will not be replaced. As a result, the industry's short-run supply curve shifts left and market price rises. Firms will continue to exit and price will continue to rise until the remaining firms can cover their total costs, that is, until they are all in the zero-profit equilibrium illustrated in Figure 12-6(ii). Exit then ceases.

Losses in a competitive industry are a signal for the exit of capital; the industry will contract, driving price up until the remaining firms are covering their total costs.

In all of this we see profits serving their function of allocating resources among the industries of the economy.

Cost in Long-Run Equilibrium

There are three major conditions for a competitive industry to be in long-run equilibrium.

First, existing firms must be doing as well as they can, given their existing plants. This means that marginal costs of production must be equal to market price.

Second, there must be no incentive for new firms to enter the industry. The absence of an incentive for entry requires that existing firms are not earning profits on their existing plants; if they were, new entrants could duplicate these facilities and earn profits themselves.

Third, existing firms must not be able to increase their profits by building plants of a different size. This implies that each existing firm must be at the minimum point of its long-run cost curve. This is a new condition and to understand it, assume that it does not hold and see that firms could then increase their profits. This is shown in Figure 12-8. Here the firm is in short-run equilibrium and just covering all costs. But there are unexploited economies of scale. By increasing its size, for example, by building a new plant with a larger capacity than its existing plant, the firm can reduce its average cost. Since in its present position average cost is just equal to price, then any reduction in average cost must yield profits.

FIGURE 12-8   Short-Run Versus Long-Run Equilibrium of a Competitive Firm

A competitive firm that is not at the minimum point on its *LRAC* curve cannot be in long-run equilibrium. A competitive firm with short-run cost curves *SRATC* and *MC* faces a market price of p_0. The firm produces q_0 where *MC* equals price and total costs are just being covered. However, the firm's long-run cost curve lies below its short-run curve at output q_0. The firm could produce output q_0 at cost c_0 by building a larger plant so as to take advantage of economies of scale. Profits would rise because average total costs of c_0 would then be less than price p_0. The firm cannot be in long-run equilibrium at any output below q^* because, with any such output, average total costs can be reduced by building a larger plant. The output q^* is the *minimum efficient scale* of the firm.

To summarize, the conditions for long-run equilibrium for a competitive industry are: (1) existing firms produce at the minimum point on their short-run average cost curves, (2) existing firms produce where marginal cost equals price, and (3) existing firms produce at the minimum point on their long-run average cost curve.[5] This is the position shown in Figure 12-9.

[5] Since all costs are variable in the long run, there is no need to distinguish long-run average variable costs (*LRAVC*) from long-run average total cost (*LRATC*). They are identical and we refer to them merely as long-run average costs (*LRAC*).

The only way in which a price-taking firm can be in long-run equilibrium with respect to its size is by producing at the minimum point on its *LRAC* curve.

The level of output where *LRAC* is a minimum is thus known as the **minimum efficient scale (MES)** or *minimal optimal scale (MOS)* of the firm.

When all firms in the industry are producing at the minimum point of their long-run average cost curve and just covering costs (i.e., are in a position shown in Figure 12-9), the whole industry is in equilibrium. Because marginal cost equals price, no firm can improve its profits by varying its output in the short run. Because *LRAC* is above price at all possible outputs except the current one, where it is equal to the price, and because there are no profits to be earned above opportunity costs, there is no incentive for entry into the industry.

In long-run competitive equilibrium the firm's cost is the lowest attainable cost, given the limits of known technology and factor prices.

We can now use our long-run theory to understand two commonly encountered, but often misunderstood, real-world situations.

Changes in Technology

Consider an industry in long-run equilibrium. Since the industry is in equilibrium, each firm must be in zero-profit equilibrium. Now assume that some technological development lowers the cost curves of newly built plants. Since price is just equal to the average total cost for the old plants, new plants will now be able to earn profits, and more of them will now be built. But this expansion in capacity shifts the short-run supply curve to the right and drives price down.

The expansion in capacity and the fall in price will continue until price is equal to the short-run average total cost of the *new* plants. At this price old plants will not be covering their long-run costs. As long as price exceeds their average variable cost, however, such plants will continue in production. As the outmoded plants wear out, they will gradually

FIGURE 12-9   The Equilibrium of a Firm When the Industry Is in Long-Run Equilibrium

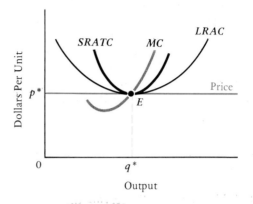

In long-run competitive equilibrium the firm is operating at the minimum point on its *LRAC* curve. In long-run equilibrium each firm must be (1) maximizing short-run profits, $MC = p$; (2) earning profits of zero on its existing plant, $SRATC = p$; and (3) unable to increase its profits by altering the size of plant. These three conditions can only be met when the firm is at *E*, the minimum point on its *LRAC* curve, with price p^* and output q^*.

disappear. Eventually a new long-run equilibrium will be established in which all plants use the new technology.

What happens in a competitive industry in which technological change occurs not as a single isolated event, but more or less continuously? Plants built in any one year will tend to have lower costs than plants built in any previous year.[6] This common occurrence is illustrated in Figure 12-10.

Industries subject to continuous technological change have a number of interesting characteristics. One is that plants of different ages and different levels of efficiency exist side by side. This characteristic is dramatically illustrated by the variety of vintages of steam turbine generators found in any long-estab-

---

[6] This statement refers to real resource costs, which tend to fall due to technological change. Of course, in times of general inflation, *money* costs of plants may well be rising. In the comparisons made here, we are assuming that costs have been adjusted for changes in the general price level.

lished electric utility. Critics who observe the continued use of older, less efficient plants and urge that "something be done to eliminate these wasteful practices" miss the point of economic efficiency.

If the plant is already there, the plant can be profitably operated as long as it can do anything more than cover its variable costs. As long as a plant can produce goods that are valued by consumers at an amount above the value of the resources currently used up for their production (variable costs), the value of society's total output is increased by using that plant to produce goods.

A second characteristic of a competitive industry subject to continuous technological change is that price is governed by the *minimum ATC of the most efficient plants.* Entry will continue until plants of the latest vintage are just expected to earn normal profits

over their lifetimes. The benefits of the new technology are passed on to consumers because all units of the commodity, whether produced by new or old plants, are sold at a price that is related solely to the *ATC* of the new plants. Owners of older plants find their returns over variable costs falling steadily as more and more efficient plants drive the price of the product down.

A third characteristic is that old plants are discarded (or "mothballed") when the price falls below their *AVC.* This may occur well before the plants are physically worn out. In industries with continuous technical progress, capital is usually discarded because it is *economically obsolete,* not because it has physically worn out. Old capital is obsolete when its average variable cost exceeds the average total cost of new capital.

FIGURE 12-10   Plants of Different Vintages in an Industry with Continuing Technical Progress

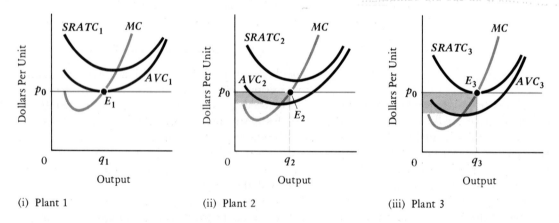

(i) Plant 1   (ii) Plant 2   (iii) Plant 3

Entry of progressively lower-cost firms forces price down, but older plants with higher costs remain in the industry as long as price covers average variable cost. Plant 3 is the newest plant with the lowest costs. Long-run equilibrium price will be determined by the average total costs of plants of this type since entry will continue as long as the owners of the newest plants expect to earn profits from them. Plant 1 is the oldest plant in operation. It is just covering its *AVC*, and if the price falls any further it will be closed down. Plant 2 is a plant of intermediate age. It is covering its variable costs and earning some contribution toward its fixed costs. In (ii) and (iii), the excess of revenues over variable costs is indicated by the shaded area.

Declining Industries

What happens when a competitive industry in long-run equilibrium begins to suffer losses due to a permanent and continuing decrease in the demand for its products? As demand declines, price falls and firms that were previously covering average total costs are no longer able to do so. They find themselves in the position shown in Figure 12-6(i). Firms suffer losses instead of breaking even, and the signal for exit of capital is given. But exit takes time.

The economically correct response to a steadily declining demand is to not replace old equipment and to continue to operate with existing equipment as long as variable costs of production can be covered. As equipment breaks down and is not repaired or replaced, the capacity of the industry will gradually shrink, slowly at first. If demand keeps declining, capacity must keep shrinking.

Declining industries typically present a sorry sight to the observer. Revenues are below long-run total costs, and as a result new equipment is not brought in to replace old equipment as it wears out. The average age of equipment in use thus rises steadily. The untrained observer seeing the industry's plight is likely to blame it on the old equipment.

The antiquated equipment in a declining industry is often the effect rather than the cause of the industry's decline.

It would not usually make sense for firms to modernize in the face of steadily falling demand even if new, improved equipment is available. To do so would increase the industry's capacity and its output, thereby making its overall plight still worse. Price would fall even more rapidly, adding further to the losses of existing firms.

A striking example of the confusion of cause and effect in a declining industry occurred during the debate over the nationalization of the coal industry in Great Britain in the period between the two world wars. The view that public control was needed to save the industry from the dead hand of third-rate, unenterprising private owners was commonly held and was undoubtedly a factor leading to its nationalization in 1946. The late Sir Roy Harrod, a leading

British economist from the 1920s to the 1960s, shocked many by taking the opposite view, arguing that the rundown state of the coal industry in some parts of England represented the correct response of the owners to the signals of the market.

> Economic efficiency does not consist in always introducing the most up-to-date equipment that an engineer can think of. . . . In not introducing new equipment, the managements may have been wise, not only from the point of view of their own interest, but from that of national interest, which requires the most profitable application of available capital . . . it is right that as much should be extracted from the inferior mines as can be done by old-fashioned methods [i.e., with equipment already installed], and that they should gradually go out of action.[7]

The general point that Professor Harrod makes is extremely important. Capital resources are scarce; to install new plant and equipment in a genuinely declining industry is to use scarce resources where they will not lead to the largest possible increases in the value of national output. It is in the public and the private interest that what appear to be antiquated methods be employed in declining industries.

The Appeal of Perfect Competition

The theory of perfect competition shows that profit-maximizing, price-taking firms, responding to prices set by the impersonal forces of supply and demand, will be motivated to provide all commodities for which total revenues are equal to or greater than total costs. They will be motivated to produce every unit for which price is greater than marginal cost, and they will thus expand production up to the point where price equals marginal cost. The entry and exit of firms will, in long-run equilibrium, push prices to the level of minimum average total costs, that is, to the lowest level attainable for the given technology and factor prices.

Consider an economy in which every industry operates as a perfectly competitive industry. For the

[7] Roy Harrod, *The British Economy* (New York: McGraw-Hill, 1963), page 54.

nineteenth century liberal economists, such a world was more than a theoretical model; it was a most attractive ideal. One of them, Bascom, glowingly characterized such an economic system as "more provocative of virtue than virtue herself." The appeal of a competitive economy has both non-economic and economic aspects. The non-economic aspects are considered briefly below. The economic aspects are discussed in detail in Chapter 14.

In a perfectly competitive economy there are many firms and many households. Each is a price taker, responding as it sees fit, freely and without coercion, to signals sent to it by the market. For one who believes in the freedom of individuals to make decisions and who distrusts all power groups, the perfectly competitive model is almost too good to be true. No single firm and no single consumer has any power over the market. Individual consumers and producers are quantity adjusters who respond to market signals.

Yet the impersonal force of the market produces an appropriate response to all changes. If tastes change, for example, prices will change, and the allocation of resources will change in the appropriate direction. Throughout the entire process, no one will have any power over anyone else. Dozens of firms will react to the same price changes, and if one firm refuses to react, there will be countless other profit-maximizing firms eager to make the appropriate changes.

Because the market mechanism works, it is not necessary for the government to intervene. Market reactions, not public policies, will eliminate shortages or surpluses. There is no need for regulatory agencies or bureaucrats to make arbitrary decisions about who may produce what, how to produce it, or how much it is permissible to charge for the product. If there are no government officials to make such decisions, there will be no one to bribe to make one decision rather than another.

In the impersonal decision-making world of perfect competition, neither private firms nor public officials wield economic power. The market mechanism, like an invisible hand, determines the allocation of resources among competing uses.

It is a noble model: No one has power over anyone, and yet the system behaves in a systematic and purposeful way. Many feel that it is a pity that it corresponds so imperfectly to economic reality as we know it today. Not surprisingly, some people still cling tenaciously to the belief that the perfectly competitive model describes the world in which we live; so many problems would disappear if only it did.

Summary

1. Market behavior is concerned with whether and how individual firms compete against one another; market structure is concerned with the type of market in which firms operate. Market structure affects the degree of power that individual firms have to influence such market variables as the price of the product. Under the market structure known as perfect competition, individual firms are price takers.

2. A profit-maximizing firm will produce at a level of output where (a) price is at least as great as average variable cost, and (b) marginal cost equals marginal revenue.

3. The two critical assumptions of the theory of perfect competition are that firms are price takers and that the industry displays freedom of entry and exit. A firm that is a price taker will adjust to different market conditions by varying its output.

4. Under perfect competition each firm's short-run supply curve is identical in shape to its marginal cost curve above average variable

cost. The perfectly competitive industry's short-run supply curve is the horizontal sum of its firms' supply curves (i.e., the horizontal sum of the firms' marginal cost curves).

5. If any profit-maximizing firm is to produce at all, it must be able to cover its variable cost. But such a firm may be making losses (price less than average total cost), making profits (price greater than average total cost), or just breaking even (price equal to average total cost).

6. In the long run, profits or losses will lead to the entry or exit of capital from the industry. Entry or exit will push a competitive industry to a long-run zero-profit equilibrium and move production to the level consistent with minimum average total cost.

7. The long-run response of a growing, perfectly competitive industry to steadily changing technology is the gradual replacement of less efficient plants and machines by more efficient ones. Older plant and equipment will be utilized as long as price exceeds average variable cost; only when average variable costs rise above price will they be discarded and replaced by more modern ones. The long-run response of a declining industry will be to continue to satisfy demand from its existing machinery as long as price exceeds *AVC*. Despite the appearance of being antiquated, this is the correct response to steadily falling demand.

8. The great appeal of perfect competition as a means of organizing production lies in the decentralized decision making of myriad firms and households. No individual exercises power over the market. At the same time it is not necessary for the government to intervene to determine resource allocation and prices.

Topics for Review

Competitive behavior and competitive market structure
Behavioral rules for the profit-maximizing firm
Price taking and a horizontal demand curve
Average revenue, marginal revenue, and price under perfect competition
Relation of the industry supply curve to firms' marginal cost curves
Entry and exit in achieving equilibrium
Short-run and long-run equilibrium of firms and industries

Discussion Questions

1. Consider the suppliers of the following commodities. What elements of market structure might you invoke to account for differences in their market behavior? Could any of these be characterized as perfectly competitive industries?
   a. Television broadcasting
   b. Automobiles

  c. Sand and gravel
  d. Medical services
  e. Mortgage loans
  f. Retail fruits and vegetables
  g. Soybeans

2. Which of the following observed facts about an industry are inconsistent with its being a perfectly competitive industry?

  a. Different firms use different methods of production.

  b. There is extensive advertising of the industry's product by a trade association.

  c. Individual firms devote 5 percent of sales receipts to advertising their own product brand.

  d. There are 24 firms in the industry.

  e. The largest firm in the industry makes 40 percent of the sales and the next largest firm makes 20 percent, but the products are identical and there are 61 other firms.

  f. All firms made large profits in 1980.

3. In which of the following sectors of the American economy might you expect to find competitive behavior? In which might you expect to find industries that are classified as operating under perfectly competitive market structures?

  a. Manufacturing

  b. Agriculture

  c. Transportation and public utilities

  d. Wholesale and retail trade

  e. Criminal activity

4. In the 1930s the U.S. coal industry was characterized by easy entry and price taking. Because of large fixed costs in mine shafts and fixed equipment, however, exit was slow. With declining demand many firms were barely covering their variable costs, but not their total costs. As a result of a series of mine accidents, the federal government began to enforce mine safety standards, which forced most firms to invest in new capital if they were to remain in production. What predictions would competitive theory make about market behavior and the quantity of coal produced? Would coal miners approve or disapprove of the new enforcement program?

5. Suppose entry into an industry is not artificially restricted, but takes time because of the need to build plants, acquire know-how, and establish a marketing organization. Can such an industry be characterized as perfectly competitive? Does ease of entry imply ease of exit, and vice versa?

6. What, if anything, does each one of the following tell you about ease of entry or exit in an industry?

  a. Profits have been very high for two decades.

  b. No new firms have entered the industry for 20 years.

  c. The average age of the firms in a 40-year-old industry is less than seven years.

  d. Most existing firms are using obsolete equipment alongside newer, more modern equipment.

  e. Profits are low or negative; many firms are still producing, but from steadily aging equipment.

7. In the 1970s grain prices in North America rose substantially relative to other agricultural products. Explain how each of the following may have contributed to this result.
   a. Crop failures caused by unusually bad weather around the world in several years
   b. Rising demand for beef and chickens because of rising population and rising per capita income
   c. Great scarcities in fishmeal, a substitute for grain in animal diets, because of a mysterious decline in the anchovy harvest off Peru
   d. Increased Soviet purchases of grain on the world market

13

Pricing in Monopoly Markets

Is Consolidated Edison a monopoly? How about IBM, U.S. Steel, the National Football League, or the Coca-Cola Company? Just as the word *competition* has both an everyday meaning and a more specialized technical one, so, too, does *monopoly*. The word *monopoly* comes from the Greek words *monos polein,* which mean "alone to sell." It is convenient for now to think of **monopoly** as the situation in which the output of an entire industry is controlled by a single seller. This seller will be called the *monopolist*. Later in this chapter we will define monopoly in a less restrictive way.

Because the monopoly firm is the only producer of a particular product, its demand curve is identical with the demand curve for that product. The market demand curve, which shows the aggregate quantity that buyers will purchase at every price, also shows the quantity that the monopolist will be able to sell at any price it sets. The importance of this is that the monopoly, unlike the firm in perfect competition, faces a downward-sloping demand curve. The firm therefore faces a trade-off between price and quantity: Sales can be increased only if price is reduced, while price can be increased only if sales are reduced.

A Single-Price Monopolist

At the outset we confine ourselves to a monopolist that charges a single price for all units of the product that are sold.

Monopoly Revenue

Given the market demand curve, the firm's average revenue and marginal revenue curves can be readily deduced. When the monopoly seller charges a single price for all units sold, average revenue per unit is identical with price. Thus, the market demand curve is also the firm's average revenue curve. But marginal revenue is less than price because the firm has to lower the price it charges on *all* units in order to sell an *extra* unit. [26] This is an important difference from the case of perfect competition; it is explored numerically in Table 13-1 and graphically in Figure 13-1.

The top part of Figure 13-2 on page 232 illustrates the average and

TABLE 13-1 The Relation of Average Revenue and Marginal Revenue: A Numerical Illustration

Price $p = AR$	Quantity q	$TR = p \times q$	$MR = \Delta TR / \Delta q$
$9.10	9	$81.90	
			$8.10
9.00	10	90.00	
			7.90
8.90	11	97.90	

Marginal revenue is less than price because price must be lowered to sell an extra unit. A monopolist can choose either the price or the quantity to be sold. But choosing one determines the other. In this example, to increase sales from 10 to 11 units, it is necessary to reduce the price on all units sold from $9 to $8.90. The extra unit sold brings in $8.90, but the firm sacrifices $.10 on each of the 10 units that it could have sold at $9 had it not wanted to increase sales. The net addition to revenue is the $8.90 minus $.10 times 10 units, or $1, making $7.90 altogether. Thus the marginal revenue resulting from the increase in sales by 1 unit is $7.90, which is less than the price at which the units are sold.

Marginal revenue is shown displaced by half a line to emphasize that it represents the effect on revenue of the *change* in output.

FIGURE 13-1 The Effect on Revenue of an Increase in Quantity Sold

For a downward-sloping demand curve, marginal revenue is less than price. A reduction of price from p_0 to p_1 increases sales from q_0 to q_1 units. The revenue from the extra amount sold is shown as the lighter shaded area. But to sell this extra amount, it is necessary to reduce the price on all of the q_0 units previously sold. The loss in revenue is shown as the darker shaded area. Marginal revenue of the extra amount is equal to the *difference* between the two areas.

marginal revenue curves for a monopolist, based on a downward-sloping straight-line demand curve.[1] In Chapter 5 we discussed the relation between elasticity of demand and total revenue. Figure 13-2 summarizes this earlier discussion and extends it to cover marginal revenue. When the demand curve is elastic, total revenue rises as quantity rises; marginal revenue must, therefore, be positive. When the demand curve is inelastic, total revenue falls as quantity rises; marginal revenue must, therefore, be negative.

Short-Run Monopoly Equilibrium

To describe the profit-maximizing position of a monopolist, we need only bring together information about the monopolist's revenues and its costs and apply the rules developed in Chapter 12 (page 214).

The key difference between firms in these two types of market structure lies in the demand conditions.[2] The firm that sells in a perfectly competitive market is faced with a perfectly elastic demand curve. This not only sets its price, but also implies that price equals marginal revenue. The firm that sells in a monopolized market faces a downward-sloping demand curve. Hence, its actions influence its price. This causes the firm's marginal revenue to differ from price; as we have seen, marginal revenue is less than price. Thus, when the monopoly firm follows the profit-maximizing rule of equating marginal revenue to marginal cost, it reaches the equilibrium

[1] It is helpful for sketching these curves to remember that if the demand curve is a downward-sloping straight line, the *MR* curve also slopes downward and is twice as steep. Its price intercept (where $q = 0$) is the same as that of the demand curve, and it cuts the quantity axis (where $p = 0$) at just half the output that the demand curve does. [27]

[2] A monopoly firm is subject to the law of diminishing returns in just the same way as is a firm that operates in a perfectly competitive market. Thus the monopoly firm will have the same type of U-shaped cost curve as has a competitive firm.

FIGURE 13-2   The Relation of Total, Average, and Marginal Revenue to Elasticity of Demand

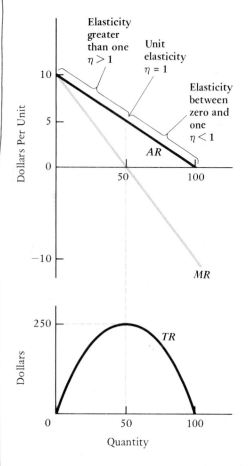

For a monopolist *MR* is always less than price; when *TR* is rising, *MR* is greater than zero and elasticity is greater than one. The monopoly firm's demand curve is its *AR* curve; the *MR* curve is below and steeper than the *AR* curve because the demand curve slopes downward.

In the example shown, for outputs from 0 to 50, marginal revenue is positive, elasticity is greater than one, and total revenue is rising. For outputs from 50 to 100, marginal revenue is negative, elasticity is less than one, and total revenue is falling.

shown in Figure 13-3, where marginal cost is less than price.

The monopoly firm produces where marginal revenue equals marginal cost. The price corresponding to that output is given by the demand curve.

Note one key respect in which the equilibrium of a monopoly differs from that of a firm in perfect competition. While a competitive firm produces at an output where $p = MC$, the monopoly firm produces at an output where p is greater than MC. We shall discuss some implications of this later.

Our earlier discussion of the relation between elasticity and revenue has one interesting implication for the monopoly equilibrium that we have just developed. Since marginal cost is always greater than zero, the profit-maximizing monopoly (which produces where $MR = MC$) will produce where marginal revenue is positive, that is, where demand is elastic. If the firm were producing where demand were inelastic, it could both increase its revenue and reduce its costs by reducing its sales.

A profit-maximizing monopoly will never push its sales of a commodity into the range over which the demand curve becomes inelastic.

Monopoly profits.   The fact that a profit-maximizing monopoly produces at an output where $MR = MC$ says nothing about how large profits will be in the short run or even whether there will be monopoly profits. Profits may exist, as shown in Figure 13-3(i), and indeed they may persist for a long time because as long as the firm retains its monopoly, entry of new firms does not push price down to the level of average total cost.

But, as Figure 13-3(ii) shows, the profit-maximizing monopolist may only break even or suffer losses. Nothing guarantees that a monopolist will make profits, and if it cannot eliminate its losses, the firm will eventually fail.

The supply curve under monopoly.   In describing the monopolist's profit-maximizing behavior, we did not introduce the concept of a supply curve, as we

FIGURE 13-3 The Profit-Maximizing Position of a Monopolist

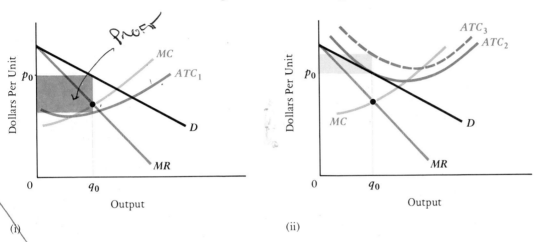

(i)   (ii)

Profit-maximizing output is q_0, where $MR = MC$; price is p_0, which is above MC at that output. The rules for profit maximization require $MR = MC$ and $p > AVC$. (AVC is not shown in the diagram, but it would be below ATC.) $MR = MC$ at output q_0.

Whether or not there are profits depends on the position of the ATC curve. In (i), where average total cost is ATC_1, there are profits, as shown by the gray shaded area. In (ii), where average total cost is ATC_2, profits are zero. If average total costs rose to ATC_3, the monopolist would suffer losses, as shown by the color shaded area.

did in the discussion of perfect competition. A supply curve relates the quantity supplied to the price offered. In perfect competition the industry short-run supply curve is known as soon as the marginal cost curves of the individual firms are known. This is because under perfect competition profit-maximizing firms equate marginal cost to price. Given marginal costs, it is possible to know how much will be produced at each price.

This is not the case, however, with monopoly.

In monopoly there is no unique relation between market price and quantity supplied.

Let us see why this is so. Like all profit-maximizing firms, a monopoly equates marginal cost with marginal revenue; but, unlike firms in perfect competition, for the monopolist marginal revenue does not equal price. Because the monopolist does *not* equate marginal cost to price, it is possible for demand curves of different shapes to give rise to the same

output, but to differing prices. If the same output can be associated with different prices, there is no unique relation between price and output that is required for a supply curve.

Long-Run Equilibrium of the Firm and Industry

When a monopolist is the only producer in an industry, there is no need for separate theories of the firm and the industry, as is necessary with perfect competition. The monopolist *is* the industry. Thus the profit-maximizing position of the firm shown in Figure 13-3 is the short-run equilibrium of the industry.

In a monopolized industry, as in a perfectly competitive one, profits provide an incentive for new firms to enter. If such entry occurs, the equilibrium position will change and the firm will no longer be a monopolist.

Entry Barriers

A monopoly will persist only if entry of new firms does not occur. Impediments that prevent entry are called **entry barriers;** they may be either natural or created.

If a monopoly is to persist in the long run, there must be barriers to entry of other firms into the industry.

When effective barriers do exist, economists speak of entry as being blockaded.

Natural barriers.   Natural barriers most commonly arise as a result of economies of scale. If the long-run average cost declines over a large range of output, big firms will have significantly lower average total costs than small firms.

Recall from Chapter 12 that the *minimum efficient scale (MES)* is the smallest size of firm that can reap all of the economies of large-scale production. It occurs at the level of output where the firm's long-run average total cost curve reaches a minimum.

Now suppose the technology of an industry is such that the typical firm's minimum efficient scale is 10,000 units a week at an average total cost of $10 per unit. Further assume that at a price of $10, the total quantity demanded is 11,000 units per week. In these circumstances there is room for only one firm operating at or near its minimum efficient scale.

A natural monopoly results when, as in the above example, the industry's demand conditions are such that only one firm can operate at the minimum efficient scale. In these circumstances if a second firm tried to enter the industry, it could not achieve sales large enough to obtain costs that were competitive with the existing firm.

Another type of natural barrier is *set-up cost.* If a firm could be catapulted full-grown into the market, it might be able to compete effectively with the existing firm. But the cost to the new firm of entering the market, developing its products, and establishing such things as its brand image and its dealer network may be such that entry is rendered unprofitable.

Created barriers.   Barriers to entry may be created by the conscious action of participants in some mar-

kets. Some are created by the government and are therefore condoned by it. Patent laws, for instance, may prevent entry by conferring on the patent holder the sole right to produce a particular commodity. A firm may also be granted a charter or a franchise that prohibits competition by law.

Other barriers are created by the existing firm itself. We shall study these in more detail in Chapter 15, but in the meantime we note that anything the existing firm can do to increase the set-up costs of new entrants will act as a barrier to entry. Of course, activities such as the threats of force, sabotage, or a price war can also deter entry, if the existing firm can make such threats credible. (The most transparent entry barriers are seen in the field of organized crime, where legal prohibitions do not prevent the use of a whole battery of crude but potent barriers to new entrants.)

The significance of entry barriers.   If there are no entry barriers, a firm would enter an industry whenever it judged that the market was sufficient to support at least one more firm. Thus in perfect competition, where there are no entry barriers, profits cannot persist in the long run. Entry will continue until profits are no longer being earned.

Profits may persist in monopoly even in the long run, but only if there are natural or created barriers to the entry of new firms. Otherwise the existence of monopoly profits will attract new firms until the profits of the original firm are eliminated. This process will, of course, eliminate the monopoly situation.

This analysis of profits and entry provides a basic insight into a two-edged driving force of the market economy:

Entry always erodes profits, while profits always attract entry.

Cartels As Monopolies

So far in this chapter we have talked about monopoly as a situation in which one firm is the single seller in an industry. A second way in which a monopoly can arise is for the firms in an industry to agree to co-operate with one another, to behave *as if* they were a single firm, and thus to eliminate competitive behavior among themselves. Such a group of firms is called a **cartel.** A cartel that includes *all* of the firms in the industry can behave in just the same way as would a single-firm monopoly that owned all of these firms. The firms can agree among themselves to restrict their total output to the level that maximizes their joint profits.

The Effects of Cartelization

To study the profit incentive to form a cartel, we will consider markets free from any form of government regulation and control. The basic result in these circumstances is:

It is always profitable for the firms in perfectly competitive equilibrium to increase their profits through an output-restricting agreement.

The reason is that the equilibrium of a perfectly competitive industry is *invariably* one in which a restriction of output, and a consequent increase in price, would raise the profits of all producers. At any competitive equilibrium each firm is producing where marginal cost equals price. (See, for example, Figure 12-3.) But as we have seen, marginal revenue for the industry is less than price and thus also less than marginal cost. Thus in competitive equilibrium the last unit sold necessarily contributes less to the industry's revenue than to its costs. Thus, restricting the industry's output must raise the industry's profits. The effect of cartelizing a perfectly competitive industry is shown in more detail in Figure 13-4.

Problems of Cartel Enforcement

Consider a cartel that includes all of the firms in a formerly competitive industry. Since before the cartel was formed, the members were separate firms in the one industry, we infer that the industry contains no overriding natural entry barriers. Thus the cartel, just as a single-firm monopoly in an industry with weak natural entry barriers, must create and maintain barriers to prevent the entry of new firms attracted by the profits that cartelization makes possible.

In addition, cartels have some special problems

FIGURE 13-4   The Effect of Cartelizing an Industry in Perfectly Competitive Equilibrium

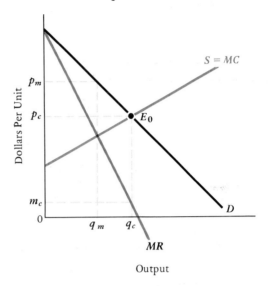

Cartelization of a perfectly competitive industry can always increase that industry's profits.
Equilibrium for a perfectly competitive industry occurs at E_0, where the supply and demand curves intersect. Equilibrium price and output are at p_c and q_c. Because the industry demand curve slopes downward, marginal revenue is necessarily less than price. In the diagram, marginal revenue is m_c at the competitive equilibrium output of q_c.

If the industry is cartelized, profits can be increased by reducing output. All units between q_c and q_m add less to revenue than to cost—the marginal revenue curve lies below the marginal cost curve. (Recall from Figure 12-5 that the industry's supply curve is the sum of the marginal cost curves of the firms in the industry.) If the units between q_c and q_m are not produced, output is reduced to q_m and price rises to p_m. This price-output combination maximizes the industry's profits because it is where marginal revenue equals marginal cost.

of their own. One key problem is how to secure cartel membership by all the firms in the industry so as to establish what is, in effect, monopoly behavior. A second problem is how to prevent the cartel's members from cheating by departing from their joint agreement to restrict output.

Individual self-interest motivates individual firms

to remain outside of the cartel or to cheat if they are inside the cartel, but their joint interest provides them with an incentive to cooperate. Every firm that enters the cartel and cooperates in restricting output is better off than it would be if all firms competed with each other. However, if firm X is the only firm to remain outside of the cartel or if it is inside but the only cheater, it is in the best of all possible situations. All other firms restrict output and drive up the industry price. They earn profits, but only by restricting output. Firm X can then reap the benefit of the other firms' restraint and sell all that it wishes at the price that is set by the actions of all of the other cooperating firms. However, if all firms cheat, price will be pushed back to the competitive level, and all firms will be back in the zero-profit position.

Cartels tend to be unstable because of the incentives for individual firms to violate the output quotas that are needed to enforce the monopoly price.

The conflict between cooperation and independent action is analyzed in more detail in Figure 13-5.

Cartels and similar output-restricting arrangements have a long history. For one example, schemes to raise farm incomes by limiting crops bear ample testimony to the accuracy of the predicted instability of cartels. Crop restriction agreements often break down and prices fall, as individuals exceed their quotas. The great bitterness and occasional violence that are sometimes exhibited against cheaters by members of crop restriction plans are readily understandable.

FIGURE 13-5   Conflicting Forces Affecting Cartels

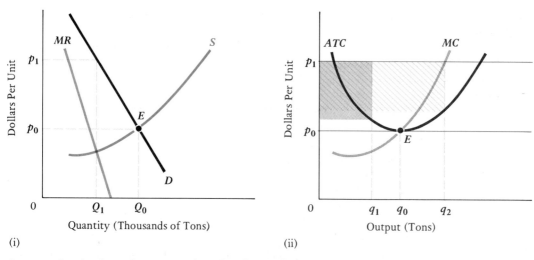

(i)

(ii)

Cooperation leads to the monopoly price, but individual self-interest may lead to production in excess of the monopoly output. Market conditions are shown in (i) and the situation of a typical firm in (ii). (Note the change of scale between the two figures.) Initially, the market is in competitive equilibrium with price p_0 and quantity Q_0. The individual firm is producing output q_0 and is just covering its total costs.

The cartel is formed and then enforces quotas on individual firms sufficient to reduce the industry's output to Q_1, the output where the supply curve cuts the marginal revenue curve. Q_1 is thus the output that maximizes the joint profits of the cartel members. Price rises to p_1 as a result. The typical firm's quota is q_1. The firm's profits rise from zero to the amount shown by the gray shaded area. Once price is raised to p_1, however, the individual firm would like to increase output to q_2, where marginal cost is equal to the price set by the cartel. This would allow the firm to earn profits shown by the diagonally striped area. But if all firms increase their outputs above their quotas, industry output will increase beyond Q_1, and the profits earned by all firms will fall.

In Chapter 15 we shall study the behavior of one of the classic cartels of modern times, the Organization of Petroleum Exporting Countries (OPEC).

The Nature and Extent of Monopoly Power

According to the theory so far developed, a monopoly firm or a cartel can set about maximizing its short-run profits unconcerned about any competition from other firms, although it must worry about the threat of entry in the long run. Such a view is, however, an extreme simplification of reality. Indeed, it is difficult to imagine any situation that would leave a firm without *any* competition, even in the short run.

There are substitutes for every product. Some products have fairly close substitutes, and even a single seller producing such a product will have close rivals. Other products may have no existing close substitute, but new products may be developed that will compete with it. For this reason it is useful to view monopoly power as a variable that can be relatively slight or nearly complete, rather than as an attribute which either does or does not exist.

Monopoly power exists to the extent that a firm is insulated from loss of sales to other firms.

Any producer who is facing a downward-sloping demand curve could choose the price-quantity combination (where $MR = MC$) that appears to maximize its profits. *But this price might not turn out to be the long-run profit-maximizing price* because the choice of a particular price-quantity combination may itself lead to changes in the behavior of other firms that in turn *shift* the original firm's demand curve.

Consider an example. The Coca-Cola Company is the sole producer of Coca-Cola and faces a downward-sloping demand curve. Suppose the demand curve for Coke shows that if the price is cut by 20 percent *and* if all other soft drink suppliers keep their prices at their present levels, sales of Coke will increase by 50 percent. Why, then, does the company not cut the price of Coke? The answer is that if it did, other soft drink prices would *not* remain unchanged—and the company knows this.

If other soft drink producers cut their prices in response, Coca-Cola's sales would not increase as much as its demand curve predicts based on the assumption of no changes in other's prices. Sales might increase by only 10 percent instead of the 50 percent predicted by the demand curve based on the assumption that other prices do not change. The company's profits would then decrease rather than increase. Thus the Coca-Cola Company, while it has a monopoly of Coca-Cola sales, does not have a monopoly of soft drink sales, although it may well have some market power over the whole soft drink market.

What the above discussion argues and the example illustrates is that the number of firms in an industry is an inadequate measure of the market power of those firms; more sophisticated measures are needed.

The larger the *shifts* in a demand curve that are induced when a firm changes its price, the less is that firm's monopoly power. Such shifts have two main sources. The first (as in the Coca-Cola example) is the price reaction of existing producers of substitute products. The second is the entry of new firms that succeed in capturing part of the sales that the monopolist included in "its" demand curve. Such shifts in the demand curve, from either cause, limit the market power of the firm and reduce its profits.

Since no firm is perfectly insulated from all competition for all time, total monopoly power never exists. Monopoly power is thus a variable.

Measuring Monopoly Power

Measuring monopoly power is not easy. Ideally, prices, outputs, and profits of firms in any industry should be compared with what they would be if all firms were under unified (monopoly) control and were fully insulated from entry. But such a hypothetical comparison does not lend itself to measurement. In practice, two alternative summary statistics are widely used to measure monopoly power: concentration ratios and profit rates.

Concentration Ratios

The **concentration ratio** is the fraction of total market sales controlled by some specified number of the largest sellers. Common types of concentration ratios cite the share of an industry's total market sales made by the largest four or eight firms but it could be any other number, such as two or ten. How well concentration ratios measure effective monopoly power is a matter of substantial debate among economists.

A first problem is to define the market with reasonable accuracy. For example, concentration ratios in national cement sales are low, but they understate the market power of cement companies because heavy transportation costs divide the cement *industry* into a series of regional *markets,* in each of which there are relatively few firms.

A second problem is the interpretation of concentration ratios. Clearly, market share is one measure of the *potential* power to control supply and set price. The inclusion in concentration ratios of the market shares of several firms rests on the possibility that large firms will, in one way or another, adopt a common price-output policy that is no different from the policy they would adopt if they were in fact under unified management.

Earlier in this chapter we defined a cartel in terms of an explicit agreement among two or more firms to act as if they were a single monopolistic firm. Such behavior is called **collusion.** Collusive behavior may occur with or without an actual agreement to collude. Where explicit agreement occurs, and a cartel is formed, economists speak of *overt* or *covert collusion,* depending on whether the agreement is open or secret. Where no agreement actually occurs, economists speak of **tacit collusion** (while lawyers speak of *conscious parallel action*). In this case all firms behave as if they were a single monopolist without an explicit agreement to do so. They merely understand that it is in their mutual interest to restrict output and not to cheat by trying to increase their sales and so drive prices downward.

Concentration ratios measure the potential for the exercise of monopoly power. The monopoly power is realized only if collusion—whether overt, covert, or tacit—actually occurs.

High concentration ratios may be necessary for the exercise of monopoly power, but they are not sufficient. They tend to show the potential for monopoly power, but not necessarily the actuality.

Profit Rates

Many economists, following the lead of Professor Joe S. Bain, use profit rates as a measure of monopoly power. By *high profits,* these economists mean returns sufficiently in excess of all opportunity costs that potential new entrants desire to enter the industry. Persistently high profits, so goes the logic, are indirect evidence that neither rivalry among sellers nor entry of new firms prevents existing firms from pricing as if they were monopolists.

Using profits in this way requires care because, as we have seen (page 168), profits as reported in firms' income statements are not what the economist calls profits—the excess of revenue over opportunity cost. In particular, allowance must be made for differences in risk and in required payments for the use of owners' capital.

While neither concentration ratios nor profit rates are ideal measures of the degree of market power that a firm, or group of firms, actually exercises, both are of value and are widely used. In fact, concentration ratios and high profit rates are themselves correlated. Because of this, alternative classifications of markets and industries, according to their monopoly power measured in these two ways, do not differ much from one another. In spite of the difficult problems of measuring monopoly power, the theory of monopoly is widely used by economists and policymakers.

A Multi-Price Monopolist: Price Discrimination

So far in this chapter we have assumed that the monopoly firm charges the same price for every unit of product no matter to whom or where it sells. But other situations are common. Raw milk is often sold at one price when it is to go into fluid milk, but at a lower price when it is to be used to make ice cream or cheese. Doctors often charge for their services according to the incomes of their patients. Movie theaters may have lower admission prices for children than adults. Railroads charge different rates per ton mile for different products. Electric companies sell electricity at lower rates for industrial than for home use. State universities charge out-of-state students higher tuition than residents. Japanese steel companies sell steel more cheaply in the United States than in Japan.

Price discrimination occurs when a producer sells different units of a specific commodity to buyers at two or more different prices, for reasons not associated with differences in cost. Not all price *differences* represent price *discrimination*. Quantity discounts, differences between wholesale and retail prices, and prices that vary with the time of day or the season of the year are not generally considered price discrimination because the same physical product sold at a different time or place or in different quantities may have different costs. If an electric power company has unused capacity at certain times of day, it may be cheaper to provide service at those hours than at peak demand hours. If the price differences reflect cost differences, they are nondiscriminatory.

However, when price differences rest merely on different buyers' valuations of the same product, they are discriminatory. It does not cost a movie theater operator less to fill a seat with a child than an adult, but it may pay to let the children in at a discriminatory low price if few of them would attend at the full adult fare.

Why should a firm want to sell some units of output at a price well below the price it gets for other units? Why, in other words, is price discrimination profitable?

Why Price Discrimination Pays

Persistent price discrimination comes about either because different buyers are willing to pay different amounts for the same commodity or because one buyer is willing to pay different amounts for different units of the same commodity. The basic point about price discrimination is that in either of these circumstances sellers may be able to capture some of the consumers' surplus that would otherwise go to buyers. (You should now review the discussion of consumers' surplus on pages 134–136.)

Discrimination among units. Look back to Table 7-2 on page 135, which showed the consumers' surplus received by one consumer if she bought eight glasses of milk at a single price. If the firm could sell her each glass separately, it could capture this consumers' surplus. It would sell the first unit for $3.00, the second for $1.50, the third for $1.00, and so on until the eighth was sold for $.30. The firm would get total revenues of $8.10 rather than the $2.40 received by selling at the single price. In this example, the firm has been able to discriminate perfectly and extract every bit of the consumers' surplus.

Of course, such perfect price discrimination may not be possible. But suppose the firm could charge two different prices, one for the first four units sold and one for the next four sold. If it sold the first four for $.80 and the next four for $.30, it would receive $4.40—less than if it could discriminate perfectly, but more than it would receive from the sale of all units at any single price.

Discrimination among buyers. Think of the demand curve in a market containing individual buyers, each of whom has indicated the maximum price he or she is prepared to pay for a single unit. Suppose for simplicity that there are only four buyers, the first of whom is prepared to pay any price up to $4, the second $3, the third $2, and the fourth $1. Suppose the product has a marginal cost of production of $1 per unit for all units. If the seller is limited to a single price, it will maximize its profits by charging $3, sell two units, and earn profits of $4. If the seller can discriminate between units, it could charge the first buyer $4 and the second $3, thus increasing profits from the first two units to $5. Moreover, it could also sell the third unit for $2 and the fourth unit for $1. Its profits would increase to $6.

Price discrimination more generally. Demand curves slope downward because different units are valued differently, either by one individual as a result of diminishing marginal utility or by different individuals. That fact, combined with a single price, gives rise to consumers' surplus.

The ability to charge multiple prices gives a seller the opportunity to capture some (or, in the extreme, all) of the consumers' surplus.

In general, the more prices that can be charged, the greater the seller's ability to increase its revenue at the expense of consumers. This is illustrated in Figure 13-6.

It follows, for any given output, that if a seller is able to price discriminate, it can increase revenues received (and thus also profits) from the sale of those units. [28] But price discrimination is not always possible, even if there are no legal barriers to its use.

When Is Price Discrimination Possible?

Discrimination among units of output sold to the same buyer requires that the seller be able to keep track of the units a buyer consumes each period. Thus the tenth unit purchased by a given buyer in a given month can be sold at a different price from the fifth unit *only* if the seller can keep track of who buys what. This can be done by the electric company through its meter readings or by the magazine publishers' distinguishing between renewals and new subscriptions. It can also be done by an establishment's giving a certificate or coupon providing, for example, a reduced price car wash for a return visit.

Discrimination among buyers is possible only if the goods cannot be resold by the buyer who faces the low price to the buyer who faces the high price. However much the local butcher might like to charge the banker's wife twice as much for hamburger as he charges the taxi driver, he cannot succeed in doing so. Madame Banker can always shop for meat in the supermarket, where her husband's occupation is not known. Even if the butcher and the supermarket agreed to charge her twice as much, she could hire the taxi driver to shop for her. The surgeon, however, may succeed in discriminating (if all reputable surgeons will do the same) because it will not do the

banker's wife much good to hire the taxi driver to have her operations for her.

Price discrimination is possible if the seller can either distinguish individual units bought by a single buyer or separate buyers into classes such that resale among classes is impossible.

Ability to prevent resale tends to be associated with the character of the product or the ability to classify buyers into readily identifiable groups. Services are less easily resold than goods; goods that require installation by the manufacturer (e.g., heavy equipment) are less easily resold than movable goods such as household appliances. An interesting example of nonresalability occurs in the case of plate glass. Small pieces are much cheaper per square foot than bigger pieces, but the person who needs glass for a 6′ × 10′ picture window cannot use four pieces of 3′ × 5′ glass. Transportation costs, tariff barriers, and import quotas separate classes of buyers geographically and may make discrimination possible.

It is, of course, not enough to be able to separate buyers or units into separate classes. The seller must be able to control the supply to each group. This is what makes price discrimination an aspect of the theory of monopoly.[3]

Positive Aspects of Price Discrimination

The positive consequences of price discrimination are summarized in two propositions.

1. For any given level of output, the most profitable system of discriminatory prices will provide higher total revenue to the firm than the profit-maximizing single price.

---

[3] For price discrimination to be profitable, the different groups must have different degrees of willingness to pay. The hypothesis of diminishing marginal utility would lead to the prediction that different valuations are placed by an individual on different units, and differences in income and tastes would lead to the prediction that different subgroups will have different elasticities of demand for a given commodity. Thus, the potential for profitable price discrimination is usually present.

FIGURE 13-6   Price Discrimination

(i) Two prices charged

(ii) Four prices charged

Multiple prices permit a seller to capture consumers' surplus. Suppose in either diagram that if a single price were charged, it would be the price p_0. Quantity q_0 would be sold, and consumers' surplus would be the entire area above p_0 and below the demand curve. In (i) two prices are charged: p_1 for the first q_1 units and p_0 for other units. Consumers' surplus is reduced to the two shaded areas, and the seller's revenue is increased accordingly. In (ii) four prices are charged: p_2 for the first q_2 units, p_1 for the units between q_2 and q_1, and so on. Consumers' surplus is further reduced to the shaded areas, and the seller's revenue is increased accordingly. At the extreme, if a different price could be charged for each unit, producers could extract every bit of the consumers' surplus, and the price discrimination would be perfect.

This proposition was illustrated in Figure 13-5. All it requires is a downward-sloping demand curve. To see that this is reasonable, remember that a monopolist with the power to discriminate *could* produce exactly the same quantity as a single-price monopolist and charge everyone the same price. Therefore, it need never get *less* revenue, and it can do better if it can raise the price on even one unit sold.

2. Output under price discrimination will generally be larger than under single-price monopoly.

Remember that a monopoly firm that must charge a single price produces less than the perfectly competitive industry because producing and selling more would drive down the price against itself. Price discrimination allows it to avoid this disincentive. To the extent that the firm can sell its output in separate blocks, it can sell another block without spoiling the market for the block already being sold. In the case of *perfect* price discrimination, where every unit of output is sold at a different price, the profit-maximizing firm will produce every unit for which the price charged can be greater than or equal to its marginal cost. It will, therefore, produce the same output as the firm in perfect competition.

Normative Aspects of Price Discrimination

The predicted combination of higher average revenue and higher output does not in itself have any *normative* significance. It will typically lead to a different distribution of income and a different level of output than when the seller is limited to a single price. The ability of the discriminating monopolist to capture some of the consumers' surplus will seem undesirable to consumers but not to the monopolist. How outsiders view the transfer may depend on who gains and who loses. For instance, when railroads discriminated against small farmers, the results aroused public anger; when doctors in private practice discriminate by giving low-priced service to poor patients, it is taken to be necessary since the poor would not be able to afford medical care if doctors charged all their patients the same fees.

Price discrimination, we have seen, tends to lead to larger output than is produced by a single-price monopoly. As we shall see in Chapter 14 this causes price discrimination to *decrease* what we will there

BOX 13-1

Is Price Discrimination Bad?

The consequences of price discrimination differ from case to case. No matter what an individual's values are, he or she is almost bound to evaluate individual cases differently from one another.

Secret rebates. A large oil-refining firm agrees to ship its product to market on a given railroad, provided that the railroad gives the firm a secret rebate on the transportation cost and does not give a similar concession to rival refiners. The railroad agrees and is thereby charging discriminatory prices. This rebate gives the oil company a cost advantage that it uses to drive its rivals out of business or to force them into a merger on dictated terms. (John D. Rockefeller was accused of using such tactics in the early years of the Standard Oil Company.)

Use of product. When the Aluminum Company of America had a virtual monopoly on the production of aluminum ingots, it sold both the raw ingots and aluminum cable made from the ingots. At one time ALCOA sold cable at a price 20 percent *below* its price for ingots. (Of course, the cable price was above ALCOA's cost of producing cable.) It did so because users of cable could substitute copper cable, but many users of ingot had no substitute for aluminum. In return for its "bargain price" for cable, ALCOA made the purchasers of cable agree to use it only for transmission purposes. (Without such an agreement, any demander of aluminum might have bought cable and melted it down.)

Covering costs. A product that many people want to purchase has a demand and cost structure such that there is no single price at which a producing firm can cover total costs. However, if the firm is allowed to charge discriminatory prices, it will be willing to produce the product and it may make a profit. This is illustrated in the figure.

Because the average total cost *(ATC)* curve is everywhere higher than the demand curve *(D)*, no single price would lead to revenues equal to costs. A price-discriminating monopolist may be able to cover cost. The total cost of output q is the area $0cbq$. The maximum revenue attainable at any output by perfect discrimination is the area under the demand curve. For output q that area, shown as gray shaded, exceeds total cost since the gray shaded triangle cda is greater than the color shaded triangle abe.

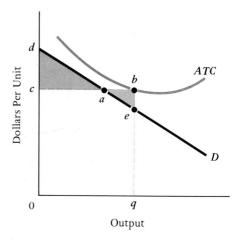

Equitable fares. For many years British railways were not allowed to discriminate among passengers in different regions. To prevent discrimination, a fixed fare per passenger mile was specified and charged on all lines, whatever their passenger traffic and whatever the elasticity of demand for the services of the particular line. In the interests of economy branch lines that could not cover costs closed down. Some lines stopped operating even though their users preferred rail transport to any alternatives and the strength of their preference was such that they would have willingly paid a price sufficient for the line to yield a profit. But the lines were closed because it was thought inequitable to discriminate against the passengers on these lines.

define as the allocative inefficiency of monopoly. Indeed, under perfect price discrimination the monopolist produces up to the point where price equals marginal cost and thus achieves allocative efficiency.

The fact that price discrimination may actually improve efficiency may seem paradoxical, for price discrimination has a bad reputation among economists and lawyers. To many people *discrimination* of any sort has odious connotations. Laws make certain kinds of price discrimination illegal. But was discrimination by airlines in giving senior citizens lower standby fares really bad? Some further examples are explored in Box 13-1.

There are two quite separate questions involved in evaluating a particular example of price discrimination. One is a question of the level of output produced; the other is a question of the distribution of that output. Economists can identify both kinds of effects, and the desirability of each can be debated. Whether an individual judges price discrimination as bad or good depends on the details of the particular example as well as on personal value judgments. Often it is the income redistribution caused by price discrimination that accounts for the strong emotional reactions to price discrimination. When it transfers income from poor to rich, price discrimination may seem bad, even if it increases total output; when it transfers income from rich to poor, it may seem good independent of its effect on output.

Systematic and Unsystematic Price Discrimination

The discussion so far has been concerned with systematic and persistent price discrimination. Systematic price discrimination most often consists of classifying buyers according to age, location, industry, income, or the use they intend to make of the product, and then charging different prices for the different "classes" of buyers. It may also take other forms, such as charging more for the first unit bought than for subsequent units, or vice versa.

Another sort of price discrimination is common. Any firm that occasionally gives a favorite customer a few cents off, or shaves its price to land a new account, is also engaged in price discrimination. If these practices are used irregularly, they are called *unsystematic discrimination*. Such discrimination is not really part of the price structure, but is instead the consequence of rivalrous behavior. Since we are here concerned with the consequences of market structure we have ignored such unsystematic discrimination. This does not mean that it is unimportant; on the contrary, unsystematic price discrimination plays a major role in the dynamic process by which prices change in response to changing conditions of supply and demand.

The causes and consequences of systematic price discrimination are very different from those of unsystematic price discrimination.

The law, however, is generally unable to distinguish between the two kinds of price discrimination and so hits at both. Legislation, motivated solely by a desire to attack systematic discrimination, may have unforeseen and possibly undesired effects on unsystematic discrimination. Because unsystematic price discrimination is important for the working of competition, prohibiting it may aid the maintenance of monopoly power.

Summary

1. In the simplest possible theory of monopoly an entire industry is supplied by a single firm that sets a single price for its product.
2. The monopoly firm's own demand curve is identical with the market demand curve for the product. The market demand curve is the monopoly firm's average revenue curve, while its marginal revenue curve always lies below its average revenue curve.
3. When the monopoly is maximizing profits, marginal revenue is positive, and thus elasticity of demand is greater than unity. The amount of profits a monopoly earns may be large, small, zero, or

negative in the short run, depending on the relation between demand and cost. For monopoly profits to persist in the long run, there must be effective barriers to the entry of other firms. Entry barriers can be natural or created.

4. Monopoly power is limited by the presence of substitute products, the development of new products, and the entry of new firms.

5. A single firm is not the only way a monopoly can occur. A group of firms may form a cartel by agreeing to restrict output and eliminate competitive behavior among themselves. If effective such a cartel becomes a monopoly. But cartels tend to be unstable because there are strong incentives for firms to violate cartel agreements.

6. The degree of monopoly power may be thought of as a quantitative variable. Two widely used measures of the degree of monopoly power are concentration ratios and the comparison of profits in one industry with those earned in other industries of similar risk and invested capital.

7. Price discrimination occurs when different buyers are charged different prices, or the same buyer is charged different prices on different units of the commodity purchased for reasons not associated with differences in costs. A successful price discriminator captures some of the consumers' surplus that would exist at a single price.

8. The conditions under which a firm can succeed in charging discriminatory prices are, first, that it can control the supply of the product offered to particular buyers and, second, that it can prevent the resale of the commodity from one buyer to another.

9. Two predictions about price discrimination are (a) for any given level of output, the best system of discriminatory prices will provide higher total revenue to the firm than the best single price, and (b) output will usually be larger than under a single-price monopoly.

10. Price discrimination affects the distribution of income and the allocation of resources. Any individual is almost certain to evaluate individual cases differently, according to his or her personal set of values and the circumstances of each case. Further, there are important differences in the effects of systematic and unsystematic price discrimination.

Topics for Review

Relationship between price and marginal revenue for a monopolist
Relationships among marginal revenue, total revenue, and elasticity for a monopolist
Potential monopoly profits in any perfectly competitive equilibrium
Minimum efficient scale *(MES)*
Natural and created entry barriers
Cartels
Measures of monopoly power
Price discrimination and price differences
Systematic and unsystematic price discrimination

1. Suppose that only one professor teaches economics at your school. Would you say this professor is a monopolist who can exact any "price" from students in the form of readings assigned, tests given, and material covered? Suppose that two additional professors are hired; has the original professor's monopoly power been decreased?

2. Imagine a monopoly firm with fixed costs but no variable or marginal costs—for example, a firm owning a spring of water that produces indefinitely, once certain pipes are installed, in an area where no other source of water is available. What would be the firm's profit-maximizing price? What elasticity of demand would you expect at that price? Would this seem to be an appropriate pricing policy if the water monopoly were municipally owned?

3. Each of the following has some "monopoly power": Xerox Corporation, Pepsico Company, Mobil Oil, and AT&T. What do you think is the basis of the monopoly power in each case? How might you decide which of the organizations listed has the greatest degree of monopoly power?

4. Which of these industries—licorice candy, copper wire, outboard motors, coal, local newspapers—would you most like to monopolize? Why? Does your answer depend on several factors or just one or two? Which would you as a consumer least like to have monopolized by someone else? If your answers to the two questions are different, explain why.

5. A movie exhibitor, Aristotle Murphy, owns movie theaters in two Indiana towns of roughly the same size, 50 miles apart. In Monopolia he owns the only chain of theaters; in Competitia there is no theater chain, and he is but one of a number of independent operators. Would you expect movie prices to be higher in Monopolia than in Competitia in the short run? In the long run? If differences occur in his prices, would Mr. Murphy be discriminating in price?

6. Airline rates to Europe are higher in summer than in winter. Some railroads charge lower fares during the week than on weekends. Electricity companies charge consumers lower rates, the more electricity they use. Are these all examples of price discrimination? What additional information would you like to have before answering?

7. Discuss whether each of the following represents price discrimination. In your view, which are the most socially harmful?
   a. Standby fares on airlines that are less than full fare
   b. Standby fares available only to bona fide students under 22 years of age
   c. First class fares that are 50 percent greater than tourist fares, recognizing that two first class seats use the space of three tourist seats
   d. Negotiated discounts from list price, where sales personnel are authorized to bargain hard and get as much in each transaction as the traffic will bear
   e. Higher tuition for out-of-state students at state-supported colleges and universities
   f. Higher tuition for law students than for history students

14

Competition and Monopoly Compared

Do the theories of perfect competition and monopoly provide a sufficient theoretical basis for analyzing price and market behavior in the real economy? Do they provide a sufficient basis for concluding that competition is more socially and economically desirable than monopoly? Today most economists would answer no to both questions, while nevertheless believing that there is a great deal of insight to be gained about both market behavior and performance by comparing them.

While we shall, in this discussion, examine the polar cases of perfect competition and complete monopoly, most of the discussion applies more broadly to all those who exercise monopoly power, not merely the single firm in an industry or the industry-wide cartel, and to competitive behavior of firms in markets with weak, rather than no, control of entry.

In this chapter we look first at the concepts of efficiency and inefficiency as they have been traditionally used by economists, assuming that technology is fixed and that there is nothing that prevents the existence of a competitive market economy. These assumptions lead to a preference for perfect competition over monopoly. Second, we look to other considerations that may lead to a modification of the previous conclusions. Third, we look at some data about the actual structure of the U.S. economy. We do so as a prelude to considering a model called *monopolistic competition* that combines elements of perfect competition and monopoly in an attempt better to explain the real economy.

Economic Efficiency in the Evaluation of Competition and Monopoly

Monopoly has long been regarded with suspicion. In *The Wealth of Nations* (1776), Adam Smith developed a ringing attack on monopolists. Since then most economists have criticized monopoly and advocated freer competition. Part of the appeal of competition and distrust of monopoly is non-economic and was discussed in Chapter 12. But much of it has to do with the allegation that competition is efficient in ways that monopoly is not. This constitutes the classic case against monopoly. In order to understand it, we must first carefully define efficiency.

246-262

The Concepts of Efficiency and Inefficiency with Known Technology

Efficiency requires avoiding the waste of resources. When labor is unemployed and factories lie idle (as occurs in serious recessions), their potential current output is lost. If these resources could be employed elsewhere, total output would be increased and hence everyone could be made better off.

But full employment of resources by itself is not enough to prevent the waste of resources. Even when resources are being fully used, they may be used inefficiently. Let us look at three examples of inefficiency in resource use.

1. If firms do not use the least costly method of producing their chosen outputs, they waste resources. For example, a firm that produces 30,000 pairs of shoes at a resource cost of $400,000 when it could be done at a cost of only $350,000 is using resources inefficiently. The lower cost method would allow $50,000 worth of resources to be transferred to productive uses.
2. If some firms produce at high cost while other firms produce at low cost, the industry's overall cost of producing its output is higher than necessary.
3. If too much of one product and too little of another is produced, resources are being used inefficiently. To take an extreme example, say that so many shoes are produced that the marginal utility of shoes is zero, while the marginal utility of coats remains high at the current level of output. Since no one places any value on the last pair of shoes produced, while people place a high value on an additional coat, no consumer will be made worse off by a reduction of the output of shoes by one or two pairs, yet some consumer will be made better off by using the resources to increase by one the production of coats.

These examples suggest that we must refine our ideas of the waste of resources beyond the simple notion of ensuring that all resources are used. Economists define rather precisely what is meant by efficiency and inefficiency in resource use.

Resources are said to be used *inefficiently* when it would be *possible* by using them differently to make at least one household better off without making any household worse off. Conversely, resources are said to be used *efficiently* when it is impossible by using them differently to make any one household better off without making at least one other household worse off.

Efficiency in the use of resources is often called **Pareto-optimality** or **Pareto-efficiency** in honor of the great Italian economist Vilfredo Pareto (1848–1923), who pioneered in the study of efficiency.

How does an economy achieve efficiency in this sense? The three sources of inefficiency given above suggest important conditions that must be fulfilled if economic efficiency is to be attained. These conditions are conveniently collected into two categories, productive efficiency and allocative efficiency.

Conditions for Productive Efficiency

Productive efficiency requires that whatever output is being produced, is being produced at the lowest attainable cost for that level of output. When this is true, the output of any one commodity entails the lowest possible opportunity cost in terms of forgone outputs of other commodities. When this is not true, an unnecessary sacrifice of other commodities is being incurred; costs could be reduced and more resources spared for the production of other commodities. (Recall that opportunity cost reflects the value of the resources in their best alternative uses.) There are two specific conditions that must be fulfilled if productive efficiency is to be achieved.

Firms must be on their relevant cost curves. The first condition is that firms be on, rather than above, their relevant cost curve. If the firm is making a short-run decision, it must be on the lowest achievable short-run cost curve. If the firm is making a long-run decision, it must choose the lowest achievable long-run cost for the output it wishes to select. If this condition is not met, there is (by definition) a less costly way for each firm to produce its present output.

This condition is met if firms are maximizing profits. Any firm that incurs more cost than is necessary will be making less profit than is possible. So it is in the interest of *all* profit-maximizing firms, no matter what type of market they sell in, to minimize their costs. This means producing on, not above, their relevant cost curve.

Although easy to state, this condition is often difficult to fulfill in practice. We know that existing firms sometimes, perhaps often, do not take advantage of all of the cost-reducing opportunities available to them. This may be so, for example, if the opportunities arise out of some new technology that existing managers have not learned about or are not trained to use. Or, it may be due to lack of access to sources of funds.

One major reason for firms being taken over by other firms is that the existing management is not achieving the lowest costs, and the acquiring firm sees a chance to raise profits by cutting costs.

All firms in an industry must have the same level of marginal cost. The second condition for productive efficiency ensures that production of any given total industry output be distributed among the producing firms so as to minimize total industry costs. This condition is fulfilled if the marginal cost of producing the last unit of output by each firm in the industry is the same for every other firm.

To see the importance of this condition, assume that it is not fulfilled. Suppose that the Jones Brothers shoe manufacturing firm has a marginal cost of $40 for the last shoe of some standard type that it produces, while Gonzales, Inc., has a marginal cost of only $35 for the same type of shoe. If the Jones plant produces one less pair of shoes while the Gonzales plant produces one more, total shoe output is unchanged, but total industry costs are reduced by $5. Thus $5 worth of resources will be freed to increase the production of other commodities.

Clearly, this cost saving can go on as long as the two firms have different marginal costs. But as the Gonzales firm produces more shoes, its marginal cost rises, while as the Jones firm produces fewer shoes, its marginal cost falls. (In producing more, the Gonzales firm is moving upward to the right along its given *MC* curve, while in producing less, the Jones firm is moving downward to the left along its given *MC* curve.) Say, for example, that after Gonzales, Inc., increases its production by 1,000 shoes per month, its marginal cost has *risen* to $37, while when

Jones Brothers has reduced its output by the same amount, its marginal cost has *fallen* to $37. Now there is no further cost saving to be obtained by reallocating production between the two firms.

Condition for Allocative Efficiency

Productive efficiency ensures that any given volume of output is produced at the lowest possible cost. Allocative efficiency concerns the appropriate mix of products. Resources must be allocated among the various goods that can be produced. **Allocative efficiency** is achieved when it is impossible to change the allocation of resources in such a way as to make someone better off without making someone else worse off. Changing the allocation of resources implies producing more of some goods and less of others, that is, changing the mix of production.

In order to understand the condition for allocative efficiency, we need to remind ourselves of a point established earlier. The price of any commodity indicates the value that each purchaser places on the last unit of the commodity that it consumes. (Recall that consumption is a flow, so that when we talk of the last unit consumed, we mean the last unit *per period of time,* such as the last orange consumed per week.) This proposition follows directly from marginal utility theory (see page 133). A household will go on increasing its rate of consumption of a commodity until the *marginal* valuation that it puts on the commodity is equal to its price. The household gets a consumers' surplus on all units except the marginal unit because it values them more than the price it has to pay. On the last, or marginal unit, however, it only "breaks even" because the valuation placed on it is just equal to its price.

Price must equal marginal cost for all products. What is the right production mix? For example, how many shoes should be produced for allocative efficiency? How many dresses? How many hats? The answer is that the economy's allocation of resources is efficient when for every good produced marginal cost of production is equated to its price.

To understand the significance of this condition assume that shoes sell for $30 a pair, but have a marginal cost of $40. If one less pair of shoes were produced, the value that households place on the pair of shoes not produced would be $30. But by the meaning of opportunity cost, the resources that would have been used to produce that pair of shoes could instead produce other goods (say, a coat) valued at $40. If society can give up something its members value at $30 and get in return something its members value at $40, the original allocation of resources is inefficient. Someone can be made better off, and no one need be worse off.

This is easy to see when the same household gives up the shoes and gets the coat. But it follows even when different households are involved, for the gaining household could compensate the losing household and still come out ahead.

Assume next that shoe production is cut back until the price of a pair of shoes rises from $30 to $35, while its marginal cost falls from $40 to $35. The efficiency condition is now fulfilled in shoe production because $p = MC = \$35$. Now if one less pair of shoes were produced, $35 worth of shoes would be sacrificed, while at most $35 worth of other commodities could be produced with the freed resources.

In this situation the allocation of resources to shoe production is efficient because it is not possible to change it so as to make someone better off without making someone else worse off. If one household were to sacrifice the pair of shoes, it would give up goods worth $35 and would then have to obtain for itself all of the new production of the alternative commodity produced just to break even. It cannot gain without making another household worse off. The same argument can be repeated for every commodity, and it leads to this conclusion:

> **The allocation of resources is efficient when each commodity's price equals its marginal cost.**

Allocative efficiency is thus assured if $p = MC$ in all industries.

Efficiency in Perfect Competition and Monopoly

How do the market structures of perfect competition and monopoly affect the ability to achieve productive and allocative efficiency?

Productive Efficiency

The monopolist's output will be different from a competitive industry's output because the monopoly restricts output to raise its price. But in either situation a firm that wishes to maximize its profits will wish to produce *whatever output it produces* at the lowest possible cost. Not to do so would be to sacrifice profits by having higher costs than necessary. Thus profit maximization ensures that firms either in monopoly or competition will be motivated to satisfy the first condition of productive efficiency by producing on, rather than above, their relevant cost curves.

What about allocating output among plants? If the monopoly had more than one plant, it will wish to ensure that its production is divided efficiently among these plants. The efficient allocation among plants becomes a matter of internal organization with a monopoly that owns all of the plants. The profit-maximizing monopolist will allocate production so that all plants produce with the same marginal cost. There is no inherent barrier to doing so.

In perfect competition this allocation occurs automatically. Since all firms are faced with the same market price, and all maximize their profits by equating marginal costs to price, all firms end up having the same marginal cost. For example, if the price of the type of shoe we have been considering is $37 a pair, all perfectly competitive, profit-maximizing firms will produce that type of shoe until the marginal cost of the last pair that they produce is $37.

Profit-maximizing behavior is all that is required to assure productive efficiency in a market economy.

Allocative Efficiency

We have already seen that perfectly competitive firms maximize their profits by equating marginal cost to price. Thus when perfect competition is the prevailing market structure across the whole economy, price is equal to marginal cost for all production, and allocative efficiency is assured.

As we have seen, the monopolist chooses an output at which the price charged is greater than marginal cost. This violates the conditions for allocative efficiency because consumers pay for the last unit an amount that exceeds the opportunity cost of producing it.

Consumers would be prepared to buy additional units for an amount greater than the cost of producing these units. Some consumers could be made better off, and none need be made worse off, by shifting extra resources into production of the monopolized commodity, thus increasing production of the product. As a consequence the monopoly produces an output that is *not* allocatively efficient.

From this follows at once the classic, efficiency-based preference for competition over monopoly:

An economy in which any output is produced under monopoly conditions will not be allocatively efficient.

This result has had important policy implications for economists and political leaders, as we shall see in Chapter 16.

Contrasts with a Command Economy

We have seen that in a free-market economy perfect competition achieves allocative efficiency by the decentralized decisions of millions of independent households and firms each responding to prices given to them by the market. We have also seen that both monopolists and perfect competitors are motivated to achieve productive efficiency by the profit motive. There are thus powerful decentralized forces pushing the economy toward efficient results.

Where a centrally planned (command) economy replaces the market mechanism and the profit motive, it must find ways to allocate resources across different products and industries and to allocate production across plants in the same industry. It must also find ways to motivate producers to minimize costs of whatever output they do produce.

These are not impossible tasks, but they have proved among the most difficult to do well in the Soviet Union, Yugoslavia, China, and other countries that have, to some degree, rejected the profit motive and the price system. Some of these problems and adaptations to them are discussed in Chapter 43.

Allocative Efficiency: An Elaboration[1]

A fuller interpretation of the normative significance of allocative efficiency can be given using the concepts of consumers' and producers' surplus.

Consumers' and Producers' Surplus

The concept of *consumers' surplus* was developed in Chapter 7. (You should review the discussion on pages 134–136 at this time, paying particular attention to Figure 7-4.) We remind you that consumers' surplus is the difference between the total value consumers place on all of the units consumed of some commodity and the payment consumers must make for purchase of that commodity. Consumers' surplus is shown in Figure 14-1.

Producers' surplus is analogous to consumers' surplus. It occurs because all units of each firm's output are sold at the same market price while, given a rising supply curve, each unit but the last is produced at a marginal cost less than the market price. **Producers' surplus** is defined as the amount producers are paid for a commodity less their total variable cost of producing the commodity. As we saw on page 187, the total variable cost of producing any output is shown by the area under the supply curve up to that output. Thus, producers' surplus is the area above the supply curve and below the line giving market price. Producers' surplus is also shown in Figure 14-1.

The Allocative Efficiency of Perfect Competition Revisited

If the sum of the consumers' and producers' surplus is not maximized, the industry could be moved to the point where it was, and the extra surplus available

---

[1] The brief discussion of allocative efficiency in the previous section is all that is strictly required for the rest of this book. The importance of the concept, however, leads us to present a fuller exposition. This section, including Figures 14-1 to 14-3, may be omitted without loss of continuity. If you wish to omit them, turn now to Beyond Allocative Efficiency in Evaluation of Market Structure on page 252.

FIGURE 14-1   Consumers' Surplus and Producers' Surplus

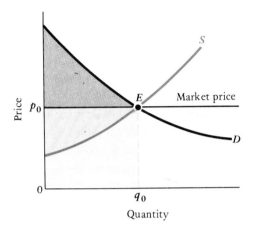

Consumers' surplus is the area under the demand curve and above the price line. Producers' surplus is the area above the supply curve and below the price line. The equilibrium price and quantity in this competitive market are p_0 and q_0. The total value consumers place on q_0 of the commodity is given by the sum of the three shaded areas. The amount they pay is p_0q_0, the rectangle consisting of the two ligher shaded areas. The difference, shown as the dark shaded area, is *consumers' surplus.*

The receipts to producers from the sale of q_0 units are also p_0q_0. The area under the supply curve, the color shaded area, is total variable cost, the minimum amount producers require to supply the output. The difference, shown as the light gray shaded area, is *producers' surplus.*

could be used to make some household better off without making anyone worse off. Thus:

Allocative efficiency occurs at the point where the sum of consumers' plus producers' surplus is maximized.

The point where the sum of consumers' plus producers' surplus is maximized is where the demand curve intersects the supply curve, that is, the point of equilibrium in a competitive market. This is shown graphically in Figure 14-2 on page 253. For any output less than the competitive output, the de-

mand curve is above the supply curve, which means consumers value the last unit at an amount greater than its marginal cost of production. Suppose, for example, the current output of shoes is such that consumers value at \$45 an additional pair of shoes that adds \$35 to costs. If it is sold at any price between \$35 and \$45, both producers and consumers gain; there is \$10 of potential surplus to be divided between the two groups. In contrast, the last unit produced and sold at competitive equilibrium adds nothing to either consumers' or producers' surplus, since consumers value it at exactly its market price, and it adds the full amount of the market price to producers' costs.

If production were pushed beyond the competitive equilibrium, the sum of the two surpluses would be diminished. Assume, for example, that firms were forced to produce and sell further units of output at the competitive market price and that consumers were forced to buy these extra units at that price. (Note that neither group would do so voluntarily.) Firms would lose producers' surplus on those extra units because their marginal costs of producing the extra output would be above the price they received for it. Purchasers would lose consumers' surplus because the valuation that they placed on these extra units, as shown by the demand curve, would be less than the price they would have to pay.

The sum of producers' and consumers' surplus is maximized *only* at the competitive output, which is thus the only output that is allocatively efficient.

If some authority wanted to "maximize the sum of producers' and consumers' surplus," it could instruct firms to produce every unit up to the point where the cost of making the last unit was just equal to the valuation the purchasers placed on that last unit. The perfectly competitive market price provides exactly that signal!

The Allocative Inefficiency of Monopoly Revisited

Since, as we have just seen in Figure 14-2, the perfectly competitive equilibrium output maximizes the sum of consumers' and producers' surplus, it follows immediately that the lower monopoly output must result in a smaller total of consumers' plus producers' surplus.

Why would producers and consumers agree to reduce their surpluses? The answer is that the monopoly equilibrium is not the outcome of voluntary agreement between the one producer and the many consumers. Instead it is imposed by the monopolist by virtue of the power it has over the market. When the monopolist reduces output below the competitive level, market price rises. As a result, consumers' surplus is diminished and producers' surplus is increased. In this way the monopoly firm gains at the expense of its customers. But that is not the whole of the story.

When output is lowered from the competitive level, there is always a *net* loss of surplus. More is given up by consumers than is gained by the monopolist. Some surplus is lost because output between the monopolistic and competitive levels is not produced. This loss of surplus is called the *deadweight loss of monopoly*. This is illustrated in Figure 14-3 on page 254.

To recapitulate, there are two effects when a monopoly replaces competition. By reducing output below the competitive level, a smaller total of consumers' plus producers' surplus is available to be shared between the consumers and the producer. But, by raising price, the monopolist gets a larger share of this smaller pie for itself. As a result, the monopolist is better off, consumers are worse off, but the two groups taken together are worse off.

Beyond Allocative Efficiency in Evaluation of Market Structure

Why Perfect Competition May Not Be Ideal

Having seen that an economy that consisted of perfectly competitive industries would achieve allocative efficiency, it would be a mistake to jump to the conclusion that perfect competition is the best of all

possible worlds and that government policy ought to do everything possible to achieve it. Let us note four important reasons why this would be a mistake.

Efficiency is not the only goal.   A competitive economy distributes output as well as produces it. A freely functioning competitive economy might produce a distribution of income consisting of 1 millionaire and 999 paupers. Such an economy may be more efficient than an economy with 1,000 persons of roughly equal income. Before one can speak of a competitive economy as being unambiguously desirable, one must consider goals other than efficiency. This matter is discussed further in Chapter 22.

Private costs may be poor measures of society's costs.   Producing a good up to the point at which the price just equals the *firms'* marginal cost is efficient from society's point of view only if the firms' private costs reflect the opportunity costs to society of using the resources. As we shall see in Chapter 22, this is often not the case because of what are called *externalities*. For example, if the firms in a competitive industry use resources they do not pay for (such as the clean air around the factories), the industry may produce too much output and too much pollution to be efficient. It does so because *its* marginal costs fail to include the value that members of society place on some of the resources (clean air) the industry uses up.

Perfect competition throughout the economy may not be compatible with productive efficiency.   Our argument about allocative efficiency rested on $p = MC$ everywhere in the economy. But there are many industries in which price does not and cannot equal marginal cost in a free-market economy, because technology makes perfect competition unattainable due to conditions of natural monopoly. In these circumstances there is no general presumption of what the effect will be of prices equaling marginal costs *somewhere* in the economy. Thus if price does not equal marginal cost in industry A, the fact that $p = MC$ in industry B may not lead to allocative efficiency.

This proposition illustrates what is known as the "theory of the second best": We may know how to

FIGURE 14-2   The Allocative Efficiency of Perfect Competition

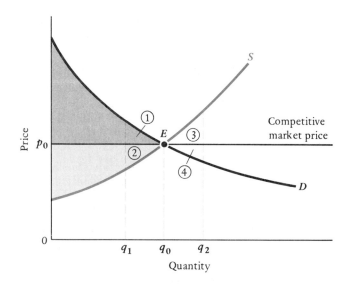

Competitive equilibrium is allocatively efficient because it maximizes the sum of consumers' plus producers' surplus. The competitive equilibrium occurs at the price-output combination, $p_0 q_0$. At that equilibrium consumers' surplus is the dark shaded area above the price line, while producers' surplus is the light shaded area below the price line.

For any output less than q_0 the sum of the two surpluses is less than at q_0. For example, reducing output to q_1, but keeping price p_0, lowers consumers' surplus by area 1 and lowers producers' surplus by area 2.

For any output greater than q_0 the sum of the surpluses is also less than at q_0. For example, if producers are forced to produce output q_2 and sell it to consumers, who are forced to buy it at price p_0, producers' surplus is reduced by area 3 (the amount by which variable costs exceed revenue on those units), while the amount of consumers' surplus is reduced by area 4 (the amount by which expenditure exceeds consumers' satisfactions on those units).

Only the competitive output, q_0, maximizes the sum of the two surpluses.

---

identify the best of all possible worlds (from the limited point of view of the optimum we are discussing), but we may have a harder task when attempting to rank two imperfect situations.

Innovation may be more rapid in one market structure than another. In a perfectly competitive industry production occurs at the lowest level of cost attainable by the competitive firm using the known technology. But it is possible that firms in a perfectly competitive industry may, for example, not innovate as rapidly as firms in another market structure. If so, cost curves will not be shifting downward in the very long run as much as they would under a more monopolistic market structure. Thus, although the competitive industry will appear productively efficient by virtue of producing on its cost curves, the cost curves themselves will not be as low as they

could be. Put differently, productive efficiency in the very long run may be different from productive efficiency with given technology.

Conditions Where Cost Determines Market Structure

The classic comparison of monopoly and competition assumed that market structure and level of cost were independent of one another. But that need not be the case.

Economies of scale. In Chapter 11 we encountered a downward-sloping long-run average cost curve, that is, a situation in which there are economies of scale. The shape of the *LRAC* curve meant that firms had to achieve a certain minimum scale of production (which was defined in Chapter 12 as minimum effi-

FIGURE 14-3   The Allocative Inefficiency of Monopoly

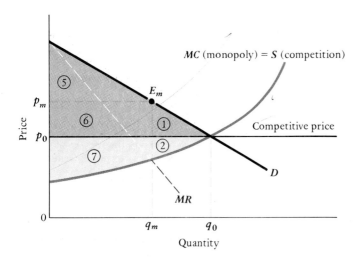

Monopoly is allocatively inefficient because it produces less than the competitive output and thus does not maximize the sum of consumers' and producers' surplus. If this market were perfectly competitive, price would be p_0, output q_0, and consumers' surplus would be the sum of areas 1, 5, and 6 (the dark shaded area). When the industry is monopolized, price rises to p_m, and consumers' surplus falls to area 5. Consumers lose area 1 because that output is not produced; they lose area 6, because the price rise has transferred it to the monopolist.

Producers' surplus in a competitive equilibrium would be the sum of areas 7 and 2 (the light shaded area). When the market is monopolized and price rises to p_m, the surplus area 2 is lost because the output is not produced. But the monopolist gains the area 6 from consumers (6 is known to be greater than 2 because p_m maximizes profits).

While area 6 is transferred from consumers' to producers' surplus by the price rise, *areas 1 and 2 are lost.* They represent the deadweight loss resulting from monopoly and account for its allocative inefficiency.

cient scale, *MES*) to reach the lowest unit costs of production. If the *MES* for a plant is sufficiently large, there may not be room in the industry for many efficient plants; at the extreme of *natural monopoly* there may be room for only one. If so, perfect competition will not persist because there will not be enough firms to have each one behave as a price taker.

If a competitive industry did exist, with each firm producing with "too small" a plant, it would pay one of them (or a new entrant) to build a bigger plant, achieve lower costs, and find itself in a position to price below the costs of the other firms (see Figure 12-8 on page 222.) Its profits would attract other firms to do the same. Eventually the competitive industry would be replaced by one with a smaller number of firms, each of which had achieved minimum efficient scale.

When minimum efficient scale is large, productive efficiency will be improved, rather than worsened, by a shift from perfect competition to a market structure with fewer firms.

Economies of scope. Even beyond any advantages of large-scale *plants,* large *firms* may be able to achieve economies, and thus lower costs, by multi-product production and associated large-scale distribution, national advertising, and large-scale purchasing. Such economies are called **economies of scope** rather than of scale.

Economies of scope cause the cost curves of large, integrated firms to be lower than the cost curves of many small firms producing the same output. In such a case the few large firms will be more productively efficient than the many small firms.

Effect of Economies of Scale or Scope

The existence of significant economies of scale or scope may mean that perfect competition will not continue to be attainable because the remaining number of firms would not continue to be price takers. If the resulting non-competitive industry's firms use their power to raise price above marginal cost, the industry will no longer be allocatively efficient. Looked at somewhat differently, allocative efficiency is now unattainable in a free market because cost minimization leads to a market structure where price exceeds marginal cost. Will consumers necessarily be worse off than if the economies of scope and scale were never achieved?

The answer is no. For example, consider a monopoly replacing a competitive industry where there are unexploited advantages of large scale or scope. The monopolist shuts some plants, reorganizes production and distribution, and thus lowers costs. The monopolist also changes price until marginal revenue equals the new (lower) level of marginal cost. If the cost savings are large enough, output may be larger and price lower than under perfect competition. This is illustrated in Figure 14-4, which shows a situation where consumers benefit from the monopolization of the industry in spite of the emergence of some monopoly profits. The reason is that cost savings are large enough so that both producers and consumers can gain.

Saying that monopolization of a competitive industry *may* lead to lower costs and prices does not mean that departures from competition usually or always lead to lower cost and prices. If there is a reduction in costs, but it is relatively small, the cost decrease may be outweighed by the increase in price due to the monopolist's reduction in output. Moreover, a monopolist protected from competition may become careless and costs may actually rise. (There may be a grain of truth in Judge Learned Hand's observation that the monopolist's greatest reward is an easy life.)

While survival of perfect competition is, in any case, unlikely once large economies of scale and scope are recognized to exist, there is still a question of whether in general we should struggle hard to maintain as much competition as is possible. The key question is factual: In what circumstances do a few large firms in less competitive market structures achieve significantly lower levels of cost than do many smaller firms in a more competitive market structure?

While the answer to this question is affected by

FIGURE 14-4   A Case in Which Monopolization Leads to Lower Prices

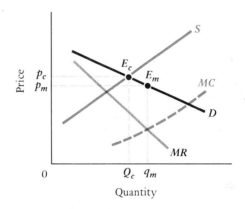

If monopolization lowers costs sufficiently, it may lead to greater output and lower price than competition. D and S are the demand and supply curves of a competitive industry that is in equilibrium at E_c with p_c and Q_c. If costs are unaffected by monopolization, S will become the monopolist's marginal cost curve and the monopolist will restrict output and raise price. However, if the monopolization reduces costs to MC, the equilibrium will be at E_m, with p_m less than p_c and q_m greater than Q_c.

economics of scale and scope, it is much more importantly affected by the effect of market structure on innovation.

Very-Long-Run Considerations

In what we have called the very long run, attention shifts from given products and a fixed technology to new products and new methods of production (see Chapter 11). Our attention shifts from operating on given cost curves to asking how rapidly the cost curves shift downward. This has two, not unrelated, aspects. One is the effect of market structure on innovation; the other is the effect of monopoly profits as an incentive to new entrepreneurs.

Market Structure and Innovation

Does market structure affect the rate of innovation? Many economists believe it does, but they do not all agree on which way.

Incentive to introduce cost-saving innovations.   Both the monopolist and the perfect competitor have a profit incentive to introduce cost-reducing innovations. A monopoly can always increase its profits if it can reduce its costs. We have seen that a cost reduction will cause the monopoly to produce more, to sell at a lower price, and to increase its profits. Furthermore, since it is able to prevent the entry of new firms into the industry, these additional profits will persist into the long run. Thus, from the standpoint of maximizing profits, a monopoly has both a short- and a long-run incentive to reduce its costs.

The firm in perfect competition has the same incentive in the short run, but not in the long run. In the short run a reduction in costs will allow a firm that was just covering costs to earn profits. In the long run other firms will be attracted into the industry by these profits. Existing firms will copy the cost-saving innovation, and new firms will enter the industry using the new techniques. This will go on until the profits of the innovator have been eliminated.

The effectiveness of profits as an incentive to reduce costs for a firm in competition will thus depend on the magnitude of the extra profits and on how long they persist. If, for example, it takes only a few months for existing firms and new entrants to copy and install the new invention, then the original innovating firm will earn profits for only a few months. These may not be sufficient to compensate for the risks and the costs of developing the innovation. In such a case the incentive to innovate will be absent from a competitive industry. On the other hand, if it takes several years for other firms to copy and install the cost-saving innovation, then the profits earned over these years by the innovating firm may be more than sufficient to compensate for all costs and risks. In this case the incentive to innovate is present in a competitive industry.

Monopolies have both a short- and long-run incentive to innovate; competitive firms have only a short-run incentive.

Funds for research and development.   So far we have considered the profit incentive to introduce new innovations. Another consideration is the availability of the resources to finance the research needed to invent new methods and new products. It is widely believed that the large profits available to firms with monopoly power provide a ready fund out of which research and development will be financed. While in principle money for research and development could come from anywhere, business practice tends to use reinvested earnings rather than borrowed funds for these purposes. To the extent that this is so, the typical competitive firm, earning only enough money to cover its costs, will have few funds to spare for research and development. If profits provide the funds for research and development, competitive firms will do little of it.

Penalties for not innovating.   Skeptics about the superiority of the monopolist as innovator often argue that competitive firms *must* innovate or they will lose out to a competitor who does so, while monopolists do not have the same urgent need because they are insulated from potential competitors by barriers to entry. In this view innovation is essential in competition and merely optional in monopoly.

Those who disagree with this argument point out that no firm, not even a complete monopolist, is shielded from competition in the very long run. It is always possible that a new firm will be able to break into the market by developing some new, similar, but superior product that overcomes existing barriers to entry. It is also the case that a firm, even a monopoly, that fails to innovate opens itself to the threat of a takeover by another firm.

Patents and the incentive to innovate.   Economists who believe that competitive market structures best serve consumers by assuring them low prices, but who worry about the possible lack of incentives to innovate under competition, believe that other institutions, such as the patent laws, can provide the necessary incentives.

Patent laws confer a temporary monopoly on the use of an easy-to-copy invention. The intent of the patent laws is to lengthen the period during which the inventor can earn profits as a reward. Once the patent expires—and sometimes even before by infringement or evasion—other firms can copy the invention and, if there are no other barriers to entry, production will expand until profits are eliminated. There is little doubt that without patent laws, many inventions would be copied sooner and the original innovators would not earn as much extra revenue to compensate them for the costs and risks of development. Thus patents do increase the rewards to invention. Just how much actual extra invention occurs is a subject of substantial debate.

Because patented items *can* be imitated, the real advantage of patents to the competitive firm should not be exaggerated. Some economists have argued that patents may be of even greater advantage to a monopolistic than to a competitive firm. A monopolist, so goes the argument, has the resources to develop, patent, and "keep on the shelf" processes that might enable a potential competitor to challenge its position.

"Creative Destruction"

An early and articulate dissenter from economists' usual opposition to monopoly was the distinguished Austrian (and later American) economist, Joseph A. Schumpeter. Schumpeter's theory relies on many of the forces just discussed. His basic argument has two main parts.

The first is that innovations which lower costs of production—by increasing output per head and creating economic growth—have a much larger effect on living standards than any "misallocation" of resources caused by too much production of one kind of commodity and too little of another at any one time.

Schumpeter believed that losses due to allocative inefficiency were small relative to the gains attributable to cost reductions. Modern empirical measures have tended to support Schumpeter in this contention. It appears unlikely that the losses due to misallocations caused by departures from competition have ever amounted to more than 2 or 3 percent of a country's national income.[2] But the national income of most countries was for many years growing at that rate each year. Thus if misallocation lets

growth continue year after year it is positively beneficial.

The second part of Schumpeter's argument is that only the incentive of profits leads people to take the great risks of innovation, and that monopoly power is much more important than competition in providing the profits that motivate innovation. The large short-run profits of the monopolist provide the incentive for others to try to usurp some of these for themselves. If a frontal attack on the monopolist's barriers to entry is not possible, then the barriers will be circumvented by such means as the development of similar products against which the monopolist will not have entry protection.

Schumpeter called the replacing of one monopoly by another through the invention of new products or new production techniques the *process of creative destruction*.

Schumpeter put part of his argument in the following words:

> What we have got to accept is that it [monopoly] has come to be the most powerful engine of progress and in particular of the long-run expansion of total output not only in spite of, but to a considerable extent through, this strategy [of creating monopolies] which looks so restrictive when viewed in the individual case and from the individual point of time. In this respect, perfect competition is not only impossible but inferior, and has no title to being set up as a model of ideal efficiency. It is hence a mistake to base the theory of government regulation of industry on the principle that big business should be made to work as the respective industry would work in perfect competition.[3]

An example of this process is discussed in Box 14-1.

Slide rules provide an example of one good product having its market destroyed by a new one, with the resulting elimination of a firm's monopoly power. Keuffel & Esser had by the 1960s achieved a dominant position in the manufacture and sale of slide rules, an essential tool of the engineer and the

---

[2] In one of the most famous of these studies, Professor Arnold Harberger of the University of Chicago puts the figure at about one-tenth of 1 percent of the U.S. national income!

[3] *Capitalism, Socialism, and Democracy,* 3rd ed. (New York: Harper & Row, 1950), page 106.

BOX 14-1

Erosion of a Monopoly

The great strength of the incentive to share in a monopoly profit can be illustrated by the case of ball-point pens, where a monopoly was created by product innovation.

In 1945 Milton Reynolds developed a new type of pen that wrote with a ball bearing rather than the then conventional nib. He formed the Reynolds International Pen Company, capitalized at $26,000, and began production on October 6, 1945.

The Reynolds pen was introduced with a good deal of fanfare by Gimbels, which guaranteed that the pen would write for two years without refilling. The price was set at $12.50. Gimbels sold 10,000 pens on October 29, 1945, the first day they were on sale. In the early stages of production the cost of production was estimated to be around $.80 per pen.

The Reynolds International Pen Company quickly expanded production. By early 1946 it employed more than 800 people in its factory and was producing 30,000 pens per day. By March 1946 it had $3 million in the bank.

Macy's, Gimbels' traditional rival, introduced an imported ball-point pen from South America. Its price was $19.98 (production costs unknown).

The heavy sales quickly elicited a response from other pen manufacturers. Eversharp introduced its first model in April, priced at $15.00. In July 1946 *Fortune* magazine reported that Sheaffer was planning to put out a pen at $15.00, and Eversharp announced its plan to produce a "retractable" model priced at $25.00. Reynolds introduced a new model, but kept the price at $12.50. Costs were estimated at $.60 per pen.

The first signs of trouble emerged. The Ball Point Pen Company of Hollywood put a $9.95 model on the market, and a manufacturer named David Kahn announced plans to introduce a pen selling for less than $3.00. *Fortune* reported fears of an impending price war in view of the growing number of manufacturers and the low of cost of production. In October Reynolds introduced a new model, priced at $3.85, that cost about $.30 to produce.

By Christmas 1946 approximately 100 manufacturers were in production, some of them selling pens for as little as $2.98. By February 1947 Gimbels was selling a ball-point pen made by the Continental Pen Company for $.98. Reynolds introduced a new model priced to sell at $1.69, but Gimbels sold it for $.88 in a price war with Macy's. Reynolds felt betrayed by Gimbels. Reynolds introduced a new model listed at $.98. By this time ball-point pens had become economy rather than luxury items, but they were still highly profitable.

In mid-1948 ball-point pens were selling for as little as $.39 and costing about $.10 to produce. In 1951 prices of $.25 were common. Within six years the power of the monopoly was gone forever. Ever since then the market has been saturated with a wide variety of models and prices of pens ranging from $.19 up. Their manufacture is only ordinarily profitable.

Of course there can still be strong incentives to gain monopoly power and profits, even if the effort is sure to fail eventually. The lag between an original monopoly and its subsequent erosion by competition may be long enough to insure large profits to the monopolist. It is estimated, for example, that Milton Reynolds earned profits as high as $500,000 *in a single month*—about 20 times his original investment.

applied scientist. Its dominant position and highly profitable operations were wiped out, not by a better slide rule, but by the pocket calculator. When first introduced in the early 1970s, pocket calculators were relatively expensive, often costing over $100. They were also relatively crude in their capabilities. None-theless they proved popular; sales and profits rose, and firms rushed to enter the lucrative new field. Competition led simultaneously to product improvement and price reduction. Today calculators that perform basic calculations can be bought for a few dollars, and sophisticated scientific and programmable pocket calculators can be bought for under $50. Few of today's college students have heard of Keuffel & Esser, but most know about Texas Instruments.

Similarly, during the 1980s microcomputers for home and office are showing signs of sweeping away the markets of many currently important products and services. For instance, in-store computers are being used to answer customer questions and decrease the need for sales people. One day computers may even displace the college textbook.

The State of the Debate

For all of the reasons discussed in this section there is no modern consensus among economists that competition is always to be preferred to monopoly. The empirical evidence seems overwhelming that perfectly competitive firms have not been leading innovators. For one example, none of the innovations that have vastly raised agricultural productivity over the last century were developed by the typical competitive farming unit; rather, they were developed by a few manufacturers of farm equipment and by researchers in universities and in government-financed research institutions. But not all firms with monopoly power have been dynamic innovators either. Thus Schumpeter's insight into the *potential* advantage of monopoly over competition does not lead economists to be unconcerned about monopoly.

Evaluating the performance of an industry requires knowing more than merely the type of market structure in which it operates.

Structure of the American Economy

Do we need more theories than monopoly and perfect competition in order to understand the real world? Texaco, Shell, and Mobil are three of the "major" oil companies. They are not, singly or collectively, monopolists, nor are they firms in perfect competition. Yet they are typical of many real firms in our economy. Similar comments apply to the Coca-Cola and Pepsi-Cola companies. We now look

at some statistics to see how well the assumptions about monopoly and competition describe the American economy.[4] Many economists believe that although the models of monopoly and perfect competition are clearly useful, there is a need for other models as well.

Two Groupings of American Industries

It is relatively easy to divide much of American industry into two broad groups, those with a large number of relatively small firms and those with a small number of relatively large firms. If these two groups are described by the two market forms we have studied so far, then perfect competition would characterize the first group and monopoly would characterize the second.

Sectors with Many Small Firms

About 65 percent of the economy's national product is produced by industries made up of a large number of small firms. This includes most agricultural production, most services (travel agents, lawyers, plumbers, television technicians, etc.), most retail trade, most wholesale trade, most construction, and industries whose major business is exchange (real estate agents, stockbrokers, etc.).

The competitive model, with the addition of government intervention where necessary, does quite well in describing many of these industries. This is obviously so where the business of the industry is exchange rather than production. Foreign exchange markets and stock exchanges are notable examples. Agriculture also fits fairly well in most ways; the individual farmer is clearly a price taker, entry into farming is easy, and exit is possible, though not in fact very rapid.[5] Many basic raw materials such as iron ore, tin, and copper are sold on world markets

---

[4] Description is not the whole of the matter, for it is the purpose of theories to abstract from the complexity of reality. Even descriptively unrealistic models may be adequate to make predictions that are confirmed by observations. But poor descriptions make one cautious.

[5] Although, as we saw in Chapter 6, the size of American farms has increased dramatically in recent years, even the largest farm is small in relation to total market demand. Thus, even the largest farmer is a price taker, not a price setter.

where prices fluctuate continually in response to changes in demand and supply.

Many other industries, however, do not seem to be described by the perfectly competitive model even though they contain many firms. In retail trade and services, for example, most firms have some influence over prices. The local grocery, supermarket, discount house, and department store not only consider weekend specials and periodic sales important to business success, they spend a good deal of money advertising them. Moreover, each store in these industries has a unique location that may give it some local monopoly power over nearby customers. In wholesaling the sales representative is regarded as a key figure—which would not be true if the firm could sell all it wished at a given market price. We are, as Professor R. L. Bishop has observed, "a race of eager sellers and coy buyers, with purchasing agents getting the Christmas presents from the salesmen rather than the other way around."

The first group of industries therefore contains some that are clearly described by the model of perfect competition and many others that are not.

Sectors with a Few Large Firms

About 35 percent of the national product is produced by industries dominated by a few large firms. The names of these firms are part of the average citizen's vocabulary. In this category fall most transportation firms (e.g., the Penn Central Railroad, the Santa Fe Railroad, United Airlines, American Airlines, Greyhound), communications (AT&T, NBC, CBS, Western Union), public utilities (American Electric Power, Consolidated Edison), and much of the largest sector of the American economy, the manufacturing sector.

A casual look at the manufacturing sector can be misleading if one does not distinguish between products and firms. In some manufacturing industries many differentiated products are produced by only a few firms. In breakfast foods, for example, a vast variety of products is produced by a mere three firms. Similar circumstances exist in chemicals, cigarettes, and numerous other industries where many more or less competing products are in each case produced by a very few firms. Clearly, these indus-

tries are not perfectly competitive. Yet neither do they appear to be monopolies, for the few firms typically compete energetically against one another.

Few American industries are easily characterized as monopolies. Many railway companies once enjoyed monopolies of service over rural areas (although seldom between major cities, which were normally served by several companies). In this century, however, both airlines and trucking have provided intense competition to the railroads. In manufacturing, examples of single-firm monopoly outside the regulated areas are few. The Aluminum Company of America was the sole producer of primary aluminum in the United States from 1893 until World War II. ALCOA and a few other companies have been described with reasonable accuracy as monopolies. The United Shoe Machinery Company had a monopoly on certain types of shoe machinery until antitrust decrees limited its exercise of monopoly power. The National Cash Register Company, the International Nickel Company, the Climax Molybdenum Company, and International Business Machines all had control, at one time or another, over more than 90 percent of the output of the industries in which they operated.

Monopolies exist in certain utility industries such as power and light and postal services. Even here, however, the monopoly sometimes exists only because of government regulation. For example, if a legal monopoly were not enforced by the government, ordinary postal and parcel delivery services would be fiercely competitive, as is suggested by the competition among Federal Express, Emery, and others for high speed, reliable delivery. In other cases a monopoly that seemed quite unassailable has not persisted. Technological breakthroughs have made voice communication an industry with significant competition in contrast to the one-time monopoly of AT&T.

Monopoly and perfect competition together do not *describe* much of the American economy. Many industries with numerous firms depart from some of the conditions of perfect competition; most industries with no more than a few firms depart from the conditions of monopoly.

TABLE 14-1   Concentration Ratios in Selected Manufacturing Industries, 1982

Industry	Four-firm concentration ratio (percentage)
Automotive	
Vehicles	92
Parts	61
Office machines	50
Tires and tubes	66
Soaps and detergents	60
Aircraft	
Planes	64
Engines and parts	72
Aluminum	
Primary	64
Rolling and drawing mills	83
Radio and television	
Sets	49
Equipment	22
Steel mills and blast furnaces	42
Chemicals	
Organic industrial	36
Plastics	22
Pharmaceutical	26
Machinery	
Farm	53
Construction	42
Forest products	
Paper mills	22
Pulp mills	45
Nonferrous wire	30
Petroleum refining	28
Foods	
Cereals	86
Bread and cake	34
Fluid milk	16
Canned fruit and vegetables	21
Soft drinks	14
Clothes	
Men's and boy's suits and coats	25
Women's and misses' dresses	6
Fur goods	12
Metal stamping	10
Commercial printing, lithography	6

Source: U.S. Department of Commerce, *1982 Census of Manufactures,* 1986.

Concentration ratios vary greatly among manufacturing industries. These data, from the 1982 census of manufactures, show the share of the industries' shipments accounted for by the four largest firms.

Patterns of Concentration in Manufacturing

Let us take a closer look at American manufacturing. Table 14-1 shows current four-firm concentration ratios in selected industries that together account for about 40 percent of all manufacturing shipments. Notice that, descriptively, few of these industries fit either of the models studied so far. Among the high-concentration industries, such as automobiles, aluminum, and cereals, the very high concentration is achieved by three or four firms in apparently vigorous rivalry with one another. That these firms have appreciable market power is undoubted; that they may be described by the monopoly model is questionable.

The competitive model conceivably fits a few of the industries near the bottom of the list, but even here there are doubts. Manufacturers of women's clothing have some control over price, contrary to the conditions of perfect competition, because of style and fashion. Metal stamping firms, print shops, and soft drink bottlers, while numerous nationally, operate in small regional and local markets in which a small number of sellers, in direct rivalry with one another, do not regard themselves as price takers.

Table 14-2 shows that in nearly three-quarters of manufacturing industries, the four largest firms control between 20 and 80 percent of the value of shipments. Such industries are not monopolies because there are several firms in the industry, and these firms engage in rivalrous behavior. Residents even of small towns will find more than one drugstore, garage, barber, and dress shop competing for their patronage. Similarly, manufacturers of computers, television sets, and chemicals belong to industries in which there are several close domestic rivals (and often foreign competitors). But neither are these firms in perfectly competitive markets. Often there are only a few major rival firms in an industry, but even when there are many, *they are not price takers.* Virtually all consumers' goods are differentiated products. Any one firm will typically have several lines of a product that differ more or less from each other and from competing lines produced by other firms. There is no market setting a single price for razor blades, or television sets, that equates overall demand to overall

TABLE 14-2 Manufacturing Industries, Classified by 1982 Concentration Ratios

Concentration ratio (percentage)	Number of industries listed by the census	Percentage of value of total shipments of all manufacturing industries
80–100	18	6
60–79	54	12
40–59	120	18
20–39	163	44
Less than 20	86	20
Total	441	100

Source: U.S. Department of Commerce, *1982 Census of Manufactures,* 1986.

Notice the importance measured both in numbers and in value of shipments of industries in the three middle groups. These data were computed from the 1982 census of manufactures. The concentration ratios are those for the four largest firms in each industry.

supply. Instead, it is in the nature of such products that *sellers must state a price at which they are willing to sell.* (Of course, a certain amount of "haggling" is possible, particularly at the retail level, but this is usually within well-defined limits set by the price initially quoted by the seller.)

The Importance of Administered Prices

Rivalrous behavior among firms that are not price takers immediately takes us out of the domain of either perfect competition or monopoly. We thus require additional market structures if we wish to explain the behavior.

In perfect competition firms face a market price that they are quite unable to influence, and they adjust their quantities to that price. In perfect competition firms are price takers and quantity adjusters. Changes in market conditions are signaled to firms by changes in the market prices that they face.

In all other market structures firms face downward-sloping demand curves and thus know that they have a choice of what price to charge for their product. Whenever different firms' products are not

perfect substitutes for other products that consumers may purchase instead, firms must decide on a price to quote. If they are unsatisfied with the sales they achieve at that price, they can change their quote, but quote a price they must. In such circumstances we say that the firm administers its price. The term **administered price** refers to a price set by the decisions of an individual firm rather than by impersonal market forces.

When a firm sets its price, the amount that it sells is determined by its demand curve. Changes in market conditions change the amount that can be sold at its administered price. The changed conditions may or may not lead the firm to change the price that it charges.

In market structures other than perfect competition, firms set their prices and then let demand determine their sales. Changes in market conditions are signaled to the firm by changes in the quantity it can sell at its administered price.

Monopolistic Competition

We have seen that the perfect competition and monopoly model do not accurately describe the American economy and that their elements do not provide all that is needed to analyze market behavior. The two theories do, however, identify key variables. One of these is the firm's view of the demand curve it faces. In monopoly the firm faces the industry demand curve; in perfect competition it faces a horizontal line at the level of market price. But what of situations where firms are not strictly price takers, but their administered prices are not independent of what other firms in the industry do? What if firms think about their rivals' reactions before setting prices? Another key variable is entry. In perfect competition entry is unimpeded, while in classic monopoly there are barriers that make entry impossible. But what of situations where entry is neither free nor totally blockaded, just more or less difficult, more or less slow to occur?

Recognition that these additional relevant dimensions of market structure are potentially important has led economists to formulate additional theoretical market structures, one of which is discussed here and others in the next chapter.

The theory of **monopolistic competition** was developed in two famous books of the early 1930s, one by the British economist Joan Robinson, the other by the American economist Edward Chamberlin.

The market envisaged in this theory is similar to perfect competition in that there are many firms with relatively easy entry and exit. But it differs in one important respect: Each firm has some power over price because each sells a product that is differentiated significantly from those of its competitors. One firm's soap might be similar to another firm's soap, but it differs in chemical composition, color, smell, softness, brand name, reputation, and a host of other characteristics that matter to customers. This is the phenomenon of **product differentiation.** It implies that each firm has a certain degree of local monopoly power over its own product. It could raise its price, even if its competitors did not, and not lose all of its sales. This is the "monopolistic" part of the theory. The monopoly power is severely restricted, however, by the presence of similar products sold by many competing firms and by easy entry and exit. As a result, the monopolistically competitive firm's demand curve is very much flatter than the industry demand curve. This is the "competition" part of the theory.

From a theoretical point of view the major difference between perfect and monopolistic competition lies in the respective assumptions of homogeneous and differentiated products. Firms in perfect competition sell a **homogeneous product,** which means a product similar enough across the industry so that no one firm has any power over price because consumers regard different firms' products as perfect substitutes for one another. Firms in monopolistic competition sell a **differentiated product,** which means a group of commodities similar enough to be called the same product, but dissimilar enough that the producer of each has some power over its own price. This dissimilarity leads to, and is enhanced by, establishment of brand names and advertising.

Assumptions of the Theory

The theory of monopolistic competition has three major assumptions. First, each firm is not a price taker. Instead, each firm faces a downward-sloping demand curve. However, the curve is highly elastic because similar products sold by other firms provide many close substitutes. The downward slope of the demand curve provides the potential for monopoly profits in the short run.

Second, there is freedom of entry and exit. This forces profits to zero in the long run. If profits are being earned by existing firms in the industry, new firms will enter. Their entry will mean that the demand for the product must be shared among more brands. Thus the demand curve for any one firm's brand will shift to the left. Entry continues until profits fall to zero.

Third, the industry contains so many firms each of which is in close competition with many others that each ignores the possible reactions of its many competitors when it sets its own price.

Predictions of the Theory[6]

While the theory of monopolistic competition has proven extremely important as a step in the development of other models of market structure, it has only one significant prediction: In an industry with differentiated products and free entry each firm will, in equilibrium, produce an output smaller than the one that would minimize its costs of production. This prediction, called the **excess capacity theorem,** is illustrated and discussed more fully in Box 14-2. In a monopolistically competitive industry there are many brands of the product each produced in smaller quantities and priced at a higher level than if the industry produced a homogeneous product and was perfectly competitive

The excess capacity theorem once aroused passionate debate. It seemed to suggest that industries

---

[6] The discussion here refers to large-group monopolistic competition, which exercised economists' imaginations in the decades after Chamberlin's and Robinson's writings. Small-group monopolistic competition is discussed in the next chapter.

BOX 14-2

The Excess Capacity Theorem

The excess capacity theorem of monopolistic competition is an implication of two of the assumptions of the theory: first, downward-sloping demand curves for each of the firms due to product differentiation and, second, free entry which pushes profits to zero at long-run equilibrium. Thus average revenue must equal average cost at some level of output, but exceed it at none. In other words, free entry pushes firms to the point at which the demand curve is tangent to the average total cost curve.

Two curves that are tangent at a point have the same slope at that point. Thus when a downward-sloping demand curve is tangent to the average total cost curve, the latter must also be downward sloping at the point of tangency. In such a situation each firm is producing an output less than the one for which its average total cost reaches its minimum point, that is, it has excess capacity.

This is illustrated in the figure. Equilibrium is at point E_0, price is p_0, and quantity is q_0. Price is greater and quantity is less than the purely competitive equilibrium price and quantity (p_1 and q_1). At equilibrium

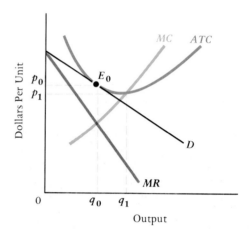

the monopolistically competitive firm has *excess capacity* of q_0q_1. Stated formally the excess capacity theorem says:

The zero-profit equilibrium of a monopolistically competitive firm occurs at an output less than the one at which average total cost is a minimum.

---

selling differentiated products are *inefficient* because they have excess capacity in long-run equilibrium and thus have a higher level of costs of production than is necessary.

But, as more modern analysis has shown, the inefficiency charge is not proven. The "excess capacity" of monopolistic competition does not necessarily indicate inefficiency (and waste of resources) because price is not the only relevant aspect of a differentiated product. People care about which brand of a product they buy. Differentiated products make a choice among several brands available to consumers. Clearly, people have different tastes; some prefer one brand and some prefer another. For example, each brand of breakfast food or running shoes has its devotees. This creates a trade-off, from the point of view of consumer welfare, between pro-

ducing more brands to satisfy diverse tastes and producing fewer at a lower cost per unit.

Monopolistic competition produces a wider range of products, but at a somewhat higher cost per unit, than perfect competition.

We cannot conclude that consumers are better off with ten brands of a differentiated product than with one standard brand, or vice versa. If consumers value variety, the extra cost that variety imposes must be matched against the benefits. Only if the costs exceed the benefits is the variety wasteful. To maximize consumers' satisfaction, the number of brands of a differentiated product should be increased until the gain from adding one more equals the loss from having to produce each existing brand at a higher cost, because less of each is produced.

The Lasting Contribution of Monopolistic Competition

The theory of monopolistic competition recognized the facts of product differentiation, the ability of firms to influence prices, and the presence of brand names and advertising. The incorporation of these factors into a new theory encouraged economists to consider the question of their effects on the operation of the price system. It rekindled economists' interest in such important things as how and when firms took each other's reactions into account, what made for easy or restricted entry, and the significance to competition of differentiated products that were similar to one another.

The reason it has not become one of the main market forms used to understand market economies is that, as economists came to realize gradually, monopolistically competitive industries are rarely, if ever, found in the economy.

This claim may sound surprising at first because there are many industries in which a large number of slightly differentiated products compete for the buyers' attention. The catch, however, is that in most such cases the industries have only a few firms, each of which sells a large number of products.

Consider the soap and detergent industry. Among the well-known brands currently on sale in the United States are Cheer, Oxydol, Tide, Dreft, Ivory Snow, Ivory Liquid, Joy, Cascade, Camay, Lava, Safeguard, Zest, Mr. Clean, Top Job, Spic and Span, Comet, and Solo. Surely this is impressive differentiation among a large number of products. This list of products might appear to provide a perfect example of monopolistic competition. But *every one* of the products is manufactured by a single company, Proctor & Gamble, which, with Lever Brothers, dominates sales of soaps, cleansers, and detergents in America. Clearly, such industries are not the large-group case envisaged by the framers of the theory of monopolistic competition. Today, product differentiation is recognized to occur mainly where

a small group rather than a large group of firms compete with each other.[7]

The modern theory of product differentiation is a direct descendant of the earlier theories of monopolistic competition. The focus remains on product differentiation and on industrial structures thought to describe the nature of the modern economy. But it is the small-group case of firms with differentiated products rather than the large-group case of monopolistic competition that seems relevant.

In the last half of the 1970s there was a great outburst of theorizing about all aspects of product differentiation.[8] In these theories, just as in the earlier ones, it pays firms to differentiate their products, to advertise heavily, and to engage in other forms of non-price competition. These are characteristics to be found in their world, but not in perfect competition. Most of the modern theory of product differentiation relates to industries with a small number of firms, such as soaps and detergents, breakfast foods, and automobiles. This is the province of "competition among the few."

A Preview of "Imperfect Competition Among the Few"

As the data in Tables 14-1 and 14-2 showed, much of American industry is characterized by small groups of firms accounting for a large fraction of an

---

[7] At first sight retailing may appear to be closer to the conditions of monopolistic competition than is manufacturing. Certainly every city has a large number of retailers selling any one commodity. The problem is that they are differentiated from each other mainly by their geographical location, each firm having only a few competing close neighbors. Thus a model with every firm in close competition with only a few neighbors seems to be a better model for retailing than the large-group monopolistic competition model, in which every firm competes directly with a large number of other firms.

[8] It is one of those regrettable confusions of life that the theory that studies market structures where a *small* number of firms compete to sell a large number of differentiated products has also taken the name *monopolistic competition*. The term now refers to any industry in which more than one firm sells differentiated products.

industry's production. In most of these industries a relatively small number of firms have enough market power that they may not be regarded as price takers (as in perfect competition), but are subject to enough rivalry that they cannot consider the market demand curve as their own (as they can in monopoly). In most of these cases entry is neither perfectly easy nor wholly prevented. In many industries a small number of firms—between three and a dozen—tend to dominate the industry, and newcomers find it hard to establish themselves. The market structure that embraces such industries is called **oligopoly,** from the Greek words *oligos polein,* meaning "few to sell."

Oligopoly is an important market structure. It applies wherever concentration ratios are high and may apply even in nationally unconcentrated industries, such as cement. A national concentration ratio is relevant where there is one national market. But if transport costs split the country into numerous regional markets, each one may contain a small number of oligopolistic firms.

Oligopolistic industries are of many types. In some there are only a few firms in the entire industry (8 in the case of cigarettes). In others there are many firms, but only a few dominate the market. For example, there are 282 petroleum refiners, but the 232 smallest firms together account for only 7 percent of the aggregate value of output. There are 108 tire and tube manufacturing companies, of which the 100 smallest supply less than 14 percent of the market. Oligopoly is not inconsistent with a large number of small sellers, called a "competitive fringe," when the "big few" dominate the decision making in the industry.

In oligopolistic industries prices are typically administered. Products are usually, but not necessarily differentiated. The intensity and nature of rivalrous behavior varies greatly from industry to industry and from one period of time to another. This variety has invited extensive theoretical speculation and empirical study. It is the topic of the next chapter.

Summary

1. Resources are said to be used efficiently when it is impossible, by using them differently, to make any one household better off without making at least one other household worse off. We distinguish two kinds of efficiency: productive and allocative.

2. Productive efficiency exists for given technology when whatever output is being produced is being produced at the lowest attainable cost for that level of output. This requires, first, that firms be on, rather than above, their relevant cost curves and, second, that all firms have the same marginal cost. Profit-maximizing behavior assures achieving productive efficiency.

3. Allocative efficiency is achieved when it is impossible to change the mix of production in such a way as to make someone better off without making someone else worse off. The allocation of resources will be efficient when each commodity's price equals its marginal cost.

4. While either an economy of monopoly or of perfect competition can be productively efficient, allocative efficiency would be achieved in an economy of perfect competition, but not in an economy with monopolies.

5. The classical economic appeal of perfect competition is that it achieves both productive and allocative efficiency. Productive efficiency is achieved because the same forces that lead to long-run equilibrium lead to production at the lowest attainable cost. Allocative efficiency is achieved because in competitive equilibrium price equals marginal cost for every product. The classical economic case against monopoly rests on its allocative inefficiency, which arises because price exceeds marginal cost.

6. The classical belief in the superiority of perfect competition should be interpreted with four qualifications in mind: (a) efficiency is not the only goal, (b) private costs may be poor measures of society's costs, (c) perfect competition throughout the economy may be incompatible with productive efficiency, (d) in the very long run cost curves may shift downward faster in market structures other than competition.

7. Levels of cost are not independent of market structures. If there are advantages of scale or scope, the minimum efficient size of the firm may be too large to be compatible with conditions of perfect competition. In such cases a shift from competition to a more concentrated market structure may lead to lower costs and increased efficiency.

8. Very-long-run considerations, such as the effect of market structure on innovation and the incentive effect of monopoly profits, are important in evaluating market structures. Joseph Schumpeter advocated the view that the incentive to innovate is so much greater under monopoly that monopoly is to be preferred to perfect competition, despite its allocative inefficiency. While few modern economists go that far, the empirical evidence suggests that technological change and innovation can to a measurable extent be traced to the efforts of large firms in concentrated industries.

9. A review of the structure of the American economy shows that while there are both large-firm and small-firm sectors, most of the industries involved have important features that differ from those assumed in the models of either perfect competition or monopoly.

10. In market structures other than perfect competition, firms tend to administer prices and sell the quantities demanded at those prices. Changes in market conditions are signaled not by changes in the prices firms' quote or face, but by changes in the quantities they can sell.

11. Monopolistic competition is a market structure in which firms sell a differentiated product. Large-group monopolistic competition does not apply to a significant number of industries in today's world. Differentiated products abound, but generally they are produced in industries that contain a small number of firms, each one of which sells many such products. This is one form of oligopoly.

Topics for Review

Productive and allocative efficiency
Consumers' and producers' surplus
Classical preference for competition over monopoly
Pareto-optimality
Economies of scale and scope
Effect of cost on market structure
Effect of market structure on costs
Creative destruction
Administered prices
Product differentiation
Monopolistic competition

Discussion Questions

1. "Suppose that allocative inefficiency of some economy amounts to 5 percent of the value of production." What does that statement mean? If it is true, would consumers be better off if policy measures succeeded in eliminating the allocative inefficiency? Why or why not?

2. If the many plants producing a given product were built at different times, have different levels of capacity, and have different cost curves, is it possible that producing the industry's output using all of them is productively efficient? Show why or why not.

3. Consider an innovation that lowers the marginal cost of production by the same amount in two industries, one of which is perfectly competitive and the other a single-firm monopoly. Show that prices will fall as a response to a change in marginal costs in each industry, but that prices and quantities will change less in monopoly than in competition.

4. "Productive efficiency or inefficiency can be evaluated at the level of an individual plant, firm, or industry. Allocative efficiency or inefficiency can be evaluated only for the economy as a whole." Discuss.

5. Is the consumer benefited by lower prices, by higher quality, by more product variety, by advertising? If trade-offs are necessary (more of one means less of another), how would you evaluate their relative importance with respect to the following products?
   a. Vitamin pills
   b. Beer
   c. Cement
   d. Bath soap
   e. Women's dresses
   f. Television programs

6. White sidewall tires cost only about $1 per tire more to manufacture than black sidewall tires, and they lower somewhat the durability of tires. At the retail level the extra cost of a white sidewall tire is at least $5 per tire. Yet 70 percent of all passenger car tires manufactured in the United States in 1986 were white sidewalls. What, if anything, do these facts tell you about the market structure of the manufacture, distribution, or marketing of automobile tires? If white sidewalls are found to be somewhat more likely to suffer blowouts, should their use be prohibited by law?

7. It is sometimes said that there are more drugstores and gasoline stations than are needed. In what sense might that be correct? Does the consumer gain anything from this plethora of retail outlets?
8. Are any of the following industries monopolistically competitive? Explain your answer.
   a. Textbook publishing (Fact: There are over 50 elementary economics textbooks in use somewhere in the United States this year.)
   b. College education
   c. Cigarette manufacture
   d. Restaurant operation
   e. Automobile retailing

15

Oligopoly

We saw in Chapter 14 that many American industries are oligopolies. Such industries have three major characteristics.

1. There are two or more competing firms—thus the industry is not a monopoly.
2. Each firm faces a downward-sloping demand curve for its own product—thus the industry is not perfectly competitive.
3. There is at least one large firm that is aware that its competitors will react to any move it makes—thus the industry is not monopolistically competitive.

In this chapter we will look at the general behavior of firms in oligopolistic industries, but first we can learn quite a bit by considering the behavior of one real world oligopoly.

OPEC As an Illustration of Oligopoly

In Chapter 13 we saw how an industry-wide cartel could result in monopoly behavior even though the firms retained their separate legal identities. The formation of a cartel that includes a substantial portion, but not all, of the producers in an industry is one way in which an oligopoly can arise.

The Organization of Petroleum Exporting Countries (OPEC) is an example of the attempted cartelization of a formerly competitive industry. It illustrates many of the problems of oligopolistic industries, and it is these aspects that we wish to emphasize now.

The pre-OPEC Energy Binge

During the half century before 1973, Americans increased their consumption of energy at a rate of about 5 percent per year, enough to double consumption every 14 years. That energy came increasingly from oil and gas.

Much of the long-term surge in energy consumption resulted from the growing use of automobiles, which, like Hollywood movies, became a distinctively American contribution to the twentieth century. Automobiles became the symbol of the American dream. As American households became richer, they tended to buy larger numbers of ever faster,

270

270 -280

bigger, and more lavishly equipped cars, to say nothing of trailers and recreational vehicles. Year by year the demand for gasoline to power their internal combustion engines rose. Yet the price of gasoline remained low, so low that until the 1970s the cost of fuel remained a minor part of the cost of owning and operating a car. (In terms of 1985 prices gasoline in 1970 cost between $.50 and $.70 a gallon, or about $.03 per mile.)

This epoch of ever-increasing demand at a constant price is analyzed in Figure 15-1. The long-run supply curve seemed to be almost perfectly elastic at a low price. For every barrel of oil produced, another was discovered. Although this could not go on forever, a rising supply price seemed far in the future. Indeed, the enormous quantities of oil being discovered and produced in the Middle East so threatened the profitability of American oil producers that the U.S. government imposed quotas that limited the imports of foreign oil. At the same time the government also gave massive tax incentives to American oil companies to find and produce more oil.

The fact that the demand curve shifted to the right year after year seemed no cause for alarm. After all, energy fueled the increasing productivity that led to ever-rising material standards of living. The United States rode the crest of a wave of prosperity based upon cheap and plentiful energy which was to a great extent provided by oil.

Americans traveling abroad were amused by the small, cramped cars they saw and rented, and they were appalled by the high cost of gasoline. The high prices abroad were due to high taxes on gasoline and led to lower gasoline consumption. Europeans drove smaller cars, waited until they reached a higher level of income before buying a car (or buying a second car), and relied more on bicycles and public transportation. The European situation during this period is also shown in Figure 15-1.

The OPEC Cartel

The oil industry in the years before 1973 was not perfectly competitive. However, there were many oil-producing countries, so many, indeed, that no one of them could significantly influence the price of oil by withholding its own output from the market.

FIGURE 15-1   Gasoline Prices in an Era of Unlimited Supply

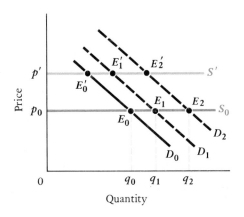

With a horizontal long-run supply curve, demand can increase year by year with no increase in price. S_0 is a long-run supply curve that is perfectly elastic at price p_0. Suppose S_0 applies to the United States in the early 1960s. The various demand curves refer to different years: D_0 for the early 1960s, D_1 for the late 1960s, and D_2 for the early 1970s. As gasoline consumption increases, the demand curve shifts to the right from D_0 to D_1 to D_2 and so on. The U.S. equilibrium is E_0 in year 0, E_1 in year 1, and E_2 in year 2. Consumption continues to grow, but this leads to no increase in price above p_0.

The supply curve S' is also perfectly elastic, at the higher price p'. Suppose it reflects the supply in European countries that have levied a high tax on gasoline. For the same set of demand curves, equilibrium consumption is much lower in European countries than in the United States, yet there, too, it increases over time with no increase in price, as shown by E_0', E_1', and E_2'.

They were price takers in the market in which they sold their oil.

OPEC did not become a cartel nor attract world attention until 1973. In that year, however, members of OPEC placed a temporary embargo on the export of Middle Eastern oil. (The embargo was in retaliation for support, particularly by the United States, for Israel in the Arab-Israeli war that broke out in that year.)

After the embargo ended, the OPEC members voluntarily restricted their outputs by negotiating quotas among themselves. At the time OPEC countries accounted for about 70 percent of the world's supply of crude oil and 87 percent of world oil exports. So, although it was not quite a complete monopoly, the cartel had substantial monopoly power. The world oil market contained one large oligopolistic producers' organization surrounded by a competitive fringe of many smaller producing countries.

Success of the Cartel

OPEC's policy of output restriction succeeded for several reasons. First, the member countries provided a large part of the total world supply of oil; second, other producing countries could not quickly increase their outputs in response to price increases; third, world demand for oil was expanding rapidly; and fourth, the world demand for oil proved to be highly inelastic in the short term.

As a result of these factors, OPEC was able to cause a substantial increase in the world price of oil. OPEC's oil production was about 31 million barrels per day in 1973; in order to raise prices within a year from an average of $3.37 per barrel to an average of $11.25 a barrel, exports had only to be restricted to 28.5 million barrels per day. What happened is analyzed in more detail in Figure 15-2.

A reduction in OPEC's exports of less than 10 percent was sufficient to more than triple the world price. The higher prices were more or less maintained for the remainder of the decade. As a result OPEC countries found themselves suddenly enjoying vast wealth, while oil-importing countries found their real incomes greatly diminished. For some underdeveloped countries the rise in prices threatened disaster, and they were helped in the short run only by loans that allowed them to meet the increased bill for the imported oil they had come to depend on.

The incentive for members to cheat on their output quotas (which we studied in Chapter 13) was not present during the early stages of OPEC. So great was the increase in the wealth of the member countries that the temptation to cheat, in order to gain even more, was small.

There was only so much that Arab sheiks and princes could spend on themselves, and there was

FIGURE 15-2   OPEC As a Successful Cartel

Given a rising non-OPEC supply curve of oil, the members of OPEC can determine equilibrium prices by choosing their contribution to total supply. The curve S_1 represents the non-OPEC supply of the product. If OPEC were prepared to supply unlimited quantities at p_0, the supply curve would be S_0 and the situation shown in Figure 15-1 would be restored. But by fixing its production, OPEC can determine the new total (OPEC + non-OPEC) supply curve S_2. OPEC can, for a given demand curve and non-OPEC supply curve, pick a price (such as p_2) and determine what quantity to supply (q_1q_2) to make that the equilibrium price. If demand is increasing, as from D_2 to D_3, the same OPEC supply will lead the price to increase, in this case from p_2 to p_3.

only so much that could be spent on their countries' economic development. Indeed, the development programs of many OPEC countries were constrained not by funds, but by limited physical facilities. For example, ships with supplies to build roads, warehouses, and other basic facilities often lay in harbor for months because of insufficient port facilities. Even when they were unloaded, supplies often sat at the harbor site for further months because of inadequate internal transport facilities. Because further funds were not urgently needed by OPEC members, the enforcement of OPEC's output quotas was an easy matter.

OPEC's ability to restrict output and keep prices high made its operation successful, but longer-term forces were working against OPEC, both from the supply side and from the demand side of the market.

Pressure on the Cartel

Monopolistic producers always face a dilemma. The closer their prices are to the profit-maximizing level, the greater their short-term profits, but also the greater the incentive for market reactions that will reduce their profits in the longer term.

Increasing World Supply

The high prices and high profits achieved by the OPEC cartel spurred major additions to the world's oil supply by non-OPEC suppliers. This was, in effect, new entry. In 1973 OPEC produced more than 70 percent of the world's oil; by 1979 its share was less than 60 percent and by 1985 only 30 percent. North Sea oil, Mexican oil, Soviet oil, and increased American and Canadian production gradually replaced output that had been withdrawn from the market by OPEC. Higher prices made profitable additional oil exploration and increased production from already proven reserves. In the United States this production trend was greatly speeded by the deregulation of oil and gas prices that occurred at the end of the 1970s. As the supply of non-OPEC oil increased, the amount of OPEC production that was consistent with maintaining a given total world supply shrank.

Declining World Demand

Any demand curve shows how the purchases will vary as the price of the commodity varies, *other things being equal*. But, other things being equal, there was little that users could do to reduce their consumption of petroleum products in response to the initial price rise. Car drivers took fewer Sunday trips, and some took a bus to work when gas prices soared. Imposition of a speed limit of 55 mph decreased gasoline consumption somewhat. Homeowners and office

managers turned their thermostats down a bit. Factories tried to economize on their fuel consumption. But, overall, the response of world demand to the price increase was modest—a reduction in rate of growth of demand rather than a decrease in demand. The reason was that the scope for short-run economizing in the use of oil was limited because so much existing machinery ran on oil products. Over a longer period of time, however, major reductions in oil consumption proved possible—as they almost always do for any product whose relative price rises greatly.

When it came time to replace the family car, many households responded to the high price of gasoline by buying smaller, more fuel-efficient cars. (Indeed, the subsequent troubles in the American automobile industry stemmed partly from the fact that this shift in consumers' demand gave sales to foreign car firms who had decades of experience in producing small cars, under the incentive of high gasoline taxes in those countries.) Homeowners and office managers found that they could greatly reduce their fuel bills by properly insulating their buildings or by turning to such alternative sources of heating as natural gas. New factories were able to use newly designed power plants that economized on fuel oil or used alternative fuels. These, and a host of other longer-term adaptations that economized on petroleum products within known technology, were gradually made.

Furthermore, even more potent very-long-run forces were unleashed. The high price of petroleum led to a burst of scientific research to develop more petroleum-efficient technologies, as well as alternatives to petroleum. Solar heating technology was advanced, as was technology for longer-term alternatives such as harnessing tidal power and capturing heat from the earth's interior. Had the price of petroleum remained at the high levels of the early 1980s, this research would have continued at an intense pace and in all likelihood would have borne increasing fruits in the decades that followed.

As a result of these developments, other things did not remain equal over the long term, and the demand curve for petroleum products began to shift to the left.

The combined effect of decreasing demand and

FIGURE 15-3   OPEC in Trouble

As demand declines and non–OPEC oil supply increases, declining OPEC production is required to
maintain the cartel price. Total supply is originally S_2,
of which S_1 is from non–OPEC sources and the quantity
q_2q_1 from OPEC. Demand is originally D_1, and the cartel
price p_1 prevails. Total quantity sold is q_1.

Now suppose demand decreases to D_2 and non-
OPEC supply increases to S_1'. If the cartel wishes to
maintain the price at p_1, it must limit total supply to q_3.
Since non-OPEC supply will be q_4, this means restricting
its own supply to q_4q_3, much less than before the shifts
occurred.

increasing supply is illustrated in Figure 15-3. The
shrinking market for OPEC oil at the high OPEC
price necessitated ever stiffer production limitations
if the cartel was to maintain its prices. By 1981
OPEC exports were only 18 million barrels per day,
two-thirds of the 1973 level, and by 1985 it was
estimated that OPEC could maintain prices only if
production were cut to 15 million barrels per day.
This created increasing problems and led, at the end
of 1985, to a complete collapse of OPEC's agreements to limit the outputs of its members.[1]

Pressure to Cheat

We have seen that as world output of oil grew,
OPEC output had to be reduced substantially to hold
prices high. As a result, incomes in OPEC countries
declined sharply. But many OPEC countries had be-

come used to their new wealth, and thus the insta-
bilities inherent in any cartel began to be felt seriously. In 1981 the cartel price reached its peak of $35
per barrel. In real terms this was about five times as
high as the 1972 price, but production quotas were
less than half of OPEC's capacity. Anxious to increase their oil revenues, many individual OPEC
members gave in to the pressure to cheat by producing in excess of their production quotas.

OPEC members met every few months to debate
quotas, deplore cheating, and argue about strategy.
Saudi Arabia, the giant of OPEC with 40 percent of
all OPEC oil reserves, maintained a semblance of
order after 1981 by a combination of threats to flood
the market with oil if cheating continued and willingness to take a lion's share of the additional cuts
required to keep prices high. Between 1981 and 1983
Saudi Arabia cut its production from 9.8 to 5.1 million barrels per day, accounting for virtually all of
the reduction in total OPEC production during those
years.

Disagreements About Strategy

The primary strategy question concerned the trade-
off between present production and future produc-

---

[1] The pressures on OPEC took a long time to build up, in part
because the governments of many countries, including the United
States, held domestic prices far below world prices in order to
cushion the blow on domestic consumers. This delayed most of
the reactions on both the demand and the supply sides. The
government exhorted people to turn their thermostats down, form
car pools, and so on, but the response was slight until the incentive
of higher domestic prices was allowed to operate.

tion. Oil taken out of the ground today is not available for sale in the future, while oil conserved for the future does not generate income now. But oil saved for the future will be valuable only as long as oil is still in heavy demand and has not been displaced—as sooner or later it will be—by some other source of energy. Deciding on the best strategy, even for a single country, is a difficult problem, for it involves a trade-off between a known present and an uncertain future. The problem is not merely one of guessing the future, but also of affecting it. The higher the price charged for using oil today, the greater will be buyers' incentive to find permanent substitutes for it.

OPEC members, representing 13 countries, did not see eye-to-eye on these questions because of vast differences among the countries, both in their needs for current oil revenues and in their proven oil reserves. Libya, Nigeria, Algeria, and Venezuela had relatively small reserves and a great need for immediate cash. The war between Iran and Iraq created pressing needs for cash in both countries. Only Saudi Arabia's willingness to reduce its own production maintained any order in the OPEC cartel after 1981. Its huge reserves, small population, and high per capita income gave it the incentive to preserve the role of oil in the future and to discourage both the development of oil substitutes and the use of high-cost oil from other sources. Thus it did not regard falling prices as an unmixed disaster, although plainly it did not wish to see prices fall to the levels that prevailed before 1973.

By late 1985 Saudi Arabia indicated it would not tolerate further cheating by its partners and demanded others share equally in quota reductions. But agreement proved impossible. In December 1985, unable to reach agreement, OPEC decided to eliminate production quotas and let each member make its own output decision.

The Future of Oil Prices

OPEC's collapse as a cartel produced a major reduction in world oil prices. Early in 1986 the price reached $20 per barrel, and fell below $9 later in the year. Some predicted that price would stabilize near the 1970 relative price, which would mean a price of around $8–9 a barrel in today's prices. Others felt new agreements then being attempted would lead to stabilization in the $12–$15 range.

The Relevance of the OPEC Experience to Oligopoly

OPEC's experience illustrates nicely the traditional problems of cartels, which OPEC did well to keep under control for most of a decade. The experience also illustrates many of the aspects of oligopoly, even when there is no formal agreement among the members of the industry. Four of the aspects illustrated are stated below.

Restriction of output below the competitive level can lead to immense profits in the short term.

This is particularly so if the demand curve turns out to be highly inelastic in the short term. There is thus substantial incentive for a group of producers to cooperate in exercising their collective market power.

Maintaining market power becomes increasingly difficult as time passes.

Supply is likely to increase as new producers find ways of overcoming entry barriers in order to share in the large profits. Demand is likely to decrease as new substitutes are invented and put into production.

Producers with market power face a basic trade-off between profits in the short term and profits in the longer term.

The closer a group of producers gets price to the monopolistic level, the higher are its short-run profits, but the greater is the incentive for longer-term market reactions from both the supply side—entry of new sources of supply—and the demand side—invention of substitutes.

Output restriction by voluntary agreement among several firms is difficult to maintain in the long run.

This is particularly so if declining demand and increasing competition from new sources or new products lead to a steadily shrinking share of the market and falling levels of profits.

OPEC illustrates many problems that are typical of oligopolies whose individual producers exercise market power. But OPEC did not face some of the problems typical of many oligopolies both because it had the power of national governments behind its output-restriction agreements and because at the outset it was the only producer with significant market power, being surrounded as it was by a host of other producing countries, each with an output that was small relative to the industry's total output.

Economists have devoted much effort to studying the behavior of all types of oligopolistic industries over the years. Three of the most important questions arising out of these studies are discussed below. First, what accounts for the observed short-run stickiness of prices set by firms in oligopolistic industries? Second, how do oligopolists make longer-term price and output decisions in the face of the interdependence among firms that typifies such industries? Third, how do oligopolists seek to protect their long-term profits by creating barriers to entry?

Short-Run Price-Output Decisions

One of the most striking contrasts between perfectly competitive and oligopolistic markets concerns the behavior of prices. In perfect competition prices change continually in response to changes in demand and supply. In oligopoly prices change less frequently. Prices for radios, automobiles, television sets, and men's suits do not change with anything like the frequency that prices change in markets for basic materials or stocks and bonds. Of course, prices in oligopolistic industries do change, but usually by significant amounts at discrete intervals of time. The basic empirical finding is:

Oligopolistic firms do not alter their prices every time demand shifts. Instead, they fix prices and let the quantity sold adjust in the short term.

This phenomenon is often referred to as the *stickiness* of oligopolistic prices. Before considering possible explanations of why prices may be sticky, it is important to recognize how and when oligopolistic prices do change.

Changing prices.   Oligopolistic prices ordinarily change when there are major changes in costs of production. Rises in raw material prices or wage rates are passed on fairly quickly by rises in product prices.[2] Also, major reductions in costs, as when a new product, such as the home computer, is being developed, are usually followed by reductions in prices. This is because of the rivalry among oligopolistic firms. If one firm fails to cut price when costs fall, another firm will do so, seeking thereby to increase its market share.

Oligopoly prices also often change in response to large unexpected shifts in demand. If an industry finds itself faced with an apparently permanent and unexpected downward shift in demand, firms will often cut prices in an attempt to retain their markets until longer-term adjustments can be made. For example, the North American car industry was faced with declining demand in 1980 to 1982 due to its lag in developing small, fuel-efficient cars that were competitive with Japanese imports. It offered big rebates that slashed prices to levels that could not have been maintained in the long run.

Sticky prices.   The rigidity of oligopolistic prices occurs mainly in the face of cyclical and seasonal fluctuations in demand. The existence of business cycles, that is, alternating periods of high and low demand for output, is well known to firms, even if the precise course of each cycle cannot be predicted in advance. Oligopolistic firms tend to hold their prices fairly constant through cyclical fluctuations in demand while allowing output to vary.

---

[2] Oligopolistic pricing may convert more or less continuous changes in input prices into discrete changes in output prices. Say that inflation is steadily raising the prices of industrial raw materials as determined in perfectly competitive markets. Firms find it expensive to change list prices every day or every week. They will therefore make discrete jumps in the prices they charge every few months, first getting output prices ahead of input prices, then slowly falling behind until a further adjustment of output prices is necessary.

Price stickiness is short-term behavior that need not affect our longer-term view of how the economy functions. Nonetheless, the stickiness is an interesting problem in its own right, and it has important implications for macroeconomics.[3] The modern explanation of this pricing behavior has two parts. The first concerns the nature of short-run cost curves in industries that are typically oligopolistic; the second concerns the costs of changing prices.

Short-Run Costs

Saucer-shaped cost curves. Ever since economists began measuring the cost curves of manufacturing firms, they have reported flat, short-run variable cost curves. The evidence is now overwhelming that in manufacturing, and in some other sectors, cost curves are shaped like the black curve in Figure 15-4, with a long, flat, middle portion and sharply rising sections at each end. For such a cost curve, which may be described as saucer-shaped, there is a large range of output over which average variable costs are constant. Over that range marginal costs are equal to average variable costs, and thus they, too, are constant per unit of output.

Given a saucer-shaped cost curve, there is no single output where average costs are minimized (in Chapter 10 we called the output that minimizes average total cost *capacity output*). Instead, we distinguish two new concepts.

Full-capacity output, which is shown as q_3 in Figure 15-4, is the maximum output that can be produced before average and marginal costs start to rise.

Normal-capacity output, a somewhat lower level shown by q_2 in Figure 15-4, is the output that the firm hopes to maintain on average. The margin between normal-capacity output and full-capacity output is available to meet unexpected, seasonal or cyclical peaks in demand. The firm expects to use it in periods of peak demand, but not in periods of average or slack demand.

[3] A major problem of macroeconomics is why in the short run it is mainly output, rather than prices, that responds to changes in the total demand for goods and services across the whole economy. The oligopolistic behavior studied in this section provides an important part of the explanation of this phenomenon.

FIGURE 15-4 Saucer-Shaped Average Variable and Marginal Cost Curves

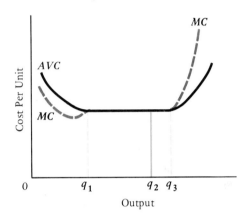

Where the AVC curve is horizontal, marginal costs coincide with average variable costs and are likewise constant per unit of output. It is possible to design a plant that achieves roughly constant variable and marginal costs over a large range of output. Such a curve is shown here. While average variable costs decrease for outputs up to q_1 and increase beyond q_3, they are constant over the large range q_1 to q_3. The level of output q_2 is normal capacity output, which is the average output the firm hopes to achieve. This is less than the highest level of output at which AVC is a minimum. With this cost curve, the firm can vary production over the whole interval from q_1 to q_3 and have constant marginal costs per unit.

Explaining the saucer shape. Why are many cost curves saucer-shaped rather than U-shaped? The answer is that firms design plants to have this property so that they can accommodate the inevitable seasonal and cyclical swings in demand for their products. As Professor George Stigler (the 1982 Nobel Laureate in Economics) was the first to point out, a firm faced with two possible average variable cost curves, such as those shown in Figure 15-5, might well prefer to build a plant that results in the flat-bottomed curve if it anticipates widely fluctuating demand. The saucer-shaped curve then leads on average to lower costs, even though at some output the U-shaped cost curve dips below it.

How does it happen that the firm has a choice of

FIGURE 15-5   U-Shaped Versus Saucer-Shaped Cost Curves

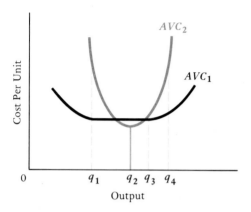

A firm anticipating fluctuating output may choose a plant with a flat-bottomed cost curve. AVC_1 and AVC_2 are alternatives based on how a plant is designed and built. While AVC_2 achieves lower unit costs than does AVC_1 if output is very close to q_2, it is much less adaptable to either higher or lower outputs. If the firm could count on producing q_2 every period, it would prefer the plant yielding AVC_2. But if it anticipated outputs ranging from q_1 to q_4, it would prefer AVC_1.

the shape of its short-run average cost curve? Consider again the law of diminishing returns first encountered in Chapter 10. The U-shaped short-run cost curve arises when a variable amount of one factor, say, labor, is applied to a fixed amount of a second factor, say, capital. Starting from zero output and zero use of the variable factor, as more of that factor is used, a more nearly optimal combination with the fixed factor is achieved. Once the optimal combination is arrived at, the use of further units of the variable factor leads to too much of the variable factor being used in combination with the fixed factor and thus to rising average variable costs. Only one quantity of labor leads to the least-cost factor proportions.

The changing combinations of fixed and variable factors must occur in the short run whenever all of the fixed factor must be used all of the time; in other words, when the fixed factor is *indivisible*. But this is not always the case. Even though the firm's plant

and equipment may be fixed in the short run, so that no more than what exists is available, it is often possible to utilize less than all the fixed capital. For that reason the flat cost curve is not inconsistent with the law of diminishing returns. The divisibility of the "fixed factor" means that diminishing returns does not apply because variations in output below full capacity are accomplished by reducing the input of both labor and capital.

Consider as a simple example a factory that consists of 10 sewing machines in a shed, each with a productive capacity of 20 units per day when operated by 1 operator for 1 shift. If 200 units per day are required, then all 10 machines are operated by 10 workers on a normal shift. If demand falls to 180, then 1 operator can be laid off. But there is no benefit to have the 9 remaining operators dashing about trying to work 10 machines. Clearly, 1 machine can be "laid off" as well, and the ratio of *employed* labor to *employed* machines held constant. Production can go from 20 to 40 to 60 all the way to 200 without any change in factor proportions for the factors in use. In this case we would expect the factory to have constant marginal and average variable costs from 20 to 200 units and only then to encounter rising costs, as production must be extended by overtime and other means of combining more labor with the maximum available supply of 10 machines.

In such a case, the fixed factor is *divisible*. Since some of it can be left unemployed, there is no need to depart from the most efficient ratio of *labor used* to *capital used* as production is decreased. Thus, average variable costs can be constant over a large range, up to the point at which all of the fixed factor is used.

The existence of plants with divisible physical capital can account for the observed saucer shape of many cost curves at the plant level.

A similar situation occurs when a firm has many plants. For example, a plywood manufacturer with 10 or more plants may choose to reduce its output by temporarily closing one or more plants while operating the rest at normal-capacity output. The *firm's* short-run variable costs tend to be constant over a large range of output because there is no need to depart from the optimal combination of labor and capital in those plants that are kept in operation.

Cost of Changing Prices

The second part of the explanation of sticky prices concerns the high costs of changing administered prices. Such costs include the costs of printing new list prices for the many products of a typical multi-product firm, the costs of notifying all customers, the accounting and billing difficulty of keeping track of frequently changing prices, and the loss of customer and retailer loyalty and goodwill due to the uncertainty caused by frequent changes in prices.

Sticky Price Behavior

The composite explanation of sticky prices is illustrated in Figure 15-6. Firms estimate their *normal*

demand curve, that is, the average of what they can expect to sell at each price over booms and slumps. Having built a plant consistent with this normal demand and with the expected fluctuations in output, they then pick the profit-maximizing price derived from their normal demand curve as their "normal price." Short-run fluctuations in demand are met by holding price constant and varying output. This avoids all the costs involved in repeated changes of prices.

The behavior just described is consistent with profit maximization. Because the cost of changing prices is high, often the best thing a firm can do is to set the price that maximizes profits for average demand and then adjust output rather than price as demand varies over the cycle.

Note, however, that this behavior is profitable only with a saucer-shaped cost curve, such as AVC_1 in Figure 15-5. If the curve were U-shaped, such as

FIGURE 15-6   A Theory of Sticky Prices in the Face of Fluctuating Demand

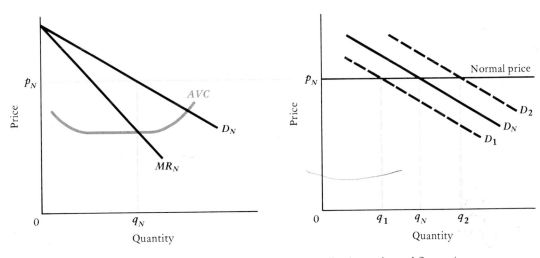

(i) Determining normal price

(ii) Adjusting to demand fluctuations

If it is costly to make price changes, a profit-maximizing firm may fix a price based on average sales and vary quantity in the face of fluctuating demand. In (i) the firm with normal capacity q_N and a normal (average) demand curve D_N with a marginal revenue curve MR_N sets p_N as the profit-maximizing price, where $MR_N = MC$. This price becomes its normal price. As shown in (ii), when demand slumps to D_1, the firm reduces output to q_1 but keeps price unchanged. When demand peaks at D_2, it also maintains prices and increases output to q_2.

AVC_2 in that figure, the firm's losses would be un-acceptable when costs soared at the extremes of lower and higher than normal output.

Holding price constant in the face of short-term fluctuations in demand can be the profit-maximizing course of action only if costs remain relatively stable over the range of output fluctuations normally encountered.

Implications of the theory.   The theory that oligopolistic firms have saucer-shaped cost curves and that it is costly for oligopolists to change prices has a number of important implications.

1. As long as output remains within the range over which the average cost curve is flat, the price charged tends to be a relatively fixed markup over the constant level of average cost.
2. Cyclical fluctuations in demand are met by quantity adjustments rather than price adjustments.
3. Cost changes in either an upward or a downward direction are passed on through price changes (although possibly with a lag because oligopolistic firms find it costly to make continuous price changes).
4. Oligopolistic firms receive signals from the economy just as do perfectly competitive firms, but the form the signals take is different. While perfect competitors receive their signals about market conditions from a price change, oligopolies receive their signals from a change in their volume of sales.

The second and the third implications are especially important when we study some current controversies in macroeconomics. We shall return to them in Chapter 39.

Long-Run Price-Output Decisions

While oligopolistic firms tend to hold prices constant in the face of expected short-term fluctuations in demand, prices do change in response to longer-term forces. How then are prices set in oligopolistic in-dustries? In competitive industries prices are set by the impersonal forces of demand and supply. But, as we have already observed, oligopolists must administer their prices. What price to charge is a decision that must be made by each individual firm and cannot be left to impersonal forces external to the firm.

Interdependence of decisions.   There is one key problem facing most oligopolistic firms that the OPEC experience does not illustrate. While there were many non-OPEC producers of oil, no one of them had anything like the output of OPEC during the 1970s. Thus, the cartel did not face another producer with substantial power to influence the world's price in response to OPEC's own decisions. Instead, OPEC was the only unified group with a large enough proportion of the total output to have real power to influence that price.

A more typical oligopolistic industry contains a few large firms, each of which is aware that it has market power. Thus, asking how prices are set under oligopoly raises a critical aspect of oligopoly theory.

The few large firms in a typical oligopolistic industry have identifiable rivals whose behavior they cannot afford to ignore.

If Bloomingdale's watches Macy's, so does Macy's watch Bloomingdale's and each firm *knows* it is being carefully watched by the other. When Bloomingdale's makes some pricing decision, it is likely to take into account how it thinks Macy's will react, and Macy's is likely to do the same with respect to Bloomingdale's. So what Bloomingdale's does may depend on what it *thinks* Macy's will do, and the outcome of Bloomingdale's actions will depend on what Macy's *actually* does do. To deal with this complexity, economists have sometimes proposed simplifying models and sometimes turned to empirical findings to suggest generalizations. We shall look at each of these approaches.

Model-Based Approaches

The first model of price setting we consider avoids the complexity of interdependence by assuming that each firm will ignore it in its decision making. The second model includes interdependence and assumes that a firm considers the reactions that it expects from its competitors when making its decisions.

Cournot-Nash Equilibrium

An important breakthrough in dealing with the oligopoly problem was made in 1838 by the French economist A. A. Cournot. He dealt with the special case of an industry containing only two firms, called a **duopoly.**

Cournot assumed that the two firms sold an identical product and that each chose its profit-maximizing output on the assumption that *the other firm would hold its output constant.* He then allowed each firm to adjust in turn to the last move made by its competitor. This gave rise to a series of adjustments: firm A chose its output given firm B's output; firm B then chose a new output given the output firm A had just selected; firm A then chose a new output given the output firm B had just selected; firm B then chose a new output given the output firm A had just selected; and so on. Cournot concluded that such behavior would lead to the following results.

1. A stable equilibrium would be reached in which the market would be divided in a determinate way between the two firms. (It would be shared equally if the two firms had identical cost curves.)
2. The resulting equilibrium price would be higher than the competitive price, but lower than the price a monopolist would charge.

These results established oligopoly as not just a mixture of competition and monopoly, but as a truly separate market form. The equilibrium Cournot analyzed has survived in modern theorizing. It is now often called the **Cournot-Nash equilibrium.** It is the equilibrium that results when each firm makes its output decisions on the assumption that all other firms' outputs will be unchanged.

Because this equilibrium is one that may occur when firms do not take their competitors' reactions into account, it is an equilibrium that arises when there is no collusion between firms. For this reason, it is often called a *non-cooperative equilibrium.* It is also a *self-policing* equilibrium in that no single firm has a profit incentive to depart from the equilibrium.

Conjectural Variations

The assumption that each firm takes its rival's behavior as given seems wrong in many small-group situations. The Ford Motor Company knows (or quickly learns) that if it slashes the prices on some of its cars, GM, Chrysler, and American Motors will react in some way, usually by adjusting their prices on comparable models. Similar considerations apply when General Mills considers changing the advertising for one of its breakfast cereals or Lever Brothers the prices of its soaps.

One way to deal with this interdependence is to assume that when it makes its decisions, an oligopolistic firm takes into account what are called *conjectural variations.* This model assumes that when making price or output decisions, each firm conjectures what variations its choices will induce its rivals to make in their prices or outputs. The firm then takes these variations into account when making its decisions. For example, firm A might assume that whatever price or output it sets, its rivals will set the same price or output. Or the firm might assume that if it raises prices, its rivals will also raise their prices, but only by half as much.

From the point of view of a simple theory, the problem with conjectural variations is that there are so many possible different ones. Thus they lead not to a single prediction but to a variety of different market outcomes. Conjectural variations are not *a* theory of oligopoly but a great number of different possible theories.

Differentiated products.   All the complexity mentioned above arises even when oligopolists sell a homogeneous product, as Cournot assumed they did. But most oligopolies sell a wide range of differentiated products. For example, one brand of running shoes sold by Nike differs not only from all other brands it sells, but also from all brands sold by Adidas and other competing companies. In such cases oligopolies face an additional set of problems. With differentiated products, each product is distinct from every other product. As a result, firms do not need to compete only by means of price; they can also use quality, advertising, and the nature of their whole product line as competitive weapons. This adds yet further to the complexity and multiplicity of model-based theories of oligopoly behavior.

Empirical Approaches

Because the problem of price-output behavior under oligopoly is so complex, some economists have sought to build a theory by generalizing from observations of the behavior of oligopolistic firms. These economists believe that we need to begin with detailed knowledge of the actual behavior of such firms. The knowledge is then used to narrow the range of theoretically possible cases by selecting those that actually occur.

Such empirically based approaches to the problem start by recognizing two limits to oligopolistic prices and profits. First, if there is no recognition of interdependence at all, a non-cooperative equilibrium will be established and profits will be much lower than they would be under a monopoly. They might even be pushed to the zero-profit position that occurs under perfect competition. Second, if the firms collude to maximize their joint profits, they might reach the upper limit and establish a monopoly price.

Although the upper limit can be attained through explicit agreement, as in the case of OPEC, such agreements are illegal for firms producing in the United States. Such a position might also arise, however, through tacit agreement based on mutual recognition of interdependence. If all firms assume that their competitors will match their own price, they will each be motivated to establish the joint profit-maximizing price and output. Because such an equilibrium can result from either actual or tacit cooperation, it is often called the *cooperative equilibrium*.

As we have already seen, however, there are forces at work to upset such a cooperative solution. Even if joint profits are maximized, there is the problem of market shares. How is the profit-maximizing level of sales to be divided among the competing firms? Competition for market shares may upset the tacit agreement to hold to joint maximizing behav-

ior. In an industry with many differentiated products and where sales are often by contract between buyers and sellers, cheating may be covert rather than overt. Secret discounts and rebates can allow a firm to increase its sales at the expense of its competitors while appearing to hold to the tacitly agreed monopoly price.

Another reason why the monopoly level of profits may not be achieved, even if the monopoly price is maintained, is that firms often compete for market shares by various forms of non-price competition such as advertising. Since such competition is costly, it will reduce industry profits.

These considerations suggest that we look at an oligopolistic industry in terms of the conflicting pressures of cooperation and competition that act on it. First, the recognition of interdependence is a force leading firms toward the monopoly price and the cooperative equilibrium of joint profit maximization. Second, the possibility of gaining at the expense of one's rivals is a force pushing toward competitive behavior which leads firms away from the cooperative equilibrium and in the direction of a non-cooperative equilibrium.

These considerations lead to the *hypothesis of qualified joint profit maximization*, first stated by Professor William Fellner.

The hypothesis of qualified joint profit maximization is that the relative strength of the tendencies toward and away from joint profit maximization varies from industry to industry in a systematic way that is associated with observable characteristics of firms, markets, and products.

Here are some of the characteristics that are hypothesized to affect the strength of the two tendencies.

1. *The tendency toward joint maximization is greater for small numbers of sellers than for larger numbers.* This characteristic involves both motivation and ability. When there are few firms, they will know that one of them cannot gain sales without inducing retaliation by its rivals. Also, a few firms can tacitly coordinate their policies with less difficulty than can many firms.
2. *The tendency toward joint maximization is greater for*

producers of similar products than for producers of sharply differentiated products. The argument here is that the more nearly identical the products of sellers, the closer will be the direct rivalry for customers and the less the ability of one firm to gain a lasting advantage over its rivals. Such sellers will tend to prefer joint efforts to achieve a larger pie to individual attempts to increase their own shares.

3. *The tendency toward joint maximization is greater in a growing rather than in a contracting market.* The argument here is that when demand is growing, firms can utilize their capacity fully without resorting to attempts to "steal" their rivals' customers. When firms have excess capacity, they are tempted to give price concessions to attract customers, but when their rivals retaliate, price cuts become general.

4. *The tendency toward joint maximization is greater when the industry contains a dominant firm rather than a set of more or less equal competitors.* A dominant firm may become a *price leader*, that is, a firm that sets the industry's price while all other firms fall into line. Even if a dominant firm is not automatically a price leader, other firms may look to it for judgment about market conditions, and its decisions may become a tentative focus for tacit agreement.

5. *The tendency toward joint profit maximization is greater when non-price rivalry is absent or limited.* If non-price competition is not limited, tacit price fixing to maximize joint profits will cause non-price competition that will take the industry away from its joint maximizing position. The argument here is that when firms seek to suppress their basic rivalry by avoiding price competition, rivalry will break out in other forms. Firms may seek to increase their market shares through extra advertising, quality changes, the establishment of new products, giveaways, and a host of similar schemes that leave their prices unchanged but increase their costs.

6. *The tendency toward joint profit maximization is greater when the barriers to entry of new firms are greater.* The high profits of existing firms attract new entrants, who will drive down price and reduce profits. The greater the barriers to entry, the less this will occur. Thus the greater the entry barriers, the closer the profits of existing firms can be to their joint maximizing level without being reduced by new entry.

The Importance of Entry Barriers

Point 6 above has taken us beyond price and output decisions and into considerations of entry. Perhaps the most important empirical observation about actual behavior of firms in oligopoly is what Professor Joe S. Bain called the *condition of entry* which relates to what we have called entry barriers.

Suppose firms in an oligopolistic industry succeed in raising prices above long-run average total costs and earn substantial profits that are not completely eliminated by non-price competition. Why do these profits not cause other firms to enter the industry, increase output, and force prices down to the zero-profit level? The answer lies in barriers to entry.

Natural barriers were discussed in Chapter 13 (see page 234). If natural barriers to entry do not exist, oligopolistic firms can earn profits in the long run only if they can create entry barriers. To the extent to which this can be done, existing firms can move toward joint profit maximization without fear of new entrants attracted by the high profits. We discuss next a few types of created barriers.

Brand Proliferation

Many products have several characteristics, which can be varied over a wide range. Thus it is possible to have many similar products, each with a somewhat different mix of characteristics. Consider the many kinds of breakfast cereals or cars. Although the multiplicity of brands is no doubt partly a response to consumers' tastes, it may also be partly an attempt to discourage the entry of new firms. When the existing firms sell a wide array of differentiated products, entry on a small scale by a new firm is difficult.

To illustrate why brand proliferation may be a formidable barrier to a small potential entrant, assume that the product is of the type where there is a substantial amount of brand switching by consumers. In this case the larger the number of brands sold by existing firms, the smaller the expected sales of a new entrant. Say that an industry contains three large firms, each selling one brand of cigarettes, and say that 30 percent of all smokers change brands in a random fashion each year. If a new firm enters the industry, it can expect to pick up 25 percent of the smokers who change brands (it has one out of the new total of four available brands). This would give it 7.5 percent (25 percent of 30 percent) of the total market the first year merely as a result of picking up its share of the random switchers, and it would keep increasing its share year by year thereafter.[4] If, however, the existing three firms have five brands each, there would be fifteen brands already available, and a new firm selling one new brand could expect to pick up only one-sixteenth of the brand switchers, giving it less than 2 percent of the total market the first year and with smaller gains in subsequent years also. This is an extreme case, but it illustrates a general result.

The larger the number of differentiated products sold by existing oligopolists, the smaller the market available to a new firm entering with a single new product.

Set-up Costs

Existing firms can create entry barriers by imposing on new entrants significant fixed costs of setting up operations in that market. This is particularly important if the minimum efficient scale occurs at an output that is low relative to total industry output, that is, there are only weak natural barriers to entry.

Advertising is one means by which existing firms can impose heavy set-up costs on new entrants. Advertising, of course, serves purposes other than creating barriers to entry. Among them, it may perform the useful function of informing buyers about their alternatives, thereby making markets work more smoothly. Indeed, a new firm may find that advertising is essential, even when existing firms do not advertise at all, simply to call attention to its entry into an industry where it is unknown.

Nonetheless, advertising can also operate as a potent entry barrier by increasing the set-up costs of new entrants. Where there is much effective brand-image advertising, a new firm will have to spend a great deal on advertising its product in order to bring the product to the public's attention. If the firm's sales are small, advertising costs *per unit sold* will be very large. Large sales allow the fixed advertising costs needed to break into the market to be spread over a large number of units. This may reduce costs per unit enough so as not to confer a significant competitive disadvantage on the new firm.

Figure 15-7 illustrates how heavy advertising can shift the cost curves of a firm with a low minimun efficient scale to make it one with a high *MES*. In essence, what happens is that a scale advantage of advertising is added to a low *MES* of production with the result that the overall *MES* is raised. Thus:

A new entrant with small sales but large set-up costs finds itself at a substantial cost disadvantage relative to its established rivals.

Any once-and-for-all cost of entering a market has the same effect as a large, initial advertising expenditure. For example, with many consumers' goods the cost of developing a new product that is similar, but not identical to, existing products may be quite substantial. Even if there are few economies of scale in the production of the product, its large fixed development cost can lead to a falling long-run average total cost curve over a wide range of output.

An application. We have seen that brand proliferation and advertising can act as entry barriers. The combined use of the two help to explain one apparent paradox of everyday life—the fact that one firm often sells multiple brands of the same product, which compete directly against one another as well as against the products of other firms.

The soap and cigarette industries provide classic examples of this behavior. Since all available scale economies can be realized by quite small plants, both industries have few natural barriers to entry. Both contain a few large firms, each of which produces an array of heavily advertised products. The array of products makes it harder for a new entrant to obtain a large market niche with one new product. The

---

[4] Because it is smaller than its rivals, it would lose fewer customers to them by random switching than it would gain from them.

FIGURE 15-7   Advertising Cost As a Barrier to Entry

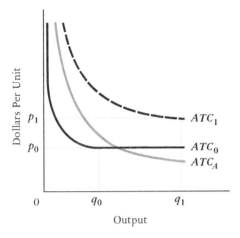

Large advertising costs can increase the minimum efficient scale (MES) of production and thereby increase entry barriers. The ATC_0 curve shows that the MES without advertising is at q_0. The curve ATC_A shows that advertising cost per unit falls as output rises. Advertising increases total cost to ATC_1 and raises MES to q_1. Advertising has given a scale advantage to large sellers and has thus created a barrier to entry.

heavy advertising, although directed against existing products, creates an entry barrier by increasing the set-up costs of a new product that seeks to gain the attention of consumers and establish its own brand image. Together multiple products and heavy advertising may provide a formidable entry barrier to any new firm.

Predatory Pricing

A firm that is considering entry will not do so if faced with certain losses after entry. One way existing firms can create such a situation is to cut prices to—or below—cost whenever entry occurs and keep them there until the entrant goes bankrupt. The existing firms sacrifice profits while doing so, but they send a discouraging message to future as well as present potential rivals.

There is much controversy concerning predatory pricing. Some economists argue that pricing policies that appear to be predatory can be explained by other motives and that existing firms only hurt themselves when they engage in such practices instead of reaching an accommodation with new entrants. Others argue that predatory pricing seems to have been observed and that it is in the long-run interests of existing firms to punish new entrants even when it is costly to do so in the short run.

Whatever the outcome of this debate among economists, the courts have taken the position that predatory pricing does occur. A number of firms have been convicted of using it in restraint of trade.

Oligopoly and the Functioning of the Economy

Oligopoly is the most commonly encountered market structure in large sectors of the U.S. economy. What does the recognition of the impossibility of achieving perfect competition and of the necessity for oligopoly over a large part of the economy do to our views of the working of the price system?

Resource Allocation

We have seen that under perfect competition prices are set by the impersonal forces of demand and supply and, when firms adjust quantities to market prices, they are responding to market conditions and helping to achieve allocative efficiency.

Firms in oligopolistic markets administer their prices. The market signaling system works slightly differently when prices are administered rather than determined by the market. Changes in the market conditions for both inputs and outputs are signaled to the perfectly competitive firm by changes in the prices of its inputs and its outputs. Changes in the market conditions for inputs are signaled to the oligopolistic firm by changes in the prices of its inputs. Changes in the market conditions for the oligopolist's output are typically signaled, however, by a change in sales at the administered price.

Rises in costs of inputs will shift cost curves upward, and oligopolistic firms will be led to raise prices and lower output. Rises in demand will cause the sales of oligopolistic firms to rise. Firms will then respond by increasing output, thereby increasing the quantities of society's resources that are allocated to producing that commodity.

The market system reallocates resources in response to changes in demand and costs in roughly the same way under oligopoly as it does under perfect competition.

Some oligopolies succeed in coming close to joint profit maximization. Others compete so intensely among themselves that they come close to competitive prices and outputs. The consequences for allocative efficiency vary accordingly.

Most oligopolistic industries charge prices that exceed marginal cost and in this respect oligopoly is similar to monopoly: It does not achieve the conditions of allocative efficiency.

Innovation

Although oligopolies do not fulfill the conditions of allocative efficiency, an important issue is how much they contribute to economic growth by engaging in innovative activity in the very long run.

An important defense of oligopoly relates to Schumpeter's concept of creative destruction (see p. 257). Some economists have theorized that intermediate market structures, such as oligopoly, would lead to more innovation than would occur in either competitive or monopolistic industries. They argue that the oligopolist is faced with clear and present competition from existing rivals and cannot afford the more relaxed life of the monopolist. At the same time, however, the oligopoly firm expects to keep a good share of the profits that it earns because of the barriers to entry and its ability to avoid excessive price competition with existing rivals.

The empirical evidence is broadly consistent with this hypothesis. Professor Jesse Markham of Harvard University concluded a survey of empirical findings by saying:

> If technological change and innovational activity are, as we generally assume, in some important way a product of organized R&D activities financed and executed by business companies, it is clear that the welfare payoffs that flow from them can to some measurable extent be traced to the doorsteps of large firms operating in oligopolistic markets.

Everyday observation provides some confirmation of this finding. Leading U.S. firms that operate in highly concentrated industries, such as Kodak, IBM, du Pont, Western Electric, Xerox, General Electric, and Minnesota Mining & Manufacturing, have been highly innovative over many years.

While Schumpeter's hypothesis has substantial credibility when applied to oligopoly, its predictions are not borne out by observations in every case. Some highly oligopolistic American industries, such as steel, appear to have lagged far behind their foreign competitors. Evidently the long, sustained absence of competition led them to become complacent and relatively inefficient.

A Final Word

Oligopoly is an important market structure in today's economy because there are many industries where the minimum efficient scale is simply too large to support a large group of competing firms. We have seen that oligopoly will not, in general, achieve the allocative efficiency of perfect competition. Rivalrous oligopoly, however, may produce more satisfactory allocative results than monopoly. Oligopoly may also be effective in producing very-long-run adaptations that develop both new products and cost-reducing methods of producing old ones.

The defense of oligopoly as a market form is that it may be the best of the available alternatives when minimum efficient scale is large. The challenge to public policy is to keep oligopolists competing and using their competitive energies to improve products and to lower costs rather than merely to erect entry barriers.

Summary

1. The OPEC cartel provides insights into the problems of oligopolies. It proved remarkably successful during the 1970s in raising the prices of oil above the previous, approximately competitive, level. At the time OPEC included a large fraction of the world's oil-exporting countries, and it succeeded for almost 10 years in holding prices high and limiting output to maintain these prices. Its initial success was due partly to the fact that neither demand nor alternative sources of supply could change quickly.

2. In the era before OPEC demand for oil products rose steadily in response to rising incomes, sustained low prices, and a highly elastic long-run supply. OPEC changed the supply situation overnight by means of an effective cartel. Using a strategy of restricting output, it converted a horizontal supply curve into a steeply rising one. From 1973 until the early 1980s OPEC managed the world price of oil and received enormous monopoly profits from its own sales.

3. OPEC's ability to control the oil market was weakened as oil-consuming countries decreased their reliance on oil and as non-OPEC sources of energy supply steadily expanded. In the early 1980s OPEC members found it necessary to accept ever larger reductions in their production and in their shares of world markets in order to maintain the high oil prices. Unable to agree on quotas or on how to enforce them, the cartel collapsed at the end of 1985 and prices tumbled toward the competitive level.

4. There are several important lessons in the OPEC experience: (a) restriction of output can lead to large short-run profits; (b) the required output restrictions become larger over time due to reductions in demand and development of other supplies; and (c) as the cartel's market shrinks, it becomes increasingly difficult to maintain output restriction agreements.

5. An important empirical finding is the relative short-run stickiness of oligopoly prices in response to seasonal and cyclical fluctuations in demand. This stickiness results from the combined influence of the flat short-run cost curves and the high costs involved in changing administered prices frequently. While prices are changed when the firms' costs change or in response to permanent shifts in demand, oligopolistic firms find it profitable to vary output, while keeping prices fixed, as demand fluctuates around its normal level.

6. A key empirical finding about oligopolistic industries, particularly in the manufacturing sector, is that short-run cost curves tend to be saucer-shaped rather than U-shaped. This reflects the decision of firms to build plants capable of being operated over a range of outputs at roughly constant marginal cost so as to keep average costs low in the face of fluctuating output. The flat cost curve does not violate the law of diminishing returns as long as the proportion in which capital and labor are used in production can be held constant for outputs below full capacity.

7. There is no simple set of predictions about the long-term outcome of oligopolistic competition. The final outcome depends on the strategies adopted by the individual firms. Therefore, instead of a single theory, there are many possible patterns of behavior. The general hypothesis of qualified joint profit maximization says that firms that recognize they are rivals will be motivated by two sets of opposing forces, one set moving them toward joint profit maximization and the other moving them away from it.

8. Oligopoly profits persist in the long run because of barriers to entry, which may be natural or created. Firm-created barriers include brand proliferation and various types of set-up costs. They may also include the threat of predatory pricing.

9. Under oligopoly the price system works to reallocate resources in response to changes in demand and costs in qualitatively the same way as it does under perfect competition. Oligopoly does not, however, fulfill the efficiency condition that marginal cost should equal price (which is achieved under perfect competition). Some economists argue that oligopoly (and monopoly) profits are conducive to rapid growth because they encourage creative destruction.

Topics for Review

Effects of OPEC cartelization
Sticky short-term prices
Saucer-shaped short-run average cost curves
Cooperative and non-cooperative equilibria
Conjectural variations
Hypothesis of qualified joint profit maximization
Created barriers to entry
Resource allocation under oligopoly

Discussion Questions

1. What bearing did each of the following have on the eventual inability of OPEC to maintain a monopoly price for oil?
    a. Between 1979 and 1985 OPEC's share of the world oil supply decreased by one-half.
    b. "Saudi Arabia's interest lies in extending the life span of oil to the longest possible period," said Sheik Yamani.
    c. The Soviet Union, in order to earn Western currency to pay for grain, increased its oil exports to the West during the late 1970s, becoming the world's second largest oil exporter.
    d. The Iran-Iraq war decreased oil production in the Middle East from 1979 to 1981 by 4.5 million barrels per day.
    e. United States government policies during the 1970s protected American consumers from oil price shocks by holding domestic prices well below OPEC levels.

2. How did these headlines, all from 1985, foreshadow the collapse of OPEC?
   a. "Saudis threaten to double oil production if OPEC does not accept its terms"
   b. "Britain's price cut adds to OPEC's predicament"
   c. "Saudi economy is ailing after three years of recession"
   d. "New oil discovery adds Colombia to world's producers"
   e. "OPEC oil ministers meet amid discord on pricing policy"
3. Do the following groups stand to gain or to lose if oil prices continue to fall in real terms over the second half of the 1980s?
   a. American consumers
   b. Coal miners in the United States
   c. People who have invested in companies developing synthetic fuels
   d. Indonesia, an oil-exporting country with small oil reserves and a large population
   e. U.S. drillers of wildcat oil wells
   f. Saudi Arabia
4. "The decade from 1975 to 1985 proved to the world that there were many available substitutes for gasoline, among them bicycles, car pools, moving closer to work, cable TV, and Japanese cars." Discuss how each of these may be a substitute for gasoline.
5. It has been estimated that if automobile companies did not change models for 10 years, the cost of production would be reduced by approximately 30 percent. In view of this fact, why are there annual model changes? Which, if any, of the reasons you have suggested depend on the industry's being oligopolistic? Should frequent model changes be forbidden by law?
6. Compare the effects on the automobile and the wheat industries of each of the following. In the light of your answers discuss general ways in which oligopolistic industries fulfill the same general functions as do perfectly competitive industries.
   a. Large rise in demand
   b. Large rise in costs of production
   c. Temporary cut in supplies coming to market due to a three-month rail strike
   d. Rush of cheap foreign imports
7. Some analysts of the beer industry believe that the big national companies are going to get bigger and the smaller companies will disappear relatively rapidly. Their reasoning is that big national brewers have decisive advantages over local and regional brewers. What are these analysts assuming about the cost and the demand conditions in the beer industry? Is this assumption consistent with the report by *Fortune* that indicated that a small regional brewery has higher labor productivity than the newest but larger plant of Anheuser Busch? If the efficient size of *plant* in the industry is small, might there be reasons to expect multi-plant firms to predominate?
8. Evidence suggests that the profits earned by all of the firms in many oligopolistic industries are less than the profits that would be earned if the industry were monopolized. What are some of the reasons why this might be so?

16

Public Policies About Monopoly and Competition

Monopolies, cartels, and price-fixing agreements have been regarded with suspicion and official hostility for at least a century. Even today in some quarters they take a large share of the blame for inflation, lagging productivity, discrimination in employment, and inequalities in income.

But competition is not always widely approved either. Protection of U.S. firms from competition occurs in many guises—protection of firms from foreign competition; protection of small firms from bigger, more efficient rivals; protection of firms generally from "unfair" competition; and protection of firms in depressed industries from the alleged danger of destructive or cutthroat competition.

In this chapter we look at a variety of ways in which American policymakers have chosen to intervene in the workings of the unregulated market economy through what is sometimes called regulation of industry and sometimes competition policy.

Antitrust Policy Against Monopoly

The theory of monopoly leads to three principal predictions. (1) Where monopoly power exists in an industry, fewer resources will be employed than under competitive conditions. (2) Firms with monopoly power will earn profits in excess of opportunity costs. (3) Their owners will thus command a larger share of the national income than they would under conditions of competition. In short, an economy where many firms exercise monopoly power will have a different allocation of resources and a different distribution of income than will an economy composed largely of competitive industries.

Antitrust laws attempt to prohibit the acquisition or exercise of monopoly power by business firms.

The first American antitrust law, the Sherman Antitrust Act, was passed in 1890, in an era when economists believed that perfect competition both produced ideal results and was the feasible alternative to monopoly. The Sherman Act prohibits monopoly, attempts to monopolize, and contracts, combinations, and conspiracies in restraint of trade.

Additional antitrust laws prohibit other commercial practices and give the courts the power to stop such practices and to impose remedies to prevent their reoccurrence.

The Nature of Antitrust Policy

The dominant theme of antitrust policy has been to foster competition against those who seek to achieve or exercise monopoly power or to restrain trade in other ways.[1] Such anticompetitive results may arise or be perpetuated in many different ways. Some are purely behavioral; others involve changing market structures. Any of them may lead to monopoly profits that will persist if there are barriers that prevent new competition from arising. Among these ways are:

1. Collusive agreements among firms to restrict output, raise prices, divide markets, or otherwise not to compete among themselves
2. Contractual agreements, such as exclusive dealing arrangements or tying contracts, that limit buyers in their choice of sellers
3. Mergers or acquisitions that reduce the number of independent firms in a market or industry
4. Predatory behavior by those with substantial market power against rival sellers to force them into bankruptcy, cooperative behavior, or merger
5. Price discrimination
6. A firm's finding monopoly "thrust upon it" (in the words of Learned Hand) either by its natural efficiency as a single producer or by successful innovation

The first five involve behavior that has been the object of antitrust legislation. All of these practices may be civil offenses and many are criminal as well. In criminal law a firm found guilty may be fined and its officers may be fined or sentenced to jail.

Civil (non-criminal) cases may be brought by the government or by private parties. A firm found in violation of the law may be required by the court to abandon certain practices, or it may be forced to dissolve itself into a number of separate companies.

---

[1] There are also non-economic motives for dealing with the "monopoly problem." Many people fear the political influence of those who have substantial economic power.

In private cases a firm may be obliged to pay injured parties an amount up to three times the amount of damages caused by the violation. Such *treble damages* were designed to provide a substantial incentive to private firms to root out violations of the law that might escape the notice of government prosecutors, as well as to provide powerful deterrence to violations.

Who Makes Antitrust Policies?

Antitrust laws prohibit certain forms of activity. The overall effect of antitrust policy at any time rests on three things: the nature of the laws themselves, the courts' interpretation of them, and the vigor with which prosecutions are brought by the government and by private plaintiffs. All three have changed over time, and as a result the overall antitrust climate has changed.

Laws Promoting Competition

The principal antitrust provisions are quoted in Box 16-1.

The Sherman Antitrust Act (1890) was enacted in response to the great growth in the size of firms during the last half of the nineteenth century. Section 1 of the act declared illegal every contract, combination, or conspiracy in restraint of trade. Section 2 made it illegal to monopolize or to attempt to monopolize. It also prohibited conspiracies or combinations that resulted in monopolization. The language of the Sherman Act was strong, but it was vague. It was some time before the courts defined the act's scope more specifically.

The Clayton Antitrust Act (1914) was an attempt to be more precise and to strengthen the powers of the antitrust prosecutors by allowing them to strike at potentially anticompetitive practices in their incipiency. It also identified certain practices as illegal "where the effect may be substantially to lessen competition." Its most important provisions were Section 7, applying to acquisition of stock in a competing company; Section 2, limiting the practice of price discrimination; and Section 3, regulating exclusive dealing and tying contracts. (A tying contract requires a buyer to purchase other items in order to

BOX 16-1

Principal Antitrust Provisions

Sherman Antitrust Act (26 Stat 209, 1890, as amended)

§1. Every contract, combination in the form of trust or otherwise, or conspiracy, in restraint of trade or commerce among the several States, or with foreign nations, is hereby declared to be illegal. . . . Every person who shall make any contract or engage in any combination or conspiracy shall be deemed guilty of a felony and on conviction thereof, shall be punished by a fine not exceeding one million dollars if a corporation, or, if any other person, one hundred thousand dollars, or by imprisonment not exceeding three years, or by both . . . in the discretion of the Court.

§2. Every person who shall monopolize, or attempt to monopolize, or combine or conspire with any other person or persons, to monopolize any part of the trade or commerce among the several States, or with foreign nations, shall be deemed guilty of a felony. . . .

§8. That the word "person," or "persons," wherever used in this act shall be deemed to include corporations.

Clayton Antitrust Act (38 Stat 730, 1914, as amended)

§2. (Including Robinson-Patman Amendments, 1948).

(a) That it shall be unlawful for any person engaged in commerce, in the course of such commerce, either directly or indirectly, to discriminate in price between different purchasers of commodities of like grade and quality . . . where the effect of such discrimination may be substantially to lessen competition or tend to create a monopoly in any line of commerce. . . . *Provided,* That nothing herein contained shall prevent differentials which make only due allowance for differences in the cost . . . resulting from the differing methods or quantities in which such commodities are . . . sold or delivered. . . .

§3. That it shall be unlawful for any person engaged in commerce, in the course of such commerce, to lease or make a sale or contract . . . on the condition, agreement,

or understanding that the lessee or purchaser thereof shall not use or deal in the . . . commodities of a competitor . . . where the effect of such . . . agreement . . . may be to substantially lessen competition or tend to create a monopoly in any line of commerce.

§4. Any person who shall be injured in his business or property by reason of anything forbidden in the antitrust laws may sue therefor . . . and shall recover threefold the damages by him sustained, and the cost of suit, including a reasonable attorney's fee. . . .

§7. (As amended by Celler-Kefauver Act of 1950.)

That no corporation engaged in commerce shall acquire . . . the whole or any part . . . of another corporation engaged also in commerce, where in any line of commerce in any section of the country, the effect of such acquisition may be substantially to lessen competition, or to tend to create a monopoly. . . .

§16. That any person, firm, corporation, or association shall be entitled to sue and have injunctive relief, in any court of the United States having jurisdiction over the parties, as against threatened loss or damage by a violation of the antitrust laws. . . .

Federal Trade Commission Act (38 Stat 717, 1914, as amended)

§5. (a)

(1) Unfair methods of competition . . . and unfair or deceptive acts or practices in or affecting commerce, are hereby declared unlawful.

(6) The Commission is hereby empowered and directed to prevent . . . using unfair methods . . . or deceptive acts or practices in commerce.

§5. (l)

Any person . . . who violates an order of the commission to cease and desist . . . shall pay a civil penalty of not more than $10,000 for each violation . . . each day of continuance . . . shall be deemed a separate offense.

---

purchase the item it wants.) An important provision in the Clayton Antitrust Act specifically exempted collective bargaining by labor unions from the antitrust provisions.

Although the Clayton Act made it sometimes

illegal to take control of another firm by purchasing its *stock,* the act neglected to prohibit taking control by purchasing the firm's *assets.* Thus, although it dealt with the trust, or "loose-knit" combination of competitors, it neglected the merger, or "close-knit" combination. In 1950 this loophole was closed by passage of the Celler-Kefauver Act, which applied the same provisions to asset acquisitions as had previously applied only to acquisitions of stock.

The Federal Trade Commission Act (1914) prohibited "unfair methods of competition" and also created a regulatory agency (FTC) with substantial powers of enforcement. The FTC has proved much less important relative to the courts than was anticipated in 1914, because the latter have appellate jurisdiction.[2]

Variation in Judicial Interpretation

The rule of reason. The first important series of antitrust prosecutions occurred at the beginning of the twentieth century. In 1911, in forcing the Standard Oil Company and the American Tobacco Company to divest themselves of a large share of their holdings of other companies, the Supreme Court enunciated the "rule of reason." Not all trusts, but only *unreasonable* combinations in restraint of trade, merited conviction under the Sherman Act.

Because the rule of reason was so broad, a conservative Court gave the Sherman Act a very narrow interpretation for 25 years. In the famous *U.S. Steel* case (1920), the Court found that the company had not violated the law, even though it found that the organizers of the company had *intended* to monopolize the industry, and even though the company had earlier conspired to fix prices. The Court held that U.S. Steel had not succeeded in *achieving* a monopoly (indeed, its vain attempts at price fixing proved that!). The fact that it was a big company controlling half the industry and with potential monopoly power was, the Court ruled, beside the point. The decision said in part, "The law does not make mere size an offense. It . . . requires overt acts."

[2] Under federal antitrust law government cases originate either within the antitrust division of the Department of Justice or within procedures of the Federal Trade Commission. Many cases never go to trial because they are settled by agreement between the Department of Justice or the FTC and the companies. Justice Department and private cases go to trial before federal district courts. FTC cases are heard first by the Commission. In all cases appeal is to the appropriate Circuit Court of Appeals and then to the Supreme Court. Supreme Court decisions, here as elsewhere, stand until modified by other decisions of this highest court.

In related decisions the Court not only reiterated that mere size was not an offense, but added that neither was the existence of unexerted monopoly power, no matter how impressive that power. These decisions reflected the business-oriented mood of the country during the 1920s, a mood shared by a highly conservative Supreme Court. Under this interpretation, which lasted until World War II, the antitrust laws were virtually unenforceable so far as attacks on the structure of heavily concentrated industries were concerned.

The "new" Sherman Act. A sharp break in this situation occurred in a series of cases prosecuted in the late 1930s, which reached the Court both before and just after World War II. A landmark decision in *United States v. Socony-Vacuum Oil Co.* (1940) enunciated a strong rule against price fixing: "Under the Sherman Act a combination formed for the purpose and with the effect of raising, depressing, fixing, pegging or stabilizing the price of a commodity in interstate commerce is illegal *per se*." Thus where price fixing was concerned, no test of reasonableness or sound social purpose would be applied.

An even more basic attack on the rule of reason was enunciated in the *Aluminum Company of America* case decided in 1945. The decision reversed the *U.S. Steel* decision and found ALCOA to be an illegal monopoly even though it had engaged in no "unreasonable behavior." The decision suggested that beyond some point mere size would in itself be an offense if the defendants had not done everything possible to avoid becoming dominant. This reversal was possible because the mood of the country—and the composition of its courts—had changed sharply.

This case and others led some people to speak of the "new" Sherman Act. Subsequent decisions have modified the strongly anti-big-business aspects of the *ALCOA* case, but the retreat from *ALCOA* has stopped well short of the *U.S. Steel* decision. The conduct of firms with massive market power, such as IBM, Kodak, and AT&T, has continued to be closely scrutinized to distinguish between competitive and monopolistic behavior.

The Warren Court. The modification of Section 7 of the Clayton Act in 1950, together with the onset of the Warren Court—so named for its chief justice, Earl Warren, a former Republican governor of California—ushered in a period of virtually unbroken triumphs for the government in its antitrust cases. Justice Potter Stewart, a frequent dissenter, wryly remarked that the only principle he could discern in the Court's decisions was that "the government always wins."

In particular, the Warren Court's antitrust decisions greatly restricted the ability of large corporations to merge. The Court's antimerger bias rested upon the implicit assumption that merger was not an appropriate way to achieve economies of scale. But the Warren Court opposed mergers even when market shares were relatively small. For example, in the *Von's Grocery* case (1965), a merger of two supermarkets was ruled illegal even though the merged firms would have had only a 7.5 percent share of the local (Los Angeles) market. The merger of Brown Shoe Company with a chain of retail stores (Kinney) was found illegal even though Kinney sold less than 2 percent of the nation's shoes and Brown supplied only 8 percent of Kinney's needs. In other areas as well, the Warren Court was highly critical of any business practice that might appear to restrain trade.

The Burger Court.   The Warren Court was replaced by the Burger Court, four of its nine members being appointed by President Nixon and one each by Presidents Ford and Reagan. This Court's views on antitrust matters were much more tolerant of normal business practices even if they are restrictive. In particular, this Court greatly reduced the list of actions that are illegal per se. In 1986 Chief Justice Burger retired and was replaced as Chief by Associate Justice William Rehnquist. Experts do not foresee a return soon to a more aggressive antitrust stance.

The Vigor of Prosecution

Courts, whatever their predilections, decide only those cases that come before them. Whether to prosecute and which cases to prosecute are matters largely decided by the antitrust division of the Department of Justice, whose head is a presidential appointee, and by private plaintiffs.

When the Sherman Act was passed in 1890, it was adopted with little discussion and attracted remarkably little attention. It was not until President Theodore Roosevelt set up the antitrust division in the Justice Department in 1903 that "trust-busting" became important. His administration initiated the series of major prosecutions that led to the *Standard Oil, American Tobacco,* and *U.S. Steel* decisions.

The rule of reason, World War I, and a sharply conservative turn in American attitudes during the 1920s and then the trauma of the Great Depression accompanied 25 years of unaggressive antitrust, from 1912 to 1937. The appointment of Thurman Arnold in 1937 to the leadership of the antitrust division marked the beginning of a most vigorous period of antitrust activity. The fruits of this activity included the *ALCOA* and *Socony-Vacuum* decisions.

Antitrust policy was pushed to the sidelines by the overriding problems of World War II, the postwar readjustment, and the Korean War. It did not begin to re-emerge until the 1950s. A relatively vigorous antitrust policy was pursued during the Eisenhower, Kennedy, and Johnson administrations. It reached a climax in the mid 1960s in the decision of the Warren Court. During the same period various barriers to private plaintiffs were greatly reduced.

During the Nixon, Ford, and Carter administrations the vigor of enforcement did not increase, but the level of both government and private prosecutions remained high. The Reagan administration began a brisk march in the other direction. Indeed, at one point the head of the antitrust division indicated his view that most restrictive practices other than price fixing were not anticompetitive.

A notable development of the 1980s was the willingness of the Reagan administration to tolerate mergers of giant corporations that would surely have been attacked a decade earlier, for example, Texaco's acquisition of Getty Oil and General Electric's acquisition of RCA. Indeed, the Secretary of Commerce went so far as to suggest repeal of Section 7 altogether, a suggestion Congress has not followed.

By the mid 1980s the antitrust pendulum had swung back from the anti-business attitude of the Warren Court; many believe it had swung too far in the other direction. The election of 1988 may have important bearing on what happens next, as will the nature of the new appointments to the Supreme Court that are expected in the next few years.

The Success of Antitrust

Economists do not generally agree on how much the *structure* of American industry has been influenced by nearly a century of antitrust policy. American industry remains highly concentrated (see Chapter 14), but empirical studies show no tendency for the concentration either to increase or to decrease drastically. Would the pattern be very different if there had been no antitrust laws, or if the existing laws had been more vigorously enforced? We do not know for sure.

Many economists and antitrust lawyers believe that U.S. antitrust laws have been quite successful in inhibiting price fixing and certain restrictive practices. At the same time the laws have done little to alter the basic structure of the economy. Whether this constitutes a signal success or a brave failure depends on one's diagnosis of the health of the American market system. Here people disagree sharply. The role of economic analysis in antitrust is discussed briefly in Box 16-2.

Public Utility Regulation of Natural Monopoly

Natural monopoly arises because of economies of scale (as was discussed on page 234). Policymakers have not wanted to compel the maintenance of several smaller, less efficient producers when a single firm would be much more efficient; neither have they wanted to give a monopolist the opportunity to restrict output, raise price, and appropriate as profits the gains made available by virtue of large-scale production.

How might these values be reconciled with the view, dominant in the late nineteenth century, that government should not interfere with the free market? The answer was to identify certain natural monopoly products as *public utilities*. The products—such as water, railroad transportation, electricity, telephone and telegraph—were ones that were con-

sidered of critical importance and therefore ones whose provision ought to be supervised by the government.

The public utility concept grew out of the recognition by economists that when there are major economies of large-scale production, protection of the public interest by competition is impractical, if not impossible.

One response to this dilemma is for government to assume ownership of the single firm and to delegate to government-appointed managers of the *nationalized* industry decisions about how much to produce and what price to charge, in each case being guided by the national interest. Many countries have done precisely that with telephone and railroad services, among others. The characteristic response in the United States since the late nineteenth century has been to allow private enterprise, but to regulate its behavior.

Public utility regulation gives to appropriate public authorities (usually specially constituted regulatory commissions) control over the the price and quantity of service provided by a natural monopoly, with the object of achieving the efficiency of a single seller without the output restriction of the monopolist.

In return for giving a company a franchise or license to be the sole producer, the public utility regulators reserve the right to regulate its behavior.

Regulation of this kind began with the establishment of the Interstate Commerce Commission (ICC) in 1887. Its primary function was to regulate railroad rates. Public utility regulation by both federal and state governments subsequently spread to other forms of transportation (airlines and pipelines) as well as to the standard utilities: telephone, electricity, water, and gas.

Although regulatory commissions were first created to deal with natural monopoly problems, most regulatory activity is no longer of that kind. In this section, however, we are concerned only with natural monopoly regulation.

BOX 16-2

Economics and Antitrust Law

Economic concepts such as competition, monopoly, and markets lie at the heart of antitrust policy. Economists are employed in the Justice Department, by the Federal Trade Commission, and by lawyers for private companies. Market definition, for example, plays a critical role in antitrust merger litigation: Section 7 of the Clayton Act requires evaluation of a merger by asking whether "in any line of commerce, in any section of the country the effect of such acquisition may be substantially to lessen competition or to tend to create a monopoly."

"Line of commerce" and "section of the country" involve product and geographical market definitions because competition occurs only within sensibly defined markets. A great many antitrust cases have turned on market definition, and some have even utilized such economic concepts as cross elasticity of demand.

Here are a few questions the courts have asked and answered:

Is cellophane in the same market as wax paper, Saran wrap, and other flexible wrapping materials? (Yes, said the Supreme Court.)

Are glass jars and tin cans in the same market? (Yes, said the Supreme Court.)

Are insulated aluminum and copper cable in the same market? (Yes, said the District Court; no, said the Supreme Court.)

Are New York and Philadelphia banks in the same market and thus in competition with one another? (No, said the courts in 1963.)

Do different grades of coal in Illinois constitute an economic market? (No, said the District Court, in part because it found the relevant market to be energy. The Supreme Court did not reverse the decision.)

Even though courts decide these matters, the matters themselves involve economic questions, and economic studies or witnesses were introduced by both parties in each of these litigations.

But while antitrust policies use economic theory and economic expertise, our antitrust laws ignore certain distinctions that economists think are important. In particular, the role of big business, even monopoly, in promoting dynamic advances, as argued by Professor Schumpeter, has many adherents, yet is largely ignored by antitrust policies. Some decisions have protected smaller competitors against larger, more efficient rivals. The distinction between injury to *competition* and injury to *competitors* has not always been made clearly by the courts. Finally, the courts have had a difficult time in coming to grips with oligopoly. Should it be regarded favorably because it is much more competitive than monopoly or unfavorably because it is much less competitive than perfect competition?

Economists themselves are divided as to whether these distinctions are important. Some believe that public policy ought to be based on things such as size and market share, without regard for actual conduct or performance. Others offer their own "rule of reason," called *workable competition*. They argue that the real choice is between more or less oligopoly and that the positive effects of a given market share, or merger, on prices, on profits, and on costs should be determined in each individual case.

This seems so reasonable; why do some people object? They object because they believe that workable competition will lead to endless studies and no action. Because economists do not speak with a unified voice on such matters, it is perhaps not surprising that the basic nature of the antitrust program has for a long time been set by lawyers. The economic point of view is, however, receiving increased attention today.

Regulation of Price

The dilemma of natural monopoly is illustrated in Figure 16-1. To achieve low costs, a single large producer is necessary, but an unregulated, profit-maximizing monopoly would restrict output, raise price, and fail to provide the large volume of output at a low price that the technology makes possible.

What price should a regulatory commission per-

FIGURE 16-1   The Problem of Natural Monopoly

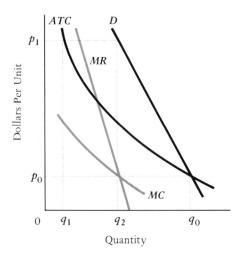

Cost conditions in a situation of natural monopoly are such that a single firm is needed to achieve the economies of scale, but a monopolist finds it profitable to restrict output to maximize profits. ATC and MC are the cost curves of an efficient firm. D is the market demand curve, and MR marginal revenue. Because ATC declines sharply, efficiency is served by having a single firm. Clearly, one firm producing at q_0 would be more efficient than several firms each producing q_1 at a cost of p_1 per unit. But an unregulated monopoly would restrict output to q_2 and charge price p_1, thereby depriving consumers of the advantages of large-scale production.

FIGURE 16-2   Pricing Strategy for a Regulatory Commission

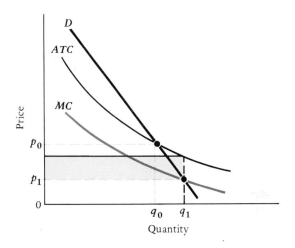

Average cost pricing is the goal of regulatory commissions that seek low prices but no losses for natural monopolies. Allocative efficiency requires a quantity q_1 where price equals marginal cost. But at the price-quantity combination p_1 and q_1, a firm would suffer losses (shown as the shaded area). A regulatory commission could not insist on price p_1 unless it was prepared to subsidize the firm. But it might require price p_0, which permits the firm to produce q_0 and cover all costs. The output q_0 achieves some, but not all of the cost advantages of large-scale output. Pricing where demand crosses ATC is called average cost pricing.

mit? It might wish to set price equal to marginal cost in order to achieve allocative efficiency ("the way it would be in perfect competition"), but such a price and quantity would surely lead to losses, for marginal cost is necessarily below average cost when average cost is falling. This is illustrated in Figure 16-2. Such a pricing scheme would require a continuing subsidy of the resulting losses.

As an alternative, regulation has often aimed at setting prices high enough to permit firms to cover all their costs, yet low enough to achieve the large sales required to reap the scale economies that characterize natural monopoly situations. If a regulatory commission knew the demand curve and the cost curves exactly, it could simply pick the price indi-

cated by the intersection of the demand curve and the average total cost curve. This is called *average cost pricing*. Average cost pricing will not, in general, lead to allocative efficiency because price is not equal to marginal cost, as is also shown in Figure 16-2. But average cost pricing would give much lower prices and larger outputs than a monopolist's.

Of course, regulators do not know exactly what demand and cost curves look like, and regulatory commissions often do not have even reasonably accurate demand and cost information. In its absence commissions have tended to judge prices according to the level of profits they produce. Generally, having set prices, regulatory agencies permit price increases when profits fall below "fair" levels and require price reductions if profits exceed such levels. Thus, what started as price regulation becomes instead profit (or what is called *rate of return*) regulation.

Problems in Regulation

While it is true that if the appropriate price is charged, only a normal rate of return will be earned, that is, profits will be zero, the reverse is not necessarily true. Profits can be zero because of inefficient operation or misleading accounting. Thus commissions that rely on rate of return as their guide to pricing must monitor a number of other aspects of the regulated firm's behavior.

Definition of costs.   If a company is to be allowed to charge a price determined as "cost plus a fair profit" (as the regulators say), and if that price is below the profit-maximizing one, it is clearly in the firm's interest to exaggerate reported costs. One major activity of regulatory commissions has been to define rules of allowable costing. Cost supervision is an important activity of public utility regulation for another reason as well. Without it, managers of the regulated industries might have little incentive to be efficient and might simply let costs drift upward.

Rate base.   Average total cost includes an appropriate rate of return on the capital invested in the business. Suppose it is agreed that a firm should be allowed to earn a rate of return of 11 percent on its capital. The **rate of return** is defined as the ratio of net profits to invested capital. What is the value of the capital to which 11 percent is to be applied? The allowable amount is called the **rate base.** There has been no more controversial area than this in public utility regulation. Should the original cost or the reproduction cost of the firm's assets be used?

It does not make much difference unless prices are changing, but in the inflationary situation of the last 35 years, reproduction cost is uniformly higher than original costs and thus leads to higher rate bases, higher permitted profits, and higher prices to users. If the major concern is to generate earnings to buy replacement equipment, reproduction cost is appropriate. If the major concern is to generate a return sufficient to compensate past capital investments,

original cost may be appropriate. Regulatory commissions (and the courts) have vacillated on this issue.

The precise nature of regulatory rules is important because the rules affect the incentives of those regulated. Economists Harvey Averch and Leland Johnson have shown that a regulated utility has less incentive to resist excessive capital costs than an unregulated one and that in some circumstances it pays the unregulated utility to buy relatively unproductive equipment. This can occur, if profits depend on the rate base, because by acquiring expensive capital goods the firm will increase its rate base. Thus the notion of "necessary and prudent investments" enters into regulatory rules. This tendency for one regulation to lead to a need for yet further regulation has been called the *tar-baby effect,* after a fictional creature that enveloped attackers in the tar of which it was made.

Fair return.   The permitted rate of return that is implicit in the theory of public utility regulation is the opportunity cost of the owners' capital, with allowances for risk. This is what economists call a position of zero profits. Regulatory commissions have paid some attention to overall earnings rates in the economy, and the level of permitted earnings has changed slightly over time. But fairness and tradition have played a much larger role than considerations of opportunity cost, and regulatory commissions have been slow to adjust permitted rates of return to changing market conditions. For decades permitted rates of return of 6 to 9 percent were employed. But when market interest rates soared to double-digit figures during the late 1970s, the traditional levels were not sufficient to induce new investment. Yet regulatory commissions were reluctant to permit the large increases in prices that would result from sharp increases in the permitted rate of return.

Curtailment of service.   While regulatory commissions regulate prices with an eye on profits, they do not guarantee any minimum rate of return. A regulated utility in a declining industry may have a serious problem. If it is failing to earn the permitted rate, it may apply for permission to increase its prices, but if its demand is elastic, a rise in rates will lead to a reduction in revenues and may reduce profits. Privately owned urban transit systems and passenger rail lines have proven unprofitable because of secularly declining demand as people shifted to substitutes: private cars and airplanes. Given elastic demand curves, when transport companies raise fares (hoping to increase revenues), they find they only lose more customers to other means of transport.

At this point a local bus company, for example, may look to its costs to see how it can avoid losses. Often it finds that some parts of its service (such as routes to outlying neighborhoods) no longer cover even the variable costs of providing them, and it proposes to the regulatory authority that this service be dropped. Often the regulators say no. The reason is that they see other considerations in abandoning the bus service (such as increased congestion in the downtown area as even more people use their own cars) that are important to the regulators, but not to the bus company.

The regulators want the regulated company to "cross-subsidize" the less popular routes with profits from the more popular routes; at the same time they do not want to force the company into bankruptcy. Thus, each time a curtailment of service is proposed, regulators must make the difficult determination of whether the company is merely trying to increase its profits and is shirking its public service responsibility or whether it is truly in trouble.

The Success of Natural Monopoly Regulation

The moral of the public utility experience is that what in theory looks like a simple and straightforward activity of regulating natural monopoly turns out in practice to be highly complex and to have spawned a maze of bureaucratic rules and procedures. In large part this is because regulated companies adapt their behavior to the rules that are imposed on them and thus begins a chain of adaptation and change by regulators and regulated companies that ends up producing a complex and cumbersome apparatus. The costs of regulation are high and include the costs of running regulatory commissions, the costs imposed on the courts by frequent appeals, and, most importantly, the costs imposed on businesses that must strive to comply with the mountains of required paperwork.

There has been a loss of confidence in natural monopoly regulation over the last decade or two. While many people believe that as long as competition is not possible, there are benefits to traditional public utility regulation, some of them doubt that the benefits exceed the costs. Such costs include not only all the regulatory red tape, but also the possible loss of the innovative zeal that unregulated firms might bring to the industries now regulated. This, Schumpeterian, view would allow short-run monopoly profits as a modest price to pay to reap very-long-run gains achieved by way of innovation.

Perhaps a more widely held view is that regulation, even when effective at first, becomes too rigid and unresponsive to change and as a result fails to recognize and to permit such competition as is possible. Given changing technology, yesterday's natural monopoly of a single railroad may become but one mode of transportation in today's competitive transportation industry. Wire telephone communications are no longer unique means of voice communication, given radio and satellites. The Post Office is not the only way to send written messages and parcels from one place to another. Thus, the scope of natural monopoly regulation keeps changing, but regulators tend to cling to, and in some cases are legally committed to, rules and assumptions that may no longer fit the world they are regulating.

An even more basic source of disenchantment with public utility regulatory commissions is that they have changed their function. They have, as we shall see, largely abandoned protection of the consumer from natural monopoly and have become protectors of firms *from* competition.

There is a growing consensus that natural monopoly regulation has failed to live up to the expectations held for it a generation or two ago.

Protection *Against* Competition

While the main thrust of antitrust policy and the original purpose of the regulatory commissions was the protection of *competition,* a parallel and, for a time, growing aspect of public policy in these areas was a shift to protection of *competitors* against the rigors of competition. To understand both the overall nature of American competition policy and the current movement toward deregulation, it is necessary to review its protectionist aspects.

Motives for Protectionism

Two different sets of motives for protecting firms from competition are easy to distinguish in principle, but virtually impossible to untangle in the real world. The first is a desire to mitigate, for certain persons or firms, the normal rigors of competition. The second is protection against "excessive" competition, competition that creates a disequilibrium that threatens to destroy firms and industries that would survive under conditions of equilibrium in competition.

The difference is easily illustrated. Suppose a particular manufacturer of women's dresses finds it is losing money and being driven toward bankruptcy by the low prices prevailing in the industry. The owner complains that, unlike last year, the competition is ruining him. This may be due (1) to that particular seller's inefficiency relative to its competitors, (2) to a growing excess of productive capacity in the industry caused by too many firms relative to demand for the product, or (3) to a price war that traps firms in a disequilibrium with prices well below the level of long-run average costs.

Does it matter which situation is occurring? In either the first or second situation, the efficient response is for the firm to leave the industry. But it may be the wrong market response in the third situation. When supply and demand are in long-run equilibrium, competition would lead to prices at the level of minimum attainable long-run average total costs; firms would generate revenues just sufficient to maintain their capital stock and to replace it as it wears out. We saw in Chapter 12 that in the short run with overall excess capacity, firms may find it profitable to operate with prices below long-run average cost as long as price exceeds average *variable* cost. This provides a signal for some firms to leave the industry, and when they have done so, prices will rise and an equilibrium will be achieved with the remaining firms covering average total costs.

Circumstances can exist, however, that cause a *chronic* tendency for firms to engage in excessive competition and result in prices that do not recover total costs in the long run. Such a situation is often described as *destructive competition,* or sometimes as *cutthroat competition.*

The plight of the dress manufacturing firm may seem to it, and to the representative in Congress from its district, worthy of relief, no matter what the cause of the plight, and thus limiting competition will be urged whether or not the competition is truly destructive.[3] If Congress acts to raise or stabilize prices, one may never know whether it was preventing competition from achieving its harsh but efficient natural selection or whether it was preserving competitors and competition against destructive forces.

Destructive Competition

Is destructive competition possible? No firm or industry would intentionally engage in practices in which all firms in an otherwise healthy industry would be sure to lose money in the long run. Yet this result is conceivable.

Destructive competition requires that long-lived capital investments play a big part in the total cost picture. For example, airlines, coal mining companies, and steamship lines often find that their average total costs are primarily fixed costs arising from large initial capital investments. In any short-run period depreciation costs can be ignored (under the bygones-are-bygones principle). Over the life of the equipment, however, unless sufficient funds are earned to replace capital as it wears out, the industry will surely shrink. In such circumstances *too much* competition could conceivably occur. It would cause severe difficulties for an industry that could prosper under less competitive conditions. The gap between total costs and variable costs combines with excess capacity to create conditions in which sellers are tempted on the one hand to collude and on the other to engage in price wars. If they are prevented from colluding by the antitrust laws and wish to avoid

---

[3] As a political tactic, advocates of protectionist policies always argue that competition is excessive, for it is easier to command support that way.

excessive competition, sellers in such industries are likely to seek help from "their" government.

Is destructive competition likely? The view of destructive competition described above was prevalent in the 1930s when excess capacity was the general rule. It led to some direct legislative attempts to exempt price stabilization activities from antitrust control and to many regulatory agencies' changing their behavior; it led President Franklin Roosevelt during his first term to encourage price-fixing activities as a cornerstone of his economic policy.

Later generations of economists have been skeptical about the occurrence or significance of destructive competition. They recognize that in major depressions there may be excess capacity, but they argue that price fixing does nothing to solve that problem. They do not deny occasional price wars, but believe that such situations tend to self-correct fairly rapidly. If some firms are bankrupted and driven from the industry, this will hasten the emergence of a healthy industry. If new firms are required, they will be motivated to enter the industry once the situation is stabilized.

However, many business people, members of Congress, and regulators are not persuaded by these economists' arguments. Severe price competition and losses seem excessive to them, and they are wary of arguments that price wars will tend to self-correct.

Whether conditions for chronic destructive competition occur frequently is an unresolved empirical question. Those who believe that they do, support government regulation to limit competition or advocate a tolerant attitude toward price-stabilizing activities. Those who believe that firms need no such protection tend to advocate leaving the market unregulated except to implement antitrust activities that discourage collusion or price fixing.

Protection Against the Rigors of Competition

The world of perfect competition is a harsh one. The best a firm can hope for in the long run is to cover all its costs. Any competitive edge in methods of production or product characteristics it may achieve will be quickly eroded by entry of new firms or by imitation by existing firms. Moreover, any failure to maintain efficiency will inexorably lead to operating losses and eventual loss of whatever investment the owner has made. Moreover, exit from an industry typically takes longer than new entry, and thus fluctuations in the general conditions of demand and supply for the industry's output are likely to be accompanied by longer periods of depressed conditions than of unusual prosperity.

Because competitive conditions are most likely to occur where there are large numbers of individual firms—in farming, in retailing, in trade—large numbers of people are likely to be affected directly. This makes them a political force to be reckoned with, and the political system has not neglected small businessmen, farmers, traders, or workers.

We have already seen, in agricultural policy, some of the devices designed to protect the incomes of such groups. Among yet other policies there is a temptation to see the *symptom* of their plight—the low prices of the things they sell—as the cause. The fallacy of this should be clear.

If excess capacity is driving prices down and thus signaling the need for resources to withdraw from the industry, artificially raising these prices only removes the signal without eliminating the cause.

Unless the policy also reduces output, the problems caused by excess capacity will reemerge in another form. One illustration of this is given in Box 16-3. But, whether futile or not, such policies have been pursued.

The Deviant Theme in Antitrust

"Antitrust" was given two meanings from its earliest days. One was antimonopoly and the other anti-big firm. Some of the supporters of the original Sherman Act saw its purposes as the protection of small, independent businessmen from the tyranny of markets in which large corporations were coming to play such a big role. When the Sherman Act was not so interpreted, they rallied behind passage of the Federal Trade Commission Act (1914), which legislated against "unfair methods of competition." From at least that time until the 1970s, when Justices Black and Douglas left the Supreme Court, the populist view had its voice on the Court, and that view often

BOX 16-3

The Price of Haircuts and the Profits of Barbers

Suppose that there are many barber shops and freedom of entry into barbering: Anyone can set up as a barber. Assume that the going price for haircuts is $10 and that at this price all barbers believe their income is too low.

The barbers hold a meeting and decide to form a trade association. The purpose of the association is to persuade the City Council (or the State) to help them by imposing a price of $14 as the price of haircuts. (Alternatively, they could get exemption from the antitrust laws and form a cartel that set the price of haircuts at $14.)

Assume that, one way or another, the barbers succeed in raising the price of haircuts to $14. What is the result?

We need to distinguish between the short-run and the long-run effects of an increase in the price of haircuts. In the short run the number of barbers is fixed. Thus, in the short run the answer depends only on the elasticity of the demand for haircuts. If demand elasticity is less than 1, total expenditure on haircuts will rise and so will the incomes of barbers; if demand elasticity exceeds 1, the barbers' revenues will fall. Thus to answer the question we need some knowledge about the size of the elasticity of demand for haircuts.

Suppose we estimate the elasticity of demand over the relevant price range to be 0.45. We then predict that barbers will be successful in raising incomes in the short run. A 40 percent rise in price will be met by an 18 percent fall in quantity of haircuts, so the total revenue of the typical barber will rise by about 15 percent.*

Now what about the long run? If barbers were just

*Let p and q be the price and quantity before the price increase. Total revenue after the increase is $TR = (1.4p)(.82q) = 1.148pq$.

covering costs before the price change, they will now be earning profits. Barbering will become an attractive trade relative to others requiring equal skill and training, and there will be a flow of barbers into the industry. As the number of barbers rises, the same amount of business must be shared among more and more barbers, so the typical barber will find business—and thus profits—decreasing.

Profits may also be squeezed from another direction. With fewer customers coming their way, barbers may compete against one another for the limited number of customers. The government (or their agreement) does not allow them to compete through price cuts, but they can compete in service. They may spruce up their shops, offer their customers expensive magazines to read, and so forth. This kind of non-price competition will raise operating costs.

These changes will continue until barbers are just covering their opportunity costs, at which time the attraction for new entrants will vanish. The industry will settle down in a new long-run equilibrium in which individual barbers make incomes only as large as they did before the price rise. There will be more barbers than there were in the original situation, but each barber will be working for a smaller fraction of the day and will be idle for a larger fraction (the industry will have excess capacity). Customers will have shorter waits even at peak periods, and they will get to read a wide choice of magazines, but they will be paying $14 for haircuts.

If the City Council agreed to the plan in order to raise the average income of barbers, it will have failed. It has created more jobs for barbers, but not a higher income for them.

The general lesson is clear: One cannot raise income by raising price above the competitive level unless one can prevent new entry or otherwise reduce the quantity of the product or service provided.

---

was protectionist in its effect. In *Chicago Board of Trade* (1918) the Court supported overnight restrictions on price competition in order to let traders enjoy a more tranquil life. In *Appalachian Coals* (1933)

effective output restriction to prevent distress price cutting was allowed by small coal producers devastated by the Great Depression. In *Von's Grocery* (1965), cited earlier, the underlying concern was the plight of the "Ma and Pa" grocery stores that were being displaced by the ever-growing presence of the chain stores.

Perhaps the easiest way to understand this protectionist theme within antimonopoly policy is to notice that the distributive aspects of monopoly have been at least as important to public policy makers as the allocative inefficiencies that so concern economists. In the industrial sectors of the economy corporate managers and stockholders typically have above average incomes. Monopoly power, when exercised by those who are relatively poor rather than relatively rich, has frequently been supported rather than opposed by the government. For example, the efforts of farmers to increase farm income have not only been approved, but actively promoted by public policies of crop restriction, price supports, and exemption of producers' cooperatives from antitrust laws. Labor unions are exempt from antitrust prosecution not because wage fixing is less anticompetitive than price fixing, but because public policymakers have chosen to help laborers increase their income by encouraging unions and giving those unions the opportunity to act as labor cartels.

The heyday of the protectionist period was the 1930s. Legislation permitted price fixing to avoid price wars and to permit manufacturers to establish and enforce minimum prices for their products in the name of "fair trade." These laws were used to prevent aggressive price competition by chain stores and by discount houses. Their most telling aspect, as anticompetitive statutes, is that a great many prosecutions under them have been brought by competitors (not customers) of the firms charged with violations.

While the most blatantly protectionist laws have been repealed, many aspects of this protectionist period survive in legal opinions that are still valid today. To many economists, they fail to distinguish between acts that injure competition (such as price fixing) and acts that injure competitors (such as cutting prices below the level of an inefficient firm's costs).

At least temporarily, protectionism in antitrust is on the wane. The Fair Trade laws have been repealed, and both Congress and the courts have restricted the FTC's ability to impose limitations on unfair competitive practices. Moreover, the Reagan administration's appointees to the antitrust division seem determined to pursue price fixing and downplay prosecution of other practices that, while apparently restrictive, may actually be pro-competitive. At the same time this backing away from explicitly protectionist attitudes has been accompanied by a general decrease in antitrust prosecutions.

Protectionist Policies of Regulatory Commissions

In antitrust, pro-competitive and anti-competitive tendencies have existed side by side. In public utility regulation, it is often argued, protection of the regulated has replaced protection of the consumer.

There seems little doubt that originally the ICC regulated railroad rates in order to keep them down. By the 1930s, however, the ICC had become concerned by the depressed economic condition of the railroads, the potentially destructive competition among them, and the emerging vigorous competition from trucks and barges. The ICC became the protector of the railroads, permitting them to establish *minimum* rates for freight of different classes, allowing price discrimination, and encouraging other restrictive practices. Moreover, it became a leading advocate of bringing motor carriers under the regulatory umbrella.

Restricting entry into trucking and setting *minimum* rates for trucks was unmistakably protectionist. The only reason for regulating the large interstate carriers was to control their competition with the railroads. The big interstate carriers were limited in where they could go and how *low* a price they could quote. As a result, they became targets for small, unregulated truckers who could cut rates and thus draw away customers without fear of retaliation. To eliminate the rate competition, regulation was extended to small truckers.

For another example consider airline regulation. When the Civil Aeronautics Board (CAB) began regulating airline routes and fares, there was arguably so little demand that competition could not have been effective. By the mid 1960s, however, the regulation was plainly protectionist and designed to shield the major carriers from competition. Supporters argued that competition was so intense that it might ruin the industry and even invite cost-cutting practices that endangered public safety. Critics argued that competition might destroy some existing airlines, but would prepare the ground for an efficient industry.

What accounted for the turn toward protectionism by regulatory commissions whose original mandate was protection of consumers from natural monopolists? One thesis is that the regulatory commissions were gradually captured by those they were supposed to regulate. Another is that the protectionist policies of the 1930s really reflected the public's mood and a genuine fear of destructive competition. The depression of the 1930s deeply affected a whole generation. It shook public confidence in many long-held beliefs, including the "received wisdom" that competition was in the public's interest. Faith in competition was greatly shaken by bank and business failures and by the massive unemployment of workers and factories. With the emergence of new generations for whom the Great Depression is but another episode in past history, not a remembered nightmare, some degree of faith in competition is returning. But it is fragile, as was demonstrated anew by the calls for more protectionism during the recession of 1981–1983.

Deregulation

Deregulation has been underway since 1980. Airlines, motor carriers, banks, natural gas producers, and long distance telephone companies are among those that have been substantially unleashed from close regulatory supervision, both of prices and of entry. The effects, and thus the wisdom of this trend, will be the subject of both economic analysis and political debate for years to come. Is deregulation a pendulum swing, soon to be reversed, or a trend that will lead

to a major increase in the scope of unrestricted market determination? We do not yet know.

More is involved in the movement for deregulation than just reversing the protectionist policies of regulatory commissions such as the ICC and FCC. It concerns, more basically, the whole question of how much interference with private decision making is desirable. Much of the regulation that is targeted for review is "social regulation" that is concerned with protection of consumers, not from high prices or monopolistic exploitation, but from other kinds of hazards. The targets of this deregulation include the Food and Drug Administration (FDA), the Securities and Exchange Commission (SEC), the Environmental Protection Agency (EPA), and the Occupational Safety and Health Administration (OSHA). These agencies are designed to protect consumers from health hazards, fraud, pollution, and occupational and product dangers rather than from excessive prices. The debate about this kind of regulation concerns "externalities," and the case for and against it will be discussed in Chapter 22.

Changes in regulation in some form or another seem likely to continue over the next decade. Some people favor rapid deregulation and reliance on market forces. Others believe that the deficiencies lie in the structure of regulation and that changing the way regulation is carried out will improve matters. Still others think that the failures of regulation require nationalization or new legislation defining a novel approach to what regulators should do.

Which of many proposed directions for regulatory reform will be followed is unclear at this stage. The movement favoring deregulation is not without opposition. Many regulatory activities, from banking to nuclear energy to pipelines, have powerful political support in Congress. Moreover, many industries subject to regulation are staunchly resisting deregulation.

Summary

1. American competition policy has had three strands: antitrust policy to prevent the acquisition or exercise of monopoly power, public utility regulation of natural monopoly, and protection of firms against excessive competition.

trust: bet. firms intending to monopolize

2. The basic tool of antitrust policy is the series of <u>laws</u> that seeks to eliminate practices that lead to monopoly. The overall effect of antitrust policy at any time rests on three things: the nature of the laws themselves, the attitude and interpretation of the courts, and the vigor with which prosecutions are brought by the government and by private plantiffs. These things have varied greatly over time and thus there have been <u>swings in the antitrust climate</u>.

3. <u>Antitrust policy</u> has been an important feature of the last forty years. Most observers believe that antitrust laws have been <u>more nearly successful in inhibiting restrictive practices than in altering the basic structure of the economy</u>.

4. The original philosophy of <u>public utility regulation</u> was to <u>grant a monopoly where necessary to achieve the advantages of large-scale production</u>, but to prevent the monopolist from restricting output and raising price. The most common regulatory approach has been to <u>regulate prices</u>. This is done by watching profits: allowing price increases only if necessary to permit the regulated utility to earn a fair return on its capital and requiring price decreases if profits rise above the approved level.

5. Implementation of this straightforward theory encounters <u>difficulties</u> because any set of <u>rules</u> becomes a set of signals that <u>induces patterns of response</u> from those regulated. Thus it has been necessary for regulators to <u>define</u> carefully "proper" costs, how the costs should be measured, the appropriate rate base, what constitutes "necessary and prudent" additions to capital equipment, and what constitutes a fair return. They have also been forced to determine when and whether utilities can discontinue providing services to groups in the community.

6. Natural utility regulation appears to most observers not to have been an unqualified success. Among the reasons are the <u>high costs of regulation</u> and the <u>loss of innovative zeal</u>. Additionally, critics charge that regulators have tended to shift their focus from protection of consumers to protection of the firms being regulated.

7. From the earliest days of antitrust and public utility regulation <u>protection of firms *from competition*</u> has been a parallel theme with protection *of competition*. During the Great Depression protectionism emerged as a dominant theme, and some believe that it has permanently transformed the regulatory environment.

8. While destructive competition may occasionally occur, there is a danger that protectionist policies will protect firms from the normal rigors of competition and thus prevent or delay the reallocations of resources that are necessary to achieve efficiency.

problems

close examination

9. The entire regulatory apparatus has come under close scrutiny in recent years. How effective deregulation has been and how far the deregulation movement will go is sure to be a major political issue of the rest of the 1980s.

Topics for Review

Purposes of antitrust legislation
Difficulties of public utility regulation
Destructive competition
Protection of competition versus protection of competitors
Deregulation

Discussion Questions

1. Would antitrust laws be necessary in an economy of perfect competition? Would they be beneficial in an economy of natural monopoly?
2. What are the arguments for and against exemption from antitrust prosecution of the following:
    a. Labor unions
    b. Farmers
    c. Professional baseball teams (but not professional football teams)
3. Evaluate the wisdom of having the antitrust division use profits as a measure of monopoly power in deciding whether to prosecute a case. Would such a rule be expected to affect the behavior of firms with high profits? In what ways might any changes be socially beneficial and in what ways socially harmful?
4. Price-fixing agreements are (with some specific exemptions) violations of the antitrust laws. Consider the effects of the following. In what way, if at all, should they be viewed as being similar to price-fixing agreements?
    a. A manufacturer "recommends" minimum prices to its dealers.
    b. A manufacturer publishes a product price list that is changed only every three months.
    c. A trade association publishes "average industry total costs of production" every month.
5. Under what circumstances might it be sensible to treat some aspect of market structure or market conduct as *illegal per se*, that is, without considering the effect in the particular case?
6. It is often asserted that when a regulatory agency such as a public utilities commission is established, it will ultimately become controlled by the people it was intended to regulate. This argument raises the question of who regulates the regulators. Can you identify why this might happen? How might the integrity of regulatory boards be protected?
7. "In a competitive market the least-cost production techniques are revealed by entry and exit, while in public utility regulation they are revealed by commission rate hearings. It is easier to fool the commission than the market. Therefore, wherever possible, competition should be permitted." Discuss.
8. The effect of the breakup of AT&T's telephone monopoly and deregulation of telephone rates is still controversial. Discuss how each of the following facts might affect the evaluation:
    a. On average, cost of telephone service has increased for residential users and decreased for large business users.
    b. The price of long distance calls has declined while that of local service has increased.

c. Prices of individual services have been brought more in line with costs of providing those services.

d. The frequency of households with one or more phones has decreased from 95 percent to about 92 percent.

9. Consider the following quotation from *The New York Times:*

> "Six huge airlines with the power to control fares and routes could emerge from turbulent forces that are reshaping the industry, many Wall Street analysts and airline executives believe.
>
> If they are right, such a concentration in a business that now has a dozen or so major participants would severely undercut the competitive forces that legislators sought to unleash when they approved deregulation of the airline industry in 1978."

Suppose the belief expressed in the first paragraph proves correct. Discuss whether it would mean that deregulation of airlines had been a mistake.

17

Who Runs the Firm and for What Ends?

Does the continuing success of the American economy depend on the initiative of healthy, independent, private firms? Does it depend instead on increased public scrutiny and control of the behavior of these firms? Does it require subsidization or protection of our firms from foreign competition? Was the economy's apparent failure to perform as well in the 1970s as it did in previous decades due to a failure of private firms? Or is it perhaps due to increasing government interference with their activities?

What light does the theory we have studied so far shed on these important questions? In standard economic theory firms are users of factors of production and producers of commodities. They face cost and demand curves that are largely determined by forces beyond their control. They seek to maximize their profits by keeping their costs as low as possible and producing to satisfy consumers' demands. They care only about profits, and their decisions are uninfluenced by their internal structure. Thus they contribute to our high living standards by producing, as cheaply as possible, goods that satisfy consumers' demands.

The ultimate source of all profits, even monopoly profits, is consumers' willingness to buy. Thus the firms that succeed are the ones that best satisfy consumers' demands, while firms that consistently do not satisfy them will eventually fail. The need for firms to respond to consumers' desires is an important part of any argument for a free enterprise system. If firms did not so respond, there would be little justification in allowing them to exert major influences on the allocation of the country's resources.

An important body of criticism disputes this standard theory of the firm. It says instead that firms have the power to control market conditions. They manipulate demand by advertising, and they do not face strong competitive pressure to produce efficiently by holding costs down. Firms, the critics continue, do not even seek to maximize profits. Instead they seek other goals that are determined by their internal structure, and these goals often cause them to behave in ways that are socially undesirable.

If true, such criticisms would support the view that firms hinder rather than advance consumer welfare and that firms need to be forced by government to act in the social interest. In this chapter we will study some of these criticisms. We begin with those that strike at the very core of the standard microeconomic theory.

Do Firms Control the Market? The Galbraith Hypothesis

John Kenneth Galbraith and consumer advocate Ralph Nader argue that it is *not* consumers' wants that create the market signals that in turn provide the profit opportunities that motivate business behavior. Instead, large corporations have the power to create and manipulate demand. Firms must plan and invest for an uncertain future, and the profitability of the enormous investments they make is threatened by the unpredictability of events. Firms try to make the future less unpredictable by actively manipulating market demand and by co-opting government agencies that are supposed to control their activities.

Manipulation of demand. The most important unpredictable events that may jeopardize corporate investments are unexpected shifts in market demand curves. To guard against unexpected declines in demand, corporations spend vast amounts on advertising to allow them to sell what they want to produce rather than what consumers want to buy. At the same time, corporations decide not to produce some products that consumers would like to buy. This reduces the risks inherent in investing in new and untried products and avoids the possibility that successful new products might spoil the market for existing products.

According to this hypothesis, consumers are the victims of the corporations; they are pushed around at the corporate whim, persuaded to buy things they do not really want and denied products they would like to have.

Corruption of public authorities. A second threat to the long-range plans and investments of corporations comes from uncontrollable and often unpredictable changes in the nature of government interference with the freedom of the corporation. According to the theory, this political threat is met by co-opting or corrupting the members of Congress, who pass laws affecting corporations, and the government agencies that are supposed to be regulating them. Corporation managers indirectly subvert public institutions, from universities to regulatory agencies.

Government, instead of regulating business and protecting the public interest, has become the servant of the corporation. It supplies the corporate sector with such essential inputs as educated, trained, healthy, socially secure workers. Government also serves the giant corporation through policies concerning tariffs, import quotas, tax rules, subsidies, and research and development. These policies protect the industrial establishment from competitive pressures and reinforce its dominance and profitability.

Corruption of our value system. Galbraith distinguishes between those who own the firm, who are capitalists, and those who run the firm, who are technically trained managers. He calls the latter technicians or technocrats and points out that they have great power. The corporations they manage earn large profits that can be reinvested to further the achievement of the values of the ruling group; a group that Galbraith calls the *technostructure*. The values of this "ruling class" emphasize industrial production, rapid growth, and materialistic aspirations at the expense of the better things of life (such as cultural and esthetic values) and the quality of the environment.

More important, the industrial managers join with the military in a military-industrial complex that utilizes, trains, and elevates the technicians to positions of power and prestige not only in industry but in the armed services, in the defense establishment, and in the highest positions of government. In so doing, the corporations and their managers threaten to dominate if not subvert our foreign as well as our domestic policies.

The new industrial state. The foregoing is an outline of what Galbraith calls the *new industrial state*.[1] If Galbraith's thesis were substantially correct, we would have to make major revisions in our ideas of how free-market economies work.

---

[1] These views did not originate with the publication in 1967 of Galbraith's book by that title nor with the formation of "Nader's raiders." Much earlier James Burnham wrote *The Managerial Revolution* and Robert Brady sounded an alarm in *Business as a System of Power*. Thorstein Veblen had predicted the technocratic takeover of society in *The Engineers and the Price System* in 1921, and Karl Marx predicted the subversion of the government bureaucrat by the businessman more than a century ago.

In Galbraith's new industrial state the largest corporations (1) largely control market demand rather than being controlled by it, (2) co-opt government processes rather than being constrained by them, and (3) utilize their substantial discretionary power against the interests of society.

The Evidence for the Hypothesis

Many facts lend superficial support to Galbraith's hypothesis. Corporations do account for nearly three-quarters of all business done in the United States today, and large corporations dominate the corporate sector. There are nearly 250,000 manufacturing corporations, but only 1 percent of them have assets of $25 million or more. These largest corporations hold 87 percent of all manufacturing assets. It takes fewer than 600 corporations to account for 75 percent of the total assets of manufacturing.

The giant corporations are well known: General Motors, Exxon, Dow Chemical, U.S. Steel, Sears Roebuck, General Electric, and so on. Many are highly profitable, and most are so widely owned that managers, rather than stockholders, exercise effective control. If power comes with size, a "few" people—several thousand strategically placed executives of a few hundred leading corporations—have great power over economic affairs. Moreover, these people are primarily white, male, wealthy, and politically conservative.

As for political influence, individual corporations and trade associations have lobbyists and exercise whatever persuasion they can. The law firms that represent them annually hire the cream of the crop of skilled young advocates. Executives of many of these corporations serve on public commissions and frequently take important government positions. They make large contributions to political campaigns. Political influence is exercised at all levels of government—Congress, the executive branch, regulatory commissions, the courts, and state and local governments.

The political activities of corporations are not confined to the United States. In the 1970s the Lockheed Corporation was implicated in scandals involving million-dollar bribes to secure foreign orders.

The list of persons involved included (among many others) a former Japanese prime minister, the husband of the ruling queen of the Netherlands, and several former Italian cabinet ministers. There is no doubt that corporations have been involved in government corruption at the highest levels—often, no doubt, merely by harnessing the corruption that was already there—and have achieved through political channels results they might never have achieved in the marketplace.

The great corporations, along with many smaller firms, spend vast amounts on advertising, as the hypothesis predicts. Today total advertising expenditure accounts for approximately 2½ percent of the value of the contribution of the private sector to the GNP. These expenditures are obviously designed to influence consumers' demand, and there is little doubt that if firms such as Lever Brothers, Gulf Oil, Schlitz, and IBM were to cut their advertising, they would lose sales to their competitors.

It is also true that much environmental pollution is associated with industries that consist of well-known large firms. If automobiles, electric power, steel, oil, industrial chemicals, detergents, and paper are the primary sources of our pollution, surely Ford, Consolidated Edison, Bethlehem Steel, Texaco, Monsanto, Procter & Gamble, and International Paper are significantly to blame. They are all among the 100 largest nonfinancial corporations.

Doubts About the Hypothesis

Sensitivity to Market Pressures

Even the largest, most powerful industries are not immune to market pressures. Ford's Edsel was a classic example of the market's rejecting a product. The penetration of small foreign cars into the North American market forced the automobile industry into first the compact car and then the still cheaper subcompacts. In spite of this, massive losses were suffered by American automobile manufacturers as consumers turned in large numbers, even in the face of heavy advertising of American cars to foreign cars whose low costs and high gas mileages they preferred. The decline of railroads for passenger travel is manifest in many ways, as the troubled financial history of once great railroading corporations shows. The Pullman Company was the nation's tenth largest firm in 1909; today it is not even in the top 300.

Changes in demand and in taste can be sudden and dramatic, but mostly they are gradual, continual, and less noticeable month by month than decade by decade. On the average, about two new firms enter the top 100 every year, and as a consequence two others leave. This means a significant change over a decade.

Turnover in the list of leading companies is revealing. Only two, U.S. Steel and Exxon (Standard Oil of New Jersey), were in the top 10 both in 1910 and in 1985. Consider these giants of 1910, none of them among the largest 250 today: International Mercantile Marine (today United States Lines), United States Cotton Oil, American Hide and Leather, American Ice, Baldwin Locomotive, Cudahy, International Salt, and United Shoe Machinery. They have slipped or disappeared largely because of the relative decline in the demand for their products. Today's giants include automobile, oil, airline, computer, and electric power companies—for the obvious reason that demand for these products is strong.

Are these demand shifts explained by the corporate manipulation of consumers' tastes through advertising or by more basic changes? Advertising has two major aspects: It seeks to inform consumers about available products, and it seeks to influence consumers by altering their demands. The first aspect, informative advertising, plays an important part in the efficient operation of any free-market system; the second aspect is one through which firms seek to control, rather than be controlled by, the market.

Clearly, advertising does influence consumers' demand. If GM were to stop advertising, it would surely lose sales to Ford, Chrysler, and foreign imports, but it is hard to believe that the automotive society was conjured up by Madison Avenue. When you are persuaded to "fly the friendly skies of United," your real alternative is not a Conestoga wagon, a bicycle, or even a Greyhound bus; more likely you are foregoing American, Delta, or Northwest Airlines.

Careful promotion can influence the success of one rock group over another, but could it sell the waltz to today's teenager? Taste making through advertising unquestionably plays a role in shaping demand, but so do more basic human attitudes, psychological needs, and technological opportunities.

Certainly, advertising shifts demands among similar products. It is hard to believe, however, that the American economy or the average American's system of values would be fundamentally changed if there were available one more or one less make of automobile or television set or brand of shoes. A look at those products that have brought basic changes to the economy—and perhaps to our value systems—suggests that these products succeeded *because consumers wanted them,* not because Madison Avenue brainwashed people into buying them. Consider a few major examples.

The automobile transformed American society and is in demand everywhere, even in Communist countries where only informative advertising exists. The Hollywood movie had an enormous influence in shaping our world and in changing some of our values; it was, and still is, eagerly attended throughout the world, whether or not it is accompanied by advertising. The jet airplane has shrunk the world. It has allowed major league sports to expand beyond the northeastern and midwestern cities that could be reached by an overnight bus or rail journey; it has made the international conference a commonplace; and it has made European, Hawaiian, and Caribbean vacations a reality for many. For better or worse, the birth control pill has revolutionized many aspects of behavior in spite of the fact that it has never been advertised in the mass media. Television has changed the activities of children (and adults) in fundamental ways. Among others, it has created national rather than regional markets in dozens of commodities.

The new products that have significantly influenced the allocation of resources and social attitudes, such as those mentioned above, have succeeded because consumers wanted them; most of those that failed did so because they were not wanted—at least not at prices that would cover their costs of production. Box 17-1 deals with a case study of a giant firm that found out the hard way just how little control it could exert over the market.

BOX 17-1

The Market Controls the Firm: The A&P Story

The Great Atlantic and Pacific Tea Company (A&P) was the world's first grocery chain store. In 1859 A&P opened 100 stores in New York City, and their large-scale purchasing and low-price policies led the company and the concept to prosper. By 1912 A&P was running a national chain of economy stores whose central policy was described as "cash and carry, no deliveries, no credit, no advertising, no telephone."

Although widely copied—Kroger's was formed in 1887 and Safeway in 1915, among many others—A&P was dominant, with over 50 percent of the chain food sales all through the 1920s and into the 1930s. The firm was so dominant in the 1930s that antitrust authorities tried to restrain it, and legislation was introduced to limit its ability to compete so effectively.

Did A&P control the market? Many in and out of the company believed that it did, but events were to show that it did not. Its first big mistake occurred in the early 1930s, when it made the decision to neglect an innovation in marketing—the supermarket. Supermarkets consisted of several departments (meat, produce, and baked goods as well as dry groceries) under one roof and relied on self-service. A&P was a *grocery* chain and used clerks. Scale efficiencies and lower labor costs enabled the supermarkets to operate much more economically than traditional clerk-operated chain grocery stores. "King Kullen the Price Wrecker" opened the first supermarket in 1930 and was extremely successful. Supermarkets spread rapidly. A&P believed that supermarkets were a passing fad, and it refused to go along. Part of this was its feeling of loyalty to its clerks, who would surely have had a difficult time finding new jobs during the depression.

But A&P's policy, whatever the motivation, meant higher labor costs and higher prices than its supermarket competitors. In 1937 John Hartford, the company president, belatedly and reluctantly decided that A&P should enter the supermarket business seriously. By then, however, A&P had lost more than half its market share.

Though A&P never regained the 50 percent market share it had in the early 1930s, its profit levels and rates rebounded as the depression ended and A&P supermarkets were opened. By the early 1950s, it had secured roughly 33 percent of the chain grocery market. Although less dominant than in its heyday, it was still the leading chain.

The second crisis of A&P's existence was the opening in the 1950s and 1960s of suburban shopping malls. A&P resisted this trend because traditional company policy had been against signing long-term leases for store locations. Long-term leases were, however, necessary to secure stores in suburban malls. Company policy clashed with market necessity, and the latter won. By the time A&P realized its mistake, the prime locations had been taken by the company's competitors.

A&P had believed that it was big and powerful enough to continue attracting customers without moving to giant stores in high-rent suburban shopping malls. In later years, as gasoline costs rose and large numbers of women entered the work force, the demand for one-stop shopping grew. When other stores increased brand coverage and started stocking nonfood items, A&P's shelves in its smaller stores were already full. Between 1953 and 1971, A&P's gross sales stayed roughly constant at between $5 and $6 billion, but its market share slid from 30 to 12 percent. By 1972 it was losing money, and over the decade of the 1970s its losses continued. Late in the 1970s, the question was not whether A&P was too powerful, but whether it would survive.

As the 1980s began, A&P was once again rebuilding—by closing many of its too small, badly located stores and by employing new marketing techniques copied from its competitors. Today is appears to have won its battle for survival and its market share is modest but stable. Nowhere is it any longer the dominant firm.

Does the firm control the market? A&P thought so and found out that it was wrong.

The evidence suggests that the allocation of resources owes more to the tastes and values of consumers than it does to corporate advertising and related activities.

Who Controls the Government?

Is government subservient to big business? Lobbying is a legal activity engaged in on a large scale by many groups. Big business has its influence, but so do farmers, labor unions, and small business.

Cases of corrupt behavior have been documented at all levels of government. It does not follow, however, that government is usually subservient to the corporations and that decision making by the former is *dominated* by the wishes of the latter.

Government contracts bolster the aerospace industry, yet Lockheed's deep financial trouble in the 1970s came in part as a result of government decisions. Tobacco companies have seen government agencies first publicize the hazards of their principal product and then restrict their advertising. Airlines finally lost their decades-long battle to prevent the introduction of cheap air fares and have now lost virtually all regulatory bolstering of fare structures and limitation of competition on routes.

These examples show that while business often succeeds in attempts to protect its commercial interests through political activity, it does so within limits. Where the truth lies between the extremes of "no influence" and "no limits" is a subject of current research. Yet it does seem safe to say that, first, corporations have much political influence and, second, there are some serious constraints on the ability of corporations to exert political influence over all levels of American government.

Neglect of the Public Interest?

One aspect of the Galbraithian critique has found a receptive public: the apparent disregard by large corporations of the adverse effects of productive activities on the environment. The problems of pollution, which we will discuss in Chapter 22, arise from the activities of both small and large corporations and the activities of government units and citizens.

Consumerism is a movement that asserts a conflict between the interests of firms and the public interest. Consumerists hold that the conflict should be removed by pressuring firms to be motivated by the public interest rather than by their stockholders' desires for maximum profits.

Consumerists believe, for example, that GM's directors must be made to recognize that automobiles pollute and cause accidents, and that GM's resources should be invested in the development and installation of safety and antipollution devices. This, they argue, is proper use of GM's funds, even if GM's stockholders do not see it that way and even if automobile purchasers do not want to pay for the extra safety and antipollution devices.

What are the main arguments *for* this view? First, only the company can know the potentially adverse effects of its actions. Second, by virtue of holding a corporate charter, the corporation assumes the responsibility to protect the general welfare while pursuing private profits.

What are the main arguments *against* the consumerist view? Managers of companies have neither the knowledge nor the ability to represent the general public interest; they are largely selected, judged, and promoted according to their ability to run a profit-oriented enterprise, and the assumption that they are especially competent to decide broader *public* questions is unjustified. Moral, as distinct from economic, decisions—such as whether to use nuclear power, to make or use internal combustion engines, to manufacture or smoke cigarettes, and to manufacture or utilize DDT or aerosol sprays—cannot properly be delegated to corporations or their executives. Some are individual decisions; others require either the expertise or the authority of a public regulatory agency. Whoever makes decisions on behalf of the public must be potentially responsible to the public.

Those opposing the consumerist view hold that most required changes in corporate behavior should be accomplished not by exhorting business leaders to behave responsibly nor by placing consumer representatives on the corporation's board of directors, but by regulations or incentives that force or induce the desired corporate behavior. Let corporations pursue their profits—subject to public laws. For example, Congress can require that all cars have seat belts or have airbags or have antipollution valves or meet specific standards of emission levels. Another alternative is to open the way for lawsuits that would either enjoin certain behavior or force corporations to pay for the damages their products cause.

The controversy is important and much of the credit for initiating and continuing it belongs to Galbraith and Nader. Should policies attempt to alter the behavior of corporations, and if so, what changes are desirable? These are major questions, whether corporations are primarily responding to market signals or are impervious to them.

What Do Firms Maximize?

Most critics of the theory of firm behavior accept what Galbraith denies: Industries face market demand curves that the firms can influence only slightly. The critics then go on to suggest that firms will behave in ways different from those suggested by profit maximizing. In effect, these theories view firms as maximizers of something other than profits.

The view that many firms maximize something other than profits is made more plausible by the changing nature of the firm. One hundred years ago the single-proprietor firm, whose manager was its owner, was common in many branches of industry. In such firms the single-minded pursuit of profits would be expected. Today, however, ownership is commonly diversified among thousands of stockholders, and the firm's managers are rarely its owners. The two theories considered below use these changes to suggest reasons why firms may no longer be profit maximizers.

The Hypothesis of Minority Control

It is quite possible for the owners of a minority of the stock to control a majority of the shares that are voted and thus to exercise effective control over the decisions of the corporation. This possibility arises because not all shares are actually voted.

Each share of common stock has one vote in a corporation. Shares must be voted at the annual meeting of stockholders, either in person or by as-

signing a **proxy** to someone attending. (The proxy authorizes the person attending to cast the shareholder's vote.) Any individual or group controlling 51 percent of the stock clearly controls a majority of the votes. But suppose one group owns 30 percent of the stock, and the remaining 70 percent is distributed so widely that few of the dispersed group even bother to vote; in this event 30 percent may be the overwhelming majority of the shares *actually voted*. In general, a small fraction (sometimes as little as 5 percent) of the shares may exercise dominant influence at meetings of stockholders.

The hypothesis of minority control is that a well-organized minority often controls the destiny of the corporation against the wishes of the majority.

Dispersed ownership and minority control are well established in the corporate sector. But the hypothesis requires more than that a minority control the voting shares; it requires that stockholders be able to exert a significant influence on the firm's behavior *and* that the controlling minority have interests and motives different from the holders of the majority of the firm's stock. If all stockholders are mainly interested in having the firm maximize its profits, then it does not matter, as far as market behavior is concerned, which set of stockholders actually influences the firm's policy.

There is no accepted evidence to show that controlling groups of stockholders generally seek objectives different from those sought by the holders of the majority of the firm's stock. Of course, disagreements between stockholder groups sometimes arise. A colorful phenomenon in corporation history is the **proxy fight,** in which competing factions of stockholders (or management) attempt to collect the voting rights of the dispersed and generally disinterested stockholders.

The Hypothesis of the Separation of Ownership from Control

A different consequence of diversified ownership was suggested by A. A. Berle and Gardiner Means. They hypothesized that, because of diversified ownership and the difficulty of assembling stockholders or gathering proxies, the managers rather than the stockholders or the directors exercise effective control over the corporation.

The hypothesis of the separation of ownership from control is that managerial control occurs and leads to different behavior than would stockholder control.

In the modern corporation the stockholders elect directors, who appoint managers. Directors are supposed to represent stockholders' interests and to determine broad policies that the managers will carry out. In order to conduct the complicated business of running a large firm, a full-time professional management group must be given broad powers of decision. Although managerial decisions can be reviewed from time to time, they cannot be supervised in detail. The links between the directors and the managers are typically weak enough that top management often truly controls the corporation over long periods of time.

As long as directors have confidence in the managerial group, they accept and ratify their proposals, and stockholders elect and re-elect directors who are proposed to them. If the managerial group does not satisfy the director's expectations, it may be removed and replaced, but this is a disruptive and drastic action, and it is infrequently employed.

Within wide limits, then, effective control of the corporation's activities resides with the managers. Although the managers are legally employed by the stockholders, they remain largely unaffected by them. Indeed, the management group typically asks for, and gets, the proxies of enough stockholders to elect directors who will reappoint it—and thus it perpetuates itself in office.

The hypothesis of the separation of ownership from control requires not only that the managers be able to exert effective control over business decisions, but that they wish to act differently from the way the stockholders and directors wish to act. One such view is found in the sales maximization theory.

Sales maximization. This theory uses the separation of management and ownership in the large corporation. The managers need to make some minimum level of profits to keep the stockholders satisfied; after that they are free to seek growth unhampered by profit considerations. This is a sensible policy on the part of management, the argument runs, because salary, power, and prestige all rise with the size of a firm as much as with its profits. Generally, the manager of a large, normally profitable corporation will earn a salary considerably higher than that earned by the manager of a small, but highly profitable corporation.

The sales maximization hypothesis says that managers of firms seek to maximize their sales revenue, subject to a profit constraint.

Sales maximization subject to a profit constraint leads to the prediction that firms will sacrifice some profits by setting price below and output above their profit-maximizing levels (see Figure 17-1).

FIGURE 17-1   Output of the Firm Under Profit Maximizing, Sales Maximizing, and Satisficing

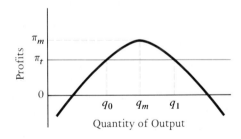

The "best" level of output depends on the motivation of the firm. The curve shows the level of profits associated with each level of output. A profit-maximizing firm produces output q_m and earns profits of π_m. A sales-maximizing firm, with a minimum profit constraint of π_t, produces the output q_1.

A satisficing firm, with a target level of profits of π_{t1}, is willing to produce any output between q_0 and q_1. Thus satisficing allows a range of outputs on either side of the profit-maximizing level, while sales maximizing results in a higher output than does profit maximizing.

Non-maximizing Theories of the Firm

Many students of large firms have been critical of economic theory for regarding modern corporations as "simple profit-maximizing computers." They believe that such firms are profit-oriented in the sense that, other things being equal, more profits are preferred to less. They do not believe, however, that firms are profit maximizers.

Non-maximization Due to Ignorance

One group of critics says that profit-maximizing theory is inadequate because firms, however hard they may try, cannot reach decisions in the way the theory predicts. We consider two such criticisms, one crude, the other more sophisticated.

Failure to understand marginal concepts.   One of the crudest criticisms is based on the observation that business people do not calculate in the manner assumed by the theory. When business people are interviewed, it is sometimes discovered (apparently to the surprise of the interviewer) that they are unaware of the concepts of marginal cost and marginal revenue. It is then argued that: (1) the theory assumes firms equate marginal cost to marginal revenue; (2) empirical observations show that many managers have not heard of marginal cost and marginal revenue; (3) therefore, the theory is refuted, because managers cannot be employing concepts of which they are unaware.

This observation, assuming it to be correct, does refute the theory that managers of firms make decisions by calculating marginal values and consciously equating them. But it does not refute the theory that firms maximize profits.

The mathematical concepts of marginal cost and marginal revenue are used by economic theorists to discover what will happen as long as, by one means or another—be it guess, clairvoyance, luck, or good judgment—firms do succeed in maximizing their profits. If firms are maximizing their profits, then the tools of economic theory allow economists to predict how firms will react to certain changes (e.g.,

the introduction of a tax), and these predictions are independent of the thought process by which firms actually reach their decisions.

Inadequate information.   More sophisticated critics point out that the information available to decision makers is simply not adequate to permit them to reach the decisions economists predict they will reach. This argument generally takes one of three forms: that firms are the victims of their accountants and base their decisions on accounting concepts, which differ from economic ones; that the natural lag between accumulating and processing data is such that important decisions must be made on fragmentary and partially out-of-date information; or that firms cannot afford to acquire as much information as economists assume them to have.

Non-maximization by Choice

Alternatives to maximizing theories are usually based on observations of actual firms. The observations, and the theories built on them, all have in common the implication that firms *choose* not to be maximizers.

Full-Cost Pricing

Most manufacturing firms are price setters: They must quote a price for the products rather than accept a price set on some impersonal competitive market. Simple profit-maximizing theory predicts that these firms will change their prices in response to every change in demand and cost that they experience. Yet students of large firms have long alleged that this much price flexibility is not observed. In the short run prices of manufactured goods do not appear to vary in response to every shift in the firm's demand. Instead, they appear to change rather sluggishly.

This short-run behavior is consistent with the hypothesis of **full-cost pricing,** which was originally advanced in the 1930s by Robert Hall, a British economist, and Charles Hitch, an American, following a series of detailed case studies of actual pricing decisions. Case studies in the intervening decades have continued to reveal the widespread use of full-cost pricing procedures.

The full-cost pricer, instead of equating marginal revenue with marginal cost, sets price equal to average cost at normal-capacity output plus a conventional markup.

The firm changes its prices when its average costs change substantially (as a result of such events as a new union contract or a sharp change in the prices of key raw materials), and it may occasionally change its markup. However, its short-run pricing behavior is rather conventional and is not characterized even by local profit maximization.

A non-maximizing interpretation of full-cost pricing.
Some modern critics of profit-maximizing theory hold that the prevalence of conventional full-cost practices shows that prices are typically not at their profit-maximizing level. They also hold that full-cost pricing shows that firms are creatures of custom that make only occasional, profit-oriented changes at fairly infrequent intervals.

A profit-maximizing interpretation of full-cost pricing.
We saw in Chapter 15 that the short-term stickiness of oligopolistic prices can be accounted for under profit-maximizing theory by saucer-shaped cost curves and by the fact that it is costly for a multi-product firm to change its list prices. The possible conflict between full-cost and profit-maximizing theory then concerns only the setting of the markup that relates prices to costs. If markups are arbitrary and only rarely revised, then there is conflict. If, however, the markup is the profit-maximizing one for normal-capacity output, then full-cost pricing can be consistent with profit maximization.

Organization Theory

A common criticism of profit-maximizing theory is that the behavior of firms is influenced seriously by their organizational structure. **Organization theory** argues that in big firms decisions are made after much discussion by groups and committees and that the structure of the process affects the substance of the decisions.

The central prediction of organization theory is that different decisions will result from different kinds of organizations, even when all else is unchanged.

One proposition that follows from this theory is that large and diffuse organizations find it necessary to develop standard operating procedures to help them in making decisions. These decision rules arise as compromises among competing points of view and, once adopted, are changed only reluctantly. Even if a particular compromise were the profit-maximizing strategy in the first place, it would not remain so when conditions changed. Thus, it is argued that profits will not usually be maximized.

Another prediction is that decision by compromise will lead firms to adopt conservative policies that avoid large risks. Smaller firms not faced with the necessity of compromising competing views will take bigger risks than large firms.

Organization theorists have suggested an alternative to profit maximization that they call **satisficing.** Satisficing theory was first put forward by Professor Herbert Simon of Carnegie-Mellon University, who in 1978 was awarded the Nobel Prize in economics for his work on firm behavior. He wrote, "We must expect the firm's goals to be not maximizing profits but attaining a certain level or rate of profit, holding a certain share of the market or a certain level of sales."

According to the satisficing hypothesis, firms will strive to achieve certain target levels of profits, but having achieved them, they will not strive to improve their profit position further. This means that the firm could produce any one of a range of outputs that yield at least the target level of profits rather than the unique output that maximizes profits. This behavior is illustrated in Figure 17-1.

Satisficing theory predicts not a unique equilibrium output, but a range of possible outputs that includes the profit-maximizing output somewhere within it and the sales-maximizing output at the upper limit.

Evolutionary Theories

The modern evolutionary theories advanced by such economists as Richard Nelson and Sidney Winter of

Yale University build on the earlier theories of full-cost pricing and satisficing. Nelson and Winter argue that firms do not—indeed, could not—behave as profit-maximizing theory predicts. They see firms operating cautiously with imperfect information in an uncertain world, and so making only gradual changes toward the profit-maximizing position. But since the conditions are constantly changing, firms are best seen as evolving toward a moving target which they never reach. Thus, although firms are profit-oriented, they never, except by accident, succeed in maximizing their profits, either locally or globally.

Evolutionary theorists have gathered much evidence to show that tradition seems to be important in firms' planning. The basic effort at the early stages of planning is directed, they argue, toward the problem of performing reasonably well in established markets and maintaining established market shares. They quote evidence to show that suggestions made in preliminary planning documents to do something entirely new in some areas, even on a 10-year horizon, are usually weeded out in the reviewing process. They believe that most firms spend little effort on plans to enter entirely new markets and still less on plans to leave or even reduce their share in long-established markets. These attitudes were illustrated by one firm which, although faced with obviously changing circumstances, reported that "We have been producing on the basis of these raw materials for more than 50 years with success, and we have made it a policy to continue to do so."

The evolutionary theory of the firm draws many analogies with the biological theory of evolution. Here are two.

The genes.   In biological theory some behavior patterns are transmitted by genes. Rules of behavior fulfill the same function in the evolutionary theory of the firm. In Professor Winter's words: "A great deal of firm decision behavior is routinized. Routinized decision procedures cover decision situations from pricing practices in retail stores to such 'strategic' decisions as advertising or R and D effort, or the question of whether or not to invest abroad." Winter talks of firms "remembering by doing" according to repetitive routines. He adds that government policymakers tend to have unrealistic expectations about firms' flexibility and responsiveness to changes in market incentives. These expectations arise from the maximizing model, whose fatal flaw, Winter alleges, is to underestimate the difficulty "of the task of merely continuing the routine performance, i.e., of preventing undesired deviations."

The mutations.   In the theory of biological evolution mutations are the vehicle of change. In the evolutionary theory of the firm this role is played by innovations. Some innovations are the introduction of new products and new production techniques. However, a further important class of innovations in evolutionary theory is the introduction of new rules of behavior. Sometimes innovations are thrust on the firm; at other times the firm consciously plans for and creates innovations.

According to maximizing theory, innovations are the result of incentives—the "carrot" of new profit opportunities. In evolutionary theory the firm is much more of a satisficer, and it usually innovates only under the incentive of the "stick" of unacceptably low profits or of some form of external prodding. Firms change routines when they get into trouble, not when they see a chance to improve an already satisfactory performance. For example, in the growing markets of the 1960s many firms continued all sorts of wasteful practices that they shed fairly easily when their profits were threatened in the more difficult economic climate of the 1970s and 1980s.

How Far Can Firms Depart from Profit-maximizing Behavior?

Many of the criticisms of modern microeconomic theory assume that firms seek to do things other than maximize their profits. Notice, however, that if the present management elects not to maximize its profits, some other management could make more money by operating the firm. A major restraint on existing managements is the threat of a stockholder revolt or a takeover bid.

A management that fails to come close to achieving the profit potential of the assets it controls becomes a natural target for acquisition. The management of the acquiring firm makes a **tender offer** (or

takeover bid, as it is sometimes called) to the stock-holders of the target firm, offering them what amounts to a premium for their shares, a premium it can pay because it believes it can increase the firm's profits. Managers who wish to avoid takeover bids cannot let the profits of their firm slip far from the profit-maximizing level because their unrealized profits provide the incentives for takeovers.

The pressure of the threat of takeovers severely limits the discretion of corporate management to pursue goals other than profit maximization.

The Significance of Non-maximizing Theories

An impressive array of evidence can be gathered in apparent support of various non-maximizing theories. What would be the implications if they were accepted as being better theories of the behavior of the economy than profit maximization?

If non-maximizing theories are correct, the economic system does not perform with the delicate precision that follows from profit maximization. But the systems described by non-maximizing theories *do* function. Firms sell more when demand goes up and less when it goes down. They also alter their prices and their input mixes when faced with sufficiently large changes in input prices.

Non-maximizing theories do not conflict with the broad generalization that the price system coordinates the response of decentralized decision makers to changes in tastes and costs.

But profit-oriented, non-maximizing firms will also exhibit a great deal of inertia. They will not respond quickly and precisely to small changes in market signals from either the private sector or government policy. Neither are they certain to make radical changes in their behavior even when the profit incentives to do so are large. This casts doubt over the efficacy of government policies that make relatively small changes in such market incentives as taxes and subsidies, hoping that firms will respond to these as profit maximizers.

When firms are oriented toward profits, but do not try to maximize profits, the price system is sensitive to large, but not to small changes in price and profit signals caused by changes in demand, costs, or public policy.

Without doubt, profits are a potent force in the life and death of firms. The resilience of profit-maximizing theory and its ability to predict the economy's reactions to many major changes (such as the dramatic variations in energy prices that have occurred over the last two decades) suggest that firms are at least strongly motivated by the pursuit of profits.

If profit-maximizing theory should eventually give way to some more organizationally dominated theory, the new theory will still be a profit-oriented theory. The search for profits and the avoidance of losses drive the economy even when firms are not continuously maximizing profits.

---

1. A sweeping attack on the traditional theory of the behavior of the firm is made by Galbraith, along with Nader and others. He argues that large corporations manipulate markets, tastes, and governments instead of responding to market and government pressures. While there is evidence about the influence of large corporations, there is also much evidence of market influence on corporate behavior.
2. In recent years serious concern has developed over whether corporations should represent the interests of their owners and managers or whether they should be responsible to a broader public interest.

Summary

Consumerists argue for the latter point of view; others prefer to rely on markets and government control to protect the public interest.

3. The widespread ownership of the modern corporation leads to the question: Who really controls the modern corporation? Attempts to answer this question have led to alternative theories that firms maximize something other than profits. Three important hypotheses have been advanced.

    a. A minority group of stockholders often controls the corporation against the wishes of the majority. The fact of minority control is widely accepted, but there is little evidence to suggest that the minority usually coerce the majority.

    b. Because of the widespread ownership of the corporation, stockholders cannot exert effective control over the managers; thus the latter have the real control of the organization and operate it for their advantage rather than that of the stockholders. This hypothesis has some serious, but by no means universal, support.

4. These and other hypotheses suggest that firms may seek to maximize something other than profits. One alternative is the hypothesis of sales maximization: Firms seek to be as large as possible (judged by sales revenue), subject to the constraint that they achieve a minimum rate of profit.

5. An alternative set of hypotheses denies that firms seek to maximize profits in any way.

    a. Some theories hold that firms do not have sufficient information to maximize their profits. Other theories hold that firms consciously choose to do something other than maximize their profits.

    b. The full-cost hypothesis states that firms determine price by adding a customary—and infrequently changed—markup to full costs. This also makes their pricing behavior relatively insensitive to short-term fluctuations in demand.

    c. Organization theorists see firms as insensitive to short-term fluctuations in market signals. The reason lies in the decision-making structure of large organizations, which must rely on routines and rules of thumb rather than on fresh calculations of profitabilities as each new situation presents itself.

    d. Evolutionary theorists build on full-cost and organizational theories. They see the firm as a profit-oriented entity in a world of imperfect information, making small, profit-oriented changes from its present situation, but being more resistant to large, "structural" changes.

6. Under both maximizing and non-maximizing theories, profits are an important driving force in the economy, and changes in demand and costs cause changes in profits, which cause firms to reallocate resources. The speed and precision, but not the general direction of the reallocations, are what is different between maximizing and non-maximizing theories.

Topics for Review

Discussion Questions

1. In 1976 the automobile manufacturers introduced their 1977 models. GM and American Motors (AMC) put major emphasis on smaller, more economical cars, and Ford and Chrysler stayed with their 1976 model sizes. Read the following news headlines (which appear in chronological order) and then discuss the light they shed on the hypothesis that firms control the market.
   a. "GM's 1977 line runs ahead of the pack. The big question: Do people want small cars?"
   b. "Ford, Chrysler, beam; AMC in trouble on sales."
   c. "GM's fuel-saving Chevette: Right car at the wrong time."
   d. "Price cuts and rebates lift sales of small AMC and GM cars."
   e. "GM confirms plans to drop the subcompact Vega."
   What do these further events reveal about the same hypothesis?
   f. In 1979 auto firms sold all the small cars they could produce. But they were left with sizable unsold inventories of large cars, and as a result they are preparing to alter their production mix in favor of small cars.
   g. Throughout the 1980s American car makers have faced growing competition from Japanese car makers, who have taken an ever-growing part of the U.S. market.

2. "Because automobile companies were interested only in profits, they would not produce the safer, less polluting, but more expensive cars that the public really wanted. Legislation was necessary, therefore, to force producers to meet consumer needs." Discuss.

3. Assume that each of the following assertions is factually correct. Taken together, what would they tell you about the prediction that big business is increasing its control of the U.S. economy?
   a. The share of total manufacturing assets owned by the 200 largest corporations has been rising steadily for the last 25 years.
   b. The number of new firms begun every year has grown steadily for the last 25 years.
   c. The share of manufacturing in total production has been decreasing for 40 years.
   d. Profits as a percent of national income are no higher now than half a century ago.

4. "Our economy, like an engine, must have fuel to operate. And the fuel our economy runs on is profit. Profits keep it going—and grow-

ing. But there is strong evidence that the economy's fuel supply is running low. Profits of U.S. corporations today are about 5 percent on sales—less than the 1965 rate.

"We Americans have become accustomed to a quality of life that can survive only through profits. For profits not only create jobs and goods, they furnish essential tax revenues. Federal, state, and local taxes finance the countless programs that our citizens demand—from paving the roads on which we drive to building our country's defense forces . . . to helping millions of Americans who need some form of assistance."

Comment on this excerpt from an Allied Chemical Corporation advertisement.

5. "The business of the businessman is to run his business so as to make profits. If he does so, he will serve the public interest better than if he tries to decide what is good for society. He is neither elected nor appointed to that task." Discuss.

6. "Our list prices are really set by our accounting department: they add a fixed markup to their best estimates of fully accounted cost and send these to the operating divisions. Managers of these divisions may not change those prices without permission of the Board of Directors, which is seldom given. Operating divisions may, however, provide special discounts if necessary to stay competitive." Does this testimony by the president of a leading manufacturing company support the full-cost pricing hypothesis?

7. The leading automobile tire manufacturers (Goodyear, Firestone, etc.) sell original equipment (OE) tires to automobile manufacturers at a price below the average total cost of all the tires they make and sell. This happens year after year. Is this consistent with profit-maximizing behavior in the short run? In the long run? If it is not consistent, what does it show? Do OE tires compete with replacement tires?

The Distribution of Income

18

Factor Mobility and Factor Pricing

Are the poor getting poorer and the rich richer, as Karl Marx thought they would? Are the rich becoming relatively poorer and the poor relatively richer, as Alfred Marshall hoped they would? Is the distribution of income affected by social changes such as the increased participation of women in the labor force? Is it affected by changes in public policy toward poverty? Should we reject the view held by Italian economist Vilfredo Pareto that inequality of income is a social constant determined by forces that are possibly beyond human understanding and probably beyond human influence?

The founders of classical economics, Adam Smith and David Ricardo, were concerned with the distribution of income among what were then the three great social classes: workers, capitalists, and landowners. They defined three factors of production: labor, capital, and land. The return to each factor was treated as the income of the respective social class.

Smith and Ricardo were interested in what determined the income of each group relative to the total national income. Their theories predicted that as society progressed, landlords would become relatively better off and capitalists would become relatively worse off. Karl Marx had a different view. He predicted that as growth occurred, capitalists would become relatively better off and workers relatively worse off (at least until the whole capitalist system collapsed).

These nineteenth century debates focused on what is now called the **functional distribution of income,** defined as the distribution of total income among the major factors of production. Table 18-1 shows data for the functional distribution of income in the United States in 1985.

Although functional distribution categories (wages, rent, profits) pervade current statistics, economists have shifted to another way of looking at differences in incomes. At the beginning of the century, Pareto studied what is now called the **size distribution of income,** the distribution of income among different households without reference to the source of the income or the social class of the household. He discovered that inequality in income distribution was substantial in all countries and, more surprisingly, that the degree of inequality was quite similar from one country to another. Tables 18-2 and 18-3 show that in the United States in 1985 there was substantial inequality in the size distibution of income.

Inequality in the distribution of income is shown graphically in Figure 18-1 on page 326. This curve of income distribution, called a **Lorenz curve,** shows how much of total income is accounted for by given proportions of the nation's families. (The farther the curve bends

TABLE 18-1   The Functional Distribution of National Income in the United States, 1985

Type of income	Billions of dollars	Percentage of total
Employee compensation	$2,373	73.8
Corporate profits	299	9.3
Proprietor's income	242	7.5
Interest	288	9.0
Rental income	14	.4
Total	$3,216	100.0

Source: Survey of Current Business, January 1986.

Income is classified here according to the nature of the factor service that earned the income. While these data show that employee compensation is about three-quarters of national income, this does not mean that workers and their families receive only that fraction of national income. Many households will have income in more than one category listed in the table.

TABLE 18-2   Incomes of American Families,[a] **1984**

Income class (thousands of dollars)	Percentage of families
Less than 12.5	20.0
12.5 to 24.9	26.7
25.0 to 34.9	19.0
35.0 to 49.9	18.4
50.0 or more	15.8

Source: Current Population Reports, Series P-60, No. 151.

[a] The census definition of a family is two or more persons related by blood, marriage, or adoption and residing together.

Although median family income in 1984 was almost $30,000, many received much less than this comfortable level of income and some a great deal more. The ranges in the income clases were chosen so that each class contained roughly one-fifth of the population. Thus 64 percent of the families had incomes between $12,500 and $50,000.

away from the diagnonal, the more unequal is the distribution of income.) Today the bottom twenty percent of all American households received just under 5 percent of all income earned. The present size

distribution of income is virtually unchanged from what it was twenty years ago.

There are good reasons why much of the attention of modern economists is devoted to the size, rather than the functional, distribution of income. After all, some capitalists (such as the owners of small retail stores) are in the lower part of the income scale, while some wage earners (such as skilled athletes) are at the upper end of the income scale. Moreover, if someone is poor, it matters little whether that person is a landowner or a worker.

In order to understand the distribution of income, we must first study how the income of households is determined. Superficial explanations of differences in income such as "People earn according to their ability," are clearly inadequate. Incomes are distributed much more unequally than any *measured* index of ability, be it IQ, physical strength, or typing skill. In what sense is Tom Watson five times as able a golfer as Dave Barr? His average score is only 1 percent better, yet he earns five times as much. However, if answers couched in terms of worth and ability are easily refuted, so are answers such as "It's all a matter of luck" or "It's just the system."

How does economic theory explain the distri-

TABLE 18-3   Inequality in Family Income Distribution, 1984

Family income rank	Percentage share of aggregate income
Lowest fifth	4.7
Second fifth	11.0
Middle fifth	17.0
Fourth fifth	24.4
Highest fifth	42.9
	100.0
Top 5 percent	16.0

Source: Current Population Reports, Series P-60, No. 151.

While far from showing overall equality, income distribution is relatively equal for the middle 60 percent of the distribution. If the income distribution were perfectly equal, each fifth of the families would receive 20 percent of aggregate income. These data are plotted in Figure 18-1.

**FIGURE 18-1   A Lorenz Curve of Family Income
in the United States**

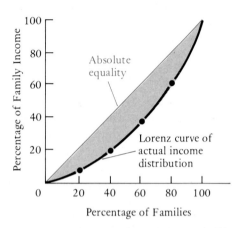

**The size of the shaded area between the Lorenz
curve and the diagonal is a measure of the inequality of income distribution.** If there were complete income equality, the bottom 20 percent of income receivers
would receive 20 percent of the income, and so forth,
and the Lorenz curve would coincide with the diagonal
line. Because the lower 20 percent receive only 5 percent
of the income, the Lorenz curve lies below the diagonal.
The extent to which it bends away from the straight line
indicates the amount of inequality in the distribution of
income.

bution of income more satisfactorily than these superficial explanations? In this chapter we provide an
answer to this question using the basic tools of supply and demand.

The Theory of Income Distribution

Every element of income has, in a purely arithmetical
sense, two components: the quantity of the income-
earning service that is provided and the price per unit
paid for it. For example, the amount a worker earns
in wages depends on the number of hours worked
and the hourly wage received.

Factor Income and Factor Prices

As with the market theory studied in Chapter 4, the
theory of distribution is concerned with *relative* magnitudes. One factor becomes "more expensive"
when its price rises relative to that of other factors.
In an inflationary world most prices are rising, but
not at the same rate, so some factors become relatively more expensive, some relatively cheaper. We
use the phrase *rise in price* to mean a rise in relative
price and the phrase *fall in price* to mean a fall in
relative price (see pages 73–74 for fuller discussion).

In this chapter we consider competitive markets.
Microeconomic theory states that the competitive
market price of any commodity or factor is determined by demand and supply. The competitive market determination of the equilibrium price and quantity, and thus the money income, of a factor of
production is illustrated in Figure 18-2. (Look again
at Figure 4-9, page 72, to see why this analysis is
familiar.) The market equilibrium, illustrated in Figure 18-2 gives rise to what is called the *neoclassical*
theory of income distribution.

**According to the neoclassical theory of distri-
bution, the problem of distribution is just a special case of the pricing of any good or service.**

The theory of factor prices is absolutely general. If one is
concerned with labor, one should interpret factor
prices to mean wages; if one is thinking about land,
factor prices should be interpreted to mean land
rents, and so on.

The Demand for Factors

Firms require inputs not for their own sake, but as
a means to produce goods and services. For example,
the demand for computer programmers and technicians is growing as we use more and more computers. The demand for carpenters and building materials rises or falls with the amount of housing
construction. Anything that increases the demand for
new housing—population growth, lower interest
rates on mortgages, and so on—will increase the
demand for the inputs required to build houses. The___

FIGURE 18-2   The Determination of Factor Price and Income in a Competitive Market

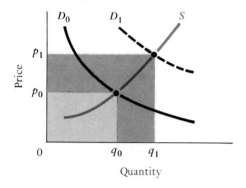

In competitive factor markets, demand and supply determine factor prices, quantities of factors used, and factor incomes. With demand and supply curves D_0 and S, the price of the factor will be p_0 and the quantity employed q_0. The total income earned by the factor is the light shaded area. A shift in demand from D_0 to D_1 raises equilibrium price and quantity to p_1 and q_1. The income earned by the factor rises by an amount equal to the dark shaded area.

demand for any input depends on the existence of a demand for the goods or services it helps produce; the demand for a factor of production is therefore called a **derived demand.**[1] Typically, one input will be used in making many commodities. Steel is used in dozens of industries, as are the services of carpenters.

The total demand for an input will be the sum of the derived demands for it in every activity in which it is used.

The theory of income distribution rests in part on the demand for land, labor, and capital as factors of production. Firms also use as inputs products produced by other firms, such as steel, plastic, and elec-

tricity. If we trace back to the production of these inputs, we may find that they, too, are made using land, labor, capital, and other produced inputs. However, if we trace back far enough, we can net out all these produced inputs and focus on the basic inputs of the economy—land, labor, and capital.

The Supply of Factors

At any one time the total supply of each factor of production is given. For example, in each country the labor force is of such and such a size; there is so much arable land available; and there is a given known supply of petroleum. However, these supplies can and do change in response to both economic and noneconomic forces. Sometimes the change is very gradual; for example, when a climate change slowly turns arable land into desert or when a medical discovery lowers the rate of infant mortality and hence increases the rate of population growth and eventually increases the supply of adult labor. Sometimes the changes can be quite rapid; for example, when a boom in business activity brings retired persons back into the labor force, when a rise in the price of oil greatly encourages the discovery of new oil supplies, or when a rise in the price of agricultural produce encourages the draining of marshes to add to the supply of arable land.

In the next chapter we return to the question of the extent to which economic forces determine the *total supply* of a factor to the whole economy. In this chapter we focus on the extent to which such forces determine the *supply available to a particular industry or use.*

Most factors have many uses. A given piece of land can be used to grow any one of several crops, or it can be subdivided for a housing development. A computer programmer in Michigan can work in one of several automobile plants or in a dozen other industries or in the physics laboratories at the University of Michigan. A lathe can be used to make many different products and requires no adaptation when it is turned from one use to another. Plainly, it is easier for any one user to acquire more of a scarce factor of production than it is for all users to do so simultaneously. One user can bid resources

---

[1] In the next chapter we look in detail at the role of marginal productivity theory in understanding the derived demand for the services of factors of production.

away from another user, even though the total supply may be fixed.

The total supply of any factor must be allocated among all the different uses to which it can possibly be put.

Factor Mobility

When considering the supply of a factor to a particular use, the most important concept is *factor mobility*. A factor that shifts easily between uses in response to small changes in incentives is said to be mobile. It will be in elastic supply in any one of its uses because a small increase in the price offered will attract many units of the factor from other uses. A factor that does not shift easily from one use to another, even in response to large changes in remuneration, is said to be immobile. It will be in inelastic supply in any one of its uses because even a large increase in the price offered will attract only a small inflow from other uses. Often a factor may be immobile in the short run, but mobile in the long run.

An important key to factor mobility is time. The longer the time interval, the easier it is for a factor to convert from one use to another.

Consider the mobility among particular uses of each of the three key factors of production.

Capital.   While some kinds of capital equipment—lathes, trucks, and computers, for example—can be readily shifted among uses, many others are comparatively unshiftable. A great deal of machinery is utterly specific: Once built, it must be used for the purpose for which it was designed, or it cannot be used at all. (It is the immobility of much fixed capital equipment that makes the exit of firms from declining industries a slow and difficult process.)

In the long run, however, capital is highly mobile. When capital goods wear out, firms may simply replace them with identical goods. But the firm has many other options. It may buy a newly designed machine to produce the same goods; it may buy machines to produce totally different goods; or it may spend its resources in other ways. Such deci-

sions lead to changes in the long-run allocation of a country's stock of capital among various uses.

Land.   Land, which is physically the least mobile of factors, is one of the most mobile in an economic sense. Consider agricultural land. Within one year one crop can be harvested and a totally different crop planted. A farm on the outskirts of a growing city can be sold for subdivision and development on short notice.

Once land is built on, its mobility is much reduced. A site on which a hotel has been built can be converted into an office building site, but it takes a large differential in the value of land use to make it worthwhile because the hotel must be torn down.

Although land is highly mobile among alternative uses, it is completely immobile as far as location is concerned. There is only so much land within a given distance of the center of any city, and no increase in the price paid can induce further land to locate within that distance. This locational immobility has important consequences, including high prices for desirable locations and the tendency to build tall buildings to economize on the use of scarce land, as in the center of large cities.

Labor.   Labor is unique as a factor of production in that the supply of the service requires the physical presence of the owner of the source of the service. Absentee landlords can obtain income from land located in remote parts of the world while continuing to live in the place of their choice. Investment can be shifted from iron mines in South Africa to mines in Labrador, while the owners of the capital commute between New York and the French Riviera. But when a worker employed by a firm in Iowa City decides to supply labor service to a firm in Atlanta, the worker must physically travel to Atlanta. This has an important consequence.

Because of the need for physical presence, non-monetary considerations are much more important in the allocation of labor than in the allocation of other factors of production.

People may be satisfied with or frustrated by the kind of work they do, where they do it, those they do it with, and the social status of their occupations. Since these considerations influence their decisions about what they will do with their labor services, they will not move every time they can earn a higher wage. Nevertheless, occupational and job movement will occur when there are changes in the wage structure.

The mobility that does occur depends on many forces. For example, it is not difficult for a secretary to shift from one company to another to to take a job in Boise instead of in Tacoma, but it can be difficult for a secretary to become an editor, a model, a machinist, or a doctor in a short period of time. Lack of ability, training, or inclination will stratify some people and make certain kinds of mobility difficult for them.

Some barriers may be virtually insurmountable for a person once his or her training has been completed. It may be impossible for a farmer to become a surgeon or for a truck driver to become a professional athlete, even if the relative wage rates change greatly. But the children of farmers, doctors, truck drivers, and athletes, when they are deciding how much education or training to obtain, are not nearly as limited in their choices as their parents, who have completed their education and are settled in their occupations.

Thus the labor force as a whole is more mobile than individual members of it. At one end of the age distribution people enter the labor force from school; at the other end they leave it through retirement or death. The turnover due to these causes is about 3 or 4 percent per year. Over a period of 10 years a society could create a totally different occupational distribution merely by directing new entrants to jobs other than the ones left vacant by workers leaving the labor force, without a single individual's ever changing jobs. The role of education in adapting people to available jobs is great. In a society in which education is provided to all, it is possible to achieve large increases in the supply of any desired labor skill within a decade or so.

Factor Price Differentials

If all units of labor were identical and if all benefits were monetary, then the price of labor would tend to be the same in all uses.[2] Workers would move from low-priced jobs to high-priced ones. The quantity of labor supplied would diminish in occupations in which wages were low, and the resulting shortage would tend to force those wages up; the quantity of labor supplied would increase in occupations in which wages were high, and the resulting surplus would force wages down. The movement would continue until there were no further incentives to change occupations, that is, until wages were equalized in all uses.

In fact, however, wage differentials commonly occur. These differentials may be divided into two distinct types: dynamic and equilibrium.

Dynamic Differentials

Some factor price differentials reflect a temporary state of disequilibrium. Such differences in factor prices, called **dynamic differentials,** or *disequilibrium differentials,* are self-correcting and disappear in equilibrium. They are brought about by circumstances such as the growth of one industry and the decline of another. The differentials themselves lead to reallocation of factors, and such reallocations in turn act to eliminate the differentials.

Consider the effect on factor prices of a rise in the demand for air transport and a decline in the demand for rail transport. There will be an increase in the airline industry's demand for factors and a decrease in the railroad industry's demand for factors. Relative factor prices will go up in airlines and down in railroading. The differential in factor prices will itself foster a net movement of factors from the railroad industry to the airline industry, and this movement will cause the dynamic differentials to lessen and eventually disappear. How long this process takes will depend on how easily factors move from one industry to the other, that is, on the degree of factor mobility.

Equilibrium Differentials

Some factor price differentials persist in equilibrium, without generating forces that eliminate them. These

[2] Similar remarks apply to all other factors of production as well.

equilibrium differentials can be explained by intrinsic differences in the factors themselves, by differences in the cost of acquiring skills, or by different nonmonetary advantages of different occupations.

Intrinsic differences.   If various units of a factor have different characteristics, the price paid may differ among these units. If intelligence and dexterity are required to accomplish a task, intelligent and manually dexterous workers will earn more than less intelligent and less dexterous workers. If land is to be used for agricultural purposes, highly fertile land will earn more than poor land. These differences will persist even in long-run equilibrium.

Acquired differences.   If the fertility of land can be increased by costly methods, then that land must command a higher price than less fertile land. If it did not, landlords would not incur the costs of improving fertility. The same holds true for labor. It is costly to acquire most skills. For example, a mechanic must train for some time, and unless the earnings of mechanics remain sufficiently above what can be earned in less skilled occupations, people will not incur the cost of training.

Nonmonetary advantages.   Whenever working conditions differ among various uses for a single factor, that factor will earn different equilibrium amounts in its various uses. The difference between a test pilot's wage and a chauffeur's wage is only partly a matter of skill; the rest is compensation for the higher risk of testing new planes compared to driving a car. If they were paid the same, there would be an excess supply of chauffeurs and a shortage of test pilots.

Academic researchers commonly earn less than they could earn in the world of commerce and industry because of the substantial nonmonetary advantages of academic employment. If chemists were paid the same in both sectors, many chemists would prefer academic to industrial jobs. Excess demand for industrial chemists and excess supply of academic chemists would then force chemists' wages up in industry and down in academia until the two types of jobs seemed equally attractive on balance.

The same forces account for equilibrium differences in regional earnings of otherwise identical factors. Welders and carpenters earn more in Point Bar-

row, Alaska, than they do in Phoenix, Arizona. Without higher pay not enough people would be willing to work in unattractive or remote locations. Similarly, if enough people prefer living in New England to living in Gary, Indiana, equilibrium wages in comparable occupations will be lower in New England than in Gary.

Differentials and Factor Mobility

The distinction between dynamic and equilibrium differentials is closely linked to factor mobility.

Dynamic differentials lead to, and are eroded by, factor movements; equilibrium differentials are not eliminated by factor mobility.

Dynamic differentials tend to disappear over time; equilibrium differentials persist indefinitely.

Maximizing net advantage.   The removal of dynamic differentials and the persistence of equilibrium differentials leads to a generalization called the *hypothesis of equal net advantage*. The hypothesis assumes that owners of factors will choose to use their factors in a way that maximizes the net advantage to themselves, where net advantage includes both monetary and nonmonetary rewards. The **hypothesis of equal net advantage** states that in eroding dynamic differentials, factor mobility serves to equalize the net advantage earned by factors in different locations and occupations.[3]

This hypothesis plays the same role in the theory of distribution as the assumption that firms seek to maximize profits plays in the theory of production. It leads to the prediction that the units of each kind of factor of production will be allocated among various uses in such a way that their owners receive the same net return in every use.

While nonmonetary advantages are important in explaining differences in levels of pay for labor in different occupations, they tend to be quite stable over time. As a result, monetary advantages, which vary with market conditions, lead to changes in *net*

---

[3] Since the central idea is maximizing behavior, we might well refer to the hypothesis of "maximum net advantage." However, the terminology in the text has become standard.

advantage. Variations in monetary advantages thus play a bigger role in reallocating resources.

A change in the relative pay of a factor between two uses will change the net advantages of the uses. It will lead to a shift of some units of that factor to the use whose rate of pay has increased.

This implies a rising supply curve for a factor in any particular use. When the price of a factor rises in that use, more will be supplied to that use. This factor supply curve (like all supply curves) can *shift* in response to changes in other variables; for example, one thing that can shift it is a change in size of nonmonetary benefits.

Policy issues.   The distinction between equilibrium and dynamic factor price differentials raises an important consideration for policy. Trade unions, governments, and other bodies often have explicit policies about earnings differentials, often seeking to eliminate them in the name of equity. The wisdom (and success) of such policies depends to a great extent on the kind of differential that is being attacked.

Consider a policy that resists a dynamic differential. Only a short time ago large differentials opened up between earnings in the Sun Belt and those in the industrial Midwest. These were *disequilibrium* differentials associated with an economic boom in the Sun Belt. Policies that sought to narrow the wage differentials may have appeared to succeed, but they would have slowed the movement of labor to the Sun Belt and thus prolonged the period during which there was excess labor in the Midwest and a shortage in the Sun Belt.

Policies that attempt to eliminate equilibrium differentials will encounter even more severe difficulties. If an equilibrium differential occurs in response to nonmonetary differences and a policy resisting the monetary differential is adopted, the nonmonetary differences will change to compensate. For example, if a policy resists a wage premium that emerged for an unattractive job—say, garbage collecting—then a shortage of garbage collectors would emerge. Companies and governments that hired garbage collectors—unable to offer higher wages—would develop non-wage benefits—longer holidays, shorter hours, better working conditions—to attract sufficient

workers. In terms of regulating the relative attractiveness of the occupation, the policy will have failed.

Factor price differentials are a natural market consequence of conditions of supply and demand. Mobility of factors tends to establish equilibrium levels of factor prices at which dynamic differentials are eliminated and equilibrium differentials are restored. Policies that seek to eliminate factor price differentials without consideration of what caused them or how they affect the supply of the factor are likely to have perverse results.

Transfer Earnings and Economic Rent

One of the most important distinctions in economics is that between transfer earnings and economic rent. The amount that a factor must earn in its present use to prevent it from moving (i.e., transferring) to another use is called its **transfer earnings.** Any excess it earns over this amount is called its **economic rent.** The distinction is crucial in predicting the effects of changes in earnings on the movement of factors.

The concept of economic rent, the surplus of total earnings over transfer earnings, is analogous to the economists' concept of profit as a surplus over opportunity cost. The terminology is confusing because economic rent is often called, simply, rent and *rent* also means the price paid to hire something, such as a machine or a piece of land. How the same term came to be used for these two different concepts is explored in Box 18-1.

The Division of Factor Earnings

In most cases the actual earnings of a factor of production are a composite of transfer earnings and economic rent. It is possible, however, to imagine cases in which earnings are all transfer earnings or are all economic rent. The possibilities are illustrated in Figure 18-3 on page 333. When the supply curve is perfectly inelastic (vertical), the whole of the payment is an economic rent. Even a price barely above zero would not lead suppliers to decrease the quantity supplied, so transfer earnings are therefore zero. The price actually paid allocates the fixed supply to those most willing to pay for it.

BOX 18-1

Origin of the Concept of Economic Rent

In the early nineteenth century there was a public debate about the high price of wheat in England. The price was causing great hardship because bread was a primary source of food for the working class. Some argued that wheat had a high price because landlords were charging high rents to tenant farmers. To pay these land rents, the prices that farmers charged for their wheat also had to be raised to a high level. In short it was argued that the price of wheat was high because the rents of agricultural land were high. Some of those who held this view advocated restricting the rents that landlords could charge.

David Ricardo argued that the situation was exactly the reverse. The price of wheat was high, he said, because there was a shortage caused by the Napoleonic wars. Because wheat was profitable to produce, there was keen competition among farmers to obtain land on which to grow wheat. This competition in turn forced up rents on wheat land. Ricardo advocated removing the tariff so that imported wheat could come into the country, thereby increasing its supply and lowering both the price of wheat and the rent that could be charged for the land on which it was grown.

The essentials of Ricardo's argument were these. The supply of land was fixed. Land was regarded as having only one use, the growing of wheat. Nothing had to be paid to prevent land from transferring to a use other than growing wheat because it had no other use. No self-respecting landowner would leave land idle as long as he could obtain some return, no matter how small, by renting it out. Therefore, all the payment to land—that is, rent—was a surplus over and above what was necessary to keep it in its present use.

Given a fixed supply of land, the price of land depended on the demand for land, which depended upon the demand for wheat. *Rent*, the term for the payment for the use of land, thus became the term for a surplus payment to a factor over and above what was necessary to keep it in its present use.

Later, two facts were realized. First, land often had alternative uses, and from the point of view of any one use, part of the payment made to land would necessarily have to be paid to keep it in that use. Second, factors of production other than land also often earn a surplus over and above what is necessary to keep them in their present use. Television stars and great athletes, for example, are in short and fairly fixed supply, and their potential earnings in other occupations are often quite moderate. But because there is a huge demand for their services as television stars or athletes, they may receive payments greatly in excess of what is needed to keep them from transferring to other occupations. This surplus is now called *economic rent*, whether the factor is land or labor or a piece of capital equipment.

When the supply curve is perfectly elastic (horizontal), the whole of the price paid is a transfer earning. If the purchaser does not pay at least this price, it will not obtain any quantity of the factor.

The more usual situation is that of a gradually rising supply curve. A rise in the factor's price serves the allocative function of attracting more units of the factor into employment, but the same rise provides additional economic rent to all units of the factor already employed. We know this increment is an economic rent because the owners of these units were willing to supply them at a lower price. This is a general result:

If a factor becomes scarce in any of its uses, its price will rise. This will serve the allocative function of attracting additional units, but it will also increase the economic rent to all units of the factor already in that employment, whose transfer earnings were already being covered.

Determinants of the Division

How much of a given payment to a factor is economic rent and how much is transfer earnings varies from situation to situation. We cannot point to a factor of production and assert that some fixed fraction of its income always is transfer earnings and the remainder is economic rent. The division depends on the mobility of the factor, that is, on the alternatives open to it.

The mobility of a factor depends on the perspective of our analysis. If we focus on a narrowly defined use of a given factor, say, the factor's use by a particular firm, then the factor will be highly mobile. Since it could readily move to another firm in the same industry, it has a number of alternatives open to it. Therefore, it will be necessary to make payments to keep it employed in a specific firm. Thus from the perspective of the firm a large proportion of the factor payment is a transfer earnings.

If we focus on a more broadly defined use, for example, the factor's use in an industry, then it is less mobile, because it would be more difficult for the factor to gain employment quickly outside the industry. From the perspective of the particular *industry* (rather than the specific *firm* within the industry), a larger proportion of the factor payment is economic rent and a smaller proportion is transfer earnings.

From the even more general perspective of a particular *occupation*, mobility is likely to be even less and the proportion of the factor payment that is economic rent is even larger.

As the perspective moves from a narrowly defined use of a factor to a broadly defined use, the mobility of the factor decreases; as mobility decreases, the share of the factor payment that is economic rent increases.

We now illustrate how these considerations apply to each of the key factors of production.

Labor.   Some labor is always able to move from job to job, and therefore something must be paid to keep a given unit of labor in its present use. This amount is transfer earnings. How much has to be paid to keep labor in its present use depends upon what the use is.

First, consider movement *among firms in one industry*. Assume, for example, that carpenters receive $160 for working a normal eight-hour day. A construction firm will have to pay $160 per day or it will not obtain the services of any carpenter. To that

FIGURE 18-3   The Division of Factor Payments Between Economic Rent and Transfer Earnings

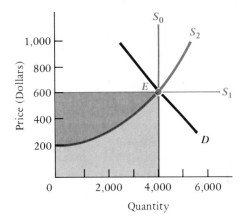

The division of total factor payments between economic rent and transfer earnings depends on the shape of the supply curve. A single demand curve is shown with three different supply curves. In each case the competitive equilibrium price is $600, and 4,000 units of the factor are hired. The total payment ($2.4 million) is represented by the entire shaded area.

When the supply curve is vertical (S_0), the whole payment is economic rent, because a decrease in price would not lead any unit of the factor to move elsewhere.

When the supply curve is horizontal (S_1), the whole payment is transfer earnings, because even a small decrease in price offered would lead all units of the factor to move elsewhere.

When the supply curve rises to the right (S_2), part of the payment is rent and part is transfer earnings. As shown by the height of the supply curve, at a price of $600 the 4,000th unit of the factor is just receiving transfer earnings, but the 2,000th unit, for example, is earning well above its transfer earnings. The aggregate of economic rents is shown by the dark shaded area and the aggregate of transfer earnings by the light shaded area.

one firm, the whole $160 is a transfer payment; if it were not paid, carpenters would not remain with that firm.

Second, consider movement *among industries*. Assume there is a decline in demand for buildings, and all construction firms reduce the wages offered to carpenters. Now carpenters cannot move to other construction firms to get more money. If they do not like the wages offered, they have to move to another industry that employs carpenters. If the best they can do elsewhere is $125 per day, they will not begin to leave the construction industry until wages in that industry fall below $125. In this case the transfer earnings of carpenters in construction is $125. When they were receiving $160 (presumably because there was a heavy demand for their services), the additional $35 was an economic rent from the point of view of the construction *industry*, even though it was a transfer earnings from the point of view of an individual firm.

Third, consider movement *among occupations*. Assume that there is a decline in the demand for carpenters in all industries. The only option a carpenter has is to move to another occupation, say, truck driving. If no carpenters are induced to leave carpentry until the wage falls to $110, then $110 is the transfer payment to carpenters in general. The wage of $110 has to be paid to persuade people to remain carpenters.

Consider how this applies to the often controversial large salaries received by some highly specialized types of labor, such as superstar singers and professional athletes. These performers have a style and talent that cannot be duplicated, whatever the training. The earnings they receive are mostly economic rent from the viewpoint of the occupation: These performers enjoy their occupations and would pursue them for much less than the high remuneration they actually receive. For example, Wayne Gretzky would choose hockey over other alternatives even at a much lower salary. However, because of Gretzky's amazing hockey skills, any team in the National Hockey League would pay handsomely to have him on its team, and he is able to command a high salary from the team he does play for. From the perspective of the firm, the Edmonton Oilers, most of Gretzky's salary is required to keep him from switching to another team and hence is properly viewed by it as a transfer payment.

Land. The analysis for land is identical to the analysis for labor. First, consider the case of an *individual wheat farmer*. In order to have the use of the land he must pay the land's going price to prevent it from being transferred to another wheat farmer. From his point of view, therefore, the whole of the payment he makes is a transfer payment to land.

Second, consider the particular *agricultural industry* that produces wheat. In order to secure land for wheat production, it will be necessary to offer at least as much as the land could earn when put to other uses. From the point of view of the wheat industry, that part of the payment made for land which is equal to what it could earn in its next most remunerative use is transfer payment. If that much is not paid, the land will be transferred to the alternative use. If, however, land particularly suitable for wheat growing is scarce relative to the demand for it, then the actual payment for the use of this land may be above the transfer earnings; the additional payment is economic rent.

Third, consider the choice between *agricultural* and *urban uses*. Land is highly mobile between agricultural uses because its location is usually of little importance. For urban uses, however, location is critical. From this point of view, land is, of course, completely immobile. If there is a shortage of land in central Chicago, any land that is available will command a high price, but no matter what the price, land in rural areas will not move into central Chicago. The high payments made to urban land are thus well in excess of what is necessary to prevent it from being transferred back to agricultural uses; the payment is thus economic rent.[4]

Capital. If a piece of capital equipment has several uses, then the analysis of land or labor can be repeated. Much equipment, however, has only one use. For capital that is virtually immobile, any income arising from its use is rent.

---

[4] From the point of view of any particular urban use, however, high rents are transfer earnings. Movie theaters, for example, account for but a small portion of the total demand for land in central Chicago; if there were no movie theaters at all, rentals of land would be about what they are now. Thus the industry faces an elastic supply of land in central Chicago, and the whole of the price it pays for its land is a transfer payment that must be paid to keep the land from transferring to other urban uses. Thus the old examination question "Is it correct to say that the price of movie seats is high in central Chicago because the price of land is high?" should be answered in the affirmative, not in the negative, as examiners often seemed to expect. The view that the prices of *all* goods and services in central Chicago are high because rents are high should, however, be denied.

Assume, for example, that when some machine was installed, it was expected to earn $5,000 per year in excess of all its operating costs, and suppose also that the machine has no scrap value. If the demand for the product falls so that the machine can earn only $2,000, it will still pay to keep it in operation rather than scrap it. Indeed, it will pay to do so as long as it yields any return at all over its operating costs.[5] Thus, all the return earned by the installed machine is economic rent because it will still be allocated to its present use—it has no other—as long as it yields even $1 above its operating costs. *Once the machine has been installed,* any net income that it earns is economic rent.

The machine will, however, wear out eventually, and it will not be replaced unless it is expected to earn a return over its lifetime sufficient to make it a good investment for its owner. Thus, over the long run some of the revenue earned by the machine is transfer earnings; if the revenue is not earned, a machine will not continue to be allocated to that use in the long run.

Do Factors Move in Response to Changes in Earnings?

The theory developed in this chapter predicts that factors move among uses, industries, and places, taking both monetary and nonmonetary rewards into account. It predicts they will move in such a way as to maximize the net advantages to the owners of factors.

We now ask: Does the world behave in the way theory predicts? Because there are impediments to the mobility of factors, there may be lags in the response of factors to changes in relative prices, but the question remains: Do adjustments occur even though there are impediments?

Land and Capital

The most casual observation reveals that the allocative system works pretty much as described by the

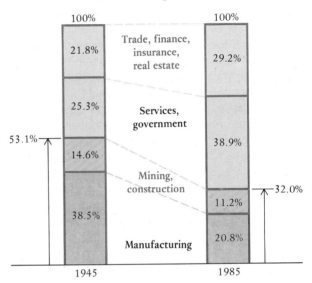

FIGURE 18-4 The Changing Composition of the Nonagricultural Labor Force

In less than half a century a major shift has occurred in labor utilization. In 1945 over 50 percent of the nonagricultural labor force was in the industrial sectors (largely blue collar), including manufacturing, mining, and construction. This figure had decreased to 32 percent by 1985. The shift was to the service-oriented sectors (largely white collar) of government, trade, finance, and other services. This process of de-industrialization was especially dramatic in the 1970s. In that period there was a net increase of 19 million jobs in the United States, 87 percent of which were in the service sector.

theory with respect to land and capital. Land is transferred from one crop to another in response to changes in the relative profitabilities of the crops. Land on the edge of town is transferred from rural to urban uses as soon as it can earn substantially more as a building site than as a cornfield. Materials and capital goods move from use to use in response to changes in relative earnings in those uses.

This is hardly surprising. Nonmonetary benefits do not loom large for factors other than labor, and the theories of both competition and monopoly predict that quantities supplied will respond to increases in earnings generated by increased demand.

[5] Recall the proposition in Chapter 12, page 214, that it pays a firm to continue in operation in the short run as long as it can cover its variable costs of production.

BOX 18-2

De-industrialization: From Big Steel to Big Mac

The growth of employment in services and retail trade over the last two decades has been dramatic. Employment in these two sectors has risen three times faster than total employment, and sixteen times faster than employment in the goods-producing sector. The growth was concentrated in three areas: eating and drinking places, health services, and business services. In the United States in 1985, *total* employment in the manufacturing of durable goods (under 11 million persons) was less than the *increase* in employment in services over the previous two decades.

This is in one sense good news, for without these new job opportunities, overall unemployment would have been far worse. But the substitution of service employment and production for industrial employment and production is a mixed blessing to the American economy. High levels of productivity and the opportunities for growth in productivity have fueled high standards of living and the growth of the economy. But productivity is lower and the opportunities for growth are much more limited in service industries than in goods-producing industries. The possibilities for substituting capital for labor are arguably less in selling hamburgers than in producing metal and metal products.

The nature of employment has also changed as a result of the changing composition of output. There is more part-time work and more contact with the public. The role of women in the work force has increased, and women are concentrated in the sectors of greatest expansion in job opportunities. In many industrial areas where men have been laid off by the steel mills and auto factories, their wives and daughters have found jobs in restaurants and offices while the men search in vain. The fact that in these areas many women are working while many men are not working reflects an important change in the American economy—and in American society—over the last decade.

Does it matter to the economy if one kind of worker (e.g., service workers) increasingly replaces another kind (e.g., industrial workers)? It is a change that worries many labor leaders and industrialists. Service jobs usually pay less than jobs in manufacturing, particularly in such basic manufacturing industries as steel and automobiles. A typical steelworker earns $10 to $12 per hour, a McDonald's kitchen worker less than $4 per hour. Because of this differential, each service job generally makes a smaller contribution to national income than each manufacturing job. Moreover, the levels of productivity and the opportunities for improvement tend to be smaller in many service industries. Of course, nothing preordains that one manufacturing job will be replaced by one service job. If enough new jobs are created in lower productivity sectors, national income may grow.

In the case of nonhuman factors—land and capital—there is strong evidence that factors move in response to earnings differentials.

Labor

Labor can be mobile in many ways. Labor can move among occupations, industries, firms, skill categories, and regions. These categories are not exclusive; to change occupation from a farm laborer to a steelworker, for example, a man will also have to change industries and probably where he lives.

There are, of course, barriers to labor mobility.

Unions, pension funds, and other institutions can and do inhibit labor mobility in various ways. State governments have erected barriers to mobility in the form of occupational licensing, differential training requirements, and the like.

Nevertheless, the documented mobility of labor is impressive. When wages on the West Coast soared during World War II, workers flocked there to take lucrative jobs in the rapidly expanding aircraft and shipbuilding industries. When new oil fields were discovered in Alaska and northern Canada, high wages attracted welders, riveters, and the many other types of labor the oil fields required.

During the period 1950 to 1970 workers migrated steadily from the South to the North in search of jobs. During the 1970s this trend slowed, and in the late 1970s and early 1980s it was reversed as the movement of industry to the Sun Belt created new jobs in the South.

Figure 18-4 on page 335 illustrates another dimension of labor mobility. The shifts among sectors that have occurred in the postwar period indicate the substantial adaptability of the labor force to changing patterns of demand for the outputs of various sectors. The process of "de-industrialization" evident in this figure is discussed further in Box 18-2.

From decade to decade, labor is highly mobile in response to changes in demand.

Of course, labor does not always move promptly and fully in response to changes in earnings. Thus not all behavior is neatly explained by the theory. For example, despite the recent relative decline in academic salaries and job opportunities, many more students persist in getting Ph.D.s in fields such as history and English than can reasonably expect to find jobs that will require or utilize their training. Economists can speculate about such behavior, for example, by saying that for many students graduate education is a consumption good as well as an investment or that the nonmonetary advantages of an academic position are large enough to be worth the gamble of finding a job. But such hypotheses go beyond elementary economics. At this stage we have to be satisfied with a theory that explains much, but not all, behavior.

Summary

1. The functional distribution of income refers to the shares of total national income going to each of the major factors of production; it focuses on sources of income. The size distribution of income refers to the shares of total national income going to various groups of households; it focuses only on the size of income, not its source.

2. The income of a factor of production is composed of two elements: the price paid per unit of the factor and the quantity of the factor used. The determination of factor prices and quantities is an application of the same price theory used to determine product prices and quantities.

3. The demand for any factor of production is a derived demand because the factor is used as an input into the production of goods and services. The total demand for a factor of production will be the sum of the individual derived demands for it in each activity where it is used. The total supply of any factor must be allocated among all the uses to which it can possibly be put.

4. Factor mobility is the ease with which a factor can move to alternative uses. Land is mobile between uses, but cannot change its geographical location. Capital equipment is durable, but firms regularly replace discarded or worn out machinery with totally different machines and so change the composition of the nation's capital stock gradually but steadily. Labor mobility is greatly affected by nonmonetary considerations. The longer the period of time, the more mobile is a factor.

5. In competitive factor markets prices are determined by demand and supply, but factor price differentials occur. Dynamic differentials in the earnings of different units of factors of production serve as signals of a disequilibrium and induce factor movements that eventually

remove the differentials. Equilibrium differentials reflect differences among units of factors as well as nonmonetary benefits of different jobs; they can persist indefinitely.

6. The hypothesis of equal net advantage is a theory of the allocation of the total supply of factors to particular uses. Owners of factors will choose the use that produces the greatest net advantage, allowing for monetary and nonmonetary advantages of a particular employment. In so doing, they will cause dynamic factor price differentials to be eliminated.

7. Transfer earnings are what must be paid to a factor to prevent it from transferring to another use. Economic rent is the difference between a factor's transfer earnings and its actual earnings. Whenever the supply curve is upward-sloping, part of the factor's total pay is transfer earnings and part is rent. The proportion of each depends upon the mobility of the factor; the more narrowly defined the use, the larger the fraction that is transfer earnings and the smaller the fraction is economic rent.

8. Factor mobility is typically greater for nonhuman factors than it is for labor. Even where impediments to mobility exist, factors (including labor) tend to move in response to persistent differences in earnings or employment opportunities.

Topics for Review

Functional distribution and size distribution of income
Derived demand
Factor mobility
Dynamic and equilibrium differentials
Hypothesis of equal net advantage
Transfer earnings and economic rent

Discussion Questions

1. Other things being equal, how would you expect each of the following to affect the size distribution of after-tax income? Do any of them lead to clear predictions about the functional distribution of income?
   a. An increase in unemployment
   b. Rapid population growth in an already crowded city
   c. An increase in food prices relative to other prices
   d. An increase in social insurance benefits and taxes

2. Consider the effects on the overall level of income inequality of each of the following.
   a. Increasing participation of women in the labor force as many women shift from work in the home to full-time jobs
   b. Increasing use by California produce growers of migrant workers who are in the United States illegally
   c. Increasing numbers of minority group members studying law and medicine

3. Distinguish between economic rent and transfer earnings in the following payments for factor services.
   a. The $750 per month a landlord receives for an apartment leased to students
   b. The salary of the President
   c. The $1,000,000 annual salary of Patrick Ewing
   d. The salary of a window cleaner who says, "It's dangerous, dirty work, but it beats driving a truck."
4. Which of the following are dynamic and which are equilibrium differentials in factor prices?
   a. Differences in earnings of football coaches and wrestling coaches
   b. A "bonus for signing on" offered by a construction company seeking carpenters in a tight labor market
   c. Differences in monthly rental charged for three-bedroom houses in different parts of the same metropolitan area
5. Equal pay for equal work is a commonly held goal. But "equal work" is hard to define. What would be the consequences of legislation enforcing equal pay for what turned out to be unequal work?
6. Rent controls often succeed in reducing rents paid by tenants in the short run, but at the cost of a growing housing shortage in the long run. What does this tell us about the nature of the earning of landlords in the short and the long run? (Consider the categories of rent and transfer earnings.)
7. Look again at the data in Figure 18-4. What economic forces might have given rise to the labor movements described there? What would you predict about the pattern of wages in the various categories in the figure? (Check the facts to see if your predictions were correct.) For those occupations that saw an increase in wages, did the increases represent increased transfer payments or economic rents?

19

More on Factor Demand and Supply

What determines whether the demand for a factor will be elastic? Why are the supplies of some factors highly inelastic, so that most of their earnings are economic rents, while the supplies of other factors are highly elastic, so that most of their earnings are transfer payments? Why do the supply and demand curves for some factors shift frequently, while the curves for other factors remain relatively stable? To deal with these and many related subjects, we need to inquire further into the determinants of the demand for and supply of factors of production.

The Demand for Factors

As we saw in Chapter 18, since the demand for any factor depends on the existence of a demand for the goods it helps produce, it is described as a *derived demand*. We now consider in detail the economic forces that influence that demand.

Marginal Productivity Theory

All profit-maximizing firms, whether they are selling under conditions of perfect competition, monopolistic competition, oligopoly, or monopoly, produce to the point at which marginal cost equals marginal revenue. Similarly, all profit-maximizing firms hire units of the variable factor up to the point at which the last unit employed adds as much to revenue as it does to cost. Thus it is a simple implication of profit maximization that firms hire units of a variable factor up to the point where the marginal cost of the factor (i.e., the addition to the total cost resulting from the employment of one more unit) equals the marginal revenue produced by the factor.

Because we use the term *marginal revenue* to denote the change in revenue resulting when the rate of product sales is increased by one unit, we shall use another term, **marginal revenue product (MRP),** to refer to the change in revenue caused by the sale of the product contributed by *an additional unit of the variable factor*. [29] Using this term, state the equilibrium condition above as:

Marginal cost of the variable = Marginal revenue product
factor of that factor

If the firm is unable to influence the price of the variable factor by buying more or less of it, that is, if the firm is a price taker when *buying*

370-348

factors, then the marginal cost of the factor is merely its price. The cost, for example, of adding an extra laborer to the firm's work force is the wage that must be paid. In these circumstances firms adjust the quantity of the variable factor they hire at the established market price, and we may state the equilibrium condition as:

$$w = MRP$$

where w is the price of a unit of the factor.

A profit-maximizing firm that is a price taker in factor markets hires a factor up to the point at which the price of the factor equals the marginal revenue product.

The proposition that in equilibrium factors will be paid the value of their respective marginal products is often called the **marginal productivity theory of distribution.**[1] This is nothing more than an implication of profit maximization. Over the years, however, the theory as been the subject of many emotional attacks and defenses and without doubt has often been seriously misunderstood. Some of these issues are taken up further in Box 19-1.

The Slope of the Demand Curve

What happens to quantity demanded when a factor's price rises? One influence operates through the link between a factor's price and the price of the good or service it helps to produce. Consider, for example, a rise in the wages of carpenters, which increases the cost of producing houses. The rise in cost shifts the supply curve of houses to the left. This leads to a rise in the price of houses and to a decrease in the number of houses sold. If fewer houses can be sold, fewer will be built and smaller quantities of factors will be needed. Thus there will be a decrease in the quantity demanded of carpenters used to produce houses.

A second influence operates through the principle of substitution. When the price of one factor goes up, other relatively cheaper factors will be substi-

[1] The way in which marginal productivity theory can be used to derive a firm's demand curve for a factor is discussed in the appendix to this chapter.

tuted. For example, if carpenters' wages rise relative to those of factory workers, some prefabricated door and window frames made by factory workers will be used to replace on-the-job carpenters.

Demand curves for factors slope downward because a change in a factor price influences the price of commodities that are produced using the factor and also gives rise to the substitution of relatively cheaper for relatively more expensive factors.

Elasticity of Factor Demand

The elasticity of demand for a factor measures the degree of the response of the quantity demanded to a change in its price. The three major forces that determine the elasticity of the demand curve for a factor, sometimes called the *principles of derived demand,* are elasticity of demand for the final commodity, ease of substitution, and importance of the factor.

Elasticity of demand for the final commodity. Other things equal, the more elastic the demand is for the commodity that the factor helps to make, the more elastic the demand for the factor will be. If an increase in the price of the commodity causes a large fall in the quantity demanded, that is, if the demand for the commodity is elastic, there will be a large decrease in the quantity of a factor needed to produce it in response to a rise in the factor's price. But if an increase in the price of a commodity causes only a small fall in its quantity demanded, that is, if the demand for the commodity is inelastic, there will be only a small decrease in the quantity of the factor required in response to a rise in its price.

Ease of substitution. The greater the ease with which one factor can be substituted for another in response to changes in relative factor prices, the greater the elasticity of demand for those factors. The ease of substitution depends on the substitutes available and technical conditions of production. Even in the short run it is possible to vary factor proportions in surprising ways. For example, in automobile manufacture and in building construction, glass and steel can be substituted for each other sim-

BOX 19-1

The Marginal Productivity Theory of Distribution

The marginal productivity theory is simply an implication of profit maximization: Any firm that is maximizing its profits must hire each variable factor up to the point at which the last unit hired adds just as much to costs (the price of the factor) as it does to revenue (the marginal revenue product). Nonetheless, misconceptions about the theory exist. (Indeed, in certain quarters marginal productivity theory is almost a dirty word.) It *seems* to say that each factor, including labor, is paid exactly the value of what it produces. It has been criticized on the grounds that it is inhumane and that it falsely implies that the market leads to factor prices that, however low they might be, are "just." Both criticisms rest on misconceptions of what the theory says and implies.

Inhumanity?

Marginal productivity theory does not take into account the differences between human services and other services. Some think the theory inhumane because it treats human labor as it treats a ton of coal or a wagonload of fertilizer.

The marginal productivity theory is only a theory of the *demand* for a factor. It predicts only what profit-maximizing employers would like to buy. It predicts that desired purchases of a factor depend on the price of the factor, the technical conditions of production, and the demand for the product produced using the factor.

Supply conditions undoubtedly differ between human and nonhuman factors, but these differences are accommodated within the theory of distribution. No evidence has been gathered to indicate that it is necessary to have separate theories of the demand for human and nonhuman factors of production.

Justice?

In a world of perfectly competitive factor markets the theory predicts that in equilibrium all factors receive payment equal to the values of their marginal products. Some eminent economists in the past spoke as if this led to a just distribution because factors were rewarded according to the value of their own contributions to the national product. "From each according to his ability; to each according to his own contribution" might have been the slogan for this group. Many critics of the low levels of wages which then prevailed reacted passionately to a theory that was claimed to justify them.

According to the marginal productivity theory, each worker receives the value of what one more worker would add to production if that worker were taken on while all other factors were held constant. If 1 million similar workers are employed, then each of the 1 million will receive a wage equal to the extra product that would have been contributed by the millionth worker if he or she had been hired while capital and all other factors remained unchanged. Whether such a distribution of the national product is or is not "just" may be debated. The marginal productivity theory does not, however, contribute to that debate; it does not say that each unit of a factor receives as income the value of *its own* contribution to production. Indeed, where many factors cooperate in production, it is generally impossible to divide total production into the amounts contributed by each unit of each factor of production.

It is possible both to hold that marginal productivity tends to determine how people get paid and to believe that government policies which change the distribution of income are desirable. Many economists hold both positions.

---

ply by varying the dimensions of the windows. Grain in the form of gasohol can substitute for oil as automobile fuel, and so on.

Nor are such direct short-run substitutions the end of the story. In the long run a factory that has a

particular technique embodied in its equipment (and thus cannot easily vary factor proportions in the short run) can be replaced. Plant and equipment are continually being replaced, and more or less capital intensive methods can be adopted in new plants in response to changes in factor prices. Similarly, engines that use less gasoline per mile are developed when the price of gasoline rises.

Importance of the factor.   The larger the fraction of total costs that are payments to a factor, the greater the elasticity of demand for the factor. Suppose that wages are 50 percent of the costs of producing a good, while raw materials account for 15 percent. A 10 percent rise in the price of labor raises the cost of producing the commodity by 5 percent (10 percent of 50 percent), but a 10 percent rise in the price of raw materials raises the cost of the commodity by only 1.5 percent (10 percent of 15 percent). The larger the increase in cost, the larger the increase in the commodity's price, and hence the larger the decrease in the quantity demanded of the commodity and the factors used to make it.[2]

The Supply of Factors

There are two important economic questions concerning the supply of factors: To what extent do economic forces determine the *total supply* of a factor to the whole economy? To what extent do economic forces determine the *supply available to a particular industry?* In Chapter 18 we largely ignored the total supply and concentrated on the supply to a particular industry. In this chapter we return to the question of the role of economic forces in determining the total supply of factors.

Let us look more closely at why total supply is not fixed, even though there is plainly a finite limit to many natural resources on earth. Although people worry about depleting natural resources, actual exhaustion of resources has not arisen often. Frequently

newly discovered or previously unexploited sources of a resource maintain the supply, although perhaps at higher cost than existing supplies. Ultimately, of course, there is an upper limit, and resources can be exhausted; worse, they can be contaminated or otherwise despoiled so as to be useless before they are consumed. But even when the supply of one resource is exhausted, substitutes are developed. The exhaustion of high-grade iron ore reserves in the Mesabi Range did not end steel production in the United States, partly because ways to use low-grade iron ores once thought worthless were discovered and partly because new supplies in Labrador and the Caribbean were developed.

Shortages often lead to their own correction. For example, as oil becomes scarce, its price will rise; users will turn to substitutes to meet their demands, synthetic oils will be developed, and oil companies will explore for new sources. A sufficient increase in the price of oil would also make it economically worthwhile to process the vast quantities of previously unexploited shale oil.

As the discussion of dynamic differentials and quasi-rents in Chapter 18 suggested, a factor may be immobile in the short run, but mobile in the long run. Similar considerations apply to the total supply of a factor.

Time is an important element in the determination of the total supply of a factor. The longer the time period, the more responsive the total supply of any factor will be to economic forces.

Consider in turn the total supply of three key factors of production.

The Total Supply of Capital

The supply of capital in a country consists of the stock of existing machines, plant, equipment, and so on. Capital is a manufactured factor of production, and its total supply is in no sense fixed, although it changes only slowly. Each year the stock of capital goods is diminished by the amount that wears out and increased by the amount that is produced. On balance, the trend has been for the capital stock to grow over the decades. In the final section of this

---

[2] This is necessarily true when there is only one variable factor of production. When there are many variable factors, we must also consider the ease of substitution. For example, copper tubing may be a small part of building costs, but if aluminum tubing is nearly a perfect substitute, the demand for copper tubing may be quite elastic. In contrast, the demand for tubing of some kind may be quite inelastic. The text statement is another example of something that is correct *other things being equal:* For a given degree of substitutability among factors, the demand for any factor will be more elastic the larger the proportion of total costs that are payments to that factor.

chapter we consider the theory of investment that describes how the stock of capital changes over time.

The Total Supply of Arable Land

If the term *land* is used to refer to the total area of dry land, then the total supply of land in a country will be almost completely fixed. It was nineteenth century practice (following Ricardo) to define land as the *original and inexhaustible powers of the soil*. But dust bowls were a phenomenon unknown to Ricardo, who also did not know that the deserts of North Africa were once fertile plains. Clearly, the supply of fertile land is not fixed. Considerable care and effort is required to sustain the productive power of land. If the return to land is low, its fertility may be destroyed within a short time. Moreover, scarcity and high prices may make it worthwhile to increase the supply of arable land by irrigation and other forms of reclamation.

The Total Supply of Labor

The total supply of labor means the total number of hours of work that the population is willing to supply. This quantity is often called the **supply of effort.** It has many obvious determinants, such as the rewards for working, the age at which people enter the labor force and retire from it, and the length of the conventional work week. It also has many less obvious ones. For one example, a social trend such as the women's liberation movement affects labor force participation. For another, the whole pattern of tax rates, unemployment insurance, and welfare payments affects the relative advantages of working and not working.

The evidence is overwhelming that such things matter. What is debated, however, is how *large* their impact is. As is discussed in Box 19-2, the evidence shows some, but relatively small, adverse effects of taxes on the supply of effort. However, welfare schemes have sometimes been a severe disincentive to work. While most people prefer working to being on welfare, it is not surprising that they respond rationally to an incentive system that severely penalizes any work done by welfare recipients.

Distribution Theory: Some Evidence

Does the theory of distribution satisfactorily explain the allocation process in our economy? In Chapter 18 we reviewed the impressive array of evidence that despite the presence of inpediments to factor mobility, such as licensing and union restrictions for labor, safety requirements for capital equipment, and zoning laws for land, factors do move in response to changes in factor earnings. In the following section we examine whether market forces do in fact play the roles predicted by the theories of competition and monopoly in determining factor prices and the allocation of resources.

Do Market Conditions Determine Factor Earnings?

Some commentators have denied the relevance of the theory of distribution outlined in this and the preceding chapter. They argue that prices of products and factors bear little relation to market conditions because prices and wages are administered by oligopolies and giant unions. Entry barriers in industry and mobility barriers for factors of production, the argument continues, prevent significant movements of resources in response to product and factor price differentials that exist or develop. Should we therefore conclude that the theory of income distribution that we have developed is irrelevant to the real world? Let us see what a careful look at the evidence says.

Capital and Land

Many nonhuman factors are sold on competitive markets. The theory predicts that changes in the earnings of these factors will be associated with changes in market conditions. The evidence overwhelmingly supports this prediction, as shown by the following examples.

The prices of plywood, tin, rubber, cotton, and hundreds of other materials fluctuate daily in response to changes in their demand and supply. The responses of factor markets to the many shortages

BOX 19-2

Taxes, Welfare, and the Supply of Effort

Taxes

Many people believe that high income taxes tend to reduce the supply of effort by lowering the incentive for people to work. Such objective evidence as exists, however, suggests that tax cuts do not always increase the supply of effort. Even when they do, the aggregate effect may be small.

A tax cut sets up two opposing forces, and the final effect on the amount of work done by people depends on the relative strengths of each. An example will suggest why this is so. Consider Barry Bluecollar, who has a job on an assembly line. He typically takes off 5 hours a week and so works only 35 hours, with a take-home pay of $8.50 an hour or $297.50 a week. Now suppose there is a tax cut so that his take-home pay rises to $10.00 an hour. He might elect to work a little more, since every hour he works now nets him $10.00 instead of $8.50. If he raises his average weekly hours to 37, he will raise his take-home pay by $72.50 to $370.00. Economists call the tendency to work more because the reward for an hour's work has risen the *substitution effect.*

However, Bluecollar might elect to work a little less, since with the rise in hourly take-home pay, he can have more income *and* get more leisure. Suppose he takes off an extra 3 hours a week. His take-home pay is now $320.00 a week (32 hours at $10.00 compared to 35 hours at $8.50 before the tax cut). Now he has 3 more hours of leisure a week *and* $22.50 more income. Economists call the tendency to work less because it is possible to have more income *and* more leisure the *income effect.*

If the substitution effect dominates, people respond to a tax cut by working more. If the income effect dominates, they work less. Either result is pos-

sible, so a tax cut may raise or lower the amount of work people want to do.

A good deal of research has been done on the effect of tax rate increases. It has shown that in response to a rise in taxes some people work fewer hours because the reward is less, while others feel poorer and work more to maintain their after-tax income. The most recent research, however, suggests at most a small net disincentive up to a level of marginal tax rate of 50 percent, such as existed in the United States until 1987. The sharp decrease in maximum rates that became effective then will provide important additional evidence within a few years.

Welfare

Do welfare payments and other aids to the poor make them less willing to take jobs? While many of those receiving payments are unable to find work, there is no doubt that some welfare rules discourage work by heavily taxing welfare recipients on much or all of any income they might earn. If a family's welfare payment of, say, $500 per month is decreased dollar for dollar by any earnings, this amounts to a 100 percent tax on the first $500 of earnings per month. The person who could earn $400 by part-time work would have no economic incentive to do so.

In recent years many welfare schemes have recognized this problem and allowed persons on welfare to keep a major fraction of any extra money they earn. (For further discussion of changes made under the Reagan administration see Chapter 21.) Thus, although some disincentives to working do exist, the disincentives can be minimized when the financial aids are structured so as to leave those who can work with some incentive to do so.

---

that seemed to characterize the American economy in the 1970s provide dramatic confirmation. When the price of agricultural commodities shot up following a grain shortage, farm income soared. When oil became scarce, prices rose and oil producers and owners of oil properties found their profits and income rising rapidly. Not only did the relative prices of oil products rise, so did the relative prices of commodities, such as chemical fertilizers and air travel, that make use of petroleum products. When oil became abundant in the early 1980s, these trends were reversed.

Land in the heart of growing cities provides another example. Such land is fixed in supply, and values rise steadily in response to increasing demand for it.[3] Land values may even be high enough to make it worthwhile to destroy durable buildings in order to convert the land to more productive uses. The skyscraper is a monument to the high value of urban land. The increase in the price of land on the periphery of every growing city is an observable example of the workings of the market.

Similar results occur in markets that are far from being perfectly competitive. In 1979 the price of power in virtually all forms rose sharply in response to the energy shortage caused by the doubling of the price of oil. Oligopolists producing key metals such as zinc, molybdenum, steel, and aluminum have raised prices when their costs of production rose or when demand outran production. Further examples can be found in almost every issue of the *Wall Street Journal,* but the point should now be clear:

The prices and earnings of nonhuman factors are successfully predicted by market theories of factor pricing.

Labor

When we apply the theory to labor, we encounter two important sets of complications. First, labor being the human factor of production, nonmonetary considerations loom large in its incentive patterns, and thus market fluctuations may have less effect. Second, the competitive and noncompetitive elements of labor markets occur in different proportions from market to market. These complications make it harder to see if market conditions determine factor earnings. Nevertheless, there is a mass of evidence to support the view that they do.

Market fluctuations. Do earnings respond to normal fluctuations of demand and supply as the theory predicts? The evidence shows that they often do. For

example, with the advent of the automobile, skilled carriage makers saw the demand for their services decline rapidly. Earnings fell, and many older workers found that they had been earning substantial economic rents for their scarce, but highly specific skills. They suffered large income cuts when they moved to other industries. Workers who acquired skills wanted in the newly expanding automotive industry found that the demands for their services and their incomes rose rapidly.

More recently there has been a large increase in the earnings of premier professional athletes. In part this has resulted from rising demand due to expansion in the number of major league teams. In part it has resulted from increased revenues to the teams and leagues from televising sports, which has increased the marginal revenue product of the athletes. And in part it has resulted from athletes' acquiring the right to offer their services to more than one employer, thereby reducing the ability of employers to hold down wages by acting as single buyers, or *monopsonists.* (Monopsony is discussed in the next chapter.)

One group that has been suffering the consequences of factor price determination on competitive markets is college graduates. In recent years the earnings of college graduates have fallen relative to other workers as employment opportunities dropped sharply, especially for new graduates. The downturn is explained partly by slackening demand due to changes in industrial structure (e.g., substituting sophisticated computers for college-trained persons) and partly by continued growth of supply as the "baby-boomers" finish college.

Wage changes induced by market conditions have little to do with abstract notions of justice or merit. If you have some literary talent, why can you make a lot of money writing copy for an advertising agency, but very little money writing poems? It is not because an economic dictator or group of philosophers has decided that advertising is more valuable than poetry. It is because in the economy there is a large demand for advertising and a small demand for poetry.

Effects of monopoly elements. A strong union— one able to bargain effectively with management and

---

[3] A friend is fond of saying, "Nobody buys land any more; its price is much too high because everybody wants it."

to control entry of labor into the field—can raise wages well above the competitive level. The high earnings attract others to the occupation or industry, and the privileged position can be maintained only if the supply of labor can be effectively restricted. Highly skilled plasterers, plumbers, and electricians have all managed to restrict entry into their trades and as a result maintain wages well above their transfer earnings. Many similar cases have been documented.

Not only can monopoly elements raise incomes above their competitive levels, they can also prevent wages from falling in response to decreases in demand. (Of course, if the demand disappears more or less overnight, there is nothing any union can do to maintain incomes.)

Consider coal mining in the years just after World War II. From 1945 to 1965 the production of coal declined as oil, gas, and electricity were steadily substituted for it. The coal that was produced was mined by ever more capital-using and labor-saving techniques. Both these forces led employment to shrink steadily. Coal mining was plainly a declining labor market from 1945 until 1965. Competitive theory would predict relatively low wages and low incomes, followed by exit of the most mobile coal miners and hard times for those who decide to stick it out.

Precisely this happened in Canada. Average wages, which in 1945 had been 36 percent above those in manufacturing, fell steadily until in 1965 they were 8 percent below those in manufacturing, and employment declined to 35 percent of its previous level. In the United States, however, this was *not* the pattern. Faced with a similar decline in production, relative wages actually rose in coal mining, from 18 percent above manufacturing in 1945 to 34 percent above it in 1965. Employment did fall; indeed, by 1965 employment was only 30 percent of the 1945 level. But those who kept jobs did relatively well.

What happened was that in the United States a powerful union, the United Mine Workers, prevented wages from falling. By raising wages despite falling demand, the union actually accelerated the decline in employment. The lower employment that accompanied the "high wage" policy of the United Mine Workers discouraged the young from waiting

for jobs in the industry. As workers left the industry because of retirement, ill health, or death, they were not replaced.[4]

All these examples support the general proposition:

Earnings of labor respond to significant changes in market conditions.

Some Efficiency Implications

The theory and evidence presented in this and the preceding chapter can be summarized in two central propositions.

1. **Factors will move between alternative uses so as to maximize the net advantage to the factor's owner.**
2. **Individual profit-maximizing employers will hire any factor up to the point where the last unit hired adds as much to costs as it does to revenue.**

Together these two propositions have a powerful implication for economic efficiency. We present the argument in terms of labor, but it also applies to capital and land. The argument is developed in stages by first considering a special case that makes the proposition considerably easier to interpret and understand.

Absence of nonmonetary advantages. Suppose that all alternative uses for labor were alike in all respects so that none had any nonmonetary benefits or disadvantages relative to any other. In this circumstance the hypothesis of equal *net* advantage would mean that labor would move between alternative jobs and occupations until the wage rates in all were equal. When there are no nonmonetary advantages, only the monetary advantage, that is, the wage, of alternatives need be equalized.

The two propositions listed above thus imply

---

[4] After 1965 the demand for coal miners rebounded as the demand for coal to produce electricity surged. As a result, in both the United States and in Canada, as theory predicts, employment *and* relative wages in coal mining rose sharply.

that, in the absence of nonmonetary advantages, the marginal revenue product of labor will be equalized in all uses. When that condition holds, the value of total output cannot be increased by shifting labor from one use to another, since the increase in the value of the output of the firm labor moves to will be exactly offset by the fall in the value of the output of the firm labor is moved from.

If there are no nonmonetary advantages to alternative uses of a factor, its marginal revenue product will be equalized in all uses; as a result, the value of total output is maximized.

Effect of nonmonetary advantages.   If alternative uses of labor involve differing nonmonetary advantages, then the value of the marginal product of labor will differ among uses by an amount reflecting the difference in nonmonetary advantages. Hence output will not reach its maximum value; output could be increased by moving labor from a use where the value of its marginal product is low (because the use has a high nonmonetary advantage) to a use where the value is high (because that use has a low nonmonetary advantage).

But the "psychic" value of output would not go up, because the increase in output of goods and services would be offset by the "psychic" cost to the worker from moving from a less preferred activity to a more preferred one. For example, a carpenter in Phoenix, Arizona, may earn a lower wage and have a lower marginal product than one in Juneau, Alaska. If she moves to Alaska, the economy's value of output of carpentry services would go up. But if the initial difference in wages, and hence in marginal products, reflected the net nonmonetary advantage to the carpenter of living in Arizona, the increase in value of output of carpentry services will be exactly matched by the decrease in nonmonetary returns to the carpenter.

The message is that factor prices reflect the value of factors in alternative uses and thus play a key role in their efficient allocation. If factors are not priced according to their scarcity, there will be no easy means of allocating them efficiently among competing uses. This is not just idle speculation. In the early years of the communist experiment in Russia, inter-est, which is the price paid for capital, was banned for ideological reasons. This led to serious waste due to the misallocation of capital. This and related ideological issues concerning interest and capital are taken up in Box 19-3.

Capital and Interest

In this section we explore a complication that applies in some measure to all factors of production, but that is most clear in the case of capital goods. The complication arises because some factors of production, such as capital goods, are durable, lasting for many years or even decades. It is convenient to think of a capital good's lifetime as being divided into shorter periods that we refer to as *production periods* or, equivalently, *rental periods*.

The Stock of Capital and the Flow of Capital Services

The durability of capital goods makes it necessary to distinguish between the capital good itself and the flow of services that it provides in a given production period. This distinction is just a particular case of the general distinction between stocks and flows first encountered on page 21.

Two Prices for Capital

The distinction between stocks and flows means that we can identify two prices for capital goods, rental price and purchase price.

Rental price.   The price paid to use a capital good for a period of time is called the *rental price of capital*. Renting a capital good entitles the renter to the services that the capital good generates over the rental period. Our earlier discussion of the marginal productivity theory of factor pricing relates directly to the services of capital and thus to the rental price of such services.

The rental price of capital is the amount a firm would pay to obtain the services of the capital

BOX 19-3

Capital, Capitalists, and Capitalism

The two most essential characteristics of capital goods are that they are produced inputs into further production rather than things found in nature, and that they tend to be durable, lasting for many periods of production.

A capitalist is one who owns capital goods. The role of the capitalist is interpreted differently in different economic philosophies. For example, to many Marxists the capitalist is a villain; to many socialists the capitalist is at best a dispensable drone; to many conservatives the capitalist is the hero who steers the economy through the risky channels that lead to ever higher living standards.

Ideology aside, if there is capital, someone must own it. Capital may be predominantly in private hands, in which case the economy is sometimes described as *capitalist,* or it may be predominantly owned by the state, in which case the economy is described as socialist or communist. In virtually all economies ownership is mixed; some capital is owned privately and some publicly.

No matter who owns the capital goods, such goods are indispensable in the productive process. A primitive society in which there are no capital goods—no spear, no lever, no stone for grinding grain, no jug for carrying water—has never occurred in recorded human history.

Since resources must be used in the manufacture of capital goods, such goods have scarcity value. Any economic system interested in maximizing production will want to allocate scarce capital to its most productive uses. One effective way of doing this is to assign a rental price to capital that reflects its opportunity cost and to allow firms to use more capital only if the capital earns enough to cover this price. Charging producers for use of capital serves such important functions that it is hard to eliminate it without serious consequences.

Early communist rulers in Russia thought differently. Payments for the use of capital were officially barred during the years following the Russian Revolution of 1917 on the ground that a communist society should purge itself of this reminder of capitalism. But this left no way of deciding how to allocate scarce capital efficiently among its many competing uses. Indeed, prices are such an efficient allocative device that today all communist states use them for allocating scarce capital among competing uses. Furthermore, their planners give a good deal of attention to setting the correct rental price for capital.

If capital is privately owned and a price is charged for its use, the payments go to the capitalists and become their income. In communist countries capital is owned by the state, and payments for its use go to the state. The desirability of private versus public ownership of the *means of production* (the term often used in socialist and communist literature to describe capital) is still debated hotly. But the issue of ownership is quite a separate issue from that of whether to charge a rental price for the use of capital.

---

good for a given rental period. It will equal the marginal revenue product of those capital services.

Capital goods may be owned by one firm and used by another. This is especially true for portable equipment with "specialty" uses that any given firm would need only occasionally. It is also obviously true for many dwellings and commercial properties where the owner is the landlord and the renter is the tenant. In such circumstances the term *rental price* refers to the actual payment made per period for the use of the capital good.

A capital good may also be used by the firm that owns it. In this case no rental price is actually paid, but the concept of the rental price is still a useful one. It represents the amount the firm would charge for the use of the good if in its role as owner it were to lease the capital good to another firm; it thus reflects the opportunity cost to the firm of using the capital good itself. The rental price also represents what the firm in its role as user of the capital good would pay if it were to lease it from another firm; it thus reflects the marginal revenue product of the capital good. Although a rental price is neither actually charged nor paid for the use of the good, there is nevertheless an implicit rental price that reflects the value of the services of the capital good to the firm during the period.

Purchase price.   The price paid to acquire ownership of a capital good is called the *purchase price of capital*. Ownership of a capital good entitles the owner to the income generated by the services of the capital good. As we shall see, the purchase price is related to the value of the capital good as an asset and reflects the total value of the benefits that accrue to the owner over the lifetime of the capital good.

As a preliminary to understanding the relationship between the purchase price and the rental price of capital, we must define the key concept of present value.

Present Value of Future Returns

In general, **present value (*PV*)** refers to the value *now* of payments to be made in the future. As we have seen, a capital good is a durable factor of production that yields a stream of payments over a number of future periods. To know what a firm would be willing to pay to own such a capital good, we must be able to calculate the present value of the stream of future payments that the capital good is expected to yield. How is this present value determined?

The present value of a single future payment.   How much would you be prepared to pay *now* to acquire the right to receive $100 in one year's time? One way to answer this question is to ask how much would you have to deposit in a savings bank now in order to have $100 a year from now? It would surely not be profitable for you to pay more than such an amount.

Suppose the interest rate is 5 percent. You have to calculate how much money *now* is equivalent to $100 in one year's time at that rate. Letting X stand for this unknown amount, we can write $X(1.05) = \$100$, and thus $X = \$100/1.05 = \$95.24$. The value

today of $100 next year is $95.24 if the interest rate is 5 percent. That sum is said to be the *present value* of $100 next year.

The particular numerical value depends on the interest rate used to *discount* (i.e., reduce to its present value) the $100 to be received one year hence. If the interest rate is 7 percent, the present value of the $100 receivable next year is $100/1.07 = \$93.46$. In general, the present value of X dollars one year hence at an interest rate of i per year is

$$PV = X/(1 + i)$$

Note that in this expression a rate of interest of 5 percent is written $i = 0.05$, so that $(1 + i) = 1.05$.

The present value of $100 *two* years hence at an interest rate of 5 percent is $100.00/(1.05)(1.05) = \$90.70$. That is, $90.70 put in a savings bank now would be worth $100 in two years. In the first year the deposit would earn interest of $(0.05)(\$90.70) = \$4.54$ and hence after one year it would be worth $95.24. In the second year interest would be earned on this entire amount; interest earned in the second year would equal $(0.05)(\$95.24) = \$4.76$. Hence in two years the deposit would be worth $100. (The payment of interest in the second year on the interest income earned in the first year is known as *compound interest*.)

In general, the present value of X dollars after t years at i percent is

$$PV = X/(1 + i)^t$$

From the formula $PV = X/(1 + i)^t$ we can conclude: The present value of a given sum payable in the future will be smaller the further away the payment date is and the higher the rate of interest.

The present value of an infinite stream of payments. Now consider the present value of a stream of income that continues indefinitely. While at first glance that might seem very high, since as time passes the total received grows without reaching any limit, the far distant payments will not in fact be highly valued now. To find the present value of $100 per year, payable forever, we need only ask how much money would have to be invested now at an interest rate of i percent per year to obtain $100 each year. This is simply $i \times X = \$100$, where i is the interest rate and X the sum required. This tells us that the present value of the stream of $100 a year forever is $100 divided by i, or

$$PV = X/i$$

If the interest rate were 10 percent, the present value would be $1,000. Here, as above, PV is related to the rate of interest: The higher the interest rate, the less the (present) value of distant payments.

The present value of a finite stream of payments. It is also possible to obtain the present value of some finite stream of income. Consider, for example, a machine that yields the following stream of gross returns: $100 now, $275 in one year, $242 in two years, $133.10 in three years, and nothing thereafter. The present value of this flow of income, if the market rate of interest is 10 percent $(1 + i = 1.1)$, is

$$PV = \$100 + (\$275/1.1) +$$
$$(\$242/1.1^2) + (\$133.10/1.1^3)$$
$$= \$100 + \$250 + \$200 + \$100$$
$$= \$650$$

But $650 invested at 10 percent interest will yield a flow of $65 per annum in perpetuity. Thus the irregular finite flow listed above has the same present value as the smooth flow of $65 forever. So in any practical problems concerning an irregular flow, we can substitute an equivalent regular flow, which can be handled with much greater ease.

Present value in general. We have now seen how to compute the present values of amounts at specific future dates and of infinite streams of income. Any income stream can be treated as the sum or difference of such streams and amounts; thus the present value of any stream of future payments can be computed.

For example, receiving $100 per year for three years can be considered either as the present value of $100 next year, plus the PV of $100 two years hence, plus the PV of $100 three years hence; or as the *difference* between the PV of $100 received each year from now to infinity and the PV of $100 received from year four to infinity. There are standard actuarial tables that make calculation of present value easy.

The Purchase Price of a Capital Good

What then determines the market price of any existing asset? The asset might be a piece of land, a machine, a contract for a baseball player's services, or an apartment house. The asset produces a stream of income given by its future marginal revenue products. The present value of this income stream is the value of the asset to whoever purchases it and hence will determine the price that a potential buyer would be willing to pay to acquire it.

The purchase price of a capital good is related to the present value of the future stream of income that the capital good is expected to produce.

The present value of the income stream is also called the **capitalized value** of the income stream.

If the capitalized value of a machine (or other capital good) is greater than the purchase price of such machines, it will pay firms to buy additional machines. As they do, given diminishing productivity, the capitalized value of additional machines will fall. Eventually it will fall to the level of the purchase price of the machines.

The previous discussion shows how the purchase price of capital and the rental price are related. Other things being equal, the higher the rental price, the higher the purchase price; for any given rental price the higher the interest rate, the lower the purchase price; and the further in the future the rental prices occur, the lower the purchase price.

The Rate of Interest and the Capital Stock

It is convenient to think of any firm, or indeed the economy, as having a quantity of capital that can be measured in physical units. The term **capital stock** refers to this total quantity of capital.[5] As with any other factor of production, there is a marginal and an average product of capital. (More precisely, there

[5] The idea of a capital stock measured by a single number is a simplification. Society's stock of capital goods is made up of a diverse array of aids to production such as factories, machines, bridges, and roads.

BOX 19-4

Productivity, Risk, and Return

The Productivity of Capital

In what sense is capital productive? To be productive it must lead to higher output than would be possible without it. The use of capital renders production processes roundabout. Instead of making what is wanted directly, producers engage in the indirect process of first making capital goods that are then used to make consumer goods.

For example, a worker may be employed in a factory that makes machines that are used in mining coal; the coal may be burned by a power plant to make electricity; the electricity may provide power for a factory that makes machine tools; the tools may be used to make a tractor; the tractor may be used by a potato farmer to help in the production of potatoes, which are the final good that may ultimately be eaten by consumers. This kind of indirect production is worthwhile when the farmer, using a tractor, can produce more potatoes than could be produced by applying all the factors of production involved in the chain directly to the production of potatoes (using only such tools as were provided by nature). In fact, the roundabout capital-using method of production often leads to more output than the direct method. The difference between the flows of output that would result from the two methods is called the productivity of capital.

The Return on Capital

Take the receipts from the sale of the goods produced by a firm and subtract the appropriate costs for purchased goods and materials, for labor, for land, and for the manager's own contributed talents. Subtract also an allowance for the taxes the firm will have to pay, and what is left may be called the **gross return to capital.**

It is convenient to divide gross return into four components.

1. **Depreciation** is an allowance for the decrease in the value of a capital good as a result of using it in production.
2. The **pure return on capital** is the amount that capital could earn in a riskless investment in equilibrium.
3. The **risk premium** compensates the owners for the actual risks to the enterprise.
4. Economic profit is the residual after all other deductions have been made from the gross return. It may be positive, negative, or zero.

The **productivity of capital,** also called the *net return on capital,* is its gross return minus the depreciation.

There is an important difference between the first three components, all of which are elements of opportunity cost, and the fourth component. In a market economy positive and negative economic profits are a signal that resources should be reallocated because earnings exceed opportunity costs in some lines of production and fall short of them in other lines. Profits, defined in this way, are thus a phenomenon of disequilibrium. In equilibrium, profits will be zero and the return to capital will be equal to the opportunity cost of capital.

It is usual to deal with a rate of return *per dollar* of capital. This concept requires placing a money value on a unit of capital (the "price of capital goods") and a money value on the stream of earnings resulting from the productivity of capital. If we let X stand for the annual value of the net return on a unit of capital and P for the price of a unit of capital, the ratio X/P may be defined as the **rate of return on capital.**

---

is a marginal and an average product of the flow of services provided by the capital stock.)

We now examine the relationship between the rate of interest in the economy and the size of its capital stock. For simplicity, in the text we only consider the case where there is no risk; Box 19-4 discusses the issues of risk and depreciation and takes up some related terminology.

Consider the simple case where an additional unit of capital gives rise to a steady stream of additional payments into the indefinite future. This makes the basic calculations simple while still conveying accurately the general principles. The purchase price of capital, which we denote by P, then equals the rental price of capital (which equals its marginal revenue product) divided by the interest rate. This condition is expressed in the equation:

$$P = MRP/i \qquad [1]$$

If the interest rate were 5 percent, it would cost 20 times as much (i.e., $1/.05$) to purchase a capital good as it would to rent it for one year. If the interest rate were 10 percent, the purchase price would be only 10 times the rental price.

The marginal efficiency of capital.   *Marginal product* (*MP*) is a *physical* measure of the additional output per period resulting from an additional unit of capital. *Marginal revenue product (MRP)* is a mixture of physical and value measures; it gives the value per period of the additional output produced by an additional unit of capital. (As we have seen, in a competitive market the rental price of capital will be set equal to the marginal revenue product.) To obtain a *value* measure we value both the additional output and the additional capital at their market prices. The ratio gives the monetary return on the marginal dollar's worth of capital and is called the **marginal efficiency of capital (MEC).** The *MEC* is defined as the marginal revenue product divided by the price of capital.

$$MEC = MRP/P \qquad [2]$$

A schedule that relates the *MEC* to the size of the capital stock is called a **marginal efficiency of capital schedule (MEC schedule).** Because capital, like any other factor, is eventually subject to diminishing returns, the value of additional output produced per dollar of additional capital employed will fall. The *MEC* schedule is thus negatively sloped, as shown in Figure 19-1.

To derive the relationship between the stock of capital and the interest rate, we can substitute the equilibrium value of the price of capital from Equa-

FIGURE 19-1   The Marginal Efficiency of Capital

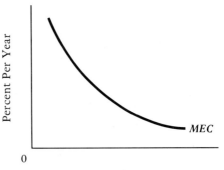

The marginal efficiency of capital (*MEC*) schedule shows the relation between the size of the capital stock and the rate of return on the marginal unit of capital. The *MEC* schedule slopes downward because of the hypothesis of diminishing returns applied to capital. Each successive unit of capital adds less to output than each previous unit. Thus the curve, which relates the value of the additional output of each additional dollar's worth of capital added to the capital stock, is downward-sloping.

tion 1 in Equation 2. This yields the important equilibrium condition:

$$MEC = \frac{MRP}{MRP/i} = i \qquad [3]$$

To see the implications of this condition that the marginal efficiency of capital equals the interest rate, it is useful to distinguish between how it applies to an individual firm and how it applies to the economy as a whole.

Equilibrium in the Individual Firm

The firm, being small relative to the economy, takes the interest rate as given. It pays a firm to purchase a capital good whenever the marginal efficiency of capital is greater than the interest rate that could be earned on the money used to buy the good.

Suppose that for $8,000 a firm can purchase a machine that yields $1,000 a year into the indefinite future. Also suppose that the firm can borrow (and lend) money at an interest rate of 10 percent. The present value of the income stream earned by the machine is $X/i = \$1,000/0.10 = \$10,000$; the present value of $8,000 now is, of course, $8,000. Clearly, the firm can make money by purchasing the machine.

Another way to see this is to suppose that the firm has only two uses for its money: to buy the machine or to lend out the $8,000 at 10 percent interest. It will pay to buy the machine, for the firm can do so and earn $1,000 per year, while if it lends the $8,000 at 10 percent it will earn only $800 per year.

Since the *MEC* declines as the firm's capital stock rises, the firm will eventually reach an equilibrium with respect to its capital stock. Equation 3 states the condition for determining the equilibrium capital stock of an individual firm.

The equilibrium capital stock of the firm is such that the *MEC* equals the (given) interest rate.[6]

This is shown in Figure 19-2. It also follows from the negative slope of the *MEC* function that a rise in the rate of interest leads to a decrease in the firm's desired capital stock.

Equilibrium in the Economy

For the economy as a whole, the relationship between the rate of interest and the capital stock is similar to the relationship in the individual firm, with one important difference. Any firm takes the interest rate as given and determines its own desired capital stock according to the relationship between the rate of interest and the *MEC* as indicated in Equation 3. In the economy as a whole the total capital stock can be changed only gradually through time. Hence at any point in time the capital stock, and hence the

FIGURE 19-2   The Equilibrium Capital Stock of a Firm

A firm's desired capital stock is negatively related to the market interest rate. The *MEC* curve is reproduced from Figure 19-1. It relates this firm's desired capital stock to the market rate of interest. Its negative slope thus reflects the diminishing marginal productivity of capital.

At an interest rate i_0 the firm's desired capital stock K_0 is that for which the *MEC* is equal to i_0. If, for example, the firm had a capital stock of only K_1, the *MEC* would exceed the interest rate and the firm would wish to expand its capital stock until it reached K_0. If the interest rate rose to say i_1, the firm would wish to reduce its capital stock to K_1.

MEC, can be taken as given. Equation 3 then determines the interest rate in the economy.

For the economy as a whole, the condition that *MEC* = *i* determines the equilibrium interest rate.

If the market interest rate were below the *MEC*, it would pay to borrow money to invest in capital. But for the economy as a whole, the stock of capital cannot change quickly, so the effect of this demand for borrowing would be to push up the interest rate

---

[6] In this chapter we assume that the rate of interest reflects the opportunity cost of capital to the firm. When the market rate of interest and the firm's own opportunity cost of capital diverge, the *MEC* must be equated to the latter, not the former.

FIGURE 19-3   The Equilibrium Interest Rate in an Economy

The equilibrium interest rate in an economy is negatively related to the stock of capital. The MEC curve is reproduced from Figure 19-2. In that figure we assumed the rate of interest was fixed (from the point of view of the firm) and used it to determine the firm's capital stock. Here we use the MEC curve to determine the interest rate for a given capital stock. It relates the equilibrium interest rate in the economy to the economy's stock of capital.

If the capital stock is K_0, the equilibrium interest rate is i_0. At an interest rate below i_0 it will pay people to borrow to invest in more capital. This will drive the interest rate up. An increase in the capital stock K_1 would cause the equilibrium interest rate to fall to i_1.

until it equaled the *MEC*. This is illustrated in Figure 19-3.

Investment in Human Capital

While capital goods are usually discussed in terms of tangible assets such as buildings or machines, the notion of a capital asset as something that produces an increase in the stream of future output suggests another sort of capital good. Consider a high school graduate who has enough schooling to get and keep a job. Instead of taking a job, however, she elects to go to college and possibly to graduate or professional school. During her college career her contribution to society's current output is small (only a summer job perhaps), but because of her education, her lifetime contribution to production may be substantially larger than it would have been had she taken a job after high school.

The choice of whether to take a job now or to continue one's education has all the basic elements of an investment decision, and it is useful to regard the student as making an investment to acquire capital. Because the value derived from such investments is embodied in a person—in terms of greater skills, more knowledge, better health, and the like—rather than in a machine, it is known as **human capital.** Major elements of human capital are health and education of all sorts. An extended education program requires, for example, that resources be withdrawn from the production of goods for current consumption. The resources include materials in the school, services of teachers, and the time and talents of pupils. The education of an individual is productive if the difference between the value of the lifetime output of the trained worker and the lifetime output of the individual without that education exceeds the value of the incremental resources used in the education process. If so, the education increases the value of total production of the economy.

The payoff to education as an investment in human capital has been studied extensively, and many investigators have concluded that investment in education pays, in the sense just defined. Of course, education also has other payoffs; it may be valued for cultural or social reasons, and it may bestow benefits or costs on individuals other than the individuals who are educated. But the fact that it may be more than a capital investment does not prevent it from being an investment.

Summary

1. The demand for any factor is derived from the demand for the commodities the factor is used to make. Factor demand curves slope downward for two reasons. First, an increase in a factor's price will raise the cost of production of goods that use the factor in their production; this will increase the price of those goods and thus reduce the amount demanded. Second, an increase in a factor price will create incentives for producers to substitute cheaper for more expensive factors.

2. A profit-maximizing firm will hire units of any variable factor until the last unit hired adds as much to costs as it does to revenue. If factors are bought in a competitive market, the addition to cost will be the price of a unit of a factor. From this comes the important condition that in competitive equilibrium, the price of a factor will equal its marginal revenue product. This is the marginal productivity theory of distribution.

3. The elasticity of factor demand will tend to be greater (a) the greater the elasticity of demand of the products it makes, (b) the greater the ease of substitution of one factor for another, and (c) the greater the proportion of the total cost of production accounted for by the factor.

4. The total supplies of most factors are variable over time and respond in some degree to economic influences. The most important influences are not the same for labor, arable land and natural resources, or capital.

5. Market conditions exert a powerful influence on factor earnings. This is most evident for nonhuman factors such as raw materials and land, but it is also true for labor, despite the greater role of nonmonetary considerations and the greater importance of noncompetitive markets.

6. The marginal productivity theory of factor demands has the important implication that factors will be allocated efficiently among competing uses.

7. Because capital goods are durable, we distinguish between the stock of capital goods and the flow of services provided by them and thus between their purchase price and their rental price. The linkage between them relies on the ability to assign a present value to future returns. The present value of a future payment will be lower the more distant is the payment and the higher is the interest rate.

8. The rental price of capital, equal to its marginal revenue product, is the amount paid to obtain the flow of services a capital good provides for a given period. The purchase price is the amount paid to acquire ownership of the capital and is equal to the present value of the future income stream earned by the capital.

9. The marginal efficiency of capital (MEC) is the ratio of the value of additional income stream to the value of the additional capital

stock that is needed to produce the increased income stream. In equilibrium, the *MEC* will equal the interest rate.

10. An individual firm will invest in capital goods as long as the *MEC* exceeds the interest rate; thus the condition that *MEC* = *i* determines the firm's equilibrium capital stock. In the economy as a whole, the size of the total capital stock, and hence the *MEC,* changes only slowly; hence the condition that *MEC* = *i* determines the interest rate.

Topics for Review

Derived demand
Marginal revenue product
Marginal productivity theory of distribution
Elasticity of factor demand
Total supplies of factors
Efficient allocation of factors
Rental price and purchase price of durable goods
Present value
Marginal efficiency of capital
The interest rate and the capital stock
Human capital

Discussion Questions

1. The demands listed below have been increasing rapidly in recent years. What derived demands would you predict have risen sharply? Where will the extra factors of production demanded be drawn from?
   a. Demand for electric power
   b. Demand for medical services
   c. Demand for international and interregional travel

2. Can the following factor prices be explained by the marginal productivity theory of distribution?
   a. The actor James Garner is paid $25,000 for appearing in a 10-second commercial. The model who appears in the ad with him is paid $250.
   b. The same jockey riding the same horse is paid 50 percent more money for winning a ¾-mile race with a $150,000 first prize than a 1½-mile race with a $100,000 prize.
   c. The manager of the New York Yankees is paid *not* to manage in the third year of a three-year contract.

3. Consider the large-scale substitution of jumbo jets, each with a seating capacity of about 350, for jets with a seating capacity of about 125. What kinds of labor service would you predict to have experienced an increase in demand and what kinds, a decrease? Under what conditions would airplane pilots (as a group) be made better off economically by virtue of the switch?

4. A recent study showed that after taking full account of differences

in education, age, hours worked per week, weeks worked per year, and so forth, professionally trained people earned approximately 15 percent less if they worked in universities than if they worked in government service. Can this be accounted for by the theory of distribution we have been studying?

5. Discuss the implications of the federal government's changing its policy of paying all its secretaries according to the same salary scale, regardless of location, to one that adapted the salary scale to local market conditions.

6. Each of the following is sometimes described as an "investment" in everyday usage. Which represent investments in capital in the economist's sense?

   a. Building of the Aswan Dam by the government of Egypt
   b. Acquisition of a law degree at Harvard
   c. Purchase of a newly discovered painting by Picasso. (Does it matter to your answer if the purchaser is the Metropolitan Museum or a private collector?)
   d. Purchase by one company of the stock or assets of another company

7. Suppose you are offered, free of charge, either one of each of the following pairs of assets. What considerations would determine your choice?

   a. A perpetuity that pays $20,000 a year forever or an annuity that pays $100,000 a year for five years
   b. An oil-drilling company that earned $100,000 after corporate taxes last year or a bond that paid $100,000 interest last year
   c. A municipal bond that provides for a tax-free interest payment of $1,000 per year or a U.S. government bond that provides a taxable interest payment of $1,200 per year

The Firm's Demand for Factors

In Chapter 19 we saw that all profit-maximizing firms will hire units of the variable factor up to the point at which the marginal cost of the factor equals the marginal revenue produced by the factor. For a firm that is a price taker in factor markets, this means that it hires a factor up to the point at which the factor's price equals its marginal revenue product.

Consider a single firm with only one variable factor, labor, and one fixed factor, capital. Assume that the average and marginal revenue products of the labor are those shown in Figure 19A-1. The firm wishes to hire the quantity of labor that will maximize its profits.

FIGURE 19A-1   The Demand for a Factor and Marginal Revenue Product

The derived demand curve for a factor is the down-ward-sloping portion of the *MRP* curve below the *ARP* curve as indicated by the black portion of the *MRP* curve. Suppose the factor in question is labor. The average revenue generated by a unit of labor, the average revenue product of labor, is shown by the curve *ARP*, while the revenue generated by a marginal increase in the labor force, the marginal revenue product of labor, is shown by the curve *MRP*. Only points on the black portion of the *MRP* curve are on the firm's demand curve for the factor.

The demand curve for a factor is the downward-sloping portion of the marginal revenue product curve where it is below the average revenue product curve.

To see why this statement is correct, let us ask a number of questions.

Why do points on the downward-sloping portion of *MRP*, such as *a* and *b* in the figure, belong on the demand curve? If the wage rate (the price of the variable factor) is w_2, the profit-maximizing firm will hire the factor up to the point where $w = MRP$, that is, up to q_2. This is point *a*. If the wage rate is w_1, the firm will hire up to q_1. This is point *b*. Points *a* and *b* are thus on the firm's demand curve for the factor.

What is the maximum wage rate the firm will pay? We saw in Chapter 12 that it will never pay to produce a product when its price is below the level of average variable cost. We also saw (see page 186) that where average product is a maximum, average variable cost is a minimum. For any wage rate above w_3, such as w_4, the average revenue generated by a unit of labor (shown by *ARP*) would be less than the variable cost of the unit of labor (its wage rate). For such a wage rate it does not pay the firm to hire any workers. In other words w_3, where average revenue product is a maximum, is the highest factor price of firm could pay and still cover variable costs.

Why is the downward-sloping, not the upward-sloping, portion of *MRP* the demand curve? Consider the wage rate w_2. Here $w = MRP$ at both q_4 (point *c*) and q_2 (point *a*). We have already seen that point *a* is on the demand curve; what about point *c*? For every unit of labor hired up to q_4, *MRP* is less than the wage rate. In other words, each unit of labor is contributing less to revenue than to cost. Thus a profit-maximizing firm would be better off hiring zero units than q_4 units. For every unit of labor from q_4 to q_2, MRP exceeds the wage rate. Thus, if a firm were hiring q_4 units, it would find each additional unit beyond q_4 (up to q_2) worth hiring. Point c, where MRP is rising when it equals the wage rate, is a point of *minimum* profit, not maximum profit. **[30]** A firm at point c would improve its profitability by moving in either direction, to hiring zero workers or to hiring q_2 workers. (We already know that q_2 is better than zero because at that quantity ARP is greater than the wage rate.)

Only points where MRP cuts the wage rate from above, that is, where MRP is downward sloping, are possible profit-maximizing quantities.

Will There Be a Downward-sloping Portion of *MRP*?

Having shown that only downward-sloping portions of MRP are relevant to the demand curve for the factor, we may ask whether we have any reason to believe MRP will slope downward. The presence of diminishing returns is sufficient to assure this result,

as can be easily shown. Marginal revenue product depends on two things: (1) the physical increase in output that an additional unit of the variable factor makes possible, multiplied by (2) the increase in revenue derived from that extra output. The first of these is called the marginal product (MP), the second is the by now familiar concept of marginal revenue:

$$MRP = MP \times MR$$

The hypothesis of diminishing marginal returns was introduced in Chapter 8. This hypothesis says that MP has a declining section over some range of output. If marginal revenue is constant (as it is in perfect competition), MRP will have the same shape as MP and must also decline.

Marginal revenue, however, may not be constant. If MR declines as output increases (as it does in monopoly and in any other situation in which the firm's demand curve declines), MRP must decline even more sharply. The hypothesis of diminishing marginal productivity thus implies diminishing MRP and a downward-sloping demand curve for the factor.

20

Wages, Unions, and Discrimination

Why do steel workers get the same pay for the same work, no matter where they work in the United States? Why do carpenters get different wages in different locations? Why do railroad employees, who work in a declining industry, get higher rates of pay than equally skilled workers in many expanding industries? How does a worker in a plant employing 5,000 people "ask for a raise"? How does a worker let her employer know that she would be glad to trade so many cents per hour in wages for a better medical insurance scheme? Why do strikes occur?

The competitive theory of factor price determination, tells us a lot about factor prices, factor movements, and the distribution of income. Indeed, for the pricing of many nonhuman factors, there is little need to modify the competitive model. Much of what is observed about labor markets is also consistent with the theory. But not all of it is.

Labor is in many ways the exceptional factor of production. The owners of capital or land need not be present when the services of those factors are utilized; indeed, the owners need not even live close to where these factors are employed. In contrast, the owner of labor must be present when labor services are used. As a result, nonmonetary factors such as location and working conditions are likely to be more important in the labor market than in markets for other factors of production.

Considerations other than material advantage enter the relationship between employer and employee, for it is a relationship between people who look for loyalty, fairness, appreciation, and justice along with paychecks and productivity. Discrimination on the basis of sex, race or age can further complicate labor markets.

Labor unions, employers' associations, collective bargaining, and government intervention in free-market wage determination are important features of the real world. They influence wages and working conditions and affect the levels of employment and unemployment in many industries.

The theory of factor price determination must therefore be extended somewhat before it can be applied to the full range of problems concerning the determination of wages.

Theoretical Models of Wage Determination[1]

In a labor market firms are the buyers and workers are the sellers. Noncompetitive elements can enter on either or both sides of the market and influence the outcome of the wage bargain.

Two extreme but relevant cases are, first, the one in which there are so many employers that no one of them can influence the wage rate by varying its own demand for labor and, second, the one in which there is a single purchaser of labor, either a single firm or an association of several firms operating as a single unit in the labor market. In the former case labor is said to be purchased under competitive conditions; in the latter case, under monopsonistic conditions. **Monopsony** means a single buyer; it is the equivalent on the purchasing side of monopoly on the selling side (a single seller). What is the effect of introducing a union into the extreme situations?

A Union in a Competitive Market

Where there are many employers and many unorganized workers there is a competitive factor market of the kind discussed in the previous chapter. Under competitive conditions the wage rate and level of employment are set by supply and demand.

Suppose a union enters such a market and sets a wage for the industry above the competitive level. By so doing it is establishing a minimum wage below which no one will work. This changes the supply curve of labor. The industry can hire as many units of labor as are prepared to work at the union wage, but no one at a lower wage. Thus the industry (and each firm) faces a supply curve that is horizontal at the level of the union wage up to the quantity of labor willing to work at that wage.

This is shown in Figure 20-1. The intersection of this horizontal supply curve and the demand curve establishes a higher wage rate and lower level of employment than the competitive equilibrium.

[1] Remember that, unless otherwise specified, we are dealing with real wages; that is, wages relative to the price level. See the discussion of the theory of price in an inflationary world on pages 73–74.

FIGURE 20-1   Union Wage Setting Above the Competitive Level

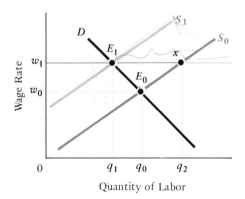

A union can raise the wages of those who continue to be employed in a competitive labor market at the expense of the level of employment. The competitive equilibrium is at E_0, the wage is w_0, and employment is q_0. If a union enters this market and sets a wage of w_1, a new equilibrium will be established at E_1. The supply curve has become $w_1 \times S_0$. At the new wage, w_1, there will be q_1q_2 workers who would like to work, but whom the industry will not hire. Employment will be q_1. The decrease in employment due to the wage increase is q_1q_0.

The wage w_1 can be achieved without generating a pool of persons seeking but unable to find work in the occupation. To do so the union must restrict entry into the occupation and shift the supply curve to the left to S_1. Employment will still be q_1.

This figure can also be used to illustrate the effect of government's imposing a minimum wage of w_1 on the market where the competitive equilibrium is at E_0. The q_1 workers who remain employed benefit by the wage increase. The q_1q_0 workers who lose their jobs in this industry suffer to the extent that they fail to find new jobs at a wage of w_0 or more.

There will be a group of workers who would like to obtain work in the industry or occupation but cannot. This presents a problem for the union if it seeks to represent *all* the employees in the industry or occupation. A conflict of interest has been created between serving the interests of the union's employed and unemployed members. Pressure to cut the wage rate may develop among the unemployed, but the union must resist this pressure if the higher wage is to be maintained.

An alternative way to achieve the higher wage level *without* the resulting unemployment is to shift the supply curve to the left. The union may be able to do this by restricting entry into the occupation by methods such as lengthening required apprenticeship periods and reducing openings for trainees. Or the union may be able to have government impose licensing or certification requirements on those who would work.

Raising wages without restricting supply will lead to unemployment. Restricting supply will tend to raise wages without creating a group of workers who are unemployed in the occupation at the going wage.

Raising wages by restricting entry is not, of course, limited to unions. Consider the professions of medicine and law. Since professional standards have long been regarded as necessary to protect the public from incompetent practitioners, doctors and lawyers have found it publicly acceptable to control supply by limiting entry into their professions.

Doctors are in short supply—and doctors' incomes are the highest of any profession—because of barriers to entry, including the difficulties of getting into an approved medical school, the high costs of creating new medical schools, long years of study, low-paid internship and residency, and various certification requirements.

Lawyers have been less successful in limiting entry into their profession (and thus in achieving high average incomes) because the supply of law schools has increased to meet the increased demand for law school admissions and because the three years of required training is relatively short. Graduates of new, even second-rate, law schools, for the most part, can satisfy certification requirements (often with the aid of "cram schools" for the bar exams) and gain access to the profession.

A Monopsonistic Market Without a Union

Consider a labor market in which there are many unorganized workers, but only a small number of firms. Imagine a case in which the firms form an employers' hiring association in order to act as a single unit so that there is a monopsony in the labor market.

While the employers' association can offer any wage rate that it chooses—the laborers must either work at that rate or find a different job—the wage rate chosen will affect the profitability of its operations. For any given quantity that the monopsonist wishes to purchase, the labor supply curve shows the price per unit it must offer; to the monopsonist, this is the *average cost curve* of labor. In deciding how much labor to hire, however, the monopsonist will be interested in the *marginal cost* of hiring additional workers.

Whenever the supply curve of labor slopes upward, the marginal cost of employing extra units will exceed the average cost. It exceeds the wage paid (the average cost) because the increased wage rate necessary to attract an extra worker must also be paid to everyone already employed. [31] For example, assume that 100 workers are employed at $4.00 per hour and that in order to attract an extra worker the wage must be raised to $4.01 per hour. The marginal cost of the one-hundred-and-first worker is not the $4.01 per hour paid to him, but $5.01 per hour—made up of the extra $.01 per hour paid to the 100 existing workers and $4.01 paid to the new worker.

The profit-maximizing monopsonist will hire labor up to the point where the marginal cost just equals the amount the firm is willing to pay for an additional unit of labor. That amount is determined by the marginal revenue product of labor and is shown by the demand curve. This is illustrated in Figure 20-2.

Monopsonistic conditions in a factor market will result in a lower level of employment and a lower wage rate than would rule when the factor is purchased under competitive conditions.

The common sense of this result is that the monopsonistic firm is aware that by trying to purchase more of the factor it is responsible for driving up the price. It will therefore stop short of the point that is

FIGURE 20-2   Monopsony in a Labor Market

A monopsonist lowers both the wage rate and employment below their competitive levels. *D* and *S* are the competitive demand and supply curves. In competition equilibrium is at E_0, the wage rate is w_0, and the quantity of labor hired is q_0. The marginal cost of labor (*MC*) to the monopsonist is above the average cost. The monopsonistic firm will maximize profits at E_1. It will hire only q_1 units of labor. At q_1 the marginal cost of the last worker is just equal to the value to the firm of that worker's output, as shown by the demand curve. The wage that must be paid to get q_1 workers is only w_1.

reached when the factor is purchased by many different firms, no one of which can exert an influence on the wage rate.

A Union in a Monopsonistic Market

What if a wage-setting union enters a monopsonistic market and sets a wage below which labor will not work? There will then be no point in the employer's reducing the quantity demanded in the hope of driving down the wage rate, nor will there be any point in holding off hiring for fear of driving the wage up. Here, just as in the case of a wage-setting union in a competitive market, the union presents the employer with a horizontal supply curve (up to the maximum number who will accept work at the union wage). The union raises wages and employment above the monopsony level. This result is demonstrated in Figure 20-3.

FIGURE 20-3   A Union Enters a Monopsonistic Labor Market

By presenting a monopsonistic employer with a fixed wage, the union can raise both wages and employment over the monopsonistic level. The monopsony position before the union enters is at E_1 (from Figure 20-2), with a wage rate of w_1 and q_1 workers hired. A union now enters and sets the wage at w_0. The supply curve of labor becomes $w_0E_0S_0$, and wages and employment rise to their competitive levels of w_0 and q_0 without creating a pool of unemployed workers. If the wage is raised further, say, to w_2, the supply curve will become w_2xS and the quantity of employment will fall below the competitive level, to q_2, while a pool of unsuccessful job applicants of q_2q_3 will develop.

This figure can also be used to illustrate the effect of the government's imposing a minimum wage of w_0 or w_2 on a monopsonistic labor market.

Because the union turns the firm into a price taker in the labor market, it can prevent the exercise of the firm's monopsony power and thus raise both wages and employment to the competitive levels.

The union may not be content merely to neutralize the monopsonist's power. It may choose to raise wages further. If it does, the outcome will be the same as that shown in Figure 20-1. If the wage is raised above the competitive level, the employer will no longer wish to hire all the labor offered at that wage. The amount of employment will fall, and unemployment will develop. This is also shown in

Figure 20-3. Notice, however, that the union can raise wages substantially above the competitive level before employment falls to a level as low as it was in the pre-union monopsonistic situation.

Minimum Wage Laws

When unions set wages for their members, they are in effect setting a minimum wage. Governments can cause similar effects by legislating specific **minimum wages,** that is wage rates that are the lowest that may legally be offered.

In the United States the federal minimum wage was $3.35 per hour in 1986. It covered about 80 percent of the labor force. For a large fraction of all employment covered by the law, this minimum wage is below the actual market wage. When this is true, the minimum wage is said to be *not binding*. But many workers are in occupations or industries where the free-market wage rate would be below the legal minimum, and there the minimum wage is said to be *binding*, or *effective*.

Minimum wages are accepted in American life but economists view their effects as less obviously beneficial than do many others. To the extent that they are effective, they raise the wages of employed workers. But, as our analysis in Chapter 6 indicated, an effective floor price (which is what a minimum wage is) may well lead to a market surplus—in this case, unemployment. Thus minimum wages will benefit some groups while hurting others. The problem is more complicated than the analysis of Chapter 6 would suggest both because not all labor markets are competitive and because minimum wage laws do not cover all employment. Moreover, some groups in the labor force, especially youth and minorities, are much more adversely affected than the average worker.

A Comprehensive Minimum Wage

Suppose first that minimum wage laws apply uniformly to all occupations. The occupations and industries in which minimum wages are effective will be the lowest-paying in the country; they usually involve unskilled or at best semiskilled labor. In most of them the workers are not members of unions. Thus the market structures in which minimum wages are likely to be effective include both those in which competitive conditions pertain and those in which employers exercise monopsony power. The employment effects of minimum wages are different in the two cases.

Competitive labor markets.   The employment consequences of an effective minimum wage are unambiguous when the labor market is competitive. By raising the wage facing employers, minimum wage legislation leads to a reduction in the quantity of labor demanded and an increase in the quantity supplied. As a result the actual level of employment falls, and unemployment is generated. This situation is exactly analogous to the one that arises when a union succeeds in setting a wage above the competitive equilibrium wage, as illustrated in Figure 20-1. The excess supply of labor at the minimum wage also creates incentives for people to evade the law by working below the legal minimum wage.

In competitive labor markets effective minimum wage laws raise the wages of those who remain employed, but also create some unemployment.

Monopsonistic labor markets.   By effectively flattening out the labor supply curve, the minimum wage law can simultaneously increase wages and employment. The circumstances in which this can be done are the same as those in which a union facing a monopsonistic employer succeeds in setting a wage above that which the employer would otherwise pay, as shown in Figure 20-3. Of course, if the minimum wage is raised above the competitive wage, employment will start to fall, as in the union case. When set at the competitive wage, however, the minimum wage can protect the worker against monopsony power and lead to increases in employment.

A Noncomprehensive Minimum Wage

Suppose a minimum wage covers only 80 percent of all jobs and that applying the minimum wage to the covered jobs does cause some unemployment in that sector. The workers displaced can move to the uncovered sector. If they do, they will shift the supply curve in the uncovered sector to the right. This will lead to lower wages and increased employment in the uncovered sector. As a general rule the increase in employment in the uncovered sector will not be large enough to offset the decrease in the covered sector.[2]

The Overall Effect of Minimum Wage Laws

Researchers have extensively studied the effect of minimum wages on employment. These studies show that the adverse employment effects of minimum wages fall most heavily on those with the least education and training. This group—which includes many teenagers, women, and blacks—has fewer job opportunities as the wage rate rises. Many of them could have found jobs at lower wages. It is estimated that for youth (aged 16 to 19) employment decreases 1 percent to 3 percent for every 10 percent increase in minimum wages. For young adults (aged 20 to 24) the employment effect is also adverse, but less so. Blacks suffer more loss of employment due to minimum wages than do whites, and females more than males.

Furthermore, this is not merely a one-time loss of jobs. Much skill acquisition occurs on the job. Employees in occupations in which such on-the-job training occurs frequently "pay" for their education by receiving low wages in the initial stages of their employment. Minimum wage legislation makes this much more difficult. Instead of being able to "apprentice" in jobs that will lead to productive careers, many teenagers, blacks, and women become trapped either in unemployment or in low-skill, short-term, or part-time employment.

In Canada several provinces responded to this kind of evidence by allowing lower minimum wages for young or inexperienced workers and for workers demonstrably in a "learning period." No exceptions

on those bases are permitted in the United States under current law, although President Reagan has talked about the need for a "youth wage."[3]

The adverse employment effect is, however, only one element in deciding whether, overall, minimum wages are beneficial or harmful. It is clear that minimum wage laws raise the incomes of many workers at the very lowest levels of pay. Some of those who benefit most are members of groups that are chronically poor, whom the government is anxious to aid by income redistribution. But it is not only the lowest paid who gain. Because union wage structures maintain differentials between skill classes, an increase in minimum wages also raises wages in a large number of occupations that are already above the minimum. Indeed, it may raise the whole wage structure.

Thus there are gainers and losers from minimum wage laws. Labor union members as a whole are gainers, as are both white and black adult males. Black and white females and teenagers are net losers because the loss of earnings due to less employment is larger than the gains due to higher wage rates. Of course, there are gainers and losers within each group. The losers are the ones without jobs, the gainers those who receive higher wages than they otherwise would.

Given this mixed result, what explains the widespread, almost uncritical belief in the power of increased minimum wages to alleviate poverty and redistribute income from the rich to the poor? Much of the explanation rests on neglect of adverse employment effects.

Organized labor finds minimum wages beneficial to most of its employed members, and labor unions have been consistently in favor of both increasing the level of minimum wages and expanding coverage. No equally powerful political force opposes them since those who do not find jobs because of the minimum wage laws are unlikely to identify these laws as the cause of their unemployment.

While many economists are critical of the mini-

---

[2] Only if the demand curve in the uncovered sector is horizontal (infinitely elastic), or if the supply curve is vertical (completely inelastic), will every displaced worker from the covered sector find employment. But these are not likely circumstances.

[3] It may be objected that such exceptions are discriminatory. But, as we saw on page 242, labeling something "discriminatory" does not necessarily mean that it is bad. The argument favoring a youth wage is that it is better to be employed at a lower wage than unemployed at a higher one.

mum wage, it is likely to remain. It is one of the hard-won labor gains dating back to President Roosevelt's New Deal, and it has great symbolic significance for labor.

The Nature and Evolution of Modern Labor Unions

Unions today represent only about 15 percent of the workers in the private sector and less than 20 percent of all workers. But union influence is greater than these percentages suggest. One reason is the impact union wage contracts have in other labor markets. When, for example, the United Auto Workers negotiate a new contract, its provisions set a pattern that directly or indirectly affects almost all the labor markets in Michigan and in many other industrial states. A second reason is the major leadership role unions have played in the last 50 years in the development of labor market practices and in lobbying for legislation that applies to all workers.

Labor Market Institutions

For the purposes of our discussion of labor markets, a **union** (or *trade union* or *labor union*) is an association of individual workers that speaks for them in negotiations with their employers. Unions negotiate with individual employers or employers' associations. American unionism has developed not only its own institutions, but also something of a specialized vocabulary, some of which is presented in Box 20-1.

The process by which unions and employers (or their representatives) arrive at and enforce their agreements is known as **collective bargaining.** This process has an important difference from the theoretical models with which we began this chapter. There we assumed that the union set the wage and the employer decided how much labor to hire. In collective bargaining the wage is negotiated. In terms of Figure 20-3 it may be that the employer wants the wage to be w_1 and the union wants w_2. Depending on each side's market power and their bargaining strength, the final agreed wage may be anywhere in between. In collective bargaining there is always a substantial range over which an agreement can be reached, and the actual result in particular cases will depend on the strengths of the two bargaining parties and on the skill of their negotiators.

Unionism today is both stable and accepted, especially in the heavy manufacturing industries and in government service. It was not always so. Within the lifetime of many of today's members, unions were fighting for their lives and union organizers and members were risking theirs. In the 1930s the labor movement evoked the loyalties and passions of people as a great liberal cause in ways that seem quite extraordinary today. Indeed, unions today often appear to many as conservative (even reactionary) groups of hard hats. Why the change and how did it come about?

The Urge to Organize

Trade unionism had its origin in the pitifully low standard of living of the average nineteenth century worker's family. Much of the explanation for the low standard of living throughout the world lay in the small size of the national output relative to the population. Even in the wealthiest countries an equal division of national wealth among all families in 1850 would have left each one in poverty by our present standards.

Poverty had existed for centuries. It was accentuated, however, by the twin processes of urbanization and industrialization. Immigrants and farmers who were moderately content working the land usually became restive and discontented when the family moved into a grimy, smoky, nineteenth century city, lived in crowded, unsanitary tenements, and took jobs in a sweatshop or a factory. Box 20-2 on page 370 provides a vivid picture of factory conditions at the turn of the present century.

The focus of resentment was usually the employer. The employer set the wages, and the wages were low. Unhappy workers had, of course, the right of all free people to quit their job—and starve. If they grumbled or protested, they could be fired and, worse, blacklisted, which meant no one else would hire them.

Out of these conditions and other grievances of working men and women came the full range of

BOX 20-1

The Vocabulary of American Unionism

Kinds of Unions

The **craft union** organizes workers with a common set of skills in a common association, no matter where or for whom they work. The craft principle of organization was and is the hallmark of the American Federation of Labor (AFL). The **industrial union** is organized along industry lines; all workers in a given plant or industry are collected into a single union. This is the pattern developed by the member unions of the Congress of Industrial Organizations (CIO). Among the prominent industrial unions are the United Automobile Workers and the United Steelworkers.

The two principles of unionism conflict. Should a carpenter employed in the steel industry be represented by the carpenters' union or the steelworkers' union? Disputes over which union shall have the right to *organize* (i.e., bring into their union) a particular group of workers are known as **jurisdictional disputes.** They have led to prolonged, bitter, and bloody battles of union against union, and they played an important role in American labor history until the merger of the AFL and CIO in 1955.

The important level for most of the economic functions of the union is the national level. The national officers do the bargaining, set the policies, and set the tone. Individual workers, however, belong to a local to which they pay dues (a part of which goes to the national). There are about 200 national unions, which have over 75,000 locals. The local for a craft union is geographical, for example, the Chicago chapter of the carpenters. The local for an industrial union is a plant or a company, for example, the Ford local of the United Automobile Workers.

The **federation** is a loose organization of national unions. Before 1955 the AFL and CIO were two separate federations; today there is one, the AFL–CIO. The federation serves an important role not in individual labor markets, but as a voice of organized labor. Its function in recent years has been largely a public relations and political one.

Kinds of Bargaining Arrangements

In an **open shop** a union represents its members, but does not have exclusive bargaining jurisdiction for all workers in the shop. Membership in the union is not needed to get or to keep a job.

Unions vehemently oppose such an arrangement. If, on the one hand, the employer yields to union demands and raises wages, the non-members ("free riders") get the benefits of the union without paying dues or sharing the risks or responsibilities. If, on the other hand, the firm chooses to fight the union, it can run its plants with the non-union employees.

If the union succeeds in raising wages above their competitive level, there will be an excess supply of labor. With an open shop, there is nothing to prevent unemployed non-union workers from accepting a wage below the union one and so undermining the

radical political movements. Out of the same conditions also came a pragmatic American form of collective action called **bread-and-butter unionism,** whose goals were higher wages and better working conditions rather than political reform.

The early industrial organizer saw that 10 or 100 employees acting together had more influence than one acting alone and dreamed of the day when all would stand solid against the employer. (The word *solidarity* occurs often in the literature and songs of the labor movement.) The union was the organization that would provide a basis for confronting the monopsony power of employers with the collective power of the workers. But it was easier to recognize solidarity as a solution than it was to achieve it. Organizations of workers would hurt the employer, and employers did not sit by idly; they, too, knew that in union there was strength. "Agitators" who tried to organize workers were fired and blacklisted; in some cases they were beaten and killed.

union's power to maintain high wages.

In a **closed shop** only union members may be employed, and the union controls its membership as it sees fit. The union can prevent its members from accepting less than the union wage and so has the power to maintain high wages in spite of the existence of excess supply.

Employers traditionally regard this as an unwarranted limitation of their right to choose their employees. The Taft-Hartley Act in 1948 prohibited the closed shop.

The **union shop** is a compromise between a closed shop and an open shop. In a union shop a firm may hire anyone it chooses at the union wage, but every employee must join the union within a specified period. This leaves employers free to hire anyone they wish, but gives the union the power to enforce its union wages because workers are prevented from accepting employment at lower wages. It is the most common union arrangement in the United States today.

Weapons of Conflict

The **strike** is the concerted refusal to work by the members of the union. It is the strike or the threat of a strike that backs up the union's demands in the bargaining process. Workers on strike are, of course, off the payroll, so many unions set aside a portion of the dues collected to have a fund for paying striking workers. **Strikebreakers** (scabs) are workers brought in by management to operate the plant while the union is on strike.

Picket lines are made up of striking workers who parade before the entrance to their plant or firm. Other union members will not, by time-honored convention, "cross" a picket line. Thus, if bricklayers strike against a construction firm, carpenters will not work on the project nor will teamsters deliver supplies to a picketed site, although they themselves may have no grievance against the firm. Pickets represent an enormous increase in the bargaining power of a small union. (Much of the bitterness against jurisdictional disputes arises from the fact that an employer may be unable to settle with either union without facing a picket line from the other union.)

A **labor boycott** is an organized attempt to persuade customers to refrain from purchasing the goods or services of a firm or industry whose employees are on strike. The boycotts organized by Cesar Chavez's United Farm Workers Union against grapes, lettuce, and bananas are prominent examples.

The **lockout** is the employer's equivalent of the strike. By closing the plant the employer locks out the workers until such a time as the dispute is settled. A **blacklist** is an employer's list of workers who have been fired for playing a role in union affairs that was regarded by the employer as undesirable. Other employers are not supposed to give jobs to blacklisted workers.

To achieve effective power over the labor market, a union had to gain control of the supply of labor and have the financial resources necessary to outlast the employer in a struggle for survival. There was no right to organize. The union had to force an employer to negotiate with it, and few employers did so willingly. Unions started in a small way among highly skilled workers and spread slowly.

Why did the union movement show its first real power among small groups of relatively skilled workers? First, it was easier to control the supply of skilled workers than unskilled ones. Organize the unskilled, and the employer could find replacements for them. But skilled workers—the coopers (barrelmakers), the bootmakers, the shipwrights—were another matter. There were few of them, and they controlled the access to their trade by apprenticeships. The original craft unions were, in effect, closed shops: One had to belong to the union to hold a job in the craft, and the union set the rules of admission.

BOX 20-2

Factory Life in the United States, 1903

Stories of workers' very real suffering during the Industrial Revolution and the years that followed could fill many volumes, but an example will at least illustrate some of the horrors that lay behind the drive for change and reform. (The quotation comes from *Poverty*, by Robert Hunter, published in 1904.)

In the worst days of cotton-milling in England the conditions were hardly worse than those now existing in the South. Children—the tiniest and frailest—of five and six years of age rise in the morning and, like old men and women, go to the mills to do their day's labor; and when they return home, they wearily fling themselves on their beds, too tired to take off their clothes. Many children work all night—"in the maddening racket of the machinery, in an atmosphere insanitary and clouded with humidity and lint." It will be long before I forget the face of a little boy of six years, with his hands stretched forward to rearrange a bit of machinery, his pallid face and spare

form showing already the physical effects of labor. This child, six years of age, was working twelve hours a day in a country which has established in many industries an eight-hour day for men. The twelve-hour day is almost universal in the South, and about twenty-five thousand children are now employed on twelve-hour shifts in the mills of the various Southern states. The wages of one of these children, however large, could not compensate the child for the injury this monstrous and unnatural labor does him; but the pay which the child receives is not enough, in many instances, even to feed him properly. If the children fall ill, they are docked for loss of time. . . . The mill-hands confess that they hate the mills, and no one will wonder at it. A vagrant who had worked in a textile mill for sixteen years once said to a friend of mine: "I done that [and he made a motion with his hand] for sixteen years. At last I was sick for two or three days with a fever, and when I crawled out, I made up my mind that I would rather go to hell than go back to the mill."

Second, employers were vulnerable to the demands of a union of workers whose skills might be indispensable to the production process. Third, because labor in a particular skilled occupation is likely to account for a relatively low proportion of total costs, the effect on the employer's overall costs of giving in to a small group's demand for a wage increase is small.

The difficulty of substituting other factors for skilled labor and a relatively small contribution to total costs combined to create an inelastic demand. This gave the unions of skilled workers an advantage in fighting the employer not enjoyed by other groups of workers. In the early days unions needed every advantage they could get since anti-unionism was for some employers a matter of principle, a crusade, and a way of life.

Even where unions gained a foothold in a strategic trade, they had their ups and downs. When employment was full and business booming, the cost of being fired for joining a union was not great because there were other jobs. However, during periods of depression and unemployment an individual worker knew that if he or she caused trouble,

unemployed members of the trade would be there to take the job. Solidarity could yield to hunger. Membership in trade unions showed a clear cyclical pattern, rising in good times and falling in bad.

The Historical Development of American Unions

The beginnings: Before 1933. The American Federation of Labor, founded in 1886 by Samuel Gompers, a cigar maker, was totally committed to organizing the skilled trades, to pursuing bread-and-butter issues, and to restricting labor supply. Gompers, himself an immigrant, led the AFL in vigorous opposition to further immigration: Restriction of supply was the key to preserving union power.

Because it was impossible to control supply, the prospects for unionization were bleak for the unskilled. Their hope lay in political reform, in socialism, in cooperatives, or in revolution. The Knights of Labor, organized in 1869, sought one big union for all workers. At its peak in 1886 it had 700,000 members. But the political climate was hostile, and the Knights collapsed in 1887 for many reasons, including some unsuccessful strikes of unskilled workers.

The AFL avoided noble causes and continued its steady growth among the skilled until the end of World War I. In 1900 it had just over half a million members (2 percent of the labor force), and by 1920 it had 5 million members, 10 percent of the labor force. By 1922, in the face of a severe recession and the strong anti-labor attitude of government and business alike, AFL membership had declined to 8 percent, and by 1933, after a decade of gradual decline, to about 6 percent of the labor force.

The New Deal: 1933–1945. The dramatic effect of the New Deal on union membership is seen in Figure 20-4. What happened? First, the monstrousness of the Great Depression created a climate of public opinion openly hostile to big business and tolerant of even violent responses of labor over this period. Second, the Wagner Act (1935) guaranteed the *right* of workers to organize and to elect, by secret ballot, an exclusive bargaining agent by majority vote of the employees. This made it possible to organize the unskilled in industrial unions which became the components of the CIO. The Wagner Act provided the means to control the supply of even unskilled labor.

The unions won—first by force and even violence and finally by law—the recognition that was required to permit workers through unions to articulate their grievances and to bargain to relieve them.

After World War II. The New Deal period and its legislation were unmistakably pro-labor. By the end of World War II attitudes had changed for several reasons, including an increasing number and the changing character of strikes. The jurisdictional strikes between rival AFL and CIO unions were less comprehensible to public and employer alike than the strikes designed to compel employers to deal with unions. An unprecedented wave of strikes in 1946 led to the loss of over 100 million worker days (about 1 percent of estimated working time), more than four times the loss of any previous year.

Congress passed the Taft-Hartley Act in 1948. Among its many provisions, unfair labor practices on the part of unions as well as management were defined and prohibited, use of the closed shop was limited, and strikes that "imperiled the national health and safety" were subject to an 80-day cooling off period. The most controversial feature of the act was the encouragement it gave to states to pass **right-to-work laws.** These laws permit the open shop—the right to work without belonging to a union.

Since 1950 union membership has continued to decline steadily as a percentage of the labor force. The major reason is the absence of employment growth in traditionally unionized industries and in industries with large concentrations of employees. The biggest question mark is the future of unionism among employees in white-collar, professional, and service fields and in government employment. In the mid 1980s over 35 percent of government employees, but only 10 percent of private employees in service occupations were members of unions.

The main development in the nature of unionization over the last three decades—besides its steady

---

FIGURE 20-4   Union Membership As a Percentage of the Labor Force in the United States, 1900–1985

The great spurt in union membership occurred after passage of the Wagner Act (1935) and before the end of World War II. Since 1960 union membership as a percentage of the nonagricultural labor force has steadily declined.

decline in fraction of workers covered—has been the stabilizing of union-management relations in industry after industry. Strikes still occur and always will, for they are a key part of the poker game of collective bargaining. The number and duration of strikes today are relatively minor compared with those of the 1930s and late 1940s. Particular strikes—for example, among teamsters, teachers, police officers, or even professional athletes—can cause real disruption in peoples' daily lives and arouse public opinion. The strikes that do occur, however, are directed overwhelmingly toward specific issues and negotiations rather than recognition or jurisdiction, and the violence and passions of a generation ago are largely gone. Labor unions are now part of the establishment.

Objectives of Modern Unions

Union constitutions are extremely democratic documents. All members have one vote, officers are elected by the vote of the membership, the rights of individual workers are fully protected, and so on. In practice, however, the relation between the members of a union and its national officers is closer to that of the relationship between stockholders and managers of a giant corporation than to that of the American people and their government. Unions tend toward one-party democracy in most cases. Union leaders are highly paid professionals whose business is to run the union, while the main business of union members is to earn a living on the job. That union members accept little participation in union decision making is understandable; they are paying dues that permit the union to pay generous salaries to union leaders to look out for the rank and file's interests—and as long as the leadership "delivers," all goes well. But delivers what and to whom?

Wages Versus Job Security

Until the 1980s people who were in their teens during the Great Depression dominated the leadership of American unions. Not surprisingly, they had a strong defensive attitude toward union members' jobs. They had lived through a period when unemployment was above 20 percent of the total labor force and nearer 50 percent in many of the hardest hit areas. They had seen people grow up, marry, and raise children on relief or part-time work.

One method of seeking job security is through *seniority rules* that require employers to lay off and rehire on the basis of years of service. This protects existing workers, and many unions have been willing to accept lower wages in order to build seniority provisions into their contracts.

A second method of seeking job security is to resist the introduction of labor-saving innovations. In a period of heavy unemployment, the installation of a labor-saving machine in a factory is likely to mean unemployment for those whose jobs are lost by the change. It is little wonder that during and after the Great Depression new machines were opposed bitterly and that job-saving restrictive practices were adhered to with tenacity.

The heritage of this fear survives in featherbedding practices such as the standby musician at the television studio and the meticulous division of tasks in the building trades that inhibit many labor-saving consolidations and reorganization of tasks.

But in the long run mechanization increases productivity and consequently the wages and profits that are earned. After World War II the attitude of many unions slowly changed from one of resisting technological change to one of collaborating with it and trying to reduce some of its costs to individuals who are adversely affected.

The return of higher unemployment rates in the late 1970s and early 1980s again heightened union interest in job security but in more constructive ways. Elimination of some restrictive practices that raised labor costs has been accepted by unions in return for company agreement to pass on savings in lower product prices and to delay planned layoffs.

The biggest change in attitude (compared with the past) is that the current generation of leaders sees the increased mechanization of Japanese, Korean, and German firms rather than their own employers as the principal threat to union workers' jobs. Many of today's labor leaders seem prepared to help their American employers improve their international competitiveness.

Wages Versus Fringe Benefits

Indirect or **fringe benefits**—such as company contributions to union pension and welfare funds, sick leave, and vacation pay, as well as required payments toward social security and unemployment compensation insurance—are estimated to make up almost a third of the total compensation of industrial workers. Why do unions and employers not simply agree to a wage and let it go at that? Why should the average employed automobile worker who earns $25,000 cost the company $40,000?

Fringe benefits appeal to employees in part because they are not subject to income taxes. Pension funds and medical benefits let employees provide for their future and that of their families more cheaply than they could by purchasing private insurance, and their benefits often protect them even when they lose their jobs. A package of fringe benefits that includes high wages and job security for the employed, and unemployment benefits for those squeezed out by high wages appeals to union leaders because it provides something for everyone.

There are also advantages to employers. For example, fringe benefits such as pension funds tend to bind the worker more closely to the company, thereby decreasing the turnover rate among employees. If employees stand to lose part of their benefits by changing jobs, they will not be so ready to move.

Wages Versus Employment

A union that sets wages above the competitive level is making a choice of higher wages for some and unemployment for others. Should the union strive to maximize the earnings of the group that remains employed? If it does, some of its members will lose their jobs and the union's membership will decline. Should it instead maximize the welfare of its present members? Or should it seek to expand employment opportunities (perhaps by a low-wage policy) so that the union membership grows?

Different unions decide these questions differently. The United Mine Workers employed a high-wage, shrinking-employment strategy for decades, and both employment and union membership declined. The longshoremen's union has achieved high wages, but chooses to ration the available jobs among its members rather than reduce its membership. It thus spreads the underemployment around. In the garment trades the demand for labor is relatively elastic, and the major unions have traditionally accepted lower wages than they could have attained in order to protect the employment of their members.

Growing competition for American manufactured goods from foreign production has led to a new recognition among major American industrial unions that high wages and high levels of layoffs and unemployment of their members often go hand in hand. Major unions in such industries as automobiles, steel, rubber, smelting, and airlines have accepted wage increases below the increases in the cost of living; many have even agreed to significant reductions in wages and other benefits under existing contracts. They did so in order to prevent further plant closings and to encourage the rehiring of unemployed union workers.

Wages versus employment poses a long-term problem as well as a short-term one. Unionization and rising wages in fruit picking have led to mechanization and a drop in the demand for labor. In the auto industry the traditional high-wage policy encouraged the major manufacturers to increase automation. There were 100,000 fewer jobs in the auto industry in 1986 than 10 years earlier for the same level of production.

The fundamental dilemma of choosing between high wages and high employment is splitting many unions and dividing the American labor movement. Barely half of the auto workers at GM approved a contract containing wage concessions by the union, despite intense lobbying for the contract by the union's leaders. Given seniority rules, it is not hard to guess which half voted yes.

Not all unions are going the same way. While steel, auto, and many others are trying to preserve jobs, the electrical workers are resolutely refusing to do so, and employment in this field is shrinking.

A recent innovation that is designed to resolve the dilemma for the present generation of union members is called two-tier pricing.

Two-tier pricing.   The objective of a two-tier wage structure is to protect the high wages of existing employees who have seniority in their unions, but at the same time permit employers to lower their labor costs by hiring new workers on a lower wage scale. This benefits the union, so goes the argument, because it assures it of a flow of new members who would otherwise not be hired. It benefits new employees *if* they would not otherwise have been hired, and it does not hurt the existing union members.

To see how it works, consider the two-tier wage agreement of 1985 between United Airlines and the Air Line Pilots Association, the union representing pilots and other flying personnel. Under the agreement, for example, a second officer (flight engineer) in his second year of service would have an unnual salary of $43,750 if already employed, but only $26,400 if hired after the contract date. In general the wage scale for new employees was 34 to 50 percent below that of existing employees with the same number of years of service. (When the agreement was ratified, United Airlines announced it was hiring 570 new second officers.)

Two-tier pricing is analogous to price discrimination in product markets, discussed in Chapter 13. It is controversial in labor unions because it violates the union tradition of "equal pay for equal work" and because it encourages employers to replace old hands with newcomers whenever possible. It has developed only where unions have contracts that provide ironclad seniority rules for layoffs.

The Persistence of Unemployment

Labor unions and the various institutions and practices that have developed in collective bargaining have long been known to make a difference in the way in which particular markets function. Recently economists have engaged in a major debate about whether—and if so, how—these institutions and practices affect the overall ability of the economy to cope with unemployment. We are now in a position to look at this question.

Neoclassical Theories of Unemployment

Competitive labor markets.   In the neoclassical theory of competitive wage determination, the wage rate adjusts to equate the demand and supply of labor. This is the sort of standard supply and demand analysis that is now familiar.

If the wage rate is free to vary, the competitive wage rate will equate demand and supply and thus "clear the market." At this wage rate there is no involuntary unemployment.

Of course, given an ordinary supply curve there are more potential workers than those employed at the competitive wage, but the extra potential workers are *voluntarily* unemployed—they do not choose to work at the competitive wage rate. **Involuntary unemployment** occurs when qualified persons seek but cannot find jobs at the going wage rate. As long as the wage-quantity combination that occurs is on the supply curve, everyone who is in the market and wants to work at the going wage rate gets a job.

It follows that persistent involuntary unemployment can occur in this world if, but only if, the real wage is held above its competitive equilibrium level. This was shown in Figure 20-1. The remedy for involuntary unemployment in the neoclassical world is thus obvious: *Reduce the real wage rate to the competitive level.* There can be no involuntary unemployment at the competitive equilibrium wage.

Noncompetitive markets.   How then could economists explain the fact of unemployment? Plainly either labor unions or monopsony or both together could lead to unemployment. For example, a wage-setting union could raise the wage rate above the market clearing level and accept the unemployment of some of its members. Similarly, monopsony could lower the level of employment below the competitive level, as was shown in Figure 20-2.

Classical economists readily accepted that either monopsony or monopoly might lead to unemployment. Thus they did not deny the existence of unemployment. *What they could not accept was that unemployment could persist in competitive markets.* Yet the evidence, accumulated in recession after recession, showed that unemployment did occur, and any doubts about its persistence were shattered during the decade of the 1930s.

New Theories of Unemployment

The Great Depression triggered a major interest in understanding the problem of persistent, involuntary unemployment. For a long time economists were satisfied with the explanation offered by early Keynesian economists. Workers would fail to appreciate the link between wages and unemployment and would in a variety of ways resist a downward movement in their money wage rate. Thus, when the real wage rate was too high, competitive forces would not reduce it by forcing money wages down because workers would stubbornly resist such a fall.

Recently economists have sought alternative explanations of persistent unemployment by re-examining the determination of wages. As a result, a new set of theories has arisen. These theories question whether forces exist in actual markets that cause wages to fluctuate quickly enough to equate the current demands for and supplies of labor. If they do not, then there is reason for supply and demand *not* to be equated for extended periods of time.

These theories start with the observation that labor markets are not auction markets in which prices always respond to excess demand or excess supply. When unemployed workers are looking for jobs, they do not knock on employers' doors offering to work at lower wages than are being paid to existing workers; instead, they answer want ads and hope to get the jobs offered, but are often disappointed. Nor do employers, seeing an excess of applicants for the few jobs available, go to their existing workers and reduce their wages until there is no one looking for a job; instead, they pick and choose until they fill their needs and then hang out a sign saying "No help wanted."

The explanation of these familiar observations that is provided by the newer theories rests on the advantages to both workers and employers of relatively long-term, stable employment relationships. Workers want job security in the face of fluctuating demand. Employers want a work force that understands the firm's organization, production, and marketing plans. Under these circumstances both parties care about things other than the wage rate, and wages become somewhat insensitive to fluctuating current economic conditions. Wages are in effect regular payments to workers over an extended employment relation rather than a device for fine tuning the supply and demand for labor. Given this situation, the tendency is for employers to "smooth" the income of employees by paying a steady money wage and letting profits and employment fluctuate to absorb the effects of temporary increases and decreases in demand for the firm's product.

Many labor-market institutions work to achieve these results. For one example, long-term contracts fix money wages for several years at a time. For another, fringe benefits providing pensions, health care, and other benefits tend to bind workers to particular employers. For yet another, the fact that pay tends to rise with years of service to the employer binds the employee to the company, while seniority rules for layoffs bind the employer to the long-term worker. Precisely such rules have become the norm in collective bargaining agreements.

These things tend to be the adhesive that leads to long-term employment despite the known fact that the marginal product of workers rises rapidly as they gain experience, reaches a peak, and then falls off as their age advances. Under gradually rising wages, experienced workers tend to get less than the value of their marginal product at earlier ages and more as they near retirement. But over the long pull they are paid, on average, the value of their marginal product, just as the theory predicts they will be. Between rising wages with age and dismissal in recessions in ascending order of seniority, employers and employees are held to each other, allowing payment of a more or less steady wage in the face of fluctuating economic circumstances.

In such labor markets the wage rate does not fluctuate to clear the market. Wages are written over what has been called the "economic climate" rather than the "economic weather." Because wages are thus insulated from short-term fluctuations in demand, any market clearing that does occur is through fluctuations in the volume of employment rather than in the wage. Of course, wages must respond to permanent shifts in market conditions, for example, the permanent and unexpected decline in the demand for the output of a particular industry.

The basic message of new theories of unemployment is that freely functioning labor markets, even those completely free from monopoly and monopsony elements, cannot be relied on to eliminate unemployment by equating current demand for labor with current supply.

Further important implications of these theories for the causes of, and cures for, persistent unemployment are discussed in detail in the macroeconomic parts of this book.

Discrimination in Labor Markets

There have been, and continue to be, large differences between the earnings of nonwhites and whites and between women and men. If we create an index of median wage and salary earnings with white males equal to 100, black males today equal about 70, white females about 60, and black females about 57. These earnings disparities have multiple causes, but they raise a concern about the existence of labor market discrimination and the extent to which discriminatory employment practices give rise to the earnings differences.

The first major labor discrimination law suit was settled in 1973 when AT&T paid $15 million in back pay and an additional $23 million a year in raises to women and minority males against whom it had allegedly discriminated in job assignments, pay, and promotions. Since then, such suits and settlements have become commonplace. Coal companies have paid fines for denying women access to high-paying underground jobs. The construction industry has agreed to quotas for black workers to remedy the past exclusion of blacks from a variety of occupa-

tions. These suits and settlements focus on what many had long suspected—that discrimination by race and by sex has often occurred in the American job market.

The economic effects of discrimination against minorities and women take many forms. Discrimination does not wholly explain, but it surely contributes to lower wages and higher unemployment rates for those discriminated against. Both lower wages and greater unemployment lead to lower incomes for the workers involved.

Discrimination may also lead to different attitudes toward the workplace and toward society. It affects not only the workers discriminated against, but their children, whose aspirations and willingness to undertake the education or training required to "succeed" may be adversely affected. Indeed, it may change their definition of success.

The problems of racial discrimination and sex discrimination are different from each other, but there are similarities as well as differences. It is helpful to look first at how either kind of discrimination produces its effects.

A Model of Discrimination

We begin by building a simplified picture of a society without discrimination and then introduce discrimination. While this reverses the real problem of reducing or eliminating discrimination, it provides insight into the effects of discrimination. We are concerned here with discrimination between two sets of workers who are in every sense equally qualified. We phrase our discussion in terms of black versus white, but it applies equally to female versus male, alien versus citizen, Catholic versus Protestant, or any other prejudicial basis for dividing workers.

Suppose there are two groups of equal size in a society. One is white; the other is black. Except for color, the groups are the same—each has the same proportion who are educated to various levels, each has identical distributions of talent, and so on. Suppose also that there are two occupations. Occupation E (for elite) requires people of above average education and skills, and occupation O (ordinary) can use anyone, but if wages in the two occupations are the same, employers in occupation O will prefer to hire the above average worker. There is no racial discrimination; everyone is color-blind. The non-monetary advantages of the two occupations are equal.

The competitive theory of distribution suggests that the wages in E occupations will be bid up slightly above those in O occupations in order that the E jobs attract the workers of above average skills. Whites and blacks of above average skill will flock to E jobs, while the others, white and black alike, will have no choice but to seek O jobs. Because skills are equally distributed, each occupation will have half whites and half blacks.

Now we introduce discrimination in its most extreme form. All E occupations are hereafter open only to whites; all O occupations are open to either whites or blacks. The immediate effect is to reduce by 50 percent the supply of job applicants for E occupations (applicants must be *both* white and above average) and, potentially, to increase by 50 percent the supply of applicants for O jobs (this group includes all blacks and the below average whites).

Wage Level Effects

Suppose, first, that there are no barriers to mobility of labor, that everyone seeks the best job he or she is eligible for, and that wage rates are free to vary so as to equate supply and demand. The analysis is shown in Figure 20-5. Wages rise sharply in E occupations and fall in O occupations. The take-home pay of those in O occupations falls, and while the O group still includes both whites and blacks, it is now approximately two-thirds black.

FIGURE 20-5   Economic Discrimination: Wage Level Effects

(i) Elite market (E)

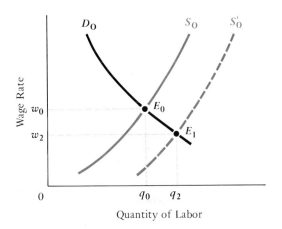

(ii) Ordinary market (O)

If market E discriminates against one group and market O does not, the supply curve will shift to the left in E and to the right in O. Market E requires above average skills, while market O requires only ordinary skills. When there is no discrimination, demands and supplies are D_E and S_E in market E, and D_O and S_O in market O. Initially the wage rate is represented by w_0 and employment by q_0 in each market. (The actual wage in market E will be slightly higher than the wage in market O.) When all blacks are barred from E occupations, the supply curve shifts to S_E' and the wage earned by the remaining workers, all of whom are white, rises to w_1. Blacks put out of work in the E occupation now seek work in the O occupation. The resulting shift in the supply curve to S_O' brings down the wage to w_2 in the O occupations. Since all blacks are in O occupations, they have a lower wage rate than many whites. The average white wage is higher than the average black wage.

Discrimination, by changing supply, can decrease the wages and incomes of a group that is discriminated against.

In the longer run further changes may occur. Notice that total employment in E industries falls. Employers may find ways to utilize slightly below average labor and thus lure the best qualified white workers out of O occupations. While this will raise O wages slightly, it will also make these occupations increasingly "black occupations." An important long-run effect may be that blacks will learn that it no longer pays to acquire above average skills since blacks are forced by discrimination to work in jobs that do not use them. Yet if blacks never acquire the skills, they will be locked into the O occupations even if the discriminatory policy is reversed. And their children may conclude that education is for whites only.

Employment Effects

For a number of reasons, labor market discrimination may have adverse employment effects that are even more important than effects on wage levels. Labor is not perfectly mobile, wages are not perfectly flexible downward, and not everyone who is denied employment in an E occupation for which he or she is trained and qualified will be willing to take a "demeaning" O job. We continue the graphical example in Figure 20-6.

If wages do not fall to the market-clearing level (say, because of minimum wage laws), the increase in supply of labor to O occupations will cause excess supply and result in unemployment of labor in O occupations. Since, in our model, blacks dominate these occupations, blacks will bear the brunt of the extra unemployment. This is illustrated in Figure 20-6(i). A similar result will occur if labor is not fully mobile between occupations, say, because many of the O occupation jobs are in parts of the country to which the workers discriminated against are unable or unwilling to move. See Figure 20-6(ii). Potential O workers who cannot move to where jobs are available become unemployed or withdraw from the labor force.

A different mechanism can produce the identical result if those persons who lose their E jobs as a result of discrimination withdraw from the labor force. They may do just this if they have the skill and training to do the more respectable and more rewarding E jobs. Indeed, it may be less demeaning to accept unemployment compensation or even welfare than to accept the only jobs that the discriminatory society offers them.

In the long term these unemployment effects may be increased by sociological and economic forces. Children of those discriminated against may well take as role models those who have made a life outside the labor force. Technological changes in the economy tend to decrease the demand for less skilled labor of the kind required in O occupations, which become increasingly oversupplied. This possibility is sketched in Figure 20-6(iii).

These theoretical possibilities have their counterparts in the real world. We shall discuss them briefly with respect to both black-white and female-male differences in the United States.

Black-White Differentials

The differences in employment and pay rates for blacks and for whites are dramatic and easily measured. By 1985, after more than two decades of vigorous equal employment activity, the median black family had earnings only 60 percent as high as those of the median white family. This figure reflects fewer jobs, lower-paying jobs, and more frequent part-time employment. Unemployment among blacks normally runs at more than twice the level for whites—roughly 13 percent to 6 percent in relatively good times—and in sharp recessions the ratio increases. Among blacks 16 to 19 years old the official unemployment rate was over 50 percent in the mid 1980s, while a rate adjusted to include those who have given up looking for work after repeated turndowns was over 60 percent!

We are talking here about averages. Of course, there are some blacks who do as well as or better than their white counterparts in employment opportunities and in pay. But this is true of too few to raise the average black to the economic position of the average white.

Even employed blacks are often disadvantaged.

FIGURE 20-6 Economic Discrimination: Employment Effects

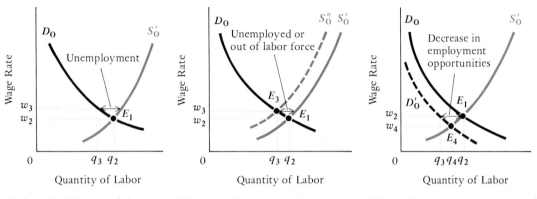

(i) Wage rigidities (or minimum wage)

(ii) Immobile labor (or withdrawal from labor force)

(iii) Declining demand

Increasing supply or decreasing demand in occupations in which those discriminated against are the major sources of labor can increase unemployment. In each part of the diagram the curves D_O and S'_O are those from Figure 20-5(ii); they show the market for O workers after the discriminatory policies are put into effect. Equilibrium is at E_1. In each case the wage w_2 would clear the market and provide employment of q_2.

(i) If the wage rate cannot fall below w_3, perhaps because of a minimum wage law, employment will fall to q_3 and unemployment will occur in the amount shown by the arrow.

(ii) If some of the potential workers in O occupation are unable or unwilling to take employment in O jobs, the supply curve will not be S'_O but S''_O. Equilibrium will be at E_3. While O wages will rise somewhat to w_3, employment will be only q_3 and a number of workers, shown by the arrow, will not be employed. Whether they are recorded as "unemployed" or as having withdrawn from the labor force will depend on the official definitions.

(iii) If demand is declining in O occupation over time, say, from D_O to D'_O, either wages and employment will fall to the new equilibrium E_4 with w_4 and q_4, or wages will be maintained but employment will fall to q_3. The arrow illustrates the latter case, where the fall in employment is q_3q_2.

Blacks tend to have less seniority than whites of similar ages, often because of past discrimination. The seniority they do have tends to be in the less skilled, lower-paid job categories. Blacks as a group have poorer health, shorter life expectancy, and shorter working lives.

All these characteristics contribute to lower economic status, but not all of them necessarily represent racial discrimination. Many of the disadvantages remain even when there is equal pay for equal work. Whites and blacks have, on average, different educational backgrounds and different sorts of professional or vocational training. Since these, too, affect employment opportunities and actual pay rates

within occupations, is it not possible that they, rather than discrimination, account for the differentials?

To answer this question it is necessary to note that discrimination might be present not only directly (e.g., refusing to hire blacks because they are black), but also indirectly (e.g., refusing to hire blacks because they are not well trained, when training has been denied them because they are black).

Direct discrimination has decreased over the last 35 years. For example, direct employment discrimination against black athletes ended in that period, and federal laws have resulted in equal pay for equal work in many industrial jobs. But blatant discrimination survives in some occupations, and a preference for whites still exists in many others. Minorities account for about 25 percent of the total work force, but only 5 percent of managerial positions.

Indirect discrimination is harder to measure. If racial prejudice and discrimination vanished from the world today, its effects would still be felt for generations. A black man whose grandfather and father were illiterate farm workers because they were denied a decent education even after they were freed from slavery is unlikely to have had the opportunity or motivation to get much education himself. For one thing, he will have been needed on the farm to help feed the family. More important, he may have been raised in a culture that failed to see in education either the path to economic opportunity or a desirable end in itself. Even when employers are prepared to treat all applicants equally, blacks are often less skilled in hearing about, applying for, and interviewing for many good jobs.

The persistence of black unemployment.   Despite both more vigorous legal enforcement of anti-discrimination laws since 1964 and substantial federal expenditures under the Comprehensive Employment Training Act (CETA), employment of blacks has not increased relative to employment of whites. Indeed, between 1980 and 1985 it actually decreased. There are a number of well-identified but not easily corrected reasons for this continuing problem. Special training programs do not have much effect on those unused to learning or without basic learning skills. Reinforcing this situation is the steady decline in employment opportunities in the unskilled and semi-skilled jobs traditionally open to those with limited education. This decline reflects both increased automation in such heavy industries as automobiles and steel and the rising importance of service industries (as compared with manufacturing).

A further cause is the lesser geographical mobility of poor blacks as many available jobs have tended to move from the central cities to the suburbs and from the older population centers of the North to the Sun Belt. Among additional reasons are rising minimum wages, which reduce employment opportunities in some unskilled occupations, and some disdain on the part of modern blacks for the lowest-paying jobs as being beneath the dignity of people who wish to be

treated equally. Finally, it seems unmistakable that the greater labor force participation of women has increased the competition for jobs. Unfortunately, blacks have often been losers in that competition.

Female-Male Differentials

While high unemployment among blacks is a key feature of black-white differentials in labor market experience, it is not the key to female-male differentials. Adult females have been steadily increasing their labor force participation. The labor force participation of adult women increased from 34 percent in 1953 to 55 percent in 1985. This occurred without any increase in the unemployment rate of females, which is approximately equal to that of males.

Getting jobs is, of course, not the whole story. It has long been clear that women and men make and are offered different occupational choices. But even here there is notable progress. Over the last two decades women have steadily increased their participation in "higher status" occupations, including managerial, sales, scientific, and technical jobs. For one example, in 1966 women accounted for 13.6 percent of the professional labor force and by 1985 that figure had risen to 36 percent.

Despite these rather dramatic changes, average earned income of females in the labor force is well below that of males of similar ages. Wages of females tend to be only about two-thirds those of males. The "salary gap" for females is due to a combination of causes: Women are still underrepresented in high-status occupations, proportionately fewer women than men reach higher-paying jobs in the occupations in which both work, and those who do reach higher-paying jobs do so more slowly. Do these facts reflect discrimination?

Discrimination within occupations.   To what extent do differences in pay levels of men and women *within* an occupation reflect discrimination against women and to what extent do they reflect such other sex-linked characteristics as the voluntary choice of different lifetime patterns of labor force participation? The statistics show that, on average, women have fewer years of education, training, and work experience than men of the same age. The average working female is less mobile occupationally and geographically than her male counterpart. At least some of these facts reflect what is called lower *labor market attachment;* for example, many women decide to withdraw from the labor force or to work only part-time in order to have and raise children.

The extent of direct discrimination in an occupation may be measured by comparing the pay status of groups with similar characteristics. Professors Mary Corcoran and Gregory Duncan analyzed pay differences between men and women and found that less than half (44 percent) of the difference could be explained by differences in education, work experience, and labor market attachment. Other studies show much the same thing and add up to 10 to 25 percent pay differences *not* explained by these variables. Analysts attribute this part of male-female pay differentials to direct discrimination.

Interoccupational discrimination. Women may have also suffered indirect discrimination as a result of being employed in a different set of occupations from men. They have been refused admission or discouraged from seeking entry into certain occupations; for example, they have traditionally been pushed into nursing rather than medicine, social work rather than law, and secretarial schools rather than managerial training programs. This is called *occupational segregation.* Similarly, girls raised in a culture in which their education seems less important than that of their brothers or in which they are trained to think of themselves as potential homemakers and urged to prepare themselves to attract and serve a husband are less likely to acquire the skills for many high-paying occupations that are wholly within their capabilities.

Differences in pay among occupations will, as we have seen, reflect differences in supply and demand, including nonmonetary factors. But may they not also reflect discrimination if one occupation is predominantly female and the other predominantly male? This is certainly possible, and many persons concerned about labor market discrimination have urged attention to interoccupational pay differences under the general term "pay equity." Determining how much observed differences reflect discrimination is extremely difficult because so many different considerations affect the pay levels of, say, firemen and librarians. A particular (but controversial) approach to this problem called *comparable worth* is discussed in Box 20-3.

Progress Against Discrimination

Laws prohibiting discrimination in pay and in employment have been in effect since the early 1960s. The civil rights and women's liberation movements have been active over the intervening years. How much progress has been made? The answer is mixed and subject to continuing debate.

Consider male-female differences. Women have, as we have seen, steadily increased their labor force participation from only about 35 percent in the 1960s to over 50 percent in the 1980s; labor force participation of males declined from 83 to 78 percent over the same period. Moreover, unemployment rates for women and men are no longer significantly different. Thus differences in ability to get and hold some kind of a job have plainly been reduced. But the pay gap has not. Partly this is differences in pay levels within occupations, partly the continued segregation of women in lower paying occupations.

Whether remaining differences in participation and the pay gap will soon be narrowed is unclear. To the extent that they rest on educational differences, they are expected to decrease. Women, especially white women, have relatively quickly closed the educational gap that led to indirect discrimination. Between 1971 and 1982 the fraction of earned doctorates awarded to women rose from 14 percent to 28 percent, and nearly half of the new graduate enrollments were women, so this upward trend is likely to continue. In 1981 17 percent of first professional degrees (law, medicine, etc.) were awarded to women, compared to 6.5 percent 10 years earlier. Current enrollments in these professional schools are roughly 30 percent women. These trends reflect affirmative action on the part of schools, changed attitudes on the part of women, and wider employment prospects for women than even 10 years before.

The black-white picture is different. While the wage gap of black males relative to white males has decreased from about 35 percent to 30 percent since 1965, the unemployment rate for blacks remains at

BOX 20-3

Comparable Worth

In 1983 a U.S. District Court judge ruled that the State of Washington had violated the Civil Rights Act of 1964 and had discriminated on the basis of sex when it paid (predominantly female) practical nurses $739 per month and (predominantly male) campus police $1,070 per month. The ruling led to retroactive pay increases that cost the State $800 million. Perhaps more important, it gave a big boost to the notion of using an occupational yardstick called *comparable worth* to evaluate sex discrimination.

While the legal status of comparable worth is in doubt, the idea has emotional and political appeal. Who, after all, would be publicly opposed to a notion that its supporters characterize as "pay equity for women"? Certainly not a politician whose electorate is half female.

The objective in measuring comparable worth is to measure the *intrinsic* value of different occupations so as to judge whether job A is worth more than job B. One method assigns each occupation "worth-points" in four categories based on interviews by a team of experts: (1) knowledge and skills, (2) mental demands, (3) accountability, and (4) working conditions. Two occupations with comparable point totals are classified as of comparable value. In Minnesota the results of such a calculation showed that librarians

and firemen were of approximately comparable worth. Since librarians (mostly female) earned less than firemen (mostly male), the conclusion was that discrimination had occurred.

Comparable Worth v. Supply and Demand

Consider, first, a situation in which pay differentials are not discriminatory, but reflect instead equilibrium differentials in a competitive market economy.

Suppose that two groups of city employees, call them librarians and firefighters, have the supply and demand curves shown below. In competitive equilibrium librarians would earn a wage w_1, firefighters w_2, that is, there is an equilibrium differential in the market-clearing wages. Now, as a result of a comparable worth study, the city is ordered to pay equal wages to the two groups.

The mayor proposes to comply by paying both groups a compromise wage, w_c, somewhat higher than the wage librarians have been receiving, but lower than that of firefighters. Librarians are pleased, and, indeed, the mayor begins to get extra applications from persons who seek to be librarians once the new wage goes into effect. (There is excess supply of librarians, q_1q_2, at w_c.) But the head of the Firemen's

more than twice the level for whites. Moreover, labor force participation of black males has dropped sharply, from about 80 percent to 70 percent, reflecting withdrawal from the labor force of many blacks after long bouts of unemployment. Thus, black

males have been substantially less successful than white women in gaining access to jobs.

What accounts for the difference? Many observers believe it lies in the fact that the economic and educational backgrounds of males and females of the

Union is burned up: "You can't cut our pay. We'll quit." Indeed, some of the firemen do quit. (At wage w_c there is excess demand of q_3q_4.) The fire chief warns the mayor he won't be able to fill the firehouse or meet all the calls for putting out fires. The mayor decides to go back to the court with her dilemma. The judge is unsympathetic: "All your problems come from the proposed cut in firefighters' pay. You may pay anything you like to firefighters; just be sure to pay the librarians the same."

The mayor then tells the state compensation director that he should raise librarians' pay to w_2, the firefighters' competitive rate.

In order to meet the extra wage bill, the city council orders libraries closed two days a week and lays off some librarians. While the firefighters do not complain, the laid-off librarians do, and so do the citizens who want the libraries open on Fridays and Saturdays. Meanwhile, the head of libraries is besieged with applications for the newly attractive library jobs.

Comparable Worth in the Public Sector

Comparable worth is usually discussed as a means of setting pay scales for *government* employment. But government pay scales cannot be wholly arbitrary, because governments must compete with the private sector for workers. If governments set the wage for one group below the equilibrium wage, they will have trouble filling vacancies, and they will eventually have to raise the pay of that group to meet their needs. But what of groups where government pay is above equilibrium? Governments will have all the workers they want, but also higher than needed expenditures.

Governments can and do sometimes pay above-market wages, ration jobs by other means, and raise taxes or cut services to pay the bill. But as those with budget responsibility look for places to cut, they will notice the excess supply in some occupations and let those wages fall behind the ones where there is a shortage. Thus, gradually, wage differentials respond to supply and demand considerations. Legislated differentials that cannot be altered in response to market needs may be right at any one moment, but they will surely be unresponsive to the changes that regularly occur.

Evaluation

Is comparable worth "progressive pragmatism," as New York Governor Mario Cuomo called it, or is it a "profoundly and irretrievably flawed" concept, as the Commission on Civil Rights concluded? The answer depends in part on whether pre-existing wage differentials are largely arbitrary or whether they reflect market conditions of supply and demand. To the extent they are equilibrium differentials, they serve to assure an adequate supply of persons in different occupations.

But suppose there *is* discrimination in existing wage scales. Some method of correction is appropriate, but any rigid system promises trouble. The right differential today will be the wrong differential next year. Comparable worth by focusing on *intrinsic* aspects of jobs and ignoring market ones—such as that with equal pay, many more people would choose to be librarians than firefighters—builds in a rigidity that will surely cause problems in resource use. Many who believe in the need for affirmative action and the reality of discriminatory pay differentials oppose anything so arbitrary and rigid as evaluation based on worth points. Most economists believe that ever-changing market conditions of supply and demand must be given a role as well.

same generation have been much more nearly equal than between blacks and whites of either sex. Moreover, cultural and motivational barriers to women can apparently be changed in a single generation, while such a change may take longer for blacks. It is

perhaps also true that sex prejudices in the labor market are less deeply ingrained than racial prejudices. But before one claims victory against sex discrimination, one must remember that the pay disadvantages of women in the labor force are still substantial, even after allowance is made for differences in education, work history, and labor force attachment.

Who Loses from Discrimination?

Obviously, the victims lose as a result of labor market discrimination. But it is a mistake to think that they are the only losers. Society loses, too, because of the efficiency losses that discrimination causes and in other ways.

Efficiency losses arise for several reasons. If women or blacks are not given equal pay with white males for equal work, the labor force will not be allocated so as to get the most out of society's resources. When people are kept from doing the jobs at which they are most productive and must instead produce goods or services that society values less, the total value of goods and services produced is reduced. And when prejudice increases unemployment, it reduces the nation's total output.

The gainers from discrimination are those who earn the higher pay that comes from limiting supply in their occupations, those who get the jobs that blacks and women would otherwise have held, and the bigots who gain pleasure from not having to work with "them" or to consume services provided by "them." But if the total output of society is less, the net losses will have to be borne by the society as a whole.

Beyond the efficiency losses that discrimination imposes on society are further economic and social costs. Increased welfare or unemployment payments may be required, and the costs of enforcing anti-discrimination laws must be paid.

The costs of discrimination also include increased crime, hostility, and violence. These things are all by-products of unemployment, poverty, and frustration. Discrimination, if not attacked and rolled back, has one more cost, perhaps the most important: a sense of shame in a society that does not do what is necessary to eliminate the barriers to equal treatment.

Summary

1. A wage-setting union entering a competitive market can raise wages, but only at the cost of reducing employment and creating a pool of unemployed former workers and others who would like to work at the going wage but are unable to gain employment in that market.

2. If the union can limit entry into the field, it can shift the supply curve to the left and achieve a higher wage without creating unemployment in the occupation.

3. A wage-setting union entering a monopsonistic market may increase both employment and wages over some range. If, however, it sets the wage above the competitive level, it will create a pool of workers who are unable to get the jobs they want at the going wage.

4. Governments set some wages above their competitive levels by passing minimum wage laws. The overall effects of minimum wages have now been extensively studied. It is clear that they raise the incomes of many employees, but they cause unemployment for many of those with the lowest levels of skills.

5. Labor markets have developed a wide variety of institutions, including labor unions and employers' associations. Such institutions greatly affect wage determination.

6. American unionism developed first in the skilled trades, along craft lines, where it was possible to control supply and prevent nonunion members from undercutting union wages. Widespread or-

ganization of the unskilled did not occur until after the legal right to organize was established by the Wagner Act in 1935. The emergence of mature collective bargaining is a relatively recent development in the stormy and sometimes bloody history of American labor unions.

7. Unions face a basic conflict between the goals of raising wages and preserving employment opportunities for members and potential members. Other trade-offs concern wages and job security, and wages and fringe benefits.

8. Labor market institutions can lead to labor markets that operate very differently from the competitive labor market of neoclassical economics. Unemployment may persist because of labor market practices that assure relatively long-term, stable employment relationships. Much of the market clearing in labor markets that occurs in the face of fluctuations in demand takes the form of fluctuations in employment rather than fluctuations in wage rates.

9. Discrimination by race and by sex has played a role in labor markets, as it has in other aspects of American life. Direct discrimination affects wages and employment opportunities by limiting the supply in the best-paying occupations and increasing it in less attractive occupations.

10. Indirect discrimination has had an effect through limiting the opportunities for education and training available to those subject to discrimination and through lowering people's aspirations in their choices of training and of careers.

11. Discrimination imposes costs on the victims of discrimination. In addition it leads to inefficiency and loss of output and is costly in other ways.

Topics for Review

Monopsony power
Union power
Effects of minimum wages
Collective bargaining
Goals of unions
Possible causes of involuntary unemployment
Labor market attachment
Wage effects and employment effects of economic discrimination
Direct and indirect discrimination
Comparable worth

Discussion Questions

1. American unions have traditionally supported laws
   a. Restricting immigration
   b. Expelling illegal aliens
   c. Raising the minimum wage and extending its coverage

How do each of these positions benefit or hurt the following groups: (1) the American consumer, (2) American workers as a whole, and (3) unionized workers with seniority in their jobs.

2. A union that has bargaining rights in two plants of the same company in different states almost always insists on "equal pay for equal work" in the two plants. It does not always insist on equal pay for men and women in the same jobs. Can you see any economic reasons for such a distinction?

3. Why were craft unions more successful than industrial unions in the late nineteenth century in the United States? What happened to change this in the 1930s?

4. Interpret the following statements or practices in terms of the subject matter of this chapter.
   a. A headline in the *New York Times*: "Two-tier wage contracts lead to surge of new hiring by major airlines."
   b. A requirement that one must pass an English language proficiency test to be a carpenter in New York City
   c. A statement by an official of a textile workers' union in Massachusetts: "Until we have organized the southern textile industry, we will be unable to earn a decent wage in New England."
   d. A statement by an official of the United Steel Workers: "Things are getting rough in our locals because the youngsters have different views about wages than the old-timers."

5. "The great increase in the number of women entering the labor force for the first time means that relatively more women than men earn beginning salaries. It is therefore not evidence of discrimination that the average wage earned by females is less than that earned by males." Discuss.

6. The American Cyanamid Corporation once had a policy of removing women of child-bearing age from, or not hiring them for, jobs that expose them to lead or other substances that could damage a fetus. Is this sex discrimination? Whether it is or not, debate whether this sort of protective hiring rule is something the government should require, encourage, or prohibit.

7. "One can judge the presence or absence of discrimination by looking at the proportion of the population in different occupations." Does such information help? Does it suffice? Consider each of the following examples. Relative to their numbers in the total population, there are
   a. Too many blacks and too few Jews among professional athletes
   b. Too few male secretaries
   c. Too few female judges

8. "Of nearly 40 million working women, 40 percent are in traditionally female occupations—secretaries, nurses, cashiers, waitresses, elementary school teachers, beauticians, maids, and sales clerks, for example. While this may result from past sex stereotyping, the notion that only women can do these jobs may also benefit women by preserving employment opportunities for them, given the high unemployment rates among black males and teenage males." Discuss this argument.

9. Consider the consequences of applying the notion of "equal pay for comparable worth" to compensation of:
   a. Football coaches and cross country coaches
   b. University presidents and network anchorpersons
   c. Fashion models and poets
   d. Police in urban ghettos and police in surburban areas
10. Compare the following policies designed to reduce pay differentials due to occupational segregation of women in lower-paid jobs.
    a. Making pay adjustments based on an analysis of the "comparable worth" of occupations
    b. Removing barriers to women's employment in traditionally male jobs
    c. Setting quotas based on the relevant population statistics for minimum fractions of females in each occupation

21

The Problem of Poverty

Possibly the most discussed aspect of distribution concerns the proportion of national income that goes to the very poor. Who are they? Why are they poor? What can—or should—we do about it?

Poverty and the means used to alleviate it play a large part in political debates. President Lyndon Johnson's so-called War on Poverty began an enormous investment in programs to aid the poor. Was the investment affordable? Did the war succeed? Those issues are as intensely debated today as they were two decades ago. The Reagan administration sharply cut back on those programs and evoked a new and bitter debate.

Poverty in the United States

There are reasons for the variations in what different individuals can earn. People differ in the talents they possess and the factors of production they own; consequently, both the quantity of factor services they can sell and the price they receive will vary. Some factor owners are in a position to respond quickly to changing opportunities. Others are immobile and suffer when events leave them in markets where no one wants what they have to sell. To what extent do such reasons account for the continuing presence of poverty in the United States?

The Concept of Poverty

One possible definition of poverty is to be poorer than most of your fellow citizens. There will, of course, always be 10 percent of the population that is poorer than the other 90 percent.

Clearly, poverty must mean more than low relative income. Some minimum family income standard is required to define the **poverty level** below which a family is said to be poor. Such a standard specifies a dollar amount based on estimates of need and the cost of living. In 1984 the American poverty level was defined by the Department of Commerce as $10,609 per year for a nonfarm family of four. This is the amount estimated to be needed to maintain "a minimum adequate standard of living."

The concept of poverty reflects the expectations and aspirations of society as a whole as to what constitutes an acceptable minimum standard of living. Less than 100 years ago, poverty would have been defined as the lack of the minimum amounts of food, shelter, and clothing needed to sustain life. At one time this condition faced (or threatened) a large portion of the world's urban and rural masses. Total output was so low that all but a privileged minority lived at or near this level, and any crop failure plunged thousands into starvation. Poverty in this sense is still present in the world, even in the United States. Starvation, hunger, and malnutrition are suffered by millions of individual Americans, and some Americans born in 1987 will starve to death.

Yet in most advanced industrial countries, as in the United States, output has risen until the average family enjoys a high material standard of living, and the provision of subsistence requirements of food, shelter, and clothing is a major problem for only a small number of families. If this is so—if mere subsistence does not define the poverty level—what does it mean to say, as the Department of Commerce did in 1984, that 33.7 million Americans live in poverty?

Consider the income of a member of a family just at the poverty level. Income of $10,609 for a family of four is $2,652.25 per person. This will not seem like a great deal to most of you, but it is above the per capita income of most of the world's population. This should not lead anyone to minimize poverty problems; the black American living in Harlem and working as a porter at LaGuardia airport needs more clothes, transportation, and other basics than an Indonesian peasant. Visit the slums of any American city and you will not lightly dismiss poverty.

While $10,609 for a family of four buys enough food, shelter, and clothing to get by, it is only about 40 percent of the average (median) income of American families, which in 1984 was $26,433. What it does not provide is enough money for the full range of commodities that almost all of us take for granted, such as having a refrigerator, and hot water, and attending an occasional movie. Many of the poor are understandably bitter and resentful that they and their children are outsiders looking in on the comfortable way of life shown in ads and on television. "I'd like, just once," one of them said to a *Newsweek* interviewer, "to buy Christmas presents the children want instead of the presents they need."

The Extent of Poverty

The extent of poverty may be measured either by the number and percentage of persons in households having incomes below the poverty level or by mea-

suring the **poverty gap:** the number of dollars per year required to raise everyone's income to this level. In 1984 over 33 million persons (14.4 percent of the population) were classified as poor, and the poverty gap was approximately $45 billion.

These figures are themselves controversial. Critics such as Stanford University economist Martin Anderson and the University of Virginia's Edgar Browning argue that the figures neglect such extras as illegal income, unreported income, and noncash benefits such as food stamps and subsidized housing. An accurate measure, they say, might count those really in poverty as only 7 million and reduce the poverty gap to somewhere between $8 to $10 billion. Others, such as Wisconsin's Robert Haveman, agree that it is appropriate to add such benefits, but say that the adjustment for extras, if done accurately, would still show 13 million people—at least 6 percent —living in poverty.

The historical trend. Whatever the deficiencies of these numbers as absolute measures of poverty, they are useful for tracing changes in the magnitude of the problem. In 1933 President Franklin D. Roosevelt spoke of a third of a nation as being in poverty. By 1959 the official definitions placed 22 percent of the nation below the poverty line. Figure 21-1 charts the course of poverty in America since then. The steady downward trend from 22 percent to just over 12 percent in the decade from 1959 to 1969 is impressive, but the trend was much flatter during the 1970s. The upturn since 1978 is a major source of concern. By 1984 the poverty percentage had risen to 14.4 percent, and was over 33 percent for blacks.

Explaining the trend. The decline in poverty shown in Figure 21-1 from 1959 to the mid 1960s was the culmination of a well-documented century-long period in which economic growth doubled average living standards every generation and reduced the incidence of poverty. Studies show that as long as 40 or 30 or even 20 percent of the population are living in poverty, economic growth is a major weapon in reducing poverty. It does so by raising average labor productivity and thus raising the real earnings of those who work.

But not all of the poor benefit from such things

FIGURE 21-1   Percentage of Americans Below the Poverty Level, 1959–1984

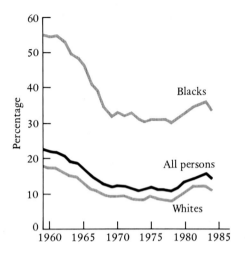

Poverty declined sharply during the 1960s, but declined much less during the 1970s and has risen since 1978. The poverty level is adjusted annually to incorporate changes in the Consumer Price Index. For 1984 a family of four with an income below $10,609 was considered poor. The frequency of poverty is much higher for blacks than for whites, and there is no suggestion in the chart that this condition is likely to change soon.

as rising wages. Those families that do not have wage earners, for example, will not benefit directly from rising wages. They are part of the so-called hard core poverty group for whom poverty will not be eliminated by mere economic growth. Estimates vary, but at least 10 percent of Americans are in the hard-core poverty group.

When by 1965 poverty was pushed down toward the hard-core level, further economic growth was no longer likely to reduce the percentage living in poverty much further. To cope with hard-core poverty would require deliberate income redistribution. The Kennedy and Johnson administrations adopted this diagnosis and began the so-called War on Poverty. The University of Wisconsin, Institute for Research on Poverty found that the policies were highly effective. Indeed they found that most of the sharp decreases in the poverty rate between 1965 and 1980

were directly due to increased payments to the poor such as food stamps and welfare payments and to increases in social security benefits. Such payments are called *transfer payments* and are discussed more generally in Chapter 23.

A widely held view among economists (which, as we shall see, the Reagan administration was to dispute) explains the level of poverty in a country at any time in terms of three influences.

1. The historical record of economic growth, which raises average productivity and can reduce poverty toward its hard-core level. Historically, economic growth has played a major role in poverty reduction.
2. The number and level of government policies that redistribute income to those in poverty. Recent experience suggests that government programs of income redistribution have become more important than economic growth in achieving further reductions in American poverty. Decreasing government transfers increase poverty.
3. The level of unemployment in the economy, with increases in unemployment leading to increases in the numbers living in poverty

As Figure 21-1 shows, even after a century of rapid growth and two decades of policies designed to eliminate poverty, the poor are still with us in significant numbers.

Who Are the Poor?

There are poor among people of all ages, races, and educational levels, among the working as well as the unemployed and the retired. Yet some groups have much higher incidences of poverty than others. Figure 21-1 shows this is true of blacks. Table 21-1 shows that poverty is also particularly high among families with minor children (particularly if they are black), those unemployed or not in the labor force, those with limited education, and those of Spanish origin.

The data in Table 21-2 permit us to look at the problem somewhat differently. Instead of focusing on the prevalence of poverty among certain subgroups in the population, we look at those who are poor and describe some of their characteristics. A

TABLE 21-1   The Incidence of Poverty Among American Families, 1984

Characteristic	Percentage below poverty line
All families	12
Race and ethnic background	
White	9
Black	31
Spanish origin	25
Families with children under 18 years of age	
All	17
White	13
Black	39
Spanish origin	31
Employment status of family head	
Employed (including armed forces)	9
Unemployed	35
Not in labor force	23
Families with female head	
All	35
White	27
Black	52
Spanish origin	54
Education of family head over 24 years of age	
Elementary school or none	22
1-3 years of high school	20
4 years of high school	10
Some college	5

Source: U.S. Department of Commerce, Bureau of the Census, *Current Population Reports,* Series P-60, No. 149.

Race and ethnic background, family status, employment, and education all affect the likelihood of poverty. The numbers show the percentage of families with the designated characteristic whose incomes fall below the poverty level. Thus, while only 5 percent of families with a family head with some college education were below the poverty level, more than half of minority families with a female head were in poverty.

TABLE 21-2   Selected Characteristics of American Families Below Poverty Level, 1984

Characteristic	White (percentage)	Black (percentage)
Employment status of family head		
Employed (including armed forces)	44	30
Unemployed	12	13
Not in labor force	44	57
	100	100
Age of family head		
Under 25 years	12	14
25-44 years	53	55
45-66 years	25	22
65 years and over	10	9
	100	100
Education of family head over 25 years of age		
Elementary school or none	29	26
1-3 years of high school	20	30
4 years of high school	33	30
Some college	18	14
	100	100
Size of family		
2 or 3 persons	57	53
4 or 5 persons	33	32
6 or more persons	10	15
	100	100

Source: U.S. Department of Commerce, Bureau of the Census, *Current Population Reports,* Series P-60, No. 149.

Escaping poverty is not merely a matter of employment status, age, education, or family status. In contrast to the previous table, this one looks at the characteristics of the poor, not the likelihood of poverty for those with a given characteristic. Many of those below the poverty level are working poor. For example, 44 percent of white families below the poverty level have an employed head. The poor are found in all age groups and in small families as well as large. Over half those in poverty are in families whose head did not finish high school.

great many of the poor are employed, many are neither very young nor very old, many did not complete high school, and many are members of small families. These data show one sharp change from a couple of decades ago, when a disporportionate number of the elderly were in poverty. Social secu-

rity and other policies have significantly decreased old age as a major correlate of being poor.

These data may also help dispose of two superficial caricatures. One is the slothful father faking a disability because he is too lazy to do an honest day's work; the other is the family with so many children that an ordinarily decent wage is spread so thin that the whole family is reduced to poverty.

Causes of Poverty

The causes of poverty are various. Poverty is almost three times as high among those families that do not have an employed head as among those who do. The fact that many of the poor are families headed by women with minor children probably results from their lesser opportunities for work; similarly, age and illness force many people out of the labor market. Other important groups suffering poverty include the rural poor, who strive in vain to earn a decent living from marginal or submarginal farmlands; the urban working poor, who simply lack the skills to command a wage high enough to support themselves and their families above the poverty level; the immobile poor, who are trapped by age and outdated skills in areas and occupations where the demand for their services is declining faster than their number; and, most important, the minority poor—blacks, Indians, Puerto Ricans, Chicanos, Chinese—who constitute only one-eighth of the population but are almost one-third of the poor.

There is no single answer to the question: What causes poverty in the midst of plenty? It is partly a result of mental and physical handicaps, partly of low motivation, and partly of the raw deal that fate gives to some. Partly it is a result of current and past prejudice. Partly it is a result of unwillingness or inability to invest in the kind of human capital that pays off in the long run. Partly it is a result of the market's valuing the particular abilities that an individual does have at such a low price that, even in good health and with full-time employment, the income that can be earned leaves that person below the poverty line. Box 21-1 on pages 394–395 provides a few profiles of individuals in poverty in the 1980s.

The extent of poverty is also affected greatly by the performance of the economy. A recession, with its increase in unemployment, pushes additional millions into poverty. (The recession of 1980–1982 did this to at least 5 million people.) Inflation continually erodes the resources of those on fixed incomes. The rapid inflation of the late 1970s outstripped increases in welfare payments and the earnings of many families at or near the poverty level and contributed to the rising trend of poverty from 1978 to 1980.

The Persistently Poor

Fluctuations in the number classified as poor that result from swings in the economy highlight the important distinction between the *occasionally poor* and the *persistently poor*. While perhaps one-third of those officially classified as being in poverty at any time are only temporarily poor, half of the rest are virtually permanently poor, according to a recent study by the University of Michigan Survey Research Center. The study defines the persistently poor as those who have been in poverty for *nine consecutive years*. It is much easier to withstand a few months (or even a few years) of poverty due to a bout of unemployment or illness than it is to be permanently poor, for the latter condition erodes hope and warps one's entire outlook on life.

The persistently poor will not be rescued by an upswing in the economy, by another decade of economic growth, or even by somewhat bigger welfare payments and less inflation. A shocking statistic from the Michigan study is that more than three-quarters of the persistently poor are black. Blacks represent 11 percent of the total population, 31 percent of those below the poverty level, and 77 percent of the persistently poor.

Black Poverty

The incidence of persistent poverty among blacks is particularly acute.

This results from two related circumstances. First, blacks are subject to discrimination, whose effects were discussed in Chapter 20. Second, blacks have many of the characteristics associated with poverty: Many of them farm in the rural South or live in areas of the North where jobs are disappearing; a disproportionate number are less well educated than the average American; working blacks are heavily concentrated in industries with declining demands for labor; and their health has often been seriously impaired by malnutrition or untreated diseases.

The two circumstances interact with and reinforce each other. Whatever the combination of reasons, and despite attempts to deal with them as a matter of public policy, a gap in incomes exists and does not show signs of being eliminated. In 1970 the average black family's income was 64 percent of the average white family's income. In 1983 it was 56 percent of that income. Moreover, the income gap is accompanied by an even greater wealth gap. Net assets of the average black family, including houses and cars, were only one-tenth as large as net assets of the average white family.

Policies Toward Poverty

Eliminating poverty is easier than eliminating air pollution or cancer, for which cures are as yet unknown. For an amount estimated at about $45 billion per year in 1985 dollars, every family now below the poverty level could be given a sufficient income supplement to bring it to that level. Congress could, in other words, close the poverty gap. Although $45 billion is a lot of money, it is less than 20 percent of the national defense budget, and it represents only about 1½ percent of the total income earned in the nation.

Should We Wage War on Poverty?

Surprisingly perhaps, a good deal of the debate about attacking poverty does not concern whether we can afford it or how best to do it, but whether we *ought* to do it.

The Case Against

Everyone concedes that there are poor people who deserve to be helped. President Reagan referred to the most deserving as the "truly needy." They are those who despite their best efforts have not been able to escape the ravages of illness, blindness, desertion, age, or obsolescence. There are as well the helpless children of the poor, who should not be made to suffer endlessly for the failings or misfortunes of their parents. But there are also the "undeserving poor," those who could work but will not as long as someone else will support them and their families.

Disincentive effects.   Not only is it unnecessary and perhaps immoral to support such people, the argument says, but their number will grow rapidly if we choose to adopt more generous programs for relieving existing poverty. Even if we thought we could afford to eliminate poverty, the attempt to do so would be self-defeating. For, the argument continues, it would destroy the present incentives of those now supporting themselves just above the level at which the government would support them. They would stop working and end up on welfare as quickly as others were raised above the poverty level.

These critics point to the decline in the work ethic that accompanies increased welfare payments, unemployment compensation, and the issuance of food stamps. There is some factual basis for this argument. Today many gladly accept unemployment compensation, welfare payments, and free goods and services—and, indeed, expect them as a matter not of charity but of basic rights. Almost every program has had its scandals, and all too many people can identify others who are relying on public assistance when in fact they could support themselves.

A second disincentive effect is on the future behavior of beneficiaries of government welfare payments. Children who grow up knowing they have a welfare safety net under them may not develop the attitudes or gain the skills needed to climb above the level of the net. This effect may be particularly noticeable in those who, because of the limitations of their abilities, could never in any case hope to climb far above that level.

A third possible disincentive effect relates to those who will be asked to pay the extra taxes that must be levied if welfare spending increases. As more people go on welfare, fewer will be left to pay the taxes, so tax rates must rise. If, in response, taxpayers work less, the total amount of income available for redistribution will shrink.

The important question is whether such effects are merely occasional horror stories or whether they are frequent and quantitatively significant. Opponents of an all-out attack on poverty believe that

BOX 21-1

Profiles of Poverty

The following are newspaper sketches of people living below the poverty level. Only the names are fictitious.

▪ A 34-year-old mother of four children ranging in age from 5 to 15 waited in the Nassau County, New York, Social Services building recently for recertification for welfare.

Divorced last year from her husband, who "lived at home on and off," Glenda Rodriguez has been on welfare for 10 years. She is entitled to $450 a month in welfare grants; of that, $271 goes for rent and $67 for heating. She works as a part-time waitress whenever she can and earns $60 in a good week.

For every $60 she earns, however, her welfare grant is reduced by $40.

"Right now, I don't know how I'll make it the next two days until Friday," she said. "I owe the oil company $400—money I haven't been able to pay. We're not starving, but my kids get a little tired of eating eggs and franks."

"I'm working and I'm trying to give my children a little better life, rather than being completely on assistance," she said, "but I'm not getting any place. I'm in the hole each month."

▪ Eddie Mason, 19 years old, drank cheap wine and smoked marijuana recently in an abandoned building on Jones Street in St. Louis's slums as he told a visitor, "I've been to the employment office and they've got jobs there only in the suburbs, and I don't have a car. It wouldn't be worth my time to pay bus fare, taxes, lunch, and stuff for a job way out in the suburbs that pays $3.35 an hour."

Mr. Mason lives with his mother and admits to just enough petty thievery "to stay alive."

▪ The slightly built woman, holding two small children by the hand, walked into the cafeteria near the Welfare Office, where she had been waiting all morning, and gazed at the menu posted on the wall.

The warmth and smell of the food set the children to clamoring, "Mamma, I want . . . " and "Mamma, can I have . . . ?" She hushed the children and looked at the prices: tuna salad, $1.65; two eggs, $.96, with ham or bacon, $1.42; deli sandwich, $1.65; hamburger, $.85; cheeseburger, $1.00.

Checking her purse she bought two frankfurters at $.60 each, two containers of milk at $.33 each, and, for herself, a cup of coffee, $.32.

---

these magnitudes are, and will be proven to be, very large.

Opportunity costs.   Some maintain that we cannot afford to eliminate poverty, given all the competing uses of public money, including the need to reduce public spending in order to reduce the national debt. They contend that welfare spending is already at excessively high levels.

Advocates of the view that total government spending is already too large often argue that there are few other items over which so much discretion may be exercised. On the one hand, less could no doubt be spent on such items as defense or schools. Many believe, however, that significant cuts in these items are either impractical or undesirable. On the other hand, a genuine option does exist with welfare expenditures. One of the few realistic hopes of keep-

ing government spending under control, so goes this view, lies in holding a tight rein on the expansion of transfer payments and in particular eliminating payments to the dishonest, the lazy, and the relatively well off, who are receiving aid without real need.

The Case For

The war on poverty had its supporters as well as its opponents. Welfare cheaters, supporters agree, should be identified, exposed, and eliminated from welfare rolls wherever possible, but the abuses should not be allowed to confuse the issue. It was one thing to put up with poverty when we had no alternative; it is another to do so when we are rich enough to spend billions on cosmetics, sports, and other frills—to say nothing of space exploration, foreign "diplomacy," and an immense nuclear arsenal.

"I don't know what I'm going to do if I'm not approved for welfare," she told the visitor at the table where she was drinking her coffee and wiping sauerkraut from her children's clothes. She said she lived in Freeport, Louisiana, with her sick husband, an unemployed carpenter.

"Things have been bad in the past," she said, "what with the high cost of everything—food, rent, clothing. But it's never been like this. We've never had to ask for help before."

▪ The old man is sitting at the bus stop, in San Francisco, "just resting." He's very old, but he's not slow witted. He's hunched a little forward, hands cupped on the top of the cane that he holds between his knees.

He wants to talk, and in a little time he covers a lot of ground. Private Julius Goldman in World War I, master sergeant in World War II, and 1929 and the depression in between. Kids, inflation, retirement, a dead wife, more inflation. The way it is and the way it was.

He is a pet food devotee. Heat it; it tastes like hash.

▪ The cab driver in Madison, Wisconsin, is glad to talk: "Call me Tommy." He's 25, has a common-law wife, Ivory, and a 2-year-old son. He gets to drive only about 80 days a year even with 2 years of seniority, but the family can almost get by on the $6,000 he earns and the welfare Ivory gets. They don't pay much in taxes. He's worried now, because it's a severe winter and fuel costs are breaking their budget. Ivory works some as a midwife, but midwifery is illegal in Wisconsin, and there's not much money in it. He dropped out of college after 2 years—it didn't seem relevant. He can't go back now, although he thinks it might make sense, because he's got a family to support. His parents could support him while he finished a degree, but they won't. His father disapproves of his long hair, his earring, and the fact that he and Ivory don't want to get married. His mother gives them money from time to time and that helps. He blames the system for forcing him to struggle in order to keep his son warm and healthy.

The shame of poverty, the argument says, is not that of the victim, but of the society that lets it continue. One great advance of modern civilization has been to lift the stigma from those who are less able and less fortunate. It is to our credit that we have replaced the poorhouse with programs of social insurance as a matter of right, not charity. To let a few cheaters plus some unsupported fears about destruction of the will to work be the excuse for not "making peace with poverty" is, they say, a real immorality in modern society.

Reducing disincentives.   Some schemes do create disincentives to work. For example, if welfare payments are reduced dollar for dollar when the recipient earns money, there is no economic incentive to take part-time or low-paid work. But this is the fault of the scheme, not of the people who are only respond-

ing rationally to it. Schemes that reduce this marginal disincentive feature can be designed. For example, reducing welfare payments by only $.30 for each dollar earned replaces a 100 percent tax on working with a 30 percent tax, and experience shows that tax rates in that neighborhood do not prevent people from taking work. Moreover, the supporters argue, the theoretical possibility of disincentive effects is far from an empirical reality. Most people who can support themselves and their families willingly do so.

Resolving the Debate

Choosing whether to expand or to contract poverty programs depends in part on value judgments of what is good and right and worth doing and in part on positive factual assessments of what can be done and how much it will cost. Positive economic research can help to narrow the range of these uncertainties, even if it cannot dictate what we should finally do.

Today a great deal of research is devoted to studying the effects of welfare expenditure on incentives. But such research will not quickly resolve the debate. To see why, consider a recent study by the University of Wisconsin, Institute for Research on Poverty, which estimated that all government transfer programs—including among others social security, unemployment insurance, Medicaid, and all welfare payments—had the effect of reducing the labor force by 4.8 percent. If an extra 4.8 percent of the labor force found productive work, a big dent could be made in the problem of poverty. If, however, there is already unemployment in a slack economy, an increase in labor supply of 4.8 percent might lead mostly to increases in the number and percent unemployed and not solve many of the problems of the poor.

Traditional Antipoverty Programs

The two underlying assumptions in the development of existing programs have been, first, that the able-bodied should work and, second, that heads of households should support their families whenever possible.

The traditional strategy for dealing with poverty is to provide job opportunities for all who are able to work and income-support programs for those unable to work.

One part of such programs provides social insurance, related to work, for temporary unemployment and for retirement. A second part provides monetary assistance and in-kind assistance to those poor who are unable to work for reasons of age, health, or family status.

Providing Employment Opportunities

Families with an employed member have much more chance of escaping poverty than those without one. Thus providing job opportunities for the unemployed and for those not even looking for work is

TABLE 21-3   Major Income-Support Programs, 1984

Program	Expenditures (billions of dollars)
Social insurance	277.4
Cash benefits	
Social Security (OASDI)	175.5
Unemployment Insurance	13.5
Worker's Compensation	13.7
Other	13.8
In-kind benefits	
Medicare	60.9
Income assistance (welfare)	80.3
Cash Benefits	
Aid to Families with Dependent Children (AFDC)	14.6
Supplementary Security Income (SSI)	10.4
Other	3.8
In-kind benefits	
Medicaid	33.3
Food stamps	10.7
Housing assistance	5.7
School lunches	1.8
Total	357.7

Source: Social Security Bulletin, April 1986, Table M-1 and U.S. Bureau of the Census, Technical Report No. 55.

In 1984 the income-support programs cost $358 billion, about 10 percent of GNP. The table shows the range and size of programs in 1984. Note that over three-quarters of the expenditures are not welfare, that is, they are not need-related, but rather are categorical entitlements to the aged, unemployed, and others regardless of their other sources of income. Only about one-quarter of the expenditures were in welfare programs targeted to the poor. AFDC and food stamps, the most publicized programs, are a relatively small part of the total cost of income-support programs. OASDI, Medicare, and Medicaid—"social security"—represent more than three-quarters of the total.

of major importance. As we have seen, providing work is not a guarantee that families will escape poverty. Over 40 percent of all poor families have a full-time working head; for these *working poor*, the problem is usually the lack of skills that command a wage that will allow them to rise above the poverty level rather than an absence of demand for the skills they have.

Programs of education, training, and retraining are designed to lessen these causes of poverty by providing better job opportunities. Such programs have proven both expensive and limited in the number of persons they can reach. Educational opportunities for the children of the poor may free them from inheriting poverty, but such progress is measured from generation to generation, not from year to year.

Social Insurance

Table 21-3 shows the major income-support programs that existed in 1984. The first prong of traditional antipoverty protection is social insurance. In 1984 such programs added up to nearly $280 billion dollars. The Social Security Act (first passed in 1935) provides Old Age and Survivors Disability Insurance (OASDI) to millions of Americans who are old and to the widows and orphans of eligible workers. Medicare provides medical expenses for those receiving OASDI benefits. Unemployment insurance is paid to those covered workers who lose their jobs. The expenditures keep millions off the poverty roles and for many others reduce the size of the poverty gap, but it should be noted that none of them is primarily a *poverty* program. Middle income and wealthy individuals also share in such benefits.

Successive increases in eligibility for coverage and in the size of benefits, including increases to match rises in the cost of living, make social insurance an increasingly effective preventative of poverty for the majority of Americans. As noted earlier, only 11 percent of the poor are over 65, largely as a result of social insurance. But these increases in coverage have created both short-term and long-term problems, which are discussed in Box 21-2.

Income Assistance (Welfare)

The second prong of traditional antipoverty protection is limited to those who fall into categories for which need is presumed. The poorest of the poor are those who have never worked or who are not currently employable. So-called income-assistance programs are designed to identify categories of the poor who cannot use labor market participation to avoid poverty, either directly by way of earnings or indirectly by way of employment-related social insurance. In 1984 these programs cost $80 billion. The largest single item is Medicaid, free medical care to the poor. Also important are the aids to nearly 5 million aged, blind, and disabled persons under the Supplemental Security Income (SSI) program, the aid to 11 million families with dependent children (AFDC), and food stamps and housing assistance.

All of these programs have certain common characteristics. They are administered by the states, which share some of the costs with the federal government. States individually determine both eligibility and levels of payment. Eligibility is limited to demonstrated cases of need; maximum payments are reduced when the family has other income.

The Size and Accomplishments of the War on Poverty Before Reagan

Public expenditures for income-support programs in 1984 totaled $358 billion. That is such a large figure that it is hard to relate to it. It came to about $1,500 for every person in the country and represented about 10 percent of GNP (gross national product) and about 30 percent of all government spending for that year. Moreover, such spending had shown great growth in a generation. In 1950 public expenditure for these purposes was 2 percent of GNP and 14 percent of government spending.

This growth reflected several developments. First, rising affluence in post-World War II America raised the level of what was defined to be a minimum adequate standard of living and also made it possible to provide benefits to those who did not achieve this level by their own efforts. Second, some programs, especially social security programs, grew automatically when more and more eligible people reached retirement ages. Third, generally liberal administrations purposely increased benefits under many existing programs. Fourth, some of the benefits were indexed to the cost of living. Fifth, a series of expensive new programs was introduced. Of these Medicare, Medicaid, and food stamps were the most important.

Many of these programs that reduce poverty—for example, social security—also provide substan-

BOX 21-2

Paying for Social Security

Late in the 1970s the American public gradually discovered what insiders had long known; unless major changes were made, the social security system was going to run out of money. It was calculated that by 1983 the system's funds would be exhausted and 36 million beneficiaries would not get their July 3, 1983, checks. Such payments represent, on average, 60 percent of the total income of the recipients. Almost all of those 36 million people were voters, and Congress and the president could no longer ignore the problem. How did all this happen? What was the solution? Will it happen again?

The Crisis of 1983

From its inception in 1935, social security was never "actuarially sound." While it was considered politically necessary to "sell" social security as merely social insurance, social security has always been a set of entitlements (benefits) and also a set of (loosely linked) taxes imposed on workers and employers. People and firms pay in via a payroll tax whatever amount Congress legislates. This amount was a maximum of $30 per worker per year each by the employee and by the employer in 1935. By 1968 the maximum was $344. In 1983 it was $2,400. While some individuals never get their contributions back, most beneficiaries eventually collect far more than they (and their employers) paid in. The average person retiring in 1980 had an actuarial claim to about $50,000. That person will withdraw $125,000 during

retirement. Since this average excess of benefits over contributions on behalf of retirees has been true for every cohort of beneficiaries, you should not be surprised to hear that social security was, and is, actuarially "unsound."

The theory has always been that this year's workers would pay in enough for this year's beneficiaries, but not for their own retirement. In the 1940s there were lots of workers and few eligible retirees, so reserves accumulated, even with modest taxes per worker. As time passed more and more people reached age 65 and began drawing benefits. Eventually the reserves stopped growing and were drawn down. By 1983 the benefits payable exceeded tax receipts by $25 billion, and there were no more reserves. Hence the crisis.

The crisis was purely financial and finite—about $150 billion to $200 billion in uncovered deficits over the period 1983–1990. From 1990 to 2015 the baby-boom generation of the 1950s and 1960s will be fully at work and would, even under the old rates of social security taxes, be paying in more than enough to meet annual costs. The interim deficits could, of course, be met by the government's diverting about $25 billion a year of other revenues into social security.

Cause and Solution of the Crisis

How did the system suddenly run out of reserves? The short answer is that Congress from 1939 until

tial transfer payments to persons who are not poor. Moreover, not all of the money aimed at the poor actually reached them due to administrative costs, graft, and even corruption. As one cynic said, "There is money in poverty."

But the fact is the expenditures did have a highly significant effect on the poverty problem. Table 21-4 on page 400 shows how, between 1965 and 1980, money and in-kind transfers reduced the number of

people living below the poverty level. Additionally, these same programs reduced the poverty gap of those below the poverty level. The War on Poverty achieved large benefits to go with its large costs. Whether the benefits justified the costs is inherently a matter of individual values and, for the nation, a political decision. The election of Ronald Reagan was widely perceived as a mandate to stop the growth and roll back the size of the whole set of government

1976 found it politically attractive to increase the benefits payable without increasing the tax rates enough to compensate. This has had several related aspects. (1) There was a shift from thinking of old age benefits as a poverty-insurance *supplement* to other sources of income for the retired, to thinking of them as the *primary source* of a decent and comfortable retirement income. Over the years Congress has steadily changed the formula to raise the benefits. (2) Since 1972 the benefits have been indexed to the cost of living, thus causing them to rise unexpectedly rapidly. (3) The eligibility for social security has been expanded until there is virtually universal coverage. (4) The benefits available to each covered worker have been sharply increased. Dependents and survivors were added in 1939, disabled workers were added in 1950, and medical coverage (Medicare) was added in 1965. These things, combined with ever greater longevity, let the deficits grow and reserves vanish.

The solution had long been obvious but politically difficult: raise taxes or reduce benefits or both. Finally, as reserves ran out a bipartisan commission was established to take the president and Congress off the hook. Its recommendations were adopted in 1983. They include accelerated social security tax increases, delay of scheduled cost-of-living adjustments, and making some social security benefits taxable income to the recipients. They also compelled some young workers not already covered to join the system, thus increasing pay-ins over the critical years to 1990.

These and related changes will generate the funds needed to cover the current annual deficits and assure the stability of the present levels of benefits well into the next century.

The Long-Run Problem

While the baby-boom generation of the 1950s and 1960s will bail out the system in 1990, what happens when that generation retires in 2015 to 2035? Recent declines in birth rates mean there will be ever fewer workers [you students!] to support ever more retirees.

In 1945 there were 42 workers supporting each retiree. By 1965 the number was 5, and by 1982 the number was 3.2. By 2030 it will be down to 2. *Every working couple will have to provide funds to support not only itself and its children, but one retired person as well.* Given generous benefits, this implies a heavy tax, maybe two or three times as high as the present 7.15 percent level.

If this burden of too many retired depending too heavily on too few workers is unacceptable, there are only a few options. One is to change retirement ages to keep people working longer. The commission report recommended gradually changing eligibility from age 65 to age 67. Another is to reduce benefits paid to retirees, encouraging them to rely more on their own savings. The alternative is to tax workers more or to find some other way to subsidize those who are not producing. The choice will be a key issue of the early years of the twenty-first century.

programs designed to provide income support and eliminate poverty by government transfer payments.

Poverty and the Reagan Administration

Ronald Reagan had long advocated, and the Reagan administration adopted, a view of the causes and solutions for the poverty problem different from those that had been in effect for decades. What were the essential differences?

Reliance on Growth Rather Than Income Transfers

Traditional antipoverty policy has been heavily dependent upon the use of income transfers to the poor.

TABLE 21-4   Effectiveness of Government Income-Assistance Programs, 1965–1984

Percent of population below poverty level, measured by

	Market income (excluding transfers)	Adjusted income (including cash and in-kind transfers)
1965	21.3	16.8
1970	18.8	—[a]
1975	22.0	—[a]
1980	21.9	10.4
1983	24.2	13.0
1984	22.0	12.2

Source: Danziger, R. Haveman, and R. Plotnick, "Antipoverty Policy: Effects on the Poor and Nonpoor," in *Fighting Poverty: What Works and What Doesn't,* edited by S. Danziger and D. Weinberg, Harvard University Press, 1986; and U.S. Bureau of the Census.

[a] Not available.

Income-assistance programs have had a major impact on the incidence of poverty since 1965. Market income includes no government transfer payments and thus provides a benchmark for evaluating the effect of transfers. Adjusted income adds both cash transfer payments (such as social security) and in-kind transfers (such as food stamps).

The data show that mere growth of the economy between 1965 and 1980, working by way of market income, had little effect. The percent falling below the poverty line fluctuated, but did not decrease. But government programs had a big effect in reducing the number living below the poverty level between 1965 and 1980. From 1980 to 1983 the increase in those in poverty (by either measure) reflects both a serious recession and a cutback in government transfer payments by the Reagan administration. The economic recovery during 1984 reduced the incidence of poverty but not enough to offset the earlier decreases in income-assistance programs.

The Reagan policies rejected this approach in principle, believing instead that the main cure for poverty lay in economic recovery and the growth of the private sector. Specifically rejected was the view that hard-core poverty requires policies of redistribution. Full employment and economic growth are all that is required. As President Reagan put it, "Our aim is to increase national wealth so all will have more, not just redistribute what we already have, which is just a sharing of scarcity."

In this view any measure that fostered economic recovery or growth, even if in the short run worsening the plight of the poor, would in the longer run lead to reductions in poverty. This reliance on growth instead of redistribution also reflected a rejection of the widely held view of the historical effectiveness of transfers, as was stated concisely by Budget Director David Stockman in 1982: "All the programs that were created out of Washington in the 1960s had almost nothing to do with the progress that was made in reducing poverty. The real war was waged by the private sector . . . with economic growth of 4, 5, 6 percent a year and with massive increases in jobs and employment."

If this controversial view is correct—and it is surely in conflict with the statistics presented in Table 21-4—it would make sense, even to those in poverty, to *reduce* the programs of income transfer if by so doing economic recovery would be fostered. Established income-support programs became a target of Reaganomics. The general economic philosophy of the administration has been that decreasing the federal government's domestic expenditures was a key to economic recovery. What better way to reduce government expenditures than to cut expensive welfare programs that had not (in any case) contributed to progress! Many of these programs were the cornerstones of the traditional antipoverty strategy. The administration sharply cut funds for food stamps, AFDC, and Medicaid in the hope that the economic recovery resulting from a reduction in government spending accompanied by reduced inflation would ameliorate the lot of the poor. Nearly 20 percent of the recipients of welfare lost some or all of their benefits. Whether or not in the long run this strategy will work, in the short run it has unmistakably increased rather than alleviated poverty.

Hard-Core Poverty

The Reagan administration recognized, as had prior administrations, that not all of the poor could be rescued by economic growth, even in the long run. The hard-core poor, or "truly needy," would always require help. Here, too, changes in philosophy became apparent. A major change was the belief that welfare and other transfers should be designed simply to assure a minimum standard of living, not to close the poverty gap. One official of the Office of Management and Budget put it succinctly: "The policy decision is that welfare is a safety-net and not an income supplement program."

What this meant was that persons whose income from other sources raised them above the threshold level of the safety net were to be cut off from eligibility for welfare, Medicaid, and food stamps. The first dollars earned above the threshold level caused major losses of benefits. The intent was to eliminate those who were not truly needy, including the welfare cheaters. But a side effect was to create a sharp disincentive to continued work by those who could raise their income above the safety net only by a combination of transfers and work.

Who Should Deal with Poverty?

Until the Great Depression and the New Deal of Franklin Roosevelt, poverty had been thought of as a family problem to be suffered through with such help as private charity might provide. Roosevelt changed all that, arguing that it was a *national* scandal that one-third of the nation was ill-housed, ill-clothed, and ill-fed. Forty years later, public programs had made the amelioration of poverty a major policy concern of local, state, and federal governments. The trend, indeed, was increasingly to make poverty a *federal* government concern, and former President Carter proposed "federalizing welfare" as the most significant possible way to provide needed economic aid to beleaguered state and local governments.

President Reagan called for an abrupt reversal of these trends. He urged increased private giving to fill any gap left by the reduction in government programs and, more importantly, he called for a return to state and local governments of the responsibility for aid to the poor.

The Impact of the Reagan Approach

The number of people living in the United States below the poverty level increased sharply between 1980 and 1985. This is not entirely attributable to the Reagan administration's poverty policy, since the poverty rate always rises when the economy suffers from a recession and the severe unemployment that accompanies it. In any case, Reagan supporters argue that the administration's policies were always designed to work not as a quick fix, but as a gradual middle- and long-run solution. In this view the real test of President Reagan's policies will have to be judged from the perspective of 1990, not 1986.

This analysis of the experience under the Reagan administration policies is, however, distinctly a minority view among economists. Studies show that less than one percentage point of the increase in poverty was related to the recession, the rest to the decrease in government programs. Most economists doubt that further economic growth will compensate for this, even in the long run.

Moreover, the shift from income-support to safety-net strategy seems likely to have significantly increased the potential disincentive effects to working. The Center for the Study of Welfare Policies of the University of Chicago found that the Reagan policies all but eliminated the economic incentive to work of the working poor. Since 40 percent of all the poor were working, the possibility of increasing the number of people who did not find it economically worthwhile to work, or to work as many days, was substantial. It is too soon to know how many people actually reduced their work effort in order to re-establish their eligibility for food stamps, Medicaid, and other forms of welfare.

Future Directions of Policy Toward Poverty

Poverty has not been eliminated. The fact that the poor are both numerous and politically aware assures that the debate about philosophy and policy will continue for many years to come.

The case for federal control rests upon defining poverty as a national problem and on the fact that there are great differences in the ability or willingness of state and local governments to cope with the problem. The poor are not distributed evenly throughout the United States—42 percent live in the South, many of the rest in northern urban slums. Much of the state and local tax base is generated in political jurisdictions in which poverty is not a major problem. Thus the tax burden of fighting poverty locally falls unevenly. Differences in ability and willingness to pay lead to great differences in programs. For example, a woman with no income and three dependent children who was eligible for aid could receive three times as much in Newark, New Jersey, as in Biloxi, Mississippi. While in each case she would remain below the poverty line, the difference in the poverty gap is enormous—and it is not explained by differences in the cost of living.

The case against federalizing welfare rests on the advantages of pluralism and local control. There are great differences in costs of living and in local standards of what constitutes an adequate minimum standard of living. Such differences cannot easily be taken into account (as a political matter) by federal bureaucrats or by Congress. Yet to provide equal welfare payments in Newark and Biloxi would also be unjust.

Part of the debate concerns one's view of whose problem poverty is. If poverty of any part of the population is viewed as a national problem and its elimination as a national goal, there is little reason to

believe a decentralized system or a reliance on voluntarism will succeed in accomplishing anything approximating a uniform set of policies. If, on the other hand, the level of income that is the minimum acceptable ought to be one of local option, then a uniform national policy will seem intrusive as well as inefficient. If poverty is merely a personal problem, then its amelioration should fall to individual effort or to family, friends, and neighbors.

Much of the debate about poverty is at the normative level. Should poverty and its elimination be a compelling national concern? Should policies distinguish between the deserving and the undeserving poor? Should welfare attempt to bring the poor to a decent standard of living or merely to a subsistence standard?

There are, of course, important positive questions as well. Which policies work best? Is there a conflict between short-run amelioration and long-run solution owing to incentive and disincentive effects? If so, how long are the lags before the present group of poor will be better off? These and other questions will occupy many economists for many years.

Summary

1. The concept of poverty involves both relative and absolute levels of income and reflects the aspirations of society as well as the income needed for subsistence alone. Today roughly 14 percent of all Americans are classified as living in poverty. Since the aggregate poverty gap is small relative to national income, it would be possible to eradicate poverty in the United States.

2. Economic growth, though it has led to a reduction of poverty, will by itself never eliminate it, for many of those in need do not share directly in the fruits of growth.

3. The incidence of poverty is much greater among some groups than among others, particularly those who are not employed and who are relatively uneducated. But there are many poor among the working, and poverty is appreciable in all ages and among those who have had considerable education.

4. Poverty is particularly acute among such minority groups as blacks and Hispanics. This reflects in part the minority groups' lower average stock of human capital—especially education and training—and in part the discrimination that has prevented utilizing more fully the skills and talents that the group's members have. Recent years have seen no significant decrease in the income disadvantage of blacks relative to whites.

5. The desirability of pursuing antipoverty policies is a matter of continuing current debate. Some people believe that it is possible and desirable to make further major reductions in poverty now. They place particular importance on income supplements to the poor regardless of why they are poor. Others believe that further attacks on poverty are undesirable both because of the burdens such government expenditures place on the economy and because of the disincentive effects generated by welfare programs.

6. The antipoverty policies that were developed between the 1930s and 1980 included attempts to expand employment opportunities for blacks and other minority groups; retraining programs intended to match people with available jobs; social insurance to help the able-bodied meet the risks of unemployment and retirement; and categorical assistance designed to serve those unable to care for themselves. The evidence is clear that these policies did greatly reduce poverty in the United States. Whether they had long-run disincentive effects is a matter of continuing debate.

7. The Reagan administration advocated and partially adopted policies that represented a sharp break with the trend of the previous half century. The underpinning of the Reagan policy was to seek economic growth by reducing government spending even if that meant decreasing income transfers to the poor. For the very poor the notion of an income supplement was to be replaced by a safety net to protect only the truly needy. Moreover, the approach of the Reagan administration was increasingly to return poverty programs to state and local control and to private charity. These controversial policies have yet to be fully implemented, and their precise long-run effect is not yet known. In the short run they have increased the incidence of poverty.

Poverty level and poverty gap
Correlates of poverty
Occasional poverty and persistent poverty
Possible disincentive effects of alleviating poverty
Social insurance versus income assistance
Alternative policies toward poverty

Topics for Review

---

1. In what ways are the problems of poverty in the United States likely to be different from the problems of poverty in an underdeveloped, poor country, such as Bangladesh? In what ways are they easier to solve in one place than in the other?
2. The official poverty level used in the United States is based only on money income. It does not take into account food stamps or subsidized housing. It does not consider the assets of the family. It does

Discussion Questions

not consider whether families with low incomes have wealthy relatives. Do these omissions lead to an exaggerated view of the poverty problem? Should the poverty level rise if average income of the American people rises, with no increase in the prices of individual items of consumption?

3. Suppose that your objectives are (first) to eradicate poverty and (second) to reduce unemployment. Evaluate the probable effectiveness of each of the following in meeting each objective.

   a. Increasing welfare payments
   b. Increasing aid to education
   c. Creating a program of public works to hire the poor
   d. Ending employment discrimination against blacks

4. A proposed program of rental allowances to the poor has been attacked in Congress as giving money to slumlords instead of to the poor and thereby worsening the distribution of income. Evaluate this position. Argue the case for and against assistance that is tied to a particular kind of expenditure rather than giving the money to the poor to spend as they think best.

5. Comment on each of the following headlines in terms of the matters discussed in this chapter:

   a. "Working poor are victims of Reaganomics"
   b. "On welfare or working: poor is poor"
   c. "Economic recovery decreases number on welfare"
   d. "War on poverty is difficult to call off"

6. In what sense does a policy that reduces welfare payments dollar for dollar for every dollar of earned income constitute "a 100 percent tax on working"? In what sense is that not accurate? (*Hint:* If the maximum welfare payment is $6,000 per family, what marginal and average "tax rate" is implicit for a welfare recipient who is offered a job that pays $8,000?)

7. News item: "On an income of $800 a month, Sharon Smith and her children cannot afford to get sick. Nor can they manage to stay well. Ms. Smith is a secretary, a single parent, who lost eligibility for AFDC, Medicaid, food stamps, and other benefits in 1981 when the Reagan budget cuts occurred. She is thinking of taking a lower paid job in order to qualify for the Medicare help her children need."

   Discuss the nature of the incentives motivating Ms. Smith and whether it "makes sense" for her to take a lower paid job.

The Market Economy: Problems and Policies

22

Benefits and Costs of Government Intervention

There are two caricatures of the American economy. One pictures the United States as the last stronghold of free enterprise, with millions of Americans in a mad and brutal race for the almighty dollar. In the other, American business people, workers, and farmers are seen strangling slowly in a web of red tape spun by the spider of government regulation. Neither is realistic.

Many aspects of economic life in the United States are determined by the operation of a free-market system. Private preferences, expressed through private markets and influencing private profit-seeking enterprises, determine much of what is produced, how it is produced, and the incomes of productive factors.

But even casual observation makes it clear that public policies and public decisions play a large role. Laws restrict what people and firms may do, and taxes and subsidies influence their choices. Much public expenditure is not market determined, and this influences the distribution of national product. The United States is in fact a mixed economy.

The general case for some reliance on free markets is that allowing decentralized decision making is more efficient in a number of ways than having all economic decisions made by a centralized planning body. This is a lesson that the governments of the USSR and Eastern Europe have learned the hard way.

The general case for some public intervention is that almost no one wants to let the market decide everything about our economic affairs. Most people's moral and practical sense argues for some state intervention to mitigate the disastrous results that the market deals out to some. Most people believe that there are areas where the market does not function well and where state intervention can improve the general social good. For such reasons, there is no known economy where the people have opted for complete free market determination of all economic matters and against any kind of government intervention.

Although many nineteenth century economists advocated a policy of **laissez faire**, the absence of any government interference with the operation of markets, the operative choice today is not between an unhampered free-market economy and a fully centralized command economy. It is instead the choice of what mix of markets and government intervention best suits a people's hopes and needs. Although all economies are mixed, the mixture varies greatly among economies and over time. Whether the existing mixture is wrong—and if so, in which direction—is debated continually.

One reason there are mixed economies lies in what an unkind critic once called the economists' two great insights: *Markets can work, and markets can fail.* A second reason is what the critic might have called the political scientists' two great insights: *Government intervention can work, and government intervention can fail.*

In this chapter we discuss the role of the government in economic markets. Why is it there at all? What does it do well, and what does it do badly? Do we need more or less government intervention?

How Markets Coordinate

Any economy consists of thousands upon thousands of individual markets. There are markets for agricultural goods, for manufactured goods, and for consumers' services; there are markets for intermediate goods, such as steel and pig iron, which are outputs of some industries and inputs of others; there are markets for raw materials such as iron ore, trees, bauxite, and copper; there are markets for land and for thousands of different types of labor; there are markets in which money is borrowed and in which securities are sold. An economy is not a series of markets functioning in isolation, but an interlocking system in which an occurrence in one market affects many others.

Any change, such as an increase in demand for a product, requires many further changes and adjustments. Should production of the product change? If so, by how much and in what manner? This in turn will require changes in other markets and will start a chain of adjustments. Someone or something must decide what is to be produced, how, and by whom and what is to be consumed and by whom.

The essential characteristic of the market system is that its coordination occurs in an unplanned, decentralized way. Millions of people make millions of independent decisions concerning production and consumption every day. Most of these decisions are not motivated by a desire to contribute to the social good or to make the whole economy work well, but by fairly immediate considerations of self-interest. The price system coordinates these decentralized decisions, making the whole system fit together and

respond to the wishes of the individuals who compose it.

The basic insight into how this system works is that decentralized, private decision makers, acting in their own interests, respond to such signals as the prices of what they buy and sell. Economists have long emphasized price as a signaling device. When a commodity becomes scarce, its free-market price rises. Firms and households that use the commodity are led to economize on it and to look for alternatives. Firms that produce it are led to produce more of it. How the price system guides these decisions has been examined at several places in this book (for example, with respect to carrots and brussels sprouts in Chapter 3, agriculture in Chapter 6, and ball-point pens in Chapter 17). When a shortage occurs in a market, price rises and profits develop; when a glut occurs, price falls and losses develop. These are *signals*, for all to see, that arise from the overall conditions of total supply and demand.

The Role of Windfall Profits and Losses

Although the free-market economy is often described as the *price system,* the basic engine that drives the economy is economic profits, often called windfall profits.[1] Economic profits and losses are symptoms of *disequilibrium,* and they are the driving force in the adaptation of the economy to change.

A rise in demand or a fall in production costs creates profits for that commodity's producers, while a fall in demand or a rise in production costs creates losses. Profits make an industry attractive to new investment. They signal that there are too few resources devoted to that industry. In search of these profits, more resources enter the industry, increasing output and driving down price, until windfall profits are driven to zero. Losses signal the reverse. Resources leave the industry until those left behind are no longer suffering losses.

---

[1] The term *windfall* has the connotation of undeserved or unearned, and this is often the case, as when a rise in demand confers profits on all producers in an industry. But whether such profits (or losses) arise this way or as a result of the firm's own efforts is immaterial. It is their existence, not their source, that matters. Windfall gains and losses were discussed in Chapter 18 in relation to all factors of production where they were referred to by their more technical name of dynamic differentials.

The importance of profits and losses is that they set in motion forces that tend to move the economy toward a new equilibrium.

Individual households and firms respond to common signals according to their own best interests. There is nothing planned or intentionally coordinated about their actions, yet when, say, a shortage causes price to rise, individual buyers begin to reduce the quantities they demand and individual firms begin to increase the quantities they supply. As a result the shortage begins to lessen. As it does, price begins to come back down, and windfall profits are reduced. These signals in turn are seen and responded to by firms and households. Eventually, when the shortage has been eliminated, there are no windfall profits to attract further increases in supply. The chain of adjustments to the original shortage is completed.

Even if profits or losses are wholly undeserved, in the sense that they result from changes over which the beneficiaries have no control, this does not mean they should be eliminated by government action. If the government taxed away *all* windfall profits and replaced by subsidy *all* windfall losses, it would effectively destroy the market economy by removing its driving force.

Because the economy is continuously adjusting to shocks, a snapshot of the economy at any given moment reveals substantial positive windfall profits in some industries and substantial windfall losses in others. A snapshot at another moment will also reveal windfall profits and losses, but their locations will be different.

The price system, like an *invisible hand* (Adam Smith's famous phrase), coordinates the responses of individual decision makers who seek only their own self-interests. Because they respond to signals that reflect market conditions, their responses are coordinated without any conscious planning.

Who Responds?

Notice that in the sequence of signal-response-signal-response no one had to foresee at the outset the final price and quantity. Nor did any government agency have to specify who would increase production and who would decrease consumption. Some firms responded to the signals for "more output" by increasing production, and they kept on increasing production until the signals got weaker and weaker and finally disappeared. Some buyers withdrew from the market when they thought prices were too high, and perhaps they re-entered gradually, when they wanted to, as prices became "more reasonable." Households and firms responding to market signals, not to the orders of government bureaucrats, "decided" who would increase production and who would limit consumption. No one was forced to do something against his or her best judgment. Voluntary responses collectively produced the end result.

Consider an example. Suppose that 10,000 families from neighboring areas decide that at existing prices they all want to move into single-family houses in the hills of Berkeley, California, overlooking San Francisco Bay. However, that beautiful residential area is already heavily populated. Suppose there are at most 1,000 vacant houses or building sites. Obviously, not all of the present and potential residents can live there. Which ones will be able to do so, and which ones will be disappointed?

The market system makes the allocation in the following way. The first impact of the great increase in demand would be a sharp rise in the asking prices of houses in the Berkeley hills. This would persuade some Berkeley residents, who previously had not intended to move, to sell their houses and move to other areas. The same rises in price would discourage many who had hoped to move into the Berkeley hills. The rising prices will also lead some owners of vacant lots to sell or develop them.

One way or the other—by reducing quantity demanded and by encouraging an increase in quantity supplied—the market will make the allocation. Of the 10,000 families who originally wanted to move in, 3,000 may end up living there, while 2,500 old residents move away and 500 of the vacant houses or lots become occupied. Which 3,000 move in? Those who value it the most. Which 2,500 move out? Those who value the extra money more than the privilege of staying in Berkeley. The market sorts them out without the need for anyone to issue orders ("you go, you stay") and without the need for a court or a board to hear appeals from those who object to the orders.

Of course, it is not *necessary* to rely on the market system to achieve coordination. Had prices not been free to rise, some other system for allocating supply would be needed. Suppose prices had been frozen by law in order to "keep Berkeley housing within the reach of the ordinary family." There would be dozens of applicants for any house that became available. The sellers would then have had great power to decide to whom to sell (and thus whom to turn down). They might exercise their prejudices, or they might find ways to get a secret payoff.

Alternatively, the city council might set up a Berkeley Authorized Waiting List (BAWL) to determine the order in which people would be permitted to become residents. This would give some public official the duty (or perhaps the privilege) of judging the relative worthiness of potential Berkeleyites and ranking them accordingly. It would also provide opportunities for bribery of those with allocative authority.

The Limited Information Required in Market Coordination

Another important characteristic of the market economy is that it functions with very limited information. As Professor Thomas Schelling put it:

> The dairy farmer doesn't need to know how many people eat butter and how far away they are, how many other people raise cows, how many babies drink milk, or whether more money is spent on beer or milk. What he needs to know is the prices of different feeds, the characteristics of different cows, the different prices . . . for milk . . . , the relative cost of hired labor and electrical machinery, and what his net earnings might be if he sold his cows and raised pigs instead.

By responding to such limited information as the costs and prices of what he buys and sells, the dairy farmer helps to make the whole economy fit together, producing more or less what people want, where and when they want it.

It is, of course, an enormous advantage that all the producers and consumers of a country can collectively make the system operate without any one of them, much less all of them, having to understand how it works. Such a lack of knowledge becomes a disadvantage, however, when people have to vote on schemes for interfering with market allocation.

Coordination in the Absence of Perfect Competition

To say that the price system coordinates is not to imply that it leads to the results that perfect competition would produce. The price system coordinates responses even to prices "rigged" by monopolistic producers or altered by government controls. The signal-response process occurs in a price system even when the prices have not been determined in freely competitive markets.

When an international cartel of uranium producers decided to reduce production and raise price, they created a current shortage (and a fear of worse future shortages) among those electric utilities that depend on uranium to fuel nuclear power plants. The price of uranium shot up from under $10 per pound to over $40 in less than a year. This enormous price rise greatly increased efforts among producers outside the cartel to find more uranium and to increase their existing production by mining poorer grade ores previously considered too costly to mine.

The increases in production from these actions slowly began to ease the shortage. On the demand side, high prices and short supplies led some utilities to cancel planned nuclear plants and to delay the construction of others. Such actions implied a long-run substitution of oil or coal for uranium. Only the fact that the OPEC cartel had also sharply raised the price of oil prevented an even more rapid reversal of the previous trend from oil to nuclear-powered generators. With the prices of both uranium and oil quadrupling, the demand for coal increased sharply, and its price and production rose. Thus the market mechanism generated adjustments to the relative prices of different fuels, even though some prices were set by cartels rather than by the free-market forces of supply and demand. It also set in motion reactions that placed limits on the power of the cartel.

The Case for the Market System

In presenting the case for free-market economies, economists have used two different approaches. One of these may be characterized as the formal defense. It is based upon showing that a free-market economy consisting of nothing but perfectly competitive industries would lead to an optimal allocation of resources. The case was discussed in Chapter 14.

The other approach, which may be characterized as the informal or intuitive defense, is at least as old as Adam Smith. It is based on variations and implications of the theme that the market system is an effective coordinator of decentralized decision making. The case is intuitive in the sense that it is not laid out in equations leading to some mathematical, maximizing result. But it does follow from some hard reasoning, and it has been subjected to some searching intellectual probing. What is the nature of this defense of the free market?

Flexible and Automatic Coordination

Defenders of the market economy argue that compared with the alternatives, the decentralized market system is more flexible and leaves more scope for adaptation to change at any moment in time and for quicker adjustment over time.

If, for example, a scarcity raises the price of oil, one household can elect to leave its heating up high and economize on its driving, while another may wish to do the reverse, and a third may instead give up air conditioning. This flexibility is surely preferable to forcing the same pattern on everyone, say by rationing heating oil and gasoline, regulating permitted temperatures, and limiting air conditioning to days when the temperature exceeds 80° F.

Furthermore, as conditions change over time, prices will change and decentralized decision makers can react continually. In contrast, government quotas, allocations, and rationing schemes are much more difficult to adjust. The great value of the market is that it provides automatic signals *as a situation develops,* so that all of the consequences of some major economic change do not have to be anticipated and allowed for by a body of central planners. Mil-

lions of adaptations to millions of changes in tens of thousands of markets are required every year, and it would be a Herculean task to anticipate and plan for them all.

Stimulus to Innovation and Growth

Major changes in resource availabilities will surely occur in all economies over the next decades. New products, new inputs, and new techniques will have to be devised in order to cope with those vast changes.

In a market economy individuals risk their time and money in the hope of earning profits. While many fail, some succeed. New products and processes appear and disappear. Some are passing fads or have little impact; others become items of major significance. The market system works by trial and error to sort them out and allocates resources to what prove to be successful innovations.

In contrast, more centralized systems have to guess which are going to be productive innovations or wanted products. Planned growth may achieve wonders by permitting a massive effort in a chosen direction, but central planners may also guess wrong about the direction and put far too many eggs in the wrong basket or reject as unpromising something that will turn out to be vital.

Relative Prices Reflect Relative Costs

A market system tends to drive prices toward the average total costs of production. When markets are close to perfectly competitive, this occurs quickly and completely; but even where there is substantial market power, it occurs as new products and new producers respond to the lure of profits and their output drives prices down toward the costs of production.

Whenever private costs to firms reflect social costs to society, there is an advantage in having relative prices reflect relative costs because market choices are then made in the light of social opportunity costs. Firms will not choose methods that use more valuable resources over methods that use less valuable resources. Households will choose commodities that use more valuable resources to produce over commodities that use less valuable ones only when they value the chosen commodities correspondingly more at the margin.

Having relative prices reflect relative costs tends to be efficient in that it encourages both producers and consumers to use the nation's resources to achieve allocative efficiency.

Self-Correction of Disequilibrium

The economic system is continually thrown out of equilibrium by change. If the economy does not "pursue" equilibrium, there will be little comfort in saying that if only it reached equilibrium, things would be bright indeed. (We all know someone who would have been a great surgeon if only he or she had gone to medical school.)

> An important characteristic of the price system is its ability to set in motion forces that tend to correct disequilibrium.

To review the advantages of the price system in this respect, imagine operating without a market mechanism. Suppose that planning boards make all market decisions. The Board in Control of Women's Clothing hears that pantsuits are all the rage in neighboring countries. It orders a certain proportion of clothing factories to make pantsuits instead of the traditional women's skirt. Conceivably the quantities of pantsuits and skirts produced could be just right, given shoppers' preferences. But what if the board guessed wrong, producing too many skirts and not enough pantsuits? Long lines would appear at pantsuit counters, while mountains of unsold skirts piled up. Once the board saw the lines for pantsuits, it could order a change in quantities produced. Meanwhile, it could store the extra skirts for another season or ship them to a country with different tastes.

Such a system can correct an initial mistake, but it may prove inefficient in doing so. It may use a lot of resources in planning and administration that could instead be used to produce commodities. Further, many consumers may be greatly inconvenienced if the board is slow to correct its error. In such a system the members of the board may have no incentive to admit and correct a mistake quickly.

Indeed, if the authorities do not like pantsuits, the board may get credit for having stopped that craze before it went too far!

In contrast, suppose that in a market system a similar misestimation of the demand for pantsuits and skirts was made by the women's clothing industry. Lines would develop at pantsuit counters, and inventories of skirts would accumulate. Stores would raise pantsuit prices and run skirt sales. Pantsuit manufacturers could earn profits by raising prices and running extra shifts to increase production. Some skirt producers would be motivated to shift production quickly to pantsuits and to make skirts more attractive to buyers by cutting prices. Unlike the planning board, the producers in a market system would be motivated to correct their initial mistakes as quickly as possible. Those slowest to adjust would lose the most money and might even be forced out of business.

Decentralization of Power

Another important part of the case for a market economy is that it tends to decentralize power and thus requires less coercion of individuals than does any other type of economy. Of course, even though markets tend to diffuse power, they do not do so completely; large firms and large unions clearly do have and do exercise substantial economic power.

While the market power of large corporations and unions is not negligible, it tends to be constrained both by the competition of other large entities and by the emergence of new products and firms. This is the process of creative destruction described by Joseph Schumpeter (pages 257–258). In any case, say defenders of the free market, even such aggregations of private power are far less substantial than government power.

Governments must coerce if markets are not allowed to allocate people to jobs and commodities to consumers. Not only will such coercion be regarded as arbitrary by those who do not like the results, but the power surely creates major opportunities for bribery, corruption, and allocation according to the tastes of the central administrators. If at the going prices and wages there are not enough apartments or coveted jobs to go around, the bureaucrat can allocate some to those who pay the largest bribe, some to those with religious beliefs, hairstyles, or political views that he likes, and only the rest to those whose names come up on the waiting list.

The Case for Intervention

The United States does not have a laissez faire economy. What has led a majority of Americans to believe that a pure private enterprise system is not the best of all possible worlds? What led them over many decades to lessen their reliance on the unrestricted workings of the free market and, in many cases, to impose regulations on markets or to substitute collective for individual action? What leads many Americans today to question whether we have gone far enough—or too far—away from free markets?

Whenever market performance is judged to be faulty, it is the practice to speak of **market failure.** The word *failure* in this context may convey the wrong impression.

Market failure does not mean that nothing good has happened, but that the *best attainable outcome* has not been achieved.

There are two somewhat different senses in which the phrase is sometimes used. One is the failure of the market system to achieve efficiency in the allocation of society's resources; the other is the failure to serve social goals other than efficiency, such as a desired distribution of income or the preservation of value systems.

As a result of market failure, many people believe it desirable to modify, restructure, complement, or supplement the unrestricted workings of the market. There are several major sources of dissatisfaction with market allocation and distribution, and it is important to understand how they arise.

Failure to Achieve Efficiency

Externalities As a Source of Inefficiency

Cost, as economists define it, concerns the value of resources used in the process of production. According to the opportunity cost principle, value is the benefit the resources would produce in their best alternative use. But who decides what resources are used and their opportunity cost? When a timber company buys a forest, it perhaps regards the alternative to cutting the trees this year as cutting them five years hence. But citizens in the area may value the forest as a nature sanctuary or a recreation area. The firm values the forest for the trees; the local residents may value the trees for the forest. The two values need not be the same.

Private and social costs.   The difference in the viewpoint of the firm and the residents illustrates the important distinction between private cost and social cost. **Private cost** measures the best alternative uses of the resources available to *the producer*. Private cost is usually measured by the market price of the resources that the firm uses. **Social cost** measures the best alternative uses of resources that are available to the whole society.

For some resources social cost may be the same as private cost; the price set by the market may well reflect the value of the resources in their best alternative use. For other resources, as will soon be clear, social cost may differ sharply from private cost.

Discrepancies between private and social cost lead to market failure from society's point of view.

The reason is that efficiency requires that prices cover social cost, but private producers, adjusting to private costs, will neglect those elements of social cost that are not included in private costs. When an element of social cost is not part of a private firm's profit and loss calculation, it is *external* to its decision-making process.

Discrepancies between social and private cost lead to **externalities,** which are costs or benefits of a transaction incurred or received by members of the society but not taken into account by the parties to the transaction. They are also called **third-party effects** because parties other than the two primary participants in the transaction (the buyer and the seller) are affected. Externalities arise in many different ways, and they may be beneficial or harmful.

Some externalities are beneficial. When I paint my house, I enhance my neighbors' view and the value of their property. When an Einstein or a Rembrandt gives the world a discovery or a work of art whose worth is far in excess of what he is paid to produce it, he confers an external benefit. Private producers will tend to produce too little of commodities that generate beneficial externalities because they bear all of the costs, while others reap part of the benefits.

Other externalities are harmful. Before we consider several examples, we can observe that private producers will tend to produce too much of commodities that generate harmful externalities because they bear none of the extra costs suffered by others.

Externalities, whether adverse or beneficial, cause market outcomes to be inefficient because they lead to the wrong allocation of resources from society's point of view.

Pollution. A major source of differences between private cost and social cost occurs when firms use resources they do not regard as scarce. This is a characteristic of most examples of pollution. When a paper mill produces pulp for the world's newspapers, more people are affected than its suppliers, employees, and customers. Its water-discharged effluent hurts the fishing boats that ply nearby waters, and its smog makes many resort areas less attractive, thereby reducing the tourist revenues that local motel operators and boat renters can expect. The firm neglects these external effects of its actions, because its profits are not affected by them.

Dumping of hazardous wastes, air pollution, and water pollution may occur as a result of calculated decisions as to what and how to produce or consume, and as a result of private producers' taking risks that prove to inflict injury on others. Even an apparent accident, such as an oil blowout or the breakup of a tanker, which is desired by no one, may be caused by a private firm's insufficient avoidance of the risk, since it bears only part of the costs.

Common-property resources. The world's oceans once teemed with fish, but today overfishing has caused a worldwide fish shortage. How could this happen?

Fish are an example of what is called a **common-property resource**, a resource that is owned by no

one and may be used by anyone. No one owns the oceans' fish until they are caught. The world's international fishing grounds are common property for all fishermen. If by taking more fish one fisherman reduces the catch of other fishermen, he does not count this as a cost, but it is a cost to society.

It is socially optimal to add to a fishing fleet until the last boat increases the value of the fleet's total catch by as much as it costs to operate the boat. This is the size of fishing fleet that a social planner would choose.

The free market will not, however, produce that result. Potential new entrants will judge entry to be profitable if the value of their own catch is equal to the costs of operating their boats. But a new entrant's catch is *partly* an addition to total catch and *partly* a reduction of the catch of other fishermen—because of congestion, each new boat reduces the catch of all other boats. Thus under free entry there will be too many boats in the fleet. Indeed, boats will continue to enter until there are no longer any profits for the marginal boat. In other words, boats will enter until the *average* value of the catch of a typical boat is equal to the cost of running that boat. At this point, however, the net addition to the *total* catch brought about by the last boat will be substantially less than the cost of operating the boat.

With common-property resources the level of activity will be too high because each new entrant will gain revenue not only from the amount that it adds to total product, but also from the amount that it takes away from the outputs of other producers.

This is not an untested theory. Fishing grounds and other common-property resources show a typical pattern of overexploitation. As a result, governments often use quotas and other restrictions in an attempt to reduce the size of the industry to what is socially optimal.

Congestion. Collisions between private planes and commercial airliners are headline news when they occur. They cannot occur unless *both* planes are in the air; this is what creates the externality. Suppose that the probability of a midair plane crash is roughly proportional to the number of planes in the air. Suppose, too, that I have the choice of flying from Phoenix to Los Angeles in my own plane or on a commercial airliner that has 100 of its 150 seats filled. In choosing to fly by myself, I decide that the slight extra risk to me of a midair collision is more than balanced by the fun or convenience of my own plane.

What I have neglected is the social cost of my action: the increased risk for every other person in the air on my route of flight that results from one more plane in the air. Since I do not consider other travelers' increased risk, my private decision may have been the wrong social decision.

Neglect of future consequences of present actions. When private producers undervalue future effects on others, they neglect an externality. A business facing bankruptcy tomorrow may be motivated to cheat on safety standards to cut costs today, even if it hurts the firm's reputation in the long term and imposes heavy future costs on others.

A less callous example is taking an action without finding out whether there are as-yet-unknown adverse externalities. One dramatic example of the neglect of future effects was the use of DDT. In 1948 the Swiss chemist Paul Mueller won the Nobel prize for his discovery of its extraordinary value as a pesticide. Gradually, however, it was confirmed that DDT did more than kill unwanted insects. Once sprayed, the chemical did not break down for years. It worked its way up the food chain from insects to birds and fish, to small mammals, and to larger and larger birds and mammals, including human beings. Arctic penguins, though thousands of miles from any sprayed areas, have measurable amounts of DDT in their bodies. DDT has thinned the egg shells of large birds to the point where breakage threatens many species, among them the peregrine falcon, the osprey, and the eagle. In 1962 Rachel Carson labeled DDT an "elixir of death," and by 1972 its use was banned in the United States.

While unavoidable ignorance of the future can never be described as market failure, unwillingness to determine whether there will be future adverse effects may be a form of market failure.

Other Sources of Inefficiency

The efficiency of the price system depends on firms' and households' receiving and responding to the sig-

nals provided by prices, costs, and windfall profits. Forces that seriously distort these signals or distort the required response to them may cause a market to fail to perform efficiently. These forces are often referred to as *market imperfections* and *market impediments*. Consider a few examples.

Moral hazard, adverse selection, and other situations of unequal information. When an individual or firm can take advantage of special knowledge to make profits while engaging in socially uneconomic behavior, **moral hazard** arises. For example, suppose a person who has ample fire insurance does not take reasonable precautions against fire; or suppose because of the availability of unemployment insurance a person refuses to accept a job he or she would otherwise have taken. In each of these cases the individuals have special knowledge that they can afford to take certain actions that impose unexpected costs on those who provide the insurance, but the insurers cannot identify them as the persons taking unintended advantage of the system. The socially valid purpose of insurance is to permit people to share given risks, not to increase the size of the aggregate risk. But in these two examples the behavior described does increase the risk and thus the social cost.

Closely related to moral hazard is the problem of **adverse selection.** A person suffering a heart attack may immediately seek to increase his life insurance coverage by purchasing as much additional coverage as is available without medical examination. People taking out insurance almost always know more about themselves as individual insurance risks than do their insurance companies. The company can try to limit the variation in risk by setting up broad categories based on variables, such as age and occupation, over which actuarial risk is known to vary. The rate charged is then different across categories based on the average risk in the category. But there must always be much variability of risk *within* any one category. Those who know they are well above average risk within their category are offered a bargain and will be led to take out more car, health, life, or fire insurance than they otherwise would. Someone who knows she is a low risk pays more than her own risk really warrants and is motivated to take out less insurance than she otherwise would.

More generally, any time either party to a transaction lacks information the other party has or is deceived by claims of the other party, market results will tend to be affected, and such changes may lead to inefficiency. Economically (but not legally) it is but a small step from such unequal knowledge to outright fraud. The arsonist who buys fire insurance before setting a fire or the business person with fire insurance who decides a fire is preferable to bankruptcy are extreme examples of adverse selection and moral hazard.

Unequal information is involved in many other situations. For example, the apparent overdiscounting of the prices of used cars because of the buyer's risk of acquiring a "lemon" is a case of differences in information between buyer and seller affecting behavior. (See the discussion of this problem on pages 139–140.)

Principal-agent issues.   A firm's managers act for the firm as *agents* of the owners, who are legally called the *principals* of the firm. If profits are the spur to efficient performance, it is clear that when a firm's managers choose to pursue their own goals rather than the *firm's* profits, they impede the functioning of the market system. A manager or a salesperson may incur unnecessary costs because the activities entailing these costs provide him or her with enjoyment. On a small scale this occurs whenever a purchasing agent is swayed by the Christmas present from a salesperson, or when a car renter is motivated to hire a more expensive car by the premium she will receive while her employer pays the bill. More serious are cases where managers regularly pursue their own goals at the expense of minimizing the costs of production. Most serious yet are outright sellouts of company interests or secrets to other firms in return for personal rewards.

Barriers to mobility.   Another kind of impediment to efficiency that occurs in the market is factor immobility. If increases in a factor's pay do not lead to increases in supply (for any of the reasons discussed in Chapters 18 and 19), the market will fail to reallocate resources promptly in response to changing demands. Monopoly power creates market imperfections by preventing resources from moving in response to the market signals of high profits. In this case, barriers to entry rather than factor immobility frustrate the flow of resources.

Collective consumption goods.   Certain goods and services, if they provide benefits to anyone, necessarily provide them to many people. Such goods are called **collective consumption goods.** National defense is the prime example of a collective consumption good. An adequate defense establishment protects all people in the country whether they want it or not, and there is no market where one individual can buy more of it and another individual less. The quantity of national defense provided must be decided collectively. Other examples of collective consumption goods are the beautification of a city, a levee to protect a city from a flood, and a hurricane-warning system.

In general, market systems cannot compel payment for a collective consumption good since there is no way to prevent a person who refuses to pay for the good from receiving its services. Governments, by virtue of their power to tax, can provide the services and collect from everyone.

Excessive or prohibitive transactions costs.   The costs incurred in negotiating and completing a transaction, such as the costs of billing or the bad-debt cost of those who never pay, are examples of **transactions costs**. They are always present to some degree, and they are a necessary cost of doing business. If buyers cannot be made to pay for the product, the producer will not be motivated to provide it. For a private firm to stay in business, it must be able to recover both production and transactions costs. If transactions costs are higher than they need to be because of imperfections in the private market, some products that it is efficient to produce will not be produced, and the market will have failed. Consider an example.

Could a private firm provide a road system for Los Angeles, covering its costs by collecting tolls? The answer is surely no (at least with today's technology).[2] It would be prohibitively expensive, both in money and in delays, to erect and staff a toll booth at every freeway exit. Requiring collection of reve-

---

[2] The warning about technology merits an additional comment. Technology changes rapidly. For example, the electronic metering of road use may make the toll booth unnecessary, just as the postage meter has made licking stamps unnecessary. Thus what a private market cannot do today, it may be able to do efficiently tomorrow.

nues via tolls would impose a prohibitive transactions cost. The users of a road system may be more than willing to pay the full costs of its construction and maintenance, but without an inexpensive way to make them pay, no private firm can produce the road. The government, collecting revenue by means of a gasoline tax, can do what the private market fails to do. (Whether it can do so without making a different mistake—producing more of the product than users are willing to pay for—is discussed below.)

Market imperfections may lead to market failure by preventing firms and households from completing transactions that are required for efficient resource allocation or by causing too much or too little production of particular goods.

Failure to Achieve Other Social Goals

Income Distribution

An important characteristic of a market economy is the *distribution* of the income that it determines. People whose services are in heavy demand relative to supply, such as television anchormen and superior football players, earn large incomes, while people whose services are not in heavy demand relative to supply, such as Ph.D.s in English and high school graduates without work experience, earn much less.

The distribution of income produced by the market can be looked at in equilibrium or in disequilibrium. In equilibrium, in an efficiently operating free-market economy, similar efforts of work or investment by similar people will tend to be similarly rewarded everywhere in the economy. Of course, dissimilar people will be dissimilarly rewarded.

In disequilibrium similar people making similar efforts are likely to be dissimilarly rewarded. People in declining industries, areas, and occupations suffer the punishment of low earnings through no fault of their own. Those in expanding sectors earn the reward of high earnings through no extra effort of their own.

These rewards and punishments serve the important function in decentralized decision making of mo-

tivating people to adapt. The "advantage" of such a system is that individuals can make their own decisions about how to alter their behavior when market conditions change; the "disadvantage" is that temporary rewards and punishments are dealt out as a result of changes in market conditions that are beyond the control of the individuals affected.

Moreover, even the equilibrium differences may seem unfair. A free-market system rewards certain groups and penalizes others. Because the workings of the market may be stern, even cruel, society often chooses to intervene. Should heads of households be forced to bear the full burden of their misfortune if, through no fault of their own, they lose their jobs? Even if they lose their jobs through their own fault, should they and their families have to bear the whole burden, which may include starvation? Should the ill and aged be thrown on the mercy of their families? What if they have no families? Both private charities and a great many government policies are concerned with modifying the distribution of income that results from such things as where one starts, how able one is, how lucky one is, and how one fares in the free-market world.

Often the goal of a more equitable distribution conflicts with the goal of a more efficient economy. Some of the problems that this can create in policy debates are further discussed in Box 22-1.

Preferences for Public Goods

Police protection, even justice, might be provided by private market mechanisms. Watchmen, Pinkerton detectives, and bodyguards all provide policelike protection. Privately hired arbitrators, "hired guns," and vigilantes of the Old West represent private ways of obtaining "justice." Yet the members of society may believe that a public police force is *preferable* to a private one and that public justice is *preferable* to justice for hire.

For another example, public schools may be better or worse than private schools, but they are likely to be different, particularly because persons others than parents, teachers, and owners influence their policies. Much of the case for public education rests on the advantages to you of having other people's children educated in a particular kind of environment

BOX 22-1

Distribution Versus Efficiency

Economists recognize that government actions can affect both the allocation of resources and the distribution of income. Because it is possible to talk about *efficient* and *inefficient* allocations, but not about *better* or *worse* distributions of income without introducing normative considerations, much of economics concerns efficiency and neglects effects on the distribution of income. Many disagreements can be understood in terms of a different emphasis on these things.

Consider the OPEC-induced rise in oil prices during the 1970s. From the point of view of efficiency alone, the correct policy was to let domestic oil prices in all oil-importing countries rise along with the world price. Instead many governments held the price down. They were concerned, among other things, with the effect of rising prices on the windfall profits earned by large oil companies and on the welfare of poorer citizens. "We just cannot let the poor find their heating bills rise so much and so fast while the profits of the oil companies soar" was a common reaction.

Here is a genuine conflict for which economics cannot provide a solution—because in the end the answer must rest on value judgments. However, economics can make the consequences of various choices apparent, and it can suggest policy alternatives. The consequences of holding down the price of oil (out of concern for the effect of higher prices on the poor) was an inefficient use of the countries' resources. Total national income was reduced, and some new investment was misdirected into high-cost (rather than low-cost) methods of production. Thus in the long run average standards of living were reduced. Whether the reduction in the average was a reasonable price to pay for shielding the poor is an open question; yet it is unlikely that the question was ever posed or the calculations made.

Can one have both efficiency and desired redistributions? One way is to let the price system do the job of signaling relative scarcities and costs, thereby ensuring some efficiency in the allocation of resources, but at the same time to use taxes or expenditures to transfer income to achieve redistributive goals. This method does not seek to help the poor (or other underprivileged groups) by subsidizing oil or any other price. Rather, it seeks to provide these groups with sufficient income by direct income transfers. Then it leaves producers and consumers free to respond to relative prices that approximately reflect relative opportunity costs.

Advocates of this method argue that it is surer, more direct, and less costly in its side effects than the method of subsidizing the prices of particular goods. Moreover, the price-subsidy method surely ends up subsidizing some who are rich and missing some who are very poor. Subsidizing gasoline prices, for example, benefits the Cadillac owner and does nothing for those too poor to own a car. Thus even in redistribution this method of subsidization is haphazard.

Supporters of redistribution through the price system usually counter with two arguments. First, it is well and good to say we *could* let oil prices rise and simultaneously subsidize the poor and tax the rich, but the political process makes it unlikely that we *will* do so. They point to the Reagan administration which deregulated prices and simultaneously *decreased* aids to the poor. Thus, say supporters of redistribution, holding prices down may be the best or even the only practical way to get a fairer distributive result.

Second, certain commodities such as food, heat, medical care, and housing are claimed to be basic to a civilized life and therefore should be provided to households cheaply, whatever their real opportunity cost. The supporters of redistribution through the price system believe that the inefficiencies resulting from prices that do not reflect opportunity costs are a burden worth bearing to ensure that everyone can afford these basics.

that is *different* from what a private school would provide. The market will be said to produce unsatisfactory results by those who believe the public product is preferable.

Protecting Individuals from Others

People can use and even abuse other people for economic gain in ways that the members of society find offensive. Child labor laws and minimum standards of working conditions are responses to such actions.

Yet direct abuse is not the only example of this kind of market failure. In an unhindered free market, the adults in a household would usually decide how much education to buy for their children. Selfish parents might buy no education, while egalitarian parents might buy the same quantity for all their children regardless of their abilities. The members of society may want to interfere in these choices, both to protect the child of the selfish parent and to ensure that some of the scarce educational resources are distributed according to intelligence rather than wealth. All households are forced to provide a minimum of education for their children, and strong inducements are offered—through public universities, scholarships, and other means—for gifted children to consume more education than they or their parents might choose if they had to pay the entire cost themselves.

Paternalism

Members of society acting through the state often seek to protect adult (and presumably responsible) individuals, not from others, but from themselves. Laws prohibiting heroin and other drugs and laws prescribing the installation and use of seat belts are intended primarily to protect individuals from their own ignorance or shortsightedness.

This kind of interference with the free choices of individuals is called **paternalism.** Whether such actions reflect the wishes of the majority of the society, or whether they reflect overbearing governments, there is no doubt that the market will not provide this kind of protection. Buyers do not buy what they do not want, and sellers have no motive to provide it.

Social Obligations

In a market system if you can pay another person to do things for you, you may do so. If you persuade someone else to clean your house in return for $35, presumably both parties to the transaction are better off: You prefer to part with $35 rather than clean the house yourself, and the person you hire prefers $35 to not cleaning your house. Normally society does not interfere with people's ability to negotiate mutually advantageous contracts.

Most people do not feel this way, however, about activities that are regarded as social obligations. For example, when military service is compulsory, contracts similar to one between you and a housekeeper could also be negotiated. Some persons faced with the obligation to do military service could no doubt pay enough to persuade others to do their tour of service for them.[3] By exactly the same argument as we used above, we can presume that both parties will be better off if they are allowed to negotiate such a trade. But such contracts are usually prohibited. Why? Because there are values other than those that can be expressed in a market. In times when it is necessary, military service by all healthy males is usually held to be a duty independent of an individual's tastes, wealth, influence, or social position. It is felt that everyone *ought* to do this service, and exchanges between willing traders are prohibited.

Military service is not the only example. Citizens cannot buy their way out of jury duty, nor legally sell their votes to another, even though in many cases they could find willing trading partners.

Even if the price system allocated goods and services with complete efficiency, members of a society may not wish to rely solely on the market if they have other goals they wish to achieve.

Government Intervention

Private collective action can sometimes remedy the failures of private individual action. (Private charities

---

[3] During the Civil War it was a common practice for a man to avoid the draft by hiring a substitute to serve in his place.

can help the poor; volunteer fire departments can fight fires; insurance companies can guard against adverse selection by more careful classification of clients.) However, by far the most common remedy for market failure is government intervention.

It is useful to ask several questions about possible government policies designed to correct market failure. First, what tools does the government have? Second, when and how vigorously should the tools be used? Third, under what circumstances is government intervention likely to fail?

The Tools of Microeconomic Policy

The legal power of the government to intervene in the workings of the economy is limited only by the Constitution (as interpreted by the courts), the willingness of Congress to pass laws, and the willingness of the executive branch to enforce them. There are numerous ways in which one or another level of government can prevent, alter, complement, or replace the workings of the unrestricted market economy. It is convenient to group these methods into four broad categories:

1. *Public provision.* Goods and services may be publicly provided in addition to or instead of private provision.
2. *Redistribution.* Public expenditures and taxes may be used to provide a distribution of income and output different from that which the private market provides.
3. *Rule making.* Rules and regulations may be adopted to compel, forbid, or specify within acceptable limits the behavior that private decision makers may engage in.
4. *Structuring incentives.* Government may alter market signals to persuade rather than force decision makers to adopt different behavior.

All four methods are frequently used, and all have great capacity to change the outcomes the unregulated market would provide. The first two will be discussed in detail in Chapter 23; the remainder of this section concerns rule making and structuring incentives.

Rule Making

Rules require, limit, or forbid certain activities and market actions. It is helpful to distinguish between *proscriptive* and *prescriptive* rules.

Proscriptive rules. Some regulations are like the Ten Commandments; they tell people and firms what they can and cannot do. Such rules require parents to send their children to school and to have them inoculated against measles and diphtheria. Laws that prohibit gambling and pornography attempt to enforce a particular moral code on the whole society. In Chapter 16 we discussed an important form of policy by prohibition—antitrust policy.

There are many other examples. Children cannot legally be served alcoholic drinks. Prostitution is prohibited in most places, even between a willing buyer and a willing seller. In most states you must buy automobile insurance. A person who offers goods for sale, including his or her own house, cannot refuse to sell because of a dislike for the customer's color or dress. There are rules against fraudulent advertising and the sale of substandard, adulterated, or poisonous foods.

Such rules set limits to the decisions that firms and households can make; they do not replace those decisions. But the allowed limits can be changed. An important means of government regulation is to change old rules or add new ones that redefine the boundary between forbidden and permitted behavior.

Prescriptive rules. Prescriptive rule making substitutes the rule maker's judgment for the firm's or the household's judgment about such things as prices charged, products produced, and methods of production. It tends to restrict private action more than proscriptive regulation because it replaces private decision making rather than limiting it to an acceptable set of decisions. Regulation of public utilities is an important example of prescriptive regulation (see Chapter 16), but prescriptive regulation goes far beyond the natural monopoly regulation we have discussed.

Federal regulatory commissions have until recently played the major role in deciding such matters as who may broadcast and on what frequencies, which airlines may fly which routes, what rates bus lines and pipeline operators may charge for different kinds of services, what prices may be paid for gasoline, how much foreign sugar may be imported into the United States, and how many miles to the gallon the average automobile sold by General Motors in 1985 must deliver. The trend toward deregulation in the 1980s has reduced but not eliminated prescriptive rule making.

Problems with rule making.   Rule making often appears to be a cheap, easy, and direct way of compelling desirable behavior in the face of market failure. But this appearance is deceptive. Rules must be enforceable and enforced, and once enforced they must be effective in obtaining the hoped for results. These conditions are often difficult and expensive to achieve.

Consider the requirement for the installation of an antipollution device that will meet a certain standard in reducing automobile exhaust emissions. Such a law may be the outcome of congressional debate on pollution control—and having passed the bill, Congress will turn to other things. Yet certain problems must be solved before the rule can achieve its purpose. Even with perfect compliance by the manufacturer, the device will not work well unless it is kept in working order by the owner. Yet it would be expensive to inspect every vehicle regularly and to force owners to keep the devices at the standard set by law.

Even a well-designed rule will work only until those regulated figure out a way to evade its intent while obeying its letter. There will be substantial incentive to find such a loophole, and resources that could be used elsewhere will be devoted by the regulated to the search—and then, in turn, by the regulators to counteracting such evasion.

Structuring Incentives

Government can change the incentives of households and firms in a variety of ways. It can fix minimum or maximum prices (as we saw in the discussion of agriculture and rent control in Chapter 6). It can adjust the tax system with exemptions and deductions. Deductible mortgage interest and real estate taxes, for example, can make owned housing relatively more attractive than rental housing. Such tax treatment sends the household different signals from those sent by the free market. Scholarships to students to become nurses or teachers may offset barriers to mobility into those occupations. Fines and criminal penalties for violating the rules imposed are another part of the incentive structure.

Internalizing Externalities

An important means of influencing incentives is to change the prices that firms and households pay in such a way as to eliminate externalities. Because externalities are a major source of market failure, much attention has been given to means of inducing decision makers to take them into account. Charging a producing firm for the pollution it causes can motivate the firm to alter its production in a socially desirable way. Procedures that make firms take account of the external effects (or extra social costs) of production are said to *internalize* them. How exactly does internalization work?

First we need to define terms. The **marginal net private benefit (MNPB)** of a unit of production is the difference between that unit's contribution to a firm's revenue and its contribution to the firm's cost. In other words, it is the contribution to profit of that unit. If we think of each unit of production as contributing to social welfare (and call that contribution **marginal social benefit**) and to social cost (defined on page 412), we can call the difference between marginal social benefit and marginal social cost **marginal net social benefit (MNSB).**

Marginal net social benefit is the key concept in judging efficiency. A unit of output should be produced if, but only if, its *MNSB* is greater than or equal to zero. To go from *MNPB* to *MNSB*, we need to add beneficial externalities and subtract adverse externalities. In the following discussion, we consider an adverse externality (such as pollution) so that *MNSB* is less than *MNPB* at each level of production.

Consider, as an a example, a private firm that

responds only to private benefits and costs. Such a firm will produce up to the point at which marginal net private benefit *(MNPB)* becomes zero. But at that output marginal net social benefit *(MNSB)* being less than *MNPB*, is necessarily negative; too much has been produced from the social point of view. This market failure can be avoided by the procedure shown in Figure 22-1. Once the firm has been forced to pay for what were previously externalities, the new net private benefit is exactly the same as net social benefit, that is, *MNPB* = *MNSB*. Thus the firm will be motivated to produce only as long as *MNSB* is not negative.

Internalization avoids the market failure caused by externalities.

There are many ways to internalize external costs. Consider two. If the amount of the external cost imposed per unit of output is known, it is possible to impose an **effluent charge,** or pollution tax, that compels the producer to pay a tax on every unit of polluting production. Such a charge might lead the producer to find a way to produce without polluting.

Another way to internalize external costs is to give legal standing to private citizens to sue for damages against polluters or to seek court injunctions against polluting activities. The legal action makes it costly for polluters; there will be damage payments if they lose and legal payments win or lose.

The Costs of Government Intervention

Consider the following argument: (1) The market system is working imperfectly; (2) government has the legal means to improve the situation; (3) therefore, the public interest will be served by government intervention.

This appealing argument is deficient because it neglects two important considerations. First, government intervention is costly. For that reason not every market failure is worth correcting. Second, government intervention may be imperfect. Just as markets sometimes succeed and sometimes fail, so government intervention sometimes succeeds and sometimes fails. In this section we consider costs of intervention, neglecting government failure. Later

FIGURE 22-1   Externalities

Internalizing an externality can correct market failure. The marginal net private benefit curve, *MNPB*, shows the benefit to the firm from producing each unit of output. The *MNPB* is the *difference between* the marginal revenue *(MR)* and the marginal cost *(MC)* associated with each unit of output. Since the firm is motivated to produce all units that make a positive contribution to its profits, its equilibrium output is q_1 where *MNPB* equals zero (i.e., *MR* = *MC*). However, this production imposes an external cost on others in society of $C per unit, as shown by the colored line. Subtracting this marginal social cost from the *MNPB* yields the marginal net social benefit curve, *MNSB*. The socially optimal output is q_2, where *MNSB* just equals zero. At this output marginal private benefit is just equal to the marginal external cost imposed on others in society by each unit of production. At q_2 the outsiders still have costs inflicted on them by the firm's production, but these costs *plus* the firm's private costs are just equal to the marginal benefit from its last unit of production.

Suppose the firm is required to pay an effluent charge of $C per unit. Its *MNPB* now becomes the *MNSB* curve. The externality hs been *internalized,* and the profit-maximizing firm is motivated to reduce its output from q_1 to q_2. It does this because any units produced beyond q_2 would now subtract from total profits.

we consider the added problem imposed by imperfect governmental intervention.

The *benefits* of government intervention are the value of the market failures averted. To evaluate governmental intervention it is necessary to consider the costs of the intervention and compare costs with benefits.

Large potential benefits do not necessarily justify government intervention, nor do large potential costs necessarily make it unwise. What matters is the balance between benefits and costs.

There are several kinds of costs of government intervention. Consider three.

Internal Costs

When government inspectors visit plants to see whether they are complying with federally imposed standards of health, industrial safety, or environmental protection, they are imposing costs on the public in the form of the salaries and expenses of the inspectors, among other ways. When regulatory bodies develop rules, hold hearings, write opinions, or have their staff prepare research reports, they are incurring costs. When the antitrust division had 40 lawyers spend 10 years preparing for and engaging in an antitrust prosecution of IBM, they were incurring costs. The costs of the judges and clerks and court reporters who hear and transcribe and review the evidence are likewise costs imposed by regulation. All these activities use valuable resources, resources that could have provided very different goods and services.

The aggregate expenditures for activities that regulate market behavior alone are large indeed. Such costs have grown greatly in the last several decades, and they represent one cause of growth in the size of government in the economy. However, they are only the most visible part of the total costs of government regulatory activities.

Direct External Costs

The nature and size of the extra costs borne by firms subject to government intervention vary with the type of regulation. A few examples are worth noting.

Changes in costs of production.   Antipollution regulations force producers not to burn high sulfur coal.

As a result, extra fuel costs are imposed on many firms. Such cost increases are directly attributable to regulation.

For 50 years (until the mid 1970s), the price of automobiles relative to other consumer goods was falling because of continuing advances in automotive engineering. Recent federal safety and emission standards have added so much to the cost of producing automobiles that since 1976 Americans have had to adjust to a steadily rising trend in the relative price of American autos, and automobile workers to the decreases in production that resulted.

Costs of compliance.   Government regulation and supervision generate a flood of reporting and related activities that are often summarized in the phrase *red tape*. The number of hours of business time devoted to understanding, reporting, and contesting regulatory provisions is enormous. Affirmative action, occupational safety, and environmental control have greatly increased the size of nonproduction payrolls. The legal costs alone of a major corporation can run into tens or hundreds of millions of dollars per year. While all this provides lots of employment for lawyers and economic experts, it is costly because there are other tasks such professionals could do that would add more to the production of consumer goods and services.

Losses in productivity.   Quite apart from the actual expenditures, the regulatory climate may reduce the incentive for experimentation, innovation, and the introduction of new products. Requiring advance government clearance before a new method or product may be introduced (on grounds of potential safety hazards or environmental impact) can eliminate the incentive to develop it. Requiring advance approval by a regulatory commission before entry is permitted into a regulated industry can discourage potential competitors.

Indirect External Costs

It has been estimated that regulatory activities decrease the growth rate of output per person in the United States by about 0.4 percent per year. This much lost growth translates into a big loss in the real living standards that could have been achieved. An extra 0.4 percent growth for 100 years would lead to a 50 percent increase in purchasing power. Such lost purchasing power is an externality of government intervention because the regulators do not take it into account. It is ironic that government intervention to offset adverse externalities can create new adverse externalities.

Consider an example. Government regulations designed to ensure the effectiveness and safety of new drugs have the incidental effect of delaying by an average of about nine months the introduction of drugs that are both effective and safe. The benefits of these regulations are related to the unsafe and ineffective drugs kept off the market. The cost includes the unavailability for about nine months of all those safe and effective drugs whose introduction was delayed.

Optimal Intervention: Benefits Versus Costs

Economic principles are useful in making decisions concerning the optimal correction of market failure. In order to develop these principles, we shall look at the question of preventing pollution.

Pollution problems range from threats to our survival to minor nuisances. Nearly all activity leaves some waste product; to say that all pollution must be removed whatever the cost is to try for the impossible and to ensure a vast commitment of society's scarce resources to many projects that will yield a low social value. But somewhere in the middle ground between trying for the impossible and maintaining a callous indifference to the problem there is a point of optimal action.

We approach the problem by assuming that government intervention is free from error. Later we shall relax this artificial assumption.

Costless intervention. We start with the easiest case. Assume that government intervention is costless except for the direct costs imposed by changes in the nature of production. All the government must do is identify the best form of pollution control, determine the right amount of it, and institute the appropriate means of achieving it. How should it proceed?

The first step is to choose the best means of pollution control. Suppose in this case a factory is emitting the noxious gas sulfur dioxide (SO_2), and it is determined that the best control method is to install filters on the smokestacks.[4]

The next step is to decide how much of the pollution should be eliminated. Suppose that simple re-circulation of the gases would reduce the discharge of SO_2 by 50 percent; after that, the cost would double for each further 10 percent reduction in the remaining SO_2. At most it would be possible to eliminate 99.44 percent of all SO_2, but the cost would be vast. In economic terms the marginal costs of removal rise sharply as the amount of SO_2 eliminated rises from 50 percent to 99.44 percent.

What percentage of the gases should be eliminated? The answer depends on the marginal benefits relative to marginal costs. The marginal benefits of pollution control are the external effects avoided. The optimal amount of prevention is the amount at which the marginal costs of further prevention equal the marginal benefits. This is illustrated in Figure 22-2.

The optimal amount of pollution prevention will be less than the maximum possible when pollution is costly to prevent. Thus the optimal amount of pollution is not equal to zero.

Costs of intervention. Next we add to our consideration the fact that government intervention brings with it enforcement costs—costs to the government, to the firm, and to third parties—of the kinds already discussed. These costs have to be added to the direct costs we have just considered.

Suppose for simplicity that enforcement costs are variable and rise as the level of pollution to be eliminated increases. The marginal costs of enforcement must be added to the marginal direct costs of prevention, thereby shifting upward the marginal costs of prevention. (This is shown by the marginal cost curves MC_2 and MC_3 in Figure 22-2.) The addition

---

[4] This choice of *means* is not trivial or always easy. Alternatives might include changing the method of production or moving people out of the path of the polluting gases. This first-step determination among alternative means is of prime importance in achieving the correct solution. A major source of "government failure" is choice of the wrong technique of control.

FIGURE 22-2   The Optimal Amount of Pollution Prevention

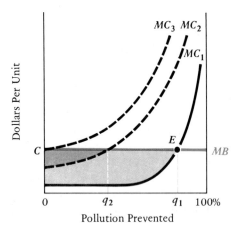

The amount of pollution prevention is optimal
when the quantity of prevention is being produced
at which marginal benefits from prevention equal
marginal costs. *MB* represents the marginal benefit
achieved by pollution prevention, assumed in this example to be constant at $\$C$ per percentage point. MC_1 rep-
resents the marginal costs of preventing pollution; it rises
sharply as more and more pollution is eliminated. The
optimal level of pollution control is q_1, where $MB =
MC_1$. *Notice that not all pollution is eliminated.* For all units
up to q_1, marginal benefits from pollution prevention exceed marginal costs. Net benefits are shown by the total
shaded area. Any further pollution elimination would
add more to costs than to benefits.

If the marginal cost curve shifts to MC_2, due, say, to
the addition of enforcement costs, the quantity of optimal prevention will decrease to q_2 and the net benefits
will be reduced to the darker shaded area. If costs increase to MC_3, the optimal amount of prevention becomes zero.

of such costs will surely decrease the amount of prevention that is optimal. If the costs are large enough,
they may even make any prevention uneconomical.

The optimal amount of government intervention to avoid market failure will be lower, the
greater are the costs of prevention and intervention.

Government Failure

All costs of intervention discussed in the previous
section would be present with a government that had
perfect foresight in defining goals, an unerring ability
to choose the least costly means of achieving them,
and intelligent and dedicated officials whose concern
was to do those things—and only those things—that
achieved the greatest possible efficiency of the economy. Government intervention usually falls short of
the high standard just described. This is not because
bureaucrats are worse than other people, more stu-
pid, more rigid, or more venal. Instead, it is because
they are like others, with the usual flaws and virtues.

Causes of Government Failure

Here are six reasons why government intervention
can be imperfect (i.e., "fail") in achieving its potential:

Imperfect knowledge or foresight.   Regulators may
not know enough to set correct standards. For example natural gas prices may, with the best of intentions, be set too low. The result will be too much
quantity demanded and too little quantity supplied,
with no automatic correction. Or the automobile
emission standards prescribed for a particular year
may be too demanding, thereby proving unexpectedly expensive to achieve, or too lax, thereby leading
to unexpected excessive pollution.

Rigidities.   Regulatory rules and allocations are hard
to change, but technology and economic circumstances change continually. Regulations that at one
time protected the public against a natural monopoly
may unnecessarily perpetuate a monopoly long after
technological changes have made competition possible. Giving AT&T a monopoly in long-distance
communication and specifying its price structure
made sense when the technology for transmitting
messages (use of cable) led to natural monopoly.
After a communications satellite had been placed in
orbit, there was room for many competitors, but the
regulatory commission was not free simply to open
up the industry to anyone. Too many people had

invested in the telephone industry and accepted limited profits on the expectation of continued regulation.

Inefficient means. Government may fail to choose the least costly means of solving a problem. It may decree a specific form of antipollution device that proves less effective and more expensive than another. It may pass a strict rule that proves all but impossible to enforce when a milder one would have achieved higher compliance at lower enforcement cost.

Myopic regulation. Regulation may become too restricted and too narrowly defined because the regulators are forced to specialize. Specialization may lead to expertise in a given area, but the regulators may lack the breadth to relate their area to broader concerns. Officials charged with the responsibility for a healthy railroad industry (dating from the time when railroads were the dominant means of transportation) may fail to see that the encouragement of trucking, even at the expense of the railroads, may be necessary for a healthy transportation industry.

Political constraints. Political realities may prevent the "right" policy from being adopted, even when it has been clearly identified. This is particularly true in a government based on checks and balances. Suppose a technically perfect tax (or tariff or farm policy) is designed by the experts. It will surely hurt some groups and benefit others. Lobbyists will go to work. The policy is likely to be modified by the cabinet, mutilated by the Senate, rebuilt in a different image by the House, and finally passed by Congress in a form the experts know is inadequate. Although the president may be aware of its flaws, he may sign it into law because it is "better than nothing."

This scenario occurs because the political process responds to political realities. "After all," the official may reason as he yields to the demands of the widget lobby (against his best judgment about the public interest), "if I'm defeated for re-election, I won't be here to serve the public interest on even more important issues next year." (Next year he will probably support widgets out of a sense of consistency!)

Decision maker's objectives. Public officials almost always wish to serve the public interest. But they have their careers, their families, and their prejudices as well. This is not unlike the principal-agent problem mentioned as a source of market failure. Public officials' own needs are seldom wholly absent from their consideration of the actions they will take. Similarly, their definition of the public interest is likely to be influenced heavily by their personal views of what policies are best.

A close relationship often exists or develops between the regulators and those they regulate. Many government regulators come from industry and plan to return to it. The broadcasting official who serves five years on the Federal Communications Commission and hopes to become a network vice-president after that term of office may view the networks' case in a not wholly disinterested way. Indeed, regulators may protect an industry in ways that would be quite illegal if done from within the industry.

The Effect of Government Failure

Suppose, for any of the reasons discussed above, the government makes a mistake in regulation. Say the government mistakenly specifies a method of pollution control that is less effective than the best method. This will increase the cost of achieving any given level of prevention. If the government insists on the level of control appropriate to the correct method, but requires the incorrect method, it can convert a social gain from control into a social loss. This is illustrated in Figure 22-3.

To generalize from the specific example, it is clear that any form of government failure adds to the costs or decreases the benefits of government intervention. Thus the lower the public's confidence in government's ability to do the right thing, the lower will be its willingness to have government intervention.

Government Intervention in the United States Today

The theoretical principles for determining the optimal amount of intervention are individually accepted

FIGURE 22-3   The Effects of Government Failure

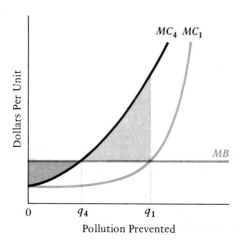

Choice of the wrong method of control will reduce the optimal amount of intervention and may convert the gains from intervention into losses. The *MB* and MC_1 curves are similiar to those in Figure 22-2. One common form of government failure is to specify the wrong method of intervention. Suppose the government specifies a method of pollution control that leads to the costs shown by MC_4. This is inefficient because costs at every level of pollution prevention are higher than necessary. Under such a method, the optimal level of prevention falls to q_4, with net benefits shown by the dark shaded area. Government failure reduces the amount of prevention that is optimal. The government will compound its failure if it insists on the level of prevention q_1 while requiring use of the inefficient method. The cost of every unit of pollution prevented beyond q_4 is in excess of its benefits, as shown by the light shaded area. Indeed, the result is worse than no intervention at all (the light shaded area is larger than the dark shaded area). While the best possible government intervention would have produced a net gain, government failure in this case produces a net loss.

by almost everyone. What they add up to, however, is more controversial. Does government intervene too little or too much in response to market failure? This question reflects one aspect of the ongoing argument about the role of government in the economy.

Much of the rhetoric of our concern with ecology

urges government intervention against heartless, profit-mad, giant corporations that destroy the environment for their own crass purposes. Such feelings lead to the demand for more—and more stringent—government regulation.

At the same time, others see the heavy hand of government regulation as burdening private companies with regulations that add to costs and impede innovation and thus keep prices and wages artificially high. Even perfect intervention would be costly, but imperfect intervention makes it much too costly. In this view, the deregulation movement that started in the 1980s was long overdue.

Evaluating the costs and the probable effectiveness of government intervention requires a comparison of the unregulated economic system as it is working (not as it might work ideally) with the pattern of government intervention as it is likely to perform (not as it might perform ideally).

The Role of Analysis

Economic analysis and measurement can help to eliminate certain misconceptions that cloud and confuse the debate. We have noted one such misconception: The optimal level of a negative externality, such as pollution, is not, as some urge, zero.

Another mistake is to equate market failure with the greed of profit-motivated corporations. Externalities do not require callous, thoughtless, or deliberately deceptive practices of private, profit-seeking firms; they occur whenever the signals to which decision makers respond do not include social as well as private benefits and costs. Such situations are not limited to private firms in a capitalist system. Cities and nationalized industries pollute just as much as privately owned industries when they neglect externalities in their operations, as they often do.

A third mistake is to think that the profits of a corporation tell something about neglected externalities. It is possible for a profitable firm (such as Dow Chemical) or an unprofitable one (such as U.S. Steel) to spend too little on pollution control or on safety, but it is also possible for it to spend too much. The existence of profits provides no clue as to which is the case.

The Role of Ideology

While positive analysis has a role to play, there are several reasons why ideology plays a bigger role in evaluating government intervention than in other areas.

First, measuring the costs of government intervention is difficult, particularly with respect to indirect costs, because some of the trade-offs are inherently uncertain. How important and how unsafe is nuclear power? Does the ban on some pesticides cause so much malnutrition as to offset the gains in the ecology it brings? What cannot be readily measured can be alleged to be extremely high (or low) by opponents (or supporters) of intervention. The numerous findings by scholars on both sides of each of these subjects has led one economist to the cynical conclusion that "believing is seeing."

Second, classifying the actual pattern of government intervention as successful or not is in part subjective. Has government safety regulation been (choose one) useful if imperfect, virtually ineffective, or positively adverse? All three views have been expressed and "documented."

Third, specifying what constitutes market failure is difficult. Does product differentiation represent market success (by giving consumers the variety they want) or failure (by foisting expensive and useless variations on them)?

In the United States in the mid 1980s it seems safe to conclude that confidence in the existing mix of free-market and government regulation is at a relatively low ebb. Not only are specific policy suggestions hotly argued, so is the whole philosophy of intervention. There is as yet no consensus as to what is wrong; the pressures for changes are strong in *both* directions.

Summary

1. The various markets in the economy are coordinated in an unplanned, decentralized way by the price system. Profits and losses play a key role in achieving a coordinated market response. Changes in prices and profits, resulting from emerging scarcities and surpluses, lead decision makers to adapt to a change in any one market of the economy. Such responses tend to correct the shortages and surpluses as well as to change the market signals of prices and profits.

2. Important features of market coordination include voluntary responses to market signals, the limited information required by any individual, and the fact that coordination will occur under any market structure.

3. A widely held argument in favor of the free market goes beyond its ability to provide automatic coordination. Many believe its flexibility and adaptability make it the best coordinator and also encourage innovation and growth. The tendency of the market to push relative prices toward the costs of production fosters efficient allocation of resources and self-correction of disequilibrium. Furthermore, the market economy tends to be impersonal, to decentralize power, and to require relatively little coercion of individuals.

4. Markets do not always work perfectly. Dissatisfaction with market results often leads to government intervention. Three main kinds of market failure are: (a) externalities arising from differences between private and social costs and benefits, (b) market imperfections and impediments, and (c) failure to achieve social goals other than efficiency.

5. Pollution is an example of an externality. An important source of pollution is producers' use of water and air that they do not regard as scarce. Since they do not pay all the costs of using these resources, they are not motivated to avoid the costs. Individual use of common-property resources, congestion, and neglect of future consequences are other sources of externalities.

6. Market imperfections and impediments are anything that prevents the prompt movement of resources in response to market signals. They include unequal information, barriers to mobility, excessive transactions costs, and the existence of collective consumption goods.

7. Changing the distribution of income is one of the roles for government intervention that members of a society desire. Others include values placed on public provision for its own sake, on protection of individuals from themselves or from others, and on recognition of social obligations.

8. Microeconomic policy concerns activities of the government that alter the unrestricted workings of the free-market system in order to affect either the allocation of resources or the distribution of income. Major tools of microeconomic policy include (a) public provision, (b) redistribution, (c) rule making, and (d) structuring incentives. (The first two are the subject of Chapter 23.) Both prescriptive and proscriptive rule making occur in a variety of forms. Incentives can be structured in a number of ways including the use of fines, subsidies, taxes, and effluent charges. Each of these is a means of internalizing the externality, and thus avoiding market failure.

9. The costs and benefits of government intervention must be considered in deciding whether, when, and how much intervention is appropriate. Among the costs are the direct costs incurred by the government; the costs imposed on those regulated, direct and indirect; and the costs imposed on third parties. These costs are seldom negligible and are often large.

10. If government intervention fails, the costs of intervention are incurred without realizing the benefits of avoiding market failure. The possibility of government failure must be balanced against the potential benefits of removing market failure. It is neither possible nor efficient to correct all market failure; neither is it always efficient to do nothing.

Market coordination
Differences between private and social valuations
Market failure
Rule making
Externalities
Internalization of externalities
Net social benefit and net private benefit
MNPB and *MNSB*
Benefits and costs of government intervention
Government failure
Optimal amount of intervention

Topics for Review

Discussion Questions

1. Should the free market be allowed to determine the price for the following, or should government intervene? Defend your choice for each.
   a. Transit fares
   b. Plastic surgery for victims of fires
   c. Garbage collection
   d. Postal delivery of newspapers and magazines
   e. Fire protection for churches
   f. Ice cream
2. The following activities have known harmful effects. In each case identify any divergence between social and private costs.
   a. Cigarette smoking
   b. Driving a car at the national speed limit of 55 mph
   c. Private ownership of guns
   d. Drilling for offshore oil
3. Suppose the facts asserted below are true. Should they trigger government intervention? If so, what policy alternatives are available?
   a. Hospital costs have been rising at about four times the rate of increase of personal income, and proper treatment of a serious illness has become extraordinarily expensive.
   b. The cost of the average one-family house in Washington, D.C., is now over $190,000, an amount that is out of the reach of most government employees.
   c. Cigarette smoking tends to reduce life expectancy of the smoker by eight years.
   d. Saccharin in large doses has been found to cause cancer in Canadian mice.
4. Consider the possible beneficial and adverse effects of each of the following forms of government interference.
   a. Charging motorists a tax for driving in the downtown areas of large cities and using the revenues to provide peripheral parking and shuttle buses
   b. Prohibiting juries from awarding large malpractice judgments against doctors

    c. Mandating no-fault auto insurance, in which the car owner's insurance company is responsible for damage to his or her vehicle no matter who causes the accident

    d. Requiring automobile manufacturers to warrant the tires on cars they sell instead of (as at present) having the tire manufacturer be the warrantor

5. Consider the following (alleged) facts about pollution control and indicate what, if any, influence they might have on policy determination.

    a. In the mid 1980s the cost of meeting federal pollution requirements was about $100 per person per year.

    b. More than a third of the world's known oil supplies lie under the ocean floor, and there is no known blowout-proof method of recovery.

    c. Sulfur removal requirements and strip mining regulations have led to the tripling of the cost of a ton of coal used in generating electricity.

    d. Every million dollars spent on pollution control creates 67 new jobs in the economy.

6. The president of Goodyear Tire and Rubber Company complained that government regulation had imposed $30 million per year in "unproductive costs" on his company, as listed below. How would one determine whether these costs were "productive" or "unproductive"?

    a. Environmental regulation, $17 million

    b. Occupational safety and health, $7 million

    c. Motor vehicle safety, $3 million

    d. Personnel and administration, $3 million

7. During a Pittsburgh air pollution alert, a 69-year-old retired steelworker was interviewed. He said, "I've got a heart condition myself, and I know that when I look out the window and see the air like it was this morning, I've got to stay inside. Yesterday, I tried to drive to the store, and I couldn't see 50 feet ahead of me, it was so thick, so I just came home. I remember that when I was young, we never thought about pollution. Everybody was working, and everybody had money, and the smokestacks were smoking, and the air was dirty, and we were all happy. I think the best air we ever had in Pittsburgh was during the Depression. That's when nobody was working." Comment on this statement in terms of the issues discussed in this chapter.

Taxation and Public Expenditure

All governments spend money, and they must raise revenue in order to do so. The American federal government is no exception. To do what the Constitution mandates, it must spend and tax. But government spending and government taxation today go far beyond the minimum required to provide such essentials as a system of justice and protection against foreign enemies. Spending and taxing are also key tools of both macroeconomic and microeconomic policy.

In this chapter we look at spending and taxing as tools of microeconomic policy. Public expenditure and public finance (raising revenue through taxation) inescapably affect both the allocation of resources and the distribution of income—sometimes intentionally, sometimes not.

There is no simple and sharp functional distinction between expenditure and tax policies. One way to deal with polluted rivers, for example, is by public expenditure to clean them up. An alternative is to use taxes to penalize polluters or to give tax concessions to firms that install pollution-abating devices. Tax concessions that seek to induce market responses are now called **tax expenditures**—that is, sacrifices of revenue by the taxing authorities that are designed to achieve purposes that the government believes are desirable.

In this chapter we are concerned with public expenditure and taxation. We ask how these activities of government affect the allocation of resources and the distribution of income. We also ask about the extent to which they are effective tools of public policy.

Taxation As a Tool of Microeconomic Policy

There is a bewildering array of taxes, some highly visible (such as sales taxes and income taxes) and others all but invisible to the consumer because they are imposed on producers of raw materials and intermediate products. People are taxed on what they earn, on what they spend, and on what they own. Firms are taxed as well as households. Taxes are not only numerous, they take a big bite. Aggregate taxes amount to roughly one-third of the total value of goods and services produced in the United States each year. The diversity and yield of various taxes are shown in Table 23-1.

TABLE 23-1   Government Tax Receipts, by Source, Fiscal Year 1983

Kind of Tax	Federal Billions of dollars	Federal Percentage	State Billions of dollars	State Percentage	Local Billions of dollars	Local Percentage	All governments Billions of dollars	All governments Percentage
Personal income	288.9	50	49.8	21	5.3	4	344.0	37
Corporate income and related	37.0	6	13.2	6	1.1	1	51.3	6
Social security and related	195.9	34	62.0	27	7.4	6	265.3	28
Subtotal (income and related)	521.8	90	125.0	54	13.8	11	660.6	71
Excise and sales	44.5	8	83.9	36	16.3	14	144.7	15
Property	0	0	3.2	1	85.8	71	89.0	10
All others	10.8	2	21.3	9	4.5	4	36.6	4
Total	577.1	100	233.4	100	120.4	100	930.9	100

Source: Facts and Figures on Government Finance, 23rd Biennial Edition (New York: Tax Foundation, 1985).

The federal government relies heavily on income taxes, state governments on income taxes and excise and sales taxes, and local governments on property taxes. The largest source of revenue for each level of government is highlighted in color.

The Tax System and the Distribution of Income

A government that taxes the rich and exempts the poor is changing the distribution of income. How much redistribution is achieved by U.S. taxes today?

Progressivity of Taxation

Rhetoric about income distribution and tax policy often invokes the important but hard to define concepts of equity and equality. Equity—fairness—is a normative concept; what one group thinks is fair may seem outrageous to another. But equality is a straightforward concept—or is it?

To tax people equally might mean several things. It might mean that everyone should pay the same amount—which would be hard on the unemployed worker and easy on Tom Watson. It might mean that each person should pay the same proportion of his or her income, say, a flat 20 percent, whether rich or poor, living alone or supporting eight children, healthy or suffering from a disease that requires heavy use of expensive drugs. It might mean that each should pay an amount of tax such that everyone's income after taxes is the same—which would remove any incentive to earn above average income. Or it might mean none of these things.

People may not agree on what redistributions are

fair, but they can agree on what redistributions actually occur. To get precise measurements of what happens, the distributional effects of taxes are usually discussed using the concept of **progressivity of taxation,** the ratio of taxes to income at different levels of income.

1. A **proportional tax** takes amounts of money from people in direct proportion to their income.
2. A **regressive tax** takes a larger percentage of income from people, the lower their income.
3. A **progressive tax** takes a larger percentage of income from people, the larger their income.

Excise and sales taxes.   An excise tax is levied on a particular commodity (e.g., liquor); a sales tax is levied on all or most sales. If two families spend the same proportion of their income on a certain commodity that is subject to a sales or an excise tax, the tax is proportional in its effects on them. If the tax is on a commodity, such as food, that takes a larger proportion of the income of lower-income families, it is regressive. If it is on a commodity, such as jewelry, on which the rich spend a larger proportion of their income than the poor, it is progressive. A general sales tax is regressive because poorer families tend to spend a larger proportion of their incomes than do richer ones.

Commodities with inelastic demands provide

easy sources of revenue. In many countries commodities such as tobacco, alcohol, and gasoline are singled out for high rates of excise taxation. Because these commodities usually account for a much greater proportion of the expenditure of lower-income than higher-income groups, the taxes on them are regressive.

The sales and excise taxes used in the United States today are as a whole regressive.

Property taxes.   The progressivity of the property tax has been studied extensively. It is well known that the rich live in more expensive houses than the poor, but all that this establishes is that the rich tend to pay more dollars in property tax than do the poor. Because the rich tend to live in different communities than the poor and thus pay taxes at different rates, and because they tend to spend a different proportion of their income for housing, the question of the progressivity of the property tax is difficult. Most studies have shown that the proportion of income spent for housing tends to decrease with income. Many, but not all public finance experts believe that the property tax tends to be regressive in its overall effect.

Personal income taxes.   The personal tax rate is itself a function of taxable income, and it is useful to distinguish between two different rates. The **average tax rate** paid by an individual or by a couple is their income tax payment divided by total income. The **marginal tax rate** is the amount of tax the taxpayer would pay on an additional dollar of income. Table 23-2 shows the applicable rates on federal income tax in 1986, before the major tax reforms of 1986 went into effect.[1]

In structure the federal personal income tax as it was from 1946 to 1986 was progressive because the average rate rose steadily with income. However,

[1] As this edition goes to press the tax reform legislation of 1986 is awaiting final congressional and presidential approval, which is expected by the end of 1986. But even when finally passed the impact of the changes will not be clear for many years. Partly this is because the changes are phased in over several years, and partly because behavior adapts only gradually. The bulk of the discussion in this chapter relies upon what we know about a tax system that has been in effect for nearly 40 years and that is now undergoing major reform.

because of the special definitions given to net income by the tax laws, the overall effect of the federal income tax was less progressive in effect than Table 23-2 suggests. To arrive at taxable income, total income was modified by certain exemptions from income, by capital gains provisions, and by deduction of certain types of expenditure from gross income.

Despite modifications, the federal income tax has traditionally been progressive in effect as well as in structure.

Corporate income taxes.   The federal corporate income tax is, for practical purposes, a flat-rate tax on profits as defined by the taxing authorities. In 1986 the rate was reduced from 46 to 34 percent, but other

TABLE 23-2   The Rate Structure of the Federal Income Tax, 1986

(1) Taxable income after deductions and exemptions	(2) Personal income tax	(3) Average tax rate, percentage (2) ÷ (1)	(4) Marginal tax rate, percentage
$ 2,400	$ 0	0	0
3,400	0	0	0
6,000	276	4.6	12
10,000	799	8.0	14
15,000	1,551	10.3	16
20,000	2,419	12.1	18
30,000	4,712	15.7	25
50,000	11,057	22.1	38
75,000	21,059	28.1	42
100,000	31,886	31.9	45
150,000	55,832	37.2	49
200,000	80,642	40.3	50
250,000	105,642	42.3	50
1,000,000	480,642	48.1	50
10,000,000	4,980,642	49.8	50

Both marginal and average tax rates rise with income; thus the personal income tax is progressive in structure. These data give the amount of federal income tax to be paid at different income levels by a married couple in 1986. The marginal tax rate (the tax on an additional dollar of income) rose through 14 brackets with income and reached 50 percent at $175,250. However, these rates were based on taxable income, not total income received. Because of a variety of deductions and exemptions, the effective average tax rates on income received were much lower than those shown in column 3.

changes in the tax laws raised the overall taxes paid by corporations. It is difficult to determine the effect of corporate taxation on income distribution, for there is great controversy over the extent to which it is "shifted" to consumers.[2] So far as the tax falls on stockholders, they as a group tend to be wealthier than individuals who do not own stock, and there is thus a tendency toward progressivity. But within the stockholder group, the results are uneven. If a dollar were paid out in dividends instead of taxes, rich stockholders would keep a much smaller share than poorer stockholders because of their high marginal personal tax rates.

The Overall Redistributive Effect of the Tax System

It is more difficult to assess the overall impact of a tax system than the impact of any particular tax, but economists often ask whether the whole array of taxes tends to increase or decrease the degree of inequality of the income distribution. One aspect of this question depends upon the mix of taxes of different kinds. Federal taxes (chiefly income taxes) tend to be somewhat progressive. State and local authorities rely heavily on property and sales taxes and thus have tax systems that are regressive.

The difficulty of determining overall progressivity is increased by the fact that income from different sources is taxed at different rates. For example, in the federal individual tax, up until 1987 income from royalties on oil wells was taxed more lightly than income from royalties on books; profits from sales of assets (called *capital gains*) were taxed more lightly than wages and salaries; and municipal bond interest was tax exempt, while most other interest income was taxed. To evaluate progressivity one needed to know the way in which different levels of income correlated with different sources of income.

The empirical evidence shows that the combined effect of all U.S. taxes, federal, state, and local, was virtually proportional in 1986 for families with incomes between $8,000 and

---

[2] The question of tax shifting is called the problem of *incidence,* that is, who really pays a tax imposed on any one group. It is discussed later in this chapter.

$100,000. Among families of very low income, the tax structure was regressive.

Can Progressivity Be Increased?

Taxes can be levied on any of three different monetary magnitudes: on assets, on incomes, and on expenditures. Inheritance taxes and gift taxes are taxes on assets; such taxes do not now play a large role in the overall revenue picture. Taxes on incomes are important and can be quite progressive. Taxes on expenditures—especially sales and excise taxes—are related to the dollar value of expenditures, not the incomes of those spending the money; they are known to be regressive.

Substantial progressivity in income taxes is required to achieve proportionality in the overall tax pattern.

Many observers have argued that to achieve overall proportionality in the tax structure is in itself a significant accomplishment. Some argue that, given the large fraction of national income that is taxed away, more progressivity cannot be achieved, since we are already forced to levy heavy taxes on average and below-average incomes simply to meet revenue requirements.

Whether or not more progressivity is desirable, is more progressivity possible?

Would Increasing Reliance on Income Taxes Increase Progressivity?

It may seem logical to conclude that, since income taxes are progressive, raising income tax rates would increase progressivity. Surprisingly, some conservative economists have argued that this is not the case. A shift to higher tax rates would raise both the average and marginal *rate* of tax on incomes, but it might not raise the total *amount* of revenue actually collected. The change in the amount would depend on the incentive effects of tax rates.

A curve that attempts to relate the government's income tax revenue yield to the level of tax rates is the **Laffer curve**, named after economist Arthur Laffer, whose views were influential during the early years of the Reagan administration. Its essential feature is that tax revenues reach a maximum at some rate of taxation well below 100 percent. (See Figure 23-1.)

The general shape of the Laffer curve is argued as a matter of simple logic. At a zero tax rate no revenue will be collected. Similarly, at a 100 percent tax rate revenues will again be zero because no one would bother to earn taxable income just to support the government. At intermediate rates people will both earn income and pay taxes. Government tax revenues will reach an upper limit at some rate of taxation below 100 percent. For rates higher than the rate that produces this maximum, every increase in tax rates will lead to a decrease in tax revenues.

Just where this maximum occurs—whether at average tax rates of 40 percent or 80 percent or 95 percent—is an important empirical matter. Laffer believed that by the 1970s the United States had already increased taxes past the point where higher tax rates yielded more revenue. As a result, he argued, any attempt to increase progressivity by raising income tax rates would be self-defeating.

Many other economists disagreed. While they might concede that some countries may have reached

such a point, they argued that this has not happened in the United States. A number of careful studies show that the current U.S. top marginal tax rate of 50 percent was still short of being self-defeating in terms of tax revenue. These studies suggest that Professor Laffer identified a potential rather than an actual problem. Box 23-1 identifies an early precursor of the Laffer curve.

Increasing Progressivity by Changing the Income Tax Structure

If the government raises income taxes for one group and lowers them for another in a way that leaves the total tax yield constant, the *structure* of the income tax will have been changed. Much repeated demand for tax reform relates to proposed changes in the structure of income taxes. Most economists believe that such changes can be made (whether or not they consider them desirable) and that if they were made, they could change the progressivity of the total tax system. Here are four important proposals, widely discussed by economists in the decades preceding the tax reform of 1986.

The negative income tax (NIT). A tax is negative when the government pays "the taxpayer" instead of the other way around. The so-called **negative income tax (NIT)** is a policy tool designed to increase progressivity and combat poverty by making taxes negative at very low incomes. Such a tax would extend progressivity to the very lowest incomes.

Many versions of the NIT have been proposed; the one described here illustrates the basic idea. The underlying belief is that a family of a given size should be allowed a minimum annual income. The aim is to guarantee this income without eliminating the incentive to become self-supporting. This is done by combining a grant with a tax. At a break-even income level, well above the minimum income guaranteed, the family neither receives money from the government nor pays any tax. Below this break-even level the family is paid by the government, that is, the family pays a negative tax. Above this level it pays a positive tax. An example based on a minimum annual income of $6,000, a break-even level of $12,000, and a marginal tax rate of 50 percent is given

FIGURE 23-1   A Laffer Curve

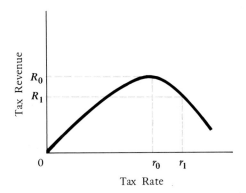

Increases in tax rates beyond some level will decrease rather than increase tax revenue. The curve relates the government's tax revenue to the tax rate. As drawn, revenue reaches a maximum level of R_0 at average tax rate r_0. If tax rates were r_1, *reducing* them to r_0 would increase revenue to the government.

BOX 23-1

The Laffer Curve 600 Years Before Laffer

In the fourteenth century the Arabic philosopher Ibn Khaldun wrote:

It should be known that at the beginning of the dynasty, taxation yields a large revenue from small assessments. At the end of the dynasty, taxation yields a small revenue from large assessments. . . .

When the dynasty follows the ways of group feeling and [political] superiority, it necessarily has at first a desert attitude. The desert attitude requires kindness, reverence, humility, respect for the property of other people, and disinclination to appropriate it, except in rare instances. Therefore, the individual imposts and assessments, which together constitute the tax revenue, are low. When tax assessments and imposts upon the subjects are low, the latter have the energy and desire to do things. Cultural enterprises grow and increase, because the low taxes bring satisfaction. When cultural enterprises grow, the number of individual imposts and assessments mounts. In consequence, the tax revenue, which is the sum total of [the individual assessments], increases.

When the dynasty continues in power and their rulers follow each other in succession, they become sophisticated. The Bedouin attitude and simplicity lose their significance, and the Bedouin qualities of moderation and restraint disappear.

As a result, the individual imposts and assessments upon the subjects, agricultural laborers, farmers, and all the other taxpayers, increase. Every individual impost and assessment is greatly increased, in order to obtain a higher tax revenue. Customs duties are placed upon articles of commerce. Gradual increases in the amount of assessments succeed each other regularly, in correspondence with the gradual increase in the luxury customs and many needs of the dynasty, and the spending required in connection with them. Eventually, the taxes will weigh heavily upon the subjects and overburden them. Heavy taxes become an obligation and tradition, because the increases took place gradually, and no one knows specifically who increased them or levied them. They lie upon the subjects like an obligation and tradition.

The assessments increase beyond the limits of equity. The result is that the interest of the subjects in cultural enterprises disappears, since when they compare expenditures and taxes with their income and gain and see the little profit they make, they lose all hope. Therefore, many of them refrain from all the activity. The result is that the total tax revenue goes down.

Finally, civilization is destroyed, because the incentive for cultural activity is gone. It is the dynasty that suffers from the situation, because it [is the dynasty that] profits from cultural activity.*

* From the Muqaddimah: An Introduction to History, translated from the Arabic by Franz Rosenthal. Bollingen Series XLIII. Copyright © 1958 and 1967 by Princeton University Press. Reprinted by permission of Princeton University Press.

---

in Figure 23-2.[3] Of course the grant is not actually given and then taxed away; thus it is spoken of as a "notional" grant.

Supporters of the negative income tax believe that it would be a particularly effective tool for reducing poverty. It provides a minimum level of income as a matter of right, not of charity, and it does so without removing the incentive to work of those eligible for payments. Every dollar earned adds to the after-tax income of the family.

As a potential replacement for many other relief programs, it promises to avoid the most pressing cases of poverty with much less administrative cost and without the myriad exceptions that are involved in most programs. An incidental advantage is that it removes whatever incentive people might have to migrate to states with better welfare programs, but it does not discourage migration to places where work may be available.

Comprehensive income taxation. Joseph Pechman of the Brookings Institution took the lead in arguing that it is possible to raise more revenue from the income tax, increase its progressivity, and at the same time *reduce* both average and marginal tax rates! This

[3] The example is unrealistic in assigning a 50 percent marginal tax at such low levels of income as $12,000. The cost to the treasury in lost revenue of an NIT would be much higher if it were combined with a sharply graduated rate structure of the sort shown in Table 23-2.

FIGURE 23-2   The Negative Income Tax

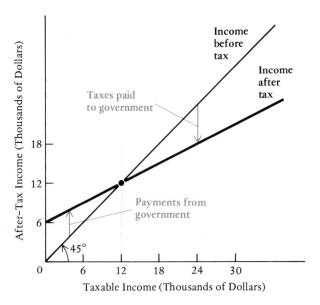

Instead of a zero income tax up to some level and a positive tax above that level, there could be a negative tax up to a break-even income and a positive tax above it. The scheme illustrated here works as if every family is given an untaxed grant of $6,000 and then taxed at a rate of 50 percent on all other income. (Of course only the *difference* between the notional grant and the tax payable actually is paid or collected.) A family with $12,000 taxable income breaks even. A family with income below $12,000 taxable is paid by the government. A family with taxable income above $12,000 pays taxes. The heavy black line shows the after-tax income for different levels of taxable income under this particular scheme. The 45° line shows the income before tax. Therefore the vertical distance between it and the heavy black curve shows the payments by or to the government at any level of income under this scheme.

sounds like magic, but it is a matter of simple arithmetic. The **tax base** is total *taxable* income. Under the pre-1986 definitions, taxable income was much less than total income because there were all sorts of deductions and exemptions. If all income were taxed, regardless of source, it would be possible to raise more revenue by applying lower rates to this larger

tax base. The idea of **comprehensive income taxation (CIT)** is to eliminate nearly all the loopholes, deductions, and exemptions that make taxable income less than total income. By eliminating some or all personal deductions, homeowner preferences, special treatment of capital gains, and exemptions for dependents, old age, and blindness, the tax base could be increased by up to 70 percent. It would then be easy to reduce tax *rates* in all income brackets.

With comprehensive income taxation it would be possible to achieve substantially more progressivity without increasing anyone's marginal tax rate at all. For example, imagine a definition of the CIT where comprehensive income is 150 percent of previous taxable income. Rates could be slightly reduced for high-income taxpayers and greatly reduced for middle- and low-income taxpayers in such amounts as to maintain the same total tax revenue but increase progressivity.

The tax reform enacted in 1986 is in the spirit of the CIT, although it does not go all the way. It will by 1988 have replaced the 14 brackets of the 1986 tax structure, ranging from 11 percent to 50 percent, with only two brackets of 15 percent and 28 percent.[4] Accompanying these rate decreases was a substantial increase in the tax base. Among the key changes were elimination of numerous tax shelters, elimination of preferential treatment of capital gains, and elimination of deductibility of many types of expenditures, including sales taxes and consumer interest payments.

At first glance these changes in tax brackets might seem to move the progressive personal income tax toward proportionality. But this may not be the case since the myriad changes in the tax code greatly increased the number of low-income persons who do not pay any tax, and increased substantially the tax paid by those with incomes over $75,000. Thus the final effect on progressivity is not known at this time.

Flat-rate tax.   An extreme form of the CIT is the *flat-rate plan,* which would tax all income above some

---

[4] Despite only two brackets, there is some greater variability in the highest rates of marginal taxation. Due to phasing out of some exemptions for those with high incomes, and other changes, the *effective* marginal tax rate can rise as high as 33 percent.

minimum per family, from any source, at a fixed rate, such as 17 percent. This use of a single tax bracket would make the personal income tax virtually a proportional tax and would surely make the overall tax system regressive unless the minimum was set quite high.

Consumption taxation.   An alternative approach to income tax reform breaks out of the annual income framework and calls for a tax on current consumption plus bequests and gifts. The household is taxed on its income minus saving. People are not taxed at all on what they earn, only on what they spend on consumption.[5]

To make sure that any income that is saved is ultimately subject to tax, there is full taxation of gifts and bequests. By not allowing intergenerational transfers of income to go untaxed, a good deal of income redistribution would occur over the long period. The authors of one such proposal, Henry Aaron and Harvey Galper of the Brookings Institution argue that such a scheme could achieve current levels of revenue with graduated rates rising to a maximum of 32 percent and at the same time encourage working, saving, and investment.

Political Barriers to Tax Reform

When major tax reform was enacted in 1986 it was hailed as something of a political miracle, resting on the immense popularity of President Reagan. Why was it so surprising? The purely political barriers to tax reform are formidable. Any proposed reform usually imposes large costs on a relatively well-identified group, while the benefits it gives are more widely diffused.

The 10 people who would each lose a million dollars from a particular tax reform are much more interested in the issue than the 10 million people who would each gain a dollar. The 10, not the 10 million, hire lobbyists and make campaign contributions. Legislators usually respond to these pressures if they want long public careers.

---

[5] Consumption taxation is not without problems of interpretation. Expenditures on higher education are one example. If viewed as investment, education expenditures would be treated as saving and would not be taxed. If viewed as consumption, such expenditures would be included in the tax base.

But, as the 1986 tax bill showed, even formidable political barriers can be overcome on occasion.

How Much Progressivity Is Desirable?

Suppose increased progressivity could be achieved; would we want it? Many say no.

Some simply oppose progressivity as a goal. A second group is motivated not by distributive considerations but by opposition to government spending. They oppose changes that would make it easier for the government to raise more money. Such people fear schemes such as CIT precisely because they do not generate tax revolts. Rates that are lowered today can be raised tomorrow. These people point to the introduction of "pay as you go" (withholding) taxes in the 1940s. The argument used then to persuade people to accept withholding was that it was more convenient and less painful to have one's employer collect the taxes on income as it was earned than to have to come up with a lump sum on a date such as April 15. But levels of taxation did not remain constant after withholding went into effect. Opponents of government spending charge that governments discovered they could exploit the system: They kept raising taxes.

A third source of opposition to increasing progressivity by means of tax reform is that every aspect of present tax policy was introduced to benefit some group whose members believe they have valid claims to special treatment. Consider one of the deductions that the 1986 tax reform reduced but did not eliminate. Tax deductibility of contributions provides incentive for gifts to churches, universities, and private charities and foundations.

Fourth, tax reform may conflict with what is seen as fair. Adjustments made in the name of equity have eroded the tax base. Special tax treatment of the aged seems fair to many in view of the probable needs by the aged for extensive medical treatment. More favorable tax treatment of families with children than of childless couples seems fair to some on the basis of need, but it seems undesirable to those who think population is already too high.

Finally, the case against tax policy as a means of achieving redistributive goals has some support even among those who favor more redistribution of income from rich to poor. They argue that it is misleading, unnecessary, and poor tactics politically to pay so much attention to *tax* progressivity. After all, how the money is spent is just as important, and often less controversial, than how it is collected. A regressive tax, say, a sales tax, may provide funds for increasing welfare payments and thus redistribute income to the poor. It is the combined overall effect of the two that is important, and it may be easier for those who want to redistribute income to the poor to get Congress to enact progressive expenditure programs than to adopt more progressive taxes.

The Tax System and Allocation of Resources

The tax system influences the allocation of resources by changing the *relative* prices of different goods and factors and the *relative* profitability of different industries and of different uses of factors of production.

While it is theoretically possible to design a neutral tax system—one that leaves all relative prices unchanged—actual tax policy, both intentionally and unintentionally, is never neutral. It leads to a different allocation of resources than would occur without it.

Intended Effects

The tax structure is often used deliberately to change incentives and thus to affect resource allocation. Taxing gasoline to discourage energy consumption is one example; an effluent charge on polluters is another.

Tax provisions may be used as a carrot as well as a stick. One way is to allow the deduction of some expenditures from income before computing the amount of taxes payable or to give tax credits for some kinds of expenditures. Every $100 spent by a wealthy family in the 28 percent marginal tax bracket on an item that is tax deductible costs it $72 in after-tax income. Every $100 it spends on items that are not tax deductible costs the full $100 in after-tax income. This encourages the family to contribute money and assets to charitable and educational institutions, for example.

Interest payments for a mortgage are tax deductible under the U.S. tax code, while payments for rental housing are not. This encourages home own-

ership by lowering the cost of buying a house relative to the cost of renting one.

Unintended Effects

Not all the allocative effects of the tax system are intended. Unintended and undesirable by-products of a tax system occur, for example, when high income taxes discourage work or induce people to spend money on tax avoidance.

Consider the tax incentives to home ownership, which were surely intended. An incidental effect of such provisions is that the incentive is much less for a poor person than for a rich one. The value of the deduction for interest is nearly twice as large to a taxpayer in the 28 percent marginal tax bracket than to someone in the 15 percent bracket. If both are paying 12 percent interest on a mortgage, the richer taxpayer pays 8.64 percent in after-tax dollars. The poorer one pays 10.2 percent. Thus the lower one's income, the less the incentive that is provided to obtain a property stake in the society. This is surely an unintended effect.

Tax Incidence

The major unresolved question about taxes and allocation is empirical: Just how different is the allocation because of tax policy? Perhaps surprisingly, there is no consensus on this question. The reason is that we are not sure who really pays the taxes that are levied. This is called the problem of **tax incidence,** or the identification of who ultimately bears the burden of a tax.

When a tax is imposed on a firm, does the firm bear the burden of the tax, or does it pass it on to the consumer in the form of higher prices? To see why this is a difficult question to answer, consider two examples.

Do Landlords or Tenants Pay the Property Tax?

Landlords characteristically protest that the crushing burden of property taxes makes it impossible for them to earn a reasonable living from renting buildings to tenants who as often as not abuse the property. Tenants are likely to reply that landlords typically shirk their responsibilities for building maintenance and that the whole burden of the tax is passed on to the tenants in the form of higher rents. Both sides cannot be right in alleging that they each bear the entire burden of the tax!

To examine the incidence, suppose that a city inposes a property tax. The thousands of landlords in the city decide to raise rents by the full amount of the tax. This scenario is shown graphically in Figure 23-3. There will be a decline in the quantity of rental accommodation demanded as a result of the price increase.

The decline in the quantity demanded without any change in the quantity supplied will cause a surplus of rental accommodations at the higher prices. Landlords will find it difficult to replace tenants who move out, and the typical unit will remain empty longer between tenancies. Prospective tenants will find alternative sites from which to choose and will become very particular in what they expect from landlords.

Some prospective tenants, seeing vacant apartments, will offer to pay rents below the asking rent. Some landlords will accept the offer rather than earn nothing from vacant premises. Once some landlords cut rents, others will have to follow suit or find their properties staying unrented for longer periods of time.

Eventually rentals will reach a new equilibrium at which the quantity demanded equals the quantity supplied. The equilibrium rental price will be higher than the original before-tax rent, but lower than the rent that passes the entire tax on to the tenants.

The incidence of the property tax is shared by landlords and tenants.

Just how it is shared by the two groups will depend on the elasticity of the demand and supply curves.[6] These elasticities, in turn, will depend on how quickly landlords and tenants can react to changes.

Notice that the question of incidence does not depend on who writes the check to pay the tax bill.

[6] We suggest you draw a series of diagrams with demand and supply curves of different slopes to see how this works. In each case, shift the supply curve up by the same vertical amount—to represent the property tax—and see what proportion of the increase is reflected in the new equilibrium price.

FIGURE 23-3   The Incidence of a Tax on Rental Housing

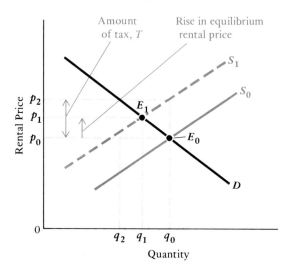

Since the equilibrium rent rises by less than the amount of the tax, landlords and tenants share the burden. The supply schedule S_0 reflects landlords' willingness to supply rental housing at different levels of rents received. Before the tax, equilibrium is at E_0. When a tax of T is imposed on landlords, the supply curve shifts up by the full amount of the tax to S_1. Suppose landlords attempt to raise rents by the full amount of the tax, from p_0 to p_2. There will be an excess supply of housing of $q_2 q_0$ at p_2, and rents will fall. At the new equilibrium E_1, with rental price p_1, landlords have succeeded in raising the rental price by $p_0 p_1$, less than $p_0 p_2$, the full amount of the tax. Thus landlords are paying $p_1 p_2$ of the total tax on each unit rented.

In many European countries, the tenant rather than the landlord is sent the tax bill and pays the tax directly to the city; even in this case, however, the landlord bears part of the burden. As long as the existence of the tax reduces the quantity of rental accommodations demanded below what it otherwise would be, the tax will depress the amount received by landlords. In this way landlords will bear part of its burden.

Notice also that this result emerges even though neither landlords nor tenants realize it. Because rents are changing for all sorts of other reasons, no one will have much idea of what equilibrium rentals would be in the absence of the tax. It does not do much good just to look at what happens immediately after tax rates are changed because, as we have already seen, landlords may begin by raising rents by the full amount of the tax. Although they think they have passed the tax on, this creates a disequilibrium. In equilibrium prices will have risen by less than the full amount of the tax.

Do Taxes on Profits Affect Prices?

Economic theory predicts that a general percentage tax on profits will have no effect on price or output, and thus the full incidence of such a tax will fall on producers. To see this quickly, suppose that one price-quantity combination gives the firm higher profits (without considering taxes) than any other. If the government imposes a 20 percent profits tax, the firm will have only 80 percent as much profits after tax as it had before; *this will be true for each possible level of output.* The firm may grumble, but it will not be profitable for it to alter its price or output.

Notice that this argument is independent of the tax rate. [32] It applies equally whether the tax rate is 10 percent or 75 percent.

A tax on corporation income.   Corporate income taxes are taxes on profits *as defined by the tax laws.* The definitions make them a tax on a combination of economic profits plus some of the return to the factors of production, capital, and risk taking.

Because such a profits tax will reduce the returns to these important factors of production, it can have significant effects on the allocation of resources and on the prices and output of goods. Suppose a risky industry requires a 24 percent return on its capital to make prospective owners willing to take the risk of investing in the industry. Suppose that every firm is earning 30 percent on its investment before taxes. A 34 percent corporate income tax will reduce the after-tax return to 19.2 percent, below the point that makes investment attractive, and resources will leave the industry. Obviously, price and output changes will occur. As firms leave the industry and as supply decreases, prices will rise until the remaining firms can earn a sufficient level of after-tax profits so that they are once again compensated for the risks in-

volved. Thus customers must bear part of the burden of the tax through a price increase.

A tax on profits, as defined by the taxing authorities, will have an effect on prices and outputs and thus will be shared by the consumer.

Because industries differ in degree of risk, the impact of a corporate income tax will be different in different industries, greater in more risky industries, smaller in less risky ones. It will thus affect the allocation of resources among industries.

Public Expenditure As a Tool of Microeconomic Policy

Public expenditure is large and growing. It affects both the distribution of income and the allocation of resources. In recent years spending by federal, state, and local government units in the United States, that is, by the public sector, has amounted to about 35 percent of the nation's expenditures. Defense, international relations, education, and social security are the largest items; collectively they make up more than half the total. Public welfare, highways, and interest on the public debt add up to another 25 percent of the total. The remainder covers everything else, from police protection and sanitation to general administration of government and space research. About 62 percent of the expenditure is made by the federal government, 15 percent by state governments, and 23 percent by local governments.

Figure 23-4 shows the changing importance of different types of federal government expenditures. Until 1974 the largest category of federal expenditures was the provision of goods and services that the market fails to provide or is not allowed to provide. Foremost among these (in volume of expenditure) are the defense and defense-related activities of the federal government; expenditures on police services, education, roads, conservation, and urban redevelopment are similar in character.

Although such purchases of goods and services are large (over $350 billion in 1985), they have remained roughly constant in real terms over the last 25 years. They have been overtaken by transfer pay-

FIGURE 23-4   The Changing Form of Major Federal Expenditures (Selected Years, 1955–1985)

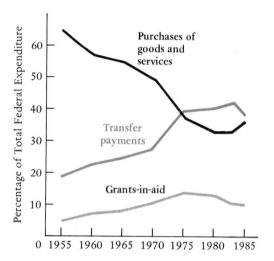

From 1955 until the "tax revolt" of the mid-1970s transfer payments and grants-in-aid grew steadily in importance. In 1955 two-thirds of all federal expenditures were purchases of goods and services. By 1980 the fraction was only one-third. Transfer payments to persons in the United States and grants-in-aid to state and local governments increased from less than one-fourth to more than one-half of the total between 1955 and 1980. The Reagan administration halted the trend. The three categories of expenditure graphed here account for 83 percent of total federal expenditures. The largest item not shown on the graph is net interest paid by the government which in 1985 was 13 percent of the total.

ments as the largest form of government expenditure. Transfer payments and grants-in-aid steadily increased in importance until the Reagan administration. Their increase from 1955 to 1980 led to important changes in both the distribution of income and the allocation of resources.

Public Expenditure and Distribution of Income

The federal government, as Table 23-1 indicates, raises most of its revenues by income-related taxes. When these federal receipts are transferred back to

individuals or to state and local governments, they have a substantial redistributive effect.

Federal Transfer Payments

Transfer payments are defined generally as payments to private persons or institutions that do not arise out of current productive activity. (They do not include intergovernment transfers, that is, transfers from one level of government to another, nor do they include interest on the national debt.) Welfare payments, social security payments, pensions, veterans' benefits, fellowships, and unemployment insurance are transfers. Some federal transfers are made to foreigners as part of foreign aid programs. Some transfer payments are private, such as private pensions and charitable contributions by individuals and corporations. Many are made by state and local governments, often using funds they have received as federal grants-in-aid.

The largest category of transfers, which we consider here, is payments by the federal government to individuals. In 1985 such transfers amounted, in the aggregate, to $366 billion. Most of these transfer payments are part of public income-maintenance programs of the kind examined in Chapter 21. The percentage of all personal income received in the form of government transfer payments increased sharply, from under 5 percent in 1955 to 7 percent in 1965 and more than 14 percent in 1983. By 1985 it had dropped to 11 percent.

The growth of transfer payments over much of the last 30 years reflected several developments. A major source of growth was the steadily increasing coverage and level of social security (including Medicaid and Medicare). While the growth of social security has had an important redistributive effect, it has been primarily from younger to older rather than from rich to poor. Because of the attempt to finance much of the cost of social security by payroll taxes, much of the cost has fallen on middle- and lower-middle-income groups.

Other sources of the growth of transfer payments since the 1960s include the War on Poverty of the 1960s and 1970s and the persistent unemployment of the 1970s and early 1980s, which greatly increased unemployment compensation payments.

Transfer payments have undoubtedly had a tendency to redistribute income toward the very poor and away from the middle income groups.

Grants-in-Aid

In addition to the federal government, there are 50 state governments, 3,000 county governments, 8,000 municipalities, and 17,000 townships in the United States. Further, there are about 20,000 districts for schools and another 20,000 for miscellaneous purposes such as sewage. Each of roughly 80,000 government units spends public money, and each must get the money to spend. Not all units have equal access to revenue, which necessitates both some division of responsibilities and intergovernment grants-in-aid.

Grants-in-aid from federal to state and local governments accounted for about 10 percent of federal expenditure in 1985, roughly double the percent of 30 years earlier. The growth in grants-in-aid was a response to a growing inability of state and local communities to manage their finances.

Grants-in-aid may be categorical or general. At present 90 percent of all federal grants are **categorical grants-in-aid,** that is, grants for specified categories of expenditure such as highways, education, and welfare payments. Not only are such grants restricted as to use, they usually require some degree of state or local matching. *General* or *noncategorical* grants-in-aid are grants with no restrictions as to use or requirements for matching funds. This return of funds to state and local units by the federal government is now called **revenue sharing.**

Many grants-in-aid programs were not designed primarily for redistribution, but do they incidentally affect distribution? Economists looking at this question do not yet know the answer. Some categorical assistance goes for inequality-reducing welfare payments and other programs of aid to the poor. But grants for highways, hospitals, and research probably tend to increase the inequality of income distribution. Revenue sharing money goes to state and local governments whose uses of the funds vary enormously and therefore have no single pattern of impact.

Many public finance specialists believe that grants-in-aid to states do not decrease inequality of income distribution and may increase it, while grants to the cities tend to reduce inequality.

The Overall Redistributive Effects of Public Expenditures

Since the tax system tends to be roughly proportional in its effect, the overall progressivity of government policies depends on the progressivity of government expenditures. The large and growing role of transfer payments to the poor and the use of many grants-in-aid to the cities (for programs that ultimately help the poor) probably assured that from the mid 1950s until 1980 there was some net redistribution of income from high- and middle-income groups to the poor. But such redistribution was never large and it came to a halt during the Reagan administration.

Changes in the degree of income inequality in the United States from decade to decade have been small.

Why does government expenditure not have a bigger effect on income distribution? One view is that government programs overall are less progressive than observers once thought because progressive programs are offset by regressive ones. Another view is that market forces exert steady pressure toward more inequality, which government programs merely offset.

To understand the second view—that one must run hard just to stay even with inequality—imagine that the government today created complete equality in wealth and income. Inevitably, market forces would produce inequality by next year, as some people and firms did well because they worked hard and long, were lucky, and invested wisely, while others did poorly or failed because they took it easy, were unlucky, or squandered their resources on a binge.

Most economists agree that there is a limit to how much inequality can be eliminated. There is controversy as to how close we are to that limit. And beyond that there is controversy as to how close it is desirable to get to "as much equality as possible," both on ethical grounds of justice and economic grounds of incentives.

Public Expenditure and Allocation of Resources

Governments spent over $800 billion in 1985 to provide goods and services. In these activities government units act like firms, using factors of production to produce outputs. Governments produce some commodities rather than leave production to the free market because the people, acting through their city councils, state legislatures, and Congress have so chosen in response to the sources of dissatisfaction with market outcomes discussed in Chapter 22.

Whether the government should be attempting to directly influence the allocation of resources is usually a subject of intense debate when a major new or expanded program is proposed. A central debate of the 1970s concerned the role of government in providing medical care to the population. It is discussed briefly in Box 23-2 on pages 446–447.

A widely debated current issue is the appropriate level of expenditure to cope with the deterioration of the country's biggest cities.

Urban Problems

Some of the biggest news stories of the late 1970s and early 1980s concerned the feared bankruptcy of such cities as New York, Philadelphia, and Cleveland. The crisis of the cities is in part a fiscal crisis because of the limited ability of local governments to raise revenues equal to their necessary expenditures. The purely fiscal crisis *could* be solved by financial help to the cities from state and federal governments. The Reagan administration, however, decreased its aid to both cities and states. States, in turn, decreased their aid to the cities. The purely fiscal crisis of the cities thus gradually worsened.

Underlying the fiscal crisis of the cities are some "real" problems that inhere in the changing character of the central cities (as distinguished from the suburbs). If urban decline is to be reversed, major changes in the allocation of resources will be required.

The Economics of Urban Decay

Urban decay reflects some major social changes and their economic consequences.

The root of the changing character of the nation's biggest cities is the change in who lives in them.

The selective flight to the suburbs (and beyond) that has triggered the urban crisis has a number of causes, among them different preferences of different groups in the population, rising incomes that permit the wealthier to move away, and sometimes prejudice. To understand why more and more families have chosen to trade the traditional advantages of the big city for cleaner neighborhoods, safer streets, and whiter schools, it is helpful to explore the dynamics of suburban migration. Much of it can be understood in economic terms. The scenario that follows suggests some causes of the urban crisis.

Flight of the wealthy. As the relatively wealthier residents of a densely populated city find their incomes rising, they often choose to spend extra income on bigger houses, more spacious lots, and tree-lined streets. Relatively high real estate prices in the central cities make extra space a luxury, but lower-cost land exists just outside the central cities. Thus suburban communities begin to be formed and are often zoned in such a way that lower-income families are excluded. As more upper-income residents move out, the proportion of lower-income residents in the city increases.

Disenchantment of the middle classes. The services required by the poor are of a different type from those sought by the middle class. More money goes to welfare, social work, and police and less to civic symphonies, schools, parks, and other amenities. At the same time, the average income per capita that is subject to taxation declines as the relatively wealthy move beyond the reach of city tax authorities. Remaining middle-class residents discover that they are paying larger taxes, but receiving fewer services of the kind they value. They find the museums closed and the park toilets unclean. Their schools curtail the "frills" in the curriculum, such as interscholastic athletics, foreign languages, and music and art. Life in the city costs more, but offers less.

Meanwhile, empty expensive houses tend to be converted to cheaper housing as three or four families move in where one used to live. The housing also deteriorates because it does not pay landlords to maintain it at its former standard. If the poor are black or Hispanic, their increasing presence in the schools, the streets, and the parks does not go unnoticed by whites.

Middle-class residents who remain see their tax burdens rising, their neighborhoods becoming more crowded, the older sections of "their" city deteriorating, the racial composition of their schools changing, and the crime rate increasing. Some move into more expensive neighborhoods or send their children to private schools; more and more flee to the suburbs.

Shift of employment opportunities.   The incentive to move increases as jobs move from the old cities of the Northeast to the Southwest and from central cities to suburbs. During the 1970s more than 3 million people moved out of the Northeast and Midwest, and many of those that remained in these areas moved to the suburbs and away from the central cities. For one example, over the 1970s Detroit's central city population decreased by 317,000 and its suburbs increased by 226,000. Stores and banks follow their customers, first by establishing branches in suburban shopping centers, later by closing central-city locations. Industry, too, moves outward, partly because of the available labor force, partly in response to the interstate highway system and the trucking industry.

The inner city becomes a ghetto.   When the jobs go, not all the workers follow. But the division of who goes and who stays is hardly random. Many poorer inner-city residents, held together by the bonds of race, language, or, indeed, poverty as well as by lack of cars and lack of middle-class aspirations, stay put. Many find housing discrimination and exclusionary zoning if they try to move away. Unemployment increases, more families need welfare,

housing deteriorates further, clean streets seem less important—and, of course, the tax base continues to shrink.

A reform mayor raises the sales tax or proposes a city income tax and finds that these measures only hasten the exodus. At this stage the city may actually be underpopulated. Existing residents abandon the worst neighborhoods as they deteriorate and move into and begin the downgrading of more expensive housing. The worst slums may become homes for new immigrants from rural areas, Cuba, or Puerto Rico, or they may be abandoned and begin to crumble. Rats, disease, crime, and decay spread.

However bleak this story seems, it comes close to representing the plight of many American cities today. One might attack urban decay by channeling efforts and funds into rebuilding the city itself. Alternatively, one might attack the problems of poverty, unemployment, and prejudice that contribute so heavily to urban deterioration. Cities, without help, can do neither.

The Fiscal Crisis of the Cities

Since greater spending on municipal services and urban renewal might halt the decline of the cities, why do cities not solve their problems simply by more spending? The answer lies in four sets of forces: (1) limited response of tax revenues of local governments to growth in average income, (2) limited ability of cities to borrow, (3) demand for local government services that rises faster than average income, and (4) rising cost per unit of providing these services. Together they contribute to local governments' steadily worsening financial situation and their urgent demand for federal assistance.

Tax revenues.   Whether government tax revenues rise as fast as the average income of residents depends on the government's ability to use income taxes. The larger the percentage of income raised by income taxes, the stronger the fiscal position of any government unit will be as income rises. While 90 percent of federal tax receipts and over 50 percent of state tax receipts today come from income taxes, only 11 percent of local taxes are so raised.

Local governments cannot readily increase their

BOX 23-2

The Rising Cost of Health Care

Health care is an emotional and provocative issue. Almost everyone would agree that in a wealthy society, such as the United States in the 1980s, some minimum level of health care should be available to all citizens by right. At the same time public concern continues at the high current cost of medical care. Economic analysis shows that these two elements— the belief in the right to free medical care and the clamor over its high social cost—are not unrelated.

Explaining the High Cost

Without health insurance, a single major operation can be an enormous financial burden and a prolonged illness will impoverish even the most prudent middle-income household. Why has health care become so costly?

One reason is that health care is highly labor intensive. The wages of nurses, laboratory technicians, and other medical service personnel have risen substantially relative to their productivity (the number of temperatures taken, beds made, and meals served per employee do not increase much over time).

A second reason is the steadily rising quality of medical care. Available knowledge, techniques, equipment, and the training of new physicians all have improved over time. Thus it becomes possible not only to provide quicker, surer cures for common and recurring ailments, but to prevent and treat other less common ailments and complications. Moreover, the demand for medical care tends to rise with rising real income. As per capita income rises, people are prepared to pay for more and better health. The demand for health care has proven to be income-elastic.

A third reason for rising medical costs is that the way medical care is provided and paid for has tended to weaken incentives to economize on its use or to keep costs down. Doctors (in their role as experts) often prescribe expensive medical care which they or other doctors provide. Will the patient contradict the doctor?

Most insurance and publicly provided medical programs have eliminated significant *marginal* charges to the patient for the incremental medical or hospital care consumed. Instead they charge either the patient or the insurance company something closer to the average cost. An individual has no incentive to economize on the quantity or quality of his or her own elective care because doing so will not significantly lower the average cost of total care. Everyone wants the very best care to which the "plan" entitles him or her.

Either free public provision or such comprehensive prepaid (or employer-paid), health insurance is virtually sure to lead to higher costs. This is an example of moral hazard, discussed in Chapter 22. In the market system individual patients would choose medical care (as they choose housing) from a wide variety of price-quality alternative forms of health care.

If patients had to pay their own bills, and if they could make fully informed choices, many might prefer to pay less and not have the best available equipment and doctors in all circumstances. But at zero marginal cost patients will naturally prefer to have the extra benefits of the best possible care, no matter what the extra cost to the insurance company, employer, or state. They will consume hospital and medical services that are free at the margin until the marginal utility from these services is zero.

Nor do doctors and hospitals have strong incentive to hold costs down. They can pass along the higher costs of advanced modern techniques to insurers in higher fees, especially if they do not have to worry that those higher fees may cause a reduction in the quantity of their services demanded. They may well reason: Our job is to give the best treatment; let others worry about the costs. Indeed unscrupulous doctors can prescribe unnecessary surgery or other medical care to increase the demand for their services. Of course, the insurance companies have to pass on higher claims in the form of higher premiums, and thus they might exercise cost control. But if the government or a giant employer pays most of the bill (as it does for many patients), insurers may not feel too much resistance to rising insurance rates, at least for a long time.

What Is the Right Quantity and Quality of Medical Care?

While everyone agrees that some minimum level of health care should be provided to all who need it, the definition of that minimum is controversial. No doubt the acceptable minimum level of health care to be provided by public support if necessary has risen over time; accordingly we have had increasing public intervention in the health sector.

The issue provokes more emotion than a discussion of housing or clothing, however. After all, human lives are at stake. True enough, but that does not end the matter. A first response is that much (although, of course, not all) medical and hospital care is elective and has almost nothing to do with life or death. By way of analogy, to say that no one should starve is not to say that all people should receive all the free food they want to eat. Nonvital attention accounts for a large part of our demand for health care. If it is offered at little or no marginal cost to users, it will be consumed beyond the point where marginal utility is equal to the cost of providing it.

But even where life is at stake, do we really always want the very best? Suppose the extra cost of the very best at all times does pay off in a small increased probability of survival. How much would we pay to have, say, 9 instead of 10 people in 10,000 die from a particular disease? Surely few would want to spend a billion dollars per life saved; most would say that the opportunity cost was too high. Yet doctors in hospitals often make a different decision implicitly by ordering the best of everything. This then passes the costs on to society as a whole through increased resource allocation to the health sector. The issue is not whether to save lives, but the opportunity cost of doing so. Money spent to save lives here is money not available to save lives (or improve the quality of life) elsewhere.

Because the issues are difficult to face, the political process has tended to avoid them. Instead of asking *how much* care we should provide, we have asked *to whom should it be provided* at substantially less than its average or marginal cost. The president and other key government officials, veterans, members of the armed forces, the very poor (via Medicaid), and the elderly (via Medicare) currently are heavily subsidized. Much of the clamor of the 1970s was to make similar subsidized coverage available to all. But lavish and expensive per capita care may be affordable only for the few, not for the many.

Controlling the Cost

Neither providers nor patients have sufficient incentive under many present schemes to keep down the costs of medical care. The most obvious solution is to place enough of a marginal charge on users so that they will ask themselves whether this doctor's visit, this extra day in the hospital, this use of the most expensive health monitoring system, is worth the cost to them.

The spread of health maintenance organizations (HMOs) that agree to provide specified levels of care for a fixed fee have created institutions with some incentives to bargain hard with doctors and hospitals to keep their costs down.

Another proposed solution is to ask the government to regulate the quantity, quality, and prices of service provided or the rates insurance companies may charge. The regulation of rates gives insurance companies the motivation to exercise cost control.

In health care, as elsewhere, if the price paid by users is kept below the marginal cost of providing the services, the private market will have excess demand. The government must either provide the services demanded directly or subsidize others to do so; or some way must be found to limit the demand to the quantity available. In countries with national health services, rationing is accomplished in part by long lines at doctors' offices and long waits for hospital admissions and in part by a lower average quality of medical services, which then reduces demand.

In adopting a policy toward health care there are at least three separable decisions: how much care to provide, how to allocate the costs of that care, and how to ration the supply. In the market system prices do all three. When we elect to have the government intervene, because we do not like the free-market results, someone has to make these decisions.

reliance on income taxes. As the percentage of personal income taken by the federal government has grown, the resistance of taxpayers to higher taxes of any kind has grown—and this is especially true of further taxes on income. Many state and local governments have tried to impose (or increase) income taxes; however, the electoral defeats of officials who advocated these taxes, and the interstate and intercity competition to attract residents and industries by having lower taxes than neighboring jurisdictions have severely limited the additional revenue that state and local governments have been able to raise in this way.

State and local governments thus rely heavily on property, sales, and excise taxes. Revenues from these taxes rise more slowly than income in the short run, and in the long run they rise only at the same rate as the income levels *of the population in their jurisdictions*. Here is where the selective outward migration of richer taxpayers has hurt so much. In most of the largest cities average real income (and thus per capita tax revenue) is falling because of the movement of higher-income families to the suburbs and the higher unemployment rates in the cities. But the problem for the cities runs deeper. Much of the tax revolt of the 1970s involved mandated *decreases* in existing levels of property taxation, on which cities rely so heavily.

Limited ability of cities to borrow.   Cities, unlike the federal government, cannot spend more than they raise in taxes, receive as gifts, or borrow from the public, for they cannot print money. In some states cities are constitutionally limited in their ability to borrow; even where this is not the case, prudence limits what is possible.

While the tax-free status of municipal bond interest has long helped cities to sell bonds, they must still pay the interest when due and repay the principal at maturity. Rising interest rates on municipal bonds—from about 3.3 percent in 1965 to over 11 percent in the early 1980s—made paying the interest an ever-growing drain on cities' current receipts. Furthermore, repaying principal requires a major revenue source when the bonds come due. Depending on how the receipts of the bond issue are used, such a source may or may not be available.

Cities borrow for two main reasons: (1) to finance long-term capital investment projects such as schools or hospitals and (2) to cover continuing current account deficits. The first reason is wholly responsible. The second is irresponsible and unacceptable to bondholders because the revenue to repay the bonds is nowhere provided for. Because of this it cannot long continue.

What happens when a city sells bonds to cover a continuing deficit? As these bonds come due, money will be needed to repay the bondholders, but there will be no current surplus available. The obvious solution is to borrow still more. Then rumors of trouble will start, and they will lead to the downgrading of the city's credit rating. Investors will become unwilling to buy new issues to replace the old ones without sharply higher interest rates. At some point the city effectively loses its ability to borrow.

Rising demand for government services.   Local government expenditures have been rising more rapidly than their residents' average income. A historically important reason is the high income elasticity of demand for city services. As societies become wealthier their residents want more parks, more police protection, better public schools and colleges, and more generous treatment of their less fortunate neighbors. This alone, combined with the limited tax sources available, would create budgetary problems for local governments in a period of rising incomes and rising expectations. Taxpayers increasingly want the social services that governments provide, but they do not want to accept the taxes required to pay for them. Elected officials arouse the public wrath when they fail to provide wanted programs, but they also do so when they provide the services and then raise taxes.

A second and, in the past two decades, much more important reason for a rise in the quantity of local government services demanded has to do, once again, with the changing character of central-city populations and the increased need for local government expenditures associated with these changes. The selective outward migration from the cities has led to an ever increasing proportion of low-income groups in the central cities. This in turn has led to more poverty and crime and thus to more demand for the welfare and public services to cope with them.

Rising relative cost of local government services.

The cost of providing services such as police and fire protection rises as the level of poverty increases, as the housing stock deteriorates, and as commuters into the city become more numerous. In addition, government services tend to use much labor of a kind whose productivity has increased less rapidly than its cost. Thus cost per unit of output has risen. While the national average of output per hour in manufacturing has risen about 50 percent in the last decade, the size of the beat covered by a police officer, the number of students taught by each schoolteacher, and the number of families that can be handled effectively by a social worker have not risen in proportion. Because wage levels tend to rise with national average productivity, the costs of services in sectors where productivity growth is low have soared.

The inevitable crisis.

The four forces just described lead inevitably to a crisis. Overall it is estimated that, on average, state and local expenditures have risen at 1.3 times the rate of increase of national income over the last 40 years and at 1.6 times the rate during the last 20 years.

Rising quantities and rising unit costs of government services cause local government expenditures to rise more than their revenues.

Eventually the city's reserves will be used up. It must then either reverse the causes of its decline, get help from the outside, or default on its obligations.

The Growing Urban Crisis

Once the interrelated processes of urban decay and movement out of the cities has begun, the city has passed the point of self-help. Only a massive dosage of money will now help. The city recognizes that it can recover its tax base if it can annex suburban areas, but those who have escaped the city's problems will reject the overtures for annexation, and their political influence in the state governments is usually suffi-

cient to prevent forced annexation. The city, unable to solve the problem itself, now tries to persuade the state or federal government to channel funds to it. Substantial funds are required simply to maintain the status quo but must compete with other demands on public budgets.

The rising level of federal contributions to state and local government during the 1970s was a response to this problem. That it was not sufficient was made clear by New York City's fiscal crisis of 1975, by the sharply worsening plights of Philadelphia, Chicago, Detroit, and other cities in the 1980s, and by the urgency with which the nation's mayors keep clamoring for more help.

The Reagan administration not only turned a skeptical ear to such pleas but actually decreased federal help to the cities. This partly reflected its philosophical commitment to returning responsibility to local communities, even though they lack the resources to deal with them, and partly reflected the fact that its expenditure cuts fell disproportionately on programs whose beneficiaries tend to be city residents. Cities responded both by raising taxes and by cutting back further on services such as police, fire, health, street maintenance, highways, sewers, and mass transit systems.

Is There a Long-Run Solution?

Cities play too vital a role in the nation's political and economic life to let them wither and to let their millions of inhabitants be overwhelmed by poverty, disease, and crime. Yet what is to be done?

One solution is a more or less permanent subsidization of the cities by taxes levied on those who live elsewhere. A great expansion in unconditional revenue sharing would give revenues to state and local governments on a per capita basis, in effect making residents of wealthy states and rich suburbs pay some part of the costs of areas densely populated by the poor.

An approach favored by many is increasingly to federalize aid to the poor wherever they reside by guaranteeing a minimum family income sufficient to permit escape from slum conditions. Others hope to provide this minimum income by manipulation of the tax structure, for example, by introducing a negative income tax, rather than by grants to individuals, categorical or otherwise.

Mayors of large cities, and many economists who specialize in urban economies, believe that the needed support to the cities is appropriately provided by state and federal governments because the key problems of the cities are those of race, poverty, and unemployment, which are *national* problems. The fact that these problems are most severe among city dwellers does not make them city problems to be ignored by those who live in the suburbs or smaller cities and villages. If this argument is accepted, regular and permanent transfers of money to the cities or their residents will be viewed not as charity to an imprudent relative, but as a regular part of public attention to persistent national problems.

An alternative view regards urban crises as the product primarily of irresponsible city governments and regards aid to the cities as a temporary necessity that perhaps has to be given "this time" but not next. These views emerged as a major point of conflict in the policy debate of the late 1980s.

As is usually the case in real debates, there is some truth in both extreme views. New York, for example, greatly compounded its problems by some irresponsible expenditure policies and fiscal maneuvering. But even a prudent city administration had trouble making ends meet in the mid 1980s, for the basic problems were still there.

Evaluating the Role of Government

Almost everyone would agree that the government has some role to play in the economy because of the many sources of possible market failure. Yet there is no consensus that the present level and role of government intervention is about right.

One aspect of the contemporary debate about the efficient level of government intervention was discussed at the end of Chapter 22. There we asked when and to what degree government is justified in attempting to modify private market behavior—say, by affecting the way a paper mill discharges its wastes. Other issues arise when government pro-

vides goods and services that the private sector does not and will not provide.

Do Benefits of Public Programs Exceed Costs?

The federal government has developed techniques of evaluation designed to provide estimates of benefits and costs in order to determine whether the former exceed the latter. If they do, the program is said to be *cost effective* and thus to be justified. For some government programs, such as flood control, there are well-defined benefits and costs, and it is relatively easy to decide whether the project is beneficial.

But consider the evaluation of a program such as the great space adventure of the 1960s—placing a man on the moon before the end of the decade. The budgetary costs were easily defined. At its peak in 1966, the program absorbed (in 1985 dollars) about $21 billion per year. Unmistakably, the project succeeded; it met its stated objective. But was the "giant step for mankind" worth the billions it cost? The benefits certainly included the psychological lift the moon walks gave the American people and the substantial advances in technology and knowledge that the space program spawned. The real costs are those things that the expenditure replaced. But what was the alternative? More arms to Vietnam? Massive urban redevelopment? A return of funds to private spenders to use as they saw fit? Most of us will evaluate the worth of the space program very differently, depending on what we see as the alternative uses of the resources involved.

Such questions can never be answered unambiguously. As a result, the evaluation of government programs is inherently political and controversial. Economic analysis of benefits and costs is involved, but it does not play the sole or even the dominant role in answering some big questions.

What Is the Correct Balance Between Private and Public Sectors?

When the government raises money by taxation and spends it on an activity, it increases the spending of the public sector and decreases that of the private sector. Since the public sector and the private sector spend on different things, the government is changing the allocation of resources. Is that good or bad? How do we know if the country has the right balance between the public and private sectors? Should there be more schools and fewer houses or more houses and fewer schools?

Because automobiles and houses are sold on the market, consumer demand has a significant influence on the relative prices and quantities produced of these commodities and thus on the allocation of the nation's resources. This is true for all goods produced and sold on the market. But there is no market that provides relative prices for private houses versus public schools; thus the choice between allowing money to be spent in the private sector and spending it for public goods is a matter to be decided by Congress and other legislative bodies.

John Kenneth Galbraith's best seller *The Affluent Society* proclaimed the "liberal" message that a correct assignment of marginal utilities would show them to be higher for an extra dollar's worth of expenditure on parks, clean water, and education than for an extra dollar's worth of expenditure on television sets and deodorants. In this view, the political process often fails to translate preferences for public goods into effective action; thus more resources are devoted to the private sector and fewer to the public sector than would be the case if the political mechanism were as effective as the market.

The "conservative" view has a growing number of supporters who agree with 1986 Nobel laureate Professor James Buchanan that society has already gone beyond the point where the value of the marginal dollar spent by the government is greater than the value of that dollar left in the hands of households or firms that would have spent it had it not been taxed away. Because bureaucrats, the conservatives argue, are spending other people's money, they regard a few million (or billion) dollars here or there as a mere nothing. They have lost all sense of the opportunity cost of public expenditure and thus tend to spend far beyond the point where marginal benefits equal marginal costs.

What Is the Role of Government Today?

One of the most difficult problems for the student of the U.S. economic system is to maintain perspec-

tive about the scope of government activity in the market economy. There are literally tens of thousands of laws, regulations, and policies that affect firms and households. Many believe that significant additional deregulation would be possible and beneficial.

But private decision makers still have an enormous amount of discretion about what they do and how they do it. One pitfall is to become so impressed (or obsessed) with the many ways in which government activity impinges on the individual that one fails to see that these only make changes—sometimes large, but often small—in market signals in a system that basically leaves individuals free to make their own decisions. In the private sector most individuals choose their occupations, earn their livings, spend their incomes, and live their lives. In this sector too, firms are formed, choose products, live, grow, and sometimes die.

A different pitfall is to fail to see that some, and perhaps most, of the highly significant amounts paid by the private sector to the government as taxes also buy goods and services that add to the welfare of individuals. By and large the public sector complements the private sector, doing things the private sector would leave undone or do very differently. To recognize this is not to deny that there is often waste, and sometimes worse, in public expenditure policy. Nor does it imply that whatever is, is just what people want. Social policies and social judgments evolve and change.

Yet another pitfall is failing to recognize that the public and private sectors compete in the sense that both make claims on the resources of the economy. Government activities are not without opportunity costs, except in those rare circumstances in which they use resources that have no alternative use.

Public policies in operation at any time are not the result of a single master plan that specifies precisely where and how the public sector shall seek to complement or interfere with the workings of the market mechanism. Rather, as individual problems arise, governments attempt to meet them by passing ameliorative legislation. These laws stay on the books, and some become obsolete and unenforceable. This is true of systems of law in general. As a result it is easy to find outrageous examples of inconsistencies and absurdities in any system. A distinguished professorship at Harvard gives its incumbent the right to graze a cow in Harvard Yard; laws still exist that permit the burning of witches.

Many anomalies exist in our economic policies; for example, laws designed to support the incomes of small farmers have created some agricultural millionaires, and commissions created to assure competition often end up creating and protecting monopolies. Neither individual policies nor whole programs are above criticism.

In a society that elects its policymakers at regular intervals, however, the majority view on the amount and type of government interference that is desirable will have some considerable influence on the interference that actually occurs. This has become one of the major political issues of the 1980s. Fundamentally, a free-market system is retained because it is valued for its lack of coercion and its ability to do much of the allocating of society's resources. But we are not mesmerized by it; we feel free to intervene in pursuit of a better world in which to live. We also recognize, however, that some intervention has proven excessive or ineffective.

Summary

1. Two of the most powerful tools of microeconomic policy are taxation and public expenditure.

2. While the main purpose of the tax system is to raise revenue, tax policy is potentially a powerful device for income redistribution because the progressivity of different kinds of taxes varies greatly. Personal income tax rates have traditionally been highly progressive, but their effect on progressivity is reduced by other provisions of the tax law. Sales and excise taxes are likely to be regressive.

3. The total American tax structure is roughly proportional except for very low-income groups (for whom it is regressive) and very high-income groups (for whom it is mildly progressive). Whether it is feasible or desirable to increase progressivity is a subject of sharp current debate.

4. Evaluating the effects of taxes on resource allocation requires first determining tax incidence, that is, determining who really pays the taxes. For most taxes, the incidence is shared. Excise taxes, for example, affect prices and are thus partially passed on, but partially absorbed by producers. The actual incidence depends on such economic considerations as demand and supply elasticities.

5. A large part of public expenditure is for the provision of goods and services that private markets fail to provide. Direct and indirect subsidies, transfer payments to individuals, and grants-in-aid to state and local governments are all rising sharply.

6. The major redistributive activities of the federal government take the form of direct transfer payments to individuals and grants-in-aid to state and local governments for economic welfare payments. While the public sector has a tendency to redistribute some income from high- and middle-income groups to the poor, the change in income inequality from decade to decade has been relatively small.

7. Government expenditure of all kinds has a major effect on the allocation of resources. The government determines how much of our total output is devoted to national defense, education, and

highways. It is also influential in areas where private provision of goods and services is common; health care is a notable example.

8. Grants-in-aid to state and local government are a key form of public expenditure policy; they lead to a different allocation of resources than would occur without them. The need for such grants-in-aid is dramatically revealed by the plight of the nation's cities.

9. The urban crisis is in large part a result of the selective migration of residents to the suburbs and out of reach of the urban taxing authorities. Such migration develops a dynamic that feeds itself, and increasingly the central cities have become occupied by the poor, with rising needs and a shrinking tax base. This leads to the urban fiscal crisis, for which state or federal assistance may be the only solution.

10. Evaluating public expenditures involves reaching decisions about absolute merit (do benefits exceed costs?) and about the relative merit of public and private expenditures.

11. The U.S. economy is a mixed economy and a changing one. Each generation faces anew the choice of which activities to leave to the unfettered market and which to encourage or repress through public policy.

Topics for Review

Tax expenditures
Progressive, proportional, and regressive taxes
Tax incidence
Transfer payments to individuals
Grants-in-aid to state and local governments
Sources of urban crises
Choosing between private and public expenditures

Discussion Questions

1. The American taxpayer is assaulted by dozens of different taxes with different incidence, different progressivity, and different methods of collection. Discuss the case for and against using at most two different kinds of taxes. Discuss the case for and against a single taxing authority that would share the revenue with all levels of government.

2. Under federal tax law certain kinds of income are tax exempt. One of these is municipal bond interest. Who benefits from such an exemption? What are its effects on the distribution of income and the allocation of resources? In what sense is this a "tax expenditure"?

3. Consider a change in the tax law that lowers every taxpayer's marginal tax rate, with the maximum rate dropping from 50 percent to 33 percent, but with an increase in the tax base that leaves total tax revenue unchanged.
   a. Is it possible that everyone's average tax *rate* will fall?
   b. Is it possible that everyone's tax *bill* will fall?

    c. Suppose contributions to universities and colleges are tax deductible under the original tax law but not under the revised one. Would you predict such contributions to increase, decrease, or remain the same?

    d. If such contributions are fully deductible under both the original and revised tax law, would the amount of such contributions be expected to increase, decrease, or remain the same?

    e. Consider now taxpayers whose marginal tax rate falls from 50 percent to 33 percent *and* whose tax bills are less after the revision. Repeat question *d*.

4. How might each of the following affect the incidence of a real estate property tax imposed on central city rental property?
    a. The residents of the community are largely blacks who face racial discrimination in neighboring areas.
    b. The city installs a good, cheap rapid transit system that makes commuting to the suburbs less expensive and more comfortable.
    c. The income tax laws are changed to eliminate the deductibility of property taxes on owner-occupied housing from taxable income for those who itemize deductions.

5. Under the federal tax laws all state and local income taxes can be deducted from income in computing the federal tax liability. Suppose, given the tax schedule shown in Table 23-2, two local communities each impose a 10 percent tax on personal incomes. Richville is composed of families who earn $100,000 per year or more. Uniontown consists mainly of workers' families who earn about $20,000 per year. Who really pays the taxes in each case? What, if anything, prevents Richville from raising its taxes?

6. Develop the case for and against having the federal government (rather than state and local governments) provide:
    a. Police protection
    b. Teachers' salaries
    c. Highways
    d. Welfare payments to the poor

7. Classify each of the following programs as transfer payment, grant-in-aid, purchase of goods and services, or none of the above. Which ones clearly tend to decrease the inequality of income distribution?
    a. Payments of wages and family living allowances to soldiers serving overseas
    b. Unemployment insurance payments to unemployed workers
    c. Payments to states for support of highway construction
    d. A negative income tax
    e. Pensions of retired Supreme Court justices
    f. An excess-profits tax on oil companies

8. The city of Miami and Dade County have gained about 200,000 new residents from Cuba in just a few years. A city official says, "Federal marshals bring in refugees, they bring them to us. We are the only jailer, we are the only public hospital. . . . We shouldn't have to pay the bill."

    In what sense is the problem one that ought to be met by the city of Miami, by Dade County, by the state of Florida, by the federal government? Why is it a *government* problem at all?

9. "I believe the spirit of volunteerism lives in America. We see examples of it on every hand: the community charity drive, the rallying around whenever disaster strikes. The truth is, we've let Government take away many things we once considered were really ours to do voluntarily, out of the goodness of our hearts and a sense of neighborliness. I believe many of you want to do those things again."

   Discuss the probable effects of getting the government out of all activities once covered by private charity. The quotation is from a speech by President Reagan.

10. Medical and health costs were 4.5 percent of GNP in 1950 and over 10 percent in 1985. Is 10 percent necessarily too much? Is it necessarily a sign that we are providing better health care? How might an economist think about what is the right percentage of GNP to devote to medical care?

PART SEVEN

National Income and Fiscal Policy

An Introduction to Macroeconomics

Inflation, unemployment, recession, and economic growth are everyday words. Governments worry about how to prevent recessions and how to increase growth. After having reduced the inflation rate in the early 1980s, governments now worry about how to keep inflation under control without letting unemployment get too large. Firms are concerned about how inflation affects their costs and how recessions affect their sales. Households are anxious to avoid the unemployment that comes with recessions and to protect themselves against the hazards of inflation.

What Is Macroeconomics?

Each of the concerns mentioned above plays a major role in macroeconomics. As we saw in Chapter 3 (see pages 50–51), economics is customarily divided into two main branches, microeconomics and macroeconomics. Now we look further at the difference between the two approaches to the economy and in more detail at what constitutes macroeconomics.

Macroeconomics studies in broad outline the flow of income in the economy (illustrated in Figure 3-1) without dwelling on much of its interesting but sometimes confusing detail. In contrast, microeconomics deals with the behavior of individual markets, such as the market for wheat, coal, or strawberries.

The following example illustrates the difference between the two branches of economics.

A microeconomic issue. For decades automobile prices fell in relation to the prices of most other commodities. Beginning in the 1970s this trend was reversed and automobiles became increasingly expensive relative to many other goods and services. In microeconomics we seek to understand the causes and effects of such changes in relative prices.

A macroeconomic issue. Over the decades, as well as changing relative to other prices, automobile prices have tended to follow the general trend of all prices to rise. The average of all prices is called the *price level.* Why does the price level stay relatively stable in some periods and rise rapidly in others? In macroeconomics we seek to understand the causes and effects of changes in the general price level.

Major Macroeconomic Issues

The economy proceeds in fits and starts rather than in a smooth pattern. Why did the 1930s see the greatest economic depression in recorded history, with up to a quarter of the American labor force unemployed and with massive unemployment in all other major industrial countries? Why were the 25 years following World War II a period of sustained boom with only minor interruptions from modest recessions? Why did the early 1980s see the onset of the worst worldwide recession since the 1930s? What fueled the recovery of the mid 1980s?

Why did the pace of inflation during the 1970s and early 1980s reach levels never before seen in peacetime in most advanced Western nations? Has our attitude toward inflation permanently changed? In the early 1970s when inflation crept up to 4 percent, concern was so great that emergency measures were introduced. By the mid 1980s the government was claiming credit for having reduced inflation to 4 percent.

Alternating bouts of inflationary boom and deflationary slump have caused many policy headaches in the past. Why were the recessions of the last decade accompanied not only by their familiar companion, high unemployment, but also by an unexpected fellow traveler, rapid inflation? Will stagflation—simultaneous high unemployment and rapid inflation—return?

Both total output and output per person have risen for several decades in many countries. These long-term trends have meant rising average living standards. Does the slowdown in worldwide growth rates over the 1970s and early 1980s represent a basic change in underlying trends, or is it just a reflection of the prolonged downturn of the last decade? Can governments do anything to affect growth rates?

Key Macroeconomic Variables

The price level, employment, and total output are key variables in macroeconomics. We hear about them on television; politicians give campaign speeches about them; economists theorize about them. Why are we concerned about them? How have they behaved over the past half century?

Index Numbers

Many key macro variables are expressed as index numbers, so our first task is to look at the general concept of an index number.

Macroeconomists frequently ask such questions as "How much have prices risen this year?" or "Has the nation's output increased this year and, if so, by how much?" There is no perfectly satisfactory way to answer these questions because all prices do not move together and because one cannot add tons of steel, pieces of furniture, and gallons of gasoline to get a meaningful total. Yet these are not foolish questions. There _are_ trends in prices and production, and thus there are real phenomena to describe. It is of little direct help to someone who wants to know about how prices have changed over some period of time to be given a list of changes in 4,682 individual prices.

Index numbers are statistical measures that are used to give summary answers to the inherently complex questions of the kind just suggested. **Index numbers** measure the percentage change that has occurred in some broad average over some particular time span. They point to overall tendencies or general drifts, not to detailed facts.

Calculating index numbers. To calculate any index number, we must have a procedure to add up the individual items that are to be included. Such a procedure involves assigning "weights" to the individual items.

Why do we bother with weights? Why not simply take the sum of all prices or add up all units of output? A moment's reflection suggests the answer. Changes in the price of bread, for example, are much more important to the average consumer than changes in the price of, say, caviar. Similarly, producing 1,000 additional automobiles is more important for the economy than producing 1,000 additional can openers. Weights are chosen to reflect the importance of each price. Usually the weights are the quantities from some particular period, called the _base period for weighting purposes_.

Once the weights are chosen, the aggregate can be calculated for each period, usually a year. For example, suppose that the sum is calculated to be $600 million in 1982, $720 million in 1985, and $900 million in 1988. Next, some **base period** for comparison purposes (or **base year**) is chosen.[1] The value of the sum for each period is then prorated by dividing it by the value for the base period and multiplying by 100. The resulting series is called an *index number series*; by construction the base period value in this series equals 100. In the example, the index would be 100 in 1982 (the base year for comparison purposes), 120 in 1985, and 150 in 1988.

Index numbers are constructed by assigning weights to reflect the importance of the individual items being combined. The value of the index is set equal to 100 in the base period.

An index number always compares two or more time periods. If a particular index number for 1985 is equal to 130, with 1982 as the base year (i.e., 1982 equals 100), then the index shows an increase between 1982 and 1985 of 30 percent in whatever is being measured.

Interpreting index numbers.   People often treat these numbers as though they had an accuracy and significance their compilers do not claim for them, but being aware of their limitations should not lead one to neglect index numbers for the useful information they can show: average changes over time. We shall learn more about index numbers in Chapter 25.

The Price Level and Inflation

The **price level** refers to an index number computed from the prices of a broad group of goods and services. It is usually denoted by the symbol P. One common index number of prices is the *Consumer Price Index,* or, as it is affectionately known, the *CPI.* It is computed by the Bureau of Labor Statistics. We will learn more about the details of how the CPI and other price indexes are constructed in the next chapter.

The **rate of inflation** is the percentage rate of increase in some price index from one period to another. In the rare event of a drop in the price level,

we speak of a *deflation*. The formula for measuring the inflation rate is:

$$\text{Inflation rate} = \frac{\text{this period's } P - \text{last period's } P}{\text{last period's } P} \times 100\%$$

If the periods being compared are not a year apart, it is common to convert the result to an *annual rate*. For example, if the CPI was 150 last month and rose by 1 percent during the month to 151.5, we might say that over the last month the price level rose at an *annual* rate of approximately 12 percent. This means that *if* the rate of increase persisted for a year, the price level would rise by 12 percent over the year. Box 24-1 identifies a source of confusion that sometimes arises from failing to distinguish other ways of calculating the annual inflation rate.

Inflation: The Historical Experience

Figure 24-1 on page 462 shows the behavior of the price level and the inflation rate for the period 1929 to 1985. In this figure, the price level is measured by the Consumer Price Index and the inflation rate by the annual rate of change of the CPI. Several facts stand out.

First, the price level is constantly changing, although by a rate that varies considerably from year to year, as reflected by the fluctuations in the inflation rate.

Second, and more important, in only 8 out of the 56 observations did the price level fall; in all 48 other years the inflation rate was positive. The cumulative effect of this sequence of small but steady price increases is quite dramatic; in 1985 the price level was more than six times higher than that in 1929.

The price level has displayed a distinct upward trend in recent decades.

Third, while it is the long-term trend that stands out when one looks at the price level, it is the short-term fluctuations that stand out when one looks at the inflation rate. The general rise in inflation from the mid 1960s through the mid 1980s is quite marked—from 1965 to 1974 inflation averaged 3.8 percent while from 1975 to 1984 it averaged 8.5 percent! The sharp swings in the inflation rate in the late 1970s and early 1980s are even more dramatic.

---

[1] Usually, but not always, the base period *for weighting purposes* and the base period *for comparison purposes* are the same. For simplicity we use the term *base period* to refer to both concepts.

BOX 24-1

Understanding Annual Rates

New values of the index numbers for many key macroeconomic variables are announced each month. But the announcements often lead to a confusing array of interpretations of what the numbers mean for the annual rate of change of the variable in question.

Consider a hypothetical example. The release of the latest monthly figure for a particular price index (PI) for some country, by that country's Bureau of Statistics, elicits the following three responses: "Inflation receding," reads a newspaper headline; "Inflation continues to rise," reports a TV newscaster; "Inflation unchanged," says the official releasing the statistic.

How can this be when all three commentators are talking about the same announcement? The different interpretations arise from different ways of converting the new monthly statistic into an annual rate of change. (The problem can arise with any index number.)

To understand what is involved, consider the hypothetical values for the PI set out in the table. According to the table, at the end of 1984 the PI (100.0) exceeded its average for the year (95.2). At the end of 1985 it was the same (100.0) as at the start of the year and equal to its average for the year; assume that it was in fact constant and equal to 100 for *each* month of 1985. In 1986 prices started to rise again.

Date	PI	Date	PI
December 1984	100.0	October 1986	106.8
1984 average	95.2	November 1986	108.9
		December 1986	110.0
December 1985	100.0	1986 average	105.0
1985 average	100.0		

Annual averages are the sum of the 12 monthly figures for the calendar year divided by 12.

Comparing annual averages. In stating that the inflation rate was unchanged, the official was comparing annual averages. Comparing the 1984 average PI (95.2) and the 1985 average (100.0) gave a change of approximately 5 percent, as did comparing the 1985 average (100.0) with the 1986 average (105.0). Thus, concludes the official, the annual inflation rate had stayed constant at 5 percent over the past two years.

Comparing this month with the same month last year. Using this procedure, the annual inflation rate in December 1986 is 10 percent; in December 1986 the PI is 10 percent higher than it was in December 1985. In November 1986 the annual inflation rate was only 9 percent, since the PI was 9 percent higher than in the previous November. Using this measure the annual inflation rate increased from 9 percent to 10 percent during the month. This procedure probably lay behind the television news report that inflation is rising.

Comparing this month with last month. Using this method the annual inflation rate in December 1986 was 12 percent; the PI had risen by 1 percent over the month and the annual rate is approximately 12 times the monthly percentage change. In November 1986 the annual inflation rate had been 24 percent, since the November PI was 2 percent higher than the October figure. This calculation would provide the basis for the newspaper headline that inflation is receding.

Which Measure Is Best?

Properly understood, all three measures give useful and complementary information.

Comparing annual averages is the least erratic. But because it focuses almost entirely on underlying trends, it is not sensitive to current changes. In our example it misses the stability in prices that prevailed throughout 1985 and the fairly sharp upturn in prices that was apparent in 1986.

Comparing this month with the same month last year is more sensitive to current events. However, it gives a lot of weight to particular events in the most recent month, events that often have little to do with the underlying trend of prices.

Comparing this month with last month is the most erratic measure. The timing of major price changes at or near the end of the month will have a substantial accidental effect on the measure. For some purposes this sensitivity may be desirable, but for understanding the underlying trend in inflation, it can be very misleading.

The three measures can be selectively used to support almost any position. But people who understand the meaning of each measure need not be fooled by such selective presentation of the data. Figures lie only to those uninformed about what a measure does and does not say.

FIGURE 24-1
The Price Level and Inflation Rate, 1929–1985

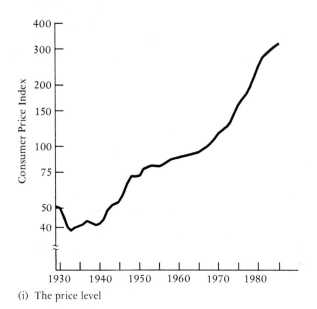

(i) The price level

(i) The overwhelming trend in the price level has been upward over the past half century. The data are for the Consumer Price Index from 1929 to 1985 with 1967 equal to 100. They are plotted on a semi-log scale where equal vertical distances represent equal percentage changes. The tendency for an accelerating rate of increase in the price level is evident from the increasing steepness of the graph. (*Source:* Department of Labor, Bureau of Labor Statistics.)

(ii) Inflation rate

(ii) The rate of inflation has varied from −10 percent to +14 percent since 1929. Prices fell dramatically during the onset of the Great Depression. They rose sharply during and after World War II and during the Korean War. The inflation rate was variable, but had no discernible trend from the end of the Korean War to the mid 1960s. The period starting in the mid 1960s experienced a strong upward trend in the inflation rate, interrupted by short-term downward fluctuations. In 1983, however, the inflation rate fell to the lowest figure since the early 1970s, and it stayed in the 3–4 percent range through 1986. (*Source:* Department of Labor, Bureau of Labor Statistics.)

The increase in the inflation rate into double-digit levels in 1974 and again in 1979 are associated with major shocks to the world price of oil and foodstuffs, while the declines in inflation that followed were delayed responses to major recessions. Note that even when the *inflation rate* falls (as it did in 1982, for example), *as long as inflation remains positive, the price level rises*.

Why Inflation Is a Matter of Concern

Changes in the price level are associated with changes in the **purchasing power of money** or **value of money**. Both terms refer to the amount of goods and services that can be purchased with a given amount of money. The purchasing power of money is negatively related to the price level. It falls with a rise in the price level. (For example, if the price level doubles, a dollar will buy only half as much.) Thus inflation, which is a rise in the general level of all prices, reduces the purchasing power of money. Conversely, the purchasing power of money rises whenever the price level falls.

Unanticipated inflation.   Any given rate of inflation tends to cause more harm when it is unforeseen than when it is foreseen. Contracts freely entered into when the inflation rate is expected to remain constant will mean hardships for some and unexpected gains for others if the inflation rate unexpectedly changes.

For example, consider a wage contract, made in the general expectation of a constant price level, that specifies wage increases of 3 percent. Both employers and workers expect that the purchasing power of wages paid will rise by 3 percent as a result of the new contract. But if the price level unexpectedly rises by 10 percent over the course of the wage contract, the workers' wages will be able to buy less than they would have before the wage increase was negotiated. A 3 percent increase in money wages combined with a 10 percent increase in prices means a reduction in the purchasing power of wages of about 7 percent.

Inflation also has different effects on borrowers and lenders. Suppose that when the price level is expected to be constant, a bank lends a customer $100 in return for a promise to repay $105 a year hence. If the price level rises during the year, the purchasing power of the $105 repaid will be less than

it was expected to be; hence the borrower benefits and the lender suffers relative to their expectations.

One of the most serious effects of inflation is what it does to anyone living on a fixed money income. If a retirement pension specifies an income as so many dollars per year, a rise in the price level lowers the purchasing power of that income. For example, anyone who retired on a fixed money income in 1970 found the purchasing power of that income reduced to about one fourth of its original value by 1985. This means that he or she could buy in 1985 only one fourth what could be bought in 1970. For such people, rapid inflation means great loss of purchasing power.

Some effects of inflation can be avoided by indexing. **Indexing** links the payments made under the terms of a contract to changes in the price level. For example, a retirement pension might specify that it will pay the beneficiary $15,000 per year starting in 1990, and that the amount paid will increase each year in proportion to the increase in some specified index of the price level. Thus, if the price index rises by 10 percent between 1990 and 1991, the pension payable in 1991 would rise by 10 percent, to $16,500.

Anticipated inflations.   Indexing provides an automatic correction that does not require anticipating future changes in the price level. However, even without formal indexing, it is possible to allow for the effects of inflation if the rise in the price level is anticipated and contracts take account of the expected rise.

Wage and price contracts are major examples. If, say, a 10 percent inflation is expected over the next year, a money wage that rises by 10 percent over that period will keep the expected purchasing power of wages at a constant level. A money wage that increases by 13 percent will provide a 3 percent increase in the expected purchasing power of wages—10 percent to preserve purchasing power in the face of the expected rise in prices and 3 percent to increase the real purchasing power of the wages.

Labor Force Variables

Employment denotes the number of adult workers (defined in the United States as workers aged 16 and

FIGURE 24-2   Labor Force, Employment, and Unemployment, 1929–1985

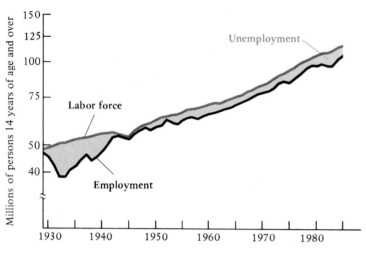

(i) Labor force, employment, and unemployment

(i) The labor force and employment have grown since the 1930s with only a few interruptions. The size of the labor force in the United States has doubled since 1930, and so has the number of the employed. These are plotted on a semilog scale. The fall in the labor force in the early 1940s was in the civilian labor force. The missing workers were in the military and the BLS definition of the labor force in use at the time did not include persons in the military. Unemployment, the gap between the labor force and employment, has fluctuated, but it has not again reached the peak of almost 13 million that occurred in 1933. As a fraction of the total labor force (see part ii), unemployment in 1933 was much higher than any recent years. *(Source: Economic Report of the President, various years.)*

(ii) Unemployment rate

(ii) The unemployment rate responds to the cyclical behavior of the economy. Booms are associated with low unemployment, slumps with high unemployment. The Great Depression of the 1930s produced record unemployment figures for an entire decade. During World War II unemployment rates fell to very low levels. Since 1945, however, the unemployment rate has demonstrated a slight upward trend. The recession of the early 1980s produced unemployment rates second only to those of the 1930s; these rates were extremely high by the standards of the post-World War II behavior of the American economy. *(Source: Economic Report of the President, various years.)*

older, including those in the military) who hold jobs. **Unemployment** denotes the number of adult workers who are not employed and are actively searching for a job. The **labor force,** is the total number of employed and unemployed. The **unemployment** **rate**, usually represented by the symbol U, is unemployment expressed as a percentage of the labor force:

$$U = \frac{\text{unemployed}}{\text{labor force}} \times 100\%$$

em — fric em
= full em

Unemployment: The Historical Experience

Figure 24-2(i) shows the trends in the labor force, employment, and unemployment since 1929. Despite booms and slumps in the economy, the main trend has clearly been growth in employment that roughly matches growth in the labor force. The growth in both reflects growth in the total population, although the labor force and employment have recently grown faster than the total population. This fact reflects the steadily increasing participation of youths and women in the labor force.

Although the long-term growth trend dominates the employment figures, some unemployment is always present. Figure 24-2(ii) shows that the short-term fluctuations in the unemployment rate have been quite marked. The unemployment rate has been as low as 1.2 percent in 1944 and as high as 24.9 percent in 1933; in the post–World War II period the unemployment rate fell as low as 2.9 percent in 1953 and rose as high as 9.7 percent in 1982.

The high unemployment rate of the Great Depression in the early 1930s tends to dwarf the fluctuations in unemployment that have occurred since then. This is unfortunate since, as we shall see, the fluctuations in unemployment in recent decades have been neither minor nor unimportant.

Unemployment can rise not only when employment falls, but also when the labor force rises. In recent decades the number of people entering the labor force has exceeded the number leaving it. The resulting rise in the labor force has meant that unemployment has sometimes grown even in periods when employment was also growing.

Consideration of employment and unemployment suggests another concept, that of *full employment.* Full employment does not mean zero unemployment. There is a constant turnover of individuals in given jobs and a constant change in job opportunities. New members enter the work force, some people quit their jobs, and others are fired. It may take some time for these people to find jobs. So at any time there is unemployment due to the normal turnover of labor that exists in any economy. Such unemployment is called **frictional unemployment**.

Full employment is defined to occur when the only existing unemployment is frictional. When the economy is at less than full employment, other types

of unemployment, including cyclical (or deficient-demand) unemployment and real wage unemployment, are present in addition to frictional unemployment. We shall study these in more detail in Chapter 35.[2]

full em — unem.

The measured unemployment rate when the economy is at full employment is often called the **natural rate of unemployment**. Estimates of the natural rate of unemployment are difficult to obtain and are often a source of disagreement among economists. Nevertheless, such estimates are a useful benchmark against which to gauge the current performance of the economy, as measured by the actual unemployment rate. Estimates indicate that the natural rate rose throughout the 1970s from around 4 percent to a high of around 7 percent in the mid 1980s, and has now stabilized or may even be declining. (We shall discuss the reasons for these changes in Chapter 35.)

Why Unemployment Is a Matter of Concern

The social and political significance of the unemployment rate is enormous. The government is blamed when it is high and takes credit when it is low. Few macroeconomic policies are planned without some consideration of how they affect it. No other summary statistic, with the possible exception of the inflation rate, carries such weight as a source of both formal and informal concern of policy as does the percentage of the labor force unemployed.

Unemployment causes economic waste and it causes human suffering. The economic waste is obvious. Human effort is the least durable of economic commodities. If a fully employed economy with a constant labor force has 120 million people willing to work in 1986, their services must either be used in 1986 or wasted. When the services of only 108 million are used because 10 percent of the labor force is unemployed, the potential output of 12 million workers is lost forever. In an economy where there is not enough output to meet everyone's needs, any waste of potential output seems undesirable and large wastes seem tragic.

The human cost of unemployment is also ob-

---

[2] In that chapter we shall also distinguish a particular type of frictional unemployment called structural unemployment.

vious. Severe hardship and misery can be caused by prolonged periods of unemployment. A person's spirit can be broken by a long period of wanting work but being unable to find it. Crime, divorce, and general social unrest usually rise with unemployment.

In the not so distant past, only private charity or help from friends and relatives stood between the unemployed and starvation. Today welfare and unemployment insurance have softened those effects. However, when an economic slump is deep and prolonged, as in the mid 1970s and again in the early 1980s, people begin to exhaust their unemployment insurance and must fall back on savings, welfare, or charity. In the early 1980s many people sank below the poverty level for the first time in their lives. They did so because they had used up their unemployment insurance, but were unable to find jobs because of a persistently high unemployment level.

Output and Income Variables

The value of a nation's total production of goods and services is called its *national product*. Since all the value that is produced must ultimately belong to someone in the form of a claim on that value, the national product is equal to the total income claims generated by the production of goods and services. Hence when we study *national product*, we are also studying *national income*.

In fact, there are several related measures of the nation's total output and total income. Their various definitions and calculations, and the relationships among them, are discussed in detail in the next chapter. In this chapter we use the generic term **national income** to refer to both the value of total output and the value of the income generated by the production of that output. National income is given the symbol Y.

Aggregating Total Output

To measure total output, quantities of a variety of different goods must somehow be added up, or *aggregated*. Just as there is a problem in obtaining an "average" of the variety of prices in the economy, so is there a problem in obtaining a measure of the total output of the wide variety of goods and services produced in the economy.

Consider this problem in terms of a single firm. If that firm produces only a single, well-defined commodity, say, loaves of French bread, then to measure its total output all we need to do is add up the number of loaves baked during the period under consideration. But if it also produces muffins, fancy pastries, cakes, and doughnuts, then we have to find a way of adding its output of these different products. The same problem arises even more prominently when we try to add the outputs of literally hundreds of thousands of different goods and services to measure the nation's total output. How can this be done?

To construct such totals, we add up values of the different products. We cannot add tons of steel to loaves of bread, but we can add the money value of steel production to the money value of bread production. Hence, by multiplying the physical output of a good by its price per unit and then summing this value for each good produced in the nation, we can find the quantity of total output *measured in dollars*.

Real and Nominal Values

The total described above gives the *money value of national output*, often called **nominal national income**. When nominal national income changes, it is important to know to what extent the change is due to a change in prices and to what extent it is due to a change in quantities produced. To answer this question we calculate *real national income*, a measure of total output in which the value of individual outputs is measured not at current prices but at the prices that prevailed in some base period chosen for this purpose.[3] Real national income is denoted by the symbol Y. Real national income tells us the value of current output measured at base period prices, that is, the sum of the quantities valued at prices ruling in the base period. Comparing the real national income for different years provides a measure of the

---

[3] Nominal national income is often referred to as *money national income* or *current dollar national income*. Real national income is often called *constant dollar national income*.

change in real output that has occurred during the interval between the years.

Since prices are held constant in calculating it, real national income changes only when output quantities change.

Since our interest is almost exclusively with the real output of goods and services, we shall take the term *national income* (and output) to refer to *real national income* unless otherwise specified. (For a concrete example of this important distinction, see Box 25-2 on page 485.)

National Income: The Historical Experience

If we are going to look at the actual experience of national income, we must choose some specific measure of this general concept. In this section we look at one of the most commonly used measures, called *gross national product*, or GNP. The details of its calculation are discussed in Chapter 25. GNP can be measured in either real or nominal terms; in this section we focus on real GNP.

Figure 24-3(i) shows real GNP produced by the American economy since 1929; Figure 24-3(ii) shows the annual percentage change in real GNP, that is, the annual rate of growth of real GNP for the same period. The series in Figure 24-3(i) shows two kinds of movement. The major one is a trend increase that resulted in a quintupling of real output in the half century from 1932 to 1982. Since the trend has generally been upward in the modern era, it is referred to as *economic growth*.

GNP— a measure of national income (Y)

Long-term growth in real national income is reflected in the trend increase in real GNP.

A second feature of the real GNP series is the short-term fluctuations around the trend, often described as the cyclical behavior of the economy. Overall growth so dominates the real GNP series that this cyclical behavior is hardly visible in Figure 24-3(i). However, as can be seen in Figure 24-3(ii), cyclical fluctuations in real GNP have not been insignificant.

The cyclical behavior of real national income is reflected in the annual fluctuations in the growth rate of real GNP.

Why National Income Is a Matter of Concern

Short-run fluctuations in national income reflect the ebbs and flows of economic activity referred to as the *business cycle*. In periods of high activity, often called *booms* or *expansions*, real GNP and employment are high and unemployment is low. In periods of low activity, or *slumps* or *contractions*, real GNP and employment are low and unemployment is correspondingly high. Policymakers care about short-term fluctuations in national income because slumps bring unwanted unemployment and output foregone, while booms may create strong inflationary pressures.

The long-run trend in real national income is also important. Not only has national income grown, but real income per person (also called real income per capita) has also grown. Indeed, it has roughly tripled in the last 60 years. When income per person grows, each generation can expect, on average, to be substantially better off than preceding ones. For example, if real income per capita grows at the relatively modest rate of 1.5 percent per year, the average person's lifetime income expectancy will be *twice* that of his or her grandparents. (Of course, although on average people are better off, it does not follow that every individual will in fact be better off.)

Potential Income and the GNP Gap

Actual national income is what the economy does in fact produce. We now introduce the important additional concept of **potential national income**, or just **potential income**, also called **full-employment national income**.[4]

---

[4] The words *real* and *actual* have similar meanings in everyday usage, but they are used quite differently in this context of describing national income. *Real* national income is distinguished from *nominal* national income, while *actual* is distinguished from *potential*. The latter both refer to real measures, so that the full descriptions are actual real national income and potential real national income.

FIGURE 24-3   National Income and Growth, 1929–1985

(i) Annual real GNP measured in constant (1982) dollars

(i) Real GNP measures the quantity of total output produced by the nation's economy over the period of a year. Real GNP, plotted in (i) in semilog form, has risen steadily since the early 1930s, with only a few interruptions. This demonstrates the growth of the American economy. Short-term fluctuations are obscured by the long-term growth trend in (i), but are highlighted in (ii), which plots changes in real GNP. (*Source: Economic Report of the President,* various years.)

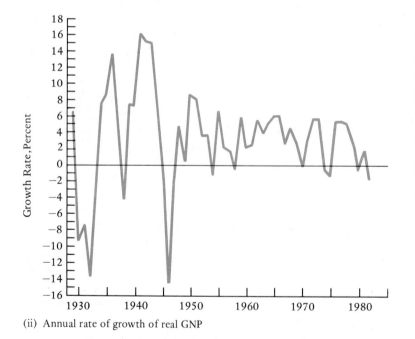

(ii) Annual rate of growth of real GNP

(ii) Fluctuations in the annual rate of growth of real GNP reflect cyclical changes in the level of activity in the economy. The growth rate fluctuates considerably from year to year. High growth rates occur during war years (such as World War II in the early 1940s and the Korean War in the early 1950s). Peacetime booms (such as the mid 1960s) are reflected by sustained periods of above average growth rates. Low growth rates occur during recessions. The long-term upward trend of real GNP still shows up in (i) because the majority of the observations in (ii) are positive. (*Source: Economic Report of the President,* various years.)

Potential national income is what the economy would produce if its productive resources were fully employed at their normal intensity of use.

This would mean in terms of labor force variables that any unemployment of labor is frictional and the unemployment rate is equal to the natural rate of unemployment. It would also mean that the nation's factories and other productive equipment are being used at their normal capacity levels.

Potential national income is represented by the symbol Y^*; it refers to potential *real* income.

The GNP Gap

If we subtract actual national income from potential income ($Y^* - Y$), we obtain a measure called the **GNP gap**. It is the difference between what could have been produced at the potential or full-employment level and what is actually produced, as measured by GNP.

When the gap is positive, that is, when potential income is greater than actual real national income, the GNP is the market value of goods and services that *could have been* produced if the economy's resources had been fully employed, but that actually went unproduced. This is sometimes referred to as the *deadweight loss of unemployment.*

Slumps in business activity are associated with large positive gaps, booms with small ones. In a major boom the gap may even become negative, indicating that actual national income exceeds the economy's potential national income. A negative GNP gap can arise because potential income is defined for a normal rate of utilization of factors of production, and there are many ways in which these normal rates can be exceeded temporarily. Labor may work longer hours than normal; factories may operate an extra shift or not close for routine repairs and maintenance. While these expedients are only temporary, they are effective in the short run.

Measuring potential national income is not straightforward since it cannot be observed directly. The problem is not only one of observation and measurement, but also of establishing acceptable definitions for such concepts as "normal level of utilization" and "full-employment capacity." Because Y^* is hard to measure, the GNP gap is correspondingly hard to measure.[5]

Potential Income and the GNP Gap: The Historical Experience

Figure 24-4(i) shows potential income for the years 1950 through 1985. The steady rising trend reflects the growth in the productive capacity of the American economy over this period. Also shown is actual real national income, which has more or less kept pace with potential income. The distance between the two is the GNP gap.

Figure 24-4(ii) shows the GNP gap for the economy over a period of years. Fluctuations in economic activity are apparent from fluctuations in the size of the gap. The deadweight loss from unemployment over any time span is indicated by the overall size of the gap over that span. It is shown in the figure by the shaded area between the curve and the horizontal line, which represents the level at which actual equals potential output.

Why Potential Income and the GNP Gap Are a Matter of Concern

Potential national income measures the economy's capacity to produce goods and services and hence its capacity to generate income for its people. Because potential income is measured at normal utilization rates of the economy's factors of production, changes in it do not reflect short-term cyclical fluctuations, but rather the long-term trend in potential level of output and income. It is this long-term trend that is important for changes in living standards from generation to generation. The low living standards at the start of the Industrial Revolution are no longer with us, primarily because economic growth has resulted in more and more output for less and less work over the last century.

The GNP gap is important because it reflects the actual performance of the economy relative to its potential. A large GNP gap means that actual national income falls short of potential, and hence the unemployment rate will be high. It is therefore indicative of economic waste and human suffering as a result of failure to use the economy's resources (including its human resources) at their normal intensity of use. A negative GNP gap, indicating that actual national income exceeds potential, also imposes serious costs. Short-run policies that involve utilizing resources at above normal levels in order to raise actual output temporarily create inflationary pressures in the economy and, as we saw earlier, inflation can impose severe costs on the economy.

---

[5] Just as the unemployment rate is not zero when the economy is at full employment, measured capacity utilization is not 100 percent. In fact, manufacturing capacity utilization has exceeded 90 percent only once in the past 35 years, and its normal value is in the 80 to 85 percent range.

FIGURE 24-4 Potential National Income and the GNP Gap, 1955–1985

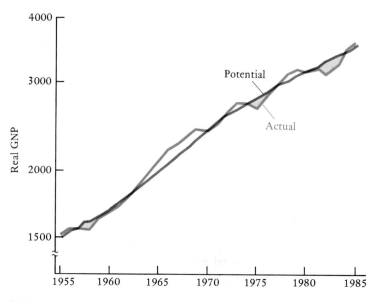

(i) Potential national income

(i) Potential and actual GNP both display an upward trend over the past half decade. Growth in the economy has been such that both potential and actual GNP have more than doubled since 1955. These are plotted in (i) in semilog form. Recall that both measures are in real terms; in the figure they are measured in 1982 dollars. The distance between the two curves represents the GNP gap. The shaded areas indicate periods when there has been a positive GNP gap.

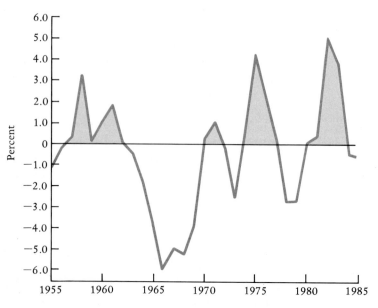

(ii) The GNP gap

(ii) The GNP gap measures the difference between the economy's potential output and its actual output; it is expressed here as a percentage of potential output. The cyclical behavior of the economy is clearly apparent from the behavior of the GNP gap from 1955 to 1985. Slumps in economic activity cause large gaps; booms reduce the gaps. The shaded area above the zero line, at which actual equals potential output, represents the deadweight loss from unemployment. (*Source: Survey of Current Business*, March 1986.)

The Relation Between Output and Employment

Output and employment (and therefore unemployment) are closely related. If more is to be produced, either more workers must be used in production or existing workers must produce more. The first change means a rise in employment; the second means a rise in output per person employed, which is called a rise in **productivity**. Increases in productivity are a major source of economic growth. (Productivity was discussed in Chapter 11 and will be discussed again in Chapter 36.)

Changes in productivity and in the labor force dominate the long-term trend of output and employment. But productivity and the labor force generally change only slowly, and thus they have little effect on the short-term behavior of the economy. As we study the main elements of macroeconomic theory over the next few chapters, we will treat both the labor force and productivity as constant. This not only greatly simplifies our discussion, it is a reasonable approximation of reality for purposes of analyzing the short-term behavior of the American economy.

Aggregate Demand and Aggregate Supply

Why are the price level, output, and employment what they are today? What causes them to change? The concepts of aggregate demand and supply help us to answer these questions.

As we have already seen in this chapter, the time series describing national income and the price level have two important properties. Both series exhibit long-term trends and short-term fluctuations around those trends. In order to focus on the short-term fluctuations, we assume in our initial discussion that the long-term trends are zero. In this case, a fluctuation that takes the price level, or national income, above its long-term trend will be indicated by an increase in its value, while a fluctuation that takes the price level, or national income, below its trend will be indicated by a decrease in its value. Later in this book, we shall examine actual long-term trends in some detail.[6]

In Chapter 4 we saw how the interaction of demand and supply can determine prices and quantities for individual commodities. If we had a single demand curve and a single supply curve for the whole economy, we could determine the economy's price level and the quantity of its total output just as we can determine price and quantity for a single product such as potatoes or coal.

This is illustrated in Figure 24-5, which assumes the existence of an aggregate demand curve and an aggregate supply curve for the entire economy. The vertical axis measures the price level and the horizontal axis measures total income (i.e., real national income). The aggregate demand curve (*AD*) shows the relation between the total amount of all output that will be purchased and the price level. The aggregate supply curve (*AS*) shows the relation between the total amount of output that will be produced and the price level.

The intersection of the aggregate demand and aggregate supply curves determines the equilibrium values of real national income and the price level.

Only at the equilibrium price level is the amount purchasers wish to buy equal to the amount producers wish to sell. At any other price level the amount demanded is not equal to the amount supplied.

The Aggregate Demand Curve

The aggregate demand curve is negatively sloped. This shape indicates that, other things being equal,

---

[6] The analysis of the next few chapters is to be understood, therefore, as establishing how the price level, and national income, will behave *relative to trend*. For simplicity, we take these trend values to be constant for the time being. When the trend is not constant, the results must be interpreted accordingly. For example, a force that causes national income to fall by 2 percent in the short term when its long-term trend is constant will cause it to increase by 1 percent when its long-term trend is an increase of 3 percent per year. Similarly, a force that causes the price level to fall by 3 percent in the short term when the long-term trend is constant will cause the price level to rise by 2 percent when its long-term trend is an increase of 5 percent per year.

**FIGURE 24-5   The Price Level and National
Income for the Whole Economy**

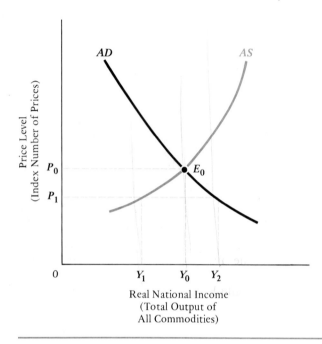

**Aggregate demand and aggregate supply determine
the price level and national income for the entire
economy.** The negatively sloped *AD* curve indicates
that the higher the price level, the smaller the total quantity of output demanded. The positively sloped *AS* curve
indicates that the higher the price level, the larger the
total quantity of output produced.

Actual output is determined by the intersection of the
aggregate demand and aggregate supply curves. Equilibrium is at E_0, with a price level of P_0 and a national
income of Y_0. At higher price levels aggregate supply
exceeds aggregate demand; at lower price levels aggregate demand exceeds aggregate supply. For example, at
price level P_1 purchasers would wish to buy Y_2 of total
output, but producers would be willing to make and sell
only Y_1. The resulting shortage would then force prices
up from P_1 to P_0.

The higher the price level, the smaller the total
quantity demanded; and, the lower the price
level, the larger the total quantity demanded.

Why does it have this slope?

The Slope of the AD Curve

Just as the individual market demand curves used in
microeconomics are negatively sloped, so, too, is the
AD curve used in macroeconomics. But the reasons
for the negative slope are quite different.

Recall that a market demand curve describes what
happens when the price of one product changes, with
the price of all other products being held constant.
What happens along a market demand curve happens, therefore, because the relation among prices is
changing, that is, the product in question is getting
cheaper or more expensive relative to all other products. The *AD* curve, however, plots aggregate demand against the *price level*. Thus what happens
along the *AD* curve depends on the average behavior

of all prices, not on the behavior of any individual
price. So the forces at work are different from those
that explain the market demand curve.

Then what does explain the negative slope of the
AD curve? One reason will emerge in Chapter 26
when we discuss what are called <u>wealth effects</u>, but
the full explanation can be given only after we have
studied money and interest rates in Chapter 32. Some
readers may decide for now just to take the aggregate
demand curve's negative slope on faith, knowing
that it will be more completely explained later. Other
readers who want a preview of this explanation now
can study Box 24-2 on pages 474–475.

The Aggregate Supply Curve

The aggregate supply curve is positively sloped. This
slope indicates that, other things being equal,

The higher the price level, the greater the total
quantity that will be produced; and, the lower

the price level, the smaller the total quantity that will be produced.

For reasons that we will soon discover, this relation is only a short-term one. To indicate its short-term nature, the positively sloped aggregate supply curve will always be referred to as the **short-run aggregate supply curve** (or *SRAS* **curve**).

The Slope of the SRAS Curve

input prices const

Suppose that firms wish to increase output above current production levels. For the moment, suppose further that the prices of all the inputs the firms use—labor, capital, and so forth—remain constant. This does not mean that either the firms' costs or output prices will remain unchanged.

Increasing output may require that less efficient standby machines and plants are used, that less efficient workers are employed, and that existing workers are given overtime hours at premium wages. Thus, even with the restriction that input prices remain constant, higher output is associated with increased costs because it requires the use of more and more costly methods of production. This increase in cost per unit of output is referred to as rising **unit costs**. Since expanding output means incurring higher unit costs, firms will produce this extra output only if it can be sold at higher prices.

Now consider what happens when firms wish to reduce their output. The forces just mentioned work in reverse. There will be cost savings as the least efficient labor is laid off and the least efficient capital is put on standby. For these reasons, the lower output will be associated with somewhat lower unit costs and hence with lower output prices.

The positively sloped *SRAS* curve shows that with input prices constant, higher output is associated with higher prices because unit costs of production increase as the level of output increases.

The relation described by the *SRAS* curve holds only in the short run. This is because it is based on the assumption that input prices are constant. Variations in output will, however, surely cause input prices to change eventually. (In Chapter 28 we shall study the effects of changing input prices on the *SRAS* curve.)

The GNP Gap Once Again

We saw in Figure 24-4 that actual national income often diverges from potential national income, the difference between the two being the GNP gap. Figure 24-6 on page 476 shows the GNP gap on the aggregate demand and aggregate supply diagram. Potential income is shown by the vertical line at Y^*. This indicates that potential income does not vary with the price level.

In Figure 24-6 the *AD* and *SRAS* curves intersect to produce a positive GNP gap. In this case, actual national income Y_0, as determined by the intersection of the *AD* and *SRAS* curves, is below potential national income Y^*. Had the *AD* and *SRAS* curves intersected at a level of national income greater than Y^*, there would have been a negative GNP gap.

Changes in Output and Prices

We have seen that the aggregate demand and aggregate supply curves determine real national income and the price level. These curves can now be used to show why those two variables change; later we will also study how government policy can influence these variables. Here is a simple overview.

Shifts in the Aggregate Curves

A shift in the *AD* curve is called an **aggregate demand shock**. A *rightward* shift in the *AD* curve represents an *increase* in aggregate demand; it means that at any given price level *more* real national income will be demanded. Similarly, a *leftward* shift in the *AD* curve represents a *decrease* in aggregate demand; it means that at any given price level *less* real national income will be demanded.

A shift in the *SRAS* curve is called an **aggregate supply shock**. A rightward shift in the *SRAS* curve represents an increase in aggregate supply; at any given price level more real national income will be supplied. A leftward shift in the *SRAS* curve repre-

BOX 24-2

The Shape of the Aggregate Demand Curve

The Fallacy of Composition

In Chapter 4 we studied the demand curves for individual products. It is tempting to think that the properties of the aggregate demand curve arise from the same behavior that gives rise to those individual demand curves. Unfortunately, life is not so simple. Let us first see why we cannot take such an approach.

If we assume that we can obtain a downward-sloping aggregate demand curve in the same manner that we derived downward-sloping individual market demand curves, we would be committing the fallacy of composition. This is to assume that what is correct for the parts must be correct for the whole.

Consider a simple example of the fallacy. Any art collector can go into the market and add to her private collection of nineteenth century French paintings provided only that she has enough money. But to assume that because any one person can do this, everyone could do so simultaneously is plainly wrong. The world's stock of nineteenth century French paintings is totally fixed. All of us cannot do what any one of us with enough money can do.

How does the fallacy of composition relate to demand curves?

The Shape of an Individual Demand Curve

An individual demand curve describes a situation in which the price of one commodity changes while the prices of all other commodities and consumers' money incomes are constant. Such an individual demand curve is negatively sloped for two reasons. First, as the price of the commodity rises, each consumer's given money income will buy a smaller *total* amount of goods, so a smaller quantity of the commodity will be bought. Second, as the price of the commodity rises, consumers buy less of it and more of the now relatively cheaper substitutes.

The first reason has no application to the aggregate demand curve, which relates the total demand for all output to the price level. All prices and total output are changing as we move along the *AD* curve. Since the value of output determines income, there is no reason to expect consumers' money incomes to be constant along this curve.

The second reason does have some, but very limited, application to the aggregate demand curve. A rise in the price level entails a rise in all domestic commodity prices. Thus there is no incentive to substitute among domestic commodities. But it does give

sents a decrease in aggregate supply; at any given price level less real national income will be supplied.[7]

What happens to real national income and to the price level when one of the aggregate curves shifts?

When one shifts, the equilibrium values of real national income and the price level also change.

A shift in either the *AD* or the *SRAS* curve leads to changes in the price level and real national income.

Aggregate Demand Shocks

Figure 24-7 on page 476 shows the effects of an increase in aggregate demand. This increase could have occurred because of, say, increased investment or government spending; it means that more national output would be demanded at any given price level.

[7] The distinction between movements along and shifts of curves first encountered in Chapter 4 is relevant here. Recall especially that the phrase "a change in quantity demanded" refers to a *movement along a demand curve*, while "a change in demand" refers to a *shift of the demand curve*. A similar distinction applies to the supply curve.

Note that for either curve a shift to the right means an *increase* and a shift to the left a *decrease*. If we speak of *upward* and *downward* shifts, however, the meaning differs for the two curves. An upward shift of the *AD* curve is an *increase* in aggregate demand, but an upward shift in the *SRAS* curve is a *decrease* in aggregate supply.

rise, as we shall see below, to some substitution between domestic and foreign goods.

The Negatively Sloped Aggregate Demand Curve

Three reasons account for the negative slope of the *AD* curve.

Wealth effect on expenditure. Bank balances, bonds, and many other assets are denominated in terms of money. When the price level rises, the real purchasing power of these assets is reduced. For example, if I hold a $1,000 bond and the price level doubles, the amount of commodities I can buy with the money I get back when the bond is redeemed falls by half. Since the bond's real value is halved, the real value of my wealth falls. This may cause me to increase my savings in order to recoup some of my lost wealth; to save more, I must spend less on current consumption.

Substitution of foreign goods. When the American price level rises, American goods become expensive relative to foreign goods, and American residents reduce their purchases of relatively expensive American goods and buy relatively cheap foreign goods instead.

Foreign consumers reduce their purchases of the increasingly expensive goods exported from America. Since the aggregate demand curve describes the demand for American goods from all sources, including foreign ones, aggregate demand falls as the American price level rises.

Interest rate effects on expenditure. The third reason the aggregate demand curve slopes downward is to be found in the effects of money on interest rates and of interest rates on total demand. The main forces are only suggested here; they will be fully apparent when the necessary links in the argument have been studied in Chapter 32.

When the price level rises, firms and households need to cover their increased money expenses between one payday and the next. With this increased demand for money, the price you have to pay to borrow it—which is the interest rate—rises. Firms that borrow money to build plants and purchase equipment, and households that borrow money to buy consumer goods, respond to rising interest rates by choosing to spend less on capital goods, housing, automobiles, and other goods. This means a decline in the aggregate quantity demanded of the nation's output.

For now we are not concerned with the source of the shock; we are interested in its implications for the price level and real national income. As is shown in the figure, following an increase in aggregate demand, both the price level and real national income rise. Figure 24-7 also shows that both the price level and real national income fall as the result of a decrease in demand. (In later chapters we take up the important distinction between unanticipated and anticipated shocks.)

Aggregate demand shocks cause both the price level and real national income to change in the same direction; both rise with an increase in demand, and both fall with a decrease.

An aggregate demand shock means a *shift* in the *AD* curve (for example, from AD_0 to AD_1 in the figure). Adjustment to the new equilibrium following an aggregate demand shock involves a *movement along* the *SRAS* curve (for example, from point E_0 to point E_1).

Several demand shocks occurred in the early 1980s. The economy entered the decade with record inflation that was widely agreed to be a major problem. In order to combat this inflation, contractionary government policy—primarily monetary restraint—was introduced, shifting the *AD* curve to the left. This led to a major recession (unemployment reached 9.7 percent and the GNP gap reached 6.2 percent) and a substantial easing of inflationary pressure. Then

FIGURE 24-6   Potential Output, Actual Output, and the GNP Gap

The GNP gap is the difference between potential output and actual output. Potential output, $Y^\star$, is shown by a vertical line because it is not influenced by the price level. Actual output, Y_0, is determined by the intersection of the AD and $SRAS$ curves. The difference between potential and actual output is the GNP gap. In the figure potential output exceeds actual, and so the GNP gap, $Y^* - Y_0$, is positive.

FIGURE 24-7   Aggregate Demand Shocks

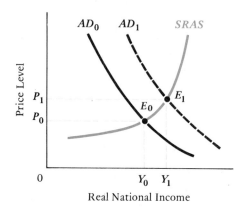

Shifts in aggregate demand cause the price level and real national income to move in the same direction. An increase in aggregate demand shifts the AD curve to the right, say, from AD_0 to AD_1. Equilibrium moves from E_0 to E_1. The price level rises from P_0 to P_1 and real national income rises from Y_0 to Y_1, reflecting a movement along the $SRAS$ curve.

A decrease in aggregate demand shifts the AD curve to the left, say, from AD_1 to AD_0. Equilibrium moves from E_1 to E_0. Prices fall from P_1 to P_0 and real national income falls from Y_1 to Y_0, again reflecting a movement along the $SRAS$ curve.

in late 1982 the AD curve started to shift to the right, fueled by increased consumer and investor confidence and by government tax cuts. As a result, output rose dramatically and inflation stabilized at roughly 4 percent.

Aggregate Supply Shocks

Figure 24-8 illustrates the effects on the price level and real national income of changes in aggregate supply. A decrease could occur because of, say, an increase in costs, which leads to less national output being supplied at any given price. As with the demand shock, we are not now concerned with the source of the supply shock. As can be seen from the figure, following the decrease in aggregate supply, the price level rises and real national income falls.

This combination of events is called **stagflation**, a rather inelegant word derived by combining *stagnation* (a term sometimes used to mean less than full employment) and *inflation*.

Figure 24-8 also shows that an increase in aggregate supply leads to an increase in real national income and a decrease in the price level.

Aggregate supply shocks cause the price level and real national income to change in opposite directions; the price level rises and income falls with an ~~increase~~ *decrease* in supply, and the price level falls and income rises with a ~~decrease~~ *increase* in supply.

An aggregate supply shock means a *shift* in the $SRAS$ curve (from $SRAS_0$ to $SRAS_1$ in the figure). Adjustment to the new equilibrium following the shock

FIGURE 24-8   Aggregate Supply Shocks

Shifts in aggregate supply cause the price level and real national income to move in opposite directions. A decrease in aggregate supply shifts the $SRAS$ curve to the left, say, from $SRAS_0$ to $SRAS_1$. Equilibrium moves from E_0 to E_1. The price level rises from P_0 to P_1, but real national income falls from Y_0 to Y_1, reflecting a movement along the AD curve.

An increase in aggregate supply shifts the $SRAS$ curve to the right, say, from $SRAS_1$ to $SRAS_0$. Equilibrium moves from E_1 to E_0. The price level falls from P_1 to P_0, but real national income rises from Y_1 to Y_0, again reflecting a movement along the AD curve.

involves a *movement along* the AD curve (from E_0 to E_1).

The first dramatic stagflation of the modern era began in 1974. One major aspect of that era was that the economy was hit with some severe supply shocks. Serious crop failures combined with the purchase of surplus wheat by the U.S.S.R. raised food prices greatly. The policies of the newly aggressive Organization of Petroleum Exporting Countries (OPEC) forced up not only the price of energy, but the prices of fertilizer, plastics, synthetic rubber, and dozens of other petroleum-based products. Since many of these are used in the manufacture of yet other commodities, costs of production rose for many firms. The rise in costs led to increases in many selling prices. Hence the $SRAS$ curve shifted to the left, meaning that at any price level less total output would be supplied. This decrease in aggregate supply caused a serious stagflation, and the economy experienced simultaneously the twin "evils" of falling output and rising prices. In the mid 1980s oil prices fell sharply; hence we might expect that, other things being equal, national output will increase while there will be deflationary pressures.

Supply-side economics.   As we have seen, an increase in aggregate supply will lead to a rise in real national income and a fall in the price level. To anyone living in economies plagued by stagflation, these conditions, which are just the opposite of stagflation, appear to be ideal. A desire to achieve just this combination lies behind "supply-side economics." Supply-siders advocate tax cuts and other incentives to increase supply in order to bring about the desirable outcome of increased output and reduced prices. "Very simple," said the advocates. "Easier said than done," replied the critics in a debate we shall take up later.

Summary

1. Macroeconomics examines the behavior of such broad aggregates and averages as the price level, national income, potential national income, the GNP gap, employment, and unemployment.

2. Index numbers are summary measures that give the average percentage change in a set of related items between a base year and another given year.

3. The price level has displayed a continual upward trend since 1929. The inflation rate measures the rate of change of the price level. Although it fluctuates considerably, the inflation rate has been consistently positive. Inflation imposes serious costs on the economy.

4. The unemployment rate is the number of adult workers who are not employed and are actively searching for a job, expressed as a percentage of the labor force. The labor force and employment have both grown steadily for the past half century. The unemployment rate fluctuates considerably from year to year. Unemployment imposes serious costs—in the form of economic waste and human suffering—on the economy.

5. The value of total production of goods and services is called national product. Since production of output generates income in the form of claims on that output, it is common to also talk of national income. One of the most commonly used measures of national income is gross national product (GNP). Nominal national income evaluates output in current prices. Real national income evaluates output in base period prices. Changes in real national income reflect changes in quantities of output produced.

6. Potential real national income measures the capacity of the economy to produce goods and services when factors of production are employed at their normal intensity of use. The GNP gap is the difference between potential and actual real national income.

7. The dominant theme of the economy is the growth of real output and employment. A secondary theme involves cyclical factors represented by fluctuations in output and unemployment around their growth trend values. In order to study these fluctuations, we focus on the unemployment rate and the GNP gap.

8. Two major tools of macroeconomics analysis are the aggregate demand and aggregate supply curves. The aggregate demand (*AD*) curve is typically negatively sloped, indicating that the lower the price level, the higher the demand for the nation's output. The short-run aggregate supply (*SRAS*) curve is typically positively sloped. The positive slope indicates that the higher the price level, the greater the output produced. *input price fixed*

9. The reasons for the negative slope of the aggregate demand curve are suggested in Box 24-2 and will be explored in subsequent chapters. The reason for the positive slope of the short-run aggregate supply curve is that increases in output entail increases in the costs of producing each unit of output and hence will be undertaken only if output prices rise.

10. Macroeconomic equilibrium occurs at the intersection of the *AD* and *SRAS* curves, thus determining the price level and real national income. Shifts in the *AD* and *SRAS* curve cause changes in the equilibrium price level and real national income.

Topics for Review

The price level and rate of inflation
Employment, unemployment, and labor force
Real and nominal national income
Potential and actual national income and the GNP gap
Aggregate demand and aggregate supply
Aggregate demand shocks
Aggregate supply shocks

Discussion Questions

1. Classify as microeconomic or macroeconomic (or both) the issues raised in the following newspaper headlines.
   a. "Lettuce crop spoils as strike hits California lettuce producers."
   b. "Analysts fear rekindling of inflation as economy recovers toward full employment."
   c. "Index of Industrial Production falls by 4 points."
   d. "Price of bus rides soars in Centersville as city council withdraws transport subsidy."
   e. "A fall in the unemployment rate signals the beginning of the end of the recession in the Detroit area."
   f. "Silicon chip technology brings falling prices and growing sales of microcomputers."
   g. "Rising costs of imported raw materials cause most American manufacturers to raise prices."
2. Using your understanding of the chapter, analyze the following recent statements made by business people.
   a. "We must be successful; our sales have increased every year for the past ten years."
   b. "I can see why prices may rise in boom times, but rising prices and falling output just don't make sense."
   c. "I can't understand why there is so much unemployment; our business is booming."
3. Explain the following by shifts in either or both the aggregate demand and aggregate supply curves. Pay attention to the initial position before the shift(s) occurs.
   a. Output and unemployment rise, while prices hold steady.
   b. Prices soar, but employment and output hold steady.
   c. Inflation accelerates even as the recession in business actively deepens.
4. In 1979-1980 the British government greatly reduced income taxes, but restored the lost government revenue by raising excise and sales taxes. This led to a short burst of extra inflation and a fall in employment. Explain this in terms of shifts in the aggregate demand and/or supply curves.
5. Indicate whether each of the following events is the cause or the consequence of a shift in aggregate demand or supply. If it is a cause, what do you predict will be the effect on the price level and on real national income?

    a. Unemployment decreases in 1984 in the United States.

    b. OPEC raises oil prices in 1979.

    c. OPEC is forced to accept lower oil prices in 1982–1983.

    d. In the late 1960s and early 1970s the United States suffers a rapid inflation under conditions of approximately full employment.

    e. In country X income and employment continue to fall while the price level is quite stable.

    f. President Reagan achieves a large increase in defense spending in 1983–1984.

6. Discuss the various reasons why two truthful people could announce that very different rates of inflation are ruling in the United States today.

7. How could unemployment rise at a time when employment was increasing rapidly? Why is unemployment not as serious a matter as it was at the beginning of this century?

8. If you thought the inflation rate was going to be 10 percent next year, why should you be unwilling to lend money at 5 percent interest? Say 5 percent was all you could get and you had money you didn't want to spend for a year. Would you be better just to hold the money? What could you do that would be better than lending your money at 5 percent?

25

Measuring Macroeconomic Variables

In Chapter 24 a number of key macroeconomic variables were introduced. Before we delve into the analysis of macroeconomic events, it will be helpful to look in some detail at the measurement and interpretation of these variables. This will give a clearer notion of the concepts. It will also provide some warning about how to avoid misusing or misinterpreting measures that play a prominent role in everyday discussion of the economy.

We focus on the two variables determined by the aggregate demand and aggregate supply curves, the price level and real national income.[1] In the first section we study the construction of price indexes and measures of real and nominal national income. In the second section we study the system of National Income Accounts which provides the framework for gathering and organizing data on the production of output and the generation of income in the economy.

Calculating Price Indexes and Measures of Aggregate Output

As we saw in Chapter 24, in order to measure aggregate variables we must assign weights to the individual components. We now examine how this is done when calculating price indexes and measures of total output.

The Price Level

The price level refers to an index number computed using some broad group of prices in the economy. A **price index** measures the price level at a *given period* relative to the *base period*. Several issues are involved in the construction of price indexes.

First, what group of prices should be used? This depends on the index. The **Consumer Price Index (CPI)** covers prices of commodities commonly bought by households. Changes in the value of the CPI are meant to measure changes in the typical household's "cost of living." Other price indexes, some of which we will encounter later in this chapter, incorporate prices of different groups of commodities.

---

[1] The measurement of labor force variables is relatively straightforward, and further details are deferred until our treatment of unemployment in Chapter 35. For present purposes it is sufficient to recall from Chapter 24 that real national income and employment tend to be positively related, while real national income and unemployment tend to be negatively related.

Second, what kind of average should be used? If all prices always changed in the same proportion, this would not matter: a 10 percent rise in each and every price would mean a 10 percent rise in the price level no matter how the index were constructed. But what if, as is always the case, different prices change in different proportions? Now it matters how much importance we give to each price change.

In calculating any price index, statisticians weight each price according to its importance. Let us see how this is done for the CPI. Government statisticians periodically survey a group of households to discover how they spend their incomes. The average bundle of goods bought is determined and the quantities in this bundle become the weights attached to the individual prices. As a result, the CPI weights rather heavily any change in prices of commodities on which consumers spend a lot of their income, and weights rather lightly any change in prices of commodities on which consumers spend only a little.

The average *change* in the price level is then calculated by comparing the cost of purchasing the typical bundle of commodities at the prices that prevailed in the base year with the cost of purchasing it at the prices prevailing in the given year. The procedure is illustrated in Table 25-1.

A price index for a given year gives the ratio of the cost of purchasing a bundle of commodities in that year to the cost of purchasing the *same* bundle in the base year, multiplied by 100. [33]

At the beginning of 1986 the CPI was approximately 330 (1967 = 100). This means that in 1986 it cost 3.3 times as much to buy the representative bundle of goods as it did in the base year of 1967. The 1986 CPI of 330 thus indicates a 230 percent *increase* in the price level since 1967. The *percentage change* in the cost of purchasing the bundle is thus the level of the price index minus 100.

A price index is meant to reflect the broad trend in prices rather than the details. This means that although the information it gives may be extremely valuable, it must be interpreted with care. Some of the potential difficulties are discussed in Box 25-1.

Measuring Aggregate Output

When we set out to measure aggregate output we wish to measure the total output of all producers in the economy. It might appear at first that this could be done simply by adding up the market value of the outputs of every producer. A problem arises, however, because production occurs in stages: One

---

TABLE 25-1   The Calculation of a Consumer Price Index Covering Three Commodities

Commodity	Quantity in fixed bundle consumption	Base year 1982		Given year 1986	
		Price in 1982	Value in 1982	Price in 1986	Value in 1986
A	500 units	$1.00	$ 500	$2.00	$1,000
B	200 units	5.00	1,000	7.00	1,400
C	50 units	2.00	100	9.60	480
			1,600		2,880

$$\text{Index value 1982} = \frac{1,600}{1,600} \times 100 = 100$$

$$\text{Index value 1986} = \frac{2,880}{1,600} \times 100 = 180$$

A price index shows the ratio of the costs of purchasing a fixed bundle of goods between two years (multiplied by 100). The cost of purchasing the fixed bundle is calculated at the prices ruling in each year. The index for year 1986 is the cost of purchasing that bundle in 1986 expressed as a percentage of the cost of purchasing the same bundle in the base year (1982 in this example). The price index is thus always 100 in the base year. The index of 180 means that prices have risen on average by 80 percent between the base year and the year in question. This index weights price changes by their *importance* in the average household's budget in the base year.

BOX 25-1

Problems in Interpreting the Consumer Price Index

First, the weights in the index refer to an average bundle of goods. This average, although typical of what is consumed in the nation, will not be typical of what each household consumes. The rich, the poor, the young, the old, the single, the married, the urban, and the rural household will typically consume different bundles. An increase in air fares, for example, will raise the cost of living of a middle-income traveler, while leaving that of a poor stay-at-home unaffected. In the example in Table 25-1, the cost of living would have risen by 100 percent, 40 percent, and 380 percent, respectively, for three different families, one of whom consumed only commodity A, one only commodity B, and one only commodity C. The index in the table shows, however, that the cost of living went up by 80 percent for a family that consumed all three goods in the relative quantities indicated.

The more an individual household's consumption pattern conforms to that of the typical pattern used to weight prices in the price index, the better the price index will reflect the average change in prices relevant to that household.

To assess the importance of this problem, separate indexes are calculated to reflect the different consumption patterns of different groups. For example, since January 1980 there has been both an all-urban CPI and a separate index for urban wage and clerical workers.

Second, households usually alter their consumption patterns in response to price changes. A price index that shows changes in the cost of purchasing a *fixed* bundle of goods does not allow for this. For example, a typical cost of living index for middle-income families at the turn of the century would have given heavy weight to the cost of maids and laundresses. A doubling of servants' wages in 1900 would have significantly increased the middle-class cost of living. Today it would have little effect, for the rising cost of labor has long since caused middle-income

families to cease to employ full-time servants. A household that has dispensed with a commodity altogether finds its cost of living unaffected by any increase in the price of that commodity, no matter how large.

A fixed-weight price index tends to overstate cost of living changes because it does not allow for changes in consumption patterns that shift expenditure away from commodities whose prices rise most and toward those whose prices rise least.

Third, as time passes, new commodities enter the typical consumption bundle and old ones leave. A cost of living index in 1890 would have had a large item for horse-drawn carriages, but no allowance at all for automobiles and gasoline.

A fixed-weight index makes no allowance for the increased importance of new products or the declining importance of old in the typical household's consumption bundle.

The longer the period of time that passes, the less some fixed consumption bundle will be typical of current consumption patterns. For this reason the Bureau of Labor Statistics makes a new survey of household expenditure patterns every 15 or 20 years and revises the weights. The base period is then usually changed to be near the year in which the new set of commodity weights was calculated. At the end of 1985 using 1967 weights the CPI stood at 322.2 (1967 = 100). This meant that the cost of purchasing the bundle of goods bought by a typical household in 1967 had risen 222 percent in the intervening 18 years. Eighteen years is a long time for fixed weights to be used, and the Bureau of Labor Statistics is currently estimating a new set of weights in order to shift the weighting year of the CPI to a more recent year.

firm may produce output that is used as inputs by other firms, and these other firms in their turn may produce output that is used as inputs by yet other firms.

Consider as an example the production of bread. If we added the total value of the sales of the wheat farmer and the value of the sales of the flour mill and the value of the sales of the baker, we would be counting the value of the wheat three times, the value of the milled flour two times, and the value of the bread once. To avoid this problem of *multiple counting* we include as each firm's output only its **value added**. This is the gross value of the firm's output minus the value of the inputs that it purchases from other firms and which were in turn the outputs of these other firms.

This concept of output as value added leads to the distinction between intermediate and final goods. **Intermediate goods** are outputs of some producers that are in turn inputs for other producers in the chain of production. **Final goods** are goods that are not, in the period of time under consideration, used as inputs by other firms. They are goods that are produced for final demand, to be sold; that is, for consumption, for investment (including inventory accumulation), for government, or for exports.

Real and Nominal National Income

We saw in Chapter 24 that prices of individual outputs are used as weights when constructing an aggregate measure of total output. While we cannot add tons of steel and loaves of bread, we can add the money value of steel produced to the money value of bread produced. When we add up money values of individual outputs, we end up with a measure of what we have called *nominal national income.*[2] Suppose that we found that our measure of nominal national income had risen by 140 percent between 1980 and 1987. If we wanted to compare *real national income* (i.e., real output) in 1987 to that in 1980, we would need to determine how much of that 140 percent increase in nominal national income was due to in-

[2] For now, we proceed as if all outputs are in fact final products. In the next part of this chapter when we encounter the "output approach" we consider outputs that are not final products.

creases in prices and how much was due to increases in quantities produced.

There are many possible approaches to distinguishing real from nominal income and many details in the procedures. But the basic principle in calculating real income is to compute the value of output in each period using a common set of (base period) prices. (The common set of prices thus form the weights used in the index of real income.) We speak of real income as being measured in *base period constant dollars.*

Total output calculated by adding values using current prices is a measure of nominal national income. Total output calculated by adding values using base period prices is a measure of real national income, measured in terms of base year constant dollars.

Any change in nominal income clearly reflects the combined effects of changes in prices and changes in outputs. But given the principle of measuring real income in different periods using a common set of base period prices, any changes in real income are due to changes in real output.

The Implicit Deflator

Any differences between nominal and real national income for a given year must be due to changes in prices between that year and the base year used in calculating real income. Such a comparison thus implies a price index relating the two years. This *implicit price index* or *implicit deflator* is defined as follows:

$$\text{Implicit deflator} = \frac{\text{nominal national income}}{\text{real national income}} \times 100\%$$

The implicit deflator is the most comprehensive index of the price level because it covers all the goods and services produced by the entire economy. While the CPI is a fixed-weight index, the implicit deflator is a variable-weight index. It uses the current year's "bundle" of production to compare the current year's prices with those prevailing in the base period. Thus the 1986 deflator uses 1986 weights, while the 1987 deflator will use 1987 weights. Box 25-2 illus-

BOX 25-2

Calculation of Nominal and Real National Income

To see what is involved in calculating nominal national income, real national income, and the implicit deflator, an example may be helpful. Consider a simple hypothetical economy that produces only two commodities, wheat and steel.

Table 1 gives the basic data for outputs and prices in the economy for two years.

Table 1   Data for a Hypothetical Economy

| | Quantity produced | | Prices | |
	Wheat (bushels)	Steel (tons)	Wheat (dollars per bushel)	Steel (dollars per ton)
Year 1	100	20	10	50
Year 2	110	16	12	55

Table 2 shows nominal national income, calculated by adding the money values of wheat output and of steel output for each year. In year 1 the value of both wheat and steel production was $1,000, so nominal income was $2,000. In year 2 wheat output rose and steel output fell; the value of wheat output rose to $1,320 and that of steel fell to $880. Since the rise in value of wheat was bigger than the fall in value of steel, nominal income rose by $200.

Table 2   Calculation of Nominal National Income

Year 1 $(100 \times 10) + (20 \times 50) = \$2,000$
Year 2 $(110 \times 12) + (16 \times 55) = \$2,200$

Table 3 shows real national income, calculated by valuing output in each year by year 2 prices; that is, year 2 becomes the base year for weighting purposes. In year 2, wheat output rose but steel output fell. Using year 2 prices, the value of the fall in steel output exceeded the value of the rise in wheat output, and real national income fell.

Table 3   Calculation of Real National Income Using Year 2 Prices

Year 1 $(100 \times 12) + (20 \times 55) = \$2,300$
Year 2 $(110 \times 12) + (16 \times 55) = \$2,200$

In Table 4 the ratio of nominal to real national income is calculated for each year and multiplied by 100. This ratio implicitly measures the change in prices over the period in question and is called the *implicit deflator* or *implicit price index.*

Table 4   Calculation of the Implicit Deflator

Year 1 $(2,000 \div 2,300) \times 100 = 86.96$
Year 2 $(2,200 \div 2,200) \times 100 = 100.00$

The implicit deflator shows the price level increased by 15 percent between year 1 and year 2.

In Table 4 we used year 2 as the base year for comparison purposes, but we could have used year 1. The implicit deflator would then have been 100 in year 1 and 115 in year 2, and the increase in price level would still have been 15 percent.

trates the calculation of real national income, nominal national income, and the implicit deflator for a simple hypothetical economy that produces only wheat and steel.

Any change in nominal income can be split into a change due to prices and a change due to quantities. For example, in 1985 American nominal income was 293 percent higher than in 1970. This increase was due to a 166 percent increase in prices and a 48 percent increase in real income. Table 25-2 gives

nominal and real income and the implicit deflator for selected years since 1940.

National Income Accounting

In the previous chapter we used the generic term *national income* to describe both the value of output produced and the income generated by that produc-

TABLE 25-2   Nominal and Real National Income

Year	Nominal national income (billions of current dollars)	Real national income (billions of 1982 dollars)	Implicit national income deflator (1982 = 100)
1940	100.4	772.9	13.0
1950	288.3	1,203.7	23.9
1960	515.3	1,665.3	30.9
1970	1,015.5	2,416.2	42.0
1980	2,732.0	3,187.1	85.7
1985	3,998.1	3,573.5	111.7

Source: Economic Report of the President, various years.

Nominal national income tells us about the money value of output; real national income tells us about changes in physical output. Nominal national income (or national income in current dollars) gives the total value of all final output in any year, valued in the selling prices of that year. Real national income (or national income in base period constant dollars) gives the total value of all final output in any year, valued in the prices ruling in one particular year, in this case 1982.

The ratio *national income in current dollars/national income in constant dollars* times 100 is the implicit deflator.

tion. In this chapter we will identify several distinct aggregate measures. Each measure helps to shed some light on specific aspects of the total being measured.

It is useful to look again at Figure 3-1, on page 52, which shows the circular flow of expenditure and income. The bottom half of the circular flow focuses on expenditure to purchase the nation's output in product markets, and the top half focuses on factor markets where the receipts of firms are distributed to those factors used in producing the nation's output.

Corresponding to the two halves of the circular flow are two ways of measuring national income: the value of what is produced and the value of incomes generated by production. We can add up the total expenditure on each of the main components of final output; this is called the *expenditure approach.* The most comprehensive measure of national income arrived at by this approach is called **gross national expenditure (GNE)**. We can also measure the incomes generated by the act of production; this is called the *income approach.* The most comprehensive measure of national income arrived at by this approach is the **gross national product (GNP)**.

Gross national expenditure and gross national product are two different ways of looking at

one magnitude: the market value of the nation's output.

GNE and GNP are conceptually identical and differ in practice only because of errors of measurement. Both approaches are of interest, however, because each gives a different and useful breakdown of national income. Also, having two independent ways of measuring the same thing provides a useful check on the statistical procedures and on unavoidable measurement errors.[3]

National income accounting is the set of rules and techniques for measuring the total flow of output (goods and services) produced and the total flow of incomes generated by this production. Gross national expenditure is the market value of all the production in the economy during any one year, while gross national product is the value of all the claims generated by that production.

[3] The use of both terms GNE *and* GNP reflects international convention. In the United States, however, the convention is to reconcile the two approaches in one table, and refer to the common sum as GNP. (See, for example, recent issues of the *Economic Report of the President* or the *Survey of Current Business.*) We retain the separate terms GNE and GNP to emphasize that the two sums are arrived at independently, using the expenditure and income approaches respectively, and *then* reconciled. The reader should be aware, however, that only the term GNP appears in the American accounts.

The conventions of double-entry bookkeeping require that all value produced must be accounted for by a claim someone has to that value.

Thus it is merely a matter of accounting convention that gross national expenditure and gross national product should be equal. (Measured values differ only to the extent that measurement errors arise. Any discrepancy arising from such errors is then reconciled so that one common total is given as *the* measure of national income.) Because both concepts have the same total value, the terms *gross national expenditure* and *gross national product* are often used interchangeably.

The Expenditure Approach AE

The expenditure approach calculates GNE as the market value of final output by adding up the expenditures made to purchase final output. Total expenditure on final output is the sum of four broad categories of expenditure: consumption, investment, government, and net exports.

Consumption Expenditure

Consumption expenditure includes expenditure on all goods and services produced and sold to households during the year (with the exception of residential housing which is counted as investment). It includes services such as haircuts, medical care, and legal advice; nondurable goods such as fresh meat, cut flowers, and fresh vegetables; and durables such as cars, television sets, and air conditioners. We denote actual, that is, measured, consumption expenditure by the symbol C^a.

Investment Expenditure

Investment expenditure is expenditure on the production of goods not for present consumption, including inventories, capital goods such as plant and equipment, and residential housing. Such goods are called **investment goods**.

Inventories. Almost all firms hold stocks of their inputs and their own outputs. These stocks are called

inventories. Inventories of inputs and unfinished materials allow production to continue at the desired pace in spite of short-term fluctuations in the deliveries of inputs bought from other firms. Inventories of outputs allow firms to meet orders in spite of temporary fluctuations in the rate of output or sales.

Inventories are an important part of the productive process. They require an investment of the firm's money, since the firm has paid for but not yet sold the goods. An accumulation of inventories counts as current investment because it represents goods produced, but not used for current consumption. A drawing down, often called a *decumulation*, counts as disinvestment because it represents a reduction in the stock of finished goods available to be sold.

Additions to inventories are a part of the economy's final production of investment goods. These are valued in the national income accounts at market value, which includes the wages and other costs the firm incurred in producing the goods and the profit the firm will make when the inventories are sold. Thus, in the case of inventories of a firm's own output, the expenditure approach measures what will have to be spent to purchase them when they are sold rather than what has actually been spent on them at the moment.

Plant and equipment. All production uses capital goods: manufactured aids to production such as tools, machines, and factory buildings. The economy's total quantity of capital goods is called the **capital stock**. Creating new capital goods is an act of investment and is called fixed business investment, or **fixed investment** for short.

Residential housing. A house is a durable asset that yields its utility over a long life. For this reason, housing construction is counted as investment expenditure rather than as consumption expenditure. This is done by assuming that the investment is made by the firm that builds the house and that the sale to a user is a mere transfer of ownership that is not a part of national income.

Gross versus net investment. The total investment that occurs in the economy is called **gross investment**. Gross investment is divided into two parts, replacement investment and net investment. **Replacement investment** is the amount of investment that just maintains the existing capital stock intact; it is called the **capital consumption allowance** or simply **depreciation**. Gross investment minus replacement investment is **net investment**. Positive net investment increases the economy's total stock of capital, while replacement investment keeps the existing stock intact by replacing what has been used up.

All of gross investment is included in the calculation of national income. This is because all investment goods are part of the nation's total output and their production creates income (and employment) whether the goods produced are a part of net investment or are merely replacement investment. Actual, that is, measured, total investment expenditure is denoted by the symbol I^a.

Government Expenditure on Goods and Services

When governments provide goods and services that households want, such as roads and air traffic control, it is obvious that they are adding to the sum total of valuable output in the same way as do private firms that produce the trucks and airplanes that use the roads and air lanes. With other government activities, the case may not seem so clear. Should expenditures by the federal government to send a rocket to Jupiter or to pay a civil servant to refile papers from a now defunct department be regarded as contributions to national income? Some people believe that many (or even most) activities "up in Washington" or "down at City Hall" are wasteful, if not downright harmful. Others believe that it is governments, not private firms, that produce many of the important things of life, such as education and pollution control.

National income statisticians do not speculate about which government expenditures are or are not worthwhile. Instead, they include all government expenditures on goods and services as part of national income. (Government expenditure on investment goods is included as government rather than investment expenditure.) Just as the national product includes, without distinction, the output of both gin and Bibles, it also includes bombers and the upkeep of parks, along with the services of CIA agents, senators, and even IRS investigators. Actual government expenditure on goods and services is denoted by the symbol G^a.

Government output is typically valued at cost rather than market value. In many cases there is really no choice. What, for example, is the market value of the services of a court of law? No one knows. But we do know what it costs the government to provide these services, so we value them at their cost of production.

Although valuing at cost is the only possible thing to do with many government activities, it does have one curious consequence. If, due to a productivity increase, one civil servant now does what two used to do, and the displaced worker shifts to the private sector, the government's contribution to national income will register a decline. On the other hand, if two now do what one used to do, the government's contribution will rise. Both changes could occur even though what the government actually does is unchanged. This is an inevitable but curious consequence of measuring the value of the government's output by the cost of the factors, mainly labor, used to produce it.

There is an important exception to the rule that all government expenditure is included in national income. **Transfer payments**, or government payments that are not made in return for factor services, do not lead directly to any increase in output, and they are not included in national income. For example, when a government agency makes welfare payments to a retired person, the government does not receive, nor does it expect to receive, any marketable services from the retiree in return for the welfare payments. The payment itself adds neither to employment of factors nor to total output. The major transfer payments are unemployment insurance, welfare payments, and interest on the national debt (which transfers income from taxpayers to holders of government bonds).

Thus when we refer to government expenditure as part of national income or use the symbol G^a, we include all government expenditure on currently produced goods and services and we *exclude* all government transfer payments. (The term government *outlays* might be used to describe all government spending, including transfer payments.)

Net Exports

The fourth category of aggregate expenditure, and one that is increasingly important to the American economy, arises from foreign trade. How do imports and exports influence the national income?

Imports. One country's national income is the total value of final commodities produced in that country. If your cousin spends $8,000 on a car made in Japan, only a small part of that value will represent expenditure on American production. Some of it goes for the services of the American dealers and transportation; the rest is the output of Japanese firms and expenditure on Japanese products. If you take your next vacation in Italy, much of your expenditure will be on goods and services produced by Italians and thus will contribute to Italian GNP.

Similarly, when an American firm makes an investment expenditure on an American-produced machine tool made partly with imported raw materials, only part of the expenditure is on American production. The rest is expenditure on the production of the countries supplying the raw materials. The same is also true for government expenditure on such things as roads and dams; some of the expenditure is for imported materials, and only part of it for domestically produced goods and services.

Consumption, investment, and government expenditures all have an import content. To arrive at total expenditure on American products, we need to subtract from total American expenditure any expenditure on imports. Actual expenditure on imports is given the symbol M^a.

Exports. If American firms sell goods to German households, the goods are a part of German consumption expenditure, but also constitute expenditure on American output. Indeed, all goods and services produced in the United States and sold to foreigners must be counted as part of American production and income; they create incomes for the Americans who produce them. To arrive at the total value of expenditure on American national product, it is necessary to add in the value of American exports. Actual exports are denoted by the symbol X^a.

It is customary to group actual imports and actual exports together as **net exports**. Net exports are defined as exports minus imports $(X^a - M^a)$. The value of net exports is usually small in relation to the total value of either X^a or M^a.

Gross National Expenditure

Gross national expenditure is the sum of the above four categories of expenditure.

The expenditure approach to measuring national income yields GNE: the sum of consumption, investment, government, and net exports expenditures.

Table 25-3 shows American national income for 1985 calculated according to the expenditure approach.

The Income Approach

The income approach calculates the value of total incomes generated in the process of production. The measure of national income obtained by the income approach is called gross national product (GNP).

The production of the nation's output generates income. Labor must be employed, land rented, and capital used. The calculation of GNP involves adding up factor payments and other claims on the value of output until all of it is accounted for. As we have already seen, because all value produced must be owned by someone, the value of production must equal the value of income claims generated by that production.

Factor Payments

National income accountants distinguish four main components of factor incomes: wages, rent, interest, and profits.[4]

Wages. Wages and salaries (which national income accountants call *compensation to employees,* but which is usually just called *wages*) are the payment for the services of labor. Wages include take-home pay, taxes withheld, social security, and pension fund contri-

---

[4] The concepts of wages, rent, interest, and profits used in macroeconomics do not correspond exactly to the concepts of the same names used in microeconomics, but the details of the differences need not detain us.

TABLE 25-3   Components of GNE, 1985

Expenditure category	Billions of dollars	Percentage of GNE
Consumption	2601	65
Government	815	20
Investment	661	17
Net exports	−79	−2
	3998	100

Source: Economic Report of the President, 1986.

GNE is measured by the expenditure approach; in 1985 it was $3,998 billion. Consumption was by far the largest expenditure category, equal to almost two-thirds of GNE. In 1985 net exports were negative so that, in fact, the other three expenditure categories added up to slightly *more* than GNE. (Note: The sum $C + I + G + (X - M)$ is referred to as GNP in official American statistics; see footnote 3 on page 486.)

butions and other fringe benefits. In total, wages represent that part of the value of production attributable to labor.

Rent.   Rent is the payment for the services of land and other factors that are rented. It includes payments for rented housing and imputed rent for the use of owner-occupied housing. For the purposes of national income accounting, homeowners are viewed as renting accommodation from themselves. This allows national income measures to reflect the value of all housing services used, whether or not the housing is owned by its user.

Interest.   Interest includes interest earned on bank deposits, interest earned on loans to firms, and miscellaneous other investment income. Hence it is one of the payments for the services of capital.

Profits.   Some profits are paid out as **dividends** to owners of firms; the rest are retained for use by firms. The former are called **distributed profits**, and the latter **undistributed profits** or **retained earnings**. Both distributed and undistributed profits are included in the calculation of GNP. For accounting purposes, total profits are reported in two separate categories—corporation profits and incomes of unincorporated businesses (mainly small businesses, farmers, partnerships, and professionals).

Net national income at factor cost.   The sum of the four components of factor incomes—wages, rent, interest, and profits—is called **net national income (NNI) at factor cost**.

Indirect Taxes Net of Subsidies

When using the income approach, we must distinguish between national income valued *at factor cost* and national income valued *at market prices*. The difference between the two is created by the effects of indirect taxes and subsidies. An important claim on the market value of output arises out of indirect taxes—taxes on the production and sale of goods and services.

If, for example, a good's value of $10 includes $1 of business excise taxes, only $9 is available as income to factors of production. One dollar's worth of market value represents the government's claim on that value. When adding up income claims to determine GNP, it is therefore necessary to add in that part of the total market value of output which is the government's claim arising out of its taxes on goods and services.

It is also necessary to subtract government subsidies on goods and services, since these allow incomes to *exceed* the market value of output. Suppose, for example, that a single proprietor receives a $5,000 subsidy from the government, and as a result his total income is $25,000. To get the market value of his output from the income side, we must take his income and subtract the government subsidy from it.

Net national product at market prices.   Adding indirect taxes to the four components of factor incomes and subtracting subsidies gives **net national product (NNP) at market prices**.

Net national product at market prices equals the sum of wages, rent, interest, profits, and indirect taxes net of subsidies.

Depreciation

Another component in the income approach arises from the distinction between net and gross investment. One claim on the value of final output is depreciation, or capital consumption allowance. This is the value of final output that embodies capital used up in the process of its production. It is part of gross profits but, being that part needed to compensate for capital used up in the process of production, it is not part of net profits. Hence it is not income earned by any factor of production. Instead it is value that must be reinvested just to maintain the existing stock of capital equipment.

Gross National Product

Adding depreciation to net national product at market prices gives **gross national product at market prices**.

The income approach measures GNP as the sum of the factor incomes generated in the process of producing final output *plus* indirect taxes net of subsidies *plus* depreciation.

The various components of GNP in the American economy in 1985 are shown in Table 25-4.

The Output Approach

There is a third way in which national income is measured: by adding up the contributions to final output of every firm in the economy. This third measure of national income, called *gross domestic product* (GDP), is then reconciled with the national income accounts.

Total output is the sum of all the final products that are produced over some period, usually a year. If every firm produced only final output, the output approach would be easy to apply: Statisticians would just add up the gross values of the outputs of all firms. This simple approach will not do because, as we have already noted, the production of commodities occurs in stages with some firms specializing in the production of intermediate products. Stages of production and the consequent interfirm sales of intermediate products make it difficult to measure national income from production data, since summing the gross value of all firms' outputs involves what we have called *double counting*. (Multiple counting would be a better term, since the same output would

TABLE 25-4 Components of GNP, 1985

Income component	Billions of dollars	Percent of GNE
Compensation to employees	2368	59
Business profits	535	13
Capital consumption allowance	437	11
Indirect taxes net of subsidies	344	9
Interest	312	8
Rental income	8	—
Statistical discrepancy	−6	—
Total	3998	100

Source: Economic Report of the President, 1986.

GNP is measured by the income, or factor payments approach; in 1985 it was $3,998 billion. The largest category, equal to almost 60 percent of GNP, was compensation to employees, which includes wages and salaries plus employers' contributions to unemployment insurance, pensions, and other similar schemes. Business profits include profits of incorporated and unincorporated business. The capital consumption allowance is that part of the earning of business sufficient to replace capital worn out during the year.

be counted every time it is sold from one firm to another.)

The problem of double counting is avoided, as we have already observed, by treating each firm's output as what it adds by its own activities to the value of final output. For example, the *value added* by a steel plant is the gross value of its output of steel minus the value of the ore that it buys from the mining company and the values of all other inputs, such as electricity and fuel oil, that it buys from other firms.

The issue of double counting and the concept of value added are further explored in Box 25-3.

Gross Domestic Product

Table 25-5 on page 493 shows the composition of American GDP by industry for 1984. It also shows the reconciliation of GDP with GNP. GDP measures the output *located in* the United States. GNP (and GNE) measure output *owned by* Americans, that is, income accruing to Americans.

The difference between GDP and GNP arises from two sources. First, some factors of production

BOX 25-3

Value Added Through Stages of Production

Because the output of one firm often becomes the input of other firms, the total value of goods sold by all firms greatly exceeds the value of the output of final products. This general principle is illustrated by a simple example in which firm R starts from scratch and produces goods (raw materials) valued at $100; the firm's value added is $100. Firm I purchases raw materials valued at $100 and produces semi-manufactured goods that it sells for $130. Its value added is $30 because the value of the goods is increased

by $30 as a result of the firm's activities. Firm F purchases the semi-manufactured goods for $130, works them into a finished state, and sells the final products for $180. Firm F's value added is $50. The value of the final goods, $180, is found either by counting only the sales of firm F or by taking the sum of the values added by each firm. This value is much smaller than the $410 that we would obtain if we merely added up the market value of the commodities sold by each firm.

	Transactions at three different stages of production			
	Firm R	Firm I	Firm F	All firms
A. Purchases from other firms	$ 0	$100	$130	$230 Total interfirm sales
B. Purchases of factors of production (wages, rent, interest, profits)	100	30	50	180 Total value added
A + B = value of product	$100	$130	$180	$410 Total value of all sales

located in the United States are owned by foreigners, and hence the income owned by those factors does not go to Americans. Second, some Americans own factors of production located in other countries, and hence they earn income not included in GDP. The United States has long been a net creditor internationally; the payment of factor income to foreigners has typically fallen short of American receipts of factor income received from abroad. However, in recent years the United States has experienced large capital inflows, so that the net receipts from abroad have fallen markedly.

Other Income Concepts

Gross national income, however measured, is the most comprehensive income concept. The next most comprehensive measure is net national product (NNP). As we saw in building up the income approaches, this is GNP minus the capital consumption allowance. NNP is thus a measure of the net output of the economy after deducting from gross output

an amount sufficient to maintain intact the existing stock of capital. It is the maximum amount that could be consumed without actually running down the economy's capital stock.

Personal income is income earned by or paid to individuals before allowance for personal income taxes. Some personal income goes for taxes, some for saving, and the rest for consumption. A number of adjustments to NNP are required to arrive at personal income. The most important are: (1) subtracting from NNP indirect taxes (net of subsidies) which are that part of the market value of output that goes directly to governments (this, as we have seen, gives net national income at factor cost), (2) subtracting from NNP business earnings retained by corporations, (3) subtracting from NNP income taxes paid by business, and (4) adding to NNP transfer payments to households. The first three are parts of the value of output not paid to households; the fourth is paid to households and thus is income that households have available to spend or to save, even though the payments are not part of GNP.

Disposable income is the amount of current

TABLE 25-5   Gross Domestic Product, 1985

	Billions of dollars	Percent of GDP
Value added by sector		
Agriculture, forestry, and fisheries	91.5	2.3
Mining	122.8	3.1
Manufacturing	795.8	20.1
Construction	182.2	4.5
Transportation and public utilities	374.4	9.5
Retail and wholesale trade	652.5	16.5
Financial insurance and real estate	626.6	15.7
Services	639.4	16.2
Government and government enterprises	477.4	12.1
Statistical discrepancy	−5.5	
GDP	3,957.0	100.0
Investment income received from nonresidents less investment income paid to nonresidents	41.2	
GNP	$3,998.1	

Source: Survey of Current Business, July 1986.

GDP measures total output, at factor cost, produced in the United States by summing the value added of each industry. As can be seen, manufacturing and trade (retail and wholesale) are major components of GDP, contributing 20 percent and 16 percent respectively. To reconcile GDP with the national income accounts; that is, to reconcile output produced in the United States with output owned by Americans (and hence income earned by Americans), it is necessary to add investment income received from nonresidents and subtract investment income paid to nonresidents. The United States has been a net creditor because of its long record of investing abroad, that is, income received from nonresidents has been larger than income paid to nonresidents.

income that households have to spend and to save; it is personal income minus personal income taxes.

Disposable income is GNP *minus* any part of it that is not actually paid to households *minus* personal income taxes paid by households *plus* transfer payments received by households.

The relations among GNP, NNP, personal income, and disposable income are shown in Table 25-6.

Interpreting National Income Measures

The information provided by measures of national income is useful, but unless carefully interpreted it

can also be misleading. Furthermore, each of the specialized measures gives different information. Thus each may be the best statistic for studying a particular range of problems.

Money values and real values.   We have seen that national income can be valued in current dollars to yield nominal income or constant dollars to yield real income. When studying the effect of inflation on national income, we need to look at nominal income. When studying changes in the economy's quantity of output, we need to look at real income.

Total values and per capita values.   The rise in real GNP during this century has had two main causes: an increase in the amounts of land, labor, and capital used in production and an increase in output per unit

TABLE 25-6   Various National Income Measures, 1985

	Billions of dollars[a]
A. GNP at market prices	$3,998
Less: capital consumption allowance	−436
B. NNP (at market prices)	3,552
Less: indirect taxes net of subsidies	−337
C. NNI at factor cost	3,215
Less: retained earnings and business taxes	−389
Plus: government transfer payments to households	+466
D. Personal income	3,294
Less: personal income taxes	−493
E. Disposable income	2,801

[a] Figures do not match because of rounding.

Each of the five related national income measures focuses on a different aspect of the national output. GNP measures the market value of total output. NNP measures the net value of output after an allowance for maintaining the capital stock. NNI at factor cost converts market price values to factor costs by adjusting for government indirect taxes net of subsidies. Personal income measures income earned or received by persons before personal income taxes. Disposable income measures after-tax income of persons; it is the amount they have available to spend or to save.

FIGURE 25-1   Disposable Income Per Capita in the United States, in Constant (1982) Dollars, 1929–1985

Disposable income per capita in constant dollars provides a measure of the real purchasing power available to the average American. Disposable income per capita fell during the early 1930s and late 1940s, but it has risen in every decade since the 1930s, including the 1970s. It underestimates the average living standard because it leaves out the contribution of government expenditure to such items as police, fire, justice, defense, and recreation. (*Source: Economic Report of the President*, various years.)

of input. In other words, more inputs have been used, and each input has become more productive. For some purposes, such as assessing a country's potential military strength or the total size of its market, we want to measure total output. For other purposes, such as studying changes in living standards, we require per capita measures, which are obtained by dividing a total measure such as GNP by the population.

There are many useful per capita measures. GNP divided by the total population gives a measure of how much GNP there is on average for each person in the country; this is called **per capita GNP**. GNP divided by the number of persons employed tells us the average output per employed worker. GNP divided by the total number of hours worked measures output per hour of labor input. A widely used measure of the purchasing power of the average person

is disposable income per capita in constant dollars. This measure is shown in Figure 25-1.

Omissions from Measured National Income

Several types of economic activity are not included in GNP and therefore are excluded from other measures based on GNP. The importance of these omissions depends on the purpose for which the data are to be used. Box 25-4 takes up some other aspects of national income accounting.

Illegal activities. GNP does not measure illegal activities, even though many of them are ordinary business activities that produce goods and services sold on the market and that generate factor incomes. The liquor industry during Prohibition (1919 to

BOX 25-4

The Significance of Arbitrary Decisions

National income accounting uses many arbitrary decisions. Goods that are finished and held in inventories are valued at market value, thereby anticipating their sale even though the actual sales price may not be known. In the case of a Ford in a dealer's showroom, this practice may be justified because the *value* of this Ford is perhaps virtually the same as that of an identical Ford that has just been sold to a customer. But what is the correct market value of a half-finished house or an unfinished novel? Accountants arbitrarily treat goods in process at cost (rather than at market value) if the goods are being made by business firms. They ignore completely the value of the novel-in-progress. While these decisions are arbitrary, so would any others be. Clearly, practical people must arrive at some compromise between consistent definitions and measurable magnitudes.

The definition of final goods provides further examples. Business investment expenditures are treated as final products, as are all government purchases. Intermediate goods purchased by business for further processing are not treated as final products. Thus, when a firm buys a machine or a truck, the purchase is treated as a final good; when it buys a ton of steel, the steel is treated as a raw material that will be used as an input into the firm's production process. But if the steel sits in inventory, it is regarded as a business investment and thus *is* a final good.

Such arbitrary decisions surely affect the size of measured GNP. Does it matter? The surprising answer, for many purposes, is no. In any case, it is wrong to believe that just because a statistical measure falls short of perfection (as all statistical measures do), it is useless. Crude measures often give estimates to the right order of magnitude, and substantial improvements in sophistication may make only second-order improvements in these estimates.

In the third century B.C., for example, the Alexandrian astronomer Eratosthenes measured the angle of the sun at Alexandria at the moment it was directly overhead 500 miles south at Aswan, and he used this angle to calculate the circumference of the earth to within 15 percent of the distance as measured today by the most advanced measuring devices. For the knowledge he wanted—the approximate size of the earth—his measurement was satisfactory. To launch a modern earth satellite, it would have been disastrously inadequate.

Absolute figures mean something in general terms, although they cannot be taken seriously to the last dollar. In 1982 GNP was measured as $3,058 billion. It is certain that the market value of all production in the United States in that year was not $100 billion nor $10,000 billion nor $500 billion, but it might well have been $3,200 billion or $2,900 billion had different measures been defined with different arbitrary decisions built in.

International and intertemporal comparisons, though tricky, may be meaningful when they are based on measures all of which contain roughly the same arbitrary decisions. American per capita GNP is a little less than three times the Spanish and 30 percent higher than the Japanese per capita GNPs. Other measures might differ, but it is unlikely that any measure would reveal that either the Spanish or the Japanese per capita production was higher than the per capita production in the United States. But the statistics also show that per capita GNP was 4 percent higher in the United States than in Sweden, a difference too small to have much meaning. American output grew at 2.8 percent per year for the 30 years following World War II; it is unlikely that another measure of output would have indicated a 6 percent increase. Further, the Japanese output grew at about 9 percent per year over the same period. It is inconceivable that another measure would change the conclusion that Japanese national output rose faster than American national output in recent decades.

1933) is an important example because it accounted for a significant part of the nation's total economic activity. Today the same is true of many forms of illegal gambling, prostitution, and the drug trade. To gain an accurate measure of the *total* demand for factors of production in the economy or of *total* marketable output, we should include these activities— whether or not we as individuals approve of particular products.[5]

The omission of illegal activities is no trivial matter. The drug trade alone is a multibillion dollar business. No one knows the exact value of its output, but a typical estimate runs around 1.5 percent of GNP, which would amount to $60 billion in 1986.

Unreported activities.   An important omission from the measured GNP is the so-called underground economy. The transactions in the underground economy are perfectly legal in themselves. The only illegal thing about them is that they are not reported for tax purposes. For example, a carpenter repairs a leak in your roof and takes payment in cash or in kind in order to avoid tax. Because such transactions go unreported, they are omitted from GNP.

There are many reasons for the growth of the underground economy. Taxes, safety regulations, minimum wage laws, anti-discrimination regulations, and social security payments may all be avoided. Its growth is also facilitated by the rising importance of services in the nation's total output. It is much easier for a carpenter to pass unnoticed by government authorities than it is for a manufacturing establishment.

Estimates of the value of income earned in the American underground economy run from 5 to 15 percent of GNP. In other countries the figures are much higher. The Italian underground economy, for example, has been estimated at close to 25 percent of that country's total GNP!

Nonmarketed activities.   If a homeowner hires a firm to do some landscaping, the value of the land-

scaping enters into GNP; if the homeowner does the landscaping herself, the value of the landscaping is omitted from GNP. Such omissions also include, for example, the services of homemakers, any do-it-yourself activity, and voluntary work such as canvassing for a political party, helping to run a volunteer day-care center, or leading a Boy Scout troop.

In most advanced industrial economies the nonmarket sector is relatively small. The omissions become serious, however, when GNP or disposable income figures are used to compare living standards in very different economies. Generally, the nonmarket sector of the economy is larger in rural than in urban settings and in less developed than in more developed economies. Be a little cautious, then, in interpreting data from a country with a very different climate and culture. When you hear that the per capita GNP of Nigeria is about $900 per year. you should not imagine living in Buffalo on that income.

Other omitted factors.   Many factors that contribute to human welfare are not included in GNP. Leisure is one. In fact, although a shorter work week may make people happier, it will tend to reduce measured GNP.

Nor does GNP allow for the capacity of different goods to provide different satisfactions. A million dollars spent on a bomber or a missile makes the same addition to GNP as a million dollars spent on a school or on candy bars—expenditures that may produce very different amounts of consumer satisfaction.

Do the Omissions Matter?

If we wish to measure the flow of goods and services through the market sector of the economy or to account for changes in the opportunities for employment for those households who sell their labor services in the market, most of these omissions will have negligible effects on our results. If, however, we wish to measure the overall flow of goods and services available to satisfy people's wants, whatever the source of the goods and services, then the omissions are undesirable and potentially serious.

---

[5] Some of them do get included because people sometimes report their earnings from illicit activities as part of their earnings from legal activities in order to avoid the fate of Al Capone, a famous Chicago gangster in the 1930s. He, having avoided conviction on many counts, was finally caught for tax evasion.

Is There a Best Measure?

To ask which is *the* best income measure is something like asking which is *the* best carpenter's tool. The answer is that it all depends on the job to be done. Which measure is used will depend on the problem at hand, and solving some problems may require information provided by several different measures or information not provided by any conventional measures. If we wish to predict households' consumption behavior, disposable income may be what we need. If we wish to account for changes in employment, constant dollar GNP is wanted. For an overall measure of economic welfare, we may need to supplement or modify conventional measures of national income, none of which measure *the quality of life*. To the extent that material output is purchased at the expense of overcrowded cities and highways, polluted environments, defaced countrysides, maimed accident victims, longer waits for public services, and a more complex life that entails a frenetic struggle to be happy, conventional measures of national income include only part of the things that contribute to human well-being.[6]

Even if we do use some new or modified measures for some purposes, we are unlikely to discard GNP (and its offspring) entirely. Economists and politicians who are interested in changes in market activity and in employment opportunities for factors of production will continue to use GNP and GDP as the measures that come closest to telling them what they need to know.

[6] Concepts that come closer to measuring economic welfare than GNP have been developed. One was worked out by Professors William Nordhaus and James Tobin. It tries to measure consumption of things that provide utility to households rather than total production; it gives value to such nonmarketed activities as leisure and makes subtractions for such "disutilities" as pollution and congestion.

Summary

1. The Consumer Price Index (CPI) is a price index constructed to reflect changes in the prices of a bundle of goods consumed by a representative household. Changes in it are taken as a measure of changes in the "cost of living."
2. Real income is a measure of total output calculated to reflect changes in quantity produced. Nominal income is a measure of total output calculated to reflect changes in both prices and quantities. Any change in nominal income can be split into a change in real income and a change due to prices. Comparing nominal and real income yields the implicit deflator.
3. Gross national expenditure (GNE) is the total market value of goods and services produced in the economy during a year. Gross national product (GNP) is the total of all income claims generated over the same period of time. By standard accounting conventions, gross national product and gross national expenditure are defined to be equal.
4. Using the expenditure approach to national income accounting, GNE = $C^a + I^a + G^a + (X^a - M^a)$. C^a is consumption expenditures of households. I^a is investment in plant and equipment, residential construction, and inventory accumulation. Gross investment can be split into replacement investment (necessary to keep the stock of capital intact) and net investment (net additions to the stock of

capital). G^a is government expenditures except transfer payments. $(X^a - M^a)$ is net exports, or exports minus imports; it will be negative if imports exceed exports.

5. The income approach measures total GNP according to who has a claim to the value arising from the production and sale of commodities. Wages, rent, interest, profits, depreciation (or capital consumption allowance), and indirect taxes net of subsidies are the major categories.

6. Gross domestic product (GDP) measures production located in the United States, and GNP measures income owned by Americans. The difference is due to income from net foreign investment.

7. Several related, but different income measures are used in addition to the GNP. Net national product (NNP) measures total output after deducting the capital consumption allowance. Personal income is income actually earned by households before any allowance for personal taxes. Disposable income is the amount actually available to households to spend or to save, that is, income minus taxes.

8. GNP and related measures of national income must be interpreted with their limitations in mind. GNP excludes production resulting from activities that are illegal, take place in the underground economy, or do not pass through markets. Moreover, GNP does not measure everything that contributes to human welfare.

9. Notwithstanding its limitations, GNP remains a useful measure for estimating the total economic activity that passes through the market and for accounting for changes in the employment opportunities that face households who sell their labor services on the open market.

Topics for Review

Index numbers and the Consumer Price Index (CPI)
Real and nominal national income
Implicit deflator
Final goods, intermediate goods, and value added
Expenditure, income, and output approaches to measuring national income
Gross national product (GNP) and gross national expenditure (GNE)
National income measured at factor cost and at market prices
Gross domestic product (GDP)
Net national income (NNI), net national product (NNP), personal income, and disposable income
Omissions from measured income

Discussion Questions

1. If Canada and the United States were to join together as a single country, what would be the effect on their total GNP (assuming that output in each country is unaffected)? Would any of the components in their GNPs change significantly?

2. "Every time you rent a U-haul, brick in a patio, grow a vegetable,

fix your own car, photocopy an article, join a food co-op, develop your own film, sew a dress, avoid purchasing a convenience food, stew fruit, or raise a child, you are committing a productive act, even though these activities are not reflected in the gross national product." To what extent are each of these things "productive acts"? Are any of them included in GNP? Where they are excluded, does the exclusion matter?

3. In measuring American GNE, which of the following expenditures are included? Why?
   a. Expenditures on automobiles by consumers and by firms
   b. Expenditures on food and lodging by tourists and by business people on expense accounts
   c. Expenditures on new machinery and equipment by American firms
   d. The purchase of one corporation by another corporation
   e. Increases in business inventories, decreases in business inventories

4. What would be the effect of the following events on the measured value of America's real GNP. Speculate on the effects of each event on the true well-being of the American people.
   a. Destruction of a thousand homes by flood water
   b. Passage of a constitutional amendment making abortion illegal
   c. Complete cessation of all imports from South Africa
   d. Outbreak of a new Arab-Israeli war in which American troops became as heavily involved as they were in Vietnam

5. In the United States a Social Security Administration study, using 1972 data, found the "average American housewife's value" to be $4,705. It arrived at this total by adding up the hours she spent cooking multiplied by a cook's wage, the hours spent with her children multiplied by a babysitter's wage, and so on. Should the time a parent spends taking children to a concert be included? Are dollar amounts assigned to such activities a satisfactory proxy for market value of production? For what, if any, purposes would such values be excluded from or included in national income?

6. Use the table on the endpaper at the back of this book to calculate the percentage increase over the most recent two decades of each of the following magnitudes. Can you account for the relative size of these changes?
   a. GNP in current dollars
   b. GNP in constant dollars
   c. Disposable income in constant dollars
   d. Disposable income per capita in constant dollars

7. Consider the effect on measured GNP and on economic well-being of each of the following.
   a. Reduction in the standard work week from 40 hours to 30 hours
   b. Hiring of all welfare recipients as government employees
   c. Increase in the salaries of priests and ministers as a result of increased contributions of churchgoers

8. A recent newspaper article reported that Switzerland was considered to be the "best" place in the world to live. In view of the fact that Switzerland does not have the highest per capita income in the world, how can it be ranked the "best"?

26

National Income and Aggregate Demand

Chapter 24 presented an overview of aggregate demand and aggregate supply. We now begin more detailed study of how these forces influence output and prices.

The Keynesian *SRAS* Curve

For the next two chapters we are going to concentrate on the influence of aggregate demand. Ultimately, we want to know what causes national income and the price level to change at the same time. But because it is easier to deal with things one at a time, we will first look at the forces that determine national income, and hence determine employment and unemployment, when the price level is treated as constant. Then in Chapters 27 and 28 we will see what happens when the price level also varies.

In this chapter we consider an economy whose national income is varying over a range substantially below potential income. Furthermore, we use an extreme version of the *SRAS* curve that is horizontal over that range. This curve is called the **Keynesian short-run aggregate supply curve,** after the English economist John Maynard Keynes, who, in his famous book *The General Theory of Employment, Interest and Money* (1936), pioneered the study of the behavior of economies under conditions of high unemployment.

The behavior that gives rise to the Keynesian *SRAS* curve can be described as follows. When real national income is below potential national income, individual firms are operating at less than normal capacity output. Firms respond to cyclical declines in demand by holding their prices constant at the level that would maximize profits if production were at normal capacity. They then respond to demand variations below that capacity by altering output. In other words, they will supply whatever they can sell at their existing prices as long as they are producing below their normal capacity. This means that the firms have horizontal supply curves and that their output is *demand determined*.[1]

Under these circumstances, the whole economy has a horizontal aggregate supply curve, indicating that any output up to potential output

---

[1] The evidence is strong that firms, particularly in the manufacturing sector, do behave like this in the short run. One possible explanation is that changing prices frequently is too costly, so firms set the best possible (profit-maximizing) prices when output is at normal capacity and then do not change prices in the face of normal cyclical fluctuations in demand. This is discussed further in Chapter 15.

will be supplied at the going price level. The amount that is actually produced is then determined by the position of the aggregate demand curve. Thus we say that real national income is demand determined.

If demand rises enough so that firms are trying to squeeze more than normal output out of their plants, their costs will rise and so will their prices. Thus the horizontal Keynesian *SRAS* curve applies only to national incomes below potential income.

Figure 26-1 shows a Keynesian *SRAS* curve. The curve is horizontal at the current price level of P_0. Given this horizontal *SRAS* curve, income is determined by the position of the aggregate demand curve. Shifts in the *AD* curve will cause equilibrium income to change.

Given a Keynesian *SRAS* curve, the questions of why national income is what it is and why it changes boil down to the questions of why the *AD* curve is where it is and why it shifts.

To answer these questions we must first look at expenditure and distinguish between desired and actual expenditure.

Desired Expenditure

In the last chapter we discussed how national income statisticians measure gross national expenditure and its components: consumption, C^a; investment, I^a; government, G^a; and net exports, $(X^a - M^a)$.

In this chapter we are concerned with a different concept. It is variously called *desired, planned,* or *intended expenditure*. Of course, everybody would like to spend virtually unlimited amounts if only they had the money. Desired expenditure does not refer, however, to what people would like to do under imaginary circumstances. It refers instead to what people, given the resources at their command, want to spend. The *actual* values of the various categories of expenditure are indicated by C^a, I^a, G^a, and $(X^a - M^a)$. We use the same letters without the superscript *a* to indicate the *desired* expenditure in the same categories: C, I, G, and $(X - M)$.

Everyone with money to spend makes expenditure decisions. Fortunately, it is unnecessary for our purpose to look at each of the millions of such individual decisions. Instead it is sufficient to place decision makers in four main groups: domestic households, firms, governments, and foreign purchasers of domestically produced products. Their actual purchases account for the four main categories of expenditure studied in the previous chapter: consumption, investment, government, and net exports.

Their desired purchases can also be divided in the same fashion: desired consumption, desired investment, desired government expenditure, and desired exports. Allowing for the fact that some of the commodities desired by each group will have an import content, we subtract import expenditure to obtain total desired expenditure on domestically produced goods and services, called **aggregate expenditure**, *AE*:

$$AE = C + I + G + (X - M)$$

Desired expenditure need not equal actual expenditure, either in total or by each individual category.

FIGURE 26-1 Income Determination with a Keynesian *SRAS* Curve

With a Keynesian *SRAS* curve the price level is fixed and real national income is demand determined. With the Keynesian *SRAS* curve any income up to the economy's potential income will be supplied at the current price level of P_0. Thus when the aggregate demand curve is AD_0, equilibrium income is Y_0.

For example, firms may not plan to invest in inventory accumulation this year but may do so unintentionally. If they produce goods to meet estimated sales, but demand is unexpectedly low, the unsold goods that pile up on their shelves are undesired, and unintended, inventory accumulation. In this case actual investment expenditure, I^a, will exceed desired investment expenditure, I.

National income accounts measure *actual expenditures* in each of the four categories: consumption, investment, government, and net exports. National income theory deals with *desired expenditures* in each of these four categories.

To develop a theory of national income determination, we need to know what determines desired aggregate expenditure. First, however, we recall the important distinction between *autonomous* and *induced* expenditure. (The distinction between autonomous and induced variables was first introduced in Chapter 2 on pages 20–21.)

Autonomous and Induced Expenditure

Components of aggregate expenditure that do *not* depend on national income are called autonomous expenditures. Autonomous expenditures can and do change, but such changes do not occur systematically *in response to changes in national income*. Components of aggregate expenditure that *do* change in response to changes in national income are called induced expenditures. As we will see, the induced response of aggregate expenditure to a change in national income plays a key role in the determination of equilibrium national income.

We need to examine the determinants of each of the components of desired aggregate expenditure. In this chapter we focus on desired consumption expenditures. Consumption is the largest single component of actual aggregate expenditure, and, as we will see, desired consumption expenditure provides the single most important link between desired aggregate expenditure and national income. We treat desired investment, government, and net exports expenditures only briefly here, but look at them in more detail later in the book.

Desired Consumption Expenditure

Households can do one of two things with their disposable income: they can spend it on consumption or they can save it. **Saving** is defined as all disposable income that is not consumed. In effect a household has only one decision to make about disposable income. Since by definition there are only two possible uses of disposable income, spending or saving, when the household decides how much to put to one use, it has automatically decided how much will go to the other.

What determines the amount that households decide to spend on goods and services for consumption and the amount they decide to save? The factors that influence this decision are summarized in the consumption function and the saving function.

The Consumption Function

The **consumption function** relates the total desired consumption expenditure of all households in the economy to the factors that determine it. It is, as we shall see, one of the central relations in macroeconomics.

While we are ultimately interested in the relationship between consumption and national income, the underlying behavior of households depends upon the income they actually have to spend—their disposable income. Therefore, we shall start with the relationship between consumption and disposable income and then go on to relate consumption to national income.

Consumption and Disposable Income

One important influence on desired consumption expenditure is household disposable income, represented by Y_d. As disposable income rises, households have more money to spend on consumption—and the evidence is that they do just that. We therefore treat desired consumption expenditure as varying positively with disposable income.

Other factors such as interest rates and inflationary expectations also exert an influence, but we shall neglect them for the moment. The simple theory of consumption focuses on changes in disposable income to explain changes in consumption. We will use the term *consumption function* to describe the relationship between consumption and disposable income. In Chapter 25 we examined the calculation of disposable income; for the purposes of this discussion all we need to know is that disposable income tends to be a relatively constant fraction of national income.

Some consumption expenditure is autonomous, but most is induced; that is, most varies with disposable and hence with national income. A schedule relating disposable income to desired consumption expenditure for a hypothetical economy appears in the first two columns of Table 26-1. In this example autonomous consumption expenditure is $100 billion, whereas induced consumption expenditure is 80 percent of disposable income. In what follows we use this hypothetical example to illustrate the various properties of the consumption function.

Average and marginal propensities to consume.   To discuss the consumption function concisely, economists use two technical expressions.

The **average propensity to consume (*APC*)** is total consumption expenditure divided by total disposable income. The third column of Table 26-1 shows the *APC*s calculated from the data in the table.

The **marginal propensity to consume (*MPC*)** relates the *change* in consumption to the *change* in disposable income that brought it about. *MPC* is the change in disposable income divided into the resulting consumption change, $MPC = \Delta C / \Delta Y_d$ (where the Greek letter Δ, delta, means "a change in"). The last column of Table 26-1 shows the *MPC*s calculated from the data in the table. [34]

The slope of the consumption function.   Figure 26-2(i) shows a graph of the consumption function plotted from the first two columns of Table 26-1. The consumption function has a slope of $\Delta C / \Delta Y_d$ which is, by definition, the marginal propensity to consume. The upward slope of the consumption function shows that *MPC* is positive; increases in income lead to increases in expenditure.

Using the concepts of the average and marginal

TABLE 26-1   The Calculation of Average Propensity to Consume *(APC)* and Marginal Propensity to Consume *(MPC) (billion of dollars)*

Disposable income (Y_d)	Desired consumption (C)	$APC = C/Y_d$	ΔY_d (Change in Y_d)	ΔC (Change in C)	$MPC = \Delta C/\Delta Y_d$
$ 0	$ 100	—			
100	180	1.800	$ 100	$ 80	0.80
400	420	1.050	300	240	0.80
500	500	1.000	100	80	0.80
1,000	900	0.900	500	400	0.80
2,000	1,700	0.850	1,000	800	0.80
3,000	2,500	0.833	1,000	800	0.80
4,000	3,300	0.825	1,000	800	0.80

***APC* measures the proportion of disposable income that households desire to spend on consumption; *MPC* measures the proportion of any *increment* to disposable income that households desire to spend on consumption.** The data are hypothetical. We call the level of income at which desired consumption equals disposable income the break-even level; in this example it is $500 billion. *APC* calculated in the third column exceeds unity, that is, consumption exceeds income, below the break-even level. Above the break-even level *APC* is less than unity and declines steadily as income rises.

The last three columns are set between the lines of the first three columns to indicate that they refer to changes in the levels of income and consumption. *MPC* calculated in the last column is constant at 0.80 at all levels of Y_d. This indicates that in this example $.80 of *every* additional $1.00 of disposable income is spent on consumption and $.20 is used to increase saving.

FIGURE 26-2
The Consumption and Saving Functions

(i) Consumption function

(ii) Saving function

Both consumption and saving rise as disposable income rises. Line C in (i) relates desired consumption expenditure to disposable income using the hypothetical data from Table 26-1. Its slope, $\Delta C/\Delta Y_d$, is the marginal propensity to consume (MPC). The consumption line cuts the 45° line at the break-even level of disposable income, $500 in this case.

Since saving is all disposable income not spent on consumption ($S = Y_d - C$), the relationship between desired saving and disposable income can be deduced from the above. This is done in Table 26-2, and the resulting relationship is shown in (ii) by line S. Its slope, $\Delta S/\Delta Y_d$, is the marginal propensity to save (MPS). The saving line cuts the horizontal axis at the break-even level of income. The vertical distance between C and the 45° line in (i) is by definition the height of S in (ii). That is, any given level of disposable income must be accounted for by the amount consumed plus the amount saved.

propensities to consume, we can summarize the properties of the short-term consumption function:

1. There is a break-even level of income at which APC equals unity. Below this level APC is greater than unity; above it APC is less than unity.
2. MPC is greater than zero but less than unity for all levels of income.

The 45° line. Figure 26-2(i) contains a line that is constructed by connecting all points where desired consumption (measured on the vertical axis) equals disposable income (measured on the horizontal axis). Since both axes are given in the same units, this line

has an upward slope of unity, or (what is the same thing) it forms an angle of 45° with the axes. The line is therefore called the **45° line.**

The 45° line makes a handy reference line. In Figure 26-2(i) it helps locate the break-even level of income at which consumption expenditure equals disposable income. The consumption function cuts the 45° line at the break-even level of income, in this instance $500. (The 45° line is steeper than the consumption function because MPC is less than unity.)

The saving function. Households decide how much to consume and how much to save. As we have said, this is a single decision: how to divide disposable income between consumption and saving. It follows that, once we know the dependence of consumption on disposable income, we also automatically know the dependence of saving on disposable income. (This is illustrated in Table 26-2.)

Two saving concepts are exactly parallel to the consumption concepts of *APC* and *MPC*. The **average propensity to save (APS)** is the proportion of disposable income that households want to save, derived by dividing total desired saving by total disposable income, $APS = S/Y_d$. The **marginal propensity to save (MPS)** relates the *change* in total desired saving to the *change* in disposable income that brought it about, $MPS = \Delta S/\Delta Y_d$.

There is a simple relation between the saving and the consumption propensities. *APC* and *APS* must sum to unity and so must *MPC* and *MPS*. Since income is either spent or saved, it follows that the fractions of incomes consumed and saved must account for all income ($APC + APS = 1$). It also follows that the fraction of any increment to income consumed and saved must account for all of that increment ($MPC + MPS = 1$). [35]

Calculations from Table 26-2 will allow you to confirm these relations in the case of the example given. *MPC* is 0.80 and *MPS* is 0.20 at all levels of income while, for example, at income of $2,000 billion *APC* is 0.85 while *APS* is 0.15.

Figure 26-2(ii) shows the saving schedule given in Table 26-2. At the break-even level of income, where desired consumption equals disposable income, desired saving is zero. The slope of the saving line $\Delta S/\Delta Y_d$ is *MPS*.

Consumption and Wealth

We have seen that disposable income is an important factor in the consumption-saving decision. A second important factor is the real value of each household's wealth. By a household's **wealth** we mean the sum of all the valuable assets it owns. This includes its car, its house and contents, the value of its money in the bank, pension fund, and any stocks, bonds, or other investments that it holds.

Households save in order to add to their wealth. Other things being equal, a rise in wealth tends to reduce the incentive to add further to wealth; that is, it reduces the incentive to save. Obviously, it is the real value of wealth that matters. Should the money value of wealth and the price level change in the same proportion, leaving real wealth unchanged, the household's incentive to save will be unchanged.

A rise in wealth tends to cause a larger fraction of disposable income to be spent on consumption and a smaller fraction to be saved. This shifts the consumption function upward and the saving function downward, as shown in Figure 26-3. A fall in wealth increases the incentive to save in order to restore wealth. This shifts the consumption function downward and the saving function upward.

Individual households experience both expected and unexpected changes in wealth. For example, either planned saving or unplanned bequests will increase wealth. Similarly either planned dissaving or unplanned losses reduce wealth.

Many unexpected changes in wealth cancel out across households and so are unimportant for the macroeconomic consumption function. We will see, however, that inflation can be an important source of unexpected changes in wealth in most households.

Planned increases in wealth as a result of past accumulation in wealth can be important for the whole society and can lead to upward shifts in the

TABLE 26-2	Consumption and Saving Schedules (billions of dollars)	
Disposable income	Desired consumption	Desired saving
0	100	− 100
100	180	− 80
400	420	− 20
500	500	− 0
1,000	900	+ 100
2,000	1,700	+ 300
3,000	2,500	+ 500
4,000	3,300	+ 700

Saving and consumption account for all household disposable income. The first two columns repeat the data from Table 26-1. The third column, desired saving, is disposable income minus desired consumption. Consumption and saving both increase steadily as disposable income rises. In this example the break-even level of disposable income is $500 billion.

FIGURE 26-3
Wealth and the Consumption Function

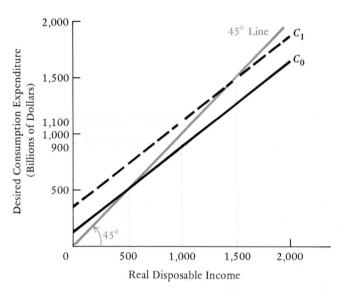

(i) The consumption function shifts up with an increase in wealth

(ii) The saving function shifts down with an increase in wealth

Changes in wealth shift consumption as a function of disposable income. In (i) line C_0 reproduces the consumption function from Figure 26-2(i). An increase in the level of wealth raises desired consumption at each level of disposable income, thus shifting the consumption line up to C_1. In the figure the consumption function shifts up by $200 so that, for example, with disposable income of $1,000, desired consumption *rises* from $900 to $1,100. As a result of the rise in wealth, the break-even level of income rises to $1,500.

The saving function in (ii) shifts down by $200 from S_0 to S_1. Thus, for example, at disposable of $1,000 saving *falls* from plus $100 to minus $100.

macro consumption function as wealth accumulates. This effect operates only slowly since wealth accumulates only slowly.

Because for the moment we are focusing on short-term issues, the consumption function used in the text does not include the effects of changes in wealth.

Consumption and National Income

We have related desired consumption to *disposable* income. For a theory of the determination of national

income, however, we need to know how consumption is related to national income.

The transition from a relation between consumption and disposable income to one between consumption and national income is readily accomplished since disposable income and national income are themselves related to each other.

The relation between disposable income and national income. On pages 492 and 493 we saw the adjustments required to derive disposable income from national income. Since transfer payments (the major addition) are smaller than total income taxes (the major subtraction), the net effect is for disposable income to be substantially less than national income. (It was about 71 percent of GNP in 1986.)

Relating desired consumption to national income. If we know how consumption relates to disposable income and how disposable income relates to national income, we can derive the relation between consumption and national income.

As an example, assume that disposable income is always 90 percent of national income. Then, whatever the relation between C and Y, we can always substitute $0.9Y$ for Y_d. Thus if changes in consumption were always 80 percent of changes in Y_d, then changes in consumption would always be 72 percent (80 percent of 90 percent) of Y. [36]

Table 26-3 shows that we can write desired consumption as a function of Y as well as of Y_d. We can then derive the marginal response of consumption to changes in Y by determining the proportion of any change in *national income* that goes to a change in desired consumption.

The marginal response of consumption to changes in *national income* ($\Delta C/\Delta Y$) is equal to the marginal propensity to consume out of *disposable income* ($\Delta C/\Delta Y_d$) multiplied by the fraction of national income that becomes disposable income ($\Delta Y_d/\Delta Y$).

We now have a function showing how desired consumption expenditure varies as national income varies. The relation is defined for real income and real expenditure (i.e., income and expenditure measured in constant dollars). For every given level of real income, measured in terms of purchasing power, households desire to spend some fraction of that purchasing power and to save the rest.

Other Expenditure Categories

To this point we have focused on desired consumption expenditure, and have seen that it has both an autonomous and an induced component. Since the induced component means that desired consumption expenditure depends on national income, desired ag-

TABLE 26-3   Consumption As a Function of Disposable Income and National Income *(billions of dollars)*

(1) National income *(Y)*	(2) Disposable income *(Y_d = 0.9Y)*	(3) Desired consumption *(C = 100 + 0.8Y_d)*
100	90	172
1,000	900	820
2,000	1,800	1,540
3,000	2,700	2,260
4,000	3,600	2,980

If desired consumption depends on disposable income, which in turn depends on national income, desired consumption can be written as a function of either income concept. The data are hypothetical. They show deductions of 10 percent of any level of national income to arrive at disposable income. Deductions of 10 percent of Y imply that the remaining 90 percent of Y becomes disposable income. The numbers also show consumption as $100 billion plus 80 percent of disposable income.

By relating columns 2 and 3, one sees consumption as a function of disposable income. By relating columns 1 and 3, one sees the derived relationship between consumption and national income. In this example the change in consumption in response to a change in disposable income (i.e., the MPC) is 0.8, while the change in consumption in response to a change in national income is 0.72.

gregate expenditure also depends upon national income. The relationship between desired aggregate expenditure and national income depends not only on desired consumption, but also on the behavior of the other major expenditure categories: I, G, and $(X - M)$. As we shall see in later chapters, changes in each of these play an important role in understanding changes in national income. For our present purposes of understanding how the equilibrium level of national income is determined, it is useful to keep things as simple as possible. Where we can, we treat these components as constant and include them in autonomous expenditure. (The one exception as we will see is imports.)

Desired investment expenditure. For the present it is convenient to study how the level of national income adjusts to a fixed level of planned real investment. So we assume that firms plan to make a constant amount of investment in plant and equipment each year and that they plan to hold their inventories constant. In Chapter 27 we shall drop these assumptions and study the important effects on national income caused by changes in the level of desired investment.

Desired government expenditure. Governments intend to spend, and succeed in spending, many billions of dollars on currently produced goods and services. In this chapter we take desired and actual real government expenditure as a constant. We assume that the real value of government expenditure does not change as the circumstances of the economy change. This assumption allows us to see how national income adjusts to a constant level of real government expenditure. In Chapter 27 we shall drop this assumption and study how national income responds to changes in desired and actual government expenditure.

Desired net exports. Exports depend on spending decisions made by foreign households who purchase American goods and services. Typically, therefore, exports will not change as a result of changes in American national income. Imports, however, depend on the spending decisions of American households. All categories of expenditure have an import content—even domestic cars, for example, use some imported components in their manufacture. Thus imports rise when the other categories of expenditure rise. Because consumption rises with income, imports of foreign-produced consumption goods and materials that go into the production of domestically produced consumption goods also rise with income.

Desired net exports are negatively related to national income because of the positive relationship between desired expenditure on imports and national income. This negative relationship between net exports and national income is called the *net export function*. Data for a hypothetical economy with constant exports and with imports that are 10 percent of national income are given in Table 26-4. In this example exports form the autonomous component and imports the induced component of the desired net export function.

TABLE 26-4 A Net Export Schedule *(billions of dollars)*

National income (Y)	Exports (X)	Imports (M = 0.1Y)	Net exports
1,000	240	100	140
2,000	240	200	40
2,400	240	240	0
3,000	240	300	−60
4,000	240	400	−160
5,000	240	500	−260

Net exports fall as national income rises. The data are hypothetical. They assume that exports are constant and that imports are 10 percent of national income. Net exports are then positive at low levels of national income and negative at high levels.

The Aggregate Expenditure Function

The aggregate expenditure function relates the level of desired real expenditure to the level of real income. Total desired expenditure on the nation's output is the sum of desired consumption, investment, government, and net export expenditures, or

$$AE = C + I + G + (X - M)$$

Table 26-5 illustrates how such a function can be calculated, given the consumption function and the levels of desired investment, government, and net exports expenditures at each level of income. The resulting aggregate expenditure function is illustrated in Figure 26-4 on page 510.

The Propensity to Spend out of National Income

Earlier we defined propensities to consume and to save that, together, account for all household disposable income. We now define propensities to spend and not to spend that together account for all national income.

The fraction of any increment to national income that will be spent on domestic production is measured by the change in aggregate expenditure divided by the change in income, and is symbolized by $\Delta AE/\Delta Y$. It is called the economy's **marginal propensity to spend.** The value of the marginal pro-

TABLE 26-5 The Aggregate Expenditure Function *(billions of dollars)*

National income (Y)	Desired consumption expenditure (C = 100 + 0.72Y)	Desired investment expenditure (I = 250)	Desired government expenditure (G = 170)	Desired net exports expenditure (X − M = 240 − 0.10Y)	Desired aggregate expenditure (AE = C + I + G + [X − M])
100	172	250	170	230	952
400	388	250	170	200	1,008
500	460	250	170	190	1,070
1,000	820	250	170	140	1,380
2,000	1,540	250	170	40	2,000
3,000	2,260	250	170	− 60	2,620
4,000	2,980	250	170	− 160	3,240
5,000	3,700	250	170	− 260	3,860

The aggregate expenditure function is the sum of desired consumption, investment, government, and net export expenditures. The table is based on the hypothetical data given in Tables 26-3 and 26-4. The autonomous components of desired aggregate expenditure are desired investment, desired government, desired export expenditures, and the constant term in desired consumption expenditure. The induced components are the second term in desired consumption expenditure $(0.72Y)$ and desired imports $(0.1Y)$.

The marginal response of consumption to a change in national income is 0.72, calculated as the product of the marginal propensity to consume (0.8) times the fraction of national income that becomes disposable income (0.9). Because this exceeds the marginal propensity to import out of national income (0.1), desired aggregate expenditure is positively related to national income, as shown in column 6. The marginal response of desired aggregate expenditure to a change in national income, $\Delta AE/\Delta Y$, is 0.62.

pensity to spend, which is something greater than zero but less than one, may be indicated by the letter z. The amount $1 - \Delta AE/\Delta Y$, is the fraction of any increment to national income that is not spent. This is the **marginal propensity not to spend**.[2] This makes the value of the marginal propensity not to spend $1 - z$.

To illustrate, suppose that the economy produces $1.00 of extra income and that the response to this is governed by the relationships in Tables 26-3 and 26-4. Since $0.10 is collected by the government as taxes, $0.90 is converted into disposable income, and 80 percent of this amount ($0.72) becomes consumption expenditure. But import expenditure also rises by $0.10, so expenditure on domestic goods, that is,

aggregate expenditure, rises by $0.62. Thus z, the marginal propensity to spend, is 0.62 (0.62/1.00). What is not spent on domestic output includes the $0.10 in taxes, the $0.18 of disposable income that is saved, and the $0.10 of import expenditure, for a total of $0.38. Hence the marginal propensity not to spend, $(1 - z)$, is 0.38, $(1 - 0.62)$.

Determining Equilibrium National Income

Now we can see how equilibrium national income is determined, *given a Keynesian SRAS curve*. To do this we study the *equilibrium conditions*, the conditions that must be fulfilled if national income is to be in equilibrium.

Table 26-6 illustrates the determination of equilibrium national income for our simple hypothetical economy. Suppose that firms are producing a final output of $1,000 and thus national income is $1,000.

---

[2] More fully, these terms would be called the marginal propensity to spend *on national income* and the marginal propensity not to spend *on national income*. Expenditures on imports are included in the latter. The marginal propensity not to spend $(1 - z)$ is often referred to as the marginal propensity to *withdraw*. Not spending a part of one's income amounts to a *withdrawal* from the circular flow of income described in Figure 3-1.

FIGURE 26-4
An Aggregate Expenditure Function

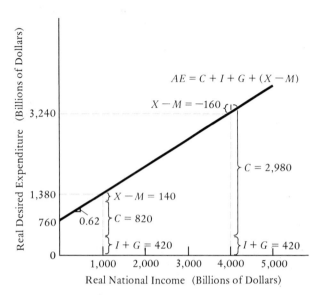

The aggregate expenditure function is derived by adding the four components of expenditure: consumption (*C*), investment (*I*), government (*G*), and net exports (*X* − *M*). The figure is drawn using the hypothetical data from Table 26-5. Substituting in the expressions from the table for each of the four components of *AE* gives:

$$AE = (100 + 0.72Y) + 250 + 170 + (240 - 0.1Y)$$

Combining these terms we get

$$AE = 760 + 0.62Y$$

Hence in the figure the *AE* function is drawn as a straight line with an intercept of 760 and a slope of 0.62. The intercept is the sum of the two constant components (*I* + *G* = 420) plus the constant terms from the other two components (100 from *C* and 240 from *X* − *M*). The slope, 0.62, is the marginal propensity to spend. It represents the marginal response of consumption to a change in national income, 0.72, net of the marginal propensity to import, 0.10.

   Two examples are illustrated. When income equals $1,000,

$$AE = 760 + (0.62 \times 1,000) = 1,380$$

If income rises by $3,000 to equal $4,000, investment and government expenditures remain at 420, consumption expenditure rises by 2,160 (0.72 × 3,000) to 2,980, and net exports fall by 300 (0.10 × 3,000) to −160. Thus *AE* rises by 1,860 to 3,240.

TABLE 26-6   The Determination of Equilibrium National Income *(billions of dollars)*

National income (Y)	Desired aggregate expenditure (*AE* = *C* + *I* + *G* + [*X* − *M*])	
100	952	Pressure on
400	1,008	income to
500	1,070	rise
1,000	1,380	↓
2,000	2,000	Equilibrium income
3,000	2,620	↑
4,000	3,240	Pressure on
5,000	3,860	income to fall

National income is in equilibrium where aggregate desired expenditure equals national income. The data are taken from Table 26-5. When national income is below its equilibrium level, aggregate desired expenditure exceeds the value of current output. This creates an incentive for firms to increase output and hence for national income to rise. When national income is above its equilibrium level, desired expenditure is less than the value of current output. This creates an incentive for firms to reduce output and hence for national income to fall. Only at the equilibrium level of national income is aggregate desired expenditure exactly equal to the value of the current output.

According to the table, aggregate desired expenditure is $1,380 at this level of income. If firms persist in producing a current output of only $1,000 in the face of an aggregate desired expenditure of $1,380, one of two things must happen.[3]

   One possibility is that households, firms, and governments will be unable to spend the extra $380 that they would like to spend, so lines or waiting lists of unsatisfied customers will appear. These will send a signal to firms that they can increase their sales if they increase their production. When the firms increase production, national income rises. Of course, the individual firms are interested only in their own sales and profits, but their individual ac-

[3] A third possibility, that prices would rise, has been excluded by assumption in this chapter by our use of the horizontal *SRAS* curve.

tions have, as their inevitable consequence, an increase in GNP that is the total of all firms' current production (i.e., the total of their values added).

The second possibility is that everyone will spend all that they wanted to spend. But then expenditure will exceed current output, which can happen only when some expenditure plans are fulfilled by purchasing inventories of goods that were produced in the past. In this example, the fulfillment of plans to purchase $1,380 worth of commodities in the face of a current output of only $1,000 will reduce inventories by $380. As long as inventories last, more goods can be sold than are currently being produced.

Eventually inventories will run out, but, before this happens, firms will increase their output as they see their inventories being drawn down. Extra sales can then be made without a further pulling down of inventories. Once again the consequence of each individual firm's behavior, in search of its own individual profits, is an increase in national income. Thus the final response to an excess of aggregate desired expenditure over current output is a rise in national income toward its equilibrium value.

At any level of national income at which aggregate desired expenditure exceeds total output, there will be pressure for national income to rise.

$AE > T \cdot O$

Next consider the $4,000 level of national income in Table 26-6. At this level, desired expenditure on domestically produced goods is only $3,240. If firms persist in producing $4,000 worth of goods, $760 worth must remain unsold. Therefore, inventories must rise. But firms will not allow inventories of unsold goods to rise indefinitely; sooner or later they will reduce the level of output to the level of sales. When they do, national income will fall.

At any level of income for which aggregate desired expenditure falls short of total output, there will be a pressure for national income to fall.

Finally, look at the national income level of $2,000 in the table. At this level, and only at this level, aggregate desired expenditure is exactly equal

to national income. Purchasers fulfill their spending plans without causing inventories to change. There is no incentive for firms to alter output. Since total output is the same as national income, national income will remain steady; it is in equilibrium.

The equilibrium level of national income occurs where aggregate desired expenditure equals total output.

This conclusion is quite general and does not depend on the numbers used in the specific example. [37]

FIGURE 26-5
Equilibrium National Income

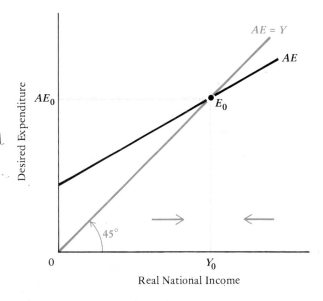

The equilibrium level of national income occurs at E_0, where the desired aggregate expenditure line intersects the 45° line. If real national income is below Y_0, desired aggregate expenditure will exceed national income and production will rise. This is shown by the arrow to the left of Y_0. If national income is above Y_0, desired aggregate expenditure will be less than national income and production will fall. This is shown by the arrow to the right of Y_0. Only when real national income is Y_0 will desired aggregate expenditure equal real national income ($AE_0 = Y_0$).

Graphical Representation of Equilibrium

Figure 26-5 on page 511 shows the determination of the equilibrium level of national income. The line labeled *AE* graphs the aggregate expenditure function. Its slope is the marginal propensity to spend. The line labeled *AE* = *Y* shows the equilibrium condition that desired aggregate expenditure, *AE*, equals national income, *Y*. Since the *AE* = *Y* line plots points where the vertical distance equals the horizontal distance, it forms an angle of 45° with the axes. Any point on this line is a possible equilibrium.

Graphically, equilibrium occurs at the level of income at which the aggregate desired expenditure line intersects the 45° line. This is the level of income where desired expenditure is just equal to total national income and, therefore, is just sufficient to purchase total final output.

We have now explained the equilibrium level of national income that arises at a *given price level*. In the next chapter we will study the forces that cause equilibrium income to change. We shall see that shifts in desired consumption and investment expenditure can cause major swings in national income. We shall also see that changes in government spending and taxation policies can do the same.

Summary

1. When the price level is fixed along a horizontal (Keynesian) *SRAS* curve, equilibrium national income is demand determined.
2. Desired aggregate expenditure includes desired consumption, desired investment, and desired government expenditures plus desired net exports. It is the amount that decision makers want to spend on purchasing the national product.
3. A change in disposable income leads to a change in consumption and saving. The responsiveness of these changes is measured by the marginal propensity to consume (*MPC*) and the marginal propensity to save (*MPS*), which are both positive and sum to one.
4. A change in wealth tends to cause a change in the allocation of disposable income between consumption and saving. The change in consumption is positively related to the change in wealth, while the change in saving is negatively related to this change.
5. Since desired imports increase as national income increases, desired net exports decrease as national income increases, other things being equal. This gives rise to a negatively sloped net export function.
6. At the equilibrium level of national income purchasers wish to buy neither more nor less than what is being produced. At incomes above equilibrium, desired expenditure falls short of national income and output will sooner or later be curtailed. At incomes below equilibrium, desired expenditure exceeds national income and output will sooner or later be increased.
7. Equilibrium national income is represented graphically by the point at which the aggregate expenditure curve cuts the 45° line, that is, where total desired expenditure equals total output.

Topics for Review

Keynesian *SRAS* curve
Desired expenditure
Consumption function

Average and marginal propensities to consume and save
The 45° line
Aggregate expenditure function
Marginal propensities to spend and not to spend
Equilibrium national income at a given price level

---

1. "The concept of an equilibrium level of national income is useless because the economy is never in equilibrium. If it ever got there, no economist would recognize it anyway." Discuss.
2. Interpret each of the following statements either in terms of the shape of a consumption function or the values of *MPC* and *APC*.
   a. "Tom Green has lost his job and his family is existing on its past savings."
   b. "The Grimsby household is so rich that they used all the extra income they earned this year to invest in a wildcat oil-drilling venture."
   c. "The widow Hammerstein can barely make ends meet by clipping coupons on the bonds left to her by dear Henry, but she would never dip into her capital."
   d. "We always thought Harris was a miser, but when his wife left him he took to wine, women, and song."
   e. "The inflation has made the Schultzes feel so poor that they are adding an extra $10 a week to their account at the Savings and Loan Society."
3. Why might an individual's marginal propensity to consume be higher in the long run than in the short run? Why might it be lower? Is it possible for an individual's average propensity to consume to be greater than unity in the short run? In the long run? Can a country's average propensity to consume be greater than unity in the short run? In the long run?
4. What relationship holds along the 45° line between total expenditures and total income? In determining equilibrium graphically, are we restricted to choosing identical vertical and horizontal scales?
5. Explain carefully why national income changes when aggregate desired expenditure does not equal national income. Sketch scenarios that fit the cases of too much and too little desired expenditure.
6. Explain how a sudden unexpected fall in consumer expenditure would initially cause an increase in investment expenditure by firms.
7. What relationship is suggested by the following 1983 newspaper headline: "Big three auto sales soar as recovery booms"?
8. State the implied impact on the *AE* curve, and hence on equilibrium national income, relating to each of the following headlines.
   a. "Washington's planned spending up 10.5%."
   b. "Soviet Union agrees to buy more wheat from America."
   c. "Major American companies expected to cut capital outlays."
   d. "President Reagan and Congress agree on a tax cut."

Discussion Questions

27

Changes in National Income I: The Role of Aggregate Demand

In Chapter 26 we investigated the conditions for national income to be in equilibrium. The equilibrium value of national income does not, however, remain unchanged. In this chapter we begin our study of why it changes. At the outset it is helpful to assume that the price level remains constant when national income changes. Later in the chapter we will study simultaneous changes in the price level and national income.

Changes in National Income with a Fixed Price Level

For any specific aggregate expenditure function there is a unique level of equilibrium national income. If the aggregate expenditure function shifts, the equilibrium will be disturbed and national income will change. Thus if we wish to find causes of changes in national income, we must look for causes of shifts in the AE function.

Shifts in the Aggregate Expenditure Function

The aggregate expenditure function shifts when one of its components shifts, that is, when there is a shift in the consumption function, in desired investment expenditure, in desired government expenditure, or in desired net exports. Such shifts were defined in Chapter 26 as changes in *autonomous* aggregate expenditure.

Increases in Autonomous Expenditure

What will happen if households permanently increase their levels of consumption spending at each level of disposable income? If the Ford Motor Company increases its rate of annual investment by $250 million in order to meet the threat from imported cars? If the U.S. government increases its defense spending? Or if U.S. grain exports soar? (In considering these questions, remember that we are dealing with continuous flows measured as so much per period of time. An upward shift in the expenditure function means that expenditure rises to and stays at a higher amount.)

Because any such increase shifts the entire aggregate expenditure function upward, the same analysis applies to all of the changes mentioned above. Two types of shift in AE occur. First, if the same addition to expenditure occurs at all levels of income, the AE curve shifts parallel to itself, as shown in Figure 27-1(i). Second, if there is a change in the propensity to spend out of national income, the slope of the AE curve changes, as shown in Figure 27-1(ii). (Recall that the slope of the AE curve is z, the marginal propensity to spend.)

Figure 27-1 shows that upward shifts in the aggregate expenditure function increase equilibrium national income. After the shift in the AE curve from AE_0 to AE_1 in Figure 27-1(i), income is no longer in equilibrium at its original level because at that level desired expenditure at point a exceeds national income by $e_1' - e_0$. This will cause an increase in

---

FIGURE 27-1   Shifts in the AE Function

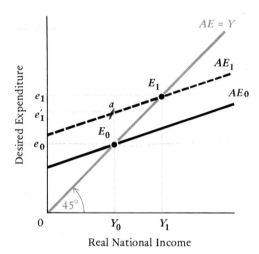

(i) A parallel shift in AE

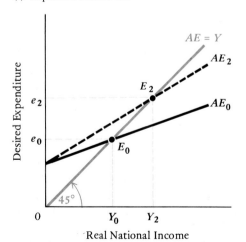

(ii) A change in the slope of AE

Upward shifts in the AE function increase equilibrium income; downward shifts decrease equilibrium income. In both (i) and (ii) the aggregate expenditure function is initially AE_0, with national income Y_0.

(i) A parallel upward *shift* in the AE curve from AE_0 to AE_1 means that desired expenditure has increased by the same amount at each level of national income. For example, at Y_0 desired expenditure rises from e_0 to e_1', and therefore exceeds national income. Equilibrium is reached at E_1, where income is Y_1 and expenditure e_1. The increase in desired expenditure from e_1' to e_1, represented by a *movement along AE_1*, is an induced response to the increase in income from Y_0 to Y_1.

(ii) A nonparallel upward shift in the AE curve, say from AE_0 to AE_2, means that the marginal propensity to spend at each level of national income has increased. This leads to an increase in equilibrium national income. Equilibrium is reached at E_2, where the new level of expenditure e_2 is equal to income Y_2.

Downward shifts in the AE function, from AE_1 to AE_0 or from AE_2 to AE_0, would lead to a fall in equilibrium income to Y_0.

MARGINAL PROPENSITY TO SPEND HAS INCREASED

national income. Equilibrium national income is now at the higher level indicated by the intersection of the new *AE* curve with the 45° line along which aggregate expenditures equals real national income. The increase in national income has induced an increase in desired aggregate expenditure (reflected in a rightward *movement along* the new *AE* curve from *a* to E_1). Thus we see that an upward *shift* of the *AE* curve will induce a *movement along* the new *AE* curve. This will not stop until a new equilibrium occurs, at which point the flow of desired expenditure again equals national income.

Decreases in Autonomous Expenditure

What will happen to national income if consumption, investment, government spending or exports decrease? All these changes shift the aggregate expenditure function downward. A constant reduction in expenditure at all levels of income shifts *AE* parallel to itself. A fall in the propensity to spend out of national income reduces the slope of the *AE* function.

Changes in Tax Rates

If tax rates change, the relationship between disposable income and national income changes.[1] For the same level of national income there will be a different level of disposable income and thus a different level of consumption. Thus, *z*, the marginal propensity to spend out of national income, will have changed.

Consider the decrease in tax rates illustrated in Table 27-1. If the government decreases its rate of income tax so that it collects 10 cents less out of every dollar of national income, disposable income rises in relation to national income. Thus consumption also rises at every level of national income. This results in an (nonparallel) upward shift of the *AE* curve, that is, a change in the slope of the curve, as shown in Figure 27-1(ii). The result of this shift will be a rise in equilibrium national income, as is also shown in Figure 27-1(ii).

---

[1] Effective tax rates can be changed either by changes in the percent of taxable income that is taken in taxes, or by changes in the percent of national income that is taxable. For simplicity, in the text we have assumed that all national income is taxable.

A rise in taxes has the opposite effect. A rise in tax rates results in less disposable income and hence less consumption expenditure at each level of national income. This results in a (nonparallel) downward shift of the *AE* curve and thus decreases the level of equilibrium national income. This, too, is illustrated in Figure 27-1(ii).

The results restated. We have now derived two important general predictions of the elementary theory of national income.

1. A rise in the amount of desired consumption, investment, government, or export expenditure associated with each level of national income will increase equilibrium national income.
2. A fall in the amount of desired consumption, investment, government, or export expenditure associated with each level of national income will lower equilibrium national income.

A change in desired consumption in relation to national income can arise, as we have seen, either because the consumption function shifts or because the relation between disposable income and national income is altered.

The Multiplier

We now know the *direction* of the changes in national income that occur in response to various shifts in the aggregate expenditure function. But what about the *magnitude* of these changes?

Economists need an answer to this question to determine the effects of changes in expenditures in both the private and public sectors. During a recession the government often takes measures to stimulate the economy. If these measures have a larger effect than estimated, demand may rise too much and full employment may be reached with demand still rising. This outcome will have an inflationary impact on the economy. If, on the other hand, the government greatly overestimates the effect of its measures, the recession will persist longer than is necessary. In this case there is a danger that the policy

TABLE 27-1   Tax Changes Shift the Function Relating Consumption to National Income

(1) National income (Y)	Disposable income equal to 80 percent of national income		Disposable income equal to 90 percent of national income	
	(2) Disposable income $(Y_d = 0.8Y)$	(3) Consumption $(C = 100 + 0.8Y_d)$	(4) Disposable income $(Y_d = 0.9Y)$	(5) Consumption $(C = 100 + 0.8Y_d)$
100	80	164	90	172
500	400	420	450	460
1,000	800	740	900	820

The consumption function shifts if the relation between disposable and national income changes. The table is based on simplified hypothetical consumption function from Table 26-1 combined with the assumption that Y_d is a constant fraction of Y. Initially, $Y_d = 0.8Y$. This yields a schedule relating consumption to national income that is given in columns 1 and 3 and described by the equation $C = 100 + 0.64Y$. Income tax rates are then decreased so that now 90 percent of national income becomes disposable income. Column 4 indicates the Y_d that corresponds at the decreased tax rate to each level of Y shown in column 1. With an unchanged consumption function, consumption at the new tax rate is given by column 5. Columns 1 and 5 give the new schedule relating consumption to national income, described by the equation $C = 100 + 0.72Y$.

will be discredited as ineffective, even though the correct diagnosis is that too little of the right thing was done.

Definition.   A measure of the magnitude of changes in income is provided by the multiplier. We have just seen that a shift in the aggregate expenditure curve will cause a change in equilibrium national income. Such a shift will be caused by a change in any autonomous component of aggregate expenditure, for example, an increase or decrease in investment or government spending. An increase in desired aggregate expenditure increases equilibrium national income by a multiple of the initial increase in autonomous expenditure. The **multiplier** is the ratio of changed income to changed expenditure, that is, the change in national income divided by the change in autonomous expenditure that brings it about.

Why the multiplier is greater than unity.   What will happen to national income if, with unchanged tax rates, the government increases its spending on road construction by $1 billion per year?

Initially the road program will create $1 billion worth of new national income and a corresponding

amount of employment for those households and firms on which the initial billion dollars is spent. But this is not the end of the story. The increase in national income of $1 billion will cause an increase in disposable income, which will cause an induced rise in consumption expenditure. Road crews and road contractors, who gain new income directly from the government's road program, will spend some of it on food, clothing, entertainment, cars, television sets, and other consumption commodities. When output expands to meet this demand, employment will increase in all the affected industries. New incomes will then be created for workers and firms in these industries. When they in turn spend their newly earned incomes, output and employment will rise further. More income will be created and more expenditure induced. Indeed, at this stage you could wonder whether the increases in income will ever come to an end. To deal with this concern, we need to consider the multiplier in somewhat more precise terms.

The simple multiplier.   Consider an increase in autonomous expenditure of ΔA, which might be, say, $1 billion per year. Remember that ΔA stands for *any* increase in autonomous expenditure; this could be an increase in investment, in government purchases, in exports, or in the autonomous component of consumption. The new autonomous expenditure shifts the aggregate expenditure function upward by that amount. National income is no longer in equilibrium at its original level since desired aggregate expenditure now exceeds income. Equilibrium is restored by a *movement along* the new *AE* curve.

The **simple multiplier** measures the change in equilibrium national income that occurs in response to a change in autonomous expenditure *at a constant price level*. We refer to it as simple because we simplify the situation by assuming that the price level is fixed. Figure 27-2 illustrates the simple multiplier and makes clear that it is greater than unity. Box 27-1 provides a numerical example.

The Size of the Simple Multiplier

The size of the multiplier depends on the slope of the *AE* function, that is, on the marginal propensity to spend, z. This is illustrated in Figure 27-3 on page 520.

A high marginal propensity to spend means a steep *AE* curve. The expenditure induced by any initial increase in income is large, with the result that the final rise in income is correspondingly large. On the other hand, a low marginal propensity to spend means a relatively flat *AE* curve. The expenditure induced by the initial increase in income is small, and the final rise in income is not much larger than the initial rise in autonomous expenditure that brought it about.

> The larger the marginal propensity to spend, the steeper the aggregate expenditure function and the larger is the multiplier.

The precise value of the simple multiplier can be derived by using elementary algebra. For those who wish to see how this is done, the derivation is given in Box 27-2 on page 521. The result is that the simple multiplier, which we call *K,* is

$$K = \frac{\Delta Y}{\Delta A} = \frac{1}{(1 - z)}$$

FIGURE 27-2   The Simple Multiplier

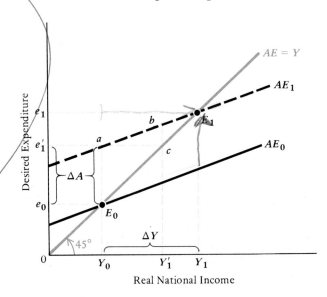

An increase in desired aggregate expenditure increases equilibrium national income by a multiple of the initial increase in autonomous expenditure. The initial equilibrium occurs at E_0 where AE_0 intersects the 45° line. At this point, desired expenditure e_0 is equal to national income Y_0. An increase in autonomous expenditure of ΔA then shifts the desired expenditure function upward to AE_1. If national income stays at Y_0, desired expenditure at point a is e_1'. Since this level of desired expenditure is greater than income, national income will rise. If income rises only by ΔA, it rises to Y_1' (point c, where $e_1' = Y_1'$). But at Y_1' desired expenditure still exceeds income by the amount bc.

Equilibrium occurs when income rises to Y_1. Here desired expenditure e_1 equals income Y_1. The extra expenditure of $e_1'e_1$ represents the induced increases in expenditure. It is the amount by which the final increase in income, ΔY, exceeds the initial increase in autonomous expenditure, ΔA. Since ΔY is greater than ΔA, the multiplier is greater than unity.

where z is the marginal propensity to spend out of national income. (z is, as we have seen, the slope of the aggregate expenditure function.)

As we saw in Chapter 26, the term $(1 - z)$ stands for the marginal propensity not to spend out of national income. For example, if $.80 of every $1.00

BOX 27-1

The Multiplier: A Numerical Example

Consider an economy that has a marginal propensity to spend out of national income of 0.80. Suppose that autonomous expenditure increases by $1 billion per year because the government spends an extra $1 billion per year on new roads. National income initially rises by $1 billion. But that is not the end of it. The factors of production involved in road building that received the first $1 billion spend $800 million. This second round of spending generates $800 million of new income. This new income in turn induces $640 million of third round spending. And so it continues, with each successive round of new income generating 80 percent as much in new expenditure. Each additional round of expenditure creates new income and yet another round of expenditure.

The table carries the process through 10 rounds. Students with sufficient patience (and no faith in

Round of spending	Increase in expenditure (millions of dollars)	Cumulative total (millions of dollars)
Initial increase	1,000.0	1,000.0
2	800.0	1,800.0
3	640.0	2,440.0
4	512.0	2,952.0
5	409.6	3,361.6
6	327.7	3,689.3
7	262.1	3,951.4
8	209.7	4,161.1
9	167.8	4,328.9
10	134.2	4,463.1
11 to 20 combined	479.3	4,942.4
All others	57.6	5,000.0

mathematics) may compute as many rounds in the process as they wish; they will find that the sum of the rounds of expenditures approaches a limit of $5 billion, which is five times the initial increase in expenditure. [38] The graph of the cumulative expenditure increases shows how quickly this limit is approached. The multiplier is thus 5, given the assumption about the marginal propensity to spend. Had the marginal propensity to spend been lower, say, 0.667, the process would have been similar, but it would have approached a limit of three instead of five times the initial increase in expenditure.

of new national income is spent ($z = 0.80$), then $.20 is the amount not spent. The value of the multiplier is then calculated as $K = 1/0.20 = 5$.

The simple multiplier can be written as the reciprocal of the marginal propensity not to spend.

From this we see that if $(1 - z)$ is very small, the multiplier will be very large (because extra income induces much extra spending). The largest possible value of $(1 - z)$ is unity, when z equals zero, indicating that all extra national income is not spent. In this case the multiplier itself has a value of unity, indicating that the increase in equilibrium national

$MPS = \Delta E_R = MUK$

FIGURE 27-3
The Size of the Simple Multiplier

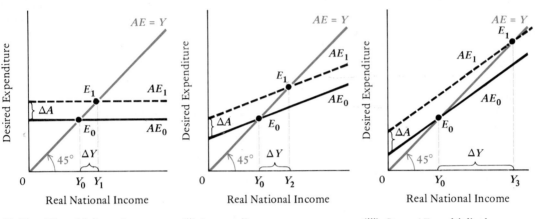

(i) Flat *AE*, multiplier unity   (ii) Intermediate case   (iii) Steep *AE*, multiplier large

The larger the marginal propensity to spend out of national income (z), the steeper the *AE* curve and the larger the multiplier. In each part of the diagram the aggregate expenditure function is AE_0, equilibrium is at E_0, with income Y_0. The *AE* curve then shifts upward to AE_1 as a result of an increase in autonomous expenditure of ΔA. ΔA is the same in each part. The new equilibrium is at E_1.

In (i) the *AE* function is horizontal, indicating a marginal propensity to spend of zero ($z = 0$). The change in income ΔY is only the increase in autonomous expenditure since there is no induced expenditure by those who receive the initial increase in income. The simple multiplier is then unity, its minimum possible value.

In (ii) the *AE* curve is upward sloping, but still relatively flat (z is low). The increase in national income to Y_2 is only slightly greater than the increase in autonomous expenditure that brought it about.

In (iii) the *AE* function is quite steep (z is high). Now the increase in income to Y_3 is much larger than the increase in autonomous expenditure that brought it about. The simple multiplier is quite large.

income is confined to the initial increase in autonomous expenditure. This is illustrated in part i of Figure 27-3.

Size of the Multiplier in the U.S. Economy

To estimate the size of the multiplier in an actual economy, we need to estimate the value of the marginal propensity not to spend out of national income in that economy. There is good reason to suppose the actual number in the U.S. economy is larger than the 0.2 we used in our example.

The various elements of national income that are "not spent," that is, that are in $(1 - z)$, include

income taxes, savings, and expenditures on imports. For the U.S. economy in the 1980s this leads to a realistic estimate of about 0.5 for z and thus also about 0.5 for $(1 - z)$. Thus the actual simple multiplier is approximately equal to 2, not the 5 as in the example.

Changes in National Income When the Price Level Changes

So far we have studied how income responds to changes in desired expenditures and derived the simple multiplier as a measure of the change, assuming a constant price level. It is time to drop the simpli-

BOX 27-2

The Multiplier: An Algebraic Approach

High school algebra is all that is needed to derive the exact expression for the multiplier. Readers who feel at home with algebra may want to follow this derivation. Others can skip it and rely on the graphical and numerical arguments given in the text.

First we derive the equation for the *AE* curve. Aggregate expenditure is divided into autonomous expenditure, *A*, and induced expenditure, *N*.* So we write

$$AE = N + A \qquad [1]$$

Since *N* is expenditure that varies with income, we can write

$$N = zY \qquad [2]$$

where *z* is the marginal propensity to spend out of national income. (It is a positive number between zero and unity.) Substituting Equation 2 in Equation 1 yields the equation of the *AE* curve.

$$AE = zY + A \qquad [3]$$

Now we write the equation of the 45° line,

$$AE = Y \qquad [4]$$

* In simple models *N* is mainly consumption expenditure, but in other models it may include other types of expenditure. All that matters is that there is one class of expenditure, *N*, that varies with income and another class, *A*, that does not.

which states the equilibrium condition that aggregate desired expenditure must equal national income. Equations 3 and 4 are two equations with two unknowns, *AE* and *Y*. To solve we substitute Equation 3 in Equation 4 to obtain

$$Y = zY + A$$

Subtracting *zY* from both sides yields

$$Y - zY = A$$

Factoring out the *Y* yields

$$Y(1 - z) = A$$

Dividing through by $(1 - z)$ yields

$$Y = A/(1 - z)$$

This tells us the equilibrium value of *Y* in terms of autonomous expenditures *A* and the propensity not to spend out of national income $(1 - z)$. The expression $Y = A/(1 - z)$ tells us that if *A* changes by ΔA, the change in *Y*, which we call ΔY, will be ΔA divided by $(1 - z)$:

$$\Delta Y = \Delta A/(1 - z)$$

Dividing through by ΔA gives the value of the multiplier, which we designate by *K*:

$$K = \Delta Y/\Delta A = 1/(1 - z)$$

---

fying assumption and study how national income responds to changes in desired expenditures when the price level is free to rise or fall. The crucial step to do so is to establish the relationship between the *AE* and the *AD* curves.

The Relation Between the *AE* and *AD* Curves

The Price Level and Aggregate Expenditure

The *AD* curve is negatively sloped because changes in the price level change desired expenditure. A rise in the price level reduces desired aggregate expenditure at every level of national income.

One channel through which a change in the price level influences aggregate expenditure is its effect on the real value of financial wealth. Much wealth is held in the form of assets with a fixed money value. This is obviously true of money itself—cash and bank deposits—and is also true of many kinds of debt such as treasury bills and bonds. A rise in the price level lowers the purchasing power of these assets and lowers the real value of wealth.

Changes in the real value of financial wealth can influence aggregate expenditure in two ways. First, there may be a *direct* effect of wealth on consumption expenditure. Second, there is an *indirect* effect on expenditure operating through interest rates. The indirect effect is quantitatively more important, but it is also much more complex to understand. Consequently, we defer detailed study of it until Chapter 32 when we will have studied the theory of money and interest rates. For now, we can understand the basic principles of the link between the price level and aggregate expenditure by focusing on the direct effect on consumption.

We saw in Figure 26-3 that a fall in the household's wealth shifts the consumption function downward. Because households have less wealth, they increase their saving (cut their consumption) so as to get back toward the wealth they wish to have for such purposes as retirement.

A fall in the consumption function shifts the whole aggregate expenditure function downward, since for any given level of real national income, people now wish to purchase a smaller quantity of goods and services. We already know that a downward shift in the aggregate expenditure function reduces equilibrium national income.

A fall in the price level has the opposite effect. To summarize briefly, the purchasing power of some existing assets is increased by the fall in prices. Households, being wealthier in the aggregate, spend more. This additional expenditure shifts the *AE* curve upward and raises equilibrium national income.

A Shift in the AE Curve Changes Aggregate Demand

The aggregate expenditure curve relates national income to desired expenditure for a given price level. The aggregate demand curve relates equilibrium national income to the price level. The relationship between the two curves is shown in Figure 27-4. Because the horizontal axes of both figures measure the same thing, real national income, they can be placed one above the other so that the level of national income on each can be directly compared.

Figure 27-4(i) describes the determination of equilibrium income at any given price level. This reviews the analysis of the first part of this chapter. For the given *AE* curve—and the fixed price level for which it is drawn—there is a unique equilibrium level of real national income. Figure 27-4(ii) plots the equilibrium income thus determined against the price level to yield one point on the *AD* curve.

The *AE* curve shows how equilibrium income is reached for a specific price level. A *point* on the *AD* curve plots that equilibrium level of national income against that given price level.

Deriving the AD Curve

Figure 27-4 shows one point on the *AD* curve. We can now show how the whole curve is derived. Figure 27-5(i) on page 524 shows how equilibrium national income changes when there are changes in the price level. The *AE* curve shifts, thus causing a new equilibrium income to be associated with the new price level. This determines a second point on the *AD* curve.

Every change in the price level leads to a new *AE* curve and a new level of equilibrium income. Each combination of equilibrium income and its associated price level becomes a particular point on the *AD* curve in Figure 27-5(ii). *A movement along the AD curve thus traces out the response of equilibrium income to a change in the price level.*

Since the *AD* curve relates equilibrium national income to the price level, changes in the price level that cause *shifts in the AE curve* cause movements along the *AD* curve.

Changes in National Income and the AD Curve

In order to analyze an economy where the price level changes, it is helpful to state in terms of the *AD* curve the analysis stated earlier in this chapter in terms of the *AE* curve.

We have just seen that the *AD* curve plots equilibrium national income as a function of the price level. Thus anything that alters equilibrium national income at a given price level must shift the *AD*

FIGURE 27-4   The Relation Between the *AE*
and the *AD* Curves

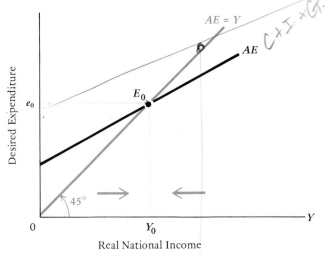

(i) Aggregate expenditure

(i) The *AE* curve determines the equilibrium level of national income for a given price level. The *AE* curve shows how desired aggregate expenditure varies with national income at the given price level P_0. The equilibrium level of income is Y_0. The forces acting to push income to Y_0 are shown by the arrows. At incomes less than Y_0 the *AE* curve lies above the 45° line, indicating that desired expenditure exceeds income; at incomes above Y_0 the *AE* curve lies below the 45° line, indicating that desired expenditure is less than income. Equilibrium occurs at Y_0 where desired aggregate expenditure equals national income.

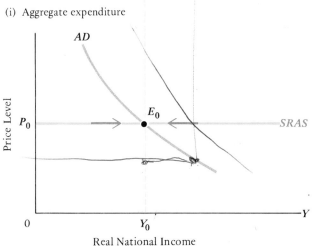

(ii) Aggregate demand

(ii) The *AD* curve plots the level of equilibrium income against the price level. For the price level P_0 the equilibrium level of income is Y_0, as determined above. Therefore, E_0 is on the *AD* curve which must intersect the Keynesian *SRAS* curve at that point. The income adjustment process described above can be suggested here, too. When income is below Y_0, there is excess demand and income rises; when income is above Y_0, there is excess supply and income falls. This is illustrated by the arrows.

curve. This allows us to restate the conclusions on page 516 as follows.

A rise in the amount of desired consumption, investment, government, or export expenditure associated with each level of national income shifts the *AD* curve to the right. A fall in any of these expenditures shifts the *AD* curve to the left.

We have seen that the simple multiplier measures the magnitude of the change in equilibrium national income when the price level is constant. It follows that the simple multiplier gives the magnitude of the

FIGURE 27-5   The Relation Between the *AE* and the *AD* Curves When the Price Level Changes

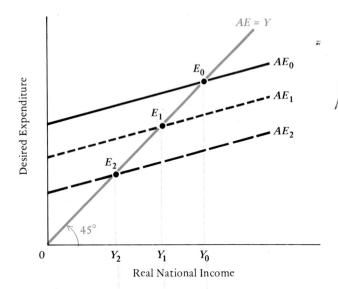

(i) Aggregate expenditure

Equilibrium income is determined by the *AE* curve for each given price level; the level of income and its associated price level are then plotted to yield the *AD* curve. Starting with the price level P_0, the *AE* curve is AE_0 and equilibrium national income is Y_0. Plotting Y_0 against P_0 yields the point E_0 on the *AD* curve.

A rise in the price level to P_1 lowers *AE* to AE_1, and this in turn lowers equilibrium income to Y_1. Plotting the new lower equilibrium income Y_1 against the new higher price level P_1 yields a second point, E_1, on the *AD* curve. A further rise in the price level to P_2 lowers the *AE* curve to AE_2 and produces the lower level of equilibrium income Y_2. Plotting Y_2 against P_2 yields point E_2 on the *AD* curve.

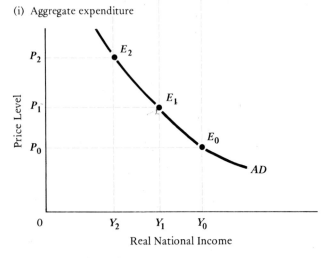

(ii) Aggregate demand

horizontal shift in the *AD* curve in response to a change in autonomous expenditure. This is shown in Figure 27-6.

The simple multiplier measures the horizontal shift in the *AD* curve in response to a change in autonomous expenditure.

When the *SRAS* curve is horizontal, indicating that firms will supply everything that is demanded at the going price level, then the simple multiplier also tells us the change in equilibrium income that will occur in response to a change in autonomous expenditure.

What if the aggregate supply curve slopes up-

FIGURE 27-6 The Simple Multiplier and Shifts in the *AD* Curve

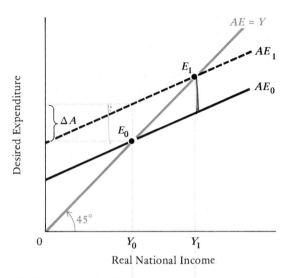

(i) Aggregate expenditure

(ii) Aggregate demand

A shift in aggregate expenditure changes equilibrium national income for any given price level, and the simple multiplier measures the resulting horizontal shift in aggregate demand. The original desired expenditure function is AE_0 in (i). Equilibrium is at E_0, with national income Y_0 at price level P_0. This yields point E_0 on the curve AD_0 in (ii).

The *AE* curve in (i) then shifts upward from AE_0 to AE_1 due to an increase in autonomous expenditure of ΔA. Equilibrium income now rises to Y_1, with the price level still constant at P_0. Thus the *AD* curve in (ii) shifts to the right to point E_1, indicating the higher equilibrium income Y_1, associated with the same price level P_0. The magnitude of the shift, ΔY, in response to ΔA is given by the simple multiplier.

A fall in desired expenditure can be analyzed by shifting the *AE* curve from AE_1 to AE_0, which shifts the *AD* curve from AD_1 to AD_0 at the price level of P_0.

$$\frac{\Delta Y}{\Delta A}$$

ward? In this case a rise in national income will be associated with a rise in the price level. But we have seen that a rise in the price level (by lowering the real value of household wealth) shifts the *AE* curve downward, which tends to lower national income. The outcome of the conflicting forces is easily seen using aggregate demand and aggregate supply curves.

The Multiplier When the Price Level Varies

Figure 27-7 shows that when the *SRAS* curve is positively sloped, the change in national income caused by a change in autonomous expenditure is no longer equal to the size of the horizontal shift in the

FIGURE 27-7   The Multiplier When the *SRAS* Curve Is Positively Sloped

The multiplier effect of a shift in aggregate demand when the *SRAS* curve is positively sloped is less than the simple multiplier. Equilibrium is initially at E_0, with real national income Y_0 and price level of P_0. An increase in autonomous expenditure shifts the *AD* curve from AD_0 to AD_1. The new equilibrium is at E_1, with income Y_1 and price level P_1. The change in real income Y_0Y_1 is smaller than Y_0Y_1', the change measured by the simple multiplier. The reason is that some of the increased demand has been absorbed by the rise in the price level.

AD curve. A shift to the right of the *AD* curve causes the price level to rise, which in turn causes the rise in national income to be less than the horizontal shift of the *AD* curve. Part of the expansionary impact of an increase in demand is dissipated in a rise in the price level, and only part is transmitted to a rise in real output. Of course, there still is an increase in output, and thus a multiplier may still be calculated, but its value is not the same as that of the simple multiplier.

When the aggregate supply curve is positively sloped, the multiplier is smaller than the simple multiplier derived for a given price level.

Why is the multiplier smaller when the *SRAS* curve is positively sloped? The answer lies in the behavior that is summarized by the *AE* curve. To

understand this, it is useful to think of the final change in national income as occurring in two stages, as shown in Figure 27-8.

First, with prices constant an increase in autonomous expenditure shifts the *AE* curve up and therefore shifts the *AD* curve to the right. The result is a change in national income given by the simple multiplier. This first stage shows up as a *shift up* of the *AE* curve in (i) and a *shift to the right* of the *AD* curve in (ii). But this cannot be the final equilibrium position because firms are unwilling to produce enough to satisfy the extra demand at the existing price level.

Second, we take account of the rise in the price level that occurs due to the positive slope of the *SRAS* curve. As we have seen, a rise in the price level via its effect on wealth and consumption leads to a downward shift of the *AE* curve. This second shift of the *AE* curve partially counteracts the initial rise in national income and so reduces the size of the multiplier. The second stage shows up as a *shift down* of the *AE* curve in (i) and an upward *movement along* the *AD* curve in (ii).

The Advantage of Using AD and AS Curves

If all we had was the *AE* curve plus the knowledge that the *AS* curve was positively sloped, we could not discover the final change in either P or Y. We would know that the initial rise in autonomous expenditure would shift the *AE* curve upward. We would also know that the consequent rise in the price level would shift *AE* back downward somewhat. But by how much? Where would the final equilibrium be in relation to the original equilibrium and the equilibrium that would occur if prices had remained constant? We cannot answer these questions unless we know by how much the price level rises. But there is nothing in Figure 27-8(i) to tell us this. The *AE*–45° line analysis is not sufficient to deal with situations in which the price level can change.

In contrast, with the *AD* curve we can determine how a change in autonomous expenditure shifts aggregate demand and then, for a given *AS* curve, how it determines changes in both national income and the price level.

FIGURE 27-8   The *AE* Curve and the Multiplier When the Price Level Varies

(i) Aggregate expenditure

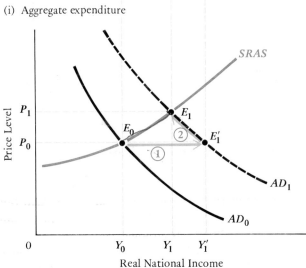

(ii) Aggregate demand

An increase in autonomous expenditure causes the *AE* curve to shift up, but the rise in the price level causes it to shift part of the way down again. Hence the multiplier effect on income is smaller than when the price level is constant. Originally, equilibrium is at point E_0 in both (i) and (ii), with real national income Y_0 and price level P_0. Desired aggregate expenditure then shifts by ΔA to AE_1', taking the aggregate demand curve to AD_1, as shown by arrow 1 in both (i) and (ii). If the price level had remained constant at P_0, the new equilibrium would have been E_1' and real income would have risen to Y_1'. The amount $Y_0 Y_1'$ is the change called for by the simple multiplier.

Instead, however, the shift in the AD curve raises the price level to P_1 because the $SRAS$ curve is positively sloped. The rise in the price level shifts the aggregate expenditure curve down to AE_1, as shown by arrow 2 in (i). This is shown as a movement along the AD curve, as shown by arrow 2 in (ii). The new equilibrium is thus at E_1. The amount $Y_0 Y_1$ is ΔY, the actual increase in real income, while the amount $Y_1 Y_1'$ is the shortfall relative to the simple multiplier due to the rise in the price level.

The multiplier adjusted for the effect of the price increase is the ratio of $\Delta Y / \Delta A$ in (i).

Summary

1. Equilibrium national income is increased by a rise in the desired consumption, investment, government, or export expenditure associated with each level of the national income. Equilibrium national income is decreased by a fall in desired expenditures.

2. Equilibrium national income is decreased by a rise in the taxes associated with each level of national income and increased by a fall in taxes.

3. The magnitude of the effect on national income of shifts in autonomous expenditure is given by the multiplier. It is defined as $K = \Delta Y/\Delta A$, where ΔA is the change in autonomous expenditure.

4. The simple multiplier is the multiplier when the price level is constant. It is equal to $1/(1 - z)$, where z is the marginal propensity to spend out of national income. Thus the larger is z, the larger the multiplier. It is a basic prediction of national income theory that the simple multiplier is greater than unity.

5. The AE curve shows desired expenditure for each level of income, at a particular price level. It shows how equilibrium national income is achieved for that price level. The AD curve plots the equilibrium level of income against the price level.

6. A change in the price level shifts the AE curve and leads to a new level of equilibrium national income. The change to the new equilibrium level of income and price level is shown by a movement along the AD curve.

7. A shift in autonomous expenditure leads to a shift in the AD curve. The simple multiplier measures the size of the horizontal shift in the AD curve. It measures the actual size of the change in equilibrium real national income *only if* the economy is on a horizontal (Keynesian) $SRAS$ curve.

8. When the $SRAS$ curve is positively sloped, part of the effect of the multiplier is dissipated in a rise in prices and only part goes to raise real income. The division of the effects between a change in national income and a change in the price level are easily discovered from AD and AS curves.

Topics for Review

Shifts of and movements along expenditure curves
Effect on national income of changes in desired expenditures
Effect on national income of a change in tax rates
The simple multiplier
Relation between size of the simple multiplier and slope of the AE curve
The multiplier when the price level varies
Relation between AE and AD curves
Effect on AE and AD curves of changes in autonomous expenditures

Discussion Questions

1. In what direction would each of the following change equilibrium national income? Which expenditure flows would be affected first?
   a. Production and sale of a new nuclear reactor
   b. Decrease in personal income taxes for low-income taxpayers
   c. Major reduction in social security payments to the elderly
   d. Spurt in consumer spending for video recorders accompanied by a reduction in savings
   e. Decrease in spending on foreign travel accompanied by an equivalent increase in saving
   f. Large increase in defense expenditure accompanied by an across-the-board tax cut
   g. Increase in spending on imported cars matched by an equal decrease in spending on domestically produced cars
2. Predict whether each of the following events will, other things being equal, increase, decrease, or leave unchanged the size of the multiplier.
   a. Shift from foreign travel to holidays at home
   b. Increase in expenditures on highways
   c. Decisions by corporations to decrease the percentage of earnings they pay out in dividends and to increase their bank balances whenever national income falls
   d. Widespread adoption by cities of a city income tax
   e. Large increase in the percentage of disposable income saved by households
3. The president of the Chamber of Commerce of Southeastern Connecticut commented on the effects in his area of a 22-week strike at a shipyard where the lost payroll was $2 million per week: "You don't just figure $2 million a week times 22 weeks; you have to multiply by four or five. That shipyard is the prime source of money in this region. Money comes into the region from Washington and then the shipyard worker's wife takes it to the grocery, and the grocery clerk takes it to the gas station, and so on until it leaves the area in taxes or some other way." Interpret his statement in terms of the analysis of this chapter.
4. Homer Hardcrust, chairman of the Council of Economic Advisors, proposes that because of the current heavy unemployment, government should prepare an austerity program and cut down government expenditures to set an example for private households. Would his policy tend to raise or lower unemployment?
5. A private research agency estimates the GNP gap to be $10 billion and recommends that it be eliminated by an increase in government expenditures of $10 billion. Does the agency's staff understand the multiplier?
6. What would happen to employment and income if, in an attempt to lower American unemployment, Congress enacted large increases in American tariff rates? What would happen if, in the face of a world-wide recession, all countries did the same?

28

Changes in National Income II: The Role of Aggregate Supply

The aggregate supply curve plays a key role in the behavior of the economy. As we saw at the end of Chapter 27, the shape of the *SRAS* curve determines how the impact of aggregate demand shocks is divided between changes in output and changes in the price level. Further, as we saw in Chapter 24, aggregate supply shocks, which *shift* the aggregate supply curve, can themselves be a major cause of changes in both output and the price level.

Aggregate Supply in the Short Run

To analyze the short-run effects of aggregate demand and aggregate supply shocks, we must first examine the shape of the short-run aggregate supply curve in more detail.

The Shape of the *SRAS* Curve

In Chapter 24 we encountered the upward-sloping *SRAS* curve. It relates the price level to the quantity of output that producers are willing to sell. Such an *SRAS* curve is reproduced in Figure 28-1. Notice two things about its shape: it has a positive slope, and the slope increases as output rises.

Positive slope. The most obvious feature of the *SRAS* curve is its positive slope, indicating that, other things being equal, a higher price level is associated with a higher volume of real output. Since the prices of all of the factors of production are being held constant along the *SRAS* curve, why is the curve not horizontal, indicating that firms would be willing to supply as much output as might be demanded with no increase in the price level?

An answer to this question was given in Chapter 24: Even though *input prices* are constant, *unit costs of production* rise as output increases because of the bottlenecks that are likely to arise as firms in the economy approach full use of their capacity. Thus a higher price level for increasing output—rising short-run aggregate supply—is necessary to compensate firms for rising costs.

The previous paragraph addresses the question "What has to happen to the price level if national output increases, with input prices held

FIGURE 28-1   A Short-Run Aggregate Supply Curve

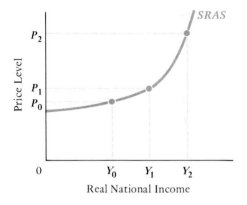

The *SRAS* **curve slopes upward, and the slope increases as real national income increases.** The upward slope of the *SRAS* curve shows that, according to the supply decisions of firms, output and the price level are positively associated. The increasing slope, especially beyond Y_0, shows that the higher the level of output, the larger the increase in the price level associated with any further increment to output. For example, the change in output in moving from Y_0 to Y_1 is the same as that in moving from Y_1 to Y_2, but the rise in prices from P_0 to P_1 (associated with the first increment to output) is smaller than the rise from P_1 to P_2 (associated with the second increment).

constant?" One may ask a different question: "What will happen to firms' willingness to supply output if product prices rise with no increase in input prices?" If there is an increase in the prices of products that firms sell, while the prices of everything that firms use to make their products remain constant, production becomes more profitable. Since firms are interested in making profits, when production becomes more profitable, they will usually produce more.[1] Thus, when the price level of final output rises while input prices are held constant, firms are motivated to increase their outputs. This is true for the individual firm and also for firms in the aggregate. This

[1] Those who have already studied microeconomics can understand this in terms of price-taking firms being faced with higher prices and thus expanding output *along* their marginal cost curves until marginal cost is once again equal to price.

increase in the amount that will be produced leads to an upward slope of the *SRAS* curve.

The higher the price level, the higher the total output that firms are willing to produce and offer for sale, other things being equal.

Thus, whether we look at how the price level will respond in the short run to increases in output or how the level of output will respond to an increase in the price level with input prices held constant, we find that the *SRAS* curve has a positive slope.

Increasing slope.   A somewhat less obvious but in many ways more important property of a typical *SRAS* curve is that its slope *increases* as output rises. It is rather flat to the left of potential output and rather steep to the right. Why? Below potential output, firms typically have unused capacity—some plant and equipment are idle. When firms are faced with unused capacity, only a small increase in the price of their output may be needed to induce them to expand production, at least up to normal capacity.

Once output is pushed far beyond normal capacity, however, unit costs tend to rise quite rapidly. Many higher cost expedients may have to be adopted. Standby capacity, overtime, and extra shifts may have to be used. Such expedients raise the cost of producing a unit of output. These higher cost methods will not be used unless the selling price of the output has risen enough to cover them. The further output is expanded beyond normal capacity, the more rapidly unit costs rise and hence the larger the rise in price needed to induce firms to increase output even further.

The increasing slope of the *SRAS* curve in Figure 28-1 has an important consequence:

Below potential national income, changes in output are accompanied by relatively small changes in the price level. Above potential national income, changes in output are accompanied by relatively large changes in the price level.

This increasing slope is sometimes called the *first important asymmetry* in the behavior of aggregate supply. (The second, "sticky wages," is discussed later in this chapter.)

Using the *SRAS* curve.   The "other things being equal" clause is the key to why we have called the upward-sloping relationship a *short-run* aggregate supply curve. Treating wages and other factor prices as constant is appropriate only when the time period under consideration is short. Hence the *SRAS* curve is used only to analyze the effects that occur in the short run. Economists sometimes call these *impact* effects.

Demand Shocks

At the end of Chapter 27, we saw that the *positive slope* of the *SRAS* curve reduced the size of the multiplier below that of the simple multiplier (see Figure 27-7). We now examine how the *increasing slope* of the *SRAS* curve influences how an aggregate demand shock is divided between changes in real output and changes in the price level.

Figure 28-2 shows an *SRAS* curve that highlights the increasing slope by exaggerating its shape at both low and high levels of national income. The curve shows three distinct ranges.

Over the *flat* range, from 0 to Y_1, any change in aggregate demand leads to *little* change in prices and, as seen earlier, a response of output nearly equal to that predicted by the simple multiplier.

Over the *intermediate range* along which the *SRAS* curve is positively sloped, from Y_1 to Y_4, a shift in the *AD* curve gives rise to appreciable changes in real income *and* in the price level. As we saw in Chapter 27, the change in the price level means that real income will change by less in response to a change in autonomous expenditure than it would if prices were constant.

Over the *steep* range, from Y_4 to Y_5, virtually nothing more can be produced, however large the demand. This range deals with an economy near its capacity constraints. Any change in aggregate demand leads to a sharp change in the price level and to virtually no change in real national income. The multiplier in this case is nearly zero.

Let us consider the nearly vertical range in more detail using Figure 28-3, and in so doing look again

FIGURE 28-2   The Effects of Increases in Aggregate Demand

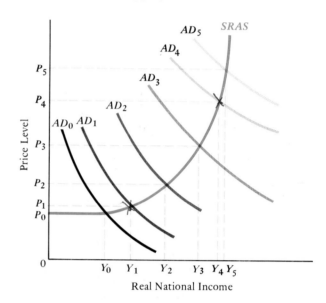

Increases in aggregate demand will have their major impact on increases in real income, increases in prices, or increases in both income and prices, depending on the shape of the *SRAS* curve.   Because of the increasing slope of the *SRAS* curve, increases in aggregate demand up to AD_0 have virtually no impact on price. When aggregate demand increases from AD_0 to AD_1, there is a relatively small increase in price, from P_0 to P_1, and a relatively large increase in output, from Y_0 to Y_1. Successive further increases bring larger price increases and relatively smaller output increases. By the time aggregate demand is at AD_4 or AD_5, virtually all of the effect is on the price level.

at the aggregate expenditure curve. An increase in autonomous expenditure shifts the *AE* curve upward, thus raising the amount demanded. But a nearly vertical *SRAS* curve means that output cannot be expanded to satisfy the increased demand. Instead, the extra demand merely forces prices up, and, as prices rise, the *AE* curve is shifted down once again. The rise in prices continues until the *AE* curve is back nearly to where it started. Thus the rise in prices offsets the expansionary effect of the original shift and leaves both *real* aggregate expenditure and equilibrium real income virtually unchanged as a result.

FIGURE 28-3 Demand Shocks When the SRAS Curve Is Nearly Vertical

(i)

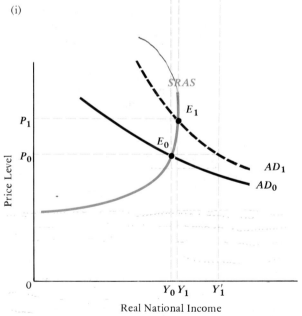

(ii)

When the *SRAS* curve is nearly vertical, the effect of an increase in autonomous expenditure is mainly a rise in the price level. An increase in autonomous expenditure shifts the AE curve up from AE_0 to AE_1, as shown by arrow 1 in (i). Given the initial price level P_0, equilibrium would shift from E_0 to E_1', and real national income would rise from Y_0 to Y_1'. (We use primes on these variables because these results cannot persist, since real national income cannot rise to Y_1'.) But the price level does not remain constant. This is shown by the $SRAS$ curve in (ii). Instead, the price level rises to P_1. This causes the AE curve to shift back down to AE_2, as shown by arrow 2 in (i), and equilibrium income increases only to Y_1. If the $SRAS$ curve were completely vertical, equilibrium income would return all the way to Y_0.

The discussion of Figures 28-2 and 28-3 illustrates the general proposition that the effect of any given shift in aggregate demand will be divided between a change in real output and a change in the price level, depending on the conditions of aggregate supply. The steeper the *SRAS* curve, the greater the price effect and the smaller the output effect.

The shape of the *SRAS* curve implies that at low levels of national income shifts in aggregate demand affect mainly output, and at high levels of national income shifts in aggregate demand affect mainly prices.

Shifts in the *SRAS* Curve

Aggregate supply is important not only because the *shape* of the *SRAS* curve determines the effects of shifts in aggregate demand, but also because *shifts* in the *SRAS* curve affect the price level and national income. Such shifts were illustrated in Figure 24-8.

Causes of Shifts

The *SRAS* curve can shift for many reasons. Two sources of shift are of particular importance.

Changes in input prices.   The fact that input prices are held constant along the *SRAS* curve suggests an important reason for the *SRAS* curve to shift. If input prices rise, firms will find that the profitability of their current production has been reduced. For any given level of output to be produced, an increase in the price level will be required. If prices did not rise, firms would react by decreasing production.[2] For the economy as a whole this would mean less output at each price level than before the input price increases. Thus if input prices rise, the *SRAS* curve shifts upward. This is what we have called a *decrease in supply*, as illustrated in Figure 28-4.

Similarly, a fall in input prices will cause the *SRAS* to shift downward (or, what is the same thing,

[2] Students who have already studied microeconomics will recognize that such an upward shift in a firm's marginal cost curve leads to a decrease in the output that is profitable for the firm to produce. This is discussed in Chapter 12.

FIGURE 28-4   Shifts in the *SRAS* Curve

A shift to the left of the *SRAS* curve reflects a decrease in supply, a shift to the right an increase in supply. Starting from P_0, Y_0 on $SRAS_0$, suppose there is an increase in input prices. At price level P_0 only Y_1 would be produced. Alternatively, to get output Y_0 would require a rise to price level P_1. The new supply curve is $SRAS_1$, which may be viewed as above and to the left of $SRAS_0$. An increase in supply, caused, say, by a decrease in input prices, would shift the *SRAS* curve down and to the right from $SRAS_1$ to $SRAS_0$.

to the right), reflecting what we have called an *increase in supply*.

Increases in productivity.   If labor productivity rises, meaning that each worker can produce more, then the unit costs of production will fall as long as wage rates remain constant. Lower costs generally lead to lower prices. Competing firms cut prices in attempts to raise their market shares, and the net result of such competition is that the fall in costs of production is accompanied by a fall in prices.[3]

Since the same output is sold at a lower price,

[3] Even a monopoly will cut its prices and raise its output when its marginal costs fall. See Chapter 14.

this causes a shift to the right in the *SRAS* curve. This shift is an *increase in supply,* as illustrated in Figure 28-4.

A change in input prices or productivity shifts the *SRAS* curve because any given output will be supplied at a different price level than previously. An increase in input prices shifts the *SRAS* curve to the left; an increase in productivity or a decrease in input prices shifts it to the right.

Effects of Shifts in the SRAS Curve

Supply shocks were briefly analyzed in Chapter 24. It will be useful to summarize the effects of short-run shifts of the kind we have been discussing.

A leftward shift in *SRAS,* brought about, for example, by an increase in the price of basic raw materials and imported oil such as occurred during the 1970s, lowers real national income and raises the price level. Stagflation, the unhappy combination of rising prices and falling real national income, can come about due to such supply shocks, as it did during the 1970s.

A rightward shift in *SRAS,* brought about, for example, by an increase in productivity with no increase in factor prices, raises real national income and lowers the price level. This happier combination is the object of government policies seeking to encourage productivity increases. It has proved hard to achieve in practice.

Aggregate Supply in the Long Run

We have been examining the behavior of aggregate supply on the assumption that factor prices remain unchanged. We need now to see what happens when they can and do change. Indeed, the key to understanding the long-run properties of aggregate supply is to see how changes in national income *induce* shifts in the *SRAS* curve. We must add to our study of impact effects, which was based on a single *SRAS* curve, a consideration of the longer-run consequences of a demand shock.

Aggregate Demand Shocks

Shifts in aggregate demand cannot be expected to leave input prices unchanged in the long run. We need to examine this question separately for expansionary and contractionary shocks, for the behavior of the economy is not symmetrical in the two kinds of situations.

Expansionary Shocks

Assume that the economy starts off in the position of full employment and a stable price level. A rise in autonomous expenditure, perhaps caused by a sudden surge in consumption, increases aggregate demand. The immediate effects are that the price level rises and that real income rises above its potential level. As is shown in Figure 28-5(i), a negative GNP gap opens up. Because the price level rises when national income exceeds Y^*, this is called an **inflationary gap**.

Firms are now producing beyond their normal capacity output, so there is a heavy demand for all factor inputs, including labor. Workers demand wage increases to compensate for the higher cost of living caused by the increase in the price level. Thus the boom generates a combination of conditions that is a recipe for sharp increases in wages—high profits for firms, heavy demand for labor, and a desire on the part of labor for wages to catch up with the price rises. This sequence is just what past experience of the economy tells us will happen.[4]

Sharp rises in wages mean sharp rises in costs. These lead to leftward shifts of the *SRAS* curve as firms seek to pass on their increases in input costs by increasing their output prices. For this reason the increases in the price level and in real output shown in Figure 28-5(i) are *not* the final effects of the demand shock. As seen in part ii of the figure, the leftward shift of the *SRAS* curve causes a further rise in the price level, but this time the price rise is associated with a fall in output. The cost increases (and the

---

[4] Wage contracts often allow for changes in prices that are *expected* to occur during the life of the contract. The role of expectations in causing the *SRAS* curve to shift plays an important role in many macroeconomic debates and will be discussed in detail in Chapter 37.

FIGURE 28-5 Demand-Shock Inflation

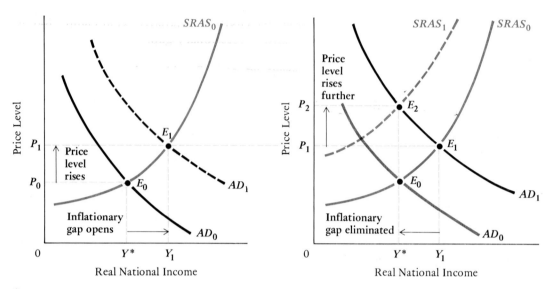

(i) Autonomous increase in aggregate demand   (ii) Induced shift in aggregate supply

A rightward shift of the *AD* curve first raises price and output along the *SRAS* curve. It then induces a shift of the *SRAS* curve that further raises prices, but lowers output along the *AD* curve. In (i) the economy is in equilibrium at E_0, at its level of potential output Y^* and price level P_0. The *AD* curve then shifts to AD_1. This moves equilibrium to E_1, with income Y_1 and price level P_1, and opens up an inflationary gap of Y^*Y_1.

In (ii) the inflationary gap results in an increase in wages and other input costs, shifting the *SRAS* curve leftward. As this happens, income falls and the price level rises along AD_1. Eventually, when the *SRAS* curve has shifted to $SRAS_1$, income is back to Y^*, the inflationary gap has been eliminated, but the price level has risen further to P_2.

---

consequent leftward shifts of the *SRAS* curve) go on until the inflationary gap has been removed, that is, until income returns to Y^*, its potential level. Only then is there no abnormal demand for labor.

This important expansionary demand-shock sequence can be summarized as follows:

1. Starting from full employment, a rise in aggregate demand raises the price level and raises income above its potential level as the economy expands along a given *SRAS* curve.
2. The expansion of output beyond its normal capacity level puts heavy pressure on factor markets; factor prices begin to rise, shifting the *SRAS* curve to the left.
3. The shift of the *SRAS* curve causes output to fall along the *AD* curve. This process continues *as long as actual output exceeds potential output. Therefore, actual output eventually falls back to its potential level.* The price level is, however, now higher than it was after the initial impact of the increased aggregate demand, but inflation will have come to a halt.

The ability to wring more output from the economy than its underlying potential output (as in summary point 2, above) is only a short-term success. Y greater than Y^* sets up inflationary pressures that tend to push national income back to Y^*.

There is a self-adjustment mechanism that brings any inflation caused by a one-time de-

mand shock to an eventual halt by returning output to its potential level and thus removing the inflationary gap.

Contractionary Shocks

Let us return to that fortunate economy with full employment and stable prices. It appears again in part i of Figure 28-6, which is similar to part i of Figure 28-5. Now assume a *decline* in aggregate demand, perhaps due to a major reduction in investment expenditure.

The impact of the decline is a fall in output and some downward adjustment of prices, as shown in part i of the figure. As output falls, unemployment rises. The difference between potential output and actual output is, as we have seen, the GNP gap. When the GNP gap is positive, as in Figure 28-6, it is called a **recessionary gap**.

Flexible wages.   Consider what would happen *if* severe unemployment caused wage rates to fall sharply. Falling wage rates would lower costs for firms and cause a rightward shift of the *SRAS* curve. As shown in Figure 28-6(ii), the economy would move along its fixed *AD* curve with falling prices and rising output until full employment was restored at potential national income Y^*. We conclude that *if* wages were to fall whenever there was unemploy-

FIGURE 28-6   Demand-Shock Deflation with Flexible Wages

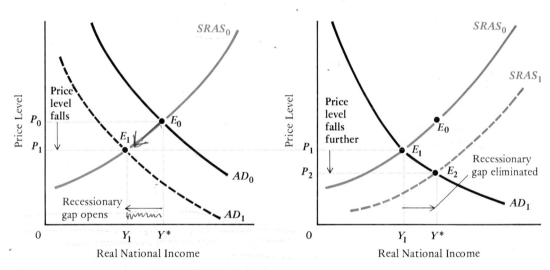

(i) Autonomous fall in aggregate demand   (ii) Induced shift in aggregate supply

A leftward shift of the *AD* curve first lowers price and output along the *SRAS* curve and then induces a (slow) shift of the *SRAS* curve that further lowers prices, but raises output along the *AD* curve. In (i) the economy is in equilibrium at E_0, at its level of potential output Y^* and price level P_0. The *AD* curve then shifts to AD_1, moving equilibrium to E_1, with income Y_1 and price level P_1, and opens up a GNP (or recessionary) gap of Y_1Y^*.

Part (ii) shows the adjustment back to full employment that would occur from the supply side of the economy if wages were sufficiently flexible downward. The fall in wages would shift the *SRAS* curve to the right. Real national income would rise, and the price level would fall further along the *AD* curve. Eventually, the *SRAS* curve would reach $SRAS_1$, with equilibrium at E_2. The price level would stabilize at P_2 when income has returned to Y^*, eliminating the recessionary gap.

ment, the resulting fall in the *SRAS* curve would restore full employment.

> Flexible wages that fell when there was unemployment would provide an automatic adjustment mechanism that would push the economy back toward full employment whenever output fell below potential.

Sticky wages. We now come to what may be called the *second important asymmetry* of the economy's aggregate supply behavior (the first being the increasing slope of the *SRAS* curve). Boom conditions with severe labor shortages do cause wages to rise rapidly, shifting the *SRAS* curve upward. But the experience of many economies suggests that wages are sticky, that is, they are not very flexible in a downward direction. Slump conditions with heavy unemployment do not cause wages to fall with anything like the corresponding speed. There are many reasons for this, including the tradition of stating labor contracts in money terms and workers' expectations that with adequate performance their wages will stay constant or rise.

If wages are sticky, unemployment has a weak and slow-acting downward effect on wages. The adjustment mechanism that depends upon rightward shifts of *SRAS* is, therefore, weak and sluggish.

The weakness of the automatic adjustment mechanism does not mean that slumps will last indefinitely. What it means is that speedy recovery back to full employment must be generated mainly from the demand side. If the economy is to avoid a lengthy stagnation, the force leading to recovery must be a rightward shift of the *AD* curve rather than a rightward drift of the *SRAS* curve.

> The *SRAS* curve shifts to the left fairly rapidly when national income exceeds Y^*, but it shifts to the right only slowly when national income falls short of Y^*.

This difference in speed of adjustment is a consequence of the second important asymmetry in the behavior of aggregate supply. This asymmetry helps explain two key facts about our economy. First, unemployment *can* persist for quite long periods without causing large decreases in wages and prices (which, if they did occur, would help to remove the unemployment). Second, booms, with labor shortages and production beyond normal capacity, cannot persist for long periods without causing large increases in wages and prices.[5]

The Long-Run Aggregate Supply (*LRAS*) Curve

The possibility of automatic adjustments gives rise to an important concept: the **long-run aggregate supply (*LRAS*) curve.** This curve relates the price level to real national income *after wage rates and all other input costs have been fully adjusted to eliminate any unemployment or overall labor shortages.*[6]

Shape of the *LRAS* curve. Once all of the adjustments required have occurred, the economy will have eliminated any excess demand or excess supply of labor. In other words, full employment will prevail and output will necessarily be at its potential level Y^*. It follows that the aggregate supply curve becomes a vertical line at Y^*.[7] (*LRAS* curves are shown in Figure 28-7.)

Notice that the vertical *LRAS* curve does not represent the same thing as the vertical portion of the *SRAS* curve (see Figure 28-2). Over the vertical range of the *SRAS* curve, the economy is at its utmost limit of productive capacity, when no more can be squeezed out, as might occur in an all-out war effort. The vertical shape of the *LRAS* curve is due to the workings of an adjustment mechanism that is assumed always to bring the economy back to its level of potential output, even though it may stray away in the short run. It is called the *long-run*

---

[5] The asymmetrical behavior is reflected in the terminology we have used. When output is above the level of potential output, we speak of an *inflationary gap*; when it is below the potential level, we speak of a *recessionary gap* (rather than a *deflationary gap*).

[6] Students who have studied microeconomics will notice that this use of the term *long run* appears to differ from its meaning in microeconomics. Note, however, the key similarity that the long run has more flexibility for adjustment than does the short run.

[7] The *LRAS* curve is sometimes called the classical aggregate supply curve because the classical economists were mainly concerned with the behavior of the economy in long-run equilibrium.

FIGURE 28-7 Long-Run Equilibrium and Aggregate Supply

(i) A rise in aggregate demand

(ii) A rise in long-run aggregate supply

When the *LRAS* curve is vertical, aggregate supply determines *Y* and aggregate demand determines *P*. In (i) a shift in the *AD* curve from AD_0 to AD_1 with the *LRAS* curve unchanged moves the equilibrium from E_0 to E_1. This raises the price level from P_0 to P_1, but leaves output unchanged at Y^* in the long run. In (ii) a shift in the *LRAS* curve from $LRAS_0$ to $LRAS_1$ with the aggregate demand curve constant at AD_0 moves the equilibrium from E_0 to E_2. This raises output from Y_0^* to Y_1^*, but lowers the price level from P_0 to P_2.

aggregate supply curve because it refers to adjustments that take a substantial amount of time.

An important implication of the vertical shape of the *LRAS* curve is that, given full adjustment of all

input prices, full employment and the level of potential income are not determined by the price level. (We shall return to the importance of this implication later.)

Long-Run Equilibrium

Figure 28-7 shows the equilibrium output and the price level determined by the intersection of the *AD* curve and the vertical *LRAS* curve. Because the *LRAS* curve is vertical, shifts in aggregate demand change the price level, but not the level of equilibrium output, as shown in part i. In contrast, a shift in aggregate supply changes both output and the price level, as shown in part ii. For example, a rightward shift of the *LRAS* curve increases national income and leads (eventually) to a fall in the price level.

With a vertical *LRAS* curve, output is determined solely by conditions of supply, and the role of aggregate demand is simply to determine the price level.

Of course, these are only long-term tendencies. To see the short-term impact of demand and supply shocks, we need to use the short-run aggregate supply curve. Since, because of wage stickiness, downward adjustments of wages and prices may take a long time, there may be long periods when the economy is not at, or even near, long-run equilibrium.

Supply-Side Economics

Both of Ronald Reagan's presidential campaigns featured a theory of economic policy that came to be known as *supply-side economics*. To some, the policy promised a quick cure for both high inflation and low growth in real national income. To others, it was an exercise in wishful thinking.

The theoretical tools developed in this chapter can be used to explore both the theory and the doubts. Although supply-side economics has many aspects, we are here concerned specifically with the effects of supply-side policies on the price level and on real national income, in an initial situation with a large inflationary gap. When Ronald Reagan became president in January 1981, the inflation rate was about 10 percent and unemployment about 7 percent; any policy that would decrease them both would have been welcomed.

How It Was Supposed to Work

The theory of supply-side economics called for adopting measures that would shift the *LRAS* curve to the right far enough and fast enough to eliminate the inflationary gap. In the most favorable case there would be no offsetting demand-side effects. This case is illustrated in Figure 28-8.

A major part of supply-side economics was the provision of tax incentives that were to increase potential national income by increasing the nation's supplies of labor and capital. Incentives were to be given to firms to increase their investment, thus increasing national productive capacity. Personal taxes

were to be cut across the board to give everyone an incentive to work more. It was argued that people already employed would be more inclined to work longer and harder when they were able to keep a larger fraction of their pre-tax earnings for themselves, and people outside of the labor force would be drawn in as a result of the higher after-tax wages. Extra tax incentives were to be given to persons at high income levels so as to increase the incentives for work and risk taking on the part of the most productive people. It was anticipated that the resulting increases in productive capacity and increases in productivity would shift the *LRAS* curve to the right.

It was also assumed that no budget deficits would result from the cuts in tax rates and increases in tax exemptions. The increase in national income, it was

FIGURE 28-8   The Theory of Anti-Inflationary Supply-Side Economics

(i) An inflationary situation

(ii) Supply–side success

Supply-side economics seeks to eliminate an inflationary gap by shifting the *LRAS* curve to the right without changing aggregate demand. Part i shows an economy in short-run equilibrium at E_0 on AD_0 and $SRAS_0$, with income Y_0 and price level P_0. As a result of the inflationary gap of $Y_0^* Y_0$, the $SRAS$ curve will shift upward, taking the equilibrium along AD_0 (as shown by the arrow), with falling national income and rising price level. Other things being equal, the inflation will come to a halt once the curve has reached $SRAS_1$ and equilibrium is established at E_1, with price level P_1 and national income at its potential level Y_0^*.

Part ii shows the same economy after supply-side measures shift the *LRAS* curve to $LRAS_1$. This makes Y_1^* the new level of potential income and removes the inflationary gap. The fall of income and rise in the price level shown in (i) are both prevented.

argued, would create a larger tax base so that even at the lower tax *rates,* total tax *revenues* (which would fall initially) would be restored. For example, if a 10 percent cut in tax rates were followed by a 10 percent increase in real national income, it would leave tax revenues approximately the same.[8]

Doubts About the Theory

One major worry of critics of the theory was that demand-side effects would swamp any supply-side effects for at least the first several years. Whatever the long-term effects on the supply side, economic theory is clear about the short-term effects of these measures on the demand side. Cuts in personal tax rates that are intended to be permanent leave households with an increase in their current and expected future disposable income. As a result they spend more, causing a rightward shift in the aggregate demand curve. Also we know that an increase in investment increases aggregate demand. In the short run the extra expenditure on capital goods creates new incomes for the factors of production that produce these goods and, through the multiplier process, new incomes for others as well.

Thus, the short-run effect of supply-side measures would surely be to shift the aggregate *demand* curve to the right. In the least favorable situation, if all the demand-increasing effects were to occur, and none of the favorable aggregate supply effects were to occur, the result will surely be an increase in the inflationary gap. This possibility is illustrated in Figure 28-9.

Neither of the extreme cases illustrated in Figures 28-8 or 28-9 is likely to occur. Supply-side measures will lead to shifts to the right of both the *LRAS* and *AD* curves and the effects of the policies will depend upon the magnitude and timing of the two shifts. For example, if the effects on demand occur first, but are followed by large increases in long-run aggregate supply, the impact effect would be to increase inflation, but the long-run effect would be for prices to come back down and for output to rise.

[8] Students who have read Chapter 23 and encountered the Laffer curve (see pages 434–435) will see that believers in that phenomenon had an even more direct reason to believe that tax cuts would increase government revenues.

FIGURE 28-9   Demand Effects of Supply-Side Measures

The effect of supply-side measures on aggregate demand is inflationary. The figure shows the economy in the same short-run initial equilibrium at E_0 as in Figure 28-8(i). However, it assumes that demand-side effects of the policy measures occur and are fully felt, before any supply-side effects come into play. The *AD* curve shifts to the right to AD_1, and the economy moves toward equilibrium at E_1, as shown by arrow 1. This gives a temporary increase in output to Y_1 at the cost of an immediate rise in the price level to P_1. But the inflationary gap is also increased, to Y^*Y_1. Now the *SRAS* curve starts to shift up, taking the equilibrium along AD_1 in the direction shown by arrow 2, with falling output and rising prices. If nothing else happens, the inflation will finally come to an end at price level P_2 and output Y^*. As a result of the supply-side measures the rise in the price level, from P_0 to P_2, is *greater* than it would have been without the measures; that is, from P_0 to P_1.

Supply-siders with training in economics surely knew that the short-term effects via aggregate demand would occur. But they believed that the supply-side shifts of long-run aggregate supply would be large enough, and quick enough, to dominate them. Critics not only doubted this view as to timing, but they also questioned whether the tax changes proposed would have the desired effects even in the long run. Economic theory makes no definite prediction about the effects of tax cuts on how much people will work. It might make them work more, because they earn more for each additional hour that they work. But it might make them work less, because the tax cut means that they can, if they wish, have both more disposable income and more leisure. For example, if in response to a 10 percent tax cut they worked 5 percent less, they would have approximately 5 percent more disposable income and 5 percent more leisure. (This is discussed in greater detail in Box 19-2 on page 345.)

Evaluating the Theory

It is difficult to resolve all the factual matters at issue in the supply-side debate on the basis of the Reagan administration's experiences. First, the proposed measures were never fully implemented. Second, the inflationary conditions postulated in the theory were changed by other policies, especially monetary pol-

icies that will be examined in Chapter 32. It is clear, however, that aggregate *demand* effects did dominate in the short run.

Beyond this, most economists would agree on at least two aspects of the experience. First, policymakers and economists are much more alert to the supply-side effects of economic policies than many of them used to be. This is an important achievement.

Second, the timing of effects is such that measures that do succeed in shifting both aggregate demand and long-run aggregate supply will surely have their initial effects through a rapid shift in the *AD* curve. Their effects through a shift in the *LRAS* curve will occur only gradually. Thus, the view of a number of Reagan supporters that supply-side measures would provide a *quick* fix to inflationary pressures is, simply, discredited. Such measures may, however, have contributed to the sustained recovery of 1983–1986.

Summary

1. The short-run aggregate supply (*SRAS*) curve, drawn for given factor prices, is positively sloped because unit costs rise with increasing output and because rising product prices make it profitable to increase output.

2. The slope of the *SRAS* curve increases as the level of output increases. This important asymmetry occurs because when output is low and firms have much unused capacity, output can be increased with little or no rise in prices; but when output is high and capacity constraints are felt, further output increases become increasingly costly, and output will be increased only if prices are increased substantially.

3. The steepness of the *SRAS* curve determines how the impact of a shift in the *AD* curve is divided between a change in output and a change in the price level. When the *SRAS* curve is flat, shifts in the *AD* curve affect mainly real national income. When the *SRAS* curve is steep, shifts in the *AD* curve affect mainly the price level.

4. A change in factor costs will cause the *SRAS* curve to shift and thus lead to a movement along the *AD* curve. A supply shock that shifts the *SRAS* curve to the left can lead to a stagflation—rising prices and falling output.

5. In the long run it is necessary to consider changes in factor prices. An expansionary demand shock will create an inflationary gap which will induce factor price increases. These will shift the *SRAS*

curve to the left, resulting in a higher level of prices, with output eventually decreasing to its potential level.

6. A contractionary demand shock will work in the opposite direction if factor prices are flexible. If, however, they are sticky, the automatic adjustment process may be slow, and a recessionary gap may not be quickly eliminated.

7. A second asymmetry of aggregate supply is that input prices, particularly wages, tend to be sticky downward, but flexible upward. As a result, an inflationary gap leads to a fairly rapid wage rise and rapid reduction of national income to the level of potential income, while a recessionary gap leads to only slowly falling wages and hence to a slow increase of national income to the level of potential income.

8. The long-run aggregate supply *(LRAS)* curve relates the price level and national income after all wages and other costs have been fully adjusted to long-run equilibrium. The *LRAS* curve is vertical at the level of potential income.

9. Because the *LRAS* curve is vertical, output in the long run is determined by the position of the *LRAS* curve, and the only long-run role of the *AD* curve is to determine the price level.

10. Supply-side economics in an inflationary situation seeks to reduce an inflationary gap and increase output by tax cuts and other incentive measures designed to shift the *LRAS* curve to the right and thus increase potential output. Whether or not this will work in the long run is a matter of current debate. In the short run such measures increase aggregate demand thus adding to inflationary pressures.

Topics for Review

Positive slope of the *SRAS* curve
Increasing slope of the *SRAS* curve
Effects of shifts in the *AD* curve
Effects of shifts in the *SRAS* curve
Long-run aggregate supply (*LRAS*)
Effects of shifts in the *LRAS* curve
Supply-side economics

Discussion Questions

1. "Starting from a full-employment equilibrium, an increase in government spending can produce more output and employment at the cost of a once-and-for-all rise in the price level."

   "Increased spending can never lead to a permanent increase in output above its full employment level."

   Discuss these two statements in terms of short- and long-run *aggregate supply curves.*

2. Following are the combinations of output and price level, given by indexes for GNP and the CPI, respectively, for some recent years. Treat each pair as if it is the intersection between an *AD* and an *AS* curve. Plot these and indicate in each case the direction of shift of the *SRAS* or *AD* curves that could have caused them. Why might you be uncertain about some of the shifts?

	CPI (1967 = 100)	GNP (Billions of 1982 dollars)
1978	195	3115
1979	217	3192
1980	247	3187
1981	272	3249
1982	289	3166
1983	298	3277
1984	311	3492
1985	322	3574

3. Identify the effects of each of the following events on the *SRAS* curve.
   a. Increase in the price of imported raw materials used in key manufacturing industries
   b. Increase in the price of imported consumption goods such as coffee or bananas
   c. Increased restrictions on pollution emissions in an attempt to combat acid rain
   d. Projections of increased federal government deficits over the next five years
   e. An improved economic outlook leading to an investment boom
   f. Increased labor force participation rate of key sectors of the population

4. Interpret each of the following news items in terms of *AD* and *SRAS* curves.
   a. "Management representative says union wage demands are irresponsible in the face of current high unemployment rates."
   b. "Administration spokesman says that although the recovery is expected to be vigorous, it will witness only modest reductions in the unemployment rate."
   c. "Inflation fell quickly in 1982 due to the 'lucky break' of reduced union strength in the automobile and steel sectors."
   d. "Wage increases have failed to keep up with inflation during the current boom."
   e. "Innovations in microelectronic technology will lead to an increase in both national output and unemployment."
   f. "Reagan's tough stance with public sector unions has vastly improved the inflation outlook over the next few years."

5. Show the effects on the price level and output of income tax cuts that make people work more in an economy currently experiencing an inflationary gap.

29

Business Cycles: The Ebb and Flow of Economic Activity

Changing, always changing; this is the dominant characteristic of the GNP for as far back as we have records. Long-term growth (which is studied in Chapters 34 and 42) appears in the upward trend in potential GNP. Short-term fluctuations are seen in oscillations of actual GNP around potential GNP. Such oscillations are caused by changes in aggregate demand and aggregate supply. They lead to changes in total real output and hence in the amount of employment and unemployment. They also affect living standards since the total amount of goods and services available varies as total output varies.

Cyclical Fluctuations

As we saw in Chapter 24, most economic series exhibit two aspects of change. The first is the long-term trend. In the case of GNP, there is an upward trend throughout the twentieth century associated with economic growth. In the case of unemployment, the series for the twentieth century is trend-free, exhibiting no long-term tendency for the unemployment rate to rise (or fall).

The second aspect of change is fluctuation around the long-term trend. These fluctuations are far from random; they exhibit a systematic pattern. A year of relatively high output is likely to occur in conjunction with other years of high output, and such groups are likely to be separated by groups of years of relatively low output. This pattern of a sequence of highs followed by a sequence of lows followed again by another sequence of highs is the source of the term *cyclical* used to describe such economic fluctuations.

The Concept of the Business Cycle

The **business cycle** refers to the continual ebb and flow of business activity that occurs around any long-term trend after seasonal adjustments have been made.[1] Such cyclical fluctuations can be seen in many economic series. For example, continual oscillations in GNP are apparent in Figure 24-3. Figure 29-1 gives a longer perspective on cyclical fluctuations.

---

[1] When economists wish to analyze monthly or quarterly data, they often try to remove fluctuations that can be accounted for by a regular seasonal pattern. This *seasonal adjustment* is made because many economic series show a marked seasonal pattern over the year. For example, logging activity tends to be low in the winter months and high in the summer, while fuel oil sales tend to have the reverse seasonal pattern.

FIGURE 29-1   American Business Activity Since 1870

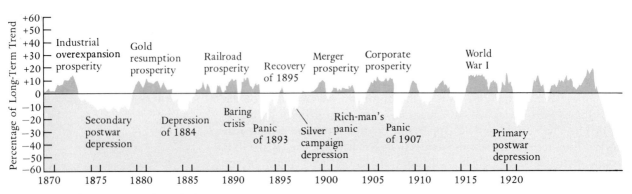

Source: The AmeriTrust Company, Cleveland, Ohio.

Cyclical ups and downs have dominated the short-term behavior of the U.S. economy at least since 1870. This chart is constructed by selecting one index of general economic activity, fitting

But the concept of the business cycle refers to fluctuations in the general pace of economic activity. This cannot be fully caught by a single statistic, even one as important as GNP. Figure 29-2 shows three other economic series. Each of these, as well as a dozen others that might be studied, tells us something about the general variability of the economy. It is clear that some series vary more than others and that they do not all move exactly together.

The picture suggested by Figures 29-1 and 29-2 is not one of occasional sharp shifts in the aggregate demand and supply curves. If it were, we would expect national income to show occasional sharp changes followed by long periods of little or no change. Instead the short-term situation is one of continual change at varying rates.

Evidently there are factors at work causing economic activity to display continual short-term fluctuations around the economy's long-term growth trend.

While all cycles are not alike in duration or intensity, each appears to have tendencies toward cumulative movements that eventually reverse themselves. This was true long before governments attempted to

intervene to stabilize their economies, and it is true still.

The late Alvin Hansen, a distinguished American authority on business cycles, once reported that there were 17 cycles in the U.S. economy between 1795 and 1937, with an average duration of 8.35 years. A shorter "inventory cycle" of 40 months' duration was also found, as well as longer cycles associated with building booms (15 to 20 years). The Russian economist Kondratieff thought he could identify long waves of 40 to 50 years associated with the introduction of major innovations. Some economists have argued that in many Western democracies there exists a political business cycle associated with the pattern of elections.

While the evidence is diverse, it is nevertheless possible to identify some basic characteristics of the pattern of business cycles:

1. **A common pattern of variation more or less pervades all economic series.**
2. **Economic series differ in their particular patterns of fluctuations.**
3. **Cycles differ substantially in the length and the size of the swings involved.**

a trend line to it, and plotting the deviations of the index from its trend value. It shows clearly the tendency for an economy to fluctuate. Major booms and slumps are unmistakable.

FIGURE 29-2 Fluctuations in Output, Selected Series, 1950–1985

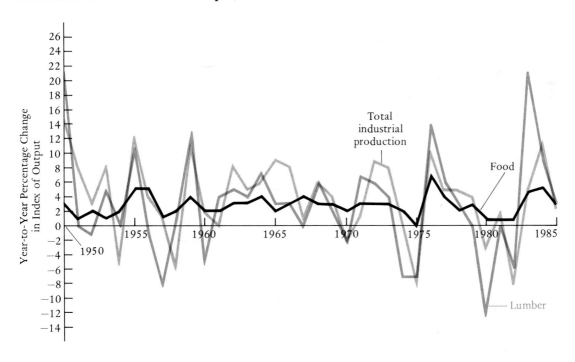

Fluctuations follow similar, but by no means identical paths for various output series. Fluctuations are easily seen in these series. Food tends to fluctuate much less and lumber somewhat more than the overall series for industrial production.

The Terminology of Business Fluctuations

Although recurrent fluctuations in economic activity are neither smooth nor regular, a vocabulary has developed to denote their different stages. Figure 29-3 shows stylized cycles that illustrate some terms.

Trough.   A trough is, simply, the bottom. A trough is characterized by high unemployment of labor and a level of consumer demand that is low in relation to the capacity of industry to produce goods for consumption. There is thus a substantial amount of unused industrial capacity. Business profits are low; for some individual companies they are negative. Confidence in the future is lacking and, as a result, firms are unwilling to risk making new investments. If a trough is deep enough, it may be called a *slump* or a **depression.**

Recovery.   When something sets off a recovery, the lower turning point of the cycle has been reached. The symptoms of a recovery (or expansion) are many: Worn-out machinery is replaced; employment, income, and consumer spending all begin to rise; expectations become more favorable as a result of increases in production, sales, and profits. Invest-

ments that once seemed risky may now be undertaken as the climate of business opinion starts to change from pessimism to optimism. As demand expands, production can be expanded with relative ease merely by re-employing the existing unused capacity and unemployed labor.

Peak.   A peak is the top of the cycle. At the peak there is a high degree of utilization of existing capacity; labor shortages may be severe, particularly in key skill categories; and shortages of essential key raw materials may develop. Output can be raised further only by investment that increases capacity. Because such investment takes time, further rises in demand are now met more by increases in prices than by increases in production. As shortages develop in more and more markets, a situation of general excess demand for factors develops. Costs rise but prices rise also, and business remains generally very profitable. A peak that exceeds the level of potential GNP may be referred to as a **boom.**

Recession.   A **recession** is a downturn from a peak of economic activity. The U.S. Department of Commerce defines a recession as a fall in the real GNP

FIGURE 29-3
A Stylized Business Cycle

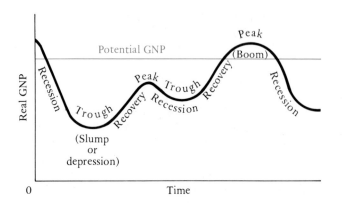

While the phases of business fluctuations are described by a series of commonly used terms, no two cycles are the same. Starting from a lower turning point, a cycle goes through a phase of recovery, or expansion, reaches an upper turning point, and then enters a period of recession. Cycles differ from one another in the severity of their troughs and peaks and in the speed with which one phase follows another. Severe troughs are called *depressions*; severe peaks are called *booms*.

for two quarters in succession. Demand falls off, and as a result production and employment fall. As employment falls so do households' incomes; falling income causes demand to fall further. Profits drop and more and more firms get into difficulties. Investments that looked profitable on the expectation of continual rising demand suddenly appear unprofitable, and investment is reduced to a low level. It may not even be worth replacing capital goods as they wear out because unused capacity is increasing steadily.

Turning points.   The point at which a recession begins is often called the **upper turning point.** The point at which a recovery begins is referred to as the **lower turning point**.

Explaining Business Cycles

An explanation of the business cycle must answer two questions. (1) What are the factors that cause GNP and other key macro variables to *fluctuate?* (2) What are the factors that cause those fluctuations to form a *cyclical* pattern? These two questions are taken up in the two main sections that follow.

Why Do Income and Employment Fluctuate?

Figure 29-4 presents an explanation of the fluctuations of GNP in terms of a fluctuating *AD* curve and a stable *SRAS* curve.

There is general agreement that over the course of U.S. economic history, the business cycle has been driven mainly by fluctuations in aggregate demand. Nevertheless, particular cycles can sometimes be explained in part by aggregate supply shocks. Indeed, events of the mid 1970s made the citizens of advanced industrial countries acutely aware of supply-side causes.

Aggregate demand shocks are a major historical source of fluctuations in GNP; aggregate supply shocks are another source.

FIGURE 29-4   A Demand-Driven Business Cycle

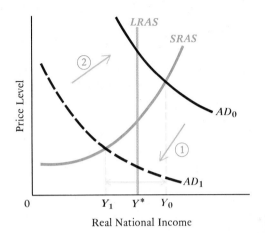

Fluctuations in aggregate demand can cause fluctuations in income and employment. Assume that over the course of the business cycle aggregate demand oscillates regularly. Starting from a high AD_0 and an income at the peak of Y_0, the curve falls continuously, as shown by arrow 1, until it reaches AD_1. Income falls through Y^* and reaches its trough at Y_1.

The *AD* curve then rises continuously, as shown by arrow 2. Income is taken back through Y^* and reaches Y_0 at the next peak.

Sources of Aggregate Demand Shocks

To say that cycles are caused mainly by fluctuations in aggregate demand only pushes the need for explanation one stage further back. What are the sources of the continual disturbances to aggregate demand? The theory of income determination suggests four main candidates—shifts in each of the four main components of aggregate expenditure.

Changes in Consumption

Consumption is the largest single component of aggregate expenditure, about two-thirds of the total. When searching for the causes of income changes, we are not concerned with changes in consumption *in response* to changes in income, but instead with *shifts* in the function relating consumption to income. Such shifts can have many causes.

Changes in tastes. In the mid 1980s there was a significant increase in the demand for American cars. If enough of the money that was spent on automobiles would have been saved instead, there would be a significant rightward shift in the aggregate demand curve. Jobs and incomes would first be gained in the auto industry. The induced increase in spending by workers in that industry would then set up a multiplier effect as increases in output, income, and spending spread throughout the economy.

Changes in expectations and interest rates. Expectations of future inflation may lead to a burst of spending to buy now while goods are cheap. On the other hand, a wave of uncertainty about the future may lead to a rise in saving and hence a cut in spending. High interest rates can be a powerful incentive to postpone buying durable goods. For example, in 1981 rates of over 20 percent helped to depress the markets for automobiles and other consumer durables, and subsequent declines in interest rates led to a boom in those markets.

In an inflationary world it is important to distinguish between the real and the nominal rate of interest. The *nominal* rate of interest is the ratio of the *amount of money* repaid to the amount of money borrowed. The *real* rate of interest concerns the ratio of the *purchasing power of the money* repaid to the purchasing power of the money borrowed. The real rate of interest is the difference between the nominal rate of interest and the rate of inflation. It is this real rate that matters for most expenditure decisions. This distinction is further elaborated in Box 29-1.

Changes in taxes. As we saw in Chapter 27, tax changes can also shift the aggregate consumption function. Income tax cuts mean that more *total* income becomes *disposable* income, leading to an increase in consumer spending. Tax increases have the opposite effect.

Changes in transfer payments. Government transfer payments amount to roughly one-eighth of personal income. Sharp changes in transfer payments could influence aggregate expenditure through their effects on personal consumption and investment.

Changes in Government Expenditures

Look again at Figure 29-1. It is obvious that every war in this century has been accompanied by a rapid expansion of economic activity. Wars result in an enormous increase in federal government expenditure as people and materials are shifted from civilian to military uses. This shift is usually reversed in the postwar period. For example, federal government purchases of goods and services (measured in constant dollars at 1982 prices) rose from $64 billion in 1940 to $723 billion in 1944 and then fell to $94 billion by 1947. Changes in government purchases of goods and services in the period from 1941 to 1946, that is, during World War II and the immediate postwar period, were the principal cause of changes in GNP during that period.

Such expenditures played a similar though less dramatic role during the Vietnam War, rising from $244 billion in 1965 to $310 billion in 1968 and falling back fairly steadily to reach $230 billion by 1973. The extra Vietnam expenditures, on top of a full-employment civilian economy, helped to open up a large inflationary gap in the late 1960s and early 1970s.

Figure 29-5 on page 552 shows the changes in real purchases of goods and services by all levels of government and compares these with changes in gross investment. The largest shifts in government expenditure occurred during the initial buildup of the Vietnam war in the latter half of the 1960s. Since that time there have been only occasional significant demand shocks caused by shifts in government expenditures, the largest being in 1984–1985. The figure makes it apparent, however, that the shocks caused by changing government expenditure have been much smaller on average than the shocks caused by changing private investment expenditure.

Changes in Net Exports

A quarter of a century ago the United States could be studied as if it were a completely closed economy, so unimportant were imports and exports. Today, trade is a significant part of American GNP. Exports, which were 5 percent of GNP in 1960, rose to just over 10 percent in the 1980s. A rise in imports,

BOX 29-1

Real and Nominal Interest Rates: An Important Distinction

If you pay me $8 interest for a $100 loan for one year, the nominal rate is 8 percent. The real rate that I earn, however, depends on what happens to the overall level of prices in the economy.

If the price level remains constant over the year, then the real rate that I earn would also be 8 percent, because I can buy 8 percent more goods and services with the $108 that you repay me than with $100 that I lent you. However, if the price level rises by 8 percent, the real rate would be *zero*, because the $108 you repay me buys the same quantity of goods as the $100 I gave up. If I am unlucky enough to lend money at 8 percent in a year in which prices rise by 10 percent, the real rate I earn would be *minus* 2 percent.

If lenders and borrowers are concerned with real costs measured in terms of purchasing power, the nominal rate of interest will be set at the rate they want as return on their money plus an amount to cover any expected rate of inflation. Consider a one-year loan that is meant to earn a real return to the lender of 5 percent. If the expected rate of inflation is zero, the nominal rate set for the loan will be 5 percent. If a 10 percent inflation is expected, the nominal interest rate will be 15 percent.

To provide a given expected real rate of interest the nominal rate will be set at the desired real rate of interest plus the expected annual rate of inflation.

Because they overlook this point, people are often surprised at the high nominal rates of interest that exist during periods of rapid inflation. For example, when the nominal interest rates rose drastically in 1979, many commentators expressed shock at the "unbearably" high rates. Most of them failed to notice that with inflation running at about 12 percent, an interest rate of 15 percent represented a real rate of only 3 percent. Had the Federal Reverse System given in to the pressure to hold interest rates to the more "reasonable" level of 10 percent, it would have been imposing a negative real rate of interest. Lenders would then have been "rewarded" for lending their money by receiving less purchasing power in interest plus principal than the purchasing power of the principal they parted with initially.

Concern about the burden of borrowing should be directed at the real, not the nominal, rate of interest.

For example, a nominal rate of 8 percent combined with a 2 percent rate of inflation is a much greater real burden on borrowers than a nominal rate of 16 percent combined with a 14 percent rate of inflation.

Cash Flow Problems

Some of the effects of inflation can be compensated for by changes in the nominal interest rate, but not all. The inflation premium on interest rates represents an early repayment of capital and hence causes cash flow problems for borrowers. Consider a simple example. A firm borrows $1,000 for 10 years at 4 percent when the price level is constant. The firm will pay $40 of interest per year and at the end of 10 years it must repay in one lump sum the capital of $1,000.

Now assume that the same bargain is struck except that a 5 percent rate of inflation will occur *and is fully expected* over the period of the loan. In this case the nominal rate of interest is set at 9 percent, and its annual interest payments will be $90.

In one sense the real situation is unchanged but in another important sense it is different. The firm is now paying an annual inflation premium of $50. This compensates the lenders for the loss of purchasing power on the principal of their loans. But for the borrowers it constitutes an early repayment of capital. Note that the $1,000 repaid at the end of the 10-year period has a much smaller real value in the second (inflationary) situation.

So the stream of real payments is very different when a 4 percent interest rate is combined with a zero inflation rate and when a 9 percent interest rate is combined with a 5 percent inflation rate.

FIGURE 29-5   **Annual Changes in Government Purchases and Real Gross Private Investment, 1961–1985** *(in 1982 dollars)*

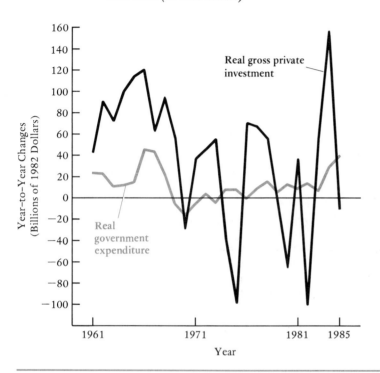

Investment shocks are typically larger than government expenditure shocks. With the exception of 1985, the last year shown, the absolute change in investment expenditure exceeded the absolute change in government expenditure. Also, while expenditure shocks have been both positive and negative, government expenditure shocks are typically positive. *(Source: Economic Report of the President, 1986.)*

resulting from, say, a preference for foreign over American automobiles, or a fall in exports, resulting from, say, a European recession, can have a major impact on American national income and employment.

Shifts in consumption, government, and export expenditures can and sometimes do cause major fluctuations in national income and employment.

Changes in Investment

Changes in investment expenditure are a major source of economic fluctuations. Consider, for example, the period 1929 to 1932. In 1929 total investment expenditure of firms and households in the U.S. economy was $16.2 billion at the then prevailing prices, almost double the amount of expenditure

needed to replace the capital goods that were used up that year in the process of producing a GNP of $103 billion. The American economy in 1929 was thus adding rapidly to its stock of capital equipment. Three years later, in 1932, total investment expenditure was $1 billion. This was less than one-sixth of the amount needed just to keep the stock of capital intact. The American economy in 1932, with GNP reduced to $58 billion, was rapidly reducing its stock of capital equipment.

As Figure 29-5 shows, investment expenditure is quite volatile. Quite large shocks due to changes in investment expenditure hit the economy frequently. The change in investment from one year to the next has been on average about three times the change in government expenditure.

Changes in investment are also quite closely correlated with changes in national income, as shown in Figure 29-6. Rising investment tends to be asso-

FIGURE 29-6   Annual Changes in Real Gross Private Investment and GNP, 1950–1985 *(in 1982 dollars)*

The fluctuations in gross private investment are sharp and closely related to changes in national income. The change in real GNP is repeated from Figure 24-3. Changes in private investment are closely related to changes in national income. *(Source: Economic Report of the President, 1986.)*

ciated with rapidly rising GNP, while falling investment tends to be associated with slowly rising or falling GNP. This is consistent with the view that investment shocks are a major cause of changes in national income.

Investment expenditures play a key role in most theories of cyclical fluctuations.

Why Does Investment Change?

The three major components of total investment expenditure are inventories, plant and equipment, and residential housing. Changes in investment are one of the prime causes of short-term fluctuations, but we do not have the whole story unless we know why investment fluctuates. In discussing the theory of income determination in Chapters 26 and 27 we talked simply of shifts in investment, not of the underlying causes of such shifts.

The Interest Rate and Investment

Empirical evidence shows that investment responds to many influencing factors. One of the most important is the rate of interest. Other things being

BOX 29-2

Many Rates of Interest

In the real world there are many different rates of interest. Speaking in terms of a single interest rate can be a valid simplification for many purposes because the whole set of rates *tends* to move upward or downward together. For some purposes, however, it is important to take into account the different rates that prevail at any one time.

At the same time that you receive an interest rate of 6 or 7 percent on deposits at a savings and loan association, you may have to pay 11 or 12 percent to borrow from that savings and loan corporation to finance your purchase of a house. Interest rates on consumer installment credit of 16 percent and 20 percent are observed. A small firm pays a higher rate on funds it borrows from banks than does a giant corporation. Different government bonds pay different rates of interest, depending on the length of the period for which the bond runs. Corporation bonds tend to pay higher interest than treasury bills, and there is much variation among bonds of different companies.

Considering the extreme mobility of money, why do such differences exist? Why do funds not flow between different uses to eliminate these differences? The answer is that money *does* flow quite rapidly between alternative assets in response to interest dif-

ferentials, but differences prevail because quoted interest rates reflect many factors.

Differences in risk.   Corporation bonds generally have higher interest rates than treasury bills because they have a greater degree of risk. For example, in mid 1985 many corporate issues were yielding more than 11 percent, while federal government bonds were paying 8 percent or less. Why? Investors were sure of the ability of the government to pay both the interest and the principal on their bonds, but they were less sure about the financial condition of private corporations.

Secured loans, where the borrower pledges an asset as collateral, tend to have lower interest rates than unsecured loans, other things being equal. Loans secured by houses (mortgages) tend to have lower interest rates than loans secured by automobiles, in part because it is harder to run away with a house than with a car and in part because a car can depreciate much more rapidly and unpredictably than a house.

Differences in duration.   The *term,* or duration, of a loan also affects its price. The same bank will usually pay a higher rate of interest on a certificate of deposit

---

equal, the higher is the interest rate, the higher the cost of borrowing money for investment purposes and the less the amount of investment expenditure. Although in basic theory we talk of "the" interest rate, reality is not so simple; Box 29-2 discusses a few of these complications.

While each dollar of investment has the same consequences for aggregate demand, different types of investment respond to different sets of causes. Thus it is useful to discuss separately the determinants of the three major types of investment expenditures, both to see why it is that the interest rate is such an important influence on investment and to determine what other factors are important.

Inventories.   Inventory changes represent only a small fraction of private investment in a typical year,

but their average size is not an adequate measure of their importance. They are one of the more volatile elements of total investment and therefore have a major influence on shifts in investment expenditure.

Studies show that the stock of inventories held tends to rise as production and sales rise. Because the size of inventories is related to the level of sales, the *change* in inventories (which is current investment) is related to the *change* in the level of sales.

A firm may decide, for example, to hold inventories of 10 percent of its sales. Thus, if sales are $100,000, it will wish to hold inventories of $10,000. If sales increase to $110,000, it will want to hold inventories of $11,000. Over the period during which its stock of inventories is being increased, there will be a total of $1,000 new inventory investment.

that cannot be redeemed at the bank (without penalty) for at least one year than on a straight savings account from which funds can be withdrawn in a matter of minutes. Yet many savers prefer savings accounts because they want to be able to withdraw their money on short notice. Except when interest rates are thought to be temporarily abnormally high, borrowers are usually willing to pay more for long-term loans than for short-term loans because they are certain of having use of the money for a longer period. Lenders usually require a higher rate of interest the longer is the time before the borrower must repay. Other things being equal, the shorter the term of a loan, the lower the interest rates.

Differences in costs of administering credit.   There is great variation in the cost of different kinds of credit transactions. It is almost as cheap (in actual dollars) for a bank to lend Western Airlines $1 billion that the airline agrees to pay back with interest after one year as it is for the same bank to lend you $14,000 to buy a new car that you agree to pay back over two years in 24 equal installments.

The installment loan to you requires many more bookkeeping entries than the loan to the airline. In addition, it is easier, and therefore less costly, to check Western Airlines' credit rating than it is to check yours. The difference in the cost *per dollar* of each loan is considerable. The bank may very well make less profit per dollar on a $14,000 loan at 20 percent per year than on a $1 billion loan at 10 percent per year. In general, the bigger the loan and the fewer the payments, the less the cost per dollar of servicing the loan. Why then do banks and finance companies usually insist that you repay a loan in frequent installments? They worry that if you do not pay regularly, you will not have the money when the loan comes due.

In the market for borrowed funds there is a structure of various interest rates for credit transactions of different kinds.

Individual rates will be set that take into account such factors as risk premiums, duration of loan, and costs of administration. Nevertheless, it is useful and usual to talk about movements of interest rate structures up and down as changes in "the" interest rate. This simplification is appropriate when the entire structure of rates moves up or down together so that changes in a single rate can capture changes in all rates.

The higher the level of production and sales, the larger the desired stock of inventories. Changes in the rate of production and sales cause temporary bouts of investment (or disinvestment) in inventories.

When a firm ties up funds in inventories, those same funds cannot be used elsewhere to earn income. At the very least the money could be lent out at the going rate of interest. Thus the higher the real rate of interest, the higher will be the cost of holding an inventory of a given size. And the higher that rate of interest, the more firms will try to lower their inventories. By causing firms to change the inventory levels that they desire to hold, a change in the rate of interest can lead to a flurry of investment or disinvestment in inventories.

The higher the real rate of interest, the lower the desired stock of inventories. Changes in the rate of interest cause temporary bouts of investment (or disinvestment) in inventories.

Residential housing construction.   Since 1970 spending on residential construction has varied between one-fifth and one-third of all gross private investment in the United States and between 2.5 percent and 5.5 percent of GNP. Because expenditures for housing construction are both large and variable, they exert a major impact on the economy.

Many influences on residential construction are noneconomic and depend on demographic or cultural considerations such as new family formation. But households must not only want to buy houses, they must be able to do so. Periods of high employment and high average family earnings tend to lead to increases in house building and those of unemployment and falling earnings to decreases in such building.

Almost all houses are purchased with money borrowed on mortgages. Interest on the borrowed money typically accounts for over one-half of the purchaser's annual mortgage payments; the remainder is repayment of principal. It is for this reason that sharp variations in interest rates exert a substantial effect on the demand for housing.

Box 29-3 provides an illustration of the importance of interest rates for housing expenditures. This importance was borne out by experiences from 1979 to 1982. During this period mortgage rates rose from less than 11 percent to just over 15 percent and housing starts fell from 1,194 thousand units to a mere 661 thousand in 1982. (Since inflation fell from 1980, the increased nominal interest rates also meant increased real rates.) The construction industry itself and its major suppliers such as the cement and the lumber industries, felt the blow of a dramatic fall in demand. Conversely, in the mid 1980s interest rates fell sharply and there was a boom in the demand for new housing.

Expenditures for residential construction tend to vary positively with changes in average income and negatively with interest rates.

Plant and equipment. Investment in plant and equipment is the largest component of domestic investment. Over half is financed by firms' retained profits (profits *not* paid out to its shareholders). This means that current profits are an important determinant of investment.

A second major determinant is the rate of interest. Much investment is financed by borrowed money. As became abundantly clear in the early 1980s, very high interest rates greatly reduce the volume of investment as more and more firms find their expected profits from investment do not cover the interest on borrowed investment funds.

A third major determinant is changes in national income. If there is a rise in aggregate demand that is expected to persist and cannot be met by existing capacity, then investment in new plant and equip-

ment will be needed. Once the new plants have been built and put into operation, however, the rate of new investment will fall.

This further illustrates an important characteristic of investment already encountered in the case of inventories: *If the desired stock of capital goods increases, there will be an investment boom while the new capital is being produced.* But if nothing else changes, and even though business conditions continue to look rosy enough to justify the increased stock of capital, investment in new plant and equipment will cease once the larger capital stock is achieved. This aspect of investment leads to the *accelerator* theory of investment, which requires a closer look.

The Accelerator Theory of Investment

According to the accelerator theory, usually called the **accelerator**, investment is related to the rate of change of national income. When income is increasing, it is necessary to invest in order to increase the capacity to produce consumption goods; when income is falling, it may not even be necessary to replace old capital as it wears out, let alone to invest in new capital.

The main insight which the accelerator theory provides is the emphasis on the role of net investment as a phenomenon of *disequilibrium*—the situation in which the actual stock of capital goods differs from what firms and households would like it to be. Anything that changes the desired size of the capital stock can generate investment. The accelerator focuses on one such source of change, changing national income. This gives the accelerator its particular importance in connection with *fluctuations* in national income. As we shall see, it can itself contribute to those fluctuations.

How the accelerator works. To see how the theory works, suppose that there is a particular capital stock needed to produce each given level of an industry's output. The ratio of the value of capital to the annual value of output is called the **capital-output ratio**. Suppose that the industry is producing at capacity and the demand for its product increases. If the industry is to produce the higher level of output, its

BOX 29-3

The Cost of Buying a House on Time

Few people who buy a house can pay cash. Most purchases are financed by borrowing money on a *mortgage*. A mortgage is a loan to the house purchaser (sometimes of as much as 85 or 90 percent of the purchase price, but 60 to 75 percent is common). In return, the borrower promises to make fixed monthly payments that cover interest on the money borrowed and repay the amount borrowed (the principal) over some agreed period, commonly 20 or 30 years. (The monthly payments often include an amount to cover insurance and taxes, but this is ignored in what follows.) The house itself acts as security for the loan. Loans of this type are said to be *amortized,* which means that fixed payments over a stated period gradually repay the principal and cover the interest on the principal outstanding.

Because the loan stretches over a long period, a great deal of the total amount paid by the borrower is interest on the outstanding loan. For example, on a 20-year mortgage for $50,000 at a nominal annual interest rate of 8 percent per year (a monthly rate of 8/12 of 1 percent), a total of $100,375 would be paid in 240 monthly installments of $418.23 each. This is

$50,000 to repay the principal of the loan and $50,375 of interest. At a 12 percent nominal annual rate (a monthly rate of 1 percent) the total payments would be $132,130, making $82,130 total interest as well as $50,000 to repay the principal.

The interest on a mortgage is calculated on the amount of the loan still outstanding. After each payment the amount outstanding is reduced so that, with fixed annual payments, most of the total amount paid goes to paying interest in the early years and to repaying principal in later years. It follows that the purchaser's equity in the house (the down payment plus the total amount of the loan that has been repaid over the years) builds up slowly at first, then more and more rapidly as the terminal date approaches.

Note in the table that when half the life of the mortgage has passed, only about a quarter of the principal has been repaid. In the first year of the mortgage, $4,965 goes as interest and only $825 to reduce the principal on the loan. In the last year, only $300 is interest and $5490 goes to repay the principal.

Breakdown of Payments in Selected Years on a 20-Year Mortgage for $50,000 at 10 Percent (*all figures to the nearest dollar*)

Year	Payments made over the year	Interest paid over the year	Principal repaid over the year	Equity (cumulative total over all the years)*
1	$5,790	$4,965	$ 825	$ 825
2	5,790	4,875	915	1,745
5	5,790	4,560	1,230	5,100
10	5,790	3,765	2,025	13,490
15	5,790	2,455	3,335	27,290
19	5,790	820	4,970	44,510
20	5,790	300	5,490	50,000

* In addition to equity due to down payment.

capital stock must increase. This necessitates new investment.

Table 29-1 provides a simple numerical example of the accelerator. Working through the data step by step leads to three conclusions:

1. **Rising levels of sales rather than high levels of sales are needed to call forth net investment.**
2. **For net investment to remain constant, sales must rise by a constant amount per year.**

TABLE 29-1   An Illustration of the Accelerator Theory of Investment

(1)	(2)	(3)	(4) Required stock of capital, assuming a capital-output ratio of 5/1	(5) Net investment: increase in required capital stock
Year	Annual sales	Change in sales		
1	$10	$0	$ 50	$ 0
2	10	0	50	0
3	11	1	55	5
4	13	2	65	10
5	16	3	80	15
6	19	3	95	15
7	22	3	110	15
8	24	2	120	10
9	25	1	125	5
10	25	0	125	0

With a fixed capital-output ratio net investment occurs only when it is necessary to increase the stock of capital in order to change output. Assume that it takes $5 of capital to produce $1 of output per year. In years 1 and 2 there is no need for investment. In year 3 a rise in sales of $1 requires investment of $5 to provide the needed capital stock. In year 4 a further rise of $2 in sales requires an additional investment of $10 to provide the needed capital stock. As columns 3 and 5 show, the amount of net investment is proportional to the *change* in sales. When the increase in sales tapers off in years 7–9, investment declines. When sales no longer increase in year 10, net investment falls to zero because the capital stock of year 9 is adequate to provide output for year 10's sales.

3. **The amount of net investment will be a multiple of the increase in sales because the capital-output ratio is greater than one.**[2]

The data in Table 29-1 are for a single industry, but if many industries behave in this way, one would expect aggregate net investment to bear a similar relation to changes in national income. This is what the accelerator theory predicts. [39]

The accelerator theory says nothing directly about replacement investment, but it does have implications for such investment. When sales are constant (no net investment required), replacement investment will be required to maintain the capital stock at the desired level. When sales are increasing from a position of full capacity, both net investment and replacement investment will be required. When sales are falling, not only will net investment be zero, but there will be a tendency to postpone replacement investment as well.

Limitations of the accelerator. Taken literally, the accelerator posits a rigid response of investment to changes in sales (and thus, aggregatively, to changes in national income). In fact, the relation is more subtle.

Changes in sales that are thought to be temporary will not necessarily lead to new investment. It is usually possible to increase the level of output for a given capital stock by working overtime or extra shifts. While this solution would be more expensive per unit of output in the long run, it is usually pref-

---

[2] In the example in the table the capital-output ratio is 5/1. Why should anyone spend $5 on capital stock to get $1 of output? It is not unreasonable to spend $5 to purchase a machine that produces only $1 of output *per year,* provided that the machine will last enough years to repay the $5 plus a reasonable return on this investment.

erable to making investments in new plant and equipment that would lie idle after a temporary spurt of demand had subsided. Thus expectations about what the required capital stock will be may lead to a much less rigid response of investment to income than the accelerator suggests.

Another limitation of the accelerator theory is that it takes a limited view of what constitutes investment. The fixed capital-output ratio emphasizes investment in what economists call **capital widening,** the investment in additional capacity that uses the same ratio of capital to labor as existing capacity. It does not explain **capital deepening,** which is the increase in the amount of capital per unit of labor that occurs, say, in response to a fall in the rate of interest. Neither does the theory say anything about investments brought about as a result of new processes or new products. Furthermore, it does not allow for the fact that investment in any period is likely to be limited by the capacity of the capital-goods industry.

For these and other reasons, the accelerator does not by itself give anything like a complete explanation of variations in investment in plant and equipment. It should not be surprising that a simple accelerator theory provides a relatively poor overall explanation of changes in investment. Yet accelerator-like influences do exist, and empirical evidence continues to suggest that they play a role in the cyclical variability of investment.

Theories of the Cycle

There are several main theories about the cycle. They do not have to be regarded as competing. Indeed, each one captures some of the forces that contribute to the cycle.

Systematic Spending Fluctuations

The most commonly accepted theory looks to systematic fluctuations in aggregate expenditure brought about by systematic alterations in spending behavior as the cause of the cycle. Several influences can cause such alterations.

The Multiplier-Accelerator Mechanism

The combination of the multiplier and the accelerator can make upward or downward movements in the economy cumulative. Imagine that the economy is settled into a depression with heavy unemployment. Then a revival of investment demand occurs. Orders are placed for new plant and equipment, which creates new employment in the capital-goods industries. The newly employed workers spend most of their earnings. This creates new demand for consumer goods. A multiplier process is now set up, with new employment and incomes created in the consumer-goods industries.

The spending of the newly created incomes in turn means further increases in demand. At some stage the increased demand for consumer goods creates, through the accelerator process, an increased demand for capital goods. Once existing equipment is fully employed in any industry, extra output requires new capital equipment, and the accelerator theory takes over as the major determinant of investment expenditure. Such investment increases or at least maintains demand in the capital-goods sector of the economy. So the process goes on, the multiplier-accelerator mechanism continuing to produce a rapid rate of expansion in the economy.

The upper turning point.   A rapid expansion can continue for some time, but it cannot go on forever. Eventually the economy will run into bottlenecks in terms of certain resources. For example, investment funds may become scarce, and as a result interest rates rise. Firms now find new investments more expensive than anticipated, and thus some become unprofitable. Or suppose that what limits the expansion is exhaustion of the reservoir of unemployed labor. The full-employment ceiling guarantees that any sustained rapid growth rate of real income and employment will eventually be slowed.

At this point the accelerator again comes into play. A slowing down in the rate of increase of production leads to a decrease in the investment in new plant and equipment. This decrease causes a drop in employment in the capital-goods industries and, through the multiplier, a fall in consumer demand.

As consumer demand falls, investment in plant and equipment is reduced to a low level because firms already have more productive capacity than they can use. Unemployment rises, and the upper turning point has been passed.

The lower turning point.   A contraction, too, is eventually brought to an end. Consider the worst depression imaginable, one in which every postponable expenditure of households, firms, or governments is postponed. Even then aggregate demand does not fall to zero. Figure 26-2 shows that as aggregate disposable income falls, households spend a larger and larger fraction of that falling income. Finally, should income fall to the break-even level, all disposable income is spent (and none is saved).

Neither does government spending fall in proportion to the fall in government tax revenues. Government expenditures on most programs continue even if tax revenues sag to low levels.

Finally, even investment expenditures, in many ways the most easily postponed component of aggregate expenditure, does not fall to zero. Industries providing basics still have substantial sales and need replacement investment. Even in the worst depression some new processes and new products appear, and these require new investment.

Taken together, the minimum levels of consumption, investment, and government expenditure will assure a minimum equilibrium level of national income that, although well below the full-employment level, will not be zero. There is a floor below which income will not fall.

Sooner or later, an upturn begins. If nothing else causes an expansion of business activity, there will eventually be a revival of replacement investment because as existing capital wears out, the capital stock eventually falls below the level required to produce current output. At this stage new machines are bought to replace those that are worn out.

The rise in the level of activity in the capital-goods industries causes, by way of the multiplier, a further rise in income. The economy turns the corner. An expansion, once started, triggers the sort of cumulative upward movement that has already been discussed.

Other Endogenous Forces

The multiplier–accelerator is one endogenous force contributing to cyclical fluctuations. Two others are inventories and construction.

Inventory cycles.   There are, as we have seen, good reasons to suppose that the required size of inventories is related to the level of firms' sales, and sales are related to the level of national income. If firms maintain anything like a rigid inventory-to-sales ratio, this will cause an accelerator-like linkage between investment in inventories and *changes* in national income.

Many observers believe that these sharp and somewhat periodic fluctuations lead to an "inventory cycle" of roughly 40 months' average duration.

Construction cycles.   Economists have noted some long-run, wave-like movements of roughly 20 years' duration in the statistics for expenditures on residential construction. These are sometimes referred to as "building cycles." Some economists suggest an accelerator-like explanation that runs from external events to demographic changes, to changes in the demand for housing and other buildings, and thence to changes in construction activity.

A major war, by taking males away from home, tends to retard family formation and thereby tends to depress the demand for private housing. When the war ends, there is typically an increase in marriages and household formation, an increase in the demand for housing, and a boom in the construction industry.

Depending on the capacity of the building industry, the boom may last many years before the desired increases in the stock of buildings of various kinds are achieved, but eventually it ends. Then, approximately 20 years after the end of the war that triggered the boom, there is likely to be a further boom in the number of marriages and births as the new generation starts its process of family formation. Wars are not the only source of such population-induced cycles; a severe depression will lead to a similar postponement of family formation.

The evidence concerning construction spending

over the past century is thought by many economists to support the theory just outlined, a theory very much like the accelerator, though with changes in demographic factors, rather than changes in income, providing the impetus.

Random Shocks and Long Lags

One other popular model of the cycle does not assume cyclical behavior from firms and households in order to generate cycles. It suggests instead that random shifts in expenditure are transformed into systematic cycles of output and employment.

This theory begins with lags. For example, if a fall in the rate of interest makes an investment in a new project profitable, it may take 6 months to plan it, 3 months to let contracts, 6 months before spending builds up to its top rate, and another 24 to complete the project. These lags mean that changes in the rate of interest will cause reactions in investment expenditure that are distributed over quite a long period of time.

These lags have important implications for key macro variables. Although the disturbances might be random or erratic, income and employment both follow a cyclical path.

Each major component of aggregate expenditure has sometimes undergone shifts large enough to disturb the economy significantly. Long lags can convert such shifts into cyclical oscillations in national income.

Policy-Induced Cycles

Yet another theory of the cycle is based on the allegation that government-induced demand shocks have sometimes caused cyclical fluctuations. Government expenditure has not often been the cause of major shocks due to sudden large changes. But government tax policy and government monetary policy have both been shifted enough to cause significant demand shocks. Why should the government administer such potentially disturbing demand shocks? Several reasons have been suggested.

A political business cycle.   As early as 1944 the Polish-born Keynesian economist Michael Kalecki warned of a political business cycle. He argued that once governments had learned to manipulate the economy, they would engineer an election-geared business cycle. In pre-election periods they would raise spending and cut taxes. The resulting expansionary demand shock would create high employment and good business conditions that would bring voters' support for the government. But the resulting inflationary gap would lead to a rising price level. So, after the election was won, the government would depress demand to remove the inflationary gap and provide some slack for expansion before the next election.

This theory invokes the image of a cynical government manipulating employment and national income solely because it wants to stay in office. Few people believe that governments deliberately do this all the time, but the temptation to do it some of the time, particularly before elections, may prove irresistible. Indeed, Professor Alan Blinder of Princeton has made a persuasive case that one such politically inspired demand shock was inflicted by the Nixon adminstration just prior to the 1972 elections.

Alternating policy goals.   A variant of the policy-induced cycle does not require a cynical government and an easily duped electorate. Instead both sides need only be rather shortsighted and have rather narrow vision.

In this theory, when there is a recession and relatively stable prices, the public and the government identify unemployment as the number one economic problem. The government then engineers an expansionary policy shock through some combination of tax cuts and spending increases. This, plus such natural cumulative forces as the multiplier-accelerator, expands economic activity. Unemployment falls and income rises, but as income rises above potential national income, the price level begins to rise. It first rises along the stable *SRAS* curve and then rises further as boom conditions raise factor prices and shift the *SRAS* curve upward. (See Figure 28-5.)

At this point the unemployment problem is declared cured. Now inflation is seen as the nation's number one economic problem. A contractionary demand shock is engineered. The natural cumulative forces again take over, causing a recession. The inflation subsides but unemployment rises, setting the stage once again for an expansionary shock to cure the unemployment problem.

Many economists have criticized government policy over the last few decades as sometimes causing fluctuations by alternately pushing expansion to cure unemployment and then contraction to cure inflation. We shall see in Chapter 37 that this charge is particularly strong against monetary policy. But whatever the policy, the charge is that policy makers have sometimes been too shortsighted in alternating their concern between unemployment and inflation.

Misguided stabilization policy. In a variant of the previous theory the government tries to hold the economy at potential national income by countering fluctuations in private-sector expenditure with offsetting changes of its own spending and taxes. The government can in principle dampen such cyclical fluctuations by its stabilization policies. But unless it is very sophisticated, bad timing may accentuate rather than dampen fluctuations. We return to this possibility in subsequent chapters.

Securities Markets (Stock Markets)

It is commonplace to observe that stock market values have sometimes displayed cumulative upward movements and at other times cumulative downward movements. The first are called *bull markets* and the second *bear markets*. Most people also know that the Great Depression of the 1930s was preceded by the great stock market crash of 1929, which caused what is still the largest percentage loss of stock values ever to be suffered by American investors.

The association between fluctuations in the stock market and in the economy is there, but is there a causal connection? Do stock market booms help to cause business cycle booms, and do stock market slumps help to cause business cycle slumps? Before we can answer this question, we need to learn a bit about such markets.

The Function of Securities Markets

When a household buys shares newly issued by a company, it becomes one of the firm's owners. The company will not return the household's money, except in the rare event that the firm is liquidated. If the household wishes to get its money back, it can only persuade someone else to buy its shares in the company.

Similarly, when a household buys a bond from a company, it cannot get its money back from the company before a specified date. If I bought a 2007 bond in 1987, the bond will be redeemed by the company (i.e., the loan will be paid back) only in 2007. If I wish to get my money back sooner, all I can do is sell the bond to someone who is willing to become one of the company's creditors.

An organized market where stocks and bonds are bought and sold is called a **securities market,** or a **stock market**. Two of the best known are the New York Stock Exchange and the American Stock Exchange. The trading of existing shares on the stock market indicates that ownership is being transferred; it does not indicate that companies are raising new investment funds from the public.

Securities markets are important because, by providing for the ready transfer of corporate securities, they make it possible for individuals to save without having to commit themselves for long periods.

Securities markets allow people to put their savings into stocks and bonds that are not themselves directly or quickly redeemable. For example, if I want to invest in a particular stock that pays an attractive yield, I may do so even though I know that I will want my money back after only a year. Given a securities market, I can be confident of my ability to sell the security a year from now. But while securities markets provide for the quick sale of stocks and bonds, they do not guarantee that securities can

FIGURE 29-7   Fluctuations in an Index of Stock Prices, 1960–1986

Stock market fluctuations are very sharp and irregular, and the last four years have witnessed a sharp increase. The chart shows quarterly variations in the Dow Jones Industrial Average of 30 leading stocks. The index grew steadily from 1962 to 1966 and then displayed very little trend over the next 15 years. Over that period the index did, however, fluctuate sharply; it is these fluctuations that make large speculative gains and losses possible. Two notable falls in the index occurred during the economic downturns in 1969 and 1974.

While the index was at approximately the same level in 1980 as it was in 1965, the Consumer Price Index (1967 = 100) has risen from 94.5 to 246.8, causing many commentators to believe that the market was "undervalued." The market then fell during the 1981 recession, but the economic recovery of 1982 to 1986 was accompanied by a dramatic sustained increase in the Dow Jones; the index rose from about 800 at the end of 1982 to over 1,900 in the summer of 1986, before falling to about 1,750 in September.

be sold at the same price at which they were bought. The price at any time is the one that equates the demand and supply for a particular security, and rapid fluctuations in stock prices are common.

Prices on the Stock Market

Figure 29-7 shows the wide swings in a well-known index of stock market prices, the Dow Jones Industrial Average. The most recent swing in the period covered in the figure began from a trough in May 1984 when the Dow Jones was about 1,100. The index then rose, almost without interruption, until in early September 1986 it reached a value of 1,919, a rise of about 75 percent in just 28 months. This long rise was then interrupted by a dramatic fall; in one week the index fell by almost 10 percent, losing over 150 points.

This was only the latest in a series of "booms" and "busts" that have periodically interrupted the long-term trend for stock market prices to rise slowly but steadily over the years. There had also been two large swings in the mid 1970s. Between 1975 and January 1977 the average stock price rose by 20 percent, yielding large gains for people who were wise or lucky enough to have bought at the beginning and sold at the end of this upswing. But then a downward movement occurred, with stock prices losing more than 25 percent of their value within a little over a year. Just a little earlier, in 1973, stocks lost 40 percent of their value and then recovered quite rapidly.

Measuring Stock Market Swings

Commentators are often careless about making the key distinction between the *number of points* by which the index changes over some period and the *percentage change* in that index over the same period. For example, when the Dow Jones Industrial Average fell by just over 150 points from a value of 1919 in one week in September 1986, newspaper reporters were quick to point out that this was the largest one-week fall measured by the number of points ever. But was it the greatest loss of stock values in any meaningful sense?

The answer is no. To see the significance for wealth holders of changes in stock market prices, we need to deal not in index points but in percentages. When we do this, the dramatic collapse of 1986 is put into perspective. Serious though it was, the loss of 10 percent in stock values was by no means unprecedented. As noted in the text, in 1973–1974 stocks lost 40 percent of their value and then recovered; in 1975–1976 they lost 25 percent of their values before recovering. These losses, as well as those of September 1986, remain dwarfed by the loss everyone hopes will never be repeated: over 80 percent of the value of stocks was lost over the three-year period from 1929 to 1933!

Causes of Stock Market Swings

What causes such rapid gains and losses, and what do they have to do with business cycles?

When investors buy a company's stocks, they are buying rights to share in the stream of dividends to be paid out by that company. They are also buying an asset that they can sell in the future at a gain or loss.

The value of that stock depends on two things: first, what people expect the stream of future dividend payments to be, and second, what capital gain or loss people expect to realize when the stock is sold.

Both things make dealing in stocks an inherently risky operation. Will the company in which you are investing pay more or less dividends over future years? Will the company's value rise or fall so that you can sell your share in it for more or less than

what you bought it for? While dividend policies of most established companies tend to be fairly stable, stock prices are subject to wide swings.

The Influence of Present and Future Business Conditions

We have observed that many influences act on stock market prices; these include the state of the business cycle and the stance of government policies.

Cyclical forces. If investors expect a firm's earnings to increase, the firm will become more valuable and the price of its stock will rise. Such influences cause stock prices to move with the business cycle, being high when current profits are high and low when current profits are low. It also causes stock prices to vary with a host of factors that influence expectations of future profits. A poor crop, destruction of trees by acid rain, announcement of new defense spending, a change in the foreign exchange value of the dollar, or a change in the political complexion of the administration can all affect profit expectations and hence affect stock prices.

Policy factors. We shall see later in this book that major alterations in monetary policy can cause major changes in interest rates. Such changes, or just the expectation of them, will have major effects on stock prices. Say, for example, that interest rates rise rapidly. Investors will see that they can now earn an increased amount by purchasing government bonds. As a result, they will wish to alter their investment portfolios to hold more bonds and less stocks. But everyone cannot do this, since there are only so many stocks, and so many bonds, available to be held at any given time. Hence, as everyone tries to sell their stocks, prices fall. The fall will only stop when the expected rate of return to investment in stocks, based on their lower purchase price, makes stocks equally attractive to bonds. Then investors will no longer be trying to shift out of bonds *en masse*.

Speculative Booms

As well as responding to a host of factors that can reasonably be expected to influence the absolute and relative earnings of companies, stock prices often develop an upward or downward movement of their own, propelled by little more than speculation that feeds on itself.

In major stock market booms, people begin to expect rising stock prices and hurry to buy while stocks are cheap. This action bids up the prices of shares and creates the capital gains that justify the original expectations. This is an example of the phenomenon of *self-realizing expectations*. Investors get rich on paper in the sense that the market value of their holdings rises. Money-making now looks easy to others who also rush in to buy, and new purchases push up prices still further. At this stage, attention to current earnings all but ceases. If a stock can yield, say, a 50 percent capital gain in one year, it does not matter much if the current earnings represent only a small percentage yield on the purchase price of the stocks. Everyone is "making money," so more people become attracted by the get-rich-quick opportunities. Their attempts to buy bid up prices still further. In such speculative booms, current earnings represent an ever-diminishing percentage yield on the current price of the stocks.

Capital gains can be so attractive that investors may buy stocks on margin—that is, borrow money to buy them, using the stocks themselves as security for the loans. In doing this, many investors may be borrowing money at a rate of interest considerably in excess of the yield from current dividends. Even if $50,000 is borrowed at 10 percent (interest payments are $5,000 per year) to buy stocks yielding a current dividend return of only 4 percent (dividend receipts are $2,000 per year), never mind, says the investor's logic, the stocks can be sold in a year or so for a handsome capital gain that will more than repay the $3,000 of interest not covered by dividends. Some people have the luck or good judgment to sell out near the top of the market, and they actually make money. Others wait eagerly for ever greater capital gains, and in the meantime they get richer and richer—on paper.

Eventually something breaks the period of unrestrained optimism. Some investors may begin to worry about the very high prices of stocks in relation not only to current yields but to possible future yields even when generous allowances for growth are made. Or it may be that the prices of stocks become depressed slightly when a sufficiently large number of persons try to sell out in order to realize their capital gains. As they offer their securities on the market, they cannot find purchasers without some fall in prices. Even a modest price fall may be sufficient to persuade others that it is time to sell. But every share that is sold must be bought be someone. A wave of sellers may not find new buyers at existing prices, causing prices to fall. Panic selling may now occur.

A household that borrowed $50,000 to buy stocks near the top of the market may find the paper value of its holdings sliding below $50,000. How will it repay its loan? Even if it does not worry about the loan, its broker will. The household may sell now before it loses too much, or its broker may "sell the customer out" to liquidate the loan. All this causes prices to fall even further, and provides another example of self-realizing expectations. If enough people think prices are going to come down, their attempt to sell out at the present high prices will create the fall in prices the expectations of which caused the selling.

This is a very simple and stylized description of a typical speculative cycle, yet it describes the basic elements of market booms and busts that have recurred throughout stock market history. It happened in the Jay Cooke panic of 1873 and in the Grover Cleveland panic of 1893. The biggest boom of all began in the mid 1920s and ended on Black Tuesday, October 29, 1929. The collapse was dramatic, with stocks losing about one-half of their value in about two months. Nor did it stop there. For three long years, stock prices continued to decline until the average value of stock sold on the New York Stock Exchange had fallen from its 1929 high of $89.10 a share to $17.35 a share by late 1933. It also happened, although less dramatically, in the booms and busts of the 1970s and 1980s discussed earlier in this section.

Stock Market Swings: Cause or Effect of Business Cycles?

Stock markets tend often to lead, and sometimes to follow, booms and slumps in business activity. In both cases the causes usually run from real business conditions, whether actual or anticipated, to stock market prices. This is the dominant theme, the stock market as reflector.

It is also possible for the stock market to be a causal factor in the business cycle. For example, some people held that the wild boom of the late 1920s tied up funds in speculative uses that would otherwise have gone to the real investment spending needed to sustain the boom into the 1930s. Such circumstances are possible, but they are only a minor theme.

Stock market fluctuations are more typically a consequence than a cause of the business cycle.

In many cases the stock market and the business cycle both reflect the common influence of other factors. For example, stock markets often react to changes in interest rates that may be caused by government policy; as we have seen, such interest rate changes can also play a causal role in cyclical fluctuations in the economy. Typically the stock market responds quicker than does the economy to such influences, and for this reason many observers look to it as a "leading indicator" of likely future economic developments.

The relationship between the stock market and the economy is further complicated by the existence of occasional speculative booms and busts. There are often real economic forces influencing expectations of stock prices, but at least for a while the prices may become dominated by speculative psychology. Unfortunately, speculative behavior causes the stock market to react to many events that turn out to have little or no enduring implications for the economy. As one wag put it, the stock market has predicted seven out of the last two recessions!

As an example, consider the long upswing that took stock prices up by about 75 percent in less than three years between early 1984 and mid 1986. At the time the United States enjoyed, almost alone among advanced industrial countries, a very strong recovery, and the rising stock prices do doubt reflected the resulting favorable profit outlook of American companies. They also reflected the fact that foreign investors saw few equally profitable investment opportunities outside of the United States. Added onto all

of that may have been a speculative component. Certainly many doubted that the full increase in stock values of over 75 percent in less than three years was justified by underlying business opportunities. Only time can tell how much, if any, of the rise in values was due to transitory speculative behavior. If any of us knew in advance, we would be able to make a killing on the market by knowing which way prices would go over the next 12–18 months!

Stock Markets: Investment Marketplaces or Gambling Casinos?

Stock markets fulfill many important functions. It is doubtful that the great aggregations of capital needed to finance modern firms could be raised under a private ownership system without them. There is no doubt, however, that they also provide an unfortunate attraction for many naive investors whose get-rich-quick dreams are more often than not destroyed by the fall in prices that follows the occasional speculative booms they help to create.

To some extent public policy has sought to curb the excesses of stock market speculation through supervision of security issues. This is handled by the Securities and Exchange Commission, which was set up in 1934. It seeks, among other things, to prevent both fraudulent or misleading information and trading by "insiders" (those in a company with confidential information). Moreover, the government can limit the ability of speculators to trade on margin.

All in all, the stock market is both a real marketplace and a place to gamble. As in all gambling situations, those who are less well informed and less clever than the average tend to be losers in the long term.

Causes of Business Cycles: A Consensus View?

Economists once argued long and bitterly about which was the best explanation of the recurrent cyclical behavior of the economy.

Today most economists agree that there is not a single cause or class of causes governing business cycles.

In an economy that has tendencies for both cumulative and self-reversing behavior, any large shock, whether from without or within, can initiate a cyclical swing. Wars are important; so, too, are major technical inventions. A rapid increase in interest rates and a general tightening of credit can cause a sharp decrease in investment. Expectations can be changed by a political campaign or a development in another part of the world. The list of possible initial impulses, autonomous or induced, is long. It is probably true that the characteristic cyclical pattern involves many outside shocks that sometimes initiate, sometimes reinforce, and sometimes dampen the cumulative tendencies that exist within the economy.

Cycles differ also in terms of their internal structure. There are variations in timing, duration, and amplitude. In some cycles full employment of labor may be the bottleneck that determines the peak. In others high interest rates and shortages of investment funds may nip an expansion and turn it into a recession at the same time that the unemployment of labor is still an acute problem. In some cycles the recession phase is short; in others a full-scale period of stagnation sets in. In some cycles the peak develops into a severe inflation; in others the pressure of excess demand is hardly felt, and a new recession sets in before the economy has fully recovered from the last trough. Some cycles are long in duration; others are short.

In this chapter we have suggested reasons why an economy that is subjected to periodic external shocks will tend to generate a continually changing pattern of fluctuations, as cumulative and then self-reversing forces alternatively come into play. In the next chapter we study how governments seek to influence the cycle and remove some of its extremes through the use of fiscal policy.

Summary

1. The economy experiences continual fluctuations. There is a self-reinforcing cumulative process that leads to a cyclical pattern of fluctuations.
2. Economists break a stylized cycle into four phases: trough, recovery, peak, and recession. These phases have certain characteristic features, although no two real-world cycles are exactly the same.
3. Short-term fluctuations in GNP are usually, though not always, the result of variations in aggregate demand. Overall, these fluctuations show a fairly clear pattern that is described as cyclical. Despite the overall pattern, the evidence is that the cycles are irregular in amplitude, in timing, in duration, and in the way they affect particular industries and sectors of the economy.
4. Any explanation of the business cycle must explain both *why* income fluctuates and *how* those fluctuations get transformed into cycles.
5. Shifts in consumption, government, and export expenditures can, and sometimes do, cause major fluctuations in American national income and employment.
6. Investment expenditure causes fluctuations in aggregate demand. The three principal components of private investment are changes in business inventories, residential construction, and investment in plant and equipment. The interest rate is an important determinant of investment spending.
7. Changes in business inventories, the smallest of the three major components of investment expenditure, often account for an important fraction of the year-to-year changes in the level of invest-

ment. They respond both to changes in the level of production and sales and to the rate of interest.

8. Residential construction shows a cyclical pattern of its own. House building responds to economic (as well as noneconomic) influences, varying directly with the level of national income and inversely with the rate of interest. The rate of interest is important because interest payments are a large fraction of the mortgage payments that greatly affect a household's ability to purchase a house.

9. Investment in plant and equipment depends on a number of variables. These include innovation, expectations about the future, level of profits, rate of interest, and changes in national income.

10. The accelerator theory relates net investment to changes in national income on the assumption of a fixed capital-output ratio. Its central prediction is that rising income is required to maintain a given level of investment. Its central insight is that net investment is a disequilibrium phenomenon that occurs when the actual capital stock is different from the desired capital stock.

11. There are several explanations of the cyclical pattern of economic fluctuations. Among these are (1) that expenditure shifts themselves are systematic; (2) that lags in the system transform random expenditure shifts into systematic cyclical changes in income; and (3) that in part the cycle is either the conscious or the accidental result of government policy.

12. Securities (stock) markets allow firms to raise new capital from the sale of newly issued securities and allow the holders of existing securities to sell their securities to other investors. Prices on the stock market tend to reflect the public's expectations both of firms' future earnings and of future changes in prices (for whatever reason). This necessarily puts a strong speculative dimension into security prices and large speculative swings do occur. Such swings are accentuated by the phenomenon of self-realizing expectations.

Topics for Review

Business cycles and economic fluctuations
Phases of the cycle
Causes of cyclical fluctuations
Components of investment
The accelerator
Interactions of the multiplier and the accelerator
Political business cycle
The stock market

Discussion Questions

1. How and in what direction might each of the following shift the function relating consumption expenditure to disposable income?
   a. Introduction of free medical care
   b. A change in attitudes so that we become a nation of conspicuous

conservers rather than conspicuous consumers, taking pride in how little we eat or spend for housing, clothing, and so on

c. Increases in income taxes

d. News that due to medical advances everyone can count on more years of retirement than ever before

e. A spreading belief that all-out nuclear war is likely within the next 10 years

f. Sharp increases in the down payments required on durable goods

2. Suppose the government wished to reduce private investment in order to reduce an inflationary gap. What policies might it adopt? If it wished to do so in such a way as to have a major effect on residential housing and a minor effect on plant and equipment expenditures, which measures might it use?

3. What effect on total investment—and on which categories of investment—would you predict as a result of each of the following?

a. Widespread endorsement of ZPG (zero population growth) by young couples

b. A sharp increase in the frequency and duration of strikes in the transportation industries

c. Forecasts of very low growth rates of real national income over the next five years

d. Tax reform that eliminates deductions for property taxes in computing taxable personal income

4. When interest rates rose sharply in the early 1980s, home construction fell dramatically, but sales of mobile homes increased. How does the rise in the sale of mobile homes relate to the notion that investment responds to the rate of interest?

5. Empirical studies show that as the volume of a firm's sales increases, the size of its inventories of raw materials tends to increase in proportion. It is common for business firms to speak of such inventories in terms of "a 20-day supply of coal" rather than "52,000 tons of coal" or "$280,000 worth of coal." Why should relative size be more important than absolute quantity or dollar value?

6. Which "cause" of business investment is being relied on in each of the following quotes?

a. An aluminum industry spokesman, justifying a $.50 a pound increase in aluminum prices: "We must have it to build the new capacity we need."

b. Bethlehem Steel, in a newspaper ad: "We need lower taxes, not cheaper money or government deficits, to help lower barriers to capital formation."

c. "The Reagan administration used a credit crunch to bring on a recession and reduce inflation."

7. Since different series behave differently, does it make sense to talk about a business cycle? Predict the comparative behavior of the following pairs of series in relation to fluctuations in the GNP.

a. Purchases of food, purchases of consumer durables

b. Tax receipts, bankruptcies

c. Unemployment, birth rates

d. Employment in New York, employment in Michigan

Check your predictions against the facts for the last decade.

30

Fiscal Policy

As we saw in previous chapters, national income fluctuates continually, primarily due to shifts in aggregate demand and short-run aggregate supply. **Fiscal policy** involves the use of government spending and tax policies to influence the *AD* curve and, to a lesser degree, the *SRAS* curve in order to damp fluctuations in the economy.

Since government expenditure increases aggregate demand and taxation decreases it, the *direction* of the required changes in spending and taxation are generally easy to determine once we know the direction of the desired change in national income. But the *timing, magnitude,* and *mixture* of the changes pose more difficult issues.

Any policy that attempts to stabilize national income at or near a desired level (usually full-employment national income) is called **stabilization policy**. This chapter deals first with the theory of fiscal policy as a tool of stabilization policy and then with the experience of using it.

There is no doubt that the government can exert a major influence on national income. Prime examples are the massive military spending during major wars. U.S. federal expenditure during World War II rose from 7.7 percent of GNP in 1940 to 47.3 percent of GNP in 1944. At the same time the unemployment rate fell from 14.6 percent to 1.2 percent. Economists agree that the increase in government spending helped bring about the fall in unemployment and the associated rise in GNP. Similar experiences occurred during the rearmament of most European countries before, or just following, the outbreak of World War II in 1939.

When used appropriately, fiscal policy can be an important tool for stabilizing the economy. In the heyday of fiscal policy from 1945 to late 1965, many economists were convinced that the economy could be adequately stabilized just by varying the size of the government's taxes and expenditures. That day is past. Today most economists are aware of the limitations of fiscal policy.

The Theory of Fiscal Policy

Fiscal policy is often referred to as the government's budgetary policy or simply as the budget.

The Budget Balance

The **budget balance** is the difference between all government revenue and all government expenditures. In this definition *government expenditure* includes both transfer payments and purchases of currently produced goods and services. Thus the budget balance is the difference between all the money the government takes in as revenue and all the money it pays out. These are called its *budget receipts* and *outlays,* respectively.

Changes in either government spending or tax policies influence the budget balance. If receipts are exactly equal to outlays, the government has a **balanced budget**. If receipts exceed outlays, there is a **budget surplus**; if receipts fall short of outlays, there is a **budget deficit**. If the government raises its outlays without raising taxes, the extra expenditure is said to be *deficit financed*. If the extra outlays are accompanied by an equal increase in tax rates that yields an equal increase in receipts, we speak of a *balanced budget change in spending*.

Financial Implications of Deficits and Surpluses

When the government spends more than it raises, where does the money come from? If the government raises more than it spends, where does the money go? The difference between expenditure and current revenue shows up as changes in the government's debt.

A deficit requires an increase in borrowing, for which there are two main sources: the central bank and the private sector. The government borrows money from these sources by selling treasury bills and bonds. A **treasury bill**, or note, is a promise to repay a stated amount at some specified date between 90 days and 1 year from the date of issue. A government *bond* is also a promise to pay a stated sum of money in the future, but in the more distant future than a bill—as much as 25 years from the date of issue.[1]

When the government borrows from the private sector, this action merely shifts funds between the two sectors. When the government "borrows" from the central bank, however, the central bank creates new money. Since the central bank can create as much money as it likes, there is no limit to what the government can "borrow" from the central bank.

A surplus allows the government to reduce its outstanding debt. Treasury bills and bonds may be redeemed from the excess tax revenue.

The Paradox of Thrift

When a government follows a balanced budget policy, as most governments tried to do during the Great Depression of the 1930s, its spending becomes procyclical. It must restrict its spending during a recession because its tax revenue will necessarily be falling at that time. During a recovery, when its revenue is rising, it must increase its spending. In other words, it rolls with the economy, raising and lowering its spending in step with everyone else.

Not long ago people generally accepted, and indeed many still fervently believe, that a prudent government should always balance its budget. This argument is based on an analogy with what seems prudent behavior for the individual household. It is a foolish household whose current expenditure consistently exceeds its current revenue so that it goes steadily further into debt. From this commonsense observation some people argue that if avoiding an ever-rising debt is good for the individual, it must also be good for the nation. But the *paradox of thrift* suggests that the analogy between the government and the household may be misleading.

The theory of national income developed in Chapters 24 through 28 predicts that if all spending units in the economy simultaneously try to increase the amount that they save, the combined increase in thriftiness will *reduce* the equilibrium level of income. The contrary case, a general decrease in thriftiness and increase in expenditure, increases national income. This prediction has come to be known as the paradox of thrift.[2]

---

[1] Bills carry a promise to return a fixed amount at maturity. Interest arises because they are initially sold at a discount; the difference between their current price and their redemption value represents interest. Bonds carry a fixed "coupon rate of interest" on their redemption value. They guarantee not only the repayment of a fixed sum on the redemption date, but also the periodic payment of fixed sums between sale and redemption.

[2] The prediction is not actually a paradox. It is a straightforward implication of the theory of the determination of income. The expectations that lead to the "paradox" are based on the fallacy of composition, the belief that what is true for the parts is necessarily true for the whole.

The policy implication of this prediction is that substantial unemployment is correctly combated by encouraging governments, firms, and households to spend more, *not* to save more. In times of unemployment and depression, frugality will only make things worse. This prediction goes directly against the idea that we should tighten our belts when times are tough. The concept that it is not just possible but acceptable to spend one's way out of a depression touches a sensitive point with people raised on the belief that success is based on hard work and frugality and not on prodigality; as a result, the idea often arouses great emotional hostility.

Applications.   As is discussed in Box 30-1, the implications of the paradox of thrift were not generally understood during the Great Depression. However, by the middle of the 1930s, many economists had concluded that the government was not making the most of its potential to control the economy in a beneficial manner. Why, they asked, should not the government try to stabilize the economy by doing just the opposite of what everyone else was doing—by increasing its demand when private demand was falling and lowering its demand when private demand was rising? At best this policy could hold aggregate demand constant even though its individual components were fluctuating.

When Milton Friedman said, "We are all Keynesians now," he was referring to (among other things) the general acceptance of the view that the government's budget is much more than just the revenue and expenditure statement of a very large organization. Whether we like it or not, the sheer size of the government's budget inevitably makes it a powerful tool for influencing the economy.

Limitations.   The paradox of thrift concentrates on shifts in aggregate demand caused by changes in saving (and hence spending) behavior. Hence it applies only in the short run, when the *AD* curve plays an important role in the determination of national income.

In the long run, when the economy is on its *LRAS* curve and hence aggregate demand is not important for the determination of national income (see Figure 28-7), the paradox of thrift ceases to apply. The more people save, the larger the supply of funds

available for investment. The more people invest, the greater the growth of potential income. Increased potential income causes the *LRAS* curve to shift to the right.

These longer-term effects are taken up in Chapter 36 in the discussion of economic growth. In the meantime we concentrate on the short-run demand effects of saving and spending.

The paradox of thrift is based on the short-run effects of changes in saving and investment on aggregate demand.

Fiscal Policy with Stable Private Expenditure Functions

A relatively easy problem faces fiscal policy makers when private-sector expenditure functions for consumption, investment, and net exports are given and unchanging. What is needed then is a once-and-for-all fiscal change that will remove any existing inflationary or recessionary gap.

Changes in tax rates or expenditure.   The necessary policies were explained in Chapter 27. A reduction in tax rates or an increase in government expenditure shifts the *AD* curve to the right, leading to an increase in GNP. An increase in tax rates or a cut in government expenditure shifts the *AD* curve to the left, leading to a decrease in GNP.

The key proposition in the theory of fiscal policy follows these results.

Government taxes and expenditure, by shifting the *AD* curve, can be used to remove GNP gaps.

Balanced budget changes.   Another policy available to the government is to make a balanced budget change by changing spending and taxes equally. Say the government increases tax rates enough to raise an extra $1 billion that it then uses to purchase goods and services. Aggregate expenditure would remain unchanged if, and only if, the $1 billion that the government takes from the private sector would otherwise have been spent by the private sector. If that is the case the government's policy would reduce private expenditure by $1 billion and raise its own spending by $1 billion. Aggregate demand, and

BOX 30-1

Fiscal Policy and the Great Depression

Failure to understand the implication of the paradox of thrift led many countries to adopt policies during the Great Depression that were disastrous. Failure to understand the role of built-in stabilizers has also led many observers to conclude, erroneously, that fiscal expansion had been tried in the Great Depression, but had failed. Let us see how these two misperceptions are related.

The Paradox of Thrift in Action

In 1932 Franklin Roosevelt was elected president on a platform of fighting the Great Depression with government policies. His actual policies did not, however, lead to an increase in aggregate demand. They were based instead on the notion that in a recession it is necessary to "tighten our belts." In his inaugural address he urged, "Our great primary task is to put people to work. . . . [This task] can be helped by insistence that the Federal, State and local governments act forthwith on the demand that their costs be drastically reduced. . . . There must be a strict supervision of all banking and credits and investments."

Across the Atlantic, King George V told the British House of Commons in 1931, "The present condition of the national finances, in the opinion of His Majesty's Ministers, calls for the imposition of additional taxation and for the effecting of economies in public expenditure."

As the paradox of thrift predicts, these policies tended to worsen, not to cure, the depression.

Interpreting the Deficit in the 1930s

The deficits that occurred following Roosevelt's election were not the result of a program of deficit-financed public expenditure. Instead, they were the result of the fall in tax yields brought about by the fall in national income as the economy sank into depression. President Roosevelt and his advisors did not advocate a program of massive deficit-financed spending to shift the aggregate demand curve well to the right. Instead, they hoped that a small amount of government spending plus numerous policies designed to stabilize prices and to restore confidence would lead to a recovery of private investment expenditure that would substantially shift the aggregate demand curve. To have expected a massive revival of private investment expenditure as a result of the puny increase in aggregate demand instituted by the federal government now seems hopelessly naive.

When we judge Roosevelt's policies from the viewpoint of modern multiplier theory, their failure is no mystery. Indeed Professor E. Cary Brown of MIT, after a careful study, concluded, "Fiscal policy seems to have been an unsuccessful recovery device in the 'thirties—not because it did not work, but because it was not tried." In 1933 the federal government was spending $2 billion for purchases of goods and services, only slightly more than the $1.3 billion it spent in 1929. This was a small drop in a very large bucket considering that GNP fell from $103 billion in 1929 to $46 billion in 1933! Given the deficits achieved, it would have taken a multiplier of 25 for the American economy to have approached full employment; in fact, the multiplier in the 1930s was closer to 2. Expenditures were wastefully small, not (as many people thought at the time) wastefully large.

Once the massive, war-geared expenditure of the 1940s began, income responded sharply and unemployment evaporated. Government expenditures on goods and services, which had been running at under 15 percent of GNP during the 1930s, jumped to 46 percent by 1944, while unemployment reached the incredible low of 1.2 percent of the civilian labor force.

The performance of the American economy from 1930 to 1945 is quite well explained by modern national income theory. It is clear that the government did not effectively use fiscal measures to stabilize the economy. War cured the depression because war demands made acceptable a level of government expenditure sufficient to remove the deflationary gap. Had the first Roosevelt administration been able to do the same, it might have ended the waste of the Depression many years sooner.

hence national income and employment, would remain unchanged.

But this is not the usual case. When an extra $1 billion in taxes is taken away from households, they usually reduce their spending on domestically produced goods by less than $1 billion. If the marginal propensity to consume out of disposable income is, say, 0.75, consumption expenditure will fall by only $750 million. If the government spends the entire $1 billion on domestically produced goods, aggregate expenditure will increase by $250 million. In this case the balanced budget increase in government expenditure has an expansionary effect because it shifts the aggregate expenditure function upward and hence shifts the *AD* curve to the right.

A balanced budget increase in government expenditure will have an expansionary effect on national income, and a balanced budget decrease will have a contractionary effect.

The **balanced budget multiplier** measures these effects. It is the change in income divided by the balanced budget change in government expenditure that brought it about. Thus, if the extra $1 billion of government spending financed by the extra $1 billion of taxes causes national income to rise by $500 million, the balanced budget multiplier is 0.5; if income rises by $1 billion, it is 1.0.

Now compare the sizes of the multipliers for a balanced budget and a deficit-financed increase in government spending. With a deficit-financed increase in expenditure, there is no increase in tax rates and hence no consequent decrease in consumption expenditure to offset the increase in government expenditure. With a balanced budget increase in expenditure, however, the offsetting increase in tax rates and decrease in consumption does occur. Thus the balanced budget multiplier is much lower than the multiplier that relates the change in income to a deficit-financed increase in government expenditure with tax rates constant.

Fiscal Policy with Shifting Private Expenditure Functions

As we saw in Chapter 29, private expenditure functions are constantly changing. Investment expenditure shifts a great deal with business conditions, and consumption functions sometimes shift upward as the public goes on a spending spree or downward as people become cautious and increase their saving. This makes stabilization policy much more difficult than it would be if it were possible simply to identify a stable inflationary or recessionary gap and then take steps to eliminate it once and for all.

What can the government reasonably expect to achieve by using fiscal policy when private expenditure functions are shifting continually? Fiscal policy might be altered often in an effort to stabilize the economy completely, or it might be altered less frequently, responding only to gaps that appear to be large and persistent while ignoring small, transitory fluctuations.

Fine Tuning

In the heyday of Keynesian fiscal policy in the 1950s and 1960s, many economists advocated the use of fiscal policy to remove even minor fluctuations in national income around its full-employment level. Fiscal policy was to be altered frequently and by relatively small amounts to hold national income almost precisely at its full-employment level. This is called **fine tuning** the economy.

Fiscal fine tuning was never really possible in the United States because of the length of the **decision lag**, the period of time between perceiving a problem and deciding how to react to it. Many things contribute to the length of this lag. Experts must study the economy and agree among themselves on what fiscal changes are most desirable. They must persuade the president to call for the action they endorse. The president must temper their advice with what he believes to be politically possible as well as desirable. Then Congress must be persuaded to enact the necessary legislation. A majority of the legislators must be convinced to vote for the measure, either because it is in the country's interests or because it would be politically advantageous to do so. The time required for this process can be very long, as much as two or three years.

While the American form of government makes the decision lag rather long, both the British system—used in the rest of the English-speaking world—and the political systems in most European countries make the decision lag very short. In such countries fine tuning has often been tried. Careful assessment of the results shows that their successes, if any, have fallen far short of what was hoped. One basic reason lies in the complexity of any economy. Although economists and policymakers can identify broad and persistent trends, they do not have detailed knowledge of what is going on at any moment, of all the forces that are operating to cause changes in the immediate future, and of all the short-term effects of small changes in the various government expenditure and tax rates.

Further difficulties for fine tuning also arise because of an **execution lag,** the time it takes to put policies in place after the decision is made, and because of lags between the introduction of a given policy measure and its effects being felt in the economy. Often by the time the effects of a given policy decision are felt, circumstances in the economy have changed and the policy is no longer appropriate.

Fine tuning often has done as much to encourage fluctuations in the economy as to remove them.

As a result of these experiences, fine tuning is currently out of favor.

Removal of Persistent Gaps

In addition to more or less continual fluctuations, the economy occasionally develops severe and persistent inflationary or recessionary gaps. For example, an inflationary gap developed in the United States in the late 1960s as Vietnam war expenditures accelerated, while a recessionary gap developed between 1981 and 1983 when America, along with many Western countries, experienced the deepest and longest-lasting recession since the 1930s. Gaps such as these may persist long enough for their major causes to be studied and understood and for fiscal remedies to be carefully planned and executed.

A persistent recessionary gap. The removal of a recessionary gap is illustrated in Figure 30-1. There are three possible ways in which the gap may be removed.

First, wages and other factor prices may eventu-

ally be forced down enough to shift the *SRAS* curve to the right by enough to reinstate full employment and potential income (at a lower price level). The evidence is, however, that this process takes a long time.

Second, the natural cyclical forces of the economy could induce a demand-side recovery for the reasons spelled out in Chapter 29. This would cause a shift to the right of the *AD* curve, moving the economy back to full employment and potential income. The evidence is that such recoveries do occur. Sometimes they happen quickly; often, however, a recession can be both deep and prolonged.

Third, government expenditure can be increased or taxes cut in an effort to shift the *AD* curve to the right. The advantage of using fiscal policy is that it may substantially shorten the length of what would otherwise be a long recession. The disadvantage is that it may stimulate the economy just before private-sector spending recovers due to natural causes. If it does, the economy may overshoot its potential output, and a serious inflationary gap may open up.

A persistent inflationary gap. Figure 30-2 on page 577 shows the three ways in which an inflationary gap can be removed.

First, wages and other factor prices may be forced upward by the excess demand. This will shift the *SRAS* curve to the left, eventually eliminating the gap, reducing income to its potential level, and raising the price level.

Second, a cyclical reduction in aggregate demand may occur for the reasons outlined in Chapter 29. This might reduce income to its potential level without the rise in the price level associated with a shift of the *SRAS* curve. But unless aggregate demand declines quickly, rising wages and other input prices will lead to a shift to the left of the *SRAS* curve and hence to rising prices.

Third, the government, by raising taxes or cutting spending, may force aggregate demand down sufficiently to remove the inflationary gap. The advantage of this approach is that it avoids the inflationary increase in prices that accompanies the first method. The disadvantage is that if private sector expenditures fall off to their more normal level, national income may be pushed below potential, thus opening up a recessionary gap.

FIGURE 30-1   Removal of a Recessionary Gap

(i) A recessionary gap removed by a rightward shift in **SRAS**

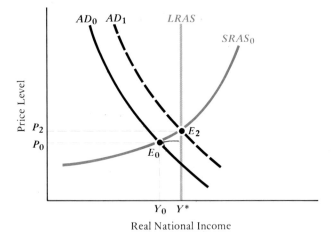

(ii) A recessionary gap removed by a rightward shift in **AD**

A recessionary gap may be removed by a (slow) rightward shift of the SRAS curve, a natural revival of private-sector demand, or a fiscal policy-induced increase in aggregate demand. Initially equilibrium is at E_0, with national income at Y_0 and the price level at P_0. The recessionary gap is $Y_0 Y^*$.

As shown in (i), the gap might be removed by a shift in the *SRAS* curve to $SRAS_1$. This increase in aggregate supply could occur as a result of reductions in wage rates and other input prices. The shift in the *SRAS* curve causes a movement down and to the right along AD_0. This establishes a new equilibrium at E_1, achieving potential income, Y^*, and lowering the price level to P_1.

As shown in (ii), the gap might also be removed by a shift of the *AD* curve to AD_1. This increase in aggregate demand could occur either because of a natural revival of private-sector expenditure or because of a fiscal policy-induced increase in expenditure. The shift in the *AD* curve causes a movement up and to the right along $SRAS_0$. This shifts the equilibrium to E_2, taking income to Y^* and the price level to P_2.

Policy. Many economists who do not believe in the value of fine tuning do feel that fiscal policy can aid in removing persistent gaps. Others believe that, even with persistent gaps, the risks that fiscal policy will destabilize the economy are still too large. They would have the government abandon any attempt at stabilization policy, instead setting its budget solely in relation to such long-term considerations as the desirable size of the public sector and the need to

obtain a satisfactory long-term balance between revenues and expenditures.

Tools of Fiscal Policy

The major fiscal tools can be classified in many ways; one important classification is the division between automatic and discretionary tools.

FIGURE 30-2   Removal of an Inflationary Gap

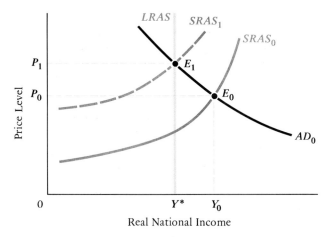

(i) An inflationary gap removed by a leftward shift in *SRAS*

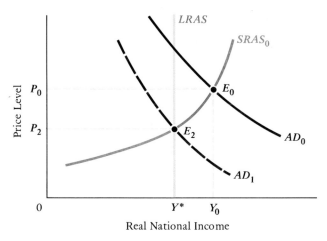

(ii) An inflationary gap removed by a leftward shift in *AD*

An inflationary gap may be removed by a leftward shift of the *SRAS* curve, a natural reduction in private-sector demand, or a policy-induced reduction in aggregate demand. Initially equilibrium is at E_0, with national income at Y_0 and the price level at P_0. The inflationary gap is Y^*Y_0.

As shown in (i), the gap might be removed by a shift in the *SRAS* curve to $SRAS_1$. This decrease in aggregate supply could occur as a result of increases in wage rates and other input prices. The shift in the *SRAS* curve causes a movement up and to the left along AD_0. This establishes a new equilibrium at E_1, reducing income to its potential level, Y^*, and raising the price level to P_1.

As shown in (ii), the gap might also be removed by a shift in the *AD* curve to AD_1. This decrease in aggregate demand could occur either because of a natural fall in private spending or because of contractionary fiscal policy. The shift in the *AD* curve causes a movement down and to the left along $SRAS_0$. This shifts the equilibrium to E_2, taking income to Y^* and the price level to P_2.

Automatic Fiscal Tools: Built-In Stabilizers

For reasons discussed in Chapter 29, the aggregate demand function is continually fluctuating. A stabilization policy for fine tuning the economy would thus require a policy that was itself ever changing. If such a conscious fine tuning policy is impossible, must we say that nothing can be done through fiscal policy except to reduce major, long-lived GNP gaps?

Fortunately, this is not so. Much of the adjustment of fiscal policy to an ever-changing economic environment is done automatically by what are called built-in stabilizers. A **built-in stabilizer** is anything that reduces the marginal propensity to spend out of national income and hence, as we saw on page 518, reduces the multiplier. Built-in stabilizers lessen the magnitude of the fluctuations in national income caused by autonomous changes in such expenditures as investment. Furthermore, they do so without the government's having to react consciously to each change in national income as it occurs.

The three principal built-in stabilizers are taxes, government expenditure on goods and services, and government transfer payments.

Taxes

Direct taxes act as a built-in stabilizer because they reduce the marginal propensity to spend out of national income. For example, if there were no taxes, every change in national income of $1 would cause a change in disposable income of nearly a dollar.[3] With a marginal propensity to consume out of disposable income (*MPC*) of, say, 0.8, consumption would change by $.80. With taxes, however, disposable income changes by less than $1; hence consumption expenditure will change by less than $.80 when national income changes by $1 (even though the *MPC* is still 0.8).

Consider, for example, the extreme case in which the marginal personal income-tax rate is 100 percent. If there is an autonomous rise of $1 billion in investment expenditure, none of the $1 billion that accrues to households will be disposable income. There are no induced rounds of secondary expenditure; the rise in national income is limited to the initial $1 billion in new investment, and the multiplier is unity.

Similarly, a drop in investment expenditure of $1 billion reduces incomes earned in the investment industry by $1 billion and hence reduces government tax revenue by $1 billion. But it does not affect disposable income. Thus there are no secondary rounds of induced contractions in consumption experience to magnify the initial drop in national income caused by the investment decline.

Table 30-1 illustrates the principle by comparing the effects of two different marginal tax rates on the marginal propensity to spend out of national income in otherwise identical situations. The general proposition can be stated as follows.

Direct taxes reduce the magnitude of fluctuations in disposable income associated with any given fluctuation in national income. Hence, for a given marginal propensity to consume out of disposable income, they reduce the marginal propensity to spend out of national income.

Tax rates have increased greatly over this century. Although citizens complain about the burden of high taxes—perhaps with good reason—few are aware that high taxes have helped to reduce the large swings in national income and employment that would have otherwise plagued all industrial economies.

Government Purchases

Government purchases of goods and services tend to be relatively stable in the face of cyclical variations in national income. Much spending is already committed by earlier legislation, so only a small proportion can be varied at the government's discretion from one year to the next. And even this small part is slow to change. In contrast, private consumption and investment expenditure tend to vary with national income.

Thus the higher the share of government spending in the economy, the lower the cyclical instability of total expenditure. The twentieth century rise in the importance of the government's role in the economy may be a mixed blessing. One benefit, however, has been to put a large built-in stabilizer into the economy.

Government Transfer Payments

Social insurance. The Old-Age, Survivors, and Disability Insurance program (popularly known as social security) is financed by taxes (called social security premiums) that are paid jointly by employers and employees. Unemployment insurance is financed by a payroll tax on employers. During recessions these tax collections decrease, and payments to the unemployed rise. Both social security and unemployment insurance support disposable income when national income falls and hold it down when national income rises.

---

[3] Undistributed profits and other minor items would still hold disposable income below national income. We ignore these in the text because taxes are the major source of the discrepancy between national income and disposable income.

TABLE 30-1   The Effect of Tax Rates on the Marginal Propensity to Spend Out of National Income

Marginal rate of tax	Change in national income (millions) ΔY	Change in tax revenue (millions) ΔT	Change in disposable income (millions) ΔY_d	Change in consumption (millions) ΔC	Marginal propensity to spend out of national income $\Delta C/\Delta Y$
0.2	$1,000	$200	$800	$640	0.65
0.4	1,000	400	600	480	0.48

The higher the marginal rate of tax, the lower the marginal propensity to spend out of national income. When national income changes by $1,000, disposable income changes by $800 when the tax rate is 20 percent and by $600 when the tax rate is 40 percent. Although the *MPC* out of disposable income is 0.8 in both examples, consumption changes by $640 in the first case and by only $480 in the second. Although that households' *MPC* out of their disposable income is unchanged, an increase in tax rates lowers the marginal propensity to spend out of national income on which the size of the multiplier depends.

Welfare payments.   Welfare payments rise with the unemployment that accompanies falling national income. Thus welfare schemes make net additions to disposable income in times of slumps. They also make net subtractions during booms when payments are low and revenues high.

Agricultural support policies.   When there is a slump in the economy, there is a general decline in the demand for all goods, including agricultural products. The free-market prices of agricultural goods fall, and government agricultural supports come into play. This means that government transfers, which support agricultural disposable income, rise as national income falls.

Transfer payments which act as built-in stabilizers tend to stabilize disposable income, and hence consumption expenditure, in the face of fluctuations in national income.

To illustrate this important proposition suppose that an investment expenditure falls by $10 billion. In the absence of transfer payments, this would reduce disposable income by $6 billion. With an *MPC* out of disposable income of 0.8, this $6 billion reduction would cause an initial induced fall in consumption expenditure of $4.8 billion. Now assume instead that the fall in national income is accompanied by an increase in transfer payments of $4 billion. Instead

of falling by $6 billion, disposable income now falls by only $2 billion. With the *MPC* out of disposable income still at 0.8, the initial induced fall in consumption expenditure is only $1.6 billion instead of $4.8 billion.

The Role of Built-In Stabilizers

Most built-in stabilizers are fairly new phenomena. Sixty years ago high marginal tax rates, high and stable government expenditures, farm stabilization policies, and large unemployment and other social security payments were unknown in the United States. Each of these built-in stabilizers was the unforeseen by-product of policies originally adopted for other reasons. The progressive income tax arose out of a concern to make the distribution of income less unequal. Social insurance and agricultural support programs were adopted more because of a concern with the welfare of the individuals and groups involved than with preserving the health of the economy. But unforeseen or not, they work. (Even governments can be lucky.)

The President's Council of Economic Advisers estimated some time ago that with the existing tax system and schedules of unemployment compensation benefits, a decline in GNP automatically produced a reduction in government receipts and an increase in transfer payments that limits the decline in after-tax income to about $.65 for each $1 of reduction of GNP, so a third of any decline is automatically offset by these two stabilizers alone. Recent tax cuts have decreased this somewhat, and the further tax cuts under consideration in 1986 promise to decrease it again.

No matter how lucky governments have been in finding built-in stabilizers, these cannot reduce fluctuations to zero. Stabilizers work by producing stabilizing reactions to changes in income. But until income changes, the stabilizer is not even brought into play.

Discretionary Fiscal Policy

Short-term, minor fluctuations that are not removed automatically by built-in stabilizers cannot, given present knowledge and techniques, be removed by consciously fine tuning the economy. We have already seen, however, that larger and more persistent gaps sometimes appear. In these cases there may be time for the government to operate a discretionary fiscal policy, that is, to institute changes in taxes and spending that are designed to offset gaps. To do this effectively an administration must periodically make conscious decisions to alter fiscal policy. The Council of Economic Advisers must study current economic trends and predict the probable course of the economy. If the predicted course is unsatisfactory, Congress must be persuaded to enact the necessary legislation.

In considering discretionary fiscal policy, we shall deal with two related questions. First, is it important that the fiscal change be easily reversible? Second, does it matter whether households and firms regard the government's fiscal changes as temporary or as long-lived?

The Need for Reversibility

To see what is involved in the issue of reversibility, assume that national income is normally at or near potential. A *temporary* slump in private investment then opens up a large recessionary gap. If the gap persists, then eventually the government decides to adopt some combination of tax cuts and spending increases to push the economy back toward full employment. If private investment recovers to its pre-

slump level and the government does not quickly reverse this policy, an inflationary gap will open up as the combination of rising investment expenditure and continuing fiscal stimulus takes national income into the inflationary range. The process is illustrated in Figure 30-3.

Alternatively, assume that starting from the same situation of approximately full employment, a temporary investment boom opens up an inflationary gap. Rather than let the inflation persist, the government reduces expenditure and raises taxes to remove the gap. If, when the investment boom is over and investment expenditure returns to its original level, the government does nothing, a recessionary gap will open up and a slump may ensue. This, too, is analyzed in Figure 30-3.

Fiscal policies designed to remove persistent GNP gaps resulting from abnormal levels of private expenditure will destabilize the economy unless the policies can be rapidly reversed once private expenditure returns to its more normal level.

In the American economy, where decision lags for changes in government spending or taxes are measured in years, rapid reversals are not easily accomplished. This fact is a powerful argument against fiscal policy, at least as it is practiced in the United States. Even if the GNP gaps persist long enough for fiscal changes to be agreed on and to be made, subsequent rapid changes in private expenditure may require a quick reversal of the fiscal stance—a reversal that cannot easily be made, given the slow political decision-making process that is built into the American constitution. As a result, many economists argue that caution dictates responding only to large GNP gaps that are expected to persist and, even then, attempting to close only part of the gap in anticipation of some stabilizing change in private expenditure.

"Temporary" Versus "Long-Lasting" Changes

Consider the attempt to remove a persistent inflationary or recessionary gap through changes in tax

FIGURE 30-3   Effects of Fiscal Policies That Are Not Reversed

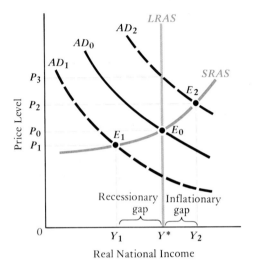

Fiscal policies that are initially appropriate may become inappropriate when private expenditure shifts. The normal level of the aggregate demand function is assumed to be AD_0, leaving income normally at Y^* and the price level at P_0. Suppose a slump in private investment shifts aggregate demand to AD_1, lowering national income to Y_1 and causing a recessionary gap of Y^*Y_1.

The government now introduces fiscal expansion to restore aggregate demand to AD_0 and national income to Y^*. Suppose that private investment recovers, raising aggregate demand to AD_2. If fiscal policy can be quickly reversed, aggregate demand can be returned to AD_0 and income stabilized at Y^*. If the policy is not quickly reversed, equilibrium will be at E_2 and an inflationary gap Y^*Y_2 will open up. This will cause wages to rise and thus shift the $SRAS$ curve leftward and eventually restore Y^* at a price level P_3.

Now suppose that starting from equilibrium E_0 a persistent investment boom takes AD_0 to AD_2. In order to stop the price level from rising in the face of the newly opened inflationary gap, the government introduces fiscal restraint, thereby shifting aggregate demand back to AD_0. Further assume, however, that the investment boom soon comes to a halt so that the aggregate demand curve shifts down to AD_1. Unless the fiscal policy can be rapidly reversed, a recessionary gap will open up and equilibrium income will fall to Y_1.

rates. Such a gap, though persistent, is unlikely to be a permanent feature of the economy. The relevant tax changes should therefore be advocated only for "the duration," that is, for as long as the administration thinks the gaps would persist without the tax changes. A discretionary fiscal policy designed to remove such a gap might take the form, say, of a surcharge on income taxes for a two-year period. For an example, the recession that began in 1974 was fought by "temporary" tax rebates that had to be renewed by Congress every six months with the clear implication that taxes would return to their "normal" levels when recovery was well under way.

Such tax changes cause changes in household disposable income and, according to the theory of the consumption function encountered in Chapter 27, would cause changes in consumption expenditure. Consumption expenditure would increase as tax rebates rose in times of recessionary gaps and would decrease as tax surcharges rose in times of inflationary gaps. This theory of the effects of short-term tax changes relies on the assumption that household consumption depends on current disposable income.

Permanent-income theories.   Many recent theories of the consumption function have emphasized what is called a household's expected **permanent income** or **lifetime income**, as the major determinant of consumption. According to such theories, households have expectations about their lifetime incomes and adjust their consumption to those expectations. When temporary fluctuations in income occur, households maintain their long-term consumption plans and use their stocks of wealth as buffers to absorb income fluctuations. Thus, when there is a purely temporary rise in income, households will save all the extra income; when there is a purely temporary fall in income, households will maintain their long-term consumption plans by using up part of their wealth accumulated through past saving.

To the extent that such behavior occurs, it will have serious consequences for short-lived tax changes. A temporary tax rebate raises households' disposable income, but households, recognizing it as temporary, would not revise their expenditure plans and instead save the extra money. Thus the hoped-for increase in aggregate expenditure would not occur. Similarly, a temporary rise in tax rates reduces disposable income, but that might merely cause a drop in saving. Thus total expenditure is again unchanged, and a temporary surcharge fails to reduce the inflationary gap.

If households' consumption expenditure is more closely related to lifetime income than to current income, tax changes that are known to be of short duration will have relatively small effects on current consumptions.[4]

Dramatic experience confirming this proposition occurred in 1968 when large military expenditures associated with the war in Vietnam gave rise to an inflationary gap. In mid 1968 a temporary tax surcharge was approved by Congress; this raised effective tax rates for a period of about 18 months and produced a substantial budget surplus. The object was to slow inflation by removing the inflationary gap. The restraining effect on inflation was disappointingly small because consumption expenditure was hardly affected.

The advantage of having households perceive tax rate changes as long lasting conflicts with the need for the reversibility of cuts and surcharges if they are not to destabilize the economy at a later date.

This conflict reduces the usefulness of changes in tax rates as a stabilizing tool.

Judging the Stance of Fiscal Policy

Governments seek to shift aggregate demand by consciously changing their fiscal policy stance. The *stance* of fiscal policy refers to its expansionary or contractionary effects on the economy. An expansionary fiscal policy increases aggregate demand and thus tends to increase national income; a contractionary fiscal policy reduces aggregate demand and tends to lower national income. In the previous chapter and earlier in this one, we looked separately at taxes,

[4] The permanent-income theory is not as devastating for fiscal policy as it may seem. This important matter is discussed further in part I of the appendix to this chapter.

purchases of goods and services, and transfer payments as means of influencing aggregate demand. But people want a summary measure, one number to express the government's effect on the economy.

The Inadequacy of the Deficit As a Measure

Not surprisingly, people tend to focus on the government's budget deficit in order to judge the stance of fiscal policy. A rising government deficit is often taken to indicate an expansionary fiscal policy, and a falling deficit is often taken to indicate a contractionary policy. But a number of problems make the deficit an unreliable guide to judging the fiscal stance.

The deficit is the difference between the government's outlays and receipts, its receipts being largely tax revenue. But tax revenue is the result of the interaction of tax rates, which the government sets, and the level of national income, which is influenced by many forces beyond the government's control.

The major tools of fiscal policy are government expenditure and tax *rates*. The budget deficit or surplus is the relation between government expenditure and tax *revenues*.

Assume, for example, that government expenditure is constant at $200 billion, and that at current tax rates the government takes 20 percent of national income in taxes. Suppose national income is $1,000 billion, so tax revenues are also $200 billion. Now assume that tax revenues sink to $150 billion, opening up a $50 billion budget deficit. This could be the result of a discretionary cut in tax rates so that they now yield only 15 percent of an unchanged national income. It could also be the result of a fall in national income itself to $750 billion, with tax rates constant. In the first case a conscious change in the government's fiscal policy causes the fall in tax revenues. In the second case a fall in national income that is not the result of fiscal policy causes tax revenue to fall; the increase in the deficit simply reflects the operation of the automatic stabilizers discussed earlier in this chapter.

This example illustrates why judging changes in the stance of fiscal policy from changes in the government's budget balance can be misleading. Doing so confuses changes in the deficit due to fluctuations in national income, which may not be the result of shifts in fiscal policy, with changes in the deficit that are the result of shifts in fiscal policy.

Cyclically Adjusted Deficit

When measuring changes in the stance of fiscal policy, it is common to calculate changes in the estimated budget balance on the assumption that national income is constant at some base level. Holding income constant ensures that measured changes in the budget balance are due to changes in policy. The base most commonly used is potential national income. Because estimating the budget balance for a given level of national income controls for cyclically induced fluctuations in expenditures and tax revenues, it is referred to as making the *cyclical adjustment;* the resulting measure is referred to as the *cyclically adjusted budget balance,* or **cyclically adjusted deficit (CAD).**[5] It is an estimate of government expenditure minus government tax revenues, not as they actually are, but as they would be if national income had been at its potential level. Table 30-2 shows the actual and cyclically adjusted deficit on an annual basis since 1969.

Changes in the cyclically adjusted deficit are an indicator of changes in the stance of fiscal policy.

Box 30-2 introduces the concept of the *budget deficit function* and discusses how it, along with the cyclically adjusted deficit, can avoid the errors that arise from using the current budget balance as an indicator of the stance of fiscal policy.

Other Problems in Measuring Fiscal Stance

In addition to the cyclical movements in the deficit, a number of other problems arise in using even the

TABLE 30-2   **Actual and Cyclically Adjusted Budget Balances for the Federal Government** *(billions of dollars, national accounts basis)*

Year	Actual deficit	Cyclically adjusted deficit
1969	8.5	4.0
1970	12.1	10.9
1971	22.0	16.8
1972	17.3	15.6
1973	5.6	13.5
1974	11.5	9.1
1975	69.3	44.4
1976	53.1	37.9
1977	45.9	42.7
1978	29.5	45.3
1979	16.1	36.3
1980	61.3	60.5
1981	63.8	55.6
1982	145.9	88.9
1983	179.4	129.5
1984	172.9	171.3
1985	199.1	202.7

Source: Survey of Current Business, March 1986.

Note: A minus indicates a surplus, that is, a negative deficit is a surplus.

Wide swings in the cyclically adjusted budget deficit indicate wide swings in the stance of fiscal policy. Because the economy operated at less than full employment during most of the 1970s, actual budget deficits were larger than cyclically adjusted deficits in most years. The large actual deficits in the mid 1970s were mainly response to low levels of national income during the recession. Variations in the cyclically adjusted deficits show the variability of the stance of fiscal policy. The sharp increases in 1975 and after 1982 indicate expansionary fiscal policy, which the decreases in 1974, 1979, and 1981 indicate contractionary policy.

[5] This concept used to be called the full-employment surplus. The change from *full employment* to *cyclically adjusted* came when the amount of unemployment associated with potential income rose rapidly in the 1970s, and referring to so much unemployment as full employment became embarrassing. The change from *deficit* to *surplus* occurred because in the 1960s people were trying to stress the depressing effects of surpluses while in the 1980s people wanted to stress the alleged harmful effects of deficits.

cyclically adjusted deficit as a measure of the fiscal stance. They arise because, while an increase in government expenditure on goods and services, a decrease in revenue, and an increase in interest payments on the debt each have the same effect on the deficit, they do not necessarily have the same effect on the economy. Three issues that arise in this context are discussed in parts II and III of the appendix to this chapter.

BOX 30-2

The Budget Deficit Function

The distinction between changes in the budget balance due to changes in the fiscal stance and those due to cyclical changes in the economy is easily seen in what is called the government's *budget deficit function*.

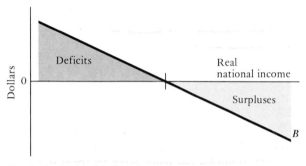

(i) The budget deficit function

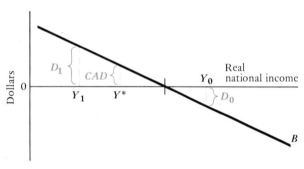

(ii) Changes in the measured deficit

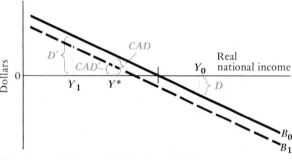

(iii) Changes in the cyclically adjusted deficit

The budget deficit function (curve B in the figure) expresses the difference between the government's expenditures and its tax revenues at each level of national income for given levels of government expenditure and tax rates. The curve in (i) shows that deficits are associated with low levels of income and surpluses with high levels of income; this is because at a given tax *rate* tax *revenue* rises with national income.

Changes in the government's budget balance induced by changes in national income are shown by *movements along* a given budget deficit function. Changes in the budget balance due to policy-induced changes in the level of government expenditure or tax rates are shown by *shifts* in the budget function. Such shifts indicate a different budget balance at each level of national income.

In part ii, a fall in national income from Y_0 to Y_1 causes the actual budget to go from a surplus of D_0 to a deficit of D_1. Government expenditure and tax rates are unchanged, that is, the fiscal policy stance is unchanged. The unchanged fiscal stance is correctly captured by the constant cyclically adjusted deficit, CAD, measured at the (constant) potential level of national income, Y^*.

Part iii illustrates a contractionary change in the stance of fiscal policy. A government expenditure cut or a tax rate increase shifts the budget deficit function from B_0 to B_1. Now there is a smaller budget deficit *at each level of national income*. This change is correctly captured by the fall in the cyclically adjusted deficit from CAD to CAD'.

To see the misleading effects of judging changes in the policy stance from changes in the measured deficit, suppose national income had fallen from Y_0 to Y_1 at the same time that the budget deficit function shifted from B_0 to B_1. In that case, the measured balance would have gone from surplus (D) to deficit (D') despite the fall in the cyclically adjusted deficit from CAD to CAD'. Thus the measured balance would have indicated an expansionary fiscal policy, while the fiscal stance was actually contractionary.

Fiscal Policy in Action

We have seen that governments inevitably have a major impact on GNP through their fiscal behavior. The very size of a government's budget guarantees that. The conscious use of the budget to influence GNP that constitutes fiscal policy is, however, by no means inevitable. Fiscal *impact* is unavoidable, but fiscal *policy* is a matter of choice.

The Fiscal Policy Record

The years following World War II were characterized in the United States by steady growth of real GNP and, once the postwar inflation had ended, only gradual inflation. As the 1950s wore on, however, economic growth became increasingly sluggish and unemployment began to creep upward, from 2.9 percent in 1953 to 6.7 percent in 1961. Many worried that the combination of rising prices and rising unemployment represented a new set of structural problems that could not easily be solved with the existing tools of macroeconomic policy. These fears did not prove justified as the 1960s turned out to be relatively buoyant years. High growth continued, although both inflation and unemployment also increased toward the end of the decade.

Since the late 1960s the American economy has undergone a series of cyclical swings that fiscal policy sometimes aggravated and sometimes resisted. The 1960s and 1970s were years of fiscal activism, if not fiscal fine tuning. Discretionary tax and expenditure changes were constantly used in an attempt to stabilize the economy. Much of the reason active fiscal policy was so in vogue was the dramatic success of tax cuts introduced in 1964. This episode, still cited by proponents of fiscal activism, is discussed in Box 30-3.

The experience of the 1970s indicated an impressive ability to manipulate aggregate demand. The stance of fiscal (and monetary) policy was changed several times, sometimes in pursuit of stabilization policy, sometimes for political motives, and sometimes because of induced effects (for example, when rapid inflation increased tax yields). Each time the response was in the direction predicted by economic theory.

However, while fiscal changes were able to influence the economy, fiscal policy was not always effective in stabilizing it. Many observers came to the conclusion that cyclical fluctuations in the economy were often caused by policy reversals.[6] For example, expansionary policies introduced in 1972 to combat unemployment soon led to concern about inflationary pressures and were then followed in 1975 by contractionary policy designed to control inflation. Then, as unemployment grew again, policy became expansionary in 1975.

This experience of policy reversals was further complicated by the emergence of stagflation, which as we have already seen was largely due to supply-side shocks caused by increases in the price of oil and other primary commodities. The simultaneous occurrence of rising inflation and unemployment led many to question the efficacy of using fiscal policy to stabilize the economy.

The resulting fall from favor of fiscal policy activism was given a further push with the election of President Ronald Reagan in 1980. The Reagan administration inherited a serious inflationary problem which it took to be economic and social enemy number one. There was a shift, however, to emphasis on monetary policy; the Reagan administration disavowed fiscal policy as a device for short-term manipulation of aggregate demand. (We shall study this episode after we have covered monetary policy in Chapter 33.)

In spite of President Reagan's commitment to a balanced budget, the deficit grew rapidly during his first term in office. At first the rising deficit reflected the operation of the automatic stabilizers. Tax revenues fell due to the 1981–1982 recession, and almost one-third of the 1982 increase in the deficit was due to the cyclical decline in the economy. Without the increase in the deficit induced by the automatic stabilizers, the decline in output and the rise in unemployment would both have been substantially larger.

But as the economy recovered in 1983 and after, with real GNP rising and unemployment falling, the deficit continued to grow. Tax cuts that had been introduced to encourage saving and investment par-

---

[6] Indeed, it is noteworthy that all four major downturns of the period have been attributed to explicit fiscal contraction.

BOX 30-3

Fiscal Drag and the 1964 Tax Cuts: A Fiscal Policy Success

Fiscal drag, first diagnosed in the early 1960s, is the problem produced by economic growth acting on stable government expenditure and fixed tax rates. In social circumstances, growth leads to a falling cyclically adjusted budget deficit. (In terms of the figure in Box 30-2, the drag is due to a movement along the budget deficit function as potential income grows.)

Throughout the 1950s potential GNP rose 2 percent to 3 percent per year because of economic growth. Such growth increases aggregate supply. But since higher output means higher income earned, aggregate demand was also shifting outward. With both demand and supply increasing, it might seem that maintaining full employment would be no problem. There was a problem, however, and it lay with the tax system.

With tax rates constant, rising national income causes rising tax revenues. These revenues are money that does not become disposable income for households. If the government spends all its extra tax revenue, aggregate demand is not depressed. Since at the time, however, there was a relatively stable level of government expenditure, rising tax revenues exerted a drag on the growth of aggregate demand by taking income away from households who would have spent it and transferring it to governments who did not. There was thus a falling cyclically adjusted deficit.

This is illustrated in the figure, where we start with the curves AD_0, $LRAS_0$, and $SRAS_0$. These yield equilibrium at E_0 and potential income Y_0^*. Economic growth now shifts the supply curves to $LRAS_1$ and $SRAS_1$. As a result of fiscal drag, however, the aggregate demand curve shifts only to AD_1 rather than to AD_2, which would have been required to sustain full employment. A GNP gap of $Y_1Y_2^*$ is thus created.

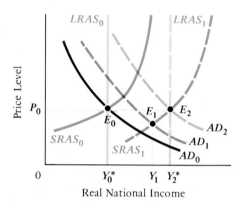

To prevent the exertion of an ever-stronger depressing effect on national income by a falling *CAD*, it is necessary to increase the deficit periodically either by increasing government spending or by reducing tax rates. This problem arose in the American economy during the 1950s. Economic growth was producing a declining *CAD*. (The terminology of the time called this a rising full-employment surplus.) As a result each cyclical upswing was weaker than the one before it, and the average level of unemployment over the cycle was creeping upward. By the beginning of the 1960s many economists were calling for a tax cut to remove the drag and restore full employment. Both the Kennedy and Johnson administrations advocated a large cut in tax rates. Their concern was not with cyclical stabilization of the economy, but with solving a problem associated with long-term economic growth.

When the 1964 tax cut was enacted, the predicted effects occurred. The tax cuts increased disposable income, causing an increase in consumption expenditure that in turn caused an increase in national income and employment.

tially offset the growth in revenues resulting from growth in the economy, while government expenditure—in particular military expenditures and debt service payments—grew. Accordingly, fiscal policy was very expansionary in this period, as indicated by the dramatic increase in the cyclically adjusted deficit. These increases reflected President Reagan's political agenda, which included cuts in personal and business taxes—with a view to improving incentives for working and saving—and increases in military spending. These changes, combined with the success of the Congress in protecting domestic social spending, contributed to the emergence of record deficits.

Ironically, despite the Reagan administration's disavowal of fiscal *policy,* its actions had significant fiscal *effects.* Many economists believe that the dramatic increase in the deficit under him played a major role in stimulating the economy and ending the recession. It also stimulated an extensive public debate about the consequences of persistent budget deficits, and Congress debated and passed legislation to try to reduce the deficit. (That legislation, called the Gramm-Rudman-Hollings Act, is discussed below.)

In the rest of this chapter we consider in more detail the issues raised by large, persistent government budget deficits.

The Economics of Budget Deficits

The average American has some idea of the size of the federal budget deficit (if not exactly how big, at least that it is too big). The average Briton or West German is not likely to have any idea of the size of the government's budget deficit or a strong opinion on whether it is too large. Why is our budget deficit so large? Why do Americans worry so much about it? Is it really such a big problem?

Facts About the Deficit

The recent emergence of record federal budget deficits is shown in Figure 30-4. Part i shows total federal spending (on goods and services and transfers) and total federal revenues since 1964, as a share of GNP. The steady trend increase in expenditures is readily apparent. Revenues display more variation and little or no trend.

Part ii shows the deficit, again measured as a share of GNP (this is the shaded area between the two lines in part i). The government budget had been in deficit prior to 1982, although the deficit had not been unusually large by historical standards. After 1982, however, the deficit increased dramatically as a share of GNP. As can be seen from Table 30-2, the cyclically adjusted deficit grew even more than the actual deficit over the period from 1982 to 1985.

Why Worry About Deficits?

It is possible to identify a set of conditions in which neither government deficits nor the public debt would matter in the economy. However, the required conditions (discussed in detail in Part II of the Appendix to this chapter) are so stringent that most economists believe that the deficit does exert important influences on the economy.

One such influence is the short-run stabilizing or destabilizing role in the economy emphasized earlier in this chapter. A second is a potential adverse long-run effect on income and welfare, to which we now turn. People worry about the long-run effects of persistent deficits for many reasons. We will look at four.

Will a deficit cause inflation?   Neither economic theory nor the available evidence suggests that deficits by themselves are sufficient to cause inflation.

The worry that persistent deficits may cause inflation arises out of the fear that a continuous deficit will lead to a continuous expansion in the money supply, that is, that it would eventually lead to pressure in the Fed to expand the money supply and thus cause inflation. This case cannot be studied in detail until Chapter 34. In the meantime we merely observe that if a deficit is financed by "borrowing" from the Fed, the money supply will be increased every year. (In effect the Fed *creates* the money to finance the deficit.) If this increase is too rapid, then it will cause inflation.

Deficits financed by the continual creation of new money may cause inflation.

No one believes that this is desirable.

FIGURE 30-4 Federal Revenues, Expenditures, and Deficits, 1964–1985 *(as a share of GNP)*

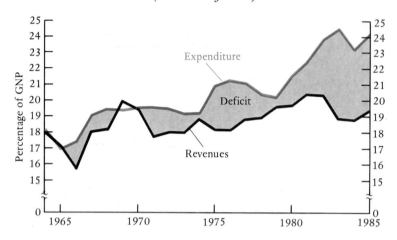

(i) Expenditures and revenues as a share of GNP

Since 1964, expenditure has grown steadily as a fraction of GNP, while revenues have fluctuated, but shown little trend. Over the period 1965 to 1970 expenditures and revenues both grew steadily. From 1970 to 1979 expenditure grew gradually, while revenues remained roughly constant. Persistent deficits emerged. Since 1979 expenditures have grown dramatically, while revenue has fallen slightly. Over that period the deficit has increased sharply.

(ii) The deficit as a share of GNP

Will the deficit crowd out private investment? People fear that deficit spending may lead to a more or less equivalent reduction in private-sector investment spending. Government borrowing to finance its deficit can absorb a significant proportion of private savings. In 1982, for example, the federal deficit was equal to about 80 percent of household savings and fully 20 percent of total private-sector savings by households and firms. The fear is that heavy government borrowing drives up the interest rate and the higher interest rate reduces private investment expenditure. This "crowding out" process is illustrated in Figure 30-5.

If government borrowing to finance the deficit drives up the interest rate, some private investment expenditure will be crowded out.

This effect is more likely when the economy is close to full employment. When there is a large recessionary gap, the rise in income will increase the volume of savings (as households move along their savings functions, as shown in Figure 26-2 on page 504). In this case the new savings generated by the rise in income helps to finance the deficit so that less crowding out of existing private-sector borrowing need occur.

Will the debt harm future generations? To the extent that government borrowing to finance current expenditures crowds out private investment, there will be a smaller stock of capital to pass on to future generations. Less capital means less output; this is the long-term burden of the debt.

Despite large deficits, investment has been sustained at high levels in the past few years. Does this mean that we do not need to worry about a burden arising from the large deficits? Unfortunately, the answer is no. While private investment has been maintained, foreign lenders have supplied much of the funds. Thus while future generations of Ameri-

FIGURE 30-5 Crowding Out of Private Investment by Government Borrowing

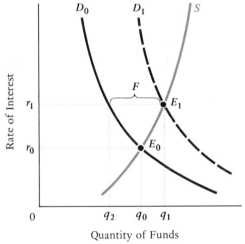

(i) Effects of government borrowing with constant national income

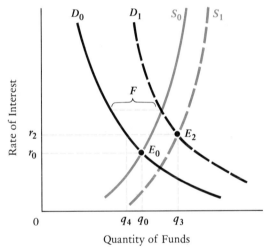

(ii) Effects of government borrowing with increased national income

Government borrowing may crowd out private-sector borrowing and investing. Part (i) of the figure shows a supply of funds available to be lent, S, that is fairly insensitive to the interest rate. Initially the demand to borrow funds is D_0, giving an equilibrium interest rate of r_0 and a quantity of funds borrowed for all purposes of q_0.

Government spending now increases by F, all of which is borrowed. This shifts the demand for funds to the right, from D_0 to D_1, taking equilibrium to E_1. The interest rate rises to r_1, and the quantity of funds borrowed rises to q_1. But q_2q_1 of these go to the government, so the private sector borrows only q_2, which is q_2q_0 less than it was able to borrow, and hence invest, before the deficit forced the government into the market.

If, however, the extra government expenditure increases national income, it will raise saving. The savings function will then shift to the right, say, from S_0 to S_1 in part (ii) of the figure. Crowding out will then be lessened. At equilibrium E_2 the interest rate rises to r_2, and private borrowing is only q_4q_0 less than before the government entered the market.

cans may well inherit a capital stock that is not significantly reduced as a result of the deficit, they will inherit an increased stock of foreign liabilities. Future payments of interest and dividends on these liabilities will lower GNP (income owned by Americans) in relation to GDP (output produced in the United States) since some income generated by the output will accrue to foreigners. These will also lower GNP relative to what it would have been in the absence of the deficits.

Borrowing from abroad entails a transfer of purchasing power to domestic residents when the borrowing occurs and a transfer back to foreigners when interest payments and repayments of principal occur.

The United States slowly built up a net creditor position over the six decades before 1980. That position was completely dissipated as a result of massive foreign borrowing during Ronald Reagan's presidency. Most economists attribute this foreign borrowing to the massive government budget deficits that occurred. If large deficits persist, America will soon become one of the world's largest debtor nations.

Does the size of the debt hamper the operation of policy?   The large interest bill on the national debt puts a strain on the budget process. For example, in 1985 a full 18.5 percent of all tax revenues went to pay interest on the national debt! The government's freedom of fiscal maneuver is obviously hampered by such a large and rising claim on the national tax revenues. When the government's interest obligations grow, it can, of course, incur an even larger deficit, at least for a while, but eventually interest on the stock of debt must be paid from new revenues. Eventually, the government must either reduce its expenditure on other programs, or it must raise taxes.

Although interest payments on the national debt have not yet reached crisis proportions, the large claim on existing government revenues is a cause for concern.

Deficits and the National Debt

The foregoing indicates that much of the concern about government budget deficits arises from their *cumulative* effect on the national debt and therefore on the government's interest obligations.

Facts About the Debt

The national debt in December 1985 was $2 trillion, almost $9,000 for every man, woman, and child in the country. About 20 percent of the debt was held by the government itself and by Federal Reserve banks; interest payments on this part of the debt are only bookkeeping transactions.[7] The debt held by the private sector at the end of 1985 was over $1.5 trillion.

The national debt of over $2 trillion represents money that the federal government has borrowed by selling bonds to American and foreign households, firms, and financial institutions.

In this sense the national debt is owed by all of us to some of us and to foreigners.

The debt in relation to GNP.   The figures for debt per person, which are often quoted in an attempt to shock the reader, require interpretation. For a government, as for a household, the significance of debt depends on what it represents and on whether the income is available to pay the interest. No one would be shocked, for example, to find that an American family of four earning $60,000 a year had a mortgage of $50,000 on a $100,000 home.

It is useful in evaluating the national debt and the government's interest payments on it to consider them *relative* to the size of the economy. The worries about the debt discussed above arise primarily when the debt grows faster than the economy; it is really the debt to GNP ratio that matters. A national debt of $2 trillion clearly has different implications when GNP is $500 billion and when it is $5 trillion.

Figure 30-6 shows historical data for the debt and interest payments on it as a proportion of GNP.

---

[7] Federal Reserve banks buy government bonds in the course of operating monetary policy (see Chapter 33). Government departments sometimes acquire government bonds when they have funds that they do not need for short, or even long, periods of time.

FIGURE 30-6   The Relative Importance of the National Debt

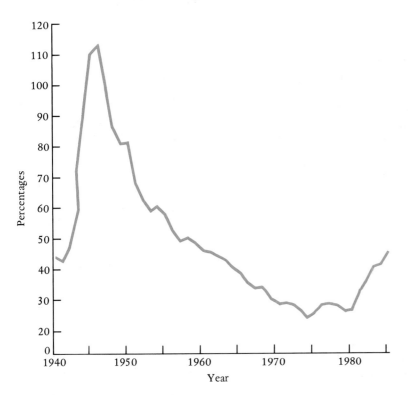

(i) National debt as proportion of GNP

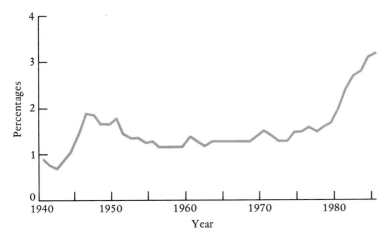

(ii) Net interest paid on national debt as proportion of GNP

The national debt has not reached alarming proportions in relation to GNP, but both the debt and interest payments on it have been growing rapidly in recent years. Stated as a proportion of the country's national income (part i), the national debt rose dramatically during World War II, and again, slightly, during the major slump of 1974 to 1976. It has been growing steadily since 1977.

Net interest payments on the national debt have been a rising proportion of GNP since 1973 (part ii). The different trends in debt and debt servicing between 1973 and 1981 are accounted for by the rising cost of servicing the debt due to rising interest rates. (*Sources:* Historical tables, budget of the United States government, fiscal year 1987. *Economic Reports of the President.*)

Figure 30-6(i) shows that national debt as a proportion of GNP started to fall at the end of World War II and continued to fall until 1976. The debt rose relative to GNP after 1977, and by 1985 the debt had reached almost 46 percent of GNP. That figure is still much less than the more than 100 percent at the postwar peak. Nevertheless, the trend is worrisome, and medium-term projections suggest that the debt to GNP ratio will continue to rise.

Consider next the interest payments on the debt, often called the *debit service payments,* shown in Figure 30-6(ii). Clearly, there is genuine cause for worry here. If the trend continues, interest payments could eventually put an intolerable burden on the government's taxing capacity. Ever-bigger deficits would occur, and with them even more borrowing.

In view of the costs imposed by a rising debt to GNP ratio, many economists and others have argued that the government's fiscal policies are imprudent and have called for a commitment to control the deficit.

Proposals to Control the Deficit

As we have seen, government deficits contribute to aggregate demand and hence can play a useful role in damping cyclical fluctuations in the economy. As we have also seen, government deficits contribute to increases in the national debt and hence in the long term might lead to a reduction in living standards of the average American. This conflict between the short-term stabilization role of deficits and the long-term adverse effects of a large public debt has been a subject of constant debate among economists and others concerned with government policy.

Views range from those who dismiss the long-run costs of the national debt and hence are not concerned about the deficit to those who wish to eschew the short-term stabilization role for the deficit entirely and impose a virtual straitjacket on the government, requiring it always to balance its budget. We now look at some of the specific proposals that have been put forward; some of the general options are illustrated in Figure 30-7.

An annually balanced budget. Much current rhetoric of fiscal restraint calls for a balanced budget. The Gramm-Rudman-Hollings bill passed in late 1985, and discussed further in Box 30-4, mandates an elimination of the federal deficit by 1991.

The discussion earlier in this chapter suggests that an annually balanced budget would be extremely difficult, perhaps impossible, to achieve. With fixed tax rates, tax revenues fluctuate as national income fluctuates. Much government expenditure is fixed by past commitments and most of the rest is hard to change quickly.

But suppose an annually balanced budget, or something approaching it, were feasible. What would its effects be? Would they be desirable?

FIGURE 30-7   Balanced and Unbalanced Budgets

(i) A cyclically unbalanced budget

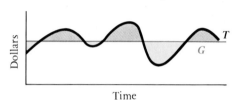

(ii) A cyclically balanced budget

(iii) A constantly balanced budget

An annually (constantly) balanced budget is a destabilizer; a cyclically balanced budget is a stabilizer. The flow of tax receipts, *T*, is shown varying over the business cycle, while in parts (i) and (ii) government expenditure, *G*, is shown at a constant rate.

In (i) deficits (dark areas) are common and surpluses (light areas) are rare because the average level of expenditure exceeds the average level of taxes. Such a policy will tend to stabilize the economy against cyclical fluctuations, but the average fiscal stance of the government is expansionary. This has been the characteristic U.S. budgetary position over the last several decades.

In (ii) government expenditure has been reduced until it is approximately equal to the average level of tax receipts. The budget is now balanced cyclically. The policy still tends to stabilize the economy against cyclical fluctuations because of deficits in slumps and surpluses in booms. But the average fiscal stance is neither strongly expansionary nor strongly contractionary.

In (iii) a balanced budget has been imposed. Deficits have been prevented, but government expenditure now varies over the business cycle, tending to destabilize the economy by accentuating the cyclical swings in aggregate expenditure.

BOX 30-4

Gramm-Rudman-Hollings: The Balanced Budget Act of 1985

In December of 1985 the U.S. Congress passed the Balanced Budget and Emergency Deficit Control Act of 1985. This potentially far-reaching bill reflected both Congress's growing frustration with its own inability to reach a satisfactory compromise with the President on budget policy and the growing perception that unchecked deficit growth will have harmful economic and political effects. Congress's frustration is easy to understand. In 1985 it had struggled to cut one program after another only to wind up with yet another huge deficit.

Referred to as Gramm-Rudman-Hollings (G-R-H), after the three senators who sponsored the legislation, the act promises to balance the budget by 1991. The idea is appealing, but the approach is subject to a number of serious criticisms.

Here is how G-R-H is supposed to work. The deficit for fiscal 1986 is projected to be $212 billion. The deficit in following years is to be reduced in equal yearly steps until it reaches zero in 1991. If the President and Congress fail to agree on how to achieve these goals, the bill requires across-the-board spending cuts, with important exceptions.

The first flaw is that aiming at zero is dangerously arbitrary. Big cuts in the deficit may be essential, but forcing a balanced budget could, depending on economic conditions, start a recession or stifle a recovery.

Second, the approach is unbalanced. The trigger mechanism would affect only spending, and not all of that. It cannot cut interest on the debt or social security and would leave considerable leeway for increases in other "uncontrollable" costs, particularly in the defense budget. No tax increases are involved and no controls apply to rising "tax expenditures."

Third, the approach is mechanical and unable to respond to changing needs and priorities. Not only does it override the potential for automatic stabilizers to dampen cyclical downturns in the economy, it threatens to hamper severely the government's ability to exercise discretion. Much of the original support for the bill came from those who believed that its options would be so unattractive that Congress and the President would both be more willing to reach a compromise on what measures to take to reduce the deficit "voluntarily." After the bill was passed, however, the fear emerged that it would have the opposite effect and replace, rather than stimulate, serious dialogue and resolution of the budget problem. Opponents say the bill is a way for Congress to avoid responsibility for measures needed to solve the problem.

A further flaw concerns credibility. Congress may solemnly demonstrate its firm resolve with legislation, but everyone knows Congress can act even faster in the opposite direction. For example, the Ninety-fifth Congress passed a law requiring a balanced budget by 1981; the Ninety-sixth repealed it.

Democratic Senator William Bradley of New Jersey, an opponent of G-R-H, stated, "This bill doesn't cut one dollar from the federal deficit. It's a procedural answer to a substantive problem. It's a promise to do later what the Congress is unwilling to do now."

Senator Rudman counters that acting to balance the budget is just what Congress has so far been unable to do. Despite its many flaws, G-R-H was at least partly responsible for the newfound optimism that surrounded much of the budget debate in April and May of 1986. In many quarters it was being given credit for breaking the paralysis that had overtaken the President and Congress, and at least some action on the deficit—whether an accord or action mandated by the bill—seemed assured.

But, the *New York Times* cautioned, "Beware. The only way to balance the budget and control the deficit is to cut spending equitably, which neither the President nor Congress seems able to do; or raise taxes, which the President refuses to do; or both. No wonder everyone's rushing to embrace this choice bit of balanced baloney."

By late 1986 it was widely held that the G-R-H act was a failure. Spending had been cut by only about $20 billion, less than half of what was required to meet the fiscal 1986 target. Yet technicalities in the law were invoked to rule out further cuts thought to be mandated by the act. Further, no one believed that the fiscal 1987 deficit would be anywhere near its $144 billion target, but there was little faith that the G-R-H cuts would emerge. One commentator wrote that, rather than halting the spiralling deficit, G-R-H was merely covering it up.

We saw earlier that a large government sector whose expenditures on goods and services are not very sensitive to the cyclical variations in national income is a major built-in stabilizer. To insist that annual government expenditure be tied to annual tax receipts would be to abandon the present built-in stability provided by the government. Government expenditure would then become a major *destabilizing* force. Tax revenues necessarily rise in booms and fall in slumps; an annually balanced budget would force government expenditure to do the same. Changes in national income would then cause induced changes not only in household consumption expenditure but also in government expenditure. This would greatly increase the economy's marginal propensity to spend and hence increase the value of the multiplier.

An annually balanced budget would accentuate the swings in national income that accompany changes in such autonomous expenditure flows as investment and exports.

A further problem is that the goal of budget *balance* is in fact stricter than is required to avoid a rising debt to GNP ratio. Growth in GNP means that some growth in the debit, and hence a (small) deficit, is consistent with a stable debt to GNP ratio. In the rest of this chapter, we shall assume that the term *budget balance* allows for this possibility.

A cyclically balanced budget.   An alternative policy, one that would prevent continual deficits (and could also inhibit the growth in the size of the government sector), would be to balance the budget over the business cycle. This would be more feasible than the annually balanced budget, and it would not make government expenditure a destabilizing force.

Although more attractive in principal than the annually balanced budget, a cyclically balanced budget would carry problems of its own. Congress might well spend in excess of revenue in one year, leaving the next Congress the obligation to spend less than current revenue in following years. Could such an obligation to balance over a period of several years be made binding? It could be made a legal

requirement through an act of Congress. But what Congress does, Congress can undo. (This has been the history of attempts to limit the size of the national debt by legal restriction.)

Perhaps even more of a problem is that there is always room for some disagreement about the current state of the business cycle. Critics of the cyclically balanced budget proposal argue that many governments have often misinterpreted long-term factors such as demographic changes which lead to an increase in the measured unemployment rate or structural change which leads to a fall in the measured rate of income growth as short-term cyclical factors which call for fiscal stimulus. Thus the critics argue that while governments can appear to accept the need for balance over the cycle, this has not in fact stopped them from running persistently large deficits and hence imprudently run up the national debt.

While a budget balanced over the course of the business cycle is in principle an acceptable way of reconciling short-term stabilization and long-term prudence, the business cycle may not be well enough defined in practice to make the proposal operational.

The Political Economy of the Debt

Almost all economists accept that if the debt got so large that it could not be serviced without either putting a crushing burden on taxpayers or forcing the government to create new money to service it, there would be serious problems. But many (in particular, those identified as Keynesians) think we are still a long way from that point. To them the overriding principle is that the debt should be changed according to the needs of stabilization policy.

An alternative view is what has come to be called *fiscal conservatism.* The conservative view takes a broad historical perspective. It says that in the eighteenth century spendthrift European rulers habitually spent more than their tax revenues and so created harmful inflation. By the end of the nineteenth century the doctrine was well established that a balanced budget was the citizen's only protection against profligate government spending and consequent wild inflation. Thus the conservatives hold that the balanced budget doctrine was not silly and irrational, as Keynes made it out to be. Instead it was the symbol of the people's victory in a long struggle to control the spendthrift proclivities of their nations' rulers.

The Keynesian revolution swept away that view. Budget deficits became, according to Keynesians, the tool by which benign and enlightened governments sought to ensure full employment. But, say the conservatives, deficit spending let the tiger out of the cage. Inflationary gaps, recessionary gaps, or full employment notwithstanding, governments spent and spent and spent. Deficits accumulated, national debt rose, and inflation became the rule.

The main premise of the conservative view is that governments are not passive agents who do what is necessary to create full employment and maximize social welfare. Instead, governments are composed of individuals—elected officials, legislators, and civil servants—who, like everyone else, seek mainly to maximize their own well-being. And their welfare is best served by government's having a big role and by a satisfied electorate. Thus they tend to favor spending and to resist tax increases. This creates a persistent tendency toward deficits that is quite independent of any consideration of a sound fiscal policy.

The debate reflects deeply held views about the role of government, the nature and motivation of public officials, and the desirability of stabilization. Keynesians tend to regard government officials as well-meaning, and substantial government intervention as essential to an effective and humane society. Fiscal conservatives regard public officials as self-serving and of limited competence and see public intervention, however well motivated, as probably inept and ultimately destabilizing. Both recognize that an interventionist government will play a large role in economic affairs. Conservatives regard that prospect with concern, Keynesians with relative equanimity.

Summary

1. Fiscal policy uses government expenditure and tax policies to influence the economy by shifting the aggregate demand curve. Changes in either government spending or tax policies also influence the budget balance.
2. The so called paradox of thrift is not a paradox at all. It applies to the short-run effects of saving and investment on aggregate demand. It predicts that severe recessions can be combated by encouraging an increase in spending.
3. When private expenditure functions are fixed, it is a relatively simple matter to increase expenditure, to cut tax rates, or to make a balanced budget increase in expenditure in order to remove a recessionary gap (and to make the opposite changes to remove an inflationary gap).
4. Fiscal policy is more difficult when, as is almost always the case, private expenditure functions are continually shifting. Fine tuning, the attempt to hold the aggregate expenditure function virtually constant by offsetting even small fluctuations in private expenditure, has been largely discredited. Many still believe, however, that large and persistent gaps can be offset by fiscal policy.
5. Short-term stabilization by fiscal policy operates largely through such automatic stabilizers as tax revenues that vary directly with national income, expenditures on goods and services that do not

vary with national income, and transfer payments that vary negatively with national income.

6. Discretionary fiscal policy is also used sometimes to attack large and persistent gaps. It must be reversible. Otherwise the economy may overshoot its target once private investment recovers from a temporary slump or falls back from a temporary boom. However, tax changes need to be perceived as relatively long-lived if they are to induce major changes in household spending patterns. (Temporary changes may merely affect the current saving rate and not expenditure.) The need to have tax changes perceived as long-lived conflicts, however, with the need to have fiscal policy easily reversible.

7. Changes in the stance of fiscal policy may be reasonably judged by changes in the cyclically adjusted deficit. This is the balance between revenues and expenditures as they would be if full employment prevailed.

8. U.S. national debt and debt service payments have risen and fallen as a percentage of national income, but they have not shown a long-term trend to grow inexorably. Recent increases in these ratios reflect the cumulative effect of the recent persistence of deficits. Persistent deficits are a cause for concern for several reasons, including inflation, crowding out of investment, and reducing national income in the long run.

9. An annually balanced budget would be unfeasible; even if it were possible, it would destabilize the economy. A cyclically balanced budget would act as a stabilizer while also curbing the growth of the government sector. Growth of GNP and some minimal acceptable inflation rate both create room for the average budget balance over the course of the business cycle to show some deficit; a deficit persistently in excess of this can be viewed as being imprudent.

10. Keynesians take a relatively sanguine view of the national debt. As long as it does not grow wildly as a proportion of national income, they view its short-term fluctuations and its long-term upward trend in absolute terms as a stabilizing device. Fiscal conservatives mistrust government and view insistence on a balanced budget as the only effective means of curtailing reckless government spending that wastes scarce resources and feeds the fires of inflation.

Topics for Review

Fiscal policy
Budget balance, balanced budget, budget surplus, and budget deficit
Fine tuning
Built-in stabilizer
Discretionary fiscal policy
The stance of fiscal policy

Actual budget balance and cyclically adjusted budget balance
National debt and debt service
Keynesian and fiscal conservative views of debt

---

1. Consider the following questions on presidential economics.
   a. President Ford in 1975 maintained that his proposed package of a $28 billion cut in federal expenditure and a $28 billion tax cut "as a short-term measure would not affect the economy in any significant way." Does this mean that President Ford believed the balanced budget multiplier was zero? If so, why then might he have proposed the package? If not, what might he have meant?
   b. President Carter in 1977 said, "There will be no new programs implemented under my administration unless we can be sure that the cost of those programs is compatible with my goal of having a balanced budget before the end of that term." Does this mean President Carter rejected fiscal policy? What might it mean?
   c. President Reagan said in 1983, "I remain committed to the idea that we can reduce budget deficits without increasing the burden on the poor, without weakening our national defense, and without destroying economic incentives by counterproductive tax increases." Are these objectives inconsistent? How does President Reagan's record stand up to his promises?
2. Which of the following would be built-in stabilizers?
   a. Food stamps for the needy
   b. Cost of living escalators in government contracts and pensions
   c. Income taxes
   d. Free college tuition for unemployed workers after six months of unemployment, provided that they are under 30 years old and have had five or more years of full-time experience since high school
3. In his first inaugural address President Franklin D. Roosevelt expounded the doctrine of "sound finance"— that the government's budget should always be balanced. During his term, however, government spending rose faster than taxes, and deficits resulted. How would the effectiveness of the New Deal on employment have been changed if Roosevelt had been successful in keeping the budget balanced throughout his first term?
4. The Employment Act of 1946 made no explicit mention of price stability as an objective of national income policy. Why do you suppose this was so? What is the relationship between fiscal policy and the price level?
5. Consider the typical annual expenditures and revenues of the organizations listed below. Comment on the appropriate debt policy for each, taking into account their respective goals, life span, and resources.
   a. Family household
   b. Two private corporations, one growing rapidly and the other a mature firm

Discussion Questions

      c. A village of 5,000 inhabitants

      d. The U.S. government

      e. The United Nations

6. Evaluate each of the following proposals to "control the deficit" in order to avoid the long-run burden of the debt.

      a. Maintaining a zero cyclically adjusted deficit

      b. Keeping the debt-to-GNP ratio constant

      c. Limiting government borrowing from the public in each year to *X* percent of the national income in that year

7. President Reagan said in 1982, "I don't place very much faith in those various deficit forecasts." Why would the president of the United States be skeptical about deficit forecasts? Does the evidence suggest that this skepticism is misplaced?

8. Discuss the following reactions to the Gramm-Rudman-Hollings bill, all taken from newspapers during the 1986 budget debate.

      a. "It's a measure that calls for compromise, yet neither side is rushing to make the first move. Instead the Hill and the White House seem locked in a game of chicken."

      b. "It sets up machinery that, if triggered, will slash the spending of the U.S. government like a mindless robot. There's no doubt this is a stupid way to do budgeting."

      c. "Balanced Budget Risks: Gramm-Rudman might precipitate the repetition of the fiscal blunders of the Depression."

      d. "The simple fact is that we are forced to cut expenditure if taxes are not to be raised."

      e. "This Bill should be called the Senate Incumbent Reelection Act of 1985."

9. How does the decision of whether to raise taxes or issue bonds in order to finance the unusually high government expenditures incurred during a war influence "who pays" for the war?

Fiscal Policy: Some Further Issues

This appendix considers three extensions to the analysis of fiscal policy presented in the text. First, the assumptions concerning behavior underlying the Keynesian consumption function are examined. Second, we look at the implications of whether government expenditure is financed by current taxes or by running a deficit. Third, we consider some further problems in using the budget deficit as a measure of the fiscal stance.

I. The Permanent-Income and Life-Cycle Hypotheses of Household Consumption

In the Keynesian theory of the consumption function, current consumption expenditure is related to current income—either current disposable income or current national income. Recent research has produced hypotheses that relate consumption to some longer-term concept of income than the income that the household is currently earning.

The two most influential theories of this type are the **permanent-income hypothesis (PIH)**, developed by Professor Friedman, and the **life-cycle hypothesis (LCH)**, developed by Professors Modigliani, Ando, and Brumberg. Although there are differences between these hypotheses, for most of the Appendix, it is their similarities that are important. In particular, we note that in both the PIH and the LCH household behavior tends to smooth the time pattern of consumption relative to that of disposable income. In part II of the appendix we shall consider a potentially important difference between the two hypotheses.

In discussing this "consumption smoothing" issue, it is important to ask: What variables do these theories seek to explain? What assumptions do they make? What are the major implications of these assumptions?

Variables

Three variables need to be considered: consumption, saving, and income. Keynesian-type theories seek to explain the amounts that households spend on purchasing goods and services for consumption. This concept is called *consumption expenditure*. Permanent-income theories seek to explain the actual flows of consumption of the *services* that are provided by the commodities that households buy. This concept is called *actual consumption*.[1]

With services and nondurable goods, expenditure and actual consumption occur more or less at the same time and the distinction between the two concepts is not important. Consumption of a haircut, for example, occurs at the time it is purchased, and an orange or a package of corn flakes is consumed very soon after it is purchased. Thus, if we knew purchases of such goods and services at some time, say, last year, we would also know last year's consumption of those goods and services.

But this is not the case with durable consumer goods. A house is purchased at one point in time, but it yields its services over a long time, possibly as long as the purchaser's lifetime. The same is true of a personal computer and a watch and, over a shorter period of time, a car and a dress. For such products, if we know purchases last year, we do not necessarily know last year's consumption of the services that the products yielded.

Thus one important characteristic of durable goods is that *expenditure* to purchase them is not necessarily synchronized with *consumption* of the stream of services that the goods provide. If in 1988 Ms. Smith buys a car for $12,000, runs it for six

---

[1] Because Keynes's followers did not always distinguish carefully between the concepts of consumption expenditure and actual consumption, the word *consumption* is often used in both contexts. We follow this normal practice, but where there is any possible ambiguity in the term we will refer to *consumption expenditure* and *actual consumption.*

years, and then discards it as worn out, her expenditure on automobiles is $12,000 in 1988 and zero for the next five years. Her consumption of the services of automobiles, however, is spread out at an average annual rate of $2,000 for six years. If everyone followed Ms. Smith's example by buying a new car in 1988 and replacing in in 1993, the automobile industry would undergo wild booms in 1988 and 1993 with five intervening years of slump, even though the actual consumption of automobiles would be spread more or less evenly over time. This example is extreme, but it illustrates the possibilities, where consumers' durables are concerned, of quite different time paths of *consumption expenditure*, which is the subject of Keynesian theories of consumption, and *actual consumption*, which is the subject of permanent-income theories.

Now consider saving. The change in emphasis from consumption expenditure to actual consumption implies a change in the definition of saving. Saving is no longer income minus consumption expenditure; it is now income minus the value of actual consumption. When Ms. Smith spent $12,000 on her car in 1988, but used only $2,000 worth of its services in that year, she was actually consuming $2,000 and saving $10,000. The purchase of a consumers' durable is thus counted as saving, and only the value of its services actually consumed is counted as consumption.

The third important variable is income. Instead of using current income, the theories use a concept of long-term income. The precise definition varies from one theory to another, but basically it is related to the household's expected income stream over a fairly long planning period. In the LCH it is the income that the household expects to earn over its lifetime, called its *lifetime income*.

Every household is assumed to have a view of its lifetime income. This is not as unreasonable as it might seem. Students training to be doctors have a very different view of expected lifetime income than those training to become schoolteachers. Both expected income streams—for a doctor and for a schoolteacher—will be different from that expected by an assembly line worker or a professional athlete. One possible lifetime income stream is shown in Figure 30A-1.

FIGURE 30A-1   Current Income and Permanent Income

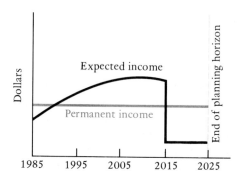

Expected current income may vary greatly over a lifetime, but expected permanent income is defined to be the constant annual equivalent. The graph shows a hypothetical expected income stream from work for a household whose planning horizon was 40 years from 1985. The current income rises to a peak, then falls slowly for a while, and finally falls sharply on retirement. The corresponding permanent income is the amount the household could consume at a steady rate over its lifetime by borrowing early against future earnings (as do most newly married couples), then repaying past debts, and finally saving for retirement when income is at its peak without either incurring debt or accumulating new wealth to be passed on to future generations.

The household's expected lifetime income is then converted into a single figure for *annual* **permanent income**. In the life-cycle hypothesis this permanent income is the maximum amount the household could spend on consumption each year without accumulating debts that are passed on to future generations. If a household were to consume a constant amount equal to its permanent income each year, it would add to its debts in years when current income was less than permanent income and reduce its debt or increase its assets in years when its current income exceeded its permanent income. Over its lifetime, however, it would just break even, leaving neither accumulated assets nor debts to its heirs. If the interest rate were zero, permanent income would be just the sum of all expected incomes divided by the number of expected years of life.[2] With a positive interest rate, permanent income will diverge from this amount because of the costs of borrowing and the extra income that can be earned by investing savings.

Assumption

The basic assumption of this type of theory, whether PIH or LCH, is that the household's actual consumption is related to its permanent rather than to its current income. Two households that have the same permanent income (and are similar in other relevant characteristics) will have similar consumption patterns even though their current incomes may behave differently.

Implications

The major implication of these theories is that changes in a household's current income will affect its actual consumption only so far as they affect its permanent income. Consider two income changes that could occur in a household with a permanent income of $20,000 per year and an expected lifetime of 30 or more years. In the first case suppose the household receives an unexpected extra income of $2,000 *for this year only*. The increase in the household's permanent income is small. If the rate of interest were zero, the household could consume an extra $66.66 per year for the rest of its expected life span; with a positive rate of interest, the extra annual consumption would be more because money not spent this year could be invested and would earn interest.[3] In the second case the household gets a toally unforeseen increase of $2,000 a year *for the rest of its life*. In this event the household's permanent income has risen by $2,000 because the household can actually consume $2,000 more every year without accumulating new debts. Although in both cases

current income rises by $2,000, the effect on permanent income is very different.

Keynesian theory assumes that *consumption expenditure* is related to current income and therefore predicts the same change in this year's consumption expenditure in each of the above cases. Permanent-income theories relate *actual consumption* to permanent income and therefore predict different changes in actual consumption in each case. In the first case there would be only a small increase in actual annual consumption; in the second there would be a large increase.

In the LCH and the PIH any change in current income that is thought to be temporary will have only a small effect on permanent income and hence on actual consumption.

Implications for the Behavior of the Economy

According to the permanent-income and the life-cycle hypotheses, actual consumption is not much affected by temporary changes in income. Does this mean that aggregate expenditure, $C + I + G + (X - M)$, is not much affected? *Not necessarily*. Consider what happens when households get a temporary increase in their incomes. If actual consumption is not greatly affected by this, then households must be saving most of this increase. But from the point of view of these theories, households save when they buy a durable good just as much as when they buy a financial asset such as a stock or a bond. In both cases actual current consumption is not changed.

Thus spending a temporary increase in income on bonds or on new cars is consistent with both the PIH and the LCH. But it makes a great deal of difference to the short-run behavior of the economy which is done. If households buy stocks and bonds, aggregate expenditure on currently produced final goods will not rise when income rises temporarily.[4] If households buy automobiles or any other durable consumer good, aggregate expenditure on currently produced final goods will rise when income rises

---

[2] In the PIH the household has an infinite time horizon and the relevant permanent-income concept is the amount the household could consume forever without increasing or decreasing its present stock of wealth.

[3] If the rate of interest were 7 percent, the household could invest the $2,000, consume an extra $161 a year, and just have nothing left at the end of 30 years.

[4] Except for such indirect effects as changes in interest rates, or in a dozen other ways.

temporarily. Thus the PIH and the LCH leave unsettled the question that is critical in determining the size of the multiplier: What is the reaction of household *expenditures* on currently produced goods and services, particularly durables, to short-term, temporary changes in income?

The PIH and LCH theories leave unanswered the critical question of the ability of short-term changes in fiscal policy to remove inflationary and recessionary gaps.

Assume, for example, that a serious recessionary gap emerges and that the government attempts to stimulate a recovery by giving tax rebates and by cutting tax rates—both on an announced temporary basis. This will raise households' current disposable incomes by the amount of the tax cuts, but it will raise their permanent incomes by only a small amount. According to the PIH, the flow of actual current consumption should not rise much. Yet it is quite consistent with the PIH that households should spend their tax savings on durable consumer goods, the consumption of which can be spread over many years.

In this case, even though actual consumption this year would not respond much to the tax cuts, expenditure would respond a great deal. Since current output and employment depend on expenditure rather than on actual consumption, the tax cut would be effective in stimulating the economy. However, it is also consistent with the LCH/PIH that households spend only a small part of their tax savings on consumption goods and seek to invest the rest in bonds and other financial assets. In this case the tax cuts may have only a small stimulating effect on the economy. It is important to note that the PIH and the LCH do *not* predict unambiguously that changes in taxes that are announced to be only short-lived will be ineffective in removing inflationary or deflationary gaps.

II. Does the Deficit Matter?

Analysts who focus on the deficit as a summary description of the government's influence on the economy presuppose that tax-financed government expenditure contributes less to aggregate demand than does bond-financed government expenditure, since the latter leads to a larger deficit. Note that deficit financing of government expenditure can be viewed as a deferral of taxes, increasing current disposable income and reducing future disposable income. This rearrangement of the timing of taxes may leave expected permanent income basically unchanged compared to the case where taxes were levied at the same time as the government expenditure occurred. While the Keynesian consumption function predicts that consumption would increase with the increase in current disposable income, the PIH studied above predicts that households' consumption is related to their lifetime or permanent income, not to their current disposable income. If the PIH is an accurate description of behavior, then deficit finance will have little effect on consumption behavior.

Thus, it is possible to identify a set of conditions which would mean that government expenditure will have the same effect on the economy whether it is financed by raising current taxes or issuing government bonds. That imaginary world, first considered by David Ricardo in 1817 and recently revived by Professor Robert Barro, is populated by far-sighted individuals whose consumption decisions depend on their 'permanent' income only. Thus changes in the time-pattern of income receipts that leave their permanent income unchanged would have no effect on private-sector expenditure decisions.

In this world government bonds would not be net wealth because the financial value of a bond would be matched exactly by a corresponding liability for future tax payments needed to service the debt. Specifically, households would be indifferent between paying $1 of current taxes and paying a stream of future taxes which has a present value of $1 when discounted at the market interest rate. In this case, the government deficit would not matter; bond rather than tax finance would merely represent a rearrangement in the timing of income receipts which the private sector could (and would) offset in capital markets. Issuing bonds now and raising taxes later would be viewed as equivalent to raising taxes now.

The theory underlying this analysis requires that

households have an infinite planning horizon, as in the PIH discussed in part I of this appendix. Otherwise taxes accruing after the household's lifetime would not offset interest payments received during the household's lifetime, and government bonds would be viewed as net wealth by the household. Hence deficits would increase household's perceived net wealth, households would increase their consumption, and deficit-financed government expenditure would be more expansionary than tax-financed expenditure.

Professor Barro's contribution was to show that debt neutrality could arise even in the context of the Life Cycle Hypothesis if the household's concern for its heirs caused its planning horizon to extend beyond its own lifetime. Suppose that the typical household, when making its own lifetime consumption plans, also plans for a positive bequest that it intends to leave to its heirs. Now consider the effects of a government decision to sell bonds rather than increase taxes in order to finance previously announced government expenditure; this of course increases the government budget deficit. (Thus we are focusing on the effects of the method of financing the expenditure, and not on the effects of the expenditure itself.) If the households wished, they could simply spend the increased disposable income that results from not having to pay current taxes to finance the government expenditure, thus leaving the next generation with a liability to pay the taxes that will have to be levied when the government redeems the bonds. If the recipients behave in this manner, the fiscal authority's decision to deficit finance will have stimulated the economy by inducing an increase in spending.

However, this behavior would reduce the net value of the bequest that the typical household would be leaving to its heirs, since the heirs now face an increased tax liability. This violates the notion that the typical household makes a rational plan that includes targets for their own consumption and for the bequest that they wish to leave to their heirs, since the government action does not change the options open to the current households. The current households could have achieved this redistribution away from future generations toward themselves without the government action simply by increasing their own consumption and reducing the value of the estate they leave to their heirs.

If they wish to preserve their initial plan, all that current households need to do is maintain their spending plans and increase saving by the full amount of the increase in their disposable income; that is, by the increase in the government budget deficit. The resulting increase in the value of the next generation's inheritance will exactly offset the increase in tax liabilities that they face. Thus a government deficit which issues bonds now and "promises" taxes in the future would have no effect even if the taxes were expected only after the current generation were dead.

Note that the level of government expenditure is still important in this model—only the method of financing is irrelevant. But there are a number of reasons to believe that future taxes that have a present value of $1 are not equivalent to present taxes of $1, and thus that this debt-neutral Ricardian model does not provide an accurate description of the working of a modern economy. (Ricardo himself rejected it.) These reasons include:

The private sector borrows on different terms than the government sector.   This is perhaps the most important reason why deficit finance is not neutral in practice. In many circumstances households, and to some extent firms, face constraints that prevent them from borrowing all that they would like to at the prevailing market interest rate. Alternatively, they may be able to borrow but at a much higher interest rate than that facing the government. Consequently when the government substitutes future taxes for present taxes by running a deficit, these "constrained" private-sector agents will feel wealthier and, consequently, will spend more.

Myopic perception.   If some households imperfectly perceive the future tax liabilities implied by the government deficit, they will not offset government dissaving with private saving.

Finite lifetimes.   Another reason why households might view future taxes as not equivalent to current taxes is that future taxes may extend beyond the expected lifetime of the household. Thus the household may anticipate escaping taxes by dying! As Barro points out, this would make no difference if households "care about their heirs"; in this case living households would simply alter any bequests they had planned to leave to their heirs by an amount equal to the expected increase in future taxes borne by their heirs. However, if currently alive households do not care or are unable to alter their bequests (perhaps because such bequests cannot be reduced below their current zero level), living households will in fact react to a change in the deficit in a manner that does not completely offset it.

Conclusions

The basic feature of the economy that makes government deficits and the public debt matter is that, to a significant extent, current private-sector expenditure is tied to current private-sector income. The government deficit influences the current income of the private sector, since for a given level of government expenditure a larger deficit means lower current taxes and hence larger current private disposable income. In the first instance, this debt finance simply causes an intertemporal rearrangement of private-sector income. But for the reasons noted above, the private sector is not indifferent to this rearrangement of its income receipts. In particular, current private-sector expenditure rises in response to the increase in current income. This influence of government deficits on private spending not only creates the potential for a stabilization role for deficits over the business cycle, it also creates the mechanism by which persistent deficits become costly and undesirable in the longer run.

III. Further Problems with the Deficit As a Measure of the Fiscal Stance

The Balanced Budget Multiplier Problem

The cyclically adjusted deficit is vastly superior to the actual budget deficit for estimating year-to-year changes in the stance of fiscal policy. But the balanced budget multiplier indicates one reason why even the cyclically adjusted deficit is not a completely reliable measure of the fiscal stance.

The balanced budget multiplier suggests that a dollar of spending will increase aggregate demand by more than a dollar of tax revenue will decrease it. Therefore, in order to properly measure the effect of fiscal actions on aggregate demand, a more sophisticated measure which takes account of these differential effects is required. Such a measure—called the *weighted cyclically adjusted deficit*—is often used by economists in detailed empirical work assessing fiscal policy.

The Inflation Adjustment

An adjustment to the government's debt service payments is often made when using the deficit to judge the fiscal stance. As we saw in Box 29-1, nominal interest rates can be divided into a real component and an inflation premium. Debt-service payments made by the government thus also have a real and an inflation premium component. While the real component constitutes a transfer from the government to holders of the government debt as payment for use of the principal, the inflation premium does not. This is because the inflation premium is exactly offset by a reduction in the real value of the principal.

Suppose the current value of the government's debt is $1,000 billion. Suppose also that in the current year the government runs a deficit of $100 billion and that the current inflation rate is 10 percent. On crude measures the government has a deficit of $100 billion; this corresponds to the increase in the nominal value of the government's indebtedness. On an inflation-adjusted basis, the deficit is zero. This is because the real value—or purchasing power—of the debt is unchanged, even though the nominal stock of debt has risen by $100 billion (i.e., by 10 percent) from $1,000 billion to $1,100 billion. Because the real value of the government's indebtedness is unchanged, the "effective," or inflation-adjusted, deficit is zero. The *inflation adjustment* is equal to the inflation premium component of government debt-service payments.

Whether making the inflation adjustment is appropriate for judging the stance of fiscal policy is a source of controversy among economists. Those who argue for the adjustment hold that the net effect on aggregate demand of this component of the deficit will be approximately zero—the government's outlay will be offset by an increase in private saving as wealth holders attempt to recoup the inflation-induced fall in their real wealth. Those who argue against the need for the adjustment hold that private-sector saving will not rise by enough to offset the inflation component completely.

PART EIGHT

Money, Banking, and Monetary Policy

The Nature of Money and Monetary Institutions

What is the significance of money to the economy, and why are economists concerned about it? Indeed, what is money, and how did it come to play its present role?

Many people believe that money is one of the more important things in life and that there is never enough of it. Yet economists argue that increasing the world's money supply would not make the average person better off. The reason is that although money allows its owners to buy someone else's output, the total amount of goods and services available for everyone to buy depends on the total output that is produced, not on the total amount of money that people possess. Increasing the world's money supply would not change the total quantity of goods produced and hence available for consumption, although it would likely cause an inflation.

The Real and Monetary Sectors of the Economy: The Classical Dichotomy

Early in the history of economics, changes in the quantity of money were seen to be associated with changes in the price level. Eighteenth century economists developed the first comprehensive theories in which the economy was conceived of as being divisible into a "real" part and a "monetary" part.

The real sector.   In such theories the allocation of resources is determined in the real sector of the economy by demand and supply. This allocation depends on *relative* prices. Whether, for example, a lot of beef is produced relative to pork depends on the relative prices of beef and pork, not on the money price of either. If the price of beef is higher than the price of pork and both commodities cost about the same to produce, there is an incentive to produce beef rather than pork. At prices of $1 a pound for pork and $3 for beef, the *relative* incentive is the same as it would be at $2 for pork and $6 for beef. As with beef and pork, so with all other commodities:

The allocation of resources among different lines of production depends on relative prices.

The monetary sector.   According to the early economists the price *level* is determined in the monetary sector of the economy. An increase in the money supply leads to an increase in all money prices. In the beef and pork example, an increase in the total money available might raise the price of pork from $1 to $2 a pound and the price of beef from $3 to $6, but in equilibrium it would leave their relative prices unchanged. Hence it would have no effect on the real part of the economy, that is, on the amount of resources allocated to beef and to pork production (or to anything else). If the quantity of money were doubled, the prices of all commodities would double; and money income would also double, so everyone earning an income would be made no better or worse off by the change.

Thus, in equilibrium, the real and the monetary parts of the economy were believed to have no effect on each other. The doctrine that the quantity of money influences the level of money prices, but has no effect on the real part of the economy is called the doctrine of the **neutrality of money.**

Because early economists believed that the most important questions—How much does the economy produce? What share of it does each group in the society get?—were answered in the real sector, they spoke of money as a "veil" behind which occurred the real events that affected material well-being.

The modern view.   Modern economists still accept the insights of the early economists that relative prices are a major determinant of the allocation of resources and that the quantity of money has a lot to do with determining the absolute level of prices. They accept the neutrality of money in long-run equilibrium when all forces causing change have fully worked themselves out. We shall see in Chapter 32, however, that they do not accept the neutrality of money when the economy is undergoing change from day to day, that is, when the economy is not in a state of long-run equilibrium.

In this chapter we look first at the experience of price level changes—one aspect of the importance of money—and then at the nature of money itself and the operation of the modern institutions that comprise the monetary system of our economy.

Historical Experience

In Chapter 24 (on pages 459–463) we discussed some important introductory material related to the price level itself and to inflations and deflations, that is, to changes in the price level. That material should be reviewed at this stage. In the figures in this chapter we present some futher details of the behavior of the price levels over very long periods of time. Figure 31-1 shows the course of producer (or wholesale) prices in the United States from 1785 through 1985. Considerable year-to-year fluctuations are apparent. Despite the large fluctuations that occurred during the nineteenth century, the price trend during that period was neither upward nor downward. In contrast, so far the twentieth century has also seen large fluctuations *and* a distinct rising trend in the price level.

Although admittedly a long time, even two centuries may still not be enough to give a clear perspective of very long-term price fluctuations. The experience of the period since 1946 looks much more dramatic and unusual when compared only with the nineteenth century than when considered in longer perspective. For an indication of the longer-term course of price levels, we can look across the Atlantic. Figure 31-2 shows the course of the price level in England over seven centuries. It shows that there was an overall inflationary trend, but that it was by no means evenly spread over the centuries.

The Nature of Money

Inflation is a monetary phenomenon in the sense that a rise in the general level of prices is the same thing as a decrease in the purchasing power of money. But what exactly is money? Probably more folklore and general nonsense are believed about money than about any other aspect of the economy. In this section we describe the functions of money and briefly outline its history. One purpose of this account is to remove some of these misconceptions. In addition, the recent revival of interest in the gold standard makes some discussion of early monetary systems relevant.

FIGURE 31-1   An Index of Producer Prices in the United States, 1785–1986 (1967 = 100)

Persistent peacetime inflation has only recently become a problem in America. While the price level has fluctuated throughout American history, no long-term trend was visible during the period from the Revolutionary War to 1930. Every major war produced an inflation that was subsequently reversed. The data are plotted on a ratio scale in which equal vertical distances represent equal percentage changes. (*Sources: Historical Statistics*, 1976, pp. 199, 201. *Historical Statistics*, 1949, p. 231. *Economic Report of the President*, 1986.)

What Is Money?

Traditionally in economics **money** has been defined as any generally accepted medium of exchange. A **medium of exchange** is anything that will be accepted by virtually everyone in a society in exchange for goods and services. But money is more than that.

Money has several functions. It acts as a medium of exchange, as a store of value, and as a unit of account.

Different kinds of money vary in the degree of efficiency with which they fulfill these functions, and different definitions of money may be required for different purposes.

A Medium of Exchange

If there were no money, goods would have to be exchanged by barter, one good being swapped directly for another. We discussed this cumbersome

FIGURE 31-2   A Price Index of Consumables in Southern England, 1275–1959

Over the last seven centuries long periods of stable prices have alternated with long periods of rising prices. This remarkable price series shows an index of the prices of food, clothing, and fuel in southern England from 1275 through 1959. The trend line shows that the average change in prices over the whole period was 0.5 percent per year. The shaded areas indicate periods of unreversed inflation. The series also shows that even the perspective of a century can be misleading because long periods of stable or gently falling prices tended to alternate with long periods of rising prices. (*Source: Lloyds Bank Review,* No. 58, October 1960.)

system in Chapter 3. The major difficulty with barter is that each transaction requires a *double coincidence of wants*. For an exchange to occur between A and B, not only must A have what B wants, but B must have what A wants. If all exchange were restricted to barter, anyone who specialized in producing one commodity would have to spend a great deal of time searching for satisfactory transactions.

The use of money as a medium of exchange removes these problems. People can sell their output for money and subsequently use the money to buy what they wish from others. The double coincidence of wants is unnecessary when a medium of exchange is used.

Without money the economic system, which is based on specialization and the division of labor, could not function, and we would have to return to primitive forms of production and exchange. It is not without justification that money has been called one of the great inventions contributing to human freedom.

To serve as an efficient medium of exchange, money must have a number of characteristics. It must be readily acceptable. It must have a high value relative to its weight (otherwise it would be a nuisance to carry around). It must be divisible, because money that comes only in large denominations is

useless for transactions having only a small value. It must not be readily counterfeitable, because if money can be easily duplicated by individuals, it will lose its value.

A Store of Value

Money is a convenient way to store purchasing power; goods may be sold today and money stored until it is needed. The money provides a claim on someone else's goods that can be exercised at a future date. The two sides of the transaction can be separated in time with the obvious increase in freedom that this confers.

To be a satisfactory store of value, however, money must have a relatively stable value. When the price level is stable, the purchasing power of a given sum of money is also stable. When the price level changes, this is not so. Such changes undermine the usefulness of money as a store of value. An extreme example is discussed in Box 31-1.

Although money can serve as a satisfactory store of accumulated purchasing power for a single individual, it cannot do so for the society as a whole. If a single individual accumulates a pile of dollars, he or she will, when the time comes to spend it, be able to command the current output of some other indi-

BOX 31-1

Hyperinflation

Can the price level ever rise so rapidly that money loses its usefulness either as a medium of exchange or as a store of value? The answer appears to be that very occasionally this has happened. Inflation rates of 50, 100, and even 200 percent or more a year have occurred year after year and proven manageable as people adjust their contracts to real terms. While there are strains and side effects, the evidence shows such situations to be possible without causing money to become useless.

Does this mean that there is no reason to fear that rapid inflation will turn into hyperinflation that will destroy the value of money completely? The historical record is not entirely reassuring. There have been a number of cases where prices began to rise at an ever-accelerating rate until the nation's money ceased to be a satisfactory store of value even for the short period between receipt and expenditure and hence ceased also to be useful as a medium of exchange.

Consider the index of wholesale prices in Germany during and after World War I given in the table. The index shows that a good purchased with one 100-mark note in July 1923 would have required *ten million* 100-mark notes for its purchase only four months later! While Germany had experienced substantial inflation during World War I, averaging more than 30 percent per year, the immediate postwar years of 1920 and 1921 gave no sign of an explosive infla-

tion. Indeed, during 1920 price stability was experienced. But in 1922 and 1923, the price level exploded. On November 15, 1923, the mark was officially repudiated, its value wholly destroyed. How could this happen?

When an inflation becomes so rapid that people lose confidence in the purchasing power of their currency, they rush to spend it. But people who have goods become increasingly reluctant to accept the rapidly depreciating money in exchange. The rush to spend money accelerates the increase in prices until people finally become unwilling to accept money on any terms. What was once money ceases to be money.

The price system can then be restored only by repudiation of the old monetary unit and its replacement by a new unit. This destroys the value of monetary savings and of all contracts specified in terms of the old monetary units. It wipes out many people's savings by destroying the value of assets denominated in money terms.

There are about a dozen documented hyperinflations in world history, among them the collapse of the continental during the American revolution, the ruble during the Russian revolution, the drachma during and after the German occution of Greece in World War II, the pengo in Hungary during 1945 to 1946, and the Chinese national currency during 1946 to 1948. Every one of these hyerinflations was accompanied by great increases in the money supply; new money was printed to give governments purchasing power they could not or would not obtain by taxation. And every one occurred in the midst of a major political upheaval in which grave doubts existed about the stability and future of the government itself.

Is hyperinflation likely in the absence of civil war, revolution, or collapse of the government? Most economists think not. And it is clear that high inflation rates over a period of time do not mean the inevitable or even likely onset of a hyperinflation, however serious the distributive and social effects of such rates may be.

Date		German wholesale price index (1913 = 1)
January	1913	1
January	1920	13
January	1921	14
January	1922	37
July	1922	101
January	1923	2,785
July	1923	74,800
August	1923	944,000
September	1923	23,900,000
October	1923	7,096,000,000
November	1923*	750,000,000,000

* The mark was repudiated on November 15, 1923.

vidual. The whole society cannot do this. If all individuals were to save their money and then retire simultaneously to live on their savings, there would be no current production to purchase and consume. The society's ability to satisfy wants depends on goods and services being available; if some of this want-satisfying capacity is to be stored up for the whole society, goods that are currently producible must be left unconsumed and carried over to future periods.

A Unit of Account

Money may also be used purely for accounting purposes without having a physical existence of its own. For instance, a government store in a truly communist society might say that everyone had so many "dollars" to use each month. Goods could then be assigned prices and each consumer's purchases recorded, the consumer being allowed to buy until the allocated supply of dollars was exhausted. These dollars need have no existence other than as entries in the store's books, yet they would serve as a perfectly satisfactory unit of account.

Whether they could also serve as a medium of exchange between individuals depends on whether the store would agree to transfer dollar credits from one customer to another at the customer's request. Banks will transfer dollars credited to demand deposits in this way, and thus a bank deposit can serve as both a unit of account and a medium of exchange. Notice that the use of *dollars* in this context suggests a further sense in which money is a unit of account. People think about values in terms of the monetary unit with which they are familiar.

Another related function of money is sometimes distinguished. It can be used as a standard of deferred payments. Payments that are to be made in the future, on account of debts and so on, are reckoned in money. Money is used as a unit of account with the added dimension of time because the account will not be settled until later.

The Origins of Money

The origins of money are lost in antiquity; most primitive tribes known today make some use of it.

The ability of money to free people from the cumbersome necessity of barter must have led to its early use as soon as some generally acceptable commodity appeared.

Metallic Money

All sorts of commodities have been used as money at one time or another, but gold and silver proved to have great advantages. They were precious because their supply was relatively limited, and they were in constant demand by the rich for ornament and decoration. Also, they do not easily wear out. Thus they tended to have a high and stable price. They were easily recognized and generally known to be commodities that, because of their stable price, would be readily accepted. They were also divisible into extremely small units.

Precious metals thus came to circulate as money and to be used in many transactions. Before the invention of coins it was necessary to carry the metals in bulk. When a purchase was made, the requisite quantity of the metal was carefully weighed on a scale. A sack of gold and a highly accurate set of scales were the common equipment of the merchant and trader.

The invention of coinage eliminated the need to weigh the metal at each transaction. The prince or ruler weighed the metal and made a coin out of it to which he affixed his own seal to guarantee the amount of precious metal it contained. If a coin was certified to contain exactly 1/16 of an ounce of gold and a commodity was priced at 1/8 of an ounce of gold, two coins could be given over without weighing the gold. This was clearly a great convenience as long as traders knew they could accept the coin at its "face value." The face value was nothing more than a statement that a certain weight of metal was contained therein.

Abuses of metallic money. The ruler's subjects, however, could not let a good opportunity pass. Someone soon had the idea of clipping a thin slice off the edge of the coin. If he collected a coin stamped as containing half an ounce of gold, he could clip a slice off the edge and pass the coin off as still containing half an ounce of gold. ("Doesn't the stamp prove it?" he would argue.) If he got away with this, he would have made a profit equal to the market value of the clipped metal.

Whenever this practice became common, even the most myopic traders noticed that things were not what they seemed in the coinage world. It became necessary to weigh each coin before accepting it at its face value; out came the scales again, and most of the usefulness of coins was lost. To get around this problem, the idea arose of minting the coins with a rough edge. The absence of the rough edge would immediately be apparent and would indicate that the coin had been clipped. The practice, called milling, survives on some coins as an interesting anachronism to remind us that there were days when the market value of the metal in the coin (if it were melted down) was equal to the face value of the coin.

Debasement of metallic money.   Not to be outdone by the cunning of their subjects, the rulers were quick to seize the chance of getting something for nothing. The power to mint placed rulers in a good position to work a *really* profitable fraud. When faced with debts that could not be paid or repudiated, rulers merely used some suitable occasion—a marriage, an anniversary, an alliance—to remint the coinage. Subjects would be ordered to bring their gold coins into the mint to be melted down and coined afresh with a new stamp. The subjects could then go away with one new coin for every old coin they had brought in. Between the melting down and the recoining, however, the rulers had only to toss some inexpensive base metal in with the molten gold to earn a handsome profit. If the coinage were debased by adding, say, one pound of new base metal to every four pounds of old coins, five coins would be made for every four turned in. For every four coins brought in, the rulers could return four and have one left as profit with which to pay off debts.

Since gold and silver are softer and more malleable than most base metals, an experienced trader could usually tell if a coin had been seriously debased by testing its hardness. This is why, in films depicting ancient markets, you will often see a merchant biting a coin to see how easily it could be bent.

The result of debasement was inflation. The sub-

jects had the same number of coins as before and hence could demand the same quantity of goods. When rulers paid their bills, however, the recipients of the extra coins could be expected to spend some or all of them, and this caused a net increase in demand. The extra demand would bid up prices. Debasing the coinage thus led to a rise in prices.

It was the experience of such inflations that led early economists to propound the *quantity theory of money and prices.* They argued that there was a relation between the average level of prices and the quantity of money in circulation, such that an increase in the quantity of money would lead to a proportionate increase in the price level. (We shall have more to say about this theory in Chapter 32.)

Gresham's law.   The early experience of currency debasement led to the observation known as **Gresham's law** after the Elizabethan financial expert Sir Thomas Gresham. Gresham's hypothesis that "bad money drives out good," has stood the test of time.

When Queen Elizabeth I of England first came to the throne in the middle of the sixteenth century, the coinage had been severely debased. Seeking to help trade, Elizabeth minted new coins containing their full face value in gold. But as fast as she fed these new coins into circulation, they disappeared. Why? Gresham reasoned as follows to the young queen.

Suppose that you possessed one new and one old coin, each with the same face value, and had a bill to pay. What would you do? Clearly, you would pay the bill with the debased coin and keep the undebased one. You part with less gold that way. Suppose that you wanted to obtain a certain amount of gold bullion by melting down the gold coins (as was frequently done). Which coins would you use? Clearly, you would use new, undebased coins because you would part with less "face value" that way. The debased coins would thus remain in circulation and the undebased coins would disappear. Whenever people got hold of an undebased coin, they would hold on to it; whenever they got a debased coin, they would pass it on. The example in Box 31-2 shows that Gresham's law is as applicable to the twentieth century as it was to the sixteenth century.

BOX 31-2

Where Has All the Coinage Gone?

Tourists traveling in Chile in the 1970s, and other countries with rapid inflation, often wondered aloud why paper currency was used even for transactions as small as the purchase of a newspaper or a pack of matches. Metallic currency in such places was scarce and sometimes nonexistent. Similarly, the silver dollar, silver half-dollar, silver quarter, and silver dime have disappeared from circulation in the United States. The reason for these things is an example of Gresham's law.

Consider a country that has three different "tokens," each of them legal tender in the amount of $.25. One is a silver quarter with $.10 worth of recoverable silver in it; a second is made of cheaper metals with $.05 worth of recoverable metal in it; the third is a $.25 bill, a brightly colored piece of paper money that says plainly on its face "legal tender for all debts public and private."

If prices are stable and the government produces all three forms of money, there is no reason why they should not all circulate freely and interchangeably. Each is legal tender, and each is worth more as money than as anything else.

However, suppose an inflation starts and prices— including proportionally the prices of silver and other metals—begin to rise sharply. By the time prices have tripled, the silver quarters will have disappeared because the silver in each one is now worth $.30, and people will hoard them or melt them down rather than spend them to buy goods priced at only $.25. While not everyone will do this, coins passing from hand to hand will eventually reach someone who withdraws them from circulation.

What about the coins made of cheaper metal? Since prices have tripled, they now contain metal worth $.15, still less than their face value. Will they too disappear? They will if there is further inflation of, say, 100 percent. This raises the market value of the metal in the coin above its face value. The coins will disappear as they are melted down. By that time, only the paper money will be in circulation. The "bad" paper money will have driven out the "good" metal money.

Thus inflation, and even the expectation of inflation, may make some money "good" and some "bad" in Gresham's sense. If it does, the bad will displace the good.

Paper Money

The next important step in the history of money was the evolution of paper currency. Artisans who worked with gold required secure safes, and the public began to deposit their gold with such goldsmiths for safekeeping. Goldsmiths would give their depositors receipts promising to hand over the gold on demand. When any depositor wished to make a large purchase, she could go to her goldsmith, reclaim some of her gold, and hand it over to the seller of the goods. If the seller had no immediate need for the gold, he would carry it back to the goldsmith for safekeeping.

If people knew the goldsmith to be reliable, there was no need to go through the cumbersome and risky business of physically transferring the gold. The buyer need only transfer the goldsmith's receipt to the seller, who would accept it, secure in the knowledge that the goldsmith would pay over the gold whenever it was needed. If the seller wished to buy a good from a third party, who also knew the goldsmith to be reliable, this transaction, too, could be effected by passing the goldsmith's receipt from the buyer to the seller. The convenience of using pieces of paper instead of gold is obvious.

Thus, when it first came into being, paper money was a promise to pay on demand so much gold, the promise being made first by goldsmiths and later by banks. Banks, too, became known for their vaults ("safes") where the precious gold was stored and protected. As long as the institutions were known to be reliable, their pieces of paper would be "as good as gold." Such paper money was *backed* by precious metal and was *convertible* on demand into this metal.

When a country's money is convertible into gold, the country is said to be on a *gold standard*.

In nineteenth century America, private banks operating initially under either federal or state charters commonly issued paper money nominally convertible into gold. **Bank notes** represented banks' promises to pay. In areas such as the American West, where banks were small and were often unreliable in meeting demands for payment in gold, bank notes had a shady reputation. The gold bag and scales persisted in America well into the second half of the nineteenth century, even after paper money became widely accepted in most parts of the country.

Fractionally backed paper money.   For most transactions individuals were content to use paper currency. It was soon discovered that it was not necessary to keep an ounce of gold in the vaults for every claim to an ounce circulating as paper money. It was necessary to keep some gold on hand because paper would not do for some transactions. If someone wished to make a purchase from a distant place where her local bank was not known, she might have to convert her paper into gold and ship the gold. Further, she might not have perfect confidence in the bank's ability to honor its pledge to redeem the notes in gold at a future time. Her alternative was to exchange her notes for gold and store the gold until she needed it.

For these and other reasons, some holders of notes demanded gold in return for their notes. However, some of the bank's customers received gold in various transactions and stored it in the bank for safekeeping. They accepted promises to pay (i.e., bank notes) in return. At any one time, then, some of the bank's customers would be withdrawing gold, others would be depositing it, and most would be trading in the bank's paper notes without any need or desire to convert them into gold. Thus the bank was able to issue more money redeemable in gold than the amount of gold held in its vaults. This was good business, because the money could be profitably invested in interest-earning loans to households and firms.

This discovery was made by the early goldsmiths. From that time to the present, banks have had many more claims outstanding against them than they actually had in reserves available to pay those claims. We say that the currency issued in such a situation is *fractionally backed* by the reserves.

In the past the major problem of a fractionally backed, convertible currency was maintaining its convertibility into the precious metal by which it was backed. The imprudent bank, which issued too much paper money, found itself unable to redeem its currency in gold when the demand for gold was even slightly higher than usual. It would then have to suspend payments, and all holders of its notes would suddenly find the notes worthless. The prudent bank, which kept a reasonable relation between its note issue and its gold reserve, found that it could meet a normal range of demand for gold without any trouble.

If the public lost confidence and en masse demanded redemption of their currency, the banks would be unable to honor their pledges. The history of nineteenth and early twentieth century banking on both sides of the Atlantic is full of examples of banks ruined by "panics," sudden runs on their gold reserves. When this happened the banks' depositors and the holders of their notes would find themselves with worthless pieces of paper.

Central banks were a natural outcome of this sort of banking system. Where were the commercial banks to turn when they had good investments but were in temporary need of cash? If they provided loans for the public against reasonable security, why should not some other institution provide loans to them against the same sort of security? Central banks evolved in response to such needs.

Fiat currencies.   As time went on, note issue by private banks became less common and central banks took control of the currency. Central banks in turn became governmental institutions. In time *only* central banks were permitted to issue notes. Originally, the central banks issued currency that was fully convertible into gold. In those days gold would be brought to the central bank, which would issue currency in the form of "gold certificates" that asserted the gold was available on demand. The gold supply thus set some upper limit on the amount of currency.

BOX 31-3

Should Currency Be Backed by Gold?

The gold standard imposed an upper limit on the quantity of convertible currency that could be issued. Now that the system has been abandoned, does it matter that the central bank is not limited to its ability to issue currency?

Gold derives its value because it is scarce relative to the demand for it (the demand being derived from its monetary and its nonmonetary uses). Tying a currency to gold meant that the quantity of money in a country was determined by such chance occurrences as the discovery of new gold supplies. This was not without advantages, the most important being that it provided a check on governments' ability to cause inflation. Gold cannot be manufactured at will; paper currency can.

There is little doubt that in the past, if the money supply had been purely paper, many governments would have attempted to pay their bills by printing new money rather than by raising taxes. Such increases in the money supply, in periods of full employment, would lead to inflation in the same way that the debasement of metallic currency did.

Thus the gold standard provided some check on inflation by making it difficult for the government to change the money supply. Periods of major gold discoveries, however, brought about inflations of their own. In the 1500s, for example, Spanish gold and silver flowed into Europe from the New World, bringing inflation in their wake.

A major problem caused by a reliance on gold is that although it is usually desirable to increase the money supply when real national income is increasing, this cannot be done on a gold standard unless, by pure chance, gold is discovered at the same time. The gold standard took discretionary powers over the money supply out of the hands of government. Whether or not one thinks this is a good thing depends on how one thinks governments would use this discretion.

In general, a gold standard is probably better than having the currency managed by an ignorant or irresponsible government, but it is worse than having the currency supply adjusted by a well-informed and intelligent one. *Better* and *worse* in this context are judged by the criterion of having a money supply that varies adequately with the needs of the economy, but does not vary so as to cause violent inflations or deflations.

But central banks could issue more currency than they had gold because not all of the currency was presented for payment at any one time. Thus even under a gold standard, central banks had substantial discretionary control over the quantity of currency outstanding.

During the period between World Wars I and II, almost all the countries of the world abandoned the gold standard; their currencies were no longer convertible into gold. Money that is not convertible by law into anything valuable depends upon its acceptability for its value. Money that is declared by government order, or fiat, to be legal tender for settlement of all debts is called a **fiat money.** Some issues raised by the abandoning of the gold standard are discussed in Box 31-3.

Today almost all currency is fiat money.

Look at any bill in your wallet—it is not convertible into anything. Until recently much American currency bore the statement, "The United States of America Will Pay to the Bearer on Demand Twenty Dollars" (or whatever the currency was worth). The notes were signed by both the secretary of the Treasury and the treasurer. If you took this seriously and demanded $20, you could have handed over a $20 bill and received in return a different but identical $20 bill! Today's Federal Reserve $20 notes simply say, "The United States of America," "Twenty dollars," and "This note is legal tender for all debts, public and private." It is, in other words, fiat money pure and simple.

Legal tender is anything that by law must be accepted when offered either for the purchase of goods or services or to discharge a debt. If you are offered something that is legal tender in payment for a debt and you refuse to accept it, the debt is no longer legally collectible.

Not only is our modern currency fiat money, so is our coinage. Modern coins, unlike their historical ancestors, contain a value of metal that is characteristically a minute fraction of the value of the coin. Modern coins, like modern paper money, are merely tokens.

Why Is Fiat Money Valuable?

Today paper money and coinage is valuable because it is generally accepted. Because everyone accepts it as valuable, it *is* valuable; the fact that it can no longer be converted into anything has no effect on its functioning as a medium of exchange.

In the early days of the gold standard, paper money was valuable because everyone believed it was convertible into gold on demand. Experience during periods of crisis, when there was often a temporary suspension of convertibility into gold, and of panic, when there were bank failures, served to demonstrate that the mere *promise* of convertibility was not sufficient to make money valuable. Gradually the realization grew that neither was convertibility necessary.

Fiat money is valuable when it will be accepted in payment for goods and for debts.

Many people are disturbed to learn that present-day paper money is neither backed by nor convertible into anything more valuable—that it consists of nothing but pieces of paper whose value derives from common acceptance and from confidence that it will continue to be accepted in the future. Most people believe their money should be more substantial than that; after all, what of "dollar diplomacy" and the "bedrock solidity" of the Swiss franc? But money is in fact made of nothing more than pieces of paper. There is no point in pretending otherwise.

If paper money is acceptable, it is a medium of exchange; if its purchasing power remains stable, it is a satisfactory store of value; and if both of these things are true, it will also serve as a satisfactory unit of account.

Modern Money

By the twentieth century private banks had lost the authority to issue bank notes. Yet they did not lose the power to create deposit money.

Deposit Money

Banks' customers frequently deposit coins and paper money with the banks for safekeeping, just as in former times they deposited gold. Such a deposit is recorded as an entry on the customer's account. A customer who wishes to pay a debt may come to the bank and claim the money in dollars, then pay the money to another person. This person may then redeposit the money in a bank.

Like the gold transfers, this is a tedious procedure, particularly for large payments. It is more convenient to have the bank transfer claims to this money on deposit. The common check is an instruction to the bank to make the transfer. As soon as such transfers became easy and inexpensive, and checks became widely accepted in payment for commodities and debts, the deposits became a form of money called **deposit money,** which is defined as money held by the public in the form of deposits in banks that can be withdrawn on demand.

When individual A deposits $100 in a bank, the bank credits A's account with $100. This is the bank's promise to pay $100 cash on demand. If A pays B $100 by writing a check that B then deposits in the same bank, the bank merely reduces A's account by $100 and increases B's by the same amount. Thus the bank still promises to pay on demand the $100 originally deposited, but it now promises to pay it to B rather than to A. What makes all this so convenient is that B can actually deposit A's check in any bank, and the banks will arrange the transfer of credits.

Checks are in some ways the modern equivalent of old-time bank notes issued by commercial banks. The passing of a bank note from hand to hand transferred ownership of a claim against the bank. A check on a deposit account is similarly an order to the bank to pay the designated recipient, rather than oneself, money credited to the account. Checks, unlike bank notes, do not circulate freely from hand to hand; thus checks themselves are not currency. The balance in the demand deposit *is* money; the check transfers money from one person to another. Because checks are easily drawn and deposited, and because they are relatively safe from theft, they are widely used. In 1985 approximately 55 billion checks were drawn in the United States. During the last decade the number of checks drawn increased at about 7 percent per year.

Thus, when commercial banks lost the right to issue notes of their own, the form of bank money changed but the substance did not. Today banks have money in their vaults (or on deposit with the central banks) just as they always did. Once it was gold, today it is the legal tender of the times—fiat money. It is true today, just as in the past, that most of the bank's customers are content to pay their bills by passing among themselves the bank's promises to pay money on demand. Only a small proportion of the transactions made by the bank's customers is made in cash.

Bank deposits are money. Today, just as in the past, banks can create money by issuing more promises to pay (deposits) than they have cash reserves available to pay out.

The Banking System

Many types of institutions make up a modern banking system such as exists in the United States today. The **central bank** is the government owned and operated institution that serves to control the banking system. Through it, the government's monetary policy is conducted. In the United States the central bank is the Federal Reserve System, nicknamed the Fed; we study it in detail in Chapter 33. *Financial intermediaries* are privately owned institutions that serve the general public. They are called intermediaries because they stand between savers, from whom they accept deposits, and investors, to whom they

make loans. In this chapter we focus on an important class of financial intermediaries, the *commercial banks*.

Modern commercial banking systems are of two main types. One type has a small number of banks, each with a large number of branch offices; the other consists of many independent banks. The banking systems of Britain and Canada are of the first type, with only a few banks accounting for the overwhelming bulk of the business. The American system is of the second type. In 1985 there were approximately 15,000 independent banks, some (such as the Bank of America) with hundreds of branches and others with only a single office. Branch banking in the United States is governed by state law. Interstate branching is not allowed. In some states banks are permitted to branch statewide. At the other extreme are "unit-bank" states that permit no branching. Yet other states permit limited branching into areas near the home office. The functioning of the banking system is, however, essentially the same in all these systems.

The Commercial Banks

The basic unit of the American banking system is the ordinary **commercial bank,** which is a privately owned, profit-seeking institution. All commercial banks have common attributes: They hold deposits for their customers, permit certain deposits to be transferred by check from an individual account to other accounts held in any bank in the country, make loans to households and firms, and invest in government securities.

It is these common features, in particular the holding of demand deposits, that distinguish commercial banks from other financial institutions, each of which may perform some but not all of these functions. Many other institutions such as credit unions, savings and loan associations, and mutual savings banks accept time deposits and grant loans for specific purposes. Finance companies make loans to households for practically any purpose. The post office and Western Union transfer money; American Express issues traveler's checks. Credit card companies extend credit so that purchases can be made on a buy-now, pay-later basis.

Commercial banks differ from one another in

many ways. Some are large (the largest, Citicorp, had deposits of $105 billion in 1985) and others are small; some are located in big cities, others in small towns; some hold charters from the federal government (national banks), others from state governments (state banks). Nearly 40 percent of the commercial banks, including most of the larger ones, are members of the Federal Reserve System. All national banks must be members, and any state bank may join the system by agreeing to abide by its regulations. However, nonmember banks are indirectly tied into the system since they are invariably *correspondents* of larger member banks, that is they have regular commercial relations with the member banks. For example, the nonmember banks keep their reserves on deposit with member banks, depend on them for loans when they are pressed for cash, and rely on them for a variety of other services that the Federal Reserve System provides for its members. In practice, then, all commercial banks, members and nonmembers alike, have always come under the effective regulatory influence of the Fed.

Interbank Activities

Commercial banks have a number of interbank cooperative relationships. These are encouraged by special banking laws because they facilitate the smooth functioning of money and credit markets.

For example, banks often share loans. Even the biggest bank cannot meet all the credit needs of an industrial giant such as General Motors, and often a group of banks will offer a "pool loan," agreeing on common terms and dividing the loan up into manageable segments. On a different scale a small bank, when approached for a loan larger than it can safely handle, will often ask a larger bank to "participate" in the loan.

Another form of interbank cooperation is the bank credit card. VISA and MasterCard are the two most widely used credit cards, and each is operated by a large group of banks.

Probably the most important form of interbank cooperation is check clearing and collection. Bank deposits are an effective medium of exchange only because banks accept each other's checks. If a depositor in bank A writes a check to someone who deposits it in bank B, bank A owes money to bank B. This, of course, creates a need for the banks to present checks to each other for payment.

There are millions of such transactions in the course of a day, and they result in an enormous sorting and bookkeeping job. Multibank systems make use of a **clearing house** where interbank debts are settled. At the end of the day all the checks drawn by bank A's customers and deposited in bank B are totaled and set against the total of all the checks drawn by bank B's customers and deposited in bank A. It is necessary to settle only the difference between the two sums. The actual checks are passed through the clearinghouse back to the bank on which they were drawn. Both banks are then able to adjust the individual accounts by a set of book entries. A flow of cash between banks is necessary only when there is a net transfer of cash from the customers of one bank to those of another. For member banks in the United States, much of this clearing function is performed by the Federal Reserve System.

Profit Seeking

Banks are private firms that start with invested capital and seek to "earn money" in the same sense as do firms making neckties or bicycles. A commercial bank provides a variety of services to its customers: a safe place to store money; the convenience of demand deposits that can be transferred by personal check; a safe and convenient place to earn a modest but guaranteed return on savings; and often financial advice and estate management services. The bank earns some revenue by charging for these services, but such fees are a small part of the bank's total earnings. The largest part (typically about five-sixths) of a bank's earnings is derived from the bank's ability to invest profitably the funds placed with it.

Principal Assets and Liabilities

Table 31-1 is the combined balance sheet of the commercial banks in the United States. The bulk of a bank's liabilities are deposits owed to its depositors. The principal assets of a bank are the *securities* it buys (including government bonds), which pay interest or dividends, and the *loans* it makes to individuals and

TABLE 31-1   Consolidated Balance Sheet of U.S. Commercial Banks, January 31, 1986 *(billions of dollars)*

Assets		Liabilities	
Reserves (cash assets including deposits with Federal Reserve banks)	$ 188.1	Deposits	
		Demand	$ 488.2
		Savings	451.9
Loans	1,600.6	Time	789.4
U.S. government securities	427.2		
Other securities	178.3	Borrowings	359.7
Other assets	30.3	Other liabilities	177.9
		Capital accounts	156.9
	$2,424.5		$2,424.0

Source: Federal Reserve Bulletin, April 1986.

Reserves are only a small fraction of deposit liabilities. If all the banks' customers who held demand deposits tried to withdraw them in cash, the banks could not meet this demand without liquidating $300.1 billion of other assets. This would be impossible without assistance from the Fed.

to businesses. A bank loan is a liability to the borrower (who must pay it back), but an asset to the bank. The bank expects not only to have the loan repaid, but to receive interest that more than compensates for the paperwork involved and the risk of nonpayment.

Banks attract deposits by paying interest to depositors and by providing them, for a fee that does not cover the banks' full cost, with services such as clearing checks and regular monthly statements. Banks earn profits by lending and investing money deposited with them for more than they pay their depositors in terms of interest and other services provided.

Competition for Deposits

Competition for deposits is active among banks and between banks and other financial institutions. Savings and loan associations (S&Ls) and mutual savings banks are important competitors of commercial banks for time deposits. These nonbank savings institutions specialize primarily in mortgage lending secured by residential real estate; their rapid postwar growth has reflected the high and growing demand for home financing.

Interest paid on demand as well as savings deposits, money-market funds, high-interest certifi-

cates of deposit (CDs), advertising, personal solicitation of accounts, giveaway programs for new deposits to existing accounts, and improved services are all forms of competition for funds. Among the special services are payroll-accounting and pension-accounting schemes for industrial customers. The "lock box" is another kind of service: banks establish locked post office boxes to which retail customers of large companies send their payments. The bank opens the remittances, deposits them to the company's account, and forwards notices of payment to the company. All these services are costly to the bank, but they serve as inducements to customers in order to gain deposits.

Reserves

The Need for Reserves

All bankers would as a matter of convenience and prudence keep sufficient cash on hand to be able to meet depositors' day-to-day requirements for cash. But just as the goldsmiths of old discovered that only a fraction of the gold they held was ever withdrawn at any given time, and just as banks of old discovered that only a fraction of convertible bank notes was actually converted, so, too, have modern banks discovered that only a fraction of their deposits will be withdrawn in cash at any one time. Most deposits of any individual bank remain on deposit with it; thus an individual bank need keep only fractional reserves against its deposits.

The reserves needed to assure that depositors can withdraw their deposits on demand will be quite small in normal times.

In abnormal times, however, nothing short of 100 percent might do the job if the commercial banking system had to stand alone. When a few bank failures cause a general loss of confidence in banks' ability to redeem their deposits, the results can be devastating. Until relatively recent times, such an event—or even the rumor of it—could lead to a "run" on banks as depositors rushed to withdraw their money. Faced with such a panic, banks would have to close until they had borrowed funds or liquidated enough assets to meet the demand or until the demand subsided. But banks could not instantly turn their loans into cash since the borrowers had the money tied up in such things as real estate or business enterprises. Neither could the banks obtain cash by selling their securities to the public since payments would be made by checks, which would not provide cash with which to pay off depositors.

The difficulty of providing sufficient reserves to meet abnormal situations can be alleviated by the central bank. Most importantly, because it controls the supply of bank reserves, the central bank can provide all the reserves that are needed to meet any abnormal situation. It can do this in two ways. First, it can lend reserves directly to the commercial banks on the security of assets which are sound but not easy to liquidate quickly. Second, it can enter the open market and buy all the securities that the commercial banks need to sell. Once the public finds that deposits can be turned into cash, the panic will usually subside and any further drain of cash out of banks will cease.

The possibility of panic withdrawals is also greatly diminished by the provision of Federal Deposit Insurance, which guarantees that depositors will get their money back even if a bank fails completely. Most depositors will not withdraw their money as long as they are *sure* they can get it when they need it.

Actual and Required Reserves

Look again at Table 31-1 and observe that the banking system's cash reserves are just a fraction of its deposits. If the holders of even 40 percent of its demand deposits had demanded cash sometime in January 1985, the commercial banking system would have been unable (without outside help) to meet the demand.

The American banking system is a **fractional reserve system,** with banks holding reserves of much less than 100 percent of their deposits. The size of the reserves reflects not only the judgment of bankers, it also reflects the legal requirements imposed on the banks by the Fed.

A bank's **reserve ratio** is the fraction of its deposits that it holds as reserves either as cash or as deposits with the central bank. Those reserves that the Federal Reserve System requires the bank to hold are called **required reserves.** Any reserves held over and above required reserves are called **excess reserves.** Reserves are required by the Fed both to assure the stability of the banking system and as part of its policy arsenal in attempting to control the money supply, as we shall discuss at the end of this chapter.

Money Creation by Banks

The fractional reserve system provides the leverage that permits commercial banks and other financial institutions to create new money. The process is important, so it is worth examining in some detail.

Some Simplifying Assumptions

To focus on the essential aspects of how banks create money, assume that banks can invest in only one kind of asset, loans, and that there is only one kind of deposit, a demand deposit.

Three other assumptions listed below are provisional. When we have developed the basic ideas concerning the bank's creation of money, these assumptions will be relaxed.

1. *Fixed required reserve ratio.* It is assumed that all banks have the same required reserve ratio, which does not change. In our numerical illustration we shall assume that the required reserve ratio is 20 percent (i.e., 0.20), that is, at least $1 of reserves for every $5 of deposits.
2. *No excess reserves.* It is assumed that all banks want to invest any reserves they have in excess of the legally required amount. This implies that they always believe there are safe investments to be made when they have excess reserves.
3. *No cash drain from the banking system.* It is assumed that the public holds a fixed amount of currency in circulation. Thus changes in the money supply will take the form of changes in deposit money.

The Creation of Deposit Money

A typical bank's balance sheet is shown in Table 31-2. The Immigrants Bank and Trust Company (IB&T Co.) has assets of $200 of reserves (all figures are in thousands of dollars), held partly as cash on hand and partly as deposits with the central bank, and $900 of loans outstanding to its customers. Its liabilities are $100 to those who initially contributed capital to start the bank, and $1,000 to current depositors. The bank's ratio of reserves to deposits is 200/1,000 = 0.20, exactly equal to its minimum requirement.

An immigrant arrives in the country and opens an account by depositing $100 with the IB&T Co. This is a wholly new deposit for the bank, and it results in a revised balance sheet (Table 31-3). As a result of the immigrant's new deposit, both cash assets and deposit liabilities have risen by $100. More

TABLE 31-2 The Initial Balance Sheet of the Immigrants Bank and Trust Company *(thousands of dollars)*

Assets		Liabilities	
Cash and other reserves	$ 200	Deposits	$1,000
Loans	900	Capital	100
	$1,100		$1,100

The IB&T Co. has a reserve of 20 percent of its deposit liabilities. The commercial bank earns money by finding profitable investments for much of the money deposited with it. In this balance sheet loans are its earning assets.

TABLE 31-3 The Balance Sheet of IB&T Co. After an Immigrant Deposits $100 *(thousands of dollars)*

Assets		Liabilities	
Cash and other reserves	$ 300	Deposits	$1,100
Loans	900	Capital	100
	$1,200		$1,200

The immigrant's deposit raises deposit liabilities and cash assets by the same amount. Since both cash and deposits rise by $100, the cash reserve ratio, formerly 0.20, increases to 0.27. The bank has more cash than it needs to provide a 20 percent reserve against its deposit liabilities.

important, the reserve ratio has increased from 0.20 to 0.27 (300/1,100). The bank now has excess reserves; with $300 in reserves it could support $1,500 in deposits.

A Single Monopoly Bank

If the IB&T Co. were the only bank in the system, it would know that any loans that it made would eventually give rise to new deposits of an equal amount. It would then be in a position to say to the next business executive who comes in for a loan, "We will lend your firm $400 at the going rate of interest." The bank would do so by adding that amount to the firm's deposit account. Table 31-4 shows what would happen in this case. The new immigrant's deposit initially raised cash assets and deposit liabilities by $100. The new loans created an additional $400 of deposit liabilities. This restored

TABLE 31-4 The Monopoly Bank's Balance Sheet After Making a $400 Loan *(thousands of dollars)*

Assets		Liabilities	
Cash and other reserves	$ 300	Deposits	$1,500
Loans	1,300	Capital	100
	$1,600		$1,600

The loan restores the reserve ratio of 0.20. By increasing its loans by a multiple of its new cash deposit, the bank restores its reserve ratio of 0.20.

the reserve ratio to its legal minimum (300/1,500 = 0.20), and no further expansion of deposit money is possible. As the bank's customers do business with each other, settling their accounts by checks, the ownership of the deposits will be continually changing. But what matters to the bank is that its total deposits will remain constant.

The extent to which a monopoly bank could increase its loans *and thus its deposits* depends on the reserve ratio. Because in this case the ratio is 1/5 (= 0.20), the bank would be able to expand deposits to five times the original acquisition of money. In general, if the reserve ratio is *r*, a monopoly bank can increase its deposits by 1/*r* times any new reserves. As we shall see, this relation holds for *any* banking system, not just for one with a single bank. **[40]**

Many Banks

Deposit creation is more complicated in a multi-bank system than in a single-bank system, but *the end result is exactly the same.* It is more complicated because, when a bank makes a loan, the recipient of the loan may pay the money to someone who deposits it in another bank.

To follow the sequence by which a multi-bank system creates deposits, we first return to Tables 31-2 and 31-3. The IB &T Co. is shown in equilibrium in Table 31-2. Then after it has received a new cash deposit as shown in Table 31-3, it is no longer in equilibrium. Whereas the monopoly bank could immediately create $400 of new deposits, one of many banks in a multi-bank system cannot do this because many of the new deposits that it creates will end up in other banks, causing a cash drain to these other banks. What now happens is most easily seen under an extreme assumption. We assume that every new borrower immediately uses the borrowed funds to pay people who deal with a different bank.

With its present level of deposits at $1,100, the bank needs only $220 of reserves (0.20 × $1,100 = $220), so it can lend the $80 excess that it has on hand. Table 31-5 shows the position after this has been done and after the proceeds of the loan have been withdrawn to be deposited to the account of a customer of another bank. The IB&T Co. once again has a 20 percent reserve ratio.

TABLE 31-5   The IB&T Co. Balance Sheet After a New Loan and Cash Drain of $80 *(thousands of dollars)*

Assets		Liabilities	
Cash and other reserves	$ 220	Deposits	$1,100
Loans	980	Capital	100
	$1,200		$1,200

The bank lends its surplus cash and suffers a cash drain. The bank keeps $20 as a reserve against the immigrant's new deposit of $100. It lends $80 to a customer who writes a check to someone who deals with another bank. When the check is cleared, the IB&T Co. suffers an $80 cash drain. Comparing Tables 31-2 and 31-5 shows that the bank has increased its deposit liabilities by the $100 deposited by the new immigrant and increased its assets by $20 of cash reserves and $80 of new loans. It has also restored its reserve ratio of 0.20.

So far deposits in the IB&T Co. have increased by only the initial $100 of new immigrant's money with which we started, as shown in Table 31-3. (Of this, $20 is held as a cash reserve against the deposit and $80 has been lent out in the system.) But other banks have received new deposits of $80 as the persons receiving payment from those who borrowed the $80 from the IB&T Co. deposited those payments in their own banks. The receiving banks are sometimes called *next-generation banks* or, more specifically according to the situation, *second-generation,*

TABLE 31-6   Changes in the Balance Sheets of Second-Generation Banks *(thousands of dollars)*

Assets		Liabilities	
Cash and other reserves	+$16	Deposits	+$80
Loans	+ 64		
	+$80		+$80

Second-generation banks receive cash deposits and expand loans. The second-generation banks gain new deposits of $80 as a result of the loan granted by the IB&T Co., which is used to make payments to customers of the second-generation banks. These banks keep 20 percent of the cash they acquire as their reserve against the new deposit, and they can make new loans using the other 80 percent. When the customers who borrowed the money make payments to the customers of third-generation banks, a cash drain occurs.

third-generation, and so on. In this case the second-generation banks receive new deposits of $80, and when the checks clear, they have new reserves of $80. Because they require an addition to their reserves of only $16 to support the new deposit, they have $64 of excess reserves. They now increase their loans by $64. After this money is spent by the borrowers and has been deposited in other, third-generation banks, the balance sheets of the second-generation banks will have changed, as in Table 31-6.

The third-generation banks now find themselves with $64 of new deposits. Against these they need hold only $12.80 in cash, so they have excess reserves of $51.20 that they can immediately lend out. Thus there begins a long sequence of new deposits, new loans, new deposits, and new loans. The stages are shown in Table 31-7. The series in the table should look familiar, for it is the same convergent process we met when dealing with the multiplier in Chapter 28.

The banking system has created new deposits and thus new money, although each banker can honestly say, "All I did was invest my excess reserves. I can do no more than manage wisely the money I receive."

If r is the reserve ratio, the ultimate effect on the deposits of the banking system of a new deposit will be $1/r$ times the new deposit. [41] This is exactly the same result reached in the monopoly bank case.[1]

Many Deposits

The two cases discussed above, the monopoly bank and a single new deposit in a many-bank situation, show that under either set of opposite extreme assumptions, the result is the same. So it is, too, in

[1] The "multiple expansion of deposits" that has just been worked through applies in reverse to a withdrawal of funds. Deposits of the banking system will fall by $1/r$ times any amount withdrawn from the bank and not redeposited at another.

TABLE 31-7 Many Banks, a Single New Deposit (*thousands of dollars*)

Bank	New deposits	New loans	Addition to reserves
IB&T Co.	$100.00	$ 80.00	$ 20.00
Second-generation bank	80.00	64.00	16.00
Third-generation bank	64.00	51.20	12.80
Fourth-generation bank	51.20	40.96	10.24
Fifth-generation bank	40.96	32.77	8.19
Sixth-generation bank	32.77	26.22	6.55
Seventh-generation bank	26.22	20.98	5.24
Eighth-generation bank	20.98	16.78	4.20
Ninth-generation bank	16.78	13.42	3.36
Tenth-generation bank	13.42	10.74	2.68
Total first 10 generations	446.33	357.07	89.26
All remaining generations	53.67	42.93	10.74
Total for banking systems	$500.00	$400.00	$100.00

The banking system as a whole can create deposit money whenever it receives new reserves. The table shows the process of the creation of deposit money on the assumptions that all the loans made by one set of banks end up as deposits in another set of banks (the next-generation banks), that the required reserve ratio (r) is 0.20, and that there are no excess reserves. Although each bank suffers a cash drain whenever it grants a new loan, the system as a whole does not, and the system ends up doing in a series of steps what a monopoly bank would do all at once; that is, it increases deposit money by $1/r$, which in this example is five times the amount of any increase in reserves that it obtains.

intermediate situations. A far more realistic picture of deposit creation is one in which new deposits accrue simultaneously to all banks, perhaps because of changes in the monetary policy of the government.

Say, for example, that the community contains 10 banks of equal size and that each received new deposits of $100 in cash. Now each bank is in the position shown in Table 31-3, and each can begin to expand deposits based on the $100 of excess reserves. (Each bank does this by granting loans to customers.)

Because each bank does one-tenth of the total banking business, an average of 90 percent of any newly created deposit will find its way into other banks as the customer pays other people in the community by check. This will represent a cash drain from the lending bank to the other banks. However, 10 percent of each new deposit created by every other bank should find its way into this bank. All banks receive new cash and all begin creating deposits simultaneously; no bank should suffer a significant cash drain to any other bank.

Thus all banks can go on expanding deposits without losing cash to each other; they need only worry about keeping enough cash to satisfy those depositors who will occasionally withdraw cash. The expansion can go on with each bank watching its own ratio of cash reserves to deposits, expanding deposits as long as the ratio exceeds 1/5 and ceasing when it reaches that figure. The process will come to a halt when each bank has created $400 in additional deposits, so that for each initial $100 cash deposit, there is now $500 in deposits backed by $100 in cash. Now *each* of the banks will have entries in its books similar to those shown in Table 31-4.

The general rule, if there is no cash drain, is that a banking system with a reserve ratio of r can change its deposits by 1/r times any change in reserves.

Excess Reserves and Cash Drains

Two of the simplifying assumptions made earlier can now be relaxed.

Excess reserves.   If banks do not choose to invest excess reserves, the multiple expansion discussed will

not occur. Turn back to Table 31-3. If the IB&T Co. had been content to hold 27 percent reserves, it might well have done nothing more. Other things being equal, banks will choose to invest excess reserves because of the profit motive. But there may be times when they believe the risk is too great. It is one thing to be offered a good rate of interest on a loan, but if the borrower defaults on the payment of interest and principal, the bank will be the loser. Similarly, if the bank expects interest rates to rise in the future, it may hold off making loans now so that it will have reserves available to make more profitable loans after the interest rate has risen.

There is nothing automatic about deposit creation; it rests on the decisions of bankers. If banks do not choose to use excess reserves to expand their investments, there will not be an expansion of deposits.

The money supply is thus at least partially determined by the commercial banks in response to such forces as changes in national income and interest rates. However, the upper limit of deposits is determined by the required reserve ratio and by the reserves available to the banks, both of which are under the influence of the central bank.

Cash drain.   Suppose firms and households find it convenient to keep a fixed *fraction* of their money holding in cash (say, 5 percent) instead of a fixed *amount* of dollars. In that case an extra $100 in money supply will not all stay in the banking system; only $95 will remain on deposit, while the rest will be added to money in circulation. In such a situation any multiple expansion of bank deposits will be accompanied by a cash drain to the public that will reduce the maximum expansion below what it was when the public was content to hold all its new money as bank deposits. Table 31-8 shows the position of a typical bank after a credit expansion of $400 and a cash drain of $20.

The story of deposit creation when all banks receive new deposits and there is a cash drain to the public goes like this. Each bank starts creating deposits and suffers no significant cash drain to other banks. But because approximately 5 percent of newly created deposits is withdrawn to be held as cash,

TABLE 31-8   The Monopoly Bank's Balance Sheet After a Credit Expansion and an Accompanying Cash Drain (*thousands of dollars*)

Assets		Liabilities	
Cash and reserves	$ 280	Deposits	$1,480
Loans	1,300	Capital	100
	$1,580		$1,580

The limit to the amount of deposit expansion is reduced by a cash drain. This example differs from that shown in Table 31-4 because, after a new deposit of $100 and a new loan of $400, 5 percent of the newly created money is withdrawn as cash to be held by the public. Cash and deposits each fall by $20 and the reserve ratio falls below 20 percent.

each bank suffers a cash drain to the public. The expansion continues, each bank watching its own ratio of cash reserves to deposits, expanding deposits as long as the ratio exceeds 1/5 and ceasing when it reaches that figure. Because the expansion is accompanied by a cash drain, it will come to a halt with a smaller deposit expansion than in the no cash drain case.[2]

The Money Supply

The total stock of money in the economy at any moment is called the **money supply** or the **supply of money.** Economists and financial analysts use several different definitions for the money supply, most of which are regularly reported in the *Federal Reserve Bulletin.* Typically, the definitions involve the sum of currency in circulation plus some types of deposit liabilities of financial institutions. Definitions vary in terms of what deposits are included. Different definitions come into or go out of favor as the importance of different types of deposits changes.

Kinds of Deposits

Most of the deposits held by the average person are either demand deposits or time deposits.

[2] It can be shown algebraically that the percentage of cash drain must be added to the reserve ratio to determine the maximum possible expansion of deposits. [42]

Demand Deposits

A **demand deposit** means that the customer can withdraw the money on demand (i.e., without giving any notice of intention to withdraw). Demand deposits are transferable by check. Such a check instructs the bank to pay without a delay a stated sum of money to the person to whom the check is made payable. Although banks now pay interest on demand deposits, they were legally prohibited from doing so until the mid 1980s.

Time Deposits

A **time deposit** is an interest-bearing deposit that is legally withdrawable only after a certain amount of notice, such as 30 days for a passbook account and up to six months on certificates of deposit. The amount of time until the deposit can be withdrawn is often called the *term* of the deposit. Until quite recently it was impossible to pay a bill by writing a check on a time deposit. A depositor wishing to use a time deposit to pay a bill had two options. Having withdrawn her money from a savings (time) account, she could then either pay the bill in cash or deposit the funds in a demand account and then write a check on the demand account. Time deposits are also often loosely referred to as saving deposits.

The Disappearing Distinction

For decades interest rates on time deposits amounted to only a few percent, and people were content to keep their savings in time deposits and their reserves of cash for ordinary transactions in demand deposits. Then, interest rates available on time deposits and other safe liquid investments grew, and it became more and more expensive (in terms of lost interest) to keep cash in demand deposits, even for a week or two. Starting in the early 1970s, several devices were invented that tended to make it easier to convert interest-bearing deposits into demand deposits transferable by check.

One of the first was the **negotiable order of withdrawal (NOW),** a checklike instruction to the savings institution to transfer funds from the depositor's time deposit to the recipient of the **NOW.**

A similar device is the **automatic transfer ser-**

vice (ATS), which allows depositors to maintain both a demand and a time deposit at the bank and to make all deposits to the time deposit. The bank automatically transfers funds to the demand deposit as needed to cover checks when they are written. This permits the customer to maintain only a small minimum amount (for example, $200) in the demand deposit account. All the rest earns interest. The ATS comes close to being both a demand deposit that pays interest and a time deposit that can be transferred by check.

Nonbank financial institutions such as brokerage firms now offer **money market mutual funds (MMMFs)** and **money market deposit accounts (MMDAs)**. These accounts earn high interest and are checkable, although some are subject to minimum withdrawal restrictions and others to prior notice of withdrawal.

Finally, the Monetary Control Act of 1980 phased out ceilings that had been imposed for decades on the interest that was allowed to be paid on various types of deposit accounts. The long-time distinction between money and other highly liquid assets used to be that, narrowly defined, money was a medium of exchange that did not earn interest, while other liquid assets earned interest but were not media of exchange (although they were easily convertible into such). Today this distinction is much less clear than it once was.

Only notes and coins are certain to bear no interest. Although non-checkable deposits and some other liquid assets are not themselves media of exchange, they are so easily (sometimes automatically) converted into a medium of exchange that the distinction between what is and is not legally a medium of exchange is of diminishing significance.

Definitions of the Money Supply

Different definitions of the money supply include different types of deposits. The narrowly defined money supply, called **M1**, includes currency and those deposits that are themselves usable as media of exhange. Broader definitions include other deposits as well.

Prior to 1980, when the distinction between demand and time deposits was quite clear, narrow money was defined simply as the sum of currency plus demand deposits. The growth in ATS, NOW, and money market accounts has led to an expanded definition of M1 to include NOW, ATS, and similar accounts at credit unions and mutual savings banks as well as the traditional currency and demand deposits.

Broader definitions include M2 and M3. **M2** is M1 plus savings and smaller time deposits of all kinds, including money market accounts and overnight loans. **M3** is M2 with the addition of several components, the most important of which are large denomination **certificates of deposit (CD).** CDs are savings deposits, the evidence for which is a slip of paper, or certificate, rather than an entry in the saver's passbook. The most important is the large denomination, negotiable CD, which is designed to attract funds from large businesses. These pay a higher rate of interest than ordinary time deposits.

M1 concentrates on the medium-of-exchange function of money. The others add in highly liquid assets that serve the temporary store-of-value function and are in practice quickly convertible into a medium of exchange at a known price ($1 on deposit in a savings account is always convertible into a $1 demand deposit or $1 in cash). Table 31-9 shows the principal elements in the money supply.

Near Money and Money Substitutes

Over the past two centuries what has been accepted by the public as money has expanded from gold and silver coins to include first bank notes and then bank deposits subject to transfer by check. Until recently, most economists would have agreed that money stopped at that point. No such agreement exists today, and an important debate centers on the definition of money appropriate to present circumstances.

If we concentrate only on the medium-of-exchange function of money, there is little doubt about what is money in America today. Money consists of notes, coins, and deposits subject to transfer by check or checklike instruments. These are the assets included in M1 as it is currently measured. No other asset constitutes a generally accepted medium of exchange; indeed, even notes and checks are not universally accepted—as you will discover if you try to

TABLE 31-9   Money Supply in the United States, 1985 (*billions of dollars*) (*annual averages of daily figures*)

Currency	171	
Demand deposits	271	
Travelers' checks	6	
Other checkable deposits	177	
M1		625
Overnight repurchase agreements and Eurodollars	73	
Money market mutual balances	176	
Money market deposit accounts	509	
Savings accounts	305	
Small denomination time deposits	878	
M2		2566
Large denomination time deposits	441	
Term repurchase agreements	76	
Term Eurodollars	77	
Institutional money market mutual funds	65	
M3		3225

Source: Economic Report of the President, 1986.

The three widely used measures of the money supply are M1, M2, and M3. The narrow definition of the money supply concentrates on what can be used directly as a medium of exchange. The broader definitions add in deposits that serve the store-of-value function and can be readily, sometimes automatically, converted to a medium of exchange on a dollar-for-dollar basis.

Note that M1 includes traveler's checks held by the public, which clearly are a medium of exchange. Within M2, RPs are funds lent out on the overnight money market, and Eurodollars are U.S. dollar-denominated deposits in American banks located outside of the United States. M2 and M3 include similar items, with the difference in most cases being that the term deposits are in M3 and the demand deposits in M2.

buy a pack of cigarettes with a $1,000 bill (or even a $100 bill in a corner grocery store). But such exceptions are unimportant.

The problem of deciding what is money arises because some media of exchange—currency that carries no interest yield and demand deposits, whose interest yield tends to be quite low—may provide relatively poor ways to meet the store-of-value function (see Table 31-10). Assets that earn a higher interest return will do a better job of meeting this function of money than will currency or demand deposits. At the same time, however, these other

TABLE 31-10   The Dollar As a Store of Value Since 1960

$1 put aside in	Had the purchasing power 5 years later of	Its average annual loss of value was
1960	$.93	1.8%
1965	.81	5.1%
1970	.72	7.9%
1975	.65	10.2%
1980	.76	6.6%

The dollar has become an increasingly less satisfactory store of value over the last two decades. The second column shows the purchasing power, measured using the Consumer Price Index, of $1 five years after it was saved (assuming it earned no interest). In order for it to have maintained its real purchasing power, it would have had to earn the annual percentage return shown in the last column. (The figures in that column assume annual compounding.)

assets are less capable of filling the medium-of-exchange function.

Near Money

Assets that fulfill adequately the store-of-value function and are readily converted into a medium of exchange but are not themselves a medium of exchange are sometimes called **near money.** Deposits at a savings and loan association are a characteristic form of near money. When you have such a deposit, you know exactly how much purchasing power you hold (at current prices) and, given modern banking practices, you can turn your deposit into a medium of exchange—cash or a checking deposit—at a moment's notice. Additionally, your deposit will earn some interest during the period that you hold it.

Why then does not everybody keep their money in such deposits instead of in demand deposits or currency? The answer is that the inconvenience of continually shifting money back and forth may outweigh the interest that can be earned. One week's interest on $100 (at 5 percent per year) is only about $.10, not enough to cover carfare to the bank or the cost of mailing a letter. For money that will be needed soon, it would hardly pay to shift it to a time deposit.

In general, whether it pays to convert cash or demand deposits into interest-earning savings deposits for a given period will depend on the inconvenience and other transaction costs of shifting funds and on the amount of interest that can be earned.

There is a wide spectrum of assets in the economy that pay interest and also serve as reasonably satisfactory temporary stores of value. The difference between these assets and savings deposits is that their capital values are not quite as certain as are those of savings deposits. If I elect to store my purchasing power in the form of a treasury bill that matures in 30 days, its price on the market may change between the time I buy it and the time I want to sell it, say, 10 days later. If the price changes, the purchasing power available to me changes. But because of the short horizon to maturity, the price will not change very much. (After all, the government will pay the bond's face value in a few weeks.) Such a security is thus a reasonably satisfactory short-run store of purchasing power. Indeed, any readily salable capital asset whose value does not fluctuate significantly with the rate of interest will satisfactorily fulfill this short-term store-of-value function.

Money Substitutes

Things that serve as a temporary medium of exchange but are not a store of value are sometimes called **money substitutes.** Credit cards are a prime example. With a credit card, many transactions can be made without either cash or a check. The evidence of credit, the credit slip you sign and hand over to the store, is not money because it cannot be used to make further transactions. Furthermore, when your credit card company takes advantage of an arrangement to have your bank pay each bill as it is presented or when it sends you a bill, you have to use money to pay for the original transaction. The credit card serves the short-run function of a medium of exchange by allowing you to make purchases even though you have no cash or bank deposit currently in your possession. But this is only temporary; money remains the final medium of exchange for these transactions when the credit account is settled.

Conclusion

Since the eighteenth century, economists have known that the amount of money in circulation is an important economic variable. As theories became more carefully specified in the nineteenth and early twentieth centuries, they included a variable called "the money supply." But for theories to be useful, we must be able to identify real-world counterparts of these theoretical magnitudes.

What is an acceptable enough medium of exchange to count as money has changed and will continue to change over time. NOW, ATS, MMMF, and MMDA accounts have broadened the spectrum. New monetary assets are continually being developed to serve some, if not all, the functions of money, and they are more or less readily convertible into money. There is no single, timeless definition of what is money and what is only near money or a money substitute. Indeed, as we have seen, our monetary authorities use several different definitions of money, and these definitions change from year to year.

Summary

1. Early economic theorists regarded the economy as being divided into a real part and a money part. The real sector is concerned with production, allocation of resources, and distribution of income— determined by relative prices. The level of prices at which all transactions take place is determined by the monetary sector, that is, by the demand for and supply of money. With the demand for money constant, an increase in the money supply would cause all equilibrium money prices to increase but relative prices, and hence everything in the real sector, would be left unaffected.

2. Traditionally in economics, money has referred to any generally accepted medium of exchange. A number of functions of money

may, however, be distinguished. The major ones are to act as a medium of exchange, a store of value, and a unit of account.

3. Money arose because of the inconvenience of barter, and it developed in stages from precious metal, to metal coinage, to paper money convertible to precious metal, to token coinage and paper money fractionally backed by precious metals, to fiat money, and to deposit money. Societies have shown great sophistication in developing monetary instruments to meet their needs.

4. The banking system in the United States consists of two main elements: commercial banks and the Federal Reserve System, which is the central bank. Each has an important effect on the money supply.

5. American commercial banks are profit-seeking institutions that allow their customers to transfer demand deposits from one bank to another by means of checks. They create and destroy money as a by-product of their commercial operations—by making or liquidating loans and various other investments.

6. Because most customers are content to pay their accounts by check rather than by cash, banks need only small reserves to back their deposit liabilities. Consequently, banks are able to create deposit money. When the banking system receives a new cash deposit, it can create new deposits to some multiple of this amount. The amount of new deposits created depends on the legal minimum reserves the Federal Reserve enforces on the banks, the amount of cash drain to the public, and whether the banks choose to hold excess reserves.

7. The money supply—the stock of money in an economy at a specific moment—can be defined in various ways. M1, the narrowest definition, includes currency, traveler's checks, and demand and other checkable deposits. M3, the widest definition, includes a number of assets, such as money market funds and overnight loans, that are readily convertible into M1 on a dollar-for-dollar basis, with or without notice.

8. Near money includes interest earning assets that are convertible into money on a dollar-for-dollar basis, but which are not currently included in the definition of money. Money substitutes are things such as credit cards that temporarily serve as a medium of exhange, but are not money.

Topics for Review

Real and monetary sectors of the economy
Functions of money
Gresham's law
Fully backed, fractionally backed, and fiat money
Creation and destruction of deposit money
Reserve ratio, required reserves, and excess reserves
Demand and time deposits
The money supply
Near money and money substitutes

Discussion Questions

1. "For the love of money is the root of all evil" (I Timothy 6:10). If a nation were to become a theocracy in which money was illegal, would you expect the level of national income to be affected? How about the productivity of labor?

2. Consider each of the following with respect to its potential use as a medium of exchange, a store of value, and a unit of account. Which would you think might be regarded as money?
   a. A $100 Federal Reserve note
   b. An American Express credit card
   c. A painting by Picasso
   d. A NOW account
   e. A U.S. Treasury bill payable in three months
   f. A savings account at a savings and loan association in Las Vegas, Nevada
   g. One share of General Motors stock
   h. A lifetime pass to Pittsburgh Steelers football games

3. When the Austrian government minted a new 1,000 shilling gold coin—worth $59 face value—the 1-inch diameter coin came into great demand among jewelers and coin collectors. By law, the number of such coins to be minted each year is limited. Lines of people eager to get the coins formed outside the government mint and local banks.
   "There is exceptional interest in the new coin," said a Viennese banker. "It's a numismatic hit and a financial success." It has disappeared from circulation, however. Explain why.

4. A Canadian who receives a U.S. coin has the option of spending it at face value or taking it to the bank and converting it to Canadian money at the going rate of exchange. When the rate of exchange was near par, so that $1 Canadian was within plus or minus $.03 of $1 U.S., American and Canadian coins circulated side by side, exchanging at their face values. Use Gresham's law to predict which coinage disappeared from circulation in Canada when the Canadian dollar fell to $.75 U.S. Why did a $.03 differential not produce this result?

5. Some years ago a strike closed all banks in Ireland for several months. What do you think happened during the period?

6. During hyperinflations in several foreign countries after World War II, American cigarettes were sometimes used in place of money. What made them suitable?

7. Assume that on January 1, 1986, a couple had $25,000 which they wished to hold for use one year later. Calculate, using library sources, which of the following would have been the best store of value over that period. Will the best store of value over that period necessarily be the best over the next 24 months?
   a. The dollar
   b. Stocks whose prices moved with the Dow Jones industrial average
   c. A Georgia Power 11¾ percent 2005 bond
   d. Gold
   e. Silver

8. If all depositors tried to turn their deposits into cash at once, they would find that there are not sufficient reserves in the system to allow all of them to do this at the same time. Why then do we not

still have panicky runs on the banks? Would a 100 percent reserve requirement be safer? What effect would such a reserve requirement have on the banking system's ability to create money? Would it preclude any possibility of a panic?

9. What would be the effect on the money supply of each of the following?
    a. Declining public confidence in the banks
    b. A desire on the part of banks to increase their levels of excess reserves
    c. Monopolizing of the banking system into a single super bank
    d. Increased use of credit cards
    e. Transfer of deposits from banks to new non-bank institutions

32

The Role of Money in Macroeconomics

At one time or another most of us have known the surprise of opening our wallet to discover that we had either more or less money than we thought. There can be pleasure in deciding how to spend an unexpected windfall in the first case just as there can be pain in deciding what expenditure to eliminate in the second.

What determines how much money people hold in their wallets and how much they keep in the bank? What happens when people discover that they are holding more, or less, money than they believe they need to hold? These turn out to be key questions for our study of the influence of money on output and prices.

Financial Assets

At any one moment households have a given stock of wealth. This wealth is held in many forms. Some of it is money in the bank or in the wallet; some is in short-term securities such as CDs or treasury bills; some is in long-term bonds; and some is in real capital, which may be held directly (in the form of family businesses) or indirectly (in the form of shares of stock that indicate ownership of a corporation's assets).

Kinds of Assets

These ways of holding wealth may be grouped into three main categories: (1) assets that serve as a medium of exchange, that is, paper money, coins, and bank deposits on which checks may be drawn, (2) financial assets, such as bonds earning a fixed rate of interest, that will yield a fixed money value at some future date (called the *maturity date*) and that can usually be sold before maturity for a price that fluctuates on the open market, and (3) claims on real capital (physical objects such as factories and machines).

To simplify our discussion, we will regroup wealth into just two categories: money and bonds. By money we mean M1 as defined in Chapter 31, and by bonds we mean all other forms of wealth. Money therefore includes currency and demand deposits and NOW, ATS, and similar accounts. Bonds include all other interest-earning financial assets *plus* claims in real capital.[1]

The Rate of Interest and the Price of Bonds

A bond is a promise by the issuer to pay a stated sum of money as interest each year and to repay the face value of the bond at some future maturity date, often many years distant. The time until the date is called the **term to maturity** or often simply the **term** of the bond. Some bonds, called perpetuities, pay interest forever and never repay the principal.

The **present value (*PV*)** of a bond, or of any asset, refers to the value now of the future payment, or payments, to which the asset represents a claim. The present value is thus the amount someone would be willing to pay now to secure the right to the future stream of payments conferred by ownership of the asset. This amount depends critically on the rate of interest as is most easily seen in the case of a perpetuity. Assume that such a bond will pay $100 per year to its holder. The *present value* of this bond depends on how much $100 per year is worth, and this in turn depends on the rate of interest.

A bond that will produce a stream of income of $100 a year forever is worth $1,000 at 10 percent interest because $1,000 invested at 10 percent per year will yield $100 interest per year forever. But the same bond is worth $2,000 when the interest rate is 5 percent per year because it takes $2,000 invested at 5 percent per year to yield $100 interest per year. The lower the rate of interest obtainable on the market, the more valuable is a bond paying a fixed amount of interest.

Similar relations apply to bonds that are not perpetuities, though the calculation of present value must allow for the lump-sum repayment of principal at maturity.

The present value of any asset that yields a stream of money over time is negatively related to the interest rate.

This proposition has two important implications: (1) if the rate of interest falls, the value of an asset producing a given income stream will rise; and (2) a rise in the market price of an asset producing a given income is equivalent to a decrease in the rate of interest earned by the asset. Thus a promise to pay $100 one year from now is worth $92.59 when the interest rate is 8 percent and only $89.29 when the interest rate is 12 percent: $92.59 at 8 percent interest ($92.59 × 1.08) and $89.29 at 12 percent interest ($89.29 × 1.12) are both worth $100 in one year's time.

The present value of bonds that are not perpetuities becomes increasingly dominated by the fixed redemption value as the maturity date approaches. Take an extreme case. The present value of a bond that is redeemable for $1,000 in a week's time will be very close to $1,000 no matter what the interest rate. Thus its value will not change much even if the rate of interest leaps from 5 percent to 10 percent during that week.

The sooner the maturity date of a bond, the less the bond's value will change with a change in the rate of interest.

For example, a rise in the interest rate from 8 to 12 percent will lower the value of $100 payable in 1 year's time by 3.6 percent, but it will lower the value of $100 payable in 10 years time by 37.9 percent.[2] (Although some assets that we included in our definition of money do earn interest, they are so short-term that their values remain unchanged when the interest rate changes.)

The above discussion should make it clear that the present value of an asset determines its market price. If the market price of any asset is greater than the present value of the income stream it produces,

---

[1] This simplification can take us quite a long way. However, for some problems it is necessary to treat debt and equity as distinct assets so that three categories—money, debt (bonds), and equity stocks—are used.

[2] The example assumes annual compounding. The first case is calculated from the numbers of the previous example: (92.58 − 89.29)/92.58. The 10-year case uses the formula

$$\text{present value} = \text{principal}/(1 + r)^n$$

which gives $46.30 with 8 percent and $28.75 with 12 percent. The percentage fall in value is thus (46.30 − 28.75)/46.30 = 0.379. Further details on the calculation of present value and on the relationship between the present value of an asset and its price, are given in Chapter 19, pages 350–351.

no one will want to buy it, while if the market value is below its present value, there will be a rush to buy it. From this it follows that:

In a free market the equilibrium price of any asset will be the present value of the income stream it produces.

The Supply of and the Demand for Money

The Supply of Money

The supply of money is a stock. (It is so many billions of dollars, *not* a flow of so much per unit of time.) In January 1986 M1 was approximately $625 billion.

We saw in the previous chapter that deposit money is created by the commercial banking system, but only within limits set by their reserves. Since, as we shall see in Chapter 33, the reserves of the commercial banking system are under the control of the Federal Reserve Board, the ultimate control of the money supply is also in the Fed's hands. In this chapter we shall simply assume that the money supply can be precisely controlled by the Fed.

The Demand for Money

The amount of wealth everyone in the economy wishes to hold in the form of money balances is called the **demand for money.** Because households have only one decision to make on how to divide their given stock of wealth between money and bonds, it follows that if we know the demand for money, we also know the demand for bonds. With *a given level of wealth* a rise in the demand for money necessarily implies a fall in the demand for bonds; if people wish to hold $1 billion more money, they must wish to hold $1 billion less of bonds. It also follows that if households are in equilibrium with respect to their money holdings, they are in equilibrium with respect to their bond holdings.

When we say that on January 2, 1986, the demand for money was $630 billion, we mean that on that date the public wished to hold money balances that

totaled $630 billion. But why do firms and households wish to hold money balances at all? There is a cost to holding any money balance. The money could instead be used to purchase bonds; it would then earn more interest.

The opportunity cost of holding any money balance is the extra interest that could have been earned if the money had instead been used to purchase interest earning assets.

Clearly, money will be held only when it provides services that are valued at least as highly as the opportunity cost of holding it. The services provided by money balances are, first, to finance purchases and sales; second, to provide a cushion against uncertainty about the timing of cash flows; and third, to provide a hedge against uncertainty over the prices of other financial assets.

The desire to hold money to obtain each of these services is summarized by the transactions, precautionary, and speculative motives for holding money. We now examine each of these motives in detail.

The Transactions Motive

Most transactions require money. Money passes from households to firms to pay for the goods and services produced by firms; money passes from firms to households to pay for the factor services supplied by households to firms. Money balances that are held to finance such flows are called **transactions balances.**

In an imaginary world, where the receipts and disbursements of households and firms were perfectly synchronized, it would be unnecessary to hold transactions balances. If every time a household spent $10 it received $10 as part payment of its income, no transactions balances would be needed. In the real world, however, receipts and disbursements are not perfectly synchronized.

Consider, for example, the balances held because of wage payments. Assume, for purposes of illustration, that firms pay wages every Friday and that households spend all their wages on the purchase of goods and services, with the expenditure spread out evenly over the week. Thus on Friday morning firms must hold balances equal to the weekly wage bill; on Friday afternoon households will hold these balances.

Over the week, households' balances will be drawn down as a result of purchasing goods and services. Over the same period, the balances held by firms will build up as a result of selling goods and services until, on the following Friday morning, firms will again have amassed balances equal to the wage bill that must be met on that day.

On the average over the week firms will hold balances equal to half the wage bill and so will households. Thus, in this example total money balances held will be equal to the total weekly wage bill. Notice that while the money circulates so that each group holds a varying balance over the week, the combined demand for balances summed over the two groups remains constant.

Our argument has been conducted in terms of the wage bill, but a similar analysis holds for all receipts and payments of households and firms. Because their receipts and payments are not perfectly synchronized, they must hold money balances to bridge the gap.

The transactions demand for money arises because of the nonsynchronization of payments and receipts.

What determines the size of the transactions balances to be held? It is clear that in the above example total transactions balances vary with the value of the wage bill. If the wage bill doubles for any reason (e.g., because twice as much labor is hired at the same wage rate or because the same amount of labor is hired at twice the wage rate), the transactions balances held by firms and households on this account will also double. As it is with wages so it is with all other transactions: The size of the balances held is positively related to the value of the transactions.

Next we ask how the total value of transactions is related to national income. Because of the "double counting" problem first discussed in Chapter 25, the value of all transactions exceeds the value of the economy's final output. When the flour mill buys wheat from the farmer and when the baker buys flour from the mill, both are transactions against which money balances must be held, although only

the value added at each stage is part of national income. Typically, the total value of transactions is many times as large as the total value of final output, which is national income.

We now make an added assumption that there is a stable, positive relation between transactions and national income. If a rise in aggregate expenditure leads to a rise in national income, it also leads to a rise in the total value of all transactions and hence to an associated rise in the demand for transactions balances. This allows us to relate transactions balances to national income. [43]

The larger the value of national income, the larger the value of transactions balances that will be held.

The Precautionary Motive

Many goods and services are sold on credit. The seller can never be certain when payment will be made, and the buyer can never be certain of the day of delivery and thus when payment will fall due. As a precaution against cash crises when receipts are abnormally low or disbursements are abnormally high, firms and households carry money balances. These are called **precautionary balances.** The larger such balances, the greater the protection against running out of money because of temporary fluctuations in cash flows.

How serious this risk is depends on the penalties for being caught without sufficient money balances. A firm is unlikely to be pushed into insolvency, but it may incur considerable costs if it is forced to borrow money at high interest rates in order to meet a temporary cash crisis.

The precautionary motive arises because households and firms are uncertain about the degree to which payments and receipts will be synchronized.

The protection provided by a given quantity of precautionary balances depends on the volume of payments and receipts. A $100 precautionary balance provides a large cushion for a household whose volume of payments per month is $800, and a small cushion for a firm whose monthly volume is $10,000. Fluctuations of the sort that create the need for precautionary balances tend to vary directly with the size of the firm's cash flow. To provide the same degree of protection as the value of transactions rises, more money is necessary.[3]

The precautionary motive also causes the demand for money to vary positively with the money value of national income.

The Speculative Motive

Firms and households hold some money in order to avoid the risks inherent in fluctuating prices of bonds. Money balances held for this purpose are called **speculative balances.** This motive was first analyzed by Keynes, and modern analysis is the work of Professor James Tobin of Yale University.[4]

When a household or firm holds money balances, it foregoes the extra interest income that it could earn if it held bonds instead. But market interest rates fluctuate and so do the market prices of existing bonds (since their present values depend on the interest rate). Because their prices fluctuate, bonds are a risky asset. Many households and firms do not like risk; they are said to be *risk averse.*

In choosing between holding money or holding bonds, wealth holders must balance the extra interest income that they could earn by holding bonds against the risk that bonds carry with them. At one extreme, if a household or a firm holds all its wealth in the form of bonds, it earns extra interest on its entire wealth, but it also exposes its entire wealth to the risk of changes in the price of bonds. At the other extreme, if the household or firm holds all its wealth in the form of money, it earns less interest income, but it does not face the risk of unexpected changes in the price of bonds. Wealth holders usually do not take either extreme position. They hold part of their wealth as money and part as bonds, that is, they *diversify* their holdings.

[3] Institutional arrangements affect precautionary demands. In the past, for example, a traveler would have carried a substantial precautionary balance in cash, but today a credit card covers most unforeseen expenses that may arise while traveling.

[4] Professor Tobin was awarded the Nobel prize in economics in 1981 for his research in monetary economics and the analysis of financial markets.

The influence of wealth.   The motivation to hold money in order to diversify wealth holdings means that the demand for money varies positively with wealth. For example, Ms. B. O'Reiley might elect to hold 5 percent of her wealth in money and the other 95 percent in bonds. If Ms. O'Reiley's wealth is $50,000, her demand for money will be $2,500. If her wealth increases to $60,000, her demand for money will rise to $3,000.

Although an individual's wealth may rise or fall rapidly, the total wealth of a society changes only slowly. For the analysis of short-term fluctuations in national income, the effects of changes in wealth are fairly small, and we shall ignore them for the present. (Over the long term, however, variations in wealth can have a major effect on the demand for money.)

The influence of interest rates.   Wealth held in cash earns no interest; hence the reduction in risk involved in holding more money carries a cost in terms of interest earnings foregone.

The speculative motive leads households and firms to add to their money holdings until the reduction in risk obtained by the last dollar added is just balanced (in each wealth holder's view) by the cost in terms of the interest foregone on that dollar.

When the rate of interest falls, the opportunity cost of holding money falls. This leads to more money being held both for the precautionary motive (to reduce risks caused by uncertainty about the flows of payments and receipts) and for the speculative motive (to reduce risks associated with fluctuations in the market price of bonds). When the rate of interest rises, the cost of holding money rises. This leads to less money being held for speculative and precautionary motives.

The demand for money is negatively related to the rate of interest.[5]

[5] When the price level is changing continually, it is necessary to distinguish the real from the nominal rate of interest. This was discussed in Box 29-1 on page 550. For now, there is no need to distinguish these two concepts of the interest rate since they are the same when the price level is constant, and they are measured by the market rate of interest.

Real and Nominal Money Balances

In referring to the demand for money, it is important to distinguish real from nominal values. Real values are measured in purchasing power units, nominal values in money units.

First, consider the demand for money in real terms. This means the number of units of purchasing power the public wishes to hold in the form of money balances. In an imaginary one-product wheat economy, this would be measured by the number of bushels of wheat that could be purchased with the money balances held. In a more complex economy it could be measured in terms of the number of weeks of national income; for example, the real value of the amount of money demanded might be equal to one month's national income.

When we come to measure the real demand for money, we measure the amount demanded in constant dollars. This means that the real demand is the nominal quantity demanded divided by an index of price level (where the base year is given a value of 1 rather than 100).

The real demand for money is the nominal quantity demanded divided by the price level.

For example, in the decade from 1975 to 1985 the nominal quantity of M1 balances held in the United States rose by 215 percent from $291 billion to $625 billion. Over the same period, however, the price level, as measured by the CPI, exactly doubled—if we let the price level be 1 in 1975, it was 2 in 1985. This tells us that the real quantity of M1 held only rose by 7 percent from $291 billion to $312 billion measured in constant 1975 dollars.

From real demand to nominal demand. The discussion of the previous few sections has identified the determinants of the demand for real money balances as real national income, real wealth, and the interest rate. Notice that the real demand for money depends, among other things, on real national income; it is not influenced by the price level. Now suppose that, with the interest rate, real wealth, and real national income constant, the price level doubles. The demand for real money balances will be unchanged. For this to be true, however, the demand for nominal balances must double. If the public used

to demand $300 billion worth of nominal money balances, they must now demand $600 billion worth. This keeps the real demand unchanged at $600/2 = $300. The constancy of the level of demand for real balances is shown in this example by the fact that $600 billion at the new, higher price level represents exactly the same purchasing power as did $300 billion at the old price level.

Other things being equal, the nominal demand for money balances varies in proportion to the price level; doubling the price level doubles desired nominal money balances.

This is a central proposition of the quantity theory of money, discussed further in Box 32-1.

The Total Demand for Money: Recapitulation

Figure 32-1 on page 641 summarizes the influences of national income, the rate of interest, and the price level, the three variables that account for most of the short-term variations in the nominal quantity of money demanded. The function relating money demand to the rate of interest is often called the **liquidity preference (LP) function.** Whatever name is used, the relation describes how the quantity of money people wish to hold varies as the rate of interest varies.

Monetary Forces and National Income

We are now in a position to examine the relationship between monetary forces and the equilibrium values of national income and the price level. The first step in explaining this relationship is a new one: the link between monetary equilibrium and aggregate demand. The second is familiar from earlier chapters: the effects of shifts in aggregate demand on equilibrium values of national income and the price level.

Monetary Equilibrium and Aggregate Demand

Monetary equilibrium occurs when the demand for money equals the supply of money. In Chapter

BOX 32-1

The Quantity Theory of Money and the Velocity of Circulation

The basic quantity theory of money can be set out formally in terms of the following four equations. Equation 1 states that the demand for money balances depends upon the value of transactions as measured by nominal income, which is real income multiplied by the price level, that is, *PY*.

$$M^D = kPY \qquad [1]$$

Equation 2 states that the supply of money, *M*, is set by the central bank.

$$M_s = M \qquad [2]$$

Equation 3 states the equilibrium condition that the demand for money must equal its supply.

$$M^D = M_s \qquad [3]$$

Substitution produces the basic relation among *P*, *M*, and *Y*, as shown in Equation 4.

$$M = kPY \qquad [4]$$

The original form of the classical quantity theory assumes that *k* is a constant given by the transactions demand for money and that *Y* is constant because full employment is maintained. Thus *M* and *P* move proportionally. Increases or decreases in the money supply lead to proportional increases or decreases in prices.

Often the quantity theory is presented using the concept of the velocity of circulation, *V*, instead of the proportion of the money income that people wish to hold in cash, *k*. The **velocity of circulation** is defined as national income divided by the quantity of money.

$$V = PY/M \qquad [5]$$

Rearranging gives what is called the *equation of exchange*.

$$MV = PY \qquad [6]$$

Velocity may be interpreted as showing the average amount of "work" done by a unit of money. Thus, if the annual national income is $1,200 billion and the stock of money is $300 billion, then on average each dollar's worth of money is used four times to create the values added that compose the national income.

There is a simple relation between *k* and *V*. One is the reciprocal of the other, as may be seen immediately by comparing Equations 4 and 6. Thus it makes no difference whether we choose to work with *k* or *V*. Further, if *k* is assumed to be constant, this implies that *V* must also be treated as being constant. An example may help to illustrate the interpretation of each.

Assume that the stock of money people wish to hold is equal to one-fifth of the value of total transactions. Thus *k* is 0.2 and *V*, the reciprocal of *k*, is 5. This indicates that if the money supply is to be one-fifth of the value of annual transactions, the average unit of money must account for $5 worth of transactions, that is, each dollar must be used on average five times.

Modern versions of the quantity theory do not assume that *k* is exogenously fixed, but nevertheless argue that it will not change in response to a change in the quantity of money.

---

4 we saw that in a competitive market for some commodity such as carrots, the price will adjust so as to ensure equilibrium. The rate of interest does the same job with respect to money demand and money supply.

The Liquidity Preference Theory of Interest

Figure 32-2 on page 642 shows how the interest rate will change in order to equate the demand for money with its supply. When a single household or firm

FIGURE 32-1   The Demand for Money As a Function of Interest Rates, Income, and the Price Level

(i)   (ii)   (iii)

The quantity of money demanded varies negatively with the rate of interest and positively with both national income and the price level. In (i) the demand for money is shown varying negatively with the interest rate along the liquidity preference function. When the interest rate rises from r_0 to r_1, households and firms reduce the quantity of money demanded from M_0 to M_1.

In (ii) the demand for money is shown varying positively with national income. When national income rises from Y_0 to Y_1, households and firms increase the quantity of money demanded from M_2 to M_3.

In (iii) the demand for money is shown varying positively with the price level. When the price level rises from P_0 to P_1, households and firms increase the quantity of money demanded from M_4 to M_5.

finds that it has less money than it wishes to hold, it can sell some bonds and add the proceeds to its money holdings. This transaction simply redistributes given supplies of bonds and money among individuals; it does not change the total supply of either money or bonds.

Now assume that all the firms and households in the economy have an excess demand for money balances. They all try to sell bonds to add to their money balances. But what one person can do, all persons cannot do. At any moment the economy's total supplies of money and bonds are fixed; there are just so much money and so many bonds. If everyone tries to sell bonds, there will be no one to buy them. Instead the price of bonds will fall.

We saw that a fall in the price of bonds means a rise in the rate of interest. As the interest rate rises, people economize on money balances because the opportunity cost of holding such balances is rising. This is what we saw in Figure 32-1(i) where the quantity of money demanded falls along the liquidity preference curve in response to a rise in the rate of

interest. Eventually the interest rate will rise enough that people will no longer be trying to add to their money balances by selling bonds. At that point there is no longer an excess supply of bonds, and the interest rate will stop rising. The demand for money again equals the supply.

Assume next that firms and households hold larger money balances than they would like. A single houschold or firm would purchase bonds with its excess balances, achieving monetary equilibrium by reducing its money holdings and increasing its bond holdings. But just as in the above example, what one household or firm can do, all cannot do. At any moment the total quantity of bonds is fixed so that everyone cannot simultaneously add to his or her holdings of bonds. When all households enter the bond market and try to purchase bonds with unwanted money balances, they bid up the price of existing bonds—the interest rate falls. Hence households and firms become willing to hold larger quantities of money; that is, the quantity of money demanded increases along the liquidity preference curve

FIGURE 32-2 The Liquidity Preference Theory of Interest

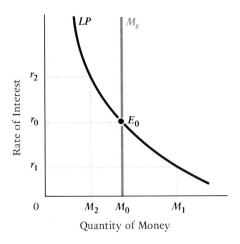

The interest rate rises when there is an excess demand for money and falls when there is an excess supply of money. The fixed quantity of money, M_0, is shown by the completely inelastic supply curve M_s. The demand for money is *LP*; its negative slope indicates that a fall in the rate of interest causes the quantity of money demanded to increase. Equilibrium is at E_0, with a rate of interest of r_0.

If the interest rate is r_1, there will be an excess demand for money of M_0M_1. Bonds will be offered for sale in an attempt to increase money holdings. This will force the rate of interest up to r_0 (the price of bonds falls), at which point the quantity of money demanded is equal to the fixed available quantity of M_0. If the interest rate is r_2, there will be an excess supply of money M_2M_0. Bonds will be demanded in return for excess money balances. This will force the rate of interest down to r_0 (the price of bonds rises), at which point the quantity of money demanded has risen to equal the fixed supply of M_0.

in response to a fall in the rate of interest. The rise in the price of bonds continues until firms and households stop trying to convert bonds into money. In other words, it continues until everyone is content to hold the existing supply of money and bonds.

Monetary equilibrium occurs when the rate of interest is such that the existing supply of money is willingly held, that is, the demand for money equals its supply.

The determination of the interest rate depicted in Figure 32-2 is often described as the *liquidity preference theory of interest* and sometimes as the *portfolio balance theory*.

As we shall see, a shift either in the demand for money or in the supply will lead to a change in the interest rate. But, as we saw in Chapter 29, desired investment expenditure is sensitive to changes in the interest rate. Here, then, is a link between monetary factors and real expenditure flows.

The Transmission Mechanism

The mechanism by which changes in the demand for and the supply of money affect aggregate demand is called the **transmission mechanism.** The transmission mechanism operates in three stages: first, the link between monetary equilibrium and the interest rate; second, the link between the interest rate and investment expenditure; and third, the link between investment expenditure and aggregate demand.

From monetary disturbances to changes in the interest rate. The interest rate will change if the supply of money changes or if there is a shift in the demand for money. For example, as shown in Figure 32-3(i) an increase in the supply of money, with an unchanged liquidity preference function, will give rise to an excess supply of money at the original interest rate. As we have seen, an excess supply of money will cause the interest rate to fall. As also shown in Figure 32-3(i), a decrease in the supply of money will cause the interest rate to rise.

As shown in Figure 32-3(ii), an increase in the demand for money, with an unchanged supply of money, will give rise to an excess demand for money at the original interest rate and cause the interest rate to rise. A decrease in the demand for money will cause the interest rate to fall.

Monetary disturbances, which can arise due to either changes in the demand for or supply of money, cause changes in the interest rate.

From changes in the interest rate to shifts in aggregate expenditure. The second link in the transmission mechanism relates interest rates to expenditure.

FIGURE 32-3 Monetary Disturbances and Interest Rate Changes

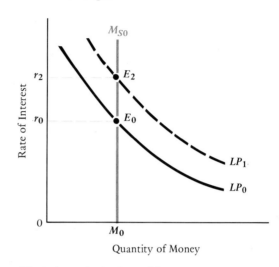

(i) A change in the supply of money

(ii) A change in the demand for money

Shifts in the supply of money or in the demand for money cause the equilibrium interest rate to change. In both parts of the figure the money supply is shown by the vertical curve M_{S0} and the demand for money is shown by the negatively shaped curve LP_0. The initial equilibrium is at E_0 with corresponding interest rate r_0.

In (i) an increase in the money supply causes the money supply curve to shift to the right from M_{S0} to M_{S1}. The new equilibrium is at E_1, where the interest rate is r_1, less than r_0. Starting at E_1 with M_{S1} and r_1, it can be seen that a decrease in the money supply to M_{S0} leads to an increase in the interest rate from r_1 to r_0.

In (ii) an increase in the demand for money causes the LP curve to shift to the right from LP_0 to LP_1. The new equilibrium occurs at E_2 and the new equilibrium interest rate is r_2, greater than r_0. Starting at E_2 we see that a decrease in the demand for money from LP_1 to LP_0 leads to a decrease in the interest rate from r_2 to r_0.

We saw in Chapter 29 that investment, which includes expenditure on inventory accumulation, residential construction, and plant and equipment, responds to changes in the rate of interest. Other things being equal, a decrease in the rate of interest makes borrowing cheaper and generates new investment expenditure.[6] This negative relation between investment and the rate of interest is called the **marginal efficiency of investment (MEI)** function.

The first two links in the transmission mechanism

are shown in Figure 32-4. We concentrate for the moment on changes in the money supply, although as we have already seen, the process can also be set in motion by changes in the demand for money. In part i we see that a change in the money supply causes the rate of interest to change in the opposite direction. In part ii we see that a change in the interest rate causes the level of investment expenditure to change in the opposite direction. Therefore changes in the money supply cause investment expenditure to change in the same direction.

An increase in the money supply leads to a fall in the interest rate and an increase in investment

[6] In Chapter 29 we saw that purchases of durable consumer goods also respond to changes in interest rates. In this chapter we concentrate on investment expenditure, which may be taken to stand for *all interest-sensitive expenditure.*

**FIGURE 32-4   The Effects of Changes in the Money Supply
on Investment Expenditure**

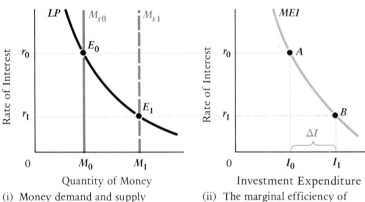

(i) Money demand and supply

(ii) The marginal efficiency of
investment

**Increases in the money supply reduce
the rate of interest and increase desired
investment expenditure.** Equilibrium is
at E_0, with a quantity of money of M_0
(shown by the inelastic money supply
curve M_{S0}), an interest rate of r_0, and an
investment expenditure of I_0 (point A). The
Fed then increases the money supply to M_1
(shown by the money supply curve M_{S1}).
This lowers the rate of interest to r_1 and
increases investment expenditure by ΔI to
I_1 (point B). A reduction in the money supply from M_1 to M_0 raises interest rates from
r_1 to r_0 and lowers investment expenditure
by ΔI, from I_1 to I_0.

expenditure. A decrease in the money supply
leads to a rise in the interest rate and a decrease
in investment expenditure.

**From shifts in aggregate expenditure to shifts in
aggregate demand.**   Now we are back on familiar
ground. In Chapter 27 we saw that a shift in the
aggregate expenditure curve can lead to a shift in the
AD curve. This is shown again in Figure 32-5.

**A change in the money supply, by causing a
change in investment expenditure and hence a
shift in the AE curve, causes the AD curve to
shift.**

An increase in the money supply causes an increase
in investment expenditure and therefore an increase
in aggregate demand. A decrease in the money supply causes a decrease in investment expenditure and
therefore a decrease in aggregate demand.
     In summary:

**The transmission mechanism connects mone-
tary forces and real expenditure flows. It works
from a change in the demand for or the supply
of money to a change in bond prices and interest
rates, to changes in investment expenditure, to
a shift in the aggregate demand curve.**

This is illustrated in Figure 32-6 for the case of an
expansionary monetary shock, that is, a shift in
money demand or money supply that tends to increase aggregate demand.

Aggregate Demand, the Price Level, and National Income

The effect of a change in the money supply.   We
have just seen that a change in the money supply
shifts the aggregate demand curve. If we want to
know what it does to real national income and to the
price level, we need to know the slope of the aggregate supply curve. This step, which is familiar from
earlier chapters, is recalled in Figure 32-7 on page
646.[7]
     The key result is that the increase in equilibrium
real income is less than the horizontal shift in the AD
curve. This is because part of this shift is dissipated
by a rise in the price level. If the aggregate demand

[7] Since the demand for money in general will depend on the level
of national income, as shown in Figure 32-1(ii), our analysis at
this stage is incomplete. The induced change in equilibrium national income will lead to a shift in the liquidity preference function in Figure 32-2. For simplicity we have assumed in the text
that the liquidity preference function does not shift in response to
a change in national income. The Appendix to Chapter 37 presents
a formal analysis in which this effect is allowed for and in which
equilibrium levels of the interest rate and national income are
determined simultaneously.

FIGURE 32-5   The Effects of Changes in the Money Supply on Aggregate Demand

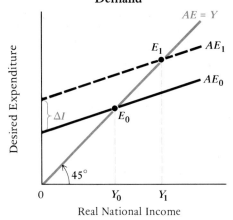

(i) Shift in aggregate expenditure

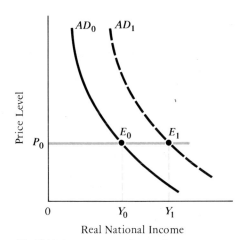

(ii) Shift in aggregate demand

Changes in the money supply cause shifts in the aggregate expenditure and aggregate demand functions. In Figure 32-4 an increase in the money supply increased desired investment expenditure by ΔI. In (i) the aggregate expenditure function shifts up by ΔI (which is the same as ΔI in Figure 32-4), from AE_0 to AE_1. At the fixed price level P_0, equilibrium income rises from Y_0 to Y_1, as shown by the horizontal shift in the aggregate demand curve from AD_0 to AD_1 in (ii).

When the supply of money falls (from M_{S1} to M_{S0} in Figure 32-4), investment falls by ΔI, thereby shifting aggregate expenditure from AE_1 to AE_0. At the fixed price level P_0, this reduces equilibrium income from Y_1 to Y_0.

FIGURE 32-6   The Transmission Mechanism for an Expansionary Monetary Shock

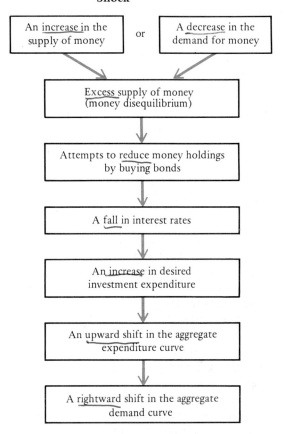

An increase in the supply of money or a decrease in the demand for money leads to an increase in aggregate demand. The excess supply of money following an expansionary monetary disturbance leads to a fall in the interest rate and an increase in investment. This causes an upward shift in the AE curve, and thus a rightward shift in the AD curve.

curve were vertical, the rise in the price level would not diminish the effect on real output; real output would rise by an amount equal to the horizontal shift of the AD curve. But because the AD curve is negatively sloped, the rise in real output is smaller.

The effect of a change in the price level. We can now use the transmission mechanism to explain the

FIGURE 32-7 The Effects of Changes in the Money Supply

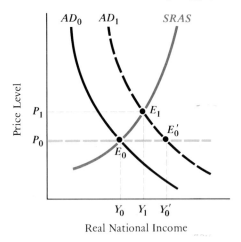

A change in the money supply leads to a change in national income that is smaller than the horizontal shift in the AD curve. An increase in the money supply causes the AD curve to shift to the right, from AD_0 to AD_1. With the price level constant, national income would rise from Y_0 to Y_0'. With the upward-sloping SRAS curve, income only rises to Y_1 while the price level rises as well—to P_1.

negative slope of the AD curve, that is, to explain why equilibrium national income is negatively related to the price level.

In Chapter 24 we gave three reasons why the AD curve was negatively sloped. In Chapter 27 we relied on the wealth effect (real balance effect) to explain this negative slope because it was simple and direct. Now that we have developed a theory of money and interest rates, we are able to understand the indirect effect that works through the transmission mechanism.

The essential feature of this indirect effect is that a rise in the price level raises the money value of transactions. This leads to an increased demand for money which brings the transmission mechanism into play. People try to sell bonds to add to their money balances, but collectively all they succeed in doing is forcing up the interest rate. The rise in the interest rate reduces investment expenditure and so reduces equilibrium national income.

This effect is important because, empirically, the interest rate is the most important link between monetary factors and real expenditure flows. Box 32-2 on pages 648–649 is for those who wish to study the reasons for the negative slope of the AD curve in more detail.

The Monetary Adjustment Mechanism

Suppose that an economy in equilibrium with real national income equal to its potential level were disturbed by an increase in the money supply. Since real national income would increase, there would be an inflationary gap, as shown in Figure 32-8(i). Let us now examine the mechanism by which such an inflationary gap is eliminated. This involves an important, but subtle, implication of the theory.

A sufficiently large rise in the price level will eliminate any inflationary gap, provided the nominal money supply remains constant.

Operation of the monetary adjustment mechanism. Because it causes excess demand in factor markets, the inflationary gap will cause factor prices to rise. This will shift the SRAS curve up and take the price level with it. This raises the money value of transactions, and the resulting increase in the demand for money raises interest rates. Hence at any level of real income, desired real expenditure falls. The fall in real expenditure as the price level rises is shown by a movement upward to the left *along* the AD curve. This reduces the inflationary gap. When the price level has risen enough, the inflationary gap disappears and the price level stops rising.

This mechanism, illustrated in Figure 32-8(ii), may be called the *monetary adjustment mechanism*. It works through the transmission mechanism.

The monetary adjustment mechanism will eliminate any inflationary gap, provided that the nominal money supply is held constant.

Thus inflationary gaps tend to be self-correcting as long as the money supply does not increase. They will cause the price level to increase, but those in-

FIGURE 32-8 The Monetary Adjustment Mechanism

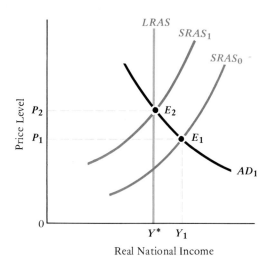

(i) Inflationary gap created

(ii) Inflationary gap eliminated

A rise in the price level will eliminate an inflationary gap. The economy is initially in long-run equilibrium at E_0 with price level P_0 and real income Y^*. In (i) some disturbance shifts the AD curve to the right, leading to equilibrium E_1 with a higher price level P_1 and an inflationary gap of Y^*Y_1.

E_1 is also shown in (ii). The inflationary gap causes wages to rise, shifting the $SRAS$ curve to the left so that the price level starts to rise. The monetary adjustment mechanism (working through a rising interest rate and falling investment) lowers aggregate expenditure so that the economy moves upward along the AD curve. Eventually, the inflationary gap is eliminated and equilibrium reached at E_2 with income at Y^* and price level P_2.

creases set in motion a chain of events in the markets for financial assets that will eventually remove the inflationary gap.

The self-correcting mechanism is the reason why price levels and the money supply have been linked for so long in economics. Many things can cause the price level to rise for some time. Yet whatever the reason for the rise, unless the money supply is expanded, the price level increase itself sets up forces that will remove the initial inflationary gap and so bring demand inflation to a halt.

Frustration of the monetary adjustment mechanism.
The self-correcting mechanism for removing an inflationary gap can be frustrated indefinitely if the money supply is increased at the same rate that prices

are rising. Say the price level is rising 10 percent a year under the pressure of a large inflationary gap. Demand for nominal money balances will also be rising at about 10 percent per year. Now suppose the Fed increases the money supply at 10 percent per year. No excess demand for money will develop, since the extra money needed to meet the rising demand will be forthcoming. The real interest rate will not rise, and the inflationary gap will not be reduced. This process is analyzed in Figure 32-9 on page 650.

If the money supply increases at the same rate as the price level rises, the real money supply and hence the real interest rate will remain constant, and the monetary adjustment mechanism will be frustrated.

BOX 32-2

The Slope of the Aggregate Demand Curve

The *AD* curve relates the price level to the equilibrium level of real national income. It is negatively sloped because the higher the price level, the lower the equilibrium national income. The main reason for this negative slope is found in the transmission mechanism.

Let us look at this process in detail. Although the argument contains nothing new, it does require that you follow carefully through several steps.

We start with an initial position depicted in part i of the figure. The liquidity preference schedule is LP_0, and the money supply is M_s. Equilibrium is at E_0 with the interest rate at r_0. The *MEI* schedule given in part

(ii) shows that, at the rate of interest r_0, desired investment expenditure is I_0. In part iii the aggregate expenditure curve AE_0 is drawn for that level of investment (I_0). Equilibrium is at E_0 with a real national income of Y_0. Plotting Y_0 against the initial price level (P_0) yields point A on the aggregate demand curve in part iv.

An increase in the price level to P_1 raises the money value of transactions and increases the quantity of money demanded at each possible value of the interest rate. As a result the liquidity preference function shifts from LP_0 to LP_1. This raises interest rates to r_1 and lowers investment expenditure by ΔI_1 to I_1.

(i) Monetary equilibrium

(ii) Marginal efficiency of investment

An inflation is said to be *validated* when the money supply is increased as fast as the price level so that the monetary adjustment mechanism is frustrated. A validated inflation can go on indefinitely, although as we shall see in Chapter 35, possibly not at a constant rate.

Controversies Over Stabilization Policy

In Chapter 33 we shall study in detail how the Fed seeks to alter the money supply in pursuit of its

monetary policy. In the present chapter we assume that the Fed can make the money supply take on any desired value. This allows us to study some points of comparison and contrast between monetary and fiscal stabilization policy. Stabilization policy aims to avoid the extremes of large inflationary and recessionary gaps by using monetary and fiscal policy to shift the aggregate demand curve. Many controversies surround the use of stabilization policy, and we are now in a position to take a look at some of them. What role has this policy played in the past? What role should be prescribed for it in the future?

The economics profession has often been deeply

(iii) Equilibrium national income

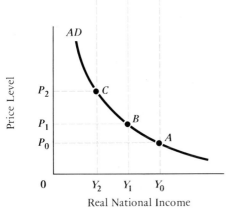

(iv) The aggregate demand curve

The fall in investment causes the *AE* curve in part iii to shift down by an equal amount to AE_1. Equilibrium income falls to Y_1. Plotting Y_1 against P_1 produces point *B* on the *AD* curve in part iv.

A further increase in the price level to P_2 shifts the liquidity preference function to LP_2, raises the interest rate to r_2, and lowers investment expenditure to I_2. The fall in investment shifts the *AE* curve in part iii to AE_2, and equilibrium income falls to Y_2. Plotting Y_2 against P_2 produces point *C* on the *AD* curve in part iv.

The negative relation between the price level and equilibrium real income shown by the *AD* curve occurs because, other things being equal, a rise in the price level raises the *demand* for money. Notice the qualification, "other things being equal." It is important for this process that the nominal money *supply* remain constant. The transmission mechanism operates because the demand for money increases when the price level rises, while the money supply remains constant. The attempt to add to money balances by selling bonds is what drives the interest rate up and reduces desired expenditure, thereby reducing equilibrium national income. (This argument is conducted in terms of the nominal supply and demand for money. Arguing in terms of the real demand and supply of money leads to identical results.) [44]

divided over how stabilization policy should be conducted. It is helpful to distinguish between two controversies that have occupied a central place in policy debates. The first concerns the relative strengths of monetary and fiscal policy. The second concerns the degree of built-in stability in the economy and hence the need to use either policy. The latter is often referred to as the debate about *policy activism.*

In both cases the profession has split into two camps, which can be identified as **monetarist** and **Keynesian.** While it is true that economists who agree on one issue tend to also agree on the other issue, there is no reason why this should be so. Here

we focus on the relative strengths of monetary and fiscal policy. Policy activism is taken up in Chapter 37.

The Relative Effectiveness of Monetary and Fiscal Policy

Fiscal policy operates *directly* on aggregate expenditure. Monetary policy influences aggregate expenditure only *indirectly* by altering the money supply and interest rates. When the Fed changes the money supply, it shifts the aggregate demand curve via the transmission mechanism.

This process is shown in Figures 32-4 and 32-5 on pages 644 and 645.

FIGURE 32–9   Frustration of the Monetary Adjustment

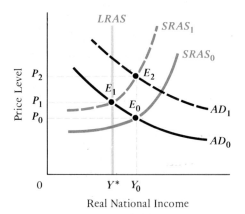

An inflationary gap can persist indefinitely if the money supply increases as fast as the price level. Suppose the economy is at E_0, with income Y_0 and price level P_0. Since potential income is Y^*, there is an inflationary gap of Y^*Y_0. The price level now rises, which tends to shift the economy upward along any given AD curve, thereby tending to reduce the excess aggregate demand. But the Fed increases the money supply so that the AD curve shifts outward, thereby tending to increase excess aggregate demand. If the two forces just balance each other, by the time the price level has risen to P_2 the curve will have shifted to AD_1, leaving the inflationary gap unchanged, with equilibrium at E_2.

Views about the key behavioral relations translate into views about the relative strengths of monetary and fiscal policies. The effects of either policy depend on the slope of the $SRAS$ curve and on how the policy affects the AD curve. Whatever the slope of the $SRAS$ curve, it is common to both policies. Hence we focus on what makes the two policies differ: their ability to shift the AD curve.

The Strength of Monetary Policy

Suppose that initially the economy is in equilibrium at less than potential income. The Fed then increases the money supply. Firms and households now hold excess money balances, and they try to buy bonds. This action forces up the price of bonds, which implies a fall in the rate of interest.

The resulting increase in desired investment expenditure shifts the aggregate demand curve rightward, thus raising equilibrium national income. This process is shown in Figures 32-4 and 32-5 on pages 644 and 645.

What happens when the Fed decreases the money supply? This creates an excess demand for money because firms and households no longer have the money balances they wish to hold at the existing level of interest rates. In an effort to replenish their inadequate holdings of money, firms and households seek to sell bonds, causing an increase in the interest rate. The increased interest rate causes a reduction in investment expenditure. This in turn shifts the aggregate demand curve leftward and lowers equilibrium income.

Monetary policy works through the transmission mechanism to shift the aggregate demand curve and so to change equilibrium national income. An increase in the money supply is expansionary, a decrease contractionary.

But how strong is this effect? If, for example, the Fed increases the money supply by 10 percent, by how much will income rise? As a first step in answering that question, we focus on the shift in the AD curve.

The size of the shift in aggregate demand in response to an increase in the money supply depends on the size of the increase in investment expenditure. This in turn depends on two factors.

The first is how much interest rates fall in response to the increase in the money supply. The more interest-sensitive the demand for money, the less interest rates will have to fall to induce firms and households to willingly hold the increase in the money supply.

The second is how much investment expenditure increases in response to the fall in interest rates. The more interest-sensitive investment expenditure, the more it will increase in response to any given fall in the interest rate.

It follows that the size of the shift in aggregate demand in response to a change in the money supply depends on the shapes of the liquidity preference and marginal efficiency of investment curves. The influ-

FIGURE 32-10   Monetarist and Keynesian Views on Monetary Policy

(i) The monetarist view

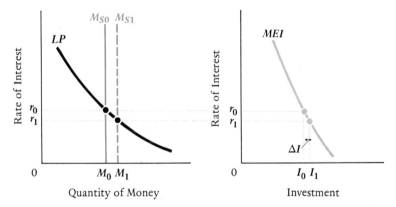

(ii) The Keynesian view

Monetarists assume that monetary policy is very effective; Keynesians assume that is is relatively ineffective. Initially the money supply is M_{S0}, and the economy is in equilibrium with an interest rate of r_0 and investment expenditure of I_0.

In both (i) and (ii) the expansionary monetary policy of the central bank shifts the money supply to M_{S1}. The rate of interest falls to r_1, causing an increase in investment expenditure of ΔI (from I_0 to I_1).

(i) In the monetarist view monetary policy is effective since it leads to a large change in investment expenditure. (ii) In the Keynesian view monetary policy is ineffective since it leads to only a small change in investment expenditure.

ence of the shapes of the two curves is shown in Figure 32-10 and may be summarized as follows:

1. **The steeper (the less interest-sensitive) the LP function, the greater the effect a change in the money supply will have on interest rates.**

2. **The flatter (the more interest-sensitive) the MEI function, the greater the effect a change in the interest rate will have on investment expenditure and hence on aggregate demand.**

The combination that produces the largest effect on aggregate demand for a given change in the money supply is a steep *LP* function and a flat *MEI* function. This combination is illustrated in Figure 32-10(i). It accords with the monetarist view that monetary policy is relatively effective as a means of influencing the economy. The combination that produces the smallest effect is a flat *LP* function and a steep *MEI* function. This combination is illustrated in Figure 32-10(ii). It accords with the view of some Keynesians that monetary policy is relatively ineffective.

Not surprisingly, much of the controversy about the effectiveness of monetary policy as a means of influencing national income has centered on the shapes of these two functions.

According to the monetarists, changes in the money supply cause large changes in interest rates that in turn cause large changes in expenditure. According to some Keynesians, changes in the money supply cause small changes in interest rates that in turn cause small or negligible changes in expenditure.

The Strength of Fiscal Policy

As with monetary policy, the amount by which a given fiscal stimulus raises national income depends upon both the *AD* curve and the *SRAS* curve. Again, we focus for the moment on the role of the *AD* curve.

We saw in Chapter 30 that the horizontal shift in the *AD* curve due to, say, an increase in government expenditure is given by the simple multiplier. In the final equilibrium when the price level has adjusted, however, the change in aggregate demand will depend on the consequent response of interest rates and investment expenditure. Disagreement over these responses cause monetarists and Keynesians to disagree over the potency of fiscal policy. This is illustrated in Figure 32-11.

Consider an increase in government expenditure. It raises national income and creates excess demand for money because, as we saw in Figure 32-1, it causes a rise in the demand for transactions balances. The interest rate rises until everyone is content to hold the existing stock of money. The rise in the interest rate lowers private investment expenditure. (A parallel analysis applies to a decline in government expenditure.)

The tendency just discussed is called the **crowding out effect.**[8] It may be defined as the offsetting reduction in private investment caused by the rise in interest rates that follows an expansionary fiscal policy. The analysis of Figure 32-11 shows that the crowding out effect is smaller (1) the flatter (more interest-sensitive) the *LP* function, so that increases in the transactions demand for money do not cause large increases in the interest rate, and (2) the steeper the *MEI* function, so that increases in the interest

rate do not cause large changes in investment expenditure.

Monetarists believe the crowding out effect is large. An increase in government expenditure will crowd out almost the same amount of private expenditure and thus have only a small net expansionary effect on aggregate demand. Keynesians believe the crowding out effect is small, at least when the economy is suffering from a substantial recessionary gap, which is when one is likely to wish to use an expansionary fiscal policy. If this is so, only a small part of any rise in government expenditure will be offset by a fall in private expenditure and fiscal policy will be successful in inducing major shifts in aggregate demand.

Monetarists hold that changes in government expenditure often induce large changes in interest rates that in turn cause large offsetting changes in private investment, leaving only a small net effect on aggregate demand.

Keynesians hold that changes in government expenditure often cause only small changes in interest rates that in turn cause small or negligible offsetting changes in investment expenditure.

The Role of the SRAS Curve

Neither monetarists nor Keynesians can assess the initial effects of monetary or fiscal policy on *real* output and employment without reference to the shape of the *SRAS* curve.

The role of the *SRAS* curve is common to both fiscal and monetary policies: for any given shift in the *AD* curve, the steeper the *SRAS* curve, the smaller the increase in national income and the larger the increase in the price level. (This should be familiar from Chapter 28; see Figure 28-2.) However, the mechanism by which the *SRAS* curve influences the outcome differs in the two policies.

Monetary policy. An increase in the money supply is expansionary because it lowers interest rates. If the expansion causes the price level to rise, the demand for money rises, damping the fall in interest rates. This means that investment does not rise as much as

---

[8] We encountered the crowding out effect in Chapter 30. See especially Figure 30-5.

FIGURE 32-11   Monetarist and Keynesian Views on Fiscal Policy

(i) The monetarist view

(ii) The Keynesian view

Keynesians assume that fiscal policy is very effective; monetarists assume that it is relatively ineffective. Initially the economy is in equilibrium, with an interest rate of r_0 and investment plus government expenditure of A_0. Suppose the government increases its expenditure by $\Delta G = A_0 A_1$. The effect on national income is given by the multiplier formula (see page 518) if the interest rate remains at r_0. But when expenditure rises the transactions demand for money rises. This shifts LP_0 to LP_1, and leads to an increase in the rate of interest to r_1. The rise in interest rates leads to a reduction in interest-sensitive investment expenditure by $A_2 A_1$. This crowding out of private investment expenditure, caused by a rise in interest rates brought about by the expansionary fiscal policy, reduces the multiplier because the decline in investment partially offsets the rise in government expenditure. The net effect of the two changes is an increase of $G + I$ from A_0 to A_2.

(i) In the monetarist view the crowding out effect is large so fiscal policy is relatively ineffective. (ii) In the Keynesian view the crowding out effect is small so fiscal policy is relatively effective.

it would have if the price level had been constant. Therefore equilibrium national income does not rise as much.

In the extreme case of a vertical aggregate supply curve, prices rise so much that the increase in money demand matches the increase in money supply, and interest rates do not fall at all. In this case investment expenditure and national income are unaffected by changes in the money supply. This is shown in Figure 28-3.

Fiscal policy.   Following an expansion induced by fiscal policy, any rise in the price level raises the demand for money even further than the initial rise

due to the expansion in national income. This then causes interest rates to rise even further, crowding out more investment expenditure. In the extreme case of a vertical *SRAS* curve, prices and interest rates rise by enough to cause investment expenditure to fall by an amount exactly equal to the rise in government expenditure. This is the case of *complete crowding out*, where national income is not influenced by fiscal policy at all.

The Present State of the Controversy

The controversy about the relative strengths of monetary and fiscal policy is no longer a central source of disagreement among economists. Few economists believe in either extreme view. The extremes are still studied since they help in understanding the important role played by the shapes of the key behavioral relations.

Indeed, although monetarist and Keynesian are convenient labels to give to the extreme views, ideas continue to evolve. Whereas 20 years ago Keynesians gave little place to monetary policy, today most Keynesians accept both monetary and fiscal policy as potent methods of influencing the economy. Traditional monetarists are still inclined to downgrade fiscal policy.

Disagreements now tend to be focused more on aggregate supply rather than on aggregate demand. One new school of thought argues that what matters more is whether policy is expected or unexpected than whether it acts through monetary or fiscal channels. This important distinction is encountered again in Chapter 37.

Summary

1. For simplicity we divide all forms in which wealth is held into money, which is a medium of exchange, and bonds, which earn a higher interest return than money and can be turned into money by selling them at a price that is determined on the open market.

2. The price of bonds varies negatively with the rate of interest. A rise in the interest rate lowers the prices of all bonds. The longer its term to maturity, the greater the change in the price of a bond for a given change in the interest rate.

3. The value of money balances the public wishes to hold is called the *demand for money*. It is a stock (not a flow), measured as so many billions of dollars.

4. Money balances are held, despite the opportunity cost of bond interest foregone, because of the transactions, precautionary, and speculative motives. They have the effect of making the demand for money vary positively with real national income, the price level, and wealth and vary negatively with the rate of interest. The nominal demand for money varies proportionally with the price level.

5. When there is an excess demand for money balances, people try to sell bonds. This pushes the price of bonds down and the interest rate up. When there is an excess supply of money balances, people try to buy bonds. This pushes the price of bonds up and the rate of interest down. Monetary equilibrium is established when people are willing to hold the fixed stocks of money and bonds at the current rate of interest. The liquidity preference (*LP*) function is the relation between money demand and the interest rate.

6. A change in the interest rate causes desired investment to change along the marginal efficiency of investment (*MEI*) function. This shifts the aggregate desired expenditure function and causes equilibrium national income to change. This means that the aggregate demand curve shifts.

7. Points 5 and 6 together describe the transmission mechanism that links money to national income. A decrease in the supply of money tends to reduce aggregate demand. An increase in the supply of money tends to increase it.

8. The negatively sloped aggregate demand curve indicates that the higher the price level, the lower equilibrium national income. The explanation lies with the monetary adjustment mechanism: The higher the price level, the higher the demand for money, the higher the rate of interest, the lower the aggregate expenditure function, and thus the lower equilibrium income.

9. The monetary adjustment mechanism that causes the aggregate demand curve to have a negative slope means that a sufficiently large rise in the price level will eliminate any inflationary gap. However, this mechanism can be frustrated if the Fed validates the price rise by increasing the money supply as fast as the price level is rising.

10. Monetary policy seeks to influence national income by creating a change in monetary equilibrium that will work through the transmission mechanism. The steeper the *LP* curve and the flatter the investment curve, the greater the effect of a given change in the money supply on aggregate demand.

11. Fiscal policy operates to shift the *AD* curve directly, but its effectiveness also depends on its indirect effects on private expenditure via changes in the interest rate. A given change in government expenditure will have larger effects on aggregate demand the flatter the *LP* curve is and the steeper the *MEI* curve is.

Topics for Review

Interest rates and bond prices
Transactions, precautionary, and speculative motives for holding money
Liquidity preference (*LP*) function
Monetary equilibrium
Transmission mechanism
Marginal efficiency of investment (*MEI*) function
Monetary adjustment mechanism
Monetarist and Keynesian views on the strength of fiscal and monetary policy

---

Discussion Questions

1. Describing a possible future "cashless society," a public report recently said, "In the cashless society of the future, a customer could insert a plastic card into a machine at a store and the amount of the purchase would be deducted from his 'bank account' in the computer automatically and transferred to the store's account. No cash or checks would ever change hands." What would such an institutional change do to the various motives for holding money balances? What functions would remain for commercial banks and for the central bank if money as we now know it disappeared in this fashion? What benefits and disadvantages can you see in such a scheme?

2. What motives do you think explain the following holdings?
   a. Currency and coins in the cash register of the local supermarket at the start of each working day
   b. The payroll account of the Ford Motor Company in the local bank
   c. Certificates of deposit that mature after one's retirement
   d. Government bonds held by private individuals

3. What would be the effects on the economy if Congress were to vote a once-and-for-all universal social dividend of $5,000 paid to every American over the age of 17, to be financed by the creation of new money?

4. What sort of situation might lead a society to have a very flat liquidity preference schedule and a very steep marginal efficiency of investment schedule? Is this a good combination for those who wish to affect the level of income by changing the money supply?

5. Suppose you alone know that the Fed is going to engage in policies that will decrease the money supply sharply starting next month. How might you make speculative profits by purchases or sales of bonds now?

6. What would happen if, starting from a situation of 10 percent rates of inflation and of monetary expansion, the Fed cut the rate of monetary expansion to 5 percent?

7. Trace the full sequence of events by which the monetary adjustment mechanism would work if, in the face of a constant money supply, workers and firms insisted on actions that raised prices continually at a rate of 10 percent per year. "Sooner or later in this situation something would have to give." What possible things could "give"? What would be the consequence of each "giving"?

8. "Bond prices pressed downward by news of M1's sharp rise, economy rebounds." Does this *Wall Street Journal* headline necessarily contradict our theory about the direct link between money supply and bond prices?

9. Paul Volcker, chairman of the board of governors of the Federal Reserve System, has recently expressed concern about the record government deficit and the growing level of debt in the economy. Why should this concern him?

33

Monetary Policy

Central Banks

All advanced free-market economies have, in addition to commercial banks, a central bank. Central banks influence the size of their country's money supply, and in doing so they operate through the transmission mechanism to influence national income and the price level. In this chapter we study how the central bank of the United States, the Federal Reserve System, has influenced the American economy through its monetary policy. Many of the world's early central banks were private, profit-making institutions that provided services to ordinary banks. Their importance, however, led to their developing close ties with government. Central banks soon became instruments of the government, though not all of them were publicly owned. The Bank of England (the "Old Lady of Threadneedle Street"), one of the world's oldest and most famous central banks, began to operate as the central bank of England in the seventeenth century, but it was not "nationalized" until 1947.

The Federal Reserve System

The Federal Reserve System (the Fed) began operation in 1914, following the passage of the Federal Reserve Act in 1913. Although the Fed appears, at first glance, to consist of a number of privately owned banks controlled by the commercial banks, it actually functions as the country's central bank. The most important thing about the Fed is this:

In its role as the central bank of the United States, the Federal Reserve System is responsible for the U.S. government's monetary policy.

The basic elements in the Federal Reserve System are (1) the board of governors; (2) the Federal Advisory Council, which has no real power, but whose 12 members advise the board of the views of commercial bankers; (3) the 12 Federal Reserve banks; (4) the Federal Open Market Committee (FOMC); and (5) the more than 25,000 member commercial banks.

The board of governors. The board consists of seven members appointed by the president and confirmed by the Senate. Members serve for 14 years. The length of term is important, for it means that each member of the board serves beyond the term of the president making the appointment. Board members are top-level public servants who often come from the world of business or banking. In 1986 a number of its members—including Henry Wallich and new appointees Manual Johnson, Wayne Angell, and Robert Heller—were economists.

The board is responsible to Congress, but works closely with the Department of the Treasury. It supervises the entire Federal Reserve System and exercises general policy control over the 12 Reserve banks.

The chairman of the board (Paul A. Volcker in 1986) is in a powerful position to influence the country's monetary policies.

The Reserve banks.   The 12 Federal Reserve banks serve the 12 districts into which the country is divided. The banks are located in Boston, New York, Philadelphia, Cleveland, Richmond, Atlanta, Chicago, St. Louis, Minneapolis, Kansas City, Dallas, and San Francisco. Each bank is nominally owned by the member banks in its district. A commercial bank that is a member of the system is required to purchase a specific amount of Reserve bank stock on which they receive a flat dividend. Each Federal Reserve bank has nine directors: three bankers elected by the member banks; three representatives of business, agriculture, or industry; and three public members appointed by the board of governors.

Although technically privately owned and operated, the Federal Reserve banks are actually operated under guidelines set down by the board of governors in what it deems to be the public interest.

The Federal Reserve banks have a strong tradition of service to the banking community within the policy guidelines laid down by the board of governors. Revenues they have earned in excess of expenses and of fixed minimum profits which they can retain for their own use must be turned over to the U.S. Treasury. Most Reserve banks, along with the office of the board of governors, engage in research and publish many bulletins of interest to the financial communities they serve.

The Federal Open Market Committee.   The Federal Open Market Committee has 12 members: the 7 members of the board of governors plus 5 presidents of various Reserve banks. This committee determines the open market policy of the system, which deals principally with how many government securities the Reserve banks should buy or sell on the open market. This is the group that determines the country's monetary policy.

Basic Functions of a Central Bank

The similarities in the functions performed and the tools used by the world's central banks are much more important than the differences in their organization. Although our attention is given to the operations of the Federal Reserve System, its basic functions are similar to those of the Bank of England, the Bank of Greece, or the Bank of Canada.

A central bank serves four main functions. It is a banker for commercial banks, a banker for the government, the controller of the nation's supply of money, and a regulator of money markets.

The first three functions are reflected by the Fed's balance sheet, shown in Table 33-1.

Banker to Commercial Banks

The central bank accepts deposits from commercial banks and will, on order, transfer them to the account of another bank. In this way the central bank provides each commercial bank with the equivalent of a checking account and with a means of settling debts to other banks. The deposits made by the commercial banks with the central bank appear in Table 33-1. The reserves of the commercial banks deposited with the central bank are *liabilities* of the central bank because it promises to pay them to the commercial banks on demand.

From their very beginnings central banks have acted as "lenders of last resort" to the commercial banking system. Commercial banks with sound investments sometimes find themselves in urgent need of cash to meet the demands of their depositors. If such banks cannot obtain ready cash, they may be forced into insolvency despite their being in a basically sound financial position. Central banks provide

TABLE 33-1 Federal Reserve Banks, Consolidated Balance Sheet, January 29, 1986
(billions of dollars)

Assets	
Gold certificates and other cash	$ 11.1
U.S. government securities	180.7
Loans to commercial banks	0.8
Other assets	36.4
	229.0

Liabilities	
Federal Reserve Notes outstanding	$174.6
Deposits of member bank reserves	24.9
Deposits of U.S. Treasury	17.1
Other liabilities	12.4
	229.0

Source: Federal Reserve Bulletin, April 1986.

The balance sheet of the Fed shows that it serves as banker to the commercial banks and to the U.S. Treasury and as issuer of our currency; it also suggests the Fed's role as regulator of money markets and the money supply. Federal Reserve notes are currency, and the deposits of member banks give commercial banks the reserves they use to create deposit money. The Fed's principal assets, holdings of U.S. government securities, arise from its open market operations designed to regulate the money supply and also from direct purchases from the Treasury.

temporary assistance to such commercial banks by making short-term loans to them.

Loans made by the Fed to commercial banks are said to be made available through the Fed's "discount window." The rate of interest the Fed charges on such loans is called the **discount rate.**

Bank for the Government

Governments, too, need to hold their funds in an account into which they can make deposits and on which they can write checks. The U.S. Treasury keeps its checking deposits at the Federal Reserve banks, replenishing them from much larger tax and loan accounts kept at commercial banks. When the government requires more money than it collects in taxes, it, too, needs to borrow, and it does so by selling securities. Most are sold directly to the public,

but when the central bank buys a new government bond on the open market, it is indirectly lending to the government. As of January 1986 the Federal Reserve System held over $180 billion in U.S. government securities.

Controller of the Money Supply

One of the most important functions of a central bank is to control the money supply. From Table 33-1 it is clear that the overwhelming proportion of a central bank's liabilities (its promises to pay) are either Federal Reserve notes or the deposits of commercial banks, which provide reserves for demand deposits owned by households and firms. Later in this chapter we shall study how the Fed seeks to control the money supply.

Regulator of Money Markets

The central bank frequently enters money markets for purposes other than controlling the money supply. For instance, it may, as an arm of the government, attempt to keep interest rates low in periods when the government is increasing its debt to reduce the government's cost of financing a given deficit.

Central banks also assume responsibility for supporting the country's financial system and preventing serious disruption by wide-scale panic and the resulting bank failures. Various institutions are in the business of borrowing on a short-term and lending on a long-term basis. Examples include savings and loan associations, which take in short-term deposits from the public and lend on long-term mortgages. Large, unanticipated increases in interest rates tend to squeeze these institutions. The average rate that they earn on their investments rises only slowly as old contracts mature and new ones are made, but they must either pay higher rates to hold on to their deposits or accept wide-scale withdrawals that could easily bring about their insolvency. The Fed sometimes helps such institutions by preventing rapid swings in interest rates. If a shortage of funds is rapidly driving up interest rates, the Fed may supply funds to the market and thus make the rise in rates more gradual.

Conflicts Among Functions

The several functions of the central bank are not always compatible. Sometimes in pursuit of an anti-inflationary policy the Fed reduces the money supply below the current demand for it. This causes interest rates to rise. The resulting squeeze makes life uncomfortable for banks and other financial institutions and makes borrowing expensive for the government. If the Fed chooses to ease those problems, say, by lending money to banks, it is relaxing its anti-inflationary policy.

The Fed must strive to balance conflicting objectives. When it wishes to raise interest rates to control the money supply, it should do so by an amount and on such a timetable as to prevent severe financial problems in money markets. Many critics think that the Fed does not always succeed in finding the right balance between its conflicting objectives.

Central Banks and the Money Supply

As we saw in Chapter 32, changes in the money supply lead to shifts in the *AD* curve, to changes in equilibrium national income and the price level. We now discuss the various ways in which monetary policy can influence the money supply and so influence national income.

Deposit money is an important part of the money supply. Demand deposits of commercial banks account for over 40 percent of M1, the narrowest definition of money, and roughly 15 percent of M3, the broadest measure in widespread use (see Table 31-9). As we have seen, the ability of commercial banks to create deposit money depends on their reserves. The ability of the central bank to affect the money supply is critically related to its ability to affect the size and adequacy of these reserves. In the following sections we shall discuss four ways in which the central bank affects the money supply.

Open Market Operations

The central bank's most important tool for influencing the supply of money is its **open market oper-**ations, the purchase or sale of government securities on the open market. At the start of 1986 the Federal Reserve held more than $180 billion in government securities. In a typical year the Fed buys and sells $20 to $40 billion worth of government securities on the open market. What is the effect of these purchases and sales?

Purchases on the Open Market

When a Federal Reserve bank buys a bond from a household or firm, it pays for the bond with a check drawn on the central bank and payable to the seller. The seller deposits this check in its own bank. The commercial bank presents the check to the Fed for payment and the central bank makes a book entry, increasing the deposit of the commercial bank at the central bank.

TABLE 33-2   Balance Sheet Changes Caused by an Open Market Purchase from a Household

Private household		
Assets		Liabilities
Bonds	− $100	No change
Deposits	+ 100	

Commercial banks		
Assets		Liabilities
Reserves (deposits with central bank)	+ $100	Demand deposits + $100

Central bank		
Assets		Liabilities
Bonds	+ $100	Deposits of commercial banks + $100

The money supply is increased when the Fed makes an open market purchase from a household. When the Fed buys a $100 bond from a household, the household gains money and gives up a bond. The commercial banks gain a new deposit of $100 and thus new reserves of $100. Commercial banks can now engage in a multiple expansion of deposit money of the sort analyzed in Chapter 31.

Table 33-2 shows the changes in the balance sheets of the several parties involved in a Federal Reserve bank purchase of $100 in government securities from a household.

The Fed has increased its assets by the value of the security it purchased and increased its liabilities in the form of the deposits of commercial banks. The commercial bank has increased its deposit liabilities and its reserves by the amount of the transaction.

The creation of excess reserves.   After these transactions are completed the commercial banks have excess reserves and are in a position to expand their loans and deposits. The household that sold the bond to the Fed has merely switched assets. Where it used to hold a bond, it now holds money. When it sold the bond, it received a check from the Fed in payment. When the household deposited this check in its own commercial bank account, its bank was placed in the same position as was the bank in Table 31-3 that received the new deposit from the immigrant. If the central bank buys many securities in the open market, the entire banking system will gain new reserves.

When the central bank buys securities on the open market, the reserves of the commercial banks are increased. These banks can then expand deposits, thereby increasing the money supply.

The response to excess reserves.   Open market purchases by the Fed provide the commercial banks with excess reserves. This permits the banks to create new deposit money by granting new loans and purchasing securities in the manner analyzed in Chapter 31. But there is nothing automatic in this. Banks often hold excess reserves as a matter of policy. For example, banks tend to hold larger excess reserves in times of business recession, when there is a low demand for loans and low interest rates, than they do in periods of boom, when the demand for loans is great and interest rates are high.

The significance of the voluntary holding of excess reserves is that it cuts the automatic link between the creation of excess reserves and money creation.

Excess reserves make it *possible* for the banks to expand the money supply if they wish to do so.

Sales on the Open Market

When the central bank sells a $100 security to a household or firm, it receives in return the buyer's check drawn against its own deposit in a commercial bank. The central bank presents the check to the private bank for payment. Payment is made by a book entry that reduces the private bank's deposit at the central bank.

The changes in this case are the opposite of those shown in Table 33-2. The central bank has reduced its assets by the value of the security it sold and reduced its liabilities in the form of the deposits of commercial banks. The household or firm has increased its holdings of securities and reduced its cash on deposit with a commercial bank. The commercial bank has reduced its deposit liability to the household or firm and reduced its reserves (on deposit with the central bank) by the same amount. Each of the asset changes is balanced by a liability change.

But the commercial bank finds that by suffering an equal change in its reserves and deposit liabilities, its ratio of reserves to deposits falls. Consider, for example, a bank with $10 million in deposits backed by $1 million cash in fulfillment of a 10 percent cash reserve ratio. As a result of the Fed's open market sales of $100,000 worth of bonds, the bank loses $100,000 of deposits and reserves. Reserves are now $900,000 while deposits are $9.9 million, making a reserve ratio of only 9.09 percent.

Banks whose reserve ratios are driven below the minimum requirement must take immediate steps to restore their reserve ratios. The necessary reduction in deposits can be accomplished by not making new investments when old ones are redeemed (e.g., by not granting new loans when old ones are repaid) or by selling (liquidating) existing investments.

When the central bank sells securities on the open market, the reserves of the commercial banks are decreased. These banks in turn are forced to contract deposits, thereby decreasing the money supply.

But what if the public does not wish to buy the securities the Fed wishes to sell? Can it force the public to do so? The answer is that there is always a price at which the public will buy. The Fed in its open market operations must be prepared to have the price of the securities fall if it insists on suddenly selling a large volume of them. As we have seen, a fall in the price of securities is the same thing as a rise in interest rates, so if the Fed wishes to curtail the money supply by selling bonds, it may well drive up interest rates.

Notice in Table 33-1 that the Fed's holdings of government securities are large relative to the reserves of commercial banks. By selling securities it can contract those reserves sharply if it chooses. Similarly, by buying securities it can expand them. In its open market operations the central bank has a potent weapon for affecting the size of member bank reserves—and thus for affecting the money supply.

Other Tools for Influencing the Money Supply

The major tool the Fed uses in conducting monetary policy is its open market operations. But other tools are available and have on occasion been used extensively.

Reserve Requirements

One way that the Fed can control the money supply is by altering the required minimum reserve ratios. Suppose the banking system is "loaned-up"; that is, it has no excess reserves. If the Fed increases the required reserve ratio (say from 20 percent to 25 percent), the dollar amount of reserves held by the commercial banks will no longer be adequate to support their outstanding deposits. Commercial banks will then be forced to reduce their deposits until they achieve the new, higher required reserve ratio.[1] This decrease in demand deposits is a decrease in the money supply. The process is illustrated in Table 33-3.

The effect of a reduction in required reserve ratios

[1] They will do this by gradually decreasing their loans or selling some of their securities. In the short term they may borrow from the Fed to give themselves time to meet the increased reserve requirements without disrupting financial markets.

is also shown in the table. The reduction first creates excess reserves. Of course, if banks choose not to increase their loans, they will not respond to this increase in excess reserves. Normally, however, the profit motive will lead most banks to respond by increasing loans and deposits—and thus lead to an increase in the money supply.

Increases in required reserve ratios force banks with no excess reserves to decrease deposits and thus reduce the money supply. Decreases in required reserve ratios permit banks to expand deposits and thus may increase the money supply.

In 1934 the Federal Reserve Board was given authority by Congress to set within limits required reserve ratios for both demand and time deposits. The Fed has frequently changed reserve requirements within the allowable limits, and Congress has from time to time changed the limits.

In recent times the use of reserve ratio changes has fallen out of favor. The chief argument against manipulating the reserve ratio is that it is a ponderous weapon for changing excess reserves. Open market policy can be applied flexibly to achieve the same effects.

The Discount Rate

The discount rate is the rate at which the Fed will lend funds to member banks who need to replenish their reserves. (When a bill is discounted, it is purchased at a *discount*, i.e., at a price below its redemption value, the difference representing an interest return to the purchaser.) As a matter of policy the Fed discourages long-term borrowing from it by commercial banks, and the reserve banks tend to accommodate requests at their "discount window" only on a short-term basis. Hence the discount rate plays a relatively minor role as a policy tool. It does, however, play an important role in helping banks meet their reserve requirements when open market sales by the Fed cause a sudden contraction of bank reserves. The banks need this temporary help to bridge the gap until they can make longer-term adjustments in their portfolios.

TABLE 33-3(a)	Balance Sheet for a Loaned-Up Banking System with a 20 Percent Reserve Ratio		
Assets		Liabilities	
Reserves	$1,000	Deposits	$5,000
Loans	4,100	Capital	100
	$5,100		$5,100

TABLE 33-3(b)	Balance Sheet for a Loaned-Up Banking System After Responding to a Change in Reserve Ratio to 25 Percent		
Assets		Liabilities	
Reserves	$1,000	Deposits	$4,000
Loans	3,100	Capital	100
	$4,100		$4,100

Increasing the required reserve ratio forces a loaned-up bank to reduce its deposits and thus decreases the supply of deposit money. The banking system in part (a) has a ratio of reserves to deposits of 0.20. If the Fed raises the required reserve ratio to 0.25, the reserves of $1,000 will support deposits of only $4,000. As shown in part (b), the banking system can reduce its deposits by reducing its loans. A reduction in reserve requirements from 0.25 to 0.20 would permit a banking system in the position of (b) to expand its loans and deposits to those of (a) with no increases in its dollar reserves.

The importance of the discount rate is as a signal of the Fed's intentions.

Changes in the discount rate are usually associated with like changes in other interest rates. It is not always clear whether the discount rate follows or leads changes in other interest rates. One reason for the discount rate's following other developments is that open market operations that apply the monetary brakes by selling bonds tend to push up interest rates. To discourage banks from turning to its discount window, the Fed must then raise the discount rate. One reason for the discount rate's leading other rates is that sharp changes in the discount rate often create expectations about the relative abundance or scarcity of funds.

Because the commercial banks do not borrow reserves from the Fed on a long-term basis, it is usual to subtract their borrowed reserves from their total reserves when judging the amount of deposit money that their reserves will maintain. **Net unborrowed reserves,** often also called **free reserves,** are the total reserves of the commercial banking system minus the reserves that have been borrowed from the Fed. Net unborrowed reserves indicate the long-term ability of the banking system to support deposit money. If these free reserves are below the legal minimum, it follows that the banks are meeting their reserve requirements using temporary borrowings from the Fed. Thus the banks will be exerting con-

tractionary pressure on the money supply. They will be trying to reduce their deposits in order to bring their unborrowed reserves up to the legal requirements so that they will be able to pay off their loans from the Fed. If, on the other hand, the banks have an excess of unborrowed reserves over the legal minimum, they are in a position to expand the supply of deposit money.

Selective Credit Controls

Monetary policy seeks to make money and credit generally scarce or plentiful, leaving the private sector to cope with the conditions it creates. **Selective credit controls,** on the other hand, allow the Fed to decide where the initial impact of tight or plentiful credit will be felt. Among the selective controls that have sometimes been used during the postwar period are margin requirements, installment-credit control, mortgage control, and maximum interest rates.

These controls can be powerful. Increasing the down payment required for an installment-plan purchase, for example, can cause a major fall in demand until households accumulate enough money to make the new, larger down payments.

Many selective controls have been used in the United States in the past, and all of them are now in use somewhere in the Western world. In the United States, however, only margin requirements were in use in 1987. Installment-credit controls were dropped after World War II, mortgage controls after 1953, and interest rate ceilings were phased out during the 1980s.

Margin requirements. Stock market speculation can be controlled by the Federal Reserve through its power to regulate the **margin requirement,** which is the fraction of the price of a stock that must be put up by the purchaser. (The balance may be borrowed from the brokerage firm through which the purchaser buys the security.) Since 1960 the margin requirement has varied between 50 percent and 90 percent. Such variations can have a substantial selective effect on stock market activity that is independent of the general credit picture. Thus, if the Federal Reserve wishes to impose moderate credit restraint generally, but is particularly apprehensive about stock market speculation, it may combine a moderate amount of open market selling with a sharp increase in margin requirements.

Moral Suasion

If the commercial banking system is prepared to cooperate, the Federal Reserve banks can operate a tight-money policy merely by asking banks to be conservative in granting loans. When the need for restriction is over, the commercial bankers can then be told that it is all right to grant loans and extend deposits up to the legal maximum.

The use of "moral suasion" does not depend on pure "jawboning." Member banks depend on the Federal Reserve banks for loans, and in the long term noncooperation with the Fed's "suggestions" can prove costly to a bank.

The Monetary Control Act of 1980

In 1980 the American banking system entered an unparalleled period of deregulation under the Depository Institutions Deregulation and Monetary Control Act. The general purpose of the act was "to facilitate the implementation of monetary policy, to provide for a gradual elimination of all limitations on the rates of interest which are payable on deposits and accounts, and to authorize interest-bearing transactions accounts." These deregulations were phased in during the first half of the 1980s.

The act phased out the interest rate ceilings that had existed for certain types of deposits. This made the banking system much more competitive. It also freed monetary policy from the need to offset distortions caused by such regulations as ceilings on deposit interest rates.

The act also set the same reserve requirements for all banks, large or small and members of the Federal Reserve System or not, thus eliminating the preferential treatment given previously to small banks who faced lower reserve requirements. A bank's reserve requirements were set at 3 percent against its first $25 million in demand deposits (and other accounts subject to direct or indirect transfer by check) and at a ratio to be determined by the Fed (between the limits of 8 percent and 14 percent) on demand deposits in excess of $25 million. The ratio on time deposits is to be set by the Fed between the limits of 3 percent and 9 percent.

The Fed was also given the power to require that all banks hold up to 4 percent additional reserves, provided that "the sole purpose of such requirements is to increase the amount of reserves maintained to a level essential for the conduct of monetary policy." This instrument is copied from one long used by the Bank of England to prevent deposit expansion when commercial banks unexpectedly find themselves with excess reserves at a time when the central bank does not deem monetary expansion desirable.

The act also initiated a phasing out of the interest rate ceilings that, as discussed above, had existed for certain types of deposits. The act made the banking system much more competitive. It also freed monetary policy from the need to offset distortions caused by such regulations as ceilings on deposit interest rates.

Instruments and Objectives of Monetary Policy

The Fed conducts monetary policy in order to influence real national income and the price level. These ultimate objectives of the Fed's policy are called **policy variables.** The variables that it controls *directly* in order to achieve these objectives are called its **policy instruments.** Variables that are neither policy variables nor policy instruments, but that nevertheless can play a key role in the execution of monetary policy are called **intermediate targets;** their importance lies in the influence they exert on the policy variables.

Policy Variables

The Fed's twin policy variables are national income and the price level. In practice the two are often lumped into a single variable, nominal national income.

Nominal national income as a policy variable. Changes in nominal national income reflect changes both in real national income and in the price level. In principle the central bank will be concerned about how a given change in nominal national income is divided between these two components.

We saw in Chapter 32, however, that monetary policy operates by influencing aggregate demand, and in the short run, the effects of a monetary policy that shifts the *AD* curve will be divided between the price level and real output in a manner determined by the slope of the *SRAS* curve. Thus, while the central bank cares about the separate reactions of the price level and of real output, there is little it can do in the short run to achieve such goals independently. For any price level response that is achieved, the real output consequence must be accepted. Alternatively, for any real output response that is achieved, the price level consequence must be accepted. Monetary policy is not capable of pursuing two objectives of pushing the price level (P) and national income (Y) toward independently determined targets. For this reason the Fed tends to focus on nominal national income (PY) as the target for monetary policy in the short run.

The price level as the policy variable in the long run. We have seen that in the long run, when the level of wages is fully adjusted to the price level, the *LRAS* curve is vertical and hence the major impact of monetary policy will be on the price level.

While monetary policy influences both real output and the price level in the short run, its main effects in the long run are only on the price level.

Policy Instruments

Having selected its policy variables and formulated targets for their behavior, the Fed must decide how to achieve these targets. How can the policy variables be made to perform in the way that the Fed wishes? Since the Fed can control neither income nor the price level directly, it must employ its policy instruments, which it does control directly, to influence aggregate demand in the desired manner.

The primary instrument used by the Fed to conduct monetary policy is open market operations.

Open market operations change the size of the Fed's monetary liabilities which are the currency in circulation plus reserves of the commercial banks. Commercial bank reserves are held on deposit with the Fed and they are the Fed's liability because it must redeem them on demand. The Fed's monetary liabilities, as we saw in Chapter 31, form the *base* on which commercial banks can expand and create deposits. For this reason their liabilities are often referred to as the **monetary base.**

The central bank cannot expect to be able to use its open market operations to control both the interest rate and the monetary base independently. This is because of the liquidity preference function, which relates the quantity of money to the rate of interest.

The Fed must therefore choose between two alternative procedures in conducting its open market operations. It may set the *price* (and hence the interest rate) at which it sells or buys bonds on the open market. In this case the quantity of bonds sold or purchased is determined by market demand. If the Fed wishes to change its policy, it must change the price at which it is willing to buy and sell bonds. This approach is called **interest rate control**, and here the interest rate is properly viewed as a policy instrument.

Alternatively, the Fed may choose to set the *quantity* of open market sales or purchases. It does this in order to set the reserves of the commercial banks. In this case it is the price of bonds, and hence the interest rate, that is determined by market demand. If the Fed wishes to change its policy, it changes the amount of its open market purchases or sales. (Of course, this means that the interest rate at which these transactions are made may also change.) In this case, where the Fed chooses to set the quantity of its open market operations, it is directly deciding how much the monetary base will change. For this reason it is said to be using **base control**, and the monetary base is properly viewed as the policy instrument.

Intermediate Targets

Major changes in the direction or method of monetary policy usually are made only infrequently. Decisions regarding the implementation of policy must, however, be made almost daily. Given the values that the Fed wishes its policy variables to take on, and given the current state of the economy, is a purchase or a sale in the open market called for? How big a purchase? Or how big a sale? At what interest rate? Such questions must be answered continually by the Fed in its day-to-day operations.

While these decisions have to be made on a day-to-day basis, daily information about the policy variables is rarely available. Inflation and unemployment rates are available only on a monthly basis and with a considerable lag. National income figures are available even less frequently; they appear on a quarterly basis. Thus the policymakers do not know exactly what is happening to the policy variables when they make decisions regarding their policy instruments.

How, then, does the Fed make decisions? Central banks have typically used *intermediate targets* to guide them when implementing monetary policy in the very short run. To serve as an intermediate target, a variable must satisfy two criteria. First, information about it must be available on a frequent basis, daily if possible. Second, its movements must be closely correlated with those of the policy variable so that changes in it can reasonably be expected to indicate that the policy variable is also changing.

The two most commonly used intermediate targets have been the money supply and the interest rate. Since the two are not independent of each other, it is important that the central bank not choose a target for one that is inconsistent with the other. By the same token, since the two are closely related, it might appear not to matter much which one is used.

For example, if the Fed wishes to remove an inflationary gap by forcing interest rates up, it will sell securities and thus drive their prices down. These open market sales will also contract the money supply. It is largely immaterial whether the Fed seeks to force interest rates up or to contract the money supply; doing one accomplishes the other. Similarly, driving interest rates down by open market purchases of government securities will tend to expand the money supply as the public gains money in return for the securities it sells to the Fed.

In spite of what we have just said, there are differences between a monetary regime where interest rates are taken as the intermediate target and a regime that uses the money supply as target.

The choice of intermediate targets.   Over the years there has been controversy over the intermediate target that the Fed should most rely upon. Throughout the earlier part of the postwar period, the Fed relied mainly on interest rates.

A long-standing attack was mounted by monetarists against the Fed's use of the interest rate as its intermediate target. These economists pointed out that, since interest rates tended to vary directly with the business cycle, rising on the upswing and falling on the downswing, it was difficult for the Fed to determine the impact of its monetary policy by observing the interest rate alone. Historical examples were pointed to where the Fed tried to restrain a boom and was lulled into thinking that its policy was pushing toward restraint by the observation that the interest rate was rising sharply. In retrospect it was concluded, however, that the expansion occurring at the time was an unusually strong one. The resulting unusually high demand for money was pushing up interest rates.

As a result of such criticisms, the Fed turned to rely almost exclusively on the narrow monetary aggregate M1. When M1 turned out to be a less than completely reliable guide, broader monetary aggregates were used.

Today, however, after a decade's experience with such aggregates, similar criticisms can be levied at the Fed's exclusive concentration on them. The reason is that changes in the money supply are reliable indicators of the direction of monetary policy *only* if the demand for money is relatively stable. Experience of the past decade suggests that the demand for money can change quite substantially and that the Fed can discover what is happening to this demand only after much time-consuming research. Critics of the use of monetary aggregates as intermediate variables can point to historical circumstances in which the Fed incorrectly thought it was exerting a restraining force on the economy through a restrictive monetary policy because monetary aggregates were growing slowly. In retrospect, however, it turned out that monetary policy had been expansionary. There was an excess supply rather than an excess demand for money, the reason being that the demand for money had fallen more than had been appreciated at the time.

Operating Regime

A central bank's **operating regime** refers to the combination that it selects of intermediate targets and policy instruments used to achieve those targets.

Table 33-4 illustrates some possible operating regimes for the central bank. If the Fed chooses the interest rate as its intermediate target, it can achieve that target directly by using interest rate control as its instrument. In this case the distinction between intermediate target and policy instrument is superfluous. If the Fed chooses the money supply as its intermediate target, it can achieve its target indirectly by means of either base control or interest rate control. The somewhat confusing multiple roles that can be played by the various economic variables are clarified in the table and summarized as follows.

Nominal national income is a policy variable. The money supply can be an intermediate target or a policy instrument. The interest rate can be a policy variable, an intermediate target, or a policy instrument.

Monetary Policy in Action

Having studied its objectives and instruments, we may now consider how monetary policy has actually worked in the period since World War II. The Federal Open Market Committee (FOMC) generally meets every four weeks; its decisions are embodied in a directive issued to the Federal Reserve Bank of New York. Open market operations are conducted in the New York Fed by the manager of the system's Open Market Account.

Changing Targets

In common with many of the world's central banks, the Fed has more than once changed the variables that are its policy objectives and its intermediate targets.

The Accord: From Interest Rate to Income and Prices As Policy Objectives

The use of monetary policy as a tool of stabilization policy in the postwar period began in 1951 with the famous Treasury–Federal Reserve Accord. Under this agreement the Federal Reserve discontinued the practice, which grew up during World War II, of supporting the prices of treasury securities so as to hold down interest rates that had to be paid on the enormous amounts of government borrowing needed to finance the war effort. This practice meant that the Fed held the interest rate down, thereby reducing the cost of servicing the debt, and that it supplied new money to buy any part of a government debt issue that the public would not buy at the fixed rate of interest. This policy made the interest rate the Fed's main policy goal. An implication was that the Fed had no control over the money supply. Indeed, whenever the government demand to borrow was too heavy to be met by private lending at the going rate of interest, the Fed expanded the money supply rapidly, with serious inflationary consequences.

The basic concern of monetary policy since the accord has been the achievement of such policy objectives as full employment and price stability. This makes real national income and the price level the policy variables. We have seen, however, that to make these broader economic objectives operational the FOMC must be able to relate them to the intermediate targets over which the Fed has a direct influence.

From the Interest Rate to M1 As Intermediate Target

Prior to 1970 the operating instructions of the FOMC were generally couched in terms of money-market conditions (that is, short-term interest rates), borrowing by member banks from the Federal Reserve, and the net unborrowed reserve position of

TABLE 33-4   Assignment of Variables Under Alternative Operating Regimes of Monetary Policy

Regime	Policy instrument	Intermediate target	Policy variable
1. Monetary targeting— base control	Open market operations: regulate volume of open market sales and purchases	Quantity of money (M1) via money supply process	
2. Monetary targeting— interest rate control	Open market operations: regulate price at which open market sales and purchases are made (i.e., regulate interest rate)	Quantity of money (M1) via liquidity preference	1. Real national income and the price level or 2. Nominal national income
3. Interest rate targeting	Open market operations: regulate intermediate target directly	Interest rates	

Even with a given set of policy variables, central banks might adopt a variety of operating regimes. The central bank could use either the quantity of money or the interest rate as its intermediate target.

When the central bank opts for monetary targeting, it can influence its target only indirectly. Through its open market operations it can control directly either the size of the monetary base or the level of interest rates. If it controls the monetary base (regime 1), the quantity of money is influenced via the money supply process, while the interest rate is determined via monetary equilibrium as in Figure 32-2. If the central bank controls the interest rate (regime 2), the influence on the quantity of money operates via the liquidity preference function.

Should the central bank choose to use the interest rate as an intermediate target (regime 3), it can achieve its target directly by using open market operations to control the interest rate. Although this appears to be a simpler process (and in terms of operation, it is simpler), many economists favor monetary targeting.

Other variables, such as the interest rate and the exchange rate, might also appear as policy variables. The interest rate could then appear as a policy instrument, an intermediate target, or a policy variable, depending on the policy regime.

member banks. Some references were made to monetary aggregates, but they were generally confined to statements concerning the desired behavior of bank credit.

In the 1970s monetary aggregates came to play a more prominent role, and the emphasis shifted from intermediate targets that were specified in terms of money-market conditions to targets specified in terms of rates of growth of the money supply. At the outset the measure used for this purpose was the narrowly defined money supply M1.

The shift to greater emphasis on controlling the money supply on the part of the Federal Reserve reflected the growing influence of the monetarist view within the economics profession.

Monetary targets are usually stated in nominal terms. The nominal money supply is targeted to grow by such and such a percent, which translates into an increase of so many dollars. To judge the expansionary or contractionary force of monetary policy over a particular period, it is often useful to look at the rate of growth of the real money supply, the nominal money supply divided by an index of the price level. In the absence of a major downward shift in the demand function for money, a reduction in the real money supply is almost certain to be contractionary. For example, if the price level rises by 14 percent and the nominal money supply rises by only 10 percent, the contraction in the real money supply almost certainly reflects a money shortage. Interest rates will rise and this will exert a contractionary pressure on the economy. On the other hand, the same money growth rate of 10 percent combined with a zero rate of inflation would, in the absence of shifts in the demand for money in excess of what would be accounted for by the growth of real income, be expansionary. It would create an excess supply of money and put downward pressure on interest rates, which would exert expansionary pressure on the economy.

From Interest Rate Control to Base Control

In 1980 the Fed also switched from a regime of interest rate control to a regime of base control. Although this policy requires that interest rates be free to find their own level, many economists did not expect the degree of interest rate volatility shown in Figure 33-1. The sharp rise in interest rates in late 1980 helped choke off the recovery that had just started. The rise in rates in early 1982 accentuated the downturn and helped turn it into the most serious recession since the 1930s. Inflation responded dra-

matically, falling from about 9 percent in 1981 to about 4 percent in 1982, and this led to a significant fall in interest rates over the last half of 1982.

From One to Many Aggregates As Intermediate Targets

Dissatisfaction with M1 as an intermediate target led the Fed, along with many other central banks throughout the world, to regard M2 as a more important intermediate variable than M1 and to watch several monetary indicators rather than just one. What were the major reasons why the Fed came to mistrust exclusive use of M1 as the intermediate target of monetary policy? They are, as we shall see next, closely related to the high degree of substitutability between M1 and other financial assets.

Misreading the effects of monetary policy.   The first effect of contractionary open market operations by the Fed is for interest rates to rise. Until recently, the rates that could be paid on demand deposits were controlled so that as interest rates rose, demand deposits became less attractive compared to other ways of holding money balances. For example, a rise in interest rates paid on savings deposits may lead people to transfer part of their transactions balances out of demand and into savings deposits (and put up with the inconvenience of having fewer demand deposits for immediate transactions purposes). This shift out of demand deposits reduces the recorded increase in M1 during the period over which it occurs. This in turn may suggest that monetary policy is more restrictive than it really is. In spite of the behavior of M1, there is in fact no shortage of money, only a slight change in the form in which transactions balances are being held.

Exclusive concentration on rigid targets for M1 could give a misleading impression that monetary policy has had an effective influence on the economy when all that the policy has done is to induce shifts of assets among M1, M2, and M3.

Inadvertent shifts in monetary policy.   An inflation is in effect a tax on non-interest bearing monetary assets whose real value, measured in purchasing

FIGURE 33-1   Monthly Short-Term Interest Rates, 1977–1986

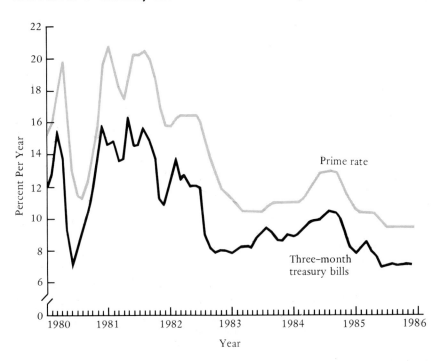

Short-term interest rates were high but variable in the period 1980 to 1982. Short-term interest rates displayed a gradual upward trend from 1978 through 1980. Tight monetary policy following the Monetary Control Act of 1980 led to sharp interest-rate cycles and high average interest rates.

power, depreciates by the amount that prices rise. When the inflation slows, the tax diminishes and people become much more willing to hold M1 balances for the convenience that they provide. When funds are transferred out of other assets and into M1, there is a large rise in the rate of growth of narrowly defined money. For example, when the inflation rate tumbled in 1982 and 1983, the demand for M1 balances rose greatly. As the public transferred funds from other financial assets into demand deposits, the quantity of existing M1 balances also rose greatly.

At that time the Fed was trying to follow a rigid target for the growth of M1. Meeting this target in the face of the transfer of funds into M1 balances would have required a very restrictive monetary policy in order to halt the rapid growth of these balances. Critics of such a policy argued that meeting

rigid M1 targets would have put major contractionary pressure on the economy because the observed growth in M1 was in response to an increase in demand for such balances, which was not in itself expansionary. These critics called for an accommodating monetary policy that would allow M1 to expand to meet the new demand. This, they argued, would put neither contractionary nor expansionary pressure on the economy because such pressures arise, as we saw in Chapter 32, from a disequilibrium between the demand for and the supply of money. Eventually, the Fed accepted the counsel of these critics. It allowed the money supply to expand to accommodate the increase in demand and, in spite of dire predictions of an inflationary expansion from some advocates of an absolutely rigid monetary target, no undue increase in aggregate demand ensued (in conformity with the predictions of the theory of the transmission mechanism).

Similar problems had arisen in earlier times. Indeed several times in the 1970s institutional innovations have caused major shifts between the demands for some of the assets that are included in the wider definitions of money but not in the narrow definition. For example, various types of money management techniques and the development of overnight markets for funds made it profitable for firms to transfer transactions balances that were unneeded even for a matter of hours out of demand deposits and into other highly liquid interest-earning assets. This led to major reductions in the demand for M1. These reductions created an excess supply of M1 which was expansionary. In these circumstances the growth of M1 balances was a poor indicator of the expansionary or contractionary force of current monetary policy. (Recall, as we saw in Chapter 32, that a fall in the demand for money can start the transmission mechanism working in an expansionary direction just as can an increase in the supply of money.)

Exclusive concentration on rigid targets for M1 can lead to inadvertent changes in monetary policy which are contractionary when the demand for M1 increases and expansionary when the demand for M1 diminishes.

The interest rate as one indicator. For all of the above reasons, concentrating on just one measure of the money supply can be misleading. Furthermore, since there are times when the demands for all the assets that are broadly defined as money are increasing or decreasing together, there are times when the current state of monetary policy needs to be gauged by measures other than money supply magnitudes. For example, all measures of money supply suggested a fairly tight monetary policy during the last half of the 1970s. But because of shifts in the demand for money that were not fully appreciated, monetary policy was much more expansionary than it seemed to be at the time. More attention to interest rates would have given an important signal of this. In 1977 and 1978, when the real money supply hardly grew at all as measured by M1 and grew only modestly as

measured by M3, short-term real interest rates were negative.[2] The rate of increase of prices exceeded the short-term interest rates so that, in purchasing power terms, lenders were paying borrowers for the privilege of lending money to them! A negative real interest rate will rarely, if ever, accompany a contractionary monetary policy. Thus although, as we argued earlier, the exclusive use of interest rates as the intermediate target can be misleading, to ignore the information that can be obtained from the behavior of interest rates can also lead to errors.

The Use of Monetary Policy Since the Accord

Figure 33-2 shows the behavior of M1 and of M2. Although the two measures differ sharply in behavior in any given year, two things stand out. First, by either measure monetary growth has shown sharp, short-period changes—from being quite expansive to being highly restrictive. Second, by either measure there was a steady upward trend in the rate of monetary expansion, which continued through the 1970s but was finally reversed sometime in the first half of the 1980s.

The Variability of Monetary Policy

From 1952 to 1967 the sharp variations in the rate of growth of the money supply resulted primarily from the Fed's attempt to use monetary policy to fine tune the economy. At best, such a policy is fraught with dangers. The problems come mainly from the lags between a change in the policy instruments and the reaction of the policy variables that the Fed wishes to control. The way in which long lags can make stabilization policy become destabilizing has already been discussed in Chapter 32 in the context of fiscal policy, and it is further discussed in Box 33-1 on pages 674–675 in the context of monetary policy.

A further telling criticism is that the policy shifts themselves were so abrupt that they added to the inherent difficulties of operating a policy of monetary

---

[2] The importance of distinguishing between nominal and real interest rates is discussed in Box 29-1 on page 550.

FIGURE 33-2 Monetary Growth, 1960–1985

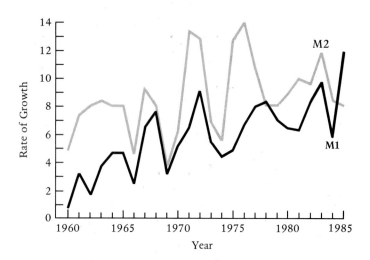

The rate of monetary expansion has shown substantial short-term variability combined with a strong long-term upward trend. The annual rate of growth is shown for money narrowly defined, M1, and the broader monetary aggregate, M2. Although for any given year fluctuations in the two are not closely related, both exhibit the same general pattern.

fine tuning. Policy typically oscillated from "full ahead" to "hard astern." The recessions of 1954–1955, 1957–1958, 1960–1961, and 1969–1970 caused the Fed to respond with expansionary monetary policies. Then when inflation increased during the later recovery phases, monetary policy typically turned sharply contractionary. Given the lags in the effects of monetary policy, it appears that what the Fed thought was a stabilizing policy actually helped to destabilize the economy, accentuating the upswings and then contributing to the downswings of the business cycle.

In 1976 and 1977 the Fed pursued an expansionary monetary policy. Then, worried about renewed inflation, it turned to a severely contractionary policy in 1979; for the three years 1979 to 1981, the rate of growth of real M1 was negative.

Most observers agree that monetary policy was often inadvertently perverse throughout the period from 1929 to 1980. A series of alternating expansionary and contractionary policies augmented the economy's natural cyclical swings.

Several economists have spoken of "this incredible series of self-inflicted wounds." In a detailed study of the mid 1970s, Professor Alan Blinder of Princeton University says that monetary policy in the period "bears eloquent witness to the monetarists' incessant complaint that policy is too variable, too apt to swing from one extreme to another. It is true that whenever monetary policy departed notably from what a fixed rule would have called for, it did so in the wrong direction and made things worse than they need to have been."[3]

The Rising Trend of Monetary Expansion, 1960–1979

As shown in Figure 33-2, fluctuations in monetary expansion from 1960 to 1979 occurred around a rising trend. This trend accompanied a similar rising trend in prices, indicating an unmistakable correlation between the rate of monetary expansion and the rate of inflation.

Monetarists believe that monetary expansion was the main cause of inflation in the 1970s, while other economists believe that the monetary expansion was mainly a passive reaction to price increases caused by

[3] Alan S. Blinder, *Economic Policy and the Great Stagflation* (New York: Academic Press, 1979), p. 201.

aggregate supply shocks in 1974 and 1979. Either way there is no doubt that the inflation of the 1970s was accompanied by monetary expansion. Most economists argued that there was little chance of reducing inflation to the relatively modest levels of the 1950s and 1960s until the rate of monetary expansion was reduced to the more modest annual rates of those years. A reduction in the rate of monetary expansion followed by a dramatic reduction in the rate of inflation is just what did happen in the first half of the 1980s.

A Contractionary Monetary Policy, 1979–1982

In 1979, concerned over the acceleration of the inflation rate, the Fed tightened its monetary policy. As already mentioned, the rate of growth of M1 balances was drastically reduced, while interest rates began a climb to unprecedented levels. For example, the *prime rate*, which is the rate charged by banks to their most favored customers, topped 20 percent in December 1980 and stayed over that figure for most of 1981. Combined with an inflation rate of about 9 percent, this represented a real rate of over 11 percent. In a sequence of events to be studied in more detail in Chapter 34, inflation came down dramatically and finally fell to levels not seen since the beginning of the 1970s. This victory was bought, however, at the cost of the most severe recession since the 1930s.

In retrospect it seems that the contractionary monetary policy was somewhat more severe than the Fed had intended. The reason lies, to some extent at least, in the unprecedented variations in the rate of growth of demand for M1 balances. The Fed used past experience to estimate how fast this demand would grow as national income grew. The Fed then set its target for the growth in the supply of M1 at a level sufficient to meet this demand at a steadily rising level of income. In this period, however, there was an unexpected surge in the growth of demand for M1 that created a severe excess demand, even though the Fed met its money supply targets. The result was rapidly rising interest rates and severe contractionary pressures on national income.

A heated debate ensued. Many observers urged the Fed to protect against a deep recession by accommodating the upsurge in money demand with an increase in supply. (Recall that an increased supply of money that merely meets an increased demand does not cause expansionary pressure through the transmission mechanism.) The Fed, however, decided to stick to its original targets and severe contractionary pressure resulted.

It is clear that the performance of monetary policy would have been improved had the monetary targets been revised to offset the *shifts* in money demand. But separating permanent shifts from temporary shifts, or just errors in the data, is possible only after intensive study. This makes the implementation of monetary policy extremely difficult. It has also made economists, and many central bankers, pessimistic not only about the role of monetary rules, but also about the usefulness of the money supply as an intermediate target. Indeed, the Fed temporarily abandoned explicit targets in late 1982. They were reinstated early in 1983, but with a change from M1 to M2 as the prime target. The hope was that the demand for M2 would prove to be more stable than that for M1 and hence that movements in M2 would prove to be more valuable as an intermediate target for monetary policy.

The Recovery Period, 1983–1986

In late 1982 the economy began a long period of recovery that, by mid 1986, had taken national income much of the way back toward its potential level. Although painfully slow, especially for those who were still unemployed, the American recovery was much more rapid than the recovery in many of the other developed industrial countries, including Australia, Canada, and most of the countries of Western Europe.

In a debate that we have discussed earlier in this section, some economists advocated that the Fed stick rigidly to long-range money growth targets even during the recovery period, but the Fed did not follow this advice. Instead, it largely accommodated the major increases in the demand for money that occurred for two separate reasons. First, the fall of inflation from two-digit to very low levels removed most of the inflationary tax on holding M1 balances

BOX 33-1

How Monetary Policy Can Be Destabilizing

In the real world the full effects of monetary policy occur only after quite long time lags, *Execution lags,* lags that occur after the decision is made to implement the policy, can have important implications for the conduct of monetary policy.

Sources of Execution Lags

1. Open market operations affect the reserves of the chartered banks. The full increase in the money supply occurs only when the banks have granted enough new loans and made enough investments to expand the money supply by the full amount permitted by existing reserve ratios. This process can take quite a long time.
2. The division of all assets into just two categories, money and bonds, is useful for showing the underlying forces at work in determining the demand for money. In fact, however, there is a whole series of assets—from currency and demand deposits to term deposits, to treasury bills and short-term bonds, to long-term bonds and equities. When households find themselves with larger money balances than they require, a chain of substitution occurs, with short-term and long-term interest rates falling as households try to hold less money and more interest-earning assets. The change in longer-term interest rates in turn affects interest-sensitive expenditures. These adjustments along a chain of interest rates can take considerable time to work out.
3. It takes time for new investment plans to be drawn up, approved, and put into effect. It may easily take up to a year before the full increase in investment expenditure builds up in response to a fall in interest rates.
4. The increased investment expenditures set off a multiplier process that increases national income by some multiple of the initiating increase in investment expenditure. This, too, takes some time to work out.

Similar considerations apply to contractionary monetary policies that seek to shift the aggregate expenditure function downward.

Furthermore, although the end result is fairly predictable, the speed with which the entire expansionary or contractionary process works itself out can vary from time to time in ways that are hard to predict.

Monetary policy is capable of exerting expansionary and contractionary forces on the economy, but it operates with a time lag that is long and unpredictably variable.

Implications of Execution Lags

To see the significance of execution lags for the conduct of monetary policy, assume that the execution lag is 18 months. If on December 1 the Fed decides that the economy needs stimulus, it can be increasing the money supply within days, and by the end of the year a significant increase may be registered.

But because the full effects of this policy take time to work out, the policy may prove to be destabilizing. By the fall of next year a substantial inflationary gap may have developed due to cyclical forces unrelated to the Fed's monetary policy. The Fed may then call for a contractionary policy, but the full effects of the monetary expansion initiated nine months earlier are just being felt, so an expansionary monetary stimulus is adding to the existing inflationary gap. If the Fed now applies the monetary brakes by contracting the money supply, the full effects of this move will not be felt for another 18 months. By that time a

and thus increased demand for M1. Accommodating this extra demand was not expansionary since its source was merely a reallocation of total demand from M3 to M1. Second, the recovery of national income toward its potential level meant an increased demand for transactions balances. Had the Fed chosen not to accommodate the increased demand, it would have put severe contractionary pressure on

the economy. This would have slowed the recovery, if not stopping it altogether.

The Fed continued to see its main policy variables behave satisfactorily during the recovery. National income rose, while inflation stayed below 4 percent. What were the most important developments over this period of sustained recovery without major inflation?

contraction may have already set in because of the natural cyclical forces of the economy. If so, the delayed effects of the monetary policy may turn a minor downturn into a major recession.

The long execution lag of monetary policy makes monetary fine tuning difficult, and it may make it destabilizing.

If the execution lag were known with certainty, it could be built into the Fed's calculations. But the fact that the lag is highly variable makes this nearly impossible. Of course, when a persistent gap has existed and is predicted to continue for a long time, monetary policy may be stabilizing even when its effects occur after a long-time lag.

A Monetary Rule?

The poor record of monetary policy as a short-run stabilizer has lent force to the monetarists' persistent criticisms of monetary fine tuning. Monetarists argue that (1) monetary policy is a potent force of expansionary and contractionary pressures; (2) monetary policy works with lags that are both long and variable; and (3) the Fed is in fact given to sudden and sharp reversals of its policy stance. Consequently, monetary policy has a destabilizing effect on the economy, the policy itself accentuating rather than dampening the economy's natural cyclical swings.

Monetarists argue from this position that the stability of the economy would be much improved if the Fed stopped trying to stabilize it. What then should the Fed do? Since growth of population and of productivity lead to a rising level of output, the Fed ought to provide the extra money needed to allow the holding of additional transactions, precautionary, and speculative balances as real income and wealth rise over time.

According to the monetarists, the Fed should expand the money supply year in and year out at a constant rate equal to the rate of growth of real income. When the growth rate shows signs of long-term change, the Fed can adjust its rate of monetary expansion. It should not, however, alter this rate with a view to stabilizing the economy against short-term fluctuations.

Economists have conducted a long debate over this monetarist recommendation. The outcome is that, at least in many standard models of the economy, the best fine tuning policy can reduce cyclical fluctuations below what they would have been under constant-rate rule. However:

Experience of the 1970s convinced many that whatever may be true of the best conceivable monetary policy, the Fed's actual policy made cyclical fluctuations larger than they would have been under a constant-rate rule.

Subsequent experience has shown, however, that the demand for money can sometimes shift quite substantially. A stable money supply rule in the face of demand instability guarantees monetary shocks, rather than monetary stability.

Insofar as one monetary magnitude was to be considered more important than the others, it became accepted that a broader magnitude than M1 was appropriate. Important changes in monetary conditions from the supply side were more likely to be reflected by changes in M2 or M3 than M1.

The search for a single monetary aggregate to be *the* correct intermediate target was slowly abandoned. Gradually, it became accepted that the economy was too complicated for a single magnitude to provide all the information that the Fed needed in developing an effective monetary policy. The high degree of substitutability among M1, M2, and M3 meant that all three magnitudes needed to be surveyed for the information that they could give to the Fed. Furthermore, institutional developments meant that the degree of substitutability was subject to continual change so that no one magnitude could be taken as a proxy for all three.

It also came to be accepted that the behavior of interest rates conveyed information that might not be available from monetary aggregates alone. For example, in the mid 1980s real interest rates were high by historical standards. A goal of monetary policy, therefore, became to create the stable conditions that would allow interest rates to return to more normal levels, but to do this without rekindling inflationary expectations. The important lesson was also drawn from the earlier period of the 1970s that, even if all the monetary aggregates are only increasing slowly, real interest rates that are low or negative, as they often were, cannot be the symptom of a tight monetary policy. Thus the combination of low rates of growth of monetary aggregates and unusually low interest rates probably indicates major reductions in the demand for money and, hence, that monetary policy is more expansionary than the behavior of any monetary aggregate would reveal.

New goals of monetary policy in addition to the traditional ones of income and price level have emerged. The two new goals of greatest importance were the health of the financial system and the behavior of the exchange rate.

1. The enormous debt that third world countries, particularly oil exporters, piled up in the 1970s became unsustainable in the 1980s. (See the further discussion in Chapter 42.) Much of this debt was owed to banks in the developed countries, with the United States being the most important single debtor country. As oil revenues fell, these oil-exporting countries found it impossible to pay the interest on their debt without further loans, let alone trying to repay any of the principal. The Fed became acutely aware that a sudden default of these debtor countries could cause a financial crisis in the banking system. It also became aware that every time the interest rate rose 1 percent, the burden on these debtor countries was measured in billions of dollars of extra payments. There is no hope that these countries can ever generate the revenues necessary to repay the principal of these loans. What the banking community of the developed world could at most try to do was to delay the final day of reckoning by re-

scheduling some of the loans and lending some of the money needed to repay the remaining interest until the major banks could adjust their portfolios sufficiently to write off enormous amounts of loans without going into insolvency.

2. The exchange rate became an important variable for the Fed in the mid 1980s. For decades most of the world's central banks have had to have exchange rate policies, but the Fed has only recently needed to be concerned with the effect of the exchange rate on the competitive position of the U.S. economy. (This issue is further discussed in Chapter 41.) The Fed can no longer worry only about domestic variables. The behavior of the exchange rate influences the health of American industries that either export or compete with imports and therefore has an important influence on domestic economic performance.

The Fed seems to have come more and more to take nominal national income as its target variable. In the past the Fed has often concentrated on the twin goals of real national income as its goal of stabilization policy (remove recessionary or inflationary gaps) and on the price level as its traditional goal of preserving the purchasing power of the nation's currency. Recently, however, the understanding has spread that Fed can, at best, influence the aggregate demand curve and how this influence divides itself between income and the price level depends on the shape of the aggregate supply curve, which is beyond the Fed's control. The Fed is still concerned with the long-term trend in the price level as its most important goal, but in the shorter term it seems to accept that it can influence nominal national income and adjust its policies to the behavior of that variable, which is a composite of changes in real income and the price level.

As the enormous Federal budget deficit is reduced, there is a need for the Fed to adopt a compensating monetary policy. The reduction in the deficit means some combination of tax increases and expenditure decreases on the part of the government. As we saw in Chapter 30, both of these changes reduce aggregate demand and tend to contract economic activity. To offset these forces, the Fed can engage in a once-and-for-all monetary expansion. As we saw in Chapter 32, this increases aggregate demand. There is no reason in theory why a change in the *mix* of macroeconomic policy to a more restrictive fiscal policy and a more expansionary monetary policy cannot leave the level of aggregate demand unchanged. This would mean that the policy changes did not significantly affect either national income or the price level. This shift in policy mix requires that the Fed be willing to play a more sophisticated role than merely following blind rules for the growth of monetary aggregates. This is a role that some would say is fraught with dangers of trying to do things that are beneficial in theory but that, given the imperfections of practical policy, may turn out to be harmful in practice—harmful in the specific way of increasing inflationary pressures. Whether or not this is a serious worry should become apparent by the end of the decade.

Monetary Policy: Agreements and Disagreements

Most economists agree that rapid changes in the money supply have major effects on aggregate demand. They also agree that avoiding rapid rates of monetary expansion is a necessary condition for avoiding rapid inflations. Furthermore, many economists hold that, given sufficient knowledge, changes in the money supply could be used to help in the government's efforts to stabilize the economy by avoiding the extremes of large inflationary and recessionary gaps.

There is disagreement, however, on a number of important issues that we summarize here and discuss in more detail in Part Ten.

1. Is control of the money supply a sufficient means of controlling inflation? Some economists answer yes. Others think not and look to causes of inflation in addition to excessive monetary expansion.
2. How strong is the influence of monetary policy on aggregate expenditure? Do small changes in the money supply yield large changes in aggregate expenditure, or are large changes in monetary magnitudes needed to induce desired changes in aggregated expenditure?
3. If stabilization policy is to be used, what are the appropriate relative roles of monetary and fiscal policies? At one extreme some economists give monetary policy a relatively minor role as a supplement to fiscal policy; at the other extreme some economists give it the exclusive role, arguing that fiscal policy is effective only to the extent that it causes changes in the money supply.
4. Although experience from the mid 1940s to the mid 1970s convinced many economists that monetary policy had in fact been a serious destabilizer, controversy continues on the conclusion to be drawn. Should we give up trying to follow a discretionary monetary stabilization policy and instead adopt a fixed rule of monetary expansion, or should we merely try to do better with discretionary policy next time?
5. With continued financial innovation and shifts in demands for various monetary assets, what are the appropriate intermediate variables for monetary policy? Will any conceivable monetary rule have a stabilizing effect on the economy? In adopting such a rule, won't the Fed then have to alter continually both the magnitude on which it is targeting and the range of values targeted?

Summary

1. The central bank of the United States is the set of Federal Reserve banks and its board of governors. Although technically private, the Reserve banks in fact belong to a system that functions as a central bank that administers the nation's monetary policy. Effective power is exercised by the board of governors, whose seven members are appointed by the president of the United States for 14-year terms.
2. The Fed can affect the adequacy of the reserves of the commercial banking system in many ways. Among other things it can change required reserves, change the rate of interest at which it will lend to commercial banks, and rely on open market operations.
3. The major policy instrument used by the Fed is open market op-

erations. The purchase of bonds on the open market is expansionary because it increases reserves, permitting (but not forcing) a multiple expansion of bank deposits and hence of the money supply. The sale of bonds on the open market reduces bank reserves, forcing a multiple contraction of bank deposits on the part of all banks that do not have excess reserves.

4. The ultimate objectives of the Fed's monetary policy are called its policy variables. In principle these include real national income and the rate of change of the price level. However, in practice nominal income is often taken to be the policy variable in the short term since the Fed cannot expect to be able to influence the composition of changes in nominal income between real growth and inflation.

5. Where the Fed cannot influence its policy variables directly, it must work through policy instruments that it can control and that will in turn influence its policy variables. Intermediate targets are used to guide decisions about policy instruments. The money supply and the interest rate may both be either intermediate targets or policy instruments.

6. National income can be influenced by open market operations. Since it cannot control both independently, the Fed must choose between the interest rate and the money supply as the intermediate target of such operations. To reduce national income the Fed sells bonds on the open market, thereby reducing bank reserves, driving up the rate of interest, and shifting the *AD* curve to the left. To increase national income the Fed buys bonds on the open market, thereby increasing reserves, driving down the rate of interest and shifting the *AD* curve to the right.

7. The modern use of monetary policy in the United States dates from the 1951 accord between the Treasury and the Fed by which the Fed's main objective ceased to be minimizing the cost of financing the government's debt by controlling interest rates. In the 1950s and 1960s the rate of interest was the main intermediate target through which the Fed sought to influence national income. In the 1970s the emphasis shifted to influencing national income through the money supply.

8. Exclusive concentration on rigid targets for M1 risks misassessing the effects of active monetary policy as the public merely shifts funds between M1 and M2 or M3. It also risks leading the Fed inadvertently into an expansionary or contractionary policy when the demand for money function shifts.

9. The Fed has been criticized for alternating too quickly between expansionary and contractionary policy and thereby contributing to cyclical swings in the economy. In the 1960s and 1970s a series of strong and abrupt changes in monetary policy exerted a destabilizing force on the economy.

10. In the early 1980s the Fed underestimated the growth in the demand for money. Meeting its money supply targets thus implied a much

tighter monetary policy than was at first intended. Monetary tightness caused high interest rates, leading to a severe recession and eventually to a sharp fall in inflation.

11. During the long recovery from the recession that broke the inflation, the Fed accommodated the increase in the demand for M1 that resulted from the fall in the inflation rate and the rise in national income.

12. It is generally agreed that rapid changes in the money supply and interest rates can have large effects on the economy. There is disagreement, however, on how much monetary policy can and should be used as a device for stabilizing national income at its potential level or coping with temporary bouts of rising prices.

Functions of a central bank
The discount rate
Open market operations
Policy variables, policy instruments, and intermediate targets
Variability of monetary policy and monetary rules
Appropriateness of monetary targets when money demand is shifting

Topics for Review

Discussion Questions

1. In the study of banking history we often see the term *elastic currency*. For example, to provide an elastic currency was a purpose behind the creation of the Federal Reserve System. What do you think this term might mean, and why might it be emphasized?

2. During the recovery of the American economy from 1983 to 1985, two different views were often expressed. Some said the adherence to a long-run constant growth rate rule for monetary growth was particularly important lest inflationary expectations be rekindled by an overly fast rate of monetary expansion. Others said that encouraging the recovery required a temporary burst of monetary expansion. Discuss these two views.

3. The Federal Reserve Board runs a facility in Culpeper, Virginia, that costs $1.8 million per year to maintain and to guard against robbery, according to Senator William Proxmire of Wisconsin. Inside this "Culpeper switch," a dugout in the side of a mountain, the government has hidden $4 billion in new currency for the purpose, it says, of "providing a hedge against any nuclear attack that would wipe out the nation's money supply." Comment on the sense of this policy.

4. Describe the chief weapons of monetary policy available to the Federal Reserve and indicate whether, and if so how, they might be used for the following purposes:
   a. To create a mild tightening of bank credit
   b. To signal that the Fed favors a sharp curtailment of bank lending
   c. To permit an expansion of bank credit with existing reserves
   d. To supply banks and the public with a temporary increase of currency for Christmas shopping

5. It is often said that an expansionary monetary policy is like "pushing on a string." What is meant by such a statement? How does this contrast with a contractionary monetary policy?
6. In what situations might the following pairs of objectives come into conflict?
   a. Lowering the cost of government finance and using monetary policy to change aggregate demand
   b. Ending a deep recession and maintaining a currently achieved target for monetary growth
   c. Maintaining stable interest rates and controlling inflation
7. Writing in 1979, Nobel Laureate Milton Friedman accused the Fed of following "an unstable monetary policy," arguing that while the Fed "has given lip service to controlling the quantity of money . . . it has given its heart to controlling interest rates." Why might the desire to stabilize interest rates create an "unstable" monetary policy?
8. Explain why each of these statements might be true under certain circumstances:
   a. Rapid tightening of monetary policy creates fear of rising interest rates.
   b. Rapid easing of monetary policy creates fear of rising interest rates in the wake of renewed inflation.
   c. Tightening of monetary policy creates expectations that actual national income will move closer to potential income.
   d. Tightening of monetary policy creates fears of widening gap between actual national income and potential income.

PART NINE

Issues and Controversies in Macroeconomics

34

Inflation

If you look again at Figure 24-1, on page 462, you will see that for 20 years following World War II inflation remained low. The only exceptions were the "bubbles" immediately following World War II and the Korean War. During the second half of the 1960s, the inflation rate slowly inched upward. It reached the double-digit range in 1973–1974. By then inflation had been declared public enemy number one. Even more worrisome, the rate stayed in the 5 percent to 7 percent range during the severe slump of 1975 to 1977 and then rose again to double digits around the turn of the decade. From a high of 13.5 percent in 1980, the inflation rate eased slightly to 10.4 percent in 1981, and then tumbled to 6.1 percent in 1982 and just below 4 percent in 1983. From then until 1986 the rate hovered around the 4 percent level. Although low by the standards of the last 15 years, 4 percent inflation is high relative to the standards of earlier times.

What are the causes of inflation? How was the great anti-inflationary battle of the early 1980s fought? Can inflation be prevented from skyrocketing into the double-digit range again? Can inflation ever be eliminated altogether?

Inflationary Shocks

We start by noting a key distinction.

It is important to distinguish between the forces that cause a once-and-for-all increase in the price level and the forces that can cause a continuing (or sustained) increase.

Some terms that are sometimes used to stress this distinction are further discussed in Box 34-1.

Any event that tends to drive the price level upward is called an *inflationary shock*. To examine the causes and consequences of such shocks, we begin with an economy in long-run equilibrium: The price level is stable and national income is at its potential, that is, full-employment, level. We then study the economy as it is buffeted by different types of inflationary shocks.

Supply Shocks

Suppose there is a decrease in short-run aggregate supply, that is, the *SRAS* curve shifts up and to the left. This might be caused, for example,

BOX 34-1

Inflation Semantics

The distinction between *once-and-for-all* and *continuing* rises in the price level is important. Some economists have sought to emphasize it by reserving the term *inflation* for a continuing or sustained rise in the price level, while using other terms such as *a rise in the price level* for a once-and-for-all increase.

One difficulty with this is that it is counter to ordinary usage, where inflation refers to any rise in the price level. Indeed, using the restricted definition causes difficulty when communicating with the public. If we were to use it, we would have to keep saying such things as "only some of the current rise in prices is an inflation, while the rest is merely a rise in the price level," and "we won't know whether or not the current rise in the price level is an inflation or not until we see if it is sustained."

In this book we use the term *inflation* as it is commonly used to mean any rise in the price level. We then make the distinction by referring to *temporary* or *once-and-for-all* inflations on the one hand and to *continuing* or *sustained* inflations on the other.

No matter of substance turns on the terms that we use to refer to clearly defined concepts. We use the terms *temporary inflation* and *once-and-for-all rise in the price level* as interchangeable. We use the term *sustained inflation* where some other economists, using the more restricted meaning of the word, might merely talk of an inflation.

This discussion is important because students need to guard against being confused by different usages. Our selection of terms reflects only a desire to keep our language as close as possible to everyday usage.

---

by a rise in the costs of imported raw materials or a rise in domestic wage costs per unit of output. The price level rises and output falls. The rise in the price level shows up as a temporary burst of inflation.

What happens next depends upon whether the shock to the *SRAS* curve is an isolated event or one of a series of recurring shocks. We choose import price increases as an example of an isolated supply shock since a couple of such shocks have occurred during the past two decades. We choose continued wage-cost push as an example of a repeated supply shock since, as we shall see later in this chapter and again in Chapter 37, this possibility has worried many economists ever since governments accepted responsibility for maintaining full employment. The decline in influence and aggressiveness of American unions in recent years has allowed this concern to recede somewhat.

What happens also depends upon how the Fed reacts. If the Fed responds by increasing the money supply, we say that the supply shock has been *accommodated*. If the Fed holds the money supply constant, the shock is not accommodated. (Notice that our terminology distinguishes between the Fed's response to a supply shock, which we describe as accommodating the shock, and its response to a demand shock, which we describe in Chapter 32 and again later in this chapter, as validating the shock.)

Isolated Supply Shocks

Suppose that the leftward shift in the *SRAS* curve is an isolated event; say it is caused by a once-and-for-all increase in the cost of imported raw materials. How does monetary policy affect the economy's response to such an isolated supply shock?

No monetary accommodation. The leftward shift in the *SRAS* curve causes the price level to rise and pushes income below its full-employment level, opening up a recessionary gap. Pressure now mounts for wages and other factor costs to fall. When they do, the *SRAS* curve shifts downward, causing a return of income to full employment and a fall in the price level. In this case the period of inflation accompanying the original supply shock is eventually followed by a period of deflation, that is, a fall in the average level of all prices. The deflation continues until the original long-run equilibrium is reestablished. This is discussed in the second paragraph of the caption to Figure 34-1. Given that wages and prices fall slowly, the recovery to full employment takes a long time.

Monetary accommodation. Now let us see what happens if the money supply is changed in response to the isolated supply shock. Suppose the Fed reacts to the fall in national income by increasing the money supply. This shifts the *AD* curve to the right and causes both the price level and output to *rise*. When the recessionary gap is eliminated, the price level, rather than falling back to its original value, has risen further. The effects are illustrated in Figure 34-1.

Monetary accommodation of a supply shock causes the initial rise in the price level to be followed by a further rise, resulting in a higher price level than if the recessionary gap were relied on to reduce costs and prices.

The monetary authorities might decide to accommodate the supply shock because relying on cost deflation to restore full employment forces the economy to suffer through an extended slump. Monetary accommodation can return the economy to full employment quickly, but at the cost of a once-and-for-all increase in the price level.

Repeated Supply Shocks

We have been assuming that a recessionary gap would be associated with downward pressure on wages. This implies that labor markets behave much like commodity markets, so that wages fall when there is excess supply and rise only when there is excess demand.

Now for one example of a repeated supply shock, assume that powerful unions are able to raise wages in the absence of excess demand for labor and even in the face of significant excess supply. Large manufacturing firms pass on these higher wages in the form of higher prices. This type of supply shock causes what is called **wage-cost push inflation:** an increase in the price level due to increases in money wages that are not associated with excess demand for labor.

FIGURE 34-1   Monetary Accommodation of a Single Supply Shock

Real National Income

Monetary accommodation of a single supply shock causes costs, the price level, and money supply all to move in the same direction. A supply shock causes the *SRAS* curve to shift leftward from $SRAS_0$ to $SRAS_1$, as shown by arrow 1. Equilibrium is established at E_1.

If there is no monetary accommodation, the unemployment would put downward pressure on wages and other costs, causing the *SRAS* curve to shift slowly back to the right to $SRAS_0$. Prices would fall and output would rise until the original equilibrium was restored.

If there is monetary accommodation, the *AD* curve shifts from AD_0 to AD_1, as shown by arrow 2. This reestablishes full employment equilibrium at E_2 but with a higher price level, P_2.

No monetary accommodation. Suppose the Fed does not accommodate these supply shocks. The initial effect of the leftward shift in the *SRAS* curve is to open up a recessionary gap, as shown in Figure 34-1. If unions continue to negotiate increases in wages, subjecting the economy to further supply shocks, prices continue to rise and output continues to fall. Eventually the trade-off between higher wages and unemployment will become obvious to everyone.

Might not really powerful unions continue to force wages up despite this realization? As long as they did so, the recessionary gap would go on growing until, finally, unemployment reached 100 percent. Of course, this would not happen because long before everyone is unemployed, unions would cease forcing up wages in order to maintain jobs for those who are still employed.

Once the wage-cost push ceases, there are two possible scenarios. First, the unions may succeed in holding on to their high wages, but not push for further increases. The economy then comes to rest with a stable price level and a large recessionary gap. Second, the persistent unemployment may eventually erode the power of the unions so that wages begin to fall. In this case the supply shock is reversed, and the *SRAS* curve shifts downward until full employment is eventually restored.

Non-accommodated wage-cost push tends to be self-limiting because the rising unemployment that it causes tends to restrain further wage increases.

Monetary accommodation. Now suppose that the Fed accommodates the shock with an increase in the money supply, thus shifting the *AD* curve to the right, as shown in Figure 34-1. In the new full-employment equilibrium both money wages and prices have risen. The rise in wages has been offset by a rise in prices. Workers are no better off than they were originally, although those who remained in jobs were temporarily better off in the transition after wages had risen (taking equilibrium to E_1 in Figure 34-1), but before the price level had risen (taking equilibrium to E_2).

The stage is now set for the unions to try again. If they succeed in negotiating further increases in money wages, they hit the economy with another supply shock. If the Fed again accommodates the shock, full employment is maintained, but at the cost of a further round of inflation. If this process goes on repeatedly, it can give rise to a continual wage-cost push inflation. The wage-cost push tends to cause a stagflation, with rising prices and falling output. Monetary accommodation tends to reinforce the rise in prices, but to offset the fall in output. This case is illustrated in Figure 34-2.

Two things are required for wage-cost push inflation to continue. First, powerful groups, such as industrial unions or government employees, must press for and employers must grant increases in

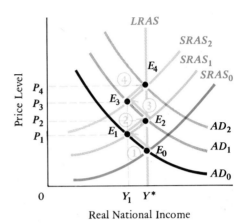

FIGURE 34-2 Monetary Accommodation of a Repeated Supply Shock

Monetary accommodation of a repeated supply shock causes a continuous inflation in the absence of excess demand. The initial equilibrium is at E_0. A supply shock then takes equilibrium to E_1, just as in Figure 34-1. This is the stagflation phase of rising prices and falling output; it is indicated by arrow 1.

The Fed then accommodates the supply shock by increasing the money supply, taking the *AD* curve to AD_1 and equilibrium to E_2. This is the expansionary phase of rising prices and rising output (arrow 2).

A second supply shock followed by monetary accommodation takes equilibrium to E_3 (arrow 3) and then to E_4 (arrow 4). As long as the supply shocks and the monetary accommodation continue, the inflation continues.

money wages, even in the absence of excess demand for labor and goods. Second, governments must accommodate the resulting inflation by increasing the money supply and so prevent the unemployment that would otherwise occur. The process set up by this sequence of wage-cost push and monetary accommodation is often called a *wage-price spiral*.

Is monetary accommodation desirable? Once started, a wage-price spiral can be halted only if the Fed stops accommodating the supply shocks that are causing the inflation. The longer the Fed waits to do so, the more entrenched will be the expectations that it will continue its policy of accommodating the shocks. These entrenched expectations may cause wages to continue to rise after accommodation has ceased. Because employers expect prices to rise, they go on granting wage increases. If expectations are firmly enough entrenched, the wage push can continue for quite some time in spite of the downward pressure caused by the rising unemployment associated with the growing recessionary gap.

Because of this possibility, some economists argue that the process should not be allowed to begin. One way to ensure this is to refuse to accommodate any supply shock whatsoever.

To some people, caution dictates that no supply shocks be accommodated lest a wage-price spiral be set up. Others are willing to risk accommodating isolated shocks in order to avoid the severe, though transitory, recessions that otherwise accompany them.

This key issue is discussed further in Chapter 37.

Demand Shocks

Now suppose that an initial equilibrium is disturbed by a rightward shift in the aggregate demand curve. This causes the price level and output to rise, as shown in Figures 34-3 and 34-4. The shift in the *AD* curve could have been caused by either an increase in autonomous expenditure or an increase in the money supply.[1] As with a supply shock, it is important to distinguish between the case in which the Fed reacts and that in which it does not. As we have seen, when the Fed reacts to the demand shock by increasing the money supply, it is said to be validating the shock.

No monetary validation.   This case is shown in Figure 34-3. Because the initial *AD* shock takes output above the full-employment level, an inflationary gap opens up. The pressure of excess demand soon causes wages and other costs to rise, shifting the *SRAS*

---

[1] As we saw in Chapter 32, an increase in the money supply works through the transmission mechanism—excess supply of money, higher price of bonds, lower interest rates, increased investment expenditure—to shift the *AD* curve to the right.

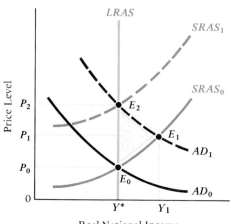

FIGURE 34-3   An Unvalidated Demand-Shock Inflation

An unvalidated demand shock raises the equilibrium price level, but leaves equilibrium income unchanged. The initial equilibrium is at E_0, with full-employment income Y^* and the price level P_0. A demand shock shifts the *AD* curve from AD_0 to AD_1, shifting equilibrium from E_0 to E_1, as shown by arrow 1. At E_1 income is Y_1 and the price level is P_1. The inflationary gap of Y^*Y_1 causes wages to rise, shifting the *SRAS* curve to the left. Equilibrium moves along AD_1 to E_2, as shown by arrow 2. At E_2, income has returned to Y^*, removing the inflationary gap, while the price level has risen to P_2.

---

curve up and to the left. As long as the Fed holds the money supply constant, the rise in the price level brings into play the monetary adjustment mechanism (discussed in detail in Chapter 32): The economy moves up and to the left along the fixed *AD* curve, and the rise in the price level acts to reduce the inflationary gap. Eventually, the gap is eliminated as equilibrium is established at a higher, but stable, price level and with income at its potential level. In this case the initial period of inflation is followed by further inflation that lasts only until the new equilibrium is reached.

Monetary validation.   Next, suppose that after the demand shock has created an inflationary gap, the

Fed frustrates the monetary adjustment mechanism by increasing the money supply when output starts to fall. This is the case illustrated in Figure 34-4.[2] Two forces are now brought into play. Spurred by the inflationary gap, the wage increases cause the SRAS curve to shift to the left. Fueled by the expansionary monetary policy, the AD curve shifts to the right. As a result of both of these shifts, the price level rises, but output need not fall. Indeed, if the shift in the AD curve exactly offsets the shift in the SRAS curve, the inflationary gap will remain constant.

Validation of a demand shock turns what would have been a transitory inflation into a sustained inflation fueled by monetary expansion.

Because of the validation process, all subsequent shifts in the AD curve that perpetuate the inflation are caused by monetary forces.

Inflation As a Monetary Phenomenon

There has been heated debate among economists about the extent to which inflation is a monetary phenomenon. Does it have purely monetary causes—changes in the demand for or the supply of money? Does it have purely monetary consequences—only the price level is affected? One slogan stating an extreme position on this issue was made popular by Milton Friedman: "Inflation is *everywhere* and *always* a monetary phenomenon."

In order to consider these issues, let us summarize what we have already learned. First, look at causes.

1. Many forces can cause the price level to rise. On the demand side, anything that shifts the AD curve to the right will cause the price level to rise. This includes such expenditure changes as an autonomous increase in investment or government expenditure and such monetary changes as an increase in the money supply or a decrease in money demand. On the supply side, anything that in-

[2] Although we distinguish between a single supply shock and a continuing one, we do not make a similar distinction with a demand shock. This is because the accommodation of a single supply shock restores full-employment equilibrium, whereas the validation of a demand shock perpetuates the disequilibrium.

FIGURE 34-4   A Validated Demand-Shock Inflation

Monetary validation will cause the AD curve to shift rightward, offsetting the leftward shift in the SRAS curve and so leave an inflationary gap in spite of the ever-rising price level. As in Figure 34-3, an initial demand shock shifts equilibrium from E_0 to E_1, taking income to Y_1 and the price level to P_1. The resulting inflationary gap then causes the SRAS curve to shift to the left. This time, however, the money supply is increased, shifting the AD curve to the right. By the time the aggregate supply curve has reached $SRAS_1$, the aggregate demand curve has reached AD_2. Now instead of being at E_2 in Figure 34-3, equilibrium is at E_2' (arrow 3). Income remains constant at Y_1, leaving the inflationary gap constant at Y^*Y_1, while the price level rises to P_2'.

The persistent inflationary gap continues to push the SRAS curve to the left, while the continued monetary validation continues to push the AD curve to the right. By the time the aggregate supply reaches $SRAS_2$, the aggregate demand has reached AD_3. The price level has risen still further to P_3, but because of the frustration of the monetary adjustment mechanism, the inflationary gap remains unchanged at $Y_1 - Y^*$. As long as this monetary validation continues, the economy moves along the vertical path of arrow 3.

creases costs of production will shift the SRAS curve to the left and cause the price level to rise.
2. Such inflations can continue for some time without any increases in the money supply.

3. The rise in prices must eventually come to a halt, unless monetary expansion occurs.

Points 1 and 2 provide the sense in which, looking at causes, a temporary burst of inflation need not be a monetary phenomenon. It need not have monetary causes, and it need not be accompanied by monetary expansion. Point 3 is the sense in which, looking at causes, a sustained inflation must be a monetary phenonomenon. If a rise in prices is to continue, it must be accompanied by continuing increases in the money supply (or decreases in money demand). This is true regardless of the cause that set the rise in motion.[3]

Second, let us summarize the consequences of an inflation on the assumption that we begin from a situation where actual national income is at its potential level ($Y = Y^*$).

1. In the short run a demand-shock inflation tends to be accompanied by an increase in national income.
2. In the short run a supply-shock inflation tends to be accompanied by a decrease in national income.
3. When all adjustments have been fully made (so that the relevant supply-side curve is the *LRAS* curve), shifts in either the *AD* or *SRAS* curve leave national income unchanged and affect only the price level.

Points 1 and 2 provide the sense in which, looking at consequences, inflation is not, in the short run, a purely monetary phenomenon. Point 3 provides the sense in which, looking at consequences, inflation is a purely monetary phenomenon from the point of view of long-run equilibrium.

We have now reached three important conclusions.

1. Without monetary accommodation supply shocks cause temporary bursts of inflation accompanied by recessionary gaps. The gaps are removed if and when wages fall, restoring equilibrium at potential income and at the initial price level.
2. Without monetary validation demand shocks cause temporary bursts of inflation accompanied by inflationary gaps. The gaps are removed as wages rise, returning income to its potential level, but at a higher price level.
3. With an appropriate response from the Fed an inflation, initiated by either supply or demand shocks, can continue indefinitely; an ever-increasing money supply is necessary for an ever-continuing inflation.

Sustained Inflation

The price level has risen in almost all years since the end of the Second World War. The decade from 1972 to 1982 was one of sustained inflation, often at rates of over 10 percent per year. In the mid 1980s the inflation rate was around 4 percent. Although this was lower than had been achieved in the previous 20 years, the rate would have been judged unsatisfactory at any time in the twentieth century before 1970. Four percent is a rate of inflation that will halve the purchasing power of money in about 18 years, less than the life expectancy of people who retire in their 60s.

Why do we have sustained inflations of either the rapid sort, as in the 1970s, or the more gradual sort, as in the 1980s? What are the costs and benefits of reducing or eliminating such inflations?

Before we can deal with these questions, we must look in greater detail at what is involved in a sustained inflation. We have already stressed the role of monetary validation in allowing the *AD* curve to shift up continually. We now focus on the forces that cause the *SRAS* curve to shift upward.

Upward Shifts in the *SRAS* Curve

A rise in the cost of producing each unit of output, which is called unit cost, will cause the *SRAS* curve to shift upward. What is it then that causes unit costs to rise?

---

[3] The statement inflation is everywhere and always a monetary phenomenon depends on a restricted and specific definition of the term *inflation*. To justify the statement a temporary burst of inflation with nonmonetary causes must be called a rise in the price level, and the term *inflation* must be reserved for increases in the price level that are sustained for long enough that they must be accompanied by monetary expansion. Variations in the use of these terms are discussed in Box 34-1.

The influence of wage rates and productivity. Does every rise in wage rates force up unit costs? The answer is no because what happens to unit costs depends on what happens to the cost of labor in relation to what happens to the productivity of labor (output per unit of labor input).

Although wages are usually the largest single element of production costs, a rise in wages is not by itself enough to raise unit costs. This is because productivity—output per unit of labor input—is usually rising as well. For example, if wages and productivity both rise by 3 percent, each unit of labor earns 3 percent more, but it also produces 3 percent more. Thus, costs per unit of output remain unchanged.

If wage increases are to cause a rise in unit costs, money wage rates must rise by more than productivity has risen.

In what follows, it is simplest to assume that productivity does not change so that a rise in money wages causes a rise in unit costs. To apply the analysis to cases where productivity is changing, the statement "wages rise" needs only to be replaced by the statement "wages rise by more than productivity rises."

Why Wages Change

Let us now ask what we know about the behavior of money wages and hence of the *SRAS* curve. Up to now it has been enough to say that an inflationary gap implies excess demand for labor, low unemployment, upward pressure on wages and, hence, an upward-shifting *SRAS* curve.

But now we need to look in more detail at three forces that can cause wage costs to change and thus shift the *SRAS* curve to the left. These are demand for labor, expectations, and random forces. Much of what we say in the case of demand forces is a recapitulation, but the points are important enough to bear repeating.

Demand Forces

The excess demand for labor associated with an inflationary gap puts upward pressure on wages.

Wages rise more rapidly than they otherwise would.

The excess supply of labor associated with a recessionary gap puts downward pressure on wages. Wages rise less rapidly (or fall more rapidly) than they otherwise would.

The absence of either an inflationary or a recessionary gap means that there is no demand pressure on wages. Demand forces do not exert any pressure on wages either to rise or to fall.

The natural rate of unemployment. We saw in Chapter 24 that when current national income is at its potential level ($Y = Y^*$), unemployment is not zero. Instead there may be a substantial amount of frictional unemployment caused by the movement of people between jobs. The amount of unemployment (all of it frictional) that exists when national income is at its potential level is called the **natural rate of unemployment (U_N)**. It follows from this definition that when current national income exceeds full-employment income (Y exceeds Y^*), current unemployment will be less than the natural rate (U less than U_N). When current national income is less than full-employment income (Y less than Y^*), current unemployment will exceed the natural rate (U exceeds U_N).

We can now use the natural rate terminology to restate the three results about the pressure that is put on wage rates, and through them on the *SRAS* curve, by inflationary and recessionary gaps.

When the unemployment rate is below the natural rate demand forces put upward pressure on wages.

When the unemployment rate is above the natural rate demand forces put downward pressure on wages.

When unemployment is at its natural rate demand forces exert neither upward nor downward pressure on wages.

The influence of demand forces on wages can be shown by a relation called the **Phillips curve,** which is discussed in Box 34-2.

BOX 34-2

The Phillips Curve and the Shifting SRAS Curve

In the early 1950s Professor A. W. Phillips of the London School of Economics was doing pathbreaking research on the pitfalls of fine tuning. He included in his early models an equation relating the rate of inflation to the difference between actual and potential income, $Y - Y^*$. Later he investigated the empirical underpinnings of this equation by studying the relation between the rate of increase of wage costs and the level of unemployment. In 1958 he reported that a stable relation had existed between these two variables for 100 years in the United Kingdom.

The relation, which came to be called the *Phillips curve*, is illustrated in the figure on the left. The curve shows money wages rising when unemployment is below the natural rate of unemployment, U_N, and falling when unemployment is above that critical level. It illustrates the effect that an inflationary gap has on wages.

Recall that the rate of unemployment is related negatively to national income: The higher national

Expectational Forces

A second force that can influence wages is *expectations*. Suppose, for example, that both employers and employees expect that a 4 percent inflation will occur next year. Unions will start negotiations from a base of a 4 percent increase in money wages, which would hold their real wages constant. Firms may also be inclined to begin bargaining by conceding at least a 4 percent increase in money wages, since they expect that the prices at which they sell their products will rise by 4 percent. *Starting from that base*, unions will attempt to obtain some desired increase in their real wages. At this point such factors as profits, productivity, and bargaining power become important.

The general expectation of an *x* percent inflation creates pressures for wages to rise by *x* percent

and hence for the *SRAS* curve to shift by *x* percent.

Other Random Forces

Wage changes are also affected by forces that are associated neither with excess demand nor expected inflation. These forces can be positive—pushing wages higher than they otherwise would go—or negative—pushing wages lower than they otherwise would go. Furthermore, they are assumed to be many in number and to be independent of each other, so that they exert an overall random influence on wages—sometimes speeding wage increases up a bit, sometimes slowing them down a bit, but having a net effect that more or less cancels out when taken income, the lower is unemployment. Thus the Phillips curve can also be drawn with national income on the horizontal axis, as in the figure on the right.

Both figures show the same information. As far as the demand effect is concerned, inflationary gaps (which correspond to low unemployment rates) are associated with rapid *increases* in wages, while recessionary gaps (which correspond to high unemployment rates), are associated with slow *decreases* in wages.

The Phillips curve must be clearly distinguished from the *SRAS* curve. The *SRAS* curve has the *price level* on the vertical axis while the Phillips curve has the *rate of wage inflation*. Therefore the Phillips curve tells us how fast the *SRAS* curve is shifting when actual income does not equal potential income.

Only when $Y = Y^*$ is the *SRAS* curve not shifting on account of demand pressures. When income is at its potential level, aggregate demand for labor equals aggregate supply; the only unemployment would thus be frictional unemployment. There would be neither upward nor downward pressure of demand on wages. Thus the Phillips curve cuts the axis at potential income Y^* and at the corresponding level of unemployment U_N.

The Phillips curve soon became famous. It provided a link between national income models and labor markets. This link allowed macroeconomists to drop the uncomfortable assumption, which they had often been forced to use in many of their earlier formal models, that money wages were rigidly fixed and neither rose nor fell as national income varied. The Phillips curve relation between money wages and national income determines (in conjunction with productivity increases) the speed at which the *SRAS* curve shifts.

Consider, for example, the situation shown in Figure 34-3, where the level of income determined by the *AD* and *SRAS* curves is Y_1. Plotting Y_1 on the Phillips curve in the left figure tells us that wage costs will be rising at ΔW_1. Then the *SRAS* curve in Figure 34-3 will be shifting upward by that amount. The same information can be seen in the right figure, where national income of Y_1 corresponds to unemployment of U_1.

To hold national income at Y_1 (and hence unemployment at U_1), the money supply must be increased at a rate sufficient to allow the *AD* curve to shift upward as fast as the *SRAS* curve.

over several years. Over the long term they may be regarded as random events and are referred to as *random shocks*.

One example of such forces occurs when an exceptionally strong union, or an exceptionally weak management, comes to the bargaining table and produces a wage increase that is a percentage point or two *above* what would have occurred under more typical bargaining conditions. Another example is when a new government policy that is favorable to management causes this year's negotiated wage rates to be a percentage point or two *below* what they would have been.

While random shocks may be important causes of temporary bursts of inflation, they are less important for sustained inflations. While they may have a large positive or negative effect in any one year,

over the period of a sustained inflation positive shocks in some years will tend to be offset by negative shocks in other years so that, in total, they contribute little to the long-term trend of the price level.

The Overall Effect

The overall change in wage costs is a result of the three basic forces just studied. We may express this as:

$$\begin{matrix} \text{percentage} \\ \text{increase in} \\ \text{money} \\ \text{wages} \end{matrix} = \begin{matrix} \text{demand} \\ \text{effect} \end{matrix} + \begin{matrix} \text{expectational} \\ \text{effect} \end{matrix} + \begin{matrix} \text{random} \\ \text{shock} \\ \text{effect} \end{matrix}$$

It is important to realize that what happens to wage costs is the net effect of all three of these forces. Consider two examples. Assume that both labor and management expect a 3 percent inflation next year and are willing on this account to allow wages to increase by 3 percent. This would leave the relation between wages and other prices unaltered. Next assume that there is a significant inflationary gap with an associated labor shortage. The demand pressure causes wages to rise by 2 percentage points more than they otherwise would have risen. Finally, assume a shock, in the form of a temporary concern on the part of labor unions with foreign competition, that moderates wage claims by 1 percentage point this year. The final outcome is that wages rise by 4 percent, which is the net effect of +3 from expectations, +2 from demand forces, and −1 from the random shock.

For the second illustration assume that there is once again a 3 percent expected inflation, but that this time there is a recessionary gap. The associated heavy unemployment puts downward pressure on wage bargains, and hence the demand effect now works to moderate wage increases, say, to the extent of 2 percentage points. Finally assume that some unusual cost-plus government contracts reduce employer resistance to wage rises to the extent of contributing an upward pressure on wage bargains of 1 percentage point. The net effect is for wages to rise by +2 percent, which is the net effect of +3 from expectations, −2 from demand forces, and +1 from shock effects.

The net effect of the three forces acting on wage costs—demand, expectations, and random shocks—determines what happens to the *SRAS* curve.

Inflationary gaps, expectations of inflation, and positive random shocks put pressure on wage rates to rise and hence on the *SRAS* curve to shift to the left. Recessionary gaps, expectations of deflation, and negative random shocks put pressure on wage rates to fall and hence on the *SRAS* curve to shift to the right. What happens to the *SRAS* curve in any one year is the net effect of all of these forces.

Accelerating Inflation

One of the reasons that policymakers worry so much about inflations is their concern that even a moderate inflation may be hard to keep under control. They worry that inflations often have a tendency to accelerate. They fear that if the Fed relaxes and is willing to accept, say, 4 percent inflation, 4 percent may soon become 5 percent, and once 5 percent becomes accepted, 5 percent may become 6 percent, and so on.

In this section, we first consider the reasons for worrying that the inflation rate will tend to drift upward unless it is held rigidly in check.

Look again at Figure 34-4, which represents a continuing inflation. The *SRAS* curve is shifting up due to the inflationary gap and the *AD* curve is shifting up because the inflation is being validated by increases in the money supply. What this analysis shows is that, if income is held above potential, the price level will be rising. We know that inflation is positive, but we do not know whether the rate of inflation is rising or falling or is constant.

One of the most important results in the theory of inflation concerns what happens to the rate of inflation when a central bank takes steps to perpetuate an inflationary gap. This is the *acceleration hypothesis* to which we now turn. The argument is in several steps.

An initial pure-demand inflation.   Suppose that initially prices are rising in the presence of neither random shocks nor expectations of inflation. This means that the inflation is due solely to the existence of excess demand. Suppose also that the level of output is held constant. For this to happen, the upward shift in the *SRAS* curve has to be accompanied by an increase in the money supply such that the *AD* curve shifts up by the same amount. When the *SRAS* and the *AD* curves are shifting at the same speed, the inflationary gap remains unchanged.

Expectational effects.   Eventually people will begin to expect that the monetary validation, and hence the inflation, will continue. As these inflationary expectations emerge, additional upward pressure will be put on wages as the inflationary effect comes into play. Now that the demand effect on wages has been augmented by an expectational effect, the *SRAS* curve will begin to shift upward more rapidly.

More rapid monetary validation required. If the Fed still wishes to hold the level of output constant, it must increase the rate at which the money supply is growing. This is because, to hold *Y* constant, the *AD* curve must be shifted more rapidly to compensate for the more rapid shifts in the *SRAS* curve.

An increasing rate of inflation. As a result of the increasingly rapid upward shifts in both the *AD* and the *SRAS* curves, the rate of inflation must now be increasing. The rise in the actual inflation rate will, in turn, cause an increase in the expected inflation rate. This will then cause the actual inflation rate to increase, which will in turn increase the expected inflation rate, and so on. The net result is a *continually increasing rate of inflation*.

Conclusion. The above analysis of the response of inflationary expectations to a persistent inflationary gap leads to what is called the **acceleration hypothesis.**

According to the acceleration hypothesis, as long as an inflationary gap persists, expectations of inflation will be rising, and this will lead to increases in the actual rate of inflation.

The tendency for inflation to increase is discussed further in Box 34-3.

Constant Inflation

Must a sustained inflation always accelerate? Or is it possible for an inflation to go on at a constant rate indefinitely?

The answer is that not all sustained inflations must accelerate. When the demand effect is absent so that all inflation is expectational, inflation can persist indefinitely at a constant rate. Let us see why this is so.

When national income is at its potential level, there is neither an inflationary nor a recessionary gap. In this case there is no demand effect operating on wage bargains. Leaving random shocks aside, the only force operating on wages is expectations. Say, for example, that both workers and employees expect a 4 percent inflation and they are prepared to raise wages by 4 percent per year to keep wages in line with everything else. Wages will rise by 4 percent per year and the *SRAS* curve will shift upward by that amount each year. If the Fed validates the resulting inflation by increasing the money supply by 4 percent each year, then the *AD* curve will also be shifting up by that amount.

This case is illustrated in Figure 34-5 on page 696. Here wage costs are rising due to expectations of inflation, and these expectations are being fulfilled.

Steady inflation with full employment results when the rate of monetary growth, the rate of wage increase, and the expected rate of inflation are all consistent with the actual inflation rate.

The key point about a pure expectational inflation at a constant rate is that there is no demand effect operating on wage bargains. Wages rise at the expected rate of inflation and that is just enough to preserve the existing relation between wages and all other prices. If there were a labor shortage, there would be pressure for wages to rise relative to other prices and this would push the rate of wage increase above the expected rate of inflation. If there were more unemployment than the normal frictional amount, there would be a tendency for wages to fall relative to other prices, and this would hold wage increases below the expected rate of inflation.

The negative demand effect of a recessionary gap is rather weak. Thus when the recessionary gap is relatively small, the demand effect may be swamped by the expectational and random shock effects so that an approximately stable inflation rate is the net result. This is what seems to have occurred in the mid 1980s, when a fairly stable inflation rate persisted for several years in spite of a modest recessionary gap.

Breaking an Entrenched Inflation

When an inflation has been going on for a long time, can it be reduced without inflicting major hardships in terms of unemployment and lost output?

BOX 34-3

The Phillips Curve and Accelerating Inflation

Professor Phillips was interested in studying the short-run behavior of an economy subjected to cyclical fluctuations (see Box 34-2). Others, however, treated the curve as establishing a long-term trade-off between inflation and unemployment.

Let the government fix income at Y_1 (and thus unemployment at U_1) in the figures and validate the ensuing wage inflation of ΔW_1 per year. By doing this the government is apparently able to choose a partic-ular combination of inflation and unemployment, with lower levels of unemployment being attained at the cost of higher rates of inflation.

In the 1960s Phillips curves were fitted to the data for many countries, and governments made decisions about where they wished to be on the trade-off between inflation and unemployment. Then, in the late 1960s, in country after country, the rate of wage and price inflation associated with any given level of un-

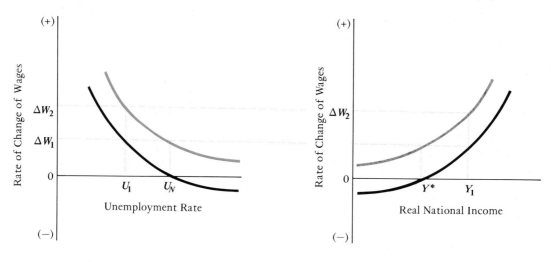

This question greatly worried policymakers in the early 1980s when they set out to break the existing two-digit inflation. It also worried those who, later in the 1980s, were unsatisfied with the 4 percent inflation rate that had persisted for several years. The issue was then, and still is, how to reduce inflation when people have come to accept the existing rate as normal and have adapted their behavior to the belief that the rate will continue.

Our analysis begins with a situation of a continuing, fully validated inflation, with actual income at its potential level ($Y = Y^*$). The inflation has been going on for some time, and people expect it to continue. Firmly held expectations of a continuation of the current inflation rate are what leads to the concept of an *entrenched inflation*. What is entrenched are the inflationary expectations.

We now suppose that the Fed decides to reduce the inflation rate by reducing its rate of monetary validation. The events that follow such a decision generally fall into three phases.

Phase 1: Removing the inflationary gap. The first phase of the anti-inflationary policy, shown in Figure 34-6(i) on page 697, consists of slowing the rate of monetary expansion below the current rate of inflation. This slows the rate at which the aggregate demand curve is shifting upward. To illustrate what happens we take an extreme case: the "cold turkey approach," where the rate of monetary expansion is cut to zero so that the upward shift in the *AD* curve is halted suddenly.

Under the combined influence of an inflationary gap and expectations of continued inflation, wages employment began to rise. Instead of being stable, the Phillips curves were shifting upward. The explanation lay primarily in a shifting relation between the pressure of demand and wage increases due to expectations, as discussed in the text.

In the text we noted that two important influences on wages are demand and expectations. It was gradually understood that the original Phillips curve concerned only the influence of demand and left out inflationary expectations. This proved to be an important and unfortunate omission. An increase in expected inflation shows up as an upward shift in the original Phillips curve drawn in Box 34-2.

The importance of expectations can be shown by drawing what is called an **expectations augmented Phillips curve,** as in the figures. The heights of the Phillips curves above the axis at Y^* and at U_N show the expected inflation rate. This is the amount that wages will rise when there is neither excess demand nor excess supply pressure in labor markets. The actual wage increase is shown by the augmented curve, with the increase in wages exceeding expected inflation when $Y > Y^*$ ($U < U_N$) and falling short of expected inflation when $Y < Y^*$ ($U > U_N$). *The demand component shown by the simple Phillips curve tells us by how much wage changes will deviate from the expected inflation rate.*

Now we can see what was wrong with the idea of a stable inflation-unemployment trade-off. Targeting on income Y_1 or unemployment U_1 in the figure is fine as long as no inflation is *expected.* But once some particular rate of inflation comes to be expected, people will demand that much just to hold their own. The Phillips curve will shift upward to the position shown in the figure. Now there is inflation ΔW_2 because of the combined effects of expectations and excess demand.

But this higher rate is above the expected rate. Once that higher rate comes to be expected, the Phillips curve will shift upward once again. *The expectations augmented Phillips curve shows that the actual rate of inflation exceeds the expected rate whenever there is an inflationary gap.* Sooner or later this will cause inflationary expectations to be shifted upward. The inflation rate associated with any given level of Y or U rises over time. This is the theory of accelerating inflation that is further studied in the appendix to this chapter.

continue to rise and the *SRAS* curve thus continues to shift. Eventually, the gap is removed and income returns to Y^*. If the only influence on wage costs were current demand, that would be the end of the story. At Y^* there is no inflationary gap and hence no upward demand pressure on wages. Wages would stop rising, the *SRAS* curve would be stabilized, and the economy would remain at full employment with a stable price level.

Phase 2: Stagflation. Governments around the world have many times wished that things were really that simple. However, instead of settling into the happy position of full employment and stable prices, economies tend to overshoot and develop a recessionary gap. The reason is, as we have already seen, that wages depend not only on current excess demand, but also on inflationary expectations. Once inflationary expectations have been established, it is not always easy to get people to revise them downward, even in the face of changed monetary policies. Thus the *SRAS* curve continues to shift to the left, causing the price level to rise and income to fall further.

Expectations may cause an inflation to persist after the original causes of the inflation have been removed. What was initially a demand inflation due to an inflationary gap becomes a purely expectational inflation fueled by the expectation that it will continue.

We have now entered phase 2, shown in Figure 34-6(ii). Even though the inflationary gap has been eliminated, the expectation of further inflation leads

FIGURE 34-5   Steady Inflation at the Natural Rate of Unemployment

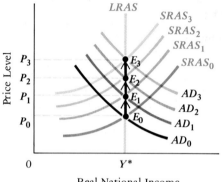

Real National Income

When income equals Y^* (and hence unemployment equals U_N) there is no demand effect on wages and steady inflation can proceed at a rate consistent with inflationary expectations. With no demand effect the *SRAS* curve shifts upward at the expected rate of inflation. If the Fed raises the money supply at the same rate, the upward shift in the *AD* curve will match that of the *SRAS* curve. Output will stay at Y^*, unemployment will be at the natural rate, and inflation will be steady. The steady inflation is shown by the rising price level as equilibrium moves along the arrows from E_0 to E_1 to E_2 to E_3 in the figure.

to further wage increases. This shifts the *SRAS* curve to the left. The price level continues to rise in spite of a growing recessionary gap. This is the stagflationary phase.

The growing recessionary gap has two effects. First, there is rising unemployment. Thus the demand influence on wages becomes negative. Second, as the recession deepens, people revise their expectations of inflation downward. When they have no further expectations of inflation, there are no further increases in wage costs and the *SRAS* curve stops shifting. The stagflationary phase is over. The inflation has come to a halt, but a large recessionary gap now exists.

Keynesian and monetarist economists have often differed strongly on what they expect in a typical phase 2 period. Keynesians tend to be pessimistic and

to expect a severe and long-lasting slump in phase 2. Monetarists tend to be optimistic and to expect a relatively mild and short-lived recession in phase 2. Indeed, in the early 1980s some monetarists argued that phase 2 would be almost nonexistent.

The main reason for these differences lies in a disagreement over what determines the expected inflation rate. Keynesians tend to believe that people adjust their expected inflation rates quite slowly, even in the face of substantial recessionary gaps. They believe, therefore, that phase 2 tends to be quite long. Monetarists are more likely to believe that downward adjustments in the expected rate can occur quite rapidly and hence that phase 2 can often be quite short. These sharply opposing views are investigated in Box 34-4 on pages 698–699.

Phase 3: Recovery.   The final phase is the return to full employment. When the economy comes to rest at the end of the stagflation, the situation is exactly the same as when the economy is hit by an isolated supply shock (see Figure 34-1). The move back to full employment can be accomplished in either of two ways. First, the recessionary gap can be relied on to reduce wages, thus shifting the *SRAS* curve to the right to eliminate the effects of the overshooting caused by inflationary expectations. Second, the money supply can be increased sufficiently to shift the *AD* curve to a level consistent with full employment. These two possibilities are illustrated in Figure 34-6(iii).

When an entrenched inflation ceases to be validated by the Fed, the inflationary gap will soon disappear but persistent inflationary expectations will produce a stagflation. The restoration of full employment and stable prices will then require the removal of the recessionary gap either by a once-and-for-all increase in the money supply or by a reduction in the levels of wages and prices.

Those economists who worry about waiting for wages and prices to fall fear that the process will take a very long time. The worry about a temporary burst of monetary expansion is that expectations of inflation may be rekindled when the Fed increases the money supply. If inflationary expectations are revived, the Fed will then have an unenviable choice.

FIGURE 34-6   Eliminating an Entrenched Inflation

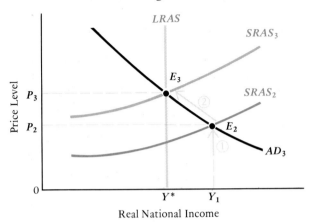

(i) Phase 1: removing the inflationary gap

(ii) Phase 2: stagflation

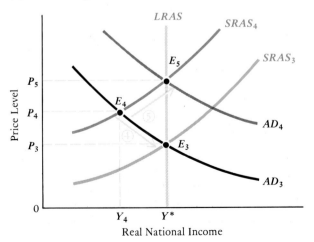

(iii) Phase 3: recovery

(i) Phase 1: The elimination of an entrenched inflation begins with a demand contraction to remove the inflationary gap. A fully validated inflation of the type shown in Figure 34-4 is taking the economy along the path shown by arrow 1 here. When the curves reach $SRAS_2$ and AD_3, the Fed stops expanding the money supply, thus stabilizing aggregate demand at AD_3. Wages continue to rise, taking the $SRAS$ curve leftward. The economy moves along arrow 2 with income falling and the price level rising. When aggregate supply reaches $SRAS_3$, the inflationary gap is removed and equilibrium is established at income Y^* and price level P_3.

(ii) Phase 2: Expectations and wage momentum lead to a stagflation, with falling output and continuing inflation. The economy moves along the path shown by arrow 3. The driving force is now the $SRAS$ curve, which continues to shift because inflationary expectations cause wages to continue to rise. The recessionary gap grows as income falls. The inflation continues, but at a diminishing rate. If wages stop rising when income has reached Y_4 and the price level P_4, the stagflation phase is over, with equilibrium at E_4.

(iii) Phase 3: After expectations are reversed, recovery takes income to Y^* and the price level is stabilized. There are two possible scenarios for recovery. In the first the recessionary gap causes wages to fall (slowly), taking the $SRAS$ curve back to $SRAS_3$ (slowly) as shown by arrow 4. The economy retraces the path originally followed in (ii) back to E_3. In the second scenario, the Fed increases the money supply sufficiently to shift the AD curve to AD_4. The economy then moves along the path shown by arrow 5. This restores potential income at the cost of a further temporary inflation that takes the price level to P_5. Full employment and a stable price level are now achieved.

BOX 34-4

Controversies Over the Length of the Stagflation Phase Needed to Break an Entrenched Inflation

Keynesian View

Keynesians cite two reasons for believing that the phase 2 stagflation in the process of breaking a sustained inflation will often tend to be long and painful. The first has to do with wage momentum and the second with expectations.

Keynesians allege the existence of a self-perpetuating momentum to wage increases. According to this view, workers are concerned about their own wage rates *relative* to rates in closely related occupations and industries. Because wage contracts fix wage rates for periods of from one to three years, any particular wage will be negotiated in a situation where many related wage rates are already fixed for some time into the future (until existing contracts expire). Thus if excess demand caused many existing wages to be raised by, say, 10 percent in contracts negotiated in the recent past, people currently negotiating new wage contracts will hold out for something close to 10 percent, even if the pressure of excess demand has weakened greatly.

This concern over wage comparability tends to give momentum to rounds of wage increases. The process is sometimes called a *wage-wage spiral*: Once started, wages tend to chase each other in a rising spiral as bargainers seek to avoid falling behind

increases that have already been agreed on for other workers.

The second main reason concerns expectations. In its simplest version, this reason is based on the so-called extrapolative theory, according to which people tend to believe that recent past trends will continue and require much new evidence before they conclude that an established inflationary trend has changed. The argument is that unless a deviation from the past trend persists, people tend to dismiss a deviation— say, a fall in the inflation rate—as a transitory change and do not let it influence their long-term wage- and price-setting behavior.

The combination of the momentum of wage increases, even in the face of large recessionary gaps, and slowly adjusting expectations means that phase 2 will be long. The stagflation will persist as rising wages shift the *SRAS* curve to the left until both the wage-wage spiral and expectations of further inflation are finally broken.

Monetarist View

Monetarists expect phase 2 to be over rapidly. Some say that under ideal circumstances it may never occur at all. They offer two reasons.

First, monetarists deny that significant wage-wage

Either it must let another severe recession develop to break these new inflationary expectations, or it must validate the inflation in order to reduce unemployment. In the latter case it is back where it started with a validated inflation on its hands.

Inflationary Experience in the 1980s

We have seen that the 1970s was a period of a rising inflationary trend. By the turn of the decade there

was a major controversy over how to reduce the inflation drastically. Everyone agreed on the goal of returning to a much lower inflation rate, zero if possible, but there was disagreement as to the means of achieving the goal. This same disagreement would occur again if the Fed advocated a policy of rapidly reducing the current rate of inflation to a much lower rate, say, as close to zero as is possible.

Monetarists advocated breaking the inflation with monetary restraint in the manner analyzed earlier in this chapter. Since they felt that there would be a short phase 2, they were willing to rely exclusively momentum exists. They believe that new wage bargains respond to current market conditions. Thus a large recessionary gap with unemployment above the natural rate will lead quickly to new wage settlements well below the expected rate of inflation. The only lag in the adjustment of wage costs to current demand conditions is caused by the length of wage contracts. Thus, it will take time for *all* wages to adjust to depressed market conditions.

Second, many monetarists argue that expected inflation falls rapidly during phase 2. They accept one version of the theory of **rational expectations**, according to which people look to the government's *current* macroeconomic policy when forming their expectations of future inflation. People are assumed to understand how the economy works and to form their expectations about future inflation rates by predicting the outcome of the monetary policies currently being followed. Their expectations need not always be correct, but the rational expectations hypothesis assumes that people do not continue to make systematic errors in forming their expectations.

Rational expectations have the effect of shortening the deflationary period. Instead of being strongly influenced by past inflation rates, people act in anticipation of the outcome of current government policies. Once they realize that the Fed has stopped validating

the inflation they will quickly revise their inflationary expectations downward, and their consequent wage- and price-setting behavior will produce a rapid slowdown in the actual inflation rate. Expected inflation falls quickly to zero, and there is no further upward push to wages arising from expectations.

This happy result occurs only if people believe the Fed is going to stick to its restrictive policies. If they are skeptical about the Fed's resolve, they may expect the inflation to continue. They will then increase wages and prices in anticipation of the inflation, and their actions will generate the very inflation that they expected. Thus, monetarists lay heavy stress on the credibility of the Fed's monetary policy.

Keynesians argue in response that sophisticated financial market operators may understand the underlying monetary causes of inflation, but the general public and most labor leaders and business managers hold different, sometimes crude, theories of inflation. They will tend, so the Keynesians argue, to extrapolate from past experiences and will not even know what the Fed is doing to the money supply, let alone base their expectations on it.

The experience of the early 1980s, and its relation to this debate, is discussed later in this chapter.

on monetary policy to bring about the transition from a high to a low inflationary environment.

Keynesians agreed that a low rate of monetary growth was a necessary condition for returning to a low rate of inflation. However, because they felt that phase 2 would be long—some talked in terms of 5 to 10 years—they were reluctant to use monetary policy alone during the transition. As a result, many Keynesians advocated using **incomes policies,** a term which covers any direct government intervention used to affect wage and price setting. They hoped that such intervention would shorten phase 2

by helping to break inflationary expectations. This potential use and other possible uses of incomes policies are discussed in Box 34-5.

The Reduction of Inflation

After some minor policy vacillations, an anti-inflationary monetary policy was initiated in mid 1981 without the addition of any incomes policy. Inflation fell from 12.4 percent in 1980 to 8.9 percent in 1981 and then to 3.9 percent in 1982. By 1983 the policy had succeeded in reducing inflation to a level not

BOX 34-5

Incomes Policies

In the past Keynesian economists have often rec-ommended the use of incomes policies as an anti-inflationary device. There is a wide range of such policy measures. Voluntary guidelines for wage and price increases can be set, as they were under the Kennedy administration in the 1960s. The govern-ment may consult labor and business leaders with a view to moderating their wage demands and price hikes, as has often been done in European countries. More drastically, compulsory controls may be im-posed on wage, price, and profit increases, such as was done under the Nixon administration in the early 1970s. A proposal commonly made in the 1970s and early 1980s was for a **tax-related incomes policy (TIP),** which would operate through the tax system to provide penalties for "excessive" wage and price hikes and rewards for moderate ones.

Incomes policies might be used for three quite distinct purposes: (1) to suppress a demand inflation, (2) to break an expectational inflation, and (3) to control a permanent wage-cost push inflation. We discuss the first two purposes in this box and the third one in Chapter 37.

Demand Inflation

One reason incomes policies have such a bad repu-tation throughout the world is that they have often been used, as they were in the United States during Richard Nixon's presidency, in a futile attempt to stop a demand inflation. To see why such an attempt is futile, consider the situation shown at E_1 in Figure 34-3 on page 686. If nothing else is done, the inflationary gap will cause the price level to rise to P_2. Wage and price controls could be used to hold the price level at P_1, but once the controls are removed, the excess demand will cause prices to rise.

In the face of an inflationary gap, wage-price con-trols can postpone an inflation, but once they are removed, the price level will rise to the value it would have attained had the controls never been used.

Expectational Inflation

When an entrenched inflation exists, incomes policies may help to break expectations and so allow the in-flation rate to drop. If they are successful, incomes policies will greatly reduce, or even eliminate, the stag-flation phase. This could happen if, once phase 1 is over and the inflationary gap has been eliminated, incomes policies were used to stop wages and prices from rising because of the expectational effect. The *SRAS* curve would not continue to shift upward and thereby open up a recessionary gap. Once expecta-tions have adjusted to the new anti-inflationary mon-etary policy and to the existing stable price level, the controls could be removed. The economy would then be at a position of stable prices and full employ-ment.

The sequence of events seems almost too good to be true. The stagflation phase is eliminated and the economy goes directly from phase 1, with an infla-tionary gap, to the final situation of an equilibrium at Y^*. If such a policy had been tried as many advocated during the early 1980s, *and if it had worked*, the recession of the early 1980s, with all of its consequent unemployment and lost output, would have been avoided.

Opponents of incomes policies believe that the costs of using incomes policies will exceed the alleged benefits. First, they argue that the benefits, in terms of shortening the stagflation phase, would be small because the policies would not be wholly successful in restraining wage and price increases. Second, they argue that the costs, in terms of direct administrative burdens and indirect frustration of the workings of the price system, would be large.

Although the Nixon administration used an in-comes policy in a futile attempt to control a demand inflation, the policy had costs similar to those that would be incurred by an incomes policy designed to break an entrenched inflation. Thus, argue the critics, the experience of Nixon's wage-price controls is rel-evant evidence about the costs of using such policies, even where the objective is not a futile one. The evi-dence of the Nixon experience suggests that when prices are set by government administrators rather than by market forces, the allocation of resources becomes increasingly arbitrary, with serious conse-quences for the efficient working of the economic system.

seen since the early 1960s, but it also produced a major recession with all of its attendent costs, including unemployment, lost output, business bankruptcies, and foreclosed mortgages.

The results came out somewhere in between the extremes that had been predicted. Keynesians were right in predicting that the anti-inflationary policies would induce a severe recession. But the inflation rate came down much faster than Keynesians had predicted. Jobs rather than wages quickly became the focus of many contract settlements. Not only were new wage agreements moderated in response to the excess supply of labor, a significant number of existing contracts were re-opened and lower wages agreed upon.

Thus, as so often happens with great debates, neither the extreme pessimists nor the extreme optimists were right. The truth lay somewhere in between.

Economists still argue about why the result turned out the way it did. Monetarists have to explain why there was a significant stagflation phase at all. They argue that it resulted from the Fed's vacillation. They claim that the Fed did not take a consistently tough line on reducing the rate of monetary accommodation. This in turn left people uncertain as to whether or not inflation really was going to be brought down. Because of this uncertainty, inflationary expectations remained high, sustaining the stagflation phase of the adjustment.

Keynesians have to explain why the stagflation phase was so much shorter than they expected. One of their main explanations is in the weakness at the time of the steel and auto industries. These industries have always had strong unions which the Keynesians claim were a major cause of the wage-price spiral. But during the early 1980s both of these industries were in deep trouble, and no matter how hard their unions pushed for wage rises, the profits out of which extra wages would have to be paid were not there as they had been in the past. Thus, say the Keynesians, for quite fortuitous reasons, the wage push was much weaker than usual and the stagflation phase was correspondingly shortened.

Whatever the reasons, there is little doubt that during the early 1980s inflation fell faster than many Keynesians had expected, and the slump was deeper and more prolonged than many monetarists had expected.

A Stable Inflation Rate

For several years following 1983, the American inflation rate stabilized at a figure around 4 percent, and it was a time of low inflation in the world as a whole. How is it that a relatively steady inflation rate persisted for several years with no clear tendency toward acceleration? The answer is that there was no inflationary gap in the economy. Thus, the inflation was purely expectational and so fulfilled the conditions for a stable, rather than an accelerating, rate.

But since there clearly was a recessionary gap, why did inflation not decelerate further? The answer here seems to be that the weak demand forces that work toward deceleration when there is excess supply were swamped by the forces of expectational inflation and random shocks. (Recall from Chapter 28 the second asymmetry of the *SRAS* curve in that it shifts rapidly upward when there is excess demand, but only slowly downward when there is excess supply.)

As the recovery proceeded through the late 1980s, concern grew that inflation could accelerate if the economy moved into the range of an inflationary gap. This concern was mitigated to some extent, however, by the collapse in oil prices in 1986 which, by reducing costs of production, helped to shift the *SRAS* curve downward.

The unfortunate inflationary experience of the 1970s and early 1980s is still fresh in the memories of policymakers, and there is a clear resolution to prevent a high rate of inflation from returning, let alone becoming entrenched in people's expectations. So it is likely that any outbreak of demand inflation in the near future would be met by contractionary fiscal and monetary policies designed to remove the inflationary gap. However, as time passes and the memory of inflation dims, the risk of inflation being rekindled increases.

Inflation in the Future

The Fed's stated policy is to reduce the existing inflation rate slowly toward zero. This objective raises a number of important policy issues on which only the future behavior of the economy can cast further evidence.

Can an inflation that is entrenched in people's expectations be slowly reduced by gradually cutting the rate of monetary expansion? The advantage of gradualism is that, if it can be made to work, it would largely avoid the stagflationary phase 2 that accompanies any more dramatic attack on the inflation. If gradualism does not work so that a more drastic reduction in the rate of monetary expansion is judged necessary to break current expectations, how long will the stagflation phase of high unemployment and lost output last?

Is a Zero Inflation Rate Attainable?

In a static world there is no reason why the goal of price-level stability should not mean just that: an unchanging price level. In a dynamic world, where relative prices are continually adjusting, a stable price level requires that some individual prices rise while others fall. Many observers believe they have identified an asymmetry in price adjustments—prices seem to rise faster in the face of excess demand than they fall in the face of excess supply. (Note that this says nothing about equilibrium, only that the speeds of adjustment are different in different markets and for different directions of change.) As relative prices adjust continually to the forces of change, if prices rise faster in markets with excess demand than they fall in markets with excess supply, then the average level of all prices will drift upward. Under these circumstances the structure of the economy causes an inflationary bias on the order of 1 to 2 percent per year. This takes the form of a slowly shifting *SRAS* curve. In these circumstances the Fed has two choices. It can accommodate the inflation to hold income at its potential level, or it can refuse to accomodate the inflation and allow the recessionary gap to slowly open up.

This is called the structural theory of inflation. It was debated throughout the 1950s when, in spite of a recessionary gap throughout the last half of that decade, the price level continued to rise, albeit slowly. If the inflation rate falls to the 1 or even 2 percent range, the debate will rekindle: Is this the best that policy can achieve, or is zero inflation possible?

Are Full Employment and Stable Prices Compatible?

A debate has raged on both sides of the Atlantic for many decades: Are full employment and a low, stable inflation rate compatible in the long term? As long as the *SRAS* curve shifts only because of demand, expectational, and random shock effects, as we assumed earlier in this chapter, the answer is yes. But what worries some observers is the possibility of a cost push that pushes wages up faster than productivity once the fear of unemployment is reduced by the continued achievement of potential income. As far back as the 1940s many Keynesians were worried that, once the government was committed to maintaining full employment, much of the discipline of the market would be removed from wage bargains. The scramble of every group trying to get ahead of every other group would lead to a wage-cost push inflation. The commitment to full employment would then lead to accommodating increases in the money supply.

There is evidence that something like this has happened periodically over the last 40 years in Britain and in many of the countries of continental Europe. Most economists are more skeptical that it has been a serious force in the United States. Nonetheless, some observers still worry that full employment and a low, stable inflation rate may in the end prove incompatible. They argue for some permanent form of incomes policy.

An interesting argument presented by some economists is that the best way to ensure that the two objectives can be obtained most of the time is for governments to make clear that a stable price level, rather than full employment, is their overriding commitment and that, whenever the two come into short-run conflict, price stability will be given priority over full employment! They argue that once this message has been accepted by the public, there will be two benefits. First, wage-cost push inflations may not occur, even at full employment. Second, incipient inflations of the supply or the demand shock varieties will be easy to quell with only minor recessions because inflationary expectations and inertias will never have a chance to become strongly entrenched. In this environment major policy-induced recessions will not be required to control an outbreak of inflation. Paradoxically, by abandoning its full-employment commitment, the government may make the maintenance of something close to full employment much more likely—at least, that is how the argument goes.

Throughout the history of economics, inflation has been recognized as a harmful phenomenon. This view was given renewed strength as a result of the worldwide experiences of high inflation rates during the last 20 years. The resolve is there, at least in advanced industrial countries, to prevent another outbreak of rapid inflation, and, should one occur for reasons of unavoidable supply-side shocks, to prevent the inflation from continuing long enough to become firmly entrenched in people's expectations. The resolve is a matter settled in the last decade; the success in fulfilling this resolve is a matter to be tested in the coming decade.

Summary

1. Either supply shocks or demand shocks can cause a temporary inflation. For either to lead to sustained inflation, it must be accompanied by a continuing expansion of the money supply so that the *AD* curve is shifting upward.
2. A sustained price inflation will also be accompanied by a closely related growth in wages and other factor costs, so that the *SRAS* curve is shifting up.
3. Factors that influence shifts in the *SRAS* curve can be divided into three main categories: demand, expectations, and random shocks.
4. The influence of demand can be expressed in terms of the inflationary and recessionary gaps, which relate national income to potential income, or in terms of the difference between the actual and natural rates of unemployment.
5. Expectations of inflation tend to cause wage settlements that preserve the expected real wage and hence lead to nominal wage increases.
6. It is impossible to have a sustained, steady inflation when income exceeds its potential level. As expectations constantly catch up to the existing inflation rate, that rate, which is the sum of the expectations and demand effects, must accelerate.
7. It is possible to have a sustained inflation at potential national income (and hence at the natural rate of unemployment). There is no demand pressure on prices, but expectations can cause wages and hence prices to grow at the same rate as the money supply.
8. Stopping an inflation through restrictive monetary policy will lead to a recession that lasts while inflation only gradually falls to a rate consistent with the new lower rate of money growth. The length and depth of the recession will depend on the strength of the downward pressure on wages and on the speed with which inflationary expectations adjust.
9. Keynesians tend to believe that the negative demand pressures on wages from a recessionary gap are weak and that expectations are sluggish to adjust. As a result, they believe that the typical stagflation phase will be deep and prolonged. Monetarists tend to believe that the negative demand pressures from a recessionary gap cause wages to respond quickly and that expectations are fast to adjust.

As a result, they believe that the typical stagflation phase will be brief.

10. In the early 1980s the rate of monetary expansion was reduced dramatically in an attempt to bring inflation down rapidly. This resulted in a larger recession than most monetarists had predicted, but also in a faster reduction in inflation than most Keynesians had predicted.

11. Some economists believe zero inflation is an achievable goal of the policy of price stability; others believe a gradual upward drift of the price level on the order of 1 to 2 percent per year must be accepted.

12. Some observers doubt that continued full employment is compatible with stable prices. They advocate permanent incomes policies to control wage inflation and so to make the two objectives compatible. Many economists are skeptical that such policies are needed in the United States and see no compelling evidence why full employment and stable prices cannot coexist in a flexible market economy.

Topics for Review

Temporary and sustained inflations
Monetary accommodation of supply shocks
Monetary validation of demand shocks
Demand inflation
Expectational inflation
Natural rate of unemployment
Accelerating inflation
Entrenched inflation
Incomes policies

Discussion Questions

1. On what source or sources of inflation do the following statements focus attention?
   a. "The one basic cause of inflation is the government's spending more than it takes in. The cure is a balanced budget."
   b. "Wage bargains currently being negotiated in autos, and several other basic industries, will soon cause inflation to accelerate."
   c. "Americans have become so accustomed to 4 percent inflation that it would be difficult for the Fed to induce the transition to 1 or 2 percent inflation."

2. When OPEC radically increased the price of oil in 1974, the world was hit with a severe supply shock. The Bank of Canada decided to accommodate this with a rapid burst of monetary expansion, while the Fed decided on a policy of non-accommodation. What do you think happened to the inflation rate and the national incomes of the two countries over the following two years?

3. When the entrenched inflation of the early 1980s was broken, the economies of many industrial countries came to rest with a relatively

stable price level and high unemployment. People who feared the outbreak of inflation opposed even a temporary increase in the rate of monetary expansion. Use aggregate demand and aggregate supply analysis to show why some people felt a *temporary* burst of monetary expansion might bring increases in employment without increases in inflation.

4. Look at the rate of increases of the money supply and the CPI over the last three years and decide whether or not the current inflation is being validated.

5. Discuss the following views expressed by two U.S. congressmen in 1986.
   a. "Now that inflation has been beaten to the ground, we can get on with reducing unemployment."
   b. "Eternal vigilance is the price of a low inflation rate."

6. What theory or theories of inflation are suggested by each of the following quotations?
   a. American newspaper headline in 1986: "February producer prices steady—fall in energy costs largest in 6 years."
   b. Newspaper editorial in Manchester, England: "If American unions were as strong as those in Britain, American inflationary experience would have been as disastrous as has Britain's."
   c. Study issued in 1980 by the Worldwatch Institute: "The nation's spiraling inflation reflects a global depletion of physical resources and therefore cannot be cured by traditional fiscal and monetary tools."
   d. Article in the London *Economist*: "Oil price collapse will reduce 1986 inflation rate."

7. Discuss the following views on the effects of inflation.
   a. Robert D. Hersy, Jr.: "The beast [of inflation] is a luminescent specter, a killer, a threat to society, public enemy No. 1."
   b. James Tobin: "In the early 1980s inflation became the national obsession. . . . the catchall scapegoat for individual and societal economic difficulties, the symptom that diverts attention from the basic maladies."

8. In an article on the harmful effects of inflation written early in the 1980s, a reporter wrote, "With the rise in mortgage interest rates to 11 percent, heaven only knows the price of what was once idealized as 'the $100,000 house.'" At the time the inflation rate was 8 percent. Did the 11 percent interest rate represent a heavy burden of inflation on the new home owner? What do you think the mortgage interest rate would have been if the inflation rate had been zero? Which situation would have meant a heavier real burden on the purchaser of a new house?

9. Discuss the apparent conflict between the following views. Can you suggest how they might be reconciled using aggregate demand and aggregate supply analysis?
   a. "A rise in interest rates is deflationary, since breaking an entrenched inflation with a tight monetary policy usually requires that interest rates rise steeply."
   b. "A rise in interest rates is inflationary, since interest is a major business cost and, as with other costs, a rise in interest will be passed on by firms in terms of higher prices."

10. Inflations cannot long persist, whatever their initiating causes, unless they are validated by increases in the money supply. Why is this so? Does it not imply that control of inflation is merely a matter of not allowing the money supply to rise faster than the rate of increase of real national income?

Sustained Inflation and the Phillips Curve

In this appendix we use the Phillips curve, introduced in Box 34-2, to analyze sustained inflations.

The Price Phillips Curve

The Phillips curve shown in Box 34-2 described a relationship between the rate of change of *wages* and the state of demand, as measured by the level of national income. As we saw, changes in wages cause the *SRAS* curve to shift, giving rise to changes in the price level. These two steps are commonly combined to produce a new curve relating the rate of change of the *price level* and the level of national income. Such a curve, often referred to as a *price Phillips curve*, is shown in Figure 34A-1.

The conditions under which it is possible to derive a price Phillips curve from the original relation between wages and national income are fairly complicated.[1] But the curve is commonly used, and we shall focus on it in this appendix. (We shall henceforth refer to the price Phillips curve simply as the Phillips curve.) The key simplification is that once the level of income has been determined—by the intersection of the *SRAS* and *AD* curves, as before—the rate of inflation can be read *directly* off the Phillips curve.

Notice that the Phillips curve in Figure 34A-1 has the *rate of change of prices* on the vertical axis. The aggregate supply curve that appears so frequently in the text has the *level of prices* on the vertical axis. Since both curves have real national income on the horizontal axis they are early confused. They must therefore be carefully distinguished.

[1] For example, at any given level of income the relationship between the rate of change of wages given by the figure in Box 34-2 and the rate of change of prices given by Figure 34A-1 depends on what is assumed about how fast the Fed is causing the *AD* curve to shift.

The Components of Inflation

Recall the three influences that cause the *SRAS* curve to shift upward and hence the price level to rise: demand, expectations, and random shocks. We encountered these on page 689. In this appendix we continue to use the terms *demand* and *shock*, but introduce the term *core inflation* as a generalization of the term *expectations* used in the text. The rate of increase of prices can now be written as the sum of the three components:

$$\Delta p = C + DE + SE$$

where Δp is the annual percentage rate of changes of prices (i.e., the rate of inflation), C refers to core inflation, DE to demand effect, and SE to shock effect. We now look at these components one at a time.

Demand Inflation

Demand inflation refers to the influence on the price level of inflationary and recessionary gaps. We have seen that an inflationary gap involves upward pressure on wages and hence on the price level, while a recessionary gap involves downward pressure. This is shown in Figure 34A-1 by the vertical distance between the Phillips curve and the horizontal axis.

The Phillips curve in Figure 34A-1 is merely a novel way of expressing relations we have used many times before. (It is important to remember, however, that Figure 34A-1 does not tell the whole story of inflation; it describes only the effects of *demand*.) These relations include the following.

1. There is neither upward nor downward pressure of demand on the price level when national income is at its potential level. Graphically, the Phillips curve cuts the axis at Y^*.

FIGURE 34A-1   A Price Phillips Curve

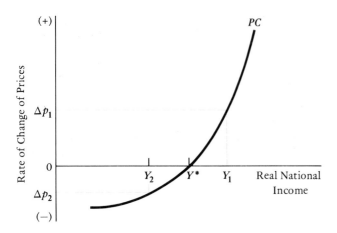

The price Phillips curve shows the positive relationship between the level of national income and rate of increase in **the price level.** An increase in national income leads to an increase in the rate of change of wages and, other things being equal, to an increase in the rate of change of prices. A fall in income leads to a decrease in the rate of change of wages and, other things being equal, to a decrease in the rate of change of prices.

With zero core inflation and output at its capacity level Y^*, inflation is zero as shown. When output is above Y^* at, say, Y_1, inflation is positive at Δp_1. When output is below Y^* at, say, Y_2, inflation is negative at Δp_2.

2. When there is an inflationary gap, wages and other costs will rise. As we have seen, this shifts the *SRAS* curve and causes the price level to rise. The inflation continues as long as the gap persists. Graphically, the Phillips curve lies above the axis where Y exceeds Y^*.
3. When there is a recessionary gap, wages and other costs will fall. This shifts the *SRAS* curve downward and causes the price level to fall. The deflation continues as long as the gap persists. Graphically, the Phillips curve lies below the axis when Y is less than Y^*.
4. The speed of the upward adjustment of the price level in the face of an inflationary gap exceeds the speed of the downward adjustment in the face of a recessionary gap. Graphically, the Phillips curve gets steeper the further to the right one moves along it. [45]

Core Inflation

The demand component cannot be the whole explanation of inflation since, if it were, inflation would only occur if national income exceeded Y^* and inflation could be quickly removed by forcing income back to Y^*. This behavior is emphatically rejected by the recent experiences of the United States and other Western economies. To explain what we observe about inflation we add the concept of core inflation. Core inflation refers to the underlying trend of inflation and it is referred to by several different names: *core* inflation, *expectational* inflation, *inertial* inflation, and the *underlying rate* of inflation.

In the text we singled out expectations as a main influence on the price level in addition to demand. But we also saw that how expectations are formed is a major source of controversy among economists. The controversy actually runs deeper than that; some question whether it is explicit expectations about the future or inertia based on past experience that really dominates wage settlements. For example, past experience may matter if recent wage increases have failed to keep up with price increases; in such circumstances current wage settlements may have a "catch-up" component.

For these and other reasons, we use the general term *core inflation* to describe those persistent effects that do not depend on current demand conditions. These include expectations and other elements that stem from both forward- and backward-looking behavior. Some elements may change quickly, others only slowly. Their total influence at any point in time is summarized in the term *core inflation.*

Core inflation operates on the *SRAS* curve

FIGURE 34A-2   Core Inflation and the Short-Run Phillips Curve

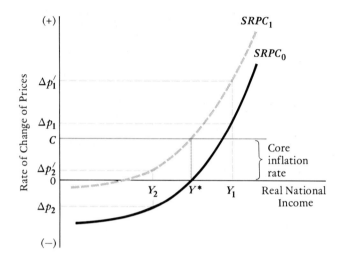

Core inflation shifts the price Phillips curve and so changes the rate of inflation that corresponds to any given level of national income. The curve $SRPC_0$, which reproduces the Phillips curve from Figure 34A-1, corresponds to a zero core inflation rate. When core inflation rises to, say, C, the Phillips curve shifts up to $SRPC_1$. The rate of inflation at Y^* rises from 0 to C. At Y_1, which is greater than Y^*, inflation rises from Δp_1 to $\Delta p_1'$. At Y_2, which is less than Y^*, inflation was initially negative at Δp_2, but now becomes positive at $\Delta p_2'$.

through the effects of wages and other costs.[2] Core inflation may also be related to *expected future changes* in wage and capital costs, since firms who plan to change prices only infrequently must set prices on the basis of their expected costs over their planning period. If that is the case, to make our concept of core inflation operative, we need a theory of how firms form their expectations of the future movement of costs. Some of the theories on how the expectations that determine the core inflation rate are formed are discussed in Chapter 37.

Graphically, the core inflation rate is added to the demand effect by shifting the Phillips curve upward by the amount of the core rate. This gives rise to a *core-augmented Phillips curve,* or more commonly an *expectations-augmented Phillips curve,* as in Figure 34A-2. At any given level of income, the height of the core-augmented Phillips curve is given by the sum of the demand effect and the core rate of inflation. For example, at $Y = Y^*$, when demand inflation is

zero, the height of the Phillips curve is given by the core rate. At any other level of income the rate of inflation differs from the demand effect by an amount equal to the core rate.

The short-run Phillips curve.   Because the Phillips curve shifts upward or downward as the core rate of inflation rises or falls, it is called a **short-run Phillips curve (SRPC)** when it is drawn at any particular height above Y^* (that is, for any given level of core inflation).

The short-run Phillips curve is drawn for a given rate of core inflation.

Shock Inflation

Shock inflation refers to once-and-for-all changes that give a temporary upward or downward jolt to the price level. These included changes in indirect taxes, changes in profit margins, changes in import prices, and all kinds of other factors often referred to as *supply shocks.* Shock inflation includes every-

---

[2] Some variations in net profit margins can and do occur. These cause price inflation to diverge temporarily from cost inflation and are included in shock inflation.

thing that is not included under demand and core inflation.

Summary

Putting all of this together, the current inflation rate depends on the influence of (1) demand as indicated by the inflationary or recessionary gap, demand inflation; (2) expected increase in costs, core inflation; and (3) a series of exogenous forces coming mainly from the supply side, shock inflation. These three components of inflation may be illustrated both numerically and graphically.

For a numerical example, assume that in the absence of any demand pressure, prices would rise by 10 percent because firms expect underlying costs to rise by 10 percent; that this price rise is moderated by 1 percentage point because costs only rise by 9 percent due to heavy unemployment; and that the price rise is augmented by 3 percentage points because large increases in indirect taxes force prices up. The final inflation is 12 percent, made up of 10 percent core inflation minus 1 percent demand inflation plus 3 percent shock inflation.

Graphically, the components of inflation are illustrated in Figure 34A-3 for two cases with a common positive core inflation component. The curve labeled *SRPC* is the expectations-augmented Phillips curve, that is, the Phillips curve shifted up by the core inflation rate. Its height above the axis at Y^* thus indicates core inflation. Points along *SRPC* where Y does not equal Y^* indicate how much the pressures of excess or deficient demand cause inflation to deviate from the core rate. The amount by which actual inflation lies above or below the *SRPC* shows the amount by which shocks cause the actual inflation rate to deviate from the sum of the core and the demand effects.

Expectations and Changes in Inflation

Originally the Phillips curve of Figure 34A-1 was thought to provide the whole explanation of inflation. When it was realized that the short-run Phillips curve shifted upward or downward, the concept of core inflation was added to explain this. Changes in the core rate cause shifts in the short-run Phillips curve. As a result we have the following conclusion.

FIGURE 34A-3   The Components of Inflation Illustrated

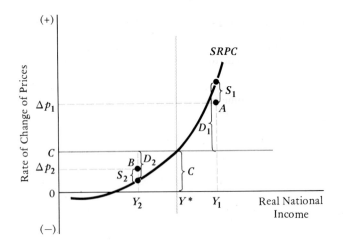

The inflation rate can be separated into three components: core inflation, demand inflation, and shock inflation. The Phillips curve is drawn for a given core rate of inflation and hence is labeled as a short-run Phillips curve. The given core rate, C, is shown by the height of the horizontal colored line.

Point A indicates a national income of Y_1 combined with an inflation rate of Δp_1. This rate is composed of the following: a core rate, C; a positive demand component, D_1 (determined by the shape of *SRPC*); and a negative shock component, S_1.

Point B indicates a national income of Y_2 combined with an inflation rate of Δp_2. This rate is composed of the following: core inflation, once again given by C; the demand component, D_2, which is now negative (since income Y_2 is less than Y^*); and a positive shock component, S_2.

There is a family of short-run Phillips curves, one for each core rate of inflation.

This is illustrated in Figure 34A-4. Let us now see what governs changes in the core rate and hence shifts in the *SRPC*.

Look at point *Z* on $SRPC_1$ in Figure 34A-5, which is reproduced $SRPC_1$ from Figure 34A-4 and corresponds to a core inflation rate of C_1. At the point *Z* shock inflation is zero and demand inflation is positive (since $Y_1 > Y^*$) so the actual inflation rate is above the core rate of C_1. Sooner or later this excess will come to be expected, the core rate will then rise, and the *SRPC* will shift upward. As long as national income is held above Y^*, the actual inflation rate will exceed the core rate and as a result sooner or later the core rate will rise. This means that the short-run Phillips curve will sooner or later shift upward, as indicated by the arrow above point *Z*.

Now look at point *W* in Figure 34A-5 where again core inflation is C_1 and shock inflation is zero. At *W* demand inflation is negative (since $Y_2 < Y^*$), so the actual inflation rate is below the core rate of C_1. Sooner or later this difference will influence ex-

pectations and the core rate will fall. As long as national income is held below Y^*, the actual inflation rate will be less than the core rate and sooner or later the core rate will fall. This means that sooner or later the short-run Phillips curve will begin to shift downward, as indicated by the arrow below *W*.

So we have a basic prediction of the theory:

A persistent inflationary gap will sooner or later cause the inflation rate to accelerate, while a persistent recessionary gap will sooner or later cause the inflation rate to decelerate.

This, of course, is the acceleration hypothesis that we have already encountered in the text. Let us now examine it in more detail.

Accelerating Inflation

Consider an economy with a core inflation of C_1 that has just experienced an increase in aggregate demand so that output is above Y^* as at point *Z* in Figure 34A-5. There is an inflationary gap with a positive inflation rate; the *SRAS* curve will be shifting upward, while monetary validation by the Fed is shift-

---

FIGURE 34A-4   A Family of Short-Run Phillips Curves

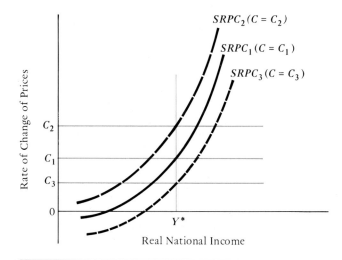

There is a separate short-run Phillips curve for each core rate of inflation. The Phillips curve of Figure 34A-3, shown here as $SRPC_1$, relates national income to inflation on the assumption that core inflation is C_1. The actual rate of inflation depends on both the core rate and the level of national income (as well as on shock inflation, assumed here to be zero).

For each positive core rate of inflation there is a short-run Phillips curve that lies above the axis at $Y = Y^*$ by the particular core rate to which it relates. If the core rate were C_2, greater than C_1, then the Phillips curve would lie above $SRPC_1$, as shown by $SRPC_2$. If the core rate were C_3, less than C_1, then the curve would lie below $SRPC_1$, as shown by $SRPC_3$.

FIGURE 34A-5   Shifts in the Short-Run Phillips Curve

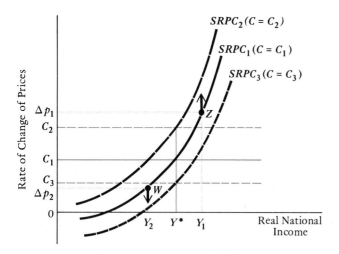

Changes in the core rate of inflation, which arise when actual inflation differs from the core rate, cause the short-run Phillips curve to shift. With a core inflation rate of C_1, the short-run Phillips curve is $SRPC_1$, reproduced from Figure 34A-4.

If income is maintained at Y_1, greater than Y^*, actual inflation will be Δp_1, greater than the core rate, as indicated by point Z. Eventually, this excess of the actual inflation rate over the core rate will cause the core rate to rise, from C_1, say, to C_2, shifting the short-run Phillips curve to $SRPC_2$, as indicated by the arrow above point Z.

If income is maintained at Y_2, less than Y^*, actual inflation will be Δp_2, less than the core rate, as indicated by point W. Eventually, the shortfall of actual inflation below the core rate will cause the core rate to fall below C_1, say, to C_3, causing the short-run Phillips curve to shift down to $SRPC_3$, as indicated by the arrow below W.

ing the *AD* curve upward. (It may be worth reiterating what is happening here: Core inflation produces the rise in prices that results from firms' expectations about the long-run trend in costs; the demand component produces the addition to inflation due to what are thought to be transitory demand factors; shock inflation is still treated as zero.

Is this situation sustainable? Only if the Phillips curve remains stable. If the short-run Phillips curve stayed put, policymakers could conclude that they had achieved a pretty good trade-off. They would have gained a permanent increase in output of Y^*Y_1 at the cost of a permanent increase in inflation from C_1 to Δp_1.

But as we have seen, this is not all that is happening. The persistence of a demand inflation will eventually cause the core inflation rate to rise and hence cause the *SRPC* to shift upward. In turn, this increases the rate at which the *SRAS* curve is shifting upward. Let us trace this process in detail.

At point Z prices and costs are rising at Δp_1 per year, and sooner or later firms and workers will stop believing that this increase from the old rate C_1 is a transitory phenomenon. They will come to expect some of this increase to persist and incorporate it

into core inflation. Let us say that after a passage of time firms come to expect wages and other costs to rise at the rate C_2 each period. This will produce a core inflation at a rate of C_2 per annum in Figure 34A-5. The short-run Phillips curve now shifts up to $SRPC_2$ in the figure. The rise in the core rate of inflation increases the actual inflation rate corresponding to each possible level of national income. If national income is maintained at Y_1 so that demand inflation remains positive, the actual inflation rate rises above Δp_1.

Now the *SRAS* curve will be shifting upward more rapidly. If output is to be maintained at Y_1, the Fed will have to increase the rate of monetary expansion. This will cause the *AD* to shift up more rapidly to match the more rapid upward shift in *SRAS*. This is illustrated in terms of the *SRAS* and *AD* curves in Figure 34-3.

The actual inflation rate, Δp_2 is well above the core rate, C_2. Sooner or later this will cause the core rate to rise again, and the short-run Phillips curve will again shift upward. As long as output is maintained at Y_1 so that demand inflation is positive, this process of growing core inflation will continue.

From this an important conclusion follows.

If the central bank validates any rate of inflation that results from Y being held above Y^*, then the inflation rate itself will accelerate continuously *and* the rate of monetary expansion required to frustrate the monetary adjustment mechanism will also accelerate.

The Long-Run Phillips Curve

Is there any level of income in this model that is compatible with a constant actual rate of inflation? The answer is yes, potential income. When income is at Y^*, the demand component of inflation is *zero*, as shown in Figure 34A-1. This means that, still letting shock inflation be zero, actual inflation equals core inflation. Since the core rate is determined by what people expect the inflation rate to be when actual inflation equals core inflation, the actual inflation rate is equal to the expected rate. There are no surprises. No one's plans are upset so no one has any incentive to alter plans as a result of what actually happens to inflation.

Providing the inflation rate is fully validated and shock inflation is zero, any rate of inflation can persist indefinitely as long as income is held at its potential level.

We now define the **long-run Phillips curve** as the relation between *national income* and *stable rates of inflation* that neither accelerate nor decelerate. This occurs when the core and actual inflation rates are equal. On the theory just described the long-run Phillips curve is vertical. This is illustrated in Figure 34A-6.

Maintaining a point on the *LRPC* leads to steady inflation at the core rate. This is illustrated in Figure 34A-7, where we show a situation with a positive core inflation rate and where there is full accommodation by the Fed. In (i) the intersection of the *SRAS* and *AD* curves determines Y at Y^*. In (ii) the Phillips curve shows the rate of inflation. There is no demand effect on inflation, so the actual and core inflation rates are equal. As a result the situation is sustainable (as long as the Fed continues to validate the core inflation). The increasingly price level in (i) reflects the positive inflation rate indicated in (ii). Note that

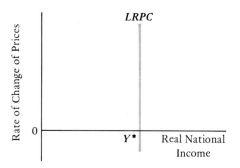

FIGURE 34A-6   The Vertical Long-Run Phillips Curve

When actual inflation equals expected inflation, there is no trade-off between inflation and unemployment. In long-term equilibrium the actual rate of inflation must remain equal to the expected rate (otherwise expectations would be revised). This can only occur at potential income Y^*, that is, along the *LRPC*.

At Y^* there is no demand pressure on the price level; hence the only influence on actual inflation is expected inflation. Any stable rate of inflation (provided it is validated by the appropriate rate of monetary expansion) is compatible with Y^* and its associated natural rate of unemployment.

in (ii), since the core rate is not changing, the *SRPC* will be stable, which means we are also on the *LRPC*.

We can now state the following general conclusion.

The long-run Phillips curve is vertical at Y^*; only Y^* is compatible with a stable rate of inflation, and any stable rate is, if fully validated, compatible with Y^*.

The Natural Rate of Unemployment

We have talked about variations of Y from Y^*, but for every level of national income there is an associated level of unemployment. Recasting these conclusions in terms of unemployment we have the following: As before, call the unemployment associated with Y^* the natural rate of unemployment. Note that unemployment can be pushed below the natural

FIGURE 34A-7   Monetary Accommodation and Steady Inflation

(i) Upward shifting *AD* and *SRAS* curves

(ii) Steady inflation

Positive core inflation means wage costs will be rising even when output is just at its capacity level; monetary accommodation can keep output constant and sustain the inflation rate. Core inflation is shown in (ii) by C, the height of the short-run Phillips curve above the axis at Y^*. This translates into an upward-shifting *SRAS* curve from $SRAS_0$ to $SRAS_1$ to $SRAS_2$ in (i). Monetary accommodation means that the *AD* curve in (i) also shifts upward, from AD_0 to AD_1 to AD_2. As drawn, the monetary accommodation just keeps output constant at Y^* so inflation persists at the core rate C.

The positive wage inflation in (ii) is reflected in an equal rate of price increase from P_0 to P_1 to P_2 in (i). Since we are on the *LRPC*, core inflation is constant and the *SRPC* is stable.

rate but only at the cost of opening up an inflationary gap. If the government seeks to maintain this lower rate of unemployment, the inflation rate will accelerate and will have to be validated by ever-increasing rates of monetary expansion.

The lowest rate of unemployment that can be maintained without a tendency for the rate of inflation to accelerate is the natural rate.

Implications for Monetary Policy

The foregoing analysis has three major implications for the understanding and conduct of monetary policy.

First, the interaction among money, inflation, and output is complex. In particular, it depends on how expectations are formulated. Monetary policies may affect expectations differently at different times. Therefore, it would be wrong to expect a simple, mechanical relationship between the money supply and the behavior of output and the price level.

Second, differences between the expected rate of inflation and the rate that is being validated by monetary policy lead to changes in the level of output and in the actual rate of inflation. Hence changes in the rate of monetary expansion can have powerful though not entirely predictable effects on the economy.

Third, in the long run GNP will move to the level indicated by the long-run aggregate supply curve and the long-run Phillips curve. This means that changes in the rate of monetary expansion will cause only temporary changes in the level of output. In the long-run changes in the rate of monetary expansion have their only influence on the rate of inflation.

Some Extensions

Shock inflation. All of the above analysis has been done on the assumption that shock inflation is zero. In today's world many shocks hit the price level. What we see is a much less regular experience than the simple combination of core plus demand inflation. The inflation rate varies quite substantially from period to period due to the action of the many shocks that impinge on it. When such shocks occur, the economy's output-inflation combination will lie off the current expectations-augmented Phillips curve—above it for a positive shock and below it for a negative shock.

Asymmetrical speeds of reaction. The shape of the Phillips curve means that it is easier to raise the core rate than to lower it. The change in the core rate from period to period depends on the discrepancy between the actual rate and the core rate. The steepness of the short-run Phillips curve above Y^* means that it is easy to create a substantial gap between the actual rate and the core rate by increasing the inflationary gap. This will tend to drag up the core rate fairly quickly. The flatness of the short-run Phillips curve below Y^* means that only a small discrepancy between the actual and the core rates can be created by even a large recessionary gap. Therefore, the core rate can be depressed only slowly by creating recessionary gaps.

It is an important prediction of this theory that the core rate of inflation can accelerate fairly quickly, but will decelerate only slowly.

Summary

We now summarize the key points of the theory of the expectations-augmented Phillips curve and indicate where there is substantial agreement and where there is controversy with competing theories.

1. *The rate of price inflation must follow the trend rate of cost inflation quite closely.* There is little disagreement over this relation, which defines the core rate of inflation. Notice, however, that it is just a matter of simple arithmetic that the major determinant of price inflation is cost inflation. This says nothing about causes. Costs could be rising because of the pressure of excess demand in factor markets or because of the exercise of arbitrary power on the part of unions.

2. *The influence of demand on inflation is asymmetrical.* Inflationary gaps cause inflation to rise well above the core rate while recessionary gaps force the actual rate only slightly below the core rate. The evidence for this asymmetry is strong, although some economists deny it.

3. *The core inflation rate falls slowly even in the face of large recessionary gaps.* There is a substantial disagreement over this point, for some economists believe the core rate can fall quite rapidly. This key controversy underlies many differences in policy recommendations.

4. *Shocks caused by such influences as changes in indirect taxes, agricultural crop failures, or increases in import prices temporarily affect the inflation rate.* Economists do not always agree on this point; at the time of the first OPEC oil-price shocks in 1974, some said that if oil-related prices rose, other prices would fall, keeping the price level constant. As a result of the evidence of the OPEC shocks, most economists now agree that supply shocks affect the price level, causing temporary deviations in the rate of inflation from what it would otherwise be. Another example of a clear supply-shock inflation was the rise in the price level that occurred in Britain in 1979–1980 after income taxes were cut and value-added taxes raised by the new Conservative government.

5. *Demand-induced rises in the inflation rate yield only temporary increases in national income.* Any departure of national income from Y^* sets in motion forces that cause a return to Y^*. Output in excess of Y^* causes an inflation that sets in motion the monetary adjustment mechanism. Frustration of the monetary adjustment mechanism by monetary expansion can sustain output above Y^*, but only if the rate of increase of wages, prices, and money is continually accelerating.

35

Employment and Unemployment

In the early 1980s worldwide unemployment rose to high levels. It remained high in many advanced industrial countries and only began to come down, and then very slowly, during the latter half of the decade. Although the experience in the United States was more favorable than in most other countries, the reduction in overall unemployment was still painfully slow. From a high of 9.7 percent in 1982 and 1983, it fell to 7.5 percent in 1984, and did not fall below 7 percent until early 1986.

Those overall American figures hide, as we shall see later in this chapter, large variations in rates for specific groups. For example, in 1985 the unemployment rate was 5.4 percent for white males over 19 years of age and 41 percent for black males between the ages of 16 and 19.

Many social policies designed to alleviate the short-term economic consequences of unemployment have been instituted since the 1930s, and their success may be counted as a real triumph of economic policy. Being unemployed, even for some substantial period of time, is no longer the economic disaster that it once was. But the longer-term effects of high unemployment rates in terms of the disillusioned who have given up trying to make it within the system and who contribute to social unrest should be a matter of serious concern to the haves as well as the have-nots.

Kinds of Unemployment

For purposes of study, the unemployed are classified in various ways. They can be grouped by personal characteristics, such as age, sex, degree of skill or education, and ethnic group. They can also be classified by geographical location, by occupation, by the duration of unemployment, or by the reasons for their unemployment.

We are concerned mainly with the reasons for unemployment in this chapter. Although it is not always possible to say why a particular unemployed person has no job, it is often possible to gain some idea of the total numbers of people unemployed for each major cause.

In Chapter 24, we distinguished two types of unemployment: *deficient-demand* unemployment, which is unemployment due to a recessionary gap, and *frictional* unemployment, which was used to account for the unemployment that exists when national income is at its potential level and hence there is neither a recessionary gap nor an inflationary gap.

For our more detailed study we will now distinguish a second reason why there is unemployment at potential income. We call this second reason *structural* unemployment. We also discuss an additional type, *real wage* unemployment.

Frictional Unemployment

Frictional unemployment refers to the normal turnover of labor. Young people enter the labor force and look for jobs. People leave jobs for many reasons. Some quit because they are dissatisfied with the working conditions; others are fired. Whatever the reason, they must search for new jobs, which takes time. Persons who are unemployed while searching for jobs are said to be frictionally unemployed.

Frictional unemployment would persist even if the structure of jobs in terms of skills, industries, occupations, and location was unchanging.

Normal turnover of labor will always produce a pool of persons who are frictionally unemployed. The search aspect of frictional unemployment is emphasized in a branch of modern theory that studies the rational behavior of people searching for jobs.

In looking at causes of unemployment, Keynes made a basic distinction between voluntary and involuntary unemployment. *Voluntary* unemployment occurs when there is a job available, but the unemployed person is not willing to accept it at the going wage rate. *Involuntary* unemployment occurs when a person is willing to accept a job at the going wage rate, but cannot find one. In Box 35-1, where we discuss search unemployment in more detail, we see that the distinction between voluntary and involuntary unemployment is not as clear as Keynes suggested.

Structural Unemployment

Structural adjustments of the economy can cause unemployment. When the pattern of demand for goods changes, the demand for labor changes. Until labor fully adjusts, structural unemployment develops.

Structural unemployment may be defined as unemployment caused by a mismatch between the structure of the labor force—in terms of skills, occupations, industries, or geographical location—and the structure of the demand for labor. In the United States today, structural unemployment exists, for example, in the automobile industry and in many of the older foundry and mill towns in the upper Midwest.

Natural causes.   Economic growth can cause structural unemployment. As growth proceeds, the mix of required inputs changes, as do the proportions in which final goods are demanded. These changes require considerable economic adjustment. Structural unemployment occurs when such adjustments are slow enough that severe pockets of unemployment develop in areas, industries, and occupations in which the demand for factors of production is falling faster than the supply.

Changes that accompany economic growth shift the structure of the demand for labor. Demand rises in such expanding areas as the Sun Belt states and falls in such contracting areas as the midwestern steel- and car-producing centers. Demand rises for workers with certain skills, such as computer programming and electronics engineering, and falls for workers with other skills, such as stenography and bookkeeping. Demand rises, say, for airline pilots and short-order cooks and falls for auto assembly line workers and crew members on transatlantic passenger liners. To meet changing demands the structure of the labor force must change. Some existing workers can retrain and some new entrants can acquire fresh skills.

Structural unemployment will increase either if there is an increase in the speed at which the structure of the demand for labor is changing or a decrease in the speed at which labor is adapting to these changes.

Policy causes.   Government policies can influence such changes. Often policies that discourage movement among regions, industries, and occupations also raise structural unemployment. Policies that discourage firms from replacing human labor with machines may protect employment in the short term. If, however, such policies lead to the decline of an

BOX 35-1

Search Unemployment

Some frictional unemployment is involuntary: No acceptable job in the person's occupational and skill category has yet been located. Often, however, it is voluntary. The unemployed person is aware of available jobs, but is searching for better options. Voluntary frictional unemployment is often called **search unemployment.**

The existence of search unemployment shows that the distinction between voluntary and involuntary unemployment is not as clear as it might seem at first sight. How, for example, should we classify an unemployed woman who refuses to accept a job at a lower skill level than the one for which she feels she is qualified? What if she turns down a job for which she is trained because she hopes to get a higher wage offer for a similar job from another employer?

In one sense people in search unemployment are voluntarily unemployed because they could find some job; in another sense they are involuntarily unemployed because they have not yet succeeded in finding the job for which they feel they are suited at a rate of pay that they believe exists.

Workers do not have perfect knowledge of all available jobs and rates of pay, and they may be able to gain information only by searching the market.

Faced with this uncertainty, it may be sensible to refuse a first job offer, for the offer may prove to be a poor one in light of further market information. Too much search—for example, holding off while being supported by others in the hope of locating a job better than that for which one is really suited—is an economic waste. Thus search unemployment is a gray area: some is useful, some wasteful.

It is socially desirable for there to be sufficient search unemployment to give unemployed people time to find an available job that makes the best use of their skills.

How long it will pay to remain in search unemployment depends on the economic costs of being unemployed. By lowering the costs of being unemployed, unemployment insurance tends to increase the amount of search unemployment. This is not necessarily undesirable. If the amount of search unemployment would otherwise be too little, then the insurance scheme can increase economic efficiency. If, however, the amount of search unemployment is already too much, then unemployment insurance will lower economic efficiency.

---

industry because it cannot compete effectively with innovative foreign competitors, serious structural unemployment can result in the long run.

One further cause of structural unemployment is the persistence of a disequilibrium structure of relative wages. Typical causes of such a structure are minimum wages, union agreements that narrow wage differentials, nationally negotiated wage structures that take no account of local market conditions, and equal pay laws where employers do not perceive that the groups concerned all contribute equally to the profitability of the enterprise. Such policies cause particular groups to lose employment because their relative wages are above their equilibrium value.

For example an elderly person may be prepared to work for $100 a week as a caretaker of an apartment. Further, the owner may believe that this person is capable of doing what is needed. But suppose

the minimum wage is $150 a week. If there were no minimum wage, the elderly person would get the job. But because of the minimum wage, the owner has to pay much more than she needs to and therefore hires someone else who can provide her with more services than she needs. She reasons that since she has to pay more, she might as well get something for it.

The same considerations apply to an inexperienced worker just out of school who would accept $100 a week for a first job. A potential employer is willing to pay this wage, but the minimum wage is $150. Once again the employer hires someone else who is overqualified for the job. A further unfortunate effect is that such young workers do not get the on-the-job training and experience that would equip them to hold down a stable, higher-paying job a year or two later.

Much empirical research supports the conclusion that imposed wage structures such as minimum wages tend to transfer employment from those whose relative wages are raised by the intervention to those whose relative wages are lowered. But do imposed wages affect overall employment? That is a difficult question but, as we discussed in Chapter 20, the evidence suggests that overall employment falls as a result of minimum wages. If such policies lead to an increase in the average wage paid, they may contribute to what we will call real wage unemployment, which we study below.

The Distinction Between Frictional and Structural Unemployment

As with many distinctions, the one between structural and frictional unemployment becomes blurred at the margin. In a sense structural unemployment is really long-term frictional unemployment. For illustration, consider a change that requires labor to reallocate from one sector to another. If the reallocation occurs quickly, we call the unemployment frictional; if the reallocation occurs slowly, we call the unemployment structural.

The major characteristic of both frictional and structural unemployment is that there is a job available, that is, an unfilled vacancy, for each unemployed person.

In the case of pure frictional unemployment the job vacancy and the searcher are matched. The only problem is that the searcher has not yet located the vacancy. In the case of structural unemployment, the job vacancy and the searcher are mismatched in one or more relevant characteristics such as occupation, industry, location, or skill requirements.

The sum of frictional plus structural unemployment is what in Chapter 34 we called the natural rate of unemployment.

Deficient-Demand Unemployment

We have called unemployment that occurs because total demand is insufficient to purchase all the output that could be produced by a fully employed labor force *deficient-demand unemployment*. It is the unemployment that exists because there is a recessionary gap. As a result there are fewer available jobs than there are unemployed persons. Deficient-demand unemployment can be measured as the number of persons currently employed minus the number of persons who would be employed at potential income. (It is thus the employment counterpart of the recessionary gap.) When deficient-demand unemployment is zero, there is some job available for every person unemployed. In this situation unemployment persists either for structural reasons or frictional reasons. This is the natural rate of unemployment.

National income theory seeks to explain the causes of and cures for unemployment in excess of frictional and structural unemployment. *Full employment* **does not mean zero unemployment; it means that all unemployment is frictional or structural.**

National income theory seeks to explain the deficient-demand unemployment associated with variations in the nation's total national income around its potential income.

Real Wage Unemployment

Unemployment due to too high a real wage is called **real age unemployment** or sometimes **classical unemployment.** This latter term is used because many economists, whom Keynes dubbed the classical economists, believed that unemployment in the 1930s was caused by high real wages. The remedy they suggested for unemployment was to reduce wages. Keynes argued that the unemployment was due to too little aggregate demand and his remedy was to raise demand, not cut wages. Keynesians won that debate, and there is now general agreement that the unemployment of the 1930s was caused by deficient aggregate demand rather than excessive real wages.

Because the debates of the 1930s aroused strong emotions, many modern Keynesians have refused to believe that *any* unemployment could be caused by high real wages. There is concern, however, that some current unemployment in Western Europe and elsewhere may be traced to excessive real wage levels.

So far in this book we have used the term *real wages* to mean the purchasing power of money wages. This is measured by deflating the money wage by the Consumer Price Index. In this section we are concerned with the real cost to the employer of hiring a worker. We call this the **real product wage.** The nominal cost to the employer includes the pre-tax wage rate, any extra benefits such as pension plan contributions, and any government payroll taxes such as employers' contributions to OASDI (social security). The real product wage is the nominal cost for a specific time period, say, per hour of labor employed, divided by the value of the output produced by labor during the same time period. Thus, for example, if it costs $20 to employ labor that produces output valued at $30, the real product wage is .666, which says that labor costs absorb two-thirds of the value of output.

Too high a real product wage can affect employment through forces operating both in the short run and in the long run. Consider the short run first. At any moment in time many industries have an array of plants, ranging from those that embody the oldest technologies in use and that can do little more than cover their variable costs to those that embody the latest technology and can make a handsome return over variable costs. A rise in the real product wage of 10 percent will mean that some plants can no longer cover their variable costs and so will close down. If, for example, a plant had wages of $.70 and other variable costs of $.25 for every $1 of sales, production would be worthwhile, since $.05 of every $1 of sales would be available as a return on already invested capital. If the product wage rose so that $.77 for every $1 of sales was paid in wages, then the plant would be shut down, since it would not even be covering its variable costs. The plant's employees would then lose their jobs. This also applies to the economy as a whole.

An economy-wide rise in real product wages, other things being equal, means that some plants and firms will no longer be able to cover their variable costs and will shut down. When they do, the unemployment rate will rise.

Now consider a period of time long enough for the demand for labor to be adjusted to the real product wage by replacing old plant and equipment with new capital that requires different capital-labor ratios. In the long run firms will adopt technologies that replace expensive labor with less expensive capital, and this will increase the amount of real wage unemployment. Thus, when the real wage is too high across the whole economy, a structural mismatch will develop between the labor force and the capital stock. This mismatch will show up as unemployment; when the capital stock is working at full capacity, there is still unemployed labor. The unemployment will continue until one of two things happen. Unemployment may force down the real wage until it pays firms to employ all of the existing labor. Alternatively, new technologies may be invented that make profitable use of the unemployed labor in spite of its high real product wage.

Experience of Unemployment

Measured and Nonmeasured Unemployment

The number of unemployed persons is estimated from the Current Population Survey conducted each month by the Bureau of the Census. Persons who are currently without a job but say they have actively searched for one during the sample period are recorded as unemployed. The total number of estimated unemployed is then expressed as a percentage of the labor force (employed plus unemployed) to obtain the figure for percentage unemployment.

The measured figure for unemployment may overstate or understate the number of people who are involuntarily unemployed.

On the one hand, the measured figure overstates unemployment by including people who are not involuntarily unemployed. For example, unemployment compensation provides protection against genuine hardship, but it also induces some to stay out of work and collect unemployment benefits for as long as they last. Such people have in fact voluntarily withdrawn from the labor force, but they are usually included in the ranks of the unemployed because, for fear of losing their benefits, they may tell the person who surveys them that they are actively looking for a job.

On the other hand, the measured figure understates involuntary unemployment by omitting some people who would accept a job if one were available, but who did not actively look for one in the sample week. For example, people who have not found jobs by the time their unemployment benefits are exhausted, may become discouraged and stop seeking work. Such people have voluntarily withdrawn from the labor force and will not be recorded as unemployed. They are, however, truly unemployed in the sense that they would willingly accept a job if one were available.

People in this category are referred to as **discouraged workers.** They have voluntarily withdrawn from the labor market because they believe they cannot find a job under current conditions.

In addition there is part-time unemployment. If some workers are working 6 hours a day instead of 8 hours because there is insufficient demand for the product they manufacture, then that group is suffering 25 percent unemployment even though no individual is reported as unemployed. Twenty-five percent of the potential manpower is going unused. Involuntary part-time work is a major source of unemployment of labor resources not reflected in the overall unemployment figures reported in the press.

The Overall Unemployment Rate

Figure 24-2 (see page 464) shows the behavior of the unemployment rate since 1930. Until 1970 unemployment among the civilian labor force fluctuated cyclically, but showed no clear rising or falling trend. During the 1950s the average rate was 4.5 percent and during the 1960s it was 4.8 percent—not a significant difference.[1] From 1970, however, the cyclical fluctuations appear to be superimposed on a rising trend. The *low* figure of 4.9 percent unemployment for 1970 to 1986 was above the *average* of 4.7 percent

---

[1] Yearly figures in this section are based on annual averages of unemployment.

for the previous two decades, while the high figure of 9.7 percent was the highest since the Great Depression of the 1930s. The low figure was achieved during the boom of 1972–1973, while the high occurred in 1982. The average rate of unemployment was 6.2 percent during the 1970s and 8.1 percent during the first six years of the 1980s. The strong recovery that developed locally in the United States by the mid 1980s still left unemployment around the 7 percent figure at the beginning of 1986.

These data reflect an important fact. The natural rate of unemployment rose some time around 1970 and remains significantly higher today than it was prior to that date. We shall see some of the reasons for this later in the chapter.

Just how much deficient-demand unemployment remains today when the overall rate is, say, 7 percent is a matter of some uncertainty. Some observers think it is no more than 0.5 percent, while others think it may be as much as 1.5 percent. Expressed as percentage points, the difference between 0.5 percent and 1.5 percent deficient-demand unemployment may not seem very big, but a reduction of one percentage point in the unemployment rate means that over 1 million more people have jobs.

It is important to know how much deficient-demand unemployment exists. Raising aggregate demand when national income is already at its potential level, and hence there is no deficient-demand unemployment, would open up an inflationary gap. This would accelerate inflation without achieving anything other than a transitory fall in unemployment.

The Relative Importance of the Various Kinds of Unemployment

At the beginning of 1986 there were about 8 million unemployed in the United States, about 7 percent of the labor force. This figure was down from the high of nearly 12 million that occurred at the end of 1982. According to the most widely accepted estimates, most of this unemployment was frictional and structural, with deficient-demand accounting for something between 0.5 and 1.5 million.

Most of the deficient-demand unemployment that existed at the end of the recession in 1982 was eliminated by the subsequent recovery, and the remainder will be eliminated *if* the recovery takes the economy all the way to its potential income. But what of the 6 million or so unemployed who will remain after deficient-demand unemployment is eliminated? To study them further we look at some of the characteristics of the unemployed.

Figure 35-1 gives some idea of the current duration of the spells of unemployment.[2] Data are given for 1982, a year of severe recession, and for 1985, when the economy was much closer to its potential income. The differences between the two sets of figures are due mainly to the reduction in deficient-demand unemployment over the period.

The figure shows that the bulk of reported unemployment is relatively short term. In 1985 fully 72 percent of the unemployed had been out of work for 14 weeks or less. Really long-term unemployment, more than half a year, accounted for only 15 percent of the unemployed in that year. These figures represent some improvement over the recession year 1982, when 67 percent of the unemployed had been without jobs for 14 weeks or less and 16.6 percent for more than 26 weeks. But the 1985 figures were not yet back to the more favorable ones for 1979, probably the last year when national income was at its potential level. In that year just less than 9 percent of the unemployed had been out of work for more than 26 weeks.

It seems that the potentially soul-destroying bouts of prolonged periods without a job are confined to a relatively small part of the labor force, but a part that rises significantly in recessions.

Figures 35-2 on page 723 and 35-3 on page 724 document some of the inequalities in unemployment rates. Males and females, the young and the experienced have very different unemployment experiences, as Figure 35-2 shows. Even more dramatic are the differences between white and black, as shown in Figure 35-3. By far the lowest unemployment

---

[2] The figures are based on the Current Population Survey, which asks currently unemployed individuals how long they have been out of work. Notice that this gives us the duration of *currently uncompleted* bouts of unemployment. It gives different and shorter figures than the duration of *completed bouts* of unemployment, which is obtained by asking people who have just found a job how long they were out of work.

FIGURE 35-1   Duration of Unemployment

☐ 1982   ■ 1985

Most measured unemployment is short term, but long-term unemployment rises during prolonged recessions. The figures refer to the length of time people who are currently unemployed have been out of a job. By far the largest single category covers those who have been out of work fewer than 5 weeks. In 1982, at the trough of a serious recession, fully 16.6 percent of the unemployed had been out of a job for more than 6 months, while in 1985, when the recovery had gone most of the way back toward potential income, the figure was still 15 percent.

---

rates in booms and slumps are recorded by white males 20 years of age and over. By far the highest rates occur for black males under 20 years of age.

Why Has the Natural Rate of Unemployment Risen?

Structural unemployment can increase because the pace of change accelerates or the pace of adjustment to change slows down. An increase in the rate of growth, for example, usually speeds up the rate at which the structure of the demand for labor is changing. The adaptation of labor to the changing structure of demand may be slowed by such diverse fac-

FIGURE 35-2   Variations in Unemployment Rates

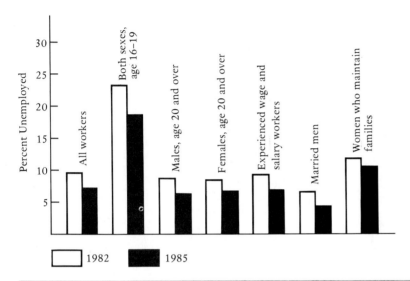

1982 ☐   1985 ■

Unemployment was unevenly divided among sex and skill groups in 1982 and again in 1985. In 1982 and 1985 overall unemployment rates of 9.5 percent and 7.1 percent, respectively, concealed large variations in the unemployment rates of different groups. The recovery from 1982 to 1985 led to a fall in unemployment rates among all groups. Unemployment among married men, who typically have favorable employment experiences, fell by 30 percent from 8.8 to 6.2 percent. Unemployment among youth reached close to 25 percent (one in four) in 1982 and fell only to 18.6 percent in 1985.

tors as a decline in education and new regulations that make it harder for workers in a given occupation to take new jobs in other states.

Demographic changes. Because people usually try several jobs before settling into one for a longer period of time, young or inexperienced workers have higher unemployment rates than experienced workers. Over the last 15 years the proportion of inexperienced workers in the labor force rose significantly as the baby boom generation of the 1950s entered the labor force along with an unprecedented number of women who elected to work outside the home. It is estimated that these demographic changes added nearly a percentage point to frictional and structural unemployment. Since birthrates were low in the 1960s and a further increase in the percentage of females entering the labor force is unlikely, there is expected to be some demographically induced fall in this type of unemployment over the next decade.

Other significant changes include the large increase in female participation rates and the related increase in the number of households with more than one income earner. In 1962 only 36 percent of white females 20 years and older were in the labor force;

in 1972 the figure was 43 percent; by 1985 it had jumped to 54 percent. (Black females have always had a higher "participation rate" in the labor force. During that 23-year period their rate rose from 50 percent to 57 percent.) When both husband and wife work, it is possible for one to support both while the other looks for "a really good job" rather than accepting the first job offer that comes his or her way.

Wage and price rigidity. Research by economists such as Professor Philip Cagan of Columbia University suggests that the speed with which wages and prices adjust to changing market conditions has slowed over the years. Anything that slows the speed of adjustment to the economy's ever-changing conditions will create a larger pool of structural unemployment.

Social insurance programs. Minimum wage laws are of real help to those who keep their jobs when their wages are forced up. They hurt those who lose their jobs as a result of the higher wage rates. They may also have a longer-term harmful effect. Employers are discouraged from hiring young people at

FIGURE 35-3   Unemployment by Age, Sex, and Race

(i) Whites

(ii) Blacks

Classification by age, sex, and race reveals large differences in the unemployment rates of these groups. Part i shows the unemployment experience of whites by age and gender; part ii shows the same data for blacks. In 1985 unemployment rates ranged from a high of 41 percent for black youths to a low of 5.4 percent for white males, age 20 and over. Similar inequalities were apparent in 1982, although the overall rate of unemployment was much higher. Youth unemployment is a serious problem among all groups—whites and blacks and males and females.

low wages while providing on-the-job training. During a period of training, employees acquire marketable skills that allow them subsequently to command a higher wage. By discouraging such practices, minimum wage laws create a pool of people without skills who alternate between low-paid jobs and bouts of unemployment, thus raising the number of people who are in structural or frictional unemployment at any one time.

Increasing structural change. The amount of resource reallocation across industries and areas seems to have increased over the last two decades. In part this is the result of the increasing integration of the U.S. economy with that of the rest of the world. Most observers feel that on balance this integration has been beneficial. But one less fortunate consequence is that changes in demand or supply conditions anywhere in the world requiring adjustments throughout the world's trading sectors increasingly affect the United States.

Internationally one of the most significant demand changes for the United States in the 1970s was the emergence of the Eastern bloc countries as major food importers. The failure of their system of collective agriculture to meet domestic demand led them to become large importers of grain. To pay for these imports, they had to become major exporters of other commodities such as natural gas.

A further demand change was the input price shocks that buffeted the world in the 1970s and early 1980s: two enormous oil price increases in the 1970s and an increase of over 200 percent in average basic materials prices in the early 1970s. Such changes have shifted competitive advantages in industrial production, leading to growth in some areas and countries and decline in others.

Changing prices have also caused changes in quantities demanded. The high cost of gas and oil led to a shift to small cars, an enormous investment program to retool U.S. industry, and major car imports from Japan and Germany that cut heavily into the demand for American cars and for their major inputs such as steel. The results were all too evident in the unemployment figures. At the beginning of 1983, when the overall unemployment rate was just

below 11 percent, unemployment was nearly 25 percent in the auto industry and nearly 30 percent in primary metals. Some of these workers were recalled as output recovered, but many had to find jobs in other industries and areas where new skills were required. Rising oil prices also led to a shift to natural gas for home heating, a large demand for insulation, and alterations in typical designs of new houses.

In the mid 1980s another set of changes more or less reversed the ones just discussed. These entailed a new and equally dramatic set of adjustments. More than a decade of high oil prices had led to a reduction in demand for oil and a great increase in its supply. Finally the OPEC countries were no longer able to control the price of oil, which tumbled in a few months during 1985–1986 to about one-third of its earlier value. The immediate effects were felt by the world's oil producers, including the United States. A rash of business bankruptcies and bank difficulties were brought on by the sudden loss of prosperity among both oil producers and those who sold to them or had lent to them. Oil users benefited greatly. Just as the high price of oil set in train a series of adjustments that economized on oil, the low price set in train the opposite series of adjustments. Once again the pattern of advantage of different technologies, products, and geographical areas changed, and major adaptations occurred.

The world food shortages in the 1970s and the accompanying high prices of foodstuffs caused a number of supply reactions to occur throughout that decade. The United States and many of the world's less-developed countries expanded their food production enormously. They were aided by technological developments which greatly increased crop yields per acre. By the mid 1980s food shortages were threatening to turn into food surpluses for many products. The emergence of the United States as the world's greatest agricultural exporter in the 1970s left American agriculture vulnerable to these changes. Difficult times for American farmers were already evident by the mid 1980s—although these were to a great extent due to over-borrowing during the earlier period of expansion. Serious slumps in world agricultural markets could have serious consequences for U.S. agriculture and would entail further major readjustments in the American economy, both among farmers and all of those who depend on farm income for their own sales.

A further factor on the cost side has been the increased use of robots in factories and computer-based processes in offices. These changes have eliminated many assembly line and clerical jobs and forced their former holders to look elsewhere for new jobs.

Another major set of forces leading to structural change arises from the shifting pattern of demand. As a result of rising income and changing social patterns, people spend a higher proportion of their income on services than they used to and a correspondingly smaller proportion on manufactured goods. Restaurant meals and day-care facilities for children are two services with rising demands. This shift is dramatically illustrated by the fact that the *increase* in employment in the fast food industry during the past two decades exceeded the total combined employment in the automobile and steel industries!

The pace of technological change over the last 15 years has contributed greatly to an increase in the level of structural unemployment.

Unemployment Policies

All kinds of unemployment have costs in terms of the output that could have been produced by the unemployed workers. Yet reducing unemployment is also costly. For example, retraining and reallocation schemes designed to reduce structural unemployment use scarce resources.

It would be neither possible nor desirable to reduce unemployment to zero. The causes of unemployment could never be removed completely, and reducing the amount of unemployment stemming from those causes is costly.

Unemployment insurance is one method of helping people live with unemployment. Certainly, it has reduced significantly the human costs of the bouts of unemployment that are inevitable in a changing society. Nothing, however, is without cost. While unemployment insurance alleviates the suffering caused by some kinds of unemployment, it can itself contribute to unemployment for, as we have observed, it encourages voluntary and search unemployment.

Supporters of unemployment insurance emphasize its benefits. Critics emphasize its costs. As with any policy, a rational assessment of the value of unemployment insurance requires a balancing of its undoubted benefits against its undoubted costs. Most Americans seem convinced that, when this calculation is made, the benefits greatly exceed the costs.

Deficient-Demand Unemployment

We do not need to say much more about this type of unemployment since its control is the subject of stabilization policy, which we have studied in several earlier chapters. A major recession that occurs due to natural causes can be countered by monetary and fiscal policy to reduce deficient-demand unemployment.

The 1970s and 1980s saw the emergence of *policy-induced* deficient-demand unemployment. This occurred when, in an attempt to combat inflation, the government adopted drastic contractionary policies that opened up large recessionary gaps. As we saw in Chapter 34, a temporary bout of deficient-demand unemployment was the price of reducing inflation.

Real Wage Unemployment

If this type of unemployment is a major problem, its cure is not an easy matter. Basically what is required is a fall in the real product wage combined with measures to increase aggregate demand so as to create enough total employment. But, as many European countries have discovered, the cure is slow and requires enough time to install new labor-using capital. The steps might be as follows.

1. The real product wage would have to fall substantially.
2. Since wages enter into disposable income and disposable income determines consumer demand, the cut in wages would tend to reduce aggregate demand and hence reduce equilibrium national income.

3. This deflationary force could then be countered by expansionary fiscal and monetary policy that would create sufficient aggregate demand to restore full employment.

Frictional Unemployment

The turnover that causes frictional unemployment is an inevitable part of the functioning of the economy. Insofar as it is caused by ignorance, increasing the knowledge of workers about market opportunities may help. But such measures have a cost, and that cost has to be balanced against the benefits.

Some frictional unemployment is an inevitable part of the learning process. One reason that there is a high turnover rate, and hence high frictional unemployment, is that new entrants have to try jobs to see if they are suitable. They will typically try more than one job before settling into one that most satisfies, or least dissatisfies, them.

Structural Unemployment

The reallocation of labor among occupations, industries, skill categories, and regions that gives rise to structural unemployment is an inevitable part of growth. There are two basic approaches to reducing structural unemployment: first, try to arrest the changes that accompany growth and, second, accept the changes and try to speed up the adjustments. Throughout history labor and management have advocated, and governments have tried, both approaches.

Resisting change. Since the beginning of the Industrial Revolution workers have often resisted the introduction of new techniques to replace the older techniques at which they were skilled. This is understandable. New techniques often destroy the value of the knowledge and experience of workers skilled in the displaced techniques. Older workers may not even get a chance to start over with the new technique. Employers may prefer to hire younger persons who will learn the new skills faster than older workers who are set in their ways of thinking. From society's point of view new techniques are beneficial because they are a major source of economic growth.

From the point of view of the workers they displace, new techniques can be an unmitigated disaster.

Here are two characteristic ways in which economic change has been resisted. First, a declining industry may be supported with public funds. If the market would support an output of X, but subsidies are used to support an output of $2X$, then jobs are provided for, say, half the industry's labor force who would otherwise become unemployed and have to find jobs elsewhere. Second, change may be accepted but agreement reached to continue to employ workers who would otherwise be made redundant by the new technology. Both these policies are attractive to the people who would otherwise become unemployed. It may be a long time before they can find another job and, when they do, their skills may not turn out to be highly valued in their new occupations.

In the long term, however, such policies are not beneficial. Agreements to hire unneeded workers raise costs and can hasten the decline of an industry threatened by competitive products. An industry that is declining due to economic change becomes an increasingly large burden on the public purse as economic forces become less and less favorable to its success. Sooner or later, public support is withdrawn and an often precipitous decline then ensues.

In assessing these remedies for structural unemployment, it is important to realize that, although they are not viable in the long run for the economy, they may be the best alternatives for the affected workers during their lifetimes.

There is often a genuine conflict between those threatened by structural unemployment, whose interests lie in preserving their jobs, and the general public, whose interest is served by economic growth, which is the engine of rising living standards.

Aiding adjustments to change. Another policy to deal with structural change is to accept the decline of industries and the destruction of specific jobs that go with it and to try to reduce the cost of adjustment for those affected. Retraining and relocation grants make movement easier and reduce structural unemployment without inhibiting economic change and growth. Retraining programs exist in the United States but have met with mixed success at best. Relocation grants are used successfully in countries such as Sweden, but have never been adopted in the United States.

By international standards the reduction in the overall level of unemployment during the recovery from the deep recession of the early 1980s was dramatic. As Figures 35-1 to 35-3 show, however, major inequalities in unemployment rates suggest that some severe structural problems will persist even when, on an overall basis, the economy is near to full employment. The Reagan administration's approach to structural unemployment has been to rely mainly on the workings of market incentives. Some schemes aimed at vocational training and retraining for youth, unemployed adults, and skilled workers in declining industries and regions were introduced, but these were given only limited funding and had correspondingly limited success.

Summary

1. Unemployment may be voluntary or involuntary. Involuntary unemployment is a serious social concern both because it causes economic waste due to lost output and because it is a source of human suffering.
2. Looking at causes, it is useful to distinguish several kinds of unemployment: (a) frictional unemployment, which is due to the time it takes to find a first job and to move from job to job as a result of normal labor turnover; (b) structural unemployment, which is caused by the need to reallocate resources among occupations, regions, and industries as the structure of demands and supplies changes; (c) deficient-demand unemployment, which is caused by too low a level of aggregate demand; and (d) real wage unemployment, which is caused by too high a real product wage. Together the amounts of frictional unemployment and structural unemployment make up what is now called the natural rate of unemployment.
3. Measured unemployment figures may overestimate or underestimate the actual number of unemployed, for they may include some who are voluntarily unemployed and omit discouraged workers who have left the labor force.
4. The natural rate of unemployment has risen in recent years. This is due in part at least to demographic changes in the work force, increasing wage and price rigidity in the economy, increasing generosity of unemployment compensation and other social insurance programs, and increasing structural change in the economy.
5. Unemployment insurance helps to alleviate the human suffering associated with inevitable unemployment. It also increases unemployment by encouraging voluntary unemployment.
6. Unemployment can be reduced by raising aggregate demand, by making it easier to move between jobs, by slowing down the rate of change in the economy, and by raising the cost of staying unemployed. However, it is neither possible nor desirable to reduce unemployment to zero.

Voluntary and involuntary unemployment
Deficient–demand unemployment
Frictional unemployment
Structural unemployment
Real wage unemployment
Effects of demographic and structural changes on unemployment

Topics for Review

Discussion Questions

1. Interpret the following statements from newspapers in terms of types of unemployment
   a. Recession hits local factory, 2,000 laid off.
   b. "A job? I've given up trying," says mother of three.
   c. "We closed down because we could not stand the competition from Taiwan," says local manager.
   d. "When they raised the minimum wage, I just could not afford to keep all of these retired policemen on my payroll as security guards," says local shopping center owner.
   e. Slack demand puts local foundry on short time.
   f. "Of course, I could take a job as a dishwasher, but I'm trying to find something that makes use of my high school training," says local teenager in our survey of the unemployed.
   g. Where have all the jobs gone? They have gone to the Sun Belt.
   h. "Thank God for the minimum wage. Without it, I couldn't earn enough to feed the kids," says single father of four.
   i. Retraining main challenge in increased use of robots.
   j. Modernization may cut U.S. textile workers.
   k. Uneven upturn: signs of recovery hit Louisville, but not all feel its effect, as joblessness stays high.
2. What differences in approach to unemployment are suggested by the following facts:
   a. Britain has spent billions on subsidizing firms that would otherwise have gone out of business in order to protect the jobs of the employees.
   b. Sweden has pioneered in spending large sums to retrain and relocate displaced workers.
3. Discuss the following views:
   a. "American workers should resist automation, which is destroying their jobs," says a labor leader.
   b. "Given the fierce foreign competition, its a case of automate or die," says an industrialist.
4. Discuss the following quotation: "There is nothing natural about the natural rate of unemployment; we should not let the inappropriate name 'natural' mislead us into believing that this amount of unemployment should be accepted as normal."
5. Use the latest *Economic Report of the President* to compare the percentage of total unemployment that is long term in the last year available with the figures for earlier years given in the text of this chapter. Can you think of any reasons why the figures have changed?

6. What theories can you suggest to explain why unemployment rates stay persistently above average for youths and for blacks and below average for males over 25?

7. It is often argued that the true unemployment figure for the United States is much higher than the officially reported figure. What are possible sources of "hidden unemployment"? On the other side, are there reasons for expecting some exaggeration of the number of people reported as unemployed? Would the relative strength of these opposing forces change over the course of the business cycle? What would you expect if a short recession turned into a long and deep depression?

8. At a time when the U.S. unemployment rate stood at close to 8 percent, the press reported, "Skilled labor shortage plagues many firms—newspaper ads often draw few qualified workers; wages over time are up." What type of unemployment does this suggest to be important?

36

Economic Growth

Popular debate is bedeviled by confusion about the various causes of change in national income. Some commentators argue that governments can spend their way into a rising national income. Others argue that while expansionary government policies may stimulate the economy in the short run, they often have adverse effects on growth in the economy in the long run.

Causes of Increases in Real National Income

Figure 36-1 illustrates some of the most important possibilities. If there is a recessionary gap, raising aggregate demand will yield a once-and-for-all increase in national income. But once potential income is achieved, further increases in aggregate demand yield only transitory increases in real income, but lasting increases in the price level.

Measures that reduce structural unemployment can also increase the employed labor force and thus increase potential income. The increase in income resulting from this change might not be very large. There would, however, be social gain resulting from the reduction in unemployment, especially the long-term unemployment that occurs when people are trapped in declining areas, industries, or occupations.

Over the long haul, however, what really raises national income is *economic growth*, that is, the increase in potential income due to changes in factor supplies (labor and capital) or in the productivity of factors (output per unit of factor input). The removal of a serious recessionary gap might raise national income by 10 percent, while the elimination of all structural unemployment might raise it by somewhat less. But a modest growth rate of 3 percent per year raises national income by 10 percent in 3 years and *doubles* it in about 24 years.

Over any long period of time economic growth rather than variations in aggregate demand or in structural unemployment exerts the major effect on real national income.

Effects of Investment and Saving on National Income

Short-Run and Long-Run Effects of Investment

The theory of income determination that we studied in Part Seven is a short-run theory. It takes potential income as constant and concentrates

FIGURE 36-1   Ways of Increasing National Income

(i) Removing deficient
     demand unemployment

(ii) Reducing structural
     unemployment

(iii) Continual economic
      growth

A once-and-for-all increase in national income can be obtained by raising aggregate demand to remove a recessionary gap or by shifting the *LRAS* curve by cutting structural unemployment. Continued increases in national income are possible by shifting the *LRAS* curve through continued economic growth. In (i) with the aggregate demand curve at AD_0, there is a recessionary gap of $Y_1 Y^*$. An increase in aggregate demand from AD_0 to AD_1 takes equilibrium to E_1, achieving a once-and-for-all change in national income from Y_1 to Y^*.

In (ii) potential output rises from Y_0^* to Y_1^* due to measures that reduce structural unemployment. The *LRAS* curve shifts from $LRAS_0$ to $LRAS_1$ because those who were formerly unemployed due to having the wrong skills or being in the wrong place are now available for employment.

In (iii) increases in factor supplies and productivity lead to increases in potential income. This *continually* shifts the long-run aggregate supply curve outward. In successive periods it moves from $LRAS_0$ to $LRAS_3$, taking potential income from Y_0^* to Y_1 to Y_2^* to Y_3^* and so on, as long as growth continues.

on the effect of investment expenditure on aggregate demand. Short-run national income theory concentrates on variations of actual national income around a given potential income. This short-term viewpoint is the focus of Figure 36-1(i).

In the long run, by adding to the nation's capital stock, investment raises potential income. This effect is shown by the continuing outward shift of the *LRAS* curve in Figure 36-1(iii).

The theory of economic growth is a long-run theory. It ignores short-run fluctuations of ac- tual national income around potential income and concentrates on the effects of investment in raising potential income.

The contrast between the short- and long-run aspects of investment is worth emphasizing. In the short run, any activity that puts income into people's hands will raise aggregate demand. Thus the short-run effect on national income is the same whether a firm invests in digging holes and refilling them or in building a new factory. The long-run growth of potential income, however, is only affected by that part of investment that adds to a nation's productive capacity; that is, by the factory but not by the refilled hole.

This point is important because some of what is classified as investment in the national income accounts is really consumption expenditure. Assume, for example, that a firm discards an adequate but dingy office building and "invests" in a lavish new head office building with superior facilities for its staff. This will count as investment in the national income data, and the expenditure will add to aggregate demand. In terms of growth, however, it is (at least in part) really disguised consumption for the firm's staff, and not investment that will increase the productivity of its labor force.

Similar observations are true of public-sector expenditure. Any expenditure will add to aggregate demand and raise national income if there are unemployed resources. But only some expenditure adds to the growth of full-employment income. Indeed, public investment expenditure that shores up a declining industry in order to create employment may have an adverse effect on growth. Such expenditure may prevent the reallocation of resources in response to shifts both in the pattern of world demand and in the country's comparative advantage. Thus in the long run the country's capacity to produce commodities that are demanded on open markets may be diminished.

Short-Run and Long-Run Effects of Saving

The short-run effects of an increase in saving are to reduce aggregate demand. If, for example, households elect to save more, this means they spend less. The resulting downward shift in the consumption function lowers aggregate demand and thus lowers equilibrium national income.

In the longer term, however, higher savings are necessary for higher investment. Firms usually reinvest their own savings, while the savings of households pass to firms, either directly through the purchase of stocks and bonds or indirectly through financial intermediaries. If full employment is more or less maintained in the long run, then the volume of investment will be strongly influenced by the vol-

ume of savings. The higher the savings, the higher the investment—and the higher the investment, the greater the rate of growth due to the accumulation of more and better capital equipment.

In the long run there is no paradox of thrift; societies with high savings rates have high investment rates and, other things being equal, high growth rates.

The Cumulative Nature of Growth

Growth is a much more powerful method of raising living standards than removing either recessionary gaps or structural unemployment *because it can go on indefinitely.* For example, a growth rate of 2 percent per year may seem insignificant, but if it continues for a century, it will lead to a more than sevenfold increase in real national income!

The cumulative effect of small annual growth rates is large.

To appreciate the cumulative effect of what seems like very small differences in growth rates, examine Table 36-1. Notice that when one country grows faster than another, the gap in their respective standards widens progressively. If countries A and B start

TABLE 36-1   The Cumulative Effect of Growth

Year	Rate of growth per year				
	1%	2%	3%	5%	7%
0	100	100	100	100	100
10	111	122	135	165	201
30	135	182	246	448	817
50	165	272	448	1,218	3,312
70	201	406	817	3,312	13,429
100	272	739	2,009	14,841	109,660

Small differences in growth rates make enormous differences in levels of potential national income over a few decades. Assume that potential national income is 100 in year zero. At a rate of growth of 3 percent, it will be 135 in 10 years, 448 after 50 years, and over 2,000 in a century. Compound interest is a powerful force!

from the same level of income, and if country A grows at 3 percent per year, while country B grows at 2 percent per year, A's income per capita will be twice B's in 72 years. You may not think it matters much whether the economy grows at 2 percent or 3 percent per year, but your children and grandchildren will! (A helpful approximation device is the "rule of 72." Divide 72 by the growth rate and the result is approximately the number of years it will take for income to double.) [46]

To dramatize the powerful long-run effects of differences in growth rates, we included in early editions of this text a table showing students of the 1960s that, if the then current growth trends continued, America would not long remain the world's richest nation, for Sweden, Canada, Japan, and many others were growing at a much faster rate. Many readers of that era rejected the notion as a textbook gimmick; deep down they knew that the material standard of living of the United States was and would remain the highest the world had ever known. Such a table is no longer even interesting, for by 1980 several industrial countries had indeed passed the United States in terms of per capita national income, and several more were within 10 percent of the U.S. level. Japan's experience is discussed in Box 36-1.

Growth, Efficiency, and Redistribution

Without any doubt, the most important single force leading to long-run increases in living standards is economic growth. To see this, let us compare the effects of growth with policies that increase economic efficiency or redistribute income. For the moment, we will consider a country with a constant population.

Making the economy more efficient can increase national income. But a once-and-for-all increase of between 5 and 10 percent would be an extremely optimistic estimate of what could be obtained by removing all economic inefficiencies.

Redistributing income can make lower-income people better off at the expense of higher-income people, but increasing the incomes of the bottom 20 percent of the people by, say, 10 percent above what

they now are would be a very optimistic prediction of what could be done with further redistribution policies. In any case, without growth the magnitude of the income gains that can be achieved for lower-income groups through redistribution is limited by the size of national income.

Economic growth, however, can go on raising national income for as long as growth continues, which can be for centuries. Even the modest rate of growth of 2 percent per year takes less than 5 years to make it possible to raise everyone's income by the 10 percent that was suggested as the maximum that could be achieved by policies that raise efficiency once-and-for-all. It takes just over 9 years for the 2 percent growth rate to raise the living standards of the poor (and everyone else) by the 20 percent that we suggested was a very high estimate of what might be obtained through redistribution policies. Furthermore, the gain continues beyond those time horizons as long as the growth persists. The 2 percent growth rate doubles average living standards about every 35 years so that average living standards will quadruple over one biblically allotted lifetime of three score years and ten.

The continued importance of efficiency and redistribution. When we say that over the long term by far the most potent force for raising living standards is economic growth rather than reducing inefficiencies or redistributing income, we are *not* asserting the unimportance of policies designed to increase economic efficiency or to redistribute income.

Consider efficiency first. If at any moment of time we could increase national income by removing certain inefficiencies, the gains would be valuable. After all, any increase in national income is welcome in a world where there is not enough to satisfy everyone's wants. Furthermore, inefficiencies may themselves serve to reduce the growth rate. For example, rent control, which we saw in Chapter 7 can be criticized for reducing the efficiency of the housing market, may also be criticized for reducing the geographic mobility of labor that is necessary for economic growth.

Now consider redistribution. It may be some consolation for the poor to know they are vastly better off—due to economic growth—than they

BOX 36-1

A Case Study of Rapid Growth: Japan, 1953–1973

The real national income of Japan was 5.4 times as large in 1973 as it was in 1953. Japan's economic growth rate was more than double the average rate in 10 North American and European countries and greatly exceeded the rate in any of them. What accounted for the extraordinarily rapid growth of Japan's economy?

To answer that question, two economists, Edward F. Denison and William K. Chung, analyzed and measured the sources of economic growth in Japan over two decades and compared the results with those for 10 Western countries. They also measured the difference between levels of output per worker in the United States and Japan in 1970 and identified its sources and magnitude. The results were published in 1976.*

They found that no single factor was responsible for Japan's high postwar growth rate. Rather, the Japanese economy benefited from several major sources of growth: an increase in quantity of labor, an increase in quantity of capital, improved technology in production, and economies of scale. Japan gained more in each of these respects than did any of the 10 other countries studied. In addition, Japan had the greatest reallocation of labor from agriculture to industry of all

* Edward F. Denison and William K. Chung, *How Japan's Economy Grew So Fast: The Sources of Postwar Expansion* (Washington, D.C.: Brookings, 1976).

the countries studied except Italy. Since productivity is generally higher in industry than in agriculture, a shift of this kind raises average productivity and thereby contributes to growth even without an increase in output per person in either sector.

The overall growth record of Japan was high partly because of a low initial *level* of productivity. It is easier to improve from a low base than a high one. At the end of the period productivity was still more than 40 percent lower in Japan than in the United States, even after eliminating the effects of differences between the countries in working hours, in composition and allocation of the labor force, in amounts of capital and land, in size of markets, and in the cyclical positions of the two economies. There was thus an obvious potential for still further Japanese growth relative to the United States.

A question was, could Japan's growth rate be sustained? The authors stressed the probability of a decline in the growth rate as the various ways of securing fast growth by "catching up" are successively exhausted. Nevertheless, they considered a fairly high rate of long-term growth in Japan—between 5 and 8 percent per year—likely for the rest of this century. (This prediction proved accurate for the decade following the period covered by their study.) By the year 2000 Japan may well be enjoying the highest standard of living of any industrialized country in the world.

---

would have been if they had lived 100 years ago. But this does not make it less upsetting if they cannot afford basic medical treatment for themselves, or schooling for their children, that is available to higher-income citizens.

Interrelations among the policies. One important implication of the above discussion is that policies to reduce inefficiencies or redistribute income need to be examined carefully for any effects they may have on economic growth. Any policy that reduces the growth rate may be a bad bargain, even if it increases the immediate efficiency of the economy or creates

a more equitable distribution of income. Consider, for example, a hypothetical redistributive policy that raises the incomes of lower-income people by 5 percent but lowers the rate of economic growth from 2 to 1 percent. In 10 years, those who gained from the policy would be no better off than if they had not received the redistribution of income while the growth rate had remained at 2 percent (and, of course, everyone who did not gain from the redistribution would be worse off from the beginning). After 20 years' time, those who had gained from the redistribution would have 5 percent more of a national income that was 12 percent smaller than it would have been if the growth rate had remained at 2 percent.

Of course, not all redistribution policies have unfavorable effects on the growth rate. Some may have no effect, and others—by raising health and educational standards of ordinary workers—may raise the growth rate.

Theories of Economic Growth

In theoretical discussions of growth it is useful to have a measure of the ability of an economy to convert its resources into goods and services. One widely used measure is output per hour of labor, or *productivity*. Obviously, productivity depends not only on labor input, but also on the amount and kind of machinery used, the raw materials available, and so on. The focus of this measure is explained by the special emphasis human beings place on labor.[1]

Economists today recognize that many different factors may contribute to or impede economic growth. Although our present knowledge of the relative importance of these factors is far from complete, modern economists look at the problems of growth more optimistically than did the Classical economists of a century or more ago. Of particular importance is the nature and source of the investment opportunities that can lead to growth. The differences between the Classical and contemporary points of view can best be understood by considering a revealing though extreme case.

Growth in a World with No Learning

Suppose that there is a known and fixed stock of projects that might be undertaken. Suppose also that nothing ever happens to increase either the supply of such projects or knowledge about them. Whenever the opportunity is ripe, some of the investment opportunities are utilized, thereby increasing the stock of capital goods and depleting the reservoir of un-

utilized investment opportunities. Of course, the most productive opportunities will be used first.

Such a view of investment opportunities can be represented by a fixed marginal efficiency of capital (*MEC*) schedule of the kind presented in Chapter 19. Such a schedule is graphed in Figure 36-2. It relates the stock of capital to the productivity of an additional unit of capital. The productivity of a unit of capital is calculated by dividing the annual value of the additional output resulting from an extra unit of capital by the value of that unit of capital. Thus, for example, a marginal efficiency of capital of 0.2 means that $1 of new capital adds $.20 per year to the stream of output.

The downward slope of the *MEC* schedule indicates that, with knowledge constant, increases in the stock of capital bring smaller and smaller increases in output per unit of capital. That is, the rate

FIGURE 36-2   The Marginal Efficiency of Capital Schedule

A declining *MEC* schedule shows that successive increases to the capital stock bring smaller and smaller increases in output and thus a declining rate of return. A fixed *MEC* schedule can represent the theory of growth in an economy with some unutilized investment opportunities but no learning. Increases in investment that increase the capital stock from K_0 to K_1 to . . . K_4 lower the rate of return from r_0 to r_1 to . . . zero. Because the productivity of successive units of capital decreases, the capital-output ratio rises.

---

[1] The discussion of productivity on pages 197–198 of Chapter 11 is relevant here. It should be read now and treated as part of this chapter. (Indeed, the whole section on the very long run, pages 196–202, could be usefully read now.)

of return on successive units of capital declines. This shape is a consequence of the law of diminishing returns.[2]

If, with land, labor, and knowledge constant, more and more capital is used, the net amount added by successive increments will diminish and may eventually reach zero. As ⟨…⟩ state of constant knowledg⟨e…⟩ down its *MEC* schedule.

In such a "nonlearning ⟨…⟩ vestment opportunities do ⟨…⟩ only so long as there are ⟨…⟩ use capital effectively to i⟨…⟩ a nonlearning world is a tr⟨…⟩ occurs as long as the soc⟨…⟩ utilized investment opport⟨…⟩

So far we have discuss⟨…⟩ of capital. The *average* eff⟨…⟩ the average amount produ⟨…⟩ per unit of capital employ⟨…⟩ cussions of the theory of ⟨…⟩ the *capital-output ratio,* whi⟨…⟩ put per unit of capital. In⟨…⟩ the capital-output ratio is ⟨…⟩

In a world without lea⟨…⟩ **capital stock will have** ⟨…⟩ **quences:**

1. **Successive increases** ⟨…⟩ **will be less and less** ⟨…⟩ **ital-output ratio wil**⟨…⟩
2. **The marginal efficie**⟨…⟩ **be decreasing and w**⟨…⟩ **to zero as the backl**⟨…⟩ **tunities is used up.**

Consequences of Learning

The steady depletion of growth opportunities with constant knowledge results from the fact that new investment opportunities are never discovered or created. However, if investment opportunities are created as well as used up with the passage of time, the *MEC* schedule will shift outward over time and the

effects of increasing the capital stock may be different. This is illustrated in Figure 36-3.

Such outward shifts can be regarded as the consequences of "learning" either about investment opportunities or about the techniques that create such opportunities. As shown in the figure, when learning ⟨oc⟩curs what matters is how rapidly the *MEC* sched⟨ule⟩ shifts relative to the amount of capital investment ⟨be⟩ing undertaken.

⟨G⟩radual reduction in investment opportunities: The ⟨Cl⟩assical view. If, as in Figure 36-3(i), investment ⟨op⟩portunities are created, but at a slower rate than ⟨th⟩ey are used up, there will be a tendency toward a ⟨fa⟩lling rate of return and an increasing ratio of capital ⟨to⟩ output. The predictions in this case are the same ⟨as⟩ those given for the world without learning.

This figure illustrates the theory of growth held ⟨b⟩y most early economists. They saw the economic ⟨p⟩roblem as one of fixed land, a rising population, ⟨an⟩d a gradual exhaustion of investment opportuni⟨ti⟩es. These conditions, they believed, would ulti⟨m⟩ately force the economy into a static condition with ⟨n⟩o growth, high capital-output ratios, and the mar⟨g⟩inal return on additional units of capital forced ⟨d⟩own toward zero.

⟨C⟩onstant or rising investment opportunities: The ⟨c⟩ontemporary view. The pessimism of the Classical ⟨e⟩conomists came from their failure to anticipate the ⟨p⟩ossibility of really rapid innovation—of technolog⟨i⟩cal progress that could push investment opportuni⟨t⟩ies outward as rapidly or more rapidly than they ⟨w⟩ere used up, as shown in parts ii and iii of Figure ⟨3⟩6-3.

⟨I⟩n a world with rapid innovation:

1. **Successive increases in capital accumulation may prove highly productive, and the capital-output ratio may be constant or decreasing.**
2. **Despite large amounts of capital accumulation, the marginal efficiency of new capital may remain constant or even increase as new investment opportunities are created.**

[2] This hypothesis was discussed on pages 182–183.

FIGURE 36-3 Shifting Investment Opportunities: Three Cases

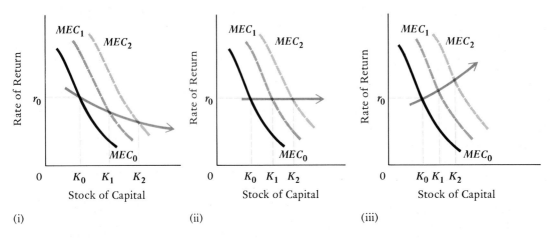

(i)   (ii)   (iii)

When both knowledge and the capital stock grow, the actual marginal efficiency of capital depends on their relative rates of growth. In each case the economy at period 0 has the MEC_0 curve, a capital stock of K_0, and a rate of return of r_0. In period 1 the curve shifts to MEC_1 and there is investment to increase the stock of capital to K_1. In period 2 the curve shifts to MEC_2 and there is new investment that increases the capital stock to K_2. It is the relative size of the shift of the MEC curve and the additions of the capital stock that are important.

In (i) investment occurs more rapidly than increases in investment opportunities and the rate of return falls along the black curve. In (ii) investment occurs at exactly the same rate an investment opportunities and the rate of return is constant. In (iii) investment occurs less rapidly than increases in investment opportunities and the rate of return rises.

The historical record suggests that outward shifts in investment opportunities over time have led to the reality of sustained growth. Evidently modern economies have been successful in generating new investment opportunities at least as rapidly as old ones were used up. Modern economists devote more attention to understanding the *shifts* in the MEC schedule over time and less to its shape under a nonlearning situation.

A Contemporary View of Growth

The classical economists had a relatively simple theory of growth because they viewed a single mechanism—capital accumulation—as decisively important. Contemporary theorists begin by recognizing a number of factors that influence growth, no one of which is necessarily dominant.

Quantity of Capital Per Worker

Human beings have always been tool users. It is still true that more and more tools tend to lead to more and more output. As long as a society has unexploited investment opportunities, productive capacity can be increased by increasing the stock of capital. The effect on output per worker of "mere" capital accumulation is so noticeable that it was once regarded as virtually the sole source of growth.

But if capital accumulation were the only source of growth, it would lead to movement down the MEC schedule and to a rising capital-output ratio and a falling rate of return on capital. The evidence does not support these predictions. The facts suggest that investment opportunities have expanded as rapidly as investments in capital goods, roughly along the pattern of Figure 36-3(ii). While capital accumulation has taken place and has accounted for much observed growth, it cannot have been the only source of growth.

Quality of Capital

New knowledge and inventions can contribute markedly to the growth of potential national income, even without capital accumulation. In order to see this, assume that the proportion of the society's resources devoted to the production of capital goods is just sufficient to replace capital as it wears out. Thus, if the old capital were merely replaced in the same form, the capital stock would be constant and there would be no increase in the capacity to produce. But if there is a growth of knowledge, so that as old equipment wears out it is replaced by different, more productive equipment, national income will be growing.

Increases in productive capacity that are intrinsic to the form of capital goods in use are called **embodied technical change.** The historical importance of embodied technical change is clear: the assembly line and automation transformed much of manufacturing, the airplane revolutionized transportation, and electronic devices now dominate the information technology industries. These innovations plus less well-known, but no less profound ones—for example, improvements in the strength of metals, the productivity of seeds, and the techniques for recovering basic raw materials from the ground—create new investment opportunities.

Less obvious, but nonetheless important changes occur through **disembodied technical change,** that is, changes in the organization of production that are not embodied in the form of the capital goods or raw materials used. One example is improved techniques of managerial control.

Most innovations involve both embodied and disembodied changes. But whatever the form of innovation, the nature of the goods and services consumed and the way they are made changes continually as innovations occur. Major innovations of the past century have resulted from the development of the telephone, the linotype, the automobile, the airplane, plastics, the assembly line, coaxial cable, xerography, computers, transistors, and silicon chips. It is hard for us to imagine life without them.

The Quality of Labor

The "quality" of labor—or what is often called *human capital*—has several aspects. One involves improvements in the health and longevity of the population. Of course, these are desired as ends in themselves, yet they have consequences for both the size of the labor force and its productivity. There is no doubt that they have increased productivity per worker-hour by cutting down on illness, accidents, and absenteeism. At the same time the extension of the normal life span with no comparable increase in the working life span has created a larger group of nonworking aged that exercises a claim on total output. Whether health improvements alone have increased output per capita in the United States is not clear.

A second aspect of the quality of human capital concerns technical training, from learning to operate a machine to learning how to be a scientist. Training is clearly required to invent, operate, manage, and repair complex machines. More subtly, there are often believed to be general social advantages to an educated population. It has been shown that productivity improves with literacy and that, in general, the longer a person has been educated, the more adaptable he or she is to new and changing challenges and thus, in the long run, the more productive. But education may also increase feelings of alienation in a society that is thought to be arbitrary or unjust.

The Quantity of Labor

The size of a country's population and the extent of its participation in the labor force are important in and of themselves, not merely because they affect the quantity of a factor of production. For this reason, it is less common to speak of the quantity of people available for work as a source of, or detriment to, growth than it is to speak of the quantity of capital or iron ore in the same way. But clearly, for any given state of knowledge and supplies of other factors of production, the size of the population can affect the level of output per capita. Every child born has both a mouth and a pair of hands; over a lifetime each person will be both a consumer and a producer. Thus, on average, it is meaningful to speak of over-populated or underpopulated economies, depending on whether the contribution to production of additional people would raise or lower the level of per capita income.

Because population size is related to income per capita, we can define a theoretical concept, *optimal population,* that maximizes income per capita.

Many countries have had, or do have, conscious population policies. America in the nineteenth century sought immigrants, as did Australia until recently. Greece in the 1950s and 1960s tried to stem emigration to Western Europe. All are examples of countries that believed they had insufficient population, though the motives were not in every case purely economic. In contrast, many underdeveloped countries of South America, Africa, and Asia desire to limit population growth.

Structural Change

Changes in the economy's structure can cause large fluctuations in its growth rate. For example, an expansion in such low-productivity sectors as agriculture and a decline in such high-productivity sectors as manufacturing will temporarily lower the measured aggregate growth rate.

When one type of energy (say, solar) supplants another type (say, oil), much existing capital stock specifically geared to the original energy source may become too costly to operate and will be scrapped. New capital geared to the new energy source will be built. During the transition, investment expenditure is high, thus stimulating aggregate demand. But there is little if any expansion in the economy's output capacity because the old capital goods have been scrapped. Gross investment is high, but net investment is low since the capital expenditure *transforms* the capital stock, but does not *increase* it. Similarly new pollution control laws will affect investment expenditure, but will not lead to growth in capacity. (The reduction in pollution may nonetheless be socially desirable.)

A rise in the international price of *imported* energy will also lower productivity. Although the same volume of goods can be produced with a given input of labor, a smaller portion of the output's value now accrues as income to domestic workers and firms

because more must be used to pay for the energy imports. The higher-priced imported energy input means that domestic *value added* falls, and with it GNP per worker. This shows up in the statistics as a decline in productivity and a temporary fall in growth rates.

These are some of the many factors that were operative in the 1970s and early 1980s. They worked to depress growth rates for some considerable period of time. But they are not permanent factors. When the structural adjustments are complete, their depressing effects will pass. Further, many of the effects were reversed when oil prices fell in early 1986, giving a boost to the productivity of many domestic factors of production.

Institutional Considerations

Almost all aspects of a country's institutions can foster or deter the efficient use of a society's natural and human resources. Social and religious habits, legal institutions, and traditional patterns of national and international trade are all important. So, too, is the political climate. In Chapter 42 many of these institutions will be discussed as potential influences on development.

Is There a Most Important Source of Growth?

The modern theory of growth tends to reject a dominant source of growth and to recognize that several different influences singly and in interaction affect the growth rate.

Among the major contributors to rapid economic growth are a capital stock that is steadily growing and improving in quality, a healthy and well-educated labor force, and a rate of population growth that is small enough to permit per capita growth in capital.

These factors are more likely to be utilized effectively in some institutional settings than in others.

A complete theory of growth would do more than list a series of influences that affect the growth rate. It would include assessments of their relative importance, the trade-offs involved in having more of one beneficial influence and less of another, and the interactions among the various influences. This poses a formidable program for further empirical research.

While much remains to be learned, an important tentative conclusion of recent studies is that improvements in *quality* of capital, human as well as physical, have played a larger role than increases in the *quantity* of capital in the economic growth of the United States since 1900. Whether quality rather than quantity of capital is also the more important source of growth for countries with different cultural patterns, more acute population problems, or more limited natural resources is a matter of continuing research.

Benefits and Costs of Growth

In the remainder of this chapter, we shall outline some more general considerations concerning economic growth. We start by looking at the benefits and then the costs of growth. Boxes 36-2 on page 742 and 36-3 on page 744 outline the popular arguments on both sides of the growth debate.

Benefits of Growth

Growth in Living Standards

A country whose per capita output grows at 3 percent per year doubles its living standards about every 24 years.

A primary reason for desiring growth is to raise general living standards.

The extreme importance of economic growth in raising income can be illustrated by comparing the real income of a father with the real income of the son who follows in his father's footsteps. If the son neither rises nor falls in the relative income scale compared with his father, his share of the country's national income will be the same as his father's. If the son is 30 years younger than his father, he can expect to have a real income nearly twice as large as

the one his father enjoyed when his father was the same age. These figures assume that the father and son live in a country such as the United States where the growth rate has been 2 or 3 percent per year. If they live in Japan, where growth has been going on at a rate of about 8 percent per year, the son's income will be about 10 times as large as his father's.

For those who share in it, growth is a powerful weapon against poverty. A family earning $9,500 today can expect an income of $14,000 within 10 years (in constant dollars) if it just shares in a 4 percent growth rate. The transformation of the life-style of blue-collar workers in America (as well as in Europe and Japan) in a generation provides a notable example of the escape from poverty that growth makes possible.

Growth and Income Redistribution

Not everyone benefits equally from growth. Many of the poorest are not even in the labor force and thus are least likely to share in the higher wages that, along with profits, are the primary means by which the gains from growth are distributed. For this reason, even in a growing economy redistribution policies will be needed if poverty is to be averted.

Economic growth makes many kinds of redistributions easier to achieve. For example, a rapid growth rate makes it more feasible politically to alleviate poverty. If existing income is to be redistributed, someone's standard of living will actually have to be lowered. However, when there is economic growth, and when the increment in income is redistributed (through government intervention), it is possible to reduce income inequalities without actually having to lower anyone's income. It is much easier for a rapidly growing economy to be generous toward its less fortunate citizens—or neighbors—than it is for a static economy.

Growth and Life-Style

A family often finds that a big increase in its income can lead to a major change in the pattern of its consumption—that extra money buys important amenities of life. In the same way the members of society as a whole may change their consumption patterns

BOX 36-2

An Open Letter to the Ordinary Citizen from a Supporter of the Growth-Is-Good School

Dear Ordinary Citizen:

You live in the world's first civilization that is devoted principally to satisfying *your* needs rather than those of a privileged minority. Past civilizations have always been based on leisure and high consumption for a tiny upper class, a reasonable living standard for a small middle class, and hard work with little more than subsistence consumption for the great mass of people. In the past the average person saw little of the civilized and civilizing products of the economy, except when he or she was toiling to produce them.

The continuing Industrial Revolution is based on mass-produced goods for you, the ordinary citizen. It ushered in a period of sustained economic growth that has raised consumption standards of ordinary citizens to levels previously reserved throughout history for a tiny privileged minority. Reflect on a few examples: travel, live and recorded music, art, good food, inexpensive books, universal literacy, and a genuine chance to be educated. Most important, there is leisure to provide time and energy to enjoy these and thousands of other products of the modern industrial economy.

Would any ordinary family seriously doubt the benefits of growth and prefer to go back to the world of 150 or 500 years ago in its same relative social and economic position? Surely, the answer is no. But we cannot say the same for those with incomes in the top 1 percent or 2 percent of the income distribution. Economic growth has destroyed much of their privileged consumption position. They must now vie with the masses when visiting the world's beauty spots and be annoyed, while lounging on the terrace of a palatial mansion, by the sound of charter flights carrying ordinary people to inexpensive holidays in far places. Many of the rich resent the loss of exclusive

rights to luxury consumption. Some complain bitterly, and it is not surprising that they find their intellectual apologists.

Whether they know it or not, the antigrowth economists—such as Kenneth Galbraith, Joan Robinson, and Ed Mishan—are not the social revolutionaries they think they are. They are counterrevolutionaries who would set back the clock of material progress for the ordinary person. They say that growth has produced pollution and wasteful consumption of all kinds of frivolous products that add nothing to human happiness. But the democratic solution to pollution is not to go back to where so few people consume luxuries that pollution is trivial; it is to accept pollution as part of a transitional phase connected with the ushering in of mass consumption, to keep the mass consumption, and to learn to control the pollution it tends to create.

It is only through further growth that the average citizen can enjoy consumption standards (of travel, culture, medical and health care, etc.) now available to people in the top 25 percent of the income distribution—which includes the intellectuals who earn large royalties from the books they write denouncing growth. If you think that extra income confers little real benefit, just ask those in that top 25 percent to trade incomes with the average citizen. Or see how hard *they* struggle to reduce their income taxes.

Ordinary citizens, do not be deceived by disguised elitist doctrines. Remember that the very rich and the elite have much to gain by stopping growth and even more by rolling it back, but you have everything to gain by letting it go forward.

Onward!

A. Growthman

---

as their average income rises. Not only do markets in a country that is growing rapidly make it profitable to produce more cars, but the government is led to produce more highways and to provide more rec-

reational areas for its newly affluent (and mobile) citizens. At yet a later stage, a concern about litter, pollution, and ugliness may become important, and their correction may then begin to account for a significant fraction of GNP. Such "amenities" usually become matters of social concern only when growth has assured the provision of the basic requirements for food, clothing, and housing of a substantial majority of the population.

National Defense and Prestige

When one country is competing with another for power or prestige, rates of growth are important. If our national income is growing at 2 percent, while another country's is growing at 5 percent, the other country will only have to wait for our relative strength to dwindle. Moreover, the faster its productivity is growing, the easier a country will find it to bear the expenses of an arms race or a program of foreign aid.

More subtly, growth has become part of the currency of international prestige. Countries that are engaged in persuading other countries of the might or right of their economic and political systems point to their rapid rates of growth as evidence of their achievements.

Costs of Growth

The benefits of growth suggest that it is a great blessing. It is surely true that, other things being equal, most people would regard a fast rate of growth as preferable to a slow one, but other things are seldom equal.

Social and Personal Costs of Growth

Industrialization can cause deterioration of the environment. Unspoiled landscapes give way to highways, factories, and billboards; air and water become polluted; and unique and priceless relics of earlier ages—from flora and fauna to ancient ruins—often disappear. Urbanization tends to move people away from the simpler life of farms and small towns and into the crowded, slum-ridden, and often darkly evil life of the urban ghetto. Those remaining behind in the rural areas find that rural life, too, has changed. Larger-scale farming, the decline of population, and the migration of children from the farm to the city all have their costs. The stepped-up tempo of life brings joys to some but tragedy to others. Accidents,

ulcers, crime rates, suicides, divorces, and murder all tend to be higher in periods of rapid change and in more developed societies.

When an economy is growing, it is also changing. Innovation renders some machines obsolete, and also leaves some people partially obsolete. No matter how well trained workers are at age 25, in another 25 years most will find that their skills are at least partially obsolete. A rapid growth rate requires rapid adjustments, which can cause much upset and misery to the individuals affected.

It is often argued that costs of this kind are a small price to pay for the great benefits that growth can bring. Even if that is true in the aggregate (which is a matter of debate), these personal costs are very unevenly borne. Indeed, many of those for whom growth is most costly (in terms of jobs) share least in the fruits of growth. Yet it is also a mistake to see only the costs—to yearn for the good old days while enjoying higher living standards that growth alone has made possible.

The Opportunity Cost of Growth

In a world of scarcity almost nothing is free. Growth requires heavy investments of resources in capital goods as well as in activities such as education. Often these investments yield no immediate return in terms of goods and services for consumption; thus they imply sacrifices by the current generation of consumers.

Growth, which promises more goods tomorrow, is achieved by consuming fewer goods today. For the economy as a whole this is the primary cost of growth.

An example will suggest the magnitude of this cost. Suppose the fictitious economy of USSA has full employment and is experiencing growth at the rate of 2 percent per year. Its citizens consume 85 percent of the GNP and invest 15 percent. The people of USSA know that if they are willing to decrease immediately their consumption to 77 percent, they will produce more capital and thus shift at once to a 3 percent growth rate. The new rate can be maintained as long as they keep saving and investing 23 percent of the national income. Should they do it?

BOX 36-3

An Open Letter to the Ordinary Citizen from a Supporter of the Growth-Is-Bad School

Dear Ordinary Citizen:

You live in a world that is being despoiled by a mindless search for ever higher levels of material consumption at the cost of all other values. Once upon a time, men and women knew how to enjoy creative work and to derive satisfaction from simple activities undertaken in scarce, and hence highly valued, leisure time. Today the ordinary worker is a mindless cog in an assembly line that turns out ever more goods that the advertisers must work overtime to persuade the worker to consume.

Statisticians and politicians count the increasing flow of material output as a triumph of modern civilization. Consider not the flow of output in general, but the individual products that it contains. You arise from your electric-blanketed bed, clean your teeth with an electric toothbrush, open with an electric can opener a can of the sad remnants of a once-proud orange, and eat your bread baked from super-refined and chemically refortified flour; you climb into your car to sit in vast traffic jams on exhaust-polluted highways. And so it goes, with endless consumption of high-technology products that give you no more real satisfaction than the simple, cheaply produced equivalent products used by your great-grandfathers: soft woolly blankets, natural bristle toothbrushes, real oranges, coarse but healthful bread, and public transport that moved on uncongested roads and gave its passengers time to chat with their neighbors, to read, or just to daydream.

Television commercials tell you that by consuming more you are happier. But happiness lies not in increasing consumption but in increasing the ratio of *satisfaction of wants* to *total wants*. Since the more you consume the more the advertisers persuade you that you want to consume, you are almost certainly less happy than the average citizen in a small town in 1900 whom we can visualize sitting on the family porch, sipping a cool beer or a lemonade, and enjoying the antics of the children as they play with scooters made out of old crates and jump rope with pieces of old clothesline.

Today the landscape is dotted with endless factories producing the plastic trivia of the modern industrial society. They drown you in a cloud of noise, air, and water pollution. The countryside is despoiled by strip mines, petroleum refineries, acid rain, and dangerous nuclear power stations producing energy that is devoured insatiably by modern factories and motor vehicles.

Worse, our precious heritage of natural resources is being fast used up. Spaceship earth flies, captainless, in its senseless orgy of self-consuming consumption.

Now is the time to stop this madness. We must stabilize production, reduce pollution, conserve our natural resources, and seek justice through a more equitable distribution of existing total income.

A long time ago Malthus taught us that if we do not limit population voluntarily, nature will do it for us in a cruel and savage manner. Today the same is true of output: If we do not halt its growth voluntarily, the halt will be imposed on us by a disastrous increase in pollution and a rapid exhaustion of natural resources.

Citizens, awake! Shake off the worship of growth, learn to enjoy the bounty that is yours already, and reject the endless, self-defeating search for increased happiness through ever-increasing consumption.

Upward!

A. Nongrowthman

Table 36-2 illustrates the choice in terms of time paths of consumption. How expensive is the "invest now, consume later" strategy? On the assumed figures, it take 10 years for the actual amount of consumption to catch up to what it would have been had no reallocation been made. In the intervening 10 years a good deal of consumption is lost, and the cumulative losses in consumption must be made up

TABLE 36-2 The Opportunity Cost of Growth

Year	(1) Level of consumption at 2% growth rate	(2) Level of consumption at 3% growth rate	(3) Cumulative gain (loss) in consumption
0	85.0	77.0	(8.0)
1	86.7	79.3	(15.4)
2	88.5	81.8	(22.1)
3	90.3	84.2	(28.2)
4	92.1	86.8	(33.5)
5	93.9	89.5	(37.9)
6	95.8	92.9	(40.8)
7	97.8	95.0	(43.6)
8	99.7	97.9	(45.4)
9	101.8	100.9	(46.3)
10	103.8	103.9	(46.2)
15	114.7	120.8	(28.6)
20	126.8	140.3	19.6
30	154.9	189.4	251.0
40	189.2	255.6	745.9

Transferring resources from consumption to investment goods lowers current income but raises future income. The example assumes that income in year zero is 100 and that consumption of 85 percent of national income is possible with a 2 percent growth rate. It is further assumed that to achieve a 3 percent growth rate, consumption must fall to 77 percent of income. A shift from (1) to (2) decreases consumption for 10 years, but increases it thereafter. The cumulative effect on consumption is shown in (3); the gains eventually become large.

before society can really be said to have broken even. It takes an additional 9 years before total consumption over the whole period is as large as it would have been if the economy had remained on the 2 percent path. [47]

A policy of sacrificing present living standards for a gain that does not begin to be reaped for a generation is hardly likely to appeal to any but the altruistic or the very young. The question of how much of its living standards one generation is prepared to sacrifice for its heirs (who are in any case likely to be richer) is troublesome. As one critic put it, Why should we sacrifice for them? What have they ever done for us?

Many governments, particularly those seeking a larger role in world affairs, have chosen to force the diversion of resources from consumption to invest-

ment. The Germans under Hitler, the Russians under Stalin, and the Chinese under Mao Tse-tung adopted four-year and five-year plans that did just this. Many less-developed countries are using such plans today. Such resource shifts are particularly important when actual growth rates are small (say, less than 1 percent), for without some current sacrifice there is little or no prospect of real growth in the lifetimes of today's citizens. The very lowest growth rates are frequently encountered in the very poorest countries. This creates a cruel dilemma, discussed in Chapter 42 as the vicious circle of poverty.

Are There Limits to Growth?

Those opposed to growth argue that sustained growth is undesirable; some even argue that it is impossible. Of course, all terrestrial things have an ultimate limit. Astronomers predict that the solar system itself will die as the sun burns out in another 6 billion or so years. To be of practical concern, a limit must be within some reasonable planning horizon. Best-selling books of the 1970s by Jay Forrester (*World Dynamics,* 1973) and D. H. Meadows et al. (*The Limits to Growth,* 1974) predicted an imminent growth-induced doomsday. Living standards were predicted to reach a peak about the year 2000 and then, in the words of Professor Nordhaus, a leading critic of these models, to "descend inexorably to the level of Neanderthal man." What lessons are there to be learned from this debate?

The Uncontroversial Fact of Increasing Pressure on Natural Resources

The years since World War II have seen a rapid acceleration in the consumption of the world's resources, particularly fossil fuels and basic minerals. World population has increased from under 2.5 billion to over 4 billion in that period, and this alone has increased the demand for all the world's resources. But the single fact of population growth greatly understates the pressure on resources.

Calculations by Professor Nathan Keyfitz of Harvard and others focus on the resources used by those who can claim a life-style of the level enjoyed by 90 percent of American families. This so-called middle class, which today includes about one-sixth of the world's population, consumes 15 to 30 times as much oil per capita and, overall, at least 5 times as much of the earth's scarce resources per capita as do the other "poor" five-sixths of the population.

The world's poor are not, however, content to remain forever poor. Whether they live in the USSR, Argentina, Korea, or Kenya, they have let their governments understand that they expect policies that generate enough growth to give *them* the higher consumption levels that all of *us* take for granted. This upward aspiration is being fulfilled to some degree in many countries. The growth of the middle class has been nearly 4 percent per year—twice the rate of population growth—over the postwar period. The number of persons realizing middle-class living standards is estimated to have increased from 200 million to 700 million between 1950 and 1980, and is predicted to almost double again by the turn of the century.

This growth is a major factor in the recently recognized or projected shortages of natural resources. Yet the 4 percent growth rate of the middle class, which is too fast for present resources, is too slow for the aspirations of the billions who live in underdeveloped countries and see the fruits of development all around them. Thus the pressure on world resources of energy, minerals, and food is likely to accelerate, even if population growth is reduced.

Another way to look at the problem of resource pressure is to note that present technology and resources could not possibly support the present population of the world at the standard of living of today's average American family. The demand for oil would increase fivefold to tenfold. Since these calculations (most unrealistically) assume no population growth anywhere in the world and no growth in living standards for the richest sixth of the world's population, it is evident that resources are insufficient.

A Tentative Verdict

Most economists agree that conjuring up absolute limits to growth based on the assumptions of constant technology and fixed resources is not warranted. Yet there is surely cause for concern. Most agree that any barrier can be overcome by technological advances—but not in an instant, and not automatically. Clearly there is a problem of timing: how soon can we discover and put into practice the knowledge required to solve the problems that are made ever more imminent by growth in population, growth in affluence, and by the growing aspirations of the billions who now live in poverty? There is no guarantee that a whole generation may not be caught in transition, with social and political consequences that promise to be enormous even if they are not cataclysmic. The nightmare conjured up by the doomsday models may have served its purpose if it helps to focus our attention on these problems and their imminence.

Summary

1. National income can increase as a result of reduction in the recessionary gap, reduction in structural unemployment, or growth in the level of potential national income.

2. Investment has short-term effects on national income through aggregate demand and has long-term effects through growth in potential national income. Such growth is frequently measured using rates of change of potential real national income per person or per hour of labor employed.

3. Savings reduce aggregate demand and therefore reduce national income in the short run, but in the long run savings finance the investment that leads to growth in potential income.

4. The cumulative effects of even small differences in growth rates become large over periods of a decade or more.

5. Understanding growth involves understanding both the utilization of existing investment opportunities and the process of creating new investment opportunities. The source of economic growth was once thought to be almost entirely capital accumulation and the utilization of a backlog of unexploited investment opportunities. Today most economists recognize that many investment opportunities can be created, and much attention is given to the sources of outward shifts in the *MEC* schedule through both embodied and disembodied technical change.

6. The most important benefit of growth lies in its contribution to the long-run struggle to raise living standards and escape poverty. It also makes more manageable the policies that would redistribute income among people. Growth also plays an important role in a country's national defense and its struggle for international prestige.

7. Growth, while often beneficial, is never costless. The opportunity cost of growth is the diversion of resources from current consumption to capital formation. For individuals who are left behind in a rapidly changing world the costs are higher and more personal. The optimal rate of growth involves balancing benefits and costs. Most people do not wish to forego the benefits growth can bring, but neither do they wish to maximize growth at any cost.

8. In addition to mere increases in quantity of capital per person, any list of factors affecting growth includes the extent of innovation, the quality of human capital, the size of the working population, and the whole institutional setting.

9. The critical importance of increasing knowledge and new technology in sustaining growth is highlighted by the great drain on existing natural resources of the explosive growth of the last two or three decades. Without continuing new knowledge, the present needs and aspirations of the world's population cannot come anywhere close to being met.

Topics for Review

Short-run and long-run effects of investment and saving
Cumulative nature of growth
Factors affecting growth
Effects of capital accumulation with and without new knowledge
Embodied and disembodied technical change
Benefits and costs of growth

Discussion Questions

1. We usually study and measure economic growth in macroeconomic terms. But in a market economy who makes the decisions that lead to growth? What kind of decisions and what kind of actions cause growth to occur? How might a detailed study of individual markets be relevant to understanding economic growth?

2. Why is rising productivity a more significant contributing factor for economic growth than simply increasing the quantity of productive resources? Define *productivity*. List all the factors that increase the productivity of labor and the productivity of capital. Comment on the differences and similarities of the two lists.

3. *Family Weekly* recently listed (among others) the following "inventions that have changed our lives": microwave ovens, digital clocks, bank credit cards, freeze-dried coffee, tape cassettes, climate-controlled shopping malls, automatic toll collectors, soft contact lenses, tubeless tires, and electronic word processors.

   Which of them would you hate to do without? Which, if any, will have a major impact on life in the twenty-first century? If there are any that you believe will not, does that mean they are frivolous and unimportant?

4. The Overseas Development Council recently introduced "a new measure of economic development based on the physical quality of life." Its index, called PQLI, gives one-third weight to each of the following indicators: literacy, life expectancy, and infant mortality. While countries such as the United States and the Netherlands rank high on either the PQLI or on an index of per capita real national income, some relatively poor countries, such as Sri Lanka, rank much higher on the PQLI index than much richer countries such as Algeria and Kuwait. Discuss the merits or deficiencies of this measure.

5. "The case for economic growth is that it gives man greater control over his environment, and consequently increases his freedom." Explain why you agree or disagree with this statement by Nobel Laureate W. Arthur Lewis.

6. Consider a developed economy that decides to achieve a zero rate of growth for the future. What implications would such a "stationary state" have for the processes of production and consumption?

7. Suppose solar energy becomes the dominant form of energy in the twenty-first century. What changes will this make in the growth rates of Africa and Northern Europe?

8. Discuss the following headlines from the *New York Times* and the *Wall Street Journal* in terms of the sources, costs, and benefits of growth.
   a. "Stress addiction: 'life in the fast lanes' may have its benefits"
   b. "Education: an expert urges multiple reforms"
   c. "Industrial radiation risk higher than thought"
   d. "Developments in the field of management design are looking ahead"
   e. "Ford urged by federal safety officials to recall several hundred thousand of its 1981–1982 front-drive vehicles because of alleged fire hazards"

9. In the late 1970s and early 1980s productivity growth was historically low, but it rebounded after 1983. How might you explain this?

37

Macroeconomic Controversies

How well do markets work? Can government improve market performance? In various guises these two questions are the basis of most disagreements over economic policy. We shall see that different answers to these questions imply big differences in macroeconomic policy prescriptions.

Alternative Views: Conservative and Interventionist

Macroeconomics is mainly concerned with the behavior of three important variables: employment (and unemployment), the price level, and the rate of economic growth. Macroeconomic policy suggests goals for each: full employment, stable prices, and a satisfactory growth rate. The advantages of full employment and a positive growth rate are obvious and not subject to serious dispute. Although most people agree that inflation is harmful, there is much debate about what can really be blamed on it.

Broadly speaking, we can identify a non-interventionist and an interventionist view with respect to each of the policy goals just specified. The non-interventionist view says that the unaided market economy can best achieve the goal. The interventionist view says that government policy can improve the economy's performance in terms of that goal. Since one can take a non-interventionist or an interventionist position with respect to each of these three goals, there are eight different possible policy combinations.[1]

Consider two extreme policy stances: *conservatives* are non-interventionist on all issues, while *interventionists* support government intervention at all times. A few people may actually be conservative or interventionist in this sense. Most, however, would favor intervention on some issues and oppose it on others. They might still identify themselves as conservative or interventionist because they were more often on one side than the other.

It is popular to identify monetarist with conservative and Keynesian with interventionist. It is true that many monetarists are on the conservative side, while many Keynesians are on the interventionist side. But it is not always so. It is, for example, quite possible to be Keynesian in accepting the Keynesian macro model as a reasonable description of the economy's macroeconomic behavior, but conservative in believing that the unaided market usually does the best job of allocating resources.

[1] Since each of the three issues breaks up into hundreds of different subissues, there are thousands of different policy stances available on one side or the other of each issue.

The Conservative View

Conservatives believe that the free-market economy performs quite well on balance. Although shocks do hit the system, they lead rather quickly, and often painlessly, to the adjustments dictated by the market system. For example, relative prices in booming sectors rise, drawing in resources from declining sectors or regions. As a result, resources (and particularly labor) usually remain fully employed, so there is no need for full-employment policies.

Conservatives hold that macroeconomic performance will be most satisfactory if it is determined solely by the workings of the free market.

Of course, few believe that the market system functions perfectly, thereby ensuring *continuous* full employment. But the view is that the market system works well enough to preclude any constructive role for policy.

In addition, many conservatives believe that policy instruments are so crude that their use is often counterproductive. A policy's effects may be so uncertain, with regard to both strength and timing, that it may often impair rather than improve the economy's performance.

In a modern economy some government presence is inevitable. Thus a stance of no intervention is impossible; rather, what is advocated by conservatives is minimal direct intervention in the market system. This involves the government's bearing responsibility for providing a *stable environment* in which the private sector can function.

The Interventionist View

Interventionists believe that the functioning of the free-market economy is often far from satisfactory. Sometimes markets show weak self-regulatory forces and the economy settles into prolonged periods of heavy unemployment. At other times markets tend to "overcorrect," causing the economy to lurch between the extremes of large recessionary and large inflationary gaps.

This behavior can be improved, argue the inter-

ventionists. Even though interventionist policies may be imperfect, they may be good enough to improve the functioning of the economy with respect to all three main goals of macro policy.

Macroeconomic Issues

Everyone agrees that the economy's performance is often less than perfectly satisfactory. Serious unemployment has been a recurring problem. Inflation was a serious problem throughout the 1970s and early 1980s. For most of that period growth rates were unsatisfactorily low. Conservatives and interventionists differ in diagnosing the causes of these economic ills.

The Business Cycle

We saw in Chapter 24 that cyclical ups and downs can be observed for as far back as records exist. Monetarists and Keynesians have long argued about the causes. As was noted in Chapter 32, monetarists often are identified with conservative views, and Keynesians with interventionist.[2]

Monetarist views. Monetarists believe that the economy is inherently stable because private-sector expenditure functions are relatively stable. In addition, they believe that shifts in the aggregate demand curve are mainly due to policy-induced changes in the money supply.[3]

The view that business cycles have mainly monetary causes relies heavily on the evidence advanced by Milton Friedman and Anna Schwartz in their monumental *A Monetary History of the United States, 1867–1960*. They establish a strong correlation be-

---

[2] The appendix to this chapter presents the widely used *IS/LM* model of the influence of monetary and fiscal policy. The *IS/LM* model expands on the theory developed in Chapter 32.

[3] The view that fluctuations often have monetary causes is not new. The English economist R. G. Hawtrey, the Austrian Nobel Laureate F. A. von Hayek, and the Swedish economist Knut Wicksell are prominent among those who have given monetary factors an important role in explaining the turning points in cycles and/or the tendency for expansions and contractions, once begun, to become cumulative and self-reinforcing. Modern monetarists carry on this tradition.

tween changes in the money supply and changes in the level of business activity. Major recessions have been associated with absolute declines in the money supply and minor recessions with the slowing of the rate of increase in the money supply below its long-term trend.

The correlation between changes in the money supply and changes in the level of business activity is now accepted by almost all economists. But there is controversy over how this correlation is to be interpreted. Do changes in money supply cause changes in the level of aggregate demand and hence of business activity, or vice versa?

Friedman and Schwartz maintain that changes in the money supply cause changes in business activity. They argue, for example, that the severity of the Great Depression was due to a major contraction in the money supply that shifted the aggregate demand curve far to the left. The Great Depression is further discussed in Box 37-1.

According to monetarists, fluctuations in the money supply cause fluctuations in national income.

This leads the monetarists to advocate a policy of stabilizing the growth of the money supply. In their view this would avoid policy-induced instability of the aggregate demand curve.

Keynesian views. The Keynesian view on cyclical fluctuations in the economy has two parts. First, it emphasizes variations in investment as a cause of business cycles and stresses the nonmonetary causes of such variations.[4]

Keynesians reject what they regard as the extreme monetarist view that only money matters in explaining cyclical fluctuations. Many Keynesians believe

that both monetary and nonmonetary forces are important in explaining the cyclical behavior of the economy. Although they accept serious monetary mismanagement as one potential source of economic fluctuations, they do not believe that it is the only or even the major source of such fluctuations. Thus they deny the monetary interpretation of business cycle history given by Friedman and Schwartz. They believe that most fluctuations in the aggregate demand curve are due to variations in the desire to spend on the part of the private sector and are not induced by government policy.

Keynesians also believe that the economy lacks strong natural corrective mechanisms that will always force it easily and quickly back to full employment. They believe that while the price level rises fairly quickly to eliminate *inflationary* gaps, the price level does not fall quickly to eliminate *recessionary* gaps. Keynesians stress the asymmetries noted in earlier chapters that imply that prices and wages fall only slowly in response to a recessionary gap. As a result, Keynesians believe that recessionary gaps can persist for long periods of time unless they are eliminated by an active stabilization policy.

The second part of the Keynesian view on cyclical fluctuations is that they accept the correlation between changes in the money supply and changes in the level of economic activity, but that their explanation reverses the causality suggested by the monetarists. The Keynesians argue that changes in the level of economic activity tend to cause changes in the money supply. They offer several reasons for this, but only the most important need be mentioned.

Keynesians point out that from 1945 to the early 1970s most central banks, including the Fed, tended to stabilize interest rates as the target variable of monetary policy. To do this they had to increase the money supply during upswings in the business cycle and decrease it during downswings. When an expansion got under way, the demand for money tended to increase, and if there was no increase in the money supply, interest rates would rise. The central bank might prevent this rise in interest rates by buying bonds offered for sale at current prices, but in so doing it would increase banks' reserves and thereby inject new money into the economy. Similarly, in a

---

[4] Like the monetarists, the Keynesians are modern advocates of views that have a long history. The great Austrian (and later American) economist Joseph Schumpeter stressed such explanations early in the present century. The Swedish economist Wicksell and the German Speithoff both stressed this aspect of economic fluctuations before the emergence of the Keynesian school of thought.

BOX 37-1

Two Views on the Great Depression

The stock market crash of 1929, and other factors associated with a moderate downswing in business activity during the late 1920s, caused the public to wish to hold more cash and less demand deposits. The banking system could not, however, meet this increased demand for liquidity without help from the Federal Reserve System. (As we saw in Chapter 31, banks are never able to meet from their own reserves a sudden demand to withdraw currency on the part of a large fraction of their depositors. Their reserves are always inadequate to meet such a demand.) The Fed had been set up to provide just such emergency assistance to banks that were basically sound, but that were unable to meet sudden demands by depositors to withdraw cash. However, the Fed refused to extend the necessary help, and successive waves of bank failures followed as a direct result. During each wave hundreds of banks failed, ruining many depositors and thereby worsening an already severe depression. In the last half of 1931 almost 2,000 American banks were forced to suspend operations! One consequence of this was a sharp drop in the money supply; by 1932 the money supply was 35 percent below the level of 1929. To monetarists these facts seem decisive.

While Keynesians accept the argument that the Fed's behavior was perverse, they argue that the cyclical behavior of investment and consumption expenditure was the major cause of the Great Depression. In support of this view, they point out that in Canada and the United Kingdom, where the central bank came to the aid of the banking system, bank failures were trivial during the Great Depression, and as a consequence the money supply did *not* shrink drastically as it did in the United States. Despite these markedly different monetary histories, the behavior of the recessionary gap, investment expenditure, and unemployment was very similar in the three countries.

---

cyclical contraction interest rates would tend to fall unless the central bank stepped in and sold bonds to keep interest rates up. Generally it did so, thereby decreasing the money supply. This behavior created the positive correlation on which the monetarists rely.

According to Keynesians, fluctuations in national income are often caused by fluctuations in expenditure decisions. Further, they believe that fluctuations in national income cause fluctuations in the money supply.

Nevertheless, most Keynesians also agree that policy-induced changes in the money supply can cause national income to change.

The Price Level

As we saw in Chapter 34, sustained inflation requires a sustained expansion of the money supply.

Motives for such excessive monetary expansions have varied from time to time and place to place. Sometimes central banks have rapidly increased the money supply in an effort to end a recession. Then when the economy expanded due to its own natural recuperative forces, the increased money supply allowed a significant inflation during the boom phase of the cycle. At other times central banks have tried to hold interest rates well below their free-market levels. To do this they buy bonds to hold bond prices up. We have seen that these open market operations increase the money supply and so fuel an inflation. At still other times central banks have helped governments finance large budget deficits by buying up the new public debt. These open market operations provide what is popularly known as *printing press finance*. The steady increase in the money supply fuels a continuous inflation.

Monetarist views.   As we have said, many monetarists hold that inflation is everywhere and always a monetary phenomenon. They thus focus on changes in the money supply as the key source of shifts in the *AD* curve.

According to monetarists, all inflations are caused by excessive monetary expansion and would not occur without it.

Keynesian views. Keynesians agree that a sustained rise in prices cannot occur unless it is accompanied by continued increases in the money supply. Keynesians also emphasize, however, that temporary bursts of inflation can be caused by shifts in the *AD* curve brought about by increases in private- or public-sector expenditure. If such inflations are not validated by monetary expansion, they are brought to a halt by the monetary adjustment mechanism.

Keynesians also accept the importance of supply-shock inflations. Again, they accept that such inflations cannot go on indefinitely unless accommodated by monetary expansion. But Keynesians argue that "temporary" inflation due to either *AD* or *SRAS* shifts can go on long enough to be a matter of serious policy concern.

Many Keynesians also take seriously the possibility of wage-cost push inflation that we studied in Chapter 34. This type of inflation, if it exists, makes full employment incompatible with a stable price level. Again, the central bank is faced with the agonizing choice of whether or not to accommodate.

Growth

Conservative views. Conservatives, and indeed most monetarists, feel that in a stable environment free from government interference growth will take care of itself. Large firms will spend much on research and development. Where they fail, or where they suppress inventions to protect monopoly positions, the genius of backyard inventors will come up with new ideas and will develop new companies to challenge the positions of the established giants. Left to itself the economy will prosper as it has in the past, provided only that inquiring scientific spirit and the profit motive are not suppressed.

Interventionist views. Interventionists, and indeed most Keynesians, are less certain than are conservatives about the ability of market forces to produce growth. While recognizing the importance of invention and innovation, they fear the dead hand of monopoly and cautious business practices that choose security over risk taking. Therefore, the state needs at the very least to give a nudge here or there to help the growth process along.

The Role of Policy

The conservative and the interventionist diagnoses of the economy's ills lead, not surprisingly, to very different prescriptions about the appropriate role of economic policy.

Conservative Prescriptions

It is not necessary to distinguish conservative policies with respect to full employment and with respect to stable prices. This is because conservatives believe that both goals will be achieved by the same basic policy: provision of a stable environment for the free-market system to operate.

Full Employment and Stable Prices: Providing a Stable Environment

Creating a stable environment, as the conservatives advocate, may be easier said than done. We focus on the prescriptions for establishing stable fiscal and monetary policies.

One major problem to keep in mind is that macro variables are interrelated. The stability of one may imply the instability of another. In such cases, a choice must be made. How much instability of one aggregate can we tolerate to secure stability in another related aggregate?

Assume, for example, that the government decides to adopt the goal of stability in the budget balance as part of the stable environment. This "stability" would require great *instability* in tax and expenditure policy. Tax revenues depend on the interaction between tax rates and the level of national income. With given tax rates, tax revenues change with the ebb and flow of the business cycle. A stable budget balance would require that the government raise tax rates and cut expenditure in slumps and lower tax rates and raise expenditures in booms.

Not only does this squander the budget's potential to act as a stabilizer, but great instability of the fiscal environment is caused by continual changes in tax rates and expenditure levels. A stable fiscal environment requires substantial stability in government expenditures and tax rates. Stability is needed so that the private sector can make plans for the future within a climate of known patterns of tax liabilities and government demand.

Any target budget balance must be some average over a period long enough to cover a typical cycle. Stability from year to year should be found in tax rates and expenditure programs, *not* in the size of the budget balance.

This in turn requires that the budget deficit vary cyclically, showing its largest deficits in slumps and its largest surpluses in booms.

Advocates of a stable monetary environment are actually advocating stable inflation. Whether a *zero* rate is feasible or not is discussed in Box 37-2. The Fed is urged to set a target rate of increase in the money supply and hold it. To establish the target, the Fed estimates the rate at which the demand for money would be growing if actual income equaled potential income and the price level were stable. As a first approximation this can be taken to be the rate at which potential income itself is growing.[5] This then becomes the target rate of growth of the money supply. The key proposition is that the money supply should be changing gradually along a stable path that is independent of short-term variations in the demand for money caused by cyclical changes in national income. This is referred to as a **k percent rule.**

Will the k percent rule really provide monetary stability? The answer is not necessarily.

[5] Such a rule assumes that members of the public wish to keep their money holdings in a fixed proportion to their real income. If other demand patterns are established, that is, if desired money holdings change as a proportion of real income as income rises, then the Fed can alter its monetary target appropriately.

Assuring a stable rate of monetary growth does not assure a stable monetary environment. Monetary shortages and surpluses depend on the relation between the supply and the demand for money.

The k percent rule looks after supply, but what about demand?

Problems for the k percent rule arise when the demand for money shifts. For example, payment of interest on checking deposits increases the demand for M1. In this event, if the Fed adheres to a k percent rule, there will be an excess demand for money and interest rates will rise. Thus contractionary pressure will be put on the economy.

Should the Fed commit itself to a specific k percent rule or merely work toward unannounced and possibly variable targets? The announced rule makes it easier to evaluate how well the Fed is doing its job. It also helps to prevent the Fed from succumbing to the temptation to fine tune the economy.

One disadvantage of the announced rule is that it sets up speculative behavior. If, for example, when weekly money supply figures are announced there is too much money, speculators know that the Fed will sell more bonds in the future to reduce the surplus. This will depress the price of bonds. Speculators are thus induced to sell bonds, hoping to rebuy them at bargain prices once the Fed acts.

Stable pre-announced M1 targets can introduce instability into interest-rate behavior.

A second disadvantage of such a rule is that the Fed, in order to preserve its credibility, may fail to take discretionary action that would otherwise be appropriate. For example, after an entrenched inflation is broken, the economy may come to rest with substantial unemployment and a stable price level (see Figure 34-6). There is then a case for a once-and-for-all discretionary expansion in the money supply to get the economy back to full employment. The k percent rule precludes this, condemning the economy to a slump.

Despite these problems conservatives believe the k percent rule is superior to any known alternative.

BOX 37-2

Is a Zero Inflation Rate a Feasible Policy Goal?

The 1950s were characterized by what would be regarded today as satisfactory price stability. But prices were not exactly steady. The inflation rate varied between 0.5 percent and 3 percent. Despite what appeared to most observers to be a slowly growing average recessionary gap throughout this period, the inflation rate never reached zero in any year. Between 1955 and 1961 there were only two years when the rate was below 1 percent: 1955 (0.4 percent) and 1961 (0.7 percent).

This creeping inflation worried observers at the time. An inflation, even a gradual one in the face of an obvious recessionary gap, seemed hard to understand.

The explanation in modern theory would be likely to come from the supply side. The combination of rising prices and recessionary gaps usually suggests a supply-shock inflation. The explanation that satisfied many observers at the time was the **structural rigidity theory** of inflation, which was indeed a supply-shock explanation.

The structural rigidity theory assumes that resources do not move quickly from one use to another and that it is easy to increase money wages and prices, but hard to decrease them. Given these conditions, when patterns of demand and costs change due to such forces as economic growth, real adjustments occur slowly. Shortages appear in potentially expanding sectors and prices rise because the slow movement of resources prevents these sectors from expanding rapidly enough. Factors of production remain in contracting sectors on part-time employment or become unemployed because mobility is low in the economy. Wages and prices are slow to move downward, so there are few significant wage and price reductions in these contracting sectors.

Thus the mere process of adjustment in an economy with structural rigidities causes inflation to occur. Prices in the expanding sectors rise; prices in the contracting sectors stay about the same; on average, therefore, the price level rises.

The inflation of the late 1950s and early 1960s was mild and the debate on its causes was inconclusive. However, this was the first suggestion of a force that later became a plaguing policy problem: inflations originating in shifts in the aggregate supply curve.

Although the structural rigidity theory cannot be a major part of the explanation of the high inflation rates of the 1970s and early 1980s, it suggests that a zero inflation rate may not be an achievable target. Of course, good luck—such as the fall in the world price of oil that occurred in early 1986, when the inflation rate was already low and perhaps still declining—can temporarily drive the inflation rate to zero, or even below zero. But if there is anything in the structural rigidity theory, then the minimum inflation rate compatible with a changing economy may be 1 percent to 2 percent rather than zero. A test of this theory might occur in the 1980s; if inflation continues to fall, will it reach zero, or get stuck in the one-to-two percent range?

Some would agree that in principle the Fed could improve the economy's performance by occasional bouts of discretionary monetary policy to offset such things as major shifts in the demand for money. But they also believe that once given any discretion the Fed would abuse it in an attempt to fine tune the economy. The resulting instability would, they believe, be much more than any instability resulting from the application of a *k* percent rule in an environment subject to some change.

Long-Term Growth

Conservatives want to let growth take care of itself. They argue that governments cannot improve the workings of free markets and that their interventions can interfere with market efficiency. Thus they push for reducing the current level of government intervention.

Given the large web of government rules, regulations, and perverse tax incentives that has grown up over many years, the conservatives' agenda for reducing government intervention is usually a long one. Such an agenda was adopted by so-called supply siders during the later 1970s and early 1980s. The supply-side, conservative view that growth is best encouraged by reducing the present degree of government intervention has already caused some significant policy changes and will no doubt always find numerous supporters.

The agenda includes *eliminating* the following policies:

Supporting declining industries.   This policy causes resources that could be more productively employed elsewhere to leave the industry more slowly. Most economists agree that such policies are costly, harmful to growth, and in the end self-defeating.

Encouraging monopolies and discouraging competition.   Most economists tend to oppose such policies, although there is disagreement over how much competition is desirable in certain industries. For example, conservatives tend to support complete deregulation of fare and route setting by airlines, while interventionists tend to worry that cutthroat competition may reduce airline quality and safety.

Taxing income rather than consumption.   Consider a woman in the 25 percent tax bracket who earns an extra $1,000 and pays $250 income tax. If she spends her after-tax income she will be able to buy $750 worth of goods. If she saves the money, she will be able to buy a $750 bond. If the bond pays a 4 percent real return, she will earn $30 interest per year. But a 25 percent tax must then be paid on the interest earnings, leaving only a $22.50 annual income. This is a 3.0 percent after-tax return on the bond and *a 2.25 percent after-tax return on the original $100 income.* Conservatives allege that this "double taxing" of saving is a serious disincentive to saving. They argue for taxes on consumption, not on income, so that any income that is saved would be untaxed. A tax would be levied only when the interest earned on the savings was actually spent on consumption.

High rates of income tax.   Conservatives allege that high taxes discourage work. But the effect of high taxes may actually be to make people work either more or less hard. Theory is silent on which is more likely, and no hard evidence has yet shown that lowering current tax rates makes people work harder. The success of tax reform in 1986 which saw tax bases broadened and tax rates reduced was a major victory for supply-side activists.

"Double taxation" of business profits.   Business profits are taxed first as income of firms and second as income of households when paid out as dividends. This and other policies that reduce business profits and hence discourage the return to investing in equities are alleged to discourage households from saving and investing in businesses that are the mainspring of economic growth.

All these policies are alleged to reduce the rate of growth below what it would otherwise be. Problems arise in assessing the existence and importance of the alleged harmful effects of each policy and also, since the government needs revenue, in finding alternative revenue sources that will have less harmful effects than the ones being criticized.

Interventionist Prescriptions

Interventionists call for different policies for the three policy goals of full employment, price stability, and growth. As we consider their prescriptions, we give their reasons for rejecting the conservative case.

Full Employment

Interventionists call for discretionary fiscal and monetary policies to offset significant inflationary and recessionary gaps. Some of the major problems associated with discretionary stabilization policy have been discussed in earlier chapters. The issues in the debate that is popularly known as "rules versus discretion" are discussed further in Box 37-3.

A Stable Price Level

Some interventionists, particularly a group called *post-Keynesians,* believe that the *k* percent rule may not be enough to achieve full employment and stable prices simultaneously. This is because they accept the

BOX 37-3

Rules Versus Discretion

Three of the main issues involved in the rules versus discretion debate are problems created by lags, type of stabilization needed, and adequacy of information.

Lags. Those hostile to discretionary policy emphasize the long and variable lags of both fiscal and monetary policy. Monetary policy can be put into effect quickly, but it takes 6 to 18 months for the full effects of a change in interest rates to be felt in terms of altered private-sector expenditures. It takes a long time to put fiscal policy into effect since both expenditure and tax changes must be passed by an often slow-moving Congress. Once the changes are made, however, their effects spread quickly through the economy.

Conservatives feel that these lags destroy the presumption that discretionary full-employment policy will usually be stabilizing. Interventionists feel that although the lags are serious, discretionary policies can be effective in reducing persistent recessionary gaps. Few interventionists, however, now call for fine tuning.

A stable climate for planning. Supporters of rules emphasize the need for a stable climate for firms and households to plan for the future. They argue that continual changes in tax rates and the money supply designed to stabilize the economy are destabilizing because they create a climate of uncertainty that makes long-term planning difficult.

Supporters of discretionary policy argue that they want discretion exercised only when the occasional serious recession develops and that large fluctuations in income and employment can be as upsetting to long-term planning as are the occasional changes in tax rates and expenditures required by stabilization policy.

Do we know enough? Discretionary stabilization policy requires that we forecast what the state of the economy will be in the absence of that policy. Generally, actual information is available only with a lag. Policymakers know approximately what GNP was last quarter and what unemployment was last month. (The first preliminary figures for many economic variables can be subject to substantial errors. Often these estimates are revised several times over subsequent months and even years.) On the basis of these data, projections of future behavior of the economy must be made and policy set.

Supporters of discretionary policy accept that errors in projections may be large in relation to the recessionary gaps created by minor recessions, but believe that the errors are small in relation to major recessions. They argue that for major recessions policy-makers will be in no doubt about the existence of a large recessionary gap and of the need for some significant stimulus, even though its exact amount cannot be precisely determined.

---

wage-cost-push theory of inflation discussed in Chapter 34.

Some Keynesians call for incomes policies to restrain the wage-cost push and so make full employment compatible with stable prices. They believe that such policies should become permanent features of the economic landscape.

Wage-price controls might work as *temporary* measures to break inflationary inertias (see Chapter 34, page 700), but as permanent features they would introduce inefficiencies and rigidities.

More permanent incomes policies might be of

two types. The first type, commonly used in Europe in the past decades but now out of favor, is often called a *social contract*. Labor, management, and the government consult annually and agree on target wage changes. These are calculated to be non-inflationary, given the government's projections for the future and its planned economic policies. Such a scheme is most easily initiated in a centralized economy such as West Germany's, where a few giant firms and unions exert enormous power, or in a country such as Britain, where the party in power during much of the period in which social contracts were used had strong official links with the labor unions.

The other main type of incomes policy is **tax-related incomes policy (TIP),** which we first encountered in Chapter 34. TIPs provide tax incentives for management and labor to conform to government-established wage and price guidelines. For example, increases in wages and prices in excess of the guidelines would be heavily taxed. TIPs have not yet been tried, although they have been strongly advocated by some American economists.

TIPs rely on tax incentives to secure voluntary conformity with wage and price guidelines, whereas wage and price controls try to impose conformity by law.

Advocates of TIPs argue that their great advantage is leaving decisions on wages and prices in the hands of labor and management while influencing behavior by altering the incentive system. Critics, however, argue that they would prove to be an administrative nightmare.

Growth

Policies for intervention to increase growth rates are of two sorts. Some policies seek to alter the general economic climate in a way favorable to growth. They typically include subsidization or favorable tax treatment for research and development, for purchase of plant and equipment, and for other profit-earning activities. Measures to lower interest rates temporarily or permanently are urged by some as favorable to investment and growth. Most interventionists support these general measures.

Some also support more specific intervention, usually in the form of what is called *picking and backing winners* in one way or another. Advocates of this view, such as Professor Lester Thurow of MIT, want governments to pick the industries, usually new ones, that have potential for future success and then to back them with subsidies, government contracts, research funds, and all of the other encouragements at the government's command.

Opponents argue that picking winners requires foresight and that there is no reason to expect the government to have better foresight than private investors. Indeed, since political considerations inevitably get in the way, the government may be less successful than the market in picking winners. If so, channeling funds through the government rather than through the private sector may hurt rather than help growth rates.

Rational Expectations and the Micro Foundations of Macroeconomics[6]

For many years Keynesian economics seemed successful both in explaining the overall behavior of the economy and in suggesting policies for controlling inflation and unemployment. As long as it appeared to work, few were interested in *how*. During the late 1960s and the 1970s, however, control of the economy by means of traditional fiscal and monetary policies seemed to become more difficult. This raised concerns about the foundations of Keynesian theory. The main question was: What behavior in the individual markets for goods and factors of production is implied by the Keynesian aggregate relationships? This question concerns what are called the *micro foundations,* or *micro underpinnings,* of macro models.

While these concerns about the Keynesian model were surfacing, the monetarist model seemed to provide an alternative for understanding the macro behavior of the economy and for prescribing appropriate policies. This elicited a debate about the merits of the two models, a debate that still rages today. Micro foundations are at the heart of the debate between monetarism and Keynesianism. The issues are important; because they are at the frontier of modern research, they are also difficult. The analysis depends on material that is treated in detail in more advanced courses. At this stage, therefore, we can discuss the issues only in broad outline.

Monetarist Micro Foundations

There is no single set of accepted monetarist micro foundations. Most monetarists, however,

---

[6] This section may be omitted without loss of continuity.

view markets as competitive.[7] One important characteristic of competitive markets is that prices and wages are flexible; they adjust to establish equilibrium at all times. When a competitive market is in equilibrium (see Chapter 4), the market is said to have *cleared*. This means that every purchaser has been able to buy all he or she wishes to buy at the going price and every seller has been able to sell all he or she wishes to sell at that price.[8] When each and every market is in equilibrium, there is full employment of all resources. The prices that clear markets are called **market-clearing prices**.

According to the monetarists, there are strong forces that ensure that departures from full-employment equilibrium are quickly rectified. That is, monetarists believe that the *automatic adjustment mechanism* works quite efficiently.

We now consider two particular monetarist views.

Traditional Monetarism

The monetarist school of thought that evolved in the 1960s was led by Professor Milton Friedman of the University of Chicago. Economists of that school, often called *traditional monetarists*, hold that the economy, when left to its own, tends to stabilize at the full-employment level. They also hold that, historically, monetary policies have been erratic. We saw in Chapter 32 that monetarists believe that monetary policy exerts a powerful influence on the economy, so they reach the following conclusion:

Traditional monetarists believe that fluctuations in the money supply are a major source of fluctuations in output and the price level.

Although monetary policy has strong effects, it operates with a long and variable lag. According to Friedman and his followers, these long and variable lags not only doom monetary policy to failure, but make it counterproductive as well. In their view monetary policy has actually served to destabilize the economy in the past. The best course for monetary policy is held to be to follow the *k* percent rule, that is, to set the rate of increase of the money supply at some given value and hold it there.

New Classical Monetarism

The *new Classical monetarists* follow Professors Robert Lucas and Thomas Sargeant in holding that temporary departures from full employment occur mainly because people make mistakes. This viewpoint can be best understood in terms of the proposition derived from microeconomics that individual supply and demand behavior depends only on the structure of relative prices.

To follow their argument, let us start by assuming that each of the economy's markets is in equilibrium; there is full employment, prices are stable, and the actual and expected rates of inflation are zero. Now suppose the government increases the money supply by 5 percent. People find themselves with unwanted money balances, which they seek to spend.[9] For simplicity, assume that this leads to an increase in desired expenditure on all commodities; the demand for each commodity shifts to the right and all prices, being competitively determined, rise. Individual decision makers see their selling prices go up and mistakenly interpret this increase as a rise in their own relative price. This is because they expect the overall rate of inflation to be zero. Firms will produce more and workers will work more; both groups think they are getting an increased *relative* price for what they sell. Thus total output and employment rise.

When both groups eventually realize that their own relative prices are in fact unchanged, output and employment fall back to their initial levels. The extra output and employment occur only while people are

---

[7] They realize, of course, that perfect competition does not exist everywhere in the economy, but they believe that the forces of competition are strong—strong enough so that analysis based on the theory of perfect competition will be close to the real behavior of the economy.

[8] Competitive markets clear only at the equilibrium price. At any other price there are either unsatisfied purchasers (excess demand) or unsatisfied sellers (excess supply).

[9] Most monetarists accept the theory of the transmission mechanism (discussed in Chapter 32) according to which the excess money balances are used to buy financial assets, thus driving down interest rates and stimulating expenditure *indirectly*. However, most monetarists tend to stress the relative importance of the *direct* expenditure effects created by excess money balances.

being fooled. When they realize that *all* prices have risen by 5 percent, they revert to their initial behavior. The only difference is that now the price level has risen by 5 percent, leaving relative prices unchanged.

According to the new Classical theory, deviations from full employment occur only because people make mistakes that cause markets to clear at more or less than full-employment output. People are not prevented from selling as many commodities or as much labor as they wish; the contraction or expansion in output is voluntary.

New Classical monetarists focus on the role of changes in relative prices in signaling appropriate information in a world where tastes and technology are constantly changing. They hold that fluctuations in the money supply will lead to increased fluctuations in all prices. This makes it hard for households and firms to distinguish changes in relative prices, to which they do wish to respond, from changes in the price level, to which they do not wish to respond. Such confusion, created by fluctuations in the money supply, thus leads to mistakes in supply and demand decisions.

This discussion highlights the importance for firms and households of distinguishing the causes of any price changes. Consider, for example, what happens if there is an unexpected and unperceived increase in the money supply. This will lead to an increase in most, if not all, prices above what most agents had expected. Most firms perceive this as an increase in the relative price of their own output and hence increase their level of production above what it normally would have been. Consequently, national income rises above the full-employment level. A similar argument shows that an unanticipated and unperceived decrease in the money supply would cause output to fall below its full-employment level.

The Lucas aggregate supply curve.   The behavior described above gives rise to the **Lucas aggregate supply curve.**

The Lucas aggregate supply curve posits that national output will vary positively with the ratio of the actual to the expected price level.

This is often also referred to as the *surprises only* supply curve since it implies that only changes in the price level that are unexpected (surprises) will give rise to fluctuations in aggregate supply.

To see this, consider what happens if there is again an increase in the money supply, but this time suppose that it has been widely expected in advance by firms and households. Again, prices will rise. Most firms will now take this to mean only that the *observed* change in the price of their own output has roughly matched the *expected* change in the average of all other prices. Hence they will not interpret it as a rise in the relative price of their own output and will maintain their production level at its normal level. National income will not rise above potential despite the rise in the general price level.

According to the new Classical theory, expected changes in the price level do not lead to fluctuations in aggregate supply.

New Classical policy views.   New Classical monetarists support the *k* percent rule, just as do the traditional monetarists. They believe that firms and households make better decisions when monetary and fiscal policies are stable than when they are highly variable. They believe that active interventionist policies designed to stabilize the economy make it harder for people to interpret the signals generated by the price system and so lead them to make more errors in forming their expectations. This then increases rather than reduces the fluctuations of output around its full-employment level and increases rather than reduces the fluctuations of unemployment around the natural rate.

According to the new Classical theory, active use of monetary policy in an attempt to stabilize the economy will lead to confusion about relative and absolute prices. This will cause people to make mistakes in their output and purchasing decisions and therefore increase aggregate output fluctuations.

This conclusion depends upon the particular view adopted by the new Classical monetarists about how people form predictions or expectations, which is a subject that has recently become an important part of macroeconomic debates.

The Theory of Rational Expectations

The new Classical model is augmented by the theory of *rational expectations*. People look to the government's current macroeconomic policy to form their expectations of future inflation. They understand how the economy works, and they form their expectations rationally by predicting the outcome of the policies being pursued. People learn fairly quickly from their mistakes; while random errors occur, systematic and persistent errors do not. In an obvious sense, such expectations are *forward looking*.

According to the theory of rational expectations, people do not make persistent, systematic errors in predicting the overall inflation rate; they may, however, make unsystematic errors.

Policy invariance. Rational expectations, combined with the Lucas aggregate supply curve, give rise to the new Classical *policy invariance*, or policy neutrality, with the result:

Systematic attempts to use monetary policy to stabilize the economy will lead to systematic changes in the price level, but will not influence the behavior of output.

Thus, according to the new Classicists, monetary policy can do harm—by creating confusion about the source of price changes—but cannot do good, except by random chance. Thus, even in the face of major recessions, laissez-faire is the best stabilization policy conceivable.

Let us review how this follows from combining the monetarist micro foundations with the theory of rational expectations.

1. According to the new classical theory's micro foundations, deviations from full employment occur only because of errors in predicting the price level (which cause workers and firms to mistake changes in the price level for changes in relative prices).
2. According to the theory of rational expectations, errors in predicting the price level are only random.
3. It follows from (1) and (2) that there is no room for active government policy to stabilize the econ-

omy. The causes of fluctuations are random.[10] It is in the nature of random fluctuations that they cannot be foreseen and offset. Thus there is no room for stabilization policy to reduce the fluctuations in the economy by offsetting the disturbances that emanate from the private sector.

Not all monetarists accept the theory of rational expectations. For those who do, however, the contrast with the Keynesians is extreme.

The most extreme monetarist attack on stabilization policy has two parts. The first is a model of an economy where deviations from full employment occur only because of errors. The second is a theory of people's expectations that predicts that persistent, systematic errors—and hence systematic deviations from full employment—will not occur.

Monetarist Conclusions

The two monetarist schools obviously do not agree with each other on everything. Both agree, however, that monetary policy should not be used actively to stabilize the economy. This is for two reasons: (1) fluctuations in the money supply are the major source of fluctuations in output and inflation, and (2) there is no long-term trade-off between inflation and national income.[11]

Most economists accept the view that monetary forces are important in influencing inflation and unemployment, but many do not agree that monetary forces are the *most* important force. Most economists also agree that inflation will tend to accelerate if income is held permanently above its full-employment level.

One aspect of the monetarist model that is particularly controversial is the belief in downward flexibility of prices, which leads to the prediction that as long as national income is below its full-employment level, the price level would *fall* at an ever-accelerating

[10] Although because of long lags, macro variables may display cyclical fluctuations, as discussed in Chapter 29.

[11] Recall that any attempt to hold income above its full-employment level will lead not to a constant rate of inflation but to a continuously accelerating inflation. This is just a restatement of the acceleration hypothesis and the natural rate hypothesis developed in detail in Chapter 34 and its appendix.

BOX 37-4

The Share Economy

Several times in this text we have noted that wage rigidity is widely perceived to be a major impediment to the efficient functioning of the American economy. In his important book *The Share Economy,* Professor Martin Weitzman of the Massachusetts Institute of Technology proposed a dramatic policy designed to restore flexibility of wages and thus enhance economic performance.

How the Share Economy Works

The basic idea is quite simple. Under Weitzman's proposal, part of the payment that any firm makes to labor would be tied directly to that firm's net revenues. This payment, which is like an annual bonus, is called the *share wage*. In addition, workers would also receive a *base wage* which is fixed for the duration of the labor contract and is much lower than their wage under existing, traditional labor contracts.

When the firm is prosperous and net revenues are high, the share wage paid to workers would be correspondingly high. In these circumstances the total wage, equal to the base wage plus the share wage, would exceed the inital wage that prevailed prior to the scheme that is being introduced. But when the firm's sales are down and thus net revenues are low, the share wage would also be low. In these circumstances the total wage would be below the initial wage.

Consider, for example, a firm that is currently paying its workers a fixed wage of $20 an hour. Now suppose that under the share contract it pays them a base wage of only $10 an hour, and that it also promises to pay workers a fixed percentage of its net revenues. Finally, suppose that this percentage is such that if net revenues are at their average or normal level, each worker will receive a combined base plus share wage of $20 an hour, just equal to the wage in the absence of the share contract.

If the firm's net revenues turn out to be above their normal level, the share wage will rise to reflect this; thus the total payment to workers will exceed $20 an hour, and the workers will share in the prosperity of the firm. If the firm's net revenues turn out to be below their normal level, the share wage will fall; in this case the total wage will be below $20 an hour, and the workers will "share" in the ill fortunes of the firm.

rate. Keynesians say that the observed downward inflexibility of the price level refutes this view. They reject the prediction that the main cause of recessionary gaps is *voluntary* reductions in employment and output due to errors in reading the signals provided by the price system. Most Keynesians do not believe that output deviates from its potential level *only* because workers and firms make mistakes.

Keynesian Micro Foundations

The Keynesian micro foundations emphasize the noncompetitive nature of the economy. Most firms are seen as setting their own prices rather than accepting those set on competitive markets. Their per unit output costs tend to be fairly constant, and they set prices by adding a relatively inflexible markup to their costs.[12] They then sell what they can at the going price. Cyclical fluctuations in aggregate demand cause cyclical fluctuations in the demand for each firm's products, which in turn cause individual firms to make cyclical variations in output and employment rather than in price.

While in the monetarist model the main impact of fluctuations in aggregate demand is on prices, in the Keynesian model their main impact is on output and employment.

[12] Complete cyclical inflexibility of markup is not necessary. What matters is that firms do not adjust prices continually and as a result are willing to sell further units at the same price. This much price inflexibility need not imply an absence of profit maximization. Instead it may follow from profit maximization when it is costly to alter prices. This is discussed further in Chapter 15.

Implications of the Share Economy

Under traditional wage-setting arrangements, rigid wages mean that a firm will lay off workers in the face of a fall in demand for its output. Under a share contract, firms will have a much smaller incentive to lay off workers during a downturn, since the total wage paid to each worker falls. Thus workers will face a more stable employment pattern with the share contract. However, workers will have to accept the risk of a fluctuating total wage compared to the initial situation in which they received a fixed wage of $20 *if they remained employed.*

Most observers feel that the situation under a share contract, where each worker bears a small part of the burden of the downturn, is more equitable than the situation under a fixed total wage, where those workers who keep their jobs bear none of the burden while the minority who get laid off bear the total burden. Further, many observers feel that the economy would operate more efficiently in the presence of the enhanced wage flexibility that the share contracts would generate.

Weitzman proposes that tax incentives be introduced to encourage firms to enter into such contracts. For example, share income could be subject to a special low tax rate, with regular tax rates still applying to any income from a fixed wage rate. Firms and workers would thus have an incentive to arrange for a large fraction of the total payment to labor to be share income.

This proposal is controversial. Some unions have criticized it, arguing that if the contract specifies a given fraction of net revenues is to be paid to all workers, firms will have an incentive to add to their work force and thus reduce each worker's share. This practice, the argument continues, will drive wages down to very low levels. Other unions reply that the expansion in employment is precisely one of the desirable features of the system, and there is no reason to expect *total* wages to fall. Some observers fear the impact on the deficit of the special tax incentives that might be required; others reply, using reasoning reminiscent of the Laffer curve (see page 434), that the improvement in the performance of the economy will be so great that total tax revenues will rise, not fall. Perhaps the highest praise of all came in a *New York Times* editorial in which *The Share Economy* was referred to as "the best idea since Keynes."

A similar argument holds for labor markets in the Keynesian model. Wages respond to the price level and productivity, but are relatively insensitive to short-term cyclical fluctuations in demand. (This is discussed in detail in Chapter 20.) A recent proposal to change wage-setting arrangements is discussed in Box 37-4.

This short-term wage inflexibility can stem from rational behavior on the part of workers. If wage rates adjust to clear labor markets, wages will vary over the cycle. *All* workers will then bear the uncertainty associated with the cyclical movements in wages. However, if wages are set in response to long-term considerations but do not vary cyclically so as to clear labor markets, cyclical fluctuations in demand will cause employment to fluctuate. Since most layoffs and rehires are based on seniority, employment fluctuations are all borne by the 10 percent or 20 percent of workers who are least senior. The majority of workers will then have little uncertainty in the face of cyclical fluctuations in demand, all the uncertainty having been placed on the minority with low seniority. Thus contracts that fix wages over the cycle and allow employment to vary may be preferable to the majority of workers compared to contracts that allow wages to vary in order to clear the labor market continually and thus prevent unemployment.

In Keynesian macroeconomics, the economy does not have a unique short-term equilibrium. Because firms would like to sell more and some workers would be willing to work more at current prices, fluctuations in aggregate demand cause output and employment to fluctuate in the short term.

The Keynesian macro model allows for systematic disturbances that can cause prolonged deflationary or recessionary gaps.

According to the Keynesians, stabilization policy can then be used to offset at least those gaps that are large and persistent.

Such policies seek to alter aggregate demand using both fiscal and monetary tools.

Differences Between the Two Models

There are many differences in the micro behavior that underlies the models. Probably the most important relates to the distinction between voluntary and involuntary unemployment.

In the monetarist model all unemployment and output below capacity is voluntary. Workers decide to be unemployed, and firms decide to produce less than capacity output as a result of errors they make in predicting the general price level (and therefore the relative price of what they sell). So if surveyed, the millions of unemployed around the world in the early 1980s would have said that they could have had a job at the going wage, but they refused to accept it because, given their expectations about inflation, the expected real wage was too low.

In the Keynesian model prices and wages do not fluctuate to clear markets. Unemployment and production below capacity are involuntary in the sense that unemployed workers would like jobs at the going wage rate, but cannot find them, and firms would like to sell more at going prices, but customers are not forthcoming.[13] So if surveyed, the millions of unemployed around the world in the early 1980s would have said that they would have accepted a job at the going wage rate, but none were available.

Major current debate centers around these two prototype models and some of their subtler off-

shoots. Issues such as what determines the degree of wage and price flexibility in the economy, the conditions under which it can be expected that people can form accurate expectations and act on them, and the potential for destabilizing the economy by pursuing an active stabilization policy are at the forefront of modern research. Views on how the economy behaves both at the micro and macro level will be influenced by the progress of the debate. So will views on the place of fiscal and monetary policy as possible ways to eliminate inflationary or recessionary gaps.

The Progress of Economics

In this chapter we have discussed a number of current controversies about the behavior of the economy and the evidence now available that relates to them. General acceptance of the view that the validity of economic theories should be tested by confronting their predictions with the mass of all available evidence is fairly new in economics.

Since 1936 when Keynes's *The General Theory of Employment, Interest and Money* was published, great progress has been made in economics in relating theory to evidence. This progress has been reflected in the superior ability of governments to achieve their policy objectives. The financial aspects of World War II were far better handled than those of World War I. When President Roosevelt tried to reduce unemployment in the 1930s, his efforts were greatly hampered by the failure even of economists to realize the critical importance of budget deficits in raising aggregate demand and in injecting newly created money into the economy. When the Vietnam War forced the government to adopt expansive fiscal and monetary policies, economists had no trouble in predicting the outcome. More involvement abroad was obtained at the cost of heavy inflationary pressure at home.

The general propositions of theories are tested in such important policy areas as running wars, curing major depressions, and coping with inflations, even if all their specific predictions are not. In some sense, then, economic theories have always been subjected to empirical tests. When they were wildly at variance

---

[13] Of course, one could still argue that this unemployment is voluntary because the workers had earlier voluntarily agreed to the contracts.

with the facts, the ensuing disaster could not but be noticed, and the theories were discarded or amended in the light of what was learned.

The advances of economics in the last 50 years reflect economists' changed attitudes toward empirical observations. Today economists are much less likely to dismiss theories just because they do not like them and to refuse to abandon theories just because they do like them. Economists are more likely to try to base their theories as much as possible on empirical observation and to accept empirical relevance as the ultimate arbiter of the value of theories. As human beings, we may be anguished at the upsetting of a pet theory; as scientists, we should try to train ourselves to take pleasure in it because of the new knowledge gained thereby. It has been said that one of the great tragedies of science is the continual slaying of beautiful theories by ugly facts. It must always be remembered that when theory and fact come into conflict, it is theory, not fact, that must give way.

Summary

1. Macroeconomic performance is judged in terms of the behavior of many variables. The key variables are (a) output, employment, and unemployment, (b) the rate of change of the price level, and (c) long-term growth.

2. Views about the role of policy in improving macroeconomic performance range between two extremes. The conservative view is that there is only a minimum role for policy; macroeconomic performance will be most satisfactory when the market system is allowed to function as freely as possible. The interventionist view is that active use of policy will improve macroeconomic performance. It is common to identify monetarists with conservatives and Keynesians with interventionists.

3. Monetarists believe that because the economy is inherently stable, the goal of damping the business cycle is best achieved by avoiding fluctuations in policy, especially monetary policy. Hence they advocate a k percent rule. Keynesians believe that the economy is inherently unstable in that expenditure functions shift regularly and the economy's self-corrective mechanisms are weak. Hence they believe in an active role for both monetary and fiscal policy to stabilize the business cycle.

4. Monetarists believe that inflation is everywhere and always a monetary phenomenon and so advocate the same conservative policies to avoid price instability as they advocate to minimize policy-induced cycles in output. They also argue that in order to control inflation, the long-term growth rate of the money supply must not be too high. Keynesians accept the view that monetary expansion is necessary for inflation to persist in the long term, but they take seriously the role of other factors in causing short-term but substantial inflation. Hence they believe in an active role for policy to offset these factors in the short term.

5. Conservatives believe that long-term growth will be maximized when the incentives provided by the profit motive are strongest. Interventionists see a need for special government programs to

channel resources into research and development and other investment expenditures designed to raise potential output.

6. Conservatives see a role for policy in terms of providing a stable
environment for individual decision makers. This involves maintaining a consistent set of "fiscal rules of the game" in terms of
expenditure and tax rates and providing a steady but gradual growth
in the money supply.

7. Interventionists have specific prescriptions for each policy variable.
They advocate active use of discretionary monetary and fiscal policy
to stabilize output and employment. Despite imperfections caused
by lags and incomplete knowledge, they believe such policies are
helpful. Similar policies can be combined with incomes policies to
stabilize the fluctuations in the price level that arise from various
sources and are subject to an upward bias. They also support policies
to promote growth through subsidization, tax favors, and more
specific intervention.

8. Monetarists view markets as competitive and hence believe that
departures from full-employment equilibrium are quickly rectified.
As a result, they believe that fluctuations in aggregate demand lead
primarily to fluctuations in the price level rather than in the level of
output. They believe that the best course for monetary policy is to
follow a *k* percent rule. For traditional monetarists, this is because
they believe that long and variable lags in the effect of monetary
policy mean that an interventionist monetary policy would destabilize output.

9. New Classical monetarists believe that departures from full-employment output occur only when people make mistakes in predicting the price level. When combined with the theory of rational
expectations, this leads to the policy invariance proposition. New
Classical monetarists support the *k* percent rule because they believe
an interventionist monetary policy will not be effective in stabilizing
output.

10. Keynesians emphasize the noncompetitive nature of the economy.
As a result they believe that fluctuations in aggregate demand lead
primarily to fluctuations in output rather than in the price level. In
this view, an interventionist stabilization policy can be effective in
stabilizing fluctuations in output.

Topics for Review

Conservatives and interventionists
Micro foundations
k percent rule
Traditional and new Classical monetarists
Lucus aggregate supply curve
Theory of rational expectations
Policy invariance proposition

1. To what extent is today's unemployment a serious social problem? If people could vote to choose between 10 percent unemployment combined with zero inflation and 2 percent unemployment combined with 10 percent inflation, which alternative do you think would win? Which groups might prefer the first alternative and which groups the second?

2. In its 1979 report the Joint Economic Committee of the Congress urged the administration to fight inflation and combat unemployment by encouraging private-sector saving and investment. How might expanded saving and investment help to reduce inflation and combat unemployment?

3. Nobel Laureate Paul Samuelson quoted a "conservative economist friend" as saying in mid 1980, "If you're contriving a teensy-weensy recession for us, please don't bother. It won't do the job. What's needed is a believable declaration that Washington will countenance *whatever* degree of unemployment is needed to bring us back on the path to price stability, and a demonstrated willingness to *stick* to that resolution no matter how politically unpopular the short-run joblessness, production cutbacks, and dips in profit might be." Discuss the "conservative friend's" view of inflation. Does experience since 1980 suggest that his advice was followed? If so, what was the consequence?

4. An ad that appeared in the *New York Times* in the early 1980s had this to say about inflation. "First [our politicians] blamed wage increases and price hikes for inflation. Then when 'voluntary guidelines' were established, the blame shifted to OPEC oil prices. Both explanations were wrong. Government policy is responsible for inflation—paying for deficit spending by 'creating money out of thin air.'" What theories of inflation are rejected and accepted by the writers of this ad?

5. In the mid 1980s a fervent national debate developed concerning the need to protect U.S. industries from foreign competition. How do the pro and con views of protectionism relate to the conservative and interventionsist policies for promoting long-term growth?

6. A number of key microeconomic policy issues that were discussed earlier in this book are listed below. Go back and review the relevant discussion of some of them, and then present both the conservative case for "letting the market work" and the interventionist case in favor of a particular policy prescription. (While the issues listed are "microeconomic" issues, their impact on the macroeconomic issues—in particular economic growth—can be important.)
   a. Rent controls (Chapter 6)
   b. De-industrialization (Chapter 18)
   c. Minimum wage laws (Chapter 20)
   d. Paying for social security (Chapter 21)
   e. Financing health care (Chapter 23)

Money in the National Income Model

We have studied the interaction between money, interest rates, and national income in terms of the apparatus in Figures 37-3 through 37-6. A loose end in that model can best be seen by considering the impact of an increase in the money supply. This leads to a fall in interest rates as shown in Figure 32-4(i), to increases in expenditure as shown in Figure 32-4(ii), and to increased national income as shown in Figure 32-5. But increased national income in turn leads to an increased need for transactions balances. This increased demand for money must then be added to the liquidity preference schedule in Figure 32-4. How is the increase in demand satisfied? Does accounting for it radically alter the conclusions of the analysis of Chapter 32?

The answer to the last question is no. This appendix provides a model that integrates monetary and expenditure factors and shows how they jointly determine the interest rate and the level of national income. The British economist Sir John Hicks (awarded the Nobel prize in economics in 1972) suggested the approach in his famous review of Keynes's *General Theory,* "Mr. Keynes and the Classics: A Suggested Interpretation." It involves identifying the relationship between income and interest rates that is imposed first by goods market equilibrium and then by money market equilibrium. We then bring the two together to determine the one combination of real national income and interest rate that satisfies both equilibrium conditions simultaneously. Finally we use the model to examine the effects of monetary and fiscal policy.

The Interest Rate and Aggregate Expenditure: The *IS* Curve

As we saw in going from Figure 32-4(ii) to Figure 32-5(i), a fall in the rate of interest is associated with a rise in the level of real national income, due to increased investment expenditures. Figure 37A-1 depicts this relationship between interest rate and na-

tional income as the negatively sloped *IS* curve. The *IS* curve shows the combinations of national income and the rate of interest for which aggregate desired expenditure just equals total production in the economy. The negative relationship is derived for *given* values of the other variables influencing the aggregate expenditure function of Figure 32-5(i).[1]

For given settings of the relationships underlying the aggregate expenditure function, the condition of goods market equilibrium—national income equals aggregate expenditure—means that the level of national income will vary negatively with the interest rate.

Fiscal Policy

Increases in the level of government expenditure raise the total level of aggregate expenditure *for any given interest rate.* As Figure 30-1 shows, this in turn leads to a multiplier effect on national income. In terms of the present model an increase in government expenditure causes the *IS* curve to shift upward and to the right, as shown in Figure 37A-1. Combinations of national income and the interest rate that were on the original *IS* curve and hence were initially positions of equilibrium in the goods market are now positions of excess demand due to the increase in autonomous government demand. Hence output must rise to satisfy the increased demand (in the process leading to the now familiar multiplier effect), or interest rates must rise to reduce investment demand, or, as IS_1 shows, some combination of both.[2]

Expansionary fiscal policy causes the *IS* curve to shift upward and to the right, creating a new

---

[1] *IS* stands for investment and saving, since the equilibrium condition is often expressed in terms of the equality between these two aggregates.

[2] A reduction in taxes, by altering the relationship between national income and disposable income, would also lead to a rightward shift in the *IS* curve.

**FIGURE 37A-1   Goods Market Equilibrium:
The *IS* Curve**

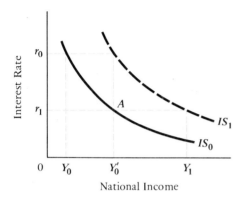

The locus of combinations of national income and
the interest rate for which aggregate expenditure
equals output is called the *IS* curve. The *IS* curve
slopes downward and to the right, indicating that a fall
in the interest rate from r_0 to r_1 leads, via increased investment, to an increase in the level of national income
from Y_0 to Y_0'. Expansionary fiscal policy creates excess
demand for output and causes the *IS* curve to shift to the
right to IS_1; from an initial position at *A*, the interest
rate must rise to r_0, or national income must rise to Y_2,
or some combination of both along IS_1 must occur.

---

locus of points for which aggregate expenditure
equals national income.

By similar reasoning, cuts in government spending or tax increases shift the *IS* curve down to the
left. [48]

Liquidity Preference and National Income: The *LM* Curve

When the money supply is held constant, if the demand for and the supply of money are to be equal
the *total* demand for money arising from the transactions, speculative, and precautionary motives must
also be constant. As we have seen, the demand for
money can be expected to vary positively with the
level of national income and negatively with the rate
of interest. If there is to be monetary equilibrium

**FIGURE 37A-2   Monetary Market Equilibrium:
The *LM* Curve**

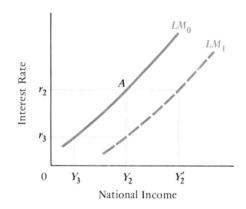

The locus of combinations of national income and
the interest rate of which total money demand
equals a given money supply is called the *LM*
curve. The *LM* curve slopes upward and to the right,
indicating that a fall in the rate of interest from r_2 to r_3,
which causes the demand for money to rise, must be accompanied by a fall in the level of national income, say,
from Y_2 to Y_3, in order to keep money demand equal to
the constant money supply. An open market purchase
creates an excess supply of money and causes the *LM*
curve to shift to the right to LM_1; from an initial position at *A*, the interest rate must fall to r_3, or national
income must rise to Y_2', or some combination of both
along *LM* must occur.

---

with a given money supply, any increase in national
income must therefore be accompanied by an increase in the interest rate to keep total money demand
constant. This is depicted by the positively sloped
LM curve in Figure 37A-2. The *LM* curve shows the
combinations of national income and interest rate for
which total money demand is constant at the level
of a given money supply.[3]

For a given money supply, the condition of
monetary market equilibrium means that the
level of national income will vary directly with
the interest rate.

[3] The *L* stands for liquidity preference (or demand for money)
and the *M* stands for money supply.

Monetary Policy

An increase in the supply of money resulting from an open market purchase by the central bank causes the *LM* curve to shift downward and to the right, as in Figure 37A-2. The combinations of national income and interest rate that were on the original curve LM_0 and hence that were initially positions of monetary equilibrium now correspond to excess supply due to the increase in the supply of money. To re-establish equilibrium, the demand for money must increase to match the larger money supply; hence national income must rise, or the interest rate must fall, or, as LM_1 shows, some combination of both.

An increase in the money supply causes the *LM* curve to shift downward and to the right, creating a new locus of points for which total money demand equals the money supply.

By similar reasoning, a decrease in the money supply causes the *LM* curve to shift upward to the left. [49]

Macroeconomic Equilibrium: Determination of National Income and the Interest Rate

The model is shown in Figure 37A-3. The intersection of the *LM* and *IS* curves indicates the only combination of national income and interest rate for which aggregate expenditure equals national income *and* the demand for money is equal to the supply.

The intersection of the *IS* and *LM* curves gives the equilibrium levels of national income and the rate of interest in a model that combines both expenditure and monetary influences.

FIGURE 37A-3   The Effects of Shifts in the *IS* and *LM* Curves

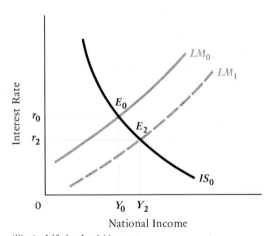

(i) A shift in the *IS* curve

(ii) A shift in the *LM* curve

Similar shifts in the *IS* and *LM* curves have similar effects on national income and opposite effects on the rate of interest. The initial levels of income and interest rate are Y_0 and r_0 in both parts of the figure. In (i) a rightward shift in the *IS* curve from IS_0 to IS_1 raises national income from Y_0 to Y_1 and raises the rate of interest from r_0 to r_1. In (ii) a rightward shift in the *LM* curve from LM_0 to LM_1 raises national income from Y_0 to Y_2 and lowers the rate of interest from r_0 to r_2. Part (i) shows the effect of an increase in government expenditure; part (ii) shows the effect of an increase in the money supply.

Figure 37A-3 shows the effects of particular shifts in the *IS* and *LM* curves. This analysis leads to four general predictions.

1. A rightward shift in the *IS* curve raises national income and the rate of interest.
2. A leftward shift in the *IS* curve lowers national income and the rate of interest.
3. A rightward shift in the *LM* curve raises national income and lowers the rate of interest.
4. A leftward shift in the *LM* curve lowers national income and raises the rate of interest.

The Effects of Fiscal and Monetary Policy

Given our analysis of the effects of government expenditure on the *IS* curve and the effects of the money supply on the *LM* curve, we can summarize the analysis in our four basic predictions about the effects of monetary and fiscal policy.

1. An increase in *G* raises national income and raises the rate of interest.
2. An increase in the money supply raises national income and lowers the rate of interest.
3. A decrease in *G* lowers national income and lowers the rate of interest.
4. A decrease in the money supply lowers national income and raises the rate of interest.

These results represent what may be called the *Keynesian synthesis*, in which both monetary and fiscal policies have an effect on national income and interest rates.[4] [50]

The Price Level and Aggregate Demand

So far we have treated the price level as given and presumed that all changes in national income were changes in *real* output. Consider now what would happen to the analysis if the price level were allowed to vary.

---

[4] As we saw in Chapters 30 and 32, a cut in tax rates has effects similar to an increase in *G*, and a fall in the demand for money has effects similar to an increase in the money supply.

Changes in the Price Level

As we saw in Box 32-2 on pages 648–649, an increase in the price level leads to an increase in liquidity preference. In order for money market equilibrium to be

---

FIGURE 37A-4   The Derivation of Aggregate Demand

(i) *IS–LM* model

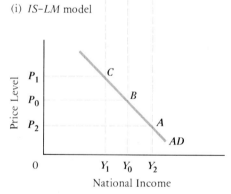

(ii) Aggregate demand

Changes in the price level shift the *LM* curve and thus change the equilibrium level of income. An increase in the price level increases the demand for money. Alternatively, it can be seen as reducing the real value of the existing money stock. The excess demand for money leads to a leftward shift in the LM_0 curve to LM_1 and a fall in national income. A fall in the price level creates an excess supply of money and a rightward shift in the LM_0 curve to LM_2. The price level and national income are inversely related, as shown by the *AD* curve in (ii).

---

preserved, the interest rate must rise or the level of income must fall or, since either leads to a reduction in money demand, some combination of both must occur. That is, the *LM* curve must shift upward and to the left.

A fall in the price level reduces liquidity preference and the *LM* curve shifts down and to the right.

Increases in the price level cause the *LM* curve to shift upward to the left; decreases in the price level cause the LM curve to shift downward to the right.

But from the previous section we know that the effect in the first case is to reduce national income, while the effect in the second case is to increase national income. This is illustrated in Figure 37A-4 on page 771.

Equilibrium in the money and goods markets combined implies that the price level and national income are negatively related, as summarized in the downward-sloping aggregate demand curve.

The negative relationship between the price level and national income summarized in the aggregate demand curve is a straightforward extension of the transmission mechanism running from liquidity preference to the rate of interest to aggregate expenditure.

Shifts in the Aggregate Demand Curve

The *AD* curve was derived on the basis of a given money supply and given relationships underlying the *IS* curve; it is a straightforward exercise to demonstrate that fiscal and monetary policies, by influencing the *IS* and *LM* curves, cause the *AD* curve to shift. [51] The mechansim by which monetary and fiscal policy cause the shift in *AD* is illustrated in Figure 32-5.

An increase in the money supply means that the *LM* curve corresponding to any particular price level shifts downward to the right. Hence that price level now corresponds to a higher level of real national income; that is, the *AD* curve shifts to the right as a result of an increase in the money supply.

An increase in government expenditure causes the *IS* curve to shift upward to the right as before; it now intersects any given *LM* curve at a higher level of national income. Again, any given price level now corresponds to a larger real national income; that is, the *AD* curve shifts to the right as a result of an increase in government expenditure.

International
Trade
and
Finance

38

The Gains from Trade

Americans buy Volkswagens, Germans take holidays in Italy, Italians buy spices from Tanzania, Africans import oil from Kuwait, Arabs buy Japanese cameras, and the Japanese depend heavily on American soybeans as a source of food. *International trade* refers to exchanges of goods and services that take place across international boundaries.

The founders of modern economics were concerned with foreign trade problems. The great eighteenth century British philosopher and economist David Hume, one of the first to work out the theory of the price system as a control mechanism, developed his concepts mainly in terms of prices in foreign trade. Adam Smith in his *Wealth of Nations* attacked government restriction of trade. David Ricardo in 1817 developed the basic theory of the gains from trade that is studied in this chapter. The repeal of the Corn Laws—tariffs on the importation of grains into Great Britain—and the transformation of that country during the nineteenth century from a country of high tariffs to one of complete free trade were to a significant extent the result of agitation by economists whose theories of the gains from trade led them to condemn all tariffs.

In this chapter we explore the fundamental question of what is gained by international trade. In Chapter 39 we will deal with the pros and cons of interfering with the free flow of such trade. Chapter 40 will consider the problems caused by different countries' using different currencies. Finally, Chapter 41 will be devoted to a brief study of the international monetary systems under which the international exchange of goods and movements of capital have functioned in the twentieth century.

Sources of the Gains from Trade

The advantages realized as a result of trade are called the **gains from trade.** The source of such gains is most easily visualized by considering the differences between a world with trade and a world without it. Although politicians often regard foreign trade differently from domestic trade, economists from Adam Smith on have argued that the causes and consequences of international trade are simply an extension of the principles governing domestic trade. What is the advantage of trade among individuals, among groups, among regions, or among countries?

Interpersonal, Interregional, and International Trade

Consider trade among individuals. Without trade each person would have to be self-sufficient; each would have to produce all the food, clothing, shelter, medical services, entertainment, and luxuries that he or she consumed. A world of individual self-sufficiency would be a world with extremely low living standards.

Trade among individuals allows people to specialize in those activities they can do well and to buy from others the goods and services they cannot easily produce. A good doctor who is a bad carpenter can provide medical services not only for his or her own family, but also for an excellent carpenter without the training or the ability to practice medicine. Thus trade and specialization are intimately connected. Without trade everyone must be self-sufficient. With trade everyone can specialize in what he or she does well and satisfy other needs by trading.

The same principles apply to regions. Without interregional trade each region would be forced to be self-sufficient. With trade each region can specialize in producing commodities for which it has some natural or acquired advantage. Plains regions can specialize in growing grain, mountain regions in mining and forest products, and regions with abundant power in manufacturing. Cool regions can produce wheat and other crops that thrive in temperate climates, and hot regions can grow such tropical crops as bananas, sugar, and coffee. The living standards of the inhabitants of all regions will be higher when each region specializes in products in which it has some natural or acquired advantage and obtains other products by trade than when all regions seek to be self-sufficient.

The same principle also applies to nations. A national boundary seldom delimits an area that is naturally self-sufficient. Nations, like regions or persons, can gain from specialization and the international trade that must accompany it. Specialization means that in any given country, more of the goods in which production is specialized are produced than residents wish to consume, while little or no domestic production is available for other goods that residents desire.

International trade is necessary to achieve the gains that international specialization makes possible.

This discussion suggests one important possible gain from trade.

With trade, each individual, region, or nation is able to concentrate on producing goods and services that it produces efficiently while trading to obtain goods and services that it does not produce efficiently.

Specialization and trade go hand in hand because there is no motivation to achieve the gains from specialization without being able to trade the goods produced for goods desired. Economists use the term *gains from trade* to embrace the results of both.

We shall examine two sources of the gains from trade. The first is differences among regions of the world in climate and resource endowment that lead to advantages in producing certain goods and disadvantages in producing others. These gains occur even though each country's costs of production are unchanged by the existence of trade. The second source is the reduction in each country's costs of production that result from the greater production that specialization brings.

The Gains from Specialization with Given Costs

In order to focus on differences in countries' conditions of production, suppose that there are no advantages arising from either economies of large scale production or cost reductions that are the consequence of learning new skills. In these circumstances what leads to gains from trade? To examine this question we shall use an example involving only two countries and two products, but the general principles apply as well to the real-world case of many countries and many commodities.

A Special Case: Absolute Advantage

The gains from trade are clear when there is a simple situation involving absolute advantage. **Absolute advantage** concerns the quantities of a single product that can be produced using the same quantity of resources in two different regions. One region is said to have an absolute advantage over another in the production of commodity X when an equal quantity of resources can produce more X in the first region than in the second.

Suppose region A has an absolute advantage over

B in one commodity, while region B has an absolute advantage over A in another. This is a case of *reciprocal absolute advantage*: Each country has an absolute advantage in some commodity. In such a situation the total production of both regions can be increased (relative to a situation of self-sufficiency) if each specializes in the commodity in which it has the absolute advantage.

Table 38-1 provides a simple example. In the ex-

TABLE 38-1   Gains from Specialization with Absolute Advantage

Part A: Amounts of wheat and cloth that can be produced with one unit of resources in America and England

	Wheat (bushels)	Cloth (yards)
America	10	6
England	5	10

Part B: Changes resulting from the transfer of one unit of American resources into wheat and one unit of English resources into cloth

	Wheat (bushels)	Cloth (yards)
America	+10	− 6
England	− 5	+10
Total	+ 5	+ 4

When there is a reciprocal absolute advantage, specialization makes it possible to produce more of both commodities. Part A shows the production of wheat and cloth that can be achieved in each country by using one unit of resources. America can produce 10 bushels of wheat or 6 yards of cloth; England can produce 5 bushels of wheat or 10 yards of cloth. America has an absolute advantage in producing wheat, England in producing cloth. Part B shows the changes in production caused by moving one unit of resources out of cloth and into wheat production in America and moving one unit of resources in the opposite direction in England. There is an increase in world production of 5 bushels of wheat and 4 yards of cloth; worldwide, there are gains from specialization. In this example the more resources are transferred into wheat production in America and cloth production in England, the larger the gains will be.

ample total world production of both wheat and cloth increases when each country produces more of the good in which it has an absolute advantage. As a result there is more wheat *and* more cloth for the same use of resources.

The gains from *specialization* make the gains from *trade* possible. England is producing more cloth and America more wheat than when they were self-sufficient. America is producing more wheat and less cloth than American consumers wish to buy, and England is producing more cloth and less wheat than English consumers wish to buy. If consumers in both countries are to get cloth and wheat in the desired proportions, America must export wheat to England and import cloth from England.

A First General Statement: Comparative Advantage

When each country has an absolute advantage over the other in a commodity, the gains from trade are obvious. But what if America can produce both wheat and cloth more efficiently than England? In essence this was David Ricardo's question, posed over 170 years ago. His answer underlies the theory of comparative advantage and is still accepted by economists as a valid statement of the potential gains from trade.

To start with assume that American efficiency increases tenfold above the levels recorded in the previous example, so that a unit of American resources can produce either 100 bushels of wheat or 60 yards of cloth. English efficiency remains unchanged (see Table 38-2). It might appear that America, which is now better at producing both wheat and cloth than is England, has nothing to gain by trading with such an inefficient foreign country. But it *does* have something to gain, as shown in Table 38-2. Even though America is 10 times as efficient as in the situation of Table 38-1, it is still possible to increase world production of both wheat and cloth by having America produce more wheat and less cloth, and England produce more cloth and less wheat.

What is the source of this gain? Although America has an absolute advantage over England in the production of both wheat and cloth, the margin of

TABLE 38-2   Gains from Specialization with Comparative Advantage

Part A: Amounts of wheat and cloth that can be produced with one unit of resources in America and England

	Wheat (bushels)	Cloth (yards)
America	100	60
England	5	10

Part B: Changes resulting from the transfer of one-tenth of one unit of American resources into wheat and one unit of English resources into cloth

	Wheat (bushels)	Cloth (yards)
America	+10	− 6
England	− 5	+10
Total	+ 5	+ 4

When there is comparative advantage, specialization makes it possible to produce more of both commodities. The productivity of English resources is left unchanged from Table 38-1; that of American resources is increased tenfold. England no longer has an absolute advantage in producing either commodity. Total production of both commodities can nonetheless be increased by specialization. Moving one-tenth of one unit of American resources out of cloth and into wheat and moving one unit of resources in the opposite direction in England causes world production of wheat to rise by 5 bushels and cloth by 4 yards. Reciprocal absolute advantage is not necessary for gains from trade.

advantage differs in the two commodities. America can produce 20 times as much wheat as England by using the same quantity of resources, but only 6 times as much cloth. America is said to have a **comparative advantage** in the production of wheat and a comparative disadvantage in the production of cloth. (This statement implies another: England has a comparative disadvantage in the production of wheat, in which it is 20 times less efficient than America, and a comparative advantage in the production of cloth, in which it is only 6 times less efficient.)

A key proposition in the theory of international trade is:

The gains from specialization and trade depend on the pattern of comparative, not absolute, advantage.

A comparison of Tables 38-1 and 38-2 refutes the notion that the absolute *levels* of efficiency of two areas determine the gains from specialization. The key is that the margin of advantage one area has over the other must differ between commodities. As long as this margin differs, total world production can be increased when each area specializes in the production of that commodity in which it has a comparative advantage.

Comparative advantage is necessary as well as sufficient for gains from trade. This is illustrated in Table 38-3, showing America with an absolute advantage in both commodities and neither country with a comparative advantage over the other in the production of either commodity. America is 10 times as efficient as England in the production of wheat and in the production of cloth. Now there is no way to increase the production of both wheat and cloth by reallocating resources within America and within England. The lower half of the table provides one example of a resource shift that illustrates this. Absolute advantage without comparative advantage does not lead to gains from trade.

A Second General Statement: Opportunity Costs

Much of the previous argument has used the concept of a unit of resources. It assumes that units of resources can be equated across countries, so that statements such as "America can produce 10 times as much wheat with the same quantity of resources as England" are meaningful. Measurement of the real resource cost of producing commodities poses many difficulties. If, for example, England uses land, labor, and capital in proportions different from those used in America, it may not be clear which country gets more output per unit of resource input. Fortunately, the proposition about the gains from trade can be restated without reference to so fuzzy a concept as units of resources.

TABLE 38-3   Absence of Gains from Specialization When There is No Comparative Advantage

Part A: Amounts of wheat and cloth that can be produced with one unit of resources in America and England

	Wheat (bushels)	Cloth (yards)
America	100	60
England	10	6

Part B: Changes resulting from the transfer of one unit of American resources into wheat and ten units of British resources into cloth

	Wheat (bushels)	Cloth (yards)
America	+100	−60
England	−100	+60
Total	0	0

Where there is no comparative advantage, no reallocation of resources within each country can increase the production of both commodities. In this example America has the same absolute advantage over England in each commodity (tenfold). There is no comparative advantage, and world production cannot be increased by reallocating resources in both countries. Therefore, specialization does not increase total output.

To do this go back to the examples of Tables 38-1 and 38-2. Calculate the *opportunity cost* of wheat and cloth in the two countries. When resources are assumed to be fully employed, the only way to produce more of one commodity is to reallocate resources and produce less of the other commodity. Table 38-1 shows that a unit of resources in America can produce 10 bushels of wheat *or* 6 yards of cloth. From this it follows that the opportunity cost of producing a unit of wheat is 0.60 units of cloth, while the opportunity cost of producing a unit of cloth is 1.67 units of wheat. These data are summarized in Table 38-4. The table also shows that in England the opportunity cost of a unit of wheat is 2.0 units of cloth foregone, while the opportunity cost of a unit

of cloth is 0.50 units of wheat. Table 38-2 also gives rise to the opportunity costs in Table 38-4.

The sacrifice of cloth involved in producing wheat is much lower in America than it is in England. World wheat production can be increased if America rather than England produces it. Looking at cloth production, we can see that the loss of wheat involved in producing one unit of cloth is lower in England than in America. England is the lower (opportunity) cost producer of cloth. World cloth production can be increased if England rather than America produces it. This situation is shown in Table 38-5.

The gains from trade arise from differing opportunity costs in the two countries.

The conclusions about the gains from trade arising from international differences may be summarized.

1. Country A has a comparative advantage over country B in producing a commodity when the opportunity cost (in terms of some other commodity) of production in country A is lower. This implies, however, that it has a comparative disadvantage in the other commodity.
2. Opportunity costs depend on the relative costs of

TABLE 38-4   Opportunity Cost of Wheat and Cloth in America and England

	Wheat (bushel)	Cloth (yard)
America	0.60 yards cloth	1.67 bushels wheat
England	2.00 yards cloth	0.50 bushels wheat

Comparative advantages can be expressed in terms of opportunity costs that differ between countries. These opportunity costs can be obtained from Table 38-1 or Table 38-2. The English opportunity cost of one unit of wheat is obtained by dividing the cloth output of one unit of English resources by the wheat output. The result shows that 2 yards of cloth must be sacrificed for every extra unit of wheat produced by transferring English resources out of cloth production and into wheat. The other three cost figures are obtained in a similar manner.

TABLE 38-5 Gains from Specialization with Differing Opportunity Costs

Changes resulting from each country's producing one more unit of a commodity in which it has the lower opportunity cost

	Wheat (bushels)	Cloth (yards)
America	+1.0	−0.6
England	−0.5	+1.0
Total	+0.5	+0.4

Whenever opportunity costs differ between countries, specialization can increase the production of both commodities. These calculations show that there are gains from specialization given the opportunity costs of Table 38-4. To produce one more bushel of wheat, America must sacrifice 0.6 yards of cloth. To produce one more yard of cloth, England must sacrifice 0.5 bushels of wheat. Making both changes raises world production of both wheat and cloth.

producing two commodities, not on absolute costs. (Notice that the examples in Tables 38-1 and 38-2 each give rise to the opportunity costs in Table 38-4.)

3. When opportunity costs are the same in all countries, there is no comparative advantage and there is no possibility of gains from specialization and trade. (You can illustrate this for yourself by calculating the opportunity costs implied by the data in Table 38-3.)

4. When opportunity costs differ in any two countries, and both countries are producing both commodities, it is always possible to increase production of both commodities by a suitable reallocation of resources within each country. (This proposition is illustrated in Table 38-5.)

Gains from Specialization with Variable Costs

So far we have assumed that unit costs are the same whatever the scale of output and have seen that there are gains from specialization and trade as long as there are interregional differences in opportunity costs. If costs vary with the level of output or as

experience is acquired via specialization, *additional* sources of gain are possible.

Economies of Scale[1]

Real production costs, measured in terms of resources used, generally fall as the scale of output increases. The larger the scale of operations the more efficiently large-scale machinery can be used and the more a detailed division of tasks among workers is possible. Smaller countries such as Canada, France, and Israel whose domestic markets are not large enough to exploit economies of scale would find it prohibitively expensive to become self-sufficient. They would have to produce a little bit of everything at very high cost.

Trade allows smaller countries to specialize and produce a few commodities at high enough levels of output to reap the available economies of scale.

Bigger countries such as the United States and the USSR have markets large enough to allow the production of most items at home at a scale of output great enough to obtain the available economies of scale. For them the gains from trade arise mainly from specializing in commodities in which they have a comparative advantage. Yet even for such countries a broadening of their markets permits achieving economies of scale in subproduct lines, such as specialty steels or blue jeans.

The importance of product diversity and specialization in specific subproduct lines has been one of the important lessons learned from patterns of world trade since World War II. When the European Common Market (now called the European Community) was set up in the 1950s, economists expected that specialization would occur according to the classical theory of comparative advantage, with one country specializing in cars, another in refrigerators, another in fashion clothes, another in shoes, and so on. This is not the way it worked out. Today one can buy French, English, Italian, and German fashion goods,

---

[1] These are discussed in detail in Chapter 11. The classic discussion of this effect is quoted in Box 3–1 on page 45. This is worth reading now, even if you have not yet studied microeconomics.

cars, shoes, appliances, and a host of other goods in London, Paris, Bonn, and Rome. Ships loaded with Swedish furniture bound for London pass ships loaded with English furniture bound for Stockholm, and so on.

What free European trade did was to allow a proliferation of differentiated products with different countries each specializing in different subproduct lines. Consumers have shown by their expenditures that they value this enormous increase in the range of choice among differentiated products. As Asian countries have expanded into American markets with textiles, cars, and electronic goods, American manufacturers have increasingly specialized their production, and we now export textiles, cars, and electronics equipment to Japan even while importing similar but different products from Japan.

Learning by Doing

The discussion so far has assumed that costs vary only with the *level* of output. They may also vary with the length of time a product has been produced.

Early economists placed great importance on a factor that we now call learning by doing. They believed that as countries gained experience in particular tasks, workers and managers would become more efficient in performing them. As people acquire expertise, costs tend to fall. There is substantial evidence that such learning by doing does occur.

The distinction between this phenomenon and the gains from economies of scale is illustrated in Figure 38-1; it is one more example of the difference between a movement along a curve and a shift of the curve.

Recognition of the opportunities for learning by doing leads to an important implication: Policymakers need not accept *current* comparative advantages as given. Through such means as education and tax incentives, they can seek to develop new comparative advantages.[2] Moreover, countries cannot complacently assume that an existing comparative advantage

will persist. Misguided education policies, the wrong tax incentives, or policies that discourage risk taking can lead to the rapid erosion of a country's comparative advantage in a particular product. So, too, can competitive developments elsewhere in the world.

A changing view of comparative advantage. The classical theory of the gains from trade, which still has many adherents, assumes given cost structures based largely on a country's natural endowments. This leads to a given pattern of international comparative advantage. It leads to the policy advice that a government interested in maximizing its citizens' material standard of living should encourage production to be specialized in those goods where it currently has a comparative advantage. When all countries follow this advice, the theory predicts that each will be specialized in a relatively narrow range of distinct products. Canadians will be producers of resource-based primary products, Americans will be factory workers, Central Americans will be banana growers, and so on.

There is today a competing view. In extreme form it says that comparative advantages are certainly there, but they are typically acquired, not nature-given—and they change. This view of comparative advantage is *dynamic* rather than static. New industries are seen to depend more on human capital than on fixed physical capital or natural resources. The skills of a computer designer, a videogame programmer, a sound mix technician, or a rock star are acquired by education and on-the-job training. Natural endowments of energy and raw materials cannot account for Britain's prominence in modern pop music nor for the leadership in ideas of Silicon Valley in California. When a country such as the United States finds its former dominance (based on comparative advantage) declining in such smokestack industries as automobiles and steel, its firms need not sit idly by. Instead they can begin to adapt by developing new areas of comparative advantage.

There are surely elements of truth in both extreme views. It would be unwise to neglect resource endowments, climate, culture, and social and institutional arrangements. But it would also be unwise to assume all of them were innate and immutable.

---

[2] Of course, they can, foolishly, use the same policies to develop industries in which they do not have, and will never achieve, comparative advantage. See the discussion in Chapter 42.

FIGURE 38-1   Gains from Specialization with Variable Costs

(i) Economies of scale

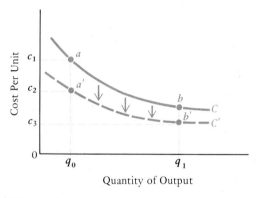

(ii) Learning by doing

Specialization may lead to gains from trade by permitting economies of larger scale output, by leading to downward shifts of cost curves, or both. Consider a country that wishes to consume the quantity q_0. Suppose that it can produce that quantity at an average cost per unit of c_1. Suppose further that the country has a comparative advantage in producing this commodity and can export the quantity q_0q_1 if it produces q_1. This may lead to cost savings in two ways. (i) The increased level of production of q_1 compared to q_0 permits it to *move along* its cost curve, C, from a to b, thus reducing costs per unit to c_2. This is an economy of scale. (ii) As workers and managements become more experienced, they may discover means of increasing productivity that lead to a downward shift of the cost curve from C to C'. This is learning by doing. The downward *shift,* shown by the arrows, lowers the cost of producing every unit of output. At output q_1 costs per unit fall to c_3. The movement from a to b' incorporates both economies of scale and learning by doing.

The Terms of Trade

So far we have seen that world production can be increased when countries specialize in the production of the commodities in which they have or can acquire a comparative advantage and then trade with one another. We now ask: How will these gains from specialization and trade be shared among countries? The division of the gain depends on the terms at which trade takes place. The **terms of trade** depend upon the quantity of imported goods that can be obtained per unit of goods exported and are measured by the ratio of the price of exports to the price of imports.

A rise in the price of imported goods, with the price of exports unchanged, indicates a *fall in the terms of trade;* it will now take more exports to buy the same quantity of imports. Similarly, a rise in the price of exported goods, with the price of imports unchanged, indicates a *rise in the terms of trade;* it will now take fewer exports to buy the same quantity of imports. Thus the ratio of prices is a proxy for the amount of exported goods needed to acquire a given quantity of imports.

In the example of Table 38-4 the American domestic opportunity cost of one unit of cloth is 1.67 bushels of wheat. In other words, if in America resources are transferred from wheat to cloth, 1.67 bushels of wheat are given up for every 1 yard of cloth gained. But if America can obtain its cloth by trade on more favorable terms, it pays to produce and export wheat to pay for cloth imports. Suppose,

BOX 38-1

The Gains from Trade Illustrated Graphically

International trade leads to an expansion of the set of goods that can be consumed in the economy in two ways: by allowing the bundle of goods consumed to differ from the bundle produced and by permitting a profitable change in the pattern of production. The key to these gains is that international trade allows the separation of production decisions from consumption decisions. Without international trade the choice of which bundle of goods to produce is the same thing as the choice of which bundle to consume. With international trade the consumption and production bundles can be altered independently to reflect the relative value placed on goods by international markets.

This proposition is illustrated graphically on page 783 for a simplified world in which there are only two goods, X and Y. The illustration is in two stages.

Stage 1: Fixed Production

In each part of the figure the black curve is the economy's production possibility boundary (such a boundary was first introduced in Figure 1-2, page 6).

If there is no international trade, the economy must consume the same bundle of goods that it produces. Thus the production possibility boundary is also the consumption possibility boundary. Suppose the economy produces and consumes at point a, with q_1 of good X and q_2 of good Y, as in part i.

Next, suppose that while production stays at point a, good Y can be exchanged for good X in international markets. The consumption possibilities are now enhanced, as is shown by the line tt drawn through point a. The slope of this line indicates the world terms of trade and reflects the quantity of Y that exchanges for a unit of X on the international market.

Although production is fixed at a, consumption can now be anywhere on the line tt. For example, the consumption point could be at b. This could be achieved by exporting ac units of Y and importing cb units of X. Since point b (and all others on line tt to the right of a) lies outside of the production possibility boundary, there are potential gains from trade. Consumers are no longer limited by *their* country's production possibilities. Let us suppose they prefer point b to point a. They have achieved a gain from trade by being allowed to exchange some of their production of good Y for some quantity of good X and thus to consume more of good X than is produced at home.

Stage 2: Variable Production

In stage 1 production was constant at a. An additional opportunity for the expansion of the country's consumption possibilities arises because, with trade, the production bundle may be profitably altered in response to international prices. The country may pro-

for example, that international prices are such that 1 yard of cloth exchanges for (i.e., is equal in value to) 1 bushel of wheat. At those prices, Americans can obtain 1 yard of cloth for 1 bushel of wheat exported. They get more cloth per unit of wheat exported than they can by moving resources out of wheat into cloth production at home. Therefore, the terms of trade favor specializing in the production of wheat and trading it for cloth on international markets.

Similarly, in the example of Table 38-4 English consumers gain when they can obtain wheat abroad at any terms of trade more favorable than 2 yards of

cloth per unit of wheat. If the terms of trade permit exchange of 1 bushel of wheat for 1 yard of cloth, the terms of trade favor English traders' buying wheat and selling cloth on international markets. Here both England and America gain from trade. Each can obtain the commodity in which it has a comparative disadvantage at a lower opportunity cost through international trade than through domestic production. The way in which the terms of trade affect the gains from trade is illustrated graphically in Box 38-1.

Because actual international trade involves many

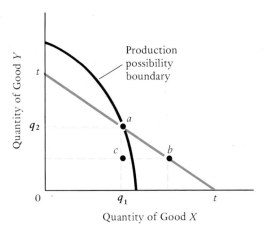

(i) Stage 1: fixed production

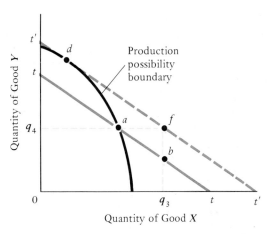

(ii) Stage 2: variable production

duce the bundle of goods that is most valuable in world markets. That is represented by the bundle *d* in part ii. The consumption possibility set is shifted to the line *t′t′* by changing production from *a* to *d* and thereby increasing the country's degree of specialization in good Y. For every point on the original consumption possibility set, *tt,* there are points on the new set, *t′t′,* which allow more consumption of both goods. Compare, for example, points *a* and *f*. Notice also that, except at the zero-trade point, *d,* the new consumption possibility set lies everywhere above the production possibility curve.

Many consumption bundles that cannot be produced domestically are made available by trade. The benefits from moving from a no-trade position, such as *a,* to a trading position such as *b* or *f* are the *gains from trade* to the country. When the production of good Y was increased and the production of food X decreased, the country was able to move to point *f* by producing more of good Y, in which the country has a comparative advantage, and trading the additional production for good X. Economists refer to such production changes as "exploiting the country's comparative advantage."

countries and many commodities, a country's terms of trade are computed as an index number:

$$\text{Terms of trade} = \frac{\text{index of export prices}}{\text{index of import prices}} \times 100$$

A rise in the index is referred to as a *favorable* change in a country's terms of trade. A favorable change means that more can be imported per unit of goods exported than previously. For example, if the export price index rises from 100 to 120 while the import price index rises from 100 to 110, the terms of trade index rises from 100 to 109. At the new terms of

trade a unit of exports will buy 9 percent more imports than at the old terms.

A decrease in the index of the terms of trade, called an *unfavorable* change, means the country can import less in return for any given amount of exports or, what is the same, it must export more to pay for any given amount of imports. For example, the sharp rise in oil prices in the 1970s led to large unfavorable shifts in the terms of trade of oil-importing countries, including the United States. When oil prices fell sharply in the mid 1980s, the terms of trade of oil-importing countries changed favorably.

Summary

1. The sources of the gains from trade between any two entities—individuals, regions, or nations—are the same.
2. One country (or region or individual) has an absolute advantage over another country (or region or individual) in the production of a commodity when, with the same input of resources in each country, it can produce more of the commodity than can the other.
3. In a situation of absolute advantage, total production of both commodities will be raised if each country specializes in the production of the commodity in which it has the absolute advantage. However, the gains from trade do not require absolute advantage on the part of each country, only comparative advantage.
4. Comparative advantage is the relative advantage one country enjoys over another in production of various commodities. World production of all commodities can be increased if each country transfers resources into the production of the commodities in which it has a comparative advantage.
5. Comparative advantage arises from countries' having different opportunity costs of producing particular goods. This creates the opportunity for all nations to gain from trade.
6. The theory of the gains from trade is: Trade allows all countries to obtain the goods in which they do not have a comparative advantage at a lower opportunity cost than they would face if they were to produce all commodities for themselves. This allows all countries to have more of all commodities than they could have if they tried to be self-sufficient.
7. As well as gaining the advantages of specialization arising from comparative advantage, a nation that engages in trade and specialization may realize the benefits of the economies of large-scale production and of learning by doing.
8. Classical theory regarded comparative advantage as largely determined by natural resource endowments and thus difficult to change. Economists now believe that comparative advantage can be acquired and thus can be changed. A country may, in this view, seek to influence its role in world production and trade.
9. The terms of trade refer to the ratio of the prices of goods exported to those imported which determines the quantities of exports needed to pay for imports. The terms of trade determine how the gains from trade are shared. A favorable change in terms of trade, that is, a rise in export prices relative to import prices, means one can acquire more imports per unit of exports.

Topics for Review

Interpersonal, interregional, and international specialization
Absolute advantage and comparative advantage
Gains from trade: specialization, scale economies, and learning by doing
Opportunity cost and comparative advantage

Dynamic comparative advantage
Terms of trade

---

1. Adam Smith saw a close connection between the wealth of a nation and its willingness "freely to engage" in foreign trade. What is the connection?
2. Suppose that the situation described in the table exists. Assume that there are no tariffs and no government intervention and that labor is the only factor of production. Let X take different values—say, $10, $20, $40, and $60. In each case in what direction will trade have to flow in order for the gains from trade to be exploited?

Country	Labor cost of producing one unit of	
	Artichokes	**Bikinis**
Inland	$20	$40
Outland	$20	$X

3. Suppose the United States had an absolute advantage in all manufactured products. Should it then ever import any manufactured products?
4. Suppose, after 1865, the United States had become two separate countries with no trade between them. What predictions would you make about the standard of living compared with what it is today? Does the fact that Canada, the United States, and Mexico are separate countries lead to a lower standard of living in the three countries than if they were united into a new country called Northica?
5. Studies of U.S. trade patterns have shown that very high wage sectors of industry are among the largest and fastest growing export sectors. Does this contradict the principle of comparative advantage?
6. Saudi Arabia has a comparative advantage over West Germany in producing oil. In what, if anything, does it have a comparative disadvantage? When Saudi Arabia lowers the price of oil, does it change the gains from trade? What does it change?
7. Predict what each of the following events would do to the terms of trade of the importing country and the exporting country, other things being equal.
   a. A blight destroys a good part of the coffee beans produced in the world.
   b. The Japanese cut the price of the steel they sell to the United States.
   c. A general inflation of 10 percent occurs around the world.
   d. Violation of OPEC output quotas leads to a sharp fall in the price of oil.
8. Heavy U.S. borrowing abroad in the early 1980s led to a high value of the dollar and thus a rise in the ratio of export prices to import prices. While this is called a favorable change in the terms of trade, are there any reasons why it may not have been a good thing for the U.S. economy?

39

Barriers to Free Trade

Conducting business in a foreign country is always difficult. Differences in language, in local laws and customs, and in currency all complicate transactions. Our concern in this chapter is not, however, with these difficulties, but with the government's policy toward international trade, which is called its **commercial policy.** At one extreme is a policy of **free trade**, which means an absence of any form of government interference with the free flow of international trade. Any departure from free trade designed to give some protection to domestic industries from foreign competition is called **protectionism.**

The Theory of Commercial Policy

Today debates over commercial policy are as heated as they were 200 years ago when the theory of the gains from trade was still being worked out. Should a country permit the free flow of international trade, or should it seek to protect its local producers from foreign competition? Such protection may be achieved either by **tariffs,** which are taxes designed to raise the price of foreign goods, or by **nontariff barriers,** which are devices other than tariffs that are designed to reduce the flow of imports. Examples include quotas and customs procedures that are deliberately made more cumbersome than is necessary.

The Case for Free Trade

The case for free trade is based on the analysis presented in Chapter 38. We saw that whenever opportunity costs differ among countries, specialization and trade will raise world living standards. Free trade allows all countries to specialize in producing commodities in which they have a comparative advantage.

Free trade allows the maximization of world production, thus making it *possible* for every household in the world to consume more goods than it could without free trade.

This does not necessarily mean that everyone *will* be better off with free trade than without it. Protectionism could allow some people to obtain a larger share of a smaller world output so that they would benefit even though the average person would lose. If we ask whether it is *possible* for free trade to be advantageous to everyone, the answer is yes. But if we ask whether free trade is in fact *always* advantageous to everyone, the answer is not necessarily so.

There is abundant evidence that significant differences in opportunity costs exist and that large gains are realized from international trade because of these differences. What needs explanation is the fact that trade is not wholly free. Why do tariffs and nontariff barriers to trade continue to exist two centuries after Adam Smith and David Ricardo stated the case for free trade? Is there a valid case for protectionism? Before addressing these questions, let us examine the methods used in protectionist policy.

Methods of Protectionism

There are three main types of protectionist policy. All three may end up affecting both the price and quantity of exports. They differ, however, in what the policy changes in the first instance.

The first policy raises the *price* of the imported commodity. A tariff, also often called an *import duty*, is the most common price-raising device. Others are rules and regulations that are costly to comply with, that do not apply to competing domestically produced commodities, and that are more than is required to meet purposes other than trade restriction.

Tariffs come in two main forms: **specific tariffs**, which are so much money per unit of the product, and **ad valorem tariffs**, which are a percentage of the price of the product. Tariffs raise revenue as well as acting as a protective device. For some less-developed countries which have limited sources of revenue, import duties can be an important revenue source. For advanced countries such as the United States, the revenue-raising function is unimportant and can be ignored.

The second type of protectionist policy restricts the *quantity* of the imported commodity. A common example is the **import quota**, by which the importing country sets a maximum on the quantity of some commodity that may be imported each year. Increasingly popular, however, is the **voluntary export restriction (VER)** by which an exporting country agrees to limit the amount it sells to a second country. VERs were negotiated between Japan and the United States to limit the sale of Japanese cars in the United States for several years in the mid 1980s.

The third type consists of domestic policies that reduce the demand for imported commodities. For example, the U.S. government recently required that all imported steel pipe be marked with its country of origin, which is both costly and alleged to reduce the quality of certain types of pipe. Whatever the apparent purpose of the legislation, its effect was to reduce the demand for imported steel pipe. Other countries restrict the ability of their citizens to purchase the foreign exchange needed to pay for the imports. This shifts the demand curve for imports to the left.

Figure 39-1 illustrates the three methods of restricting trade. Although each method achieves a reduction in imports, each has different side effects. Some of these are examined in Box 39-1 on pages 790–791.

In what follows, we concentrate on tariffs, which are one of the most important tools of trade restriction.

In addition to devices designed to restrict imports for protectionist purposes, there is also a series of devices designed to prevent what are called "unfair trade practices" by foreign firms or governments. The two most common of these are *antidumping duties* and *countervailing duties*. Although not intended as tools of protection, they can be used as such, and we shall consider them later in the chapter.

Nominal and Effective Rates of Tariff

The rate of tariff charged on each commodity, called the **nominal rate of tariff**, does not necessarily show the degree of protection given to that commodity. Nominal rates frequently understate the degree of protection offered to domestic manufacturing industries and a better measure is provided by what is called the effective tariff rate.

The distinction between nominal and effective rates of tariff arises whenever imported raw materials or semi-finished goods carry a different rate of duty than do imports of the final manufactured goods that embody these intermediate products. When the final good is made abroad, the duty for manufactured goods is applied to the entire price of that good, even though the price includes the values of the raw materials and semi-finished goods that it embodies. When the final good is produced domestically, the

FIGURE 39-1   Three Ways of Reducing Imports

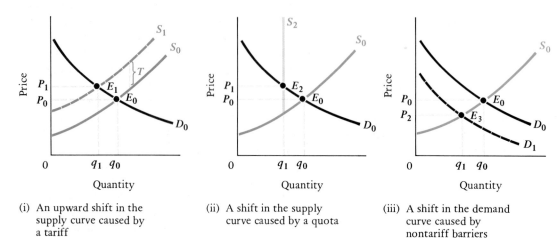

(i) An upward shift in the
     supply curve caused by
     a tariff

(ii) A shift in the supply
      curve caused by a quota

(iii) A shift in the demand
       curve caused by
       nontariff barriers

The government can restrict imports by policies that raise the price of the commodity, that directly reduce the quantity imported, or that reduce the demand for the commodity. In all the diagrams, D_0 is the domestic demand, while S_0 is the foreign supply to the domestic market of some commodity that is not produced domestically. P_0 and q_0 are the equilibrium price and quantity, but the government wishes to reduce the quantity of imports, and hence the quantity of consumption, to q_1.

In (i) the government adopts a specific tariff that raises by T per unit the price at which any quantity will be supplied. This shifts the supply curve vertically by the amount of the tariff to S_1 and achieves a new equilibrium at E_1.

In (ii) the government sets a maximum quantity of q_1 that can be imported. The new supply curve follows the old curve S_0 between 0 and q_1, but then follows the vertical line S_2 at quantity q_1. The new equilibrium is at E_2.

In (iii) the government causes demand to shift leftward to D_1 by such policies as limiting importers' rights to purchase either the commodity or the foreign exchange needed to pay for it. In this case a new equilibrium occurs at E_3.

---

raw materials and semi-finished goods enter at the lower rate of tariff. For this reason a tariff of, say, 10 percent on the final good will protect a domestic producer that is much more than 10 percent less efficient than its foreign competitor.

To illustrate this important point, consider an example. A product is manufactured in both Canada and the United States using a Canadian raw material. The raw material is assumed to enter the United States duty free, but the manufactured good is subject to a 10 percent tariff. Further assume that when the product is manufactured in Canada, the raw material accounts for half the cost of the final product

and the other half is value added by the Canadian manufacturer. Because of the 10 percent tariff, a unit of output that costs $1 to produce in Canada will sell in the United States for $1.10.

Now consider the position of a U.S. manufacturer who is assumed to be less efficient than the Canadian manufacturer. Let the American firm's production costs be 20 percent higher than those of the Canadian firm. Thus to produce one unit of output, the raw material costs the U.S. firm $.50, but its other costs—including the opportunity costs of its capital—are $.60 (i.e., 20 percent higher than the Canadian manufacturer's costs of $.50.) This gives the U.S. firm a final price of $1.10, which is just low enough to compete against the tariff-burdened Canadian import.

In this example, a tariff of 10 percent on the value of the final product is sufficient to protect a U.S. firm that is 20 percent less efficient than its Canadian competitor. To measure this effect, the **effective rate of tariff** expresses the tariff as a percentage of the *value added* by the exporting industry in question. Thus the effective American rate of tariff on the Canadian manufacturing industry in the above example is 20 percent, whereas the nominal tariff on manufactured goods is only 10 percent.

The Case for Protectionism

Two kinds of arguments for protection are commonly offered. The first concerns national objectives other than output; the second concerns the desire to increase domestic national income possibly at the expense of world national income.

Objectives Other Than Maximizing National Income

It is quite possible to accept the proposition that national income is higher with free trade and yet rationally oppose free trade because of a concern with policy objectives other than maximizing per capita national income. For example, comparative advantage might dictate that a country should specialize in producing a narrow range of commodities. The government might decide, however, that there are distinct social advantages to encouraging a more diverse economy. Citizens would be given a wider range of occupations, and the social and psychological advantages of diversification would more than compensate for a reduction in living standards by, say, 5 percent below what they could be with complete specialization of production according to comparative advantage.

Specialization also involves the risk of cyclical fluctuations in the prices of basic commodities, which may face depressed prices for years at a time and then enjoy periods of very high prices. The national income of a country specializing in the production of such commodities will be subject to wide fluctuations. Even though the average income level over a long period might be higher if specialization in the production of a few basic commodities were allowed, the serious social problems associated with a widely fluctuating national income may make the government decide to sacrifice some income in order to reduce fluctuations. The government might use protectionist policies to encourage the expansion of several less cyclically sensitive industries.

Yet another reason for protectionism is the desire to maintain national traditions. For example, many Canadians are passionately concerned with maintaining an identity separate from that of the United States and believe that their restrictions on trade and investment help them to do this. They would be prepared, if necessary, to tolerate, say, a 10 percent differential in living standards in order to maintain this independence.

The most frequently cited noneconomic reason for protectionism concerns national defense. It has traditionally been argued, for example, that the United States needs an experienced merchant marine in case of war and that this industry should be fostered by protectionist policies even though it is less efficient than the foreign competition. Another example is the perceived need for protection of the petroleum industry in order to reduce dependence on foreign energy sources.

Other things being equal, most people prefer more income to less. Economists cannot, however, say that it is irrational for a society to sacrifice some income in order to achieve other goals. Economists can, however, do three things when faced with such reasons for adopting protectionist measures. First, they can ask if the proposed measures really do achieve the ends suggested. Second, they can calculate the cost of the measures in terms of lowered living standards. Third, they can see if there are alternative means of achieving the stated goals at lower cost in terms of lost output.

The Objective of Maximizing National Income

Next we consider four important arguments for the use of tariffs when the objective is to make national income as large as possible.

BOX 39-1

Import Restrictions on Japanese Cars: Tariffs or Quotas

In the early 1980s imports of Japanese cars seriously threatened the automobile industries of the United States, Canada, and Western Europe. While continuing to espouse relatively free trade as a long-term policy, the U.S. government argued that the domestic industry needed short-term protection. This protection was to tide it over the period of transition it faced as smaller cars became the typical American household's vehicle. Once the enormous investment needed to transform the American auto industry had been made and new American models had gained acceptance, free trade could be restored and the American industry asked to stand up to foreign competition.

But how was the temporary protection to be achieved? Politically, voluntary export restrictions (VERs) mutually agreed upon by the two governments seemed the easiest route. An agreement was reached severely limiting the number of Japanese cars to be exported to the United States. (A similar agreement was reached between the Canadian and the Japanese governments.)

What does theory predict to be the economic difference between VERs and tariffs? In both cases im-

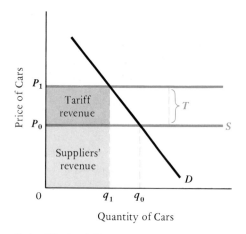

(i) Tariff of *T* dollars per car

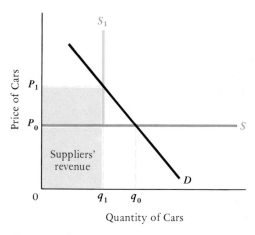

(ii) Quota of q_1 cars

To alter the terms of trade. Trade restrictions can be used to turn the terms of trade in favor of countries that produce and export a large fraction of the world's supply of some commodity. They can also be used to turn the terms of trade in favor of countries that constitute a large fraction of the world demand for some commodity that they import.

When the OPEC countries restricted their output of oil in the 1970s, they were able to drive the price of oil up relative to the prices of other traded goods. This turned the terms of trade in their favor; for every barrel of oil exported, they were able to obtain a larger quantity of imports. When the output of oil

grew greatly in the mid 1980s, the relative price of oil fell dramatically, and the terms of trade turned unfavorably to the oil-exploring companies. These are illustrations of how changes in the quantities of exports can affect the terms of trade.

Now consider a country that provides a large fraction of the total demand for some product that it imports. By restricting its demand for that product through tariffs it can force the price of that product down. This turns the terms of trade in its favor because it can now get more units of imports per unit of exports.

Both of these techniques lower world output.

ports are restricted and the resulting scarcity supports a higher market price. With a tariff the extra market value is appropriated by the government of the importing country—in this case the U.S. government. With a VER the extra market value accrues to the goods' suppliers—in this case the Japanese car makers and their U.S. retailers.

Both cases are illustrated in the figure. We assume that the U.S. market provides a small enough part of total Japanese car sales to leave the Japanese willing to supply at their fixed list price all the cars that are demanded in the United States. This is the price P_0 in both parts of the figure. Given the American demand curve for Japanese cars, D, there are q_0 cars sold before restrictions are imposed.

In (i) the United States places a tariff of T per unit on Japanese cars, raising their U.S. price to p_1 and lowering sales to q_1. Suppliers' revenue is shown by the light shaded area. U.S. government tariff revenue is shown by the dark shaded area.

In (ii) a VER of q_1 is imposed, making the supply curve vertical at q_1. The market-clearing price is P_1. The suppliers' revenue is the whole shaded area (P_1 times q_1).

In both cases the shortage of Japanese cars drives up their price, creating a substantial margin over costs. Under a tariff the U.S. government captures the margin. Under a VER policy, however, the margin accrues to the Japanese manufacturers.

Although this is a simplified picture, it catches the essence of what actually happened. First, while American manufacturers were keeping prices as low as possible and sometimes offering rebates on slow-selling models, Japanese cars were listed at healthy profit margins. Second, while it was always possible for the buyer of an American car to negotiate a good discount off the list price, Japanese cars usually sold for their full list price. Third, since Japanese manufacturers were not allowed to supply all the cars they could sell in the United States, they had to choose which types of cars to supply. Not surprisingly, they tended to satisfy fully the demand for their more expensive cars, which have larger profit margins, and to restrict exports to the United States of the less expensive cars with lower profit margins. This change in the "product mix" of Japanese cars exported to the United States raised the average profit per car exported. The VERs were thus very costly to American consumers and an enormous profit boon to Japanese car manufacturers.

There was nothing immoral or even surprising about these developments. They are the natural responses of sellers whose markets are restricted by quotas. Indeed, they were fully predictable in advance by economic theory.

They can, however, make it possible for a small group of countries to gain because they get a sufficiently larger share of the smaller world output. However, if foreign countries retaliate by raising their tariffs, the ensuing tariff war can easily leave every country with a lowered income.

To protect against "unfair" actions by foreign firms and governments. Tariffs may be used to prevent foreign industries from gaining an advantage over domestic industries by use of predatory practices that will harm domestic industries and hence lower national income. Two common practices are subsidies paid by foreign governments to their exporters and dumping by foreign firms. Such practices are called "unfair trade practices" and the laws that deal with them are called "fair trade laws." The circumstances under which dumping and foreign subsidization provide a valid argument for tariffs are considered in detail later in this chapter.

To protect infant industries. The oldest valid argument for protectionism as a means of raising living standards concerns economies of scale. It is usually called the **infant industry argument.** If an industry has large economies of scale, costs and prices will be high when the industry is small, but will fall as the industry grows. In such industries the country first in the field has a tremendous advantage. A newly developing country may find that in the early stages of development its industries are unable to compete with established foreign rivals. A trade restriction may protect these industries from foreign competition while they grow up. When they are large enough, they will be able to produce as cheaply as foreign rivals and thus be able to compete without protection.

To encourage learning by doing.   Learning by doing, which we discussed in Chapter 38, suggests that the existing pattern of comparative advantage need not be taken as immutable. If a country can learn enough by producing commodities in which it currently is at a comparative disadvantage, it may gain in the long run by specializing in those commodities and developing a comparative advantage in them as the learning process lowers their costs.

Learning by doing is an example of what in Chapter 38 we called dynamic comparative advantages. The successes of such *newly industrializing countries* (the so-called NICs) as Brazil, Hong Kong, Korea, Singapore, and Taiwan seems to many observers to be based on acquired skills and government policies that create favorable business conditions. This gave rise to the theory that comparative advantages can change and can be developed by suitable government policies.

Protecting a domestic industry from foreign competition may give its management the time to learn to be efficient and its labor force the time to acquire needed skills. If so, protection of the industry against foreign competition, while a dynamic comparative advantage is being developed, may pay in the very long run.

Some countries have clearly succeeded in developing strong comparative advantages in targeted industries, but others have failed. One reason such policies sometimes fail is that protecting local industries from foreign competition may make the industries unadaptive and complacent. Another reason is the difficulty of identifying the industries that will be able to succeed in the long run. All too often the protected infant grows up to be a weakling requiring permanent tariff protection for its continued exis-

tence. Or else the rate of learning is slower than for similar industries in countries that do not provide protection from the chill winds of international competition. In these instances the anticipated comparative advantage never materializes.

How Much Protectionism?

So far we have seen that there is a strong case for allowing free trade in order to realize the gains from trade, but that there are also some reasons for departing from completely free trade.

It is not necessary to choose between free trade on the one hand and absolute protectionism on the other. A country can have some trade and some protectionism, too.

Free Trade Versus No Trade

It would undoubtedly be possible to grow coffee beans in American greenhouses and to synthesize much of the oil we require in our factories (as Germany did during the Second World War). But the cost in terms of other commodities foregone would be huge because these artificial means of production require lavish inputs of factors of production. It would likewise be possible for a tropical country, currently producing foodstuffs, to set up industries to produce all the manufactured products that it consumes. But for a small country without natural advantages in industrial production, the cost in terms of resources used could be enormous. It is thus clear that there is a large gain to all countries in having specialization and trade. The real output and consumption of all countries would be very much lower if each chose to produce domestically all the goods it consumed.

In an all-or-nothing choice, almost all countries would choose free trade over no trade.

A Little More Trade Versus a Little Less Trade

Today we have trade among nations, but that trade is not perfectly free. Table 39-1 shows the levels of tariffs on selected commodities in force today.

TABLE 39-1 Tariffs on Selected Commodity Groups (*ad valorem rates*)

Commodity	United States	European Community	Japan
Weighted average of all manufactured items	4.4	5.5	3.6
Fruits, vegetables	1.7	3.4	14.5
Tea, coffee, and spices	5.3	1.8	34.1
Paper, paperboard	0.3	4.0	1.4
Textiles	15.9	9.0	8.0
Transport vehicles	2.5	6.2	2.1
Tobacco	13.0	0.0	54.3
Petroleum and coal products	0.0	6.3	1.4
Oil and natural gas	4.0	0.0	0.0
All commodities (trade weighted)	3.2	3.7	5.4

Source: Post-Tokyo Round tariff rates, courtesy Special Trade Representatives Office, U.S. government.

The United States is a low-tariff country overall, yet tariffs on selected items are plainly designed to be protective of important domestic industries. These tariffs, the lowest in history, result from the General Agreement on Tariffs and Trade (GATT) Tokyo Round negotiations. They were phased in over the 1980s. Notice the U.S. use of tariffs for protection on textiles and tobacco. In Japan the high tariffs on tobacco, tea, coffee, and spices are for revenue since Japan does not produce these commodities.

Would we be better off if today's barriers to trade were reduced or increased a little bit? This question shifts the focus of our discussion considerably, for it is quite a jump from the proposition that "Free trade is better than no trade" to the proposition that "A little less trade restriction than we have at present is better than a little more."

To see this latter issue, compare the effects of a 20 percent uniform effective rate of tariff with those of free trade. Tariffs of 20 percent will protect industries that are up to 20 percent less efficient than foreign competitors. If the costs of the various tariff-protected industries were spread out evenly, some would be 20 percent less efficient than their foreign competitors and others only 1 percent less efficient. Their average inefficiency would be about half the tariff rate, so they would be on average about 10 percent less efficient than their foreign competitors.

Suppose that as a result of tariffs, approximately 20 percent of a country's resources are allocated to industries different from the ones to which they would be allocated if there were no tariffs. This means that about 20 percent of a country's resources would be working in certain industries only because of tariff protection. If the average protected industry is 20 percent less efficient than its foreign rival, approximately 20 percent of a country's resources are producing on average about 10 percent less efficiently than they would be if there were no tariffs. This causes a reduction in national income on the order of 2 percent as a result of tariff protection.[1]

Suppose the economic costs of existing tariffs are 2 percent of our national income. Is the sacrifice of national income implied by existing tariffs large or small? Expressed as a percentage of GNP, the loss seems small, yet in 1985 prices it was $80 billion *per year* in the United States. That amount every year forever could buy a lot of hospitals, schools, medical research, solar energy research—or even imported oil.

The previous calculations refer to gains from exploiting comparative advantage when costs are given and constant. More recent calculations allow for unexploited economies of scale in specific product lines and for some forms of dynamic comparative advantages. They show gains from reducing the world's remaining tariffs that are much larger than the small ones suggested above. These gains can approach 10 percent of the national incomes of small and middle-sized countries; although for large countries such as the United States, the gains tend to be somewhat smaller—because many of the scale and dynamic economies can be exploited within the large domestic market.

Longer run considerations. Some may be tempted to conclude that the seemingly small economic costs of the current amount of protectionism make it worthwhile to give in to the clamor to provide more protection for America's hard-pressed industries. Before rushing to that conclusion, however, some long-run political and economic possibilities need to be considered. The world prosperity of recent decades has been built largely on a rising volume of

[1] The above rough calculation is meant only to give some intuitive understanding of why the many careful measures of the cost of moderate tariffs commonly lead to figures closer to 2 than to 10 percent of the United States' national income.

relatively free international trade. There are real doubts that such prosperity could be restored if the volume of trade were to shrink steadily because of growing trade barriers. Yet the pressure to use trade restrictions in troubled times is strong. If countries give in and begin to raise barriers moderately when the initial economic costs are not large, so strong are the political forces involved that there is no telling where the process, once begun, will end.

In today's world a country's products must stand up to international competition if they are to survive. Protection, by conferring a national monopoly, reduces the incentive for industries to fight to hold their own internationally. If any one country adopts high tariffs unilaterally, its domestic industries will become less competitive. Secure in their home market because of the tariff wall, they are likely to become less and less competitive in the international market. However, as the gap between domestic and foreign industries widens, *any* tariff wall will provide less and less protection. Eventually, the domestic industries will succumb to the foreign competition. Meanwhile, domestic living standards will fall relative to foreign ones as an increasing productivity gap opens between domestic tariff-protected industries and foreign, internationally oriented ones.

While restrictive policies have sometimes been pursued following a rational assessment of the approximate cost, it is hard to avoid the conclusion that, more often than not, such policies are pursued for flimsy objectives or on fallacious grounds, with little idea of the actual costs involved. The very high tariffs in the United States during the 1920s and 1930s are a conspicuous example. The current clamor for the government to do something about the competition from Japan, Korea, and other countries of the East may well be another.

Fallacious Trade Policy Arguments

We have seen that there are gains from a high volume of international trade and specialization. We have also seen that there can be valid arguments for a moderate degree of protectionism. There are also many claims that do not advance the debate. Fallacious arguments are heard on both sides, and they color much of the popular discussion. These arguments have been

around for a long time, but their survival does not make them true. We will examine them now to see where their fallacies lie.

Fallacious Free Trade Arguments

Free trade always benefits all countries.   This is not necessarily so. We saw above that a small group of countries may gain by restricting trade in order to get a sufficiently favorable shift in their terms of trade. Such countries would lose if they gave up these tariffs and adopted free trade unilaterally.

Infant industries never abandon their tariff protection.   It is argued that granting protection to infant industries is a mistake because these industries seldom admit to growing up and will cling to their protection even when fully grown. But infant industry tariffs are a mistake *only* if these industries never grow up. In this case permanent tariff protection would be required to protect a weak industry never able to compete on an equal footing in the international market. But if the industries do grow up and achieve the expected scale economies, the fact that like any special interest group they cling to their tariff protection is not a sufficient reason for denying protection to genuine infant industries. When economies of scale are realized, the real costs of production are reduced and resources are freed for other uses. Whether or not the tariff or other trade barriers remain, a cost saving has been effected by the scale economies.

Fallacious Protectionist Arguments

Prevent exploitation.   According to the exploitation theory trade can never be mutually advantageous; one trading partner *must* always reap a gain at the other's expense. Thus the weaker trading partner must protect itself by restricting its trade with the stronger partner. But the principle of comparative advantage shows that it is possible for both parties to gain from trade and thus refutes the exploitation doctrine of trade. When opportunity cost ratios differ in two countries, specialization and the accompanying trade make it possible to produce more of all commodities and thus make it possible for both parties to consume more as a result of trade than they could get in its absence.

Keep the money at home.   This argument says, If I buy a foreign good, I have the good and the foreigner has the money, whereas if I buy the same good locally, I have the good and our country has the money, too. Abraham Lincoln is said to have made this argument, and it is still heard today.

The argument is based on a misconception. It assumes that domestic money actually goes abroad physically when imports are purchased and that trade flows only in one direction. But when American importers purchase Italian-made goods, they do not send dollars abroad. They (or their financial agents) buy Italian lire and use them to pay the Italian manufacturers. They purchase the lire on the foreign exchange market by giving up dollars to someone who wishes to use them for expenditure *in the United States*. Even if the money did go abroad physically—that is, if an Italian firm accepted a shipload of dollars—it would be because that firm (or someone to whom it could sell the dollars) wanted them to spend in the only country where they are legal tender, the United States.

Dollars ultimately do no one any good except as purchasing power. It would be miraculous if green pieces of paper could be exported in return for real goods; after all, the Fed has the power to create as much new money as it wishes. It is only because the green paper can buy American commodities and assets that others want it.

Protect against low-wage foreign labor.   Surely, the argument says, the products of low-wage countries will drive U.S. products from the market, and the high U.S. standard of living will be dragged down to that of their poor trading partners. Arguments of this sort have swayed many voters through the years.

As a prelude to considering them, stop and think what the argument would imply if taken out of the international context and put into a local one, where the same principles govern the gains from trade. Is it really impossible for a rich person to gain from trading with a poor person? Would the local millionaire be better off if she did all her own typing, gar-

dening, and cooking? No one believes that a rich person cannot gain from trading with those who are less rich. Why then must a rich group of people lose from trading with a poor group? "Well," you say, "the poor group will price their goods too cheaply." Does anyone believe that consumers lose from buying in a discount house or a supermarket just because the prices are lower there than at the old-fashioned corner store? Consumers gain when they can buy the same goods at a lower price. If the Koreans pay low wages and sell their goods cheaply, *Korean* labor may suffer, but we will gain because we obtain their goods at a low cost in terms of the goods that we must export in return. The cheaper our imports are, the better off we are in terms of the goods and services available for domestic consumption.

Stated in more formal terms, the gains from trade depend on comparative, not absolute, advantages. World production is higher when any two areas, say the United States and Japan, specialize in the production of the goods for which they have a comparative advantage than when they both try to be self-sufficient.

Might it not be possible, however, that Japan will undersell the United States in all lines of production and thus appropriate all, or more than all, the gains for itself, leaving the United States no better off, or even worse off, than if it had no trade with Japan? The answer is no. The reason for this depends on the behavior of exchange rates, which we shall study in Chapter 40. As we shall see, equality of demand and supply on foreign exchange market ensures that trade flows in both directions.

Imports can be obtained only by spending the currency of the country that makes the imports. Claims to this currency can be obtained only by exporting goods and services or by borrowing. Thus, lending and borrowing aside, imports must equal exports. All trade must be in two directions; we can buy only if we can also sell.

In the long run trade cannot hurt a country by causing it to import without exporting.

Trade then always provides scope for international specialization, with each country producing and exporting those goods for which it has a comparative advantage and importing those goods for which it does not.

Exports raise living standards; imports lower them.
Exports add to aggregate demand; imports subtract from it. Thus, other things being equal, exports tend to increase national income and imports to reduce it. Surely then, it is desirable to encourage exports and discourage imports. This is an appealing argument, but it is incorrect.

Exports raise national income by adding to the value of domestic output, but they do not add to the value of domestic consumption. In fact, exports are goods produced at home and consumed abroad, while imports are goods produced abroad and consumed at home. The standard of living in a country depends on the goods and services available for *consumption*, not on what is produced.

If exports were really good and imports really bad, then a fully employed economy that managed to increase exports without a corresponding increase in imports ought to be better off. Such a change, however, would result in a reduction in current standards of living, because when more goods are sent abroad and no more are brought in from abroad, the total goods available for domestic consumption must fall.

The living standards of a country depend on the goods and services consumed in that country. The importance of exports is that they permit imports to be made. This two-way international exchange is valuable because more goods can be imported than could be obtained if the same goods were produced at home.

Create domestic jobs and reduce unemployment.   It is sometimes said that an economy with substantial unemployment, such as that of the United States in the 1930s or in the early 1980s, provides an exception to the case for freer trade. Suppose that tariffs or import quotas cut the imports of Japanese cars, Korean textiles, Italian shoes, and French wine. Surely, the argument maintains, this will create more employment for Detroit auto workers, Georgia textile workers, Massachusetts shoe factories, and California farm workers. The answer is that it will—initially. But the Japanese, Koreans, Italians, and French can buy from America only if they earn American

dollars by selling goods in America. The decline in their sales of autos, textiles, shoes, and wine will decrease their purchases of American machinery, aircraft, grain, and vacations in America. Jobs will be lost in our export industries and gained in those industries that formerly faced competition from imports. The likely long-term effect is that overall unemployment will not be reduced, but merely redistributed among industries.

Industries and unions that compete with imports favor protectionism, while those with large exports favor more trade. Most economists are highly skeptical about the government's ability to reduce overall unemployment by protectionism.

To offset an overvalued exchange rate.   To complete the list of fallacious arguments for protection, we must add a point that we cannot study in detail until Chapter 41, when we have learned about the forces that determine a country's exchange rate.

In the mid 1980s the U.S. dollar had an extremely high value on the foreign exchange market. This made it difficult for American firms to sell in foreign markets, but easy for foreign firms to sell in the American market. The pressure on American industries led to growing pressure in Congress—a pressure that was opposed by the Reagan Administration—to alleviate the plight of American manufacturers by raising trade restrictions. As we shall see in Chapter 41, the need to import foreign capital to finance the American government's budget deficit led to the overvalued exchange rate of the U.S. dollar. Until the government's deficit is made low enough to be financed out from domestic rather than foreign borrowing, no amount of tariffs could help to bring down the exchange rate and so aid American exporters.

Trade Policy in the World Today

The Importance of Trade and Tariffs

Figure 39-2 shows how tariffs have been used in U.S. history. The government of the United States has

FIGURE 39-2   Tariffs in the United States, 1828–1985

U.S. tariffs have been lower in the post-World War II period than in any other period of comparable length in American history. Throughout its history the United States has alternated between being a high-tariff country and being a modest-tariff country. The average rate of tariff has been lower since World War II than ever before. The rate fell below 10 percent in 1971 and below 5 percent when the Tokyo Round tariff reductions came into full effect in the mid 1980s. (*Statistical Abstract of the United States,* selected years.)

often paid less attention to economists's arguments for freer trade than to the protests of producers who would be hurt by tariff reductions. Part of the reason was the relative unimportance of trade to the American economy; for example, in 1985 only about 6 percent of the economy's output was exported in the form of goods. However, this figure underestimates the importance of trade for two main reasons. First, the overvalued dollar was holding exports well below their normal value in that period. The normal figure would be somewhere between that 6 percent figure and the 9 percent figure for imports expressed as a percentage of national income. Second, these figures cover only merchandise trade. Trade in services has been growing in importance and now accounts for a significant part of all of U.S. exports.[2]

In contrast, trade is extremely important to the economies of many countries. Sweden, Great Britain, and Canada all export between 20 and 25 percent of their GNP. The loss of their foreign trade would have a devastating effect on their standards of living.

America would also suffer from the loss of its foreign trade, but to a lesser degree.

Although foreign trade is not a large fraction of total American national income, it is very important to particular industries. Large quantities of certain materials—petroleum, bauxite, coffee beans, iron ore, lumber, and newsprint—are imported. The loss of any of these supplies would cause serious difficulties in some industries, and some would cause major disruptions in the whole economy—as we have learned from even the temporary interruptions in oil supplies.

Foreign trade contributes substantially to the standards of living of many countries. Even the United States, with its low dependence on trade, would have its living standard significantly lowered if it refused to participate in the gains from trade among nations.

Nontariff Barriers

While the United States generally imposes low tariffs, it uses many nontariff barriers to protect particular domestic industries that were losing ground to foreign competition in the mid 1980s. Some of these

[2] Trade is more important in the United States today than it was half a century ago, in the heyday of prohibitive tariffs. In 1929 exports were less than 5 percent of GNP.

restrictions have been negotiated, with the U.S. government's putting pressure on another country to accept VERs. Others have been imposed unilaterally. Let us consider one example of each.

A **nontariff barrier** is anything other than an import duty that restricts the flow of trade. It may take any of the three forms illustrated in Figure 39-1 by raising the price of the imported good, directly restricting its quantity, or shifting the demand for imports. In recent years protectionist-minded countries have made increasing use of nontariff barriers to replace tariff barriers that have been reduced by international agreement.

In the late 1950s the textile and clothing industries in many advanced industrial nations saw their market shares reduced by a rising volume of trade from Hong Kong, Korea, the Philippines, and other newly industrializing nations. In response to a United States' initiative, international meetings were held in 1961. Out of these meetings came the *multi-fiber agreements* (MFAs), providing maximum annual quotas for each exporting textile-producing country for a 20-year period. Starting in 1981 many of these agreements were renegotiated, generally leading to more, rather than less, restrictive policies.

Similar "orderly marketing agreements" have been accepted by foreign countries with respect to footwear in 1977, color television sets in 1977, and citizens band radio sets in 1978. Lobbyists for many other industries have urged similar agreements for their products. One of the most recent agreements, which limited Japanese car exports to the United States, is considered in Box 39-1.

Why, one may ask, would a country such as Korea agree voluntarily to limit its profitable exports to the United States when it needs the revenue and foreign exchange that its exports earn? The answer, one may surmise, is that the United States is so needed and valued an ally that its "requests" have the weight of veiled threats. In any case, the Commerce Department has proven to be quite persistent and persuasive once it has set out to negotiate an agreement.

Unilaterally Imposed Antidumping Rules

The American steel industry has suffered badly from competition from Japan, which (it is charged) is selling steel in the United States at lower prices than it is selling steel at home. This is called **dumping,** and it is a form of price discrimination of the kind studied in the theory of monopoly (see Chapter 15). The steel industry has asked the United States government for help, and it has received it. To understand the issues, we need to understand a bit more about dumping.

Possible motives for dumping. Japanese producers dump steel in the United States because it is profitable for them to do so. There are several reasons why it might pay them to sell more cheaply here than at home.

1. It may be a sensible long-term strategy because of economies of large-scale production and the fact that the Japanese home market is permanently too small to support an industry of efficient size. In such circumstances, to have an efficient industry requires an export market; but to achieve that market, a low-price policy may be required. By selling cheaply abroad, the country can generate sufficient demand to justify an efficient-size industry. Dumping in this case benefits both its domestic and its foreign customers by making it possible to produce output at the lowest possible cost per unit.

2. It may be a sensible middle-term strategy to provide a market for efficiently produced steel for a period, say 5 or 10 years, until Japanese manufacturers will be able to absorb the entire output of Japanese production. In this scenario home sales would gradually replace export sales. Dumping permits an efficient-size industry now, without waiting for Japanese demand to grow.

3. It may be a sensible cyclical strategy, providing a market for output in periods when Japanese demand is low, and thereby utilizing the capacity required to meet maximum Japanese demands in periods of boom and expansion. In this scenario sales in the export market are simply sporadic "white sales" that permit Japanese production to continue on an even level over the cycle.

4. It may be a predatory strategy designed to destroy the foreign industry. In this scenario, after foreign plants have shut down and the foreign industry's work force has dispersed, prices can be raised to exploit the foreigner's new dependence on imports.

Effects on the buying country. Suppose America is the "beneficiary" of dumped Japanese steel, that is, steel sold at less than the Japanese home price and (let us suppose) below the average cost of production in the United States. If such sales continue, they will either eliminate the U.S. industry or force it to become competitive by becoming more efficient. However unfair this may sound to American steel makers, it will benefit American steel buyers for as long as they are able to buy cheaper steel. Cheaper steel will lead to less expensive buildings, refrigerators, nails, and all other products that use steel.

No matter what the Japanese producers' motives, the American steel industry and the United Steelworkers of America will want the U.S. government to stop this, for it threatens profits and their jobs.

Suppose the government chooses to look beyond the political pressures of the moment and to do what is best for the national interest. Here it matters which of the four motives explains the dumping. If the Japanese are prepared to supply cheap steel on a permanent basis, it would surely benefit Americans to buy Japanese steel and use American resources to produce something in which we have a comparative advantage. This is the case for doing nothing to protect the domestic steel industry and instead helping it to become more efficient or encouraging an orderly shift of its workers and resources into other industries. However, if cheap Japanese steel would destroy the American industry without replacing the need for it—that is, for any of the other listed motives—then sufficient protection to preserve a viable industry may be required. This is the valid case for protectionism.[3]

The problem for policy is to diagnose what is happening and to adopt rules that will preserve needed industries without depriving American buyers of cheaper sources of supply. Currently there is controversy about what is really happening in Japanese steel production. Many economists are not persuaded that protection is required to preserve American national interests.

Antidumping laws and procedures. Under current American law any American producer, or the gov-

ernment itself, can file suit before the U.S. International Trade Commission (ITC) alleging that a foreign producer is dumping. Antidumping duties will be levied only if the U.S. producers can demonstrate that they have been injured by the dumped imports.

Two features of the antidumping system now in effect make it highly protectionist. First, *any* price discrimination is classified as dumping and thus subject to penalties. Thus the foreign prices become, in effect, minimum prices below which no foreign producer can risk selling. Thus the provisions inhibit foreign competition and serve as nontariff barriers to trade, both where dumping is beneficial to American interests and where it is not.

Second, U.S. law calculates the "margin of dumping" as the difference between the price charged in the American market and the foreign producer's "full allocated cost" (what economists call average total cost, including a normal return on capital). This means that if there is global excess demand so that the profit-maximizing price for all producers is below average total cost (but above average variable cost), foreign producers can be convicted of dumping in the U.S. market, even though their American selling prices are the same as their own domestic selling prices. This latter provision makes U.S. antidumping laws highly protectionist, especially in periods of slack demand.

During the period starting in 1982, a number of developing countries that were under heavy pressure to export in order to earn the foreign currency needed to service their foreign debts were hit heavily by these antidumping duties. These countries were forced to restrict their exports to the United States as a result of the provision that they could not sell below their average total cost even where they were doing so at home. Among other countries, Brazil, Argentina, and Guatemala were hurt by this measure.

Countervailing Duties

Throughout the 1980s one of the most potent American measures affecting trade has been countervailing duties. These duties were not designed to act as nontariff barriers, but rather as a means of creating a "level playing field" on which fair international competition could take place. American firms rightly complain that they cannot compete against the bot-

---

[3] The fact that three of the four motives listed lead to the protectionist position does not mean that they are three times as likely to apply as the other motive.

tomless purses of foreign governments. Subsidized foreign exports can be sold indefinitely in the United States at prices that would guarantee losses in the absence of the subsidy. The object of countervail is to counteract the effect on price of the presence of such foreign subsidies.

If a U.S. firm suspects the existence of such a subsidy and registers a complaint, the American government is then required to make an investigation. For a countervailing duty to be levied, the investigation must find, first, that the foreign subsidy to the specific industry in question does exist and, second, that it is large enough to be a potential injury to competing American firms.

There is no doubt that countervailing duties have sometimes been used to remove the effects of "unfair" competition caused by foreign subsidies. Foreign governments complain, however, that countervail is also sometimes used as a thinly disguised barrier to trade. For example, a countervailing duty was placed on Canadian pork and hog exports to the United States after the finding that Canadian agricultural policy conferred a subsidy to Canadian producers of $.05 a pound, notwithstanding the fact that U.S. policies gave a subsidy to American producers of something between $.10 and $.15 a pound. Commenting on this case, one observer said, "In allowing a countervailing duty based on the existence of any foreign subsidy, rather than on the net difference between the foreign and the American subsidy, countervail has proved itself to be a one-eyed referee."

Foreign subsidies to industries exporting to the United States are not necessarily harmful from the point of view of all U.S. citizens. Such subsidies can lower the price of U.S. imports and thus improve the national terms of trade. Economists would suggest that countervailing duties should be focused on subsidies that could have predatory effects. As with dumping, the only time foreign subsidies are a significant problem to the country as a whole is when U.S. producers are driven out of business and the foreign producer subsequently obtains a monopoly position.

Many U.S. industries, however, have lobbied for broader, not narrower, application of countervailing duties. Alleging that foreign trade is "unfair" provides a political rationale for obtaining protection from foreign competition.

Overall Importance of Nontariff Barriers in the United States

Judged by the level of trade restrictions, American trade policy remains relatively unprotectionist. Judged by recent changes, however, American trade policy has been moving rapidly in a protectionist direction. Furthermore, in selected industries—textiles and steel among them—the combined effect of nontariff and tariff barriers is significant. Many economists who have seen American policy become less and less protectionist over the last 50 years are now concerned about the spread of protectionism via nontariff barriers. They see American policymakers, unable to find a short-run solution to pockets of unemployment, being unable to resist the protectionist views of the lobbyists for industries hurt by foreign competition.

International Agreements Concerning Trade and Tariffs

In the past any country could impose any desired set of tariffs on its imports. But when one country increases its tariffs, the action may trigger retaliatory changes by its trading partners. Just as an arms race can escalate, so can a tariff war; precisely this happened during the 1920s and early 1930s. Extended negotiations may then be required to undo the damage.

The General Agreement on Tariffs and Trade (GATT)

One of the most notable achievements of the post-World War II world in retreating from the high-water mark of protectionism in the 1930s was the General Agreement on Tariffs and Trade (GATT). Under this agreement GATT countries meet periodically to negotiate bilaterally on mutually advantageous cuts in tariffs. They agree in advance that any tariff cuts negotiated in this way will be extended to all member countries. Significant tariff reductions have been effected by the member countries.

The two most recent rounds of GATT agreements have each reduced tariffs by about one-third. The Kennedy Round negotiations were completed in 1967, and new rates were phased in over a five-year period ending in 1972. The Tokyo Round negotiations began in 1975 and were completed in 1979. The reductions began to take effect in 1981 and were completed in 1986.

Ironically, as that new round of reductions began, pressure was mounting in many countries to protect jobs at home through trade restrictions. Protectionist policies grew alarmingly in Europe. As time passed, even GATT itself came under attack. The worldwide recession that began in late 1981 was undoubtedly the main cause of this pressure. In addition, protectionist pressures in many countries were also created by the decline in the international competitiveness of traditional industries due to sharp changes in terms of trade. Also, under the impact of the high value of the U.S. dollar, protectionist pressures grew throughout the 1980s in the United States.

Although GATT has produced large reductions in *tariffs*, the results are a bit misleading in terms of the freedom of trade because of the growing use of nontariff barriers. One important feature of the Tokyo Round was the agreement, for the first time, on some very limited steps to restrict the growth of nontariff barriers.

In 1986 a preliminary meeting was held as a beginning towards a new round of GATT negotiations. This round will grapple with two pressing issues: the growing worldwide use of nontariff barriers to trade and the need to develop rules for liberalizing trade in services, which is the most rapidly growing component of foreign trade.

Common Markets

A **common market** is an agreement among a group of countries to eliminate barriers to free trade among themselves and to present a common trading front to the rest of the world in terms of common tariff or nontariff barriers to trade. The most important example came into being in 1957 when the Treaty of Rome brought together France, Germany, Italy, Holland, Belgium, and Luxembourg in the European Economic Community (EEC). The original six were joined in 1973 by the United Kingdom, the Republic of Ireland, and Denmark; Greece entered in 1983 and Spain in 1986.

This organization, now known as the European Community (EC), is dedicated to bringing about free trade, complete mobility of factors of production, and the eventual harmonization of fiscal and monetary policies among the member countries. All tariffs for manufactured goods have been eliminated and much freedom of movement of labor and capital achieved. Movement toward the harmonization of economic and social policies and creation of a common monetary system seems now, however, to be stalled.

Other common markets have been formed, such as the Central American Common Market and the East African Community, but none has yet achieved the success of the EC, and some have collapsed.

Free Trade Associations

A **free trade association** allows for tariff-free trade between the member countries but, unlike a common market, it leaves each member free to levy its own tariffs on imports from other countries. As a result, members must maintain customs points at their common border (if they have one) to make sure that imports into the free trade area do not all enter through the country levying the lowest tariff on each item.

The first important free trade association in the modern era was the European Free Trade Association (EFTA). It was formed in 1960 by a group of European countries unwilling to join the European Community because of its all-embracing character. Not wanting to be left out of the gains from trade, they formed an association whose sole purpose was to remove tariffs among themselves and subsequently also with the members of the EC.

American interest in forming free trade associations arose in the 1980s when the United States became frustrated with what it saw as European and Japanese protectionism and as the subversion of GATT liberalization agreements through the use of nontariff barriers. In an effort to put pressure on GATT members for further multilateral liberalization, the U.S. administration advocated concluding bilateral trade-liberalizing agreements. In 1985 a free trade association was signed with Israel. In 1986 negotiations began over the formation of a free trade association between the United States and its largest trading partner, Canada.

Summary

1. The case for free trade is that world output of all commodities can be higher under free trade than when protectionism restricts regional specialization.

2. Free trade among nations may be restricted intentionally by protectionist policies which seek to raise prices, lower quantities, or reduce the demand for imports.

3. Protection can be urged as a means to ends other than maximizing world living standards. Examples of such ends are to produce a diversified economy, to reduce fluctuations in national income, to retain distinctive national traditions, and to improve national defense.

4. Protection can also be urged on the grounds that it may lead to higher living standards for the protectionist country than would a policy of free trade. Such a result might come about through exploiting a monopoly position or by developing a dynamic comparative advantage by allowing inexperienced or uneconomically small industries to become efficient enough to compete with foreign industries.

5. Almost everyone would choose free trade if the only alternative were *no* trade. Cutting existing tariff barriers offers gains that may seem small expressed as a percentage of GNP, but are large in terms of the total of goods and services involved.

6. Some fallacious free trade arguments are that (a) because free trade maximizes world income, it will maximize the income of every individual country and (b) because infant industries seldom admit to growing up and thus try to retain their protection indefinitely, the whole country necessarily loses by protecting its infant industries.

7. Some fallacious protectionist arguments are that (a) mutually advantageous trade is impossible because one trader's gain must always be the other's loss; (b) buying abroad sends our money abroad, while buying at home keeps our money at home; (c) our high-paid workers must be protected against the competition from low-paid foreign workers; (d) imports are to be discouraged because they lower national income and cause unemployment.

8. Trade is vitally important in the national incomes of many countries. It is relatively less important to the United States. Nonetheless trade is vital to particular American industries, and few economists doubt that American living standards would be lowered significantly if America tried to make itself fully self-sufficient.

9. Although the United States today has low tariffs, its recent tendency to institute nontariff barriers either by negotiation (as in textiles) or by unilateral policies (such as the misuse of antidumping and countervailing duties) causes concern that the 50-year trend to ever freer trade is being reversed.

10. International agreements and negotiations have succeeded in lowering trade barriers from the high levels of 50 years ago. After

World War II the GATT began a series of multinational rounds of tariff reduction that have greatly lowered tariffs and are now trying to address nontariff barriers as well. Nevertheless the recent clamor for protection in many trading nations threatens the free-trade trend GATT has fostered. Regional common markets, such as the EC, have created substantial areas where free trade exists.

Topics for Review

Free trade and protectionism
Tariff and nontariff barriers to trade
Countervail and voluntary export agreements
Fallacious arguments for free trade
Fallacious arguments for protectionism
Dumping and antidumping duties
General Agreement on Tariffs and Trade (GATT)
Common markets and free trade associations

Discussion Questions

1. "Pay $68,000, save a shoemaker," said a 1985 editorial in the *New York Times* pointing out that a quota on shoe imports would save only 33,000 American jobs at a cost in higher shoe prices of $68,000 per job. Do consumers pay the cost? What alternatives are there to protecting jobs in the shoe industry?
2. "What unfair trade had done to an American community" was the headline of a recent full-page ad in the *New York Times*. The ad claimed that subsidized and "dumped" steel imports from unstated foreign countries were unfairly driving American steel plants out of business. What foreign practices might justify this claim? What apparent dumping might represent perfectly fair competition? What American legislation or other practices could provide relief, whether justified or not, to the U.S. firms?
3. "U.S. consumer is seen as big loser in new restraints on imported steel," said the *Wall Street Journal* in 1985. The big gainers from the quota limitations on imported steel were predicted to be U.S. producers, who would sell more, and foreign producers, who would sell less but at a higher price; the big losers would be U.S. consumers. Expain carefully why each of these groups might gain or lose.
4. Suppose America had imposed prohibitive tariffs on all imported cars over the last three decades. How do you think this would have affected the following?
   a. The U.S. automobile industry
   b. The American public
   c. The kinds of cars produced by U.S. manufacturers
5. Lobbyists for many industries argue that their products are essential to national defense and therefore require protection. Suppose that supplies of a certain commodity are indeed essential in wartime. How does restricting imports solve the problem? Are there alternatives to import restrictions? If so, how might the alternatives be evaluated?
6. Import quotas are often used instead of tariffs. What real difference (if any) is there between quotas and tariffs? Explain why lobbyists

for some American industries (cheese, sugar, shoes) support import quotas, while lobbyists for others (pizza manufacturers, soft drink manufacturers, retail stores) oppose them. Would you expect labor unions to support or oppose quotas?

7. "The only pro-tariff argument that is likely to be valid for the whole world taken as an economic unit (rather than for a particular nation at a particular time) is the infant industry argument." Explain why you agree or disagree with this statement.

8. The United States has greatly reduced tariffs since Congress passed trade legislation authorizing the president to negotiate tariff concessions with foreign countries. Why might Congress find it desirable to give the president this authority rather than reserve the authority to itself?

9. When France increased tariff restrictions on foreign poultry, seriously hurting American chicken exporters, the United States reversed tariff reductions that had been made on brandy. When the United States put a tariff on Canadian shingles and shakes, Canada retaliated with a tariff on American books. Do these kinds of "trade war" make any sense?

10. "An issue of *American Heritage* [reminds us] that Karl Marx was a firm, even fervent, free trader. (When he was the London correspondent for Horace Greeley's *New York Tribune*, Marx—the wicked communist—advocated free trade while Greeley—the avid capitalist—exposed protectionism.)" Reflect on what factors might have caused Marx and Greeley, given their political persuasions, to hold these views (as reported in the July 26, 1983, issue of the *Wall Street Journal*).

11. Classical economists favored free trade among nations as a means of interlocking their economies so they could not afford to fight each other. President Reagan has opposed interlocking the economies of the Eastern and Western block on the grounds that this gives too much power of blockage to the Eastern countries. Discuss the "political economy" of these two opposing views.

40

Exchange Rates and the Balance of Payments

In the mid 1980s American exporters and importers were concerned about the high value of the U.S. dollar on foreign exchange markets. The high value made it hard for American firms to sell abroad and easy for foreign firms to sell in the United States. The value of the dollar also concerned such varied groups as Japanese firms wanting to build factories in the United States, Americans wanting to buy French government bonds, German exporters sending automobiles to the United States, and Americans hoping to sell computers in Saudi Arabia. It also mattered to American tourists cashing their dollar traveler's checks in London, Athens, or Bangkok.

In this chapter we are concerned with what it means to speak of the "price of the dollar" and what causes that price to change. The discussion will bring together material on three topics studied elsewhere in this book: the theory of supply and demand (Chapter 4), the nature of money (Chapter 31), and international trade (Chapter 38).

The Nature of Foreign Exchange Transactions

We have seen that money, which consists of any accepted medium of exchange, is vital in any sophisticated economy that relies on specialization and exchange. Yet money as we know it is a *national* matter, one closely controlled by the national governments. If you live in Sweden, you will earn kronor and spend kronor; if you run a business in Austria, you borrow schillings and meet your payroll with schillings. The currency of a country is acceptable within the bounds of that country, but it will not usually be accepted by households and firms in another country. The Stockholm bus company will accept kronor for a fare, but not Austrian schillings. The Austrian worker will not take Swedish kronor for wages, but will accept schillings.

American producers require payment in dollars for their products. They need dollars to meet their wage bills, pay for their raw materials, and reinvest or distribute their profits. There is no problem when they sell to American purchasers. However, if they sell their goods to Indian importers, either the Indians must exchange their rupees to acquire dollars to pay for the goods or the U.S. producers must accept rupees. They will accept rupees only if they know that they can exchange the rupees for the dollars that they require. The same holds true for producers in all countries; they must eventually receive payment for the goods that they sell in terms of the currency of their own country.

In general, trade between nations can occur only if it is possible to exchange the currency of one nation for that of another.

The exchange rate.   International payments that require the exchange of one national currency for another can be made in a bewildering variety of ways, but in essence they involve the exchange of currencies between people who have one currency and require another. Suppose that an American firm wishes to acquire £3,000 for some purpose (£ is the symbol for the British pound sterling). The firm can go to its bank or to some other seller of foreign currency and buy a check that will be accepted in the United Kingdom as £3,000. How many *dollars* the firm must pay to purchase this check will depend on the price of pounds in terms of dollars.

The exchange of one currency for another is part of the process of foreign exchange. The term **foreign exchange** refers to the actual foreign currency or various claims on it, such as bank deposits or promises to pay, that are traded for each other. The **exchange rate** is the price at which purchases and sales of foreign currency or claims on it take place; it is the amount of home currency that must be paid in order to obtain one unit of the foreign currency. For example, if one must give up $2.00 to get £1.00, the exchange rate is 2.[1]

A rise in the price of foreign exchange (i.e., a rise in the exchange rate) is a **depreciation** of the home currency. *Foreign currencies have become more expensive; therefore the relative value of the home currency has fallen.* A fall in the price of foreign exchange (i.e., a fall in the exchange rate) is an **appreciation** of the home currency. *Foreign currencies have become cheaper; therefore, the relative value of home currency has risen.* For example, when the dollar price of sterling rises from

$2.00 to $2.50 (in other words, the sterling price of the dollar falls from £0.50 to £0.40), the dollar has *depreciated* and the pound has *appreciated*.

The mechanism of foreign exchange transactions. Let us see how foreign exchange transactions are carried out. Suppose that an American firm wishes to purchase a British sports car to sell in the United States. The British firm that made the car requires payment in pounds sterling. If the car is priced at £3,000, the American firm will go to its bank, purchase a check for £3,000, and send the check to the British seller. Let us suppose this requires that the firm pay $5,000.[2] (The exchange rate in this transaction is £1.00 = $1.67, or $1.00 = £0.60.) The British firm deposits the check in its bank.

Now assume that in the same period of time a British wholesale firm purchases 10 American refrigerators to sell in Britain. If the refrigerators are priced at $500 each, the American seller will have to be paid $5,000. To make this payment the British importing firm goes to its bank, writes a check on its account for £3,000 and receives a check drawn on a U.S. bank for $5,000. The check is sent to America and deposited in an American bank. The effects of these transactions are shown in Table 40-1.

The two transactions cancel each other out, and there is no net change in international liabilities. No money need pass between British and American banks; each bank merely increases the deposit of one domestic customer and lowers the deposit of another. Indeed, as long as the flow of payments between the two countries is equal (Americans pay as much to British residents as British residents pay to Americans), all payments can be managed as in the above example, and there will be no need for a net payment from British banks to American banks.

All these calculations involve comparing magnitudes measured in different currencies. These comparisons are done using the exchange rate. We now turn to an analysis of how such exchange rates are determined.

---

[1] This expresses the relative values of the two currencies in terms of the dollar price of one pound sterling. Alternatively, one could consider the pound sterling price of $1.00 which in this example is £0.50.

[2] Banks charge a small commission for making currency exchanges, but we shall ignore this and assume that parties can exchange moneys back and forth at the going exchange rate.

TABLE 40-1   Changes in the Balance Sheets of Two Banks As a Result of International Payments

U.K. bank			U.S. bank		
Assets	Liabilities		Assets	Liabilities	
No change	(1) Deposits of car exporter	+£3,000	No change	(1) Deposits of car importer	−$5,000
	(2) Deposits of refrigerator importer	−£3,000		(2) Deposits of refrigerator exporter	+$5,000
	Net change	0		Net change	0

International transactions involve a transfer of deposit liabilities among banks. The table records two separate international transactions at an exchange rate of $1.00 = £0.60: (1) an American purchase of a British car for £3,000 (= $5,000) and (2) a British purchase of American refrigerators for $5,000 (= £3,000). The American's import of a car reduces deposit liabilities to U.S. residents and increases deposit liabilities to British residents. The Britisher's import of refrigerators does the opposite. When a series of transactions are equal in value, there is only a transfer of deposit liabilities among individuals within a country. The American refrigerator manufacturer received (in effect) the dollars the American car purchaser gave up to get a British-made car.

The Determination of Exchange Rates

For simplicity we shall consider an example involving trade between the United States and the United Kingdom and the determination of the exchange rate between their two currencies, dollars and sterling. The two-country example simplifies things, but the principles apply to all foreign transactions. *Thus sterling stands for foreign exchange in general, and the dollar price of sterling stands for the foreign exchange rate in general.*

We can relate our example to the demand and supply analysis of Chapter 4. To do so, we need only to recognize that *in the market for pounds sterling* the American firm that wants pounds is a demander of pounds and the British firm that is selling pounds to buy dollars is a supplier of pounds. We can also look at the *same* transaction in the market for dollars: The American firm is a supplier of dollars, and the British firm is a demander of dollars.

Because one currency is traded for another on the foreign exchange market, it follows that to desire (demand) dollars implies a willingness to offer (supply) foreign exchange, while an offer (supply) of dollars implies a desire (demand) for foreign exchange.

When £1.00 = $1.67, a British importer who offers to buy $5.00 with pounds must be offering to sell £3.00. Similarly, an American importer who offers to sell $5.00 for pounds must be offering to buy £3.00. For this reason a theory of the exchange rate between dollars and pounds can deal either with the demand for and the supply of dollars or with the demand for and the supply of pounds sterling; both need not be considered. We shall concentrate on the demand, supply, and price of dollars (quoted in pounds).

The Demand for Dollars

Sources of Demand for Dollars

American exports.   One important source of demand for dollars in foreign exchange markets is people who do not currently hold dollars, but who wish to buy American-made goods and services. The British importer of refrigerators is such a purchaser; an Austrian couple planning to vacation in the United States is another; the Soviet government seeking to buy American wheat is a third. All are sources of demand for dollars arising out of international trade. Each potential buyer wants to sell its own currency and buy dollars for the purpose of purchasing American exports.

Long-term capital flows.   A second source of a demand for dollars comes from foreigners who wish to purchase American assets. In recent years foreign households and firms have invested billions of dollars in American securities and real estate. This required the conversion of foreign currencies into U.S. dollars. The resulting transactions are called *long-term capital movements* or *flows*. In order to buy American assets, holders of foreign currencies must first buy dollars on foreign exchange markets.

Short-term capital flows.   When interest rates in the United States soared in the early 1980s, floods of "foreign money" came to the United States to buy short-term treasury bills and notes, certificates of deposit, and so on. The buyers of these securities were seeking a high return on their liquid assets. But first these buyers had to convert their lire, guilder, marks, and francs into dollars on the foreign exchange market. When people sell financial assets in one country for foreign exchange that they then use to buy short-term financial assets in another country, the transactions are called *short-term capital movements* or *flows*.

A medium of exchange.   One other type of transaction may be noted. Certain currencies, the most important of them the American dollar, have come to be accepted by nations, banks, and ordinary people as an international medium of exchange. These currencies are readily acceptable among buyers and sellers who might be less willing to trade with each other using less well-known kinds of money. Thus a Norwegian exporter of smoked fish to a Turkish wholesaler may quote prices in dollars and expect payment in dollars. Most of the oil sold by the OPEC countries must be paid for in dollars, so a French purchaser of oil must convert francs to dollars to buy oil from Saudi Arabia.

There is therefore a demand for currencies that act as an international medium of exchange. Some of the trading in the U.S. dollar exists to provide a medium of exchange quite independent of the flow of American imports or exports.

Reserve currency.   Firms, banks, and governments often accumulate and hold currency reserves just as individuals maintain savings accounts. The government of Nigeria, for example, has foreign exchange reserves. It may decide to increase its holdings of dollars and reduce its holdings of pounds; if so, it will be a demander of dollars (and a supplier of pounds) on foreign exchange markets.

The Total Demand for Dollars

The demand for the dollar by holders of foreign currencies is the sum of the demands for all the purposes discussed above—for purchases of American exports, for long- or short-term capital movements, for purchases of the dollar to use in other transactions, or for adding to currency reserves.

Furthermore, since people, firms, and governments in all countries purchase goods from and invest in many other countries, the demand for any one currency will be the aggregate demand of individuals, firms, and governments in a number of different countries. Thus the total demand for dollars, for example, may include Germans offering marks, British offering pounds, Greeks offering drachmas, and so on.

The demand for any one currency comes from many sources, and the supply of that currency comes from many holders of that currency, including banks, individuals, and businesses in many different countries. For simplicity, however, we continue with our two-country example with only Britain and the United States.

The Shape of the Demand Curve for Dollars

The demand for dollars in terms of pounds is represented by a downward-sloping curve such as that shown in Figure 40-1. This figure plots the price of dollars (measured in pounds) on the vertical axis and the quantity of dollars on the horizontal axis. Moving down the vertical scale, the dollar becomes cheaper, that is, it is worth fewer pounds; its value is depreciating on the foreign exchange market. Moving up the scale the dollar becomes more expensive; its value is appreciating.[3]

---

[3] Since we have chosen to work with the demand and supply of dollars, the vertical axis measures the pound sterling price of dollars, which is the inverse of the exchange rate as we have defined it. Thus the exchange rate falls as we move up the vertical axis.

FIGURE 40-1   An Exchange Rate Determined on a Competitive Market

The equilibrium exchange rate equates demand and supply on the foreign exchange market. The quantity of dollars demanded is originally equal to the quantity supplied at a price of £0.80 per dollar (or £1.00 = $1.25). If the demand for dollars rises to D_1 the equilibrium exchange rate will change to £0.82 per dollar, that is, the dollar appreciates in value and the pound depreciates.

Why does the demand curve for dollars slope downward? Consider the demand derived from purchases of American exports. If the dollar depreciates in value, the sterling price of American exports will fall. The British will buy more of the cheaper U.S. goods and will require more dollars for this purpose. The quantity of dollars demanded will rise. In the opposite case, when the dollar rises in value, the price of American exports rises in terms of foreign currency. The British will buy fewer U.S. goods and thus demand fewer U.S. dollars.

Similar considerations affect other sources of demand for dollars. When the dollar is cheaper, American assets or securities become attractive purchases, and the quantity purchased will rise. As it does, the quantity of dollars demanded to pay for the purchases will increase.

The demand curve for dollars on the foreign exchange market is downward sloping when plotted against the sterling price of dollars.

The Supply of Dollars

Because of the symmetrical nature of foreign exchange markets, the sources of supply of dollars are merely the opposite side of the demand for pounds. (Recall that the *supply* of dollars by people seeking pounds is the same as the *demand* for pounds by holders of dollars.) Who wants to sell dollars? Americans seeking to purchase foreign goods and services or assets will be supplying dollars and purchasing foreign exchange for the purpose. Holders of American securities may decide to sell their American holdings and shift into foreign assets. If they do, they will try to sell dollars, that is, they will be supplying dollars to the foreign exchange market. Similarly, a country with large dollar reserves of foreign exchange may decide the dollar is "weak" and try to sell dollars in order to buy another currency.

Once again, from many sources and for many purposes, people will be wishing to give up dollars and acquire foreign exchange, but for simplicity, we continue with our two-country example.

What about the shape of the supply curve of dollars? When the dollar depreciates, the effective price of British exports to the United States rises. It takes more dollars to buy the same British good, so Americans will buy fewer of the now more expensive British goods. The amount of dollars being offered in exchange for pounds sterling in order to pay for British exports (American imports) will fall.[4]

In the opposite case, when the dollar appreciates, British exports to the United States become cheaper, more are sold, and more dollars are spent on them. Thus more dollars will be offered in exchange for pounds in order to obtain the foreign exchange needed to pay for the extra imports. Precisely the same argument used for commodities applies to purchases and sales of assets.

---

[4] As long as the elasticity of demand for imports is greater than one, the fall in the volume of imports will swamp the rise in price and hence fewer dollars will be spent on them. This elasticity condition is related to a famous, long-standing issue in international economics. In what follows, we adopt the standard case of the condition's being met. In a more general form, it is called the *Marshall-Lerner condition* after two famous economists who first studied the problem.

The supply curve of dollars on the foreign exchange market is upward sloping when plotted against the sterling price of dollars.

Equilibrium Exchange Rates in a Competitive Market

Consider a rate of exchange that is set on a freely competitive market. Like any competitive price, this rate fluctuates according to the conditions of demand and supply.

Assume that the current price of dollars is so low (say, £0.76 in Figure 40-1) that the quantity of dollars demanded exceeds the quantity supplied. Dollars will be in scarce supply, some people who require dollars to make payments to America will be unable to obtain them, and the price of dollars will be bid up. The value of the dollar vis-à-vis the pound will appreciate. As the price of the dollar rises, the sterling price of U.S. exports to the United Kingdom rises and the quantity of U.S. dollars demanded to buy British goods decreases. However, as the dollar price of imports from the United Kingdom falls, a larger quantity will be purchased and the quantity of U.S. dollars supplied will rise. Thus a rise in the price of the dollar reduces the quantity demanded and increases the quantity supplied. Where the two curves intersect, quantity demanded equals quantity supplied—and the exchange rate is in equilibrium.

What happens when the price of dollars is above its equilibrium value? The quantity of dollars demanded will be less than the quantity supplied. With the dollar in excess supply, some people who wish to convert dollars into pounds will be unable to do so. The price of dollars will fall, fewer dollars will be supplied, more will be demanded, and an equilibrium will be reestablished.

A foreign exchange market is like other competitive markets in that the forces of demand and supply tend to lead to an equilibrium price in which quantity demanded equals quantity supplied.

Changes in Exchange Rates

What causes exchange rates to vary? The simplest answer to this question is changes in demand or supply in the foreign exchange market. Anything that shifts the demand curve for dollars to the right or the supply curve for dollars to the left leads to an appreciation of the dollar. Anything that shifts the demand curve for dollars to the left or the supply curve for dollars to the right leads to a depreciation of the dollar. This is nothing more than a restatement of the laws of supply and demand, applied now to the market for foreign currencies.

But what causes the shifts in demand and supply that lead to changes in exchange rates? There are many causes, some of them transitory and some persistent; we shall mention several of the most important ones.

A Rise in the Domestic Price of Exports

Suppose the dollar price of American electronic equipment rises. What this will do to the demand for dollars depends on the foreign elasticity of demand for the American product. If the demand is elastic, perhaps because other countries supply the same product in world markets, the total amount spent will decrease and thus fewer dollars will be demanded. That is, the demand curve for dollars will shift to the left and the dollar will depreciate.

If the demand is inelastic, say because America is uniquely able to supply the product for which there are no close substitutes, more will be spent, the demand for dollars to pay the bigger bill will shift the demand curve to the right, and the dollar will appreciate.

A Rise in the Foreign Price of Imports

Consider the effects of a large rise in the price at which some important import is supplied. Assume that the sterling price of Scotch whisky increases sharply. Assume also that American drinkers have an elastic demand for Scotch because they can easily switch to bourbon, rye, and other relatively close substitutes. They thus end up spending fewer pounds for Scotch whisky than they did before. Hence, they must supply fewer dollars to the foreign exchange market. The supply curve of dollars shifts to the left, and the price of the dollar tends to rise.

Changes in the Overall Price Levels

Suppose that instead of a change in the price of a specific export, such as electronic calculators, there is a change in all prices due to inflation. What matters here is the change in our price level *relative* to the price levels of our trading partners. (In our two-country example, the United Kingdom stands for the rest of the world.)

An equal percentage change in the price level in both countries. Suppose there is a 10 percent inflation in both the United States and the United Kingdom. In this case, the sterling prices of British goods and the dollar prices of U.S. goods both rise by 10 percent. At the existing exchange rate the dollar prices of British goods and the sterling prices of American goods will each rise by 10 percent. Thus the relative prices of imports and domestically produced goods will be unchanged in both countries. There is now no reason to expect a change in either country's demand for imports at the original exchange rate, so the inflations in the two countries leave the equilibrium exchange rate unchanged.

This argument forms the basis of what is called the *purchasing power parity* theory of exchange rates, a theory we shall study below.

A change in the price level of only one country. What will happen if there is inflation in the United States, while the price level remains stable in the United Kingdom? The dollar price of U.S. goods will rise, and American goods will become more expensive in the United Kingdom. This will cause the quantity of American exports, and therefore the quantity of dollars demanded by British importers in order to pay for American goods, to diminish.

At the same time British exports to America will have an unchanged dollar price, while the price of American goods sold at home will have been increased by the inflation. Thus British goods will be more attractive compared with American goods (because they have become *relatively* cheaper), and more British goods will be bought in America. At any exchange rate the quantity of dollars supplied in order to purchase pounds will be increased.

An American inflation unmatched in the United Kingdom causes the demand curve for dollars to shift to the left and the supply curve of dollars to shift to the right. As a result the equilibrium price of dollars must fall; there is a depreciation in the value of the dollar relative to that of the pound.

Inflation at unequal rates. The two foregoing examples are, of course, just limiting cases of a more general situation in which the price levels change in both countries. The arguments can readily be extended when one realizes that it is the *relative* size of the changes in prices in two countries that determines whether home goods or foreign goods look more or less attractive. If country A's inflation rate is higher than country B's, country A's exports are becoming relatively expensive in B's markets, while imports from B are becoming relatively cheap in A's markets. This will shift the demand curve for A's currency to the left and the supply curve to the right. Each change causes the price of A's currency to fall.

If the price level of one country is rising relative to that of another country, the equilibrium value of its currency will be falling relative to that of the second country.

Capital Movements

Major capital flows can exert strong influences on exchange rates. For example, an increased desire to invest in British assets will shift the supply curve for dollars to the right and depreciate the value of the dollar.

A movement of investment funds has the effect of appreciating the currency of the capital-importing country and depreciating the currency of the capital-exporting country.

This statement is true for all capital movements, short term or long term. Since the motives that lead to large capital movements are likely to be different in the short and long terms, however, it is worth considering each.

Short-term capital movements. A major motive for short-term capital flows is a change in interest rates. International traders hold transactions balances just as domestic traders do. These balances are often lent out on short-term loan rather than being left idle. Naturally, the holders of these balances will tend to lend them, other things being equal, in those markets where interest rates are highest. Thus if one major country's short-term rate of interest rises above the rates in most other countries, there will tend to be a large inflow of short-term capital into that country to take advantage of the high rate, and this will tend to appreciate the currency. If these short-term interest rates should fall, there will most likely be a sudden shift away from that country as a source of transactions balances, and its currency will tend to depreciate.

A second motive for short-term capital movements is speculation about a country's exchange rate. If foreigners expect the dollar to appreciate, they will rush to buy assets that pay off in dollars; if they expect the dollar to depreciate, they will be reluctant to buy or hold American securities.

Long-term capital movements.   Such movements are largely influenced by long-term expectations about another country's profit opportunities and the long-run value of its currency. A British firm would be more willing to purchase an American factory if it expected that the dollar profits would buy more sterling in future years than the profits from investment in a British factory. This could happen if the American firm earned greater profits than the British firm, with exchange rates unchanged. It could also happen if the profits were the same but the British firm expected the dollar to appreciate relative to the pound.

Structural Changes

An economy can undergo structural changes that alter the equilibrium exchange rate. *Structural change* is an omnibus term for a change in cost structures, the invention of new products, or anything else that affects the pattern of comparative advantage. For example, when a country's products do not improve as rapidly as those of some other country, consumers' demand (at fixed prices) shifts slowly away from the first country's products and toward those of its foreign competitors. This causes a slow depreciation in the first country's currency because the demand for its currency is shifting slowly leftward.

Loss of Confidence in the Dollar As a Reserve Currency

In the period since 1944 many nations, banks, and even private firms have come to hold dollars as a major part of their foreign exchange reserves. In 1970 more than $500 billion was held for that purpose. If for any reason these holders come to believe that the dollar will depreciate in world markets, they may decide that it would be shrewd to shift some of their dollar holdings to sterling, marks, or even gold. This happened during the 1970s. When there are large dollar holdings, attempts to "get out of dollars" in a hurry can lead to large rightward shifts of the supply curve and rapid depreciation of the dollar.

The Balance of Payments

Balance-of-Payments Accounts

In order to know what is happening to the course of international trade, governments keep track of the transactions among countries. The record of such transactions is made in the **balance-of-payments accounts.** Each transaction, such as a shipment of exports or the arrival of imported goods, is classified according to the payments or receipts that would typically arise from it. Table 40-2 shows the major items in the American balance-of-payments accounts for 1984.

Current Account

The **current account** records payments arising from trade in goods and services and from income in the form of interest, profits, and dividends arising from capital owned in one country and invested in another. The current account is divided into two main sections.

The first is variously called the **visible account, the trade account,** and the **merchandise account.** It records payments and receipts arising from the import and export of tangible goods such as computers, cars, wheat, and shoes. American imports

---

TABLE 40-2   U.S. Balance-of-Payments, 1984
(billions of dollars)

Current account	
Merchandise exports	+ 220
Merchandise imports	− 334
Trade balance	− 114
Services balance	+ 18
Government grants and other transfers	− 11
Balance on current account	− 107
Capital account	
Net change in U.S. investments abroad (increase −, decrease +)	− 11
Net change in foreign investments in United States (increase +, decrease −)	+ 94
Balance on capital account	+ 83
Balance on capital plus current accounts	− 24
Official financing	
Changes in liabilities to foreign official agencies (increase +, decrease −)	− 3
Use of official reserves (increase −, decrease +)	+ 4
Statistical discrepancy[a]	+ 23
Overall balance of payments	Always zero

[a]In balance-of-payments accounts there is a "statistical discrepancy" item that results from the inability to measure accurately some items. For example, many capital transactions are not recorded.

The overall balance of payments always balances, but the individual components do not have to. In this example the U.S. shows a negative (deficit) trade balance (imports exceed exports) and a smaller negative (deficit) balance on current account. There is a positive (surplus) balance on capital account because capital imports exceeded capital exports. This is because the U.S. has in recent years been a large net borrower of funds from abroad. The capital *plus* current account surplus is what is commonly referred to as the *balance of payments*. It is exactly matched by the balance in the official accounts. Note the very large statistical discrepancy of a size that is commonly found in recent years, but not in earlier ones. Evidently, some major international transactions are not now being recorded in the payments statistics.

---

require the use of foreign exchange and hence are entered as debit items on the visible account. American exports earn foreign exchange and hence are recorded as credit items.

The second section of the current account is called the **invisible account** or the **service account**. It records payments arising out of trade in services and payments for the use of capital. Trade in such services as insurance, shipping, and tourism is entered in the invisible account, as are payments of interest, dividends, and profits made for capital used in one country but owned by residents of another country.

Those items that use foreign exchange, such as purchases by American residents of foreign insurance and shipping services, travel abroad by Americans, and payments to foreign residents of interest earned in the United States, are entered as debit items. Those items that earn foreign exchange, such as foreign purchases of American insurance and shipping services, foreign travel in the United States, and payments to American residents of interest earned abroad, are entered as credit items.

Capital Account

The second main division in the balance of payments is the **capital account**, which records transactions related to international movements of financial capital. The export of funds from the United States, called a *capital export*, uses foreign exchange and so is entered as a debit item in the U.S. payments accounts. The import of funds into the United States, called a *capital import*, earns foreign exchange and so is entered as a credit item in the payments statistics.

It may seem odd that, while a merchandise export is a credit item on current account, the export of capital is a debit item on capital account. To see that there is no contradiction between the treatments of goods and capital, consider the export of American funds for investment in a German bond. The capital transaction involves the purchase, and hence the *import*, of a German bond, and this has the same effect on the balance of payments as the purchase, and hence the import, of a German good. Both items involve payments to foreigners and both use foreign exchange. Both are thus debit items in American balance of payments accounts.

The capital account often distinguishes between movements of short-term and long-term capital. Short-term capital is money held in the form of highly liquid assets, such as bank accounts and short-term treasury bills. If a non-resident merchant buys dollars and places them in a deposit account in New York, this represents an inflow of short-term capital into the United States, and it will be recorded as a credit item on short-term capital account. Long-term capital represents funds coming into the United States (a credit item) or leaving the United States (a debit item) to be invested in less liquid assets such as long-term bonds or physical capital such as a new car assembly plant.

The two major subdivisions of the long-term part of the capital accounts are direct investment and portfolio investment. **Direct investment** relates to changes in non-resident ownership of domestic firms and resident ownership of foreign firms. Thus one form of direct investment in the United States is capital investment in a branch plant or subsidiary corporation in the United States in which the investor has voting control. Another form is a takeover in which a controlling interest in a firm previously controlled by residents is acquired by foreigners. **Portfolio investment,** on the other hand, is investment in bonds or a minority holding of shares that does not involve legal control.

Official Financing Account

The final section in the balance-of-payments account represents transactions in the *official reserves* held by a country's central bank. These transactions reflect the financing of the balance on the remainder of the accounts. The central banks of most countries hold reserves of funds to use in order to buy and sell in the foreign exchange market. Some of these reserves are held in gold, some in foreign exchange, some as claims on various major foreign currencies, and some in an international currency called special drawing right, or SDR (which we study in Chapter 41).

The Federal Reserve Board, operating on behalf of the government, can intervene in the market for foreign exchange to influence the dollar's exchange rate. For example, to prevent the price of dollars from falling, the Fed must buy dollars. This means it must sell gold or foreign exchange. It can do so only if it holds reserves of these media. When the Fed wishes to stop the dollar from rising in value, it enters the market and sells dollars. In this case, the Fed buys foreign exchange which it then adds to its reserves.

The Meaning of Payments Balances and Imbalances

We have seen that the payments accounts show the total of receipts of foreign exchange (credit items) and payments of foreign exchange (debit items) on account of each category of payment. It is also common to calculate the *balance* on separate items or groups of items. The concept of the balance of payments is used in a number of different ways. These can be confusing, so we must approach this issue in a series of steps.

The Balance of Payments Must Balance Overall

Notice two things about the payments accounts. First, they record *actual* payments, not *desired* payments. Second, they record *all* payments, whatever the reason for which they were made.

It is quite possible that, at the existing exchange rate between dollars and yen, holders of yen want to purchase more dollars than holders of dollars want to sell in exchange for yen. In this situation, the quantity of dollars demanded exceeds the quantity supplied. But holders of yen cannot actually buy more dollars than holders of dollars actually sell; every yen that is bought must have been sold by someone, and every dollar that is sold must have been bought by someone.

It follows that, if we add up all the receipts arising from (1) payments received by U.S. residents on account of American exports of goods and services, (2) capital imports, and (3) purchase of foreign exchange or gold by the Fed, these must be exactly equal to all payments made by holders of dollars arising from (1) American imports of goods and services, (2) exports of capital, and (3) sale of foreign exchange or gold by the Fed.

This relation is so important that it pays us to write it out in symbols. We let C, K, and F stand for current account, capital account, and official financing account and use a P for payments (debit items) and *R* for receipts (credit items). Now we can write

$$C_R + K_R + F_R = C_P + K_P + F_P \qquad [1]$$

All this tells us is that, if we add up across all transactions, they must balance in total.

Although the relation given in the above equation is necessarily true, it often worries students who feel that it need not be true. To help clarify the issue some apparent exceptions are considered in Box 40-1.

Payments on Specific Parts of the Accounts Do Not Need To Balance

Although the overall total of payments must equal the overall total of receipts, the same zero balance does not have to hold on subsections of the overall accounts. We now look at the balances on parts of the accounts, balances that may be positive or negative. We do this first in relation to particular countries and then in relation to particular subsectors of the account.

Country balances.   When all foreign countries are taken together, a country's balance of payments must balance, but a country can have bilateral surpluses or deficits with individual foreign countries, or groups of countries. In general, the **multilateral balance of payments** refers to the balance between one country's payments to and receipts from the rest of the world. When all items are considered, every country must have a zero multilateral payments balance with the rest of the world, although it can have bilateral surpluses or deficits with individual countries. This important principle is illustrated in the second part of Box 40-1.

Subsection balances.   The balance on visible, or merchandise, account refers to the difference between the value of U.S. exports of goods and the value of imports of goods. A surplus occurs when exports of goods exceed imports of goods, while a deficit occurs when imports exceed exports. The balance on invisibles refers to the difference between the value of receipts on invisibles and the value of payments for invisibles. The **balance of payments on current account** is the sum of the balances on

the visible and invisible accounts. It gives the balance between payments and receipts on all income-related items.

As a carryover from a long-discredited eighteenth century economic doctrine called mercantilism, a credit balance on current account (receipts exceed payments) is called a **favorable balance**, while a debit balance (payments exceed receipts) is called an **unfavorable balance**.

Mercantilists, both ancient and modern, hold that the gains from trade arise only from having a favorable balance of trade. This misses the whole point of the doctrine of comparative advantage, which states that countries can gain from a balanced increase in trade between themselves because of the opportunity it provides for each country to specialize according to its comparative advantage. The modern resurgence of mercantilist views is discussed in Box 40-2 on page 818.

The balance on capital account gives the difference between receipts of foreign exchange and payments of foreign exchange arising out of capital movements. A surplus, or "favorable" balance, on capital account means that a country is a *net* importer of capital, while a deficit, or "unfavorable" balance, means that the country is a *net* exporter of capital.

Notice that a deficit on capital account, which is referred to as an unfavorable balance, merely indicated that a country is investing abroad. For a rich country to invest abroad and accumulate assets that will earn income in the future may be a desirable situation. So once again we observe that there is nothing necessarily unfavorable about having an "unfavorable" balance on any of the payments accounts.

A credit balance on official settlements account means that the Fed has bought more gold and foreign exchange that it has sold. This adds to its reserves of foreign exchange. A deficit balance means that the Fed has sold more gold and foreign exchange than it has bought. This reduces its foreign exchange reserves.

The Relation Between Various Balances

Two important points should be noticed at this point. First, since overall payments must balance,

BOX 40-1

An Illustration of How the Balance of Payments Always Balances

Trade Between Two Countries

Suppose that the sole international transaction made this year by a small country called Myopia was an export to the United States of Myopian coconuts worth $1,000. Further suppose that the Myopian central bank issues a local currency, the stigma, but does not operate in the foreign exchange market, so there is no official financing. Finally, suppose that Myopia's self-sufficient inhabitants want no imports. Surely, then, you might think Myopia has an overall favorable balance of $1,000, which is a current account receipt (C_R) with no balancing item on the payments side?

To see why this is wrong, we must ask what the exporter of coconuts did with the dollars he received for his coconuts. If he deposited them in a New York bank, this transaction represents a capital export from Myopia. Myopians have accumulated claims on foreign exchange which they hold in the form of a deposit with a foreign bank. Thus there are two entries in the Myopian accounts—one a credit item for the export of coconuts (C_R = $1,000) and the other a debit item for the export of capital (K_P = $1,000).

The fact that the same firm made both transactions is irrelevant. Although the current account shows a credit balance, the capital account exactly balances this with a debit item. Hence, looking at the *balance of payments as a whole*, the two sides of the account are equal. The balance of payments has balanced—as it must always do.

Consider now a slightly more realistic case. If the coconut exporter wants to turn his $1,000 into Myopian stigmas so that he can pay his coconut pickers in local currency, he must find someone who wishes to buy his dollars in return for Myopian currency. But we have assumed that no one in Myopia wants to import, so no one wants to sell Myopian currency for current account reasons. Assume, however, that a wealthy Myopian landowner would like to invest $1,000 in New York by buying shares in an American firm. To do so, he needs $1,000. The coconut exporter can sell his $1,000 to the landowner in return for stigmas. Now he can pay his local bills. The landowner sells his stigmas to the exporter in return for dollars. Now he can buy the American shares.

Once again the Myopian balance of payments will

---

the terms "a balance-of-payments *deficit*" and "a balance-of-payments *surplus*" refer to the balance on some part of the payments accounts. Second, because of the necessity for the balance of payments to balance overall, a deficit on any one part of the accounts implies an offsetting surplus on the rest of the accounts. We now consider two important applications of this second statement. The first application concerns the balances on current and capital accounts, while the second concerns the balances on official settlements account and the remainder of the total accounts.

The current and capital account balances. To make the relation between current and capital balances clear, let us assume that the Fed does not engage in any foreign exchange transactions. This means that

the official settlements account is zero because both F_R and F_P in Equation 1 are zero.

Now any deficit or surplus on current account must be matched by an equal and opposite surplus or deficit on capital account. For example, if a country has a credit balance on current account, the foreign exchange earned must appear as a debit item in the capital account. The foreign exchange may be used to buy foreign assets or merely stashed away in foreign bank accounts. In either case there is an outflow of capital from the United States. It is recorded as a debit item because it uses foreign exchange.

We can see this clearly if we return to Equation 1 and set F_R and F_P equal to zero to indicate no transactions by the Fed. This gives us

$$C_R + K_R = C_P + K_P \qquad [2]$$

show two entries, equal in size but opposite in sign. There is a credit item for the export of coconuts (the sale of coconuts earned foreign exchange) and a debit item for the export of capital (the purchase of the American shares used foreign exchange).

Trade Involving Many Countries

In the above example Myopia had what is called a bilateral payments balance with the United States. The *bilateral balance of payments* between any two countries is the balance between the payments and receipts flowing between them. If there were only two countries in the world, their overall payments would have to be in bilateral balance, that is, one country's payments to the other would be equal to its receipts from the other. But this is not true when there are more than two countries.

Suppose that in the year following the one discussed above, Myopia again sells $1,000 worth of coconuts to the United States, that the landowner does not wish to invest further in the United States, but that the Myopian people wish to buy 200,000

yens' worth of parasols from Japan. (Assume also that on the foreign exchange market $1 trades for 200 yen.) Finally, assume that a Japanese importer wishes to buy $1,000 worth of skateboards from an American company.

Now what in effect happens is that the Myopian coconut exporter sells his $1,000 to the Japanese skateboard importer for 200,000 yen, which the coconut dealer then sells to the Myopian parasol importer in return for Myopian stigmas. (In the real world the exchanges are all done through banks, but the above is what happens in effect.) Now the Myopian payments statistics will show a $1,000 bilateral payments surplus with the United States—receipts of $1,000 from the United States on acccount of coconut exports, and no payments to the United States—and a bilateral deficit with Japan of 200,000 yen (equal to $1,000)—$1,000 of payments to Japan on account of parasol imports and no receipts from Japan. But when both countries are considered, Myopia's multilateral payments are in balance.

Now subtract C_P and K_R from both sides of the equation to get

$$C_R - C_P = K_P - K_R. \qquad [3]$$

This expresses in equation form what we have just stated in words: A surplus on current account must be balanced by a deficit on capital account (i.e., an outflow of capital), while a deficit on current account must be matched by a surplus on capital account (i.e., an inflow of capital).

One important implication relates to capital transfers. A country that is importing capital has a surplus on capital account and so it *must* have a deficit on current account. This is the position that the United States was in during the mid 1980s. Because of the borrowing requirements of a massive government budget deficit, and because the boom made the United States an attractive place in which to invest,

there was a massive capital inflow into the United States. This inflow made a current account deficit inevitable. As long as the capital inflow persisted, no policy measure could remove the current account deficit. This issure is considered in more detail in Chapter 41.[5]

Official financing and the rest of the accounts. When people speak of a country as having an overall balance-of-payments deficit or surplus, *they are usually referring to the balance of all accounts excluding official financing.* A balance-of-payments surplus means that

[5] If we allow for the Fed's transactions, the relation given in Equation 3 does not need to hold exactly. The current and capital account balance can diverge from zero by the balance on official settlements account $(F_R - F_P)$. Since this balance is almost always small relative to net payments on current and capital account, the relation between the two major accounts, shown in Equation 3, is approximately true.

BOX 40-2

The Volume of Trade, the Balance of Trade, and the New Mercantilism

Media commentators, political figures, and much of the general public often judge the national balance of payments as they would the accounts of a single firm. Just as a firm is supposed to show a profit, the nation is supposed to secure a balance-of-payments surplus, with the benefits derived from international trade measured by the size of that surplus.

This view is related to the exploitation doctrine of international trade. Since one country's surplus is another country's deficit, one country's gain, judged by its surplus, must be another country's loss, judged by its deficit.

People who hold such views today are echoing an ancient economic doctrine called *mercantilism.* The mercantilists were a group of economists who preceded Adam Smith. They judged the success of trade by the size of the trade balance. In many cases this doctrine made sense in terms of their objective, which was to use international trade as a means of building up the political and military power of the state rather than raising the living standards of its citizens. A balance-of-payments surplus allowed the nation (then and now) to acquire foreign exchange reserves. (In those days the reserves took the form of gold. Today they are a mixture of gold and claims on the currencies of other countries.) These reserves could then be used to pay armies, composed partly of foreign mercenaries; to purchase weapons from abroad; and generally to finance colonial adventures.

People who advocate this view in modern times are called *neo-mercantilists.* Insofar as their object is to increase the power of the state, they are choosing means that could achieve their ends. Insofar as they

are drawing an analogy between what is a sensible objective for a business interested in its own material welfare and what is a sensible objective for a society interested in the material welfare of its citizens, their views are erroneous, for the analogy is false.

If we take the view that the object of economic activity is to promote the welfare and living standards of ordinary citizens, rather than the power of governments, then the mercantilist focus on the balance of trade makes no sense. The law of comparative advantage shows that average living standards are maximized by having individuals, regions, and countries specialize in the things they can produce comparatively best and then trading to obtain the things they can produce comparatively worst. The more specialization, the more trade.

On this view the gains from trade are to be judged by the volume of trade. A situation in which there is a *large volume* of trade but where each country has a *zero balance* of trade can thus be regarded as quite satisfactory. Furthermore, a change in commercial policy that results in a balanced increase in trade between two countries will bring gain, because it allows for specialization according to comparative advantage even though it causes no change in either country's trade balance.

To the business interested in private profit and to the government interested in the power of the state, it is the balance of trade that matters. To the person interested in the welfare of ordinary citizens, it is the volume of trade that matters.

the central bank is adding to its holdings foreign exchange reserves; a balance-of-payments deficit means that the central bank is reducing its reserves.

If the central bank does not operate in the foreign exchange market, there can be no overall balance-of-payments deficit or surplus on current plus capital account. Suppose that holders of dollars are trying

to buy more foreign exchange than holders of foreign currencies wish to sell in return for dollars. There will be an excess supply of dollars and an excess demand for foreign exchange. The dollar will depreciate on the foreign exchange market until demand equals supply. At this point both desired and actual international payments are in balance.

If exchange rates are completely free to vary, balance-of-payments deficits and surpluses will be eliminated though exchange rate adjustments.

In today's world, while no country need have a balance-of-payments problem, many still do have them. As long as governments intervene in foreign exchange markets, there will be balance-of-payments deficits and surpluses. Surpluses will occur whenever the currency is held below its equilibrium level. Persistent deficits will cause persistent loss of reserves; they are evidence that the government is trying to resist longer-term trends for changes in the exchange rate.

Summary

1. International trade can occur only when it is possible to exchange the currency of one country for that of another. The exchange rate between two currencies is the amount of one currency that must be paid in order to obtain one unit of another currency. Where more than two currencies are involved, there will be an exchange rate between each pair of currencies.

2. The determination of exchange rates in the free market is simply an application of the laws of supply and demand studied in Chapter 4; the item being bought and sold is a nation's money.

3. The demand for dollars arises from American exports of goods and services, long-term and short-term capital flows into the United States, and the desire of foreign banks, firms, and governments to use American dollars as an international medium of exchange or as part of their reserves.

4. The supply of dollars to purchase foreign currencies arises from American imports of goods and services, capital flows from the United States, and the desire of holders of dollars to decrease the size of their holdings.

5. A depreciation of the dollar lowers the foreign price of American exports and increases the quantity of dollars demanded; at the same time, it raises the dollar price of imports from abroad and thus lowers the quantity of dollars supplied to buy foreign exchange to be used to purchase foreign goods. Thus the demand curve for dollars is downward sloping and the supply curve of dollars is upward sloping when the quantities demanded and supplied are plotted against the price of dollars measured in terms of a foreign currency.

6. A currency will tend to appreciate on foreign exchange markets if there is a shift to the right of the demand curve or a shift to the left of the supply curve for its currency. Shifts in the opposite directions will tend to depreciate the currency. Such shifts are caused by such things as the prices of imports and exports, the rates of inflation in different countries, capital movements, structural changes, expectations about future trends in earnings and exchange rates, and the level of confidence in the currency as a source of reserves.

7. Actual transactions among the firms, households, and governments of various countries are kept track of and reported in the balance-of-

payments accounts. In these accounts any transaction that uses foreign exchange is recorded as a debit item and any transaction that produces foreign exchange is recorded as a credit item. If all transactions are recorded, the sum of all credit items necessarily equals the sum of all debit items since the foreign exchange that is bought must also have been sold.

8. Major categories in the balance-of-payments account are the balance of trade (exports minus imports), current account, capital account, and official financing. The so-called balance of payments is the balance of the current plus capital accounts; that is, it excludes the transactions on official account. Ignoring official settlements, a balance on current account must be matched by a balance on capital account of equal magnitude but opposite sign.

9. There is nothing inherently good or bad about deficits or surpluses. Persistent deficits or surpluses cannot be sustained because the former will eventually exhaust a country's foreign exchange reserves and the latter will do the same to a trading partner's reserves.

Topics for Review

Foreign exchange and exchange rates
Appreciation and depreciation
Sources of the demand for and supply of foreign exchange
Effects on exchange rates of capital flows, inflation, interest rates, and expectations about exchange rates
Balance of trade and balance of payments
Current and capital account
Official financing items
Mercantilist views on the balance of trade and volume of trade

Discussion Questions

1. What is the probable effect of each of the following on the exchange rate of a country, other things being equal?
   a. The quantity of oil imports is greatly increased, but the value of imported oil is lower due to price decreases.
   b. The country's inflation rate falls well below that of its trading partners.
   c. Rising labor costs of the country's manufacturers lead to a worsening ability to compete in world markets.
   d. The government greatly expands its gifts of food and machinery to underdeveloped countries.
   e. A major boom occurs with rising employment.
   f. The central bank raises interest rates sharply.
   g. More domestic oil is discovered and developed.
2. In the mid 1980s the United States became a major importer of capital, partly to finance the large internal budget deficit and partly because the American boom and the European slump made the United States a highly attractive place in which to invest foreign funds. Predict the effects of this large capital inflow on the U.S.

dollar exchange rate and on the balance of payments on current account. Would these developments have anything to do with the upsurge of protectionist sentiment in the Congress during the latter part of the 1980s?

3. In recent years money wages have risen substantially faster in Canada than in the United States. Many Canadians have expressed the fear that their rapidly rising costs will price them out of U.S. markets. Did this fear make sense when the Canadian exchange rate was fixed relative to the American dollar? Does it make sense today when exchange rates are free to vary on the open market?

4. Indicate whether each of the following transactions increases the demand for dollars, the supply of dollars, or neither on foreign exchange markets.
   a. IBM moves $10 million from bank accounts in the United States to banks in Paris to expand operations there.
   b. The U.S. government extends a grant of $3 million to the government of Peru, which Peru uses to buy farm machinery from a Chicago firm.
   c. Canadian investors, responding to higher profits of U.S. rather than Canadian corporations, buy stocks through the New York Stock Exchange.
   d. Several countries stop interest payments on their large debts to U.S. banks.
   e. Lower interest rates in New York than in London encourage British firms to borrow in the New York money market, converting the proceeds into pounds sterling for use at home.

5. "The necessity of the government to stabilize the balance of payments through the settlement account is a relic of the past. It was a by-product of the adherence to a policy of fixed exchange rates." Do you agree?

6. "If a country solves its balance-of-payments problems, it will have solved its foreign trade problems." Discuss.

7. Outline the reasoning behind the following summer 1983 newspaper headline: "Sterling tumbles as British interest rates weaken."

41

Alternative Exchange Rate Systems

The nations of the world have tried many different international monetary systems. No system has been fully satisfactory, and periods of crisis have alternated with periods of stability.

The twentieth century began with a system of fixed exchange rates under the gold standard. This system suffered periodic crises in the post-World War I years, but did not collapse until the onset of the Great Depression. The 1930s was a period of experimentation with flexible, market-determined exchange rates. This ended with World War II, when governments fixed exchange rates.

In 1944 the fixed exchange rate regime was formalized by international agreement at a conference in Bretton Woods, New Hampshire. The Bretton Woods system lasted for over a quarter of a century, but its shortcomings and the periods of crisis it induced finally prevailed over its advantages and the periods of stability it afforded. After several attempts to patch it up in the 1970s, the system finally broke down and was gradually abandoned as countries turned one by one to market-determined, flexible exchange rates.

Fixed and Flexible Exchange Rates

Among the principal international monetary systems two extremes can be distinguished. The first is a system in which exchange rates are fixed at announced par values. The gold standard was such a system and so was Bretton Woods. (The operation and decline of both systems are discussed in the appendix to this chapter.)

The second is a system of freely fluctuating rates determined by market demand and supply in the absence of government intervention. Some countries have come close to this system, first in the 1930s and then since 1971.

Between these two "pure" systems there is a variety of possible intermediate cases. The two that we will encounter are known as the *adjustable peg* and the *managed float*. In the adjustable peg system, governments set and attempt to maintain par values for their exchange rates, but they explicitly recognize that circumstances may arise in which they will change the par value. In a managed float, the central bank seeks to have some stabilizing influence on the exchange rate, but does not try to fix it at some publicly announced par value.

The International Monetary Fund (also called the IMF and the Fund) was created as part of the Bretton Woods system. Under its original charter the Fund had several tasks. It tried to ensure that countries kept their exchange rates fixed in the short run. It was supposed to ensure that any exchange rate change was really needed to remove a persistent payments disequilibrium and that a single devaluation did not set off a self-canceling round of devaluations. It also made loans—out of funds subscribed by member nations—to governments to support their exchange rates in the face of temporary payments deficits.

The Bretton Woods system has been abandoned, but the Fund survives, although its tasks have changed. For example, the Jamaica Agreement of 1976 amended the IMF charter to ratify the adoption of floating exchange rates and deemphasize gold as a basis for the international payments system.

A Fixed Exchange Rate System

In a system of **fixed exchange rates,** each country's central bank intervenes in the foreign exchange market to prevent that country's exchange rate from going outside a narrow band on either side of its par value.

This system presents one immediate difficulty in that one country must take a passive role with respect to its exchange rate. This is because there is one less exchange rate to be determined than there are countries. In a two-country world containing only Japan and the United States, for example, if the Bank of Japan fixes the exchange rate at 150 yen to the dollar, the U.S. Federal Reserve cannot fix a different rate making the dollar worth, say, 200 yen. Under the Bretton Woods system, all foreign countries fixed their exchange rate against the U.S. dollar. The Fed adopted the passive role; it was the only central bank in the world that did not have to intervene to support a particular value of its currency.

Having picked a fixed exchange rate for its currency against, say, the U.S. dollar, each foreign central bank then had to manage matters so that the chosen rate could actually be maintained. The bank had to be prepared to offset imbalances in demand and supply by government sales or purchases of foreign exchange. In the face of short-term fluctuations in market demand and supply, each central bank could maintain its fixed exchange rate by entering the market and buying and selling as required.

To do this the central bank has to hold reserves

of acceptable foreign exchange. When there is an abnormally low demand for its country's currency on the market, the bank keeps the currency from depreciating by selling foreign exchange and buying up domestic currency. This depletes its reserves of foreign exchange. When there is an abnormally high demand for its country's currency on the foreign exchange market, the bank prevents the currency's appreciating by selling domestic currency in return for foreign exchange. This augments its stocks of foreign exchange.

As long as the central bank is trying to maintain an exchange rate that equates demand and supply for its currency on average, the policy can be successful. Sometimes the bank will be buying and other times selling, but its reserves will fluctuate around a constant average level.

If, however, there is a permanent shift in demand for or supply of a nation's currency on the foreign exchange market, the long-term equilibrium rate will move away from the **pegged rate**, that is, its par value. It will then be difficult to maintain the pegged rate. For example, if there is a major inflation in France while prices are stable in the United States, the equilibrium value of the franc will fall. In a free market the franc would depreciate and the U.S. dollar would appreciate. But a fixed exchange rate is not a free-market rate. If the Bank of France persists in trying to maintain the original exchange rate, it will have to meet the excess demand for U.S. dollars by selling from its reserves. This policy can persist only as long as the bank has reserves that it is willing to spend to maintain an artificially high price of francs. But the bank cannot do this indefinitely. Sooner or later the reserves that it has, and those that it can borrow, will be exhausted.

The management of a fixed rate is illustrated in Figure 41-1. The example used is the maintenance by the Bank of England of a fixed exchange rate between sterling and the U.S. dollar.

When the fixed rate is not near the free-market equilibrium rate, controls of various sorts may be introduced in an attempt to shift the demand curve for foreign exchange so that it intersects the supply curve at a rate close to the fixed rate. This is usually done by restricting imports of goods and services or by restricting the export of capital. If the central bank

FIGURE 41-1   A Fixed Exchange Rate

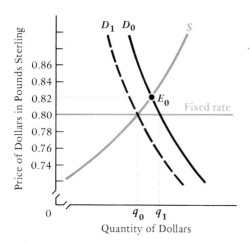

When an exchange rate is fixed at other than the equilibrium rate, either excess demand or excess supply will persist. Suppose demand and supply curves of dollars in the absence of government controls are D_0 and S; equilibrium is at E_0, with a price of £0.82 per dollar. The equilibrium price of the pound is $1.22. Now the British authorities peg the price of the pound at $1.25; that is, they fix the price of the dollar at £0.80. They have overvalued the pound and undervalued the dollar. As a result there is an excess of dollars demanded over dollars supplied of q_0q_1. To maintain the fixed rate it is necessary to shift either the demand curve or the supply curve (or both) so that the two intersect at the fixed rate. For example, demand might be shifted to D_1 by the British government's limiting imports. If the curves are not shifted, the fixed rate will have to be supported by the British government's supplying dollars in the amount of q_0q_1 per period out of its reserves.

cannot shift demand and supply in order to keep the equilibrium rate approximately as high as the fixed rate, it will have no alternative but to devalue its currency.

Problems with Fixed Exchange Rates

Three problems typically arise in a system of fixed exchange rates: (1) providing sufficient reserves, (2) adjusting to long-term trends, and (3) dealing with speculative crises.

Reserves.   Reserves are needed to accommodate short-term balance-of-payments fluctuations arising from the current and the capital accounts. On current account, trade is subject to many short-term variations, some systematic and some random. This means that even if the value of imports does equal the value of exports on average over several years, there may be considerable imbalances over shorter periods.

With a market-determined exchange rate, fluctuations in current and capital account payments would cause the exchange rate to fluctuate. To prevent such fluctuations when rates are fixed, the monetary authorities buy and sell foreign exchange as required. These operations require the authorities to hold reserves of foreign exchange. If they run out of reserves, they cannot maintain the pegged rate.

As discussed in the appendix, the Bretton Woods system had difficulty providing sufficient reserves. This was because the ultimate reserve was gold and there was not enough of it. As a result, the world's central banks held much of their reserves in U.S. dollars and British pound sterling. Currencies that are widely held for this purpose are called **reserve currencies**.

This system worked well enough as long as these reserve currencies had a stable value. However, in the mid 1960s fear of an impending devaluation of sterling arose, and in the early 1970s a similar fear arose regarding the U.S. dollar. In both cases the fears were well founded: Sterling was devalued in late 1967, and the dollar was devalued in 1971 and again in 1973.

The devaluation of a reserve currency reduces the value of the reserves of that currency held by the world's central banks. Fear that a devaluation will occur reduces the acceptability of a currency as a means of holding reserves. This is discussed further in Box 41-1.

The problem of providing reserves, although serious, need not be insurmountable in any future system of fixed rates. After all, a balanced portfolio composed of some holdings of a number of currencies could be held as reserves. This would reduce the risks from holding reserves, since whenever one currency falls in value against a second currency, the second currency rises in value against the first.

BOX 41-1

Problems for Nations Whose Currency Is Held As a Reserve

Under the Bretton Woods system the supply of gold was augmented by reserves of the key currencies, the U.S. dollar, and the British pound sterling. While it is prestigious to have one's currency held as a reserve currency—and even advantageous as long as other countries are willing to increase their holdings of one's paper money without making claims on current output—there are both disadvantages and hazards for the country whose currency is involved.

Such a country is placed under great pressure not to devalue its currency. If it does devalue, all countries holding that currency will find the value of their reserves diminished. If it tries to avoid devaluation, the fear that it may be unable to do so will in any case impair the usefulness of the currency as a reserve because other countries will become reluctant to hold it. The result may well be that the domestic policy of the country whose currency is the reserve becomes unduly subservient to the overriding need to maintain its exchange rate.

The Loss of Confidence in the U.S. Dollar As a Reserve Currency

In the 1950s and 1960s America ran frequent deficits on its overall balance of payments. This resulted largely from American loans, investments, and contributions to other nations who were rebuilding their economies after World War II. As long as other nations were willing to accumulate dollar holdings, this caused no problem; indeed, the buildup of dollars provided the growth in foreign exchange reserves that was needed to finance the growing volume of world trade.

The effect of the dollar devaluations of the early 1970s.   Had everyone believed that the devaluations of 1971 (7.9 percent) and 1973 (11 percent) were just isolated adjustments, they might well have licked their wounds and gone on as before. But no fundamental changes arose either in American policy or in international financial arrangements. Thus many believed that these devaluations were but preludes to inevitable future ones.

Fear of further devaluations not only made holders of U.S. dollars reluctant to increase their holdings, but actually led many prudent holders to want to decrease reliance on such a shaky reserve. As people tried to get rid of U.S. dollars, the exchange rate began to slide. Between 1970 and 1973 the U.S. dollar declined 22 percent against the yen and 30 percent against the mark. The lower value of the U.S. dollar reduced the adequacy of most countries' dollar reserves and threatened their financial stability.

Attempts to flee from the dollar.   While one country (or one bank) can readily reduce its holdings of U.S. dollars by buying gold or other currencies, for everyone to do so requires major changes in the value of the dollar and its alternatives. In the late 1970s the dollar fell sharply relative to the yen and the mark, and one cause of the startling rise in the price of gold in 1979–1980 from $250 to over $900 an ounce was the attempt of many holders of U.S. dollars to flee to gold.

The return to stable prices in the United States restored some faith in the dollar; indeed in the period 1981 to 1984 most observers felt that the dollar was overvalued so that its sharp decline in 1984 was welcomed. While the use of SDRs and other currencies has increased, the dollar still remains "the" key currency and the problems discussed in this box remain.

Long-term disequilibria. With fixed exchange rates long-term disequilibria can be expected to develop because of lasting shifts in the demands for and supplies of foreign exchange. There are three important reasons for these shifts. First, different trading countries have different rates of inflation. Chapter 40 explained how these varying rates produce changes in the equilibrium rates of exchange; if the rate is fixed, these would produce excess supply or excess demand in each country's foreign exchange market. Second, changes in the demands for and supplies of imports and exports are associated with long-term economic growth. Because the economies of different countries grow at different rates, their demands for imports and their supplies of exports can be expected to shift at different rates. Third, structural changes, such as major new innovations or a change in the price of oil, cause major changes in imports and exports.

The associated shifts in demand and supply on the foreign exchange market imply that there is no reason to believe that the exchange rate consistent with equilibrium in the market for foreign exchange will be unchanged.

The exchange rate consistent with balance-of-payments equilibrium will change over time; over a decade the change can be substantial.

Government may react to long-term disequilibria in at least three ways.

1. The exchange rate can be changed whenever it is clear that a balance-of-payments deficit or surplus is the result of a long-term shift in demands and supplies in the foreign exchange market and not the result of some transient factor.

2. Domestic price levels can be allowed to change in an attempt to make the present fixed exchange rates become the equilibrium rate. To restore equilibrium, countries with overvalued currencies need to have deflations and countries with undervalued currencies need to have inflations. But changes in domestic price levels have all sorts of domestic repercussions. Deflations are difficult and costly to accomplish (e.g., reductions in aggregate demand intended to lower the price level are likely to raise unemployment), and often the explicit goal of government policy is to avoid inflation. One might ex-

pect governments to be more willing to change exchange rates than to try to change their price levels.

3. Restrictions can be imposed on trade and foreign payments. Imports and foreign spending by tourists and governments can be restricted, and the export of capital can be slowed or even stopped. Surplus countries are often quick to criticize such restrictions on international trade and payments. But as long as exchange rates are fixed and price levels prove difficult to manipulate, deficit countries have little option but to restrict the quantity of foreign exchange their residents are permitted to obtain.

Since restrictions on trade and foreign payments are undesirable in a world economy characterized by large-scale international trade and foreign investment, and since deflations of the price level are difficult and costly to bring about, most countries will want to preserve the possibility of making occasional changes in their exchange rates even if fixed rates are the main rule of the day.

Under the Bretton Woods system, although most countries defended their exchange rates in the face of crises, there were still major rounds of exchange rate adjustments. Because exchange rates did have to be changed from time to time, the system of fixed rates under the Bretton Woods agreement was called an **adjustable peg system**.

Handling speculative crises. When enough people begin to doubt the government's ability to maintain the current exchange rate, speculative crises develop. The most important reason for such crises is that, over time, equilibrium exchange rates get further and further away from any given set of fixed rates. When the disequilibrium becomes obvious to everyone, traders and speculators come to believe that a realignment of rates is due. There is a rush to buy currencies expected to be revalued and a rush to sell currencies expected to be devalued. Even if the authorities take drastic steps to remove the payments deficit, there may be doubt that these measures will work before the exchange reserves are exhausted. Speculative flows of funds can reach large proportions, and it may be impossible to avoid changing the exchange rate under such pressure.

Under an adjustable peg system, opportunities often arise for speculators to make large profits;

this occurs when everyone knows the direction in which an exchange rate will be changed if it is to be changed at all.

As the equilibrium value of a country's currency changes, possibly under the impact of high inflation, it becomes obvious that the central bank is having more and more difficulty holding the pegged rate. So when a crisis arises, speculators sell the country's currency. If it is devalued, they can buy it back at a lower price and earn a profit. If it is not devalued, they can buy it back at the price at which they sold it and lose only the commission costs on the deal. This asymmetry, with speculators having a chance to make large profits by risking only a small loss, eventually destroyed the Bretton Woods system.

During the Bretton Woods period governments tended to resist changing their exchange rates until they had no alternative. This made the situation so obvious that speculators could hardly lose, and their actions set off the final crises that forced exchange rate readjustments. If changes could be made more frequently and before they became inevitable, the number of speculative crises might diminish, and the system of fixed exchange rates might appear more viable. Such changes, however, would remove the day-to-day certainty that was one of the chief advantages of this system. Moreover, a surprise change might lead to suspicion that a devaluation was made to gain a competitive advantage for a country's exports rather than to remove a fundamental disequilibrium. After all, governments are not supposed to devalue under an adjustable peg system until it is *clear* that they are faced with a fundamental disequilibrium. If this is clear to them, it is also clear to ordinary traders and speculators.

Flexible Exchange Rates

Under a system of flexible exchange rates, demand and supply determines the rates without any government intervention. (This was illustrated in Figure 40-1 on page 809.) Such rates are called free or **flexible** or **floating exchange rates**. Since the foreign exchange market always clears, the government can turn its attention to domestic problems of inflation and unemployment, leaving the balance of payments

to take care of itself—at least so went the theory before flexible rates were introduced.

For reasons that we shall analyze later in this chapter, this optimistic picture did not materialize when the world went over to flexible exchange rates. Free-market fluctuations in rates were far greater, and hence potentially more upsetting to the performance of national economies and to the flow of international trade, than many economists had anticipated. As a result, central banks have felt the need to intervene quite frequently and extensively to stabilize exchange rates.

Managed Floats

A major difference between the present system and Bretton Woods is that central banks no longer publicly announce values for exchange rates that they are committed in advance to defend even at heavy cost. Central banks are thus free to adjust their exchange rate targets as circumstances change. Sometimes they leave the rate completely free to fluctuate, and at other times they interfere actively to alter the exchange rate from its free-market value. Such a system is called a **managed float** or a **dirty float**.

Some countries have opted for what is called a *currency block* by pegging their exchange rates against each other and then indulging in a joint float against the outside world. The best-known currency block is the European **snake**. Under this arrangement the countries of the EC, with the exception of the United Kingdom, maintain fixed rates among their own currencies, but allow them to float as a block against the dollar.

What Determines the Exchange Rate in a Floating System?

One surprise to supporters of floating exchange rates has been the degree of exchange rate volatility. Why have rates been so volatile?

The average value of exchange rates over the long term depends on their **purchasing power parity (PPP)** values. The PPP exchange rate is the one that holds constant the relative price levels in two countries *when measured in a common currency*. For example, assume that the U.S. price level rises by 20 percent, while the German price level rises by only 5 percent over the same period. The PPP value of the German mark then appreciates by approximately 15 percent. This would mean that in Germany the prices of all goods (both German-produced and imported American goods) would rise by 5 percent measured in German marks, while in the United States the prices of all goods (both American-produced and imported German goods) would rise by 20 percent measured in U.S. dollars.

The PPP exchange rate adjusts so that the relative price of the two nations' goods (measured in the same currency) is unchanged because the change in the relative values of two currencies compensates exactly for differences in national inflation rates.

If the actual exchange rate equals the PPP rate, the competitive positions of producers in the two countries will be unchanged. Firms located in countries with high inflation rates will still be able to sell their outputs on international markets, since the exchange rate adjusts to offset the effect of the higher domestic prices.

Figure 41-2 shows that the exchange rate between U.S. dollars and sterling has followed the PPP rate over the long run. But notice also the large fluctuations around the PPP rate.

During the Bretton Woods period of fixed exchange rates, the advocates of floating rates argued that speculators would stabilize the actual rates within a narrow band around the PPP rates. The argument was that since everyone knew the normal value was the PPP rate, speculators seeking a profit when the rate deviated from its PPP level would

FIGURE 41-2   Actual and PPP Exchange Rate, U.S. Dollar and Pound Sterling, 1972–1986

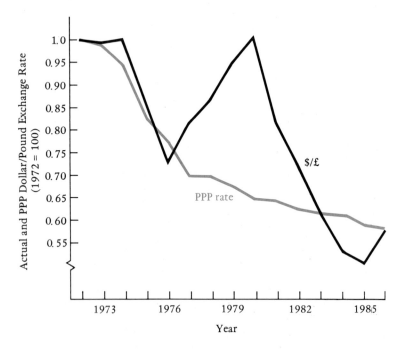

The actual exchange rate follows the trend value of the PPP exchange rate, but fluctuates substantially around it. The black line shows the dollar/pound exchange rate; the colored line shows the ratio of the U.S. CPI to the British CPI. (Both series are set to 1.00 in 1972. The figures for 1986 are those for the exchange rate at the end of April.)

The continual decline of the PPP exchange rate reflects the United Kingdom's higher inflation rate relative to that of the United States. Until 1976 the relative value of the pound fell in accordance with the PPP rate, but after 1976 the pound appreciated sharply through 1980. (Many observers associate this appreciation with the onset of production from large oil deposits in the North Sea and with high interest rates in 1979–1980.) In 1980 the relative value of the pound began to fall, bringing it back toward its PPP value. In 1983 the pound fell below its PPP value, and in 1985 it started to rise again towards its PPP value. (*International Financial Statistics.*)

quickly force the rate back to that level. To illustrate, suppose the PPP rate is U.S. $1.25 = £1.00 and that the actual rate falls to U.S. $1.15 = £1.00. Speculators would rush to buy pounds at U.S. $1.15 each, expecting to sell them for U.S. $1.25 when the rate returns to its PPP level. This very action would raise the demand for sterling and help push its value back toward U.S. $1.25.

Such speculative behavior would stabilize the exchange rate near its PPP value if speculators could be sure that the deviations would be small and short-lived. But in practice the swings around the PPP rate have been wide and have lasted for long periods. Thus, if sterling fell to U.S. $1.15, speculators would know that it could go as low as U.S. $1.05 and stay there for quite a while before returning to U.S. $1.25. In that case it might be worth speculating on a price of U.S. $1.10 next week rather than a price of U.S. $1.25 in some indefinite future.

The wide swings in exchange rates that have occurred show that speculative buying and selling cannot be relied on to hold exchange rates close to their PPP values.

But why have these wide fluctuations occurred? There are many reasons, and one of the most important is associated with international differences in interest rates.

Exchange Rate Overshooting

Suppose that American interest rates rise above those ruling in other major financial centers. A rush to lend money at the profitable rates found in the United States will lead to an appreciation of the U.S. dollar.

This process will stop only when the rise in value of the U.S. dollar on foreign exchange markets is large enough that investors expect the dollar subsequently to fall in value. This expected future depreciation then just offsets the interest premium from lending funds in U.S. dollars.

To illustrate, assume that interest rates are 4 percentage points higher in New York than in London due to a restrictive monetary policy in the United

States. Investors believe the PPP rate is U.S. $1.25 = £1.00 but, as they rush to buy dollars to take advantage of the higher U.S. interest rates, they drive the rate to, say, U.S. $1.10 = £1.00. (Since £1.00 now buys fewer U.S. dollars, sterling has depreciated, and since it takes fewer U.S. dollars to buy £1.00, the dollar has appreciated.) They do not believe this rate will be sustained and instead expect the U.S. dollar to lose value. If foreign investors expect it to depreciate at 4 percent per year, they will be indifferent between lending money in New York and doing so in London. The extra 4 percent of interest they earn in New York per year is exactly offset by the 4 percent they expect to lose when they turn their money back into their own currency.

Any policy that raises domestic interest rates above world levels will cause the external value of the domestic currency to appreciate enough to create an expected future depreciation sufficient to offset the interest differential.

A central bank that is seeking to meet a monetary target may have to put up with large fluctuations in the exchange rate. If, in the example above, the high U.S. interest rates were the result of a restrictive monetary policy, the overshooting of the U.S. dollar beyond its PPP rate may put export- and import-competing industries under temporary but severe pressure from foreign competition.

The other side of this coin is that the high value of the U.S. dollar creates inflationary pressure in other countries. U.S. goods become much more expensive abroad, thus putting upward pressure on foreign prices and wages. Authorities in those countries are faced with the uncomfortable choice of accepting this increased inflation or raising their own interest rates and thus maintaining their exchange rates in terms of the U.S. dollar. In the early 1980s many foreign central banks chose this latter option, and the tight U.S. monetary policies were quickly imitated in other countries. This combined monetary contraction contributed to the severity of the world recession, as discussed further in Box 41-2.

The overvaluation of the dollar meant that the recession was particularly severe in the United States,

BOX 41-2

Beggar-My-Neighbor Policies Past and Present

The Great Depression of the 1930s brought an end to the long-standing stability of the gold standard and ushered in a period of experimentation in exchange regimes. Experiments were tried with both fixed and fluctuating rates.

But the overriding feature of the decade was that considerations of massive unemployment came to dominate economic policies in almost every country, and all devices, including exchange rate manipulations, seemed fair game for dealing with them. Many of the policies adopted at this time were acts of desperation that would have made long-term sense only if other countries had not also been in crisis. Governments tended not to consider the long-term effects on trade or on their trading partners of the policies they adopted, hoping to gain short-term advantages before their policies provoked the inevitable reaction from others.

The use of devaluations to ease domestic unemployment rested on a simple and superficially plausible line of analysis: If a country has unemployed workers at home, why not substitute home production for imports and thus give jobs to one's citizens instead of to foreigners? One way to do this is to urge, say, Americans to "buy American." Another, probably more effective, way is to lower the prices of domestic goods relative to those of imports. The devaluation of one's currency does this by making foreign goods that much more expensive. (A 10 percent devaluation, means that it will take 10 percent more domestic money to buy the same imports; this is equivalent to a 10 percent rise in the prices of all foreign goods.)

Of course, if this policy works other countries will find *their* exports falling and unemployment rising as a consequence. Because such policies attempt to solve one country's problems by inflicting them on others, they are called **beggar-my-neighbor policies** and are described as attempts to "export one's unemployment."

In a situation of inadequate world demand, a beggar-my-neighbor policy on the part of one country can work only in the unlikely event that other countries do not try to protect themselves. A situation in which all countries devalue their currencies in an attempt to gain a competitive advantage over one another is called a situation of **competitive devaluations**.

This is what happened during the 1930s. One country would devalue its currency in an attempt to reduce its imports and stimulate exports. But because other countries were suffering from the same kinds of problems of unemployment, they did not sit idly by. Retaliation was swift, and devaluation followed devaluation. But the simultaneous attempt of all countries to cut imports without suffering a comparable cut in exports is bound to be self-defeating.

When unemployment is due to insufficient world aggregate demand, it cannot be cured by measures designed to redistribute among nations the fixed and inadequate total of demand.

and that U.S. export- and import-competing industries suffered enormously. Not surprisingly, this spurred many calls for protectionist measures to save jobs in those sectors. The relatively low values of many foreign currencies, and in particular Japanese yen, contributed to the view that foreign competition in such traded-goods sectors was indeed unfair and hence protection was justified.

As the U.S. economy recovered in 1983 and after, it might have been expected that the pressures for protection would have subsided. But the U.S. dollar remained high, and the pattern of recovery was uneven. Growth was concentrated in the service sector, in new high-tech sectors, and in industries that benefited directly from the expansion in military spending. Many of the traditional, trade-oriented sectors, such as steel and other "smokestack" industries, remained weak. As a result the pressure for protectionism remained strong. We discuss these protectionist pressures next.

These policies, along with other restrictive trade policies such as import duties, export subsidies, quotas, and prohibitions, led to a declining volume of world trade and brought no relief from the worldwide depression. Moreover, they contributed to a loss of faith in the economic system and in the ability of either economists or politicians to cope with economic crises.

To avoid a recurrence of the beggar-my-neighbor policies of the 1930s, trading nations designed some important institutions. The International Monetary Fund (IMF) was supposed to reduce the chances of competitive devaluations, and the General Agreement on Tariffs and Trade (GATT) was to reduce the chances of competitive increases in tariffs and other trade restrictions. These institutions worked well for over 30 years.

In 1980 the United States embarked on tight monetary policy, driving up U.S. interest rates and the external value of the U.S. dollar. Just as expansionary monetary policy in the face of world recession tends to "export unemployment" by leading to a depreciation of the home currency and reducing the demand for foreign goods, tight monetary policy in the face of the world inflation tends to "export inflation" by leading to an appreciation of the home currency and raising the demand for foreign goods.

Most other governments, notably Germany and Japan, were worried about the implications of this for their own inflation rates and reacted by also adopting tight monetary policies. This monetary tightness helped to lead the world into the serious recession of 1981 to 1983.

Under the extreme pressures of this difficult economic situation, beggar-my-neighbor pressures surfaced, and many governments found them hard to resist politically. Throughout the 1980s American voters have shown strong support for advocates of increased tariffs. Many countries negotiated unofficial quotas restricting the importation of Japanese cars. European agricultural protectionism nearly wrecked the GATT negotiations in December 1982, and have been the focus of considerable debate in the United States for the past few years. Less-developed countries sought covert ways of protecting their own infant industries and complained, with some justice, that the developed nations paid lip service to, rather than really acting on, the slogan of "trade not aid." It was clear that great pressure was being put on the whole postwar fabric designed to encourage trade and discourage beggar-my-neighbor policies. As the world recovered in the period from 1983 to 1986, some but not all of the pressures abated. But in the rest of the world in mid 1986, most observers were still worried about the threat of protectionist, beggar-my-neighbor policies, and the protectionist mood in the United States was stronger than ever.

Current Problems[1]

The Lack of an Alternative to the Dollar As a Reserve Currency

Governments operating dirty floats need reserves, just as do governments operating adjustable pegs.

The search for an adequate supply of reserves has continued unabated since the demise of the Bretton Woods system.

One major form in which reserves are held is U.S. dollars; another, and one that is growing in size, is the **special drawing rights (SDRs)** held with the IMF. First introduced in 1969, SDRs were designed to provide a supplement to existing reserve assets. The Special Drawing Account of the IMF was set up and kept separate from all other operations of

---

[1] The rest of this chapter can be omitted without loss of continuity.

the Fund. Each member country was assigned an SDR quota that was guaranteed in terms of a fixed gold value. Each country could use its quota to acquire an equivalent amount of convertible currencies from other participants. SDRs could be used without prior consultation with the Fund, but only to cope with balance-of-payments difficulties. SDR allocations grew from about $10 billion in 1970 to over $50 billion in 1985.

The commitment to lower inflation initiated by the Reagan administration in 1981 has restored some confidence in the U.S. dollar as a reserve asset. But overall these developments have not been seen as long-term solutions to the reserve problem. While it is possible that some other national currencies will take over the reserve role played by the U.S. dollar, this is not likely.

Why does the world not turn to an international paper reserve system based on SDRs or some similar creation? Such a solution has much support from academic economists, who see an appropriate international institution managing the supply of international currency to accommodate growth and to avoid inflation.

Critics of such a system—among them most of the world's central bankers—distrust the concept of an international paper currency, pointing out that few countries have managed their own money supplies effectively. However difficult the task of the U.S. Federal Reserve may be, the task of a World Reserve Bank would be more difficult. Further, private acceptance and use of the SDR has been virtually nonexistent, indicating the enormous difficulties inherent in creating a new currency.

Some who are skeptical of an international paper monetary standard have urged a return to the gold standard. This approach has critical disadvantages. In fact, the IMF and the U.S. government have at various times taken the lead in the attempt to "demonetize" gold completely.

For the moment at least, the world cannot agree on an international monetary reserve. Until it does, there will be crises whenever there is a desire to shift from one to another of the multiple sources of reserves: dollars, gold, SDRs, marks, francs, and yen. The speculative opportunities inherent in such a system remain large, as evidenced by the recent behavior of the price of gold shown in Figure 41-3.

FIGURE 41-3   The Price of Gold

Gold soared in value and proved highly volatile after convertibility of the dollar was suspended in 1973. The two devaluations of the U.S. dollar in terms of gold that occurred under the adjustable peg system are barely visible. (These devaluations are discussed in the appendix to this chapter.) The effects of speculation on the price of gold is seen in subsequent experience. The price of gold more than quadrupled from 1977 to 1979, reaching a peak of over $900 per ounce. It subsequently fell to around $300 by 1981 and then started to rise again.

The Impact of OPEC

One issue affecting the future payments system—and indeed the whole of international economic relations—is the variability of the price of oil.

Oil Price Increases

The OPEC cartel raised the price of oil dramatically in 1974 and again in 1979. In total these events led to a tenfold increase which generated an unprecedented imbalance in the international economic system in the form of a massive payments surplus for the oil producers and a corresponding deficit for the oil-importing countries. The excess purchasing power in the hands of oil producers has come to be called **petrodollars**. The cumulative stock of petrodollars may well have exceeded $500 billion. Petrodollars caused several different kinds of problems, some of them short term, others long term in nature.

Short-term problems of industrialized countries. Most petrodollars were eventually used for the purchase of consumption goods and services or investment goods from industrialized countries. But the oil-producing countries could not spend their oil revenues on goods and services as fast as they were earned in the late 1970s.[2] Nor could the industrialized oil-consuming countries produce the goods and services at the rate necessary for all the oil revenues to be spent without creating enormous inflationary pressures.

Thus, in the short term the OPEC countries had excess dollars. They also had an understandable desire to earn a return on those funds. One way was to invest their surplus revenues in the advanced industrialized nations, thereby returning on capital account the purchasing power extracted from the current accounts of the oil-importing nations. This creates many serious problems.

One of the most important concerns the havoc brought to foreign exchange markets when surplus oil funds are invested in liquid assets and switched between currencies in response to changes in interest rates and expected capital gains arising from possible exchange rate alterations. Surplus petrodollars can also be used speculatively, and many observers believe that a good part of the wild rise and sudden fall in gold prices in 1979 to 1980 was due to just such a use of petrodollars.

Short-term problems of underdeveloped countries. Consider an oil-importing country such as Kenya, for which the OPEC price increase turned a small trade surplus into a massive deficit overnight. The country was unable to generate revenues quickly enough to pay its oil bill, yet it could sharply decrease its use of oil only at the cost of a great slowdown in its domestic economy.

The IMF stepped in with loan arrangements to help countries most severely affected by the rising oil prices, the repayments of maturing loans were deferred, and the OPEC nations established a fund for short-term loans to such countries. Thus the purely short-term problems can be, and have been, solved through international cooperation and recognition of the need for accommodation on the part of creditor nations.

Oil Price Decreases

Many oil-exporting countries also borrowed heavily on the expectation of rising oil prices. In early 1983, however, OPEC had lost control of the market and the price of oil started to fall. In early 1986 the price of crude oil fell sharply from over $30 a barrel to around $12. Many international loans were threatened, including those made by large private banks to less-developed countries such as Mexico, which is heavily dependent on oil exports for repayment. The risk of a major default hangs over the system, and the IMF again finds itself facing the problem of rescheduling repayments of large international loans. (This is discussed further in Box 42-1 on pages 860–861.)

Nevertheless, lower oil prices generally contributed to a reduction of interest rates and an increase in economic growth among the industrialized countries. Both of these contribute to the long-run health

---

[2] There is a limit to the speed with which any country can absorb foreign goods, and many oil-producing countries were at that limit. Ships sometimes wait months to unload for want of dock capacity, unloaded goods sometimes sit in wharfside stockpiles for months, even years, for want of transportation capacity, and so on.

of the less-developed countries, whether oil exporting or not.

The Dollar and Protectionism

The dollar became overvalued during the period of
tight monetary policy that began in 1980. If a temporary overshooting of the exchange rate was all that
was involved in that overvaluation, the dollar would
have come down shortly thereafter. Many expected
it to do so, but in fact it remained high throughout
1981–1985.

Most observers believe that the dollar remained
high because this period witnessed enormous capital
inflows into the United States. These capital inflows
were partly a result of the record government budget
deficit. That deficit exceeded $200 billion in 1985
(over 5 percent of GNP); some of this was financed
by domestic savings, but much also had to be financed by foreign borrowing, thus resulting in capital inflows. The large capital inflows that occurred
were also responding to the combination of low inflation and relative prosperity in the United States,
which made the country a safe and profitable place
in which to invest.

As we saw in Chapter 40, equilibrium in the
foreign exchange market means that the capital inflow is *necessarily* matched by a current account deficit (see page 817). Only when these two are equal
will the demand for dollars by foreign investors
wishing to buy American capital assets be matched
by the supply of dollars by those Americans wishing
to import foreign goods and services. The large capital inflows thus meant that there also had to be a
current account deficit; from this perspective, the
high value of the dollar was simply the mechanism
by which the required current account deficit was
brought about.

The high value of the dollar placed American
firms that produce traded goods (i.e., goods for export and goods that face competition from imports)
at a cost/price disadvantage relative to foreign producers. Falling production, rising unemployment,
and many business failures resulted. These events,
combined with the increase in the demand for imports resulting from the fall in their relative price,

contributed to the growth of the current account
deficit.

As noted earlier in this chapter, in spite of the
vigorous expansion of the macro economy from
1984 through 1986, these traded goods sectors remained depressed; the recovery was focussed in the
non-traded sectors. Not surprisingly, the plight of
the import-competing and export sectors led to a call
for protection. Pressure was put on Japan, Germany,
and Canada to reduce their current account surpluses,
and the United States itself took many steps to curb
imports. Some steps were specific, such as the tariff
imposed in May 1986 on Canadian cedar shakes and
shingles. Further, at the beginning of 1987, many
protectionist trade bills were being considered in
both the Congress and the Senate, where the newly
elected Democratic majority was expressing strong
protectionist sentiments.

While the motivation for these protectionist measures was easy enough to understand, most economists felt that the measures were seriously misguided. First, the measures threatened to upset the
fabric of international trading relations and cooperation built up through multilateral negotiation during the post-World War II period. The growing
protectionist sentiment in Congress led to a split
between the administration and Congress; in late
1985 President Reagan, an avowed "free trader,"
warned of a "mindless stampede to protectionism."

Second, the measures were likely to be largely
ineffective in terms of their goal of reducing the
current account deficit. As we have seen, the current
account deficit was a necessary counterpart to the
capital inflows that the U.S. economy was experiencing. Unless the root causes of the capital inflows
were dealt with, the current account deficit would
persist with or without protectionist measures. If the
government deficit remained large, and if the United
States remained attractive to foreign investors, the
current account would have to remain in deficit in
order to match the capital inflows.

To see this very important point, assume that
import tariffs, surcharges, and quotas succeeded in
bringing the current account into balance, but that
people still wished to bring capital into the United
States. With a balanced current account, there would
not be anyone willing to supply the dollars to the
would-be capital importers, and consequently the

dollar would start to appreciate. This would then lead to a reduction in exports and an increase in imports until the original current account deficit was re-established.[3]

The United States as a debtor nation. Over the first three quarters of the twentieth century, a continual pattern of capital outflows and investment abroad led the United States to become the world's largest creditor nation. In the 1980s, as a result of the Reagan administration's massive budget deficits, so much capital was imported from abroad that by mid 1986 the cumulative effects of almost a century of capital outflows were reversed and the United States became a debtor nation. Further, in the absence of a dramatic reduction in the deficit relative to its 1986 level, by 1988 the United States will have become the world's largest debtor. Over the same period, persistent current account surpluses will have caused Japan to replace the United States as the world's largest creditor nation.

The fall in the dollar. In late 1985 and early 1986, the dollar fell dramatically against the Japanese yen and the German mark. This may have reflected the operation of "market fundamentals" returning the exchange rates towards their PPP values, but the fall was no doubt helped by the September 1985 "Plaza Accord" in which the leaders of the five major industrialized countries (France, Germany, Japan, the United Kingdom, and the United States) announced their commitment to policies which would bring about an orderly fall of the dollar. Further, the Gramm-Rudman-Hollings Bill (see Box 30-4 on page 593) led people to believe that the budget deficit, and hence the current account deficit, was going to be reduced; as a result, the dollar was expected to fall.

Despite the fall in the dollar in terms of the yen and the major European currencies, the United States' current account did not turn around right away. (The fall in the dollar may not have been as large as comparing it against these major currencies suggests—over this period it actually rose against some major trading partners such as Mexico and remained stable against others such as Canada—but there is little question that the dollar did depreciate considerably.) One reason for the lack of current account adjustment was that the government deficit remained large, and hence there remained a need for capital inflows. Further, there are lags, due to contracts and other inertias, before exports start to rise and imports fall following a depreciation. But as foreigners discover that American goods are now cheaper, and Americans learn that imports are now more expensive, there will be some response of the current account, although it may be years before the full response is felt.

The permanent harm to the world's trading arrangements from this experience cannot yet be assessed. Protectionist measures are easiser to introduce than to remove. The irony is that the United States led the world in pressing for trade liberalization for 30 years after World War II, and as a result laid the ground work for the prosperity built on the growth in world trade that characterized the postwar period. Now the United States is a leader in the surge to protectionism. Whether the fall in the dollar and any subsequent improvement in the current account would prove sufficient to stem the protectionist tide was a major unresolved question at the beginning of 1987.

The Challenge for the Next Ten Years

The 1970s witnessed the replacement of a system of managed fixed exchange rates by a system of managed flexible exchange rates. The problems of the latter may have been revealed by the events of the decade, but they cannot be said to have been solved. Officials understand the need to devise workable guidelines for managing flexible rates and to enhance cooperation more generally.

The Management of Exchange Rates

Managing floating rates poses several potential problems for the international monetary system. Three key problems are discussed next:

---

[3] Of course, to the extent that the tariffs create revenue and therefore reduce the government deficit, more domestic private saving would be available to finance domestic investment, and capital inflows and the current account both could be reduced correspondingly.

BOX 41-3

Proposals for International Monetary Reform, 1986

The high degree of variability and persistent misalignment of exchange rates that plagued the flexible exchange rate system for over the first decade of its operation led in the mid 1980s to a number of proposals for reform.

Fixed Exchange Rates

Some observers advocated a return to fixed exchange rates. In fact, some even wanted the new system to be based on gold or some other group of commodities. This proposal was apparently motivated by the belief that *ruling out* exchange rate changes would allow some of the problems noted in the text to be avoided.

This proposal has not received wide support among economists since most believe that the flaws that led to the demise of the Bretton Woods system were indeed fatal, and that a system of fixed exchange rates would have performed worse, not better, than flexible exchange rates did in the face of the shocks that disturbed the world economy in the decade since Bretton Woods was abandoned. Proponents of fixed exchange rates counter that many of those shocks were in fact the result of bad policies that were made possible only by the freedom for independent domestic policy that exists under flexible exchange rates. They argue that the discipline imposed by fixed exchange rates would have improved the performance of policy over the period.

Target Exchange Rate Zones

Another proposal was for establishing *target zones* for exchange rates. Some advocates proposed "hard" zones, that is, narrowly defined zones with automatic intervention required whenever exchange rates moved outside the defined limits. This amounts to a fixed exchange rate system, and, not surprisingly, debate on this type of proposal paralleled that on fixed exchange rates.

Alternatively, some advocates proposed "soft" zones, defined more loosely and departures from which simply served as a signal to authorities that some policy reaction might be appropriate. While these soft zones were more acceptable to some observers, many expressed a good deal of skepticism about what such weak arrangements might accomplish.

Objective Indicators

Other participants in the debate promoted the idea that "objective indicators" be calculated to provide a signal to authorities when policies become mutually inconsistent. Such indicators, which might involve measures of performance such as real growth and inflation as well as policy measures such as money growth rates and fiscal deficits, are an extension of the soft zone for exchange rate targets in that they serve merely as an indicator and do not themselves trigger automatic policy responses.

While many commentators were sympathetic to this idea, there is little consensus as to how to calculate such indicators and how exactly they might work to avoid the problems in the system. Indeed, proponents of all these reforms concede that the high variability and persistent misalignment of exchange rates are really just symptoms of the real problems in the international economy; and that any real reform must address the root causes of such problems. While many of those root causes are beyond the control of policymakers, some of the problems result from undesirable economic policies in the industrialized countries. Recognizing this, Western leaders attending the Economic Summit held in Tokyo in May 1986 reached an agreement to establish objective indicators in an effort to improve international cooperation in formulating economic policies.

Inconsistent exchange rate policies. Different governments may try to fix their exchange rates at levels that are inconsistent with each other. For example, if the Fed is targeting that the U.S. dollar should be worth 150 yen while the Bank of Japan is targeting that the yen should be worth U.S. $0.005, both of these policies cannot succeed. If both banks persist in trying to meet such inconsistent targets, they can destabilize exchange markets.

Competitive devaluations. Countries may get involved in bouts of competitive devaluations similar to those that sometimes destabilized exchange markets in the 1920s and 1930s. For example, if one country devalues its currency in order to get a competitive advantage for its exports and other countries respond by devaluing their currencies, the rounds of successive devaluations will destabilize the exchange market without giving any country's exports a permanent advantage.

Destabilizing speculation. Speculative behavior can destabilize exchange markets. Before the system of floating exchange rates was adopted, many economists felt that rates would stay fairly close to their equilibrium values. Economists expected that speculators would then stabilize rates even further by buying currencies that seemed temporarily low in price and selling those that seemed temporarily high. In that event, however, very large and persistent deviations of exchange rates from the long run equilibrium values occurred. This left speculators less clear on which way a particular rate was likely to go in the near future. When a particular currency started to fall in value, speculators might conclude that a large and persistent fall was just beginning. In this case their rush to sell the currency before its expected further fall would bring the fall about.

To help avoid these problems, the IMF has issued guidelines for exchange rate management. The guidelines emphasize that exchange rate policy is a matter for international consultation and surveillance by the IMF and that intervention practices by individual central banks should be based on three principles: (1) Exchange authorities should prevent sudden and disproportionate short-term movements in exchange rates and ensure an orderly adjustment to

longer-term pressures. (2) In consultation with the IMF, countries should establish a target zone for the medium-term values of their exchange rates and keep the actual rate within that target zone. (3) Countries should recognize that exchange rate management involves joint responsibilities and is not just the responsibility of the individual country in question.

The experiences of the 1970s have underlined one of the most important unsolved problems of managed floating rates: coping with the massive volume of short-term funds that can be switched rapidly between financial centers. Short-term capital flows forced the abandonment of exchange rates that had been agreed on in 1971 and have often caused violent fluctuations in floating rates since then. Severe "currency misalignments" have arisen and persisted, rendering uncompetitive on world markets the export- and import-competing sectors in countries with overvalued currencies, while creating enormous profit opportunities in countries with undervalued currencies.

Capital flows often prevent the quick return of exchange rates to their PPP values. Various attempts have been made to limit such capital flows. Italy has adopted a two-tier foreign exchange market, with one price for foreign exchange to finance current account transactions and another price (and another set of controls) for foreign exchange to finance capital movements. Germany has used direct controls on overseas borrowing. There has also been a considerable extension of arrangements under which central banks in surplus countries lend the funds they are accumulating back to central banks in deficit countries. Through such arrangements, the ability of banks to maintain stable exchange rates in the face of short-term speculative flights of capital is enhanced.

The major problem in managing speculative flows is to identify them accurately. Experience suggests that exchange rate management can smooth out temporary fluctuations but cannot resist underlying trends in equilibrium rates caused by relative inflation rates, structural changes, and persistent nonspeculative capital flows. In day-to-day management it is not always easy to distinguish among them.

Nevertheless, the excessive variability and persistent misalignment of exchange rates that continued to plague the flexible exchange rate system led to a number of proposals for reform. These are discussed further in Box 41-3 on page 836.

The Need for Cooperation

One of the most impressive aspects of the international payments history of the last 30 years has been the steady rise of effective international cooperation. When the gold standard collapsed and the Great Depression overwhelmed the countries of the world, "every nation for itself" was the rule of the day. Rising tariffs, competitive exchange rate devaluations, and all forms of beggar-my-neighbor policies abounded.

After World War II the countries of the world cooperated in bringing the Bretton Woods system and the IMF into being. The system itself was far from perfect, and it finally broke down as a result of its own internal contradictions. But the international cooperation that was necessary to set up the system survived. The joint cooperative actions of central banks allowed them to weather speculative crises in the 1970s that would have forced them to devalue their currencies in the 1950s.

Thus the collapse of Bretton Woods did not plunge the world into the same chaos that followed the breakdown of the gold standard. The world was also better able to cope with the terrible strains caused by the sharp rise in oil prices in the 1970s. Of course, enormous oil-related problems remain, and they are matters for continuing international dialogue. Further, it is not yet clear how well the world economy will weather the upsurge of American protectionism of the mid 1980s. Prior to this upsurge, the United States provided essential leadership in working for lower restrictions on international trade. It is a serious question, then, whether or not other nations will now follow the American lead to *increased* protectionism, and thus join in a mutually destructive round of competitive tariff increases and other restrictions.

Whatever the problems of the future, the world has a better chance of solving them—or even just learning to live with them—when its countries cooperate through the IMF and other international organizations than when each country seeks its own solution without concern for the interests of others.

Summary

1. Various systems of international monetary arrangements have been tried. All involve aspects of the two extremes of fixed exchange rates and flexible exchange rates.

2. Under fixed exchange rates the central bank intervenes in the foreign exchange market to maintain the exchange rate at or near an announced par value. To do this the central bank must hold sufficient stocks of foreign exchange reserves. Reserves have historically been held in the form of gold or reserve currencies, particularly the U.S. dollar. The SDR is a relatively new international paper money meant to provide additional international reserves linked neither to gold nor to the U.S. dollar.

3. Any fixed exchange rate system will face three major problems: (1) providing sufficient international reserves, (2) adjusting to long-term trends in receipts and payments, and (3) handling periodic speculative crises.

4. Under a system of flexible, or floating, exchange rates, the exchange rate is market-determined by supply and demand for the currency.

5. Since their adoption in the mid 1970s, flexible exchange rates have fluctuated substantially. As a result central banks have often inter-

vened to stabilize the fluctuations. Thus the present system is called a managed, or dirty, float.

6. Fluctuations in exchange rates can be understood as fluctuations around a trend value that is determined by the purchasing power parity (PPP) rate. The PPP rate adjusts in response to differences in national inflation rates.

7. Current problems include the need to find an adequate reserve not tied to a national currency, to accommodate both the short-term and the longer-term impact of OPEC, and to develop rules for managing flexible exchange rates. A continuing commitment to international cooperation will help the world cope with these problems.

Topics for Review

Fixed and flexible exchange rates
Managed floats
Adjustable peg
Bretton Woods system
International Monetary Fund
Exchange rate overshooting
Petrodollars

Discussion Questions

1. As the 1986 elections loomed close, Congress passed a number of measures designed to reduce the value of the current account deficit by restricting imports. If imports had actually fallen, what would have happened? Why did many economists argue that this result was unlikely as long as the government budget deficit remained large?

2. The U.S. dollar is no longer convertible into gold because of a change in U.S. policy. Does this lack of conversion make the dollar any less useful as an international medium of exchange?

3. Are Americans benefited or hurt when the U.S. dollar is the standard form of international reserves?

4. "Under a flexible exchange rate system no country need suffer unemployment, for if its prices are low enough there will be more than enough demand to keep its factories and farms fully occupied." The evidence suggests that flexible rates have not generally eliminated unemployment. Can you explain why? Can changing exchange rates ever cure unemployment?

5. The OPEC oil price increases during the 1970s caused grave problems in international payments and increased the need for IMF loans. Why did market adjustment of exchange rates not solve the problem?

6. In November 1985 the five major industrialized countries (G-5) met and agreed that a major realignment of the world's currencies was appropriate. Why? What did they do about it? What was the result?

7. What role in international payments does or did gold play under (a) the gold standard, (b) the adjustable peg Bretton Woods system, and (c) the present system?

8. Might a person who regards inflation as the number one economic danger favor a return to the pre-1914 gold standard? Would you predict non-inflationary results if in order to restore the gold standard, the price of gold had to be set at U.S. $1,600 per ounce, either all at once or gradually?

The Gold Standard and the Bretton Woods System

Two episodes with fixed exchange rates were experienced in the twentieth century. Each ultimately failed. The gold standard, whose origins are as old as currency itself, was used until the late 1920s and early 1930s. The Bretton Woods system, which was the only payments system ever to be designed and established by conscious action, was born out of World War II and collapsed a little less than 30 years later. Their histories are instructive, not the least because many people continue to propose returning to one or the other of these systems.

The Gold Standard

The gold standard was not *designed;* it just happened. It arose out of the general acceptance of gold as the commodity to be used as money. In most countries paper currency was freely convertible into gold at a fixed rate. In 1914 the U.S. dollar was worth 0.053 standard ounces of gold, while the British pound sterling was worth 0.257 standard ounces. This meant that the pound was worth 4.86 times as much as the dollar in terms of gold, thus making £1 worth U.S. $4.86. (In practice the exchange rate fluctuated within narrow limits set by the cost of shipping gold.) As long as all countries were on the gold standard, a person in one country could be sure of being able to make payments to a person in another.

The Gold Flow, Price Level Mechanism

The gold standard was supposed to maintain a balance of international payments by causing adjustments in price levels within individual countries. Consider a country that had a balance-of-payments deficit because the value of its imports (i.e., purchases) from other countries exceeded the value of its exports (i.e., sales) to other countries. The demand for foreign exchange would exceed the supply on this country's foreign exchange market. Some people who wished to make foreign payments would need to convert their domestic currency into gold and ship the gold. Therefore, some people in a surplus country would receive gold in payment for exports. They would deposit this to their credit and accept claims on gold—in terms of convertible paper money or bank deposits—in return. Thus deficit countries would be losing gold, while surplus countries would be gaining it.

Under the gold standard, the whole money supply was linked to the supply of gold. The international movements of gold would therefore lead to a fall in the money supply in the deficit country and a rise in the surplus country.[1] If full employment prevails, changes in the domestic money supply will cause changes in domestic price levels. Deficit countries would thus have falling price levels, while surplus countries would have rising price levels. The exports of deficit countries would become relatively cheaper, while those of surplus countries would become relatively more expensive. The resulting changes in quantities bought and sold would move the balance of payments toward an equilibrium position.

Actual Experience of the Gold Standard

The half century before World War I was the heyday of the gold standard. During this relatively trouble-free period, the adjustment mechanism described above seemed to work well.

Subsequent research has suggested, however, that the gold standard succeeded during the period mainly because it was not called on to do much work. No

---

[1] When the person who received gold deposited it in a bank, the bank would be in the position of the Bank in Table 31-2 on page 623, and a multiple expansion of deposit money would ensue.

major trading country found itself with a serious and persistent balance-of-payments deficit, so no major country was called upon to restore equilibrium through a large change in its domestic price level. Short-run fluctuations were ironed out either by movements of short-run capital in response to changes in interest rates or by changes in national income and employment.

In the 1920s the gold standard was called on to do a major job. It failed utterly, and it was abandoned. How did this happen? During World War I most belligerent countries had suspended convertibility of currency (i.e., they went off the gold standard). Most countries suffered major inflations, but the degree of inflation differed from country to country. As we have seen, this will lead to changes in the equilibrium exchange rates.

After the war countries returned to the gold standard (i.e., they restored convertibility of their currencies into gold). For reasons of prestige, many insisted on returning at the prewar rates. This meant that some countries' goods were overpriced and other countries' goods were underpriced. Large deficits and surpluses in the balance of payments inevitably appeared, and the adjustment mechanism required that price levels should change in each of the countries in order to restore equilibrium. Exchange rates were not adjusted, and price levels changed very slowly. By the onset of the Great Depression, equilibrium price levels had not yet been attained. The financial chaos brought on by the depression destroyed the existing payments system.

Major Disabilities of a Gold Standard

One may ask whether an altered gold standard, based on more realistic exchange rates, might not have succeeded. While some modern economists, notably Robert Mundell of Columbia University, think it would, most believe the gold standard suffered from key weaknesses.

Like any other exchange rate system, it required a mechanism for orderly adjustment to changes in the supply and demand for a nation's currency. The price adjustment process worked too slowly and too imperfectly to cope with large and persistent disequilibrium.

Furthermore, gold as the basis for an international money supply suffered several special disadvantages. These included a limited supply that could not be expanded as rapidly as increases in the volume of world trade required, an uneven distribution of existing and potential new gold supplies among the nations of the world, and a large and frequently volatile speculative demand for gold during periods of crisis. These factors could cause large, disruptive variations in the supply of gold available for international monetary purposes.

The Bretton Woods System

The one lesson that everyone thought had been learned from the 1930s was that a system of either freely fluctuating exchange rates or fixed rates with easily accomplished devaluations was a sure route to disaster. In order to achieve a system of orderly exchange rates that would facilitate the free flow of trade following World War II, representatives of most of the countries that had participated in the alliance against Germany, Italy, and Japan met at Bretton Woods, New Hampshire, in 1944. In the words of Charles Kindleberger of MIT, the Bretton Woods meeting was "the biggest constitution-writing exercise ever to occur in international monetary relations."

The Bretton Woods system had three objectives: to create a set of rules that would maintain fixed exchange rates in the face of short-term fluctuations; to guarantee that changes in exchange rates would occur only in the face of "fundamental" deficits or surpluses in the balance of payments; and to ensure that when such changes did occur, they would not spark a series of competitive devaluations. The basic characteristic of the system was that U.S. dollars held by foreign monetary authorities were made directly convertible into gold at a price fixed by the U.S. government, while foreign governments fixed the prices at which their currencies were convertible into U.S. dollars. It was this characteristic that made the system a **gold exchange standard.** Gold was the ultimate reserve, but other currencies were held as reserves because directly or indirectly they could be exchanged for gold.

As we saw in the text, a system with a rate that

is pegged against short-term fluctuations but that can be adjusted from time to time is called an adjustable peg system. In order to maintain the convertibility of their currencies at fixed exchange rates, the monetary authorities of each country had to be ready to buy and sell their currency in foreign exchange markets to offset imbalances at the pegged rates.[2]

In order to be able to support the exchange market, the monetary authorities had to have reserves of acceptable foreign exchange. In the Bretton Woods system the authorities held reserves of gold and claims on key currencies, mainly the American dollar and the British pound sterling. When a country's currency was in excess supply, its authorities would sell dollars, sterling, or gold. When a country's currency was in excess demand, its authorities would buy dollars or sterling. If they then wished to increase their gold reserves, they would use the dollars to purchase gold from the Fed, thus depleting the U.S. gold stock.

The problem for the United States was to have enough gold to maintain fixed-price convertibility of the dollar into gold as demanded by foreign monetary authorities. The problem for all other countries was to maintain convertibility (on either a restricted or unrestricted basis) between their currency and the U.S. dollar at a fixed rate of exchange.

Problems of the Adjustable Peg System

Here we see how the three problems of the Bretton Woods system discussed in the text actually worked out in the period after World War II.

Reserves to accommodate short-term fluctuations.
It is generally believed that the average size and frequency of the gaps between demand and supply on the foreign exchange market created when central banks peg their exchange rates will increase as the volume of international payments increases. Since there was a strong upward trend in the volume of overall international payments, there was also a

strong upward trend in the demand for foreign exchange reserves.

The ultimate reserve in the Bretton Woods system was gold. The use of gold as a reserve caused two serious problems during the 1960s and early 1970s. First, the world's supply of monetary gold did not grow fast enough to provide adequate reserves for the expanding volume of trade. As a result of the fixed price of gold, rising costs of production, and rising commercial uses, the world's stock of monetary gold during the 1960s was rising at less than 2 percent per year, while trade was growing at nearly 10 percent per year. Gold, which had been 66 percent of the total monetary reserves in 1959, was only 40 percent in 1970, and had fallen to 30 percent by 1972. Over this period reserve holdings of dollars and sterling rose sharply. Clearly, the gold backing needed to maintain convertibility of these currencies was becoming increasingly inadequate.

Second, the country whose currency is convertible into gold must maintain sufficient reserves to ensure convertibility. During the 1960s the United States lost substantial gold reserves to other countries that had acquired dollar claims through their balance-of-payments surpluses with the United States. By the late 1960s the reduction in U.S. reserves had been sufficiently large to undermine confidence in America's continued ability to maintain dollar convertibility.

Adjusting to long-term disequilibria.
The second characteristic problem of a fixed rate system is the adjustment to long-term disequilibria that develops because of secular shifts in the demands for and supplies of foreign exchange.

These disequilibria did slowly develop. At first they led to a series of speculative crises as people expected a realignment of exchange rates to occur. Finally they led to a series of realignments that started in 1967. Each occurred amid quite spectacular flows of speculative funds that thoroughly disorganized normal trade and payments.

Speculative crises.
The adjustable peg system often leads to situations in which speculators are presented with one-way bets. In these disequilibria situations, there is an increasing chance of an exchange rate

---

[2] The exchange rates were not quite fixed; they were permitted to vary by 1 percent on either side of their par values. Later the bands of permitted fluctuation were widened to 2.25 percent on either side of par.

adjustment in one direction, with little or no chance of a movement in the other direction. Speculators then have an opportunity to secure a large potential gain with no corresponding potential for loss. Speculative crises associated with the need to adjust to fundamental disequilibria were the downfall of the system.

Collapse of the Bretton Woods System

The Bretton Woods system worked reasonably well for nearly 20 years. Then it was beset by a series of crises of ever-increasing severity that reflected the system's underlying weaknesses.

Speculation against the British pound.   Throughout the 1950s and 1960s, the British economy was more inflation prone than the U.S. economy, and the British balance of payments was generally in deficit. Holders of sterling thus had reason to worry that the British government might not be able to keep sterling convertible into dollars at a fixed rate. When these fears grew strong, there would be speculative rushes to sell sterling before it was devalued.

The crises in the 1960s were of this kind. By the mid 1960s it was clear to everyone that the pound was seriously overvalued. Finally, in 1967 it was devalued in the midst of a serious speculative crisis. Many other countries with balance-of-payments deficits followed, bringing about the first major round of adjustments in the pegged rates since 1949.

Speculation against the American dollar.   The U.S. dollar was not devalued in 1967. The lower prices of those currencies that were devalued in 1967 plus the increasing Vietnam War expenditures combined to produce a growing deficit in the American balance of payments. This deficit led to the belief that the dollar itself was becoming seriously overvalued. People rushed to buy gold because a devaluation of the U.S. dollar would take the form of raising its gold price. (Under the Bretton Woods system, the dollar was devalued by raising the official price at which the Fed would convert dollars into gold.)

The first break in the Bretton Woods system came in 1968 when the major trading countries were forced to stop pegging the free-market price of gold. Speculative pressure to buy gold could not be re-

sisted, and from that point there were two prices of gold: the official price at which monetary authorities could settle their debts with each other by transferring gold and the free-market price, determined by the forces of private demand and supply independent of any intervention by central banks. The free-market price quickly rose far above the official U.S. price of $35 an ounce (see Figure 41-3).

Once the free-market price of gold was allowed to be determined independently of the official price, speculation against the dollar shifted to those currencies that were clearly undervalued relative to the dollar.[3] The German mark and the Japanese yen were particularly popular targets, and during periods of crisis billions and billions of dollars flowed into speculative holdings of these currencies. The ability of central banks to maintain pegged exchange rates in the face of such vast flights of funds was in question; on several occasions all exchange markets had to be closed for periods of up to a week.

Devaluation of the dollar.   By 1971 the American authorities had concluded that the dollar would have to be devalued. This uncovered a problem, inherent in the Bretton Woods system, that had so far gone virtually unnoted. Because the system required each foreign country to fix its exchange rate against the dollar, the American authorities could not independently fix their exchange rate against other currencies.[4]

But when the U.S. economy began to inflate rapidly, it became necessary to devalue the U.S. dollar relative to most other currencies. Any other country in this situation would merely unilaterally devalue its currency. But the only way that the required U.S. devaluation could be brought about was for all

---

[3] When the free-market price of gold was held the same as the official price, a devaluation of the dollar entailed a rise in the free-market price—and hence profit for all holders of gold. Once the free-market price was left to be determined by the forces of private demand and supply independent of any central bank intervention, there was no reason to believe that a rise in the official price of gold would affect the (much higher) free-market price. Speculators against the dollar then had to hold other currencies whose price was sure to rise against the dollar in the event of the dollar's being devalued.

[4] If, for example, the British authorities pegged the pound sterling at $2.40, as they did in 1967, then the dollar was pegged at £0.417, and the Fed could not independently decide on another rate. Similar considerations applied to all other currencies.

other countries to agree to revalue their currencies relative to the dollar.

Prompted by continuing speculation against the dollar, President Nixon suspended gold convertibility of the dollar in August 1971. He also announced the intention of the United States to achieve a de facto devaluation of the dollar by persuading those nations whose balance of payments were in surplus to allow their rates to float upward against the dollar.

By ending the gold convertibility of the dollar, the U.S. government brought the gold exchange standard aspect of the Bretton Woods system officially to an end. The fixed exchange rate aspect of the system lasted a little longer.

The immediate response to the announced intention of devaluing the dollar was a speculative run against that currency. The crisis was so severe that for the second time that year foreign exchange markets were closed throughout Europe. When the markets re-opened after a week, several countries allowed their rates to float. The Japanese, however, announced their intention of retaining their existing rate. Despite severe Japanese controls, $4 billion in speculative funds managed to find its way into yen in the last two weeks of August, and the Japanese were forced to abandon their fixed rate policy by allowing the yen to float upward.

After some hard bargaining, an agreement among the major trading nations was signed at the Smithsonian Institution in Washington, D.C., in December 1971. The main element of the agreement was that all countries consented to a 7.9 percent devaluation of the dollar against their currencies.

The de facto dollar standard. Following the Smithsonian agreements, the world was on a de facto **dollar standard**. Foreign monetary authorities held their reserves in the form of dollars and settled their international debts with dollars. But the dollar was not convertible into gold or anything else. The ultimate value of the dollar was given not by gold, but by the American goods, services, and assets that dollars could be used to purchase.

One major problem with such a system is that the kind of American inflation that upset the Bretton Woods system is no less upsetting to a dollar standard because the real purchasing power value of the world's dollar reserves is eroded by such an inflation.

The final breakdown of fixed exchange rates. The Smithsonian agreements did not lead to a new period of international payments stability. This doomed the hope that a de facto dollar standard could provide the basis for an international payments system free of crises and devaluations.

The U.S. inflation continued unchecked, and the U.S. balance of payments never returned to the relatively satisfactory position that had been maintained throughout the 1960s. Within a year of the agreements speculators began to believe that a further realignment of rates was necessary. In January 1973 speculative movements of capital once again occurred. In February the United States proposed a further 11 percent devaluation of the dollar. This was to be accomplished by raising the official price of gold to $42.22 an ounce and by not keeping other currencies tied to the dollar at the old rates. Intense speculative activity followed the announcement.

Five member countries of the European Economic Community then decided to stabilize their currencies against each other, but to let them float together against the dollar. This joint float was called the *snake*. Norway and Sweden later joined the snake with this arrangement. The other EEC countries (Ireland, Italy, and the United Kingdom) and Japan announced their intention to allow their currencies to float in value. In June 1972 the Bank of England abandoned the de facto dollar standard with the announcement that it had "temporarily" abandoned its commitment to support sterling at a fixed par value against the U.S. dollar. The events of 1973 led "temporarily" to become "indefinitely."

Fluctuations in exchange rates were severe. By early July the snake currencies had appreciated about 30 percent against the dollar, but by the end of the year they had nearly returned to their February values.

The dollar devaluation formally took effect in October. Most industrialized countries maintained the nominal values of their currencies in terms of gold and SDRs, thereby appreciating them in terms of the U.S. dollar by 11 percent. The devaluation quickly became redundant, for despite attempts to restore fixed rates, the drift to flexible rates had become irresistible by the end of 1973.

Economic Growth and Comparative Systems

42

Growth and the
Less-Developed Countries

It is only about 10,000 years since human beings became food *producers* rather than food *gatherers*. It is only within the last few centuries that a significant proportion of the world's population could look forward to anything but a hard struggle to wrest subsistence from a reluctant nature. The concept of leisure, combined with high consumption standards as a right to be enjoyed by all, is new in human history.

The Uneven Pattern of Development

There are more than 4.5 billion people alive today, but the wealthy parts of the world—where people work no more than 40 or 50 hours per week, enjoy substantial leisure, and have a level of consumption at or above *half* of that attained by the citizens of the United States—contain less than 15 percent of the world's population. Many of the rest struggle for subsistence. Many exist on a level at or below that enjoyed by peasants in ancient Egypt or Babylon.

Data on per capita income levels throughout the world (as in Table 42-1) cannot be accurate down to the last $100.[1] Nevertheless, such data do reflect enormous real differences in living standards that no statistical discrepancies can hide. The *development gap*—the discrepancy between the standards of living in countries at either end of the distribution—is real and large.

There are many ways to look at inequality of income distribution among the world's population. One way is a Lorenz curve, as in Figure 42-1 on page 850. The more the curve bends away from the straight, 45° line, the greater is the inequality in income distribution. The Lorenz curve of income distribution among people in the United States gives perspective on the disparity in income among countries. It is much closer to equality than the world distribution.

Another way of looking at inequality is to look at the geographical distribution of income per capita, as in Figure 42-2 on page 851. Recent political discussions of income distribution have distinguished between richer and poorer nations as "North" versus "South." The map reveals why.

---

[1] There are many problems in comparing national incomes across countries. For example, home-grown food is vitally important to living standards in underdeveloped countries, but it is excluded, or at best imperfectly included, in the national income statistics of most countries. So is the contribution of a warm climate.

TABLE 42-1   Income and Population Differences Among Groups of Countries, 1983

Classification (based on gross domestic product per capita in 1980 U.S. dollars) Group level	(1) Number of countries[a]	(2) GDP (billions)	(3) Population (millions)	(4) GDP per capita	(5) Percentage of world GDP	(6) Percentage of world population	(7) Growth rate[b]
I $400 or less	15	$ 548	2,099	$ 241	4.6	49.8	1.3
II $401–1,000	18	274	421	690	2.3	10.0	0.1
III $1,001–5,000	31	1,619	635	2,420	13.4	15.1	1.7
IV $5,001–10,000	13	4,175	613	6,794	34.7	14.5	2.0
V More than $10,000	16	5,417	448	13,251	45.0	10.6	1.4

Source: IMF International Financial Statistics Yearbook, 1985. Handbook of Economic Statistics, 1984.

[a] Countries for which data are not available, and are therefore not represented in the table, account for about 9 percent of the world's population and are mostly in the poorer categories.

[b] Average annual percentage rate of growth of real GDP per capita, 1975–1983.

Over half of the world's population lives in poverty. Many of the very poorest are in countries that have the lowest growth rates and thus fall ever farther behind. The unequal distribution of the world's income is shown in columns 5 and 6. Groups I and II, which have about 60 percent of world population, earn less than 10 percent of world income. Groups IV and V, with 25 percent of world's population, earn 80 percent of world income. Column 7 shows that the poorest countries are not closing the gap in income between rich and poor countries.

The Consequences of Underdevelopment

The consequences of low income levels can be severe. In a rich country such as the United States variations in rainfall are reflected in farm output and farm income. In poor countries such as those of the Sahel area of Africa variations in rainfall are reflected in the death rate. In these countries, many live so close to subsistence that slight fluctuations in the food supply bring death by starvation to large numbers. Other less dramatic characteristics of poverty include inadequate diet, poor health, short life expectancy, illiteracy, and, importantly, an attitude of helpless resignation to the caprice of nature.

For these reasons, reformers in underdeveloped countries, now often called **less-developed countries (LDCs)**, feel a sense of urgency not felt by their counterparts in rich countries.[2] Yet, as the first two rows of Table 42-1 show:

[2] The terminology of development is often confusing. *Underdeveloped, less developed,* and *developing* do not mean the same thing in ordinary English, yet each has been used to describe the same phenomenon. For the most part we shall refer to the underdeveloped countries as the *less-developed countries,* or LDCs. Some of them are making progress, that is, developing; others are not.

The development gap for the very poorest countries has been widening.

As we will see, this is a problem of both output and population. It is also an international political problem.

Incentives for Development

Obviously underdevelopment is nothing new. Concern with it as a remediable condition, however, is recent; it has become a compelling policy issue only within the present century. One incentive behind this new attention to development has been the apparent success of planned programs of "crash" development, of which the Soviet experience is the most remarkable and the Chinese the most recent (see Chapter 43). Leaders in other countries ask, If they can do it, why not us?

Demonstration effects should not be underestimated. It has been said that the real secret of the atomic bomb was that it *could* be made, not how. Much the same is true of economic development. Observing other developing countries, people see

FIGURE 42-1   Lorenz Curves Showing Inequalities Among the Nations of the World and Within the United States

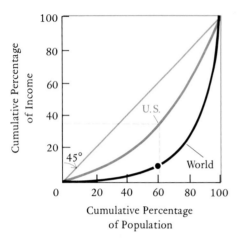

There is much less inequality in the distribution of income within the United States than among all the nations of the world. In a Lorenz curve a wholly equal distribution of income is represented by the 45° line: 20 percent of the population would have 20 percent of the income, 50 percent of the population would have 50 percent of the income, and so on. The curve for the world indicates a very unequal distribution of income. For example, 60 percent of the world's population live in countries that earn only 10 percent of the world's income, as shown by the black dot. Contrast this with the distribution of income within the United States. The poorest 60 percent of the American population earn 36 percent of the nation's income. This is not equality, but it is much less unequal than the world distribution.

that it is possible to achieve better lives for themselves and their children. It is bad enough to be poor, but it is doubly galling to be poor when others are escaping poverty.

A second incentive for development has come from the willingness of developed countries to aid less-developed countries. We shall discuss such programs and their motivation later.

A third incentive for development results from the emergence of a relatively cohesive bloc of LDCs within the United Nations. The bloc is attempting to use political power to achieve economic ends.

What are the causes of underdevelopment, and how may they be overcome?

Barriers to Economic Development

Income per capita grows when aggregate income grows faster than population. Many forces can impede such growth.

Population and Natural Resources

Rapid Population Growth

Population growth is a central problem of economic development. If population grows as quickly as national income, per capita income does not increase. Many less-developed countries have rates of population growth that are nearly as large as their rates of growth of gross domestic product (GDP).[3] As a result, their standards of living are barely higher than they were a hundred or even a thousand years ago. They have made appreciable gains in aggregate income, but most of the gains have been literally eaten up by the increasing population. This is shown in Table 42-2 on page 852.

The population problem has led economists to talk about the *critical minimum effort* that is required not merely to increase capital, but to increase it fast enough so that the increase in output outpaces the increase in population. When population control is left to nature, nature often solves it in a cruel way. Population increases until many are forced to live at a subsistence level; further population growth is halted by famine, pestilence, and plague. This grim possibility was perceived early in the history of economics by Thomas Malthus.

In some ways the population problem is more severe today than it was even fifty years ago because advances in medicine and in public health have brought sharp and sudden decreases in death rates. It is ironic that much of the compassion shown by

[3] GDP is output produced in a country and differs from GNP as a result of such things as foreign interest or dividends paid or received.

FIGURE 42-2   Countries of the World, Classified by Per Capita GNP, 1985

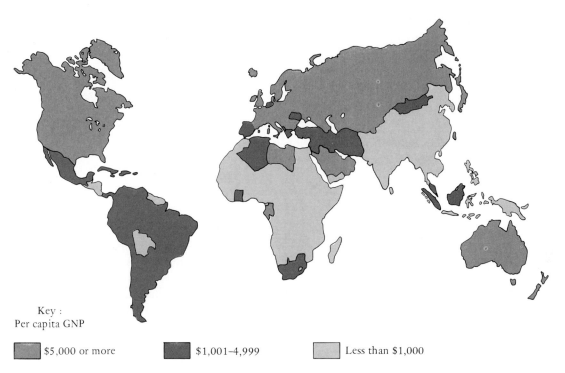

Key :
Per capita GNP

$5,000 or more $1,001–4,999   Less than $1,000

There is a sharp geographical division between "North" and "South" in the level of income per capita. The nations of the world are classified here according to three levels of measured per capita GNP. The poorest group, shown in light gray, represents 31 percent of the world's population. The middle group, shown in dark gray, represents about 41 percent of world population. The wealthiest group, shown in color, includes all of North America, Europe, the Soviet Union, and Japan and represents only 25 percent of the world's population. Areas in white indicate no data available. See Table 42-1 for more detail.

wealthier nations for the poor and underprivileged people of the world has traditionally taken the form of improving their health, thereby doing little to avert their poverty. We praise the medical missionaries who brought modern medicine to the tropics, but the elimination of malaria has doubled population growth in Sri Lanka. Cholera, once a killer, is now largely under control. No one argues against controlling disease, but other steps must also be taken if the child who survives the infectious illnesses of infancy is not to die of starvation in early adulthood.

Figure 42-3 illustrates actual and projected world population growth. The population problem is not limited to underdeveloped countries, but about seven-eighths of the expected growth in the world's population is in Africa, Asia, and Latin America, those areas where underdevelopment is the rule rather than the exception.

Insufficient Natural Resources

A country with ample fertile land and a large supply of easily developed resources will find growth in

TABLE 42-2   The Relation of Population Growth to Per Capita Income, 1975–1983 *(percentages)*

Classification of countries (based on GDP per capita in 1980 U.S. dollars)			Average annual growth rate of			Population growth as percentage of real GDP growth
Group	Average income level	Percentage of world population	Real GDP	Population	Real GDP per capita	
I–II	$1,000 or less	59.8	3.2	2.6	0.6	81
III–IV	$1,001–10,000	29.6	3.6	1.8	1.8	50
V	More than $10,000	10.6	2.7	1.3	1.4	48

Source: Calculated from *IMF International Financial Statistics Yearbook,* 1985. *Handbook of Economic Statistics,* 1984.

Growth in per capita real income depends on the difference between growth rates of real national income and population. The very poorest countries spend much of their increase in income on a rising population. Thus their increase in income per capita is less than half of the countries which are already richer.

income easier to achieve than one poorly endowed with such resources. Kuwait has an income per capita above that of the United States because by accident it sits on top of the world's greatest known oil field.

FIGURE 42-3   World Population Growth, 1400–2000

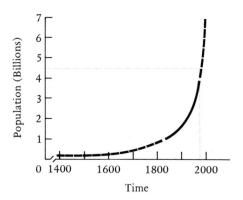

The trend of growth in the world's population is explosive. The solid line reflects present measurements. The dashed line involves projections from observed trends. It took about 50,000 years from the emergence of modern human beings for the world's population to reach 1 billion. It took 100 years to add a second billion, 30 years to add the third billion, and 15 years to add the fourth billion. If these trends continue, the population will reach 7 billion by the year 2000.

A lack of oil proved a devastating setback to many LDCs when the OPEC cartel increased oil prices tenfold during the 1970s. Without oil their development efforts would be halted, but to buy oil took so much scarce foreign exchange that it threatened to cripple their attempts to import needed capital goods.

The amount of resources available for production is at least in part subject to control. Badly fragmented land holdings may result from a dowry or inheritance system. When farm land is divided into many small parcels, it may be much more difficult to achieve the advantages of modern agriculture than it is when the land is available in huge tracts for large-scale farming.

Lands left idle because of lack of irrigation or spoiled by lack of crop rotation are well-known examples of barriers to development. Ignorance is another. The nations of the Middle East sat through recorded history alongside the Dead Sea without realizing that it was a substantial source of potash. Not until after World War I were these resources utilized; now they provide Israel with raw materials for its fertilizer and chemical industries.

Inefficient Use of Resources

Low levels of income and slower than necessary growth rates may result from the inefficient use of resources as well as the lack of key resources.

FIGURE 42-4   Allocative Inefficiency Versus X-inefficiency

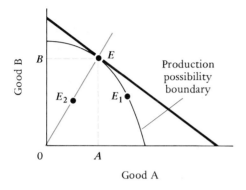

Good A

Allocative inefficiency places the society at an inappropriate point on its production possibility boundary, while X-inefficiency places the society inside this boundary. The thinner black curve represents a society's production possibilities between two goods, A and B. The slope of the thicker black line represents the opportunity cost of good B in terms of good A as given by prices set on world markets. The efficient output of A and B is represented at point E, and the country can trade to achieve any position on the thicker line. Point E_1 is inefficient in the allocative sense. The economy is operating on its production possibility boundary, but it is producing too much A and too little B for the given opportunity cost. In contrast, at point E_2 the proportions of B and A are the same as at E, but the economy is operating inside its boundary. This is X-inefficiency.

It is useful to distinguish between two kinds of inefficiency. An hour of labor would be used inefficiently, for example, if a worker, even though working at top efficiency, were engaged in making a product that no one wanted. Using society's resources to make the wrong products is an example of *allocative inefficiency.*

In terms of the production possibility boundary encountered in Chapter 1, allocative inefficiency represents operation at the wrong place on the boundary. It will occur if the signals to which people respond are distorted (both monopoly and tariffs are commonly cited sources of distortions) or if market imperfections prevent resources from moving to their best uses.

A second kind of inefficiency has come to be called **X-inefficiency,** following Professor Harvey Leibenstein. X-inefficiency arises whenever resources are used in such a way that even if they are making the right product, they are doing so less productively than is possible. One example would be workers too hungry or too unmotivated to concentrate on their tasks. X-inefficiency may be the price societies pay when they give more weight to friendship, loyalty, and tradition than to productivity.

The distinction between allocative inefficiency and X-inefficiency is illustrated in Figure 42-4.

Inadequate Human Resources

A well-developed entrepreneurial class, motivated and trained to organize resources for efficient production, is often missing in less-developed countries. Its absence may be a heritage of a colonial system that gave the local population no opportunity to develop; it may result from the fact that managerial positions are awarded on the basis of family status or political patronage; it may reflect the presence of economic or cultural attitudes that do not favor acquisition of wealth by organizing productive activities; or it may simply be due to the absence of the quantity or quality of education or training that is required.

Poor health is likewise a source of inadequate human resources. When the labor force is healthy less time is lost and more effective effort is expended. The economic analysis of medical advances is a young field, however, and there is a great deal to be learned about the drag of poor health on the growth of an economy.

Institutional and Cultural Patterns

Inadequate Infrastructure

Key services, called **infrastructure,** such as transportation and a communications network, are necessary to efficient commerce. Roads, bridges, railroads, and harbors are needed to transport people, materials, and finished goods. The most dramatic confirmation of their importance comes in wartime, when belligerents always place high priority on destroying each other's transportation facilities.

Reasonable phone and postal services, water supply, and sanitation are essential to economic development. The absence, whatever the reason, of a dependable infrastructure can impose severe barriers to economic development.

Unstable Financial Institutions

The lack of an adequate and trusted system of financial institutions is often a barrier to development. Investment plays a key role in growth, and an important source of funds for investment is the savings of households and firms. When banks and other financial institutions do not function well and smoothly, the link between private saving and investment may be broken and the problem of finding funds for investment greatly intensified.

Many people in LDCs do not trust banks, sometimes with good reason, more often without. Either they do not maintain deposits or they panic periodically, drawing them out and seeking security for their money in mattresses, in gold, or in real estate. When banks cannot count on their deposits being left in the banking system, they cannot engage in the kind of long-term loans needed to finance investments. When this happens, increases in savings do not become available for investment in productive capacity.

Developing countries must not only create banking institutions, they must create enough stability and reliability that people will trust their savings to those who wish to invest.

Cultural Barriers

Traditions and habitual ways of doing business vary among societies, and not all are equally conducive to productivity. Max Weber argued that the "Protestant ethic" encouraged the acquisition of wealth and hence encouraged more growth than systems of belief that directed activity away from the economic sphere.

Often in LDCs, personal considerations of family, past favors, or traditional friendship or enmity are more important than market incentives in motivating behavior. One may find a too-small firm struggling to survive against a larger rival and learn that the owner prefers to remain small rather than expand because expansion would require use of nonfamily capital or leadership. To avoid paying too harsh a competitive price for built-in inefficiency, the firms' owners may then spend much of their energies in an attempt to influence the government to prevent larger firms from being formed or to try to secure restrictions on the sale of output—and they may well succeed. Such behavior will inhibit economic growth.

In an environment where people believe that it is more important who your father is than what you do, it may take a generation to persuade employers to change their attitudes and another generation to persuade workers that times have changed. In a society in which children are expected to stay in their fathers' occupations, it is more difficult for the labor force to change its characteristics and to adapt to the requirements of growth than in a society where upward mobility is itself a goal.

Structuring incentives is a widely used form of policy action in market-oriented economies. But if people habitually bribe the tax collector rather than pay taxes, they will not be likely to respond to policies that are supposed to work by raising or lowering taxes. All that will change is the size of the bribe.

There is lively debate on how much to make of the significance of differing cultural attitudes. Some believe that traditional considerations dominate peasant societies to the exclusion of economic responses; others suggest that any resulting inefficiency may be relatively small.

The fact that existing social, religious, or legal patterns may make growth more difficult does not in itself imply that they are undesirable. Instead it suggests that the benefits of these patterns must be weighed against the costs, of which the limitation on growth is one. When people derive satisfaction from a religion whose beliefs inhibit growth, when they value a society in which every household owns its own land and is more nearly self-sufficient than in another society, they may be quite willing to pay a price in terms of growth opportunities foregone.

Some Basic Choices

There are many barriers to economic development that, singly and in combination, can keep a country poor.

Economic development policy involves identifying the barriers to the level and kind of development desired and then devising ways to overcome them. Although the problems and strategies vary greatly from country to country, there are common basic choices that all developing countries must face.

How Much Government Control?

How much government control over the economy is necessary and desirable? Practically every shade of opinion from "The only way to grow is to get the government's dead hand out of everything" to "The only way to grow is to get a fully planned, centrally controlled economy" has been seriously advocated.

The extreme views are easily refuted by historical evidence. Many economies have grown with very little government assistance: Great Britain in the industrial revolution, Holland during the heyday of its colonial period, Singapore, Hong Kong, and Taiwan during modern times. Others, such as the Soviet Union and Austria, have sustained growth with a high degree of centralized control. Other countries have successfully used almost every conceivable mix of state and private initiative.

The Case for Planning

The case for active government intervention in the management of a country's economy rests on the real or alleged failure of market forces to produce satisfactory results. The major appeal of such intervention is that it is expected to accelerate the pace of economic development.

Many barriers to development may be lowered by appropriate government actions.

For example, when living standards are low, people have urgent uses for their current income, so savings tend to be low. Governments can intervene in a variety of ways and force people to save more than they otherwise would in order to ease a shortage of investment funds.

Compulsory saving has been one of the main aims of most development plans of centralized governments, such as those of the USSR and China. The goal of such plans is to raise savings and thus lower current consumption below what it would be in an unplanned economy. A less authoritarian method is to increase the savings rate through tax incentives and monetary policies. The object is the same: to increase investment in order to increase growth, and thus to make future generations better off.

Authoritarian central governments can be particularly effective in overcoming some of the sources of X-inefficiency. A dictatorship may suppress social and even religious institutions that are barriers to growth, and it may hold on to power until a new generation grows up that did not know and does not value the old institutions. It is much more difficult for a democratic government, which must command popular support at each election, to do currently unpopular things in the interests of long-term growth. Whether the gains in growth that an authoritarian government can achieve are worth the political and social costs is, of course, an important value judgment.

The Case for the Market

Most people would accept that government must play an important part in any development program, especially in programs concerning education, transportation, and communication. But what of the sectors usually left to private enterprise in advanced capitalist countries?

The advocates of relying on market forces in these sectors place great emphasis on human drive, initiative, and inventiveness. Once the infrastructure has been established, they argue, an army of entrepreneurs will do vastly more to develop the economy than will an army of civil servants. The market will provide the opportunities and direct their efforts. People who seem lethargic and unenterprising when held down by lack of incentives will show bursts of energy when given sufficient self-interest in economic activity.

Furthermore, the argument goes, individual capitalists are far less wasteful of the country's capital than civil servants. A bureaucrat investing capital that is not his own (raised perhaps from the peasants by a state marketing board that buys cheap and sells dear) may choose to enhance his own prestige at the public's expense by spending too much money on cars, offices, and secretaries and too little on truly productive activities. Even if the bureaucrat is genuinely interested in the country's well-being, the incentive structure of a bureaucracy does not encourage creative risk taking. If his ventures fail, his head will likely roll; if they succeed, he will receive no profits—and his superior may get the medal. Thus he will be cautious about taking risks.

What Sorts of Education?

Most studies of less-developed countries suggest that undereducation is a barrier to development and often urge increased expenditures on education. This poses a choice: whether to spend educational funds on erasing illiteracy and increasing the level of mass education or on training a small cadre of scientific and technical specialists.

To improve basic education requires a large investment in school building and in teacher training. This investment will result in a visible change in the level of education only after 10 or more years, and it will not do much for productivity even over that time span. The opportunity cost of basic education expenditures always seems high. Yet it is essential to make them because the gains will be critical to economic development a generation later.

Many developing countries have put a large fraction of their educational resources into training a small number of highly educated men and women, often by sending them abroad for advanced study, because the results of acquiring a few hundred doctors or engineers or Ph.D.s are relatively more visible than the results of raising the school-leaving age by a year or two, say, from age 10 to age 12. It is not yet clear whether the policy of "educating the few" pays off, but it is clear that it has some drawbacks.

Many of this educated elite are recruited from the privileged classes on the basis of family position, not merit; many regard their education as the passport to a new aristocracy rather than as a mandate to serve their fellow citizens; and an appreciable fraction emigrate to countries where their newly acquired skills bring higher pay than they do at home. Of those who return home, many seek the security of a government job, which they may utilize to advance their own status in what is sometimes a self-serving and unproductive bureaucracy.

What Population Policy?

The race between population and income has been a dominant feature of many less-developed countries.

Where population is growing rapidly, there are only two possible ways for a country to win this race. One is to make a massive effort to achieve an income growth rate well in excess of the population growth rate. The other is to control population growth.

The problem *can* be solved by restricting population growth. This is not a matter of serious debate, but the means of restricting it are, for considerations of religion, custom, and education are involved.

The consequences of different population policies are large. The birthrate in Sweden is 12 per thousand, in Venezuela it is 42 per thousand, and the two countries have similar death rates. The variations in birthrates have economic consequences. In Venezuela the net increase of population per year is 33 per thousand (3.3 percent), but it is only 3 per thousand (0.3 percent) in Sweden. If each country were to achieve an overall rate of growth of output of 3 percent per year, Sweden's living standards would be increasing by 2.7 percent per year, while Venezuela's would be falling by 0.3 percent per year. In 1983 Sweden's income per capita ($8,400) was two and one-half times as high as Venezuela's ($3,400)—and Venezuela is the wealthiest country in South and Central America. The gap will widen rapidly if present population trends continue.

Population control can take forms as mild as public education programs designed to alter attitudes toward family size and to encourage the avoidance of involuntary pregnancies. At the other extreme are massive programs of compulsory sterilization, such as Prime Minister Indira Gandhi attempted in India in the mid 1970s. Between these extremes are many possibilities, most of which use various economic and legal incentives or penalties to encourage a lower birthrate.

Customs can be changed to raise the average marriage age and hence lower the birthrate. Prohibition of child labor and the establishment of compulsory education alters the costs and benefits of having children and reduces desired family size. Changing the role of women and providing career alternatives outside the home can also lower the birthrate.

University of Maine Professor Johannes Overbeck reported recently that a comprehensive family planning program—involving the provision of a broad selection of birth control techniques, a broad range of social services, and accelerated research to develop more effective and cheaper contraceptives—would have an annual cost of $1 per capita in a typical less-developed country. Excluding mainland China, this amounts to around $2 billion per year for all LDCs combined, a relatively modest sum compared with the over $500 billion currently spent annually on armaments. If this estimate is roughly accurate, population policy offers an extremely high return on spending to promote per capita growth in LDCs.

Different countries have adopted very different positions with respect to population. Kenya, with a birthrate of 50 per thousand, until recently rejected any serious national policy of population control. Mexico, with nearly as high a birthrate in the early 1970s, began to dispense free contraceptives and family planning information and saw its annual rate of population growth drop from 3.2 percent to 2.5 percent in less than five years.

The Chinese—today a quarter of the world's population—have reduced their rate of population increase from more than 3 percent to less than 1 percent in the last 25 years by promoting later marriages and exhorting parents to value daughters as well as sons and thus to be content with fewer children. In 1980 China began more aggressive steps in an announced attempt to achieve zero population growth by the year 2000. Families that have only one child receive bonuses and preferential treatment in housing and in education for their offspring. (Housing space is allocated to all families as though they had one child.) Families that do not comply with the policy have their salaries decreased and are promoted more slowly.

The political, religious, and cultural dimensions of population policy lead some governments to resist population control. Positive economics cannot decide whether population control is desirable, but it can describe the consequences of any choice. Economic development is much easier to achieve with population control than without it.

How to Acquire Capital?

A country can raise funds for investment in three distinct ways: from the savings (voluntary or forced) of its domestic households and firms, by loans or investment from abroad, and by contributions from foreigners.

Capital from Domestic Saving: The Vicious Circle of Poverty

If capital is to be created at home by a country's own efforts, resources must be diverted from the production of goods for current consumption. This means a cut in present living standards. If living standards are already at or near the subsistence level, such a diversion will be difficult. At best, it will be possible to reallocate only a small proportion of resources to the production of capital goods.

Such a situation is often described as the *vicious circle of poverty*: Because a country has little capital per head, it is poor; because it is poor, it can devote few resources to creating new capital rather than to producing goods for consumption; because little new capital can be produced, capital per head remains low, and the country remains poor.

The vicious circle can be made to seem an absolute constraint on growth rates. Of course it is not; if it were, we would all still be at the level of Neanderthal man. The grain of truth in the vicious circle argument is that some surplus must be available somewhere in the society to allow saving and investment. In a poor society with an even distribution of income, where nearly everyone is at the subsistence level, saving may be very difficult. But this is not the common experience. Usually there is at least a small middle class that can save and invest if opportunities for the profitable use of funds arise. Also in most poor societies today the average household is above the physical subsistence level. Even the poorest households will find that they can sacrifice some present living standards for a future gain. For example, presented with a profitable opportunity, villagers in Ghana planted cocoa plants at the turn of the century even though there was a seven-year growing period before any return could be expected!

An important consideration is that in less-developed countries one resource that is often *not* scarce is labor. Profitable home or village investment that requires mainly labor inputs may be made with relatively little sacrifice in current living standards. However, this is not the kind of investment that will appeal to planners mesmerized by large and symbolic investments such as dams, nuclear power stations, and steel mills.

Imported Capital

Another way of accumulating the capital needed for growth is to borrow it from abroad. When a poor country borrows from a rich country, it can use the borrowed funds to purchase capital goods produced in the rich country. The poor country thus accumulates capital and needs to cut its current output of consumption goods only to pay interest on its loans. As the new capital begins to add to current production, it is possible to pay the interest on the loan and also to repay the principal out of the increase in output. This method has the great advantage of giving a poor country an initial increase in capital goods far greater than it could possibly have created by diverting its own resources from consumption industries.

However, many countries, developed or undeveloped, are suspicious of foreign capital. They fear foreign investors will gain control over their industries or their government. The extent of foreign control depends on the form foreign capital takes. When foreigners buy bonds in domestic companies, they do not own or control anything. When they buy common stocks, they own part or all of a company, but their control over management may be small.

When foreign companies establish plants and import their own managers and technicians, they have much more control. Finally, when foreign firms subsidize an LDC government in return for permission to produce, they may feel justified in exacting political commitments.

Whether foreign ownership of one's industries carries political disadvantages sufficiently large to outweigh the economic gains is a subject of debate. In Canada, for example, there is serious political opposition to having a large part of Canadian industry owned by U.S. nationals. Many other countries actively seek increased foreign investment.

During the period 1974 to 1984 reliance on foreign borrowing exploded to the point where it became a serious international problem, for both LDCs and their creditors. During the 1970s the rising cost of oil to many oil-importing less-developed countries combined with overly optimistic income expectations and led to massive borrowing by the LDCs. High interest rates in the 1980s greatly raised the cost of servicing this debt. World recession and rising protectionism in the developed world made it more difficult to earn the money necessary to pay interest on, let alone repay, the principal. For oil-importing countries the collapse of oil prices in 1985 provided some relief, but for oil exporters such as Mexico the oil price decline made things much worse. This problem had reached the dimensions of a crisis by the mid 1980s and is discussed with reference to Mexico in Box 42-1 on pages 860–861.

Contributed Capital

Investment funds for development are being received today by LDCs from the governments of the developed countries. These governments sometimes act unilaterally (for example, the program of the U.S. Agency for International Development and a similar Soviet program) and sometimes act through international agencies such as the World Bank, the Export-Import Bank, and the OPEC Fund established in January 1980. These funds are not really outright gifts, but are "soft" loans, where repayment is not demanded in the near future. It is common to label them *contributed capital* to distinguish them from hard loans, where repayment is expected under normal commercial terms.

The heyday of contributed capital was the post World War II cold war period, when the United States, the Soviet Union, and others sought to win the allegiance of Third World LDCs by making soft loans and outright gifts. (See Box 42-2 on page 862 for further discussion.)

Development Strategies

In the search for development individual LDCs have a number of policy options. The choice of options is in part a matter of what the planners believe will work and in part a question of the nature of the society that will be created once development has occurred.

The noneconomic aspects of the choice of a development strategy may be illustrated by the Greek government's explicit decision in the mid 1960s to change the direction of its growth. At that time Greece was achieving rapid growth largely because of a booming tourist trade and the emigration of many young Greeks to West Germany to work in factories there. The emigrants had been earning incomes in Greece that were substantially below the Greek average, and their remittances home to their families increased both domestic income and foreign exchange reserves. Although these events were helpful to the Greek growth rate, they threatened an image of life that visualized "Greece for the Greeks." Even at the prospect of some loss in growth, Greek planners recommended the restriction of emigration, the moderation of the size of the tourist role in the economy, and the development of new industry for the Greek economy.

There may also be economic reasons for choosing a different pattern of growth than the free market would provide. An important role of planning is to direct growth in a different direction, one that the planners guess will have the greatest chance of long-run success.

Unplanned growth will usually tend to exploit the country's present comparative advantages; planners may choose a pattern of growth that involves trying to change the country's future comparative advantages.

One reason planners seek to do so is their belief that they can evaluate the future more accurately than the countless individuals whose decisions determine market prices. A country need not passively accept its current comparative advantages. Many skills can be acquired, and fostering an apparently uneconomic domestic industry may, by changing the characteristics of the labor force, develop a comparative advantage in that line of production.

The Japanese had no visible comparable advantage in any industrial skill when Commodore Matthew Perry opened that feudal country to Western influence in 1854, but they became a major industrial power by the end of the century. Their continuing gains relative to the United States in fields such as steel, automobile production, and electronics do not need to be called to anyone's attention today. (Neither, however, were the gains primarily centrally planned.) Soviet planners in the 1920s and 1930s chose to create an industrial economy out of a predominantly agricultural one and succeeded in vastly changing the mix between agriculture and industry in a single generation. Soviet planning is discussed further in Chapter 43.

These illustrations suggest why the choice of which development strategy to adopt is crucial. Governments must choose between agricultural and industrial emphases, between different kinds of industrial development, and between more or less reliance on foreign trade. Several possibilities have been widely advocated, and each has been tried. None is without difficulties.

Agricultural Development

Everyone needs food. An LDC may choose to devote a major portion of its resources to stimulating agricultural production, say, by mechanizing farms, irrigating land, and utilizing new seeds and fertilizers. If successful, the country will stave off starvation for its current population, and it may even develop an excess over current needs and so have a crop available for export. A food surplus can earn foreign exchange to buy needed imports.

Among the attractions of the agricultural strategy are that it does not require a great deal of technical training or hard-to-acquire know-how nor does it

BOX 42-1

Debt and the LDCs

The 1970s and early 1980s witnessed explosive growth of the external debt of many LDCs. Recently a number of these countries have experienced difficulties in making the payments required to service their debt. "Debt reschedulings"—that is, putting off until tomorrow payments that cannot be made today—have been common, and by 1985 many observers felt that major defaults were inevitable.

The trend to increased debt started when OPEC quadrupled the world price of oil in 1973. Because many LDCs relied on imported oil, their balance of trade moved sharply into deficit. At the same time, the OPEC countries developed massive trade surpluses. Commercial banks helped *recycle* the deposits of their OPEC customers into loans to the deficit LDCs. These loans financed some necessary adjustments and worthwhile new investment projects in the LDCs. However, not all of the funds were used wisely; wasteful government spending and lavish consumption splurges occurred in a number of borrowing countries.

A doubling of energy prices in 1979 led to a further increase in LDC debt. The severe world recession that began in 1981 reduced demand for the exports of many of the LDCs. As a result, the LDCs were unable to achieve many benefits from the adjustments and investment expenditures they had made. Furthermore, sharp increases in real interest rates led to increased debt service payments; as a result, many of the LDCs could not make their payments.

The lending banks had little choice but to reschedule the debt—essentially lending the LDCs the money to make interest payments while adding to the principal of the existing loans. The IMF played a central role in arranging these reschedulings, making further loans and concessions conditional on appropriate policies of adjustment and restraint. These conditions presumably were intended to limit wasteful government expenditure and consumption and thus increase the likelihood that the loans would eventually be repaid. Critics of the IMF's role, however, argued that much of the restraint resulted in reduced investment, and thus the IMF conditions were counterproductive.

In the mid 1980s, the world economy recovered and interest rates fell. As a result, the LDC's export earnings grew, their debt service obligations stabilized, and the crisis appeared to subside. The sharp *fall* in the price of oil, which started in late 1985, further eased the problems of the oil-importing LDCs, but it also created a new debt problem.

Thoughout the period of rising energy prices, a number of *oil-exporting* LDCs—including Mexico, Venezuela, and Indonesia—saw in those high prices new opportunities for investment and growth. Based on their high oil revenues, their ability to borrow improved. Their external debt grew, and they were able to avoid many of the adjustments that the oil-importing LDCs had been forced to undertake. When oil prices fell, these oil-exporters found themselves in a very difficult position.

Mexico provides an illustrative case study. Its oil revenues doubled from around $8 billion in 1978 to $16 billion by 1982. This increased earning capacity led to increased borrowing, and its external debt also doubled in the same period, from $40 billion in 1978 to $80 billion in 1982. Even with its high oil revenues,

place the country in direct competition with highly industrial countries.

India, Pakistan, Taiwan, and other Asian countries have achieved dramatic increases in food production by the application of new technology and the use of new seed in agricultural production. Increases of up to 50 percent have been achieved in grain production, and it has been estimated that with adequate supplies of water, pesticides, fertilizers, and modern equipment, production could be doubled or tripled. This has been labeled the *green revolution*.

Big, rural, poor countries are usually well advised to start with policies designed to increase agricultural output in order to utilize the existing labor force and however, not all was well; in the words of the *Economist* magazine, "Mexico officially opened the international debt crisis in 1982."

For a number of reasons, including bad investment decisions and the world recession, Mexico's export earnings did not increase as fast as its debt. Soaring real interest rates meant that by 1982 Mexico was unable to service its debt. Only a major debt rescheduling, conditional on severe fiscal restraint and a devaluation to stimulate exports, prevented a probable default.

Continued borrowing, much of it necessary just to service its existing debt, meant that Mexico's debt continued to rise; by 1986 the debt had risen to $100 billion. For much of this period, the spending restraint in Mexico combined with the recovery in the world economy and the fall in world interest rates led to a gradual improvement in Mexico's prospects for growing out from under its debt burden. But in 1986 world oil prices fell, and Mexico's oil revenues plummeted to around $8 billion. A new crisis emerged.

The 1986 situation was different from the situation in 1982 in several important ways. The world economy and the international financial system were both healthier. Lower real interest rates and lower oil prices meant that other LDCs were able to repay their loans; hence there was less fear of a collapse of the international financial system.

But for Mexico the 1986 crisis was worse than the 1982 one. Domestic restraint had been pushed virtually to the limit; the government deficit had been cut by over 6 percent of GNP in just two years. Headlines in the international press proclaimed, "With Mexico Focusing on Debt Repayment, Ports and Roads Suffer," and "Mexican Children Scrounge for Food as Schools Drop Free Lunch."

Projections showed that Mexico would require major foreign borrowing if it were to continue to meet its interest obligations on existing debt. Commercial banks were not anxious to lend any more on their own initiative. The IMF tried to negotiate a loan package based on further restraint, and U.S. Secretary of the Treasury James Baker proposed a plan with renewed lending conditional on major economic adjustment. But further restraint and rapid adjustment seemed politically impossible in a country already racked by massive restraint and plummeting export revenues; many economists argued that restraint would in any event retard growth and prove counterproductive.

A major impasse thus arose. Using the threat of default, Mexico demanded major concessions on the terms of its new borrowing. The "crisis" situation stimulated innovative proposals. One proposal was for the banks to forgive some debt in return for equity participation in Mexico's oil and other industries; this would reduce the burden of Mexico's debt service payments while sharing some of the risks of the Mexican situation between Mexico and its creditors.

In late July an agreement was reached providing for major new borrowing; for the first time in IMF history, the terms not only included conditions that appropriate adjustment policies be undertaken but also a provision for repayment linked to the price of the borrowing country's exports, in this case oil. This provision is intended to forestall further crises by allowing the required payments to fluctuate with the country's ability to pay.

---

increase standards of living. But the gains from this strategy, while large at first, are subject to diminishing returns. Further gains in agricultural production have an ever higher opportunity cost, in the resources needed to irrigate land and to mechanize production. Critics of sole reliance on agricultural output argue that underdeveloped economies must start at once to develop other bases for economic growth.

One problem with heavy reliance on the agricultural strategy is that it frequently requires heavy initial subsidization of agricultural production and also some means of subsidizing consumption of increased quantities of food by a poor population. A common

BOX 42-2

"Aid," "Trade," or "Restitution"

The motivations behind international giving are the subject of debate. Do developed nations give aid for humanitarian reasons, because it serves their political objectives, or because it is economically self-serving? Of course, all three motives can play a role, but which one dominates? Should LDCs demand aid, accept it gratefully, or reject it?

LDCs more or less chronically lack capital and lack wealth. Typically they have large foreign debts as a result of past borrowing. In these circumstances, one might think that foreign aid, whether from a single country or from an international agency, would be eagerly sought and gratefully received. This is not always so; there is some significant resistance to accepting aid.

The slogan "Trade, not aid" reflected political opposition to U.S. economic aid in certain recipient countries in the 1950s. Yugoslavia turned down much aid proffered by the Soviets after 1948, and China accepted no foreign aid after 1960. In 1975 Colombia made the decision to forego further U.S. aid on the grounds that it bred an unhealthy economic dependency.

The primary explanation of this attitude lies in a country's noneconomic goals. It may suspect the motives of the givers and fear that hidden strings may be attached to the offer. Independent countries prize their independence and want to avoid either the fact or the appearance of being satellites. Pride—a desire to be beholden to no one—is also a factor.

One response was to do without aid, no matter how badly it was needed. Another, increasingly the pattern in the 1970s, was to reject "aid" but to demand "wealth transfers," not as a matter of charity but as a matter of "restitution" or redress for past sins by colonial powers against their former colonies. The obvious problem of asserting such claims against noncolonial powers such as the United States and the USSR has been no deterrent. There is a generalized

sense that the inhabitants of the "North" exploited the nations of the "South" in past centuries and that present generations should redress the balance. The paradoxical aspect of this is that while "restitution, not charity" makes LDCs willing to accept aid, precisely that claim decreases the willingness of developed countries to offer it.

What *are* the motives of givers of aid? The Scandinavian Nobel Prize winning economist Gunnar Myrdal argued that humanitarian considerations have played a large role. The evidence for the existence of humanitarian motives is in part the success of voluntary appeals in developed countries for food, funds, and clothes for persons in stricken areas of the world. As per capita incomes have risen in the Western world, so have contributions, private as well as public. It is the policy of the governments of most of the so-called Western democracies to devote some resources to alleviating poverty throughout the world.

Professor Edward S. Mason, among others, has argued that such aid can best be understood by looking to political and security motives. He points to the substantial U.S. congressional preference for military assistance over economic assistance, the denial of aid to countries such as Sri Lanka that traded with Communist countries, the fostering of Yugoslavia *because* of its anti-Soviet stand—all of which reveal a strong political motive. Many critics of OPEC think its contributions were designed to quiet opposition among LDCs to the oil price hikes that proved so profitable to the oil producers and so painful to oil users, LDCs and developed countries alike.

Should motives and attitudes, either of givers or of receivers, matter? After all, it is economically beneficial to receive aid when you are poor. Economists cannot say that fears, aspirations, pride, and "face" are either foolish or unworthy; they can only note that they do have their cost.

device is to provide artificially high prices to producers and artificially low prices to consumers. Once such a program is put in place it creates a serious potential dilemma. Continuation of the artificially

high prices for producers and low prices for consumers creates a substantial drain on the government's finances. Lowering the subsidy to producers risks a rural revolution; eliminating the subsidy to consumers risks an urban revolution. The government finds itself with an untenable policy, but with no room for maneuver.

Specialization in a Few Commodities

Many LDCs have unexploited resources such as copper, uranium, or opportunities for tourism. The principle of comparative advantage provides the traditional case for the desirability of relying on such resources. By specializing in producing those products in which it has the greatest comparative advantage, the country can achieve the most rapid growth in the short run. To neglect these opportunities will result in a lower standard of living than would result from specialization accompanied by increased international trade.

These are cogent reasons in favor of *some* specialization. But specialization involves risks, and it may be worthwhile to reduce the risks by maintaining diversification even at the cost of loss of some income. Specialization in a few commodities makes the economy highly vulnerable to cyclical fluctuations in world demand and supply. For example, a recession in developed countries or fear of terrorism decreases overseas travel and creates problems for an LDC that has relied on tourism for foreign exchange.

The problem is not only short run. When technological or taste changes render a product partially or wholly obsolete, a country can face a major calamity. Just as individual firms and regions may become overspecialized, so too may countries.

Import Substitution Industrialization

During the Great Depression the collapse in world agricultural prices caused the value of the exports of agricultural countries to decline drastically relative to the prices of goods those countries imported. During World War II many countries found that the manufactured goods they wished to import were unavailable. In each of those situations dependence on foreign trade for necessities was unattractive. During the 1970s, the rising prices of fuel and other imports created enormous balance-of-payments problems for many LDCs. Such countries were forced to reduce imports, increase exports, or resort to foreign borrowing.

Much of the industrialization by LDCs in the 1950s and 1960s was directed toward **import substitution industry (ISI),** that is, industry to produce home goods that were previously imported. It is often necessary both to subsidize the home industry and to restrict imports to allow the ISI time to develop.

LDCs sometimes pursue certain lines of production on a subsidized basis for prestige purposes or because of a confusion between cause and effect. Because most wealthy nations have a steel industry, the leaders of many underdeveloped nations regard their countries as primitive until they develop a domestic steel industry. Because several LDCs have succeeded in producing consumer durables, many others assume that they should try to do so. However, if a country has a serious comparative disadvantage in steel or in making consumer durables, fostering such industries will make that country even poorer.

The ISI strategy has many problems. It fosters *inefficient* industries, and in the long run countries do not get rich by being inefficient. It aggravates inequalities in income distribution by raising the prices of manufactured goods relative to agricultural goods and by favoring profits over wages.

Export Development

Most development economists believe that industrialization ought to be encouraged only in areas where the country can develop a reliable and efficient industry that can compete in world markets.

Obviously, if Tanzania or Peru could develop steel, shipbuilding, and manufacturing industries that operated as efficiently as those of Japan or West Germany, they might share in the rapid economic growth enjoyed by those industrial countries. Indeed, if a decade or two of protection and subsidization could give infant industries time to mature and become efficient, the price might be worth paying. After all, within living memory Japan and Russia were underdeveloped countries.

Industrialization for export can sometimes be done by employing inexperienced workers in simple, labor-intensive enterprises, such as sewing clothing. But it often means devoting resources for a long period to education, training, infrastructure development, and overcoming any cultural and social barriers to efficient production. While this is hard, it is not impossible. Indeed, there have been some spectacular success stories. Brazil, Korea, Hong Kong, and Taiwan are charter members in the category of **newly industrializing countries (NIC)** that are providing vigorous competition in manufactured goods in world markets.

Their success has led to a further (and bitterly resented) problem for the industrialization strategy. When an LDC succeeds, it is likely to find the developed countries trying to protect *their* home industries from the new competition.

Import substitution and export development do not need to be seen as alternative development strategies. Many now successful trading countries used import substitution in the first stages of their development strategy. The intention was to create the domestic industrial base, and the human capital that were needed for industrial success. Once that base was in place, emphasis could be shifted to export encouragement.

Canada used import substitution to build its industries behind high tariff walls in the first half of the twentieth century. Then, throughout the second half of the century, it has lowered tariffs to integrate its developing export industries into the world economy. Singapore and Korea used import substitution policies in their early stages of development. Japan also did so in selected industries. The most recent example was in semiconductors (which include the chips that drive computers) where the domestic industry developed behind a prohibitive Japanese tariff and then went on to lead the world in exports of semiconductors.

The challenge is not, therefore, to choose at an early stage of growth between import substitution and export development policies for all time. The challenge, if import substitution policies are adopted first, is to be able to shift into export encouraging policies at a later stage. Such a shift will not occur if the wrong industries are chosen for import substitution so that they remain sickly infants indefinitely, or if strong vested interests in the sheltered industries are able to prevent the country's later transition to an export-oriented strategy.

Cartelization

When all or most producers of a commodity can agree on price and output levels, they can achieve monopoly profits not available in competitive markets. Many LDCs are heavily committed to the production and export of one or more basic commodities such as bananas, bauxite, cocoa, coffee, copper, cotton, iron ore, jute, manganese, meat, oil, phosphates, rubber, sugar, tea, tropical timber, and tin. Why do not all producers of, say, bananas get together and create an effective cartel that gives producers the enormous profits that are potentially available?

Cartelization has been tried many times in history. Until OPEC it has always failed, yet everyone knows that OPEC transformed a handful of formerly poor LDCs into the wealthiest of nations.[4] OPEC's success was substantial, but proved impossible to sustain. The special reasons for its success for almost 10 years and its eventual failure are discussed in Chapter 15.

Wheat, coffee, cocoa, tin, rubber, and copper have all been suggested as potential subjects for similar commodity price stabilization agreements, but they lack the small number of politically cohesive producers and inelastic short-run demand and supply conditions that gave the OPEC cartel its initial successes.

Some Controversial Unresolved Issues

There are some lively current controversies among development economists. Among them are the following.

A New International Economic Order (NIEO)

In May 1974 the General Assembly of the United Nations adopted (over the objections of the devel-

---

[4] This has added to the terminological confusion. It was once fashionable to speak of a nonaligned *third world* as another term for LDCs, the first two "worlds" being the developed capitalist and developed socialist countries. Now some commentators divide the LDCs into a richer (oil-producing) *third world* and a still poor *fourth world*.

oped countries) a Declaration on the Establishment of a New International Economic Order. This represented an attempt on the part of LDCs to use collective *political* power to achieve a larger share of the world's goods.[5]

The NIEO proposals are aimed basically at wealth transfers instead of wealth creation; they are concerned with a more equal distribution of existing wealth rather than economic development.

The major proposals were threefold. First, marketing boards for primary products exported by the developing nations should be established. These, modeled along the lines of OPEC, would reduce output, raise prices, and thus create monopoly profits for producers. Second, exports of manufactured goods from developing countries should receive preferential tariffs or quotas in the markets of developed countries. Third, the enormous debts of the developing countries, incurred partly to finance development projects and partly to finance the increased cost of oil imports during the 1970s, should be partly forgiven and partly rescheduled to provide for longer repayment periods and easier terms of finance.

Thus far, the NIEO demands have produced few results, although attention to the debt burdens of LDCs has occurred in response to other forces. The NIEO proposals have been discussed extensively, but little major redistribution of wealth has resulted. To most market-oriented economists, NIEO has two major flaws. First, it focuses too much on redistribution and too little on seeking real growth in world output. Second, it relies on bureaucratic allocations of wealth, trade, and natural resources rather than on market mechanisms. Nothing in the world's experience to date suggests that this will increase total world output, indeed, it will probably decrease it.

The Pace of Development

Reformers in less-developed countries often think in terms of transforming their economies within a gen-

eration or two. The sense of urgency is quite understandable, but unless it is tempered by some sense of historical perspective, totally unreasonable aspirations may develop, only to be dashed all too predictably.

Many underdeveloped countries are probably in a stage of economic development analogous to that of medieval England, having not yet achieved anything like the commercial sophistication of the Elizabethan era. It took 600 years for England to develop from the medieval economic stage to its present one. Such a change would be easier now, for much of the needed technology can be imported rather than invented. But what is the proper pace? To effect a similar growth within 50 or 100 years would require a tremendous achievement of the kind accomplished by America, Japan, and a handful of other countries; to aspire to do it in 20 or 30 years may be to court disaster—or to invite repressive political regimes.

The View of Population Policy

The view presented in this chapter of population growth as a formidable barrier to development is neo-Malthusian and constitutes much of current conventional wisdom on underdevelopment.

This view allows little place for the enjoyment value of children by their parents. Critics point out that the psychic value of children should be included as a part of the living standards of their parents. They also point out that in rural societies even young children are a productive resource, and in societies where state help for the aged is negligible, fully grown children provide old-age security for their parents.

The neo-Malthusian theory is also criticized for assuming that people breed blindly, as animals do. Critics point out that traditional methods of limiting family size have been known and practiced since the dawn of history. Thus they argue that large families in rural societies are a matter of choice.

The population explosion came not through any change in "breeding habits," but as a result of medical advances that greatly extended life expectancy (which surely must be counted as a direct welfare gain for those affected). Critics argue that once an urban society has developed, family size will be reduced voluntarily. This was certainly the experience

---

[5] An excellent introduction to this development is Rachel McCulloch's *Economic and Political Issues in the NIEO* (International Institute for Economic Research, 1979).

of Western industrial countries; why, critics ask, should it not be the experience of the developing countries?

The Cost of Creating Capital

Is it true LDCs must suffer by sacrificing current consumption if they wish to grow? A recent criticism of this conventional wisdom questions the alleged heavy opportunity cost of creating domestic capital. Production of consumption and capital goods are substitutes only when factor supplies are constant and fully employed. But, critics say, the development of a market economy will lead people to substitute work for leisure.

For example, the arrival of Europeans with new goods to trade led the North American Indians to collect furs and other commodities needed for exchange. Until they were decimated by later generations of land-hungry settlers, the Indians' standard of living rose steadily with no immediate sacrifice. They created the capital needed for their production—weapons and means of transport—in their abundant leisure time. Thus their consumption began to rise immediately.

This, the argument says, could happen in less-developed countries if market transactions were allowed to evolve naturally. The spread of a market economy would lead people to give up leisure in order to produce the goods needed to buy the goods that private traders are introducing from the outside world. In this view it is the pattern of development chosen, rather than development itself, that imposes the need for heavy sacrifices.

Is There a Best Strategy for Development?

Each of the five strategies discussed—agricultural development, specialization, import substitution, export development, and cartelization—has been tried, and each has problems. Because countries differ, there is no single best strategy, but a substantial consensus is being reached among experts that rapid economic development requires at least three simultaneous thrusts: (1) sufficient agricultural development to provide a healthier, better fed population and work force, (2) sufficient restraint on population growth to permit rising per capita income, and (3) sufficient development of export commodities to allow the country to trade for those essentials it must import. Whether the export commodities should be agricultural, natural resources, light manufactures, heavy manufactures, or services depends on a country's comparative advantage.

Import substitution policies that do not lead eventually to industries that can compete in world markets, and price stabilization agreements, seem much less promising strategies than they did a decade ago, although there may be specific situations in which each of those policies may be helpful.

Finally, a word of warning is in order. The view presented in this chapter is perhaps the mainline view of economists in developed economics such as our own. Problems look different when viewed from the inside out, and they look different from the perspective of socialist nations than they do from market-oriented economies.

Summary

1. Sustained economic development is relatively recent in history and has been highly uneven. About one-fourth of the world's population still exists at a level of bare subsistence, and nearly three-fourths are poor by American standards. The gap between rich and poor is large, keenly felt, and not decreasing.

2. Incentives for economic development include the demonstration effect of other countries' successful transformation from peasant economy to industrial power, and the opportunity to receive aid from developed countries.

3. Impediments to economic development include population growth, resource limitations, inefficient use of resources, and institutional and cultural patterns that make economic growth difficult.

4. A series of basic choices face LDCs as they contemplate development. How much should governments intervene in the economy and how much should the economy be left to operate on the free market? History has demonstrated that growth is possible with almost any conceivable mixture of free-market and central control. Centralized planning can change both the pace and direction of economic development; it can also prove highly wasteful and destroy individual initiative.

5. Educational policy, while vitally important to the long-run rate of economic development, yields its benefits only in the future. Improvement of basic education for the general populace is sometimes bypassed for the more immediate visible results of educating a selected technical and political elite.

6. The race between output and population is a critical aspect of development efforts in many countries. Different countries have different attitudes toward limiting population growth and have chosen different population policies.

7. Capital for development is invariably a major concern in development. It can be acquired from domestic savings, but the vicious circle of poverty may arise: A country that is poor because it has little capital cannot readily forego consumption to accumulate capital because it is poor. Importing capital rather than using domestic savings permits heavy investment during the early years of development, but imported capital is available only when the LDC has opportunities that are attractive to foreign investors. Much foreign capital for LDCs in the last three decades has been in the form of soft loans or contributions by foreign governments and international institutions.

8. Development involves choices among different strategies: agricultural development, specialization based on natural resources, development of import substitution industries, development of new export industries, and cartelization. None of these strategies is without problems and risks.

9. Most experts in development believe that the most appropriate approach is a multipronged strategy that includes at least some agricultural development, some development of new export commodities, and some restraint on population growth.

10. Among controversial unresolved issues is the appropriateness of attempting to solve problems of underdevelopment by wealth transfers rather than wealth creation. This is the thrust of the NIEO proposals. Other controversies concern the pace of development, the neo-Malthusian view of population growth as a problem, and the cost of creating capital in terms of sacrifices of current consumption.

Topics for Review

Gap between LDCs and developed countries
Barriers to development
Infrastructure
Role of planning in development
Alternative development strategies
Wealth creation versus wealth transfers

Discussion Questions

1. Each of the following is a headline from the *New York Times*. Relate them to the problem of economic development.
   a. "Black Africa: Economies on the brink of collapse because of OPEC"
   b. "Hungary reforming economy to attract tourists"
   c. "Goodyear to build plant in Congo for $16 million"
   d. "Algeria's 4-year plan stresses industrial growth"
   e. "India: Giant hobbled by erratic rainfall"
   f. "Foreign banks to finance New Guinea copper mine"
   g. "Not all benefit by green revolution"
   h. "OPEC nations provide loans to underdeveloped nations to pay for oil imports"

2. If you were a member of a U.S. foreign aid team assigned to study needed development projects for a poor recipient country, to which of the following would you be likely to give relatively high priority, and why?
   a. Birth control clinics
   b. A national airline
   c. Taxes on imported luxuries
   d. Better roads
   e. Modernization of farming techniques
   f. Training in engineering and business management
   g. Primary education
   h. Scholarships to students to receive medical and legal training abroad

3. China requires 5 million tons more grain each year just to keep up with its annual population growth of 17 million people. This is about five times Canada's wheat supply at present. What policy choices do these facts pose for the Chinese government? How should it resolve those choices?

4. "This natural inequality of the two powers of population and of production in the earth . . . form the great difficulty that to me appears insurmountable in the way to perfectability of society. All other arguments are of slight and subordinate consideration in comparison of this. I see no way by which man can escape from the weight of this law which pervades all animated nature. No fancied equality, no agrarian revolutions in their utmost extent, could remove the pressure of it even for a single century" (T. R. Malthus, *Population: The First Essay,* Chapter 1, page 6).

   Discuss Malthus's "insurmountable difficulty" in view of the history of the past 100 years.

5. To what extent does the vicious circle of poverty apply to poor families living in developed countries? Consider carefully, for example, the similarities and differences facing a poor black family living in Arkansas and one living in Ghana, where per capita income is less than $400 per year. Did it apply to immigrants who arrived on the New York docks with $10 in their pockets?

6. The president of an LDC said in 1980, "A decision by OPEC members to raise petroleum prices should be applauded by all third world countries. It represents the irrevocable decision to dignify the terms of trade, to revalue raw materials and other basic products of the third world." Can you predict whether that country was an oil exporter or importer? Might an underdeveloped country that is an oil importer want to see OPEC succeed in raising oil prices?

7. "High coffee prices bring hope to impoverished Latin American peasants" reads the headline. Mexico, Kenya, and Burundi, among other LDCs, have the right combination of soil and climate to increase greatly their coffee production. Discuss the benefits and risks to them if they pursue coffee production as a major avenue of their development.

43

Comparative Economic Systems: The Economies of China and the USSR

Economics is concerned with basic questions of what is produced, how it is produced, and how the product is distributed. So far we have examined these questions in the context of a free-market economy in which private firms and households interact in markets with some assistance and interference from the government. We have studied this kind of economy because it is the kind of economy *we* live in and because it is the economic environment in which the serious study of economics was born and has grown.

However, over one and a quarter billion people, about a third of the world's population, live in the Soviet Union and China, countries that explicitly reject many aspects of our economic system. At least another third of the world's population live in countries whose economies have not yet developed to the point where the model of either the free market or the managed economy fits closely.

Can the theories we have studied in this book be applied to such different economies as those of China and the Soviet Union? The answer is yes, at least to a great extent. The same economic principles about resource allocation and human behavior are applicable under a variety of assumptions about ends, means, or incentive systems.

In Chapter 1 we discussed some general characteristics of different economic systems. (We suggest you reread pages 7–11 at this time.) In this chapter we look briefly at the economies of China and the Soviet Union.

The Economy of China

The People's Republic of China dates from 1949, when the Chinese Communists defeated the Nationalist forces of General Chiang Kai-Shek. Initially the People's Republic sought to adopt an economic system patterned along Soviet lines and embodying both Marxist principles of ownership and control of resources and a Stalinist strategy of rapid industrialization managed by a highly centralized, command economy. As it has evolved, however, the Chinese economy today is much less of a command economy than the Soviet economy, with greater use of market incentives and decentralized decision making. It is, however, still a highly planned socialist economy very different from the economy of the United States.

The economic system in China today did not develop smoothly and gradually over the decades since the Nationalist defeat. Rather it is the product of many political and ideological struggles within the government. Although purely ideological issues have played a role in the development of the economic system, there is little doubt that economic performance has been a major factor. Thus economic setbacks have tended to be followed by political upheavals and reforms of the economic system.

The current government reflects the emerging dominance since 1976 (when Mao died and the Gang of Four was overthrown) of the pragmatists (sometimes described as the right wing) over the ideologues (described as the left wing). The Chinese government, with a billion mouths to feed, is evidently no longer willing to encourage ideologically pure, but productively inefficient, methods.

There are many underlying economic reasons why the Chinese economy has developed along lines different from those of the Soviet economy. Perhaps most important is that the vast majority of the population is rural and depends on agriculture for its existence. While 30 percent of Americans and 39 percent of Soviets live in rural areas, over 75 percent of Chinese do so. As agriculture prospers or suffers, so does China. Drought, crop failure, or mismanagement of agricultural production leads to large-scale poverty. Another reason for the difference from the Soviet experience is that this huge country is even now lacking an integrated system of communication and transportation. This makes centralized planning and operation much less effective than it would otherwise be and has inevitably led to substantial decentralization in the planning process.

Finally, China in 1949 was a truly underdeveloped country close by two major industrialized nations, the Soviet Union and Japan, that were also historical enemies. In 1949 most of the population lived near the subsistence level and used primitive tools and methods of production.

The Development of the Chinese Socialist Economy

When the Communists took power in 1949 they inherited an economy in total disarray as the result of World War II, the lengthy revolution, and the corrupt administration of the displaced Chinese Nationalist government. The Communists promised to be a unifying force and more honest than the notorious Nationalists.

1949–1958: The First Decade

The initial economic moves were along classical Marxist-Leninist lines. As Chou En-lai, later to be premier, put it, "The present of the Soviet Union is the future of China." The properties of the displaced Nationalist government, of its supporters, and of foreign capitalists were confiscated and nationalized. Large landholdings were broken up and distributed in small plots to peasants. The central government took firm control of the economy as well as of the political system.

By 1953 a first five-year plan was launched with Soviet guidance and massive Soviet economic assistance. It was Russian in orientation, emphasizing development of heavy industry through forced saving designed to limit consumption and generate high levels of investment. The Russians even physically moved whole factories from the Soviet Union to China.

This first plan neglected agriculture. Encouraged by the favorable harvest of 1955, however, the plan was modified to begin the collectivization of agriculture. When agriculture did poorly in 1956, collectivization was postponed until 1958, when output was once again at a satisfactory level.

1958–1960: The Great Leap Forward

By the end of the first five-year plan the failure to achieve most of the plan's targets, and especially the lack of success in agriculture, led to a major internal split. Out of this Mao Tse-tung emerged as the victorious leader. Mao believed that Communist ideology, not capitalist incentives, would provide the means to the economic development of China's sleeping giant.

Mao also believed China's large underemployed population to be its greatest asset. He thought that mobilizing it was critical for economic growth. Only 2.5 percent of the labor force worked in industry at the time of the revolution, and the Great Leap Forward was to be founded on a massive mobilization of labor for industrial as well as agricultural development.

Labor was brought to the newly created factories in the urban areas and the establishment of small labor-using industries in the rural areas was encouraged. Initially this campaign involved the creation of millions of backyard workshops and furnaces used to smelt steel in workers' and peasants' spare time. However, these small-scale steel mills were soon abandoned as a serious waste of resources. A more important and lasting part of the campaign was the development in rural areas of small-scale factories that produced goods such as the fertilizer and machinery needed in those areas. These plants, scattered about rural China, employed as many as 20 million people. Tens of millions of peasants were also engaged during the slack agricultural season in thousands of irrigation projects designed to increase agricultural productivity.

A major feature of the Great Leap Forward was a tremendous increase in the size of the collective unit of production in agriculture. The 740,000 cooperatives, originally set up in the collectivization that occurred between 1956 and 1958, were re-organized into 24,000 communes averaging 5,000 households each, with communal ownership and organization. The communes were more than agricultural producing units. They represented a tight-knit form of both government and economic management that was involved in everything from crafts to the militia to education. By providing collective child care they freed 90 million women for productive activity outside the home. The communes provided the focus for a substantial regional decentralization of planning and control organized around provincial governments.

The Great Leap Forward was a massive economic failure. By the end of 1960 agricultural output had dropped 20 percent below its 1957 level. Among the causes of this failure were the bitter resistance of peasants to the communes, bad weather, and a political rift with the Soviet Union that led to an abrupt withdrawal of Soviet advisers and economic aid. Perhaps, too, the proposed changes were too massive to be adopted so suddenly, particularly since there was no trained, efficient government bureaucracy to implement new orders in the face of traditional ways.

In any event Mao yielded power to a more pragmatic, less ideological group, with Liu Shaoqi as its dominant figure.

1961–1965: The Period of Readjustment, Consolidation, and Repair

The pragmatists shifted the emphasis from mobilizing workers to increasing productivity in agriculture. They did so in part by allowing commune members to develop private plots and sell the output in farm markets and in part by having the industrial sector greatly alter its focus so that production of fertilizers and farm machinery could be increased. Within three years agricultural output returned to the levels achieved in the years preceding the Great Leap Forward. Some modest private incentives were also introduced within the industrialized sector.

1966–1975: The Cultural Revolution and the Four Modernizations

With the aid of revolutionary youth, Mao regained power in 1966 in a massive political coup and purged the government of its moderate pragmatists. In the name of ideological purity, education was denounced and scientists and technicians banished to rural labor. On the economic front all traces of capitalist influence were eliminated: private plots were confiscated, rural markets closed, and material incentive plans for industrial workers eliminated. The political and personal repressions of this period of Chinese history have only recently been exposed.

The program was another economic disaster. The levels of industrial and agricultural output began to decline almost immediately. In 1968 real GNP was well below its level during the first year of the Cultural Revolution. In response, Mao gave greater power to the more moderate Chou En-lai.

Chou did a remarkable job, by reinstating experienced administrators and increasing imports of vitally needed machinery and equipment among other things. He proposed a long-run strategy called the Four Modernizations for the gradual, simultaneous development of agriculture and industry. However, his death in January 1976 and the emergence of the Gang of Four, Mao's ultra-left-wing colleagues, led to an abrupt reversal and a return of the uncompromising ideology of the Cultural Revolution.

1976 to the Present: The Emergence of Deng Xiaoping

Mao's death in 1976 and the arrest of the Gang of Four brought to power a new government whose dominant figure became Deng Xiaoping.

This government has now ruled China for over a decade, with the aging Deng (born in 1904) still its leader in 1986. Over this period there has been an end to the abrupt reversals of policy that characterized the two preceding decades. The pragmatists have moved steadily and rapidly toward increased reliance on material incentives in both agriculture and industry, improvements in technology, increased foreign trade, and encouragement of foreign investment in China. This has led to a notable (and increasingly noted) reliance on private enterprise, foreign capitalist investment, and other devices of capitalism. Of course, the leaders continue to advocate enhancing socialism and attaining communism as the ultimate goal.

China in the 1980s

The Chinese economic system has been changing so rapidly that any written account is almost certain to be partially out of date by the time it is published. In what follows we describe the situation as it existed in 1986.

Organization of Agriculture

The latest development in agricultural policy has been to dismantle the collective farms that were a key feature of the Great Leap Forward. This decollectivization occurred in two stages.

Teams.   In the first stage, achieved in the late 1970s, the *team* of about 33 households replaced the commune of 5,000 households as the primary unit of production and ownership. The team owned the land it cultivated (about 50 acres) and the machinery and draft animals that were its capital. The team was given production targets, or quotas, by the com-

mune. Prices for agricultural inputs and for quota outputs were set by the central government. If the team exceeded its output quotas, it could sell the extra output on farm markets at whatever price it could get.

Team income was distributed to individual households by formula. Peasants were awarded *work points* for their work for the collective, either on the basis of the hours worked, with different work points awarded for different tasks, or on the basis of the quantity and quality of output produced. The value of each work point was determined annually by dividing the net income of the commune by the total number of work points awarded to its members. During the year all peasants and their family members were given a grain ration on a per capita basis. At the end of the year the value of their grain ration was deducted from the value of their work points. They received cash for any work points they had after this deduction was made and owed a debt to the commune if they ended up with a negative balance.

The contract responsibility system.   In the second stage of agricultural decollectivization the team was replaced by the household as the primary unit of production in what is called the contract responsibility system.[1] This system has now spread to over 98 percent of agricultural households. The household enters into a contract with the team to use a specified amount of the team's land and machinery to produce a fixed amount of output. Anything produced above that amount is generally shared by the household and the team, with the greater part going to the household for its own use or for sale on farm markets.

Allowing the household to keep the revenues from extra output has proven a powerful incentive to increase productivity. Households are encouraged to invest in machinery, fertilizer, and other means of increasing productivity. The central government can increase or decrease the incentive to do so by varying the prices it charges for the inputs. Industries run as sidelines by people primarily working on farms continue to be an important feature of rural life, but they have changed. They no longer smelt steel as in Mao's

---

[1] In some cases a small group of households or an individual peasant rather than a single household is the relevant unit.

time, but produce simpler goods such as bricks, leather products and textiles. Such sideline activities today account for about 20 percent of rural income, but the number is rising rapidly. (See Box 43-1, pages 876–877.)

The various rural administrative units are run by elected representatives who are paid salaries for the time they put in. They are not bosses or managers in the Western sense, but carry supervisory authority for as long as they are elected. It is too early to know if a permanent managerial class will emerge, but the signs point in that direction, with Communist party membership and loyalty to the party major criteria for success.

One important freedom that is absent in China is labor mobility. Workers must stay in their village or township unless given permission to leave. While some movement to neighboring villages does occur, migration to distant regions or the cities is uncommon. Consequently, there is often substantial underutilization of labor but little labor mobility in response.

The disadvantage of this policy is the loss of personal freedom that it entails. The advantage is the avoidance of the human misery that is so prevalant on the fringes of major cities in many newly developing countries. On the fringes of such cities such as Calcutta, Mexico City, and Lagos vast slums are populated by persons from rural areas who came seeking urban employment only to end as malnourished and unemployed, eking out a miserable subsistence in the hope that sooner or later some job will become available.

Organization of Urban Industry

China's industrial base has three main parts: a relatively small, but rapidly growing, private entrepreneurial sector employing about 15 million persons; cooperative-owned enterprises employing about 30 million persons; and state-owned enterprises employing about 88 million persons.

Most modern, capital-intensive industry is in the state sector; more traditional, small-scale, labor-intensive industry is in the cooperative sector; and many services and crafts are in the private sector. However, the basis for the division is not so much dependent on the current function of an enterprise as

on its historical origins. During China's socialization process major industrial enterprises were taken over by the state, while craftspeople and artisans were organized into producer cooperatives. As the political climate changed, the cooperatives' freedom to form, to expand, and to capitalize was encouraged. Reasons for this development were that the emphasis on light industry, the importance given to worker participation, and the labor-intensive nature of cooperative production allowed it better to absorb China's unemployed and underemployed persons than can the capital-intensive state industries.

Private entrepreneurs.   No one is sure just how many private enterprises exist because they come and go, but the number is growing rapidly. In 1981 the estimate was 1 million, by 1983 over 2 million, by 1985 over 10 million. Most are single-person shops selling raw and prepared food or providing services such as tailoring and shoe repair. Their capital is largely human, with perhaps a sewing machine or a shack that serves as a store. Such enterprises may receive permission to employ up to five people if the owners can demonstrate that they will do so in "nonexploitative ways." (This rule is characteristic of the ever-present mixture of Communist ideology and increasing emphasis on market incentives.)

Cooperatives.   The number and nature of cooperative enterprises is also changing rapidly. In 1979 and 1980 they operated "in the plan," that is, their operations were closely integrated with state activities. They bought their inputs from state enterprises (at fixed prices), depended on the state for credit and for funds for investment, and sold much of their output (at fixed prices) to the state. In this arrangement they had assured markets for their outputs and a fixed margin between input and output prices.

Since 1981 cooperatives have been permitted to operate "out of plan" and buy inputs and sell outputs wherever they please at uncontrolled prices. While some have played it safe and have stayed in the plan, most have chosen the riskier route, leaving the plan in order to get higher prices available on the market. To do this they have had to pay nonsubsidized market prices for many inputs, but they have been willing to do so in order to avoid bureaucratic delays such as having to wait one's turn for inputs that are in short supply at state-controlled prices.

While some cooperative enterprises have failed, the overall economic boom of the 1980s has led to high and rising profits for most out-of-plan coops. These enterprises must pay taxes, including a share of any profits, to the state, but what remains is distributed to workers or reinvested.

While the government has removed restrictions on cooperative enterprises and given them virtual free-market discretion, managers are exhorted to remain faithful to socialist ideals and methods.

State enterprises.   The most closely planned and controlled activities are in the state-owned enterprises. According to regulations each enterprise is given detailed instructions about quantity, quality, and variety of output as well as targets for permissible amounts of inputs, including capital. This implies expected levels of productivity. Output and input prices are also set by the state. Thus there are "profit" targets for each enterprise. Basic wages are also set by the state. There are eight basic grades, depending on difficulty of job, working environment, and the individual's skills.

These regulations overstate the degree of central control actually practiced, even in the state enterprises. More and more state enterprises have been given permission to sell any outputs they produce above their assigned targets and to keep a share of the profits they earn from these above-target sales. They may invest any retained earnings and keep the first two years' return from such investment. They may also brand their products and advertise to create a market for their above-target production. They may even apply for permission to sell above-quota outputs in export markets. Within limits an enterprise's management committee may alter the methods of production. Its worker-management group may recruit, hire, and (recently and to a limited degree) fire workers. Bonuses may be paid to individual workers from the enterprise's retained earnings. Workers' total compensation consists of basic wages, bonuses paid to the workshop by the state for cost reduction and innovation, and welfare benefits. Perhaps as much as 50 percent of total compensation comes as supplements to the basic wages.

Because these experiments have led to increased output, they have been extended. Some Western observers even believe that they will soon become the norm for all of China's state-owned industry. The Chinese authorities are discussing plans to put the housing industry, now completely state controlled, under the free market. Were this to be done, rental prices would soar and there would be a resulting burst of housing construction by private contractors. Socialist distributional objectives would be met by giving housing certificates to lower-income households. These certificates would allow people to rent housing at the market price, paying with certificates that the state would redeem from landlords.

Of course, even if all presently discussed schemes are implemented, the Chinese economy is still far from a free-market one. The basic decisions about major investments and about what to produce in what quantities and varieties remain with the state. The prices of outputs and raw materials and the basic wage levels—all of which are set by the state—substantially limit the discretion of the local enterprise managers. Moreover, prices are often quite arbitrary, reflecting relative prices that were appropriate decades earlier or the values of central planners.

Consumption Decisions

Perhaps the most visible change in the Chinese economic system in the post-Mao years has been the greater scope given to consumption and to consumption choices. While Western tourists, especially in Shanghai and Beijing (Peking), comment on the rampant Westernization, with everything from Coca-Cola to Frisbees to electronic games in evidence, the bulk of the Chinese continue to live at low levels of income, with consumption patterns to match. But the Stalinist philosophy of sacrificing everything for industrial growth has given way to a substantially more consumer-oriented economy, which benefits the present generation.

The progression toward a consumer orientation is seen in the slogans. Under Mao citizens were offered Five Guarantees: housing, clothing, grain, employment, and burial. In 1978 people spoke of the Four Musts: bicycle, radio, watch, and sewing machine. By the mid 1980s talk was of the Eight Big

BOX 43-1

In a Chinese Village

A Buddhist saying goes: "See the universe through a grain of sand." From the story of a small, rather insignificant village, one may be able to glimpse some important aspects of the vast modernization movement that is sweeping through China today and fundamentally changing the livelihood of one-fourth of mankind.

Hungshan: Pre-industrialization

Hungshan is a collective farm of 845 families about 100 miles south of Shanghai. Until 1969 Hungshan was a salt marsh, with a few households eking out a living by drying seawater for salt. In 1969, during the height of the Cultural Revolution, a decree was issued to turn the marsh into arable land for growing food grains. In the spirit of those daring times the decree was carried out with no consideration of the costs involved. Hordes of laborers were mobilized to build dikes, dig drainage trenches, plant legumes that thrive on salt (thus removing salt from the soil), and construct irrigation canals. Three years' hard work achieved the decree's objective: The salt marsh was turned into high-yielding rice fields.

Out of the huge investment in labor and capital arose the newly established Hungshan Collective Farm of a few hundred desperately poor households. One reason for their poverty was that the government set farm product prices so low relative to industrial prices that farm income barely reached a subsistence level. The system of regulated prices in effect taxed farmers to keep down the urban cost of living. Another reason was that farm production was carried out by work brigades. Workers were paid by the hours put in, with no regard to productivity or individual initiative. The net result was that the rural standard of living remained far below that of the urban, and a nationwide household registration system kept rural populations from migrating into the cities.

Industrial Take-off

In 1978 the new national leadership launched the Modernization drive. Under the new policy market incentives were to replace ideological fervor as the motive force for economic activities. Bureaucratic controls over the economy were to be loosened to give private enterprises more latitude in making decisions. Individuals were to be rewarded for their productivity and initiative. A market mechanism was to be activated to help allocate resources in a fundamentally socialist economic system.

The new wind reached Hungshan in 1980. A new team of village leaders decided that the time had come for the village to pull itself out of poverty through industrialization. Seeing the widespread shortage of building materials, they hit upon the idea of building a cement factory. A group was sent to procure technical advice from cement plants elsewhere. The collective's meager surplus fund was used as initial capital, plus a small capital loan from a government bank at zero interest. In addition, advance payments were asked of customers, who were eager to comply in order to ensure future delivery of much needed cement.

The factory started operation in 1980 and was a spectacular financial success by the very next year. Emboldened, the farm plowed profits into starting a ceramic tile factory, a slate-polishing factory, a cloth-dyeing factory, a clothes-making factory, a plastic-molding factory, a television shell factory, and a farm-machinery parts factory in the succeeding years. By late 1984 a total of 18 enterprises had been established.

The collective farm was replaced by the Hungshan Agricultural-Industrial-Commercial Development Corporation, which served as the holding company for the 18 separate enterprises. Whereas in 1978 the collective farm depended mostly on farming, five years later the corporation generated 84 percent of its revenue from industry, 6 percent from commerce, and only 10 percent from agriculture. During the same period agricultural employment fell from 80 percent of total employment to 37 percent, and industrial employment rose from 16 percent to 58 percent.

With a more diversified industrial structure came the problem of securing future supplies of energy and raw materials. Given the inadequate distribution system and the distorted price structure in China, ensuring a steady supply of energy was the first requirement for sustained industrial growth. The village corporation's managers contracted to make a substantial capital investment in a small coal mine in a distant

Source: Adapted with permission from "In a Chinese Village" by Hang-Sheng Cheng, in Federal Research Bank of San Francisco *Weekly Letter,* November 1, 1985.

province to ensure an adequate supply of coal for the village in future years.

Industrialization raised the village's income at a dizzying rate. From 1978 to 1983 its total net income increased 470 percent. After deducting for tax payments and the corporation's surplus funds, per capita distribution in 1983 was about $300—triple the amount in 1978.

Welfare

With the higher income came improved living conditions, including handsome two-story prefabricated concrete houses, decorated extensively with locally produced ceramic tiles and polished slate, that contained spacious and airy rooms and traditional farm-kitchen facilities (that used dried rice stalks for fuel). Inside, the houses were remarkably clean and well-furnished—looking suspiciously like model homes in U.S. new housing developments. The hosts proudly showed this visitor the new television sets, refrigerators, and bicycles.

In addition, the village also built a four-story school building. Education from kindergarten through junior high school was free. The village did not have a high school, but provided scholarships for students who were accepted into high schools elsewhere and for those who entered universities.

The village also paid for 70 percent of medical expenses up to $10 per illness and 100 percent above that amount. For families of a single child, it paid an annual bonus for up to 14 years. The village claimed not to have had a new family with more than one child in the past six years.

Incentive Versus Equity

A great deal of credit for the village's spectacular economic success goes to entrepreneurship, and entrepreneurship has been richly rewarded. In 1983 the cement factory was contracted out to a five-person management team with a target profit twice the amount that was realized in 1982. Under the contract each worker was paid a flat wage rate of $12.50 per month plus a floating bonus depending on the amount by which the factory's target profit was exceeded. That year the workers averaged over $1,000 income per person, and the five-man management team each received more than $3,500.

The clothing factory suffered losses in 1982. In 1983 the factory switched to the new incentive system. It was contracted out to a young man from a neighboring village who had had six years of clothing-sales experience. Through innovative management methods and the introduction of new products (new-style shirts and ski jackets), the factory realized a profit in 1983. The manager received a total of $10,000 that year, including bonus, and became the highest paid person in the village. In a country where per capita income was about $140 a year, these remunerations were indeed astronomical.

Newspapers reported these income disparities with approval and relish. These cases were cited as successes of the new incentive system. It was the government's proclaimed policy to permit a few people to get rich first in order to help everybody else get rich later.

Conclusions

Hungshan village and its story symbolize the ideals of the nation's new leaders. In a fundamental sense these ideals are perhaps not that different from those that had prevailed for thirty years before the new leaders came into power. However, in terms of the means for achieving the goals the departures from the old path have been significant.

From this viewpoint the story is noteworthy because it helps highlight some points about China's Modernization drive. First, it demonstrates that by giving free rein to industrial development outside the rigidly controlled state-enterprise sector, a vast reservoir of entrepreneurship and creative energy can be released to propel the country's economic growth.

Second, the deliberate allowance of income disparity has provided a large incentive for individual initiative that was absent in the old regime.

Third, rural industrial development has continued to be distinctly socialist: The enterprises are collectively owned by village or township corporations and not by private individuals.

Fourth, by encouraging rural industrial development—and thereby providing jobs where the majority of the population resides—China may be able to mitigate the ills of urban concentration that have plagued many developing nations.

Things: color television, refrigerator, stereo, camera, motorcycle, tape recorder, washing machine, and electric fan.

State control of the amount and nature of consumption occurs through its control of income distribution, prices, and, for some goods, ration tickets. A primary tool of income distribution has been the state-controlled relationship of wages and bonuses to prices of consumer goods. By keeping certain prices low and allowing wages to rise, the central government has created a significant amount of discretionary income for consumers. Furthermore, the opportunity to earn, and keep, incentive pay and bonuses has steadily increased. This has meant refraining from high taxation of marginal income and limiting the share of total national income devoted to new investment. (How much this will reduce long-run economic growth is currently a hotly debated issue.) Additionally, by raising farm prices relative to industrial prices and by encouraging rural free enterprise, the government has increased the ability of the large, relatively poorer rural population to earn incomes above the subsistence level.

The prices of consumer goods that are not set in the free market are deliberately controlled. "Essentials" are priced at or below the cost of production. These goods are characteristically rationed, with ration tickets issued to households according to the number and age of household members, the type of work the members engage in, and the region of residence.

The combination of subsidized consumption of necessities and rationed availability is taken by the Chinese to be an ideological triumph of their system. Everyday necessities, such as coal, are priced at something like average total cost, and the objective is to produce a quantity sufficient to meet the demand at the controlled prices. Secondary needs are priced well above cost, with the exact markup determined by the central government's desire to encourage or limit consumption. Some of these secondary-need commodities, such as wristwatches, bicycles, and toothpaste, are rationed by means of waiting lists for the limited available supplies. They tend, however, to be more readily available in large cities than in rural areas. Consequently, below-market clearing prices are being charged at least in some areas of the country.

The fact that both food and industrial products are available to some degree in private markets limits the state's ability to control consumption decisions by setting the structure of official prices. Of course, it can control consumption indirectly by limiting the production of individual commodities and by reducing the amount of discretionary income households have. But substantial consumer choice is presently being encouraged and is being exercised. The increased opportunity for consumption has reinforced the incentive to earn extra income. There are worthwhile things to work for and to buy.

Economic Reform

The Maoist period accomplished many things, some good and some bad for the health of the economy. Some of its more harmful consequences are listed below. Some are harmful practices introduced by Mao that have persisted. Others represent the long-lasting effects of now-discontinued policies that must still be lived with.

1. A highly centralized planning system put great power into a few hands, leaving few effective methods for challenging or even modifying decisions.

2. The growth policy, which was adapted from the early Russian model, was based on high rates of capital accumulation and a concentration on heavy industry. This tended to foster an attitude of growth for its own sake.

3. The so-called iron-rice-bowl policy means that a worker receives tenure on his first day of work. Under this system it was virtually impossible to fire anyone. While the policy has been officially abandoned, it remains in practice since firms are unwilling to fire anyone.

4. Managers of state enterprises have been controlled too closely by central directives and given too little scope, or incentive, to exercise initiative on their own.

5. Pricing policies are extremely inefficient in a number of ways. First, capital is often provided freely to enterprises and usually does not have to be repaid. As a result, fixed capital is inefficiently utilized, and many firms carry excessive inventories. Second, Chinese pricing policies put great emphasis on price stability. As a result, many relative prices bear no relation to current costs of production or to

current scarcities. So even when producers are allowed some profit incentive, the incentives tend to encourage them to produce the wrong commodities. Third, the shortages caused by disequilibrium relative prices are countered by rationing schemes that themselves impose added costs and reduce consumer satisfaction. Fourth, food prices of such staple commodities as rice are kept very low. This transfers income from rural to urban areas and greatly diminishes the incentives for increased agricultural production of the commodities whose prices are controlled.

To attack some of these problems, reforms have either been introduced or proposed. Many reforms, such as increased incentives, less emphasis on heavy industry, and some relaxation of total job security, are already coming into effect.

In the opinion of many economists, however, the reforms that are the most important are changes in pricing policies to move prices of outputs and inputs closer to efficient, market-clearing levels. In the absence of major price reform, most of the other reform measures will fail to achieve their objectives or, still worse, result in further misallocations of resources. In 1985 the first major increases in prices of staple foods were announced, thus decreasing sharply the subsidy to food consumption. Whether this signals the long awaited price reform is unclear at this time.

The Chinese are currently discussing moving towards a system that they call *parametric planning*. By this they mean that they will plan, and control, such broad macroeconomic magnitudes as total investment, total capital expenditure on transportation, and total consumption. But, within these broad macro controls, market forces will be allowed to allocate resources and so to decide how much of each individual commodity is to be produced.

Performance of the Chinese Economy

Growth

Since 1949 the Chinese economy has grown at an average rate of nearly 8 percent per year and in per capita terms at about 3.6 percent per year. Most of the growth in the period from 1949 to 1977 was in the industrial sector, which showed an annual aver-

age growth rate of 12 percent. These are impressive growth rates by Western standards, but the comparison may be misleading. China started from a very low base. After decades of occupation, war, and civil unrest, almost any kind of peacetime economy would have shown growth. In every five-year period, except that of the Great Leap Forward, income grew, as did both industrial and agricultural output.

China's growth has been smaller than that of Japan, Korea, Hong Kong, and Singapore, but above that of many other Asian countries, such as India, Burma, and Indonesia. The pattern of growth has been uneven; it has tended to be higher in the pragmatic, relatively market-oriented periods and lower in the Maoist, culturally oriented ones. It has tended, at least until recently, to be greater in industry than in agriculture, despite the critical need for and the great emphasis on agricultural output.

Since 1978 growth has slowed in the industrial sector to about 7 percent per year, but it has risen in agriculture. Thus the overall growth rate has been maintained while progress was being made in restoring balance among the sectors of the economy. This balance should remove one of the major inhibitions to sustained future growth: bottlenecks that have resulted from the unbalanced growth strategies of the past. How much of the credit belongs to the increased use of market incentives, how much to the increased role of foreign trade, how much to the relative political stability, and how much to other factors is a matter for current debate. But Western experts on the Chinese economy believe the prospects for continued rapid growth are good.

Population Control

As the rise in per capita income suggests, China has had some recent success in limiting its population growth. Everything from posters that proclaim "An only child is a happy child" to incentives that make it very expensive to have a second child to much more repressive measures has been used.

In any event and from all sources, population control is occurring. A recent study cites over 50 million abortions between 1980 and 1985. But overpopulation continues to be a problem. Every person of working age is assigned to a job, whether in a factory or farm or elsewhere, or is classified as "waiting for employment assignment" (a euphemism for unemployment). Underemployment in rural areas is evident, and is kept from becoming urban unemployment only by restrictions that prevent people from leaving their villages. Urban underemployment also exists, but is largely concealed in the cooperative and small-business sectors, which have more workers or helpers than fully paid employees.

Living Standards

When living standards are considered, especially in socialist countries, it is important to include the contribution of nonwage as well as wage income. Until the past few years rural measured income in China changed little. Standards of living, however, have risen steadily since the mid 1950s through increased literacy, availability of such public services as libraries, schooling and medical care, growth of income security at all stages of life, and a spectacular increase in life expectancy. (Life expectancy in rural areas rose from about 40 years in 1950 to over 60 years in 1985. Of all the countries or regions in the world with China's approximate per capita income, only Sri Lanka and the State of Kerala in India appear to have achieved as high a life expectancy.) Since 1981 growth of private incomes of rural households has added to the growth in living standards.

Similar remarks apply to urban areas. Here, there is in addition the great increase in female labor force participation rates, which has meant that the average household has more workers and hence more income.

Income Distribution

A study by the World Bank suggested that the percentage of real income received by the poorest two-fifths of the income distribution is no higher in China than in Thailand, India, or Indonesia. While many believe that recent reforms have changed this situation, income disparities surely are substantial even today. This is the result of many factors, but one of the most important is the absolute control exercised over internal migration. This has permitted the emergence of large income differentials between rural and urban areas that in a freer society would have caused a large shift of population into the cities and towns.

Prognosis for the Future

It is too early to know how far the recent changes in economic management will move China along the path of long-term economic development. On the one hand it is easy to find in the recent Chinese experience evidence that economic incentives, individual discretion, and foreign trade have proven more productive than mass enthusiasm, self-reliance, the class struggle, and a tightly controlled command economy—all aspects of Maoist doctrine. On the other hand, Chinese communism has often succeeded in tapping the vast potential energy and enthusiasm of the masses.

Has the Chinese experience proven that Maoist-Marxist philosophy is in error in assuming that ideology is more important than material incentives? Many observers feel that it would be premature to answer yes to this question. That philosophy is directed primarily to goals other than material well-being, goals that include achieving a classless society with a more equal distribution of income, income security, and guaranteed employment. China under Mao and still to a degree under Deng is pursuing noneconomic goals even if they conflict with maximum economic growth. Which goals to pursue and with what intensity are always important social choices. At the moment China is leaning toward the material, but there are many in China who believe this is wrong. A leading American student of China believes that latent Marxist sentiments are consistent with Chinese traditions and are still important to millions of Chinese. Those who hold these beliefs most strongly could return to power within a decade of Deng's death. China's future—economic, political, and cultural—will change sharply if they do.

The Economy of the Soviet Union

The modern *economic* history of the Soviet Union is usually taken to have begun in 1928, 11 years after the Bolshevik revolution. At the time of World War I, Russia was a large and in most ways backward country with an enormous, poor, largely ignorant and illiterate peasantry, who were to prove as sullenly hostile to their new Bolshevik rulers as they had been to the czars. Backward and poor though Russia was, by 1917 industrialization had been under way for three decades; the nucleus of heavy industry and of an industrial labor force already existed.

During its first decade of existence the new regime hung on by its teeth, contending with recurring famines, internal power struggles, and invasion by the Western powers. By the late 1920s Joseph Stalin emerged as an effective strong man ready to undertake the economic task of lifting the Soviet Union from an underdeveloped giant to a major industrial power. Whatever the costs—and they have been enormous—the economic rise of the Soviet Union in six decades is a major achievement.

Stalin's economic policy had three strategies: (1) to consolidate management over all economic resources in such a way that they would respond surely and quickly to the needs of the regime; (2) to constrict consumption drastically so that the maximum possible rate of capital accumulation, and thus growth, could be achieved; (3) to channel growth into the areas of heavy industrial development required for a major military power.

Neither the sacrifices imposed on the people as consumers nor the Herculean efforts asked of them as producers were borne without complaint or opposition. Stalin is perhaps best remembered for his "terrors," dramatized by the purges in which thousands were exiled or killed. Whatever its primary purposes, this regime of terror had the two effects of enforcing centralized power and providing a powerful set of incentives to carry out the orders of the regime.

The famous five-year plans began the rapid industrial development that was to transform the Soviet Union into a major military power by World War II and a major world power in the postwar period. The twelfth five-year plan, covering the period 1986 to 1990, was only the fourth to put major emphasis on production of consumer goods.

Ownership

With certain limited exceptions the central government—the state—owns all land, all natural resources, all capital goods, all business enterprises, and most urban housing.

In the industrial sector state ownership is virtually complete. In the retail fields state stores make up about two-thirds of the total sales. The bulk of the remainder is accounted for by rural cooperatives, with a small amount of farm produce sold in free "farmers' markets." Most rural housing and perhaps a third of urban housing is privately owned (and officially restricted to personal use); the rest is publicly owned.

About a third of all agricultural production comes from farms (called *sovkhos*) that are owned and managed by the state. Another half of all production comes from collective farms that, while nominally cooperatives into which peasants were once forced, are in fact so closely controlled by the state that their differences from the sovkhos are minor. The remainder of the agricultural output is produced on privately owned farms and by members of collective farms on garden plots they are allowed to cultivate in their spare time.

Private enterprise is profitable where it is permitted—in agriculture and in personal services of various kinds from psychiatric counseling to carpentry. The official figures probably underestimate the private sector by ignoring the illegal black market in privately produced goods and services.

The black market is a response by households (who are permitted to own savings deposits and personal possessions) to the restricted supply of officially available goods. They are glad to buy goods and services from others, who in turn are glad to earn extra money by producing them.

The Organization of Production

In the industrial sector of the Soviet economy production is predominantly organized around individual plants that are managed by a director. The director is appointed by the government with the approval of the local Communist party group. Directors may appear omnipotent to the workers, but decisions about how and what to produce and how and when to replace equipment or expand operations are handed down from higher up in the planning hierarchy. Directors are in fact more bureaucrats than entrepreneurs.

Production decisions are made in a highly organized pyramidal bureaucracy. The overall planning agency, the USSR GOSPLAN, develops broad plans that are translated into orders for regional GOS-PLANs, which in turn hand down directives to particular ministries. Ministries may be either at the industry level or in control of a particular resource. Ministries' instructions ultimately take the form of orders to individual plant directors, who then do their best to carry them out.

The industrial firm's targets include quotas with respect to total output and output of individual commodities. The wages a firm can offer are fixed by the government, and there is no open market on which the firm's manager can acquire scarce commodities. Within limits, workers are free to choose any job they are offered, and labor mobility is not really restricted, except that workers on collective farms have not been allowed to leave them at will. Despite rather large occupational wage differences, labor mobility has tended to be low.

Industry is governed by the many rules of a command economy. Directives cover many aspects of a firm's operations, though, of course, they cannot cover all contingencies. *Within* the guidelines of the plan as it is sent down to the given firm, the firm is instructed and encouraged to be efficient and, where possible, to make "above-plan profits." Planned profits go to the state; part of above-plan profits may be retained in the firm and used for the benefit of the employees. Thus there is some scope for maneuver, but the constraints are much tighter than those that face a typical American or Chinese firm. A Soviet enterprise cannot usually experiment with new products or new methods of production without first securing permission. Indeed, because there is such emphasis on meeting or exceeding plan quotas, *quantity* of output becomes more compelling than cost savings or quality.[2]

Western observers—and Soviet observers, too—have often noted that many microeconomic inefficiencies result from the command principle. Among them are excessive stockpiles of some commodities,

shortages of others, and poor quality of many goods. Similar inefficiencies have been shown to exist in many American government activities, such as military procurement, where centralized command systems are in use. This suggests that inefficiencies of these kinds are inherent in highly centralized systems in which incentives are mainly to fulfill output quotas rather than to earn profits.

Despite inefficiencies the Soviet system clearly works. It has produced a growing flow of armaments, goods, machines, and space vehicles. Soviet industry has met the major demands placed on it; its inefficiencies have been serious, but not crippling.

One of the sharpest critics of the inefficiencies of overcentralization and rigid control structure is a Soviet professor, E. Liberman. Some socialist countries, such as Yugoslavia, have responded to his criticisms more than the USSR, but there is currently within the USSR a great debate on this very issue, and numerous reforms have been aimed at decentralization over the last two decades.

Soviet managers have little incentive to innovate by experimenting with new products or new ways of producing old products but they have often been successful in copying capitalist products and techniques. One of the severest critics of the stultifying effects on invention and innovation exerted by a highly centralized economy has been the distinguished Soviet physicist and Nobel prize winner A. K. Sakharov. (Since 1980 Sakharov has been banned from Moscow as a result of his too persistent criticisms.)

Agricultural production (which in 1928 absorbed 80 percent of the Soviet labor force and today absorbs about 25 percent) is almost as centralized as manufacturing. The results have been much less successful than those in the industrial sector. The collective farms were designed to provide cheap and adequate food supplies, but the coercion required to bring unwilling individual peasants into the collective farms did not generate cooperative responses. Many observers believe that the lack of incentives and rewards is responsible. Meeting steel quotas wins bonuses, medals, praise, and pay raises for steelworkers; meeting grain quotas is likely to lead to even higher quotas for the next period.

Collective farmers do not receive wages; rather,

---

[2] Because prices are specified by the state and are spelled out in the directive, the firm can earn above-plan profits only by exceeding output quotas. Many critics both outside and inside the system have noticed an overconcentration on physical output—on technological rather than economic efficiency.

they share in the income of the farm. But the government's policy, designed to keep food prices down by keeping farm prices low, has kept farm income low, too. In any case, low morale and the inability of farm labor to find other jobs have not led to high productivity, and agricultural production has been a chronic trouble spot in the Soviet economy.

Probably the biggest single failure of the Soviet system is its agricultural policy. Communist theorists, who were mainly urban in their origin and experience, sought to make collective farms resemble factories and regarded peasants as if they were assembly line workers. But throughout the world a farmer's job is tougher than that of an assembly line worker. Farming is not a 9-to-5 job nor is it limited to five days a week. The evidence suggests that the constant, backbreaking toil required of farmers is provided efficiently only when the fruits of that toil accrue to the farmers themselves. Whenever, as in China, socialist governments have allowed peasants to own their land, have allowed them to keep much of the proceeds of the crops they sell, and have made the necessary agricultural equipment available, food output has risen dramatically. Whenever, as in the Soviet Union, the peasants do not own their land and cannot keep much of the return from marketing their crops, production languishes because peasants are not motivated to apply the necessary effort.

Household Incentives and the Distribution of Goods

Both the nature and quantity of the goods to be produced are specified by the central planners. Those for consumers are placed in the state-owned shops or in cooperatives, to be sold at government-specified prices that include an important "turnover tax" (See Box 43-2.)

Households are free to spend their incomes on these goods. Individual choice rather than "command" is at work, but even here the function of a market is restricted. For instance, if too many consumers want a particular item, supplies will run out, but no price rise signals the higher demand to producers. The shortage is not an effective signal because producers are not motivated to respond to it. As a result there is no assurance that production will be increased. There is no automatic feedback indicating what consumers want and would buy that has any effect on the goods and services actually produced.

The use of the market, rather than direct allocation, in the distribution of consumer goods is explained by the need to avoid the impossible administrative burden of deciding who gets what, rather than by a philosophical desire to let consumers be sovereign. There is a difference between consumer sovereignty, which allows consumer choices to help determine *what is produced,* and consumer freedom to choose from among goods of *predetermined* quantity, quality, and price.

Until the 1970s Soviet planners were reluctant to respond to such clear consumer signals as shortages of particular goods. The consumer riots in Poland in December 1970 changed this. After that Soviet planners began to take account of shortages and surpluses of particular consumer goods at existing prices in setting new production targets. To the extent that this occurs, consumer sovereignty has been introduced into the system.

Recently there has been increased pressure for, and some experimentation with, a two-phase system. The system would allow planners to decide what proportion of the nation's resources to devote to the production of consumer goods. It would also allow consumers, through a decentralized market-decision mechanism, to exert an influence on how those resources are allocated among various lines of production.

Household incomes come from the state principally in the form of wages and salaries. "To each according to his need" was the Marxist ideal, but in the Soviet Union scientists, engineers, ballet dancers, and athletes apparently need more than do laborers and teachers. Wage *differentials* are in fact much larger than in the United States; skilled workers characteristically earn four times more than unskilled workers (in contrast to one and a half times more in the United States).

But wages are not the only determinant of the distribution of income. Many goods and services, such as medical care, higher education, and old-age pensions, are provided free to those who qualify. State housing is provided at low cost. Large families receive special money allowances and special hous-

BOX 43-2

Planning in the Soviet Union

Plans to Specify Growth Objectives

Five-year plans.   Five-year plans are, roughly, blueprints for later detailed implementation. They contain no orders to individual plants and no detailed quotas of goods to be produced, but they do prescribe both the level of aggregate income that is to be achieved and the *structure* of the economy by major sectors and industries.

Every five-year plan has included decisions about how drastically to curtail consumption in order to release resources for investment. Each has also decided how much effort is to be devoted to developing educational and technical resources that will be needed in the future. Decisions are also made about such matters as the form capital investment should take, and the state-controlled banking system lends only to those enterprises whose expansion the planners want to encourage.

One-year plans.   Planning details are spelled out in the one-year plans. They are extremely complex exercises that work out the myriad microeconomic implications of certain broad objectives. The one-year plans translate the objectives of the five-year plans into detail sufficient to enable individual plants (or farms) to meet them and to ensure that the required supplies of needed resources are made available.

This is obviously an enormous coordinating job. Tentative plans are sent to lower bureaucratic levels for comments and suggestions before being issued as final orders. Actual quotas are to some degree negotiated between the directors at the operating levels, who want to hold down the quotas expected of them, and the higher-level planners, who must achieve apparent miracles to satisfy overall growth objectives.

Prices in the Planning Process

Factor pricing.   For internal productive use, "prices" of commodities or resources are designed to measure the scarcity value of the resources, compared to alternative uses. If the efficient use of resources is to occur, the charge for using, say, the services of a carpenter anywhere should reflect the value of his or her marginal product elsewhere.

But the state may wish to pay carpenters a higher wage than this, either because it has embarked on a program of income redistribution in which carpenters are to be favored or because the state wishes to denote carpentry as a "prestige" occupation. To avoid productive inefficiency, the planners assign *two* wage rates for carpenters. One is charged as a cost of production; the other (which may be higher or lower) is actually paid out to carpenters and becomes the source of their income.

With one important exception, this dual treatment of factor prices has long been part of the Soviet planning procedure. The exception concerns the cost of capital. Because "interest" is traditionally a payment to private owners of capital in capitalist societies, interest rates were odious to Marx and to early Marxist planners. Soviet planners were reluctant to assign a real scarcity-value interest rate to funds allocated for investment until a series of studies showed that investment allocation was among the least efficient aspects of Soviet planning. Today a number very much like an interest rate is used to measure the cost of capital.

Consumer prices and the turnover tax.   Consumer prices are made up of two parts: the full cost of the good produced, using the correct internal accounting prices for factors, plus a **turnover tax.** This is an excise tax, which varies tremendously from commodity to commodity.

The amount of the turnover tax is a means by which planners can encourage or discourage consumption of certain goods. In part it is a means for redistributing income; goods consumed by low-income groups may have low turnover taxes.

Revenue from the turnover tax is used by the state for new investment. By changing the turnover tax, the planners can affect the relative size of consumption and investment. By varying the tax rate on different kinds of commodities, the state can affect the relative sacrifice in consumption among different kinds of consumers.

ing. Thus standards of living in the Soviet Union are considerably less unequal than wage differentials suggest. In contrast to the United States, there are fewer extreme incomes at either end but a somewhat greater spread in the incomes of the middle and upper middle income groups.

Income distribution in the USSR is very much a matter of conscious policy decisions. Through wages, allowances, free and subsidized goods, and the turnover tax, the party hierarchy can effectively impose *their* views as to the appropriate pattern of output and distribution of income.

Sources of Investment Funds

The tax revenues of the Soviet state are an important source of state revenues. In addition the central bank (GOSBANK) can expand the money supply and absorb any government deficit it is asked to absorb. If it prints too much money, it will, of course, create an inflationary gap. With such a gap, there will be longer lines, more shortages, and more grumbling. These results can be avoided only by raising prices—by letting the inflation occur. Another aspect of the money supply is the ability of firms to borrow in order to expand. GOSBANK lends only to those enterprises whose expansion the planners want to encourage. It thus becomes a further device for implementing planners' objectives.

Unlike most Western central banks, GOSBANK is a monopoly commercial bank with thousands of branches. Since the central bank controls the commercial banking system completely, it does not use any of the indirect tools, such as open-market operations, used by Western central banks.

Comparative Performance: The United States and the Soviet Union

In judging the performance of an economy, there are many different criteria and many different ways of viewing it. Moreover, comparing the actual performances of only two economies can be misleading. For example, during the last 40 years the Soviet Union has experienced twice as great a growth rate

as the United States. But before concluding that this demonstrates a growth advantage of communism over capitalism, the even higher growth rates achieved in West Germany and Japan—capitalist countries—should be noted. With this warning in mind, we shall compare elements of the economic performances of the United States and the Soviet Union.

The Standard of Living in the 1980s

Most national income acountants and students of the Soviet economy judge the level of real purchasing power per capita in the Soviet Union to be about 50 percent of that in the United States. This kind of statistic is difficult to interpret. Clearly, most Americans would feel poor if their present incomes were cut in half. But American real incomes a generation ago were half what they are today, and at that time the United States was the richest nation in history. The perceived adequacy of one's income depends on what everyone else's income is and on past and future expectations. The Soviet citizens' standard of living is so much higher than it was even a decade ago, and is rising so rapidly, that it probably seems comfortable to them.

Nevertheless, it is clear that Soviet citizens are poorer than their American counterparts. Not only is housing worse and clothing in shorter supply and less elegant, but the average citizen has to work more hours to earn the cost of a pair of shoes or an evening dinner. A small car in 1985 cost about twice the annual salary of the average Muscovite, and even at that price there was a three-year wait for delivery. Not surprisingly, the Soviet worker buys less, works longer hours, and has shorter vacations.

Notice, however, that these comparisons reflect in good part *our* social values. An observer might note that the Soviet citizen can see better chess, better gymnastics, and better soccer than an American counterpart and can see them more cheaply. Another observer might note that Soviet citizens need not worry about providing medical and dental care for their families, the possibility of unemployment due to a severe economic slump, or providing for their retirement or the support of their dependents after their own death. A comprehensive set of welfare programs covers all these contingencies for all Soviet citizens.

Growth

From 1928 to 1975 the Soviet Union achieved an overall rate of growth of more than 4.5 percent per year notwithstanding some major disasters, particularly the famines of the 1930s and the devastating impact of World War II. During the 1960s the Soviet rate of growth was twice the U.S. rate. In more recent times, however, the growth rate has declined (although it is still higher than the U.S. rate). Recent growth experience is shown in Table 43-1.

As we noted, this remarkable growth record has not been costless. It was achieved by sacrificing current consumption for investment that led to greater production in the future. The relative prosperity of today's Soviet citizens is owed to their parents' and grandparents' forced forbearance. To sustain this growth rate for another generation, present-day cit-

TABLE 43-1   Estimates of Growth of GNP in the USSR, by Sector of Origin

	Average annual growth rate (percent)			
	1966–1970	1971–1975	1976–1980	1981–1983
Agriculture	3.9	−0.4	1.2	3.4
Industry	6.4	5.9	3.2	2.7
Construction	5.8	5.6	1.9	2.1
Transportation	6.7	6.5	3.5	2.5
Communications	8.9	7.3	5.8	3.8
Trade	7.0	4.6	2.9	1.8
Services	4.3	3.4	2.8	2.3
Total GNP	5.3	3.7	2.6	2.6

Source: Handbook of Economic Statistics, 1984, Central Intelligence Agency, Directorate of Intelligence, Table 41.

Growth rates in all sectors of the Soviet economy, except agriculture, slowed sharply after 1975.
Growth rates vary significantly from sector to sector. Agriculture, long the slowest growing sector, has shown a recent revival. The overall growth rate in the Soviet Union since 1976 is no longer far above that of the United States.

izens may well have to continue to forego many of the comforts available to Americans. There is little general enthusiasm for such policies, and the regime has eased the restrictions on the consumer sector even at the cost of its growth rate. But the Soviet economy has demonstrated how an underdeveloped country can develop in one lifetime, if it will pay the price and if it has the unexploited resources on which to base an expansion.

Economic Stability

If growth has been the great triumph of the Soviet experience, economic stability has been a small one. A highly planned economy, if it is insulated from the outside world, need have no deficient-demand unemployment, no unintended inflation or deflation, and no cyclical phenomena. If it must engage heavily in foreign trade, it is not so easily insulated. In this regard the Soviet Union during its period of rapid growth was fortunate. It is a large country with ample and varied natural resources (like the United States), and it did not have to rely heavily on foreign trade. Moreover, much of what it did need after 1945 was provided from within the Soviet system by the satellite countries of Eastern Europe.

The failure of Soviet agriculture to increase output sufficiently to keep pace with demand has led to increasingly large imports of foodstuffs from the West. Imports of high technology products, a field in which the Soviet Union has not kept pace with the West, have also been increased to meet a growing demand. As a result the Soviets have been faced with an increased need to earn foreign exchange to pay for these imports.

Although unemployment due to deficient aggregate demand need not and does not occur in the Soviet system, frictional and structural unemployment can occur. The state's ability to control the movement of people away from the farms (through a system of work permits and internal passports) has led to much disguised unemployment in the agricultural sector. There is little doubt that if people had been free to move from the farms, they would have moved in great numbers to the cities in search of the excitement and higher living standards there, and they would have moved at a faster rate than industry could have absorbed them. In a market economy this would have led to substantial urban overcrowding and unemployment and would have served to depress the wages of those who were successful in finding work. The Soviet policy has been to hold these people on the farms where they are underemployed and to allow them to move to the cities no faster than they could be absorbed into jobs there.

Again, a potential clash of values can be seen. Western observers are inclined to stress what to them is the severe loss of personal freedom, while Soviet observers tend to emphasize the gains to the economy of an orderly relocation of labor. In particular, they see the advantages to urban workers of not having their wages depressed by the unemployed migrants from the farm and the advantage to the farm dwellers in being detained on the farm, where they can be fed and housed at lower cost and in greater comfort until jobs are available in the city.

The Soviets have had less success in controlling inflation than in controlling unemployment. Like the princes discussed in Chapter 31, they found increasing the money supply too easy a way to finance public expenditures, particularly during World War II. The high wartime expenditures resulted in a dangerously inflationary piling up of private money balances. But the response of a command economy can be quick and sure, if harsh. When monetary reform came, the state confiscated the bulk of private monetary balances and repudiated some of the public debt that workers had accepted in lieu of part of their wages. Thus workers who thought they had been saving found they really had been taxed.

All belligerent countries faced the same problem at the end of World War II. Wartime savings and deferred consumption created an enormous backlog of demand. After the war this demand for goods was far in excess of the supply. The Soviet response was to destroy the backlog of purchasing power by monetary reform; the Western answer was to allow people to try to exercise it and accept the inevitable inflation. This reduced the real value of accumulated purchasing power to a level commensurate with the goods actually available for purchase. Both systems achieved the same end of reducing the real value of purchasing power to what was available. To Western eyes, the Soviet solution (confiscation) seems harsh

and autocratic; to Soviet eyes, the Western solution (inflation) seems arbitrary and highly inequitable.

Shortcomings of the Soviet Economic Experience

In at least three major ways, a Soviet-type planned economy compares unfavorably to a Western market economy. First, it is accompanied by what most observers agree to be far more numerous and more serious microeconomic inefficiencies. Many small interdependent decisions have to be made that are difficult or impossible to make quickly, consistently, and efficiently, given a centralized decision hierarchy. The shortages, gluts, misshipments, and shortfalls of key quotas that have annoyed Soviet industry and plagued Soviet agriculture are neither surprising nor wholly avoidable. They are periodically denounced as the "planning errors" of a previous regime. Such errors, however, are apparently a cost of choosing to replace an automatic mechanism (whose implicit values the planners have rejected) by a deliberate mechanism that permits the planners to introduce their own values. In recent years some pressure has developed within Soviet-type economies to retreat from complete planning and to allow market or market-like mechanisms to do more of the allocating.

A second deficiency has been in the detailed planning process itself, which makes enormous demands on time and energy. When labor was abundant, and when alternative uses of those with the planners' skills were not numerous, this transactions cost of planning was perhaps not serious. Increasingly, however, the Soviet bureaucracy has been absorbing a large quantity of the energies of valuable, highly trained men and women in plan formation and implementation. The Soviets have come to recognize this as a real cost. The major surge of interest in techniques of mathematical programming, input-output analysis, and simulation reflects an official effort to substitute capital for high-priced labor in the "production function of planning." They hope both to save resources and to avoid some microeconomic inefficiencies and mistakes.

A third deficiency is that the goods and services produced reflect planners' preferences rather than those of citizens, for there is no effective market mechanism by which consumers can signal their preferences. Not every family wants the same size apartment, but if the family is allocated space according to family size and occupation, there is no way that family *preferences* will play a role.

Source and Costs of the Achievements

A planned, command economy has certain advantages over a market economy: The leaders can set up whatever priorities they wish, and they can then use the full power of the state to implement them. In such economies the power of the state has been used to achieve forced saving to permit capital formation and rapid growth. It has also been used to prevent widespread unemployment. It may well be that the Soviet growth record could not have been achieved had it depended on popular or majority support, for it is by no means clear that the growth benefited the Soviet population of the 1930s and 1940s.

This rapid growth has had costs—costs not only in current consumption foregone, but also the costs of coercing individuals, of their loss of freedom, and of substituting centralized for individual judgments.

Because these costs cannot readily be measured, the question of whether the benefits justify the costs is debatable. Most citizens of Western countries are content to have foregone both the benefits and the costs; contemporary Russians may feel they have been justified. Different people and different governments in the rest of the world come down on different sides.

Politically, the present government is in many ways highly repressive, particularly to those expressing dissent. Indeed, some regard it as a monstrous tyranny. It is not necessary to assume, however, that tyranny *must* accompany any command economy. After all, the tradition of Russian political tyranny stretches well back into the time of the czars. Other command economies have had regimes less repressive than that of the USSR. However, command economies must by their very nature be more authoritarian than free-market economies. An important and unsettled question concerns the minimum repression of individual freedom that is consistent with a highly centralized planned economy of the Soviet type.

Summary

1. The economies of China and the Soviet union are different from one another and from our own, but all these economies must find ways to allocate scarce resources and to solve other common problems.

2. The building of the socialist economy of the Peoples Republic of China began after the victory of the Communists over the Nationalists in 1949. The first decade saw Russian-style planning with emphasis on heavy industry and neglect of agriculture. The Great Leap Forward in 1958 to 1960 was a failure of doctrinaire socialist views, which included the collectivization of agriculture. From 1961 to 1965 the pragmatists introduced reforms relying on market incentives and decentralization of economic power. From 1966 to 1975 another doctrinaire experiment, called the Cultural Revolution, produced economic chaos by its rejection of all market values as well as scholarship, learning, and technological innovation. Since 1976 the pragmatists have been in power and less centralized control is the rule of the day.

3. Agriculture and related activities employ 75 percent of the Chinese population. Collectivization has proven a failure, as it has through-

out the communist world. Chinese pragmatists have been giving ever more scope to the private profit motive to influence agricultural decisions.

4. Industry is partly state owned and controlled and partly left to individual initiative. Again, the pragmatists are introducing more decentralization of decision making in industry.

5. The performance of the Chinese economy has been mixed, but population control now seems to be finally a matter of serious policy attention and standards of living—as measured by such factors as absence of famine, greatly increased life expectancy, free medical and hospital care for all, universal old-age security, and a relatively stable price level—have risen significantly under the Communist government.

6. The Chinese economy is characterized by many inefficiencies that various reforms are trying to remedy. By far the most serious are the inefficiencies caused by policies with respect to prices which have been set to meet planners objectives rather than to promote efficient resource allocation. In particular, food prices have been kept far below free market levels, and the price of using capital is below its opportunity cost. As a result scarcities have been common, and rationing and subsidies have been required.

7. Reform is occurring both through the increased reliance on free markets and through recent decisions to allow prices in controlled markets to move closer to market-clearing level.

8. Central planning plays a major role in the Soviet economy. Long-term goals are outlined in five-year plans, which in turn are implemented by highly detailed one-year plans. Most of the key decisions are made centrally by the various GOSPLANs, but prices are used both for internal accounting and to affect the distribution of goods and incomes.

9. A comparison of relative performance between the United States and the Soviet Union reveals that the United States has higher levels of real output per capita, but a much less impressive growth record. The Soviet Union has suffered less than the United States from unemployment, but has not avoided inflationary pressures. Microeconomic inefficiencies have been numerous in the Soviet experience, and agriculture has been a serious, chronic problem.

10. The use of coercion by the state has permitted the Soviet economy to achieve certain objectives, including extremely rapid capital formation, monetary reform, and the orderly movement of labor from farm to city.

---

1. How might the economies of the United States, the Soviet Union, and China attempt to achieve each of the following results? Which system would be likely to do it most easily?

Discussion Questions

    a. Achieve full employment

    b. Redistribute income from rich to poor

    c. Choose the appropriate mix between tractor production and residential construction

    d. Determine the relative pay of carpenters and school teachers

    e. Avoid a shortage or surplus of men's shirts

    f. Increase the rate of saving

2. "What the world of economics needs is an end to ideology and *isms*. If there is a best system of economic organization, it will prove its superiority in its superior ability to solve economic problems." Do you agree with this statement? Would you expect that if the world survives for another 100 years, a single form of economic system would be found superior to all others? Why or why not?

3. Explain each of the following statements in terms of the economic system of China. Which, if any, of these statements might (with appropriate name changes) be applicable in the Soviet Union? In the United States?

    a. "Deng asserts that ties to the West are vital to fight poverty."

    b. "Canton is booming on Marxist free enterprise."

    c. "Equality of wages saps incentives."

    d. "The Chinese get credit cards."

4. Capital is used in the heavy industries of both the United States and the Soviet Union and in roughly equal amounts. In what sense is the United States capitalist and Russia socialist? Who supplies the capital in a Communist economy?

5. In an economic report to the twenty-fifth Communist Party Congress, then Soviet Prime Minister Aleksei Kosygin said that the crisis of capitalism was marked by inflation and unemployment, in contrast to the Soviet Union's full employment and stable retail prices. How do the Soviet Union and China avoid the problems of inflation and unemployment? In doing so, do they encounter problems not faced by capitalist countries?

6. According to the mayor of Moscow, that city could never have problems of the kind that plague New York and other American cities. "In my country the city government owns and operates not only schools, hospitals, and other nonprofit enterprises but also such profitable enterprises as all the restaurants, stores, movie theaters, bakeries, food processing factories, manufacturers of consumer goods, construction companies, and trucks in the city." These activities generate 80 percent of the revenues needed to run the city. The rest of the revenue is raised by taxes collected by the central government and paid to the city. Is a socialist country uniquely able to avoid or solve the problems of its biggest cities? Compare the things the U.S. government might do to help New York meet its deficit with those done for Moscow.

7. During World War II, the U.S. government (a) rationed steel, aluminum, and copper; (b) put price controls on most goods and services but rationed only meat, sugar, shoes, and gasoline; (c) used the draft to raise armed forces of 11 million but deferred workers in key industries; (d) purchased about half of the goods and services comprising the GNP; and (e) increased income taxes and introduced an excess profits tax.

   Would you classify the United States as a command economy at that time? Explain. Can you see reasons for each of the five measures outlined above, given the economic goals of the time?

Mathematical Notes

1. Since it is impermissible to divide by zero, the ratio $\Delta Y/\Delta X$ cannot be evaluated when $\Delta X = 0$. But the limit of the ratio as ΔX approaches zero can be evaluated, and it is infinity.

$$\lim_{\Delta X \to 0} \frac{\Delta Y}{\Delta X} = \infty$$

2. Many variables affect the quantity demanded. Using functional notation, the argument of the next several pages of the text can be anticipated. Let Q^D represent the quantity of a commodity demanded and

$$T, \overline{Y}, N, Y^*, p, p_j$$

represent, respectively, tastes, average household income, population, income distribution, its price, and the price of the jth other commodity.

The demand function is

$$Q^D = D(T, \overline{Y}, N, Y^*, p, p_j), \quad j = 1, \ldots, n$$

The demand schedule or curve looks at

$$Q^D = q(p) \Big|_{T, \overline{Y}, N, Y^*, p_j}$$

where the notation means that the variables to the right of the vertical line are held constant.

This function is correctly described as the demand function with respect to price, all other variables held constant. This function, often written concisely $q = q(p)$, shifts in response to changes in other variables. Consider average income. If, as is usually hypothesized, $\partial Q^D / \partial \overline{Y} > 0$, then increases in average income shift $q = q(p)$ rightward and decreases in average income shift $q = q(p)$ leftward. Changes in other variables likewise shift this function in the direction implied by the relationship of that variable to the quantity demanded.

3. Quantity demanded is a simple, straightforward, but frequently misunderstood concept in everyday use, but it has a clear mathematical meaning. It refers to the dependent variable in the demand function from note 2 above:

$$Q^D = D(T, \overline{Y}, N, Y^*, p, p_j)$$

It takes on a specific value, therefore, whenever a specific value is assigned to each of the independent variables. A change in Q^D occurs whenever the specific value of any independent variable is changed. Q^D could change, for example, from 10,000 tons per month to 20,000 tons per month as a result of a *ceteris paribus* change in any one price, in average income, in the distribution of income, in tastes, or in population. Also it could change as a result of the net effect of changes in all of the independent variables occurring at once. Thus a change in the price of a commodity is a sufficient reason for a change in Q^D but not a necessary reason.

Some textbooks reserve the term *change in quantity demanded* for a movement along a demand curve, that is, a change in Q^D as a result of a change in p. They then use other words for a change in Q^D caused by a change in the other variables in the demand function. This usage gives the single variable Q^D more than one name, and this is potentially confusing.

Our usage, which corresponds to that in all intermediate and advanced treatments, avoids this confusion. We call Q^D *quantity demanded* and refer to any change in Q^D as a *change in quantity demanded*. In this usage it is correct to say that a movement along a demand curve is a change in quantity demanded. But it is incorrect to say that a change in quantity demanded can occur only because of a movement along a demand curve (since Q^D can change for other reasons, for example, a *ceteris paribus* change in average houshold income).

4. Continuing the development of note 2, let Q^S represent the quantity of a commodity supplied and

$$G, X, p, w_i$$

represent, respectively, producers' goals, technology, the product's own price and the price of the ith input.

The supply function is

$$Q^S = S(G, X, p, w_i), \quad i = 1, 2, \ldots, m$$

The supply schedule and supply curve looks at

$$Q^S = s(p) \Big|_{G, X, w_i}$$

This is the supply function with respect to price, all other variables held constant. This function, often written concisely $q = s(p)$, shifts in response to changes in the variables G, X, w_i.

5. Continuing the development of notes 2 through 4, equilibrium occurs where $Q^D = Q^S$. *For specified values of all other variables,* this requires that

$$q(p) = s(p) \qquad [1]$$

Equation 1 defines an equilibrium value of p; hence although p is an *independent* variable in each of the supply and demand functions, it is an *endogenous* variable in the economic model that imposes the equilibrium condition expressed in Equation 1. Price is endogenous because it is assumed to adjust to bring about equality between quantity demanded and quantity supplied. Equilibrium quantity, also an endogenous variable, is determined by substituting the equilibrium price into either $q(p)$ or $s(p)$.

Graphically, Equation 1 is satisfied only at the point where demand and supply curves intersect. Thus supply and demand curves are said to determine the equilibrium values of the endogenous variables, price and quantity. A shift in any of the independent variables held constant in the q and s functions will shift the demand or supply curves and lead to different equilibrium values for price and quantity.

6. The definition in the text uses finite changes and is called *arc elasticity*. The parallel definition using derivatives is

$$\eta = \frac{dq}{dp} \times \frac{p}{q}$$

and is called *point elasticity*. Further discussion appears in the Appendix to Chapter 5.

7. The propositions in the text are proven as follows. Letting TR stand for total revenue, we can write:

$$TR = pq$$

$$\frac{dTR}{dp} = q + p \frac{dq}{dp} \qquad [1]$$

But from the equation in note 6

$$q\eta = p \frac{dq}{dp} \qquad [2]$$

which we can substitute in Equation 1 to obtain

$$\frac{dTR}{dp} = q + q\eta = q(1 + \eta) \qquad [3]$$

Because η is a negative number, the sign of Equation 3 is negative if the absolute value of η exceeds unity (elastic demand) and positive if it is less than unity (inelastic demand).

8. The axis-reversal arose in the following way. Marshall theorized in terms of "demand price" and "supply price," these being the prices that would lead to a given quantity being demanded or supplied. Thus

$$p^d = D(q) \qquad [1]$$

$$p^s = S(q) \qquad [2]$$

and the condition of equilibrium is

$$D(q) = S(q)$$

When graphing the behavioral relations expressed in Equations 1 and 2, Marshall naturally put the independent variable, q, on the horizontal axis.

Leon Walras, whose formulation of the working of a competitive market has become the accepted one, focused on quantity demanded and quantity supplied *at a given price.* Thus

$$q^d = q(p)$$

$$q^s = s(p)$$

and the condition of equilibrium is

$$q(p) = s(p)$$

Walras did not use graphical representation. Had he done so, he would surely have placed p (his independent variable) on the horizontal axis.

Marshall, among his other influences on later generations of economists, was the great popularizer of graphical analysis in economics. Today we use his graphs, even for Walras' analysis. The axis reversal is thus one of those historical accidents that seem odd to people who did not live through the "perfectly natural" sequence of steps that produced it.

9. The distinction made between an incremental change and a marginal change is the distinction for the function $Y = Y(X)$ between $\Delta Y/\Delta X$ and the derivative $\frac{dY}{dX}$. The latter is the limit of the former as ΔX approaches zero. Precisely this sort of difference underlies the distinction between arc and point elasticity, and we shall meet it repeatedly—in this chapter in reference to marginal and incremental *utility* and in later chapters with respect to such concepts as marginal and incremental *product, cost,* and *revenue.* Where Y is a function of more than one variable—for example, $Y = f(X, Z)$—the marginal relationship between Y and X is the partial derivative $\frac{\partial Y}{\partial X}$ rather than the total derivative.

10. The hypothesis of diminishing marginal utility requires that we be able to measure utility of consumption by a function $U = U(X_1, X_2, \ldots, X_n)$ where $X_1, \ldots, X_n$ are quantities of the n goods consumed by a household. It really embodies two utility hypotheses. First, $\frac{\partial U}{\partial X_i} > 0$,

which says for some levels of consumption the consumer can get more utility by increasing consumption of the commodity. Second, $\frac{\partial^2 U}{\partial X_i^2} < 0$, which says that the marginal utility of additional consumption is declining.

11. The relationship of the slope of the budget line to relative prices can be seen as follows. In the two-commodity example, a change in expenditure (ΔE) is given by the equation

$$\Delta E = p_F \Delta F + p_C \Delta C \qquad [1]$$

Expenditure is constant along a budget line, that is, $\Delta E = 0$. Thus, along such a line,

$$p_F \Delta F + p_C \Delta C = 0 \qquad [2]$$

whence

$$-\frac{\Delta C}{\Delta F} = \frac{p_F}{p_C} \qquad [3]$$

The ratio $-\Delta C/\Delta F$ is the slope of the budget line. It is negative because, with a fixed budget, to consume more F, one must consume less C. In other words, Equation 3 says that the negative of the slope of the budget line is the ratio of the absolute prices (i.e., the relative price). While prices do not show directly in Figure 8-2, they are implicit in the budget line. Its slope depends solely on the relative price, while its position, given a fixed money income, depends on the absolute prices of the two goods.

12. Because the slope of the indifference curve is negative, it is the absolute value of the slope that declines as one moves downward to the right along the curve. The algebraic value, of course, increases. The phrase *diminishing marginal rate of substitution* thus refers to the absolute, not the algebraic, value of the slope.

13. Marginal product as defined in the text is really incremental product. More advanced treatments distinguish between this notion and its limit as ΔL approaches zero. Technically, *MP* measures the rate at which total product is changing as one factor is varied. The marginal product is the

partial derivative of the total product with respect to the variable factor. In symbols,

$$MP = \frac{\partial TP}{\partial L}$$

14. We have referred specifically both to diminishing *marginal* product and to diminishing *average* product. In most cases eventually diminishing marginal product implies eventually diminishing average product. This is, however, not necessary, as the accompanying figure shows.

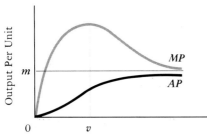

Units of the Variable Factor

In this case marginal product diminishes after v units of the variable factor are employed. Because marginal product falls toward, but never quite reaches, a value of m, average product rises continually toward, but never quite reaches, the same value.

15. Let q be the quantity of output and L the quantity of the variable factor. In the short run

$$TP = q = f(L) \qquad [1]$$

We now define

$$AP = \frac{q}{L} = \frac{f(L)}{L} \qquad [2]$$

$$MP = \frac{dq}{dL} \qquad [3]$$

We are concerned about the relation between these two. Whether average product is rising, at a maximum, or falling is determined by its derivative with respect to L.

$$\frac{d\frac{q}{L}}{dL} = \frac{L\frac{dq}{dL} - q}{L^2} \qquad [4]$$

This may be rewritten:

$$\frac{1}{L}\left(\frac{dq}{dL} - \frac{q}{L}\right) = \frac{1}{L}(MP - AP) \qquad [5]$$

Clearly, when MP is greater than AP, the expression in Equation 5 is positive and thus AP is rising. When MP is less than AP, AP is falling. When they are equal, AP is at a stationary value.

16. The mathematically correct definition of marginal costs is the rate of change of total cost, with respect to output, q. Thus $MC = dTC/dq$. From the definitions, $TC = TFC + TVC$. Fixed costs are not a function of output. Thus we may write $TC = K + f(q)$, where $f(q)$ is total variable costs and K is a constant. From this, we see that $MC = df(q)/dq$. MC is thus independent of the size of the fixed costs.

17. This point is easily seen if a little algebra is used:

$$AVC = \frac{TVC}{q}$$

but

$$TVC = L \times w$$

and

$$q = AP \times L$$

where L is the quantity of the variable factor used and w is its cost per unit. Therefore

$$AVC = \frac{L \times w}{AP \times L} = \frac{w}{AP}$$

Since w is a constant, it follows that AVC and AP vary inversely with each other, and when AP is at its maximum value, AVC must be at its minimum value.

18. A little elementary calculus will prove the point:

$$MC = \frac{dTC}{dq} = \frac{dTVC}{dq}$$

$$= \frac{d(L \times w)}{dq}$$

If w does not vary with output

$$MC = \frac{dL}{dq} \times w$$

But, referring to note 15, Equation 3,

$$\frac{dL}{dq} = \frac{1}{MP}$$

Thus,

$$MC = \frac{w}{MP}.$$

Since w is fixed, MC varies negatively with MP. When MP is a maximum, MC is a minimum.

19. As we saw in note 16, $MC = \frac{dTVC}{dq}$. If we take the integral of the MC from zero to q_0 we get:

$$\int_0^{q_0} MC\ dq = TVC_{q_0} + K$$

The first term is the area under the marginal cost curve, while the constant of integration, K, is fixed cost.

20. Strictly speaking, the marginal rate of substitution refers to the slope of the tangent to the isoquant at a particular point while the calculations in Table 11A-1 refer to the average rate of substitution between two distinct points on the isoquant. Assume a production function

$$Q = Q(K, L) \qquad [1]$$

Isoquants are given by the function

$$K = I(L, \overline{Q}) \qquad [2]$$

derived from Equation 1 by expressing K as an explicit function of L and Q. A single isoquant relates to a particular value $(\overline{Q})$ at which Q is held constant. Define Q_K and Q_L as an alternative, more compact notation for $\partial Q/\partial K$ and $\partial Q/\partial L$, the marginal products of capital and labor. Also, let Q_{KK} and Q_{LL} stand for $\partial^2 Q/\partial L^2$ and $\partial^2 Q/\partial K^2$, respectively. To obtain the slope of the isoquant, totally differentiate Equation 1 to obtain

$$dQ = Q_K dK + Q_L dL$$

Then, since we are moving along a single isoquant, set $dQ = 0$ to obtain

$$\frac{dK}{dL} = -\frac{Q_L}{Q_K} = MRS$$

Diminishing marginal productivity implies Q_{LL}, $Q_{KK} < 0$ and hence, as we move down the isoquant of Figure 11A-1, Q_K is rising and Q_L is falling, so the absolute value of MRS is diminishing. This is called the *hypothesis of a diminishing marginal rate of substitution*.

21. Formally, the problem is maximize $Q = Q(K, L)$ subject to the budget constraint

$$p_K K + p_L L = C$$

To do this, form the Lagrangean

$$Q(K, L) - \lambda(p_K K + p_L L - C)$$

The first-order conditions for finding the saddle point on this function are

$$Q_K - \lambda p_K = 0; \ Q_K = \lambda p_K \qquad [1]$$

$$Q_L - \lambda p_L = 0; \ Q_L = \lambda p_L \qquad [2]$$

$$-p_K K - p_L L + C = 0 \qquad [3]$$

Dividing Equation 1 by Equation 2 yields

$$\frac{Q_K}{Q_L} = \frac{p_K}{p_L}$$

that is, the ratio of the marginal products, which is (-1) times the MRS, is equal to the ratio of the prices, which is (-1) times the slope of the isocost line.

22. For this note and the next two it is helpful first to define some terms. Let

$$\pi_n = TR_n - TC_n$$

where π_n is the profit when n units are sold.

If the firm is maximizing its profits by producing n units, it is necessary that the profits at output q_n are at least as large as the profits at output zero. If the firm is maximizing its profits at output n, then

$$\pi_n \geq \pi_0 \qquad [1]$$

The condition says that profits from producing must be greater than profits from not producing. Condition 1 can be rewritten

$$TR_n - TVC_n - TFC_n \geq TR_0 - TVC_0 - TFC_0 \qquad [2]$$

But note that by definition

$$TR_0 = 0 \qquad [3]$$
$$TVC_0 = 0 \qquad [4]$$
$$TFC_n = TFC_0 = K \qquad [5]$$

where K is a constant. By substituting Equations 3, 4, and 5 into Condition 2, we get

$$TR_n - TVC_n \geq 0$$

from which we obtain

$$TR_n \geq TVC_n$$

This proves Rule 1.

On a per unit basis it becomes

$$\frac{TR_n}{q_n} \geq \frac{TVC_n}{q_n} \qquad [6]$$

where q_n is the number of units produced.

Since $TR_n = q_n p_n$, where p_n is the price when n units are sold, Equation 6 may be rewritten

$$p_n \geq AVC_n$$

23. Using elementary calculus, Rule 2 may be proved.

$$\pi_n = TR_n - TC_n$$

each of which is a function of output q. To maximize π it is necessary that

$$\frac{d\pi}{dq} = 0 \qquad [1]$$

and that

$$\frac{d^2\pi}{dq^2} < 0 \qquad [2]$$

From the definitions

$$\frac{d\pi}{dq} = \frac{dTR}{dq} - \frac{dTC}{dq} = MR - MC \qquad [3]$$

From Equations 1 and 3 a necessary condition of maximum π is $MR - MC = 0$, or $MR = MC$, as is required by Rule 2.

24. Not every point where $MR = MC$ is a point of profit maximization. Continuing the equations of the previous note,

$$\frac{d^2\pi}{dq^2} = \frac{dMR}{dq} - \frac{dMC}{dq} \qquad [4]$$

From Equations 2 and 4 a necessary condition of maximum π is

$$\frac{dMR}{dq} - \frac{dMC}{dq} < 0$$

which says that the slope of MC must be greater than the slope of MR. Taken with the previous result, it implies that, for q_n to maximize π, $MR_n = MC_n$ at a point where MC cuts MR from below.

25. Marginal revenue is mathematically the derivative of total revenue with respect to output, dTR/dq. Incremental revenue is $\Delta TR/\Delta q$. But the term *marginal revenue* is loosely used to refer to both concepts.

26. To prove that, for a downward-sloping demand curve, marginal revenue is less than price, let $p = p(q)$. Then

$$TR = pq = p(q) \cdot q$$
$$MR = \frac{dTR}{dq} = q\frac{dp}{dq} + p$$

For a downward-sloping demand curve dp/dq is negative by definition, and thus MR is less than price for positive values of q.

27. These propositions are easily proved using calculus. Let $p = a - bq$, which is the general equation for a downward-sloping straight line $(b > 0)$

$$TR = pq = aq - bq^2$$

and

$$MR = \frac{dTR}{dq} = a - 2bq$$

28. A monopolist selling in two or more markets will set its marginal cost equal to marginal revenue in each market. Thus, the condition $MC = MR_1 = MR_2$ is a profit-maximizing condition for a monopolist selling in two markets. In general, equal marginal revenues will mean unequal prices, for the ratio of price to marginal revenue is a function of elasticity of demand: the higher the elasticity, the lower the ratio. Thus equal marginal revenues imply a higher price in the market with the less elastic demand curve.

29. The marginal revenue produced by the factor involves two elements: first, the additional output that an extra unit of the factor makes possible and second, the change in price of the product that the extra output causes. Let Q be output, R revenue, and L the number of units of labor hired. The contribution to revenue of additional labor is $\frac{\partial R}{\partial L}$. This in turn depends on the contribution of the extra labor to output $\frac{\partial Q}{\partial L}$ (the marginal product of the factor) and $\partial R/\partial Q$, the firm's marginal revenue from the extra output. Thus

$$\frac{\partial R}{\partial L} = \frac{\partial Q}{\partial L} \cdot \frac{\partial R}{\partial Q}$$

We define the left-hand side as marginal revenue product, *MRP*. Thus

$$MRP = MP \cdot MR$$

30. The condition that for profit maximization *MRP* be downward-sloping at the point where $w = MRP$ is just an application of the proposition (proved in math notes 23 and 24) that for profit maximization *MC* must cut *MR* from below. Consider the output added by the last unit of the variable factor. Its marginal cost is w, and its marginal revenue is *MRP*. Thus w must cut *MRP* from below. Since w is a horizontal line, *MRP* must be falling.

Putting the matter in standard mathematical terms,

$$w = MRP \tag{1}$$

is a first order condition of *either* maximizing or minimizing. The second order condition for maximization is

$$\frac{dw}{dq} > \frac{dMRP}{dq} \tag{2}$$

Since

$$\frac{dw}{dq} = 0 \tag{3}$$

the slope of *MRP* must be negative to satisfy [2], that is, it must be declining.

31. The proposition that the marginal labor cost is above the average labor cost when the average is rising is essentially the same proposition proved in math note 15. But let us do it again, using elementary calculus.

The quantity of labor depends on the wage rate: $L = f(w)$. Total labor cost is wL. Marginal cost of labor is $d(wL)/dL = w + L(dw/dL)$. Rewrite this as $MC = AC + L(dw/dL)$. As long as the supply curve slopes upward $dw/dL > 0$, therefore $MC > AC$.

32. Let t be the tax rate applied to the profits, π, of the firm. Thus, after-tax profits are $(1 - t)\pi$, where π is a function of output, q. To maximize profits after tax it is necessary that

$$\frac{d(1 - t)\pi}{dq} = 0 \quad \text{or}$$

$$(1 - t)\frac{d\pi}{dq} = 0$$

Dividing through by $(1 - t)$ we now see that $d\pi/dq = 0$ depends on the level of q and is independent of that tax rate.

33. Calculating the ratio of the cost of purchasing a fixed bundle of commodities in two periods is the same thing as calculating the percentage change in each price and then averaging these by weighting each price by the proportion of total expenditure devoted to the commodity. The following expression illustrates the equivalence of these two procedures for the two-commodity case:

$$\frac{q^A p_1^A + q^B p_1^B}{q^A p_0^A + q^B p_0^B} = \frac{p_1^A}{p_0^A} \left(\frac{q^A p_0^A}{q^A p_0^A + q^B p_0^B} \right)$$
$$+ \frac{p_1^B}{p_0^B} \left(\frac{q^B p_0^B}{q^A p_0^A + q^B p_0^B} \right)$$

The qs are fixed quantity weights, while the ps are prices. The superscripts A and B refer to two commodities; the subscripts 0 and 1 refer respectively to the base period and some subsequent time period. The expression on the left is the fixed bundle q^A and q^B valued at given year prices divided by its value in base year prices. The first term in the expression on the right gives the ratio of the price of good A in the given and the base year multiplied by the proportion of total expenditure in the base year devoted to good A. The second term does the same for good B. Simple multiplication and division reduces the right-hand expression to the left-hand one.

34. In the text we define *MPC* as an incremental ratio. For mathematical treatments it is sometimes convenient to define all marginal concepts as derivatives: $MPC = dC/dY_d$, $MPS = dS/dY_d$, and so on.

35. The basic relation is

$$Y_d = C + S$$

Dividing through by Y_d yields

$$Y_d/Y_d = C/Y_d + S/Y_d$$

or $1 = APC + APS$

Next take the first-difference of the basic relation to yield

$$\Delta Y_d = \Delta C + \Delta S$$

Dividing through by ΔY_d gives

$$\Delta Y_d/\Delta Y_d = \Delta C/\Delta Y_d + \Delta S/\Delta Y_d$$

or $1 = MPC + MPS$

36. This involves using functions of functions. We have $C = C(Y_d)$ and $Y_d = f(Y)$. So by substitution $C = C[f(Y)]$. In the linear expressions used in the text, $C = a + bY_d$, where b is the marginal propensity to consume. $Y_d = hY$, so $C = a + bhY$, where bh is thus the marginal response of C to a change in Y.

37. The elementary theory of national income can be described by the following set of equations (or model).

$Y = AE$ (equilibrium condition)   [1]
$AE = C + I + G + (X - M)$
          (definition of AE)   [2]
$C = a + hY$ (consumption function)   [3]
$M = mY$ (import function)   [4]
$Y_d = hY$ (disposable income)   [5]

where I, G, and X are all treated as constant. Substituting Equations 3, 4, and 5 and collecting terms in Y, we can obtain the aggregate expenditure function relating desired expenditure to income.

$$AE = (a + I + G + X) + (bh - m)Y$$

where the first term (in parentheses) is autonomous expenditure and the second term is induced expenditure. Using Equation 1, the equilibrium level of income can be derived by solving

$$Y = (a + I + G + X) + (bh - m)Y$$

to obtain

$$Y = \frac{1}{(1 - bh + m)} (a + I + G + X) \qquad [6]$$

The example in Table 26-6 has these values: $a = 100$, $I = 250$, $G = 170$, $X = 240$, $b = 0.80$, $h = 0.90$, and $m = .1$. Substituting into Equation 6 yields

$$Y = \frac{1}{(1 - .72 + .10)} (100 + 250 + 170 + 240)$$
$$= \frac{1}{(.38)} (760) = 2,000.$$

38. The total expenditure over all rounds is the sum of an infinite series. Letting A stand for the initiating expenditure and z for the marginal propensity to spend, the change in expenditure is ΔA in the first round, $z\Delta A$ in the second,

$z(z\Delta A) = z^2\Delta A$ in the third, and so on. This can be written

$$\Delta A(1 + z + z^2 + \ldots + z^n)$$

If z is less than 1, the series in parentheses converges to $1/(1 - z)$ as n approaches infinity. The change in total expenditure is thus $\Delta A/(1 - z)$. In the example in the box, $z = 0.80$; therefore the change in total expenditure is five times ΔA.

39. The accelerator may be stated as a general macroeconomic theory. Define I_n as the volume of net investment this year and ΔY as the increase in national income from last year to this year. The accelerator theory is the relationship between I_n and ΔY.

Assume that the capital-output ratio is a constant.

$$K/Y = \propto$$

or
$$K = \propto Y$$

If Y changes, K must be changed accordingly:

$$\Delta K = \propto \Delta Y$$

But the change in the capital stock (ΔK) is net investment, so

$$\Delta K = I_n = \propto \Delta Y$$

40. This is easily proven. In equilibrium the banking system wants sufficient deposits (D) to establish the legal ratio (r) of deposits to reserves (R). This gives $R/D = r$. Any change in D of ΔD has to be accompanied by a change in R of ΔR of sufficient size to restore r. Thus $\Delta R/\Delta D = r$, so that $\Delta D = \Delta R/r$, and $\Delta D/\Delta R = 1/r$.

41. Proof: Let r be the reserve ratio. Let $e = 1 - r$ be the excess reserves per dollar of new deposit. If X dollars are deposited in the system assumed in the text, the successive rounds of new deposits will be $X, eX, e^2X, e^3X. \ldots$ The series

$$X + eX + e^2X + e^3X \cdots$$
$$= X[1 + e + e^2 + e^3 + \cdots]$$

has a limit

$$X\frac{1}{1 - e} = X\left[\frac{1}{1 - (1 - r)}\right] = \frac{X}{r}$$

42. Suppose the public desires to hold a fraction, v, of deposits in cash. Now let the banking system receive an initial increase in its reserves of ΔR. It can expand deposits by an amount ΔD. As it does so, the banking system suffers a cash drain to the public of $v\Delta D$. The banking system can increase deposits only to the extent the required reserve ratio r makes possible. The maximum deposit expansion can be calculated from

$$r\Delta D = \Delta R - v\Delta D$$

which, collecting terms, can be written

$$(r + v)\,\Delta D = \Delta R$$

Hence

$$\Delta D = \Delta R/(r + v)$$

43. The argument is simply as follows, where prime marks stand for first derivatives:

$$M^D = F_1(T), \quad F'_1 > 0$$
$$T = F_2(Y), \quad F'_2 > 0$$

therefore,

$$M^D = F_1[F_2(Y)]$$
$$= H(Y), \quad H' > 0$$

where H is the function of the function combining F_1 and F_2.

44. Let $L(Y, r)$ give the real demand for money measured in purchasing power units. Let M be the supply of money measured in nominal units and P an index of the price level so that M/P is the real supply of money. Now the equilibrium condition requiring equality between the demand for money and the supply of money can be expressed in real terms as

$$L(Y, r) = M/P \qquad [1]$$

or by multiplying through by P in nominal terms as

$$PL(Y, r) = M \qquad [2]$$

In Equation 1 a rise in P disturbs equilibrium by lowering M/P, and in Equation 2 it disturbs equilibrium by raising $PL\ (Y,\ r)$.

45. This is expressed in functional notation as

$$DE = f(Y - Y^*)$$

where the restrictions are (i) that $f(0) = 0$ so when $Y = Y^*$ there is no demand effect; and (ii) $f' > 0$ so that as Y rises, the demand effect rises. Together (i) and (ii) imply that $DE > 0$ when $Y > Y^*$ and $DE < 0$ when $Y < Y^*$.

   Often, the further restriction is added that $f'' > 0$; that is, the Phillips curve gets steeper as Y rises.

46. The "rule of 72" is an approximation derived from the mathematics of compound interest. Any measure X_t will have the value $X_t = X_0 e^{rt}$ after t years at a continuous growth rate of r percent per year. Because $X_1/X_0 = 2$ requires $rt = 0.69$, a "rule of 69" would be correct for continuous growth. The "rule of 72" was developed in the context of compound interest, and if interest is compounded only once a year the product rt required for X to double is approximately 0.72.

47. The time taken to break even is a function of the *difference* in growth rates, not their level. Thus, in the example, had 4 percent and 5 percent or 5 percent and 6 percent been used, it still would have taken the same number of years. To see this quickly, note that we are interested in the ratio of two growth paths: $e^{r1t}/e^{r2t} = e^{(r1 - r2)t}$.

48. The equation for the IS curve is given by

$$y = c(y - T) + I(r) + G \qquad [1]$$

where $c'\ (y - T) > 0$ is the marginal propensity to consume $[c'(y - T) = b]$, $I_r < 0$ is the response of investment to a change in the interest rate, and T is taxes. Substituting $T = T_0 + ty$ into [1], and differentiating, we get

$$wdy = -b\ (dT_0 + ydt) + I_r dr + dG \qquad [2]$$

where w is equal to $[1 - b\ (1 - t)]$, the marginal propensity not to spend. The IS curve is drawn for $dT_0 = dt = dG = 0$. Its slope is therefore

$$\left.\frac{dr}{dy}\right|_{IS} = \frac{w}{I_r} < 0 \qquad [3]$$

The horizontal shift in the IS curve due to a change in any of the exogenous variables (T_0, t, or G) can be calculated from [2] by setting $dr = 0$. For example, a change in G shifts the IS curve by

$$\left.\frac{dy}{dG}\right|_{dr\ =\ 0} = \frac{1}{w} > 0$$

while a change in tax rates causes a shift of

$$\left.\frac{dy}{dt}\right|_{dr\ =\ 0} = \frac{-by}{w} < 0$$

49. The equation for the LM curve is given by

$$M = PL(y,r) \qquad [1]$$

where $L(y,r)$ represents the demand for real money balances which depends positively on income ($L_y > 0$) and negatively on the interest rate ($L_r < 0$). Differentiating Equation 1 we get

$$dM = L(y,r)dP + PL_y + PL_r dr \qquad [2]$$

The LM curve is drawn for $dM = dP = 0$. Its slope is therefore

$$\left.\frac{dr}{dy}\right|_{LM} = -\frac{L_y}{L_r} > 0 \qquad [3]$$

The horizontal shift in the LM curve due to a change in the money supply can be calculated from Equation 2 by setting $dr = 0$.

$$\left.\frac{dy}{dM}\right|_{dr\ =\ 0} = \frac{1}{PL_y} > 0 \qquad [4]$$

50. Equations 2 from each of the two previous math notes can be combined to give two relationships between dy and dr. Solving them simultaneously we can derive the following expressions for the effects of monetary and fiscal policy on national income and interest rates. Restricting our analysis of fiscal policy to the effects of government expenditure (so $dT = dt = 0$), and holding $dP = 0$, these are as follows:

$$\frac{dy}{dM} = \frac{-I_r}{D} > 0 \qquad \frac{dr}{dM} = \frac{-w}{D} < 0$$

$$\frac{dy}{dG} = \frac{-PL_r}{D} > 0 \qquad \frac{dr}{dG} = \frac{Pl_y}{D} > 0$$

where $D = -(I_r PL_y + wPL_r) > 0$.

51. The aggregate demand curve can be written by solving Equations 1 from each of the math notes 48 and 49 to eliminate the interest rate, thus leaving a relationship between P and y. The relationship between *changes* in P and y can be written

$$Ddy = I_r L(y, P)dP - PL_r dG - I_r dM \qquad [1]$$

where D is as defined in note 50.

The AD curve is drawn from $dG = dM = 0$, so its slope is given by

$$\frac{dP}{dy}\bigg|_{AD} = \frac{I_r L(y, P)}{D} < 0 \qquad [2]$$

The horizontal shift in AD can be calculated from Equation 1 by setting $dP = 0$, so that the effects of monetary (dM) and fiscal (dG) policy with a constant price level can be written as follows:

$$\frac{dy}{dM}\bigg|_{dr=0} = \frac{-I_r}{D} > 0$$

$$\frac{dy}{dG}\bigg|_{dr=0} = \frac{-PL_r}{D} > 0$$

which, of course, are as in math note 50.

Glossary

absolute advantage   The advantage one nation has over another in the production of a commodity when the same amount of resources will produce more of the commodity in that nation than in the other.

absolute price   The amount of money that must be spent to acquire a unit of a commodity. Also called *money price*.

acceleration hypothesis   The hypothesis that when national income is held above potential, the persistent inflationary gap will cause inflation to accelerate; and when national income is held below potential, the persistent recessionary gap will cause inflation to decelerate.

accelerator   The theory that relates the level of investment to the rate of change of national income.

actual GNP   The gross national product that the economy in fact produces.

adjustable peg system   A system in which exchange rates are fixed in the short term but are occasionally changed in response to persistent payments imbalances.

administered price   A price set by the conscious decision of the seller rather than by impersonal market forces.

ad valorem tariff   An import duty that is a percentage of the price of the imported product.

ad valorem tax   See *excise tax*.

adverse selection   Self-selection, within a single risk category, of persons of above average risk.

AE   See *aggregate expenditure*.

aggregated data   Data for broad totals, such as all investment expenditure in the U.S. economy; in contrast to disaggregated data, such as investment by General Motors.

aggregate demand   Total desired purchases by all the buyers of an economy's output.

aggregate demand (*AD*) curve   A curve showing the combination of real national income and the price level that makes aggregate desired expenditure equal to national income and the demand for money equal to the supply of money; the curve thus relates the total amount of output that will be demanded to the price level of that output.

aggregate demand shock   A shift in the aggregate demand curve.

aggregate expenditure (*AE*)   Total expenditure on final output of the economy; $AE = C + I + G + (X - M)$, representing the four major components of aggregate desired expenditure.

aggregate expenditure (*AE*) function   The function that relates aggregate desired expenditure to national income.

aggregate supply   Total desired output of all the producers of an economy's output.

aggregate supply (*AS*) curve   A relation between the total amount of output that will be produced and the price level of that output.

aggregate supply shock   A shift in the aggregate supply curve.

allocation of resources   The distribution of the available factors of production among the various uses to which they might be put.

allocative efficiency   A situation in which no reorganization of production or consumption could make everyone better off (or, as it is sometimes stated, make at least one person better off while making no one worse off).

allocative inefficiency   The absence of allocative efficiency. A situation in which either production or consumption could be reorganized so as to make everyone better off (or, as it is sometimes stated, make at least one person better off while making no one worse off).

annuity   A given sum of money paid at stated intervals for a specific period of time or (in case of an *infinite annuity*) forever.

antitrust laws   Laws designed to prohibit the acquisition and exercise of monopoly power by business firms.

appreciation   A rise in the free-market value of domestic currency in terms of foreign currencies.

a priori   Literally, "at a prior time" or "in advance"; knowledge that is prior to actual experience.

arc elasticity   A measure of the average responsiveness of quantity to price over an interval of the demand curve. For analytical purposes it is usually defined by the formula

$$\eta = \frac{\Delta q / q}{\Delta p / p}$$

An alternative formula often used where computations are involved is

$$\eta = \frac{(q_2 - q_1)/(q_2 + q_1)}{(p_2 - p_1)/(p_2 + p_1)}$$

where p_1 and q_1 are the original price and quantity and p_2 and q_2 the new price and quantity.

With negatively sloped demand curves elasticity is a negative number. Sometimes the above expressions are therefore multiplied by -1 to make measured elasticity positive.

automatic transfer service (ATS)   A savings deposit from which funds are transferred automatically to the depositor's demand deposit to cover checks as they are drawn.

autonomous expenditure   In macroeconomics, elements of expenditure that do not vary systematically with other variables, such as national income and the interest rate, but that are determined by forces outside of the theory. Also called *exogenous expenditure*.

autonomous variable   See *exogenous variable*.

average cost (AC)   See *average total cost*.

average fixed cost (AFC)   Total fixed costs divided by the number of units of output.

average product (AP)   Total product divided by the number of units of the variable factor used in its production.

average propensity to consume (APC)   The proportion of income devoted to consumption; total consumption expenditure divided by disposable income ($APC = C/Y_d$).

average propensity to save (APS)   The proportion of income devoted to saving; total saving divided by disposable income ($APS = S/Y_d$).

average revenue (AR)   Total revenue divided by quantity sold.

average tax rate   The ratio of total tax paid to total income earned.

average total cost (ATC)   Total cost of producing a given output divided by the number of units of output; it can also be calculated as the sum of average fixed costs and average variable costs. Also called *cost per unit, unit cost, average cost*.

average variable cost (AVC)   Total variable costs divided by the number of units of output. Also called *direct unit cost, avoidable unit cost*.

balanced budget   A situation in which current revenue is exactly equal to current expenditures.

balanced budget multiplier   The change in income divided by the tax-financed change in government expenditure that brought it about.

balanced growth policy   A policy designed to produce simultaneous growth in all sectors of the economy.

balance-of-payments accounts   A summary record of a country's transactions that involve payments or receipts of foreign exchange.

balance-of-payments deficit   A situation in which a country's receipts on current and capital account fall short of its payments (ignoring transactions on the official settlements account).

balance-of-payments surplus   A situation in which a country's receipts on current and capital account exceed its payments (ignoring transactions on the official settlements account).

balance of trade   The difference between the value of

exports and the value of imports of visible items (goods).

balance sheet   A financial report showing a firm's assets and the claims against those assets at a moment in time.

bank notes   Paper money issued by commercial banks.

barter   A system in which goods and services are traded directly for other goods and services.

base control   The use of the monetary base as the instrument by which the central bank attempts to influence its target variables. See also *interest rate control*.

base period   A year or other point in time chosen for comparison purposes in order to express or compute index numbers or constant dollars. Also called *base year*.

beggar-my-neighbor policies   Policies designed to increase a country's prosperity (especially by reducing its unemployment) at the expense of reducing prosperity in other countries (especially by increasing their unemployment).

blacklist   An employer's list of workers who have been fired for union activity.

black market   A situation in which goods are sold illegally at prices above a legal price ceiling.

bond   An evidence of debt carrying a specified amount and schedule of interest payments as well as a date for redemption of the face value of the bond.

bondholders   Creditors of a firm, whose evidence of debt is a bond issued by the firm.

boom   A period in the business cycle characterized by high demand and increasing production at a level that exceeds potential GNP.

boycott   A concerted refusal to buy (buyers' boycott) or to sell (producers' or sellers' boycott) a commodity.

bread-and-butter unionism   A union movement whose major objectives are better wages and conditions of employment rather than political or social ends.

break-even level of income   The level of disposable income where total consumption expenditure equals total disposable income (saving is zero).

budget balance   The difference between total government revenue and total government expenditure.

budget deficit   The shortfall of current revenue below current expenditure.

budget deficit function   A function relating the size of the government's budget deficit (expenditure minus revenue) to the level of national income. (Deficits are shown as negative surpluses.)

budget line   Graphic representation of all combinations of commodities or factors that a household or firm may obtain if it spends a given amount of money at fixed prices of the commodities or factors. Also called *isocost line*.

budget surplus   The excess of current revenue over current expenditure.

built-in stabilizer   Anything that tends to adjust government revenues and expenditures automatically (i.e., without an explicit policy decision) so as to reduce inflationary and recessionary gaps whenever they develop.

business cycle   More or less regular, long-term patterns of fluctuations in the level of economic activity.

C   *consumption expenditure.*

capacity   The level of output that corresponds to the minimum short-run average total cost. Also called *plant capacity.*

capital   A factor of production consisting of all manufactured aids to further production.

capital account   A part of the balance-of-payments accounts that records payments and receipts arising from the import and export of long-term and short-term financial capital.

capital consumption allowance   An estimate of the amount by which the capital stock is depleted through its contribution to current production. Also called *depreciation.*

capital deepening   Adding capital to the production process in such a way as to increase the ratio of capital to labor and other factors of production.

capitalist   One who owns capital goods.

capitalist economy   An economy in which capital is predominantly owned privately rather than by the state.

capitalized value   The value of an asset measured by the present value of the income stream it is expected to produce.

capital-labor ratio   A measure of the amount of capital per worker in an economy.

capital-output ratio   The ratio of the value of capital to the annual value of output produced by it.

capital stock   The aggregate quantity of a society's capital goods or the total of a firm's capital goods.

capital widening   Adding capital to the production process in such a way as to leave factor proportions unchanged.

cartel   An organization of producers who agree to act as a single seller, thus limiting competition among themselves, in order to maximize joint profits.

categorical grant-in-aid   A federal grant to a state or local government for a specified category of expenditure, such as highways or welfare payments.

ceiling price   See *price ceiling.*

central bank   A bank that acts as banker to the commercial banking system and often to the government as well. In the modern world, usually a government owned and operated institution that controls the banking system and is the sole money issuing authority.

certificate of deposit (CD)   A negotiable time deposit carrying a higher interest rate than that paid on ordinary time deposits.

ceteris paribus   Literally, "other things being equal"; usually used in economics to indicate that all variables except the ones specified are assumed not to change.

change in demand   An increase or decrease in the quantity demanded at each possible price of the commodity, represented by a shift in the whole demand curve.

change in quantity demanded   An increase or decrease in the specific quantity bought at a specified price, represented by a movement along a demand curve.

change in supply   An increase or decrease in the quantity supplied at each possible price of the commodity, represented by a shift in the whole supply curve.

change in quantity supplied   An increase or decrease in the specific quantity supplied at a specified price, represented by a movement along a supply curve.

civilian labor force   The total number of employed, including those serving in the armed forces, plus the number of unemployed.

classical unemployment   See *real wage unemployment.*

cleared market   A market in which buyers have been able to buy all they wish and sellers have been able to sell all they wish at the going price.

clearing house   An institution where interbank indebtedness arising from transfer of checks between banks are computed, offset against each other, and net amounts owing are calculated.

closed shop   A place of employment in which a union has exclusive bargaining jurisdiction for all employees in a shop and only union members can be employed.

coefficient of determination (r^2 or R^2)   A measure of how closely a relationship between two variables holds. A coefficient showing the fraction of the total variance of the dependent variable that can be associated with the independent variables in the regression equation; r^2 is used for two variables and R^2 for three or more variables.

collective bargaining   The process by which unions and employers arrive at and enforce agreements.

collective consumption goods   Goods or services that, if they provide benefits to anyone, necessarily provide benefits to a large group of people, possibly everyone in the country.

collusion   An agreement among sellers to act as though there were a single seller, for example, by setting a common price. Collusion may be overt or covert, explicit or tacit.

command economy   An economy in which the decisions of the government (as distinct from households and firms) exert the major influence over the allocation of resources.

commercial bank   Privately owned, profit-seeking institution that provides a variety of financial services, such as accepting deposits from customers, which it agrees to transfer when ordered by a check, and making loans and other investments.

commercial policy   Restrictions on the free flow of goods and services among nations.

commodities Marketable items produced to satisfy wants. Commodities may be either *goods,* which are tangible, or *services,* which are intangible.

common-property resource A natural resource that is owned by no one and may be used by anyone.

common stock A form of equity capital usually carrying voting rights and a residual claim to the assets and profits of the firm.

comparative advantage The ability of one nation (region or individual) to produce a commodity at a lesser opportunity cost of other products foregone than another nation.

comparative statics Short for comparative static equilibrium analysis; the derivation of predictions by analyzing the effect of a change in some exogenous variable on the equilibrium position.

competitive devaluations A round of devaluations of exchange rates by a number of countries, each trying to gain a competitive advantage over the other and each failing to the extent that other countries also devalue.

complement Two commodities are complements when they tend to be used jointly with each other; the degree of complementarity is measured by the size of the negative cross elasticity between the two goods.

comprehensive income taxation (CIT) Use of a very broad tax base by defining taxable income to include income from most sources and thus eliminating most exemptions and deductions.

concentration ratio The fraction of total market sales (or some other measure of market occupancy) controlled by a specified number of the industry's largest firms, four-firm and eight-firm concentration ratios being most frequently used.

conglomerate merger See *merger.*

conscious parallel action See *tacit collusion.*

constant-cost industry An industry in which costs of the most efficient size firm remain constant as the entire industry expands or contracts in the long run.

constant dollar GNP Gross national product valued in prices prevailing in some base year; year-to-year changes in constant dollar GNP reflect changes only in quantities produced. Also called *real GNP.*

constant returns A situation in which output increases proportionately with inputs as the scale of production is increased.

consumerism A movement that asserts a conflict between the interests of firms and the public interest.

Consumer Price Index (CPI) A measure of the average prices of commodities commonly bought by households; compiled monthly by the Bureau of Labor Statistics.

consumers' durables See *durable good.*

consumers' surplus The difference between the total value consumers place on all units consumed of a commodity and the payment they must make to purchase the same amount of the commodity.

consumption The act of using commodities, either goods or services, to satisfy wants.

consumption expenditure In macroeconomics, household expenditure on all goods and services except housing. Represented by the symbol C as one of the four components of aggregate expenditure.

consumption function The relationship between total desired consumption expenditure and all the factors that determine it; in a more specific sense, the relationship between desired consumption expenditure and disposable income.

corporation A form of business organization in which the firm has a legal existence separate from that of the owners and ownership and financial responsibility are divided, limited, and shared among any number of individual and institutional shareholders.

cost (of output) To a producing firm, the value of inputs used in producing output.

cost minimization An implication of profit maximization that the firm will choose the method that produces specific output at the lowest attainable cost.

Cournot-Nash equilibrium An equilibrium that results when each firm makes its decisions on the assumption that the behavior of all other firms will remain unchanged, also called the *non-cooperative equilibrium.*

CPI See *Consumer Price Index.*

craft union A union organized to include workers with a specified set of skills or occupations, regardless of where or in what industry they are employed.

credit rationing Rationing of available funds among borrowers in a situation of excess demand for loans at prevailing interest rates.

cross elasticity of demand (η_X) A measure of the responsiveness of the quantity of a commodity demanded to changes in price of a related commodity, defined by the formula

$$\eta_X = \frac{\text{percentage change in quantity demanded of } X}{\text{percentage change in price of } Y}$$

cross-sectional data Several different measurements or observations made at the same point in time.

crowding out effect The offsetting reduction in private expenditure caused by the rise in interest rates that follows an expansionary fiscal policy.

current account A part of the balance-of-payments accounts that records payments and receipts arising from trade in goods and services and from interest and dividends earned by capital owned in one country and invested in another.

current dollar GNP Gross national product valued in prices prevailing at the time of measurement; year-to-year changes in current dollar GNP reflect changes both in quantities produced and in market prices. Also called *nominal GNP.*

cyclically adjusted deficit (CAD) An estimate of the government budget deficit (expenditure minus tax revenue) not as it actually is but as it would be if national income were at its potential level.

debt Amounts owed to one's creditors, including banks and other financial institutions. That portion of a firm's money capital that has been borrowed from persons or institutions who are not owners of the firm.

decision lag The period of time between perceiving some problem and reaching a decision on what to do about it.

decreasing returns A situation in which output increases less than proportionately to inputs as the scale of production increases. A firm in this situation, with fixed factor prices, is an *increasing cost* firm.

demand The entire relationship between the quantity of a commodity that buyers wish to purchase per period of time and the price of that commodity.

demand curve The graphic representation of the relationship between the quantity of a commodity that buyers wish to purchase per period of time and the price of that commodity, other things equal.

demand deposit A bank deposit that is withdrawable on demand (without notice of intention to withdraw) and transferable by means of a check.

demand for money The total amount of money balances that the public wishes to hold for all purposes.

demand inflation Inflation arising from excess aggregate demand, that is, when national income exceeds potential income.

demand schedule A table showing for selected values the relationship between the quantity of a commodity that buyers wish to purchase per period of time and the price of that commodity, other things equal.

deposit money Money held by the public in the form of demand deposits with commercial banks.

depreciation (1) The loss in value of an asset over a period of time due to physical wear and tear and obsolescence. (2) The amount by which the capital stock is depleted through its contribution to current production. (3) A fall in the free-market value of domestic currency in terms of foreign currencies.

depression A period of very low economic activity with very high unemployment and high excess capacity.

derived demand The demand for a factor of production that results from the demand for products it is used to make.

differentiated product A product sufficiently distinguishable from others within an industry that the producer of each has some power over its own price; the products of firms in monopolistically competitive industries.

diminishing marginal rate of substitution The hypothesis that the marginal rate of substitution changes systematically as the amounts of two commodities being consumed vary.

direct investment In balance-of-payments accounting, foreign investment in the form of a takeover or capital investment in a branch plant or subsidiary corporation in which the investor has voting control.

dirty float See *managed float*.

disaggregated data Detailed data, such as investment by a single firm or all firms in one industry; in contrast to aggregated data, such as total investment by everyone in the economy.

discount rate (1) In banking, the rate at which the central bank is prepared to lend reserves to commercial banks. (2) More generally, the rate of interest used to discount a stream of future payments to arrive at their present value.

discouraged workers People who would like to work but have ceased looking for a job and hence have withdrawn from the labor force, because they believe that no suitable jobs are available.

discretionary fiscal policy Fiscal policy that is a conscious response (not according to any predetermined rule) to each particular state of the economy as it arises.

disembodied technical change Technical change that raises output without the necessity of building new capital to embody the new knowledge.

disequilibrium The absence of equilibrium. A market is in disequilibrium when there is either excess demand or excess supply.

disequilibrium price A price at which quantity demanded does not equal quantity supplied.

disposable income (Y_d) The income that households have available for spending and saving; GNP minus any part of it not actually paid to households minus personal income taxes paid by households.

distributed profits Profits paid out to owners of a firm. For incorporated firms the distributed profits are called *dividends*.

dividends That part of profits paid out to shareholders of a corporation.

division of labor The breaking up of a production process into a series of repetitive tasks, each done by a different worker.

dollar standard A system under which countries hold reserves in and settle debts with U.S. dollars, but the dollar is not backed by gold or any other physical source of monetary value.

double counting In national income accounting, adding up the total outputs of all the sectors in the economy so that the value of intermediate goods is counted in the sector that produces them and every time they are purchased as an input by another sector.

dumping In international trade, the practice of selling a commodity at a lower price in the export market than in the domestic market for reasons not related to differences in costs of servicing the two markets.

duopoly An industry that contains only two firms.

durable good A good that yields its services over an

extended period of time. Often divided into the sub-categories *producers' durables* (e.g., machines, equipment) and *consumers' durables* (e.g., cars, appliances).

dynamic differential   A difference in factor prices caused by disequilibrium that will tend to lead to corrective movements of resources and will be eliminated in equilibrium. Also called *disequilibrium differential*.

economic efficiency   The least costly method of producing any output.

economic growth   Increases in real, or constant dollar, potential GNP.

economic profits or **losses**   The difference between the revenues received from the sale of output and the opportunity cost of the inputs used to make the output. Negative economic profits are economic losses. Also called simply *profits* or *losses*.

economic rent   That part of the payment to a factor in excess of its transfer earnings.

economies of scale   Reduction of costs per unit of output resulting from an expansion in output; falling *LRAC* over a range of increasing output.

economies of scope   Economies achieved by a firm that is large enough to engage efficiently in multi-product production and associated large-scale distribution, advertising, and purchasing.

economy   A set of interrelated production and consumption activities.

effective rate of tariff   The tax charged on any imported commodity expressed as a percentage of the value added by the exporting industry.

effluent charge   A fee, fine, or tax on a producer for polluting activity, usually on a per unit basis.

elastic demand   The situation in which for a given percentage change in price there is a greater percentage change in quantity demanded; elasticity greater than unity.

elasticity of demand (η)   A measure of the responsiveness of quantity of a commodity demanded to a change in market price, defined by the formula

$$\eta = \frac{\text{percentage change in quantity demanded}}{\text{percentage change in price}}$$

With negatively sloped demand curves, elasticity is a negative number. Sometimes the above expression is multiplied by -1 to make measured elasticity positive. Also called *demand elasticity, price elasticity*.

elasticity of supply (η$_s$)   A measure of the responsiveness of the quantity of a commodity supplied to a change in the market price, defined by the formula

$$\eta_s = \frac{\text{percentage change in quantity supplied}}{\text{percentage change in price}}$$

embodied technical change   Technical change that can be utilized only when new capital, embodying the new techniques, is built.

employment   The number of adult workers (16 years of age and older) who hold full-time jobs.

endogenous expenditure   See *induced expenditure*.

endogenous variable   A variable that is explained within a theory.

entry barrier   Legal or other artificial impediment to entry into an industry, such as patents, economies of scale, and established brand preferences.

envelope curve   Any curve that encloses, by being tangent to, a series of other curves. In particular, the *envelope cost curve* is the *LRAC* curve, which encloses the *SRAC* curves by being tangent to each without cutting any of them.

equilibrium condition   A condition that must be fulfilled if some market or sector of the economy or the whole economy is to be in equilibrium.

equilibrium differential   A difference in factor prices that would persist in equilibrium, without any tendency for it to be removed.

equilibrium inflation   The rate of inflation that arises when there is no shock inflation, when output is held at potential so there is no demand inflation, and when there is monetary accommodation of expectational inflation.

equilibrium price   The price at which quantity demanded equals quantity supplied.

equity capital   Funds provided by the owners of a firm the return on which depends on the firm's profits.

excess capacity   The amount by which actual output falls short of capacity output (which is the output that corresponds to the minimum short-run average total cost.

excess capacity theorem   The proposition that equilibrium in a monopolistically competitive industry will occur where each firm has excess capacity.

excess demand   A situation in which, at the given price, quantity demanded exceeds quantity supplied. Also called a *shortage*.

excess reserves   Reserves held by a commercial bank in excess of the legally required minimum.

excess supply   A situation in which, at the given price, quantity supplied exceeds quantity demanded. Also called a *surplus*.

exchange rate   The price in terms of one currency at which another currency, or claims on it, can be bought and sold.

excise tax   A tax on the sale of a particular commodity; may be a *specific tax* (fixed tax per unit of commodity) or an *ad valorem tax* (fixed percentage of the value of the commodity).

execution lag   The time it takes to put policies in place after the decision is made.

exogenous expenditure   See *autonomous expenditure*.

exogenous variable   A variable that influences other variables within a theory but is itself determined by factors outside the theory. Also called *autonomous variable*.

expectational inflation Inflation that occurs because decision makers raise prices (so as to keep their relative prices constant) in the expectation that the price level is going to rise.

expectations augmented Phillips curve The relationship between unemployment and the rate of increase of money wages or between national income and the rate of increase of money prices that arises when the demand and expectations components of inflation are combined.

externalities Effects, either good or bad, on parties not directly involved in the production or use of a commodity. Also called *third-party effects*.

factor markets Markets in which the services of factors of production are sold.

factor mobility The ease with which factors can be transferred between uses.

factors of production Resources used to produce goods and services to satisfy wants; frequently divided into the basic categories of land, labor, and capital.

falling-cost industry An industry in which the lowest costs attainable by a firm fall as the scale of the industry expands.

favorable balance of payments A credit balance on some part of the international payments accounts (receipts exceed payments); often refers to a favorable balance on current plus capital account (that is, everything except the official settlements account).

federation In respect to labor unions, any loose organization of national unions.

fiat money Paper money or coinage that is neither backed by nor convertible into anything else but is accepted as legal tender.

final goods Goods that are not used as inputs by other firms, but are produced to be sold for consumption, investment, government, or exports.

final output Total output of goods and services excluding what is sold to other firms for use as a component in producing their output.

fine tuning The attempt to maintain national income at or near its full-employment level by means of frequent changes in fiscal or monetary policy.

firm The unit that employs factors of production and produces goods and services to be sold to households, other firms, or the government.

fiscal drag The tendency for a GNP gap to open up because tax revenues rise faster than government expenditure as full-employment income rises due to economic growth.

fiscal policy The use of the government's revenue-raising and spending activities in an effort to influence the behavior of such macro variables as the GNP and total employment.

fixed cost A cost that does not change with output. Also called *overhead cost, unavoidable cost*.

fixed exchange rate An exchange rate that is maintained within a small range around its publicly stated par value by the intervention of a country's central bank in foreign market operations. Also called a *pegged rate*.

fixed factors An input that cannot be increased in the short run.

fixed investment Investment in plant and equipment.

flexible exchange rate An exchange rate that is left free to be determined by the forces of demand and supply on the free market with no intervention by the monetary authorities. Also called *floating exchange rate*.

floating exchange rate See *flexible exchange rate*.

floor price A minimum permitted price.

foreign exchange Actual foreign currency or various claims on it, such as bank balances or promises to pay, that are traded for each other.

45° line In macroeconomics, the line that graphs the equilibrium condition that aggregate desired expenditure should equal national income ($AE = Y$).

fractional reserve system A banking system in which commercial banks are required to keep only a fraction of their deposits in cash or on deposit with the central bank.

freedom of entry and exit The absence of legal or other artificial barriers to entering into production or withdrawing assets from production.

free good A commodity for which the quantity supplied exceeds the quantity demanded at a price of zero; therefore a good that does not command a positive price in a market economy.

free-market economy An economy in which the decisions of individual households and firms (as distinct from the government) exert the major influence over the allocation of resources.

free reserves See *net unborrowed reserves*.

free trade The absence of any form of government intervention in international trade, which implies that imports and exports must not be subject to special taxes or restrictions levied merely because of their status as "imports" or "exports."

frictional unemployment Unemployment caused by the fact that it takes time for labor to move from one job to another.

fringe benefits Compensation other than wages for the benefit of labor, such as company contributions to pension and welfare funds, sick leave, and paid holidays.

full-cost pricing Setting price equal to average total cost at normal-capacity output plus a fixed markup.

full employment Employment sufficient to produce the economy's potential output; all unemployment is frictional and structural.

full-employment GNP (Y^*) See *potential GNP*.

full-employment national income (Y^*) See *potential GNP*.

function Loosely, an expression of a relation between two or more variables. Precisely, Y is a function of the variables $X_1, \ldots, X_n$ if for every set of values of the variables $X_1, \ldots, X_n$, there is associated a unique value of the variable Y.

functional distribution of income   The distribution of income by major factors of production.

G   See *government expenditure*.

gains from trade   The increased consumption that results from specialization and trade as opposed to self-sufficiency.

Giffen good   An inferior good for which the negative income effect outweighs the substitution effect so that the demand curve is positively sloped.

given year   A year for which an index number measures a change in some variable that has occurred since some earlier year, called the base year. (More generally referred to as *given period* to include other time units.)

GNP deflator   See *implicit GNP deflator*.

GNP gap   The difference between GNP that could have been produced at the potential or full-employment level and what is actually produced; that is potential GNP minus actual GNP.

gold exchange standard   A monetary system in which U.S. currency is directly convertible into gold and other countries' currencies are indirectly convertible by being convertible into the gold-backed U.S. dollar at a fixed rate.

goods   Tangible commodities, such as cars or shoes.

government   All public officials, agencies, and other organizations belonging to or under the control of state, local, or federal government.

government expenditure   Includes all government expenditure on currently produced goods and services and does not include government transfer payments. Represented by the symbol G as one of the four components of aggregate expenditure.

Gresham's law   The theory that "bad," or debased, money drives "good," or undebased, money out of circulation because people keep the good money for other purposes and use the bad money for transactions.

gross domestic product (GDP)   National income as measured by the output approach; equal to the sum of all values added in the economy or, what is the same thing, the values of all final goods produced in the economy.

gross investment   The total value of all investment goods produced in the economy during a stated period of time.

gross national expenditure (GNE)   National income as measured by the expenditure approach; equal to the sum of expenditures on consumption, investment, government production, and net exports.

gross national income   The sum of all the claims on income generated in the process of producing total output (equal to GNP).

gross national product (GNP)   National income as measured by the income approach; equal to the sum of all factor incomes earned plus depreciation plus (to get the valuation at market prices) indirect taxes minus subsidies.

gross return on capital   The receipts from the sale of goods produced by a firm less the cost of purchased goods and materials, labor, land, manager's talents, and taxes.

homogeneous product   In the eyes of purchasers every unit of the product is identical to every other unit.

horizontal merger   See *merger*.

household   All the people who live under one roof and who make, or are subject to others making for them, joint financial decisions.

human capital   The capitalized value of productive investments in persons; usually refers to value derived from expenditures on education, training, and health improvements.

hypothesis of equal net advantage   The hypothesis that owners of factors will choose the use of their factors that produces the greatest net advantage to themselves and therefore will move their factors among uses until net advantages are equalized.

hypothesis of diminishing returns   The hypothesis that if increasing quantities of a variable factor are applied to a given quantity of fixed factors, the marginal product and average product of the variable factor will eventually decrease. Also called *law of diminishing returns, law of variable proportions*.

I   See *investment expenditure*.

implicit GNP deflator   An index number derived by dividing GNP measured in current dollars by GNP measured in constant dollars and multiplying by 100. In effect, a price index with current-year quantity weights measuring the average change in price of all the items in the GNP. Also called *gross national product deflator*.

import quota   A limit set by the government on the quantity of a foreign commodity that may be shipped into that country in a given period.

import substitution industry   Domestic production for sale in the home market of goods previously imported; usually involves some form of protection or subsidy.

imputed costs   The costs of using factors of production already owned by the firm, measured by the earnings they could have received in their best alternative employment.

income-consumption curve   (1) A curve showing the relationship for a commodity between quantity demanded and income, *ceteris paribus*; (2) a curve drawn on an indifference curve diagram and connecting the points of tangency between a set of indifference curves and a set of parallel budget lines, showing how the consumption bundle changes as income changes, with relative prices held constant.

income effect The effect on quantity demanded of a change in real income.

income elasticity of demand A measure of the responsiveness of quantity demanded to a change in income, defined by the formula

$$\eta_Y = \frac{\text{percentage change in quantity demanded}}{\text{percentage change in income}}$$

income statement A financial report showing the revenues and costs that arise from the firm's use of inputs to produce outputs over a specified period of time.

incomes policy Any direct intervention by the government to influence wage and price formation.

increasing returns A situation in which output increases more than in proportion to inputs as the scale of a firm's production increases. A firm in this situation, with fixed factor prices, is a *decreasing cost* firm.

incremental cost See *marginal cost.*

incremental product See *marginal product.*

incremental revenue See *marginal revenue.*

indexing The automatic change in any money payment in proportion to the change in the price level.

index number An average that measures changes over time of variables such as the price level and industrial production; conventionally expressed as a percentage relative to a base period assigned the value 100.

indifference curve A curve showing all combinations of two commodities that give the household an equal amount of satisfaction and between which the household is thus indifferent.

indifference map A set of indifference curves based on a given set of household preferences.

induced expenditure In macroeconomics, elements of expenditure that are explained by variables within the theory. In the aggregate desired expenditure function it is any component of expenditure that is related to national income. Also called *endogenous expenditure.*

industrial union A union organized to include all workers in an industry, regardless of skills.

industry A group of firms producing similar products.

inelastic demand The situation in which for a given percentage change in price there is a smaller percentage change in quantity demanded; elasticity less than unity.

infant industry argument for tariffs The argument that new domestic industries with potential economies of scale need to be protected from competition from established low-cost foreign producers so that they can grow large enough to achieve costs as low as those of foreign producers.

inferior good A good for which income elasticity is negative.

inflation A rise in the average level of all prices. Sometimes restricted to prolonged or sustained rises.

inflationary gap A negative GNP gap, that is, a situation in which actual national income exceeds potential income.

infrastructure The basic installations and facilities (especially transportation and communications systems) on which the commerce of a community depends.

injections Income earned by domestic firms that does not arise out of the spending of domestic households and income earned by domestic households that does not arise out of the spending of domestic firms.

innovation The introduction of an invention into methods of production.

inputs Materials and factor services used in the process of production.

interest The payment for the use of borrowed money.

interest rate The price paid per dollar borrowed per year; expressed either as a proportion (e.g., 0.06) or as a percentage (e.g., 6 percent) See also *real interest rate.*

interest rate control The use of the interest rate as the instrument by which the central bank attempts to influence its target variables. See also *base control.*

intermediate goods All outputs that are used as inputs by other producers in a further stage of production.

intermediate targets Variables that the government cannot control directly and does not seek to control ultimately, yet that have an important influence on policy variables.

internalization A process that results in a producer's taking account of a previously external effect.

invention The discovery of something new, such as a new production technique or a new product.

inventories Stocks of raw materials, goods in process, and finished goods, held by firms to mitigate the effect of short-term fluctuations in production or sales.

investment expenditure Expenditure on the production of goods not for present consumption.

investment goods Goods produced not for present consumption, i.e., capital goods, inventories, and residential housing.

invisible account A form of balance-of-payments account that records payments and receipts arising out of trade in services and the use of capital. Also called *service account.*

invisibles All those items of foreign trade that are intangible; services as opposed to goods.

involuntary unemployment Unemployment due to the inability of qualified persons who are seeking work to find jobs at the going wage rate.

isocost line See *budget line.*

isoquant A curve showing all technologically efficient factor combinations for producing a specified output.

isoquant map A series of isoquants from the same production function, each isoquant relating to a specific level of output.

jurisdictional dispute Dispute between unions over which has the right to organize a group of workers.

Keynesians A label attached to economists who hold the view, derivative from the work of John Maynard Keynes, that active use of monetary and fiscal policy can be effective in stabilizing the economy. Often the term encompasses economists who advocate active policy intervention in general.

Keynesian short-run aggregate supply curve A horizontal aggregate supply curve indicating that when national income is below potential, changes in national income can occur with little or no accompanying changes in prices.

k percent rule The proposition that the money supply should be increased at a constant percentage rate year in and year out, irrespective of cyclical changes in national income.

labor A factor of production consisting of all physical and mental contributions provided by people.

labor boycott An organized attempt to persuade customers to refrain from purchasing the products of a firm or industry whose employees are on strike.

labor force See *civilian labor force.*

labor union See *union.*

Laffer curve A graph relating the revenue yield of a tax system to the marginal or average tax rate imposed.

laissez faire Literally, "let do"; a policy advocating the absence of government intervention in a market economy.

land A factor of production consisting of all gifts of nature, including raw materials and "land" as conventionally defined.

law of demand The assertion that market price and quantity demanded in the market vary inversely with one another, that is, that demand curves slope downward.

law of diminishing returns See *hypothesis of diminishing returns.*

law of variable proportions See *hypothesis of diminishing returns.*

legal tender Anything that by law must be accepted for the purchase of goods and services or in discharge of a debt.

less-developed countries (LDCs) The lower-income countries of the world, most of which are in Asia, Africa, and South and Central America. Also called *underdeveloped countries, developing countries,* the *South.*

life-cycle hypothesis (LCH) A hypothesis that relates the household's actual consumption to its expected lifetime income rather than (as in early Keynesian theory) to its current income.

lifetime income See *permanent income.*

limited liability The limitation of the financial responsibility of an owner (shareholder) of a corporation to the amount of money he or she has actually made available to the firm by purchasing its shares.

limited partnership Limited partners do not participate in management and their personal liability for the debts of the firm is limited to the amount each has invested.

limit price The minimum price at which a new firm can enter a market without incurring a loss; equal to its minimum average total cost.

liquidity The degree of ease and certainty with which an asset can be turned into the economy's medium of exchange.

liquidity preference (LP) function The function that relates the demand for money to the rate of interest.

lockout The closing of a plant by an employer during a bargaining dispute; the employer's equivalent of a strike.

logarithmic scale A scale in which equal proportional changes are shown as equal distances (for example, 1 inch may always represent doubling of a variable, whether from 3 to 6 or 50 to 100). Also called *log scale, ratio scale.*

long run A period of time in which all inputs may be varied, but the basic technology of production cannot be changed.

long-run aggregate supply (LRAS) curve The curve indicating total supply that is forthcoming when all wages and prices have adjusted; a vertical line at $Y = Y^*$.

long-run average cost (LRAC) curve The curve relating the least-cost method of producing any output to the level of output. Also called *long-run average total cost (LRATC) curve.*

long-run industry supply (LRS) curve The curve showing the relation of the quantity supplied to prices with quantities of all factors freely variable, and allowing time for firms to achieve long-run equilibrium.

long-run Phillips curve (LRPC) The relation between national income and the price level when all goods and factor markets are in long-run equilibrium.

Lorenz curve A graph showing the extent of departure from equality of income distribution.

lower turning point The bottom point of the business cycle where a contraction turns into an expansion of economic activity.

Lucas aggregate supply curve A curve expressing the hypothesis that national output varies positively with the ratio of the actual to the expected price level.

M Imports; a country's total expenditure on imports.

M1 Currency plus demand deposits plus other checkable accounts.

M2 M1 plus money market mutual balances, money market deposit accounts, savings accounts, and small denomination time deposits.

M3 M2 plus large denomination time deposits, term repurchase agreements, and money market mutual funds held by institutions.

macroeconomics The study of the determination of

economic aggregates and averages, such as total output, total employment, the price level, and rate of economic growth.

managed float Intervention in the foreign exchange market by a country's central bank to respond to particular circumstances in pursuit of an unofficial exchange rate target, but not to maintain an announced par value. Also called *dirty float*.

marginal cost (MC) The increase in total cost resulting from raising the rate of production by one unit. Mathematically, the rate of change of cost with respect to output. Also called *incremental cost*.

marginal efficiency of capital (MEC) The marginal rate of return on a nation's capital stock. The rate of return on one additional dollar of net investment, i.e., an addition of one dollar's worth of new capital to capital stock.

marginal efficiency of capital schedule A schedule relating *MEC* to the size of the capital stock.

marginal efficiency of investment (MEI) The function that relates the quantity of investment to the rate of interest.

marginal net private benefit (MNPB) The difference between the contribution of a unit of production to a firm's revenue and its contribution to the firm's cost.

marginal net social benefit (MNSB) The difference between marginal social benefit and marginal social cost.

marginal physical product (MPP) See *marginal product*.

marginal product (MP) The change in quantity of total output that results from using one unit more of a variable factor. Mathematically, the rate of change of output with respect to the quantity of the variable factor. Also called *incremental product* or *marginal physical product* (*MPP*).

marginal productivity theory of distribution The theory that factors are paid the value of their marginal products so that the total earnings of each type of factor of production equals the value of the marginal product of that factor multiplied by the number of units of that factor that are employed.

marginal propensity to consume (MPC) The change in consumption divided by the change in disposable income that brought it about; mathematically, the rate of change of consumption with respect to disposable income ($MPC = \Delta C/\Delta Y_d$).

marginal propensity not to spend The fraction of any increment to national income that is not spent on domestic production (1 − the marginal propensity to spend; i.e., 1 − $\Delta AE/\Delta Y$).

marginal propensity to save (MPS) The change in saving related to the change in disposable income that brought it about; the rate of change of saving divided by disposable income ($MPS = \Delta S/\Delta Y_d$).

marginal propensity to spend The fraction of any increment to national income that is spent on domestic production; it is measured by the change in aggregate expenditure divided by the change in income ($\Delta AE/\Delta Y$).

marginal rate of substitution (MRS) (1) In consumption, the slope of an indifference curve, showing how much more of one commodity must be provided to compensate for the giving up of one unit of another commodity if the level of satisfaction is to be held constant. (2) In production, the slope of an isoquant, showing how much more of one factor of production must be used to compensate for the use of one less unit or another factor of production if production is to be held constant.

marginal revenue (MR) The change in a firm's total revenue arising from a change in its rate of sales by one unit. Mathematically, the rate of change of revenue with respect to output. Also called *incremental revenue*.

marginal revenue product (MRP) The addition of revenue attributable to the last unit of a variable factor. $MRP = MP \times MR$. Mathematically, the rate of change of revenue with respect to quantity of the variable factor.

marginal social benefit The contribution of a unit of production to social welfare.

marginal tax rate The amount of tax a taxpayer would pay on an additional dollar of income, i.e., the fraction of an additional dollar of income that is paid in taxes.

marginal utility The additional satisfaction obtained by a buyer from consuming one unit more of a good; mathematically, the rate of change of utility with respect to consumption.

margin requirement The fraction of the price of a stock that must be paid in cash, while putting up the stock as security against a loan for the balance.

market A concept with many possible definitions. (1) An area over which buyers and sellers negotiate the exchange of a well-defined commodity. (2) From the point of view of a household, the firms from which it can buy a well-defined product. (3) From the point of view of a firm, the buyers to whom it can sell a well-defined product.

market-clearing price Price at which quantity demanded equals quantity supplied so that there are neither unsatisfied buyers nor unsatisfied sellers; that is, the equilibrium price.

market economy A society in which people specialize in productive activities and meet most of their material wants through exchanges voluntarily agreed upon by the contracting parties.

market failure Failure of the unregulated market system to achieve optimal allocative efficiency or social goals because of externalities, market impediments, or market imperfections.

market rate of interest The actual interest rate in effect at a given moment.

market sector That portion of an economy in which

commodities are bought and sold and in which producers must cover their costs from sales revenue.

market structure   Characteristics of market organization that affect behavior and performance of firms, such as the number and size of sellers, the extent of knowledge about each other's actions, the degree of freedom of entry, and the degree of product differentiation.

markup   The amount added to cost to determine price.

medium of exchange   Anything that is generally acceptable in return for goods and services sold.

merchandise account   See *visible account.*

merger   The purchase of either the physical assets or the controlling share ownership of one company by another. In a *horizontal* merger both companies produce the same product; in a *vertical* merger one company is a supplier of the other; if the two are in unrelated industries, it is a *conglomerate* merger.

microeconomic policy   Activities of governments designed to alter resource allocation and/or income distribution.

microeconomics   The study of the allocation of resources and the distribution of income as they are affected by the workings of the price system and by government policies.

minimum efficient scale (*MES*)   The level of output at which long-run average cost is at a minimum. The smallest size of firm required to achieve the economies of scale in production and/or distribution.

minimum wages   Legally specified minimum rate of pay for labor in covered occupations.

mixed economy   An economy in which some decisions about the allocation of resources are made by firms and households and some by the government.

monetarists   A label attached to economists who stress monetary causes of cyclical fluctuations and inflations and who believe that an active stabilization policy is not normally required. Often the term encompasses conservative economists who oppose active policy intervention in general.

monetary base   The sum of currency in circulation plus reserves of the commercial banks.

monetary equilibrium   A situation in which the demand for money equals the supply of money.

monetary policy   An attempt to influence the economy by operating on such monetary variables as the quantity of money and the rate of interest.

money   Any generally accepted medium of exchange.

money capital   The funds used to finance a firm, including both equity capital and debt.

money income   Income measured in monetary units per period of time.

money market deposit account (MMDA)   See *money market mutual fund.*

money market mutual fund (MMMF)   Liquid financial instruments that earn high yields, are checkable, but are subject to minimum transaction restrictions.

money rate of interest   See *interest rate.*

money substitute   Something that serves as a temporary medium of exchange but is not a store of value.

money supply   The total quantity of money in an economy at a point in time.

monopolistic competition   (1) A market structure of an industry in which there are many sellers and freedom of entry but in which each firm has a product somewhat differentiated from the others, giving it some control over its price. (2) More recently, any industry in which more than one firm sells differentiated products.

monopoly   A market situation in which the output of an industry is controlled by a single seller.

monopsony   A market situation in which there is a single buyer.

moral hazard   A situation in which an individual or firm takes advantage of special knowledge while engaging in socially uneconomic behavior.

multilateral balance of payments   The balance between one country's payments to and receipts from the rest of the world.

multiple regression analysis   See *regression analysis.*

multiplier   The ratio of the change in national income to the change in autonomous expenditure that brought it about.

Nash equilibrium   See *Cournot-Nash equilibrium.*

national debt   The current volume of outstanding federal government debt.

national income   In general, the value of total output and the value of the income generated by the production of that output.

national income accounting   The set of rules and techniques for measuring the total flow of output produced and incomes generated by this production.

natural monopoly   An industry characterized by economies of scale sufficiently large that one firm can most efficiently supply the entire market demand.

natural rate of unemployment   The rate of unemployment (due to frictional and structural causes) consistent with potential national income (Y^*). It is the rate of unemployment at which there is neither upward nor downward demand pressure on the price level.

natural scale   A scale in which equal absolute amounts are represented by equal distances.

near money   Liquid assets that are easily convertible into money without risk of significant loss of value and can be used as short-term stores of purchasing power, but are not themselves media of exchange.

negative income tax (NIT)   A tax system in which households with incomes below taxable levels receive payments from the government based on a percentage of the amount by which their income is below the minimum taxable level.

negotiable order of withdrawal (NOW)   A checklike

device for transferring funds from one person's time deposit to another person.

net exports Total exports minus total imports. Represented by the expression $(X - M)$ as a component of aggregate expenditure, where X is total exports and M is total imports.

net investment Gross investment minus replacement investment.

net national income (NNI) at factor cost The sum of the four components of factor incomes (wages, rent, interest, and profits).

net national product (NNP) at market prices Sum of wages, rent, interest, profits, and indirect taxes minus subsidies.

net private benefit (*NPB*) The difference between private benefits and private costs.

net social benefit (*NSB*) The difference between social benefits and social costs. Where private production produces externalities, it is net private benefit plus external benefits and minus external costs.

net unborrowed reserves The total reserves of the commercial banking system minus required reserves minus the reserves that have been borrowed from the central bank. Also called *free reserves*.

neutrality of money The doctrine that the money supply affects only the absolute level of prices and has no effect on relative prices and hence no effect on the allocation of resources or the distribution of income.

newly industrializing countries (NIC) Formerly underdeveloped countries that have become major industrial exporters since World War II.

nominal GNP See *current dollar national income*.

nominal national income Total output measured in dollars; the money value of national output. Also called *money national income* or *current dollar national income*.

nominal rate of interest See *interest rate*.

nominal rate of tariff The tax charged on any imported commodity.

nonmarket sector That portion of an economy in which commodities are given away and producers must cover their costs from some source other than sales revenue.

nonprice competition Competition by sellers for sales by means other than price cutting, such as advertising, product differentiation, trading stamps, and other promotional devices.

nontariff barriers to trade Restrictions, other than tariffs, designed to reduce the flow of imported goods.

normal capacity output The level of output that a firm hopes to maintain on average over the business cycle; typically, somewhat less than full capacity output.

normal good A good for which income elasticity is positive.

normal profits A term used by some economists for the imputed returns to capital and risk taking just necessary to keep the owners in the industry. They are included

in what the economist, but not the businessman, sees as *total costs*.

normative statement A statement or theory about what ought to be, as opposed to what is, was, or will be true.

note See *treasury bill*.

NOW See *negotiable order of withdrawal*.

oligopoly A market structure in which a small number of rival firms dominate the industry.

open market operations The purchase and sale on the open market by the central bank of securities (usually short-term government securities).

open shop A place of employment in which a union represents its members but does not have bargaining jurisdiction for all workers in a shop and membership in the union is not a condition of getting or keeping a job.

operating regime The combination of intermediate targets and policy instruments used to achieve those targets selected by a central bank in order to reach its policy goals.

opportunity cost The cost of using resources for a certain purpose, measured by the benefit given up by not using them in their best alternative use.

organization theory A set of hypotheses that predicts that the substance of the decisions of a firm is affected by its size and form of organization.

outputs The goods and services that result from the process of production.

Pareto-efficiency See *Pareto-optimality*.

Pareto-optimality A situation in which it is impossible by reallocation of production or consumption activities to make all consumers better off without simultaneously making others worse off (or, as it is sometimes put, to make at least one person better off while making no one worse off). Also called *Pareto-efficiency*.

partnership A form of business organization in which the firm has two or more joint owners, each of whom is personally responsible for all of the firm's actions and debts.

paternalism Intervention in the free choices of individuals by others (including governments) to protect them against their own ignorance or folly.

pegged rate See *fixed exchange rate*.

per capita GNP GNP divided by total population.

perfect competition A market structure in which all firms in an industry are price takers and in which there is freedom of entry into and exit from the industry.

permanent income The maximum amount that a household can consume per year into the indefinite future without reducing its wealth. (A number of similar but not identical definitions are in common use.) Also called *lifetime income*.

permanent-income hypothesis (PIH) A hypothesis that relates actual consumption to permanent income rather than (as in the original Keynesian theory) to current income.

personal income Income earned by individuals before allowance for personal income taxes on that income.

petrodollars Money earned by the oil-exporting countries and held by them in short-term, liquid investments.

Phillips curve Originally, a relation between the percentage of the labor force unemployed and the rate of change of money wages. Now often drawn as a relation between the percentage of the labor force employed and the rate of price inflation or between actual national income and the rate of price inflation.

picket line Striking workers parading at the entrances to a plant or firm on strike; a symbolic blockade of the entrance.

point elasticity A measure of the responsiveness of quantity to price at a particular point on the demand curve. The formula for point elasticity of demand is

$$\eta = \frac{\Delta q}{\Delta p} \times \frac{p}{q}$$

With negatively sloped demand curves elasticity is a negative number. Sometimes the above expression is multiplied by -1 to make elasticity positive.

point of diminishing average productivity The level of output at which average product reaches a maximum.

point of diminishing marginal productivity The level of output at which marginal product reaches a maximum.

policy instruments The variables that the government can control directly to achieve its policy objectives.

policy variables The variables that the government seeks to control, such as real national income and the price level.

political business cycle Cyclical swings in the economy generated by fiscal and monetary policy for the purpose of winning elections.

portfolio investment In balance-of-payments accounting, foreign investment in bonds or a minority holding of shares that does not involve legal control. See also *direct investment*.

positive statement A statement or theory about what is, was, or will be true, as opposed to what ought to be.

potential GNP (Y^*) The real gross national product the economy could produce if its productive resources were fully employed at their normal intensity of use. Also called *full-employment GNP, full-employment national income*.

potential income See *potential GNP*.

potential national income See *potential GNP*.

poverty gap The number of dollars per year required to raise everyone's income that is below the poverty level to that level.

poverty level The official government estimate of the annual family income required to maintain a minimum adequate standard of living.

precautionary balances Money balances held for protection against the uncertainty of the timing of cash flows.

preferred stock A form of equity capital with a preference over common stock to receipt of dividends up to a stated maximum amount; may be voting or nonvoting.

present value (PV) The value now of one or more payments to be received in the future; often referred to as the *discounted present value* of future payments.

price ceiling A maximum permissible price.

price-consumption line A line connecting the points of tangency between a set of indifference curves and a set of budget lines where one absolute price is fixed and the other varies, money income being held constant.

price control policy Any government policy that regulates the price at which a commodity can be bought and sold; often used to refer to the imposition of maximum prices on one or more commodities.

price discrimination The sale by a single firm of different units of a specific commodity to buyers at two or more different prices for reasons not associated with differences in cost.

price elasticity of demand See *elasticity of demand*.

price floor A minimum permissible price.

price index A number that shows the average percentage change that has occurred in some group of prices over some period of time; price indexes can be used to measure the price level at a given time relative to a base period.

price leader A firm that sets a price for its product and is followed by other firms in establishing and changing that price.

price level The average level of a broad group of prices; it is usually measured by an index number.

price parity The ratio of prices farmers receive for products they sell to the prices they pay for products they buy, compared with some base period; a basic concept in U.S. farm policy.

price taker A firm that can alter its rate of production and sales without significantly affecting the market price of its product.

price theory The theory of how prices are determined; competitive price theory concerns the determination of prices in competitive markets by the interaction of demand and supply.

principle of substitution The prediction that as the relative prices of the inputs vary, the proportions in which various inputs are used will vary so as to use relatively more of the cheaper inputs.

private cost The value of the best alternative use of resources used in production as valued by the producer.

private sector That portion of an economy in which the organizations that produce goods and services are owned and operated by private units such as households and firms.

producers' cooperative An organization of producers of a commodity usually formed to serve as a joint selling organization for the producers and often operated as a cartel.

producers' durables See *durable good*.

producers' surplus The difference between the total amount producers receive for all units sold of a commodity and the total variable cost of producing the commodity; it can be calculated by finding the difference between the marginal cost and marginal revenue associated with the production and sale of each unit of output and summing over all units of output.

product differentiation The existence of similar but not identical products sold by a single industry such as the breakfast food and the automobile industries.

production The act of making commodities, either goods or services.

production function A functional relation showing the maximum output that can be produced by each and every combination of inputs.

production possibility boundary A curve that shows which alternative combinations of commodities can just be attained if all available productive resources are used; it is thus the boundary between attainable and unattainable output combinations.

productive efficiency Production of any output at the lowest attainable cost for that level of output.

productivity Output produced per unit of resource input; frequently used to refer to *labor productivity,* measured by output per hour worked or per worker.

product markets Markets in which outputs of goods and services are sold.

profit (1) In ordinary usage, the difference between the value of outputs and the value of inputs. (2) In microeconomics, the difference between revenues received from the sale of goods and the value of inputs, which includes the opportunity cost of capital, so that profits are *economic profits*. (3) In macroeconomics, profits exclude interest on borrowed capital, but do not exclude the return on owner's capital.

progressive tax A tax that takes a larger percentage of income the higher the level of income.

progressivity of taxation The ratio of taxes to income as income increases. If the ratio decreases, the tax is *regressive;* if it remains constant, *proportional;* if it increases, *progressive.*

proportional tax A tax that takes a constant percentage of income at all levels of income and is thus neither progressive nor regressive.

protectionism Government intervention to provide partial or complete protection of domestic industries from foreign competition in domestic markets by use of tariff or nontariff barriers to trade.

proxy A document authorizing the holder to vote one's stock in a corporation.

proxy fight A struggle between competing factions in a corporation to obtain the proxies for a majority of the outstanding shares.

public sector That portion of an economy in which production is owned and operated by the government or bodies appointed by it such as nationalized industries.

public utility regulation Regulation of such things as prices and profit rates in industries that have been deemed to be natural monopolies.

purchasing power of money The amount of goods and services that can be purchased with a unit of money. Decreases in the purchasing power of money are measured by increases in a price index. Also called *value of money.*

purchasing power parity (PPP) exchange rate The exchange rate between two currencies that adjusts for relative inflation rates.

pure rate of interest The rate of interest that would rule in equilibrium in a riskless economy where all lending and borrowing is for investment in productive capital.

pure return on capital The amount capital can earn in a riskless investment; hence the transfer earnings of capital in a riskless investment.

quantity actually bought The amount of a commodity that households succeed in purchasing in some time period.

quantity actually sold The amount of a commodity that producers succeed in selling in some time period.

quantity demanded The amount of a commodity that households wish to purchase in some time period. An increase (decrease) in quantity demanded refers to a movement down (up) the demand curve in response to a fall (rise) in price.

quantity exchanged The identical amount of a commodity that households actually purchase and producers actually sell in some time period.

quantity supplied The amount of a commodity producers wish to sell in some time period. An increase (decrease) in quantity supplied refers to a movement up (down) the supply curve in response to a rise (fall) in price.

random sample A sample chosen from a group or population in such a way that every member of the group has an equal chance of being selected.

rate base The total allowable investment to which the rate of return allowed by a regulatory commission is applied.

rate of inflation   The percentage rate of increase in some price index from one period to another.

rate of return   The ratio of return on capital earned by a firm to total invested capital.

rate of return on capital   Sometimes used synonymously with *rate of return*. Frequently used to refer to a specific capital good; the annual return to capital produced by a capital good, expressed as a percentage of the price of the good.

rational expectations   The theory that people understand how the economy works and learn quickly from their mistakes, so that while random errors may be made, systematic and persistent errors are not made.

ratio scale   See *logarithmic scale*.

real capital   Physical assets of a firm, including plant, equipment, and inventories. Also called *physical capital*.

real GNP   See *constant dollar GNP*.

real income   A household's or firm's income expressed in terms of the purchasing power of the income, that is, the quantity of goods and services that can be purchased with the income; it can be calculated as money income deflated by a price index.

real product wage   The proportion of each sales dollar accounted for by labor costs (including the pre-tax nominal wage rate, benefits, and payroll taxes).

real rate of interest   The money rate of interest corrected for the change in the purchasing power of money by subtracting the inflation rate.

real wage unemployment   Unemployment caused by too high a real product wage. Also called classical unemployment.

recession   In general, a downswing in the level of economic activity. Defined by the Department of Commerce as a fall in real GNP for two successive quarters.

recessionary gap   A positive GNP gap; that is, a situation in which actual national income is less than potential income.

regression analysis   A quantitative measure of the systematic relationship between two or more variables. *Simple regression* concerns the relation between Y and a single independent variable, X_1; *multiple regression* concerns the relation between Y and more than one independent variable, $X_1, \ldots, X_n$. Also called *correlation analysis*.

regression equation   An equation describing the statistically determined best fit between variables, or best estimate of the average relationship between variables in regression analysis.

regressive tax   A tax that takes a lower percentage of income the higher the level of income.

relative price   The ratio of the money price of one commodity to the money price of another commodity; that is, a ratio of two absolute prices.

replacement investment   The amount of investment that just maintains the existing capital stock intact.

required reserves   The minimum amount of reserves a bank must, by law, keep either in currency or in deposits with the central bank.

reserve currencies   Currencies (such as the U.S. dollar) commonly held by foreign central banks as international reserves.

reserve ratio   The fraction of its deposits that a bank holds as reserves in the form of cash or deposits with a central bank.

resource allocation   The allocation of an economy's scarce resources among alternative uses.

retained earnings   See *undistributed profits*.

return to capital   The total amount available for payments to owners of capital; the sum of pure returns to capital, risk premiums, and economic profits.

revenue sharing   The return of some of the revenue collected by the federal government to a state or local government for unrestricted expenditure; a noncategorical or general grant-in-aid.

right-to-work laws   State laws that prohibit a closed or union shop, that is, that give an individual the right to work in an organized plant without belonging to the union that is the collective bargaining agent of the workers.

rising-cost industry   An industry in which the minimum cost attainable by a firm rises as the scale of the industry expands.

rising supply price   A rising long-run supply curve, caused by increases in factor prices as output is increased or by diseconomies of scale.

risk premium   The return on capital necessary to compensate owners of capital for the risk of loss of their capital.

sample   A small number of items, chosen from a larger group or population, that is intended to be representative of the larger entity.

satisficing   A hypothesized objective of firms to achieve target levels of satisfactory performance rather than to *maximize* some objective.

saving   All disposable income that is not spent on consumption.

scarce good   A commodity for which the quantity demanded exceeds the quantity supplied at a price of zero; and therefore a good that commands a positive price in a market economy.

scatter diagram   A graph of statistical observations of paired values of two variables, one measured on the horizontal and the other on the vertical axis. Each point on the coordinate grid represents the values of the variables for a particular unit of observation.

search unemployment   Unemployment caused by people continuing to search for a good job rather than accepting the first job they come across when unemployed.

sectors   Parts of an economy.

securities market   See *stock market*.

selective credit controls Controls on credit imposed through such means as margin requirements, restrictions on installment buying, and minimum down payments on mortgages.

sellers' preferences Allocation of commodities in excess demand by decisions of those who sell them.

service account See *invisible account*.

services Intangible commodities, such as haircuts or medical care.

short run A period of time over which the quantity of some inputs cannot, as a practical matter, be varied.

short-run aggregate supply (SRAS) curve A relation between the price level of final output and the quantity of output supplied on the assumption that all input prices (including wage rates) are held constant.

short-run equilibrium Generally, equilibrium subject to fixed factors or other things that cannot change over the time period being considered. For a competitive firm, the output at which market price equals marginal cost; for a competitive industry, the price and output at which industry demand equals short-run industry supply and all firms are in short-run equilibrium. Either profits or losses are possible.

short-run Phillips curve (SRPC) A relation between unemployment and the rate of wage inflation or between national income and the rate of price inflation, drawn for a given state of expectations about the future rate of inflation.

short-run supply curve A curve showing the relation of quantity supplied to prices, with one or more fixed factors; it is the horizontal sum of marginal cost curves (above the level of average variable costs) of all firms in an industry.

simple multiplier The ratio of the change in equilibrium national income to the change in autonomous expenditure at a constant price level.

single proprietorship A form of business organization in which the firm has one owner, who is personally responsible for all of the firm's actions and debts.

size distribution of income The distribution of income among households by amount, without regard to source of income or social class of households.

slope The ratio of the vertical change to the horizontal change between two points on a straight line.

Snake An agreement among the countries of the European Community (except the U.K.) to fix exchange rates among their own currencies and then let their joint rate float against the dollar.

social benefit The contribution an activity makes to the society's welfare.

social cost The value of the best alternative use of resources available to society as valued by society. Also called *social opportunity cost*.

special drawing rights (SDRs) Financial liabilities of the IMF held in a special fund generated by contributions of member countries. Members can use SDRs to maintain supplies of convertible currencies when these are needed to support foreign exchanges.

specialization of labor An organization of production in which individual workers specialize in the production of particular goods or services (and satisfy their wants by trading) rather than produce everything they consume (and satisfy their wants by being self-sufficient).

specific tariff An import duty of a specific amount per unit of the product.

specific tax. See *excise tax*.

speculative balances Money balances held as a hedge against the uncertainty of the prices of other financial assets.

stabilization policy Any policy designed to reduce the economy's cyclical fluctuations. Attempts by the government to remove inflationary and recessionary gaps when they appear.

stagflation The coexistence of high rates of unemployment with high, and sometimes rising, rates of inflation.

stockholders The owners of a corporation who have supplied money to the firm by purchasing its shares.

stock market An organized market where stocks and bonds are bought and sold. Also called *securities market*.

strike The concerted refusal of the members of a union to work.

strikebreakers Nonunion workers brought in by management to operate the plant while a union is on strike (derisively called *scabs* by union members).

structural rigidity theory The theory that downward inflexibility of money prices means that the adjustment of relative prices necessary in any changing economy will cause an upward drift in the average level of all prices (i.e., a gradual inflation).

structural unemployment Unemployment due to a mismatch between characteristics required by available jobs and characteristics possessed by the unemployed labor.

substitute Two commodities are substitutes for each other when both satisfy similar needs or desires; the degree of substitutability is measured by the magnitude of the positive cross elasticity between the two.

substitution effect A change in quantity of a good demanded resulting from a change in its relative price, eliminating the effect on real income of the change in price.

supply The entire relationship between the quantity of some commodity that producers wish to make and sell per period of time and the price of that commodity, other things being equal.

supply curve The graphic representation of the relation between the quantity of some commodity that producers wish to make and sell per period of time and the price of that commodity, other things being equal.

supply of effort The total number of hours of work

that the population is willing to supply. Also called *total supply of labor*.

supply of money   See *money supply*.

supply schedule   A table showing for selected values the relation between the quantity of some commodity that producers wish to make and sell per period of time and the price of that commodity, other things being equal.

surplus function   See *budget surplus function*.

tacit collusion   The adoption, without explicit agreement, of a common policy by sellers in an industry. Also called *conscious parallel action*. See also *collusion*.

takeover bid   See *tender offer*.

tariff   A tax applied on imports.

tax base   The aggregate amount of taxable income.

tax-related income policy (TIP)   Tax incentives for labor and management to encourage them to conform to wage and price guidelines.

tax expenditures   Tax concessions, such as exemptions and deductions from taxable income and tax credits, designed to induce market responses considered to be desirable. They are called expenditures because they have the same effect as having no concessions and then spending money on subsidies and other transfers to the groups getting the concessions.

tax incidence   The location of the burden of a tax; that is, the identify of the ultimate bearer of the tax.

technological efficiency   The ratio of quantity of output to quantity of inputs (real resources) achieved by a method of production. Also called *technical efficiency*.

tender offer   An offer to buy directly some or all of the outstanding common stock of a corporation from its stockholders at a specified price per share, in an attempt to gain control of the corporation. Also called *takeover bid*.

term   See *term to maturity*.

terms of trade   The ratio of the average price of a country's exports to the average price of its imports.

term to maturity   The period of time from the present to the redemption date of a bond. Also called simply the *term*.

third-party effects   See *externalities*.

time deposit   An interest-earning bank deposit, legally subject to notice before withdrawal (in practice the notice requirement is not normally enforced) and until recently not transferable by check.

time series   A series of observations on the values of a variable at different points in time.

time-series data   A set of measurements or observations made repeatedly at successive periods (or moments) of time. Contrasted with *cross-sectional data*.

total cost (TC)   The sum of the opportunity costs of the factors used to produce that output, it can be divided into total fixed costs and total variable costs of producing at a given level of output.

total fixed cost (TFC)   Total costs of producing that do not vary with level of output.

total product (TP)   Total amount produced during a given period of time by all the factors of production employed over that time period.

total revenue (TR)   Total receipts from the sale of a product; price times quantity.

total utility   The total satisfaction resulting from the consumption of a given commodity by a consumer in a period of time.

total variable cost (TVC)   Total costs of producing that vary directly with level of output.

trade account   See *visible account*.

trade union   See *union*.

transactions balances   Money balances held to finance payments because payments and receipts are not perfectly synchronized.

transactions costs   Costs incurred in effecting market transactions (such as negotiation costs, billing costs, and bad debts).

transfer earnings   That part of the payment to a factor in its present use that is just enough to keep it from transferring to another use.

transfer payment   A payment to a private person or institution that does not arise out of current productive activity; typically made by governments, as in welfare payments, but also made by businesses and private individuals in the form of charitable contributions.

transmission mechanism   The channels by which a change in the demand or supply of money leads to a shift of the aggregate demand curve.

treasury bill   The characteristic form of short-term government debt. A promise to pay a certain sum of money at a specified time in the future (usually 90 days to 1 year from date of issue). Although they carry no fixed interest payments, holders earn an interest return because they purchase them at a lower price than their redemption value. Also called *treasury note*.

trigger price   In U.S. trade policy, a price for an imported commodity set by the U.S. government on the basis of average total cost of the low-cost producing nation. A foreign country that sells below a trigger price is subject to proceedings under antidumping laws.

turnover tax   An excise tax levied on the gross value of all sales (not just value added), sometimes used in socialist countries.

unbalanced growth   The growth of different sectors of the economy at substantially different rates, which usually implies a changing pattern of international trade.

undistributed profits   Earnings of a firm not distributed to shareholders as dividends, but retained by the firm. Also called *retained earnings*.

unemployment   The number of persons 16 years of age and older who are not employed and are actively searching for a job.

unemployment rate   Unemployment expressed as a percentage of the labor force.

unfavorable balance of payments   A debit balance on some part of the payments accounts (payments exceed receipts); often refers to the balance on current plus capital account (that is, everything except the official settlements account).

union   An association of workers authorized to represent them in bargaining with employers. Also called *trade union, labor union*.

union shop   A bargaining arrangement in which the employer may hire anyone at union wages, but every employee must join the union within a specified period of time (often 60 days).

unit costs   Costs per unit of output, equal to total cost divided by total output. Also called *average cost*.

upper turning point   The top point of the business cycle where an expansion turns into a contraction of economic activity.

utility   The satisfaction that results from the consumption of a commodity.

value added   The value of a firm's output minus the value of the inputs that it purchases from other firms.

value of money   See *purchasing power of money*.

variable   A magnitude (such as the price of a commodity) that can take on a specific value, but whose value will vary with time and place.

variable cost   A cost that varies directly with changes in output. Also called *direct cost, avoidable cost*.

variable factor   An input that can be varied in the short run.

velocity of circulation   National income divided by quantity of money.

vertical merger   See *merger*.

very long run   A period of time in which the technological possibilities open to a firm are subject to change.

visible account   A form of balance-of-payments account that records payments and receipts arising from the import and export of tangible goods. Also called *trade account*, and *merchandise account*.

visibles   All those items of foreign trade that are tangible; goods as opposed to services.

voluntary export restriction (VER)   An agreement by an exporting country to limit the amount of a good exported to another country.

wage and price controls   Direct government intervention into wage and price formation with legal power to enforce the government's decisions on wages and prices.

wage-cost push inflation   An increase in the price level caused by increases in labor costs that are not themselves associated with excess aggregate demand for labor.

wealth   The sum of all the valuable assets owned minus liabilities.

windfall profit   A change in profits that arises out of an unanticipated change in market conditions such as a sudden increase in demand. Negative windfall profits are sometimes called *windfall losses*.

withdrawals   Income earned by households and not passed on to firms in return for goods and services purchased, and income earned by firms and not passed on to households in return for factor services purchased.

X   Exports; the value of all domestic production sold abroad.

X-inefficiency   The use of resources at a lower level of productivity than is possible, even if they are allocated efficiently, so that the economy is at a point inside its production possibility boundary.

X − M   See *net exports*.

Index